CARTRIDGES OF THE WORLD

A COMPLETE AND ILLUSTRATED REFERENCE FOR OVER 1500 CARTRIDGES

11th Edition

By Frank C. Barnes / Edited by Stan Skinner

©1965, 1969, 1972, 1980, 1985, 1989, 1993, 1997, 2000, 2003, 2006 by
Frank C. Barnes and
Krause Publications
Published by

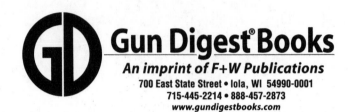

Gun Digest®Books

An imprint of F+W Publications
700 East State Street • Iola, WI 54990-0001
715-445-2214 • 888-457-2873
www.gundigestbooks.com

Our toll-free number to place an order or obtain
a free catalog is (800) 258-0929.

Library of Congress Control Number: 2005906863

ISBN 13: 978-0-89689-297-2
ISBN 10: 0-89689-297-2
1st Edition: 1965
2nd Edtion: 1969
3rd Edition: 1972
4th Edition: 1980
5th Edition: 1985
6th Edition: 1989
7th Edition: 1993
8th Edition: 1997
9th Edition: 2000
10th Edition: 2003
11th Edition: 2006

Designed by Patsy Howell
Edited by Ken Ramage

Printed in the United States of America

STAFF

Field Research Editor	Editor	Editor, Gun Digest Books
Bill Ball	**Stan Skinner**	**Ken Ramage**

About the Covers

Front Cover

Recently, Hornady's been busy developing new cartridges and innovative solutions to certain limitations on existing favorites. Here are examples *(clockwise from top)* of the most recent releases.

The LeverRevolution line of ammunition for lever-action rifles greatly improves the ballistic performance of traditional flat-point lever-gun cartridges by incorporating a pointed elastomer tip on the bullet that greatly improves the exterior ballistics, yet is safe to load in tubular magazines because the elastomer tip flattens when pressed against the cartridge primer ahead of it. Hornady reports their 30-30 loading is traveling 450 fps faster than comparable lever-gun loads from other ammunition companies. The LeverRevolution line currently includes the 30-30 Winchester, 35 Remington, 444 Marlin, 45-70 Government and the 450 Marlin.

The SST shotgun slug is now available in both 20- and 12-gauge loadings. The SST slug is intended for rifled shotgun barrels and delivers 100-yard groups under two inches, according to Hornady. The pointed projectile design delivers the flattest trajectory on any slug loading on the market.

The Hornady 17 HMR *(longest)* and 17 Mach 2 *(shortest)* are two rimfire cartridges that offer rimfire shooters high-performance ammunition at affordable prices. The 17 HMR is the faster of the two, and is available in two bullet weights. The 17 Mach 2 delivers tack-driving accuracy and a trajectory much flatter than that of the standard high-velocity 22LR cartridge.

Hornady's TAP FPD line of personal defense ammunition is specifically designed for personal protection and law enforcement use. The line includes pistol, rifle and shotshell cartridges in the popular law enforcement calibers: 9mm, 40 S&W and 45 ACP, 223 Remington and 308 Winchester, and a 12-gauge loading of OO buck.

The Custom line of Hornady ammunition now includes the big 460 S&W and 500 S&W *(shown)* cartridges. The 500 S&W has three bullet options, the 300-grain Evolution, 350-grain XTP MAG or the 500-grain FP-XTP. Other chamberings in the line include the 44 Magnum, 45ACP, 454 Casull, 475 Linebaugh and 480 Ruger.

Back Cover

Founded in 1949, Hornady's early offerings were bullet jackets and complete bullets made by converting spent 22 rimfire cases. The bullet line grew and the company moved to its present location in 1958.

Hornady's Frontier line of loaded ammunition was born just six years later, in 1964.

Today Hornady is a well-established shooting sports company involved in a number of areas: bullets, ammunition, muzzleloading, metallic reloading and shotshell reloading.

For more information, go to www.hornady.com or call 800-338-3220 to request a catalog.

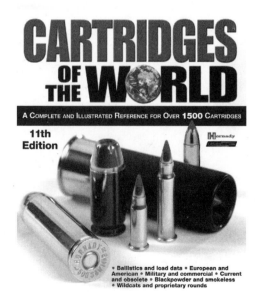

By Frank C. Barnes / Edited by Stan Skinner

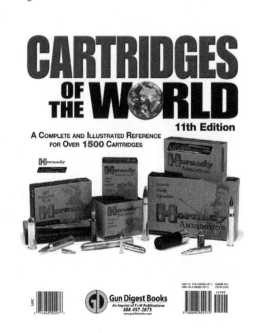

FOREWORD

SPORTSMEN AND firearms enthusiasts in general are fond of indulging in a timeless, endless discussion that usually begins something like this: "If you had the opportunity to hunt all over the world, but due to space-weight limitations could carry only one gun, what would it be?" This simple assumption is good for hours or even days of lively debate. Also, on occasion, a few fist fights. This is mentioned, not to engage in any phase of this classic argument, but because it is apropos to a summary of this book.

Let me put it this way: If you were traveling to Mars or some other planet by rocket ship, and because of space-weight limitations could only carry one book on cartridges, what would it be? We sincerely hope it would be this one, because it contains more usable information per pound than any other single book on the subject.

As of this writing there is no record of any copies of CARTRIDGES OF THE WORLD having been carried to other worlds, although the effort did get off the ground here on earth. The many letters received by the author and editors indicate that we certainly followed the right path in our treatment of the many known cartridges. The word used most often in describing this book is "useful." We consider this a high compliment because it describes our original objective — to publish a useful cartridge book. We sincerely believe the buyer of this edition will also find it so.

Frank C. Barnes

DEDICATION

To my parents, Clifford and Margaret Barnes – whose encouragement of my boyhood dreams and ambitions made all that came later possible – this book is wholeheartedly dedicated. F.C.B.

ACKNOWLEDGMENTS

For this 11th Edition of CARTRIDGES OF THE WORLD, we wish to give special thanks to the following people and organizations for their contributions toward the various improvements and additions:

Bill Ball, freelance journalist
Randy Brooks, CEO, Barnes Bullets
Steve Comus, Publications Director, Safari Club International
Kevin Howard, President, Howard Communications
Tim Janzen, Chief Ballistician, Barnes Bullets
J.D. Jones, President, SSK Industries
Mike Jordan, Senior Account Executive, Howard Communications
Dr. Ken Oehler, Oehler Research, Inc.
Jeff Patterson, Swanson Russell Agency
Carroll Pilant, Ballistician, Sierra Bullets

CONTENTS

Introduction

THE ORIGINAL philosophy worked out by myself and the late John T. Amber (the original editor) was to assemble a practical and useful book that would appeal to as broad a spectrum of the shooting fraternity as possible. The sales record of the book over the years indicates that this was the proper approach. The 11th Edition carries on in the same tradition as the previous editions in offering both something new as well as retaining old data that is either useful or of general interest. There is really not much that can be done in the area of, say, obsolete cartridges because nothing changes except that occasionally one or two of the old-timers will be reintroduced. This requires moving such cartridges back into the chapter covering modern cartridges, or on the other hand, some commercially loaded number will be discontinued and relegated to the obsolete chapter. Such changes are updated in the next edition. We have retained the encyclopedic reference format and are continuing to present the information from a shooter's and hunter's point of view.

Included is information covering handgun, rifle, shotgun, obsolete blackpowder, European, British, military, wildcat and proprietary cartridges, along with data on the guns that shoot these cartridges. There is something for everybody.

The information contained in CARTRIDGES OF THE WORLD was obtained from many sources, including textbooks, new and old catalogs, periodicals and individuals. Amber supplied many out-of-print and rare cartridge catalogs from his extensive library. Much information is from the author's and editor's files, as well as other original sources, and will not be found elsewhere. Practical experience also weighs heavily in the balance. Barnes had more than 50 years of hunting, shooting, reloading and collecting experience. Amber was a gun collector with extensive hunting experience in North America, Europe and Africa. Ken Warner, successor to Amber and former editor of GUN DIGEST, is also a collector, hunter and shooter with many years of experience. This collective experience is reflected in the pages of this book.

The book is divided into chapters based on each category of ammunition: Current American Rifle, Obsolete American Rifle, Handgun, Military, etc. Ballistics and basic loading data have been included with each cartridge listing if possible. Extensive dimensional charts and tables are found at the end of each chapter. Dimensional data is presented in this manner, rather than with the individual cartridges, in order to simplify the identification of unknown cartridges. Cartridges are listed in the order of increasing bullet diameter, or if caliber is the same, by length or power. One of the more difficult facts to establish with certainty is the date of origin for older obsolete cartridges. This is a matter of some importance to historians and occasionally archaeologists digging into our recent past when they happen to find spent cases or cartridges in graves or on old battlefields. It can be useful when attempting to determine the caliber of certain guns or the relationship between firearms, ammunition and historical events. Those who write western novels or make similar movies might be well served if they would peruse the pages of this book so that they would not constantly be placing the wrong guns in the wrong time period. It might surprise them to discover that the U.S. Cavalry in the 1870s did not carry either Model 1892 or 1894 Winchester lever-action carbines. These guns were unavailable then, and none of the cartridges those rifles chambered were ever adopted by the military. The date of origin, insofar as can be determined, has been included with the historical notes.

Many law-enforcement agencies, military organizations and defense ordnance groups have found CARTRIDGES OF THE WORLD to be a worthwhile reference source. It is also used as a basic text in colleges and universities for firearms identification courses. Firearms identification involves working with cartridges as much as working with firearms. CARTRIDGES OF THE WORLD even made it into television when it showed up in one episode of the once-popular cop show, "Miami Vice."

Under the heading "General Comments," an effort has been made to rate the various cartridges for hunting purposes. Admittedly any such ratings are highly subjective, since there is no quantitative formula for determining what cartridge is suitable for what game. Evidence (or lack thereof), observations in the hunting field and personal opinion inevitably enter this process. If the reader takes issue with the author or editor regarding the efficacy of a particular cartridge for some specific purpose, it doesn't necessarily follow that someone is wrong. Rather, the problem is evaluated from different points of view. I remember reading several years ago about a fellow in Africa who fired a 22 Long Rifle at an elephant in an effort to scare it away from his garden. Unfortunately, he hit the poor beast and dropped it in its tracks with a single, misplaced round, and then really had a hell of a time getting it out. I hardly think that this qualifies the 22 Long Rifle as an elephant round, although some might think so. Also, many years ago, I ran into an old-time trapper in the Yukon Territory of Canada who had a much-used Savage Model 99 lever-action rifle chambered for the 303 Savage. He handloaded all his ammunition with hand-cast 190-grain bullets at a muzzle velocity of about 1,950 feet per second. He insisted that this 30-30 class combination was more than adequate for moose, grizzly bear or anything else, and with his experience as a woodsman, trapper and hunter, it was. However, not many present-day gun writers would agree. So ideas about what's good for what in the world of hunting cartridges depends a good deal on personal experience, skill and opinion. In any event, the ratings of various cartridges for hunting purposes is, in all cases, based on the assumption that the hunter properly places the correct type of bullet into the intended target.

Finally we come to the subject of which cartridges should or should not be included within the pages of CARTRIDGES OF THE WORLD. Obviously this book does not include every known cartridge in the world. If it did, it would have to be divided into many volumes. From time to time, certain readers write rather irate letters wondering why such-and-such a cartridge has not been included, or on the other hand, why we bothered to include certain cartridges. Admittedly, there must be hundreds of cartridges and variations, including obsolete, military, European, etc., that have been excluded. There are several reasons for this. First, editorial constraints on the number of pages and contents don't leave sufficient room to include everything in one volume. The book has to be kept in balance to appeal to a general, rather than a specific, audience. Second, while most gun nuts are casual cartridge collectors, only a few shooters are avid cartridge collectors. In other words, not many people have even a remote interest in all the obsolete and little-known cartridges that have been available at one time or another. There are already a large number of excellent books aimed specifically at the cartridge collector per se, such as those written by Charles Suydam, Herschel Logan, Fred Datig and others. The criteria used in this book to determine what cartridges to include are based largely on what the author and editor perceive as being of greatest general interest, what has historical significance or is of unusual interest. A survey has demonstrated, for example, that 98 percent of readers are interested in modern cartridges and many purchase the book for that information alone. Chapter 2 is based on commercially loaded ammunition readily available through most gun stores. Obsolete cartridges (Chapter 3) include all the better-known smokeless and blackpowder cartridges no longer commercially loaded, but not every known obsolete cartridge. In other words, there has to be some sort of cutoff or the whole thing could get out of hand. A number of currently popular wildcat cartridges have always been included. In this edition, we have greatly expanded the chapter on wildcats because of new developments and renewed interest in this area. The reader will note a considerable reorganization in Chapter 11: Shotgun Shells, including a new dimensional table. As information, samples and illustrations become available, we intend to further expand this chapter. In this edition, we have expanded the proprietary cartridge chapter. This reflects the growing popularity of this class of custom chamberings. Also, we have included a master dimensional table, Chapter 20, organized by bullet diameter and case length to ease identification of unknown cartridges or spent cartridge cases by measuring them. Finally, we have reorganized the index at the back of the book to ease location of information on a cartridge, once its name is known. The author and the editor have tried to please as many potential readers as possible, but remember, as in the biblical parable of the man and his donkey, it is impossible to please everybody.

—F.C.B.

Chapter 1

Cartridge Nomenclature

IT IS difficult or impossible for the novice to follow the action without some knowledge of cartridge caliber designation. Even the individual experienced with standard American ammunition may be ignorant of British, European or even obsolete American cartridge nomenclature. The subject, regrettably, is full of inconsistencies and confusion.

With the majority of American, British or European (metric) cartridges, the caliber (indicating bore land diameter in 1/100-inch) is the first figure given. However, there are exceptions that will be pointed out later. Caliber may be given in terms of bullet or bore diameter (land or groove), and is neither accurate nor consistent. For example, the 307 Savage cartridge, which uses the same .308-inch diameter bullet as the 308 Winchester. Then there is the 458 Winchester Magnum and the 460 Weatherby Magnum, both of which are loaded with the same .458-inch diameter bullet. Other similar examples abound. In the latter example, the Weatherby people didn't want anyone to get their round mixed up with the Winchester design so they changed the figures a little. That is one reason some cartridges do not follow in normal caliber designation in the dimensional tables. There are others.

The second figure, if there is one, is usually some distinguishing feature such as case length or powder charge. Cartridges of European origin are, almost without exception, designated in metric units by caliber and case length. Obsolete American cartridges, or any that have a blackpowder origin, are designated by caliber and powder charge weight; or caliber-powder charge-bullet weight (the last two in grains weight). Smokeless powder charges vary so widely with the powder type and grain structure that this system is no longer used. However, there are again such exceptions as the 30-30 Winchester and 30-40 Krag. Here, the second figure represents the original smokeless powder charge although it no longer has anything to do with it. With blackpowder cartridges the designation 45-70 Springfield means a 45-caliber bullet with 70 grains of blackpowder; or 45-70-405 spells out the same cartridge with 405-grain bullet to distinguish it from such other bullet loadings as the 45-70-500. But then there was the 45-56-405 Carbine load in the same case!

The truth of the matter is that the American "system" of cartridge nomenclature really hasn't any system to it, and can only be learned through reading and experience. Otherwise, you simply never know what is meant. For example, take the 30-06, a very popular military and sporting round. Here, the first figure shows the caliber, the second last two numbers are the date of origin. In other words, a 30-caliber cartridge — model of 1906. Or again, the 250-3000 Savage (25-3000 just simply lacked that special "ring" the advertising folks wanted). This translates out as a 25-caliber cartridge firing a bullet at 3,000 fps muzzle velocity. The bullet diameter is actually .257-inch and muzzle velocity varies with bullet weight from 2,800 to over 3,000 fps. Some of the older blackpowder cartridges included the case length and type; thus the 44-90

Sharps 2 5/8-inch necked, or 45-120 Sharps 3 1/4-inch straight. As you can see, cartridge nomenclature isn't a system at all — it's a code.

The British, to a large extent, follow the same "system" as we do. However, they add to the general confusion with such cartridges as the 577/450 or 500/465. Here, the second figure gives the approximate bullet diameter in 1/1000-inch, and what is meant is the 577 case necked to 450-caliber and a 500 case necked to 465-caliber. They may also add the case length. At this point it is necessary to point out that some American wildcat (noncommercial) cartridges dreamed up by individual experimenters are designated by a similar but opposite system. Here, we have such cartridges as the 8mm-06, 30-338 and 25-06. These work out as an 8mm based on the 30-06 case, a 30-caliber based on the 338 Winchester case and a 25-caliber based on the 30-06 case. Confusing indeed!

The Europeans have evolved the only real system of cartridge designation that is consistent and somewhat meaningful. Dimensions are in millimeters, including bore-land diameter, case length and type. The 7x57mm Mauser is a cartridge, for example, for use with a 7mm bore-land size (7.21mm groove size) with a 57mm rimless case. The 9.3x74Rmm is a 9.3mm caliber and a 74mm rimmed case. The R denotes the rimmed type, its absence a rimless case. The name of the originator or manufacturer may follow. This is a relatively simple and straightforward system, but unfortunately it isn't perfect either. The Germans used two rim types in some of their older cartridges, and this resulted in duplicate designation of cartridges that differ only in the rim (9.05x36.4R, 10.85x24.9R, etc.), and there must be at least three 9.3x72mm cartridges that differ only in case configuration. This is all something of a mess and probably too late to change. Mr. Barnes, in an effort to straighten things out or perhaps add to the confusion, developed two wildcat cartridges which he designated as the 308x1.5-inch and 458x2-inch.

To further elucidate, the reader needs to know that there are two major classifications of cartridges — centerfire and rimfire. The former is fired by a primer located in the center of the case head; the latter by the priming compound distributed around the entire inside of the rim's outer diameter. The modern centerfire cartridge primer is removable and replaceable so that the case can be reloaded after it is fired. It is possible, but not practicable to reload rimfire cases after they have been fired. Centerfire cartridges are subdivided into two types based on the primer, Berdan and Boxer. The Berdan-primed case has the anvil as a separate protrusion, or teat, in the bottom of the primer pocket. The Boxer primer is completely self-contained and the anvil is a part of the primer. All American-made ammunition is normally Boxer-primed, whereas much British and European ammunition is Berdan-primed. Most foreign-made ammunition manufactured for the American market has the Boxer-type primer.

Rim Types

There are four common types of centerfire cartridge cases based on rim type. These are: rimmed, rimless, semi-rimmed and belted. The British equivalents are: flanged, rimless, semi-flanged and belted. There is a fifth type, not widely used, which is the rebated rimless in which the rim is of smaller diameter than the base of the case. Only one American rifle cartridge is of this type, the 284 Winchester. The 41 Action Express pistol cartridge is also rebated. The purpose of the rebated rim is to allow the use of a standard diameter bolt with a larger diameter cartridge. In the past, there have been a few rimless cases without the usual extractor groove.

Both centerfire and rimfire cartridges may be of straight or necked type. Contrary to popular opinion, the necked case was not designed to provide greater velocity for smokeless powder cartridges. It evolved back in blackpowder days as a means of getting the same powder charge in a shorter case, thus allowing the repeating actions of the day to handle cartridges of the same power as the single shots with their long, straight cartridges. Some of the very early rimfire cartridges were of the necked type.

The latest fad in cartridges is the caseless, or combustible type, an idea not really very new that dates back to the early 1800s or before. The original used a nitrated paper or cloth container for the powder charge and sometimes also the bullet. The entire package was loaded into the gun, and the powder and its container consumed in firing. During World War II, the Germans began an intense research and development program to perfect caseless ammunition and design weapons to shoot it. The principal motivating factor at the time was the severe shortage of brass and other metal for cartridge cases. The Germans are known to have had at least partial success, and some insist complete success. United States military ordnance facilities as well as private industry have been working on the problem of caseless ammunition for the past 50 years or more. There has been considerable success in developing caseless and partially-caseless artillery rounds, but there are still many problems in the small arms field. Obturation is a big problem, as is ejecting a misfired round from the chamber of a repeating action. Modern caseless ammunition usually consists of compressed powder grains fastened to the base of the bullet, or the powder may be encased in a plastic case made of the same material as the propellant. Ignition may be percussion or electrical, and there is, in some types, a booster charge extending through the center of the powder charge.

Cartridge Collectors

Though this book is not a collectors' manual, it includes nonetheless considerable material of use and interest to collectors, or any serious student of cartridges and related weapons. The tables of dimensions are organized to facilitate cartridge identification. The key to this is bullet diameter and case type. The reader must understand that in measuring cartridge dimensions, certain manufacturing tolerances must be allowed, and these can affect the last, or even the second, decimal figure. Dimensional tolerances can be rather

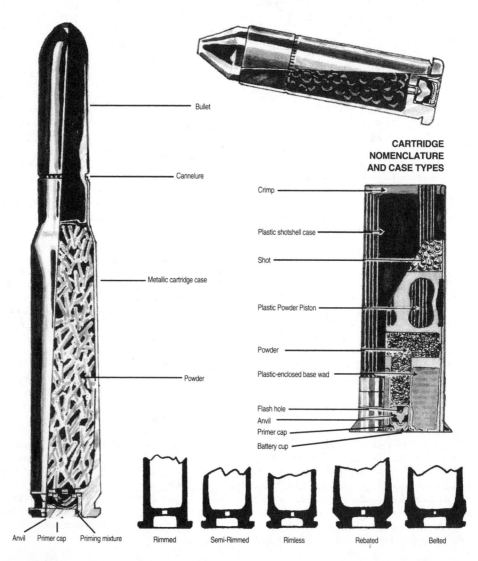

Bullet

Cannelure

Metallic cartridge case

Powder

Anvil   Primer cap   Priming mixture

CARTRIDGE NOMENCLATURE AND CASE TYPES

Crimp

Plastic shotshell case

Shot

Plastic Powder Piston

Powder

Plastic-enclosed base wad

Flash hole

Anvil

Primer cap

Battery cup

Rimmed   Semi-Rimmed   Rimless   Rebated   Belted

considerable with old blackpowder cartridges and the modern bottlenecked numbers. Also, the true diameter of the obsolete paper-patched bullet should include the patch, not just the lead slug protruding from it. Minor variations in dimensions should not be mistaken for errors or the existence of an unknown caliber. The dimensional tables can also be used to identify the caliber of a gun if the chamber dimensions are known. This can best be determined by means of a chamber cast and the means of doing this is explained in Chapter 3. If you own an obsolete or foreign gun for which ammunition is not available, the tables of dimensions will assist in determining whether ammunition can be made by reforming some similar existing case.

Metallic Cartridge Development

The self-contained metallic cartridge is a fairly modern development, only perfected about 1850. The use of blackpowder as a propellant in guns in the western world goes back something like 650 years, and the knowledge of gunpowder over 700 years. The Chinese knew about gunpowder 500 or 600 years before it was introduced to Europeans, although they used it as fireworks and not as a propellant any earlier than the Europeans. The centerfire cartridge, a necessary prerequisite to our modern ammunition, evolved during the 1860s and 1870s. Smokeless powder and high-velocity cartridges only date back to the 1890s. Improvements since the turn of the century have been more in the area of improved ignition, powder chemistry and bullet construction rather than cartridge design. Charles Newton designed cartridges back around 1910 that, had modern powders been available, would have equaled the performance of present-day high-velocity developments of similar caliber and type. Smokeless powder military cartridges designed between 1888 and 1915 were so good that improvement was possible only after more advanced types of powder became available, and many of these cartridges were still in use through World War II. As the result of this situation, many modern innovations in the gun and cartridge field turn out, after a little investigation, to be a reintroduction of something really quite old.

A few examples of the not-really-very-new among modern cartridges are worth pointing out. The 244 Remington (6mm) makes a good case to start out with. Introduced in 1955, it is based on the 257 Roberts case, necked down, which in turn is the 7x57mm Mauser, slightly modified. Back in 1895, or thereabout, the Germans had a 6x57mm, made by necking-down the 7x57mm Mauser. With the exception of a slight (insignificant) difference in the shoulder angle, the 244 Remington is a carbon copy of this much-older cartridge.

The 7mm Remington Magnum is another brilliant "design" that is really just a modification of a much-older cartridge. It is very similar to the 275 Holland & Holland Magnum introduced around 1912 or 1913. However, the H&H round didn't have a good American smokeless powder of later development to bring out its full potential. On the other hand, there are a number of wildcat 7mm short-belted magnums practically identical to the 7mm Remington Magnum that pre-date it by quite a few years and are identical in performance.

Yet another Remington innovation is the 280 Remington, a rimless cartridge based on the 30-06 case, necked-down. This is a dead ringer for the 7x64mm Brenneke introduced in 1917. It is also practically identical to the wildcat 7mm-06 developed around 1928, so there is nothing very original here. However, none of these cartridges are interchangeable.

The commercial manufacturers are not alone in their design duplication; many individuals have inadvertently done the same thing. One of the most popular wildcat cartridges anyone has thought up is the 35 Whelen, introduced about 1922 and adopted as a commercial standard by Remington in 1987. This

is simply the 30-06 case necked-up to 35-caliber and was originated by the late Col. Townsend Whelen. It is a very close copy of the German 9x63mm, which dates back to about 1905. As a matter of fact, a number of wildcat cartridges are nothing more than a duplication of some much older British or European designs. In fairness, it must be stated that the originator of the wildcat version probably was completely unaware of the existence of a parallel cartridge at the time of his bright idea.

Some companies and wildcatters go to considerable trouble to complete the circle, often coming up with something that duplicates a long-forgotten cartridge. If they were more familiar with the history of cartridge development, they could save a lot of time. The 444 Marlin, introduced during 1964, is a good case in point. To begin with, it is a poorly disguised copy of the wildcat 44 Van Houten Super that pre-dates it by at least three years. According to Parker Ackley, in his *Handbook for Shooters and Reloaders*, the 44 VHS is made by necking up the 30-40 Krag case, trimming it to 2 inches, and turning down the rim. When this is done, we end up with a near carbon copy of the 10.3x65Rmm Swiss cartridge (DWM 237A) that originated around 1900 or earlier. The only difference is in the fact that the 10.3mm case is 0.3-inch longer than the 44 VHS or 0.2-inch longer than the 444 Marlin. However, that's not all there is to the story because the 10.3x65Rmm cartridge is based on the brass .410 shotgun shell loaded with a conical bullet and fired in a rifled barrel. It is possible to make the 444 Marlin from brass .410 cases and the new originators could have done the same thing in the beginning.

Cartridges don't just happen — they evolve in response to some need or use requirement. Our Western frontier dictated American cartridge development for 50 years or more. Its influence is still an important factor in directing the imagination of the modern hunter. British rifle cartridges, in the main, were designed for conditions existing in other parts of the world such as Africa and India rather than the home island. European cartridges were developed on one hand because of hunting conditions and available game on the European continent, and on the other to compete with American and British innovations. Since the end of World War II, there has been considerable blending and standardization of the various worldwide cartridge designs. More British and European rifles and cartridges are used by American gun buffs than ever before, and they, in turn, have adopted many of our ideas.

Modern Ammunition

The most important factor influencing the ammunition available at any given time is economics. The ammunition manufacturers are willing to produce anything that will sell, but, obviously, are most reluctant to tool up and turn out something for which there is little or no demand. Military developments, as illustrated by the 30 Carbine, 30-06, 7.62mm NATO (308 Winchester), 5.56mm (223 Remington), 45 ACP and that old standby, the 45-70, have almost always provided a good long-term sales record when introduced in sporting version. For this reason the ammunition companies have usually been quick to adopt these. They have not been quite so enthusiastic in their attitude toward cartridges developed by individuals or wildcatters. However, Remington has been the leader in introducing commercial versions of what were originally wildcat cartridges. They initiated the trend with the 257 Roberts back in 1934, and since 1945 have added a number of others including the 17 Remington, 22-250 Remington, 6mm Remington, 25-06 Remington, 7mm-08, 7mm Remington Magnum and the 8mm Remington Magnum, to name most of them. Actually, we must recognize that Winchester adopted the 22 Hornet (an original wildcat development) in 1930. Also the 300 Winchester Magnum and possibly the 358 Winchester were around in wildcat versions before the company decided to develop something similar. The 444 Marlin is another cartridge based on an original wildcat innovation. Since most of these have had good sales records, it would not be surprising to see some of the other more popular wildcats introduced in commercial version as time goes on. This is a healthy trend, and we hope it will continue.

Nostalgia is another factor that is now exerting considerable influence on ammunition and firearms trends. Shooting muzzleloading and blackpowder cartridge guns of all types is a solidly-established facet of the shooting game. Although there have always been a few muzzleloading clubs and a small core of blackpowder devotees, the current popularity of this sport has given birth to a whole new industry specializing in the manufacture of replica arms. Muzzleloading clubs with several hundred members are now common and most states have special muzzleloading big game hunting seasons. As an example of the magnitude of this development, Colt Firearms once again sold its cap-and-ball revolvers, Harrington & Richardson offered replicas of the U.S. 1873 Trapdoor cavalry carbine, Shiloh Rifle Mfg. will sell you 1874 Sharps carbines and rifles and one can buy any number of Hawken-type muzzleloading replicas. What is mentioned here is only a very small portion of what is available to blackpowder shooters. If you are interested in the full extent of the offerings in this field, I suggest you buy the latest edition of GUN DIGEST (Krause Publications) and look in the catalog section in the back of the book.

How does all this affect modern cartridges? The nostalgia syndrome is responsible for the reappearance of a number of long obsolete cartridges, or at least new reloadable cases, although admittedly this is as yet on a rather limited or custom basis for most of the old-timers. Dixie Gun Works, for example, is offering new, reloadable cases in the old 50-70 Government caliber and has recently brought in the 41 Rimfire. The development of modern cartridges is a dynamic rather than a static process, although it does move in a series of starts and stops, depending on fads and trends at any given time. These, then, are the factors that shape our modern ammunition and this includes some very exciting innovations (some old and some new) since the first edition of CARTRIDGES OF THE WORLD came off the press.

Cartridge Loading Data

Basic loading data has been furnished as part of the general information on each cartridge, except in those cases where such information was unavailable and test rifles or cartridges unobtainable. Insofar as possible, the loads listed are for those powders that provide the most efficient velocity and energy for the caliber and bullet weight involved. With old blackpowder cartridges or obsolete smokeless powder numbers, the objective has been to supply data that more or less duplicates the original factory performance figures. The cartridge loading data has been gathered from various published sources and the extensive experience of the author and various editors. The data selected for inclusion in COTW provides a good starting point for the handloader, but there are many more good powders available for loading each cartridge than can possibly be presented here. It is therefore recommended that the serious reloader obtain one or more of the very fine reloading manuals published by Krause Publications, Lyman, Speer, Hornady, Hodgdon, Sierra, Nosler, P.O. Ackley and others. Loading data listed here does not necessarily agree with that published elsewhere as to the velocity obtainable with a given

charge of powder because the test conditions and equipment are not the same. There is no such thing as absolute loading data and all published loads reflect the conditions of test firing, which includes a number of important variables such as barrel length, chamber configuration, temperature, components used, test equipment, etc. Test firings conducted by the author some years ago with different makes and models of 30-06 rifles demonstrated that there can be a variation of more than 300 fps between different rifles firing the same, very carefully loaded ammunition.

All loading data, wherever published, should be used with caution and common sense. If you are not sure or don't know what you are doing, DON'T DO IT!!! Since neither the author, editor or publisher has any control over the components, assembly of the ammunition, arms it is to be fired in, the degree of knowledge involved or how the resulting ammunition might be used, no responsibility, either implied or expressed, is assumed for the use of any of the cartridge loading data in this edition of COTW.

Cartridge Dimensional Data

The reader should understand that the tables of cartridge dimensional data at the end of each chapter are based on actual cartridge measurements and not derived from SAAMI or other drawings. In some instances, data is based on measurement of a single specimen; in others, it may be an average taken from several cartridges of different manufacture. The tables are intended primarily to assist the reader in identifying cartridges, and their use for the purpose of chambering rifles is not recommended unless checked carefully against manufacturers' chamber dimensions. The reason for this is that there are far greater differences in cartridge dimensions between different makes and lots than most people realize. There are differences in the third decimal place even within most 20-round boxes, in fact.

This brings up another point. From time to time, the author or editor will receive letters from readers complaining that their measurement of some cartridge dimension does not agree with ours, and therefore we must be wrong. I have, for example, two letters before me — one claiming that a certain figure is too high, the other stating that the very same figure is too low. The differences are all in the third decimal place. This is not a matter of anyone being wrong, but rather variances in manufacturing tolerance.

As a more specific example of the tolerance factor, I acquired a box of 10mm pistol ammunition for the Bren 10 and other semi-autos and in measuring several rounds, found some discrepancy in the rim diameters. Just to see what the minimum and maximum figures were, I measured the entire 20-round box. It turned out that the minimum rim diameter was 0.419-inch and the maximum was 0.426-inch or a difference of 0.007-inch. Is that a sufficient range to cause the pistol to malfunction? I hardly think so, but people have written letters over a difference of 0.002-inch or even 0.001-inch between their measurements and mine.

All of this is just to get the subject of cartridge dimensions into proper perspective. In any event, if your measurements don't match someone else's by a few thousandths of an inch, don't get excited and don't get the idea you may have discovered a new and heretofore unknown cartridge. You may be dealing with maximum and the other guy with minimum dimensions.

— Frank C. Barnes

Chapter 2

Current American Rifle Cartridges

(Centerfire Sporting)

THE CRITERION used to determine which cartridges should be included in Chapter 2 is the requirement that the cartridge be currently manufactured and available to the American sportsman through local dealers either on an over-the-counter basis, or by special order, since no gun store carries every single item of ammunition that is manufactured.

The cartridges listed here include not only the most modern developments, but also some that are ancient and obsolete by any standard. The characteristic they share is that they are manufactured on a commercial basis, still used, and rifles are available chambered for the round, although perhaps not made by the major American arms companies. Two of the oldest American centerfire cartridges are included in this group, the 44-40 Winchester and the 45-70 Government, both of which originated in 1873 and have been in continuous use since. Several replica rifles are now chambered for the 44-40, and the 45-70 has staged a remarkable comeback. Both modern and replica rifles are being chambered for the 45-70. The popularity of this grand old military and sporting cartridge continues to increase.

One thing that can be said about many cartridges in Chapter 2 is that they have stood the test of time and include among their number the best and most useful designs available to the American shooter. Those that ended up in second place, often for good reasons but sometimes for no reason anyone could reasonably understand or explain, will be found in Chapter 3: Obsolete American Rifle Cartridges. Interestingly, nostalgia is in the process of moving a few of these back into Chapter 2.

For many years, the new trend in cartridge and rifle design has been toward high velocity and flat trajectory, often at the expense of almost any other consideration. It appears to be the fashionable thing in some circles to show up on a big-game hunt with the largest caliber or most powerful rifle in the crowd. This odd psychosis is partly responsible for the success of the Weatherby line of rifles and cartridges, although prestige and owning a perceived superior product also enter into this. The major gun manufacturers in the United States were slow in recognizing this as a fact of life, but have since closed the gap. Modern high-velocity magnum cartridges can cancel out some small measure of poor judgment in estimating range or lead if the shooter can handle the added recoil and muzzle blast without flinching. (Editor's Note: Recently this trend has slowed with many new chamberings now middle-of-the-road offerings.)

The author has, at various times, owned and shot most of the modern magnum rifles and handguns and has a very high regard for their capabilities, but has reservations as to any real need for the larger calibers under normal North American hunting conditions. A great deal depends, of course, on what is to be hunted and under what conditions. Is there any actual advantage, for example, in owning a 300 Magnum if your hunting area is confined to, say, southern California? What game would one encounter there so large or so dangerous that would require all this extra power? Yes, I understand the magnum might provide an extra 100-yard sure-hit range. But with a little practice in range estimation, wouldn't something like the 257 Roberts, 270 Winchester or the 30-06 do just as well? However, one should never disparage a man's wife, his automobile or his favorite hunting rifle. Therefore, far be it for me to make enemies by casting aspersions on those who favor the magnum cartridges for whatever reason. My only point is that one doesn't need a magnum to kill a mouse, not that there is anything wrong with doing so. In any event, if you are looking for the latest and the most powerful, it will be found in Chapter 2.

The reader who is trying to determine which of the current American rifle cartridges best suits his hunting needs should first determine what game animals he intends to hunt. Second, he should decide which type of rifle action is preferred: bolt-, lever-, semi-auto, pump- or single-shot action. Next, sit down with a copy of GUN DIGEST or a variety of gun catalogs to see what calibers are available for the different actions. Finally, give some careful and realistic thought as to how the gun is to be used, type of cover, average range and the variety of game animals to be legally hunted. Once you have all of these factors in hand, check through the cartridges listed in this chapter and pick the one that matches your particular needs and situation. Don't select the most powerful or the one with the highest velocity in the ballistics tables unless this actually offers some real advantage to you. Bear in mind that high velocity and flat trajectory offer no advantage if the bulk of your hunting is confined to brush or heavy timber with ranges that average only 50 yards or so. On the other hand, a big, heavy, slow bullet won't put meat in the freezer if you are shooting antelope at 300 yards and beyond. Always bear in mind that the 20 foot-pounds of recoil energy produced by cartridges in the 30-06 class is about all the average person can stand without flinching badly. In other words, use a little common sense and be realistic in your choice of hunting calibers. All the velocity, energy and killing power in the world is of no value if you can't hit anything with the rifle.

From time to time, readers write and ask me what my favorite hunting calibers are or what type rifle action I prefer. I happen to be very partial to the 257 Roberts and the 30-06 for the simple reason that I have always had extremely good results with both, and they will (if you reload) allow great flexibility in the variety of game or pests that can be hunted. If you handload, the 30-06 can be adapted to shoot anything from varmints right on up to moose and brown bear under most hunting situations. However, I also happen to like the 45-70 and have been shooting rifles of this caliber since I was 14 years old when an uncle gave me an 1873 Trapdoor Springfield rifle as a birthday present. Actually, I have fired, at one time or another, nearly every cartridge listed in Chapter 2. I don't really have anything against any of them for their intended purpose. As for rifle actions, I prefer the bolt-action, single-shot and lever-action, in about that order. One thing about cartridges: There is certainly sufficient variety to please just about anyone. As the saying goes, "Whatever turns you on." — F.C.B.

17 Remington

Historical Notes The 17 Remington was introduced in 1971 as a new caliber for Remington's 700 series bolt-action rifles. It is the smallest caliber centerfire rifle cartridge offered on a commercial basis to date. The case is based on the 223 Remington necked-down to 17-caliber, with the shoulder moved back .087-inch to lengthen the neck while retaining the same shoulder angle. The 17 Remington is similar to, but not identical with, the 17-223 wildcat developed about 1965. Experiments with 17-caliber rifles go back to 1944 when P.O. Ackley, the well-known gunsmith and experimenter, developed the 17 Ackley Bee based on necking-down the improved 218 Bee case. There are a number of other 17-caliber wildcat cartridges made by necking-down 22-caliber centerfire cases such as the 221 Remington Fireball, 222 Remington, etc. Remington, Ultra Light Arms, Wichita, and Sako offer rifles in this caliber.

General Comments The 17 Remington has had a steady, though unspectacular, sales record since its introduction. Its greatest drawback is that it is a special-purpose cartridge suited almost exclusively for varmint shooting. For the sportsman who wants a rifle only for that purpose, this is not a disadvantage, however those requiring a rifle for both varmint and deer hunting would be better served with some other caliber.

With the 25-grain hollowpoint bullet loaded by Remington and similar bullets available for handloading by Hornady, the 17 Remington must be rated as a short-range varmint cartridge. On the other hand, it has certain advantages such as minimal recoil, ricochet probability, and a very flat trajectory due to the high initial velocity of over 4000 fps. Disadvantages include: rapid barrel fouling, extreme sensitivity to slight charge weight variation and limited component availability. Factory loaded ammunition is available only from Remington. (New advances, such as moly-plated bullets and cleaner-burning powders, could eliminate the rapid fouling problem.)

17 Remington Loading Data and Factory Ballistics

Bullet (grains/type)	Powder	Grains	Velocity	Energy	Source/Comments
25 HP	IMR-4064	22.5	3800	801	Hornady
25 HP	IMR-4320	24.7	4000	888	Hornady
25 HP	IMR-4895	23.8	3900	845	Hornady
25 HP	IMR-3031	21.6	3800	801	Hornady
25 HP	N135	22.8	4040	906	Vihtavuori
20 AccuTip	FL		4250	802	Remington factory load
25 HP	FL		4040	906	Remington factory load

Note: Remington cases and Remington 7 1/2 primers used in all loads.

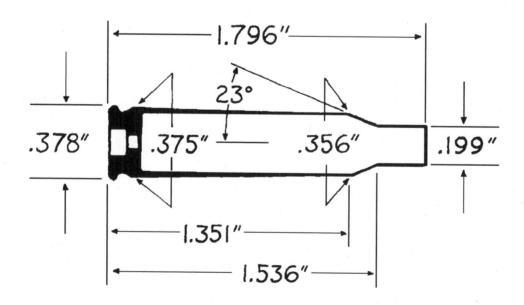

204 Ruger

Historical Notes Introduced in 2004 as a joint Hornady-Ruger project for varmint and target shooting, the 204 Ruger became the first 20-caliber cartridge to be produced on a large commercial scale. The 204 Ruger is the fastest production cartridge ever offered. Remarkably, it also offers excellent barrel life. After shooting approximately 500 prairie dogs with the Ruger and Dakota rifles chambered for the 204 Ruger, the field research editor found it to be an accurate, low-recoil round, superbly suited for long-range varminting. The 204 Ruger received the Academy of Excellence 2004 Cartridge of the Year Award.

General Comments The 204 Ruger uses the 47mm-long 222 Remington Magnum as its parent case, necking it down to accept .204 bullets and changing the shoulder angle to 30-degrees. It performs best with 26-inch barrels using a 1-12 rifling twist. The cartridge is available in Ruger, Dakota, Remington, and Savage bolt action rifles, Thompson Center and SSK Industries Contender single shot rifles, and AR-15 style rifles. Hornady, Remington and Winchester offer loaded ammunition.

204 Ruger Loading Data and Factory Ballistics

Bullet (grains/type)	Powder	Grains	Velocity	Energy	Source/Comments
32 V-Max	FL		4225	1268	Hornady
40 V-Max	FL		3900	1351	Hornady
32 V-Max	BL-C(2)	30.7	4081		Hodgdon
32 V-Max	Benchmark	28.0	4047		Hodgdon
40 V-Max	BL-C(2)	30.0	3774		Hodgdon

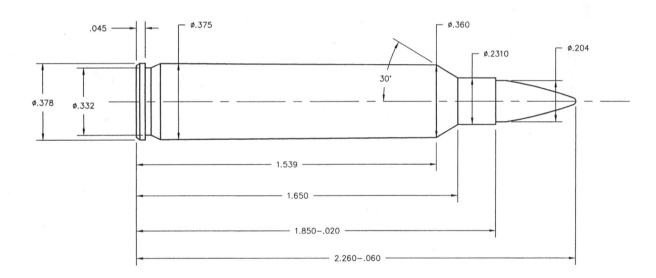

22 Hornet (5.6 x 36Rmm)

Historical Notes The 22 Hornet, based on the blackpowder 22 WCF, was developed during the late 1920s by a group of experimenters at Springfield Armory—Col. Townsend Whelen, Captain G. L. Wotkyns, and others. Winchester produced the first commercial ammunition in 1930. Within a few years the Hornet had been standardized by all American manufacturers. The original rifles were based on Springfield M1903 military and Martini single shot actions. Winchester announced its Model 54 bolt action in 22 Hornet caliber in 1932, but rifles did not actually reach the market until early 1933. Savage Model 23-D bolt-action rifles were available in 22 Hornet by August 1932. The Stevens single shot Model 417 "Walnut Hill" target and 417 1/2 sporting rifles were advertised in 22 Hornet caliber in 1933. During World War II, military survival rifles were made for the Hornet. At present, Anschutz, Ruger and Meacham chamber rifles for the Hornet and Thompson/Center has the Contender in the caliber. In Europe, the Hornet is known by the metric designation 5.6x35Rmm.

General Comments The 22 Hornet was the pioneer small-bore, high-velocity cartridge marketed in the United States primarily for varmint and small game shooting. It has never been commercially available in anything but bolt-action and single-shot rifles. For this reason, it quickly established a reputation for superb accuracy. No other cartridge of this type has ever caught on so fast or achieved such wide popularity.

Although not quite as powerful as the 218 Bee, it is a perfectly adequate small game and varmint cartridge. It remains popular, but suffers in comparison with the 223 Remington and the 22-250. It remains a fine choice for economical shooting at ranges between 100 and 150 yards. Due to its reduced powder capacity, the Hornet won't do as well with heavier bullets of 50 or 55 grains as will the 218 Bee. It is a good cartridge for use in settled areas because of the light report and low incidence of ricochet. Early rifles had bores requiring bullets of .223-inch diameter. Sierra still offers such bullets. Later rifles had normal bores for .224-inch diameter bullets. Most bullet manufacturers offer special bullets for loading the Hornet. The improved "K" Hornet is among the best known wildcats based on the Hornet and most common of all Improved chamberings. Loaded ammunition is available from Remington, Winchester and Norma.

22 Hornet Loading Data and Factory Ballistics

Bullet (grains/type)	Powder	Grains	Velocity	Energy	Source/Comments
35 V-Max	FL		3200	795	Hornady factory load
35 V-Max	H-110	11.2	3060	725	Hodgdon
40 SP	2400	10	2700	648	Sierra
40 SP	IMR 4227	11.4	2700	648	Speer, Sierra
45 SP	2400	9.2	2500	725	Hornady, Sierra
45 SP	IMR 4227	11	2600	678	Nosler, Hornady, Sierra
50 SP	2400	9	2400	640	Sierra, Hornady, Nosler
50 SP	IMR 4227	11	2550	694	Hornady, Nosler, Sierra
55 SP	IMR 4227	10.8	2400	704	Sierra, Hornady
55 SP	IMR 4198	12	2400	704	Sierra
45 SP	FL		2690	723	Factory load

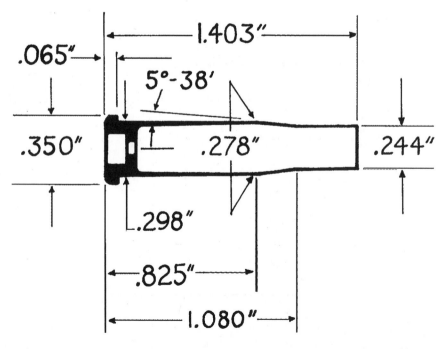

218 Bee

Historical Notes The 218 Bee, introduced by Winchester in 1938, was originally chambered in the Model 65 lever-action rifle, a modernized version of the Model 1892. Considerable enthusiasm greeted the announcement of this cartridge, and many magazine articles were devoted to comparing its superior killing power and range to the 22 Hornet. Although criticized as inaccurate, some Model 65s were capable of minute-of-angle accuracy. After WWII, Winchester brought out the Model 43 bolt-action rifle in 218 Bee. Mechanical troubles developed in some early models, and the rifle was discontinued. For a time, one or two European manufacturers, such as Sako and Krico, furnished small Mauser-type rifles in 218 Bee. The 218 Bee is based on the 32-20 case necked-down to 22-caliber. Cases can be made by necking-down 25-20 or 32-20 cases, then fire-forming.

General Comments The 218 Bee has a larger case and somewhat greater powder capacity than the 22 Hornet. It provides higher velocity and a greater effective range than the Hornet, and in a good single-shot or bolt-action rifle, is just as accurate. It is one of the most economical small game or varmint cartridges available. On small varmints it can be counted on out to 200 yards, but on coyote,

bobcat or the like, it cannot be depended on for one-shot kills farther than 150 yards. On rabbits or other edible game it is necessary to use full-jacketed bullets or reduced loads, otherwise it ruins much of the meat.

The Bee is easy to reload, and one can duplicate anything from the 22 Short up to and exceeding the 22 Hornet. With modern powders, the factory performance can be improved safely. By using heavier bullets of 50 or 55 grains, its killing power and range can be increased.

Although still a fine cartridge and useful for many purposes, the 218 Bee has been largely displaced by the 223 Remington and 22-250 Remington. The 218 Bee, like the 22 Hornet, has a relatively mild report compared to the more powerful 22 centerfires and can be used under circumstances in which the larger cartridges would not be acceptable. It is a better performer than the 22 Hornet and its lack of popularity has always been something of a mystery to me.

The Bee is the basis of several useful wildcats. Ackley's version approximately equals 222 Remington performance. The 17 Bee Improved offers impressive short-barrel performance. Factory loaded ammunition is available from Winchester.

218 Bee Loading Data and Factory Ballistics

Bullet (grains/type)	Powder	Grains	Velocity	Energy	Source/Comments
40 HP	2400	12	2800	697	Sierra
40 HP	IMR-4227	11.7	2600	601	Hornady, Sierra
45 SP	2400	11.6	2700	729	Sierra
45 SP	IMR-4227	13	2800	784	Nosler, Sierra
50 SP	2400	10.5	2500	694	Sierra, Nosler
50 SP	IMR-4227	12	2700	810	Hornady, Sierra
55 SP	2400	10	2300	646	Sierra
55 SP	IMR-4198	14	2500	763	Sierra
55 SP	IMR-4227	12.5	2500	763	Sierra
46 SP	FL		2760	778	Winchester

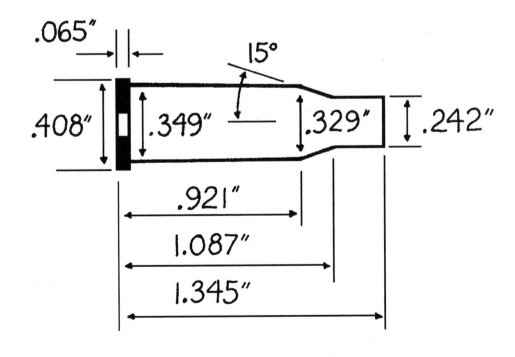

222 Remington

Historical Notes The 222 Remington was introduced by Remington in 1950 for the 722 bolt-action rifle which was later superseded by the current 700 series. For a short time, the Remington Model 760 pump-action repeater was also available in this caliber. Much of the credit for the 222 is due to Mike Walker, a longtime Remington employee. The cartridge became very popular with benchrest competitors in the 1970s and varmint hunters also found its performance excellent. But by the early 1990s the 222 Remington had lost much of its popularity to the 223 Remington.

General Comments The 222 Remington is in about the same class as the older 219 Zipper, but is rimless and adapted to modern bolt-action rifles. It is not based on any older case necked-down, but is of original design. It is a more or less scaled-down version of the 30-06, and fills the gap between the 218 Bee and the 220 Swift. It is well suited to the needs of the average person who desires a high-velocity 22. A great many benchrest matches have been won with the 222 Remington, and it has a reputation for superb accuracy. It is an excellent 200-yard cartridge for the full range of varmint and small game animals up to, but not including, deer. It has been outlawed for big game in many of the 50 states because, like the 220 Swift, you can't always depend on it to kill large animals humanely. I have seen several deer and antelope killed very cleanly with the 222 handloaded with heavier-jacketed 55- and 60-grain bullets. Range was about 125 yards. This caliber is offered by all large domestic ammunition manufacturers and several foreign companies.

222 Remington Loading Data and Factory Ballistics

Bullet (grains/type)	Powder	Grains	Velocity	Energy	Source/Comments
35 V-Max	H4198	22.0	3591	1000	Hodgdon
40 HP	IMR 4198	20	3300	967	Speer, Sierra
40 HP	W748	26.3	3400	1027	Speer, Sierra
45 SP	H335	24.5	3100	960	Hornady, Speer
45 SP	IMR 4198	21	3300	1088	Hornady, Speer, Sierra, Nosler
50 SP	W748	25.8	3100	1067	Speer, Sierra, Hornady
50 SP	RE 7	20.9	3150	1102	Hornady, Speer, Sierra
50 SP	IMR 4198	20	3200	1132	Speer, Hornady, Sierra
55 SP	H335	24	3200	1174	Sierra, Speer, Hornady, Nosler
55 SP	IMR 4320	25	3000	1099	Hornady, Speer
55 SP	IMR 4895	24.5	3000	1099	Speer, Hornady, Sierra
55	Varget	25.0	2095	1170	Hodgdon
60 HP	IMR 4895	23	2900	1121	Nosler, Hornady, Speer
50 SP	FL		3140	1094	Factory load
55 FMJ	FL		3020	1114	Factory load

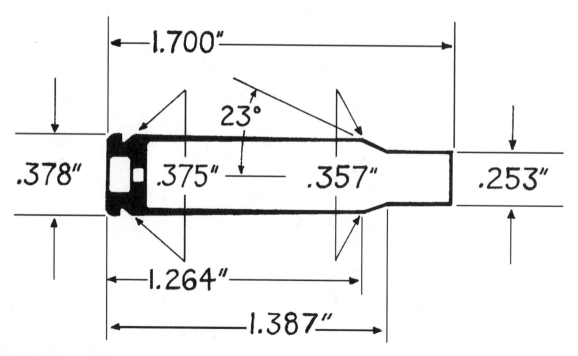

223 Remington (5.56x45mm)

Historical Notes The 223 Remington first appeared in 1957 as an experimental military cartridge for the Armalite AR-15 assault rifle. In 1964, it was officially adopted by the U.S. Army as the 5.56mm Ball cartridge M193. It is used in the selective-fire M16 rifle which is based on the original AR-15 design. The cartridge was the work of Robert Hutton, who was technical editor of *Guns & Ammo* magazine and had a rifle range in Topanga Canyon, California. One of the requirements for the cartridge was that the projectile have a retained velocity in excess of the speed of sound (about 1,080 fps at sea level) at 500 yards, something you could not achieve with the 222 Remington. Working with Gene Stoner of Armalite, Bob Hutton designed a case slightly longer than the 222 and had Sierra make a 55-grain boattail bullet. This combination met the design requirements. All this was documented in the 1971 issue of the *Guns & Ammo Annual*.

Originally an alternative military cartridge, the 223 (5.56x45mm) is now the official U.S. and NATO military round. Additional information will be found in Chapter 6 covering military cartridges. We should note here that NATO forces, including the United States, have standardized a new 5.56x45mm round with a heavy bullet and the M193 is no longer standard.

Shortly after the military adopted this cartridge, Remington brought out the sporting version, which has largely replaced both the 222 Remington and Remington Magnum in popularity. Practically every manufacturer of bolt-action rifles has at least one model chambered for the 223. In addition, there are a large number of military-type semi-auto rifles available in this caliber. At one time, the Remington Model 760 pump-action was available in 223.

General Comments The 223 Remington is nearly identical to the 222 Remington Magnum, the only difference being that the 223 has a slightly shorter case. The two are not interchangeable, although the 223 will chamber in a 222 Magnum rifle. The result, though, is to create a gross headspace condition, and the 223 case can rupture if fired in the 222 Magnum chamber.

The 223 has proven to be an effective military cartridge for fighting in jungle or forested areas and for close-in fire support, and has been improved lately by NATO with heavier (SS109 designed by FN of Belgium) bullets fired through fast-twist (1 in 7-inch) barrels. As a sporting round, it is just as accurate as any of the other long-range, centerfire 22s. Military brass cases are sometimes heavier than commercial cases, so maximum loads should be reduced by at least 10 percent and approached cautiously. That is because the reduced case capacity results in a higher loading density and, increased pressure with the same powder charge. The 223 Remington can be classed as an excellent medium-range varmint cartridge at ranges out to 250 yards.

In 1979, SAAMI cautioned shooters that 5.56x45mm military chambers and throats differ from 223 Remington sporting rifle chambers. Therefore military ball ammo may produce high chamber pressures in sporting rifles.

223 Remington Loading Data and Factory Ballistics

Bullet (grains/type)	Powder	Grains	Velocity	Energy	Source/Comments
40 SP	IMR 3031	25	3300	1140	Sierra, Speer
40 SP	IMR 4198	22	3200	995	Sierra, Speer
40 Nos BT	Varget	28.0	3674	1195	Hodgdon
45 SP	IMR 3031	25	3300	1162	Hornady, Sierra
45 SP	IMR 4198	22	3200	965	Hornady, Sierra, Speer
50 SP	IMR 3031	25.2	3250	1250	Sierra, Nosler, Hornady, Speer
50 SP	IMR 4198	21.5	3200	1155	Nosler, Hornady, Speer, Sierra
55 SP	IMR 3031	24.5	3200	1330	Hornady, Nosler, Sierra
55 SP	W748	25	3000	1110	Hornady, Nosler, Sierra
55	Varget	27.5	3384	1395	Hodgdon
60 HP	IMR 3031	24	3100	1130	Hornady, Sierra
80	Varget	25.0	2869	1460	Hodgdon
55 SP	FL		3240	1280	Factory load
55 FMJBT	FL		3250	1290	Military load
40 HP	FL		3650	1185	Federal factory load
60 HP	FL		3100	1280	Remington factory load
64 SP	FL		3020	1296	Winchester factory load
69 HP	FL		3000	1380	Federal factory load

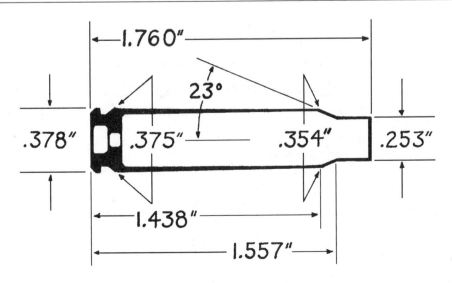

22 PPC

Historical Notes The 22 PPC was developed in 1974 by Dr. Louis Palmisano and Ferris Pindell, primarily as a benchrest cartridge. Although originally a wildcat, Sako of Finland introduced commercial rifles and ammunition late in 1987. Norma followed suit in 1993 with loaded ammunition. Since it is an American development, it is listed here as a current American rifle cartridge rather than as a European cartridge. The cartridge is based on the 220 Russian case which is a necked-down version of the 7.62x39mm Soviet military cartridge. The Wichita Engineering and Supply Co. made the first rifles for both the 22 and 6mm PPC cartridges. Many custom rifles have been turned out in this caliber. In 1993 Ruger announced their No. 1V and M77 varmint rifles in this caliber.

General Comments The originators altered the 220 Russian case by giving it a 10-degree body taper and 30-degree shoulder angle, as well as expanding the neck to accept the standard .224-inch diameter bullet used in the U.S. The cartridge cases are made in Finland by Sako or in Sweden by Norma and use Small Rifle primers. Although the 22 PPC is a short, rather stubby case only 1.51 inches long, it nevertheless develops ballistics superior to some larger, longer cartridges such as the 222 and 223 Remington. The 52-grain bullet can be pushed out of the muzzle at over 3,500 fps, and this definitely places the 22 PPC in the varmint and small game class. A 1 in 14-inch twist has become pretty much standard for these rifles, although 1 in 12-inch twist will sometimes be found.

22 PPC Loading Data and Factory Ballistics

Bullet (grains/type)	Powder	Grains	Velocity	Energy	Source/Comments
40 Nos BT	Varget	29.5	3560	1125	Hodgdon
52 HP	BL-C2	28.3	3400	1335	Speer
52 HP	W748	28.0	3300	1258	Speer, Nosler, Hornady
55 SP	H-335	27.0	3200	1251	Speer, Nosler
55 SP	W748	28.0	3200	1251	Hornady, Nosler, Speer
52 HP	FL		3400	1335	Sako factory load

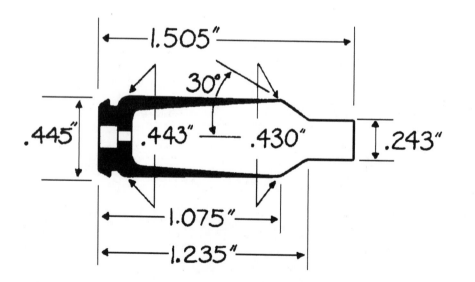

Sako Varmint (Heavy Barrel)

225 Winchester

Historical Notes The 225 Winchester was officially announced in June 1964. Both the standard and a heavier-barreled varmint version of the Model 70 bolt action were offered for this round. The 225 replaced the older 220 Swift in the Winchester lineup. It is a semi-rimmed case with an unusually large rim for this type of cartridge. The 220 Swift never achieved great popularity and neither did its replacement, the 225. The last Winchester catalog to list the cartridge as a caliber available for the Model 70 rifle was in 1972. No other manufacturer picked it up as a standard chambering because the already popular 22-250 was standardized by Remington in 1965, and it was just common sense to adopt the 22-250 instead. Winchester still loads 225 ammunition, but this cartridge did not have a very long life, being semi-obsolete in only eight years.

General Comments The 225 is a fine varmint cartridge with performance similar to the 224 Weatherby or the 22-250. But the 22-250 was already established as a popular wildcat with an outstanding reputation, and it was inevitable that it would dominate the field. Those who purchased 225 Winchester rifles have no need to feel bad or trade them off for anything else because the 225 cartridge is just as accurate and will do anything that the more popular 22-250 will do. It simply turned out to be a design or idea whose time had not yet arrived. As a matter of fact, it might be well to hang on to your 225 because not a great many were sold and eventually some gun writer will rediscover it as the greatest 22 varmint cartridge conceived by the mind of man, and at that point all your shooting friends will wish they had one, too. The 225 has an edge over both the 222 and the 223 Remington for long-range varmint shooting because of the increased muzzle velocity. At one time, Winchester was supposed to furnish a 50-grain loading at 3800 fps and a 60-grain at 3,500 fps, along with the standard 55-grain at 3650 fps (now reduced to 3570 fps), but these loads never materialized. For handloaders, this cartridge is nothing more than a slightly modified 30-30. Neck down the 30-30 to 22 caliber, shorten the case slightly, turn the rim to '06 dimensions and slightly improve and you have the 225 Winchester.

225 Winchester Loading Data and Factory Ballistics

Bullet (grains/type)	Powder	Grains	Velocity	Energy	Source/Comments
40 Speer SP	BL-C(2)	36.0	4020	1435	Hodgdon
40 HP	IMR 4064	31.5	3400	1027	Speer, Sierra
45 SP	IMR 4064	33	3600	1295	Hornady, Speer
50 SP	IMR 3031	31	3400	1284	Speer, Nosler, Hornady
50 SP	IMR 4895	33	3600	1439	Sierra
55 SP	IMR 4320	34.5	3700	1672	Hornady
60 HP	IMR 4064	31.8	3500	1632	Hornady
70 SP	IMR 4350	34.5	3000	1399	Speer
55 SP	FL		3570	1556	Winchester factory load

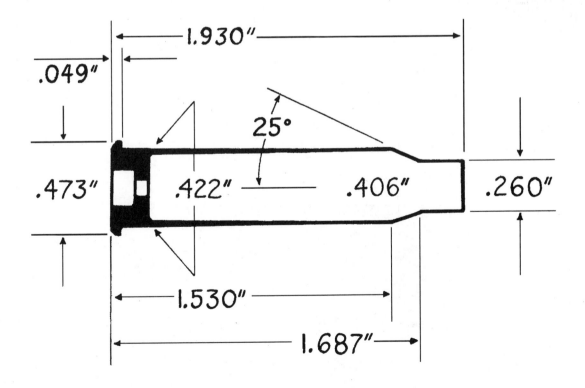

22-250 Remington (22 Varminter, 22 Wotkyns Original Swift)

Historical Notes The 22-250 Remington was adopted early in 1965 as one of the calibers for the Remington 700 series bolt-action rifles, and also for the Model 40XB match rifle. Browning bolt-action rifles were offered in 22-250 two years earlier. This is not a factory design, but rather a popular wildcat that has been around for many years and made good. However, Remington's adoption of the round moved it into the commercial classification.

There is some confusion regarding date of origin of the 22-250 which is based on the 250-3000 Savage case necked to 22-caliber. Its moniker is derived from the caliber (22) and the parent case name (250). The parent cartridge was introduced in 1915 and a 22 version may have been made up experimentally shortly thereafter. Harvey Donaldson, Grosvenor Wotkyns, J.E. Gebby, J.B. Smith and John Sweany all worked on versions of the 22-250 between 1934 and 1937. J.E. Gebby and J.B. Smith are usually credited with having developed the present configuration in 1937. However, there are different versions of this cartridge and much depends on which one is referred to. The Gebby version was named the 22 "Varminter," and he obtained a copyright on the name. Other gunsmiths renamed it the 22-250. The Wotkyns version was the forerunner of the 220 Swift, although Winchester ended up using the 6mm Lee Navy case rather than the 250 Savage.

At the present time, all of the major American and European rifle makers furnish bolt-action rifles in 22-250 chambering. In addition, the Ruger, Thompson/Center, and other single shots are available in this caliber.

General Comments The 22-250 is one of the best balanced and most flexible of the high-powered 22 centerfires. It is also the most popular of the long-range 22 varmint cartridges, effective to ranges of 400 yards or more. The 22-250 also has a reputation for outstanding accuracy and has been used with some success for benchrest shooting. Many individuals who have had experience with both the 22-250 and the 220 Swift report that the former gives significantly longer case life with full loads than the latter. The 22-250, as with most of the other high-powered 22s, is not recommended for use on deer or other medium game. The reason, of course, is that the light varmint bullets are made to expand quickly and will not offer sufficient penetration on a large animal. Based on personal experience, and purely as a matter of opinion, I would rate the 22-250 as the best all-round, long-range 22 varmint cartridge available today.

In a 2000 press release, Remington announced availability of electronic ignition 22-250 ammunition for use in its new EtronX rifle. The initial loading uses a 50-grain Hornady V-Max, polymer-tipped bullet. Owing to the unique primer, this ammunition will not work in a conventional rifle (conventional ammunition will not work in the EtronX rifle). Except for the primer, this ammunition uses conventional components.

22-250 Remington Loading Data and Factory Ballistics

Bullet (grains/type)	Powder	Grains	Velocity	Energy	Source/Comments
40 HP	IMR 4895	36	3900	1345	Speer, Sierra
40 HP	IMR 3031	35	3900	1345	Sierra, Speer
40	Varget	39.5	4135	1515	Hodgdon
45 SP	IMR 4064	37	3900	1520	Speer, Sierra
45 SP	IMR 3031	32	3500	1224	Hornady, Speer
50 SP	IMR 4064	36	3700	1520	Hornady, Speer, Sierra
50 SP	IMR 3031	34.5	3700	1520	Speer, Hornady, Sierra
55 SP	IMR 4064	35	3600	1580	Hornady, Speer, Sierra
55 SP	RL-7	29	3500	1496	Sierra
55 SP	IMR 4320	35	3500	1496	Nosler, Hornady, Sierra
60 HP	RL-7	28	3300	1451	Sierra
60 HP	IMR 4320	34	3500	1630	Hornady, Nosler, Sierra
70 SP	IMR 4064	33	3300	1690	Speer
70 SP	N205	41	3300	1690	NA
40 HP	FL		4000	1420	Federal factory load
55 SP	FL		3680	1655	Factory load

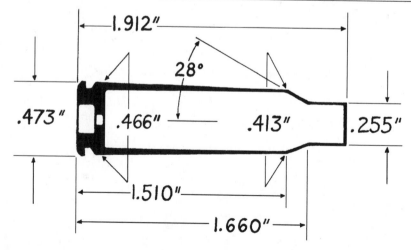

220 Swift

Historical Notes The 220 Swift was developed by Winchester and introduced in 1935 as a new caliber for the Model 54 bolt-action rifle. When the Model 70 Winchester bolt action was first issued in 1936, the 220 Swift was one of the standard calibers offered and continued to be until 1964, when it was discontinued. Now the Savage Model 112V, the Ruger Model 77 and the Ruger No. 1V single shot are offered in the 220 Swift chambering. The Model 70 Winchester is no longer made in this caliber. Norma of Sweden lists the 220 Swift with a 50-grain bullet at 4110 fps, and it also sells unprimed brass cases for reloading. Hornady/Frontier offers a 55-grain SP and a 60-grain HP loading.

The prototype for the 220 Swift was developed in 1934-35 by Grosvenor Wotkyns, who necked-down the 250-3000 Savage as a means of achieving very high velocities. However, the final commercial version developed by Winchester is based on the old 6mm Lee Navy cartridge necked-down. It is a semi-rimmed case.

General Comments The 220 Swift was and still is the fastest commercial cartridge in the world. It is also one of the most accurate super-velocity 22 cartridges ever developed. Its popularity has been somewhat retarded by the fact that ammunition in this caliber is expensive. Swift barrels have never been noted for long life, but this factor has been negated to a large degree by development of modern, erosion-resistant barrel steels since World War II. Factory ammunition has always featured the 48-grain and 50-grain bullets, but the Swift will handle the 55-grain or heavier bullets quite well, at slightly reduced maximum velocity. The 220 Swift is considered adequate on all animals up to deer-size. There is certainly plenty of field evidence to demonstrate that on occasion it will give fantastic one-shot kills on deer and antelope. However, the 220 Swift tends to be erratic in its performance on large animals, and most states will not permit its use on big game of any kind. Properly constructed bullets would almost certainly solve this problem on animals to mule deer size. In any case, factory bullets are designed for quick expansion on light animals. Most varmint hunters agree that the 220 Swift is the best varmint cartridge made. It remains sufficiently popular that various manufacturers occasionally chamber it.

In a 2000 press release, Remington announced availability of electronic ignition 220 Swift ammunition for use in its new EtronX rifle. The initial loading uses a 50-grain Hornady V-Max, polymer-tipped bullet. Owing to the unique primer, this ammunition will not work in a conventional rifle (conventional ammunition will not work in the EtronX rifle). Except for the primer, this ammunition uses conventional components.

220 Swift Loading Data and Factory Ballistics

Bullet (grains/type)	Powder	Grains	Velocity	Energy	Source/Comments
40 HP	IMR 4064	39	4000	1421	Speer, Sierra
40	Varget	40.5	4113	1500	Hodgdon
45 HP	IMR 4350	41.5	3600	1295	Hornady, Speer, Sierra
45 SP	IMR 3031	37	4000	1599	Hornady, Speer, Sierra
45 SP	IMR 4895	38.5	3900	1520	Sierra
45 SP	H-380	43	3850	1481	Speer, Sierra
50 SP	IMR 4320	39	4400	1689	Sierra
50 SP	IMR 3031	37	4000	1777	Sierra
55 SP	IMR 4350	44	3800	1764	Speer, Hornady
55 SP	IMR 4320	40	3000	1955	Sierra
55 SP	H-380	42	3800	1764	Nosler, Sierra, Speer
60 HP	IMR 4895	33	3400	1541	Hornady, Sierra
*48 SP	FL		4110	1800	Factory Load
50 SP	FL		4110	1877	Norma factory load
55 SP	FL		3650	1627	Hornady/Frontier factory load
60 HP	FL		3600	1727	Hornady/Frontier Factory load

* Discontinued loading.

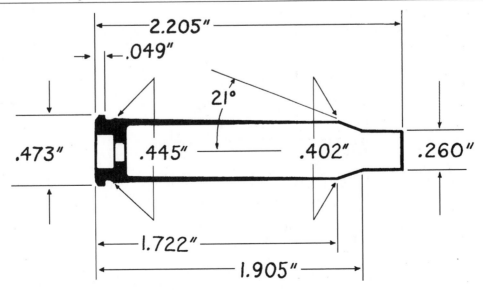

22 Accelerator

(30-30 version shown)

Historical Notes The 22 Accelerator is not a new cartridge, but rather a special loading of 30-30, and 30-06 cartridges using a sub-caliber .224-inch diameter bullet held in a discarding 30-caliber plastic sabot. These loadings were introduced by Remington, the 30-06 in 1977 and the 30-30 and the 308 in subsequent years. The 308 version has subsequently been dropped. All versions employ a 55-grain .224-caliber softpoint bullet retained in a 7-grain, six-fingered, plastic sabot with a hollow base. According to the 1979 Remington catalog, the rifling of the barrel imparts spin, which, combined with air resistance, causes the bullet and sabot to separate approximately 14 inches from the muzzle. The 30-30-224 Accelerator has a muzzle velocity of 3400 fps and the 30-06-224 the impressive muzzle velocity of 4080 fps. The existence of two different 30-caliber Accelerator rounds seems to indicate commercial success. Remington originally intended to offer other Accelerator calibers but these never materialized.

General Comments The author's experience shooting Accelerator cartridges indicated that accuracy is not as good as when the same 55-grain bullet is fired in one of the high-velocity centerfire 22 rifles, such as the 222 Remington, 22-250, etc. Most of these rifles, when properly tuned, will deliver minute-of-angle groups or better. Shooting at 100 yards and using various rifles, I was unable to print any groups with the 30-30 Accelerator that ran under 2 1/2 inches or under 2 inches with the 30-06 (five-shot groups). Actually, the Accelerator cartridges appear to group about the same as the standard 30-caliber cartridge does in the same rifle. This is just what the factory says it will do. In other words, if your rifle ordinarily makes 3-inch five-shot groups at 100 yards, it isn't going to do any better with the Accelerator. However, from a practical point of view, the Accelerator loads will allow one to use a regular 30-30 or 30-06 big game rifle for varmint shooting. The lack of MOA accuracy might restrict effective range to 200 yards or less, but this will vary greatly with individual rifles. The Accelerator concept is of greater usefulness to the shooter who does not reload than to the fellow who can cook up his own varmint loads with light 110-grain 30-caliber bullets. After firing, the plastic sabots are usually found anywhere from 40 to 100 feet in front of the muzzle. Remington has applied an old principle to modern sporting ammunition and come up with a very useful innovation.

Sabotted military loads, both as new loadings for old chamberings and for sabot-specific guns, are most effective. Likely, sabot-specific sporting guns could be accurate enough for sporting purposes and external ballistics could be most impressive.

The 308 Winchester version is now obsolete.

22 Accelerator Loading Data and Factory Ballistics

Bullet	Grains	Velocity	Energy	Source/Comments
30-30 Accelerator	55 SP	3400	1412	Remington factory load
30-06 Accelerator	55 SP	4080	2033	Remington factory load

30-06

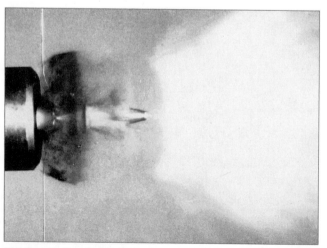

Remington Accelerator bullet leaving muzzle at 4080 feet per second.

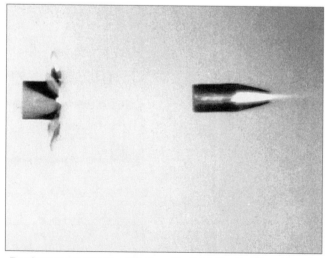

Remington Accelerator sabot and bullet 18 inches from muzzle.

223 Winchester Super Short Magnum

Historical Notes Announced in 2002, the 223 WSSM is intended to deliver a new level of long-range performance and accuracy to the 223 family of chamberings. Cartridge overall length is 2.36 inches, a half-inch shorter than the 2.8-inch length of existing short-action cartridges. The 223 WSSM will be chambered in super short rifle actions, which should improve receiver stiffness and accuracy. A new Browning bolt-action rifle, the Super Short Magnum A-Bolt, weights six pounds, and uses a shorter action for the 2.36-inch cartridge. Winchester Firearms also plans a shorter-action rifle for this round, the Winchester Super Short Magnum Model 70.

General Comments The 223 WSSM case does not employ a belt; it headspaces on the case shoulder. For efficient and consistent powder burning, it retains the short-fat cartridge case geometry of the Winchester Short Magnum line. Cartridges will be available in three bullet types: 55-grain Ballistic Silvertip and Pointed Soft Point, and 64-grain Power-Point. WSSM velocities are targeted at roughly 200 fps faster than the 22-250 Remington offerings. It is suitable for long-range varmint shooting, and for light thin-skinned game, a good combination cartridge with light recoil.

223 Winchester Super Short Magnum Factory Ballistics

Bullet (grains/type)	Powder	Grains	Velocity	Energy	Source/Comments
55 BST	FL		3850	1810	Winchester/Olin
55 PSP	FL		3850	1810	Winchester/Olin
64 PP	FL		3600	1841	Winchester/Olin

6mm PPC

Historical Notes The 6mm PPC is an outgrowth of the 22 PPC and based on the same case configuration with the neck expanded to take 6mm (.243-inch) bullets. This cartridge was also developed by Dr. Louis Palmisano and Ferris Pindell and based on the 220 Russian case, which is a variation of the 7.62x39mm (M43) Soviet military cartridge. The original rifles were made by Wichita Engineering and Supply Co. in 1975. Many custom rifles have been made up in this caliber in both sporter and benchrest types. Although originally a benchrest wildcat, Sako of Finland began turning out commercial bolt-action rifles and supplying loaded ammunition late in 1987. In 1993, Ruger announced that its M77 Varmint and No. 1 Varmint rifles would be offered in this caliber, and at the same time, Norma announced factory-loaded ammunition. The 6mm PPC is one of the top competitive benchrest cartridges. In addition to loaded ammunition and factory cases, many handloaders make their own cases by fireforming 220 Russian cases or necking-down and reforming 7.62x39mm brass.

General Comments Chronograph tests by various individuals have demonstrated that the 6mm PPC gives very uniform velocity readings, which accounts for its fine accuracy. On the other hand, practically all rifles chambered for the cartridge are heavy-barrel accuracy jobs, and that must also be a factor. Rifles for match shooting usually have a 1 in 14-inch twist, although a few are turned out with a 1 in 12-inch twist. The 6mm PPC is not only an outstanding benchrest cartridge, but gives very good results on small game and varmints. It is only slightly less powerful than the 243 Winchester, despite the much smaller case. It should also do well on deer or antelope at moderate ranges. The velocity with the 90-grain bullet is only some 100 to 150 fps less than the 243 Winchester. Popularity of this caliber is growing beyond benchrest shooting; varmint hunters are now taking it up as well. Look for continued growth here.

6mm PPC Loading Data and Factory Ballistics

Bullet (grains/type)	Powder	Grains	Velocity	Energy	Source/Comments
60 Sierra HP	H4895	29.0	3218	1375	Hodgdon
60 HP	H322	28.4	3200	1365	Sierra
70 HP	H335	29	3100	1494	Hornady, Sierra
75 HP	H-322	26.7	3100	1601	Hornady, Speer, Sierra
80 SP	W748	29	2800	1393	Speer
85 SP	H-335	28.0	3000	1699	Speer
90 SP	H-335	29	3000	1799	Speer
70 SP	FL		3140	1535	Sako factory load

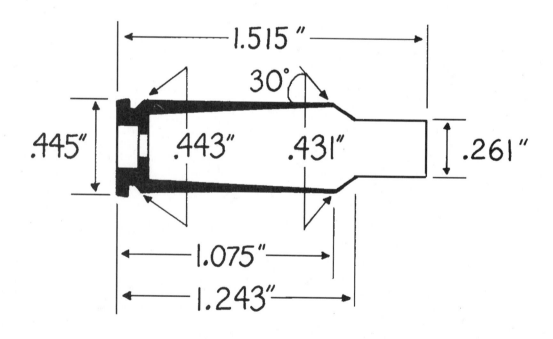

6mm Norma BR

Historical Notes In February 1996, Norma introduced this "new" cartridge. While case dimensions are identical to the 6mm BR Remington, chambering specifications differ. Remington perceived this cartridge as a traditional benchrest number. Therefore, they designed chambering specifications around bullets of about 70 grains. Conversely, with considerable prodding from the late Roger Johnston, Norma recognized the long-range target potential of this basic case. They standardized a chambering specification appropriate for very low drag (VLD) bullets exceeding 100 grains. Therefore, the Norma chamber has a much longer neck. While there are no case differences, CIP (the European counterpart to SAAMI) requires a new designation for any cartridge or chambering differing in any way from any previous version. Therefore, Norma was required to apply a new name.

General Comments While the 6mm BR Remington has failed to become a world-beater in traditional benchrest, with heavy VLD bullets, Norma's version has established itself as a force to be reckoned with in the long-range game. It is also a superior long-range varminting choice. Given a 28-inch barrel and loaded with any of the better 95- to 115-grain VLD moly-plated bullets, this cartridge can achieve sufficient velocity for 1000-yard benchrest shooting. Owing to the high BCs of these bullets, 1000-yard retained velocity is surprisingly high—often exceeding 1400 fps.

For cartridges of this genre, such loads generate unusually light recoil, which contributes to precise shooting. However, unless conditions are unusually good, those using larger-bored rifles usually fare better. While those rifles generate more recoil, which effectively reduces intrinsic accuracy, the longer bullets exhibit less wind drift and, therefore, reduce the error associated with imperfections in the shooter's ability to properly dope the wind.

6mm Norma BR

Bullet (grains/type)	Powder	Grains	Velocity	Energy	Source/Comments
68 Berger Match	N202	32.0	3393	1735	Norma (26-inch Bbl)
80 Hornady	N203	32.1	3232	1855	Norma (26-inch Bbl)
95 Nosler	N203	30.1	2914	1790	Norma (26-inch Bbl)

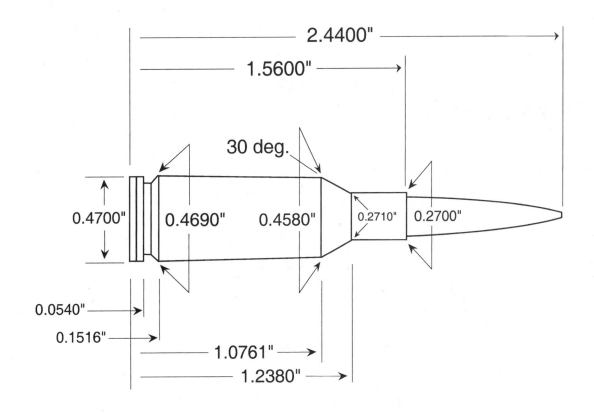

243 Winchester

Historical Notes The 243 Winchester was introduced by Winchester in 1955 for their Model 70 bolt-action and Model 88 lever-action rifles. The 243 was quickly adopted by Savage for their Model 99 lever- and Model 110 bolt-action rifles. All of the British and European manufacturers began chambering bolt-action rifles for this round. In fact, even Remington, who developed their own 6mm, had to recognize the popularity of the 243 and start chambering their rifles for it. The 243 (6mm) Winchester is nothing more than the 308 Winchester case necked-down. Original development and publicity was due largely to the efforts of gun writer, the late Warren Page, who along with other wildcatters worked out a similar version before Winchester. The 243 is probably chambered in more different rifles than any other cartridge, except possibly the 30-06 Springfield. All other manufacturers of rifles offer this caliber.

General Comments The 243 Winchester represents a successful effort to develop a light deer rifle caliber that could hold its own with the high-velocity 22s for long-range use on small targets and still be adequate for larger animals. The 243 does this job well. It eliminates the need to own two different rifles for anything from small game and pests up to and including deer and antelope. The 80-grain bullet is intended primarily for varmint and small game and the 100-grain bullet for deer-size animals. The 257 Roberts and the 250-3000 Savage are supposed to cover the same range and certainly do. All major domestic and overseas manufacturers of commercial ammunition offer this caliber. Its popularity as a deer caliber has prevailed over its varmint capabilities.

(***Editor's note:*** *The 243 has garnered a reputation among ballisticians for erratic performance. Handloaders should keep this firmly in mind.*)

In a 2000 press release, Remington announced availability of electronic ignition 243 Winchester ammunition for use in its new EtronX rifle. The initial loading uses a 90-grain Nosler Ballistic Tip bullet. Owing to the unique primer, this ammunition will not work in a conventional rifle (conventional ammunition will not work in the EtronX rifle). Except for the primer, this ammunition uses conventional components.

243 Winchester Loading Data and Factory Ballistics

Bullet (grains/type)	Powder	Grains	Velocity	Energy	Source/Comments
55 Nos BT	H4895	44.5	4058	2010	Hodgdon
75 HP	IMR 4064	40	3300	1814	Hornady, Speer
80 SP	IMR 4320	38	3000	1599	Speer, Hornady
85 SP	H-380	38.5	3100	1814	Sierra
90 SP	IMR 4831	44	3000	1799	Speer, Sierra
95 SP	IMR 3031	35	2900	1775	Nosler
100 SP	IMR 4350	42	2900	1868	Sierra, Hornady
80 SP	FL		3550	1993	Factory load
85 SP	FL		3320	2080	Factory load
100 SP	FL		2960	1945	Factory load
105 SP	FL		3100	2133	Factory load

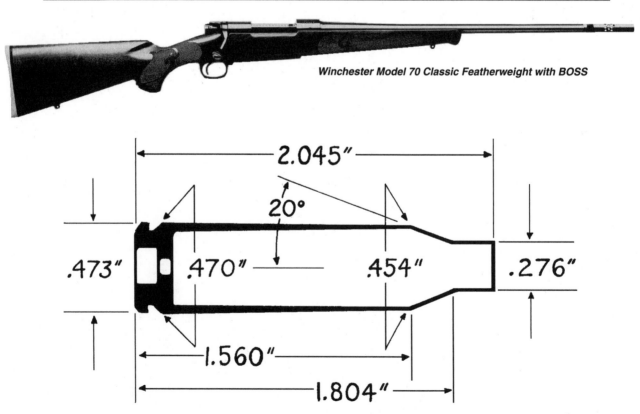

Winchester Model 70 Classic Featherweight with BOSS

6mm Remington (244 Remington)

Historical Notes The 6mm Remington has exactly the same case dimensions as the 244 Remington. They differ only in the fact that the 6mm Remington is loaded with bullets of up to 100 grains, whereas the 244 Remington was never loaded with bullets of more than 90 grains. Ammunition marked 244 Remington can be fired in 6mm Remington chambers and vice versa. However, rifles marked 244 Remington will not always stabilize the 100-grain bullet. The difference in the two is that 244 rifles (if manufactured by Remington) have a 1 in 12-inch rifling twist and rifles marked 6mm have a 1 in 9-inch twist. When Remington introduced the 244 in 1955, it selected the 1 in 12-inch twist as best suited to long-range accuracy with bullets of 75-90 grains. That was correct, except that most shooters wanted to be able to use bullets of 100 to 105 grains in order to cover the range of game from varmints through deer with the same rifle. To correct this misjudgment, Remington renamed the cartridge 6mm Remington and changed to a 1:9 twist. To have retained the 244 designation and simply changed the twist would have brought on complaints from purchasers of the original 244s with the slower twist when they tried to use the new 100-grain

load. The change in cartridge nomenclature to 6mm and the faster twist occurred in 1963. The Remington 700 series and 788 bolt-action rifles as well as the firm's autoloaders and the slide actions have been available in 6mm.

General Comments The original 6mm Remington was loaded only with the 100-grain bullet. However, it is now available with 80-, 90- and 100-grain bullets, which greatly extends its flexibility. Although the older 244 lost out to the 243 Winchester, the 6mm Remington is gradually picking up a following. It is an excellent choice for the varmint hunter who also wants to use his rifle for deer and antelope. Although the 6mm has a slightly larger powder capacity than the 243, the difference in performance is negligible as far as killing power is concerned. Nevertheless, this small advance in ballistics appeals to some people and so does the longer neck of the 6mm case, which many handloaders consider desirable. This caliber is commercially loaded by Federal and Winchester as well as Remington.

6mm Remington Loading Data and Factory Ballistics

Bullet (grains/type)	Powder	Grains	Velocity	Energy	Source/Comments
55 Nos BT	H4895	45.5	4115	2065	Hodgdon
60 HP	H-335	42	3700	1824	Sierra
70 SP	IMR 4350	47	3400	1797	Sierra, Hornady
75 HP	IMR 4064	41	3500	2041	Speer, Nosler
75 HP	IMR 4350	47	3450	1983	Nosler, Speer, Sierra
80 SP	IMR 4350	45	3200	1820	Hornady
80 SP	IMR 4831	47	3200	1820	Hornady, Speer
90 HP	IMR 4350	45	3200	2047	Speer, Sierra
90 HP	IMR 4831	45	3100	1921	Speer, Sierra
100 SP	IMR 4350	42	2900	1868	Hornady, Speer, Sierra, Nosler
100 SP	IMR 4831	44	2900	1868	Speer, Sierra, Hornady
100	H1000	51.0	3111	2145	Hodgdon
105 SP	IMR 4350	42	2950	2030	Speer
105 SP	IMR 4064	37	2900	1961	Speer
80 SP	FL		3470	2139	Factory load
90 SP	FL		3190	2133	Factory load
100 SP	FL		3100	2133	Factory load

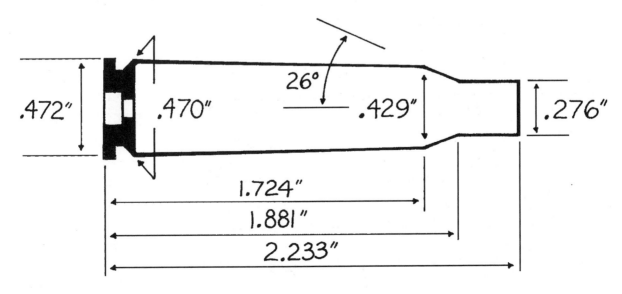

243 Winchester Super Short Magnum (243 WSSM)

Historical Notes Announced in 2002, the 243 WSSM is intended to deliver a new level of long-range performance and accuracy to the 243 family of chamberings. Cartridge overall length is 2.36 inches, a half-inch shorter than the 2.8-inch length of existing short-action cartridges. The 243 WSSM will be chambered in super short rifle actions, which should improve receiver stiffness and accuracy. A new Browning bolt-action rifle, the Super Short Magnum A-Bolt, weighs six pounds, and uses a shorter action for the 2.36 length cartridge. Winchester Firearms also plans a shorter-action rifle for this round, the Winchester Super Short Magnum Model 70.

General Comments The 243 WSSM case does not employ a belt — it headspaces on the case shoulder. For efficient and consistent powder burning, it retains the short-fat cartridge case geometry of the Winchester Short Magnum line. Cartridges will be available in three bullet types: 55-grain Ballistic Silvertip, 95-grain Ballistic Silvertip, and 100-grain Power Point. The 243 WSSM shares the same basic cartridge case with the 223 WSSM, also announced in 2002. Like its small-diameter brother, it is suitable for long-range varmint shooting, and for light thin-skinned game — a good combination cartridge with light recoil.

243 Winchester Super Short Magnum Factory Ballistics

Bullet (grains/type)	Powder	Grains	Velocity	Energy	Source/Comments
55 BST	FL		4060	2013	Winchester/Olin
95 BST	FL		3250	2258	Winchester/Olin
100 PP	FL		3110	2147	Winchester/Olin

240 Weatherby Magnum

Historical Notes The 240 Weatherby was added to round out the Weatherby proprietary magnum line in 1968. It differs from other 6mms in having a belted case with somewhat greater powder capacity. It is very similar to the 240 Belted Rimless Nitro-Express introduced by Holland & Holland around 1923. Thus far, it is available only in the Weatherby Mark V bolt-action rifle or through custom gunsmiths. It is an excellent cartridge and will push the 100-grain 6mm bullet with about 200 fps greater muzzle velocity than the 6mm Remington and around 300 fps faster than the 243 Winchester. However, a considerable portion of this ballistic advantage results from increased barrel length and loading pressure. It is important to allow plenty of barrel cooling time with this, and all, high-intensity cartridges. The principal detraction regarding the 240 Weatherby Magnum is that ammunition is expensive and difficult to find. The 240 case has about the same capacity as the 30-06 and rim diameter is also the same.

General Comments The 240 Weatherby is among the most powerful of the 6mm cartridges. It represents the maximum performance that one can squeeze through a 6mm tube with modern powders. The 244 H&H Belted Rimless Magnum, based on necking-down the 375 H&H Magnum case, will hold more powder but doesn't produce any improvement in ballistics. The late Roy Weatherby built a successful proprietary gun business on the basis of a good product plus the all-important element of ballistic one-upmanship. The Weatherby magnum cartridges have traditionally offered higher velocity and energy than their standard factory counterpart. The 240 was born of this same tradition. Of course, Remington, Winchester, Norma, etc., have their own magnum lines in various calibers, and Winchester offered the 300 and 375 H&H Magnums before World War II. However, Roy Weatherby was the first to really popularize this British innovation in the United States. He convinced the American shooters that it was something they truly needed.

240 Weatherby Magnum Loading Data and Factory Ballistics

Bullet (grains/type)	Powder	Grains	Velocity	Energy	Source/Comments
60 HP	IMR 4350	53	3800	1924	Sierra
70 HP	IMR 4350	52	3700	2128	Hornady, Nosler
75 HP	IMR 4320	50.5	3800	2405	Hornady
80 SP	IMR 4831	52.5	3500	2177	Hornady, Speer
85 SP	IMR 4350	51	3450	2247	Nosler, Speer, Sierra
90 SP	IMR 4831	52	3400	2311	Speer, Hornady, Sierra
95 SP	IMR 4350	47	3050	1963	Nosler
100 SP	IMR 4831	52	3300	2419	Hornady
105 SP	IMR 4831	49.5	3150	2314	Speer
70 HP	FL		3850	2304	Weatherby factory load
87 SP	FL		3500	2366	Weatherby factory load
100 SP	FL		3395	2559	Weatherby factory load

25-20 Winchester (25-20 WCF)

Historical Notes The 25-20 Winchester Center Fire was developed for the short action of the Winchester Model 1892 lever-action rifle. The case is based on the 32-20 necked-down. There is a difference in opinion as to when it was actually introduced. Some authorities say 1893, others 1895. In any event, it was quickly adopted by a majority of the gun manufacturers and achieved considerable popularity. The Winchester lever-action 1892 and modernized Model 65, Remington pump-action Model 25, Marlin pump-action 27 and lever-action Model 94, and the Savage bolt-action repeater Model 23, were all available in 25-20 WCF. Marlin has reintroduced the 25-20 WCF in their Model 1894CL lever action. Winchester also loaded this same chambering with a slightly different bullet shape and headstamped it 25-20 Marlin.

General Comments Prior to the 22 Hornet and the 218 Bee, the 25-20 WCF was one of the most popular small game and varmint cartridges. It was also advertised as being suitable for deer and similar animals. No doubt it has killed plenty of deer, but it is not a satisfactory big game cartridge by any standard. Today, it is universally outlawed for big game hunting. On smaller animals, the 60-grain bullet is quite effective for 100- to 150-yard varmint shooting. The 86-grain softpoint or lead bullet does a fine job on rabbit or turkey to 125 yards. A great many rifles were made in this caliber and are still in use by trappers, ranchers and farmers. Under certain conditions, the 25-20 repeater is still a useful small game

number. It will probably be around for a good many more years. With the growing popularity of Cowboy Action Shooting, the 25-20 is destined for renewed popularity.

The 25-20 is another old-timer the author has played around with at various times. Ownership of a Winchester Model 1892 lever action and later a Winchester Low Wall single shot in this caliber allowed ample opportunity to test its potential for small game and varmint hunting. It will do the job, but has serious range limitations due in part to bullet design. The 60-grain high-velocity load achieves its maximum expansion at a range of between 50 and 70 yards. Beyond that, good bullet placement is essential for quick kills. At ranges out to 50 yards, bullet expansion will ruin most of the edible meat on small game. The 86-grain bullet is a better load for meat hunting, although the lower velocity requires good distance judgment at ranges much beyond 75 yards.

On the other hand, the 25-20 is one of those cartridges that can be improved to a satisfying degree by handloading. The 86-grain bullet can be loaded to deliver around 1,700 fps, but the 60-grain bullet can't be improved much over the factory load. The 25-20 is also capable of very good accuracy when fired in a single shot or bolt-action rifle. My Winchester single shot would do better than 2-inch groups at 100 yards with handloads. Both Winchester and Remington continue to offer this caliber only with the 86-grain bullet.

25-20 Winchester (25 WCF) Loading Data and Factory Ballistics

Bullet (grains/type)	Powder	Grains	Velocity	Energy	Source/Comments
60 Win OPE	680	13.0	2300	700	Hodgdon
60 SP	2400	9.6	2200	645	Hornady
60 SP	H-4227	11	2200	645	Hornady
60 SP	FL		2250	675	Factory load
86 SP	FL		1460	407	Factory load

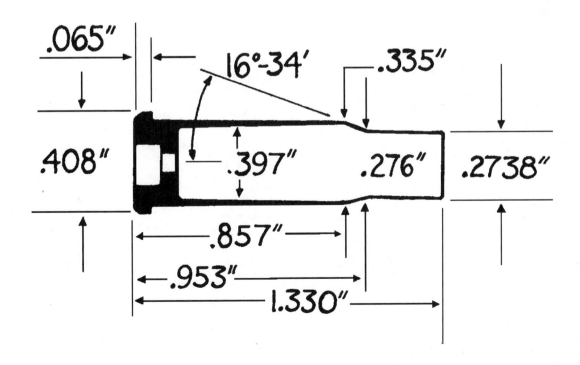

25-35 Winchester
(25-35 WCF)

Historical Notes The 25-35 was developed by Winchester and introduced in 1895 for the Model 94 lever-action rifle. Along with the 30-30, it was one of the first small-bore, smokeless powder, sporting cartridges developed in the United States. Winchester, Marlin and Savage all chambered repeating lever-action rifles for this cartridge. Quite a few single-shot rifles also chambered the 25-35, and in Europe it was used in combination-type arms. No American rifles have been made for the 25-35 since the end of World War II.

General Comments The 25-35 is one of the most accurate cartridges available in the older lever-action rifles. In a good solid-frame single-shot, it will shoot about as accurately as any 25 ever developed. It does not have sufficient velocity for long-range

shooting. It has never been noted for great stopping power on deer or similar animals. In fact it is illegal for this purpose in many states. There are still a large number of 25-35 rifles in use, but it is more or less obsolete. It is not nearly as effective as the 250-3000 Savage, 257 Roberts or any of the more modern 6mm cartridges. However, it does have moderate recoil and will do a good job on small game and varmints at medium ranges. Modern powders would allow significant ballistic improvement if loads were at the same pressure as the current 30-30 factory ammunition. Loaded thus, this cartridge might not appear quite so anemic and would be better suited to deer hunting. Ackley's improved version provides impressive performance. Winchester is the only remaining manufacturer of this ammunition.

25-35 Winchester (25 WCF) Loading Data and Factory Ballistics

Bullet (grains/type)	Powder	Grains	Velocity	Energy	Source/Comments
60 SP	IMR 4064	30.5	2800	1045	Hornady
60 SP	IMR 4320	32	2900	1120	Hornady
117 SP	IMR 3031	25.5	2300	1375	Hornady
117 SP	IMR 4320	27	2200	1258	Hornady
117 SP	FL		2230	1292	Winchester factory load

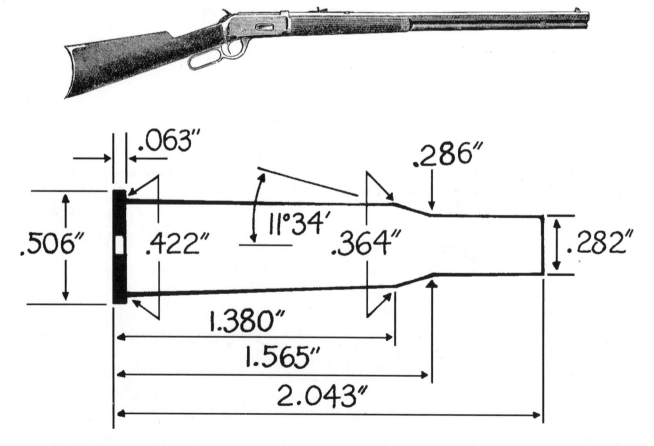

Winchester Repeating Rifle, Model 1894.

Made For .25-35 And .30 W. C. F., .32 W. S., .32-40 And .38-55 Cartridges.

250 Savage (250-3000)

Historical Notes Designed by Charles Newton, the 250 Savage was introduced by the Savage Arms Co. as a high-velocity round for the Model 99 lever-action rifle. The original loading used an 87-grain bullet at 3,000 fps muzzle velocity, and Savage named it the 250-3000. One suspects the 87-grain bullet was chosen because it could be safely driven at 3,000 fps with the powders then available. This allowed Savage to introduce it with the ever-so-sexy name 250-3000. Remember in 1915, when this cartridge was introduced, riflemen were still marveling at cartridges achieving 2000 fps. About 1932, the 100-grain bullet load was marketed by Peters Cartridge Co. and later the velocity of the 87-grain bullet was slightly increased. Now it is simply called the 250 Savage. The Savage Model 20 and 40 bolt-action rifles also chambered the round, as did the Winchester Model 54 and 70 bolt actions. Late in 1971, Savage announced that the Model 99 would again be available in this caliber. Others, such as Ruger and Remington, have made rifles in this caliber also.

General Comments Flat trajectory, outstanding accuracy and good killing power on anything up to and including deer are established characteristics of the 250 Savage. It was, and is, excellent on varmints through deer. In the past few years, it has been edged out by the 257 Roberts and the new 6mm cartridges. It is far superior as a deer cartridge to the 30-30 or anything in that class, regardless of what some 30-30 addicts claim. Because of its light recoil, it is an excellent choice for youths and women. The 250-3000 is the basis of one of Ackley's best wildcats, the 250 Ackley Improved. Both Remington and Winchester continue to load this caliber. However, the 87-grain and 120-grain bullets are no longer factory loaded.

250 Savage (250-3000) Loading Data and Factory Ballistics

Bullet (grains/type)	Powder	Grains	Velocity	Energy	Source/Comments
60 Hdy SP	H4895	40.0	3667	1790	Hodgdon
60 SP	IMR 4064	39	3500	1632	Hornady
87 SP	IMR 4895	36.5	3200	1979	Sierra
87 SP	IMR 4064	35	3100	1857	Sierra
100 SP	IMR 4320	36	2800	1741	Nosler
117 SP	IMR 4064	32.5	2700	1894	Hornady
87 SP	FL		3030	1770	Factory load
100 SP	FL		2820	1765	Factory load
120 SP	FL		2645	1865	Factory load

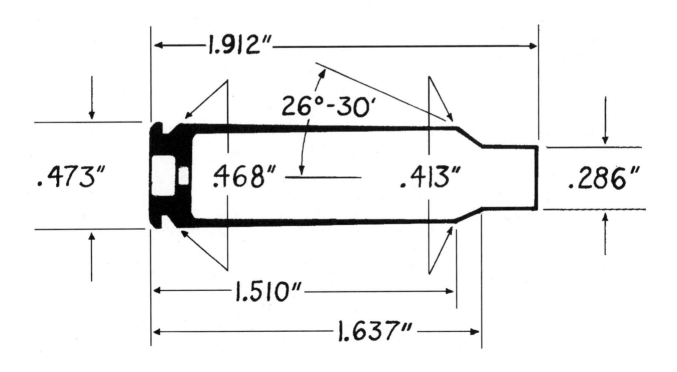

257 Roberts (257 Roberts +P)

Historical Notes The commercial version of the 257 Roberts was released by Remington in 1934 chambered in its Model 30 bolt-action rifle. It was quickly picked up by Winchester for its Model 54 and the later Model 70. The Remington 722 bolt-action and the 760 pump-action models were also available in 257-caliber. In recent years, many American manufacturers have discontinued it, although Ruger continues to offer it in the Model 77 bolt action. The original cartridge was designed by N.H. Roberts (a well-known experimenter and gun writer during the 1920s and '30s) and is based on the 7x57mm Mauser necked-down. Remington changed the Roberts' shoulder angle from 15 to 20 degrees. The name of the cartridge was adopted to honor its original developer. Custom rifles in this caliber were made by the Niedner Rifle Co. as early as 1928.

General Comments The 257 Roberts has often been referred to as the "most useful rifle cartridge ever developed." That is not very far wrong. It is suitable for a wide range of hunting under a variety of conditions. As a long-range varmint cartridge, it is as good as they come, being only slightly inferior to the newer 6mms. On deer,

antelope, black bear, sheep or goat, it is as good as any other cartridge available. Naturally, it is not as powerful as the 270 Winchester or 30-06, but it has ample power for the game mentioned at all practical ranges.

The 257 was underloaded by ammunition companies. However, in the late 1980s, higher pressure +P loads were introduced, which enabled factory-loaded 257 Roberts ammunition to reach full potential. With modern powders, the handloader can improve performance safely in all bullet weights. With 117- or 120-grain boattail bullets at velocities of around 2,800 fps, the 257 can be used successfully on elk and caribou. It is at this end of the scale that it has an advantage over the 6mms. The author has used it for many years and it is one of his favorite calibers for western hunting.

Ackley's improved version of the 257 Roberts practically duplicates the ballistics of the longer 25-06. Winchester, Federal and Remington all offer this cartridge. The 87- and 100-grain bullets are no longer factory loaded.

257 Roberts (257 Roberts +P) Loading Data and Factory Ballistics

Bullet (grains/type)	Powder	Grains	Velocity	Energy	Source/Comments
60 Hdy SP	H335	46.0	3885	2010	Hodgdon
60 SP	IMR 4064	44	3600	1727	Hornady
75 HP	IMR 4064	42	3300	1814	Sierra
75 Hdy HP	H4895	44.0	3561	2110	Hodgdon
87 SP	IMR 4320	37.5	3000	1739	Hornady
87 SP	H-380	46	3200	1979	Sierra, Hornady
100 SP*	IMR 4831	45.5	3100	2134	Nosler, Speer
100 SP	IMR 3031	34	2800	1741	Hornady, Sierra
117 SP	IMR 4320	36	2600	1757	Sierra
117 SP	IMR 4064	34.5	2600	1757	Hornady, Sierra
120 SP*	IMR 4831	42.5	2800	2091	Nosler
120 SP	IMR 4350	38.5	2600	1802	Hornady
87 SP	FL		3200	1980	+P factory load
100 SP	FL		3000	1998	+P factory load
117 SP	FL		2780	2009	+P factory load
120 SP	FL		2645	1865	Factory load

* +P data

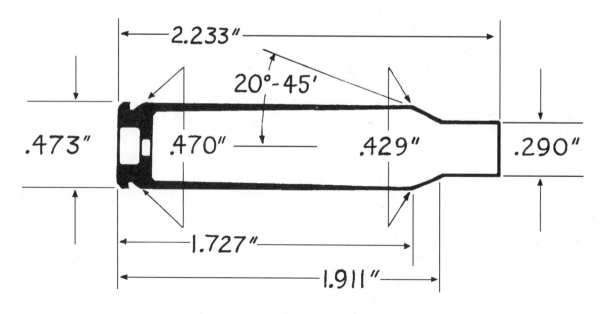

25 Winchester Super Short Magnum

Historical Notes Tailored for use in a shorter action rifles, the 25 WSSM uses a short and fat cartridge case to equal 25-06 ballistics with 14-percent less powder and less perceived recoil. Winchester® significantly re-directed the shape of magnum cartridges through the 2000 introduction of the Winchester short magnum and later, the Winchester super short magnum families. Introduced in 2005, the 25 WSSM is intended as a versatile, dual purpose (varmint and medium game) hunting cartridge.

General Comments The WSSM case is a half-inch shorter than the Winchester Short Magnum cases used for the 300, 7mm and 270 WSM cartridges. The "short and fat" design improves interior ballistics of the 25 WSSM cartridge. Exposing more propellant surface area to the primer results in more consistent ignition. The beltless cartridge case headspaces off the shoulder to provide better centering of the bullet in the chamber. Winchester and Browning super short rifle actions for this cartridge are stiffer, reducing accuracy inhibiting vibrations. Winchester offers 25 WSSM unprimed cartridge cases for reloaders.

25 Winchester Super Short Magnum Loading Data and Factory Ballistics

Bullet (grains/type)	Powder	Grains	Velocity	Energy	Source/Comments
85 BST	FL		3470	2273	Winchester
120 AccuBond	FL		3100	2347	Winchester
115 BST	FL		3060	2392	Winchester
120 PEP	FL		2990	2383	Winchester
75 V-Max	BL-C(2)	49.3	3775		Hodgdon
85 Nos BT	BL-C(2)	47.5	3547		Hodgdon
100 Spr BT	H4350	48.5C	3233		Hodgdon
120 SP	H414	44.7	2985		Hodgdon

25-06 Remington

Historical Notes The 25-06, originally a wildcat cartridge, was picked up by Remington and added to its commercial line late in 1969. The wildcat version dates back to 1920, when it was introduced by A.O. Niedner. Remington has stuck to his original configuration of simply necking-down the 30-06 case. The Remington Model 700 series bolt-action rifles were the first to be offered in the newly-adopted caliber. At the present time, Remington, Interarms, Ruger, Savage, Winchester, Weatherby, Sako and almost every other manufacturer of bolt-action rifles offer at least one version in 25-06. In addition, the Ruger single shot is available in this caliber. This round became a very popular number, but that has waned recently.

General Comments The 25-06 is a fine 25-caliber wildcat. Its emergence as a standardized factory load was welcomed by many.

As a varmint cartridge with the 87-grain bullet, some have claimed it is unsurpassed. However, a comparison of factory ballistics and a little chronographing can be most informative. Comparing factory data, we see that as a varmint cartridge, both the 6mm Remington and 270 Winchester beat anything the 25-06 can offer in every category that matters. Amazingly, in spite of its much smaller case, the 6mm Remington, 100-grain load is only marginally behind the 25-06, 120-grain load in retained energy at long range. There really isn't any comparison between hunting loads in the 25-06 and the 270 Win. Chronograph results suggest that factory data is equally representative of what each can realistically do. So just exactly what does the 25-06 offer? Evidently something, because many laud the 25-06 as among the best. Federal, Winchester and Remington offer this cartridge in several bullet weights.

25-06 Remington Loading Data and Factory Ballistics

Bullet (grains/type)	Powder	Grains	Velocity	Energy	Source/Comments
75 Hdy V-Max	H4350	62.0	3700	2275	Hodgdon
75 HP	IMR 4350	55	3500	2041	Hornady, Sierra
87 SP	IMR 4831	57	3500	2367	Hornady
100 SP	IMR 4831	54.5	3300	2419	Sierra, Speer
120 SP	IMR 4064	44	3000	2399	Hornady
120 SP	IMR 4831	50	3000	2399	Nosler, Speer
87 SP	FL		3500	2370	Factory load
90 SP	FL		3440	2364	Factory load
100 SP	FL		3230	2316	Factory load
117 SP	FL		2990	2320	Factory load
120 SP	FL		2940	2382	Factory load

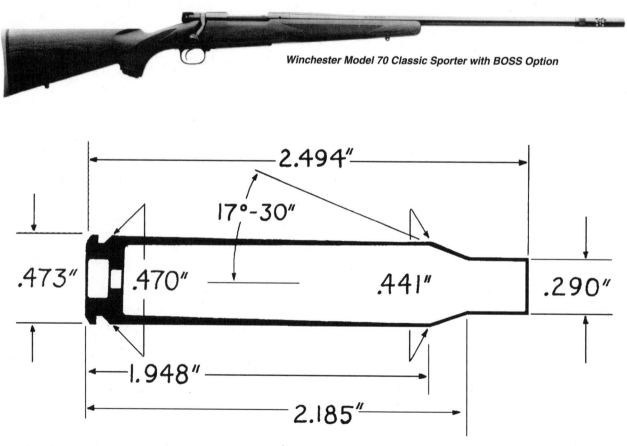

Winchester Model 70 Classic Sporter with BOSS Option

257 Weatherby Magnum

Historical Notes This cartridge was designed by Roy Weatherby in 1944, a year before he went into the commercial gun business. Like most other Weatherby cartridges, it is based on the necked-down and blown-out 300 H&H case. Commercial ammunition under the Weatherby name has been available since 1948. These have been based on Norma components since 1951. There are a number of wildcat versions of the 300 H&H Magnum necked-down to 25-caliber, but the Weatherby cartridge has largely displaced these.

General Comments The 257 WM was one of the first modern, ultra-velocity, small-bore rifle cartridges to be produced on a commercial basis that developed and retained a degree of popularity. It is accurate and well-suited for long-range varmint shooting, but also delivers sufficient velocity and energy to take on almost any North American big game. A superb deer, antelope,

sheep, goat or black bear cartridge, it has also been used successfully on elk, moose, brown bear, lion, buffalo and zebra. Many authorities insist that it is much too light for heavy game, but high-velocity advocates insist that with proper bullets, it is adequate for anything except the largest game in close cover. However, like most of its ilk, this number can be extremely hard on its barrel, especially if insufficient time is allowed between shots for the barrel to cool or if the barrel has not been cleaned adequately. And, like all high-intensity chamberings, it loses a great deal of velocity with barrels shorter than 26 inches. It is in its element for long-range plains or mountain hunting. The author used a custom Model 70 Winchester and later a Weatherby Mark V in this caliber, and it is dynamite on deer-size animals. For long-range varmint shooting, it can only be described as spectacular.

257 Weatherby Magnum Loading Data and Factory Ballistics

Bullet (grains/type)	Powder	Grains	Velocity	Energy	Source/Comments
75 HP	IMR 4350	66.5	3800	2405	Hornady
87 SP	IMR 4831	71	3700	2645	Speer
100 SP	IMR 4831	66.5	3400	2568	Sierra, Speer, Nosler
117 SP	IMR 4831	61.5	3100	2497	Hornady, Sierra
120 SP	IMR 4350	59	3200	2729	Hornady
87 SP	FL		3825	2827	Weatherby factory load
100 SP	FL		3602	2882	Weatherby factory load
120 SP	FL		3305	2911	Weatherby factory load

Weatherby Mark V Sporter with Weatherby Supreme 3-9x44 Scope installed on Buehler Mounts

260 Remington
6.5-08 A-Square

Historical Notes Inclusion of this cartridge presents us with a bit of a problem. Along about 1996, A-Square—a bona fide member of SAAMI—submitted drawings, chambering specifications, chambering reamers, sample cartridges and all other necessary materials and data describing a new factory chambering to be adopted into the SAAMI fold. A-Square requested that the chambering be named "6.5-08 A-Square," as specified on the sample cartridge headstamp. Many months later, Remington submitted a memo to SAAMI wherein it mentioned that it intended to eventually standardize a 6.5mm version of the 308 Winchester as the 260 Remington. Since SAAMI subsequently chose to christen this chambering as "260 Remington," a disinterested observer would have to conclude that something was a bit rank, somewhere.

General Comments This cartridge has precisely two things to recommend it. First, it is a superior choice for long-range target shooting, particularly in the NRA Highpower game, where reduced recoil with lighter bullets is valuable for the shorter-range events and where barrel life is an issue—a serious competitor can wear out several barrels each year. Second, for those who want or need a very light hunting rifle and are honest enough to admit that they cannot tolerate much recoil, this chambering is a superior choice.

Hunting load ballistics far exceed what the 243 Winchester can produce but are not insurmountably far behind the 7mm-08 Remington. Nevertheless, this would seem to be a minimal chambering for use on any North American big game. Those intending to use this cartridge for elk hunting should consider only the best premium bullets, such as bonded-core and partition designs and the 100-grain Barnes X.

260 Remington/6.5-08 A-Square Factory Ballistics

Bullet (grains/type)	Powder	Grains	Velocity	Energy	Source/Comments
120 Nosler BT	FL		2890	2226	Remington factory load
125 Nosler Partition	FL		2875	2294	Remington factory load
140 PSP Core-Lokt	FL		2750	2351	Remington factory load

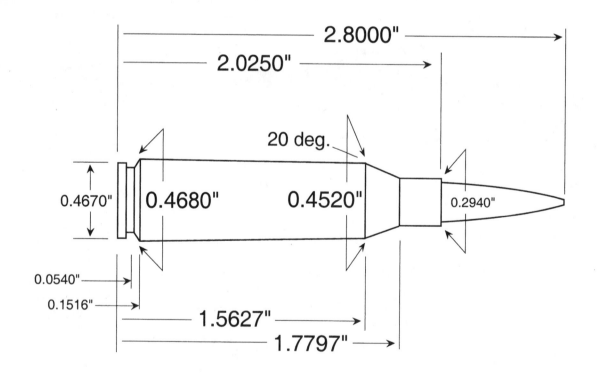

6.5x55 Swedish Mauser

Historical Notes Jointly developed by Norway and Sweden, this cartridge was adopted by both countries as an official military chambering in 1894. Originally both countries loaded and used essentially identical ammunition. Later, the Swedes modified dimensions and loaded to a higher pressure for use in their Mauser rifles, while the Norwegians kept the original version for use in the Krag rifle. In 1990, the National Rifle Associations of Denmark, Norway and Sweden agreed on a standardized set of drawings and specifications, renaming the cartridge 6.5x55 SKAN. This cartridge remained in active Swedish military service until quite recently. It is quite popular throughout Scandinavia for hunting all types of game, including moose. It is also a popular choice for 300-meter target shooting and other forms of rifle competition. Prior to World War II, the 6.5x55 Swedish was almost unknown in the United States. After the war, Canadian and U.S. sportsmen became acquainted with this chambering through the thousands of surplus Swedish Mauser rifles sold in North America. Many of these excellent rifles were sporterized in their original chambering. Canadian sportsmen were first off the mark to appreciate the virtues of this cartridge in the 1950s and 1960s. Later, U.S. sportsmen arrived at the same conclusions in the 1970s and 1980s. Other than imported rifles from Scandinavian countries, few sporting rifles in this chambering

were available in the U.S. until the 1990s. This has now changed as Winchester has offered its Featherweight M70 rifle and Ruger its M77 rifle in this chambering.

General Comments The 6.5x55 is one of the few 6.5mm calibers ever to catch on in the United States. For many years, Norma of Sweden was the only manufacturer of this cartridge until 1991-92 when Federal Cartridge Co. added this cartridge to its Premium product line. This cartridge continues to gain popularity as surplus Swedish Mauser rifles are still being imported. Two reasons for its growth in popularity are low recoil and superb accuracy. It is an excellent deer and antelope cartridge and is also suitable for bear and elk under good conditions at moderate ranges. Because of its flat trajectory, it is an outstanding choice for hunting sheep and goat in mountainous terrain using lightweight rifles. Lack of suitable bullets and handload data handicapped the full potential of this cartridge for many years. This has changed as good bullets and reloading data are now available from most component manufacturers. The 140-grain bullets are best for most types of hunting and are also the most accurate. The 6.5x55 Swedish Mauser case is not related to typical Mauser cartridge cases.

6.5x55mm Swedish Mauser Loading Data and Factory Ballistics

Bullet (grains/type)	Powder	Grains	Velocity	Energy	Source/Comments
85 Sierra HP	H4895	44.0	3370	2140	Hodgdon
85 HP	IMR 4320	47	3100	1814	Sierra
100 HP	H-380	43.5	3000	1999	Hornady
120 SP	H-4350	47	3000	2399	Nosler, Barnes
129 SP	H-380	43.5	2800	2246	Hornady
140 SP	IMR 4831	47	2600	2102	Speer, Barnes
140 Speer SP	H1000	51.5	2651	2185	Hodgdon
160 SP	H-4831	44	2600	2402	Speer
140 SP	FL		2550	2020	Federal factory load

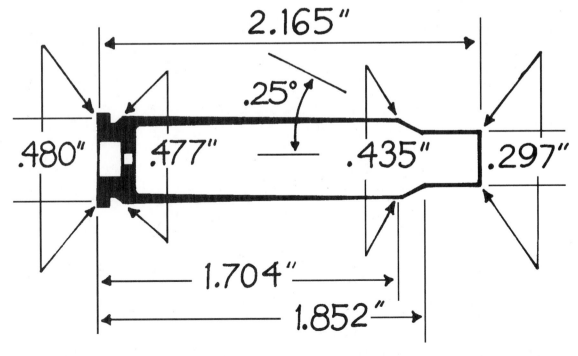

6.5-284 Norma

Historical Notes Hornady now produces cases and will produce ammunition (depending upon rifle manufacturing) for this long-time popular wildcat chambering. Originally, this version of the 284 Winchester was designed simply to offer a shorter hunting cartridge that approximates 6.5-06 ballistics; the long-range accuracy potential was recognized much later. This chambering has been used extensively in NRA Highpower and elsewhere when accuracy and barrel life are important. Peak pressure specification for this thoroughly modern cartridge is comparatively high.

General Comments A 28-inch barrel loaded with any of the better VLD (Very Low Drag) moly-plated bullets between 130 and 155 grains in this cartridge easily achieves sufficient velocity for accurate 1,000-yard benchrest shooting. These combinations generate much less recoil than any effective 30- or 33-caliber 1,000-yard match combination. This contributes to precise shooting. However, unless conditions are unusually good, those using larger-bored rifles usually fare better. While those rifles generate more recoil, which effectively reduces intrinsic accuracy, the longer bullets those bigger bores can accurately fire exhibit less wind drift and, therefore, reduce the error associated with imperfections in the shooter's ability to properly dope the wind.

Owing to a relatively high working pressure, ballistic potential is not too different from that for the 270 Winchester, making this a fine hunting cartridge and one that will function in medium-length actions. One only hopes that current gun writers treat the 6.5-284 Norma more fairly than their forebears did its progenitor. Of course, since I had some hand in the standardization of this number, I might be a bit prejudiced; nevertheless, I believe this is a very fine new cartridge for its intended purposes.

6.5-284 Norma Loading Data

Bullet (grains/type)	Powder	Grains	Velocity	Energy	Source/Comments
120 Sierra/Nosler	RI-25	59.4	3217	2755	Norma (26-inch Bbl)
140 Match	RI-25	57.4	3028	2850	Norma (26-inch Bbl)

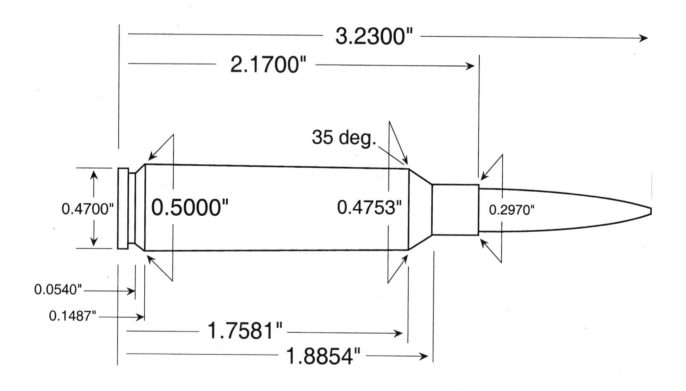

264 Winchester Magnum

Historical Notes This cartridge was officially announced by Winchester in 1958. The 264 Magnum is one of a series of cartridges based on the original Winchester 458 belted case, necked-down. It is historically significant as it is the first American 6.5mm cartridge since the long-defunct 256 Newton was announced back in 1913. It was originally available only in the Winchester bolt-action Model 70 Westerner with a 26-inch stainless steel barrel. For a time, the Remington 700 Series was offered in 264-caliber, as was the Ruger M77.

General Comments The 264 Winchester is a fine, ultra-velocity cartridge with excellent long-range capabilities and ballistics superior to the time-tried 270 Winchester. Its development may well have been suggested by the 257 Weatherby Magnum, for the two are quite similar. The 264 is able to equal the 257 WM, but with the added advantage of the heavier 140-grain bullet for larger species of big game. The 100-grain bullet is intended for animals in the deer and antelope class, the 140-grain for elk and above. The rifling twist used by Winchester is not quick enough to stabilize spitzer bullets of more than 140 grains. The handloader has a wide choice of bullets ranging from 87 to 160 grains. All things considered, the 264 Magnum is adequate for any North American big game. It is a plains and mountain cartridge. Like most of its ilk, this number can be extremely hard on its barrel, especially with either careless shooting, inadequate barrel cooling between shots or inadequate cleaning. (Joyce Hornady said the company went through three barrels for this chambering just trying to work up the data for three bullets with a few powders each. They were tipped off to a problem when the maximum charge for the 140-grain bullet turned out to be quite a bit higher than the maximum charge for the 120-grain bullet with the same powder.) And, like all high-intensity chamberings, it loses a great deal of velocity with barrels shorter than 26 inches. To quantify this: Best-possible safe 264 Winchester Magnum loads from 22-inch barrels produce less energy than best-possible 270 Winchester loads from a 22-inch barrel with equal-weight bullets. Both Remington and Winchester still offer this loading. However, only the 140-grain bullet is available.

264 Winchester Magnum Loading Data and Factory Ballistics

Bullet (grains/type)	Powder	Grains	Velocity	Energy	Source/Comments
85 Sierra HP	H4831	78.0	3812	2740	Hodgdon
85 SP	IMR 4895	57	3700	2585	Sierra
100 SP	IMR 4831	65	3500	2721	Hornady
120 SP	IMR 4350	60	3200	2729	Nosler, Sierra
129 SP	IMR 4350	57	3100	2753	Hornady
140 SP	IMR 4831	61	3100	2988	Hornady
140 Nosler Part.	H870	73.0	3163	3110	Hodgdon
160 SP	IMR 4831	54.5	2700	2591	Hornady
140 SP	FL		3030	2854	Factory load

Loads shown are for the factory 26-inch barrel, using Winchester-Western cases.

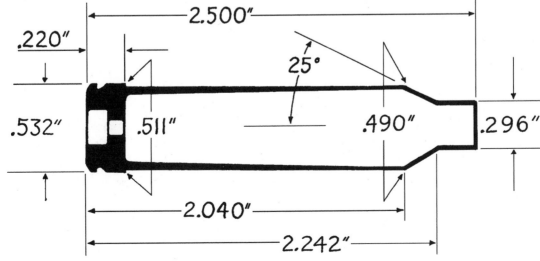

Remington Model 700 Classic Bolt-Action Centerfire Rifle

6.8mm Special Purpose Cartridge (6.8 SPC)

Historical Notes Anecdotal reports from U.S. forces involved in combat in Iraq and Afghanistan in recent years indicate the six-decade old 7.62x39 cartridge and AK47 rifle may be more effective in combat than the U.S. M4 carbines firing the 5.56x45 cartridge. In 2003, Steve Holland and Cris Murray, individuals associated with special forces and marksmanship units, developed a special purpose cartridge to improve combat effectiveness in short-barreled (16.5-inch) M4 carbines used for special operations. The resulting 6.8 SPC (Special Purpose Cartridge) achieved favorable results in actual usage, but has not been officially adopted by the U.S. Army as of 2005. The cartridge is under review by the U.S. Marine Corps and FBI.

General Comments Intended to launch heavier bullets than the standard U.S. 5.56 round, the 6.8 SPC uses the 1906–vintage 30 Remington cartridge shortened and necked down to accept a .270-caliber (6.8mm) bullet. Holland and Murray selected the 30 Remington as a parent case for two reasons. First, bolts for the M-16 family of rifles and carbines can readily be manufactured to accept the 30 Remington's case head diameter (.420). Second, standard 20-round and 30 round M-16 magazines can accept the 6.8 SPC without change. After extensive test firings into ordnance gel blocks, and on military firing ranges with the 30 Remington cases sized for .30, 7mm, .270, 6.5mm and 6mm bullets, 270-caliber bullets delivered the best balance of velocity, accuracy and terminal performance. Hornady and Remington offer loaded 6.8 SPC ammunition. The cartridge is chambered by Barrett, DPMS and PRI in AR15 rifles; by both SSK Industries and Thompson Center in Contender, G2 and Encore single shot actions; by Remington in bolt action rifles; and by custom gunsmiths on CZ-527 bolt actions. It is a good whitetail deer cartridge.

6.8mm Special Purpose Cartridge (6.8 SPC) Loading Data and Factory Ballistics

Bullet (grains/type)	Powder	Grains	Velocity	Energy	Source/Comments
110 V-Max	FL		2550	1588	Hornady
115 MC	FL		2800	2002	Remington
90 Spr HP	H4198	28.6C	3012		Hodgdon
110 V-Max	Benchmark	27.0	2518		Hodgdon
115 Sierra HPBT	H322	28.2C	2608		Hodgdon

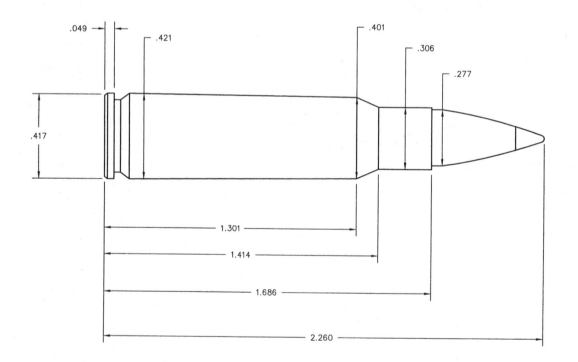

270 Winchester

Historical Notes Designed by Winchester in 1925 for its Model 54 bolt-action rifle, the 270 caused quite a stir in shooting circles. It has remained somewhat controversial ever since. At the time of introduction, it offered better long-range performance than any big game cartridge available on the American market. It has now been adopted by practically every manufacturer of standard bolt-action, high-powered sporting rifles in the world. The Remington pump-action and Remington and Browning semi-autos are also available in 270-caliber. The cartridge is based on the 30-06 case necked-down to .277-inch. (It is just possible that Winchester chose a 0.277-inch bullet to avoid paralleling anything European or British and they could possibly have been inspired by a Chinese cartridge that used a 0.277-inch bullet. We will likely never know.) The case neck is 0.050-inch longer but, except for the neck and headstamp, the 270 Winchester is otherwise identical to the 30-06. This cartridge was a long-time favorite of well-known gun writer the late Jack O'Connor, who probably contributed more to popularizing the 270 than any other individual. Today, the 270 Winchester is one of the most popular calibers on the market.

General Comments Along with the 30-06, this is one of the most accurate and effective all-round American big game cartridges. Its reputation and popularity have increased steadily since its introduction. Although not intended as a varmint cartridge, the 270 will serve very well in that capacity when loaded with bullets of 90 to 110 grains. It is generally conceded to be a better long-range varmint cartridge than its parent, the 30-06. The 130-grain bullet at 3,100 fps muzzle velocity is considered adequate by many experienced hunters for any North American big game. When first introduced, some deer hunters complained that the 130-grain bullet had such an explosive effect that it ruined too much meat. To satisfy the demand for a deer load, Winchester brought out a 150-grain bullet at a reduced velocity of 2,675 fps. However, it was short-lived because the people who demanded it wouldn't buy it. The present 150-grain bullet at 2,860 fps is intended for maximum penetration on heavier animals such as elk, moose or bear. Some disagree, but current evidence reinforces the conclusion that the 270 is adequate for any North American big game and some African plains game as well. Assuming the hunter uses the proper bullet for the job at hand, the 270 will deliver reliable performance. In any comparison of the 270 with the 30-06, much depends on intended use and hunting conditions. For some reason, many individuals shoot better with the 270 than the 30-06. The 270 is flatter shooting than the 30-06, and thus makes a better varmint/big game rifle where this is a consideration. The 30-06, with its 180-, 200- and 220-grain bullets, must be conceded as a better heavy game cartridge. In accuracy and general performance, there isn't a great deal to argue about. Anyone trying to make a big case for one against the other is beating a pretty dead horse. The 270 Winchester is commercially loaded by all large domestic and most foreign ammunition manufacturers.

270 Winchester Loading Data and Factory Ballistics

Bullet (grains/type)	Powder	Grains	Velocity	Energy	Source/Comments
90 Sierra HP	H4350	62.0	3603	2590	Hodgdon
100 Speer SP	RI-19	64.0	3510	2735	Hodgdon
110 Hornady HP	H4350	57.0	3267	2605	Hodgdon
130 Speer SP	RI-19	60.0	3160	2880	Hodgdon
135 Sierra SPBT	H1000	63.0	3011	2715	Hodgdon
140 Swift SP	H1000	63.0	2979	2755	Hodgdon
150 SP	IMR 4831	54	2800	2612	Speer, Sierra, Hornady
150 Sierra SPBT	RI-22	58.5	3010	3020	Hodgdon
160 Nosler Part.	H1000	59.0	2765	2715	Hodgdon
180 Barnes JRN	RI-22	53.0	2762	3045	Barnes
100 SP	FL		3480	2612	Factory load
130 SP	FL		3060	2702	Factory load
150 SP	FL		2850	2705	Factory load

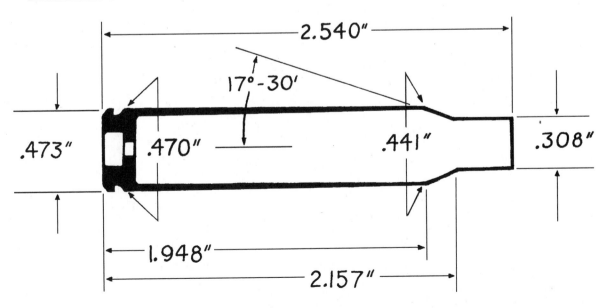

270 Winchester Short Magnum (270 WSM)

Historical Notes Introduced in 2001 and intended for riflemen preferring the 270 family of cartridges, the 270 WSM is crafted from the instantly popular 300 WSM case, necked down to accept .277-inch diameter bullets. Compared to the long-popular 270 Winchester the late Jack O'Connor held in high esteem, the 270 WSM is a modern magnum upgrade, suitable for short-action rifles, and offering higher performance—approaching 270 Weatherby magnum velocity levels with similar weight bullets. SSK Industries also re-barrels the AR-10 self-loading rifle for 270 WSM.

General Comments For efficient and consistent powder burning, the 270 WSM continues the short-fat cartridge case geometry Winchester first popularized in the 300 WSM, a benchrest-proven concept for nearly three decades. Retaining the 35-degree shoulder of the parent 300 WSM case, the 270 WSM headspaces on the shoulder, which should provide for tighter headspacing tolerances, and improved accuracy potential.

270 Winchester Short Magnum Loading Data and Factory Ballistics

Bullet (grains/type)	Powder	Grains	Velocity	Energy	Source/Comments
130 BST	FL		3275	3096	Winchester/Olin
140 Fail Safe	FL		3175	3035	Winchester/Olin
150 P PT	FL		3275	3096	Winchester/Olin
140 Fail Safe	WXR	63.8	3020		Winchester/Olin 56,500 psi
150 BST	WXR	65.5	3100		Winchester/Olin 61,900 psi

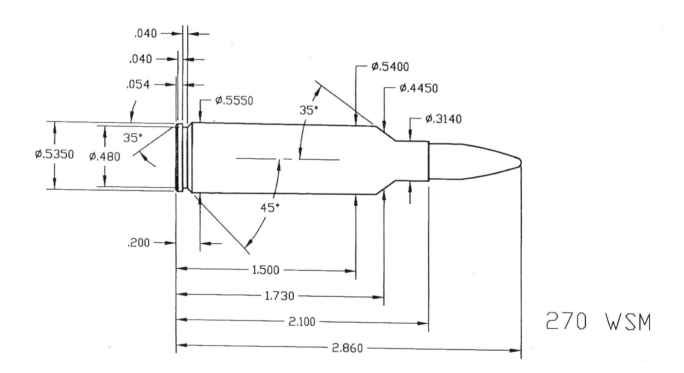

270 WSM

270 Weatherby Magnum

Historical Notes Most shooting enthusiasts think that the 270 Weatherby was developed to satisfy a demand for this caliber after the popularity of the 300 Weatherby Magnum had been established. As a matter of fact, the 270 is the first of the line developed by Roy Weatherby on the necked-down 300 H&H case. This was in 1943, after experiments with an improved 220 Swift that Weatherby called the 220 Rocket. It was largely actual hunting experience with the 270 WM that started Weatherby on the high-velocity trail. This culminated in his starting a commercial gun business in September 1945.

General Comments The popularity of the 270 Winchester made it almost mandatory for Weatherby to include this caliber in his line of commercial magnum rifle cartridges. The 270 WM has been used extensively, and successfully, on all species of North American big

game. It has also achieved notable success on African plains game. Those who have used it claim the 270 Weatherby provides flat trajectory, excellent long-range stopping power on all thin-skinned game and noticeably less recoil than the famous 300 WM. As an added attraction, the 270 WM is not impractical for varmint shooting. The 100-grain bullet is excellent for this purpose, thus making the 270 WM a very versatile all-round caliber. However, it is important to allow plenty of barrel-cooling time with this and all high-intensity cartridges. The 270 WM is easy and economical to reload, and empty cases are available for it. Like the other large-capacity magnum cases, it does not lend itself to reduced loads and is at its best with full or nearly full charges. It is a very fine choice for the hunter who wants to include varmint-hunting potential in a big-game rifle. It has been one of the most popular calibers that Weatherby offers.

270 Weatherby Magnum Loading Data and Factory Ballistics

Bullet (grains/type)	Powder	Grains	Velocity	Energy	Source/Comments
90 HP	IMR 4350	73	3800	2886	Sierra
100 SP	IMR 4350	71	3600	2878	Speer
100 SP	H-4831	76.5	3500	2721	Hornady
130 SP	IMR 4350	68	3300	3144	Speer, Sierra, Nosler
130 SP	IMR 4831	70	3300	3144	Sierra, Speer
140 SP	IMR 4350	66.5	3100	2988	Nosler
150 SP	IMR 4350	66	3000	2998	Hornady, Speer
150 SP	IMR 4831	67	3000	2998	Nosler, Sierra
160 SP	IMR 4831	65	2900	2989	Nosler
100 SP	FL		3760	3139	Weatherby factory load
130 SP	FL		3375	3283	Weatherby factory load
150 SP	FL		3245	3501	Weatherby factory load

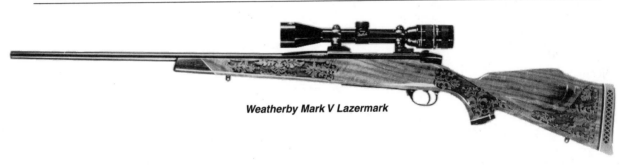

Weatherby Mark V Lazermark

7-30 Waters

Historical Notes The 7-30 Waters was introduced in 1984 for the U.S. Repeating Arms Model 94XTR Angle Eject rifle and carbine. The cartridge was the work of Ken Waters, a well-known gun writer and ballistics expert. He began planning the cartridge in 1976 as a high-velocity, flat-trajectory round for short, handy, lever-action carbines. There are many problems to be overcome by those who would improve on the performance of the 30-30 cartridge class in lever-action rifles. Severe restrictions are imposed by tubular magazines, the length of the action and permissible working pressures. However, by 1982, Ken had developed a cartridge that would push the 139-grain 7mm bullet at 2600 fps. At this point, U.S. Repeating Arms Co. became interested in the project and decided in 1983 to produce Model 94 lever-action rifles for this new cartridge. Federal Cartridge Co. then completed the final version of the cartridge by making various dimensional changes and opting for a lighter 120-grain bullet to achieve higher velocity at less pressure. The current commercial loading uses a 120-grain Nosler Partition bullet that develops a muzzle velocity of 2700 fps when fired from a 24-inch barrel.

General Comments The 7-30 Waters does offer improved performance for those who like lever-action carbines or rifles. This should make a good deer and black bear-class cartridge. However, the majority of 30-30 lever-action shooters prefer the short carbine, since most are woods hunters. The 7-30, with its light 120-grain bullet is unlikely to best the 30-30, 32 Special, 38-55, etc. with shots at close range. Also, it is not going to be the answer for the long-range plains or mountain hunter. When fired from a 20-inch barrel, its performance is considerably reduced. So anyone interested in this cartridge will be better served if they buy the rifle rather than the carbine. The light recoil of this cartridge makes it an excellent choice for a woman, boy or anyone who is recoil sensitive. The 7-30 is at its best in broken country with shots varying from patches of brush and trees to open areas with shots ranging from 75 to 175 yards.

7-30 Waters Loading Data and Factory Ballistics

Bullet (grains/type)	Powder	Grains	Velocity	Energy	Source/Comments
120 Nosler FP Part.	H414	42.0	2757	2025	Hodgdon
120 SP	H-335	28.5	2500	1666	Nosler
130 SP	H-335	33	2600	1952	Speer
139 Hornady FP	RI-15	34.7	2540	1990	Hodgdon
140 SP	W748	35	2500	1943	Hornady
140 SP	H-335	34	2600	2102	Hornady
145 SP	748	34	2400	1855	Speer
154 Hornady NR	H414	37.0	2347	1835	Hodgdon
120 SP	FL		2700	1940	Federal factory load

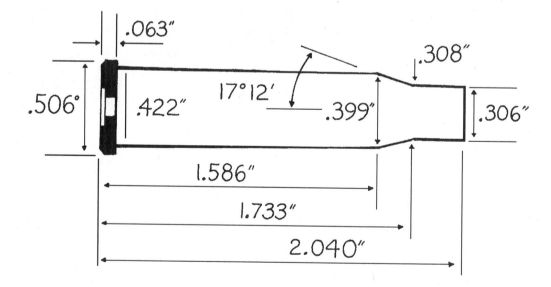

7mm Mauser (7x57mm)

Historical Notes Developed by Mauser as a military cartridge, the 7x57mm was introduced in 1892. Shortly afterward, this caliber was adopted by the Spanish government and chambered in a limited quantity of Model 92 Mauser bolt-action rifles. In 1893, Spain adopted a new model Mauser rifle in this same cartridge. This rifle has been called the Spanish Mauser ever since, although it was also adopted by Mexico and a number of South American countries. Remington chambered its rolling block and Lee rifles for the 7mm about 1897, and later the Model 30. The Winchester Model 54 and 70 also chambered it. Recently, the Ruger Model 77 and Winchester Featherweight bolt action, plus the Ruger No. 1 single shot, offer the 7mm as standard. Also, most European-made bolt-action rifles and combination guns chamber the 7mm Mauser, as do many custom-made rifles each year.

General Comments Although originally a military cartridge, the 7x57mm Mauser has proven to be one of the best all-round sporting rounds ever developed. It is particularly useful in lightweight rifles because it delivers good killing power with moderate recoil. It has been used successfully on every species of big game on earth. However, it is no dangerous game cartridge in the true sense of the term. Its success in the field is due largely to the ability of the hunters who have used it. Ballistically, it is only slightly less powerful than the 270 Winchester or the 280 Remington. It is adequate for most American big game, but is perhaps on the light side for large bear or moose. The 7mm Mauser was once discontinued by American gun manufacturers (about 1940) due to lack of popularity. Since the end of World War II, it has become increasingly common due to the influx of surplus 7mm military rifles. The wide selection of 7mm bullets now available for handloading has also contributed to an increase in popularity. The 7x57mm Mauser is commercially loaded by all domestic and most foreign ammunition manufacturers.

7mm Mauser (7x57mm) Loading Data and Factory Ballistics

Bullet (grains/type)	Powder	Grains	Velocity	Energy	Source/Comments
100 HP	W748	52.6	3300	2419	Hornady
115 SP	IMR 3031	46	3000	2299	Speer
120 SP	IMR 4064	46	2900	2241	Hornady
130 SP	IMR 4350	52	2850	2345	Speer
139 SP	IMR 4064	45	2800	2420	Hornady
150 SP	IMR 4064	41.5	2700	2429	Sierra, Nosler, Hornady
160 Sierra SPBT	RI-22	50.0	2690	2570	Hodgdon
175 SP	IMR 4895	42	2500	2430	Hornady
175 SP	IMR 4064	39	2450	2333	Nosler, Sierra
140 SP	FL		2660	2199	Factory load
145 SP	FL		2690	2334	Factory load
154 SP	FL		2690	2475	Factory load
175 SP	FL		2440	2313	Factory load

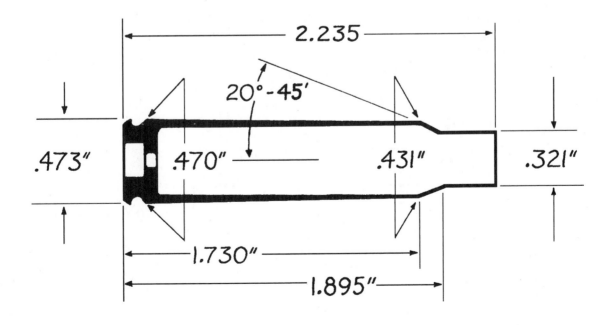

7mm-08 Remington

Historical Notes Remington introduced this medium-capacity rifle cartridge to the marketplace in 1980. It is based on the 308 Winchester case necked-down to 7mm and was loaded with a 140-grain bullet at 2860 fps. Remington advertised this cartridge as the "...first modern 7mm round designed for use in short-action rifles." This is an interesting claim in view of the fact that the 284 Winchester, designed for the same purpose, arrived on the scene in 1963. Furthermore, the 7mm-08 is a direct copy of the 7mm/308 wildcat dating back to 1958 and earlier. This is not meant to denigrate a fine cartridge, but to demonstrate that there really isn't much new under the sun despite advertising claims. The 7mm-08 is chambered in exactly the same actions as the 284 Winchester, but cannot equal 284 ballistics.

Original rifles chambered for the 7mm-08 were the Remington Model 788 and 700BDL Varmint Special bolt actions. Current Remington catalogs list the 700 series and Model Seven bolt actions as available in this chambering. Other makers have chambered it.

Remington has hung its hat on the 7mm caliber and with considerable success. It now offers six chamberings: 7mm BR, 7mm-08, 7x57mm Mauser, 7mm Express (280 Remington), 7mm Remington Magnum and 7 STW. The 7mm BR originated as something of a semi-wildcat based on the 308x1.5-inch necked-down. Remington has contributed more than any other company to the belated recognition of the ballistic advantages of the 7mm caliber by U.S. shooters.

General Comments Owing partly to a more pointed bullet shape, the 7mm-08 140-grain load surpasses the 308 Winchester 150-grain load downrange, according to Remington tests from a 24-inch barrel. This appears to be true. At 500 yards, the 7mm-08 bullet has an edge of 238 fps and 750 foot-pounds of energy over the 308 bullet. This would make quite some difference in potential killing power and also help in better bullet placement at unknown distances. There is not sufficient difference to cause owners of 308-caliber rifles to rush down and trade them off for 7mm-08s, but it does illustrate the ballistic advantages of the smaller caliber loaded with more streamlined bullets.

The 7mm-08 is a great favorite with many metallic silhouette shooters, and I have heard many glowing reports regarding its accuracy on the range, particularly with handloads. It is also building a good reputation as a long-range deer and antelope cartridge. When handloaded with bullets heavier than 140 grains, it is also suitable for heavier game such as elk. Unfortunately, the two factory bullet weights do not make for a very flexible big game cartridge. On the other hand, by handloading, this cartridge can be adapted to anything from varmint shooting through elk.

Case capacity of the 7mm-08 is slightly less than the 7x57mm Mauser and performance with the heavier bullets of around 175 grains is about 100 to 150 fps less, which is not anything to get really excited about. The fact of the matter is that the 7mm-08 is adequate for most North American hunting, but is handicapped by only two commercial bullet loadings. Remington has been joined by Federal in offering factory loaded ammunition in this caliber.

7mm-08 Remington Loading Data and Factory Ballistics

Bullet (grains/type)	Powder	Grains	Velocity	Energy	Source/Comments
100 HP	H-335	40.5	3000	1999	Hornady
120 SP	IMR 4320	41	2700	1943	Hornady, Sierra, Nosler
130 SP	IMR 4064	45	3000	2599	Speer
140 SP	IMR 4895	44	2900	2615	Sierra
150 SP	IMR 4320	38	2400	1919	Hornady, Sierra
160 SP	IMR 4350	44	2650	2496	Nosler, Sierra, Speer
175 SP	IMR 4350	44	2600	2627	Speer
120 SP	FL		3000	2398	Factory load
140 SP	FL		2860	2542	Factory load

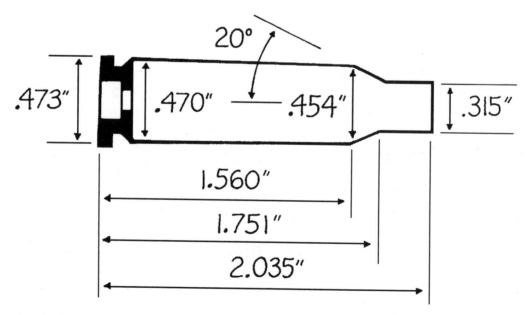

7x64mm Brenneke

Historical Notes This cartridge was developed by Wilhelm Brenneke in Germany in 1917. Although nearly unknown in the United States, this caliber rivals the 7mm Remington Magnum for popularity in Europe. Unlike the 7mm Remington Magnum, the 7x64 is not belted, although is has virtually the same case length. The 7x64 is dimensionally similar to the 280 Remington. Although it is not recommended, the 7x64 can be chambered in most 280 rifles, but not vice versa.

The 7x64 is unique in that it is one of the few cartridges in modern times made by American manufacturers to meet European demand without a significant demand in the United States. In 1991-92, Federal Cartridge Co. added the 7x64 to its Premium product line.

General Comments Ballistically, the 7x64 is very similar to the 284 Winchester. However, the 7x64 is outclassed by the 7mm Remington Magnum, which offers 11 percent more muzzle velocity and 22 percent more muzzle energy. This explains why American sportsmen prefer the 7mm Remington Magnum. Still, higher velocity is not always better and the 7x64 is an excellent choice for hunting deer, antelope, and other medium game at longer ranges. If you do wish to handload, cases for this cartridge cannot be formed from standard Mauser-type cartridge cases. However, cases are commercially available for the 7x64 from Remington, Federal and Norma.

7x64mm Brenneke Factory Ballistics

Bullet (grains/type)	Powder	Grains	Velocity	Energy	Source/Comments
120 Hornady SP	N160	59.9	3230	2780	VihtaVuori
139 Hornady SP	N140	48.6	2890	2575	VihtaVuori
154 Hornady SP	N160	58.0	2890	2855	VihtaVuori
160 Nosler	N160	57.3	2900	2985	VihtaVuori
175 Hornady SP	N160	56.8	2760	2960	VihtaVuori
160 SP	FL		2650	2495	Federal factory load

Reinhart Fajen stocked F.N. Mauser in 7x64 Brenneke

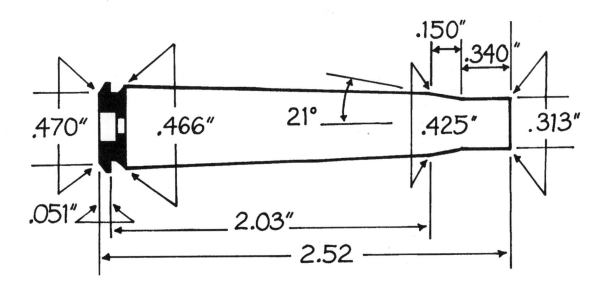

284 Winchester

Historical Notes The 284 was introduced by Winchester in 1963 for its Model 88 lever-action and Model 100 semi-auto rifles. Both have since been discontinued. This is the first American commercial cartridge to have a rebated, or undercut rim of smaller diameter than the body of the case, though British and European designers used this type of case years ago. For a short time, the Savage Model 99 lever action and Browning's BLR were available in 284. No major gun makers now offer this chambering.

General Comments The 284 Winchester has the rim diameter of the 30-06 and the body diameter of the belted magnums. This provides increased case capacity in a relatively short case. The cartridge is designed for short actions and will increase the performance of these short, light rifles. Ballistics are practically identical to the 280 Remington. There is no difference in killing power, range or capability between the two. (Except in some gun writer's imagination!) The 284 Winchester should be a good long-range cartridge for any North American big game. It could also be adapted for varmint shooting. This cartridge has recently staged a well-deserved comeback and continues to prosper, particularly as a basis for short-action wildcats.

284 Winchester Loading Data and Factory Ballistics

Bullet (grains/type)	Powder	Grains	Velocity	Energy	Source/Comments
100 HP	IMR 4350	60.5	3200	2274	Sierra
120 Hornady SP	RI-19	60.5	3265	2840	Hodgdon
130 SP	IMR 4350	58	3100	2775	Speer
140 SP	IMR 4350	55	3000	2799	Hornady
140 SP	IMR 4895	46	2800	2438	Sierra
145 Speer SP	RI-19	55.0	2940	2780	Hodgdon
150 SP	IMR 4350	53.5	2800	2612	Sierra
160 Sierra SPBT	RI-19	54.0	2885	2955	Hodgdon
175 SP	IMR 4350	50	2600	2627	Hornady, Sierra, Speer
150 SP	FL		2860	2724	Winchester factory load

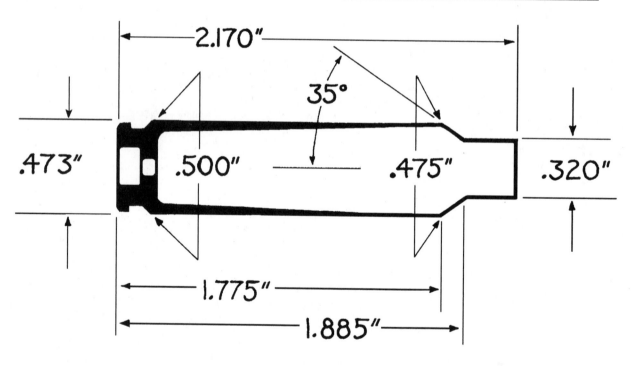

280 Remington/7mm Express Remington

Historical Notes The 280 Remington was introduced by that company in 1957. Initially it was chambered in the Remington Model 740 autoloader, later in the 760 pump-action and the 721 and 725 bolt-actions. The Remington 700 series bolt-action rifles originally included the 280 chambering. In an effort to increase sales, from 1979 to 1980 Remington cataloged the 280 as the 7mm Express Remington. But too much confusion resulted and Remington went back to the original 280 moniker. The 280 Remington, actually a 7mm with a bullet diameter of 0.284-inch, is based on the 30-06 case necked-down. It is very similar to the wildcat 7mm-06 which has been around for a good many years. In 1979, Remington introduced a new 150-grain loading.

General Comments This is a 30-06 case necked-down and with the shoulder moved forward 0.050-inch to prevent it from being chambered in 270 Winchester rifles. Had this been possible, the oversized neck might not have had room to open enough to free the bullet and the results could have been extremely dangerous. However, by moving the shoulder forward, Remington created an even more dangerous situation. The 270 Winchester cartridge, which is visually almost indistinguishable from the 280 Rem., chambers effortlessly in 280 Remington rifles. Should the extractor catch the case during loading and then allow it to slip forward when

the firing pin strikes the primer, or should the striker reach the primer of a load that was chambered ahead of the extractor, the results would be a 0.050-inch headspace problem with almost certain head separation and the resulting flood of 50,000 psi gas in one's face. Not a pretty thought. Remington could have solved the original problem and eliminated the one it created by simply enlarging the case at the shoulder or increasing the shoulder angle.

The 280 Remington is slightly more powerful than the 270 Winchester. It would be stretching a point to say that the 280 is better than the 270 Winchester, although it is probably a little more versatile due to the wider variety of factory bullets available. If you are a handloader, any difference would be one of personal preference. The 280 is certainly adequate for any North American big game and would also lend itself for use on large varmints. It is another case of a good wildcat cartridge finally emerging in a commercial version. It has picked up a modest following among 7mm fans since its introduction. Loaded with the 120-grain or new 100-grain varmint bullets, the 280 becomes an excellent varmint cartridge. The 150-grain bullet at 2,970 fps brings out some of the latent potential of this cartridge, which is truly an excellent long-range big game cartridge. Both Remington and Winchester commercially load this cartridge.

280 Remington Loading Data and Factory Ballistics

Bullet (grains/type)	Powder	Grains	Velocity	Energy	Source/Comments
100 Sierra HP	VarGet	51.3	3433	2615	Hodgdon
120 Barnes XFB	H4350	56.0	3114	2580	Hodgdon
130 SP	IMR 4350	57	3100	2775	Speer
140 Nosler Part.	H4831	58.5	2927	2660	Hodgdon
150 SP	IMR 4831	48	2900	2802	Sierra, Nosler
160 Sierra SPBT	RI-22	55.7	2795	2775	Hodgdon
175 SP	IMR 4350	52	2650	2730	Speer, Hornady
120 SP	FL		3150	2643	Factory load
150 SP	FL		2890	2781	Factory load
165 SP	FL		2820	2913	Factory load
140 SP	FL		3050	2799	Factory load

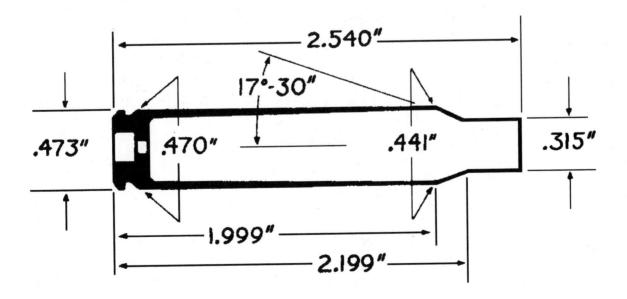

7mm Remington Magnum

Historical Notes Introduced by Remington during 1962, the 7mm Remington Magnum was brought out at the same time as the improved, bolt-action 700-series rifles, which replaced the earlier Models 721, 722 and 725. Most other manufacturers have since added this popular caliber to their lines. It took American firearms manufacturers nearly 40 years to realize that the 275 Holland & Holland (made long ago by Western Cartridge Co.) is a first-rate, medium-game, long-range cartridge. The long line of 7mm wildcats is much like the old 275 H&H which came out in 1912. Remington chose to ignore the classic 7mm bullet — 160-grain spitzer — in its 7mm Magnum loads.

General Comments The 7mm Remington Magnum is a fine, long-range, big game cartridge. There is a good selection of factory loaded 7mm bullets available and the handloader could make it do just about anything. It has ample power for any North American big game and most thin-skinned African varieties. However, it is an open-country, plains or mountain cartridge rather than a woods or brush number. Many will compare it with the 7mm WM or the 7x61mm Sharpe & Hart Super. Bitter arguments will ensue as to which is the best or most powerful. This will be akin to the ancient Greek pastime of discussing how many spirits can dance on the head of a pin. However, any difference in these cartridges will be strictly a matter of opinion or imagination. They all have nearly the same case capacity and none will do anything the others can't duplicate. In fact, the 7mm Remington is hardly a new or brilliant design. It is largely a commercial version of several wildcat short-belted 7mm magnums (Ackley, Luft, Mashburn, etc.). Its principal advantage lies in the fact that it is a standard factory product that is widely distributed and available in well-made, moderately priced rifles. Come to think of it, that's quite a bit to a lot of people. However, don't trade off your present 7mm Magnum with the idea that the Remington round is going to provide some mysterious extra margin of power or knockdown. The 7mm Rem. Mag. can be somewhat hard on barrels, especially with either careless shooting, inadequate barrel cooling between shots or inadequate cleaning. And, like all similar chamberings, it loses significant velocity with barrels shorter than 24 inches. Actual ballistics may be closer to the 7mm Weatherby Magnum than factory data suggests. Ammunition in 7mm Remington Magnum caliber is available in a wide variety from all domestic and most foreign ammunition manufacturers.

7mm Remington Magnum Loading Data and Factory Ballistics

Bullet (grains/type)	Powder	Grains	Velocity	Energy	Source/Comments
100 HP	IMR 4831	71.5	3500	2721	Hornady
115 HP	IMR 4831	71	3400	2953	Speer
120 SP	IMR 4350	66	3350	2991	Sierra, Nosler
130 SP	IMR 4350	63	3200	2957	Speer
140 SP	IMR 4350	64	3100	2988	Nosler, Sierra, Hornady
150 SP	IMR 4831	62	3000	2998	Nosler, Sierra
160 SP	IMR 4831	62.5	3000	3198	Sierra, Nosler, Speer
175 SP	H-450	64.5	2900	3269	Sierra
140 SP	FL		3175	3133	Factory load
150 SP	FL		3110	3221	Factory load
160 SP	FL		2950	3090	Factory load
165 SP	FL		2900	3081	Factory load
175 SP	FL		2860	3178	Factory load

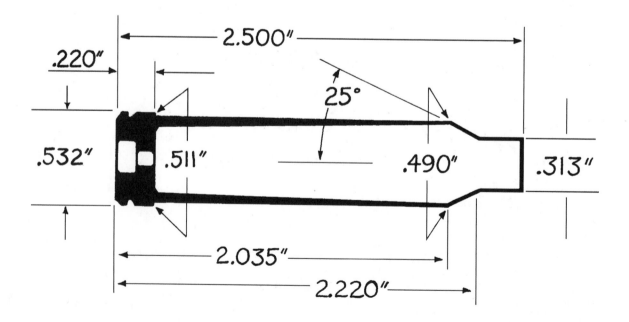

7mm Remington Short Action Ultra Magnum

Historical Notes In 2001, Remington introduced the 7mm Remington Short Action Ultra Magnum cartridge as a competitor to Winchester's 7mm Winchester Short Magnum. Ballistic performance of the Remington and Winchester offerings is similar. The 7mm Remington Short Action Ultra Magnum easily exceeds or equals 7mm Remington Magnum performance while fitting into easy-carrying, fast-handling rifles such as the short-action Remington Model 7.

General Comments Based on a shortened 300 Ultra Magnum case, which is itself derived from a slightly modified 404 Jeffery

cartridge of African fame, the 7mm Remington Short Action Ultra Magnum is slightly shorter and smaller in diameter than its Winchester counterpart. Short, fat cases burn powder very efficiently, since the primer's flash ignites a larger area of the packed gunpowder. The case is unbelted and headspaces on the shoulder for improved shoulder tolerances. Remington barrels for this cartridge use a twist rate of 1:9-1/4. Shooters are cautioned never to fire a 7mm Remington Short Action Ultra Magnum in a 7mm WSM-chambered rifle, as the headspace would be excessive, leading to possible injury or firearms damage.

7mm Remington SA Ultra Magnum Loading Data and Factory Ballistics

Bullet (grains/type)	Powder	Grains	Velocity	Energy	Source/Comments
140 PSP	FL		3175	3133	Remington factory load
150 PSP	FL		3110	3221	Remington factory load
160 Nosler Partition	FL		2960	3112	Remington factory load

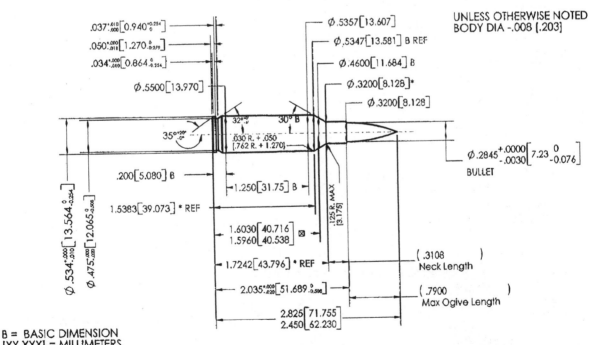

B = BASIC DIMENSION
[XX.XXX] = MILLIMETERS
REF = REFERENCE DIMENSION
* = DIMENSIONS ARE TO THEORETICAL INTERSECTION OF LINES
ALL CALCULATIONS APPLY AT MAXIMUM MATERIAL CONDITION (MMC)

7mm Winchester Short Magnum (7mm WSM)

Historical Notes Introduced in 2001 and intended for ranks of riflemen preferring 7mm calibers, the 7mm WSM is crafted from the instantly popular 300 WSM case, necked down to accept .284-inch diameter bullets. Also, the 7mm WSM shoulder was lengthened by .038-inch to prevent any possibility of chambering in a 270 WSM rifle. The 7mm WSM is the modern, short-action equivalent of the 7mm Remington Magnum, a cartridge that showed untold numbers of hunters just how effective a flat-shooting, highly efficient 284 cartridge could be for North American and large African plains game. SSK Industries also re-barrels the AR-10 self-loading rifle for 7mm WSM.

General Comments For efficient and consistent powder burning, the 7mm WSM continues the short-fat cartridge case geometry Winchester first popularized in the 300 WSM, a benchrest-proven concept for nearly three decades. Omitting a belt on the case, the 7mm WSM headspaces on the shoulder, which should provide for tighter headspacing tolerances, and improved accuracy potential. Shooters are cautioned never to fire the slightly shorter, physically similar 7mm Remington Short Action Ultra Magnum in a 270 WSM- or 7mm WSM-chambered rifles, as the 270 bore is smaller, and the headspace would be excessive, leading to possible injury or firearms damage.

7mm Winchester Short Magnum Loading Data and Factory Ballistics

Bullet (grains/type)	Powder	Grains	Velocity	Energy	Source/Comments
140 BST	FL		3225	3233	Winchester/Olin
150 P Pt	FL		3200	3410	Winchester/Olin
160 Fail Safe	FL		2990	3176	Winchester/Olin
140 BST	WXR	70.0	3200	3184	Winchester/Olin
					61,500 psi
140 SP	WXR	66.5	3220	3224	Winchester/Olin
					63,900 psi
150 SP	WXR	68.0	3145	3295	Winchester/Olin
					61,600 psi
160 BST	WXR	60.5	2915	3020	Winchester/Olin
					61,700 psi

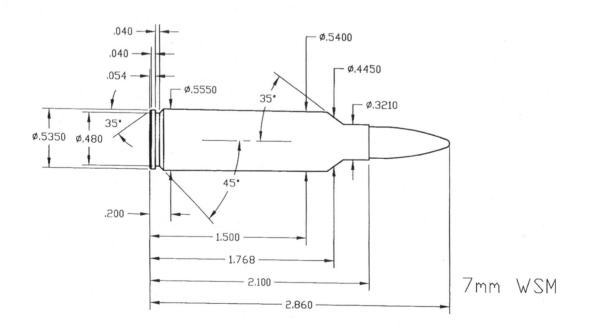

7mm WSM

7mm Weatherby Magnum

Historical Notes The 7mm Weatherby Magnum was developed in 1944 as one of a series of cartridges based on the necked-down 300 H&H case (it is the 270 WM necked up 0.007-inch, although it does use a longer overall cartridge length). There are several similar wildcat versions, but Weatherby's design is the most popular due to the availability of commercial ammunition.

General Comments The 7mm (or 284 caliber) has long been popular in the United States in various wildcat cartridges, yet the original 7mm Mauser never generated any great enthusiasm. The 7mm Weatherby Magnum, offered as a maximum-performance cartridge, is probably the best known and widely used of the current 7mm Magnums with the single exception of the 7mm Remington Magnum. This is due in part to the availability of factory-loaded ammunition with a good selection of bullet weights. The 7mm Weatherby has a slight edge over the 270 Weatherby on tough or dangerous game because it can use heavier bullets and churns up greater energy. However, if long-range varmint shooting is on the

agenda, the 270 is the better choice. The 7mm WM is adequate for any North American big game and all thin-skinned African game. The 7mm Weatherby Magnum has, to a large extent, lost popularity to the 7mm Remington Magnum because the Remington version is available in a wider variety of rifles generally less expensive than the Weatherby. Like most high-intensity cartridges, the 7mm WM can be somewhat hard on its barrel, especially with either careless shooting, inadequate barrel cooling between shots or inadequate barrel cleaning. And, like all similar chamberings, it loses significant velocity with barrels shorter than 24 inches. Ammunition in this caliber is now available from Remington and PMC as well as Weatherby. For many years now, Norma has loaded Weatherby ammunition in all calibers under the Weatherby brand name. In 1992, Norma began offering Weatherby calibers under the Norma brand name. Norma ammunition is distributed in the United States by Dynamit.Nobel.

7mm Weatherby Magnum Loading Data and Factory Ballistics

Bullet (grains/type)	Powder	Grains	Velocity	Energy	Source/Comments
100 HP	IMR 4350	73.5	3600	2878	Hornady
115 HP	IMR 4831	76	3600	3310	Speer
120 SP	IMR 4350	70	3400	3081	Sierra, Nosler, Hornady
130 SP	IMR 4320	63	3300	3144	Speer
139 SP	IMR 4350	68	3200	3161	Sierra, Nosler, Hornady
154 SP	IMR 4350	67	3100	3287	Hornady
160 SP	IMR 4350	65	3000	3198	Sierra, Speer
175 SP	IMR 4350	65	2800	3047	Speer, Hornady
195 SP	IMR 7828	61	2500	2707	Speer
139 SP	FL		3340	3443	Weatherby factory load
154 SP	FL		3260	3633	Weatherby factory load
175 SP	FL		3070	3662	Weatherby factory load

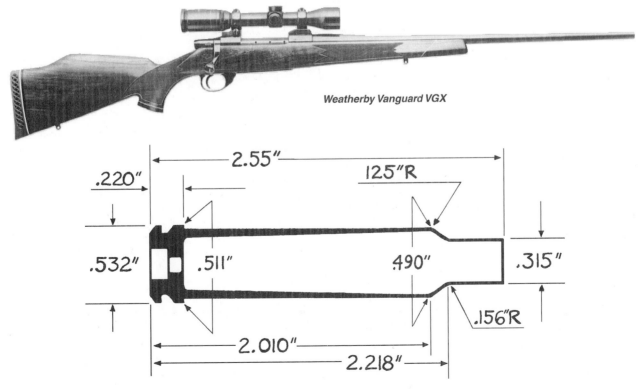

Weatherby Vanguard VGX

7mm Shooting Times Westerner (7mm STW)

Historical Notes This original wildcat chambering was designed in 1989 by Layne Simpson, a gun writer for *Shooting Times* magazine. This design includes a slight decrease in body taper, compared to the original 8mm Remington Magnum case. This provides clean rechambering of 7mm Remington Magnum chambers. Throat design was also changed to include a straight section. This improves accuracy potential. This cartridge takes advantage of the 3.65-inch magazine length of the long-action Remington Model 700. The 7mm STW was adopted as a SAAMI cartridge about 1996, an unusually quick transition from wildcat to factory offering.

General Comments The 7mm STW has impressive velocity potential and can deliver good ballistics with a variety of bullets and powders. A-Square provides ammunition and data for a few of the more popular bullet weights and types. It is likely that the slowest handloader powders would show improved performance in this chambering. Barrel life can be very limited, especially for those who are incautious about barrel cooling between shots or proper cleaning.

7mm Shooting Times Westerner (7mm STW) Loading Data

Bullet (grains/type)	Powder	Grains	Velocity	Energy	Source/Comments
140 Nosler BT	H4831	75.0	3234	3250	A-Square/maximum load
140 Nosler SP	RI-22	79.0	3410	3615	A-Square/maximum load
140 Nosler BT	IMR 7828	83.0	3413	3620	A-Square/maximum load
160 Nosler Part.	RI-22	72.0	3084	3380	A-Square/maximum load
160 Nosler Part.	H4831	75.0	3200	3635	A-Square/maximum load
160 Nosler Part.	IMR 7828	77.0	3211	3660	A-Square/maximum load
160 Sierra SBT	IMR 7828	75.0	3093	3400	A-Square/maximum load
160 Sierra SBT	RI-22	75.5	3115	3445	A-Square/maximum load
160 Sierra SBT	H4831	75.0	3138	3500	A-Square/maximum load
140 Nosler SBT	FL		3450	3700	A-Square factory load
160 Sierra SBT	FL		3250	3750	A-Square factory load
160 Nosler SBT	FL		3250	3750	A-Square factory load

7mm Remington Ultra Magnum

Historical Notes The 7mm Remington Ultra Magnum, draws upon a large capacity case to become a serious contender for the title of *flattest-shooting factory big game cartridge on the planet*. The performance-driven popularity of the 300 Remington Ultra Magnum cartridge following its 1999 introduction led Remington to offer a family of cartridges based on this beltless magnum-sized case. Shooting flatter than the 7mm STW, the 7mm Ultra Mag delivers a flatter trajectory with a 140-grain bullet than a 22-250 does with a 55-grain bullet. At 300 yards, it produces 24-percent more energy than the standard 7mm Remington Magnum and 12-percent greater energy than the 7mm STW.

General Comments In suitably equipped rifles, such as the Remington 700, and the hands of a skillful hunter, the 7mm Ultra Magnum is a superb choice for long-range antelope, deer and sheep. Except for bullet diameter, the technical details of this cartridge are identical to the 300 Remington Ultra Magnum cartridges. *(See separate listing).*

7 mm Remington Ultra Magnum Factory Ballistics

Bullet (grains/type)	Powder	Grains	Velocity	Energy	Source/Comments
140 PSP	FL		3425	3646	Remington factory load
140 Nosler Partition	FL		3425	3646	Remington factory load
160 Nosler Partition	FL		3200	3637	Remington factory load

30 Carbine (30 M1 Carbine)

Historical Notes In 1940, the U.S. Ordnance Department concluded that a light carbine would have advantages over the 45-caliber pistol in many combat situations. Various designs were submitted by a number of private manufacturers and, in the end, Winchester's offering was selected. The semi-auto 30 M1 Carbine was officially adopted in 1941. The cartridge, a modification of the 32 Winchester Self-Loading round of 1906, was hardly a revolutionary new design, but it served the purpose. At about the same time, the Germans developed their StG 44 assault rifle and the 7.92mm Kurz cartridge. The M1 Carbine is not an assault rifle. The military insists it was designed to fulfill a different purpose.

For a few years, starting in 1966, the Marlin Model 62 Levermatic was available in 30 Carbine caliber. Iver Johnson, Plainfield and others manufactured several versions of the M1 carbine for the sporting trade. Federal, Remington and Winchester load softpoint sporting ammunition. One version of the Ruger Blackhawk single-action revolver is available in 30 Carbine.

General Comments In mid-1963, the government began releasing 30-caliber M1 Carbines for sale to civilians through the National Rifle Association at the moderate price of around $20. Thousands of these guns are, as a result, used for sporting purposes. The 30 Carbine cartridge is in the same class as the 32-20 WCF. It is wholly a small game and varmint number, despite contrary claims by those who love the short, light, handy M1 Carbine. The accuracy of the carbine combined with the ballistics of the cartridge limit the effective sporting accuracy range to about 150 yards maximum. The author used an M1 Carbine to hunt small game and deer as early as 1943, before most people could get their hands on one, so he had a pretty good idea of the capability of the cartridge. Remember that the 32 Winchester Self-Loading round became obsolete in 1920 because it was more or less useless for sporting purposes. The 30 Carbine was derived from it and shares the same shortcomings. Because of inadequate energy, the 30 Carbine is illegal for deer hunting in most states. It is, however, effective against the smaller deer species when shots are at short range. It is ideal for hunting smaller game such as peccary. Had the military chosen to adopt this round with a modern, full-pressure standard, performance would have been about 40 percent better and we might have a different opinion.

30 Carbine Loading Data and Factory Ballistics

Bullet (grains/type)	Powder	Grains	Velocity	Energy	Source/Comments
85 Sierra RN	H110	17.5	2458	1140	Hodgdon
100	H-110	14.5	1950	845	Speer
100	H-110	16.5	2200	1075	Hornady
110 SP	H-110	14	1900	882	Hornady, Speer
110 FMJ	FL		1900	882	Military load
110 SP	FL		1990	967	Factory load

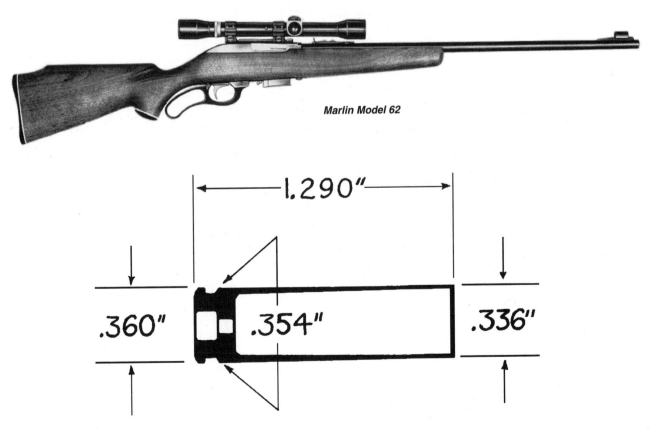

Marlin Model 62

1.290"

.360"   .354"   .336"

30-30 Winchester (30-30 WCF/30 Winchester)

Historical Notes The 30-30, or 30 WCF, was the first American small-bore, smokeless-powder sporting cartridge. It was designed by Winchester and first marketed in early 1895 as one of the chamberings available for the Model 1894 lever-action rifle. The original loading used a 160-grain softpoint bullet and 30 grains of smokeless powder. Thus the name 30-30 for 30-caliber bullet and 30 grains of powder. This is really an older way of describing a caliber based on blackpowder. Muzzle velocity was 1970 fps.

It was adapted to the Winchester Model 54 bolt action as well as various versions of the original 1894 action such as the Models 55 and 64. Marlin chambered it in the Model 1893 lever action, the improved 36 and the Model 336. At one time, the Savage Model 99 lever action was made in 30-30, and Savage also chambered the old Model 40 bolt action for it, as well as Model 340. The Remington rolling block and Winchester single shot were also at one time available in this caliber. In Europe, the 30-30 is known as the 7.62x51R and is popular in single shot and combination guns. Modern factory loads in this caliber are assembled with 150- or 170-grain bullets. Despite the designation, .308-inch diameter bullets are used.

General Comments The 30-30 has long been the standard American deer cartridge, and it is still the yardstick by which the performance of all others is compared. To say that a cartridge is in the 30-30 class means that it is suitable for game up to and including deer and black bear at moderate ranges. Its popularity is due to the fact that this cartridge has always been available in short, light rifles or carbines. It is extremely popular in Mexico and Latin America. So much so that in many backcountry areas, the "treinta-treinta" is the only high-powered cartridge anyone knows or has heard of. It was, and to a large extent still is, the most popular small-bore sporting cartridge. Despite this popularity, the 30-30 is no wonder cartridge with regard to accuracy or killing power. For larger deer, the 170-grain bullet is a good choice and the 170-grain Nosler Partition or the Barnes 150-grain XPF are the best choices for those who wish to tackle elk. For smaller species, 125- to 150-grain bullets give adequate penetration with reduced recoil. In no case is it suited to shots beyond about 200 yards. Although sometimes reloaded with bullets of 80 to 110 grains, it has neither the velocity nor the accuracy (in most rifles) to make a very good varmint round. Despite its faults, it is a perfectly adequate deer cartridge if properly used by a good shot. The author's first modern high-powered rifle was a 30-30 Model 1894 Winchester carbine, and it served for many useful and game-filled years. All major domestic ammunition companies offer this cartridge.

30-30 Winchester Loading Data and Factory Ballistics

Bullet (grains/type)	Powder	Grains	Velocity	Energy	Source/Comments
100 SP	IMR 3031	33	2600	1394	Speer
110 Speer FP	H335	38.0	2684	1755	Hodgdon
125 Sierra JFP	Rl-7	30.0	2630	1920	Hodgdon
150 Sierra JFP	Rl-15	36.0	2450	1995	Hodgdon
170 Hornady JFP	Rl-15	34.1	2330	2045	Hodgdon
150 SP	FL		2390	1902	Factory load
170 SP	FL		2200	1827	Factory load

Always use round- or flat-pointed bullets in tubular magazine rifles; sharp-pointed bullets might set off other cartridges in the magazine.

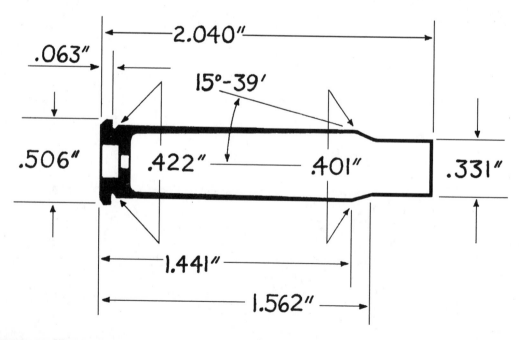

300 Savage

Historical Notes Developed and introduced by Savage Arms Co. for the Model 99 lever-action rifle in 1920, the 300 Savage was later chambered in the Savage Models 20 and 40 bolt actions. The 300 Savage was intended as a cartridge that would work through medium-length actions and deliver ballistics similar to the 30-06. Remington chambered it in the Model 81 autoloader, 760 pump-action and 722 bolt-action. The cartridge achieved considerable popularity, but has now lost out to the superior 308 Winchester.

General Comments The 300 Savage provided lever-, pump-action and semi-auto fans with performance close enough to the 30-06 to make rifles of this type useful for most American big game. The original factory load used a 150-grain bullet and matched the original 30-06 sporting load at 2,700 fps. If loaded to original factory pressure levels with IMR-4064, it can significantly but safely exceed that velocity. It is not fully adequate for moose or brown bear, but it is a fine deer and elk cartridge. It is a better choice than the 30-30 for deer under any conditions. The 308 Winchester fulfills the same function as a short-action cartridge and has somewhat more power, so it has gradually replaced the 300 Savage. However, many thousands of 300 Savage-caliber rifles are still in use so the cartridge will continue to be loaded for many more years. In a bolt-action rifle, it is as accurate as any other 30-caliber. All the major domestic ammunition companies offer this ammunition.

300 Savage Loading Data and Factory Ballistics

Bullet (grains/type)	Powder	Grains	Velocity	Energy	Source/Comments
100 SP	IMR 4064	46	3000	1999	Speer
110 SP	IMR 4895	43	2800	1915	Speer, Sierra
110 SP	BL-C2	42	2800	1915	Hornady, Speer, Sierra
125 SP	IMR 4895	43.5	2800	2177	Sierra
130 SP	IMR 4064	43	2700	2105	Speer, Hornady
150 SP	IMR 4064	41.5	2600	2252	Sierra, Hornady, Speer
150 SP	IMR 4895	40.5	2600	2252	Sierra
150 SP	IMR 4064	44.0	2800	2610	Hornady
165 SP	IMR 3031	37.8	2500	2290	Hornady, Sierra
180 SP	IMR 4350	46	2400	2303	Hornady, Speer
180 SP	IMR 4895	39.5	2400	2303	Sierra
150 SP	FL		2630	2303	Factory load
180 SP	FL		2350	2207	Factory load

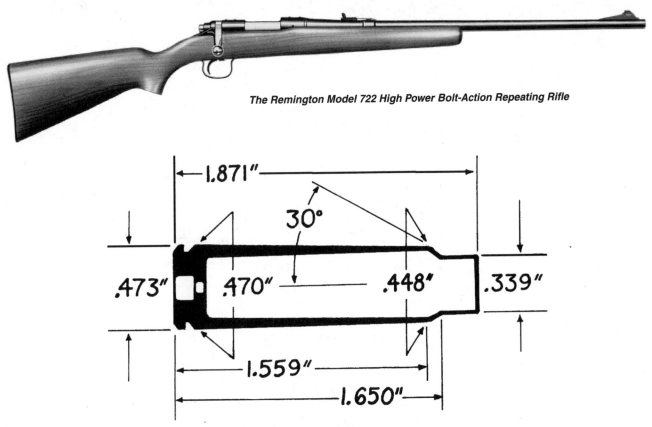

The Remington Model 722 High Power Bolt-Action Repeating Rifle

7.62x39 (7.62x39mm Soviet)

Historical Notes This cartridge is the standard military chambering for the Russian armed forces. It has become a modern favorite of U.S. sportsmen by virtue of the thousands of new and used SKS and AK 47-type carbines being imported and sold at very low prices. Ruger, Sako, and others are now making sporting rifles in this chambering. For example, the Ruger Mini Thirty semi-auto carbine and bolt-action M77 rifle are both offered in 7.62x39mm.

All major American ammunition manufacturers now offer this cartridge with a softpoint bullet, brass case, and non-corrosive Boxer primer. Imported, low-cost, surplus military ammunition from present and former Communist countries is usually steel cases with corrosive Berdan primers.

General Comments While previous military cartridges generally made suitable hunting rounds with proper bullets, many writers condemn the 7.62x39 out of hand as being unsuited for hunting anything beyond small game. In short, they claim it is very much like the M1 Carbine cartridge — fine for military use, but useless for hunting. However, best 125- and 150-grain spitzer loads in this cartridge typically match best 30-30 FP or RN load energy at 100 yards, and at 200 yards, there is no comparison — this little round bests the 30-30 by 20 percent.

Still, the 7.62x39 is definitely a close-range number suitable for deer, javelina and the like. With the best handloads and the proper bullet, it can do even better. It can be loaded to good advantage with 150-grain bullets and then becomes a very good 30-30 class deer rifle. Youthful shooters and women will appreciate its low recoil and mild report. Aftermarket bullet manufacturers now offer suitable bullets. Bore diameter is nominally .311-inch but .308-inch diameter bullets can be used with good results and most reloading dies will accommodate this by including expander balls for both bullet sizes.

7.62mm Soviet Loading Data and Factory Ballistics

Bullet (grains/type)	Powder	Grains	Velocity	Energy	Source/Comments
110 SP	IMR 4727	42	2500	1527	Speer
125 SP	RL-7	26.5	2400	1599	Hornady, Sierra
125 Speer SP	H335	31.5	2408	1605	Hodgdon
135 SP	IMR 4227	22.5	2200	1451	Sierra
150 SP	IMR 4198	22	2100	1469	Hornady
150 Hornady SP	H322	28.5	2192	1600	Hodgdon
123 SP	FL		2300	1445	Federal factory load
123 SP	FL		2365	1527	Winchester factory load
125 SP	FL		2365	1552	Remington factory load

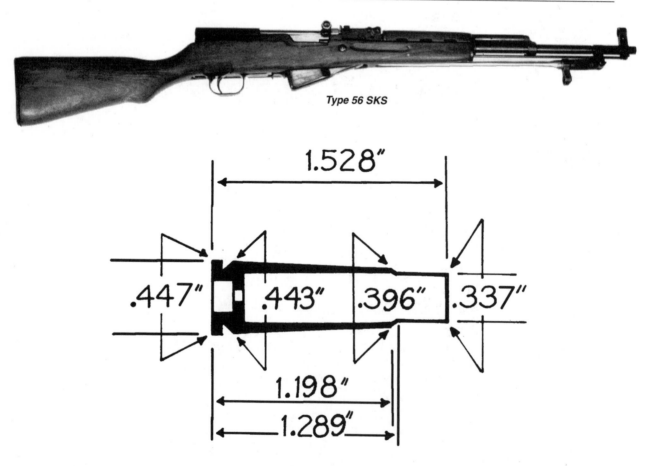

Type 56 SKS

30-40 Krag (30 Army)

Historical Notes The 30 U.S. Army, or 30-40 Krag — the first United States small-bore military cartridge — was adopted in 1892. (The first smokeless sporting cartridge, the 30-30, did not arrive until three years later, in 1895.)

The Winchester high-wall single shot was the first commercial rifle in the United States produced for a small-bore, smokeless-powder cartridge. This happened when the 30-40 Krag was added to the available calibers during 1893. The Remington-Lee bolt-action, Remington rolling block, Winchester Model 95 lever-action and high-wall single shot were the first commercial sporting rifles to offer this chambering. No commercial rifles used the cartridge from 1936 to 1973. From 1973 until 1977, the Ruger No. 3 single shot was chambered for the 30-40 Krag, thus stimulating a renewed interest in the cartridge. A rimless version headstamped as 30 USA and loaded by United Metallic Cartridge was offered for use in the Blake rifle.

General Comments The 30-40 (30-caliber/40 grains of the original smokeless powder load) Krag holds the unusual distinction of being the cartridge used to take what was until recently the world's record Rocky Mountain elk in 1899. This cartridge has retained its popularity primarily because large numbers of fine sporting conversions of the Krag military rifles and carbines chambered for it are still in use. This speaks highly for both cartridge and gun. If there is or has been a smoother working bolt-action rifle, I have not seen it.

Although not quite as powerful as either the 30-06 or the 308 Winchester, the 30-40 is well suited for use against North American big game. Just as with any cartridge, marksmanship and bullet choice are important, especially when going after the biggest and the meanest species on this continent. The Krag earned its reputation with the 220-grain loading, but it can be loaded to great advantage with lighter bullets for smaller species.

Interestingly, most authorities consider the 1895 Winchester chambering to be safe with loads at a somewhat higher pressure than the Krag rifle. However, both actions have limitations and one should be particularly circumspect in this regard. Bountiful loading data can be found in current manuals. The 30-40 is the basis of an entire genre of powerful Ackley Improved chamberings particularly suited to strong single-shot rifles. Winchester is the only remaining manufacturer of this ammunition. Only the 180-grain bullet is still offered.

30-40 Krag Loading Data and Factory Ballistics

Bullet (grains/type)	Powder	Grains	Velocity	Energy	Source/Comments
100 SP	H-322	45	3000	1999	Speer
110 SP	IMR 4320	47	2700	1781	Sierra, Speer
125 SP	IMR 4895	44.5	2600	1877	Sierra
130 SP	IMR 4064	45.5	2900	2428	Hornady, Speer
150 SP	IMR 4895	40	2400	1919	Nosler, Sierra
165 SP	IMR 4350	47	2500	2290	Hornady, Nosler, Sierra
180 SP	IMR 4350	46	2450	2400	Nosler, Sierra, Speer
180 SP	IMR 4895	39	2200	1935	Sierra
200 SP	IMR 3031	34	2100	1959	Nosler, Speer, Sierra
220 SP	IMR 4350	42	2100	2155	Hornady, Speer, Nosler
180 SP	FL		2430	2360	Factory load
220 SP	FL		2200	2360	Factory load

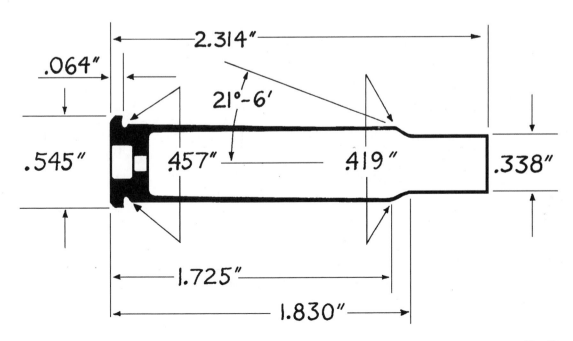

307 Winchester

Historical Notes The development of the rimmed 307 Winchester began in 1980, with the first public announcement in December 1982. However, the cartridge and the Model 94 XTR Angle Eject carbine chambered for it were not available until early 1983. The Marlin Model 336ER in 307 chambering introduced at the same time is no longer offered. The Angle Eject feature is a design modification of the beefed-up Model 94 XTR that ejects spent cartridge cases to the side rather than straight up, the same as earlier Model 94 actions. This was accomplished by changing the position of the extractor and ejector and lowering the right receiver sidewall.

The 307 caliber designation is to avoid confusing this cartridge with the other 30 calibers. It actually uses standard .308-inch bullets. The 307 Winchester is essentially a rimmed 308 Winchester although there is a difference in the overall cartridge length. Original factory loadings had 150- and 180-grain bullets.

General Comments The popular Model 1894 Winchester lever action has always suffered from two major deficiencies: The design did not allow center mounting of a scope sight, and the tubular magazine required use of flat-point bullets to prevent one cartridge from setting off others in the magazine under recoil. These factors combined to relegate the Model 1894 to largely short-range use. The new XTR Angle Eject redesign eliminates the scope-mounting problem and modernizes an old-but-popular action.

The 307 Winchester will certainly enhance the range and power of lever-action rifles so chambered. It is, based on factory ballistic figures, faster than the 30-30 by some 375 fps in muzzle velocity. Although the 307 Winchester has the same general configuration as the rimless 308 Winchester, there are slight differences that prevent it from achieving the full power of the 308. For one thing, the bullet is seated slightly deeper to maintain an overall length compatible with the length of the Model 1894 action. The result is that for any given barrel length with the same bullet weight, the 308 will deliver approximately 60 to 110 fps more muzzle velocity. Also, with its pointed bullet, the 308 will lose velocity at a slower rate than the 307 flat-point.

It is possible to chamber and fire 308 cartridges in some 307 rifles. However, for various reasons, this is an unsafe practice that could result in damage to the rifle and possible injury to the shooter.

The 307 has slightly less velocity at 200 yards than the 30-30 has at 100 yards. If the 30-30 is an adequate 100-yard-plus deer cartridge, then the 307 is certainly a 200-yard deer cartridge. It is not likely to replace the 30-30 as America's favorite deer cartridge, but it is a more versatile cartridge and certainly takes the Model 94 carbine out of the woods, bush and short-range class. Although it has been reported that the 307 Winchester has thicker case walls and, therefore, reduced internal volume, measurements do not verify this. Winchester is the only manufacturer of ammunition in this caliber. Only the 180-grain bullet is still offered.

307 Winchester Loading Data and Factory Ballistics

Bullet (grains/type)	Powder	Grains	Velocity	Energy	Source/Comments
110 Sierra HP	H322	44.0	3000	2195	Hodgdon
130 Speer FP	H4895	43.0	2762	2200	Hodgdon
150 Hornady RN	H4895	42.0	2604	2255	Hodgdon
170 Hornady FP	BI-C (2)	44.0	2535	2425	Hodgdon
170 SP	IMR4064	41.0	2500	2360	Hornady
150 SP	FL		2760	2538	Factory load
180 SP	FL		2510	2519	Factory load

*In tubular magazine rifles, load only flat-point bullets.

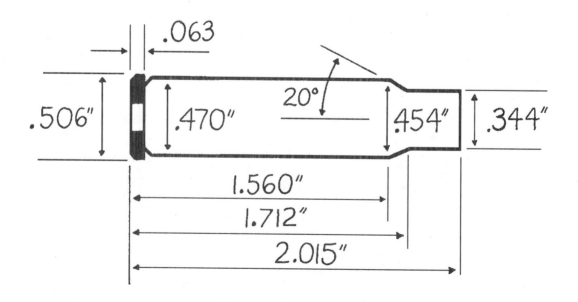

308 Winchester (7.62x51mm NATO)

Historical Notes Introduced by Winchester as a new sporting cartridge in 1952, the 308 is nothing more than the NATO 7.62x51mm military round. This was a very smart move, to tack the Winchester name on what was sure to become a popular sporting number. Practically every manufacturer of high-powered sporting rifles chambers the 308, since it will work through medium- or standard-length actions. The Model 70 bolt-action and 88 lever-action Winchester were the first American sporting rifles so chambered. It was adopted as the official U.S. military rifle cartridge in 1954, although guns for it were not ready until 1957.

General Comments In power, the 308 Winchester is superior to the 300 Savage and almost equal to the 30-06. It delivers about 100 fps less muzzle velocity than the larger 30-06 with any given bullet weight. Most authorities consider the 308 suitable for most North American big game, although it's on the light side for moose or brown bear. This chambering is a favorite of target shooters and has a reputation for excellent accuracy. It is the basis for a number of wildcat cartridges that have been adopted as factory chamberings: 243 Winchester, 6.5-08, 7mm-08 Remington, 358 Winchester and the rimmed versions 307 Winchester and 356 Winchester. All major domestic and foreign ammunition companies offer this cartridge.

308 Winchester Loading Data and Factory Ballistics

Bullet (grains/type)	Powder	Grains	Velocity	Energy	Source/Comments
110 SP	IMR 4064	50	3200	2502	Sierra
110 SP	IMR 4895	48	3200	2502	Hornady, Sierra
125 SP	W748	51.5	3100	2668	Sierra, Nosler
150 SP	IMR 4064	46	2800	2612	Nosler, Sierra, Speer
150 SP	IMR 4895	44	2700	2429	Nosler, Speer, Sierra
165 SP	IMR 4064	43	2600	2477	Sierra, Speer, Nosler, Hornady
180 SP	IMR 3031	41	2500	2499	Nosler
180 SP	IMR 4064	41.5	2500	2499	Nosler, Sierra, Hornady
190 SP	IMR 4064	41.5	2500	2637	Hornady, Speer, Sierra
200 SP	IMR 4064	41.5	2400	2559	Sierra
150 SP	FL		2820	2648	Factory load
168 HPBT	FL		2600	2180	Factory load
180 SP	FL		2620	2743	Factory load

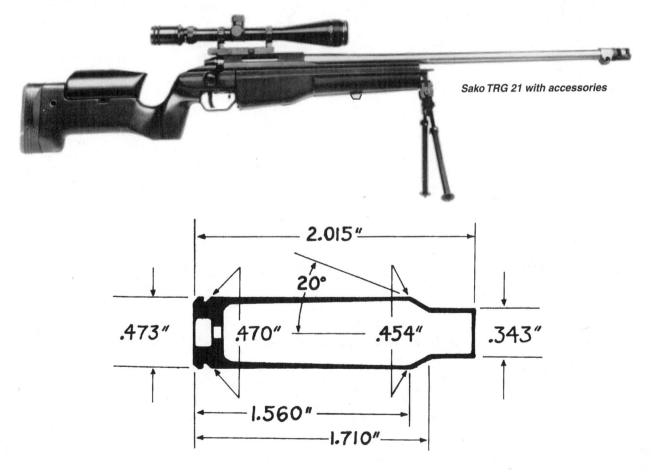

Sako TRG 21 with accessories

30-06 Springfield (7.62x63mm/ 30 Government M'06)

Historical Notes The 30-06 Springfield is a United States military cartridge adapted from the 30-03 by adopting a lighter, streamlined bullet and making other minor changes. In this, it parallels other military cartridge developments of the era, with French and German developments leading the way. It was adopted in 1906 for the Model 1903 Springfield service rifle, which was based on the Mauser bolt-action system. The Winchester Model 1895 lever action appears to have been the first sporting rifle chambered for the 30-06. The cartridge was added to the line in 1908. The Remington bolt-action Model 30, introduced in 1921, and the Winchester bolt-action Model 54 brought out in 1925 both offered the 30-06, among other chamberings. The Savage bolt-action Model 40 and 45 Super-Sporter rifles were also so chambered when introduced in 1928. At present, in addition to the many bolt-action rifles, the Remington Model 7600 pump-action and 7400 semi-auto, as well as the Browning semi-auto, include the 30-06 as standard chamberings. The Ruger Number 1 single-shot rifle is also offered in 30-06. A number of British and European side-by-side or over/under double rifles can be ordered in this chambering, and so can some European rifle-shotgun combination guns.

General Comments The 30-06 is undoubtedly the most flexible, useful, all-round big game cartridge available to the American hunter. For many years, it has been the standard by which all other big game cartridges have been measured. To say that a cartridge is in the 30-06 class means it is suitable for any game in North America. The secret of success when using this cartridge is to select the right bullet for the game and hunting conditions at hand. Lighter bullets of 100 to 130 grains should be used only for varmint and small game hunting. While these bullets can be driven at impressive velocities (well over 3,000 fps), they are designed to expand rapidly on small game and will not penetrate properly on large game. For deer, antelope, goats, sheep, black or brown bear, under most hunting conditions, the 150- or 165-grain bullet is proper and a good compromise for those seeking one load for medium to heavy game. For heavier game such as elk, moose or brown bear, the 165-, 180-, 200- or 220-grain bullets are the best choice. The '06 performs impressively with handloads using 250-grain bullets. Many experienced hunters consider the 180-grain bullet the most satisfactory all-round loading for the 30-06 because it can be used effectively on anything from deer to the heaviest game under almost any hunting conditions. As a matter of fact, the 30-06 will give a good account on all but the heaviest or most dangerous African or Asiatic species under average hunting conditions. The 220-grain bullet is generally recommended for African game although the 180-grain also has a good reputation there. With the proper bullet, this cartridge can be adapted to any game or hunting situation in North or South America, whether in the mountains, plains, woods or jungles. Few other cartridges can claim equal versatility.

30-06 Springfield Loading Data and Factory Ballistics

Bullet (grains/type)	Powder	Grains	Velocity	Energy	Source/Comments
100 SP	IMR 4064	59	3400	2568	Speer
110 SP	IMR 4064	54.5	3300	2660	Sierra, Hornady
110 SP	H-380	56	3300	2660	Sierra
125 SP	IMR 3031	50	3100	2668	Sierra
130 SP	IMR 4350	58	3000	2599	Hornady, Speer
150 SP	IMR 4350	59	3000	2998	Nosler, Speer, Sierra, Hornady
150 SP	IMR 4895	51	2900	2802	Nosler
165 SP	IMR 4320	50.5	2800	2873	Sierra
180 SP	IMR 4320	48.5	2700	2910	Sierra, Nosler
180 SP	IMR 4831	57	2750	3023	Speer, Nosler, Sierra
190 SP	IMR 4350	54	2700	3076	Hornady, Speer, Sierra
200 SP	IMR 4320	47	2400	2559	Nosler, Sierra
220 SP	IMR 4350	50.5	2400	2854	Hornady, Sierra, Barnes
220 SP	IMR 4831	54	2500	3054	Hornady, Sierra
250 SP	IMR 4831	47	2100	2499	Barnes
55 SP	FL (Accelerator)		4080	2033	Remington factory load
125 SP	FL		3140	2736	Factory load
150 SP	FL		2920	2839	Factory load
165 SP	FL		2800	2873	Factory load
168 HPBT	FL		2700	2720	Factory load
180 SP	FL		2700	2913	Factory load
220 SP	FL		2410	2837	Factory load

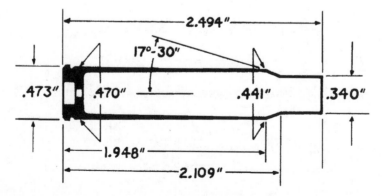

300 Holland & Holland Magnum (300 H&H Super)

Historical Notes The 300 H&H Magnum was introduced in 1925 by the British firm of Holland & Holland as "Holland's Super 30." The Western Cartridge Co., the first American company to load this round commercially, offered it here in 1925. No American-made commercial rifles were chambered for the 300 H&H until 12 years after its introduction. However, Griffin & Howe and other custom rifle makers turned out rifles for it almost as soon as the British. In 1935, Ben Comfort won the 1000-yard Wimbledon Cup Match with this cartridge, and overnight it became the new sensation. The Model 70 Winchester was chambered for the 300 H&H in 1937, and the Model 721 and succeeding Model 700 Remingtons were also available in this chambering. Most European bolt-action rifles chambered it as standard.

General Comments Since 1935, the 300 H&H has enjoyed a limited popularity in the United States. Many shooters consider it the best all-round 30-caliber available to the American hunter; others insist it is hardly better than the 30-06. Regardless of which side one favors, this is an accurate cartridge and adequate for any North American big game. Its most useful range is from elk on up, but it is also a very fine long-range cartridge for antelope, sheep or goats. It is popular in Africa as an all-round caliber for plains game. Lately, its popularity has suffered considerably from competition with the 300 Weatherby and 300 Winchester Magnums. It is no longer used for match competition. Derived from the earlier 375 H&H, the 300 H&H is the direct progenitor of an entire family of belted magnums. With modern powders and best handloads, the 300 H&H is very close ballistically to even the biggest 300 Magnums. Winchester, Remington and Federal all load this cartridge.

300 Holland & Holland Magnum Loading Data and Factory Ballistics

Bullet (grains/type)	Powder	Grains	Velocity	Energy	Source/Comments
110 HP	IMR 4350	76	3600	3166	Sierra, Hornady
130 SP	IMR 4320	64	3400	3338	Hornady
150 SP	IMR 4831	73	3300	3628	Nosler, Sierra, Speer
165 SP	IMR 4350	69	3100	3522	Sierra, Speer, Hornady
180 SP	IMR 4831	68	2900	3362	Sierra, Speer
190 SP	H-380	65.5	3000	3798	Hornady
200 SP	IMR 4831	67.5	2800	3483	Sierra, Speer
220 SP	IMR 4350	63	2700	3562	Hornady, Sierra
150	FL		3190	3390	Factory load
180	FL		2880	3315	Factory load
220	FL		2620	3350	Factory load

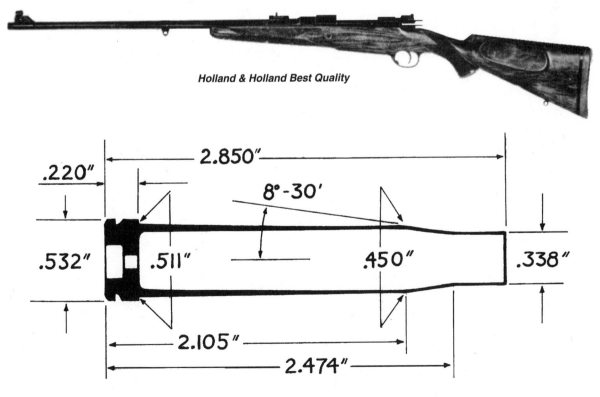

Holland & Holland Best Quality

300 Remington Short Action Ultra Mag

Historical Notes In 2001, Remington introduced the 300 Remington Short Action Ultra Magnum cartridge as a competitor to Winchester's 300 Winchester Short Magnum. Ballistic performance of the Remington and Winchester offerings is similar.

General Comments Based on a shortened 300 Ultra Magnum case, which is itself derived from a slightly modified 404 Jeffery cartridge of African fame, the 300 Remington Short Action Ultra Magnum is slightly shorter and smaller in diameter than its

Winchester counterpart. Short, fat cases burn powder very efficiently, since the primer's flash ignites a larger area of the packed gunpowder. The case is unbelted and headspaces on the shoulder for improved shoulder tolerances. Remington barrels for this cartridge use a twist rate of 1:10. Shooters are cautioned never to fire a 300 Remington Short Action Ultra Magnum in a 300 WSM-chambered rifle as the headspace would be excessive, leading to possible injury or firearms damage.

300 Remington SA Ultra Magnum Loading Data and Factory Ballistics

Bullet (grains/type)	Powder	Grains	Velocity	Energy	Source/Comments
150 PSP	FL		3200	3410	Remington factory load
165 PSP	FL		3075	3464	Remington factory load
180 Nosler Partition	FL		2960	3501	Remington factory load
180 Scirocco	FL		3250	4221	Remington factory load

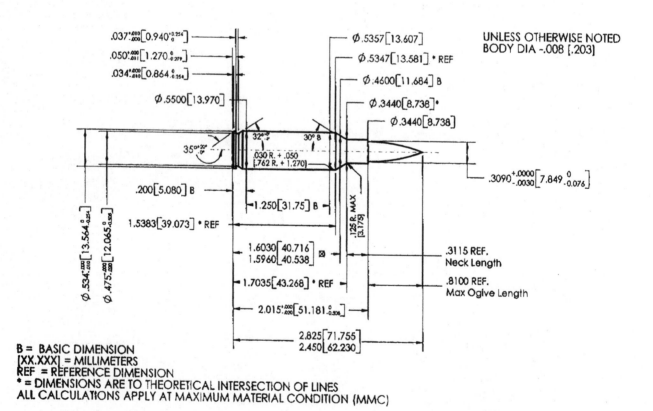

B = BASIC DIMENSION
[XX.XXX] = MILLIMETERS
REF = REFERENCE DIMENSION
* = DIMENSIONS ARE TO THEORETICAL INTERSECTION OF LINES
ALL CALCULATIONS APPLY AT MAXIMUM MATERIAL CONDITION (MMC)

300 Winchester Short Magnum (300 WSM)

Historical Notes At the start of the 21st century, cartridge designs diverged. One direction was longer, fatter cartridges chambered in long-action rifles. Winchester took another path with new chubby, stubby cartridges sized to fit the more rigid short-action rifles. Introduced in 2000 and chambered in short, light Browning and Winchester rifles, the 300 Winchester Short Magnum demonstrated a remarkably accurate ability to duplicate 300 Winchester Magnum velocities while consuming about 10 percent less powder. SSK Industries also re-barrels the AR-10 self-loading rifle for 300 WSM.

General Comments The 300 WSM, an original Winchester cartridge case design, fits handily into bolt actions sized for a cartridge length of 2.860 inches. Officially a rimless cartridge, the case rim is slightly rebated by .020-inch, and the case rim sized to fit existing magnum bolt face dimensions. For highly efficient and consistent powder burning, the 300 WSM employs a short-fat powder column geometry, a concept revered by accuracy obsessed benchrest shooters for nearly three decades. Eschewing a belt on the case, the 300 WSM headspaces on the 35-degree shoulder, which should provide tighter headspacing tolerances, and improved accuracy potential. Shooters are cautioned never to fire the slightly shorter, physically similar 300 Remington Short Action Ultra Magnum in a 300 WSM-chambered rifle, as the headspace would be excessive, leading to possible injury or firearms damage.

300 Winchester Short Magnum Loading Data and Factory Ballistics

Bullet (grains/type)	Powder	Grains	Velocity	Energy	Source/Comments
150 BST	FL		3300	3628	Winchester/Olin factory load
180 Fail Safe	FL		2970	3526	Winchester/Olin factory load
180 P Pt	FL		2970	3526	Winchester/Olin factory load
150 BST	WW760	71.0	3250	3519	Winchester/Olin 60,000 psi
165 Fail Safe	WW760	68.5	3130	3590	Winchester/Olin 63,300 psi
168 BST	WW760	69.8	3090	3563	Winchester/Olin 60,300 psi
180 SP	WW760	66.9	2960	3503	Winchester/Olin 60,500 psi
180 Fail Safe	WW760	68.0	2940	3456	Winchester/Olin 60,200 psi

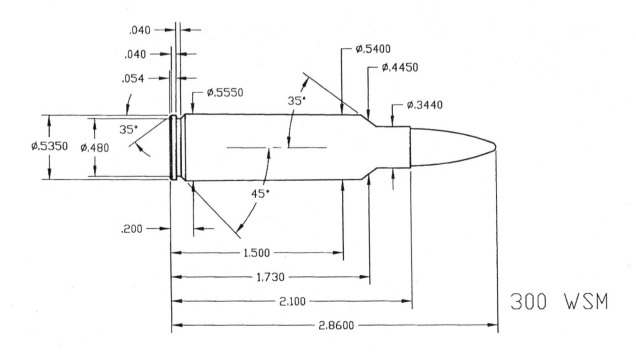

300 Winchester Magnum

Historical Notes This cartridge was introduced in 1963 for the Winchester Model 70 bolt-action rifle. Rifles chambered for the 300 Winchester Magnum have since been introduced by most domestic and European manufacturers.

General Comments Arrival of the 300 Winchester Magnum was rather anti-climatic because everyone had been predicting it from the day the 338 Winchester Magnum was brought out in 1958. The 30-338 wildcat quickly followed. The newer 300 Winchester Magnum has a slightly longer body (by about 0.12-inch) and a shorter neck than its predecessors. This short neck is considered a poor feature as it means the heavy bullets have to project back into the powder space quite a bit. The 308 Norma Magnum, introduced

in 1960, is nearly identical to the 338 Winchester Magnum necked-down. If that chambering had not been offered before Winchester was ready to produce its own 30-caliber Magnum, it is possible the company would simply have necked the 338 to 30-caliber. In any event, the 300 Winchester Magnum is a fine long-range, big game cartridge in the same class as the 300 Weatherby and suitable for any North American species. Actual factory-load ballistics may be closer to 300 Weatherby Magnum ballistics than published data suggests. With cartridges in this class and above, recoil becomes a factor for many shooters. It is loaded by all domestic and many foreign ammunition manufacturers.

300 Winchester Magnum Loading Data and Factory Ballistics

Bullet (grains/type)	Powder	Grains	Velocity	Energy	Source/Comments
110 HP	IMR 4350	80	3600	3166	Hornady, Sierra
125 SP	IMR 4350	77	3400	3209	Sierra
130 SP	IMR 4064	66	3300	3144	Speer, Hornady
150 SP	IMR 4350	76	3300	3628	Sierra
150 SP	IMR 4895	62	3150	3306	Speer, Sierra
150 SP	IMR 4350	76	3200	3412	Speer, Sierra
165 SP	IMR 4831	76	3200	3753	Speer, Sierra
180 SP	IMR 4350	71	3000	3598	Sierra
190 SP	IMR 4831	74	3150	4187	Speer
200 SP	IMR 4350	68	2950	3866	Nosler
220 SP	IMR 4350	60	2500	3054	Hornady, Sierra
150 SP	FL		3290	3605	Factory load
180 SP	FL		2960	3501	Factory load
200 SP	FL		2825	3544	Factory load
220 SP	FL		2680	3508	Factory load

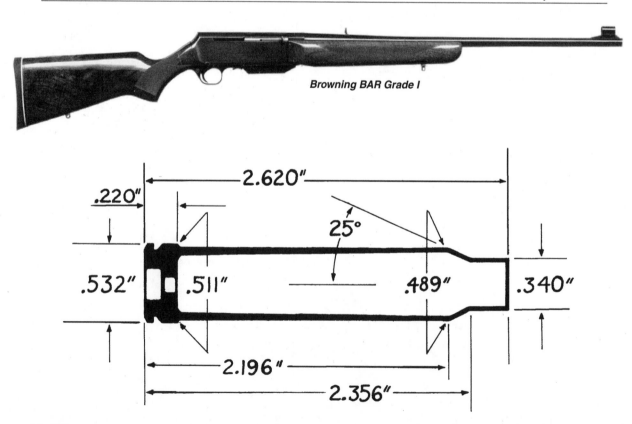

Browning BAR Grade I

300 Weatherby Magnum

Historical Notes The 300 Weatherby Magnum is the most popular and well-known cartridge of the Weatherby line. At the same time, it is one of the most controversial. It was developed in 1944. Commercial ammunition has been available since 1948, under the Weatherby label. Weatherby brand ammunition is loaded by Norma of Sweden. The Weatherbys were the only U.S. rifles chambered for this round on a commercial basis, but it is a popular caliber among custom rifle makers. In 1989, Remington offered the Model 700 Classic in 300 Weatherby and other makers have since followed suit. Recently, several ammo manufacturers have begun offering ammunition in this caliber.

General Comments Until the advent of the 30-378 Weatherby, the 300 Weatherby Magnum was the biggest of the commercial 300 belted magnums. Barrel life can be short, some might classify recoil as severe, and ballistics suffer greatly when shorter barrels are tried. None of these limitations matter to many who use it strictly for big game hunting and seldom fire it more than a few dozen times a year. It can be adapted to long-range varmint shooting if one can develop an accurate enough load, but it is not very flexible in that regard. For the hunter who wants one rifle suitable for any species of non-dangerous big game worldwide, the 300 WM is an excellent choice. However, because of caliber restrictions, local game laws may prohibit its use, even against non-dangerous species. This is another case of archaic regulations, where the law might allow one to use an entirely inappropriate loading from a much less powerful big-bore; where, given the right choice of bullets, the 300 WM would be much more effective and humane.

300 Weatherby Magnum Loading Data and Factory Ballistics

Bullet (grains/type)	Powder	Grains	Velocity	Energy	Source/Comments
110 HP	IMR 4064	79.5	3800	3528	Hornady, Sierra
125 SP	IMR 4831	87.5	3500	3401	Sierra
150 SP	H-380	77	3300	3628	Sierra
150 SP	IMR 4350	80.5	3200	3412	Hornady, Speer
165 SP	IMR 4831	82	3200	3753	Speer, Sierra
180 SP	IMR 4350	76.5	3000	3598	Hornady, Speer, Nosler, Sierra
180 SP	MRP	84	3100	3842	Speer
200 SP	IMR 4350	75	2900	3736	Speer, Sierra
220 SP	H-450	77	2800	3831	Hornady
250 SP	IMR 7828	69	2350	3066	Barnes
150 SP	FL		3600	4316	Factory load
165 SPBT	FL		3450	4360	Factory load
180 SP	FL		3300	4352	Factory load
190 SPBT	FL		3030	3873	Factory load
220 SP	FL		2905	4122	Factory load

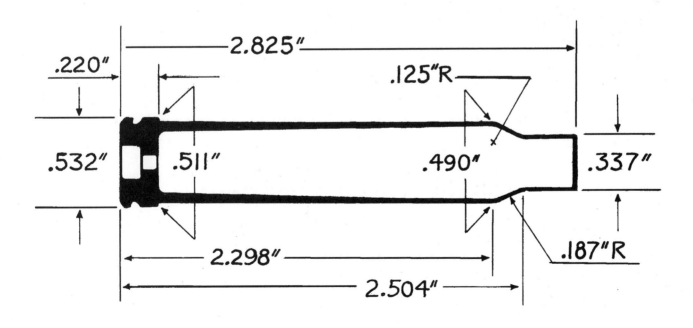

300 Remington Ultra Magnum

Historical Notes When it debuted the 300 Remington Ultra Magnum cartridge in 1999, Remington joined an increasingly popular trend toward big, beltless rounds. Popular from the onset, the 300 Remington Ultra Magnum launched a whole family of non-belted, high performance magnums, which includes the 7mm, 338, and 375 Remington Ultra Magnums. When tested by Remington at 200 yards, the 300 Ultra Mag delivered nearly 18-percent greater retained energy than the 300 Weatherby Mag and almost 27-percent greater retained energy than the 300 Winchester Magnum.

General Comments The velocity and energy performance of Remington Ultra Mag cartridges comes from an innovative case design. Modifying the 404 Jeffery case with a rebated rim to fit Model 700 rifle bolt faces *(for magnum cartridges)*, increased body taper and 30 caliber-sized neck, Remington's resulting case allows about 13-percent more internal capacity than the 300 Weatherby. It offers a similarly sized ballistic advantage. The result is a "non-belted magnum" with a larger case diameter, which allows for dramatically increased powder capacity. Headspacing on the shoulder of the case, rather than the use of a belt, promotes better accuracy due to precise bore alignment. At a Newfoundland moose camp with a 100-percent success rate in the 2002 season, the editor picked up a fired 300 Ultra Magnum case—a solid reminder of its eminent suitability for big game anywhere in North America, and for non-dangerous game in Africa.

300 Remington Ultra Magnum Factory Ballistics

Bullet (grains/type)	Powder	Grains	Velocity	Energy	Source/Comments
150 Scirocco	FL		3450	3964	Remington factory load
180 PSP	FL		3250	4221	Remington factory load
180 Nosler Partition	FL		3250	4221	Remington factory load
180 Scirocco	FL		3250	4221	Remington factory load
200 Nosler Partition	FL		3025	4063	Remington factory load

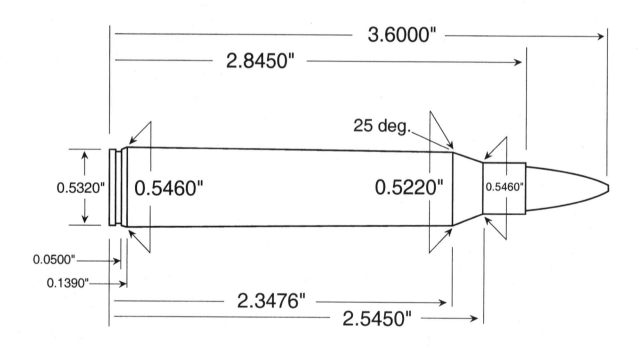

30-378 Weatherby

Historical Notes This cartridge was developed specifically for use in 1000-yard benchrest competition. It was created by simply necking the 378 Weatherby case to accept 30-caliber bullets. The standard design retains the trademark Weatherby double-radius shoulder. Weatherby asked Norma to develop factory ammunition about 1996. This chambering was more-or-less factory standardized about 1998.

General Comments The 30-378 case can hold more than 120 grains of powder, compared to about 90 grains for the 300 Weatherby. With the advent of new slower-burning powders, increased capacity promises a useful advantage to the handloader. (Recent availability of 250-grain, match-grade bullets served to increase potential benefit and demand for a chambering with increased powder capacity.) The 30-378 Weatherby certainly delivers on this promise: It is a simple matter to load 250-grain Sierra MatchKing bullets to produce almost 3,000 fps muzzle velocity without exceeding 30-06 pressure levels — from a 26-inch barrel! Lighter bullets can be driven faster but with those this chambering offers less advantage over standard 300 Magnum chamberings. When bullets lighter than 200 grains are fired from a 26-inch barrel, this cartridge is only marginally superior to the 300 Weatherby. Recently, tests have demonstrated that lighter bullet (150- to 180-grain) ballistics are markedly improved by use of slower rifling twist (1:13 to 1:15 works well), compared to the factory 1:10 twist. However, with 30-inch barrels installed, ballistic difference is significant with all bullet weights. Those looking for the ultimate long-range hunting rifle for smaller species might give this chambering a hard look. A single-shot rifle equipped with a 30-inch tube offers reasonable handling ease and, if chambered for this cartridge, would deliver huge doses of energy to a distant target with the flattest trajectory available. Accurate Arms data shows the 250-grain MK generating the same muzzle energy as the 458 Winchester Magnum when loaded to about the same pressure! How about a 300-grain VLD launched from a 30-inch barrel at 2800 fps? In any case, useful barrel life can be extremely limited.

30-378 Weatherby Loading Data (26-inch barrel)

Bullet (grains/type)	Powder	Grains	Velocity	Energy	Source/Comments
180 Barnes-X	AA 8700	118.0	3283	4310	Accurate
200 Nosler Partition	AA 8700	117.0	3208	4570	Accurate
200 Sierra HPBT	AA 8700	117.0	3163	4440	Accurate
220 Sierra HPBT	AA 8700	115.0	3050	4545	Accurate
250 Sierra HPBT	AA 8700	111.0	2954	4840	Accurate

303 British

Historical Notes The 303 British was the official military rifle cartridge of England and the British Empire from its adoption in 1888 until the 7.62 NATO came along in the 1950s. The original loading was a 215-grain bullet and a compressed charge of blackpowder — cordite became the propellant in 1892. Manufacture in the United States began about 1897. Remington chambered its Lee bolt-action magazine rifle for this cartridge and Winchester did likewise in its Model 95 lever action. No American rifle has chambered the 303 British since 1936. However, Winchester, Federal and Remington continue to load this popular cartridge.

General Comments The 303 British has always been popular in Canada and other parts of the British Empire. In the United States it has not been as widely used because of its performance similarity to the 30-40 Krag. However, since the end of World War II, the importation of large numbers of British Lee-Enfield military rifles has altered this situation. At the present time, the 303 is more popular than the 30-40 Krag. Norma imports 130- and 180-grain loads that greatly increase the flexibility and usefulness of this cartridge for the American hunter. The 215-grain bullet has always had a good reputation for deep penetration and is a favorite for moose and caribou in the Canadian backwoods. The 303 is suitable for anything the 30-40 Krag is in the way of game. In Australia, a number of popular sporting cartridges are based on necking-down and/or reforming the 303 case.

*(**Editor's Note:** Although often classed with the 30-40 Krag, this cartridge is loaded to higher pressures and delivers superior ballistics. Foreign factory loads place it very close ballistically to the 308 Winchester and measurably above any factory 30-40 load, though handloads for the 30-40 in the Model 95 Winchester can match the 303 British.)*

303 British Loading Data and Factory Ballistics

Bullet (grains/type)	Powder	Grains	Velocity	Energy	Source/Comments
123 Hornady SP	RI-15	49.8	3015	2480	Hodgdon
150 SP	IMR 4064	43	2600	2252	Speer, Hornady
150 SP	IMR 4895	42	2400	1919	Sierra, Speer
150 SP	IMR 4064	43	2600	2252	Speer, Sierra
150 Speer SP	RI-15	46.2	2755	2525	Hodgdon
180 SP	IMR 4895	42	2400	2303	Sierra
180 SP	IMR 4350	46	2400	2303	Speer, Hornady
180 Sako SP	N140	41.7	2540	2575	VihtaVuori
130 SP	FL		2789	2246	Factory load
150 SP	FL		2690	2400	Factory load
180 SP	FL		2460	2420	Factory load
215 SP	FL		2180	2270	Factory load

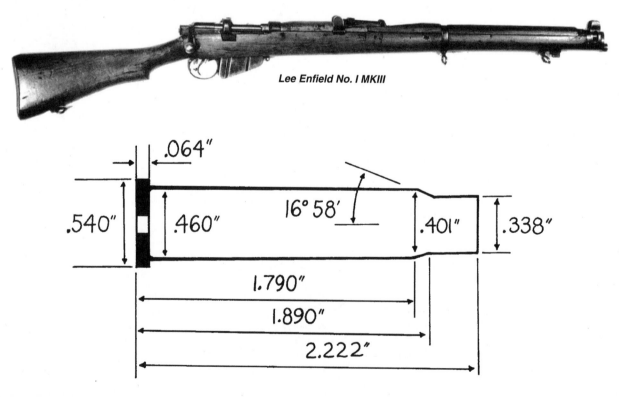

Lee Enfield No. I MKIII

.064"

.540" .460" 16° 58' .401" .338"

1.790"

1.890"

2.222"

32-20 Winchester (32-20 WCF)

Historical Notes Introduced by Winchester in 1882 for the Model 73 lever-action rifle, the 32-20 quickly attained considerable popularity as a medium-power cartridge in both rifle and revolver. Practically all American makers have chambered rifles for the 32-20 in lever-, pump- or bolt-action, and most single-shot rifles have also chambered it. Colt, Smith & Wesson and Bayard made revolvers in this caliber. Marlin reintroduced it for their Model 94CL lever action in 1988. Winchester once offered a lighter 100-grain bullet blackpowder load for the 32 Colt Lightning magazine rifle, headstamped 32 C.L.M.R. A similar 100-grain loading specifically for Marlin rifles was headstamped 32-20. Both Remington and Winchester still offer factory-loaded ammunition.

General Comments Although recently semi-obsolete, the 32-20 still enjoys modest popularity with farmers, ranchers, trappers and pot hunters. It can be reloaded easily and at moderate cost. In addition, it delivers good killing power on small and medium game at ranges out to 100 yards without destroying all the edible meat.

Winchester once advertised it as a combination small game and deer cartridge. However, it is much too underpowered for deer-size animals. It is, nonetheless, a useful small game and varmint cartridge at short ranges, and it is quite accurate in a bolt-action or solid-frame single-shot.

The author had considerable personal experience with the old 32-20, having owned and hunted with several rifles of this caliber. These included (in chronological order) a Winchester Model 1892 lever action, Savage Model 23C bolt action, Remington Model 25A slide action and a rechambered Greener single-shot Cadet rifle.

The Savage bolt action with a scope sight would shoot very consistently into 1 to 1-1/4 inches at 100 yards. This was a very nice little varmint and small game combination at ranges of 100 to 125 yards. I used this in the immediate post-World War II era when nothing else was available, and it worked out very well within its range limitations. I have also used the 25-20, but always considered the 32-20 a better all-around cartridge in this class. It's a better killer on just about anything at practical ranges.

In a strong single-action revolver, the 32-20 can be loaded to 1,050 to 1,100 fps from a 6-inch barrel, which makes a very effective field gun. Trouble is, the cartridge is too long for most modern revolver cylinders. The 32 H&R Magnum is shorter and will serve to fill the requirement for a high-performance 32-caliber handgun round. The 357 Magnum revolver cartridge chambering in a rifle will out perform the 32-20 by a substantial margin. In any event, the author always liked the 32-20 for certain purposes. The advent of Cowboy Action Shooting has given this round a new lease on life. The 32-20 is the basis for the 25-20 and the 218 Bee.

32-20 Winchester Loading Data and Factory Ballistics

Bullet (grains/type)	Powder	Grains	Velocity	Energy	Source/Comments
85 SP	2400	12.5	2100	833	Rifle only — Hornady
85 SP	IMR 4227	17	2300	999	Rifle only — Hornady
85 SP	H-110	14	2100	833	Rifle only — Hornady
110 SP	IMR 4227	15	2000	977	Rifle only — Hornady
110 SP	H-110	15.5	2100	1077	Rifle only — Hornady
110 SP	2400	10.5	1700	706	Rifle only — Hornady
80 SP	FL		2100	780	Factory load
100 SP	FL		1210	325	Factory load

WARNING: Do not use rifle loads in revolvers; pressures develop beyond what the average handgun is designed to withstand.

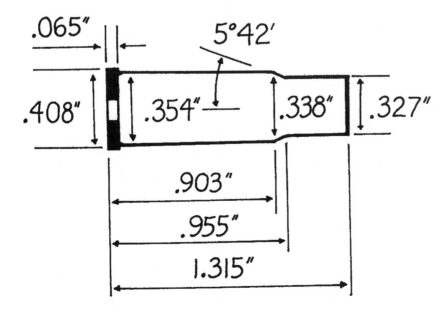

32 Winchester Special (32 WS)

Historical Notes Introduced in 1902 for the Winchester Model 1894 lever action, the 32 Special was an original smokeless powder design. Because it is a rimmed shell, it has never been used in anything but lever-action and single shot rifles. Remington brought out a rimless version to function in their bolt and semi-auto rifles. Winchester and Marlin were the principal American companies to chamber the 32 Special. Federal, Remington and Winchester continue to offer factory loaded ammunition until quite recently.

General Comments In the 1916 catalog, Winchester had this to say about the 32 Special: "The 32 Winchester Special, which we have perfected, is offered to meet the demand of many sportsmen for a smokeless powder cartridge of larger caliber than the .30 Winchester and yet not so powerful as the .30 Army." It goes on to explain that the 32 Special meets these requirements and the 1916 ballistics chart shows it generating 10.6 percent more energy than the 30-30 at the muzzle and retaining an edge to any reasonable hunting range.

Today, it is still loaded to higher velocity, and if loaded to equal pressure, it easily beats the 30-30 by over 100 fps. However, bullet selection is limited. Speer's 170-grain flat point, the most streamlined available, actually has a higher ballistic coefficient than most 170-grain 30-30 bullets. For those whose 32 Special rifle has a truly shot-out barrel, Hornady's 170-grain round-nose 0.323-inch bullet works wonderfully. There has been a mountain of bunk written about the 32 Special answering the demand of handloaders who wanted to use blackpowder. Since the same rifle was originally chambered for the 32-40 at about one-half the price of the nickel steel 32 Special version, this seems fantastic. Those writers would have us believe that the man wanting to save money on ammunition would for no reason spend the price of two rifles for the privilege. The fact that blackpowder can be used successfully in the 32 Special, and the fact that Winchester once provided a blackpowder-height rear sight for the rifle certainly do not prove that the cartridge was invented to allow folks to do what they could already do with the much cheaper 32-40 Model 94.

Much ink has also been spilled claiming the 32 Special just wouldn't shoot straight after the barrel got a bit of wear. I have experimented with two 32 Special carbines, a very early Winchester and a 1936 Marlin. With bullets that fit, both shoot inside 3 inches at 100 yards with open sights. The Winchester had been so abused that its rifling hardly showed until we thoroughly cleaned it. The bore is pitted but it shoots just fine.

32 Winchester Special Loading Data and Factory Ballistics

Bullet (grains/type)	Powder	Grains	Velocity	Energy	Source/Comments
170 SP	RL7	31.0	2283	1965	Lyman
170 SP	W748	36.2	2240	1890	Winchester
170 SP	FL		2250	1910	Factory load

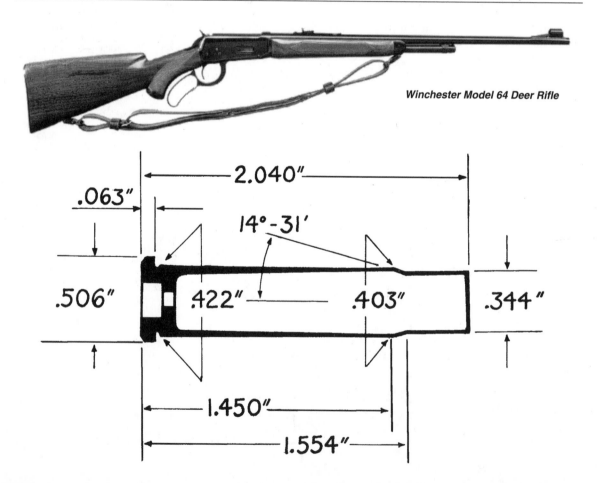

Winchester Model 64 Deer Rifle

8mm Mauser (7.92mm Mauser/8x57mmJ/8x57mmI/ 8x57mmS/8x57JS)

Historical Notes The 8mm or 7.92 Mauser was the German military rifle cartridge through both world wars. It was officially adopted in 1888 with a bullet diameter of 0.318-inch. In 1905, the bullet diameter was increased to 0.323-inch. In Europe, the 8mm Mauser and several other 8mm cartridges are available in both sizes. The larger size is always designated as S or JS bore. In the United States, ammunition companies load only the .323-inch diameter or "S" bullet. The 8mm Mauser is widely chambered in European sporting rifles, but American gunmakers have not adopted it as a standard sporting caliber. The "J" or "I" in the name denotes infantry ammunition. The German capital "I" was mistaken for a capital "J" by U.S. military interpreters after World War I and the "J" misnomer came into common use here and even in Europe thereafter!

General Comments The 8mm Mauser had not been very popular in the United States prior to World War II. However, the large number of obsolete, surplus 8mm military rifles sold here since the end of the war has increased its use substantially. American cartridge companies only put out one loading; the 170-grain bullet at 2360 fps or so. As loaded by Norma and by other European companies, such as RWS, it is in the same class as our 30-06. It is adequate for any North American big game if the proper bullets and full loadings are used. A large variety of good .323-inch bullets is now available for the individual handloader, and this has increased the usefulness of the 8mm Mauser for the American shooter.

8mm Mauser (8x57mm JS) Loading Data and Factory Ballistics

Bullet (grains/type)	Powder	Grains	Velocity	Energy	Source/Comments
125 SP	H-4198	44	3100	2668	Hornady
125 SP	IMR 3031	49	3100	2668	Hornady
150 SP	IMR 4320	53.5	2900	2802	Hornady
150 SP	IMR 3031	49	2750	2519	Speer
175 SP	IMR 3031	45.5	2600	2627	Sierra
200 SP	IMR 4831	54	2400	2559	Speer
220 SP	IMR 4831		2200	2365	Hornady
159 SP	FL		2723	2618	European factory load
170 SP	FL		2360	2100	U.S. factory load
196 SP	FL		2526	2778	European factory load
198 SP	FL		2625	3031	European factory load
200 SP	FL		2320	2390	European factory load
227 SP	FL		2330	2737	European factory load

WARNING! Many J-bore (0.318-inch) rifles still exist and will fire S-bore (0.323-inch) cartridges, creating dangerous pressures. When in doubt, check bore diameter CAREFULLY!

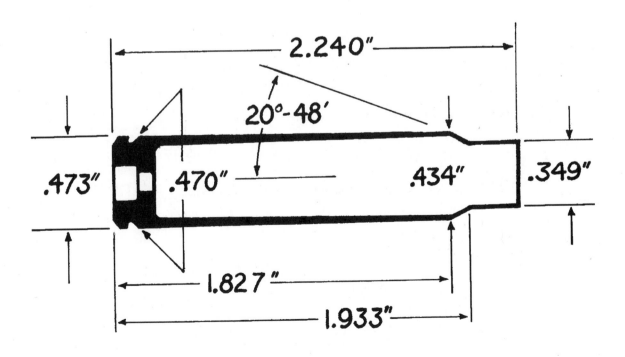

8mm Remington Magnum

Historical Notes This cartridge was a Remington development announced in 1978 for the Model 700 BDL bolt-action rifle. The 8mm Magnum is something of a departure from the usual belted, short magnum configuration favored by Remington in the past (a design that will work through the standard-length bolt action). The 8mm Magnum is based on the full-length 375 H&H case blown out, thus requiring a 0.375-inch longer bolt travel than the standard 30-06.

Again, this is not an entirely original design, since it was preceded by similar developments in years past. The 8x68mm (S) Magnum, for example, originated in Germany around 1940, and a number of 8mm wildcat magnums such as the 8mm Ernst, 8x62 Durham, 323 Hollis, 8mm PMM, etc., date back to the late 1950s and early 1960s. However, this is the first commercial 8mm magnum cartridge introduced by an American company. Remington originally offered two loadings: a 185-grain bullet at a muzzle velocity of 3,080 fps and a 220-grain at 2,830 fps. The 220-grain load has since been dropped. There is a good selection of 8mm (0.323-inch diameter) bullets available for handloading this cartridge.

General Comments Comparing either handloaded or factory ballistics for the 338 Winchester Magnum and the 8mm Remington Magnum, one can easily see why the latter failed to garner any great following. Any minuscule ballistic advantage it might have just doesn't justify the increased cartridge length and recoil resulting from a heavier powder charge. Add to that a more limited bullet selection and the 8mm Remington Magnum dims even further. With lighter recoil and potentially flatter trajectories, the various 300 Magnums have it beaten on that side; with heavier bullets shooting almost as flat and delivering more energy, the 338 Winchester Magnum and the 340 Weatherby Magnum have it beaten on the other side. This is a classic example of a cartridge that fails to fill any useful niche. Due to its large powder capacity, this cartridge is another that is particularly sensitive to barrel length.

8mm Remington Magnum Loading Data and Factory Ballistics

Bullet (grains/type)	Powder	Grains	Velocity	Energy	Source/Comments
125 SP	IMR 4064/76		3600	3598	Hornady
150 SP	IMR 4350/	79.5	3300	3628	Speer, Hornady, Sierra
175 SP	IMR 4831	80	3100	3735	Speer, Sierra, Hornady
200 SP	IMR 4831	78	3050	4132	Nosler, Speer
220 SP	IMR 4831	76	2800	3831	Sierra, Hornady
250 SP	IMR 7828	72	2550	3611	Barnes
185 SP	FL		3080	3896	Remington factory load
220 SP	FL		2830	3912	Remington factory load

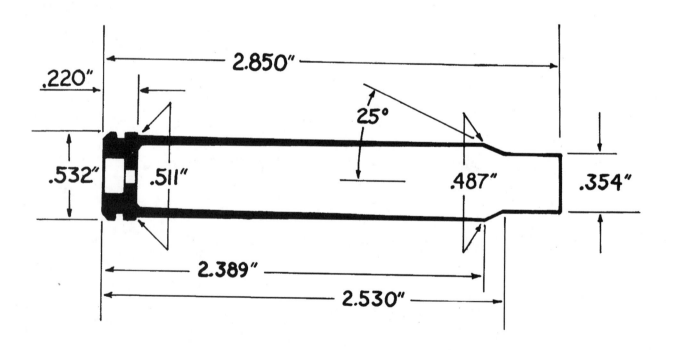

325 Winchester Short Magnum (325 WSM)

Historical Notes After introducing their short magnum family of cartridges in 2000, Winchester® recognized the need for another cartridge capable of launching 200-grain bullets (and heavier) with high inherent accuracy, energy capable of stopping the largest North American game, and lower perceived recoil. After considering different calibers, Winchester engineers determined the 325-caliber provided the best performance using the short magnum case. Released in 2005, the new 325 WSM cartridge delivers similar energies as the 338 Winchester Magnum while using a smaller case.

General Comments In addition to delivering excellent ballistics, the 325 WSM also exhibits exceptional accuracy. Initially, Winchester fielded three loads for the 325 WSM—a 200-grain Nosler Accubond® CT®, a Winchester 220-grain Power-Point® bullet, and a 180-gain Ballistic Silvertip®. Hunters can expect delayed, controlled expansion and deep penetration through thick, tough skin, heavy muscle tissue and bone, with ballistic coefficients ranging up to .477 for the 200-grain Nosler bullet. The 325 WSM is well suited for elk, bear, moose or other large and dangerous game where a lightweight short magnum rifle is desired.

325 Winchester Short Magnum Factory Ballistics

Bullet (grains/type)	Powder	Grains	Velocity	Energy	Source/Comments
180 BST	FL		3060	3743	Winchester
200 Nos AccuBond	FL		2950	3866	Winchester
220 Win PP	FL		2840	3941	Winchester

338 Federal

Historical Notes In collaboration with Sako Rifles, Federal Cartridge's engineers and ballisticians have developed the 338 Federal, which necks up the proven 308 Winchester case to accept a .338 caliber bullet. This design, which is the first to bear the name "Federal" on the headstamp, is intended to provide big-bore wallop with moderate recoil for today's light weight, short bolt-action rifles. The 338 Federal should be available in 2006 in Federal's Premium line of ammunition.

General Comments The 338 Federal bears more than a passing resemblance to the 358 Winchester cartridge, which was introduced in 1955. Like the 358 Win, the 338 Federal offers excellent performance on big game without magnum recoil. Its muzzle energy exceeds the 30-06 with a similar weight bullet, equaling the ME of the 7mm Remington Magnum. Its muzzle velocity ranges to approximately 200 fps greater than its parent 308 Winchester with similar weight bullets. Leaving nothing to chance, Federal offers three loads for the 338 Federal, each tipped with a premium-grade bullet that is proven to deliver devastating results on game ranging from deer to elk to bear.

The 358 Winchester, having been introduced in a time when ever-higher velocities were the craze, languishes in obscurity. Given the current interest in lightweight rifles and efficient cartridge designs, one hopes that the 338 Federal will fare better with the shooting public.

338 Federal Factory Ballistics

Bullet (grains/type)	Powder	Grains	Velocity	Energy	Source/Comments
180 Nos AccuBond	FL		2830		Federal
185 Barnes TSX	FL		2750		Federal
210 Nos Part	FL		2630		Federal

338-06 A-Square/338-06

Historical Notes In 1945-1946, Charles O'Neil, Elmer Keith and Don Hopkins developed a cartridge they named the 333 OKH, which was based on the 30-06 case necked-up to 333 caliber. It was a very good big game cartridge, but today it suffers from the lack of good, readily available 0.333-inch diameter bullets. When the 338 Winchester Magnum was introduced in 1958, it was followed immediately by a variety of commercial 0.338-inch diameter bullets. Shortly thereafter, several individuals at different places conceived the idea of either altering the 333 OKH or necking-up the 30-06 to accept 0.338-inch diameter bullets. Any difference in performance between the 333 OKH and the 338-06 is purely academic and almost invisible. The latter uses a commercial bullet of standard diameter, which has the advantage of being readily available through handloading-supply dealers. The two cartridges are so nearly alike that one can use loading data from the 333 OKH in the 338-06 with virtually the same results. A-Square standardized the 338-06 as a factory round in 1998 and, about 2001, Weatherby began chambering rifles in 338-06. With typical Weatherby honesty, their catalogs list the cartridge as the 338-06 A-Square.

General Comments The 30-06 case is necked up to accept 338-diameter bullets, and retains the original 17.5-degree shoulder. The 338-06 delivers about 85 percent of the performance of the 338-caliber magnum cartridges, but without the recoil, cigar-sized cases or magnum-length actions. Most 30-06 bolt-action rifles can be rebarreled to the 338-06, and the wide range of available bullets makes the 338-06 a flexible hunting alternative to its ballistic near-twin, the 35 Whelen. Weatherby uses Norma brass and powders, matching them with bullets well suited for the intended purpose; their catalog lists just one bullet for the 338-06, the Nosler Partition. Weatherby offers Mark V Super Big Game Master and Ultra Lightweight rifles in 338-06 A-Square, both well suited for North American game.

338-06 A-Square Loading Data and Factory Ballistics

Bullet (grains/type)	Powder	Grains	Velocity	Energy	Source/Comments
200 SP	IMR 3031	48.0	2465	2700	NA
200 SP	IMR 4320	54.0	2610	3020	NA
250 SP	IMR 4064	56.0	2585	3730	NA
250 SP	IMR 3031	47.0	2370	3130	NA
275 SP	IMR 4350	55.0	2305	3250	NA
275 SP	IMR 4895	50.0	2275	3165	NA
210 Nosler Partition	FL		2750	3527	Weatherby factory load

338 Winchester Magnum

Historical Notes Announced in 1958, the 338 is another of the series based on the 458 Winchester necked-down. Initially available only in the Winchester Model 70 "Alaskan" bolt-action rifle, Remington adopted it for the 700 Series bolt action. Some of the European rifle makers also chamber it, as does Ruger for the Model 77 and No. 1 rifle and many custom and semi-custom rifles. Browning's autoloader, lever- and pump-action rifles also chamber it.

General Comments With proper bullets, the 338 Winchester Magnum shoots almost as flat across 500 yards as similar loads in the various 30-caliber magnums — the difference amounts to only a few inches more drop. Designed to handle the heaviest North American big game, the 338 has also done well in Africa on the larger varieties of plains game. Although slightly less powerful than the 375 H&H Magnum, the 338 is better suited for North American hunting conditions and game. It is a well-balanced cartridge for anything from elk through moose and grizzly bear under almost any situation. It could also serve very well for deer or antelope, even though it is overly powerful for this class. Like the 300 WM, the 338 Winchester would make an excellent one-gun cartridge for the worldwide hunter who has to travel light. The 338 is automatically barred in some African countries in which the 375 is the minimum caliber. Lately, the 338 has enjoyed a renewed and well-deserved popularity. Winchester, Remington and Federal all load this ammunition.

338 Winchester Magnum Loading Data and Factory Ballistics

Bullet (grains/type)	Powder	Grains	Velocity	Energy	Source/Comments
175 SP	IMR 4895	67.5	3200	3980	Barnes
180 Nosler BT	H4350	74.5	3157	3980	Hodgdon
200 SP	IMR 4350	71.5	2900	4048	Speer, Hornady
210 SP	IMR 4350	73	2900	3923	Nosler
225 Hornady SP	RI-19	75.3	2865	4100	Hodgdon
250 SP	IMR 4831	71	2700	4048	Speer, Sierra
250 SP	IMR 4350	70	2700	4048	Sierra
275 SP	IMR 4831	68	2500	3817	Speer
275 SP	IMR 4064	58	2400	3518	Speer
300 SP	IMR 7828	70	2500	4164	Barnes
200 SP	FL		2960	3890	Factory load
225 SP	FL		2780	3860	Factory load
250 SP	FL		2660	3921	Factory load

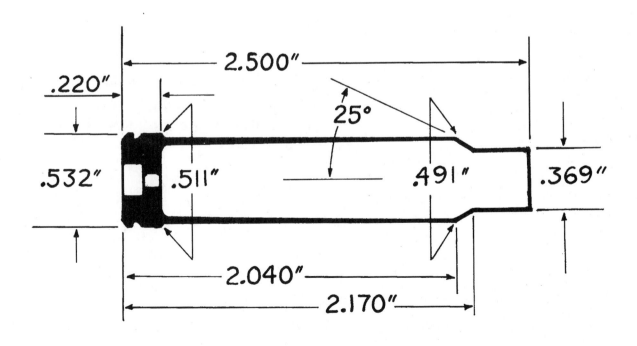

340 Weatherby Magnum

Historical Notes The growing popularity of the 338 Winchester Magnum for elk and larger game undoubtedly influenced the development of the 340 Weatherby. First announcement of the new caliber came in 1962. John Amber had one of the first 340 WM rifles and reported 100-yard groups of 2 inches or less — quite good for such a heavy-caliber hunting rifle of that era.

General Comments With its larger case, the 340 Weatherby develops higher velocity with any given bullet weight than the 338 Winchester. Velocities of 3,260 fps with the 200-grain bullet and 2,980 with the 250-grain are impressive. This means around 4,700 foot-pounds of energy with either bullet. This should be quite effective on African game. A 210-grain Nosler bullet loading is also available with a muzzle velocity of 3,250 fps (all from 26-inch

barrels). The cartridge is suitable for all North American big game and most African species as well. Weatherby ammunition is loaded by Norma of Sweden. Handloaders will find that case life with older Weatherby (Norma) cases is very limited with top handloads because of soft case heads. This problem can be eliminated by reforming 8mm Remington Magnum cases, but these require a significant reduction in charge because of a much-reduced capacity. Nevertheless, such loads can surpass any safe load in older Norma cases because Remington cases can safely withstand somewhat higher pressures and because the lost powder space was not necessary anyway. Ballistics are greatly handicapped if shorter barrels are used.

340 Weatherby Magnum Loading Data and Factory Ballistics

Bullet (grains/type)	Powder	Grains	Velocity	Energy	Source/Comments
175 SP	IMR 4350	85.5	3250	4105	Barnes
200 SP	IMR 4350	82	3000	3998	Speer, Hornady
200 SP	IMR 4350	84	3200	4549	Hornady
210 SP	IMR 4350	83.5	3200	4776	Nosler
225 SP	IMR 4831	83	3000	4498	Hornady
250 SP	IMR 4350	77	2800	4353	Sierra, Speer, Hornady
250 SP	IMR 4831	80	2800	4353	Sierra, Hornady, Speer
275 SP	IMR 4350	76	2600	4129	Speer
275 SP	IMR 7828	88	2750	4619	Speer
300 SP	IMR 7828	77.5	2550	4333	Barnes
200 SP	FL		3260	4719	Weatherby factory load
210 SP	FL		3250	4924	Weatherby factory load
250 SP	FL		2980	4931	Weatherby factory load

Federal 215 primers used in all cases.

338 Remington Ultra Magnum

Historical Notes The 338 Remington Ultra Mag is one of the most powerful 338-caliber rounds available, delivering 25-percent greater muzzle energy than the 338 Winchester Magnum and retains a flatter trajectory all the way out to 500 yards. Remington introduced this cartridge in 2002 as a member of the Ultra Magnum family of cartridges.

General Comments In suitably equipped rifles, such as the Remington 700, and the hands of a skillful hunter, the 338 Ultra Magnum is an excellent choice for bear, elk and moose. Except for bullet diameter and a slightly shorter case length, technical details of this cartridge are identical to the 300 Remington Ultra Magnum. *(See separate listing).*

338 Remington Ultra Magnum Factory Ballistics

Bullet (grains/type)	Powder	Grains	Velocity	Energy	Source/Comments
250 PSP	FL		2860	4540	Remington
250 Swift A-Frame	FL		2860	4540	Remington

338 Lapua Magnum
8.58x71mm (Finland)

Historical Notes In 1983, Research Armament Co. in the U.S. began development of a new, long-range sniper cartridge capable of firing a 250-grain, 0.338-inch diameter bullet at 3000 fps. After preliminary experiments, a 416 Rigby case necked down to 0.338-inch was selected. Brass Extrusion Labs Ltd. (then of Bensenville, Illinois) made the cases, Hornady produced bullets and Research Armament built the gun under contract for the U.S. Navy. Subsequently, Lapua and Norma have put this cartridge into production. It is now a CIP standard chambering; since CIP and SAAMI have reciprocal agreements in place (at least in theory), that makes it a standard SAAMI chambering as well.

General Comments You have to burn a lot of powder to launch a 250-grain bullet at 3000 fps. The 338 Lapua Magnum, as it is known commercially, or the 8.58x71mm, does just that. The full metal jacket, boattail military bullet is reportedly very effective at 1500 meters. The commercial softpoint bullet is intended for hunting very heavy game. Cartridge cases are brass with Boxer primers. Guns for this cartridge are bolt-actions but at least one gas-operated M-16-style rifle has been developed (RND Machining, 14311 Mead Street, Longmont, CO — 303-623-2112).

338 Lapua Magnum Factory Ballistics

Bullet (grains/type)	Powder	Grains	Velocity	Energy	Source/Comments
250 FMJ-BT Ball	FL		2950	4830	Factory load
250 SP			2855	4525	Military load

338-378 KT/
338-378 Weatherby

Historical Notes The 338-378 Keith-Thompson was developed specifically to deliver heavy bullets to distant big game animals with a flat trajectory. Elmer Keith always advocated the 33 bore as minimum for elk hunting. The advent of the 378 Weatherby case gave him ready access to a larger-capacity case that would allow equal-weight bullets to be launched several hundred feet per second faster than was safely possible with existing 0.338-inch Magnums. Evidently, Keith could not pass up this opportunity. Belatedly recognizing the superior big game hunting potential of this cartridge, Weatherby finally offered it as a factory chambering about 1999.

General Comments The 338-378 KT holds more than 120 grains of powder, compared to about 90 grains for the 340 Weatherby — once the largest commercial 0.338-inch case. With the advent of slower-burning powders suitable for handloading in this cartridge, the 338-387 KT should gain added support among the "Bigger is Better" genre of hunters. Should loading data become available for some of the newer powders between H4831 to H870 in burning rates, this cartridge could soon gain new popularity. The only data we could find is for H4831, which burns too fast for this number. Still, velocities exceed what the 340 Weatherby can offer by about 10-percent, when loaded to similar pressures. Properly loaded with a somewhat slower powder, this chambering should be able to gain about 100 fps more velocity advantage. When combined with the more aerodynamic hunting bullets available, this number can easily deliver substantially more energy at one-quarter of a mile than the 30-06 produces at the muzzle. The KT and Weatherby versions differ slightly in both case length and overall cartridge length.

338-378 KT Loading Data (26-inch barrel)

Bullet (grains/type)	Powder	Grains	Velocity	Energy	Source/Comments
250	H4831	98.0	3009	5030	Hodgdon
275	H4831	95.0	2859	4990	Hodgdon
300	H4831	90.0	2731	4965	Hodgdon

348 Winchester

Historical Notes The 348 was developed by Winchester for the Model 71 lever-action rifle and introduced in 1936. No other rifle has ever been commercially available for this cartridge and the Model 71 was discontinued in 1958. In 1987, Browning marketed a limited number of reproduction Model 71s that were made in Japan. At this writing, only Winchester still loads the 348, and the 200-grain bullet load is the lone survivor. The Model 71 was the smoothest lever action ever built.

General Comments One of the more powerful rimmed cartridges available for the lever-action rifle, the 348 was supposedly made obsolete by the newer 358 Winchester and the more modern Model 88 lever-action rifle (now also discontinued). The 348 is an excellent cartridge for any North American big game at close range.

Due to the flat-point bullets required by the tubular magazine of the Model 71 rifle, it is not a particularly good long-range cartridge. The 150-grain bullet has very poor ballistic properties due to its short, flat shape, and the 200- or 250-grain bullets are preferred for anything beyond 100 yards. Winchester dropped the 150-grain and 250-grain loads in 1962 but still offers the 200-grain loading. Remington no longer loads the round. The 348 is the basis of an entire list of improved cartridges. Perhaps the best of these, a somewhat improved 45-caliber version — which is very close to 458 Winchester Magnum performance — is still prized as among the best combination ever invented for use in Alaska against heavy game in close quarters.

348 Winchester Reloading Data and Factory Ballistics

Bullet (grains/type)	Powder	Grains	Velocity	Energy	Source/Comments
200 SP	H-4895	53	2500	2776	Hornady
200 SP	IMR 4350	60.5	2500	2776	Hornady
200 SP	IMR 4064	51	2400	2559	Hornady
250 SP	IMR 4350	55	2300	2937	Barnes
150 SP	FL		2890	2780	Factory load
200 SP	FL		2520	2820	Winchester factory load
250 SP	FL		2350	3060	Factory load

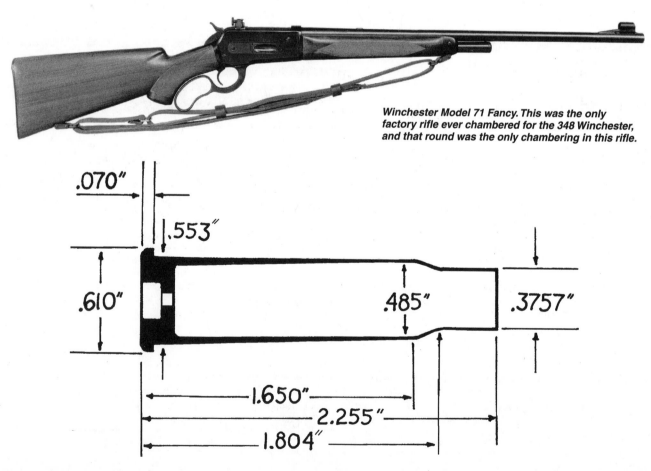

Winchester Model 71 Fancy. This was the only factory rifle ever chambered for the 348 Winchester, and that round was the only chambering in this rifle.

.070"
.553"
.610"
.485"
.3757"
1.650"
2.255"
1.804"

35 Remington

Historical Notes Introduced with the Remington Model 8 semi-automatic rifle in 1906, the 35 Remington was later also chambered in the Remington Models 14 and 141 pump-action, the Model 81 semi-auto, Model 30 bolt-action, and for a short time, in the Winchester bolt-action Model 70. At one time, the Marlin 336 lever-, Mossberg 479 lever- and Savage 170 pump-action rifles were offered in 35 Remington. Currently, only the Marlin is still available in rifles; Remington's XP-100 was and Thompson/Center's handgun is still chambered for the 35 Remington.

General Comments The 35 Remington is the only one of the Remington rimless line of medium-powered cartridges still alive. It has proven itself over the years as a reliable short-range woods cartridge on deer or black bear. It has far better knockdown power than the 30-30 under any conditions and at any range. The velocity and energy figures are not very different from the 30-30, but the larger, heavier bullet has greater shock and makes a more severe wound. The 35 Remington, with its moderate recoil, is a good cartridge for light rifles or carbines at short ranges (150 yards or less). It was originally the Remington counter to the much more powerful 35 Winchester. When I was a boy, my "hunting uncle" used a Model 8 Remington rifle in 35 Remington with great success. However, I don't think he ever chanced a shot at much more than 150 yards, and that probably had a great deal to do with it. Remington, Winchester and Federal offer this ammunition.

35 Remington Loading Data and Factory Ballistics

Bullet (grains/type)	Powder	Grains	Velocity	Energy	Source/Comments
125 SP	W680	32	2400	1599	Speer
140 HP	RL-7	40	2500	1943	Speer
158 SP	IMR 3031	37	2200	1698	Hornady, Speer
180 Speer FP	H4895	39.0	2232	1990	Hodgdon
200 Hornady RN	VarGet	39.5	2139	2030	Hodgdon
220 Speer FP	H4895	36.3	2010	1970	Hodgdon
150 SP	FL		2300	1762	Factory load
200 SP	FL		2080	1921	Factory load

For light loads for small game or varmint shooting at short range, use any 150-160-gr. lead, gascheck or half-jacketed 38 revolver bullet and 15 grs. of 2400. MV will be about 2200 fps.

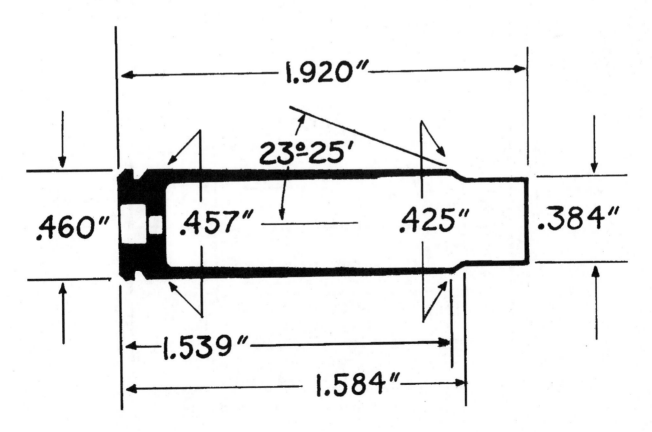

356 Winchester

Historical Notes The 356 Winchester is a rimmed cartridge developed concurrently with the 307 Winchester for the Winchester Model 94 XTR Angle Eject lever-action carbine. Development of both cartridges began in 1980. Guns and ammunition were sold early in 1983. Marlin introduced the lever-action Model 336ER in 356-caliber at about the same time the Winchester hit the market. The Winchester Model 94 XTR is a beefed-up version of the original Model 94 lever action to allow the use of higher-pressure cartridges. The angle-eject feature is an additional modification to eject spent cartridge cases to the side instead of straight up. This feature allows center mounting of a scope sight, something not possible with the original 1894 action. This was accomplished by repositioning the extractor and ejector and lowering the right sidewall of the receiver slightly.

The 356-caliber designation was used to avoid confusion with the rimless 358 Winchester. In fact, the 356 is little more than a rimmed 358 and uses them same diameter bullets. The 356 and the 358 are not identical, since the 356 not only has a rim, but also the bullet is seated deeper to reduce overall length. It's possible to chamber 358 cartridges in 356 rifles, but firing them is an unsafe practice that could damage the gun and cause serious injury to the shooter.

General Comments The ballistics of the 356 are slightly below the older rimless 358. Although it has been reported that the 356 Winchester and 307 have thicker case walls than the corresponding rimless 308 and 358 cartridges (and therefore reduced internal volume), measurements do not verify this. However, the 356 delivers performance superior to the 35 Remington by a significant margin. Factory-published ballistics data show that the 35 Remington 200-grain bullet has a muzzle velocity of 2,080 fps, whereas the 356 Winchester delivers 2,460 fps with the same bullet weight, both from a 24-inch barrel.

While the 35 Remington is largely a short-range cartridge for deer or black bear, the 356 Winchester would be adequate for larger game up to elk at longer ranges. One should consider, though, that both the Winchester and Marlin lever-action carbines with their short 20-inch barrels are intended primarily as light, handy guns for use in heavy cover. A hunter armed with one of the 356 carbines could probably take on just about anything likely to be encountered in the continental United States at short to moderate ranges. The 358 Winchester never achieved great popularity, and the 356 does not appear to be doing much better. Winchester is the only commercial manufacturer of this cartridge.

356 Winchester Loading Data and Factory Ballistics

Bullet (grains/type)	Powder	Grains	Velocity	Energy	Source/Comments
158 SP	H-322	49	2600	2372	Speer
180 SP	H-322	48	2600	2703	Speer
180 Speer FP	H4198	43.0	2600	2700	Hodgdon
220 SP	IMR 4064	46	2300	2585	Speer
250 Hornady RN	BL-C(2)	48.0	2163	2595	Hodgdon
200 SP	FL		2460	2688	Factory load
250 SP	FL		2160	2591	Factory load

In tubular-magazine rifles, load only flat-point bullets.

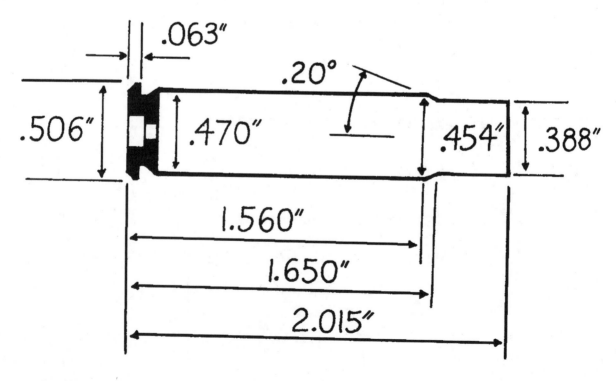

358 Winchester

Historical Notes Introduced in 1955 by Winchester for its Model 70 Lightweight bolt-action and Model 88 lever-action rifles, the 358 Winchester is based on the 308 Winchester case necked-up. It is known in Europe as the 8.8x51mm. Many European rifle makers chamber the round. In the United States, only the Browning BLR lever-action is currently chambered for this cartridge. The Model 99 Savage was also once available in 358.

General Comments The 358 Winchester is one of the best commercial (non-magnum) 35-caliber cartridges turned out by any American manufacturer. It is a big improvement over the 35 Remington, slightly more powerful than the old 35 Winchester, and more useful than the 348 Winchester. As the 308 Winchester is a shortened version of the 30-06, by the same token the 358 is a shortened 35 Whelen. With its spitzer-pointed bullets, the 358 is a good medium- to long-range cartridge with capabilities out to 250 yards on big game. Although a good woods number, it is definitely beyond the short-range, deer-only class. In fact, the 358 is adequate for any North American big game. With the 250-grain bullet, it is better than the 30-06 on heavy game at close ranges. The 358 in a bolt-action rifle with a good scope sight is as accurate as any hunting cartridge available. Performance can be improved by handloading. Winchester is the only remaining manufacturer of this ammunition.

358 Winchester Loading Data and Factory Ballistics

Bullet (grains/type)	Powder	Grains	Velocity	Energy	Source/Comments
158 SP	RL-7	48	2850	2850	Speer
180 SP	IMR 3031	51	2700	2914	Speer
200 SP	IMR 4320	50.5	2500	2776	Hornady, Sierra
200 SP	H-4198	40.5	2500	2776	Hornady
220 SP	BL-C2	49	2500	3054	Speer
250 SP	IMR 3031	41.5	2200	2687	Hornady, Speer
250 SP	IMR 4064	44	2250	2811	Speer
300 SP	IMR 4895	43	2200	3225	Barnes
200 SP	FL		2490	2753	Factory load
250 SP	FL		2250	2810	Factory load

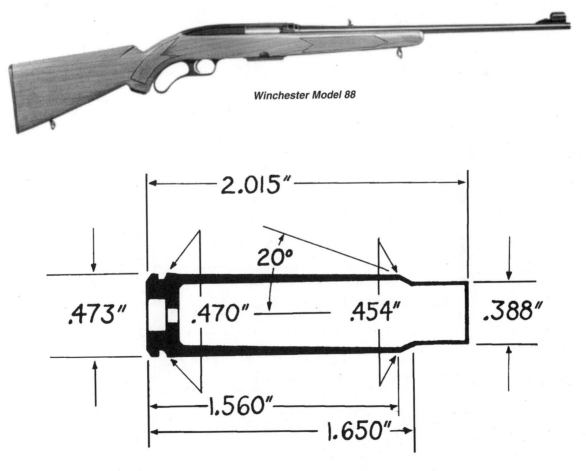

Winchester Model 88

35 Whelen

Historical Notes Facts uncovered in recent research suggest that Col. Townsend Whelen may, after all, have been intimately involved in the creation of this cartridge which has generally been heretofore attributed to James Howe of Griffin & Howe, whom it was said developed it and named it after the famous writer, hunter and gun authority. The 35 Whelen is simply the 30-06 case necked up without any other change. Ackley championed an improved version, which features less body taper and a sharper shoulder. The improved version has two significant advantages. First is about 10 percent more usable capacity, providing a similar increase in ballistics. The second is the more distinct shoulder which completely solves the poor headspacing problem 35 Whelen rifles have, resulting from a too narrow, steeply sloping shoulder. One is hard pressed to explain why Remington chose to standardize the inferior version when they adopted the 35 Whelen as a factory chambering in 1987.

General Comments Remington has been active in adding popular wildcats to their line of commercial cartridges. The 35 Whelen is another example. The author has had considerable past experience with the 35 Whelen, and it is an excellent cartridge for any North American big game and most African species as well. A pump-action rifle chambered for 35 Whelen makes a good combination. The 35 Whelen is one of the best balanced and most flexible medium bores for North American big game. There is a large variety of 35-caliber bullets available to the handloader, ranging from 110 to 300 grains in weight. The popularity of this round has waxed and waned over the years, reaching a peak during the 1920s and again shortly after World War II. Only Remington manufactures this ammunition.

35 Whelen Loading Data and Factory Ballistics

Bullet (grains/type)	Powder	Grains	Velocity	Energy	Source/Comments
180 SP	IMR 4895	59	2700	2914	Hornady
180 SP	IMR 4320	56	2700	2914	Nosler
200 SP	IMR 4064	58.5	2600	3003	Hornady
225 SP	IMR 4320	56	2500	3123	Sierra
250 SP	IMR 4895	52.5	2500	3470	Hornady
250 SP	IMR 4064	54.5	2400	3198	Hornady
250 SP	RL-15	55	2400	3198	Hornady
200 SP	FL		2675	3177	Remington factory load
250 SP	FL		2400	3197	Remington factory load

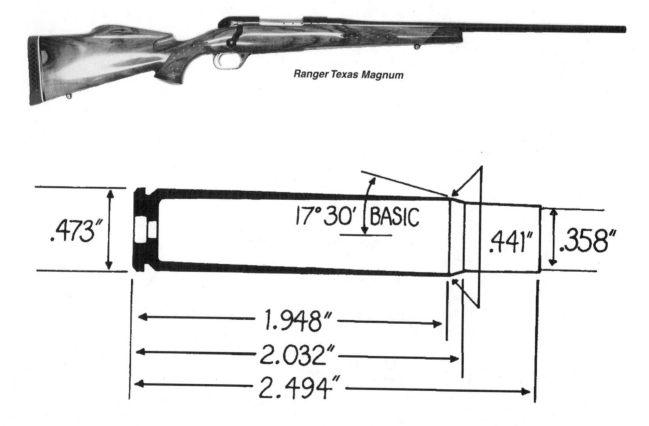

Ranger Texas Magnum

.473"   17° 30' BASIC   .441" .358"

1.948"

2.032"

2.494"

350 Remington Magnum

Historical Notes Remington reintroduced the 350 Remington Magnum in 2002, chambered in its new Model 673 bolt-action rifle. The 350 Remington Magnum first appeared in the 1965 Remington catalog concurrently with the Model 600 Magnum bolt-action carbine that chambered it. The original carbine had an 18-inch barrel, but in 1968, this was lengthened to 20 inches as the Model 660 Magnum carbine. By 1971, the Model 600 and 660 Magnum carbines had been discontinued, but the 350 Magnum was continued as a standard chambering for the Model 700 bolt-action rifle until 1974. For a short time, the Ruger Model 77 bolt-action rifle was available in 350 Magnum. Currently, Remington offers the 350 Remington Magnum in the Model 673 Guide Rifle, which is a near-look-a-like M600 based on the Model Seven action. The cartridge is unique in having a somewhat short, fat, belted case with somewhat more capacity than the 30-06. This allows for its use in short-action rifles that can be made a bit lighter and handier than those based on the standard-length bolt action.

General Comments With bullets of moderate weight, the 350 Remington Magnum can nearly duplicate 35 Whelen ballistics in a much shorter barrel and it can be chambered in short bolt-action rifles. This is a significant advantage for those preferring a light, handy rifle with plenty of punch. Also, many find the short-throw bolt to be much easier to use and master. For those preferring heavier bullets, the round-nose design doesn't take up so much of the powder space and, therefore, can safely develop better muzzle energy. For use where shots will not be long, these may be the best choice. For those with 350 Remington Magnum rifles in full-length actions, heavy spitzers can sometimes safely be seated to exceed the nominal 2.80-inch length for the cartridge and increased muzzle energy can be achieved. Here though, it is hard to see much advantage over the 35 Whelen, which generally feeds smoother from a magazine holding two additional cartridges. The 350 Remington Magnum is adequate for any North American big game at short to medium ranges.

350 Remington Magnum Loading Data and Factory Ballistics

Bullet (grains/type)	Powder	Grains	Velocity	Energy	Source/Comments
125 HP	IMR 4895	60	2850	2255	Speer
158 SP	IMR 3031	58	2850	2850	Speer
180 SP	IMR 4064	62	2900	3362	Speer
200 SP	IMR 4320	60	2700	3238	Hornady, Sierra
220 SP	IMR 4895	60	2650	3431	Speer
250 SP	IMR 4895	53	2350	3066	Speer, Nosler
300 SP	IMR 4064	52	2300	3525	Barnes
200 SP	FL		2710	3261	Factory load

375 Winchester

Historical Notes Developed by Winchester, the 375 was announced in 1978 as a new cartridge for the Model 94 Big Bore lever-action carbine. The gun is a strengthened version of the standard Model 94 action and can be distinguished by the beefed-up rear quarter of the receiver as opposed to the flat sides of the regular Model 94. The cartridge is based on a shortened (about 1/10-inch) 38-55 case, although 375 Winchester cases are heavier and stronger than those of the 38-55. Two carbines were initially available in this caliber: the Winchester Model 94 Big Bore and the Ruger Number 3 single-shot. This is a rimmed case and not well suited to Mauser-type bolt actions. Two bullet weights are offered: a 200-grain at 2,200 fps muzzle velocity and a 250-grain at 1,900 fps, as advertised by Winchester.

General Comments The 375 Winchester fills a gap in the line of cartridges available for the popular Winchester Model 1894 lever-action series. Many hunters who hunt in heavy cover prefer large- or medium-caliber rifles firing heavy bullets as the best combination for their particular hunting environment. Such a combination was not available for the Winchester Model 1894. The 375 helps offers competition to lever-actions chambered for the 35 Remington and the 444 Marlin. Comparisons will be made between this 375 and the other popular woods cartridges such as

the 35 Remington, 44 Magnum, 444 Marlin and the 45-70. Ballistically, the 444 Marlin with its 240-grain bullet and 2,400 fps muzzle velocity has the edge on all the others in the group. However, all of these cartridges have one common failing: They are used in lever-action rifles with tubular magazines. This requires a flat-pointed bullet so that under recoil, one cartridge won't set off the one ahead of it in the magazine. These blunt bullets offer high air resistance. No matter what the initial velocity, they all slow down quite rapidly. The result is that at 200 yards or less they all end up with about the same energy, which varies from 1000 to 1100 foot pounds. All of these brush cartridges, then, are at their best at ranges of 150 yards or less.

Certainly the 375 Winchester is a fine deer or black bear cartridge and would probably also do well on heavier game such as moose or brown bear. Within its range limitations, it would also serve as a good meat-getter on thin-skinned African species. The 375 cartridge can be chambered in 38-55 rifles, but must never be fired in any rifle except those specifically marked for it because it develops much higher pressure than the older 38-55. To fire it in any of the old blackpowder rifles would almost certainly result in a wrecked gun and serious injury to the shooter. Winchester is the only commercial manufacturer of this ammunition.

375 Winchester Loading Data and Factory Ballistics

Bullet (grains/type)	Powder	Grains	Velocity	Energy	Source/Comments
200 Sierra JFP	H4198	38.0	2480	2730	Hodgdon
220 Hornady JFP	RL-7	36.0	2260	2495	Hodgdon
220 SP	RL-7	38	2200	2365	Hornady
235 SP	IMR 4198	32	2000	2088	Speer
235 SP	RL-7	35	1950	1985	Speer
255 SP	IMR 3031	36	1900	2045	Barnes
200 SP	FL		2200	2150	Winchester factory load
250 SP	FL		1900	2005	Winchester factory load

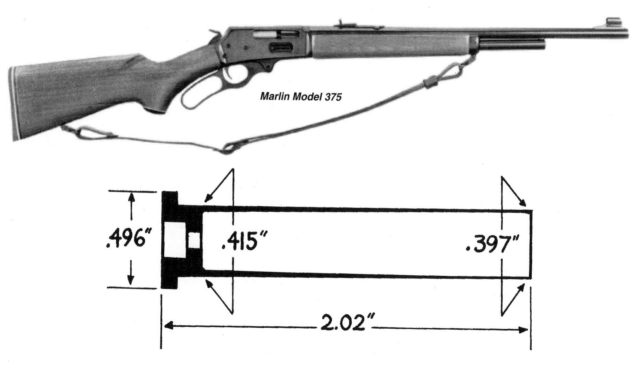

Marlin Model 375

.496" .415" .397"

2.02"

376 Steyr

Historical Notes Hornady and Steyr announced this chambering at the 2000 SHOT Show. Jeff Cooper has long heralded the "Scout Rifle" concept. Basically, this is a short, lightweight bolt-action rifle that is essentially designed for equipping with a forward-mounted, compact, long-eye-relief scope of low magnification. Hence, the Scout Rifle is a package deal. Mr. Cooper wanted a chambering for his creation that would do in a pinch for stopping practically any game on earth. The specific critter of actual concern is the Cape buffalo, long noted for bad temper, tenacity and terminally effective retaliation. From this backdrop grew the 376 Steyr. Using bullets of up to 300-grains and easily generating as much as 4000 foot pounds of muzzle energy, it would seem that the 376 Steyr should fulfill Jeff's wishes.

General Comments This case, while an essentially new design, shares characteristics with several earlier numbers. Base diameter, at 0.500-inch, is just about the same as the 284 Winchester (nominally 0.496-inch) or the 9.3x64mm Brenneke (nominally 0.504-inch). The rim, at 0.494-inch, is sufficiently smaller than the case body as to qualify this as a (slightly) rebated rim design.

Shoulder angle is quite shallow, to facilitate smooth feeding from the magazine. Case and cartridge length (2.35-inch & 3.075, respectively) are both intermediate between traditional "short-action" and "long-action" numbers. Capacity and maximum pressure specification are sufficient to accommodate substantial performance. With the ready availability of a wide selection of bullets of various quality levels and weights, this should be a very versatile chambering. I predict that it will also form the basis of an entire genre of new wildcat cartridges. To establish precedence, I will take this opportunity to declare my intentions to adjust neck diameter and length on the 376 Steyr case to produce cartridges appropriate to both 2.8-inch and 3.2-inch actions in every feasible bore size from 6mm to 41-caliber.

For those who prefer the style, the Scout Rifle is a very fine design for hunting dangerous game. However, with the proposed Steyr rifle weighing in at far under 8 pounds — making it significantly heavier would seem to defeat Mr. Cooper's design intent — recoil is no small matter.

376 Steyr

Bullet (grains/type)	Powder	Grains	Velocity	Energy	Source/Comments
225 Hornady SP	FL		2560	3325	Hornady, Steyr Specified Loading
270 Hornady SP	FL		2560	3990	Hornady

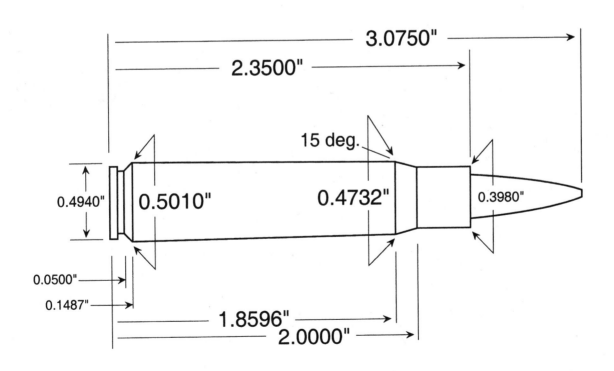

375 Holland & Holland Magnum (375 H&H Magnum)

Historical Notes Originated by the British firm Holland & Holland in 1912, this is one of the original belted, rimless, magnum-type cartridges. It has been used as the basis for numerous wildcats and most of the Weatherby cartridges. H&H furnished it in a magnum Mauser action and Griffin & Howe chambered rifles for it beginning about 1926. The Western Cartridge Co. first offered it in 1925. At present, Federal, Remington and Winchester load the 375. The first commercial rifle of American make to chamber the round was the Model 70 Winchester in 1937; Weatherby rifles were at one time available in 375 H&H as was the Remington Model 725 "Kodiak." At present, several American manufacturers list the 375 H&H as standard including Ruger, Winchester and Remington.

General Comments Long considered the best all-round African caliber, the 375 H&H is overpowered for North American big game. However, many Alaskan hunters and guides prefer it for moose and grizzly bear. It isn't a very flexible cartridge for the American hunter unless he expects to hunt the heaviest species and spend time in Africa or Asia. John Taylor, in his 1948 book *African Rifles and Cartridges*, Georgetown, S.C., rates the 375 as the best of the medium bores for African hunting. It is his candidate for the most effective, all-round cartridge. This cartridge was the basis for H&H's latter 300 H&H Magnum and is therefore the great-grandfather of almost all modern belted magnum chamberings. It can certainly be said that it inspired the entire genre.

375 Holland & Holland Magnum Loading Data and Factory Ballistics

Bullet (grains/type)	Powder	Grains	Velocity	Energy	Source/Comments
200 SP	IMR 4064	80	3200	4549	Sierra
220 SP	SR4759	42	2300	2585	Hornady
235 SP	IMR 4064	77	3000	4697	Speer
270 SP	RL-15	74	2700	4372	Hornady
270 SP	IMR 4064	70	2600	4054	Hornady
285 SP	IMR 4831	85	2700	4615	Speer
300 SP	IMR 4064	68	2500	4164	Hornady
300 SP	IMR 4350	77	2600	4504	Sierra, Hornady
350 SP	IMR 4320	65.5	2400	4478	Barnes
270 SP	FL		2690	4340	Factory load
300 SP	FL		2530	4265	Factory load

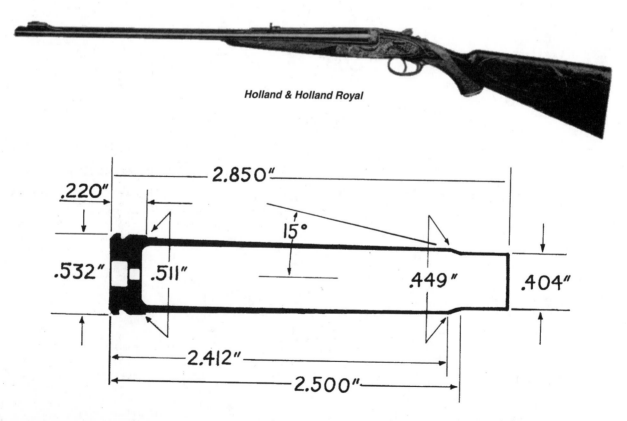

Holland & Holland Royal

375 Weatherby Magnum

Historical Notes The 375 Weatherby Magnum was developed by the late Roy Weatherby between 1944 and 1945, and was chambered only in Weatherby rifles. There are several similar wildcat versions such as the 375 Ackley Improved Magnum, but the 375 WM had the advantage of commercial ammunition loaded by Weatherby using Norma cases. Although brass cases are available, Weatherby no longer loads ammunition or chambers rifles for this cartridge.

Its popularity lasted until the more powerful, harder-recoiling 378 Weatherby displaced it about 1953, but returned to the Weatherby line when many hunters demanded something that recoils less than the 378 Weatherby, but with more power than the 375 H&H.

General Comments The 375 WM is a full-length, blown-out and improved cartridge based on the 375 H&H case. It holds more powder and delivers higher velocity with the same bullets, compared to the parent cartridge. It is really overpowered for North American big game. On African game, it will qualify for just about anything and is considered a fine all-round cartridge, particularly for dangerous game. The 270-grain bullet approximates 30-06 trajectories and is a fine long-range load for large North American game and for thin-skinned African animals. Commercial chambers are freebored in the Weatherby tradition; this increases the charge required to achieve any given pressure and velocity.

Out of production for several decades, the 375 Weatherby was reintroduced in 2001, and is available in Weatherby's Mark V Dangerous Game Rifle and Fibermark composite rifles. Some factory 375 H&H rifles can be rechambered to the 375 Weatherby.

375 Weatherby Magnum Loading Data and Factory Ballistics

Bullet (grains/type)	Powder	Grains	Velocity	Energy	Source/Comments
235 SP	IMR 4064	84.0	3015	4745	Ackley
270 SP	IMR 4064	80.0	2795	4685	Ackley
300 SP	IMR 4350	86.0	2675	4770	Ackley
270 SP	FL		2940	5181	Weatherby factory load
300 SP	FL		2800	5223	Weatherby factory load
300 Nosler Partition	FL		2800	5224	Weatherby factory load

375 Remington Ultra Magnum

Historical Notes With the flat trajectory of a 150-grain 270 Winchester load, the 375 Remington Ultra Magnum is one of the hardest-hitting 375 chamberings available. Introduced in 2002 and based on Remington's Ultra Magnum cartridge family, the 375 Ultra Mag has 23-percent more energy at the muzzle than the 375 H&H, and delivers more energy at 200 yards than does the 375 H&H at 100 yards

General Comments In suitably equipped rifles, such as the Remington 700, and the hands of a skillful hunter, the 375 Ultra Magnum is an excellent choice for African and Alaskan game, noted for their fangs, teeth, claws and attitude. Except for bullet diameter, technical details of this cartridge are identical to the 300 Remington Ultra Magnum. *(See separate listing.)*

375 Remington Ultra Magnum Factory Ballistics

Bullet (grains/type)	Powder	Grains	Velocity	Energy	Source/Comments
270 SP	FL		2900	5041	Remington factory load
300 Swift A-Frame	FL		2760	5073	Remington factory load

378 Weatherby Magnum

Historical Notes Another development by the late Roy Weatherby dating back to 1953, this is an original design not based on any existing cartridge, although it is hard to miss the similarity in all critical dimensions to the 416 Rigby. It was first field-tested in the spring of 1953 by Weatherby, who downed an elephant with one shot. The Federal Cartridge Co. 215 Magnum large rifle primer was originally developed for this cartridge, as existing primers did not properly ignite the large quantity of powder used. Only the Weatherby line of rifles is commercially chambered for this round.

General Comments According to the Weatherby catalog, the 378 WM was designed for deep penetration on heavy, thick-skinned game. It is also intended to furnish an extra margin of insurance when facing dangerous game such as rhino, Cape buffalo, elephant or lion in thick cover. Field reports indicate that it lives up to these expectations. However, for proper performance at the velocities developed, it is necessary to use bullets with a very heavy jacket. Although considerably overpowered for any North American big game, it is nonetheless a fine cartridge for the hunter who requires optimum stopping power. Recoil of these cartridges is extremely heavy, so one should be sure such power is really needed before selecting anything in this class.

378 Weatherby Magnum Loading Data and Factory Ballistics

Bullet (grains/type)	Powder	Grains	Velocity	Energy	Source/Comments
235 SP	H-4831	115	3200	5345	Barnes
250 SP	H-4831	113	3050	5165	Barnes
270 SP	IMR 4350	108	3100	5763	Hornady
300 SP	H-4831	112	2900	5604	Sierra, Nosler
350 SP	H-4831	102	2650	5459	Barnes
270 SP	FL		3180	6062	Weatherby factory load
300 SP	FL		2925	5701	Weatherby factory load

38-55 Winchester (38-55 Ballard)

Historical Notes Like the smaller 32-40, the 38-55 was originally a Ballard-developed target cartridge. The present commercial version was introduced in 1884 as one of the cartridges for the Ballard Perfection No. 4, which was originally chambered for the 38-50 Everlasting. According to Satterlee in his *Catalog of Firearms*, 2nd Ed., Detroit, 1939, the Union Hill Nos. 8 and 9 were also chambered for the 38-55 Ballard in 1884. The external dimensions of the 38-55 Everlasting and the 38-55 Winchester & Ballard are nearly identical, but the heavier, thicker Everlasting version was a handloading proposition. The implication in Saterlee's book is that the original Everlasting case was introduced when Marlin Fire Arms Co. took over Ballard in 1881. The 38-55 Everlasting is nothing more than a 1/10-inch longer case than the 38-50 that Ballard introduced in 1876.

The Marlin Model 93 and Winchester 94 lever-action repeaters were available in 38-55, as was the Remington-Lee bolt-action, Colt's new Lightning pump-action, Stevens, Remington and Winchester single-shot rifles and also the Savage Model 99. No commercial rifles were available after Winchester dropped the 38-55 from the Model 94 list of calibers in 1940. However, Winchester has reintroduced the cartridge in several versions of the Model 94 in recent years, and it also has been offered in the H&R Handi-Rifle and others. The 225 Winchester, 22 Savage High Power, 25-35 Winchester, 32-40 Winchester, 30-30 Winchester, 32 Winchester Special, 375 Winchester and a host of wildcat cartridges are based on this case.

General Comments The 38-55 built up a reputation for fine accuracy at ranges out to 200 yards. It also developed a modest popularity with deer and black bear hunters. It gave good knockdown on deer-size animals with the 255-grain bullet at velocities of over 1,500 fps. At one time, factory-loaded cartridges were available with the 255-grain bullet at a muzzle velocity of 1,700 fps. At these higher velocities, it is a better deer cartridge than the 30-30. Present factory loading more or less duplicates blackpowder ballistics. In old Ballard and Stevens single-shot rifles, it is not safe to use loads developing velocities over 1,500 fps. Discontinued in 1970, the 38-55 is again listed in Winchester ammunition catalogs. Proper bullet diameter for cast bullets is 0.379-inch.

The growing popularity of Cowboy Action Shooting has breathed new life into this fine, old cartridge.

38-55 Winchester & Ballard Loading Data and Factory Ballistics

Bullet (grains/type)	Powder	Grains	Velocity	Energy	Source/Comments
200 FN	XMP5744	25.5	1853	1525	Accurate Arms
220 SP	RL-7	31	1600	1257	Hornady
220 SP	IMR 3031	33	1600	1251	Hornady
220 SP	IMR 3031	34.5	1700	1412	Hornady
220 SP	IMR 4198	26	1600	1251	Hornady
220 SP	RL-7	29.5	1400	958	Hornady
240 Lead	XMP5744	22.0	1601	1365	Accurate
222 FN	XMP5744	23.5	1648	1325	Accurate
255 SP	H-4895	35	1700	1637	Barnes
255 SP	FL		1320	987	Winchester factory load

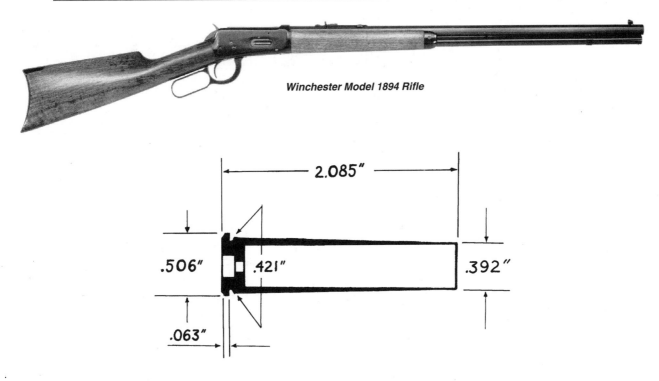

Winchester Model 1894 Rifle

2.085"

.506" .421" .392"

.063"

38-40 Winchester (38-40 WCF)

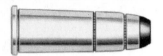

Historical Notes The 38-40 was developed by Winchester as a companion cartridge to its 44-40 and introduced in 1874. It is based on the 44-40 case necked-down to what is actually 40-caliber (0.401-inch). It was originally a blackpowder cartridge chambered in the Winchester Model 73 lever action. About 1878, Colt began chambering revolvers for it. It was later offered in the Remington Model 14 1/2 pump-action, Winchester 92 and Marlin 94 lever-actions, plus a number of single-shot rifles. No rifles have been chambered for the 38-40 since 1937. Winchester loaded a slightly different version especially for the Colt Lightning magazine rifle, headstamped 38 C.L.M.R. Another version was loaded with the same 180-grain bullet as the 38 Winchester, but with 40-grains of blackpowder instead of Winchester's standard load of 38 grains and was headstamped 38-40 instead of 38 W.C.F. This raises the intriguing possibility that the name we now use, 38-40, came from 38 grains of blackpowder and a 40-caliber bore.

General Comments The 38-40 was at one time a popular medium-power cartridge. Winchester used to load a high-velocity rifle version with a 180-grain bullet at 1775 fps. This was considered a pretty good short-range deer number, but was not intended for old blackpowder rifles or revolvers. It was discontinued because it caused a lot of trouble for people who never read labels. The present factory loading is strictly for revolvers, and it is necessary to handload in order to realize the full potential in a rifle. With proper load and bullets, the 38-40 can be used on small game, varmints, medium-size game or even deer at short range. Rifle loads should not be used in revolvers, as these loads develop pressures beyond safe limits.

The author's experience with the 38-40 is limited to one Remington Model 14 1/2R pump-action carbine that was used for several years before being traded off for something more useful. Although it was a nice, handy little rifle, I was not particularly impressed with the cartridge. The 38-40 is a bit much for most varmint and small game shooting and really not adequate for deer-size animals. In any event, it is quite limited in its effective range on whatever you happen to be using it for. This lack of enthusiasm notwithstanding, the 38-40 enjoyed a certain popularity from its inception until about 1920, after which it declined in sales volume and was finally discontinued in 1937. Actually, there is no great difference in performance between the 38-40 and the 44-40, although some considered the 38-40 a better cartridge for a woman or young boy because it had less recoil. Honestly, neither one has any great recoil, and I could never tell much difference between the two in that regard.

The 38-40 made a better revolver cartridge than it did a rifle cartridge. The present factory load with the 180-grain bullet at 1160 fps (Winchester) cannot be considered adequate for deer, and only by handloading can one achieve acceptable performance for much of anything except self-defense, for which it is formidable.

38-40 Winchester Loading Data and Factory Ballistics

Bullet (grains/type)	Powder	Grains	Velocity	Energy	Source/Comments
155 SP	2400	15	1200	496	Hornady
155 SP	IMR 4227	19.5	1200	496	Hornady
180 HP	2400	14.5	1100	484	Hornady
180 HP	Unique	9	1100	484	Hornady
180 HP	IMR 4227	18.5	1100	484	Hornady
200 HP	Unique	8.4	1000	444	Hornady
200 HP	2400	13.5	1050	490	Hornady
180 SP	FL		1160	538	Winchester factory load

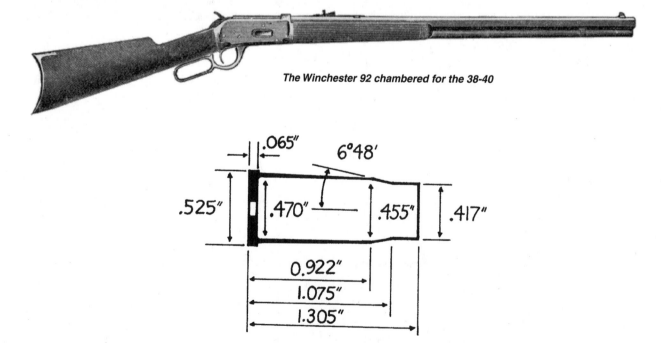

The Winchester 92 chambered for the 38-40

.065"   6°48'

.525"   .470"   .455"   .417"

0.922"

1.075"

1.305"

416 Remington Magnum

Historical Notes Officially announced in November 1988, the 416 Remington Magnum is the first American cartridge for dangerous game introduced since the 458 Winchester Magnum back in 1956. The 416 is based on the 8mm Remington Magnum necked-up to 416 caliber. It was initially available with either a 400-grain pointed softpoint or a 400-grain solid bullet loaded to a muzzle velocity of 2,400 fps and a muzzle energy of 5,115 foot-pounds. The company says that the 400-grain solid is exactly that, turned from solid brass and not a lead core with a heavy jacket. The cartridge was available in the Remington Model 700 Safari bolt-action rifle. Other rifle manufacturers have picked up the 416 Remington. It is available in a variety of bolt-action and single-shot rifles, including Ruger. It has proved to be a fairly popular cartridge.

General Comments There has been a persistent call by those who hunt dangerous game for a cartridge to fill the gap between the 375 Holland & Holland Magnum and the 458 Winchester Magnum. The 416 Rigby accomplished this rather well, but both rifles and ammunition became increasingly difficult to obtain until Federal began offering that cartridge in the late 1980s. This problem was then solved to some extent by a number of wildcat cartridges such as the 416 Taylor, 416 Hoffman and the 425 Express. These cartridges all more or less duplicated the performance of the 416

Rigby. The 416 Remington does pretty much the same thing. However, the Remington version has one great advantage in that it is available as a commercial loading in a proven commercial rifle. The combination will be much easier and less expensive to come by than a custom rifle for wildcat or proprietary cartridges.

Although the 416 bullet is 100 grains lighter than the 458 Winchester, it starts out with almost 300 fps higher velocity. That, combined with better sectional density and a superior aerodynamic shape, gives it certain ballistic advantages. It not only has a higher initial velocity, but it also increases its retained velocity over the 458 as the range increases. According to the factory figures, it has an 11 percent advantage in muzzle energy, and this increases to 18 percent at 100 yards and 30 percent at 200 yards.

The 416 Remington should be ideal for dangerous game including Cape buffalo, elephant, lion and brown bear. It would also do well on moose and elk. The 416 Remington has a trajectory very similar to the 375 H&H and is a better long-range cartridge than the 458 Winchester for use against thin-skinned game. For the man who has to travel light, the 416 would be a good one-gun cartridge choice for use in Africa. To date, only Remington loads ammunition in this caliber.

416 Remington Magnum Loading Data and Factory Ballistics

Bullet (grains/type)	Powder	Grains	Velocity	Energy	Source/Comments
300 SP	H-4895	78	2850	5412	Barnes
350 SP	H-4895	80	2700	5667	Barnes
400 SP	IMR 4064	78	2400	5117	Hornady
400 SP	IMR 4895	76.5	2400	5117	Hornady
300 SP	FL		2530	4262	Remington factory load
350 SP	FL		2520	4935	Remington factory load
400 SP	FL		2400	5115	Remington factory load

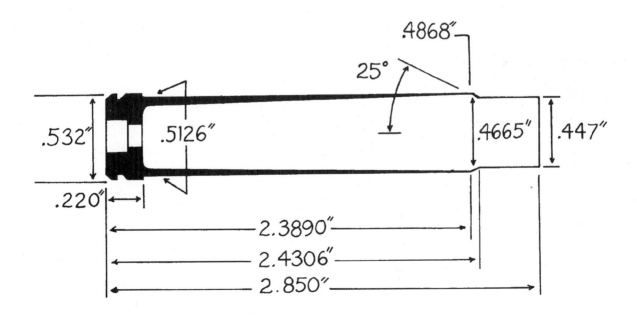

416 Weatherby Magnum

Historical Notes There has been a moderate, but persistent, interest in 40-caliber, dangerous-game cartridges for a good many years. The demand has been filled by several wildcat cartridges, but the call for a factory 40-caliber intensified in the 1980s. Remington was the first to exploit this potential market with its 416 Remington Magnum in 1988. This was followed by the 416 Weatherby Magnum (which is based on the 378 Weatherby Magnum) in 1989. In the game of cartridge one-upmanship, the Weatherby version was bound to be somewhat more powerful than an ordinary 416.

General Comments The 416 Weatherby Magnum offers 300 fps more initial velocity than the 416 Remington Magnum with the same bullet weight. How useful this will be in the field is difficult to assess, because both cartridges are adequate for the intended purpose, which is to dispatch large and/or dangerous game with a minimum of fuss. On the other hand, Weatherby rifles carry a certain prestige, and there is nothing wrong with having a little extra power when the crucial moment arrives. The choice between the two will probably be a matter of personal preference. However, recoil is rather brisk with any such chambering, and more powder pushing the same bullet faster translates into more recoil.

416 Weatherby Loading Data and Factory Ballistics

Bullet (grains/type)	Powder	Grains	Velocity	Energy	Source/Comments
300 SP	IMR 4831	115	3000	5997	Barnes
350 SP	IMR 4831	110	2800	6095	Barnes
400 SP	IMR 4831	110.5	2700	6477	Hornady
400 SP	H-450	119	2700	6477	Hornady
400 SP	IMR 7828	117	2600	6006	Hornady
400 SP	FL		2700	6474	Weatherby factory load

416 Rigby

Historical Notes Introduced by John Rigby of London, the 416 Rigby is a good example of a sound design that refuses to die. Until quite recently, less than 10,000 rifles in this caliber had been made. However, most of the older rifles in that chambering are still in use. In 1992, Ruger added this number to its rifle product line. Ruger thus increased the total number of guns in this chambering by 10 percent in one year, and continues to produce it. In 1989, Federal Cartridge Co. added the 416 Rigby to its Premium product line. In so doing, Federal became the first major American manufacturer to offer this classic African cartridge. By their actions, both Ruger and Federal took much of the momentum from the new 416 Remington Magnum cartridge. Their efforts in reintroducing the 416 Rigby have been successful and sales remain brisk. This only goes to show that not all new-product success stories use totally new products.

General Comments The 416 Rigby is a great favorite today of African game wardens and professional hunters alike. It is an excellent choice for the man who wishes to take only one rifle to Africa. Federal ballistics are identical to previous British loads, so the point of impact with express sights will be the same. Breech pressures of the 416 are only about 40,000 CUP in order to avoid sticky extraction because of high pressures on very hot days. This is strictly good sense based on many years of African experience. Remington has chosen to load the 416 Remington Magnum to pressure levels of 50,000 CUP, which makes one wonder if extraction at very high temperatures has been adequately tested. In any case, handloaders should resist the urge to improve the 416 Rigby ballistics for this reason. Bullets and brass for handloading are available from Huntington's in Oroville, Calif.

416 Rigby Loading Data and Factory Ballistics

Bullet (grains/type)	Powder	Grains	Velocity	Energy	Source/Comments
300 Barnes XFB	RL-22	103.0	2590	4470	Hodgdon
350 Barnes XFB	H4350	102.0	2518	4925	Hodgdon
400 Hornady FMJNR	H4831	106.0	2422	5210	Hodgdon
410 SP/FMJ	FL		2370	5115	Federal factory load

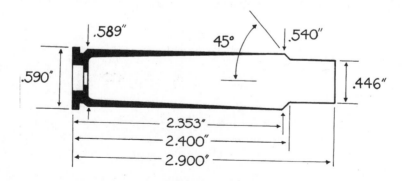

444 Marlin

Historical Notes News and data on the 444 Marlin round was released to the public in June 1964. The cartridge was designed for the Marlin Model 336 lever-action rifle. Initially, the rifle was manufactured with a 24-inch Micro-Groove barrel, two-thirds length magazine and recoil pad. The straight-grip stock had a Monte Carlo cheekpiece. Original ammunition was made by Remington.

The 444 Marlin is somewhat similar to the 44 Van Houten Super. The 44 VH was developed by E.B. Van Houten and "Lucky" Wade of Phoenix, Ariz. It was made by necking-up 30-40 Krag brass, trimming it to 2 inches and turning down the rims slightly. It was designed for the 336 Marlin or 94 Winchester actions. It predates the Marlin round by at least three years. Ballistics of the two rounds are nearly identical.

General Comments The 44 Magnum revolver cartridge achieved popularity as a rifle round. However, anyone using it discovers quite quickly that it has a rainbow-like trajectory, and its killing power on heavier game such as elk and moose is adequate only at close range. Consequently, there was need for a somewhat more powerful option. The 444 Marlin extends both the effective range and killing power inherent in the 44 Magnum. This round fires the same 240-grain softpoint bullet, at 2330 fps as compared to 1850 for the average 44 Magnum rifle. The 444 Marlin is substantially more powerful than the old 30-30 or the 35 Remington at short ranges. It develops about the same energy as the 348 Winchester and slightly more than the later 358 Winchester. However, with its larger diameter bullet it should provide better knockdown power. It is a short- to medium-range cartridge and should be adequate for any North American big game. It would also be effective on most thin-skinned African game, except dangerous varieties. Its advantage over the above-named cartridges is at ranges out to 150 yards. Beyond that, due to better bullet shape and sectional density, those all catch up to and finally surpass the 444 in retained velocity and energy. The 444 Marlin was formerly available as a superb all-round hunting load with a 265-grain bullet. Remington and Buffalo Bore now offer ammunition, with the latter firm offering several superior-performance, heavy-bullet loads.

444 Marlin Loading Data and Factory Ballistics

Bullet (grains/type)	Powder	Grains	Velocity	Energy	Source/Comments
180 HP	IMR 4198	51	2500	2499	Sierra
220 SP	IMR 4198	49	2350	2698	Sierra
240 HP	IMR 4198	46.5	2300	2820	Hornady, Sierra
240 HP	H-322	53	2300	2820	Hornady, Sierra
250 SP	IMR 4198	47	2250	2811	Sierra
265 Hornady JFP	H-4198	47.0	2273	3040	Hodgdon
275 SP	RL-7	47	2250	3092	Barnes
280 Swift HP	H322	49.5	2120	2790	Hodgdon
300 SP	RL-7	46	2150	3080	Barnes
300 Swift HP	H4198	42.5	2082	2885	Hodgdon
240 SP	FL		2330	2942	Remington factory load

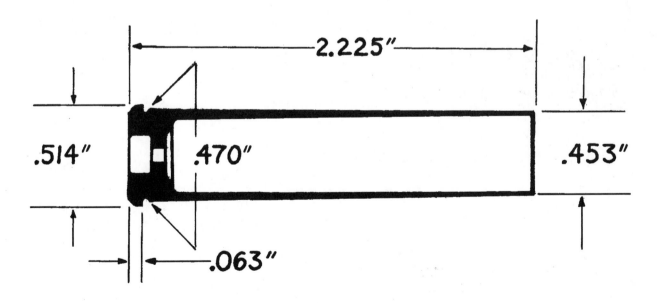

44-40 Winchester
(44 WCF, 44 Winchester)

Historical Notes This was the original cartridge for the famous Winchester Model 1873 lever-action repeating rifle. By 1878, Colt began offering revolvers in 44-40-caliber. At one time or another, just about every American arms manufacturer has offered some kind of gun chambered for this cartridge. The Colt-Burgess lever-action rifle of 1883 was made for the 44-40 and so was the 1885 Colt Lightning pump-action rifle. The Remington Model 14 1/2 pump-action used it, as did the Winchester 92 and Marlin 94, both lever-action repeaters. Most of the single-shot rifles made in the United States had a 44-40 model at one time or another. In Spain, there was a copy of the Winchester Model 92 in 44-40 caliber manufactured for police and civil guard use. No American-made rifles have chambered the round since 1937, but Colt revolvers retained it until 1942. Several foreign-made replicas of the Henry Carbine and the Winchester Model 66 and 73 are currently available in 44-40, as are new revolvers.

Winchester once loaded a 217-grain bullet in two separate headstamps: 44 C.L.M.R., for the Colt Lightning Magazine Rifle, and 44-40 for Marlin rifles. They also offered a 34-grain blackpowder load behind a 115-grain bullet for the Marble Game Getter rifle, which was headstamped 44 G.G.

General Comments The 44-40 is one of the all-time great American cartridges. It is said that it has killed more game, large and small, and more people, good and bad, than any other commercial cartridge ever developed. In its original blackpowder loading, it was the first effective combination cartridge that could be used interchangeably in rifle or revolver, and was a great favorite in the early days of the American West.

With proper handloads used in strong rifles, the 44-40 can safely propel the 200-grain jacketed bullet at 1,800 fps. Compared to the standard 30-30 load with a 170-grain bullet at about 2,100 fps, this is a superior combination against deer at short range. It was once offered in a high-velocity loading specifically designed to take advantage of the Model 92 Winchester's strength. Like many other high-velocity loadings of yesteryear, it had to be discontinued because certain types just insisted on chambering anything that would fit in whatever gun was at hand. The 44-40 became obsolete in the revolver with the advent of the 357 and 44 Magnums, and in the rifle by the 30-30 and similar cartridges that have a flatter trajectory at ranges beyond 100 yards. Present factory loads by Remington and Winchester are intended for revolvers and it is necessary to handload in order to get top performance from the rifle. Many 44-40 rifles have been rebarreled for the 44 Magnum. The rise of Cowboy Action Shooting has rekindled the 44-40's popularity.

44-40 Winchester Loading Data and Factory Ballistics

Bullet (grains/type)	Powder	Grains	Velocity	Energy	Source/Comments
180 SP	2400	18	1250	625	Hornady
180 SP	SR4756	11	1150	529	Hornady
180 SP	2400	16.5	1000	400	Hornady
180 SP	Unique	10.4	1150	529	Hornady
200 SP	IMR 4227	20	1100	537	Hornady
200 SP	2400	15.3	1000	444	Hornady
200 SP	Unique	9.5	1050	490	Hornady
200 SP	FL		1190	629	Factory load

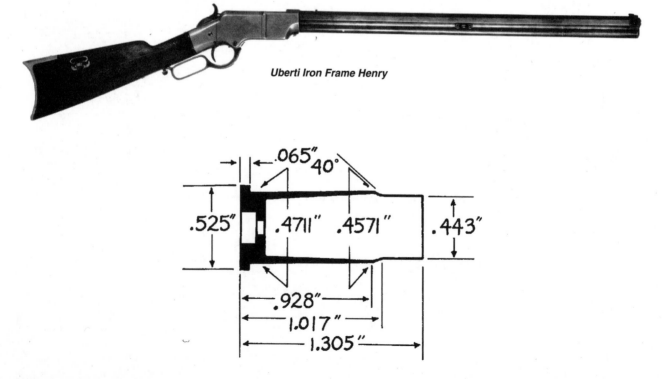

Uberti Iron Frame Henry

45-70 Government (45-70-330/45-70-350/ 45-70-405/45-70-500)

Historical Notes Adopted by the U.S. military in 1873 with the single shot "Trapdoor" Springfield rifle, this continued as the official service cartridge for 19 years. It was replaced in 1892 by the 30-40 Krag. The 45-70 Government was also a popular cartridge for sporting use and many repeating and single-shot rifles were chambered for it — the Remington rolling block, Remington-Keene, Remington-Lee, Marlin Model 81, Winchester Model 86 and Hotchkiss, plus many others. Though the Krag officially replaced the 45-70 in 1892, all volunteer Spanish-American War regiments — with the reported sole exception being Teddy Roosevelt's Rough Riders — were equipped with the Trapdoor 45-70. Many state militias were armed with the 45-70 Springfields well beyond 1900. American companies dropped the 45-70 as a rifle chambering in the early 1930s. However, it has staged a major comeback in popularity, and currently Marlin, Ruger and Browning chamber rifles for the 45-70. Winchester once loaded many versions of the basic 45-70 case with different bullet weights, shapes and blackpowder charges. They also loaded one variant of the 45-70-

405 Winchester load expressly for the Marlin 1881 lever-action rifle. It featured a differently shaped 405-grain bullet and was headstamped 45-70 Mar.

General Comments "Old soldiers never die," and apparently neither do old military cartridges. The 45-70 has been with us for more than 125 years and is still very much alive. As a short-range cartridge for anything from deer to grizzly bear, the 45-70 will hold its own with most of our more modern developments. Its greatest fault is the curved trajectory that makes it difficult to place shots beyond 150 yards with any certainty. Unfortunately, the U.S. Springfield and most of the other blackpowder rifles won't stand pressures over 25,000 psi or so. This prevents using heavy loads of smokeless powder. In late Model 86 Winchester or other smokeless powder rifles, the 45-70 can be loaded to deliver very impressive performance on the heaviest species of big game. Winchester, Remington, Federal, Cor-Bon and Buffalo Bore offer 45-70 ammunition.

45-70 U.S. Government Loading Data and Factory Ballistics

Bullet (grains/type)	Powder	Grains	Velocity	Energy	Source/Comments
300 HP	IMR 4198	34	1400	1306	Hornady, Sierra
300 HP	IMR 4227	29	1400	1306	Hornady, Sierra
300 HP	IMR 3031	43	1400	1306	Hornady
300 HP	SR 4759	27	1400	1306	Hornady
Loads for Modern Smokeless Powder Rifles Only					
300 HP	IMR 4198	46	2000	2665	Hornady
300 HP	IMR 4227	43	2100	2938	Sierra
350 Hornady JFP	H4198	54.0	2191	3730	Hodgdon
400 SP	H4198	50.5	2002	3555	Hodgdon
400 SP	IMR 3031	54	1800	2878	Speer
300 SP	FL		1880	2355	Factory load
405 SP	FL		1330	1590	Factory load

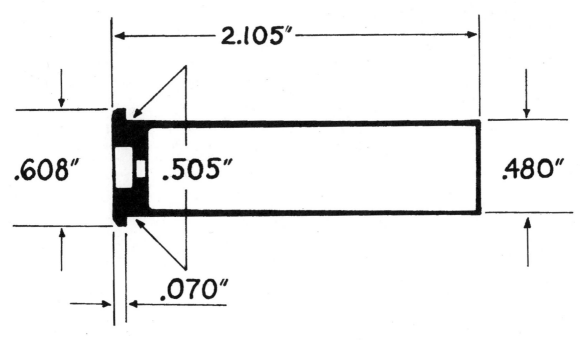

450 Marlin

Historical Notes Hornady and Marlin announced the 450 Marlin at the 2000 SHOT Show. This is the first new chambering from Marlin since the introduction of the 444 Marlin in mid-1964. This editor was among those who long advocated that Marlin should introduce a "Magnum" chambering for the Model 1895. The motivation for this cartridge is simple; handloaders have been souping up 45-70 loads for use in Marlin's modern 1895 since the day that gun was introduced. My own efforts along that path culminated in a combination that safely generates more than 4,000 foot pounds of energy in a specially modified version of this rifle. More recently, several ammunition producers have offered Magnum-level loadings. Owing to the many weaker 45-70 rifles still in use, Marlin could not condone this practice, nor could they stop it. Something had to give. Some have asked why Marlin did not simply lengthen the 45-70 case, and standardize a new higher-pressure cartridge. That alternative was not tenable because such a cartridge would have chambered in older (potentially weaker) rifles designed for the 45-90, 45-110, etc.

General Comments In my humble opinion, when one considers a simple approach that could have been taken, this cartridge design is a poor second-best choice for chambering in the new M-1895 Marlin. The simple adoption of an "Ackley Improved" version of the 45-70, would have provided a superior case design with a cartridge that would function better through the Marlin rifle and would not chamber in any older factory rifle. In any case, the 450 Marlin offers lever-action fans a factory chambering with significant ballistic potential. Shooters in this country have a long history of fascination with large-bore, lever-action rifles. Except for caliber, Marlin's new number is quite reminiscent of Winchester's circa-1903, 50-110 Winchester High Velocity load, which originated for the same reason — muzzle energy is essentially identical. This cartridge and rifle make a fine and versatile combination for those who hunt dangerous game under the worst possible conditions. Given correct bullet choice and shot placement, this is a capable performer for any task.

450 Marlin Factory Ballistics

Bullet (grains/type)	Powder	Grains	Velocity	Energy	Source/Comments
350 Hornady FP	FL		2100	3427	Hornady factory load

458 Winchester Magnum

Historical Notes The 458 Winchester Magnum was introduced in 1956 for a dressed-up version of the Model 70 rifle called the "African." The Remington 700 Safari is available in 458 and so are many other American- and European-made rifles such as the A-Square, Dakota 76, BRNO and the Ruger 77. The 458 has become a world standard and many factories and individual makers provide hunting arms for it. Ruger also chambers the 458 in its No. 1 single-shot rifle.

General Comments With an increasing number of American sportsmen making the trek to Africa, and with the Weatherby Magnum line of cartridges selling rather well, Winchester decided to get into the act. The result is the fine 458, a cartridge suitable for any of the most dangerous game in the world. This cartridge has been tested thoroughly in Africa and has proven itself adequate for the toughest game found there. It is as powerful as most of the oversized English big-bore elephant cartridges. Although overpowered for North American big game, it has nonetheless found favor with many hunters as a woods and brush cartridge when reloaded with lighter than standard factory bullets. With the 300-, 350- or 405-grain bullets, it can be loaded to duplicate the 45-70 at any level, and to cover a wide range of game and hunting conditions. As a factory load, it is not good for anything but the biggest and toughest. But then that is what it was intended for. Federal, Winchester and Remington offer ammunition.

458 Winchester Loading Data and Factory Ballistics

Bullet (grains/type)	Powder	Grains	Velocity	Energy	Source/Comments
300 SP	RL-7	58	2100	2938	Hornady
300 SP	IMR 4198	49	2100	2938	Hornady, Sierra
350 SP	IMR 4198	70.5	2500	4859	Hornady
400 SP	IMR 4198	64	2250	4498	Speer
400 SP	IMR 4320	77	2200	4300	Speer
500 SP	IMR 3031	70	2100	4897	Hornady
350 SP	FL		2470	4740	Factory load
400 SP	FL		2380	5031	Factory load
500 FMJ	FL		2040	4620	Factory load
510 SP	FL		2040	4712	Factory load

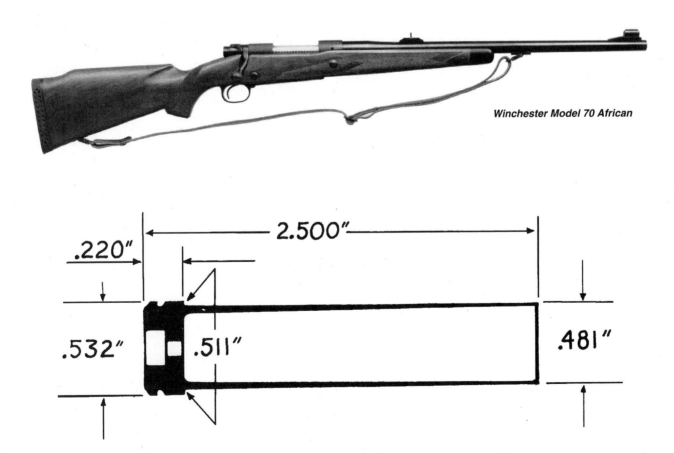

Winchester Model 70 African

.220"

2.500"

.532" .511" .481"

458 Lott

Historical Notes When a twice-shot African buffalo energetically squashed Jack Lott, dissatisfaction with his 458 Winchester's performance led to the creation, in 1971, of a more capable 458 cartridge, the 458 Lott. By using a case 2.8 inches long, the 458 Lott was able to achieve 2,150 fps with a 500-grain bullet. The genius of the late Mr. Lott's design is that 458 Lott rifles also chambered and fired 458 Winchester Magnum ammo. On the downside, the wildcat 458 Lott was strictly a handloading and custom rifle proposition. Then in 2002, Hornady decided to produce factory ammunition, and Ruger chambered their Model 77 MKII in 458 Lott.

General Comments The 458 Winchester is advertised as developing 2,040 fps with the 500-grain bullet when fired from a 24-inch barrel. In reality, poorly constructed factory loads often produce little more than 1,900 fps in 22-inch barreled rifles. The 458 Lott will do an honest 2,300+ fps from a 22-inch barrel. It has been field-tested in Africa and has chalked up an impressive number of one-shot kills on elephants and buffalo. It is similar to the 450 Watts, which is also based on the full-length 375 H&H case expanded to 458-caliber, but is shorter. Rifles chambered for the 458 Lott will also safely shoot 458 Winchester ammo. Since Hornady has adopted this cartridge as a factory loading, availability of ammo and brass should improve markedly. Numerous bullet makers make bullets suitable for the 458 Lott, ranging from 350 grains to 600 grains. With factory ammo and production rifles now readily available, the 458 Lott continues to be a superb choice for virtually any dangerous game worldwide.

458 Lott Loading Data and Factory Ballistics

Bullet (grains/type)	Powder	Grains	Velocity	Energy	Source/Comments
500 SP	IMR 4320	85.0	2330	6020	NA
500 SP	IMR 4064	79.0	2230	5520	NA
500 RN	FL		2300	5873	Factory load

460 Weatherby Magnum

Historical Notes This big, potent caliber was brought out in 1958 for the avowed purpose of providing the world's most powerful commercial rifle cartridge. It was developed by necking the 378 Weatherby case up to 45 caliber. Rifles and ammunition are available only through Weatherby on a commercial basis, but custom-made rifles based on Mauser-type bolt actions are occasionally chambered for this round.

General Comments Until the advent of the 700 Nitro Express, which is just barely in the ranks of commercial cartridges, the 460 Weatherby Magnum was among the most powerful available. Recent factory ballistics have been toned down a bit, but it still delivers better than 7,500 foot pounds of muzzle energy, which far exceeds most dangerous game loads. The big 460 is overly powerful for any North American big game, but it does provide that ultimate bit of insurance against the dangerous African or Asiatic varieties under adverse conditions. It would, of course, be preferable to be caught slightly overgunned than to be eaten by a lion or trampled by an elephant. Two wildcat cartridges, the 450 and 475 Ackley, are in the same class as the 460 WM insofar as energy is concerned. The 475 A&M Magnum reportedly develops a muzzle energy of some 10,000 foot-pounds. However, none of these are commercial cartridges. Recently, many new A-Square and proprietary numbers have exceeded the 460 Weatherby.

460 Weatherby Magnum Loading Data and Factory Ballistics

Bullet (grains/type)	Powder	Grains	Velocity	Energy	Source/Comments
300 SP	IMR 4320	112	3000	5997	Barnes
350 SP	IMR 4064	111	2900	6538	Hornady
500 SP	IMR 4350	123.5	2650	7799	Hornady
500 SP	IMR 4320	108	2550	7221	Hornady
500 SP	IMR 3031	99	2500	6941	Hornady
500 SP	H-4831	125	2650	7799	Barnes
500 SP/FMJ	FL		2600	7507	Weatherby factory load

470 Nitro Express (470 NE)

Historical Notes Since its introduction in 1907, the 470 Nitro Express has proven to be one of the most popular and long lived of the British Nitro Express cartridges. Guns in this chambering are not excessively heavy and recoil, while heavy, is acceptable. This makes a good combination for the hunter who wants to use one cartridge for all African game without fear of being under-gunned. For this reason, most guns in this cartridge are the tried-and-true double rifles, such as the English-made H&H, Purdey, J. Rigby & Co., Westley Richards, Powell and a few others. Production of such rifles is also abundant in Europe, with Beretta of Italy, Francotte of Belgium, and Heym of Germany offering models priced from

$10,000 on up. The 5,130 foot-pounds of muzzle energy generated by the 500-grain, steel-jacketed solid bullet is the stuff from which myths are made in the hot-stove league.

General Comments In 1989, Federal Cartridge Co. added this caliber to its Premium product line, making it the first British Nitro Express caliber offered by a major American manufacturer. The 470 is generally too powerful for most North American game, but works well on medium to large game worldwide. Many 470 shooters reload the cartridge because of the high cost of factory ammo. Federal's factory loads can provide cases, and Barnes offers bullets.

470 Nitro Express Loading Data and Factory Ballistics

Bullet (grains/type)	Powder	Grains	Velocity	Energy	Source/Comments
500 Barnes SP	H4831	119.0	2159	5175	Hodgdon
600 Barnes SP	H4831	105.0	1941	5020	Hodgdon
500 SP/FMJ	FL		2150	5130	Federal factory load

Custom Ruger No. 1

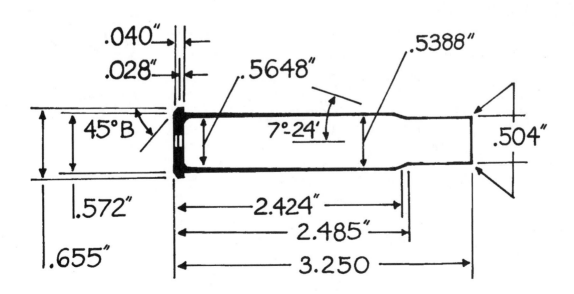

50 Browning Machine Gun (50 BMG)

Historical Notes The 50 BMG was invented by its namesake and adopted into United States military service in 1918 for John M. Browning's famous heavy machinegun. Browning's attentions in this area were prompted by a battlefield need recognized during World War I. There have been other developments and at least once the Pentagon was considering dropping the 50 BMG in favor of more modern and generally bigger chamberings. However, the 50 BMG has remained. The advent of saboted loads, generating 4,500 fps muzzle velocities with devastating armor-penetration capabilities, and its performance in the Gulf War has seemed to cement its continued existence as a stable part of NATO's arsenal.

Battlefield use is against light-armored vehicles to ranges of a mile or more, and used against the unprotected, it is effective to several times that range.

General Comments There has long been interest in the 50 BMG as a quasi-sporting round. Today, the most significant sporting use for this chambering is long-range accuracy shooting with some competitions exceeding one mile. The 1000-yard 50-caliber record, as of this writing, is a five-shot group of just under 3 inches on centers. Several bolt-action rifles are currently available for the big fifty. The 50 BMG easily launches the 750-grain bullets available for it at 2,700 fps. The lighter 647-grain bullets available can be launched at 3000 fps. For obvious reasons, sporting rifles chambered for the big fifty uniformly feature muzzlebrakes and weigh 20 pounds or more. Recoil is a bit harsh until the rifle's weight approaches 30 pounds.

The only commercial ammunition that has ever been available for the 50 BMG is from PMC. Components and specialized tools and equipment to handload this cartridge are available to the advanced reloader.

50 Browning Machine Gun Loading Data and Factory Ballistics

Bullet (grains/type)	Powder	Grains	Velocity	Energy	Source/Comments
750	H870	225.0	2769	12,775	Barnes
800	AA8700	215.0	2675	12,720	Barnes
660	FL		3080	13,910	PMC factory load

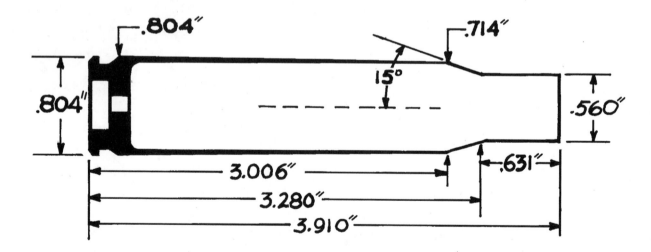

CURRENT AMERICAN RIFLE CARTRIDGES
Centerfire Sporting
Dimensional Data (SAAMI Maximum Cartridge Data)

Cartridge	Case Type	Bullet Dia.	Neck-Dia.	Shoulder Dia.	Base Dia.	Rim Dia.	Rim Thck.	Case Length	Ctge. Length	Twist	Primer
17 Remington	C	.172	.198	.355	.374	.377	.041	1.79	1.86	9	S
204 Ruger	C	.204	.229	.360	.373	.375	.045	1.850	2.260	12	S
22 Hornet	**A**	**.223**	**.242**	**.274**	**.294**	**.345**	**.060**	**1.40**	**1.72**	**16**	**S**
218 Bee	A	.224	.241	.331	.349	.408	.060	1.35	1.68	16	S
223 Remington	C	.224	.249	.349	.373	.375	.041	1.76	2.10	12	S
22 PPC	C	.224	.245	.430	.440	.441	.050	1.52	1.96	1-14	S
225 Winchester	A	.224	.260	.406	.422	.473	.045	1.93	2.50	14	L
22-250 Remington	C	.224	.254	.412	.466	.470	.045	1.91	2.33	14	L
220 Swift	G	.224	.260	.402	.443	.472	.045	2.20	2.68	14	L
223 WSSM	C	.224	.254	.544	.555	.535	.040	1.670	2.360	14	L
6mm PPC	**C**	**.243**	**.260**	**.430**	**.441**	**.442**	**0.50**	**1.50**	**2.12**	**1-12**	**S**
6mm Norma BR	C	.243	.271	.458	.469	.470	.051	1.56	2.44	8	S
243 Winchester	C	.243	.276	.454	.470	.470	0.49	2.05	2.71	10	L
6mm Remington	C	.243	.276	.454	.470	.472	.045	2.23	2.91	9	L
244 Remington	C	.243	.276	.429	.470	.472	.045	2.23	2.825	12	L
243 WSSM	C	.243	.276	.544	.555	.535	.040	1.670	2.360	12	L
25-20 Winchester	**A**	**.257**	**.274**	**.329**	**.349**	**.405**	**.060**	**1.33**	**1.60**	**13-14**	**S**
25-35 Winchester	A	.257	.280	.355	.420	.500 (.506)	.059	2.04	2.53	8	L
250 Savage	C	.257	.286	.413	.468	.470	.045	1.91	2.52 (2.515)	14	L
257 Roberts (257 Roberts +P)	C	.257	.290	.430	.468	.473	.045	2.23	2.74	10-12	L
25 WSSM	C	.257	.299	.544	.555	.535	.040	1.670	3.260	10-12	L
25-06 Remington	C	.257	.287	.441	.470	.471	.045	2.49	3.00	10-12	L
6.5-08 A-Square/260 Rem	**C**	**.264**	**.294**	**.452**	**.468**	**.467**	**.045**	**.025**	**2.80**	**9-10**	**L**
6.5x55 Swedish	C	.264	.297	.435	.480 (.477)	.480 (.479)	.050	2.16	3.15	7.9	L
6.5-284 Norma	I	.264	.297	.475	.500	.470	.051	2.17	3.23	8-9	S
264 (6.5mm) Win. Magnum	E	.264	.289	.490	.515 (.5127)	.532	.047	2.52	3.29	9	L
6.8 SPC	**C**	**.277**	**.306**	**.401**	**.421**	**.417**	**.049**	**1.686**	**2.260**	**10**	**L**
270 Winchester	C	.277	.307	.440	.468	.470	.045	2.54	3.28	10	L
7-30 Waters	A	.284	.306	.399	.422 (.4215)	.506	.058	2.04	2.52	9.5	L
7mm Mauser	C	.284	.320	.420 (.4294)	.470	.474	.046	2.24 (2.235)	3.06	8-10	L
7mm-08 Remington	C	.284	.315	.454	.470	.473	.050	2.04 (2.035)	2.80	9	L
7x64 Brenneke	C	.284	.313	.422	.463	.468	.045	2.51	3.21		L
284 Winchester	I	.284	.320	.465 (.4748)	.495 (.500)	.470	.049	2.17	2.75	10	L
280 Remington (7mm Express Remington)	C	.284	.315	.441	.470	.472	.045	2.54	3.33	10.5	L
7mm Remington Magnum	E	.284	.315	.490	.511	.525	.047	2.50	3.24	9.5	L
7mm Weatherby Magnum	E	.284	.312	.490	.511	.530	.048	2.55	3.25	12	L
7mm STW	E	.284	.316	.487	.513	.532	.048	2.85	3.65	9-9.5	L
30 Carbine	**D**	**.308**	**.335**		**.355**	**.360**	**.046**	**1.29**	**1.65**	**16**	**S**
30-30 Winchester	A	.308	.328	.402	.422 (.4215)	.502	.058	2.03 (2.039)	2.53	12	L
300 Savage	C	.308	.339	.443 (.4466)	.470	.470	.045	1.87	2.62	12	L
30-40 Krag	A	.308	.338	.415 (.419)	.457 (.4577)	.540	.059	2.31	3.10 (3.089)	10	L
307 Winchester	G	.308	.344	.454	.470	.506	.059	2.02 (2.015)	2.60 (2.56)	12	L
308 Winchester	C	.308	.344	.454	.470	.470	.049	2.01 (2.015)	2.75	12	L

Cartridge	Case Type	Bullet Dia.	Neck-Dia.	Shoulder Dia.	Base Dia.	Rim Dia.	Rim Thck.	Case Length	Ctge. Length	Twist	Primer
30-06 Springfield	C	.308	.340	.441	.470	.473	.045	2.49	3.34	10	L
300 H&H Magnum	E	.308	.338	.447	.513	.530	.048	2.85	3.60	10	L
300 Winchester Magnum	E	.308	.334	.4891	.5126	.530	.046	2.60 (2.62)	3.30	10	L
300 Weatherby Magnum	E	.308	.337	.495	.513 (.5117)	.530	.048	2.82 (2.825)	3.56	12	L
300 Rem. UltraMag	I	.308	.344	.525	.550	.532	.050	2.845	3.60	10	L
7.62x39mm	C	.311	.340 (.337)	.344 (.396)	.438 (.433)	.440	.053	1.52 (1.528)	2.20	9.4	S
303 British	**A**	**.311**	**.338**	**.401**	**.458**	**.530**	**.062**	**2.21 (2.222)**	**3.05 (3.075)**	**10**	**L**
32-20 Winchester	A	.312	.326	.338 (.3424)	.353	.405	.058	1.32 (1.315)	1 59	20	S
32 Winchester Special	A	.321	.343	.396 (.4014)	.422 (.4219)	.506	.058	2.04	2.55 (2.565)	16	L
325 WSM	**C**	**.323**	**.358**	**.538**	**.555**	**.535**	**.054**	**2.10**	**2.560**	**9-10**	**L**
8mm Remington Magnum	E	.323	.351 (.3541)	.485 (.4868)	.509 (.5126)	.530	.047	2.85	3.57 (3.600)	10	L
338 Federal	**C**	**.338**	**.369**	**.454**	**.470**	**.473**	**.049**	**.201**	**2.75**	**10**	**L**
338 Winchester Magnum	E	.338	.369	.480 (.491)	.515 (.5127)	.530	.047	2.49 (2.50)	3.30 (3.34)	10	L
338 Rem. UltraMag	I	.338	.371	.526	.550	.532	.050	2.76	3.60	10	L
338 Lapua Mag	C	.338	.370	.540	.590	.590	.060	2.72	3.60		L
348 Winchester	**A**	**.348**	**.379 (.3757)**	**.485**	**.553**	**.610**	**.062**	**2.26 (2.255)**	**2.80 (2.795)**	**12**	**L**
35 Remington	C	.358	.384	.419 (.4259)	.458 (.4574)	.460	.046	1.92	2.52	16	L
356 Winchester	G	.358	.388	.454	.4703	.508	.058	2.02 (2.015)	2.56	12	L
358 Winchester	C	.358	.388	.454	.4703	.473	.048	2.01 (2.015)	2.78	12	L
35 Whelen	C	.358	.388	.441	.470	.473	.045	2.50 (2.494)	3.34	12-14	L
375 Winchester	**B**	**.375**	**.400**		**.415 (.4198)**	**.502**	**.046**	**2.02**	**2.56**	**12**	**L**
376 Steyr	I	.375	.398	.472	.501	.494	.048	2.35	3.075	12	L
375 H&H Magnum	E	.375	.402	.440 (.4478)	.521	.530	.046	2.85	3.60	12	L
38-55 Winchester 38-55 Ballard	B	.379	.392	.3938	.422	.506	.058	2.12 (2.085)	2.51	18	L
38-40 Winchester	A	.401	.416	.438 (.4543)	.465	.520	.058	1.30	1.59	36	L
408 Cheytac	**C**	**.408**	**.438**	**.601**	**.637**	**.640**	**.065**	**3.04**	**4.307**		**L**
416 Remington Magnum	**E**	**.416**	**.447**	**.487**	**.509**	**.530**	**.046**	**2.85**	**3.60**	**14**	**L**
416 Rigby	C	.416	.445 (.4461)	.539 (.5402)	.589	.586	.058	2.90	3.75	16.5	L
44-40 Winchester	**A**	**.427/ .429**	**.443**	**.4568**	**.471**	**.525**	**.058**	**1.31**	**1.92**	**20-36**	**LP**
444 Marlin	B	.429	.453	.4549	.469	.514	.058	2.16 (2.225)	2.57	38	L
45-70 Government	**B**	**.458**	**.475 (.480)**	**.4813**	**.500**	**.600 (.608)**	**.065**	**2.105**	**2.55**	**18-22**	**L**
450 Marlin	F	.458	.480		.511	.532	.047	2.09	2.55	22	L
458 Winchester Magnum	F	.458	.478 (.4811)	.4825	.513	.532	.046	2.50	3.34	14-16	L
470 Nitro Express	A	.475	.504	.528 (.5322)	.5728	.655	.037	3.25	3.98	20	L
50 BMG	C	.510/ .511	.560	.714	.804	.804	.080	3.91	5.545	16	50 BMG

Case Type: A = Rimmed, bottleneck. B = Rimmed, straight. C = Rimless, bottleneck. D = Rimless, straight. E = Belted, bottleneck. F = Belted, straight. G = Semi-rimmed, bottleneck. H = Semi-rimmed, straight. I = Rebated, bottleneck. J = Rebated, straight. K = Rebated, belted bottleneck. L = Rebated, belted straight.

Primer Type: S = Small rifle (0.175"). SP = Small pistol (0.175"). L = Large rifle (0.210"). LP = Large pistol (0.210"). 50 BMG = CCI-35/VihtaVuori-110/RWS-8212. B-1 = Berdan #1. B-2 = Berdan #2.

Other codes: Belt/Rim Diameter. Unless otherwise noted, all dimensions in inches. Twist (factory) is given as inches of barrel length per complete revolution, e.g., 12 = 1 turn in 12", etc. Unless otherwise noted, all dimensions are in inches. Data in parenthesis represents SAAMI maximum specifications. Bullet upset performance of the 264 Winchester Magnum 140 gr. Power Point at ranges of 100, 200, 300, 400 and 500 yards.

Chapter 3

Obsolete American Rifle Cartridges

(Centerfire Sporting—Blackpowder and Smokeless Powder)

CHAPTER 3 covers obsolete rifle cartridges: those no longer loaded by American ammunition manufacturers or those no longer chambered in commercially available rifles. Sometimes such ammunition is still available out of dealers' old stocks. Both smokeless powder and blackpowder cartridges are included in this section. The total number of old blackpowder sporting cartridge types is quite large. Many of those are now collectors' items.

Some authorities are bound to disagree with a few of the cartridges placed in the obsolete category. For example, wildcat experimenters have kept the Newton cartridge line alive over the years, and it might be argued that those belong in that classification. A wildcat cartridge is usually defined as one that is not loaded, chambered or available on a commercial basis. Strictly speaking, this would make wildcats of almost all the cartridges listed in this chapter. However, these have one common, differentiating characteristic — all were at one time available as true commercial cartridges. Furthermore, used rifles and ammunition out of old stock are sometimes still available for the majority of smokeless powder types. These are also listed in old catalogs and ballistics tables, and it might create confusion to call these wildcats.

The cartridges in Chapter 3 can be considered as commercial innovations that have not stood the test of time. This is as true of the Newton cartridges as the others, but in addition, the Newton designs must be recognized as too advanced for their day. If Charles Newton were alive and his cartridges were introduced today, they would be hailed as brilliant and modern in every respect. Unfortunately, modern powders and entirely suitable actions were not available back around 1910, nor was the sporting world quite ready to accept high-intensity cartridges. The general big game hunting conditions at that time made the benefits of this development of doubtful value. The trouble with being ahead of the times is that people do not appreciate your genius during your lifetime. Posthumous recognition must be of precious little comfort to the individual involved. The late Roy Weatherby, on the other hand, arrived on the scene at the right time. He was also a far better promoter and businessman than Charles Newton. Result? Ultra-velocity Weatherby rifles are a commercial success and his ideas are accepted the world over by all but a few die-hards.

The principal importance of obsolete commercial cartridges to today's sportsman is that rifles for many of these are still floating around, particularly the smokeless powder types. It is well to be aware of its existence and disadvantages before some sharpy unloads an obsolete rifle on you. Obtaining ammunition for any of these chamberings is going to be an ever-increasing problem. Of course, certain handloaders like to play around with obsolete cartridges just to be different or to try to improve performance. If you belong to this group, well and good, you probably know what you are doing. However, cartridges in Chapter 2 will serve the average sportsman better. Up to this point, we have aimed most of these remarks toward obsolete smokeless powder cartridges. The true blackpowder types are a different story. Many of the old blackpowder rifles are now quite valuable, and we find a considerable and growing trend toward use of these old rifles for target shooting, hunting and Cowboy Action Shooting.

Cartridge Development

Blackpowder cartridges discussed in this chapter cover arms development from about 1868 to 1895. Ideas and experiments of this interval were a necessary prerequisite to perfection of modern, high-powered rifles and ammunition. This was also one of the most romantic periods of American history — the consolidation and settling of the western frontier.

The first successful, self-contained metallic cartridge produced on a commercial basis in the United States was the 22 rimfire Short, introduced by Smith & Wesson for its small tip-up revolver in 1857. Commercial cartridge production from then until after the close of the Civil War was mostly in the rimfire field. Patents issued to George W. Morse in 1856 and 1858 covered the essential features of the modern centerfire cartridge. His design incorporated an anvil, formed out of a wire, soldered inside the case. A perforated rubber disc held at the base of the case by this wire supported the primer (or cap, as was the common name at that time).

American Col. Hiram Berdan perfected his priming system, with the anvil formed in the bottom of the primer pocket, during 1866. British Col. Edward Boxer developed his self-contained primer and anvil in 1867. (Oddly, European manufacturers use the Berdan type extensively while American manufacturers use the Boxer primer almost exclusively.) Frankford Arsenal initiated experiments to develop a satisfactory centerfire system as early as 1858. The Union Metallic Cartridge Co. (now Remington) began manufacturing Berdan centerfire cartridges in 1868, about a year after formation of the company. The first of the American outside-primed, Berdan-type cartridges were probably the 50-70 Govt. and 50 Remington Navy rounds.

After 1870, development and introduction of improved centerfire cartridges was quite rapid. In 1885, the French chemist, Vielle, developed the first practical smokeless powder, and in 1886, the French adapted this to the new 8mm Lebel military cartridge. The United States military adopted its first smokeless powder small-bore cartridge in 1892 for the Krag bolt-action rifle. Winchester developed the first smokeless powder sporting round, the 30 Winchester Center Fire (now known as the 30-30 Winchester), during 1895. Popularity of blackpowder cartridges did not begin a serious decline in the United States until after about 1910. Both Remington and Winchester were still loading blackpowder in some of the old cartridges as late as 1936 or 1937. Many blackpowder centerfire cartridges, such as the 32-20, 32-40, 38-55, 38-40, 44-40, 45 Colt and 45-70 survived the change to smokeless powder. Several manufacturers load one or more of these but now with smokeless powder. (Cor-Bon offers a limited production of blackpowder Cowboy Action loads in 45 Colt and 45-70.) We cover those early rounds still produced in other chapters, as appropriate.

Cartridge Designation Confusion

Two great sources of confusion with blackpowder sporting cartridges are the method of nomenclature and the manufacturer's habit of sticking its name on any cartridge it manufactured or for which that company chambered guns. Two or three numbers were normally used to designate a particular cartridge and loading, e.g., 45-70 Govt. or the 45-70-500 Govt. The first numeral represents caliber (approximate bullet diameter in hundredths of an inch); the second numeral signifies blackpowder charge (grains); the third numeral specifies bullet weight (grains). The manufacturer often tacked on its name after the final numeral. Worse, sometimes, a manufacturer would offer several interchangeable cartridges but with distinct names. For example, Winchester offered two essentially identical 45-70 loadings, one called 45-70-350 WCF, the other (offered for Marlin rifles) called 45-70-300 Marlin. As a matter of confusing fact, the Sharps Rifle Co. designated this same 45-70 Govt. round as the 45/2.1-inch Sharps. Winchester introduced the tapered-case 40-65 WCF; for its rifle, Marlin loaded the same case with 60 grains of blackpowder and called the resulting round the 40-60 Marlin. Despite the distinct names, these two cartridges are nearly identical and are fully interchangeable. However, Winchester also introduced its own 40-60 WCF, a shorter and entirely different case than the "so-called" 40-60 Marlin. Then consider the following trio: 50-100, 50-105 and 50-110 Winchester. Some references have listed these as different cartridges, but these are, in reality, just different loadings of the same case, which Winchester originally offered as the 50-110-300 WCF. Confusing!

To add a bit more difficulty to this mess, consider the "Everlasting," a heavy reloadable-type case, which was popular for many years. Often, these cases were so thick and heavy that the original powder charge would not fit. Manufacturers solved this problem by making the case slightly longer than standard. This practice gave rise to all manner of different cartridges, which are simply a slightly lengthened version of something else. Trying to tie the standard original and the longer reloadable version together is often difficult. We have attempted to unravel this confusion as much as possible.

Most cartridge-book authors list bullet diameter, based upon that portion protruding from the case mouth. This is OK for identification purposes, but not much help to the handloader. Bullet diameter, as given here, is that recommended for loading and shooting and is based upon average groove diameter. We obtained this by measuring bullets removed from factory ammunition or from old Ideal catalogs or manufacturers' specifications. Ideal catalogs had a reference table listing various cartridges and the loading tool and standard bullet furnished. This is a good index for bullet diameter in any given cartridge, but old rifle bores exhibited considerable variation. It is a good idea to measure bore diameter before you order a mould, just to be on the safe side.

If you cannot figure out the chambering of your rifle, have it checked by a gunsmith or make a chamber cast and measure it. A comparison of chamber dimensions with the cartridge dimensions in this or other chapters should allow you to determine chambering of almost any rifle. These cartridge dimensions will also assist in making up ammunition for the old-timers, or determining the proper name of unmarked cases.

Chamber Casting

In making chamber castings, one can use lead alloy (not recommended), sulphur, a low melting point bismuth alloy or paraffin wax.

Flowers of sulphur, obtainable at any drugstore, is satisfactory. However, sulphur casts are extremely brittle and prone to breakage during removal from the chamber or during later handling. The tinker must heat a sulphur solution (4 ounces of sulphur, a pinch of lampblack and about a teaspoon of camphor) very slowly with continuous stirring. As soon as this becomes fully molten, it is ready for pouring into the chamber. It should be poured quickly and allowed to cool thoroughly before attempting to remove the cast.

The chamber must be thoroughly cleaned and lightly oiled before pouring. The bore should be plugged, just forward of the chamber, thus also giving you a cast of the bore for measurement. A good method is to drive a piece of wire through a bore-fitting cork and leave this wire extending from the breech. A finger loop on the end of this wire mandrel aids in removing the cast.

For a simple, albeit less precise but nonetheless perfectly useful casting, prepare the chamber the same way, then plug the bore with a paper wad or other similar device and fill the chamber with molten paraffin. After thorough cooling, this casting will easily come free from the chamber. This provides a very good casting but will always shrink a few thousandths of an inch in every dimension. Nevertheless, this will usually be adequate to distinguish correct chambering designation.

The most satisfactory and durable chamber casts are accomplished with chamber cast metal available from gunsmith supply houses (such as Brownells: 800-471-0015). These are bismuth alloys. The user can repeatedly re-melt and reuse casts made from this material. Lightly oil the chamber and throat as above. One of the typical bismuth alloys used for chamber castings is Cerrosafe. This alloy has a pouring temperature of 190-degrees Fahrenheit, significantly below the boiling point of water. You should be cautious to avoid overheating this material, as doing so will destroy its reusability. Cerrosafe shrinks slightly for a few minutes after it hardens, which simplifies removal of large or long castings. Measurements made approximately one hour after removal give truest dimensions. Surfaces of bismuth alloy casts are very smooth, unlike those of lead alloy, which often wrinkle badly.

Blackpowder Loads and Shooting

Although considerable difference in knockdown or killing power exists among blackpowder sporting cartridges, little variation in effective range exists. Stories abound about market-era buffalo hunters killing game at ranges of 1/2-mile or more, and, no doubt, this sometimes happened. Competitors used some of the big-bore match cartridges for 1,000- and even 1,400-yard target shooting. Buffalo hunters were generally professionals who had spent years in the field and must have developed a keen ability for estimating distances. On the target range, distance was known and the rifle sighted-in before the match started. Many people cannot tell 100 feet from 100 yards in the field and that is why blackpowder rifles, with their rainbow-like trajectories, are restricted to an effective game range of not much beyond 150 yards. An experienced hunter, or anyone who has practiced with his rifle and knows how to judge distance with reasonable accuracy can, of course, do better. Blackpowder cartridges below about 38-caliber are mostly for small or medium game. Larger calibers include many good short- to medium-range deer and black bear cartridges. The big and long 45- to 50-caliber numbers would knock the stuffing out of the largest moose or grizzly bear that ever lived. All you have to do is place the shot correctly.

Loading ammunition for blackpowder rifles requires caution if you intend to use smokeless powder. As a matter of safety, velocity and pressure must be kept at the original level in most rifles.

Jacketed bullets and high velocity are out of the question unless you have a modern action and a steel barrel designed for use with smokeless powder loads. While a few of the old actions are strong enough to be re-barreled to modern chamberings, most are not. Among the strongest are the Peabody-Martini, Remington rolling block & Hepburn, Sharps-Borchardt, Stevens 44-1/2 and the Winchester single-shot. Late models of these are as strong as many modern actions, but early models do not have the improved "smokeless powder steel" and caution is advisable.

The weakest of the lot are the U.S. 1866 and 1873 Springfield, Kennedy, Whitney, and Winchester Models 1873 and 1876. In these, use blackpowder or very light smokeless powder loads.

Also, do not use a smokeless powder charge given for one bullet weight with a heavier bullet, as this will raise pressure, perhaps beyond safe limits. Old cartridge cases are often of the folded-head (balloon) type, which are not particularly strong. Furthermore, since blackpowder residue is corrosive to brass, inspect your cases very carefully. It is safer to use modern-made cases in original or reformed sizes when possible. Non-corrosive primers do not leave chloride salts in the bore, hence, reduce that corrosion. However, these can also raise pressure — a fact to bear in mind when working up loads. Shooting blackpowder rifles and cartridges is lots of fun, and it can be just as safe as shooting modern rifles. On the other hand, it requires common sense and knowledge of what you are trying to do. If in doubt, do not do it! Ask a good gunsmith and follow his advice — in the end, that practice will be cheaper.

Shooting old blackpowder rifles has become such a popular pastime that furnishing ammunition for these obsolete guns is a growing business. As a further aid in obtaining ammunition, get a copy of the book, *Cartridge Conversions*, by the late Maj. George C. Nonte, Jr. This will tell you how to make, via re-forming, most of the non-existent blackpowder cartridges. An article in the 1962, 16th Edition of GUN DIGEST by Nonte introduces this subject. The *Lyman Reloaders Handbook* and the NRA's *Illustrated Reloading Handbook* (out of print) also have much valuable information on making and loading obsolete cartridges. It is not surprising to find reproductions (identical in every important way to the originals) and replicas (dimensionally and functionally similar to the origi-

nals) of some of the more popular blackpowder cartridge rifles are being manufactured. This follows the success of percussion replica arms. Bell Basic Brass (formerly Brass Extrusion Laboratories, and then called M.A.S.T. Technologies) made 45- and 50-caliber brass cases from which many obsolete blackpowder cartridges could be formed. Further information can be found under individual cartridges in this chapter. Red Willow Tool and Armory and Bertram Bullet Co. have recently manufactured many obsolete American and British cartridges. These can be obtained from Huntington's (601 Oro Dam Blvd., Oroville, CA 95965) or The Old Western Scrounger (now owned by the Gibbs Rifle Co.).

— FCB

22-15-60 Stevens

Historical Notes One of a number of cartridges for the Stevens 44 or 44-1/2 series of single-shot rifles, this cartridge was introduced by Stevens in 1896. Actual design is credited to Charles H. Herrick of Winchester, Mass. It did not enjoy a particularly long life as most shooters preferred the 25-21 or some of the larger calibers. Many shooters claimed the 22-15 Stevens gave better accuracy than the 22 WCF.

General Comments This is an improved centerfire 22 of substantially better killing power than other 22s of its day. With the heavy 60-grain bullet, it would shoot relatively flat for 125 yards or

so. As a target or match cartridge, most of the blackpowder 22s fouled the bore badly and required frequent cleaning. Most shooters preferred the larger calibers of 25 on up. The 22-15-60 was displaced by the 22 WCF and smokeless powder developments in the rimfire group. Original primer was the 1-1/2 size, the same as our modern Small Rifle or Pistol primer of 0.175-inch diameter. Charge was 15 grains of FFFFg or FFFg. Lyman No. 22636 or 22637 in 54- to 60-grain weight is the proper bullet. Therefore, if you should have one of these old rifles in shooting condition, you can still shoot it — if you can find cases.

22-15-60 Stevens Loading Data and Factory Ballistics

Bullet (grains/type)	Powder	Grains	Velocity	Energy	Source/Comments
60 Lead	Unique	3.4	1070*	152	Lyman No. 22636
60 Lead	blackpowder (FFg)	15.0	1150	176	Factory load
*Estimated					

22 Extra Long Centerfire (Maynard)

Historical Notes The 22 Extra Long centerfire is one of a series of cartridges for the Model 1882 Maynard single-shot hunting and gallery rifles. It is, in effect, a centerfire version of the 22 rimfire Extra Long. It originally used the small number 0 primer, which has not been manufactured for many years. It was replaced by the longer 22 centerfires and the 22 WCF. Ballard and Stevens rifles were also available in this caliber.

General Comments Powder charge varied from 8 to 10 grains of FFFg or FFFFg blackpowder or semi-smokeless powder. Case lengths of 1-15/32 inches to 1-1/4 inches will be encountered. Three or 4 grains of IMR 4756 shotgun powder makes a satisfactory load. Lyman's No. 228151 (45-grain) bullet is proper for this cartridge.

22 Extra Long Centerfire (Maynard) Factory Ballistics

Bullet (grains/type)	Powder	Grains	Velocity	Energy	Source/Comments
45 Lead	blackpowder (FFFg)	8.0-10.0	1100	122	Factory load

22 Winchester Centerfire (22 WCF)

Historical Notes The 22 WCF was introduced in 1885 as one of the original cartridges for the famous Winchester single-shot rifle, first manufactured that year. It was also chambered in the Remington No. 7 rolling block rifle in 1904. It was actually too long for most of the short repeating actions of the day, although Winchester once cataloged it for the Model 1873, so its use was confined mostly to single-shot rifles. It is the predecessor of the 22 Hornet.

General Comments The 22 WCF enjoyed considerable popularity as a target, small game and varmint cartridge until 1925. Winchester advertised it as a 200-yard cartridge, but with its mid-range trajectory of some 13.5 inches, it was more of a 100- to 125-yard number. Although originally a blackpowder cartridge, it was loaded in a smokeless powder version with identical ballistics. In Europe, it was stepped up to about 1700-1800 fps and used in drillings or other combination guns. The 22 WCF was discontinued in 1936.

22 Winchester Centerfire Loading Data and Factory Ballistics

Bullet (grains/type)	Powder	Grains	Velocity	Energy	Source/Comments
45 SP	Unique	4.0	1500	226	
45 SP	2400	6.0	1650	273	
45 Cast	blackpowder (FFg)	13.0	1560	244	Lyman No. 228151
45 Lead	blackpowder (FFFg)	13.0	1540	240	Factory load

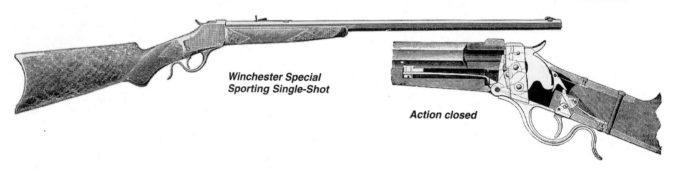

Winchester Special Sporting Single-Shot

Action closed

222 Remington Magnum

Historical Notes The 222 Remington Magnum was originally developed as an experimental military cartridge in a cooperative effort between Remington and Springfield Arsenal. Since it was never adopted by the military, Remington introduced it as a sporting round in 1958 as one of the calibers for its Model 722 bolt-action rifle, and also for a time in the later 700 series bolt-action rifles. At present, no Remington rifles are available in this caliber. None of the other major American sporting arms manufacturing companies currently offer the 222 Remington Magnum.

General Comments In comparison to the standard 222 Remington, the magnum version has about 20 percent greater case capacity, and consequently delivers 100 or so fps higher muzzle velocity and an effective range of between 50 and 75 yards greater than the 222. Though its case capacity is 4 to 5 percent greater than the 223

Remington, the performance of these two is indistinguishable because the 222 Remington Magnum is factory loaded to a lower maximum pressure. The 222 Magnum is nearly 1/10-inch longer than the 223 in overall case length and it is also slightly longer in body length. As a result, the two are not interchangeable, and although the 223 can be chambered and fired in a 222 Magnum rifle, a dangerous headspace condition exists and case rupture is almost certain to occur when the round is fired. The 222 Remington Magnum is probably every bit as accurate as the standard 222 or the 223 and is certainly adequate for anything up to, but not including, deer. It never achieved the popularity of the standard 222 and has been largely superseded by the 223 Remington. It is, nevertheless, a very fine long-range varmint cartridge.

222 Remington Magnum Loading Data and Factory Ballistics

Bullet (grains/type)	Powder	Grains	Velocity	Energy	Source/Comments
40 Sierra SP	BL-C(2)	30.0	3818	1290	Hodgdon
45 SP	H-380	29.5	3400	1125	Hornady
45 SP	BL-C2	27	3400	1236	Hornady, Sierra
45 SP	IMR 4895	27	3400	1082	Speer, Hornady
50 SP	H-380	30	3400	1180	Hornady
50 SP	BL-C2	26	3300	1190	Nosler, Hornady, Speer
50 SP	IMR 3031	26	3300	1204	Speer
55 SP	H-380	29	3200	1234	Hornady
55 SP	RL-7	22	3200	1170	Sierra
55 SP	IMR 3031	26	3300	1332	Speer
55 SP	IMR 4064	26	3300	1340	Hornady
60 HP	IMR 4895	25	3000	1242	Nosler, Hornady
55 SP	FL		3240	1282	Remington factory load

22 Savage High-Power (22 High-Power, 22 Imp)

Historical Notes Designed by Charles Newton and introduced, as a commercial cartridge, by Savage Arms Co. in its Model 99 lever-action rifle about 1912. The cartridge was first called the "Imp." In the United States, only Savage produced a commercial rifle in this chambering, although a great many custom rifles were chambered for it. In England, the BSA Martini single-shot was chambered for it about 1912. In Europe, it is known as the 5.6x52Rmm and has been chambered in various drillings or combination rifle and shotgun arms. The 22 Savage is based on the 25-35 case necked-down. It has been obsolete here since the 1930s. Norma still manufactures this ammunition.

General Comments The 22 Savage High-Power enjoyed considerable popularity through the early 1900s. However, accuracy was often marginal for small game and the bullets sometimes failed to penetrate adequately on larger game. No doubt, considering the general quality of jacketed bullets of that era, the Imp was greatly handicapped by poor bullet quality. Nonetheless, the 22 Savage was used in Africa and Asia on such unlikely beasts as lion and tiger, with some glowing reports on its effectiveness. It is a perfectly adequate small game and varmint cartridge, but no big-game number by any standard. It has been rendered obsolete by new and much improved modern cartridges such as the 222 Remington. For single-shot rifles, most modern shooters prefer the 225 Winchester because of the availability of ammunition and cases, plus the fact that the 225 uses standard 0.224-inch diameter bullets, as opposed to the 0.228-inch bullets of the 22 Savage High-Power.

22 Savage High-Power Loading Data and Factory Ballistics

Bullet (grains/type)	Powder	Grains	Velocity	Energy	Source/Comments
55 SP	IMR 4895	27.0	2870	1106	
55 SP	IMR 3031	30.0	3260	1291	
55 SP	H380	29.0	3200	1249	
70 SP	RI-7	23.0	2900	1308	Hornady
70 SP	IMR 4198	23.0	3000	1399	Hornady
70 SP	IMR 3031	27.0	3100	1494	Hornady
71 SP	FL		2790	1228	Norma factory load

224 Weatherby Magnum

Historical Notes The Weatherby line of proprietary cartridges was somewhat incomplete for lack of an ultra-velocity 22. The previous 220 Weatherby Rocket was actually an improved wildcat based on the 220 Swift case, and Weatherby never manufactured ammunition of this caliber. The 224 Varmintmaster was introduced in 1963, but according to the late Roy Weatherby, development work went back 10 years prior to this. Introduction of the cartridge was delayed because of lack of a suitable action. The caliber was offered in a reduced-size version of the Weatherby Mark V rifle, but is no longer available.

General Comments The 224 Weatherby lies ballistically between the 223 Remington and the 220 Swift. It is a belted case with the advantages and disadvantages inherent in this type of construction. For the handloader, it mitigates certain headspace and case-stretch problems and should provide maximum case life. It is an excellent long-range varmint cartridge with performance similar to the 22-250 Remington. Its popularity was determined largely by economic factors. One could buy a Remington, Ruger or Winchester bolt-action in 22-250 caliber for much less than a 224 Weatherby. It was the smallest belted case manufactured commercially.

224 Weatherby Magnum Loading Data and Factory Ballistics

Bullet (grains/type)	Powder	Grains	Velocity	Energy	Source/Comments
40 HP	IMR 4198	28.5	4100	1493	Sierra
45 SP	IMR 4198	28	3900	1520	Sierra
50 SP	IMR 4064	32.8	3800	1604	Hornady, Sierra
50 SP	IMR 4895	33	3800	1604	Hornady
53 HP	IMR 4064	32	3600	1526	Hornady, Sierra
55 SP	IMR 4064	32	3600	1583	Sierra, Hornady
55 SP	IMR 4895	32	3600	1583	Hornady
55 SP	FL		3650	1627	Factory load
60 HP	IMR 4895	31.5	3500	1632	Hornady

219 Zipper

Historical Notes The 219 Zipper was brought out in 1937 by Winchester for its Model 64 lever-action rifle, which was a modernization of the Model 94. This combination (as with the 218 Bee in the Model 65) did not prove sufficiently accurate for long-range shooting on small targets and in addition did not allow the proper mounting of telescopic sights. Winchester discontinued the Model 64 after World War II. The last commercial rifle chambered for this cartridge was Marlin's Model 336 lever-action, discontinued in this chambering in 1961. A number of custom-made single-shot and Krag-Jorgensen rifles have been made for the 219 Zipper. It is not and never has been very popular. It is based on the necked-down 25-35 WCF case. Winchester dropped the 219 Zipper in 1962, and Remington followed shortly thereafter.

General Comments In a good solid-frame, single-shot or bolt-action rifle, the 219 Zipper is just as accurate as any other high-velocity 22 in its class. Since it was designed for tubular magazines, all factory-loaded ammunition is furnished with flat- or round-nosed bullets, and this causes rapid velocity loss. Although overshadowed by the 222 Remington, it is still an entirely satisfactory small game, varmint or target cartridge. Given carefully prepared ammunition in a carefully prepared lever-action, performance of this cartridge and rifle combination is limited more by the necessary use of blunt bullets than by intrinsic accuracy constraints. Such a combination is certainly capable of 200-yard shots on vermin, which is stretching what most shooters can do with iron sights; beyond that range, velocity drops off so fast that trajectory limits usefulness, even given a telescopic sight. This is one of the few American cartridges that functions well through the British Lee-Enfield action. Some of these rifles have been rebarreled and altered to handle the Zipper. Anecdotal information from several serious shooters who have bothered to wring out the cartridge's accuracy in the Model 64 suggests that Winchester should have spent more effort on ammunition quality.

219 Zipper Loading Data and Factory Ballistics

Bullet (grains/type)	Powder	Grains	Velocity	Energy	Source/Comments
45 SP	IMR 4320	30.0	3600	1295	Hornady
45 SP	BL-C	27.0	3400	1152	Hornady
45 SP	H380	30.5	3500	1224	Sierra
50 SP	IMR 3031	26.0	3400	1284	Sierra
50 SP	H380	31.0	3500	1360	Sierra, Hornady
55 SP	IMR 4320	29.0	3300	1330	Hornady, Sierra
55 SP	H380	30.0	3300	1330	Hornady, Sierra
55 SP	IMR 4320	27.0	3300	1330	Sierra
60 SP	IMR 4064	28.0	3300	1451	Hornady
60 SP	H380	31.0	3300	1451	Hornady
55 SP	FL		3110	1200	Factory load

6mm Bench Rest Remington (6mm BR Remington)

Historical Notes The 6mm BR Remington is one of eight cartridges based on the 308x1 1/2-inch case necked either up or down. It is impossible to determine who first came up with the 6mm version because a number of individuals claim the honor, dating back to 1962 and 1963, shortly after the author introduced the 308x11/2-inch. However, Mike Walker of Remington Arms deserves credit for standardizing dimensions and configuration in 1978. This allowed the cartridge to be adopted as a standard commercial cartridge. In late 1988, Remington announced that the 6mm BR would be produced as loaded factory ammunition. Prior to that, it was a sort of factory wildcat. Cases had to be formed from Remington BR brass, which is actually a modified 308 Winchester with a Small Rifle primer pocket, comparatively thin walls and annealing to facilitate reforming. The factory load has a 100-grain bullet with a muzzle velocity of 2,550 fps and muzzle energy of 1,444 fps. The 6mm BR was intended primarily as a benchrest cartridge, but it also makes a good varmint number. It was available as one of the chamberings for the Remington XP-100 single-shot pistol. (Editor's note: Since the 6mm BR was in use before it was a factory round, there will be some chamber confusion. The original chambers were mostly intended for cases with turned necks.)

General Comments The 6mm BR is similar to the 6mm PPC, except that the case is of larger diameter and has about 10 percent greater capacity. The 6mm PPC is loaded somewhat hotter than the 6mm BR, with some loading manuals listing the 90-grain bullet at around 3,000 fps. There is no reason why the 6mm BR can't do anything the 6mm PPC can. And the availability of factory ammunition should increase its popularity. This will also help overcome one of the problems with the 6mm PPC — the matter of obtaining suitable brass on an over-the-counter basis and at a reasonable price. Remington was the only manufacturer to take up commercial production of this caliber, briefly.

6mm BR Remington Loading Data and Factory Ballistics

Bullet (grains/type)	Powder	Grains	Velocity	Energy	Source/Comments
60 Sierra HP	H322	32.0	3481	1610	Hodgdon
70 SP	W748	32	3200	1592	Hornady
75 HP	W748	33	3200	1706	Hornady
80 SP	W748	31.5	3100	1708	Hornady
80 SP	RL-7	24	2900	1494	Hornady
80	Varget	32.5	3159	1740	Hodgdon
87 SP	W748	31	3000	1739	Hornady
87 SP	H-322	25.5	2800	1515	Hornady
100 SP	FL		2550	1444	Remington factory load

244 Remington

Historical Notes The 244 Remington was introduced by Remington in 1955 in its Model 722 bolt-action rifle. The cartridge is based on the 257 Roberts necked-down to 6mm. It was actually originated as a wildcat by Fred Huntington of Oroville, Calif. The wildcat version preceded the factory design by several years and was called the 243 Rockchucker. Only Remington chambered the 244 among American manufacturers, but several European-made bolt-action rifles were available in this chambering.

General Comments The 244 Remington is ballistically almost identical to the 243 Winchester. The only notable difference is that Remington made its 6mm rifles with a 12-inch twist (one turn in 12 inches), whereas Winchester adopted a 10-inch twist for its 6mm. The faster twist rate of the Winchester enabled use of 100-grain spitzer bullets, whereas the slower twist of the Remington did not. The net result is that the 244 Remington will not stabilize spitzer bullets heavier than about 90 grains in weight, while the 243 Winchester does very well with all 100- and even 105-grain bullets. Remington looked on the 6mm as largely a varmint and small game development and concluded that anything beyond the 90-grain bullet was unnecessary. Winchester, on the other hand, decided the 6mm was very much a big game cartridge and therefore heavier bullets would be highly desirable. Who was right? It appears as if something like ten 243 Winchester-chambered rifles were sold for each 244 Remington-chambered gun. Remington changed to a 9-inch twist at the last, but too late to rescue the 244 from oblivion. What Remington did to extricate themselves from this dilemma was to change the name of the 244 to the 6mm Remington and make all such rifles with a 1-in-9-inch twist. (Since, with lighter bullets, the 6mm Remington is interchangeable with the 244 Remington, then strictly speaking, only the headstamp is obsolete.)

244 Remington Loading Data and Factory Ballistics

Bullet (grains/type)	Powder	Grains	Velocity	Energy	Source/Comments
75 HP	IMR 4831	48.0	3300	1814	Speer, Hornady
75 HP	IMR 4350	47.0	3400	1926	Nosler, Sierra
75 HP	H380	42.0	3150	1653	Hornady
90 SP	IMR 4831	47.0	3200	2047	Speer, Sierra, Hornady
90 SP	IMR 4350	44.5	3100	1921	Sierra, Speer, Hornady
90 SP	H380	39.0	3000	1799	Sierra, Speer
90 SP	IMR 3031	36.6	3000	1799	Sierra
75 SP	FL		3500	2040	Remington factory load
90 SP	FL		3200	2050	Remington factory load

The 244 Remington was initially chambered in Remington's Model 722 in 1955.

6mm Lee Navy

Historical Notes The 6mm Lee cartridge (also known as the 236 Navy) was used in the 1895 Lee Straight Pull bolt-action military rifle manufactured by Winchester for the United States Navy. About 15,000 of these rifles were made and used by the Navy on a trial basis. Winchester, Remington and Blake also chambered sporting rifles for this cartridge. No factory-loaded ammunition has been available since 1935.

General Comments The 244 or 6mm caliber was revived in two cartridges introduced by Remington and Winchester in 1955, the 244 (now the 6mm Remington) and the 243. The 6mm Lee cartridge died out mainly because it was too far ahead of its time. The powders available in 1895 were not suitable to this small caliber. A few shooters who have old rifles for this round reload and use it for hunting. It is a good varmint, medium game, deer, black bear and antelope cartridge at moderate ranges. It is not as powerful as the 6mm Remington or the 243 Winchester. By increasing the rim to fit the standard Mauser bolt face and necking the case to accept 0.224-inch bullets, Winchester created the 220 Swift.

6mm Lee Navy Loading Data and Factory Ballistics

Bullet (grains/type)	Powder	Grains	Velocity	Energy	Source/Comments
75 SP	IMR 3031	37.0	3300	1809	Ackley
95 Cast	Unique	5.0	1200	305	Lyman No. 244203
100 SP	IMR 4895	34.0	2680	1595	
112 SP	IMR 3031	30.0	2650	1895	Ackley
112 SP	IMR 4895	34.0	2670	1946	
112 SP	FL		2560	1635	Factory load

25-20 Single Shot

Historical Notes Designed by J. Francis Rabbeth — a gun writer at the turn of the century who used the pen name of J. Francis — the 25-20 Single Shot first appeared about 1882, and was one of the first centerfire, 25-caliber wildcats. The first commercial cartridges were loaded by Remington (UMC), and shortly thereafter, Maynard, Remington, Stevens and Winchester chambered single-shot rifles for the round. No commercial rifles have been available in this chambering since the late 1920s and the manufacturers stopped loading this number in the mid '30s. Bell Basic Brass (contact Buffalo Arms/208-263-6953/www.buffaloarms.com for brass. Successor to M.A.S.T. Technologies and Brass Extrusion

Laboratories, Ltd.) turned out at least one run of 25-20 Single Shot brass in 1987 and 1988.

General Comments The 25-20 Single Shot was too long to work through the action of the Winchester Model 1892, so Winchester designed the 25-20 WCF or Repeater version with a shorter, more bottlenecked case. The 25-20 SS is quite accurate and was used almost entirely in single-shot rifles. As a varmint or small game cartridge, it is in the same class as the 25-20 WCF. At one time there was a good deal of leftover ammunition on dealer shelves, but as this cartridge is the base for forming the once-popular 2R Lovell wildcat, most of this was bought up by 2R fans. Most rifles for this cartridge have been rechambered for the still-available 25-20 WCF.

25-20 Single Shot Loading Data and Factory Ballistics

Bullet (grains/type)	Powder	Grains	Velocity	Energy	Source/Comments
60 SP	2400	8.0	1535	310	Ackley
65 Cast	2400	8.0	1620	380	Lyman No. 257420
86 SP	IMR 4227	8.5	1400	370	Ackley
86 SP	FL		1410	380	Factory load

25-20 Marlin

Historical Notes This cartridge was loaded for the Marlin repeating rifle Model 1894. Winchester loaded the 25-20 Marlin beginning at the turn of the century and until about World War I. It is nothing more than a special version of the 25-20 Winchester, except perhaps for the bullet nose shape, seating depth and the 25-20 Marlin headstamp. It is otherwise identical to the current 25-20 Winchester. In 1916, Winchester offered five versions of this cartridge: lead, blackpowder (86 grains, 17 grains); softpoint, smokeless powder; full-patch, smokeless powder; high-velocity softpoint; and high-velocity, full-patch.

General Comments Sales of Marlin's Model 1894 rifles evidently generated sufficient demand for special-cartridge versions of the

rifle's typical chamberings, or perhaps cartridges with slightly different bullet shapes or loading lengths were found to function better in it. There must have been some good reason, for Winchester's 1916 catalog shows separate cartridge loadings with the following names: 25-20 Marlin, 32-20 Marlin, 38-40 Marlin and 44-40 Marlin. It is possible the 25-20 Marlin was somehow unique from the 25-20 Winchester, because the catalog does not specify adaptation to Winchester rifles, as it does with the others. In addition, Winchester showed the same blackpowder load and bullet weight for both the 25-20 Winchester and the 25-20 Marlin. The 32-20, 38-40 and 44-40 were unique loadings.

Marlin Model 1894 Lever-Action

25-21 Stevens

Historical Notes The 25-21 Stevens was developed about 1897 as a shortened version of the slightly older 25-25. First introduced for the 44 Stevens rifles and later available in the 44-1/2 series, it was designed by Capt. W.L. Carpenter of the 9th U.S. Infantry, who also designed the 25-25 Stevens. The Remington-Hepburn was available in various models for the 25-21, and it was a popular target and small game number. Many shooters of the period disliked the bottlenecked case and the 25-21 was intended as a straight-case version of the 25-20 SS.

General Comments The 25-21 was noted as a very accurate cartridge, reportedly capable of 1/2-inch, 100-yard groups. It gave about the same performance as the 25-20 SS, but was much too long for the standard repeating actions. It is easy to reload and quite pleasant to shoot. Use Lyman No. 25720 flat-point or No. 25727 hollowpoint cast bullets. The former weighs 86 grains, the latter 75 grains. Twenty to 23 grains of FFFg blackpowder, or the light smokeless powder loads listed below can be used.

25-21 Stevens Loading Data

Bullet (grains/type)	Powder	Grains	Velocity	Energy	Source/Comments
86 Lead	2400	9.0	1610	498	NA
86 Lead	Unique	5.0	1500	434	NA
88 Cast	Unique	5.5	1440	406	Lyman No. 257231

25-25 Stevens

Historical Notes The 25-25 was the first straight shell manufactured for Stevens. Designed by Capt. Carpenter in 1895, Stevens introduced it for its Model 44 single-shot rifles and for the 44-1/2 series after this action was marketed in 1903. It was also a standard chambering for some of the Remington-Hepburn target rifles. It was somewhat popular, but the shorter 25-21 developed practically the same performance and was a little cleaner shooting.

General Comments A very freakish-appearing cartridge with its excessive length-to-diameter ratio, it is the 25-21 with about 1/2-inch added to its overall length. The late Phil Sharpe wrote (*The Rifle in America*, 1938) that the 25-25 caused much extraction trouble and that is why the shorter 25-21 was developed. However, modern users say this is not so, although the 25-25 fouls the bore a little more than the 25-21. It is highly probable the 25-21 was developed because it was found that 20 or 21 grains of powder gave practically the same ballistics as the extra 4 grains or so. You can use any cast 0.257-inch diameter bullet of 60 to 86 grains weight; the gascheck type is preferable with smokeless powder.

25-25 Stevens Loading Data and Factory Ballistics

Bullet (grains/type)	Powder	Grains	Velocity	Energy	Source/Comments
86 Lead	Unique	5.5	1525	448	NA
86 Lead	IMR 4198	10.2	1520	446	NA
86 Lead	FL		1500	434	Factory load

25-36 Marlin

Historical Notes This cartridge, adopted by Marlin in 1895 for its lever-action Model 93 rifle, was designed by William V. Lowe a year or so prior and originally called the 25-37. It was probably inspired by the 25-35 Winchester. The two are very similar but not interchangeable although the 25-35 can be fired in the slightly longer 25-36 chamber. The 25-36 Marlin was loaded in a smokeless powder version and survived until the early 1920s.

General Comments The 25-36 and the 25-35 WCF are similar; however, many rifles for the Marlin cartridge were not strong enough to withstand maximum loads safely. In general, one should not exceed 2000 fps velocity with the 25-36. It is not an adequate deer cartridge, and its use should be confined to small or medium game. It did not acquire a reputation for outstanding accuracy.

25-36 Marlin Loading Data and Factory Ballistics

Bullet (grains/type)	Powder	Grains	Velocity	Energy	Source/Comments
87 SP	IMR 3031	20.0	2010	770	NA
117 SP	IMR 3031	20.0	1800	845	NA
117 SP	FL		1855	893	Factory load

Marlin Model 1893 Special Lightweight Rifle

256 Winchester Magnum

Historical Notes The 256 Winchester Magnum was announced in 1960 as a new handgun cartridge; however, the only handgun that chambered it was the single-shot, enclosed-breech Ruger "Hawkeye" introduced in late 1961. The 256 Winchester Magnum is listed as a rifle cartridge because Marlin produced its Model 62 lever-action rifle in this chambering and Universal Firearms made the semi-auto "Ferret" on the M-1 Carbine action. The Marlin rifle was available about a year after the Ruger "Hawkeye" and both were discontinued after a relatively short production life. The Thompson/Center Contender, a single-shot pistol, was also available for this round. The cartridge is based on the necked-down 357 Magnum revolver case.

General Comments As a rifle cartridge, the 256 is considerably more potent than the 25-20 and several jumps ahead of the 22 Hornet or the 218 Bee. The factory-loaded, 60-grain bullet develops over 2760 fps muzzle velocity when fired from a 24-inch rifle barrel. This offers 1015 foot-pounds of muzzle energy, which is well above the Hornet or Bee. The 256 Magnum is an effective varmint cartridge out to ranges of 200 yards. It can be handloaded with heavier 75- or 87-grain bullets to velocities of 2500 and 2230 fps, respectively. Although a good varmint and small game chambering, it is not an adequate deer cartridge and most states will not allow its use for this purpose. Winchester was the only commercial manufacturer to offer the 256 Winchester Magnum. It was discontinued in the early 1990s.

256 Winchester Magnum Loading Data and Factory Ballistics

Bullet (grains/type)	Powder	Grains	Velocity	Energy	Source/Comments
60 SP	H4227	14.0	2500	833	Hornady
60 SP	H4227	16.0	2800	1045	Hornady
60 SP	2400	14.0	2600	901	Hornady
75 HP	H4227	14.0	2400	958	Hornady
75 HP	IMR 4227	15.5	2500	1041	Sierra
87 SP	IMR 4227	14.0	2200	935	Sierra
87 SP	H4227	14.0	2200	935	Hornady
60 SP	FL		2760	1015	Winchester factory load

25 Remington

Historical Notes The 25 Remington is one of a series of rimless cartridges developed for the Model 8 Autoloading rifle and later used in other Remington rifles. It was introduced in 1906. The Remington Model 14 pump-action, Model 30 bolt-action and the Stevens Model 425 lever-action also used the 25 Remington. No rifles have chambered this cartridge since 1942, and the ammunition companies stopped loading it about 1950.

General Comments The 25 Remington is nothing more than a rimless version of the 25-35, but differs slightly in shape. The two

are not interchangeable. Since the Remington line of rifles, particularly the Model 30 bolt-action, would stand higher pressures than the lever-action, it is possible to get slightly better performance out of the 25 Remington. However, the difference is not sufficient to make the rimless version anything but a barely adequate deer cartridge. It will do for varmints and small to medium game quite well and deer in a pinch, provided the hunter is a good shot. The 30-30 is a better cartridge for anything, and the 25 Remington is hardly in the same class as the 250 Savage or the 257 Roberts.

25 Remington Loading Data and Factory Ballistics

Bullet (grains/type)	Powder	Grains	Velocity	Energy	Source/Comments
60 SP	H4895	31.0	2900	1121	Hornady
60 SP	IMR 4320	32.0	2900	1121	Hornady
117 SP	H4895	26.5	2200	1258	Hornady
117 SP	IMR 3031	25.5	2300	1375	Hornady
100 SP	FL		2330	1216	Factory load
117 SP	FL		2125	1175	Factory load

Remington Model 8 Rifle

256 Newton

Historical Notes One of several high-velocity, rimless cartridges designed by Charles Newton for his bolt-action rifles, the 256 Newton was introduced in 1913 by the Western Cartridge Co. Until the 264 Winchester Magnum came along in 1958, this was the only American-designed 6.5mm to be offered on a commercial basis. The last of the Newton rifle companies failed in the early 1920s, and Western quit loading Newton cartridges in 1938. The 256 Newton is based on the 30-06 case necked-down.

General Comments The 256 Newton has hung on as a wildcat cartridge and occasionally custom rifles are made for it. Cases can be made by necking-down, reforming and shortening 30-06 brass. This is a good cartridge and is adequate for practically all North American big game, but it is not as effective as the 270 Winchester. With modern, slow-burning powders, its performance can be improved over original factory ballistics.

256 Newton Loading Data and Factory Ballistics

Bullet (grains/type)	Powder	Grains	Velocity	Energy	Source/Comments
120 SP	IMR 4350	55.0	2980	2362	NA
130 SP	IMR 4895	46.0	2900	2425	NA
140 SP	IMR 4831	57.0	2890	2598	NA
129 SP	FL		2760	2180	Western factory load

6.5mm Remington Magnum

Historical Notes The 6.5mm is a Remington innovation introduced in 1966 for its Model 600 carbine. The 6.5mm Remington Magnum is based on the 350 Remington Magnum case necked down to 6.5mm (0.264-inch). The Remington Model 600 carbine had an 18 1/2-inch barrel and the later 660 carbine a 20-inch barrel. Neither of these carbines allowed the cartridge to develop its full velocity potential and both were discontinued. By 1971, only the Remington Model 700 and 40-XB target rifle with 24-inch barrels were cataloged as available in 6.5mm Magnum chambering. For a short time, the Ruger Model 77 was offered in this chambering. All of the rifles referred to are bolt-actions. Currently, no one offers rifles chambered for the 6.5mm Remington Magnum.

General Comments The 6.5mm Remington Magnum has greater case capacity and develops higher velocity than any of the European military 6.5s. It is an excellent cartridge for North American big game and can double as a varmint cartridge by handloading the lighter bullets. Probably one reason it never achieved great popularity was that the chambering's rifles had short magazines, which required deep seating of heavier bullets with a consequent loss in powder capacity and performance. Combined with the short barrels of the Remington Model 600 and 660 carbines, this added up to ballistics well below the 30-06 class of cartridges. In a standard long action that will allow seating heavier bullets farther out, one can approach the performance of the 270 Winchester. With the proper bullet, the 6.5mm Magnum is adequate for North American big game at moderate ranges under normal hunting conditions. Unfortunately, this is another case of a good cartridge that did not catch on. At one time, Remington offered two bullet weights, a 100-grain bullet at an advertised muzzle velocity of 3450 fps and a 120-grain bullet at 3220 fps. The older 6.5mm cartridges gained its reputation with heavier bullets of 140 to 160 grains; the lack of such a factory load is very likely another reason for the demise of the Remington version. Early factory-advertised ballistics were based on a longer-than-standard barrel and were, therefore, unrealistic.

6.5mm Remington Magnum Loading Data and Factory Ballistics

Bullet (grains/type)	Powder	Grains	Velocity	Energy	Source/Comments
85 SP	IMR 4350	57.0	3100	1814	Sierra
100 SP	H4831	56.2	3200	2274	Hornady
100 SP	H380	51.5	3100	2134	Sierra
120 SP	IMR 4831	55.0	3000	2399	Speer
129 SP	H4831	54.0	3000	2579	Hornady
140 SP	IMR 4831	52.0	2750	2352	Speer
160 SP	H4831	54.5	2800	2786	Hornady
120 SP	FL		3210	2745	Remington factory load

275 Holland & Holland Magnum (275 H&H Magnum)

Historical Notes First loaded in Great Britain about 1912; this cartridge was introduced in the United States by Western Cartridge Co. in 1926. Western loaded this cartridge with only the 175-grain bullet until production was discontinued in 1939.

General Comments The 275 H&H was never particularly popular in this country. It resembled the 280 Ross, but did not give the velocity of the Ross. Its chief advantage over other 7mm cartridges was its ability to handle a 175-grain bullet at increased velocity. The Western cartridge loading, with a 175-grain softpoint boattail bullet, gave a muzzle velocity of 2690 fps, a muzzle energy of 2810 and a mid-range (iron-sight) trajectory at 100 yards of 0.7-inch. Impressive performance, considering the powders then available. See Chapter 8 for additional information.

275 H&H Magnum Loading Data

Bullet (grains/type)	Powder	Grains	Velocity	Energy	Source/Comments
140	IMR 4064	48.0	2810	2455	Ackley
160	IMR 4350	59.0	3050	3305	Ackley
180	IMR 4350	58.0	2850	3245	Ackley
195	IMR 4350	52.0	2671	3090	Ackley

7x61mm Sharpe & Hart Super

Historical Notes The 7x61mm was developed in the United States by Philip B. Sharpe and Richard F. Hart. Its design was originally based on a rimless, experimental French 7mm semi-auto military cartridge. It was copyrighted and made available on a commercial basis in the Schultz & Larsen rifle in 1953. Ammunition was loaded and imported by Norma. The final version had a belted case with "Super" added to its name. Ammunition loaded with a 154-grain bullet (instead of the original 160-grain) was recently offered by Norma.

General Comments The 7x61mm Sharpe & Hart (now listed as the S&H Super) is very similar to the 275 H&H Magnum, a belted case that was chambered and loaded in England. It is in the short 7mm magnum class and its performance is the same as a number of other wildcat cartridges, based on the blown out and shortened 300 H&H

Magnum case. However, the Sharpe & Hart case has a slightly larger base diameter than the 300 H&H. This cartridge is quite popular in Canada, but its popularity in the United States was limited by competition from the 7mm Weatherby Magnum, the 7mm Remington Magnum and various wildcats. The 7mm S&H is, nonetheless, a fine cartridge for any North American game and most African plains game.

Like any of this ilk, this number can be somewhat hard on its barrel, especially with either careless shooting, not allowing plenty of time between shots for barrel cooling, or inadequate cleaning. Moreover, like all similar chamberings, it loses significant velocity with barrels shorter than 24 inches. Actual ballistics may be closer to the 7mm Weatherby than factory data suggests.

7x61mm Sharpe & Hart Super Loading Data and Factory Ballistics

Bullet (grains/type)	Powder	Grains	Velocity	Energy	Source/Comments
120 SP	IMR 4350	64.0	3300	2902	Sierra
140 SP	IMR 4831	63.0	3100	2988	Sierra
140 SP	IMR 4350	62.5	3200	3184	Hornady, Sierra
150 SP	IMR 4831	64.5	3100	3202	Sierra
160 SP	IMR 4350	58.0	2900	2989	Hornady, Sierra
175 SP	IMR 4350	60.5	2900	3269	Hornady
154 SP	FL		3060	3200	Norma factory load (latest)
160 SP	FL		3100	3410	Norma factory load (original)

---

280 Rimless (Ross)   See Chapter 8.

28-30-120 Stevens

Historical Notes The 28-30 was probably the first American-designed, commercial 7mm cartridge. Introduced by the J. Stevens Arms & Tool Co. in 1900, it was designed by Charles H. Herrick of Winchester, Mass. Both 44 and 44-1/2 Stevens rifles were chambered for the round. It was an early favorite of Harry M. Pope, who made up and fitted barrels to a variety of single-shot actions in this chambering. As a match cartridge, it established a reputation for exceptional accuracy.

General Comments Remington made the first factory loads for the 28-30, and these used the 120-grain bullet and 30 grains of Fg

blackpowder. By 1918, it was no longer listed in the Remington catalog. Some match shooters who used the 28-30 considered it superior to the 32-40 out to 300 yards. It makes a good 150-yard small game or varmint cartridge. Lyman No. 285222 or 285228 is the proper cast bullet, but one can use any standard cast 7mm bullet up to 180 grains weight. Do not use jacketed bullets in the old blackpowder barrels as they will wear the bore excessively and the fine accuracy may be destroyed within a few hundred rounds. Gas-checked bullets are OK.

28-30-120 Loading Data and Factory Ballistics

Bullet (grains/type)	Powder	Grains	Velocity	Energy	Source/Comments
135 Lead	blackpowder (Fg)	28.0	1410	602	
135 Lead	IMR 4198	17.0	1500	605	
120 Lead	FL		1500	605	Factory load

30-30 Wesson

Historical Notes The 30-30 Wesson was used in rifles designed and marketed by Frank Wesson of Worcester, Mass., who operated from the 1860s into the late 1880s. During the Civil War, the government purchased about 150 Wesson military carbines in caliber 44 rimfire. Some of the state militia also purchased Wesson carbines. His sporting rifles were marketed, in rimfire types, as early as 1861. As near as can be determined, the 30-30 Wesson was probably developed sometime around 1880. Frank Wesson was a brother of Daniel B. Wesson, co-founder of Smith & Wesson. Both Remington and Winchester made bullets and cases for this cartridge, and U.S. Cartridge Co. catalogs listed it. Usable cases can probably be fabricated from 357 Maximum cases.

General Comments The most common Wesson rifle was a single-shot with a double trigger arrangement. The forward trigger unlatched the breech, allowing the barrel to be tipped up for loading and unloading. Several models were marketed, including sporting and target types. There were, in addition, under-lever, falling-block solid-frame types that are quite scarce, as are the Wesson cartridges. The 30-30 Wesson is not the same as the 30-30 Winchester, and there is nothing to indicate that it had any influence on the design of the 30-30. Smokeless powder loads would not be advisable in this rifle.

30-30 Wesson Loading Data and Factory Ballistics

Bullet (grains/type)	Powder	Grains	Velocity	Energy	Source/Comments
165 Lead	blackpowder (Fg)	30.0	1250	1010	Factory load

30 Remington

Historical Notes A rimless version of the 30-30, the 30 Remington was introduced by Remington in 1906 for its Model 8 autoloader. When the Model 14 pump-action came out in 1912, it was also chambered for the 30 Remington, as was the Model 30 bolt-action introduced in 1921. The Stevens lever-action Model 425 and the Standard gas-operated rifle also used the 30 Remington. No new rifles have chambered this round since immediately after World War II. Some domestic ammunition companies continued to load it until recently. There are a large number of rifles for this caliber still in use. The original rifles were marked 30-30 Remington. (*Editor's note: Imagine the confusion that must have arisen when Remington originally called this cartridge the 30-30 Remington. One wonders how many hunters found themselves in the wilderness with a box of Remington-brand 30-30 Winchester ammunition and a Model 8 rifle that those would not fit. The simple*

request to "give me a box of Remington 30-30s" was bound to lead to this problem.)

General Comments Identical to the 30-30 in performance, the 30 Remington is strictly in the small-, medium- and deer-size game class. Its advantages are in the nature of the guns that chambered it. It is possible to use spitzer bullets in most 30 Remington rifles, which help retain velocity at longer ranges. The 30 Remington can be reloaded to better performance than the 30-30 Winchester. Interestingly, handloading data has seldom, if ever, reflected this possibility. Similarly, factory ammunition has uniformly downplayed the Remington rimless series with loads rated a full 100 fps slower than their rimmed counterparts. However, the difference is not great enough to take the 30 Remington out of the 30-30 class. Note: The nominal bullet diameter is given as 0.307-inch.

30 Remington Loading Data and Factory Ballistics

Bullet (grains/type)	Powder	Grains	Velocity	Energy	Source/Comments
150 SP	IMR 4895	35.5	2350	1840	Lyman
150 SP	IMR 4320	36.0	2320	1794	Lyman
170 SP	IMR 3031	30.0	2115	1690	Lyman
170 SP	IMR 4895	33.0	2145	1735	Lyman
170 SP	FL		2120	1696	Remington factory load

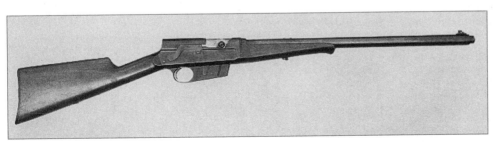

Remington Model 8A

30 USA/30-40 Rimless

Historical Notes We have little information on this cartridge. It was used in the Blake rifle and ammunition was produced by United Metallic Cartridge for a time. No doubt, considerable confusion ensued in that era of rapid development and the nascent exposure of U.S. shooters to rimless chamberings. We include this number here as a demonstration that the Europeans were not the only ones to muddy up the water with rimless and rimmed versions of otherwise identical or nearly identical cartridges.

General Comments For ballistic data refer to Chapter 2.

30-03 Springfield
30-03 Government

Historical Notes In 1903, the U.S. government adopted a new military loading to replace the 30 Army (30-40 Krag), which had been adopted in 1892. Like the 30-40 Krag, this new (30-Caliber, Model of 1903) cartridge featured a 220-grain round-nosed, full-metal-jacket bullet. However, the '03 increased muzzle velocity by about 100 fps, although the M1903 rifle featured a significantly shorter barrel. The rimless cartridge design, generously borrowed from Mauser, was also an improvement as it featured superior feeding from a box magazine. Nevertheless, as seems to have been typical in that era, the U.S. Army was slow to the task of modernizing. As the 30-03 was standardized, all other world powers were in the process of adopting spitzer-bullet military loadings. The brand new 30-03 became instantly obsolete. A crash program was instituted and in 1906, a modified version of this basic cartridge was adopted as the 30 Caliber, Model of 1906. That loading featured a lighter spitzer bullet and a shorter case neck. The spitzer bullets had a much shorter bearing surface, so the existing rifles were modified by turning back the barrels two threads and recutting the chambers.

General Comments Despite its short life, this cartridge, like the 30-06, found application in John M. Browning's Winchester Model 1895. Considering the ambitious pressure levels common in the early days of these chamberings, that was perhaps not such a good idea. For the handloader, case life could be extremely limited, owing to case stretching, because of the rear lockup on those rifles. Compared to the 30-06, the 30-03 offers no advantage as a sporting round. Ammunition was available at least until World War I. By today's standards that is remarkable, for there were very few sporting rifles chambered for this cartridge and very soon after 1906, virtually all 1903 Springfields had been converted to 30-06.

Winchester Model 1895 rifle

30 Newton

Historical Notes The 30 Newton was originally designed for Fred Adolph, and was called the "Adolph Express" when introduced in 1913. It was not until several years later that Charles Newton produced rifles for his own brainchild, and it received the gun inventor's name. The Western Cartridge Co. produced the 30 Newton cartridge. No commercial rifle other than the Newton ever chambered it. Production of rifles ceased in the early '20s, and Western dropped the cartridge about 1938.

General Comments The 30 Newton is a rimless, magnum-type cartridge similar to the 30-06, but larger in diameter. Neither ammunition nor cases are readily available since it has been obsolete for more than 50 years. However, brass can be readily formed from RWS 8x68mm. A limited quantity of new cases was manufactured right after World War II by Richard Speer. The 30 Newton is powerful enough for any North American big game. The 300 H&H Magnum and 300 Weatherby Magnum outperform it, although its performance can be improved by handloading with modern powders.

30 Newton Loading Data and Factory Ballistics

Bullet (grains/type)	Powder	Grains	Velocity	Energy	Source/Comments
150 SP	IMR 4320	67.0	3175	3361	NA
150 SP	IMR 4831	76.0	3100	3206	NA
180 SP	IMR 4320	62.0	2840	3235	NA
180 SP	IMR 4831	73.0	2890	3350	NA
200 SP	IMR 4350	66.0	2730	3318	NA
180 SP	FL		2860	3270	Western factory load

308 Norma Magnum

Historical Notes The 308 Norma Magnum was introduced in 1960 by Å.B. Norma Projektilfabrik of Åmotfors, Sweden. In its original form, this cartridge was something of a semi-wildcat, because only unprimed brass cases were available and no commercial rifles were chambered for it. However, about 18 months after it was introduced, Norma began producing factory ammunition. Several European manufacturers chamber the round as standard or on order.

General Comments The 308 Norma Magnum is practically identical to the wildcat 30-338, which is the 338 Winchester Magnum necked-down to 30-caliber. However, the two cases are not interchangeable because of a difference in body length. Almost any standard-length 30-06 rifle can be rechambered to take the 308

Norma cartridge. This cartridge is also similar to a number of 30-caliber wildcat magnums based on the blown-out and shortened 300 H&H case, and known collectively as the 300 short magnum group. The 30 Luft, 300 Apex and Ackley Short 30 Magnum are representative of this class. The 308 Norma Magnum is adequate for any North American big game and should do well on African plains game. Powder capacity is only a hair greater than the 300 H&H, but the shape of the case is radically different. This is a proprietary cartridge of European origin designed specifically for the American market. It is placed with the American cartridges because most U.S. readers will look for it here. Technically, it belongs in the chapter covering European cartridges.

308 Norma Magnum Loading Data and Factory Ballistics

Bullet (grains/type)	Powder	Grains	Velocity	Energy	Source/Comments
100 SP	H380	70.0	3500	2721	Speer
110 SP	IMR 4350	75.5	3400	2824	Sierra, Hornady
125 SP	IMR 4350	76.0	3400	3209	Sierra, Hornady
150 SP	IMR 4350	72.0	3200	3420	Hornady, Nosler, Sierra, Speer
150 SP	IMR 4831	73.0	3150	3306	Nosler, Speer
165 SP	IMR 4350	71.0	3100	3522	Sierra, Speer, Nosler
180 SP	IMR 4831	73.0	3000	3598	Sierra
220 SP	IMR 4350	68.0	2800	3831	Hornady
180 SP	FL		3100	3842	Norma factory load

Remington M700AS Rifle

32-40 Remington

Historical Notes The 32-40-150 (2 1/8-inch) Remington was one of the cartridges for the single-shot, rolling block Sporting Rifle No. 1, introduced in 1870. This cartridge appears to have been introduced shortly after the rifle, about 1871-72. The 32-40 Remington was also one of the cartridges for the No. 3 Hepburn, and some of the Farrow single-shot rifles. Other than this, no one else seems to have adopted it. Remington quit loading it in 1910.

General Comments This is a very odd-looking cartridge, with a long tapered shoulder that merges imperceptibly with an elongated neck. It is usually listed as a straight case, but it is not straight and is not exactly necked. It might best be described as a "taper-necked"

case. On the dimensional chart, it is shown as type "A", or rimmed, bottleneck, but this is not totally correct either. The shoulder diameter is arbitrary, since it is difficult to decide just where the shoulder begins. Although called a 32-caliber, true bullet diameter is 0.308- or 0.309-inch; hence, it is really a 30-caliber. It was both a hunting and target round of limited popularity. It lost out to the 32-40 Ballard, which was available in both single-shot and repeating rifles. It was a small to medium game cartridge, but was probably also used to some extent for hunting deer-size animals. Usable cases might be formed from either 30-40 Krag or 303 British cases.

32-40 Remington Loading Data and Factory Ballistics

Bullet (grains/type)	Powder	Grains	Velocity	Energy	Source/Comments
150 Lead	IMR 4198	14.5	1350	607	Lyman No. 308156
150 Lead	FL125		1350	607	Factory load

303 Savage

Historical Notes Originally developed as a potential military cartridge in 1895, the 303 Savage was later introduced commercially as one of several chamberings for the popular Savage Model 1899 lever action. Savage discontinued this chambering when rifle production was resumed after World War II. In England, it is known as the 301 Savage. No new rifles are chambered for this round at present.

General Comments Dogma holds that the 303 Savage is not a true 303 but instead uses standard 0.308-inch bullets. However, current SAAMI specifications call for a bullet of 0.311-inch. Measurements of bullets on three lots of each of two makes of World WarII-era factory loads yields mixed results. Some were 0.308-inch+, others 0.310-inch+. The 303 is similar to the 30-30 in size, shape and performance, but the two are not interchangeable.

With its 190-grain bullet, many old woods hunters swore by it. With the relatively heavy bullet at moderate velocity, it gave good penetration on deer-size animals. However, it is ballistically no more powerful than the 30-30, so its use should be restricted to deer at short ranges. Unfortunately, Savage never took advantage of the fact that the 99 rifle is particularly suited to the use of spitzer bullets. Proper loadings of 150-grain spitzers in the 303 could have moved it completely out of the 30-30 class and might have come a long way toward increasing its popularity. As it has always been loaded, it is effective only at close range. This need not have been the case. Many handloaders still use the 303 Savage with 150-grain spitzer bullets loaded to about 2,500 fps. It is still no long-range wonder, but such a load gives it a decided edge over any other 30-30-class chambering.

303 Savage Loading Data and Factory Ballistics

Bullet (grains/type)	Powder	Grains	Velocity	Energy	Source/Comments
150 SP	IMR 4064	36	2400	1919	Lyman
170 SP	IMR 3031	31	2170	1778	Lyman
180 SP	FL		2140	1830	Factory load
190 SP	FL		1890	1507	Winchester factory load

Savage Model 99A

32-20 Marlin

Historical Notes This cartridge was loaded for the Marlin 1894 repeating rifle. Winchester loaded this cartridge beginning around the turn of the century and until about World War I. It is nothing more than a special version of the 32 WCF (32-20 Winchester). Compared to the Winchester round, it was loaded with a lighter bullet, 100 grains versus 117 grains. With the exceptions of perhaps bullet nose shape, seating depth and headstamp, this loading appears to have been otherwise identical to the 32-20 Winchester. In 1916, Winchester offered three versions of this cartridge: lead and blackpowder (100 grains, 20 grains); softpoint (117 grains) and smokeless powder; and full-patch (117 grains) and smokeless powder. High-velocity loadings were not offered.

General Comments Evidently sales of Marlin's Model 1894 rifle generated sufficient demand for special versions of the cartridges for which that rifle was nominally chambered. Perhaps cartridges with slightly different bullet shapes or loading lengths were found to function better in it. Whatever the reason, the 1916 catalog shows separate cartridge loadings with these names: 25-20 Marlin, 32-30 Marlin, 38-40 Marlin and 44-40 Marlin. Winchester says this cartridge was adapted to both Winchester and Marlin rifles, as were the 38-40 and 44-40 Marlin cartridges.

32-30 Remington

Historical Notes This bottleneck cartridge, similar to the 32-20 WCF, was one of the chamberings available for the Remington-Hepburn No. 3 series single-shot rifle introduced in 1880. The cartridge was first made in November of 1884. Not a true 32, bullet diameter is 0.312-inch.

General Comments The Remington-Hepburn was billed as a "long-range hunting and target rifle," but the 32-30 is hardly a long-range cartridge. It is only a notch or so above the 32-20 WCF. It was not a popular cartridge, and died out in 1912. Like most other single-shot cartridges, this one was too long for the short repeating actions such as the Model 92 Winchester. These were, in addition, too small for the larger actions. This in-between position eliminated these as the repeater gained popularity. Rifles for the 32-30 are comparatively rare today. Ammunition can be made by reforming 357 Magnum or 357 Maximum cases.

32-30 Remington Loading Data and Factory Ballistics

Bullet (grains/type)	Powder	Grains	Velocity	Energy	Source/Comments
111 Lead	IMR 4198	14.0	1650	676	Lyman No. 311316
115 Lead	blackpowder (FFg)	35.0	1430	528	NA
125 Lead	FL		1380	535	Factory load

32-35 Stevens & Maynard

Historical Notes A match cartridge introduced by J. Stevens Arms & Tool Co. in the mid-1880s, this was one of the chamberings available for the New Model Range Rifle Nos. 9 and 10, which first appeared in 1886. These were on a tip-up, single-shot action and some of the earlier models of this type might have chambered the 32-35. Later rifles based on the 44 and 44-1/2 under-lever single-shot actions were available in 32-35.

General Comments This was one of the most accurate of the Stevens target cartridges, and many records were established with it. The 32-40 was responsible for the 32-35's gradual obsolescence. Best accuracy usually was obtained by seating the bullet in the chamber 1/16-inch or so ahead of the case; the case, full of powder with a wad to prevent powder spillage, was then inserted in the chamber behind the bullet. Lyman's No. 3117 bullet of 153 grains was popular with many riflemen. The correct charge of blackpowder was 35 grains of Fg or FFg.

32-35 Stevens & Maynard Loading Data and Factory Ballistics

Bullet (grains/type)	Powder	Grains	Velocity	Energy	Source/Comments
153 Lead	IMR 4198	14.0	1410	683	NA
165 Lead	IMR 4227	11.0	1380	696	NA
165 Lead	FL		1400	683	Factory load

32-40 Bullard

Historical Notes This is the smallest cartridge of a series designed for the Bullard single-shot and repeating rifles. Bullard patents were granted in 1881, and manufacture of its rifles is believed to have started during 1882 or 1883. Exact date of introduction of the individual cartridges is difficult to establish, but all were available by 1887.

General Comments The Bullard lever-action repeating rifle resembled the Winchester, but employed a different rack-and-pinion mechanism. The loading port in the magazine was located on the bottom, unlike the Winchester's side port. The single-shot was of the under-lever type and quite strong. Although Bullard rifles and cartridges were as good as any of contemporary manufacture, they did not endure beyond 1900. Some Bullard cartridges were made by Remington and Winchester. Performance of the 32-40 Bullard is the same as the 32-40 Winchester and Marlin. Both are scarce items. Usable cases can be easily formed from 357 Remington Maximum cases.

32-40 Bullard Loading Data and Factory Ballistics

Bullet (grains/type)	Powder	Grains	Velocity	Energy	Source/Comments
150 Lead	IMR 4198	15.0	1470	719	Lyman No. 311241
155 Lead	2400	13.0	1400	674	NA
150 Lead	FL		1492	750	Factory load

32 Long (CF)

Historical Notes This centerfire, reloadable version of the 32 Long rimfire with an outside-lubricated bullet was introduced in 1875 in a variety of light-frame single-shot rifles and the Marlin Models of 1891 and 1892. Some of these were constructed so that both rimfire and centerfire ammunition could be used by changing the firing pin or hammer.

General Comments The 32 Long was not a satisfactory or effective cartridge. A longer case was soon used, called the "Extra Long," in order to increase range and killing power on small game. Eventually the 32 Long was replaced by such numbers as the 32-20 WCF, 32 Ideal and the 32-35 Stevens. It is very similar to the 32 Colt revolver cartridge. The standard load consisted of 13 grains of FFFg blackpowder and an 80- to 85-grain bullet. Muzzle velocity was only about 800 to 900 fps, depending on load and barrel length. The 32 S&W Long or 32 Long Colt will work in most old rifles in this chambering. These cartridges are now collector's items.

32 Long (CF) Loading Data and Factory Ballistics

Bullet (grains/type)	Powder	Grains	Velocity	Energy	Source/Comments
85 Lead	FL		850	136	Factory load

32 Ballard Extra Long

Historical Notes The 32 Extra Long is an elongated version of the 32 Long centerfire, the latter being one of the chamberings available for the J.M. Marlin 1876 Ballard No. 2 Sporting Rifle. The 32 Extra Long cartridge appeared in 1879. This was after Marlin Fire Arms Co. began manufacturing Ballard rifles. They introduced (or continued) the Sporting Rifle No. 2 in 1881. Stevens, Remington, Wurfflein and other single-shot rifles were also available in this chambering. It was popular, but lost out to the 32-20 WCF. Most companies stopped loading it by 1920. Rifles chambered for this cartridge will usually chamber and fire both the 32 S&W Long and 32 Long Colt.

General Comments This is essentially a centerfire version of the 32 Extra Long rimfire, and ballistics are practically identical. It was used as a target and small game cartridge throughout the late 1800s. It is very similar in performance to the blackpowder loading of the 32-20 WCF. Most of the old rifles for this cartridge will not safely withstand heavy loads of modern smokeless powder. An outside-lubricated bullet of the same diameter as the case neck was first used.

32 Ballard Extra Long Loading Data and Factory Ballistics

Bullet (grains/type)	Powder	Grains	Velocity	Energy	Source/Comments
115 Lead	IMR 4198	9.0	1360	473	NA
115 Lead	blackpowder (FFg)	20.0	1200	372	Factory load

32 Winchester Self-Loading (32 WSL)

Historical Notes This is the second of two cartridges developed for the Winchester Model '05 self-loading rifle, which was introduced in 1905-1906. It became obsolete when the rifle was discontinued in 1920. The case is of the semi-rimmed type similar to the 35 SL, which was the original cartridge for the Model '05 rifle. The 32 Winchester SL was probably the prototype of the 30 U.S. Carbine cartridge. The two are very similar except for bullet diameter and the fact that the 30 Carbine cartridge is rimless.

General Comments The 32 Winchester SL cartridge is in the same class as the 32-20 Winchester, strictly a small to medium game number at close range. However, it is not nearly as flexible as the 32-20 because of the semi-automatic rifle in which it was used. This was never a very popular cartridge. Not only was the cost of ammunition relatively high, but in addition, the cartridge is not well-suited to reloading, even if you could find the empty cases after being ejected from the action. Some might consider this cartridge the best candidate for the title: "World's Most Useless Centerfire Rifle Cartridge."

32 Winchester Self-Loading Loading Data and Factory Ballistics

Bullet (grains/type)	Powder	Grains	Velocity	Energy	Source/Comments
155 Cast	2400	9.5	1270	556	Lyman No. 321298
165 SP	2400	12.0	1450	775	NA
165 SP	IMR 4227	12.5	1440	760	NA
165 SP	FL		1400	760	Winchester factory load

32-40 (32-40 Ballard/ 32-40 Winchester)

Historical Notes Originally developed as a blackpowder match or target cartridge for the single-shot Ballard Union Hill Rifle, Nos. 8 and 9, the 32-40 was introduced in 1884 loaded with a 165-grain lead bullet in front of 40 grains of Fg blackpowder. It established a reputation for fine accuracy and Winchester and Marlin added it to their lines of lever-action repeating and single-shot rifles late in 1886 *et seq*. The late Harry Pope's favorite cartridge was the 32-40 and his variant, the 33-40. Ammunition has been discontinued by major companies. However, in the early 1980s, Winchester loaded this cartridge to boost sales of its John Wayne Commemorative rifle.

General Comments In a good solid-frame rifle, the 32-40 will shoot as well as any modern high-powered match cartridge out to 200 or 300 yards. It was a popular hunting cartridge for medium game and deer, and while it has certainly killed its share of deer, the factory loading barely qualifies in that class. However, in a strong action it can be handloaded to equal the 30-30. For small to medium game or varmints, it will do very well at moderate ranges. Do not use high-velocity loadings in the old Ballard or Stevens 44 rifles. A number of modern copies of old Sharps single-shot rifles and a special commemorative M1894 Winchester have been chambered for the 32-40 in recent years. Usable cases can easily be formed from 30-30, 32 Special or 38-55 cases.

32-40 Loading Data and Factory Ballistics

Bullet (grains/type)	Powder	Grains	Velocity	Energy	Source/Comments
155 Lead	2400	13.0	1460	786	
165 Lead	H4895	16.0	1410	729	OK for old rifles – Hodgdon
165 Lead	H4198	14.0	1340	658	OK for old rifles – Hodgdon
165 Lead	H4895	22.0	1865	1275	Not for old rifles – Hodgdon
165 Lead	H335	23.0	1890	1309	Not for old rifles – Hodgdon
170 Lead	AA 5744	20.0	1802	1226	Accurate Arms
165 SP	FL		1440	760	Winchester factory load
165 SP	FL		1752	1125	Winchester factory load high velocity

32 Remington

Historical Notes Another of the Remington rimless line of medium high-power rifle cartridges; this one is a rimless version of the 32 Winchester Special. Introduced in 1906, it was originally chambered in the Model 8 autoloader and later available in Remington pump-action and bolt-action rifles. The ammunition companies discontinued it many years ago.

General Comments Remington felt some need to counter the popular series of rimmed cartridges chambered in Winchester's Model 94 lever-action. The incentive was great enough to persuade Remington to invent substitutions for Winchester's rimmed 25-, 30- and 32-caliber cartridges. It could be argued that the 35 Remington was an answer to Winchester's 38-55. A bit of reflection suggests that the folks at Remington were confused. It was not the cartridges that made Browning's invention successful – it was Browning's invention that made the cartridges successful. The 32 Remington is, nonetheless, perfectly adequate for any task to which the 30-30 or 32 Special are suited.

32 Remington Loading Data and Factory Ballistics

Bullet (grains/type)	Powder	Grains	Velocity	Energy	Source/Comments
170 SP	IMR 4895	33.0	2070	1578	Lyman
170 SP	IMR 3031	30.0	2020	1546	NA
170 SP	IMR 4198	26.0	1992	1718	NA
170 SP	FL		2220	1860	Remington factory load

32 Ideal

Historical Notes One of the chamberings available for the single-shot Stevens 44 and 44-1/2 rifles, as well as for other single-shot rifles, this cartridge was introduced in 1903 and was quite popular for 20 years or so.

General Comments The 32 Ideal is an improvement over the older 32 Extra Long Ballard in having inside lubrication and better performance. It is cleaner to handle and easier to reload. It was also quite accurate and an adequate 150-yard small or medium game

number. Use of bullets lighter than standard provides room for more powder and gives higher velocity. Sometimes called the 32-25-150, the 32 Ideal uses a bullet diameter of 0.323-inch and, as pointed out in early Ideal Hand Books, it offered new life, via reboring and rerifling, to "thousands of 32-caliber, Short, Long and Extra Long, Rim and Center Fire rifles that have been shot out or rusted…"

32 Ideal Loading Data and Factory Ballistics

Bullet (grains/type)	Powder	Grains	Velocity	Energy	Source/Comments
115 Lead	blackpowder (FFg)	38.0	1425	524	Lyman No. 32359
150 Lead	blackpowder (Fg)	25.0	1250	526	Lyman No. 32360
150 Lead	IMR 4198	12.0	1330	596	NA
150 Lead	blackpowder (FFg)	25.0	1250	526	Factory load

33 Winchester

Historical Notes Introduced in 1902 for the Winchester Model 86 lever-action rifle and discontinued along with the rifle in 1936, it was replaced by the 348 Winchester developed for an updated version of its '86, the Model 71 rifle. It was also chambered in Marlin's Model 95 lever-action and in the Winchester Model of 1885 single-shot. This round was dropped in 1940.

General Comments The 33 Winchester earned a good reputation as a deer, black bear and elk cartridge when used in the woods at moderate ranges. Its paper ballistics are no better than the 35

Remington rimless, but it uses a smaller diameter bullet with better sectional density than the 200-grain 35-caliber. It gave good penetration and satisfactory killing power when properly used. It is still a good cartridge for anything up to and including elk, and it can be improved safely with modern powders. In any case, it is not quite as powerful as the 348 Winchester and early Model 86 actions are not quite as strong as the Model 71. Cases can be formed from 45-70 cases.

33 Winchester Loading Data and Factory Ballistics

Bullet (grains/type)	Powder	Grains	Velocity	Energy	Source/Comments
200 SP	H4895	45.0	2200	2150	Hornady
200 SP	IMR 3031	40.0	2100	1959	Hornady
200 SP			2200	2150	Winchester factory load

35 Winchester
Self-Loading (35 WSL)

Historical Notes The 35 SL was the original cartridge for the Winchester Model '05 semi-auto rifle introduced in 1905. The Model '05 was the only rifle that ever chambered it, and the cartridge was such a poor one that it was discontinued by 1920.

General Comments The 35 SL cartridge was unsuitable for anything but small to medium game at very close ranges. However,

it was too expensive for such shooting. It is too underpowered for deer, and ranks right along with the 32 SL as a rather useless cartridge. It is semi-rimmed, and can be fired in the 38 Special or 357 Magnum revolver if reloaded with 0.357-inch diameter lead bullets. Just what value this might have is difficult to imagine, but it is an interesting fact, just in case the reader did not already know it.

35 Winchester Self-Loading Loading Data and Factory Ballistics

Bullet (grains/type)	Powder	Grains	Velocity	Energy	Source/Comments
180 SP	IMR 4227	13.5	1440	834	NA
180 SP	2400	13.0	1430	823	NA
165 Lead	2400	8.0	920	312	NA
180 SP	FL		1452	842	Winchester factory load

351 Winchester Self-Loading (351 WSL)

Historical Notes Introduced in 1907 to replace the underpowered 35 SL, the 351 Self-Loading is a more powerful round for the improved Model 1907 Winchester autoloading rifle. This cartridge was used to a very limited extent by the French in both World War I and II as a military cartridge. The rifle was discontinued in 1957.

General Comments The 351 SL does not have much to offer, although it is an improvement over the older 35. It does not qualify as a suitable deer cartridge, although it has been used for that purpose. It is a good medium-game cartridge for coyote, mountain lion or animals in that class, but is too powerful for small game. It is expensive, not accurate enough and too limited in range for varmint shooting. Nevertheless, it far surpasses even the best 357 Magnum rifle loads and comes very close to duplicating the 357 Remington Maximum. It has been popular for Latin American jungle hunting because at the short ranges involved it has sufficient power for the game encountered there. Here in the United States, the 351 WSL and the handy Model 1907 semi-automatic rifle in which it was introduced were used extensively by prison guards. The rifle is notorious as one of the guns used in the killing of Bonnie and Clyde. It has been used from low-flying, light aircraft in the western United States for pest control. Like the 35, the 351 SL is semi-rimmed. The principal differences are a 0.24-inch longer case used in the 351 and higher loading pressures. Winchester was the last company to offer ammunition.

351 Winchester Self-Loading Loading Data and Factory Ballistics

Bullet (grains/type)	Powder	Grains	Velocity	Energy	Source/Comments
177 Cast	IMR 4227	16.0	1550	947	Lyman No. 351319
180	2400	19.0	1793	1280	Medium game only; Lyman
180	IMR 4227	19.5	1751	1225	NA
180	FL		1850	1370	Factory load

350 Griffin & Howe Magnum

Historical Notes The 350 G&H Magnum was developed by Griffin & Howe in the early 1930s. It is also known as the 350 Holland & Holland Magnum, since that company chambered it in its rifles for a number of years. In the United States, ammunition was loaded by Western Cartridge Co. It is based on the 375 H&H case necked-down and is similar to a number of 35-caliber wildcats that came along years later. It did not achieve popularity and died out by the end of the 1930s. Today it is largely a collector's item.

General Comments The 350 G&H Magnum used standard 0.357-inch-diameter bullets and so could be handloaded with a variety of weights and types. It is a good big game cartridge for either North American or African hunting. However, it is obsolete and the 358 Norma Magnum or one of the 35-caliber short magnums would be a better choice. Cases are easy to make and plenty of good bullets are available.

350 Griffin & Howe Loading Data and Factory Ballistics

Bullet (grains/type)	Powder	Grains	Velocity	Energy	Source/Comments
220 SP	IMR 4350	88.0	3120	4762	NA
250 SP	IMR 4831	93.0	2950	4848	NA
250 SP	FL		2700	4055	Western factory load

35 Winchester

Historical Notes Developed by Winchester for its Model 1895 lever-action rifle, the 35 Winchester was introduced in 1903. The Remington-Lee bolt-action rifle also chambered this round. It was discontinued in 1936 along with the Model 95 rifle. It was listed in the 1962 British Kynoch ammunition catalogs.

General Comments The 35 Winchester is a more powerful cartridge than the 33 Winchester, but is not as potent as the 348 or the 358 Winchester. It had a good reputation as a short-range number for elk, moose or brown bear. It is certainly powerful enough for any North American big game, but has little to offer as

compared to more modern cartridges. It can be improved by using modern powders, but pressures in the old 1895 lever-action should be kept to about 45,000 psi. This cartridge, like the 405 Winchester, is based on the same basic case as the 30-40 Krag. Here, by moving headspace control to the case shoulder, it is feasible to form perfectly useful cases from 30-40 Krag cases. The case neck will be somewhat shorter than with original cases, but this poses no problem because it is not necessary to crimp the case mouth in cartridges used in the M-95.

35 Winchester Loading Data and Factory Ballistics

Bullet (grains/type)	Powder	Grains	Velocity	Energy	Source/Comments
200 SP	IMR 4895	52.0	2480	2738	NA
200 SP	IMR 4064	45.0	2220	2182	NA
204	IMR 4227	18.0	1550	1091	Lyman No. 358315
250 SP	IMR 4895	50.0	2290	2920	NA
250 SP	IMR 4320	48.0	2190	2670	NA
250 SP	FL		2195	2670	Winchester factory load

35 Newton

Historical Notes The 35 Newton was listed in the Newton Rifle Co. catalog in 1915, which presumably is the year it was introduced. It is the 30 Newton case necked-up to 35-caliber. The Western Cartridge Co. listed it until 1936, but no commercial rifles other than the Newton chambered this round.

General Comments The 35 Newton is more powerful, in some loadings, than the 375 H&H Magnum. The factory load listed below was the last one offered by the Western Cartridge Co., but at one time, other loads were available. This cartridge is somewhat

overpowered for most North American big game. It has been used in Africa with considerable success, although the Newton rifle was much too light and poorly stocked for such a powerful cartridge. Cases can be readily formed from RWS 8x68mm brass or by necking-up the 30 Newton, itself a scarce item. Performance is similar to the later 358 Norma Magnum, which would be a far better choice because ammunition has been recently offered and handloading is easier (through simple conversion of readily available cases).

35 Newton Loading Data and Factory Ballistics

Bullet (grains/type)	Powder	Grains	Velocity	Energy	Source/Comments
200 SP	IMR 3031	78.0	3030	4100	NA
250 SP	IMR 4064	70.0	2650	3918	NA
250 SP	IMR 4320	75.0	2815	4410	NA
250 SP	FL		2660	3930	Western factory load
250 SP	FL		2975	4925	Western factory load

358 Norma Magnum

Historical Notes This cartridge was developed by Norma and introduced in the United States in 1959. At the start, no rifles were chambered for the 358 Norma Magnum. However, empty cases and loaded ammunition were available. The Schultz & Larsen Model 65 and the Husqvarna bolt-action were made available in this chambering early in 1960. No mainstream American gun manufacturer ever chambered this cartridge. Like the 308 Norma Magnum, it is a proprietary cartridge and perhaps should be listed under European cartridges. However, it was designed for the American market and is listed here because many custom rifles were made here.

General Comments The 358 Norma Magnum is a short, magnum-type cartridge intended to work through standard-length actions. It is nearly identical to the wildcat 35 Ackley belted, short magnum. It is also nearly identical to the wildcat 35-338, which is the 338 Winchester necked-up to 35-caliber.

The 358 Norma Magnum delivers the same performance as the slightly larger 375 H&H Magnum and would be suitable for the same range of game. It is overpowered for most North American big game, but would be an excellent choice for the big Kodiak bears. It is another good all-around number for the person who wants to be prepared for hunting anything, anywhere, at any time. A-Square has reintroduced this ammunition.

358 Norma Magnum Loading Data and Factory Ballistics

Bullet (grains/type)	Powder	Grains	Velocity	Energy	Source/Comments
180 SP	IMR 4895	69.0	3100	3842	Speer
200 SP	IMR 3031	66.5	2900	3736	Hornady
225 SP	IMR 4350	75.0	2900	4203	Nosler
250 SP	IMR 4320	68.0	2800	4353	Hornady
250 SP	IMR 4350	76.0	2700	4048	Speer
250 SP	Norma MRP	78.0	2500	3470	Speer
300 SP	IMR 4350	71.0	2600	4504	Barnes
250 SP	FL		2790	4322	Norma factory load

35-30 Maynard (1882)

Historical Notes The 35-30 was one of a series of cartridges designed for and introduced with the Model 1882 Maynard single-shot rifle. The Improved Hunters Rifle Nos. 7 and 9, along with the Target & Hunting No. 10 and Improved Target No. 16 were available in this chambering.

General Comments Maynard rifles were used during the Civil War. After the war, the company manufactured sporting rifles. The Maynard rifle used a tip-up breech linked to an under-lever. These were smooth operating, safe and possessed excellent accuracy. 35-30 ammunition can be made from 38-55 cases. Nominal 0.358-inch case bullets can usually be used as cast (without sizing). Lyman's 165-grain No. 358429 bullet usually works well. A version with an unusually wide rim was also made. Such cases are available from Ballard Rifle & Cartridge Co. (307-587-4914).

35-30 Maynard 1882 Loading Data and Factory Ballistics

Bullet (grains/type)	Powder	Grains	Velocity	Energy	Source/Comments
165 Lead	IMR 4198	16.0	1320	645	Lyman No. 350293
165 Lead	2400	13.0	1450	787	Lyman No. 350293
250 Lead	FL		1280	918	Factory load

35-40 Maynard (1882)

Historical Notes This an elongated version of the 35-30 and used in the Model 1882 Maynard rifles.

General Comments The 35-40 provides greater powder capacity than the shorter 35-30. The case dimensions are not identical, but cases can be made from 38-55 cases, just as with the 35-30. The long case is probably superior for hunting, but since both are strictly small- to medium-game numbers, any advantage would be a matter of opinion. Any cast 0.358-inch rifle or revolver bullet can be sized to work. The Lyman No. 358429 (165 grains) would be a good choice.

35-40 Maynard Loading Data and Factory Ballistics

Bullet (grains/type)	Powder	Grains	Velocity	Energy	Source/Comments
165 Lead	IMR 4198	18.0	1400	725	Lyman No. 358429
250 Lead	FL		1355	1018	Factory load

38-45 Stevens

Historical Notes One of the special Stevens "Everlasting" cartridges, this one was introduced with the 1875 tip-up models. It was not very popular and was discontinued within a few years. Today it is one of the rarer Stevens cartridges.

General Comments Another of the 38-40 class cartridges, the 38-45 used a heavier bullet, but ballistics are similar. The 38-40 and 38-55 made most of these in-between cartridges obsolete. Original loading called for 45 to 50 grains of Fg blackpowder and a bullet of 210 to 255 grains. It should be possible to convert 303 British cases to work in these rifles.

38-45 Stevens Loading Data and Factory Ballistics

Bullet (grains/type)	Powder	Grains	Velocity	Energy	Source/Comments
210 Lead	IMR 4198	16.0	1340	845	Lyman No. 36275
210 Lead	FL		1420	947	Factory load

35-30 Maynard (1865)

Historical Notes This unusual, externally ignited "cartridge" was chambered in the Model of 1865 Maynard rifle. This was a forerunner to all centerfire cartridges because it featured a central flash hole in the base of the case. This was also forerunner to the 35-30 Maynard cartridge used in Model 1873 and 1882 rifles. While Maynard rifles saw Civil War usage, this particular combination came along quite late in that conflict.

General Comments This rifle combines what appears to be a more-or-less conventional cartridge case with external priming. The base of the case has a centered, small-diameter flash hole. This hole carries the flash from a conventional cap into the charge. Conceptually, it is a very small step from this design to one combining the cap and the case into one unit.

One could argue that this "cartridge" falls outside the purview of this book because it does not incorporate a self-contained primer – it is not a complete cartridge in the modern sense. It is, however, much closer to the modern cartridge than its forerunners, the paper-cased "cartridge." Therefore, since this rifle and cartridge represent a significant step toward perfection of the self-contained cartridge, we feel that this number is worthy of mention here. Fully functional 35-30 Maynard pinfire cases are available from Ballard Rifle & Cartridge Co. (307-587-4914).

38-40 Remington-Hepburn

Historical Notes Although listed as the 38-40 Remington-Hepburn, this cartridge was available in the No. 1 Sporting Model rolling block rifle that preceded the Hepburn action by 10 years. The No. 1 rifle was also chambered for the 38-40 WCF shortly after Winchester introduced it during 1873-1874. It is likely that this cartridge was intended as a straight-case version of the bottlenecked Winchester round. The 38-40 Remington-Hepburn appeared about 1875.

General Comments Rifle and ammunition manufacturers went all out to please every segment of the trade during the 1800s. Some riflemen did not cotton to the bottlenecked cases, so all kinds of straight, tapered and bottleneck designs appeared in the same caliber and with the same powder charge. This may have provided a great lift to the men using these, but it is very confusing. The 38-40 Remington and 38-40 Winchester are a case in point. Neither could do anything the other would not, but the Winchester round won out in company with the repeating rifle. The Remington cartridge is a good target or small to medium game number. The original bullet is slightly heavier than the 38 WCF, but loading data for one will give similar results in the other. It is possible to convert 30-40 Krag cases to load this cartridge.

38-40 Remington-Hepburn Loading Data and Factory Ballistics

Bullet (grains/type)	Powder	Grains	Velocity	Energy	Source/Comments
190 Lead	IMR 4198	16.0	1427	865	Lyman No. 373164
250 Lead	2400	15.0	1300	937	NA
245 Lead			1200	790	Remington factory load

38-45 Bullard

Historical Notes This is another of the special cartridges for the Bullard lever-action, single-shot and repeating rifles. It was introduced approximately 1887. Remington once loaded this round, but it was never a very popular number.

General Comments Very few rifles in this chambering still exist. Ballistically it is similar to the 38-40 WCF. It was an accurate cartridge, suitable primarily for small or medium game at close ranges. These cartridges are now collector's items. It should be possible to convert 44 Remington Magnum cases to work in these rifles.

38-45 Bullard Loading Data and Factory Ballistics

Bullet (grains/type)	Powder	Grains	Velocity	Energy	Source/Comments
175 Lead	2400	16.0	1480	883	Lyman No. 37582
250 Lead	Unique	10.0	1200	797	NA
190 Lead	FL		1388	822	Remington factory load

38 Long, Centerfire (38 Long, CF)

Historical Notes The 38 Long is another old-timer designed to replace a similar rimfire cartridge. It was introduced in 1875-76 and used in a number of single-shot rifles including the Ballard, Stevens, Remington and others. It was obsolete by 1900 and, oddly, the original rimfire version outlived the centerfire.

General Comments The 38 Long, like the 32 and 44, was not very effective and had a short life. It was an alternative to the rimfire and many of the old rifles could, by a simple adjustment, fire either. The 38 Long Colt or 38 S&W Special can be used to make ammunition. Standard load was 20 to 25 grains of blackpowder and a 140- to 150-grain bullet.

38 Long, Centerfire Loading Data and Factory Ballistics

Bullet (grains/type)	Powder	Grains	Velocity	Energy	Source/Comments
145 Lead	FL		950	291	Factory load

38 Ballard Extra Long

Historical Notes This centerfire version of the 38 Extra Long rimfire was introduced in 1885-86 as one of the chamberings for the Ballard No. 2 Sporting Model. It also was used by many other companies. It had the old No. 1 primer that has not been made for many years. Some of these rifles were furnished with a changeable firing pin or hammer arrangement so they could fire the rimfire or centerfire version with only a minor adjustment.

General Comments The 38 Extra Long was designed to furnish a reloadable case to those who favored the 38 Extra Long rimfire ballistics. It was a nice little plinking, small game or target cartridge for those who wanted economy. Any 0.358-inch bullet of suitable weight can be used. Using Lyman No. 358161 (145 grains) and 31 grains of FFg blackpowder will work fine. The 357 Remington Maximum case can be converted to work in the 38 Ballard Extra Long chamber.

38 Ballard Extra Long Loading Data and Factory Ballistics

Bullet (grains/type)	Powder	Grains	Velocity	Energy	Source/Comments
150 Lead	Unique	6.0	1160	450	Lyman No. 358160
146 Lead	FL		1275	533	Factory load

38-35 Stevens

Historical Notes Introduced in 1875 for the Stevens tip-up single-shot rifles, this was one of the special Stevens "Everlasting" cartridges. It was not very popular, so it was dropped after a few years. In its original form, it is occasionally referred to as the 38-33.

General Comments Stevens "Everlasting" shells were sold as separate components and the older, less popular numbers are seldom encountered as loaded rounds. These cases, intended to give very long reloading life, were necessarily thick and heavy.

About six of these special chamberings survived. Loadings were not standard, and they may be found with a variety of bullet weights in both grooved and paper-patched form. A load of 35 grains or so of Fg blackpowder and any bullet of 180 to 255 grains can be used in this cartridge. It should be possible to chamber and safely shoot either 41 Short Colt or the 41 Long Colt lead bullet loads in these rifles. The softer oversize bullet will safely swage down to bore diameter.

38-35 Stevens Loading Data and Factory Ballistics

Bullet (grains/type)	Powder	Grains	Velocity	Energy	Source/Comments
180 Lead	blackpowder (Fg)	35.0	1350*	729	NA
215 Lead	blackpowder (Fg)	35.0	1255	758	Factory load
* Estimated					

38-50 Maynard (1882)

Historical Notes The 38-50 Maynard is practically identical to the 38-55 Ballard and Winchester, and uses a bullet of similar diameter. It was not popular because it was so similar to the Winchester number.

General Comments To reload the 38-50, one can make cases by resizing and trimming 38-55 cases and loading 38-caliber cast rifle

bullets sized to correct diameter. The 38-55 would only hold 48 to 50 grains of blackpowder after the ammunition companies began using heavier, solid-head cases. For all practical purposes, there is no performance difference between the 38-50 Maynard and the 38-55.

38-50 Maynard Loading Data and Factory Ballistics

Bullet (grains/type)	Powder	Grains	Velocity	Energy	Source/Comments
149 Lead	IMR 4198	10.0	1100	420	Lyman No. 37583
250 Lead	IMR 4198	16.0	1320	974	Lyman No. 375248
255 Lead	FL		1325	990	Factory load

38-50 Ballard

Historical Notes This cartridge was the forerunner of the 38-55. It was introduced in 1876 for the Ballard Perfection No. 4 and Pacific No. 5 rifles, but was also available in other models. It is an "Everlasting" type case, heavier than the standard 38-55 and 3/16-inch shorter. It was replaced by the 38-55 when that cartridge was introduced in 1884.

General Comments Standard bullet diameter for most 38-caliber rifles was 0.375-inch, but many had a groove diameter of 0.379-inch, requiring a larger bullet. It is wise to measure the bore diameter before ordering a bullet mould for these old rifles. Lyman moulds are available in a variety of 38 rifle bullets, from 150 grains to more than 300 grains. Modern 38-55 cases can be used in 38-50 rifles by shortening the case to the proper length. Performance and usefulness are on a par with the 38-55 (see Chapter 2).

38-50 Ballard Loading Data and Factory Ballistics

Bullet (grains/type)	Powder	Grains	Velocity	Energy	Source/Comments
145 Lead	IMR 4198	14.0	1300	550	Lyman No. 37583
250 Lead	IMR 4198	17.0	1350	1020	Lyman No. 375248
255 Lead	FL		1321	989	Factory load

38-50 Remington-Hepburn

Historical Notes Introduced in 1883 as one of the chamberings for the Remington-Hepburn match rifles, this was too similar to the popular 38-55 to gain much of a following and was discontinued after a few years.

General Comments Loading data for the 38-55 Winchester and Marlin can be applied to this cartridge. There is no difference in usefulness or performance. It should be possible to convert 303 British or 30-40 Krag cases to work in these rifles.

38-50 Remington-Hepburn Loading Data and Factory Ballistics

Bullet (grains/type)	Powder	Grains	Velocity	Energy	Source/Comments
255 Lead	IMR 4198	23.0	1580	1421	NA
250 Lead	Unique	10.0	1200	797	NA
255 Lead	FL		1320	989	Factory load

38-56 Winchester

Historical Notes Introduced in 1887 for the Model 1886 Winchester repeater, this cartridge was also used in the single-shot and the 1895 Marlin. The 38-56 made the transition into the smokeless powder era and was loaded until about 1936. The Colt New Lightning pump-action, magazine rifles also used this cartridge.

General Comments Design of this cartridge was intended to develop increased velocity without lengthening the case. It is a sort of super 38-55 in conception, but not in fact. With smokeless powder, and within allowable pressures, there is not any real performance difference. It is a bottlenecked case and will not interchange with others of similar designation. Although advertised as a powerful big game number, it is little more than a deer or black bear cartridge. With maximum handloads, it might do OK for elk at short range. Cases can be made from 45-70 cases.

38-56 Winchester Loading Data and Factory Ballistics

Bullet (grains/type)	Powder	Grains	Velocity	Energy	Source/Comments
255 Lead	IMR 3031	36.0	1830	1908	NA
265 Lead	IMR 4198	25.0	1600	1512	Lyman No. 375296 gas checked
255 SP	FL		1395	1105	Factory load

38-90 Winchester Express (38 Express)

Historical Notes Introduced in 1886 as one of many chamberings for the successful Winchester Model 1885 single-shot, this was not a popular cartridge, and by 1904 it had been discontinued.

General Comments This is a long, bottlenecked case with a light bullet for cartridges of this class. Since it is designated an "Express" cartridge, it was probably intended to develop superior velocity for a 38-caliber rifle. Old Ideal catalogs list bullet No. 375248 as standard with the No. 3 loading tool for this cartridge, but any of the lighter 38-55 bullets can be used. A charge of 90 grains of Fg blackpowder was the original factory loading.

38-90 Winchester Express Loading Data and Factory Ballistics

Bullet (grains/type)	Powder	Grains	Velocity	Energy	Source/Comments
218 Lead	IMR 4198	21.0	1350	886	Lyman No. 37584
218 Lead	IMR 4198	23.0	1470	1045	Lyman No. 37584
217 Lead	FL		1595	1227	Winchester factory load

38-70 Winchester

Historical Notes Introduced in 1894 for the Model 1886 Winchester lever-action repeater, the 38-70 did not catch on and was discontinued within a few years.

General Comments This cartridge offers little if any improvement over the 38-55. It is of bottlenecked design but is not the same as the 38-56 or the 38-72 Winchester. The older Lyman catalogs indicated it used the standard 38-55 bullet of 0.379-inch. Although the 38-70 case is longer than that of the 45-70, usable, short-necked cases could be made from the 45-70. However, the basic 45 cases now available will make perfect replacement cases.

38-70 Winchester Loading Data and Factory Ballistics

Bullet (grains/type)	Powder	Grains	Velocity	Energy	Source/Comments
250 Lead	IMR 4198	26.0	1710	1625	NA
265 Lead	IMR 3031	41.0	1700	1698	NA
255 Lead	FL		1490	1257	Factory load

38-72 Winchester

Historical Notes This round was designed for, and introduced with, the Model 1895 Winchester lever-action, box magazine repeater. Both gun and cartridge were obsolete by 1936. The 38-72 was only moderately popular.

General Comments This is a nearly straight case with a very slight neck. Some cases have a pronounced groove around the neck to prevent the bullet from receding under recoil. This tends to obscure the slight neck. This is another 38-caliber cartridge touted as being very powerful when, in fact, it is nearly the same as the 38-55 (see Chapter 2). The 38-72 case has the same basic body as the 30-40 Krag, but because headspacing is on the rim, it may not be possible to safely use that case to make the 38-72, except for very low pressure loads.

38-72 Winchester Loading Data and Factory Ballistics

Bullet (grains/type)	Powder	Grains	Velocity	Energy	Source/Comments
255 Lead	IMR 3031	33.0	1735	1715	NA
275 Lead	IMR 4198	27.0	1350	1120	Lyman No. 375167
275 Cast	blackpowder (Fg)	72.0			Lyman No. 357167
275 SP	FL		1475	1330	Winchester factory load

38 Colt Lightning and 38-40 Marlin   See 38-40, Chapter 2

40-50 Sharps (Straight)

Historical Notes Introduced in 1879, this is the smallest of the Sharps cartridges. There is a similar, necked version. In addition to Sharps rifles, the Winchester single-shot was available in this chambering, as was the Remington rolling block. This is also known as the 40-1 7/8-inch Sharps.

General Comments Although listed as the 40-50, this cartridge was actually loaded with 40 or 45 grains of powder and was identical in performance to the 40-40 Maynard and other similar

rounds. Standard diameter of most 40-caliber rifle bullets is 0.403-inch and almost any bullet of that diameter can be used. These chambers were cut to use bore diameter paper-patch bullets; groove diameter is typically 0.408-inch to 0.411-inch. It should be possible to convert the 30-40 Krag case to work in these rifles. However, the rim is 0.010-inch too thin, so only very light loads should be used. Better to get the correct case from Buffalo Arms Co. (208-263-6953).

40-50 Sharps (Straight) Loading Data and Factory Ballistics

Bullet (grains/type)	Powder	Grains	Velocity	Energy	Source/Comments
260 Lead	IMR 4198	21.0	1450	1220	Lyman No. 403169
265 Lead	FL		1410	1168	Factory load

40-50 Sharps (Necked)

Historical Notes Also known as the 40-1 11/16-inch, this cartridge was introduced in 1869 for that model of Sharps Sporting rifle. It was available with several bullet weights, including 265, 285 and 296 grains. The Remington rolling block and other single-shot rifles also chambered this cartridge.

General Comments The 40-50 bottlenecked cartridge is shorter than the straight version, but there is little difference in ballistics.

The 40-50 Sharps (Straight) and 40-50 Sharps (Necked) are not interchangeable. Proper bullet diameter is 0.403-inch, and several Lyman bullet moulds are available in this size. These chambers were cut to use bore-diameter paper-patch bullets; groove diameter is typically 0.408-inch to 0.411-inch. This is largely a medium game, deer or intermediate-range target cartridge. It should be possible to convert 45-70 cases to work in these rifles.

40-50 Sharps (Necked) Loading Data and Factory Ballistics

Bullet (grains/type)	Powder	Grains	Velocity	Energy	Source/Comments
260 Lead	IMR 4198	21.0	1500	1308	Lyman No. 403169
265 Lead	FL		1460	1262	Factory load

40-60 Marlin

Historical Notes The 40-60 is one of the chamberings for Marlin 1881 and 1895 lever-action repeaters. The 1895 uses the same basic system as the 1893 and 1894 models, but is larger and longer. This appears to be the same case as the 40-65 Winchester, but with a slightly different loading. The pump-action Colt New Lightning rifles also used the Marlin loading of this cartridge.

General Comments During the late 1800s, the same cartridge often went under various names, depending on who loaded it or whose rifle it was used in. It was also common practice to change the name if you furnished more than one load or bullet in the same

case; that is what happened here. The 40-60 Marlin and the 40-65 Winchester are interchangeable and either can be used in the same gun. However, the old Ideal catalog states the 40-60 Marlin "must not be confused with the 40-60 Winchester as they are not the same." This, of course, is true. If the reader is not thoroughly confused by now, he should be. Go ahead. Read it through a few more times and it will clear up. Converting 45-70 cases into 40-60 Marlin cases is easily done. Marlin 40-caliber rifles often have significantly oversize bores. Groove diameters as large as 0.414-inch are noted.

40-60 Marlin Loading Data and Factory Ballistics

Bullet (grains/type)	Powder	Grains	Velocity	Energy	Source/Comments
260 Lead	IMR 4198	23.0	1500	1308	Lyman No. 403170
260 Lead	IMR 3031	35.0	1480	1263	NA
260 Lead	FL		1385	1115	Factory load

40-60 Colt

Historical Notes At a casual glance, this cartridge appears to be identical to both the 40-60 Marlin and the 40-65 Winchester (except bullet diameter). However, this cartridge includes a definite shoulder, while the other two are true tapered designs. The value or need for a cartridge so similar to the 40-60 Marlin seems moot. Almost certainly, the Marlin round would chamber and fire normally in the Colt rifle.

General Comments It seems that this version must have been created in response to a request from Colt for a cartridge that was

specifically intended for use in its rifle. Winchester displayed this number for at least one year on its product advertisement board but it was not found in any catalog listing between 1879 and 1910 or in the 1916 catalog. Therefore, it seems unlikely that it was ever actually offered for sale — at least not directly from Winchester. We present it here in an effort to try to demonstrate just how confusing such research can become. Unless this number was loaded with a different bullet weight, which seems unlikely, ballistics would have been identical to the 40-60 Marlin (see ballistics table).

40-63 and 40-70 Ballard

Historical Notes These two cartridges have identical length and outside dimensions, so are listed together. The 40-63 is actually just a heavier-case version of the 40-70 factory cartridge. Both are, in turn, an outgrowth of the original 40-65 Ballard Everlasting case, which had to be handloaded. The 40-63 and 40-70 were first listed for the Ballard Perfection No. 4 and Pacific No. 5 after the Marlin Fire Arms Co. took over manufacture of these rifles in 1881.

General Comments This was a popular cartridge among Ballard rifle fans and was as good as similar cartridges offered by Winchester and others. However, cartridges designed for repeating

rifles tended to survive longer than those intended for single-shots. These were used more as match cartridges than anything else, but these also made good deer, black bear or elk numbers. Their performance is identical to the 40-70 Sharps Straight or the 40-72 Winchester. The 444 Marlin case should work in these rifles; however, the rim is generally too small to properly engage the extractor. These chambers were cut to use bore-diameter (0.403-inch), paper-patch bullets; groove diameter is typically 0.408-inch to 0.411-inch.

40-63/40-70 Ballard Loading Data and Factory Ballistics

Bullet (grains/type)	Powder	Grains	Velocity	Energy	Source/Comments
330 Lead	IMR 4198	22.0	1310	1260	Lyman No. 403149 — 1/20 or 1/30 tin-lead
330 Lead	FL		1335	1318	Factory load

40-65 Ballard Everlasting

Historical Notes The 40-65 Ballard Everlasting was introduced in 1876 as one of the original chamberings for the Perfection No. 4 and Pacific No. 5 rifles, and in 1879 it was added to the Hunter No. 1-1/2. These were all the same basic, under-lever, single-shot action. This cartridge was used in the J.M. Marlin Ballards, and after the Marlin Fire Arms Co. took over, it was altered to the 40-70 and 40-63.

General Comments The 40-70 or 40-63 Ballard can be chambered in the older 40-65 rifles, but the 40-65 case will not fit the other chamber. Note that firing the smaller diameter cases could result in a case wall rupture, so this is not a good idea. It is a much heavier case of slightly larger diameter, although all have the same length. Ballistics of all are the same for practical purposes, and the loading data shown for the 40-63 will give the same results in any of the cases. The 40-65 Everlasting is one of the rarer Ballard cartridges and is seldom encountered. It should be possible to convert 444 Marlin cases to work in these rifles.

40-70 Sharps (Straight)
40-65 Sharps (1876)

Historical Notes This is the 40-2 1/2-inch straight case introduced in 1876. It is sometimes referred to as the 40-65, because with heavy, reloadable cases, that is all the powder it would hold unless a lighter bullet was used. Remington and Winchester single-shots also chambered this round.

General Comments This is another cartridge with ballistics similar to a half-dozen others of different make or origin. There are actually more than a dozen 40-caliber cartridges with powder charges of around 40 to 70 grains and none offer any stupendous advantage over the others. Like other 40 Sharps numbers, this one used a 0.403-inch bullet, weighing 330 or 370 grains. These chambers were cut to use bore-diameter bullets (often paper-patched). Groove diameter is typically 0.408-inch to 0.411-inch. A number of Lyman bullet moulds are available in this size. Although longer, this case has the same basic body as the 30-40 Krag. However, because headspacing is on the rim, it may not be possible to safely use that case to make the 40-70 except for very-low-pressure loads.

40-70 Sharps (Straight) Loading Data and Factory Ballistics

Bullet (grains/type)	Powder	Grains	Velocity	Energy	Source/Comments
330 Lead	IMR 4198	23.0	1250	1150	Lyman No. 403149
330 Lead	FL		1258	1160	Factory load

40-70 Sharps (Necked)

Historical Notes This is the 40-2 1/4-inch bottlenecked Sharps that was brought out in 1871 for the Model 1871 Sporting rifle. It was used in other single-shot rifles also.

General Comments The 40-70 necked cartridge had a reputation for fine accuracy and was popular as a match cartridge as much as for hunting. While many people regard the Sharps rifles as strictly buffalo guns, Sharps also made match rifles that gained worldwide respect on the range — whence the name, Sharps-shooter. The best marksmen were given Sharps rifles in a special squad and its notoriety grew until the single word "sharpshooter" was synonymous with accurate rifle fire. It should be possible to convert the 45-70 case to work in these rifles but the neck would be very short. The 45 Basic will make perfect cases. These rifles have chambers that were cut to use a bore-diameter (0.403-inch), paper-patched bullet. Groove diameter is typically 0.408-inch to 0.411-inch.

40-70 Sharps (Necked) Loading Data and Factory Ballistics

Bullet (grains/type)	Powder	Grains	Velocity	Energy	Source/Comments
330 Lead	IMR 4759	26.0	1510	1671	NA
330 Lead	IMR 4198	27.0	1450	1542	Lyman No. 403139
330 Lead	FL		1420	1482	Factory load

40-85 Ballard
40-90 Ballard

Historical Notes The 40-85 and the 40-90 Ballard are the same case with different loadings. L.D. Satterlee lists the 40-90 Everlasting with the J.M. Marlin Ballard Pacific No. 5 and Sporting No. 4-1/2 (introduced in 1878). He shows the 40-85 chambering for the Pacific No. 5 after the Marlin Fire Arms Co. took over manufacture in 1881.

General Comments The 40-90 Everlasting case is heavier and about 1/8-inch longer than the regular 40-90 or 40-85 case. Many of the 40-90 Everlasting cases were nickel plated. This is a hunting cartridge very similar to the 40-90 Sharps straight. The same loading data can be used for both, however these are not interchangeable. Although the case of the 40-85 Ballard is longer, it has the same basic body as the 444 Marlin case. It should be possible to make usable, albeit shorter, cases from those. These rifles had chambers designed to use a 0.403-inch (bore-diameter), paper-patched bullet. Groove diameter typically ran 0.408-inch to 0.411-inch.

40-85/40-90 Ballard Loading Data and Factory Ballistics

Bullet (grains/type)	Powder	Grains	Velocity	Energy	Source/Comments
370 Lead	IMR 4198	28.0	1400	1615	Lyman No. 40395
370 Lead	FL		1427	1672	Factory load

40-90 Sharps (Straight)

Historical Notes Sharps catalogs do not list this cartridge, although Sharps rifles (and others) chambered for it are known. It was introduced about 1885. The Remington-Hepburn No. 3 single-shot was advertised in this chambering and UMC and Winchester manufactured cases and ammunition.

General Comments The so-called "Everlasting," or reloadable case, was popular with hunters and target shooters during the 1880-90 period. These heavy cases could be reused repeatedly. In fact, they were made so heavy that powder capacity was often reduced by 5 or 10 grains. To get around this, the "Everlasting" case was often made longer than the standard. UMC cases of the 40/3-1/4 inch are usually of very heavy, reloadable construction.

The reason for mentioning this is that it might have a bearing on the origin of this cartridge. Physical measurements of the so-called 40-90 Sharps Straight are practically identical to the 40-90 Ballard, except for the length. It is possible that the design of the 40-90 Sharps straight is based on lengthening the Ballard cartridge to create an "Everlasting" version with the same capacity and ballistics. Anyway, the idea is worth mentioning and would probably occur to anyone who compared the two. Although longer, this case has the same basic body as the 444 Marlin. It should be possible to make usable, albeit much shorter, cases from those. These rifles had a chamber cut to use a bore-diameter (0.403-inch), paper-patched bullet; groove diameter was 0.408-inch to 0.411-inch.

40-90 Sharps (Straight) Loading Data and Factory Ballistics

Bullet (grains/type)	Powder	Grains	Velocity	Energy	Source/Comments
370 Lead	IMR 4198	30.0	1400	1612	Lyman No. 403171
370 Lead	FL		1387	1582	Factory load

40-90 Sharps (Necked)

Historical Notes The 40-90 Sharps was introduced in 1873 for the Sharps side-hammer model rifles. There was also another loading, referred to as the 40-100 Sharps, which used a 190-grain hollowpoint bullet. However, it used the same 2 5/8-inch long case.

General Comments This became one of the more popular Sharps cartridges. The hollowpoint Express bullets made by Sharps were designed to accept a 22 rimfire blank, which was supposed to provide explosive expansion and better knockdown. The author has experimented with bullets of this type, and they do not work as they are intended to. An ordinary hollowpoint or a properly constructed softpoint will do as much damage. Perfect cases can be made from the 45 Basic case.

40-90 Sharps (Necked) Loading Data and Factory Ballistics

Bullet (grains/type)	Powder	Grains	Velocity	Energy	Source/Comments
370 Lead	IMR 4198	28.0	1450	1735	Lyman No. 403171
370 Lead	FL		1475	1800	Factory load

40-110 Winchester Express (40 Express)

Historical Notes Designed for the Winchester single-shot rifle and introduced in 1886, the 40-110 was intended to compete with the big Sharps cartridges.

General Comments In its original form, the 40-110 used a copper-tubed bullet. The Ideal catalog lists bullet No. 403169 (260 grains) as proper for reloading. The 50 Basic will make perfect cases.

40-110 Winchester Express Loading Data and Factory Ballistics

Bullet (grains/type)	Powder	Grains	Velocity	Energy	Source/Comments
260 Lead	FG	110.0	1617	1509	NA
260 Lead	IMR 4198	32.0	1650	1580	Lyman No. 403169
260 SP	FL		1617	1509	Winchester factory load

40-60 Winchester

Historical Notes The 40-60 Winchester is a sharply tapered, slightly necked cartridge for the Model 1876 Winchester rifle, which is a heavier version of the lever-action Model 1873 designed to handle more powerful cartridges. Rifle and cartridge were marketed from 1876 until 1897. This was a popular cartridge and Winchester continued to load it up to 1934.

General Comments The big powerful cartridges available for the Sharps and other single-shot rifles forced Winchester to bring out a more potent line for its repeaters. The cartridges for the Centennial Model marked the beginning of such a trend. This is not the same as the 40-60 Marlin. It is a better hunting choice than the old 44-40 WCF. The 45-70 case can be easily converted to make 40-60 Winchester cases.

40-60 Winchester Loading Data and Factory Ballistics

Bullet (grains/type)	Powder	Grains	Velocity	Energy	Source/Comments
210 Lead	IMR 4198	21.0	1520	1083	Lyman No. 403168
210 Lead	FL		1562	1138	Winchester factory load

40-70 Winchester

Historical Notes This cartridge was developed for the Model 1886 Winchester repeater and was used in the Winchester single-shot. It was introduced in 1894, but never became popular or widely used. The Marlin Model 1895 repeating rifle was also available in this chambering.

General Comments This is a bottlenecked case generally similar to the 38-70 Winchester. It provides a larger, heavier bullet in a cartridge suitable to the same action as the 38 caliber. This case is not the same as that of the 40-72 Winchester. However, the ballistics are nearly identical. It should be possible to convert 45-70 cases to work in these rifles, but the neck would be short. The 45 Basic will make perfect cases. Although groove diameter was typically 0.408-inch, original bullets were 0.406-inch diameter.

40-70 Winchester Loading Data and Factory Ballistics

Bullet (grains/type)	Powder	Grains	Velocity	Energy	Source/Comments
330 Lead	IMR 4759	26.0	1540	1738	
330 Lead	IMR 4198	25.0	1380	1050	Lyman No. 406150
330 Lead	FL		1383	1333	Factory load

40-70 Remington

Historical Notes Although listed as the 40-70 Remington, this cartridge is really Remington's version of the 40-70 Sharps necked. The Remington rolling block No. 1 Sporting Model chambered it and so did the Hepburn No. 3. It was added to the Remington line in 1880.

General Comments Two versions of this cartridge were available: one with a regular brass case, the other with a special reloading case with a brass body and steel head. The steel head fastened to the brass body with an inside screw, which served as a primer anvil and had a flash hole drilled through it. Steel head cases in 1880! There really is nothing new under the sun. The 40-70 was used more for match shooting than for hunting. It should be possible to convert 45-70 cases to work in these rifles, but the neck would be very short. The 45 Basic will make perfect cases.

40-70 Remington Loading Data and Factory Ballistics

Bullet (grains/type)	Powder	Grains	Velocity	Energy	Source/Comments
330 Lead	IMR 4198	27.0	1450	1542	Lyman No. 403139
330 Lead	FL		1420	1482	Remington factory load

40-65 Winchester

Historical Notes The 40-65 Winchester & Marlin was introduced in 1887 for the Model 1886 Winchester rifle. The Winchester single-shot also chambered it and so did the Marlin Model 1895. The 40-65 Winchester was loaded in both blackpowder and smokeless powder versions, and Winchester catalogs listed it to 1935.

General Comments The 40-65 was a further effort to put more steam in the repeating rifles' cartridges so they would be competitive with similar single-shot cartridges. This one, reasonably popular, continued for almost 50 years. Rifles in this chambering are common and ammunition can be made by reforming 45-70 cases. Although groove diameter was typically 0.408-inch, original load bullets were 0.406-inch diameter.

40-65 Winchester Loading Data and Factory Ballistics

Bullet (grains/type)	Powder	Grains	Velocity	Energy	Source/Comments
260 Lead	IMR 4198	23.0	1500	1308	Lyman No. 403169
260 Lead	IMR 3031	44.0	1720	1708	NA
260 Lead	AA 5744	26.0	1651	1573	Accurate Arms
300 Lead	AA 5744	24.0	1515	1528	Accurate Arms
260 Lead	FL		1420	1165	Factory load

40-72 Winchester

Historical Notes Introduced for and with the Winchester Model 1895 lever-action, box-magazine repeater, the 40-72 was not very popular, but was loaded until 1936.

General Comments This cartridge uses a smaller diameter, 30-grain heavier bullet, compared to the much more powerful 405 Winchester. The latter was preferred by most purchasers of the Model 1895. Blackpowder cartridges of the 1890s suffered from competition with the newly introduced smokeless powder cartridges of that era. Most blackpowder cartridges introduced at that time had no chance to establish any degree of popularity. Although longer, this case has the same basic body as the 30-40 Krag. Because headspacing is on the rim, it may not be possible to safely use that case to make the 40-72, except for very low-pressure loads.

40-72 Winchester Loading Data and Factory Ballistics

Bullet (grains/type)	Powder	Grains	Velocity	Energy	Source/Comments
330 Lead	IMR 3031	40.0	1435	1510	Lyman No. 406150
300 Lead	FL		1425	1350	Winchester factory load
330 Lead	FL		1407	1451	Winchester factory load

40-82 Winchester

Historical Notes Introduced in 1885 for the Winchester single-shot and also available for the Model 1886 lever-action repeater, this cartridge was popular enough to make the transition into the smokeless powder era. It was loaded up to 1935.

General Comments The 40-82 WCF gained a favorable reputation on elk and heavy game. It developed a higher muzzle velocity than many other blackpowder cartridges, which made it easier to hit with over unknown distances. Despite the relative popularity, rifles in

this chambering are seldom encountered. Most of the original single-shots and Model 1886s have been rebarreled to some more modern chambering. It should be possible to convert the 45-70 case to work in these rifles, but the neck would be very short. The 45 Basic will make perfect cases. Although groove diameter was typically 0.408-inch, bullets used in original loads were only 0.406-inch diameter.

40-82 Winchester Loading Data and Factory Ballistics

Bullet (grains/type)	Powder	Grains	Velocity	Energy	Source/Comments
260 Lead	IMR 4198	28.0	1425	1180	Lyman No. 403169
260 Lead	FL		1490	1285	Winchester factory load

401 Winchester Self-Loading (401 WSL)

Historical Notes The 401 was introduced by Winchester in 1910 for its new Model 10 Autoloading rifle, which was a minor modification of the Model 1907. Both the cartridge and the rifle were discontinued in 1936, but the ammunition was loaded by most ammunition companies until after World War II. It is another obsolete "Self-Loading" cartridge.

General Comments The 401 is the most powerful of the Winchester Autoloading line, and the only one suitable for deer. The 401 found favor with many hunters as a quick, short-range number

for hunting deer and black bear. Velocity is too low and the trajectory too high for this to be a useful cartridge beyond about 150 yards. It can be reloaded, but like all cartridges used in semi-auto guns, it is necessary to stick to the factory ballistics or the rifle action may not function properly. Proper bullet diameter is 0.406-inch, but 0.410-inch revolver bullets can sometimes be used safely — verify chamber clearance. With a bit of lathe work, 35 Remington cases can be converted to work perfectly in 401 WSL chambered rifles.

401 Winchester Loading Data and Factory Ballistics

Bullet (grains/type)	Powder	Grains	Velocity	Energy	Source/Comments
200 SP	2400	24.7	1915	1625	Lyman
212 Lead	IMR 4227	29.0	2074	2025	Lyman
240 Lead	IMR 4227	27.5	1968	2150	Lyman
200 SP	FL		2135	2020	Winchester factory load
250 SP	FL		1870	1940	Winchester factory load

40-70 Peabody "What Cheer"

Historical Notes Made for the Peabody-Martini rifles (made by the Providence Tool Co.), this is one of a series of cartridges named for the "What Cheer" rifle range outside Providence, R.I., which opened in 1875. The first of the Peabody sporting and target rifles was said to have been exhibited at the opening celebration. The 40-70 cartridge actually was not introduced until 1877 or 1878. The Union Metallic Cartridge Co. loaded the round and so did Winchester.

General Comments This is an odd-shaped cartridge with a long, tapered shoulder and short body. Most samples have Berdan priming. Bullet diameter is 0.408-inch, but most nominal 0.406-inch bullets will cast sufficiently oversize to meet this diameter. This is not a common cartridge in collections, and rifles in this chambering are rare. For these low-pressure loads, 348 Winchester cases could be converted to work in this chamber.

40-70 Peabody "What Cheer" Loading Data and Factory Ballistics

Bullet (grains/type)	Powder	Grains	Velocity	Energy	Source/Comments
330 Lead	IMR 4198	22.0	1350	1340	Lyman No. 406150
380 Lead	FL		1420	1710	Factory load

40-90 Peabody "What Cheer"

Historical Notes This unusually shaped cartridge was for the Peabody-Martini Rifle No. 3, introduced in 1877-78. This rifle was a fancy model similar to the No. 2 "Creedmoor," but was designated the "What Cheer". This was in line with the Peabody policy of naming its rifles after famous target ranges of the day.

General Comments The 40-90 Peabody is a bottlenecked case similar to the other "What Cheer" cartridges. This was a popular match cartridge until the early 1900s. Proper bullet diameter is 0.408-inch. Cast bullets intended for the 405 Winchester can be sized down and used in this round. No one lists a mould for a 500-grain bullet for this cartridge. For these low-pressure loads, 348 Winchester cases could be converted to work in this chamber.

40-90 Peabody "What Cheer" Loading Data and Factory Ballistics

Bullet (grains/type)	Powder	Grains	Velocity	Energy	Source/Comments
330 Lead	IMR 4198	27.0	1450	1550	Lyman No. 406150
500 Lead	FL		1250	1735	Factory load

405 Winchester

Historical Notes The 405 is another of the rimmed cartridges developed for the Winchester Model 1895 lever-action rifle. Introduced in 1904, the rifle became obsolete in 1936 but has been reproduced recently in limited runs; most were chambered for cartridges that are somewhat more modern but one run was promised in 405. The Winchester single-shot also chambered the 405, and a number of double rifles were turned out in this chambering in England and Europe. The Remington-Lee bolt-action rifle was available in 405 caliber between 1904 and 1906. The old Eley-Kynoch catalog lists the 405 Winchester with a 300-grain softpoint bullet at standard factory-load velocity.

General Comments The 405 Winchester is the most powerful rimmed cartridge ever developed for the lever-action rifle. It is adequate for any North American big game at short- to medium-range and has been used successfully in Africa on all species. In the old Model 1895 Winchester, with its curved buttplate and poorly-designed stock, it had a reputation for punishing recoil. Theodore Roosevelt used the 405 in Africa and thought very highly of it as a lion cartridge. However, John Taylor in his excellent book, *African Rifles and Cartridges*, rates it as a poor choice compared to other available chamberings for African use. The short, fat, 300-grain round-nosed bullet loses velocity rapidly and lacks the sectional density necessary for deep penetration of heavy game. Nevertheless, it is quite adequate for any North American animals at ranges of 100 to 150 yards. Although longer, this case has the same basic body as the 30-40 Krag. However, because headspacing is on the rim, it is not possible to safely use that case to make 405s, except for very-low-pressure loads (which this editor has done). With modern jacketed pistol bullets, one can thus make perfectly adequate short-range deer loads. A-Square has recently reintroduced 405 ammunition. Buffalo Arms (208-263-6953) offers modified 30-40 cases that are the correct length and have a modified rim to give the correct headspace.

405 Winchester Loading Data and Factory Ballistics

Bullet (grains/type)	Powder	Grains	Velocity	Energy	Source/Comments
290 Cast	IMR 3031	40.0	1500	1449	Lyman No. 412263
300 SP	IMR 4895	56.0	2230	3321	NA
300 SP	IMR 3031	57.0	2250	3380	NA
300 SP	FL		2200	3220	Winchester factory load

40-75 Bullard

Historical Notes Introduced in 1887 for the Bullard lever-action repeating rifle and available for the single-shot, the 40-75 was the same case with a different bullet weight and powder charge as the 40-60 Bullard.

General Comments This is a big game cartridge similar in performance to the 40-60 Marlin or the 40-65 Winchester. Winchester's cartridge achieved the greatest popularity of these three. Proper diameter for a cast bullet is 0.413-inch, which is significantly larger than many of the other 40-caliber cartridges, which used a bullet of 0.403-inch diameter. The old Bullard catalog states that the 40-60 Marlin can be fired in guns of the above chambering. If so, then the 40-65 WCF could also be used, as it is the same case as the Marlin round. It should be possible to convert 45-70 cases to work in these rifles.

40-75 Bullard Loading Data and Factory Ballistics

Bullet (grains/type)	Powder	Grains	Velocity	Energy	Source/Comments
260 Lead	blackpowder (Fg)	75.0	1513	1315	Lyman No. 412174
260 Lead	IMR 4198	20.0	1500	1302	Lyman No. 412174
258 Lead	FL		1513	1315	Factory load

40-90 Bullard

Historical Notes This rather odd bottlenecked cartridge was developed for the Bullard single-shot and repeating rifles, introduced in 1886-87. Both Winchester and Remington manufactured this round for a number of years.

General Comments This is a rather large, fat cartridge with ballistics similar to other 40-caliber cartridges of the period such as the 40-82 Winchester. There was not a lot to choose from regarding performance between any of these. Cartridges designed by the big manufacturers for its rifles were more widely advertised and distributed, and consequently won the popularity race. Cartridges like the Bullard line gradually faded into the background. The 40-90 Bullard was undoubtedly an effective big game cartridge, particularly if the now-rare 400-grain loading was used. Considering the low-pressure loads used, it should be possible to convert 50-90 Sharps cases for safe use in rifles so chambered.

40-90 Bullard Loading Data and Factory Ballistics

Bullet (grains/type)	Powder	Grains	Velocity	Energy	Source/Comments
300 Lead	blackpowder (Fg)	90.0	1569	1648	Lyman No. 415175
300 Lead	IMR 4198	29.0	1450	1405	Lyman No. 415175
300 Lead	FL		1569	1648	Factory load

40-40 Maynard (1882)

Historical Notes A cartridge for the Maynard 1882 rifle, Improved Hunting or Target No. 9 and the Mid Range Target or Hunting No. 10, it was advertised as a combination hunting and target cartridge.

General Comments In performance, the 40-40 is similar to the 44-40 WCF. Maynard made only two bullet weights in 40-caliber; the 330-grain was intended for the longer 40-60, but was sometimes used in the 40-40. Bullet diameter of these cartridges is not the same as the 0.403-inch of most Sharps and Winchester cartridges. The Maynard Co. sold moulds or factory-made bullets for its rifles. The 40-caliber Maynard bore is usually 0.415- to 0.417-inch diameter. It should be possible to convert 303 British cases to work in these rifles.

40-40 Maynard 1882 Loading Data and Factory Ballistics

Bullet (grains/type)	Powder	Grains	Velocity	Energy	Source/Comments
260 Lead	IMR 4198	24.0	1400	1140	Lyman No. 413174
270 Lead	FL		1425	1222	Factory load
330 Lead	FL		1260	1168	Factory load

40-60 Maynard (1882)

Historical Notes This is an intermediate-range match cartridge for the 1882 Maynard Models 10, 12 and 13 Hunting and the Models 15-16 Target rifles. It does not use the same case as the longer 40-70 Maynard.

General Comments The 40-60 Maynard is an elongated version of the 40-40 and differs mainly in the longer case length. Unfortunately, it duplicated the performance of similar Marlin, Sharps and Winchester cartridges, and for that reason, it did not become popular or widely used. It should be possible to convert 303 British cases to work in these rifles.

40-60 Maynard 1882 Loading Data and Factory Ballistics

Bullet (grains/type)	Powder	Grains	Velocity	Energy	Source/Comments
300 Lead	IMR 4198	26.0	1370	1248	Lyman No. 413175
330 Lead	FL		1370	1380	Factory load

40-70 Maynard (1882)

Historical Notes This has the longest case of the three 40-caliber cartridges chambered in the 1882-type Maynard single-shot rifle, which was available in both target and hunting models.

General Comments Some publications show the 40-70 Maynard to be the same as the 40-60, but with a different load. Others indicate that it is identical except for length. Actually, it has a little longer case (0.21-inch) with a slightly larger rim and base diameter. The 40-60 can be fired in a 40-70 chamber, but the reverse is not true. In overall length, this is the shorter of the two cartridges because of the lighter bullet seated farther down in the case. This is more of a hunting cartridge, although it was also available in the target rifle models. It should be possible to convert 303 British cases to work in these rifles.

40-70 Maynard (1882) Loading Data and Factory Ballistics

Bullet (grains/type)	Powder	Grains	Velocity	Energy	Source/Comments
260 Lead	IMR 4198	27.0	1450	1211	Lyman No. 413174
270 Lead	FL		1645	1620	Factory load

44 Evans Short

Historical Notes This is the cartridge for the various Old Model Evans rifles introduced in 1875. Winchester loaded the ammunition until the early 1920s.

General Comments The Evans rifle was designed for military use, but when it was turned down by the U.S. Ordnance Department, it was manufactured as a sporting number. The Evans had a magazine capacity of 34 cartridges held in the four-column tubular magazine located in the butt. This was an odd-looking lever-action rifle. Evans rifles were once somewhat common items and box lots of ammunition could be purchased until 1940-41. This is not a particularly strong action, so only use blackpowder loads. A load of 28 grains of Fg or FFg was used in the original round. Cases can be made by cutting off 303 Savage cases and perhaps thinning the rim, as required. (As in similar rim-thinning situations, pistol primers may have to be used, but those work well in most blackpowder or blackpowder pressure loads anyway.) Also, either the case mouth must be thinned or an undersized bullet must be used to provide adequate case-neck to chamber-wall clearance.

44 Evans Short Factory Ballistics

Bullet (grains/type)	Powder	Grains	Velocity	Energy	Source/Comments
215 Lead	FL		850	350	Winchester factory load

44 Evans Long

Historical Notes The 44 Evans Long was developed for the 1877 New Model Evans sporting rifle. It is sometimes referred to as the 44-40 Straight or the 44-40-300 because of its different loadings.

General Comments The New Model Evans rifle was similar to the Old Model except for the change to a longer, more powerful cartridge. The magazine capacity was only (!) 26 rounds compared to 34 for the Old Model. Again, this is not a strong action, so it is advisable to use only blackpowder loads. The cartridge was loaded with 275- to 300-grain bullets and 40 to 43 grains of blackpowder. Although this case is somewhat larger in diameter, usable cases might be made by cutting off 303 Savage cases as with the Henry Center Fire Flat. As with all similar numbers, it is best to load only with blackpowder or Pyrodex. Also, either the case mouth must be thinned or an undersized bullet must be used to provide adequate case-neck to chamber-wall clearance.

44 Evans Long Factory Ballistics

Bullet (grains/type)	Powder	Grains	Velocity	Energy	Source/Comments
280 Lead	FL		200	903	Factory load

44 Henry Center Fire Flat

Historical Notes This is a centerfire version of the rimfire 44 Henry Flat. In 1891, 1020 M1866 Winchester rifles wee chambered for this cartridge and shipped to Brazil.

General Comments Rifles for this cartridge are extremely rare. The 1866 Henry rifle was not very strong. Those who want to shoot one of these should stick to blackpowder. The proper charge is 26 or 28 grains of FFg or FFFg. Cast bullets for the 44-40 WCF can be used. Cases can be made by cutting off 303 Savage cases and, perhaps thinning the rim, as required. (As in similar rim thinning situations, pistol primers may have to be used, but these are preferable in almost every blackpowder or blackpowder pressure load anyway.)

44 Henry Factory Ballistics

Bullet (grains/type)	Powder	Grains	Velocity	Energy	Source/Comments
200 Lead	FL		1150	594	Factory load
227 Lead	FL		1200	725	Factory load

44 Game Getter
44-40 Marlin
44 Colt Lightning

Historical Notes In 1908, Marble Arms Corp. introduced its Game Getter, a double-barrel, over/under pistol with a removable skeleton buttstock. The upper barrel was rifled and chambered for the 22 rimfire cartridge; the lower barrel was smoothbore and chambered for the 44 Shot cartridge. The introduction of this pistol bolstered the popularity of the several varieties of 44 Shot cartridges.

The Stevens Model 101 "Featherweight" rifle (1914-16) was chambered for this cartridge as well as the 44 XL and 44 WCF shot cartridges. The 44 WCF Shot cartridge was a crimped case with cardboard wadding; others were loaded with a wood or paper "bullet" that enclosed the shot. The Marble catalog of 1914 stated, "Shot cartridges with paper or wooden ends are especially adapted to rifled barrels. However, they can be used in the Game Getter, but give uncertain results." UMC loaded a 44 Round Ball cartridge before the introduction of the Game Getter, using 34 grains of blackpowder and a 115-grain round lead ball. This combination of gun and cartridge became very popular and Winchester and U.S. Ammunition Co. began to offer it, calling it the 44 Game Getter.

General Comments The 44-40 is, of course, still loaded today, but during its life span as a blackpowder cartridge (and the early smokeless powder days) it was available in a variety of loads that are now obsolete.

The standard load of 40 grains of blackpowder and a 200-grain bullet of the 44 WCF was altered slightly (a 217-grain bullet was used) and the resulting cartridge was called the 44-40 Marlin or the 44 Colt Lightning Magazine Rifle. All are nothing more than load variations on the standard 44-40 Winchester – some rifles may require shorter overall cartridge lengths.

Also obsolete today are the high-velocity smokeless powder loads that were offered for rifles with stronger actions.

44-40 Extra Long

General Comments The 44-40 Extra Long is listed in various publications and sample rounds are common. It has a longer body and neck than the standard 44-40 WCF. The author was unable to find any record indicating the gun for which this cartridge was designed. It is listed so the reader will not confuse it with the straight Ballard or Wesson Extra Long 44 cartridges. These are not the same. Some believe this is the 44-40 shot case with a conical bullet. According to William R. Small of Ojo Caliente, N.M., the Stevens Model 101 "Featherweight" rifle (1914 to 1916) chambered this round as well as the 44 XL and 44 WCF shot cartridges. Cases can be made by shortening and necking 444 Marlin cases.

44 Long Center Fire (Ballard)

Historical Notes The 44 Long CF, was introduced in 1875-76 as one of the chamberings for the J.M. Marlin Ballard Sporting Rifle No. 2. It was also used in a number of other single-shot rifles, including those of Frank Wesson. It was replaced by the 44 Extra Long CF, before both were phased out by the more popular 44-40 WCF. It is the centerfire equivalent of the 44 Long rimfire.

General Comments This is a more-or-less transitional cartridge from the rimfire to the better centerfires. Most early breech-loading rifles were developed for rimfire cartridges and it was a simple matter to bring out a similar centerfire for the same basic rifle. This allowed the shooter to reload; however, most of these cartridges were no more effective than the rimfire they replaced and so these did not last long. The original load used 35 grains of blackpowder and a 227-grain bullet. Muzzle velocity was low — only about 1,100 to 1,200 fps. As with the 44 Evans Long, Short or Henry Flat Center Fire, cases can be made by cutting off 303 Savage cases, but stick to blackpowder and cast bullets.

44 Extra Long Center Fire (Ballard)

Historical Notes This cartridge is sometimes listed simply as the 44 Extra Long. It is a straight case and is the centerfire version of the 44 Rimfire Extra Long. As near as can be determined, it was introduced in 1876 for the J.M. Marlin Ballard Sporting Rifle No. 2. It was only available for a few years, before being replaced in the Ballard rifles by the 44-40 WCF. Rifles in this chambering are rare today.

General Comments The 44 Extra Long was not a popular Ballard number because there were too many better 44-caliber cartridges available. The 44-40 WCF was already popular by the time the Ballard round hit the market and the 44 Extra Long was available only in the single-shot. It did, however, provide a reloadable case for those used to the 44 EL rimfire, and quite a few of the old rimfire rifles were probably converted to use the centerfire type. Remington loaded this with 50 grains of blackpowder and a 265-grain bullet. Cases can be made by cutting off 303 Savage cases as mentioned in the discussion about the 44 Henry Flat Center Fire.

44 Extra Long (Ballard) Factory Ballistics

Bullet (grains/type)	Powder	Grains	Velocity	Energy	Source/Comments
265 Lead	FL		1320	1030	Remington factory load

44 Wesson Extra Long

Historical Notes Made for the Frank Wesson tip-up rifles, this cartridge appears to be identical to the 44 Extra Long Ballard except for the shape of the bullet. The Wesson bullet shows two grease grooves when loaded in the case, while the Ballard shows only one.

General Comments Many of the Wesson tip-up rifles were furnished with a patented adjustable hammer, permitting the use of both rim- and centerfire cartridges. Lyman No. 419182 (240-grain) or 424100 (170-grain) bullets can be adapted to this cartridge. Original load used 48 to 50 grains of blackpowder. Wesson rifles in this chambering are very rare. As discussed with the 44 Henry Flat Center Fire, cases can be made by cutting off 303 Savage cases.

44 Wesson Extra Long Factory Ballistics

Bullet (grains/type)	Powder	Grains	Velocity	Energy	Source/Comments
250-257 Lead	FL		1340	1010	Factory load

44-90 Remington Special (Necked)

Historical Notes The 44-90 Remington Special looks like the 44-90 Sharps, but on closer inspection it has a shorter case with slightly larger body diameter so these are not interchangeable. The 40-90 was introduced as a match cartridge for the Remington rolling block Creedmoor series in 1873. Remington catalogs listed empty cases and bullets for this cartridge as late as 1910.

General Comments The 44-77 Sharps had a 2 1/4-inch case, the 44-90 Sharps a 2 5/8-inch case. The 44-90 Remington Special case was 2 7/16-inch or 2.44-inch long. The Remington cartridge was regularly loaded with a 550-grain patched or lubricated lead bullet, which is heavier than the normal bullet used in Sharps cartridges. Remington probably designed its 44-90 so a heavy bullet and 90 grains of powder could be used without increasing the overall length of the cartridge. The loaded length is actually less than the similar Sharps cartridges. This is primarily a match cartridge, but would also be effective on almost any big game. Lighter bullets and more powder could be used to increase blackpowder ballistics for hunting. The only safe source of cases (those that have been extensively modified from 348 Winchester size) is Buffalo Arms (208-263-6953).

44-90 Remington Special Loading Data and Factory Ballistics

Bullet (grains/type)	Powder	Grains	Velocity	Energy	Source/Comments
470 Lead	IMR 4198	30.0	1270	1688	Lyman No. 446187
470 Lead PP	blackpowder (Fg)	90.0			Factory load, early paper patch
550 Lead	blackpowder (Fg)	90.0	1250	1812	Remington factory load

44-100 Remington "Creedmoor" /44-90 Remington Straight

Historical Notes The 44-100 cartridge was for the Remington-Hepburn or No. 3 Long-Range Creedmoor rifle. It was introduced in 1880. This special 2 6/10-inch shell had various loadings and bullets plus the usual variety of designations for the same round. As if to add more confusion, a 2 4/10-inch version was also made. This may have been designed to furnish a straight case as an alternative to some of the necked Sharps 44 cartridges.

General Comments Also known as the 44-2 6/10-inch and 44-90 Remington Straight, this was designed as a match cartridge for long-range shooting out to 1,000 and even 1,400 yards. It was moderately popular, but rifles in this chambering are scarce. The cartridge is a collector's item. Remington manufactured a number of match rifles designated "Creedmoor," and this is the correct spelling of the Creedmoor, Long Island rifle range. However, the company also made various cartridges under the "Creedmore" label (note the different spelling). Ammunition so designated had a target-type bullet and very often was intended for rifles that the manufacturer had never called "Creedmoor." This has caused much confusion, although Remington changed the spelling to try to prevent it. Both Remington and Winchester furnished empty cases and bullets for handloading. Cases can be converted from the 45 Basic.

44-100 Remington "Creedmoor" Loading Data and Factory Ballistics

Bullet (grains/type)	Powder	Grains	Velocity	Energy	Source/Comments
470 Lead	IMR 4198	27.0	1410	2080	Lyman No. 446187
520 Lead	FL		1435	2380	Remington factory load
550 Lead	FL		1380	2338	Remington factory load

44-95 Peabody "What Cheer"

Historical Notes The 44-95 Peabody also had a 100-grain loading and was occasionally referred to as the 44-100 Peabody. It is the largest of the Peabody "What Cheer" cartridges. It was the original chambering for the Peabody-Martini Long-Range Creedmoor Rifle. The straight stock version was the No. 3 "What Cheer" and eventually the cartridge was given this name. Some authorities say it was introduced in 1877, but it may have made its debut as early as 1875. It was popular primarily as a target round.

General Comments Peabody and Peabody-Martini rifles were manufactured by the Providence Tool Co. of Providence, R.I. The action was patented by H.L. Peabody of Boston, Mass., in 1862. Peabody-Martini military rifles were manufactured for the Turkish government during 1873 and something like 600,000 were delivered. The original Peabody pivoting block action had a side-hammer, but the Swiss Martini modification did away with this, employing an internal lock. The British Martini-Henry rifle is based on this modified American design. This is one of the strongest of the old single-shot actions.

44-95 Peabody "What Cheer" Loading Data and Factory Ballistics

Bullet (grains/type)	Powder	Grains	Velocity	Energy	Source/Comments
470 Lead	blackpowder (Fg)	100.0	1380	1990	Lyman No. 446187
470 Lead	IMR 4759	21.0	1380	1990	Lyman No. 446187
550 Lead	FL		1310	2100	Factory load

44-70 Maynard (1882)

Historical Notes Introduced for the 1882-type Maynard single-shot rifle, the 44-70 was also available for the Hunters Model No. 11 and the Creedmoor No. 14 match rifle.

General Comments The 44-70 Maynard is a 44-caliber version of the popular 45-70 Government military round. Many riflemen of

the late 1880s preferred the 44-caliber over the larger 45 bore, although there is little difference in bore dimensions. The Maynard company furnished a 430-grain bullet for hunting and general shooting and a 520-grain for target work. Although somewhat too short, 45-70 cases will work in these rifles.

44-70 Maynard (1882) Loading Data and Factory Ballistics

Bullet (grains/type)	Powder	Grains	Velocity	Energy	Source/Comments
470 Lead	IMR 4198	26.0	1300	1768	Lyman No. 446187
430 Lead	FL		1310	1640	Factory load

44-75 Ballard Everlasting

Historical Notes The 44-75 is one of the rarer Ballard cases. Seldom found in collections and not mentioned in most cartridge books, L.D. Satterlee * lists it as available for the J.M. Marlin Ballard Perfection No. 4, Pacific No. 5 and Schuetzen No. 6, all introduced in 1876. He gives case length as 2 1/4-inch.† This chambering is not listed in the Marlin Fire Arms Co. after Marlin began making Ballard rifles in 1881. James J. Grant ** says this was one of the special Marlin Everlasting cases using the shallow Berdan-type No. 2 primer similar to the 40-65. He also has specimens using Large Rifle primers.

General Comments The 44-75-2 1/2-inch can be made by trimming and sizing Sharps 45-2 6/10-inch cases. This must have been intended as both a target and hunting cartridge since it was

available in rifles of both types. Marlin and Ballard catalogs listed a patched 405-grain, 44-caliber bullet, which was probably one of the weights used in the 44-75. Bullets for 44-caliber Sharps cartridges of 0.446-inch diameter can be adapted to the 44-75 Ballard. No factory ballistics are available, so it is probable that only empty cases and bullets were furnished.

---

*op. cit.
**More Single Shot Rifles (New York, 1959).
†John T. Amber owned a fine No. 7 Ballard in 44-75 chambering, complete in case with hunting and target sights, etc., and including a score or more of cases. All were 2 1/2 inches long, not 2 1/4 inches, and were Berdan-primed Everlasting type.

44-100 Ballard

Historical Notes The 44-100 Ballard Everlasting was one of the chamberings introduced with the various J.M. Marlin Ballard rifles. It is first listed for the 1876 Model Pacific No. 5 and Long Range No. 7A. It was discontinued about 1880 and does not appear as a standard chambering in later Marlin Fire Arms Co. catalogs. However, the 1888 Marlin & Ballard catalog again lists brass shells under obsolete sizes at 12 cents each. The 45-100 Ballard, which came out later, is based on this same case with the neck reamed out to accept the larger-diameter bullet.

General Comments This is another rare Ballard cartridge. It was an accurate target number and had considerable knockdown power for big game. Ballard rifles were manufactured by several companies. The best known of these were made by the Marlin Fire Arms Co. after it was incorporated in 1881. Most of its models and

cartridges are not particularly scarce. John M. Marlin organized the Marlin Fire Arms Co., but prior to that, he turned out Ballard rifles under the name of J.M. Marlin (1875 to 1881). The first Ballard arms were for rimfire cartridges, and these were introduced by Ball & Williams in 1861, and continued until 1866 under its brand. From 1866 to 1869, these were made by Merrimack Arms & Manufacturing Co., and from 1869 to 1873 by Brown Manufacturing Co. Some of these early models and cartridges are rare and valuable. Although the 44-100 Ballard is larger and somewhat longer in diameter, it might be possible to form 45-70 cases to work in these rifles. Basic 45s could be cut to the proper length. In either case, one might have to turn down the rim to fit the chamber.

44-100 Ballard Loading Data and Factory Ballistics

Bullet (grains/type)	Powder	Grains	Velocity	Energy	Source/Comments
365 Lead	blackpowder (Fg)	110.0	1500	1830	Lyman No. 446109
365 Lead	IMR 4198	26.0	1350	1480	Lyman No. 446109
535 Lead	FL		1400	2328	Factory load

44-100 Wesson

Historical Notes As with the 44-85 Wesson, this one was found on a U.S. Cartridge Co. advertising sheet printed in 1881-82. This is also a straight case with the length listed as 3-3/8 inches. The bullet is seated deeply so the total length of the loaded cartridge is 3-9/10 inches. The load is given as 100 or 120 grains of blackpowder with a 550-grain, paper-patched bullet.

General Comments What date and what rifle? There is no information given on this. As previously stated, all 44-caliber Sharps cartridges are necked, and perhaps this is intended as the

straight case counter to the necked 44-100 or 105 (2 5/8-inch) Sharps. This is speculation, but many shooters of this period did prefer the straight case. The 44-100 Wesson is not listed in any previous cartridge book, and now that its existence has been brought to the attention of collectors, additional information may be forthcoming. Muzzle velocity of this combination would be approximately 1350 to 1400 fps, depending on charge, barrel length, etc.

44-77 Sharps & Remington

Historical Notes This is the 2 1/4-inch Sharps bottlenecked case introduced in 1869 for the Model 1869 Sharps breech-loading sporting rifle. It was also one of the chamberings available for the Remington-Hepburn or No. 3. It was a popular target round, used more for this purpose than hunting. The design of the 44-77 is said to have been based on a combination of the 42 Russian and the 43 Spanish military cartridges.

General Comments A variety of factory loadings were turned out for the 44-77, with bullet weights from 300 grains to 470 grains. It is sometimes listed as the 44-70 or 44-75, depending on the powder charge used. Remington made an unusual two-piece reloadable case with a steel head and brass body.

44-77 Sharps & Remington Loading Data and Factory Ballistics

Bullet (grains/type)	Powder	Grains	Velocity	Energy	Source/Comments
365 Lead	IMR 4198	28.0	1480	1782	Lyman No. 446109
470 Lead PP	blackpowder (Fg)	77.0			Factory load, early paper patch
365 Lead	FL		1460	1730	Factory load

44-85 Wesson

Historical Notes The 44-85 Wesson is another of the mysterious and little-known Wesson cartridges. The little information available was gathered from a United States Cartridge Co. (U.S.C.C.) advertising sheet printed in 1881-82. The 44-85 is a straight case with a length of 2 7/8 inches. All 44-caliber Sharps cartridges were necked, so it is not similar to any of those. There is nothing to indicate which Wesson rifle it was for, but with that length, it was probably meant for the Creedmoor models.

General Comments It is well to point out that during the late 1800s, many riflemen did not like bottlenecked cases. It may be that Frank Wesson introduced this cartridge because all the Sharps 44 cases were necked and some individuals wanted the same performance in a straight case. The U.S.C.C. load had a 390-grain patched bullet backed by 85 grains of Fg blackpowder. This would have developed a muzzle velocity of approximately 1,450 fps in the average rifle.

44-85 Wesson Factory Ballistics

Bullet (grains/type)	Powder	Grains	Velocity	Energy	Source/Comments
390 Lead	blackpowder (Fg)	85.0	1450	1821	Factory load

44-90 Sharps Necked (44-100 Sharps 2-5/8"/ 44-105 Sharp Necked)

Historical Notes This is the 44-90 Sharps 2 5/8-inch case of larger capacity than the 44-77 Sharps. It was the chambering for the Sharps 1873 Creedmoor rifle made by the old Sharps Rifle Manufacturing Co., before its reorganization in 1875-76, and was chambered in later side-hammer models. Advertisements list it as early as June of 1873. Sharps rifles of 44 caliber were discontinued during 1878 in favor of the more popular 45 caliber.

General Comments These are just different loadings and bullet weights. Ammunition was available with bullets weighing 277, 450, 470, 500 and 520 grains. It was not as popular for hunting as some of the other Sharps chamberings, but was used for 1,000-yard match shooting. A version with a 0.19-inch shorter case also existed. Both are listed in the 1910 Winchester catalog. The only safe source of cases is Buffalo Arms — They extensively modify 348 Winchester cases to properly fit these chambers (208-263-6953).

44-90 Sharps (Necked) Loading Data and Factory Ballistics

Bullet (grains/type)	Powder	Grains	Velocity	Energy	Source/Comments
470 Lead	IMR 4198	28.0	1300	1630	Lyman No. 446187
520 Lead	FL		1270	1860	Factory load

44-60 Sharps & Remington (Necked)

Historical Notes This 1 7/8-inch 44 case was loaded by Remington and Winchester. It was introduced in 1869 for the 1869 Sporting Rifle and used in Sharps, Winchester and Remington single-shot rifles.

General Comments This was a general purpose cartridge for hunting or target shooting. It was listed by Remington and labeled as one of its "Creedmore" types (note the difference in spelling), which has caused some confusion identifying the round. Sharps match rifles for long-range shooting were named after the famous range at Creedmoor, Long Island. Other rifle makers also used this name. Remington applied the name to cartridges not originally chambered in the Sharps Creedmoor line. It is interesting to compare this cartridge with the 42 Russian Berdan Carbine round. Except for bullet diameter, the two are practically identical. This suggests the possibility that the 44-60 was developed by expanding the neck of the Russian Carbine cartridge, much as some modern wildcats are made. The 44-60 necked Peabody, Winchester, Remington, etc. appear to be the same as the 44-60 (1 7/8-inch) Sharps cartridge.

44-60 Sharps (Necked) Loading Data and Factory Ballistics

Bullet (grains/type)	Powder	Grains	Velocity	Energy	Source/Comments
315 Lead	IMR 4198	24.0	1300	1188	Lyman No. 446110
396 Lead	FL		1250	1375	Factory load

45-50 Peabody (Sporting)

Historical Notes A sporting cartridge for the Peabody-Martini single-shot rifle, the 45-50 was introduced in 1873-74, shortly after the Martini modification of the Peabody action was adopted.

General Comments The 45-50 bears a close resemblance to the Peabody 45-55 Turkish carbine cartridge. It is probable that it is a modification of the Turkish military round, adapted to sporting use. Physical measurements of the two are not identical, but very close. This is a rare cartridge and rifles in this chambering are seldom encountered. Almost any 45-caliber rifle bullet can be sized down to

0.454-inch diameter and used; the Lyman No. 456191 (300-grain) will work fine. Powder charge can be varied from 50 to 55 grains of Fg blackpowder, depending on bullet weight and seating depth. For smokeless powder loads, use 22 to 23 grains of Du Pont (IMR) 4198. This will more-or-less duplicate original blackpowder ballistics. It could be possible to cut and form 45-70 cases to work in these rifles. This is one of the few Peabody designs that is close enough to common current chamberings to offer hope of conveniently shooting the rifle chambered for it.

45-50 Peabody (Sporting) Loading Data and Factory Ballistics

Bullet (grains/type)	Powder	Grains	Velocity	Energy	Source/Comments
255 Lead	IMR 4198	25.0	1350	1080	Lyman No. 454190
300 Lead	blackpowder (Fg)	50.0	1285	1080	Lyman No. 456191
290 Lead	FL		1295	1085	Factory load

44-60 Winchester
44-60 Peabody "Creedmoor"

Historical Notes This cartridge is for the Peabody-Martini "Creedmoor" rifle introduced in 1877-78. It is not a well-known cartridge and apparently was of limited popularity. Winchester loaded this round under its own name, which it introduced in 1874-75. This is the same as the Sharps 44-60-1 7/8-inch necked cartridge.

General Comments Examination of these cartridges in comparison with the 42 Russian Carbine indicates they are identical except for neck and bullet diameter. The 44-60 was likely developed by expanding the neck of the Russian cartridge, very much as some of our modern wildcats are made. The Russian Carbine cartridge is a shortened version of the 42 Berdan.

44-60 Peabody "Creedmoor" Loading Data and Factory Ballistics

Bullet (grains/type)	Powder	Grains	Velocity	Energy	Source/Comments
365 Lead	blackpowder (Fg)	65.0	1280	1410	Lyman No. 446109
395 Lead	FL		1250	1375	Winchester factory load

45 Remington Thompson

Historical Notes This cartridge was developed for use in the Thompson M-1923 "Military Model" submachinegun. While this cartridge has been described as a stretched 45 Automatic, this is not precisely correct. Both case and bullet diameter are smaller than in the 45 Automatic (0.472- versus 0.476-inch and 0.447- versus 0.451-inch, respectively). The sample cartridge is headstamped "REM-UMC" over "45 ACP." Development was in 1923 as a joint venture of Remington Arms and Auto Ordnance Corp. Intended application was a long-barreled version of the Thompson that could

provide significantly improved ballistics over the standard 45 Automatic-chambered versions.

General Comments When one considers that this number generated ballistics exceeding any standard 44 Magnum factory loading fired from a pistol, this was, indeed, a significant ballistic improvement, compared to the 45 Automatic. However, it seems likely that the Thompson, despite its significant weight and good design, must have been something of a handful when firing such loads fully automatic.

45 Remington Thompson

Bullet (grains/type)	Powder	Grains	Velocity	Energy	Source/Comments
250	FL		1450	1165	Factory load

45-60 Winchester

Historical Notes The 45-60 is one of several cartridges designed for the Winchester 1876 Centennial Model rifle. The 45-60 cartridge was introduced in 1879. Winchester continued production of this cartridge until 1935, although the rifle was discontinued in 1897. The Kennedy lever-action repeating rifle used this cartridge, as did the Colt Lightning pump-action repeater.

General Comments The 45-60 was brought out, with others of the Model 1876 cartridge line, to provide greater power than the 44-40

and other short cartridges used in the Model 1873 Winchester. The 45-60 design was probably influenced by the 45-70 Government round. The Model 1876 rifle had a medium-length action that would not handle the long cartridges used in the single-shots of the period. The 45-60 would be a better deer cartridge than the 44 WCF, but would not be suitable for larger game. Rifles for this cartridge are not strong, so one should not attempt to exceed original ballistics. It should be easy to form 45-70 cases to work in these rifles.

45-60 Winchester Loading Data and Factory Ballistics

Bullet (grains/type)	Powder	Grains	Velocity	Energy	Source/Comments
300 Lead	IMR 4198	25.0	1450	1410	Lyman No. 456191
300 Lead	FL		1315	1152	Winchester factory load

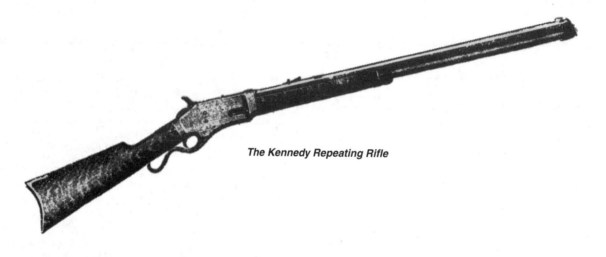

The Kennedy Repeating Rifle

45-75 Winchester (Centennial)

Historical Notes The 45-75 Winchester was the original chambering for the Model 1876 Centennial rifle. Other chamberings were added later. The Kennedy repeating rifle also used this round. Winchester continued to produce this cartridge until 1935. The Canadian Northwest Mounted Police adopted the '76 Winchester in 45-75 chambering and used it for 27 years.

General Comments To compete with the big Sharps and other single-shot cartridges, Winchester needed a longer repeating action. The Model 76 was designed to fill that need. However, as

produced it was not long enough to handle cartridges with an overall length exceeding 2 1/4 inches. The 45-75 gives performance equal to, or slightly better than, the 45-70 Government by use of a shorter, fatter, bottlenecked case. The Model 76 action is not noted for great strength and heavy smokeless powder charges should be avoided. The 45-75 would be a good short-range deer or black bear cartridge by modern standards. It was favored by Theodore Roosevelt for grizzly bear. Usable cases can be made from 348 Winchester cases.

45-75 Winchester Loading Data and Factory Ballistics

Bullet (grains/type)	Powder	Grains	Velocity	Energy	Source/Comments
350 Lead	IMR 4198	24.0	1380	1480	Lyman No. 456192
350 Lead	FL		1383	1485	Factory load

45-100 Ballard

Historical Notes Satterlee * indicates that this cartridge was introduced in 1878 with the Ballard Sporting No. 4-1/2 rifle. However, Grant first shows it with the 1882 (Marlin Fire Arms Co.) Pacific No. 5. Manufacture of Ballard single-shot rifles was discontinued between 1888 and 1890. The 45-100 cartridge was still listed as a standard chambering in the 1888 Marlin & Ballard catalog. This was the last catalog that advertised the Ballard, according to some authorities.

General Comments The 45-100 is not a common cartridge, although it was available up to the time Ballard rifles were discontinued. It is the same case as the 44-100 Ballard, but the inside of the neck was reamed, to accommodate the larger 45-caliber bullet. Almost any 45-caliber lead rifle bullet can be sized to

fit this case. The company offered 45-caliber bullets in 285, 405, 420, and 550 grains for loading this and other cartridges. Lighter bullets left room for up to 120 grains of blackpowder. This was used as both a target and hunting round and was equal in power to some of the big Sharps and Winchester cartridges of similar capacity. The old Ballard action is not particularly strong and caution is advised when using smokeless powder. Although the base is a bit smaller than the 45-70, one suspects usable cases could be made from 45-70 cases. If so, Basic 45 cases could be cut to the proper length to duplicate this cartridge, which is very similar to the 45-90 Winchester, only longer.

*op. cit.

45-100 Ballard Loading Data and Factory Ballistics

Bullet (grains/type)	Powder	Grains	Velocity	Energy	Source/Comments
500 Lead	blackpowder (Fg)	100.0	1400	2180	Lyman No. 457125
500 Lead	IMR 4198	22.0	1250	1740	Lyman No. 457125
550 Lead	FL		1370	2300	Factory load

Ballard No. 5 Pacific Rifle

45-125 Winchester (45 Express)

Historical Notes Introduced in 1886 as a special-order chambering for the Winchester single-shot rifle, the 45-125 was not widely used and was discontinued after a few years. Winchester continued to load this ammunition until 1916.

General Comments The 45-125 has a long bottlenecked case and was furnished with the 300-grain copper-tubed, "Express" bullet. Lyman No. 456191 is the proper bullet for reloading. In

appearance, this cartridge resembles the British 500/465 Nitro, but they are not the same and can be distinguished by head markings, bullet diameter, etc. This is a powerful blackpowder number and would do for most big game in North America. One reason it became obsolete is that the 45-90 WCF will do the same thing with a smaller case and less powder.

45-125 Winchester Loading Data and Factory Ballistics

Bullet (grains/type)	Powder	Grains	Velocity	Energy	Source/Comments
300 Lead	IMR 4198	35.0	1475	1456	Lyman No. 456191
300 SP	FL		1690	1903	Winchester factory load

45-70 Van Choate

Historical Notes This cartridge was originally designed for the experimental Van Choate military bolt-action rifle made by the Brown Manufacturing Co. in 1872. It is similar to the 45-70 Government, but has a case length of 2-1/4 inches instead of 2-1/10 inches. It was used in other rifles as well because it was listed in Remington and Winchester catalogs as late as 1910-12. The paper patched bullet weighed 420 grains.

General Comments There are a number of variations of the basic 45-70 Government cartridge. Most of these vary by bullet weight, but a few use a different case length. One of these was the 45-78-475 Wolcott with a 2.31-inch case. There was also a 45-80 Sharpshooter cartridge that was used in special target rifles. This had a 2 4/10-inch case that was very similar, if not identical, to the Sharps 2 4/10-inch case. Although these cartridges are identical in all dimensions except length, a rifle would have to be chambered to accept the extra-long case, so these would not be interchangeable. Just what the originators hoped to gain from these variations is hard to imagine. It was probably done to allow a full or increased powder charge with a heavier or longer-than-standard bullet. Most of these variations have an odd-shaped bullet. For any of these, one can use the same bullets and loading data given with the 45-70. Standard 45-70 cases chamber in these rifles. To duplicate the original case, trim Basic 45s to the proper length.

45-75 Sharps (Straight)
45-70 Sharps 2 1/10"

Historical Notes This cartridge is identical to the 45-70 Government. It represents another instance of a manufacturer adding his name to a cartridge when chambered for his rifles. Also known as the 45-70 Sharps, it was added to the company product line early to mid-1875. It was one of the loadings of what was designated as the Sharps 45-2 1/10-inch case.

General Comments Use the same loading data as that given for the 45-70 Government. Most original Sharps rifles have blackpowder steel barrels so it is advisable to stick to lead bullets to reduce wear on the bore. Any load safe for the 1873 "Trapdoor" Springfield will be OK in Sharps rifles of any vintage.

45-75 Sharps (Straight) Factory Ballistics

Bullet (grains/type)	Powder	Grains	Velocity	Energy	Source/Comments
400 Lead	FL		1330	1580	Factory load

45-100 Remington (Necked)

Historical Notes The 45-100 Remington necked cartridge is listed in the 1880-81 United States Cartridge Co. advertising sheet. It must have been a special-order chambering for Remington single-shot rifles because there are no references to it concerning a specific rifle. It was also available as a special order item for some of the late Sharps rifles, for it is listed in the 1875 Sharps catalog as the 45-2 1/4-inch case.

General Comments The 45-100 Remington uses a 2 5/8-inch necked case, which appears to be identical to the 44-90 Remington except for the larger diameter and longer neck. As we have mentioned before, some shooters liked the straight case, while others preferred the necked case. All Sharps 45-caliber cases are straight. Perhaps Remington offered a choice to the man who wanted a necked 45-caliber cartridge. Since the U.S. Cartridge Co. shows this as loaded ammunition, at least a moderate demand must have existed. Although shorter, 348 Winchester cases can be modified for use in these rifles.

Sharps Model 1877 Rifle

45-82 Winchester
45-85 Winchester
45-90 Winchester
45-90 Winchester High Velocity

Historical Notes These designations are often listed separately, giving different case dimensions. However, these are nothing more than different loads and bullet weights in the same basic 45-90 case. All loads were for the Winchester Model 1886 repeater or the 1885 single-shot. The 45-90 was introduced in 1886. The other loads followed. The Marlin Model 1895 was also chambered for the group. The smokeless powder 45-90 came out in 1895 and was discontinued about 1936.

General Comments For many decades after its introduction, the 45-90 was a popular sporting cartridge. Once offered in a high-velocity loading with its standard 300-grain bullet at nearly 2,000 fps and generating over 2,900 foot pounds of energy, it was no doubt a good killer. With a 200 fps advantage over the high-velocity 45-70-300 load, it would shoot a bit flatter and give, perhaps, 50 yards more usable range.

The 45-90 case is practically identical to the 45-70, only longer. It is common practice to fire the 45-70 in these rifles when the proper ammunition is not available. The 45-90 is adequate for any North American big game at moderate ranges. Use standard 0.458-inch diameter bullets for loading. For handloading, use only lead bullets to avoid excessive barrel wear.

45-82, 45-85, 45-90 Winchester Loading Data and Factory Ballistics

Bullet (grains/type)	Powder	Grains	Velocity	Energy	Source/Comments
300 Lead	IMR 4198	38.0	1530	1565	NA
405 Lead	IMR 4198	32.0	1410	1790	Lyman No. 457483 gas checked
405 Cast	IMR 3031	40.0	1500	2023	Lyman No. 457124
300 Lead	FL		1554	1609	Factory load
350 Lead	FL		1510	1775	Factory load
405 Lead	FL		1468	1938	Factory load

Extra Light Weight Rifle, Model 1886

45-90 Sharps (Straight)
45-100 Sharps (Straight)
45-110 Sharps (Straight)
45 Sharps Special

Historical Notes When the Sharps company adopted the 45-caliber, it developed a variety of loads and case lengths. The first of these was introduced in mid-1876 (2-7/8 inches), and different case lengths were added late in 1876 (2-6/10 inches) and mid-1877 (2-4/10 inches). The principal difference in these cartridges was in bullet weight, powder charge and case length. Other dimensions are the same. Some are heavy reloadable cases that had to be lengthened slightly to hold the same charge as the originals.

General Comments The 45-100 (2-4/10 inches), 45-100 (2-6/10 inches), 45-90 (2-3/4 inches), 45-100 (2-7/8 inches) and the 45-110 (2-7/8 inches) all appear to be identical except for loading and/or case length. The 45-2 3/4-inch case, listed in the 1876 catalog, is otherwise unknown. There is no point listing all of these separately because of slight differences. However, the reader should know that each exists, as these are encountered in literature referring to Sharps rifles or loading data for those. The 45-90 Winchester case can be fired in any of the above chambered rifles by seating the bullet well out of the case. With cast bullets, 45-70 cartridges can be fired in these rifles. These cases can be made from Basic 45 cases and many custom bullet moulds are currently available.

45-90 Sharps (Straight), 45-100 Sharps (Straight), 45-110 Sharps (Straight)
Loading Data and Factory Ballistics

Bullet (grains/type)	Powder	Grains	Velocity	Energy	Source/Comments
485 Lead	IMR 4198	24.0	1300	1822	Lyman No. 451112
550 Lead	FL		1360	2240	Factory load

45-120 (3 1/4")
Sharps (Straight)
45-125 (3 1/4")
Sharps (Straight)

Historical Notes The 45-caliber 3 1/4-inch case is the largest Sharps cartridge of this caliber. Because of differences in case thickness, it usually came in two versions: the 45-120 and the 45-125. It was introduced in 1878-79 for the Sharps-Borchardt rifles, although there is no documentary evidence that the Sharps factory produced rifles in this chambering or any of the 3 1/4-inch cases, either 40, 45 or 50. Original rifles in this chambering and original ammunition are collector's items. The Sharps Rifle Co. failed in 1881, so the big 3 1/4-inch case did not have a particularly long life, although other single-shot rifles could be (and were) chambered for it. In 1991-92, Eldorado Cartridge made a run of cases and loaded this ammunition.

General Comments The 45-120 Sharps is a very powerful blackpowder cartridge adequate for any North American big game. It is usually considered one of the big buffalo cartridges, but it could not have participated in the slaughter of these animals to any great extent because it arrived on the scene very late. Western buffalo hunting reached its peak in 1875-76 and by 1880 was on the wane. The last of the great herds was destroyed in 1884 and the need for the big, powerful buffalo rifles and cartridges passed with the last of these animals. The repeating rifle and the small-bore, high-velocity cartridge would, within a decade, give them the final shove into obsolescence. Most of the Sharps-Borchardt single-shot rifles in this and other chamberings have been rebarreled and made into modern small-bore varmint rifles.

45-120 (3 1/4") Sharps (Straight), 45-125 (3 1/4") Sharps (Straight)
Loading Data and Factory Ballistics

Bullet (grains/type)	Powder	Grains	Velocity	Energy	Source/Comments
485 Lead	IMR 4198	26.0	1360	2000	Lyman No. 451112
500 Cast	Blackpowder (FFg)	85.0	1299	1873	Lyman No. 457125
500 Lead	FL		1520	2561	Factory load

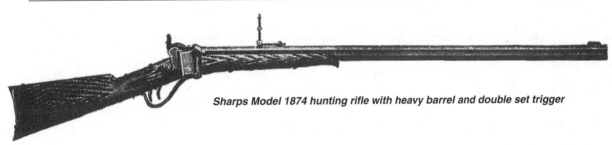

Sharps Model 1874 hunting rifle with heavy barrel and double set trigger

50-90 Sharps
50-100 Sharps
50-110 Sharps

Historical Notes The 2 1/2-inch, 50-caliber Sharps was introduced in the 1872 Sharps catalog, which also listed the 50-70, among others. This period was the heyday of buffalo hunting. There was a strong demand for more potent loads in all game chamberings. The 50-90 offered more power. When western writers refer to the "Big 50" Sharps buffalo rifle and cartridge, this is the cartridge they mean, whether they know it or not. The longer Sharps (3 1/4-inch) 50-caliber cartridge did not arrive on the scene until after the buffalo were finished.

General Comments Soon after its introduction, it was the "Big Fifty" or "Poison Slinger." The 50-90 is also called the 50-100 or 50-110, depending on what bullet weight and powder charge was used. Sharps discontinued its 40- and 50-caliber cartridges except on special order when it adopted the 45-caliber. Correct bullet diameter is 0.509-inch; several Lyman moulds in this size are available. One should not confuse various loadings of this cartridge with the 50-110 Winchester. Cases are readily available from several sources.

50-90 Sharps, 50-100 Sharps, 50-110 Sharps Loading Data and Factory Ballistics

Bullet (grains/type)	Powder	Grains	Velocity	Energy	Source/Comments
365 Lead	AA 5744	37.0	1652	2210	Accurate Arms
422 Cast	IMR 4198	25.5	1129	1194	Lyman No. 515141
440 Lead	AA 5744	33.0	1418	1965	Accurate Arms
465 Lead	IMR 4198	30.0	1320	1804	Lyman No. 509133
550 Lead	AA 5744	30.0	1275	1985	Accurate Arms
335 Lead	FL		1475	1630	Factory load
473 Lead	FL		1350	1920	Factory load

50-140 (3 1/4")
Sharps
50-140 Winchester
Express

Historical Notes This is another special-order Sharps cartridge. It was introduced in 1880, but specific reference is lacking. Dimensions, except for length, are the same as the 50-90 Sharps. Some authorities believe rifles were made by rechambering 50-90s. None of the Sharps catalogs lists this cartridge or chambering.

General Comments Winchester loaded the 50-140 with a 473-grain bullet, but many handloaders used the 700-grain paper-patched type, which could be purchased on a commercial basis. UMC also offered empty cases. Rifles chambered for this round are rare, and cartridges are collector's items. This was the most powerful of the Sharps "buffalo" cartridges, but it was introduced after most of the great herds were long gone. By 1880, buffalo hunting had almost ended, though it continued sporadically until 1884, when the last remaining herd was destroyed. Buffalo hunting for scattered individuals or small groups was not economically feasible. Sharps rifles used 0.509-inch diameter bullets, while Winchester used 0.512-inch diameter. The Basic 50 duplicates this case.

50-140 Sharps, 50-140 Winchester Express Loading Data and Factory Ballistics

Bullet (grains/type)	Powder	Grains	Velocity	Energy	Source/Comments
422 Cast	IMR 4198	39.0	1386	1780	Lyman No. 515141
440 Lead	AA 5744	55.0	1978	3820	Accurate Arms
550 Lead	AA 5744	50.0	1736	3680	Accurate Arms
465 Lead	IMR 4198	33.0	1450	2190	Lyman No. 509133
700 Lead	AA 5744	48.0	1529	3635	Accurate Arms
473 Lead	FL		1580	2520	Winchester factory load
700 Lead	FL		1355	2850	Factory load

50-115 Bullard

Historical Notes This, the largest of the Bullard cartridges, was introduced in 1886. It is unique in being both the first semi-rimmed and solid-head cartridge produced in the United States. It was chambered in the repeating Bullard rifles and possibly the single-shot. No other rifle makers used it.

General Comments The 50-115 Bullard has a slight shoulder. With its larger body diameter, it is shorter than similar 50-caliber cartridges. It delivers the same performance as the longer 50-110 Winchester. It is another rare cartridge and would be difficult to duplicate out of some other case because of the semi-rim construction, although one could turn down the rim on the 470 Nitro Express to make usable cases.

50-115 Bullard Loading Data and Factory Ballistics

Bullet (grains/type)	Powder	Grains	Velocity	Energy	Source/Comments
290 Lead	blackpowder (Fg)	115.0	1539	1580	Lyman No. 512139
290 Lead	IMR 4198	32.0	1570	1647	Lyman No. 512139
300 Lead	FL		1539	1583	Factory load

50-100 Winchester
50-105 Winchester
50-110 Winchester
50-110 Winchester High Velocity

Historical Notes Here we have another example of different loadings in the same case causing confusion, as if they had been used in differently chambered guns. These are all variations of the original 50-110 Winchester, introduced in or before 1916 for the Model 1886 repeating rifle. The original 50-110 was cataloged in November 1887, the 50-100-450 version was offered in August 1895 and the High Velocity version came along sometime after 1910, but is shown in the 1916 catalog. This chambering was also available for the single-shot. Winchester listed cartridges until 1935.

General Comments Originally a blackpowder number, both a standard- and high-velocity smokeless powder version also were developed. The high-velocity load pushed the 300-grain bullet at 2,225 fps and developed 3,298 foot-pounds of energy at the muzzle. This was quite a potent number, being comparable to some of the British African cartridges. For loading, use the Lyman No. 512139 (290-grain) hollowpoint, No. 512138 (450-grain), or one of those bullets listed with the loading data. In spite of being a bit shorter, straightened 348 Winchester cases should work in most rifles.

50-100, 50-105, 50-110 Winchester Loading Data and Factory Ballistics

Bullet (grains/type)	Powder	Grains	Velocity	Energy	Source/Comments
285 Lead	blackpowder (Fg)	110.0	1600	1710	Lyman No. 518144
285 Lead	IMR 4198	39.0	1750	2045	Lyman No. 518144
450 Lead	blackpowder (Fg)	100.0	1475	2190	Lyman No. 515141
300 Lead	FL		1605	1720	Winchester factory load, standard
300 Lead	FL		2225	3298	Winchester factory load, high velocity

50-50 Maynard (1882)

Historical Notes This is the Maynard version of the 50 U.S. Carbine cartridge. It was used in the 1882 Model Maynard single-shot rifle.

General Comments Some of the 50-50 Maynard cartridges have a smaller base diameter than that listed, but this is more a matter of manufacturing tolerance than design difference. Ammunition for old rifles of this chambering can be made by trimming 50-70 cases to the correct length. Powder charge is 50 to 60 grains of blackpowder, depending on bullet weight and type. Lyman No. 518144 (285-grain) or 518145 (350-grain) make good cast bullets for these old rifles. By shortening and possibly thinning the rim, 348 Winchester cases can be used in these rifles.

50-50 Maynard Factory Ballistics

Bullet (grains/type)	Powder	Grains	Velocity	Energy	Source/Comments
350 Lead	FL		1270	1260	Factory load
400 Lead	FL		1210	1305	Factory load

50-95 Winchester
50-95 Winchester Express

Historical Notes The 50-95 is another of the short-necked cartridges developed for the Winchester 1876 Centennial Model repeater. This is the big bore of the group and was introduced in 1879. It was not as popular as some of the others and had a relatively short production life. The Colt New Lightning pump-action rifle was also available in this chambering.

General Comments The 50-70 Government cartridge gained a certain following among buffalo hunters of the period and the 50-95 is essentially an improved, repeating rifle version of that cartridge. Lyman hollowpoint bullets No. 512137 (350 grains) or 512139 (290 grains) can be used for loading. It is advisable to stick to blackpowder or low-pressure smokeless-powder loads for the Model 76 Winchester. It is not a strong action, although entirely adequate for any blackpowder load. Shortened 348 Winchester cases should work in most rifles, with very light loads. Cases from the 50-90 Sharps can be converted into perfectly fitting 50-95 WCF cases.

50-95 Winchester Loading Data and Factory Ballistics

Bullet (grains/type)	Powder	Grains	Velocity	Energy	Source/Comments
285 Lead	IMR 4198	26.0	1420	1302	Lyman No. 518144
350 Lead	IMR 4198	23.0	1350	1420	Lyman No. 518145
300 Lead	FL		1557	1615	Winchester factory load

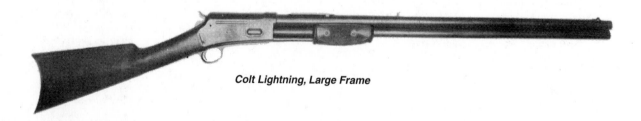

Colt Lightning, Large Frame

50 U.S. Carbine (50 Carbine)

Historical Notes Introduced as a carbine loading for the 1870 "Trapdoor" Springfield single-shot rifle or carbine, this is a centerfire modification of similar rimfire types developed during and immediately after the Civil War.

General Comments The 50 Carbine round is a short-case variation of the standard 50-70 military cartridge. It can be fired in the rifle, but the standard 50-70 case is too long to fit in carbines. The carbine load consisted of a 400-grain bullet and 45 to 50 grains of Fg blackpowder. Lyman No. 518144 (285 grains) is a good bullet for loading these old shells. If your gun will not take the regular 50-70, just trim the case to the proper length. The 1870 Springfield has a weak action so do not try any hot smokeless powder loads. Cases can be converted from 50-90 Sharps cases.

50 U.S. Carbine Loading Data and Factory Ballistics

Bullet (grains/type)	Powder	Grains	Velocity	Energy	Source/Comments
400 Lead	IMR 4198	22.0	1200	1285	NA
400 Lead	FL		1200	1285	Factory load

50-70 Musket (50 Govt.)

Historical Notes The 50-70 was the United States military rifle cartridge from 1866 to 1873. It was the first centerfire cartridge in general use by the U.S. military. The design was derived from the 50-60-400 Joslyn rimfire. It was used in various models and modifications of the single-shot Springfield rifle until replaced by the 45-70 in 1873. It was also chambered in the Remington single-shot military rifle and in a variety of sporting rifles, both single-shot and repeating. The original cartridge had the inside, Benet-type primer. It has been obsolete since the turn of the century.

General Comments The 50-70, or 50 Government, was a popular cartridge through the 1870s and '80s. It was said to be very effective on buffalo and other heavy game. It was the popularity of this cartridge that induced Winchester to bring out the 50-110, which was, in effect, an improved and more powerful version of the 50-70. Very few rifles in this chambering remain in use and ammunition is almost non-existent. However, it would be adequate for any North American big game at short range. Cases with the later Boxer-type priming can be reloaded. Most 50-70 rifles were intended for blackpowder; only very light charges of smokeless powder can be considered safe. In 1934, Francis Bannerman & Sons of New York City advertised both 50-70 Springfield rifles and ammunition. Rifles were still available as late as 1940. Until recently, no sporting rifles chambered this round since the early 1900s. The rise of Cowboy Action Shooting and Blackpowder Silhouette competition has renewed interest in this number. Cases and guns have recently been produced. There was also a carbine version with a shorter case (1.35-inch instead of 1.94-inch).

50-70 Musket (50 Govt.) Loading Data and Factory Ballistics

Bullet (grains/type)	Powder	Grains	Velocity	Energy	Source/Comments
350 Lead	IMR 3031	38.0	1310	1333	Lyman No. 518145
422 Cast	IMR 4198	25.5	1129	1194	Lyman No. 515141
425 Lead	AA 5744	30.0	1419	1900	Accurate Arms
550 Lead	AA 5744	25.0	1208	1780	Accurate Arms
450 Lead	IMR 3031	36.0	1270	1611	Lyman No. 515141
450 Lead	IMR 4198	26.0	1410	1987	NA
425 Lead	FL		1275	1535	Factory load
450 Lead	FL		1260	1488	Factory load

55-100 Maynard

Historical Notes This cartridge is for the Maynard Improved Hunters Rifle No. 11, 1882-type. The 55-100 listed here was introduced the same year as the rifle. This is a little known and seldom encountered round. There was also a shotshell version.

General Comments Some Maynard rifles were available as combination guns with interchangeable shot or rifled barrels. The 55-100 was one of the cartridges for this arrangement. Shells for both shot-and bullet-loading were advertised in its catalog. This is an odd bullet diameter (0.551-inch) and no one makes a suitable mould. However, some of the 54-caliber musket balls or Minié bullets could probably be resized to work. Although significantly undersized at the base, for the low pressures of blackpowder loading in this cartridge, the 470 Nitro Express case could probably be converted for safe use in one of these rifles.

55-100 Maynard Factory Ballistics

Bullet (grains/type)	Powder	Grains	Velocity	Energy	Source/Comments
530 Lead	FL		1410	2340	Factory load

58 Carbine (Berdan)

Historical Notes This is the carbine version of the 58 Berdan Musket cartridge introduced in 1869. The two differ only in case length and powder charge. The carbine case is 1-1/2 inches long, whereas the musket case is 1-3/4 inches long. There is no other difference except the powder charge.

General Comments Rifles for 58 Berdan cartridges are scarce items. Proper load for the carbine version is 40 to 45 grains of Fg blackpowder. Use Lyman No. 585213 (476-grain) bullet. For a good smokeless powder load, try 22 grains of Du Pont (IMR) 4198.

58 Berdan Carbine Factory Ballistics

Bullet (grains/type)	Powder	Grains	Velocity	Energy	Source/Comments
530 Lead	FL		925	1012	Factory load

58 U.S. Musket (Berdan)

Historical Notes Introduced in 1869 for use in the Berdan breech-loading conversion of the Springfield rifled musket, this cartridge was produced in both a rifle version (listed here) and a carbine version (listed above). Bullet weight is the same in both cartridges. This cartridge was never officially adopted by the United States armed forces, but was used experimentally. The centerfire cartridge evolved from earlier rimfire and inside-primed types. The Springfield muzzle-loading musket used a 500-grain bullet and 60 grains of powder for 950 to 1,000 fps, before conversion to breech loading.

General Comments Col. Hiram Berdan, noted chiefly for his part in organizing and leading Berdan's Sharpshooters during the Civil War, was also a firearms designer of considerable importance in the post-war period. The breech-loading conversion system he designed

was not used by the United States, but was adopted by Spain, Russia and other European powers. His Berdan I (hinged cam-lock) and Berdan II (bolt-action) single-shot rifles were both officially adopted and used by Russia for a number of years. In 1895, his widow was awarded a judgment for patent infringement in a suit filed against the U.S. government. The 1866 Springfield rifle used a breech system that copied essential features of the Berdan design.

In 1870, Col. Berdan developed the priming form that bears his name, the Berdan system that is used almost universally outside the United States. Evidently, Berdan was truly unappreciated by his homeland. The Boxer primer used here was invented by an Englishman who seems to have been equally unappreciated at home. The 58 Musket cartridge is common, but arms in this chambering are scarce.

58 U.S. Musket (Berdan) Loading Data and Factory Ballistics

Bullet (grains/type)	Powder	Grains	Velocity	Energy	Source/Comments
476 Lead	blackpowder (Fg)	80-85	1230	1608	Lyman No. 585213
476 Lead	IMR 4198	25.0	1230	1608	Lyman No. 585213
530 Lead	blackpowder (Fg)	80-85	1100	1420	Factory load

70-150 Winchester

Historical Notes The 70-150 cartridge appeared on the 1888 Winchester cartridge boards. Some say it was an advertising novelty for display only. According to Paul Foster (GUN DIGEST, 1952, 6th Edition p. 173), the only gun chambered for it was a specially-made Model 1887 shotgun with rifled barrel. It was never produced on a commercial basis.

General Comments The 70-150 is based on the brass 12-gauge shotshell shortened and necked slightly. It is mentioned only to

complete the record. No guns were produced for it; therefore, no loading or ballistics data is available. However, the case would hold about 150 grains of powder and bullets of this caliber could weigh anywhere from 600 to 900 grains. The muzzle velocity this combination could develop would be approximately 1,300 to 1,500 fps, depending on bullet weight. This would suggest a muzzle energy of about 4,000 foot pounds!

70-150 Winchester Ballistics

Bullet (grains/type)	Powder	Grains	Velocity	Energy	Source/Comments
600 Lead			1500	3000	Theoretical ballistics
900 Lead			1300	3380	Theoretical ballistics

OBSOLETE AMERICAN RIFLE CARTRIDGES
Centerfire Sporting – Blackpowder & Smokeless Powder
Dimensional Data

Cartridge	Case Type	Bullet Dia.	Neck Dia.	Shoulder Dia.	Base Dia.	Rim Dia.	Rim Thck.	Case Length	Ctge. Length	Twist	Primer
219 Zipper	A	.224	.252	.364	.421	.497	.058	1.94	2.26	16	L
22-15-60 Stevens	B	.226	.243		.265	.342		2.01	2.26	12	S
22 Extra Long (Maynard)**	B	.228	.252		.252	.310		1.17	1.41	16	S-O***
22 Winchester CF	A	.228	.241	.278	.295	.342	.058	1.39	1.61	16	S
222 Remington	C	.224	.253	.355	.375	.375	.041	1.70	2.15	14	S
222 Remington Magnum	C	.224	.253	.355	.375	.375	.041	1.85	2.21	14	S
22 Savage High Power	A	.228	.252	.360	.416	.500	.056	2.05	2.51	12	L
6mm Bench Rest Remington	**C**	**.243**	**.263**	**.457**	**.466**	**.468**	**.045**	**1.52**	**2.19**	**12**	**S**
244 Remington	C	.243	.276	.429	.470	.472	.045	2.23	2.90	12	L
6mm Lee Navy	C	.244	.278	.402	.445	.448		2.35	3.11	7.5	L
25-20 Single Shot	**A**	**.257**	**.275**	**.296**	**.315**	**.378**		**1.63**	**1.90**	**12-15**	**S**
25-20 Marlin	A	.257	.274	.329	.349	.405		1.33	?	13-14	S
25-21 Stevens	B	.257	.280		.300	.376		2.05	2.30	14	S
25-25 Stevens	B	.257	.282		.323	.376		2.37	2.63	14	S
25-36 Marlin	A	.257	.281	.358	.416	.499	.056	2.12	2.50	9	S
256 Winchester Magnum	A	.257	.283	.370	.378	.440	.055	1.30	1.53	14	S
25 Remington	C	.257	.280	.355	.420	.421	.045	2.04	2.54	10	L
256 (6.5mm) Newton	C	.264	.290	.430	.469	.473	.045	2.44	3.40	10	L
6.5 Remington Magnum	E	.264	.300	.490	.512	.532	.047	2.17	2.80	9	L
275 H&H Magnum	**E**	**.284**	**.375**	**.375**	**.513**	**.532**	**.048**	**2.50**	**3.30**	**9.5**	**L**
7x61 Sharpe & Hart	E	.284	.320	.478	.515	.532	.048	2.40	3.27	12	L
28-30-120 Stevens	B	.285	.309		.357	.412		2.51	2.82	14	L
30-30 Wesson	**A**	**.308**	**.329**	**.330**	**.380**	**.440**		**1.66**	**2.50**	**12**	**L**
30 Remington	C	.307	.328	.402	.420	.421	.045	2.03	2.525	12	L
30 USA Rimless	C	.308	.333	.417	.454	.456	.054	2.31	3.10	?	L
30-03 Government	C	.308	.340	.441	.470	.473	.045	2.54	3.34	10	L
30 Newton	C	.308	.340	.491	.523	.525		2.52	3.35	10-12	L
308 Norma Magnum	E	.308	.340	.489	.514	.529	.048	2.56	3.30	10-12	L
32-40 Remington	**A**	**.309**	**.330**	**.358**	**.453**	**.535**		**2.13**	**3.25**	**16**	**S**
303 Savage	A	.308/ .311	.334 (.3322)	.408 (.4135)	.439	.501	.058	2.00 (2.015)	2.52	12	L
32-20 Marlin	**A**	**.312**	**.326**	**.338**	**.353**	**.405**		**1.32**	**?**	**20**	**S**
32-30 Remington	A	.312	.332	.357	.378	.437		1.64	2.01	16	S
32-35 Stevens & Maynard	B	.312	.339		.402	.503		1.88	2.29	16	S
32-40 Bullard	A	.315	.332	.413	.453	.510		1.85	2.26	16	S
32 Long, CF*	B	.317	.318		.321	.369		0.82	1.35	20	S
32 Ballard Extra Long*	B	.317	.318		.321	.369		1.24	1.80	22	S
32 Winchester SL	**H**	**.320**	**.343**		**.346**	**.388**		**1.28**	**1.88**	**16**	**S**
32-40 Ballard & Winchester	B	.320	.338		.424	.506	.058	2.13	2.59	16	L
32 Remington	C	.320	.344	.396	.420	.421	.045	2.04	2.57	14	L
32 Ideal	B	.323	.344		.348	.411		1.77	2.25	18	S
33 Winchester	A	.333	.365	.443	.508	.610	.065	2.11	2.80	12	L
35 Winchester SL	**H**	**.351**	**.374**		**.378**	**.405**	**.045**	**1.14**	**1.64**	**16**	**S**

Cartridge	Case Type	Bullet Dia.	Neck Dia.	Shoulder Dia.	Base Dia.	Rim Dia.	Rim Thck.	Case Length	Ctge. Length	Twist	Primer
351 Winchester SL	H	.351	.374	.378	.407	1.38	.045	1.91	?	16	S
350 Griffin & Howe Mag.	**E**	**.357**	**.382**	**.446**	**.511**	**.528**	**.048**	**2.848**	**3.64**	**12**	**L**
35 Winchester	A	.358	.378	.412	.457	.539		2.41	3.16	12	L
350 Remington Magnum	E	.358	.388	.495	.5126	.532	.046	2.17	2.80	16	L
35 Newton	C	.358	.383	.498	.523	.525	2.52	3.35	12	L	
358 Norma Magnum	E	.358	.384	.489	.508	.526	.048	2.52	3.22	12	L
35-30 Maynard (1882)	B	.359	.395		.400	.494		1.63	2.03	16-18	S
35-40 Maynard (1873)	B	.360	.390		.400	.492		2.06	2.53	16-18	S
35-40 Maynard (1882)	B	.360	.390		.400	.492		2.06	2.53	16-18	S
38-45 Stevens	B	.363	.395		.455	.522		1.76	2.24	16-18	S
35-30 Maynard 1873	B	.364	.397		.403	.765		1.63	2.10	16-18	B-1
35-30 Maynard 1865	B	.370	.397		.408	.771/ 1.076	.037	1.53	1.98	16	ext. primed
38-40 Remington-Hepburn	**B**	**.372**	**.395**		**.454**	**.537**		**1.77**	**2.32**	**16**	**S**
38-45 Bullard	A	.373	.397	.448	.454	.526		1.80	2.26	16-18	S
38 Long, CF*	B	.375	.378		.379	.441		1.03	1.45	36	S
38 Ballard Extra Long*	B	.375	.378		.379	.441		1.63	2.06	36	S
38-35 Stevens	B	.375	.402		.403	.492		1.62	2.43		S
38-50 Maynard (1882)	B	.375	.415		.421	.500	.069	1.97	2.38		S
375 Weatherby Magnum	E	.375	.403	.495	.513	.530	.048	2.86	3.69	12	L
38-50 Ballard	B	.376	.395		.425	.502		2.00	2.72	20	S
38-50 Remington-Hepburn	B	.376	.392		.454	.535		2.23	3.07	16	S
38-56 Winchester	A	.376	.403	.447	.506	.606	.065	2.10	2.50	20	L
38-90 Winchester Express	A	.376	.395	.470	.477	.558		3.25	3.70	26	L
38-70 Winchester	A	.378	.403	.421	.506	.600		2.31	2.73	24	L
38-72 Winchester	A	.378	.397	.427	.461	.519		2.58	3.16	22	L
38 Colt Lightning	A	.401	.416	.438	.465	.520	.058	1.30	?	36	S-L
38-40 Marlin	A	.401	.416	.438	.465	.520	.058	1.30	?	36	S-L
40-50 Sharps (Straight)	**B**	**.403**	**.421**		**.454**	**.554**	**.078**	**1.88**	**2.63**	**18**	**B-1**
40-50 Sharps (Necked)	A	.403	.424	.489	.501	.580		1.72	2.37	18-20	B-1
40-60 Marlin	B	.403	.425		.504	.604		2.11	2.55	20	S
40-60 Colt	A	.403	.425	.445	.504	.604	.065	2.09	2.55	?	S
40-63 (40-70) Ballard	B	.403	.430		.471	.555		2.38	2.55	20	S
40-65 Ballard Everlasting	B	.403	.435		.508	.600		2.38	2.55	18-20	B-1
40-70 Sharps (Straight)	B	.403	.420		.453	.533	.078	2.50	3.18	18-20	L
40-70 Sharps (Necked)	A	.403	.426	.500	.503	.595		2.25	3.02	18-20	L
40-85 (40-90) Ballard	B	.403	.425		.477	.545		2.94	3.81	18-20	S
40-90 Sharps (Straight)	B	.403	.425		.477	.546		3.25	4.06	18	B-1
40-90 Sharps (Necked)	A	.403	.435	.500	.506	.602		2.63	3.44	18-20	B-1
40-110 Winchester Express	A	.403	.428	.485	.565	.651		3.25	3.63	28	L
40-60 Winchester	A	.404	.425	.445	.506	.630		1.87	2.10	40	S
40-70 Winchester	A	.405	.430	.496	.504	.604		2.40	2.85	20	L
40-70 Remington	A	.405	.434	.500	.503	.595		2.25	3.00	18-20	L
40-65 Winchester	B	.406	.423		.504	.604		2.10	2.48	20-26	L
40-72 Winchester	B	.406	.431		.460	.518		2.60	3.15	22	L
40-82 (40-75) Winchester	A	.406	.428	.448	.502	.604	.060	2.40	2.77	28	L
401 Winchester SL	H	.406	.428		.429	.457	.055	1.50	2.00	14	L

Cartridge	Case Type	Bullet Dia.	Neck Dia.	Shoulder Dia.	Base Dia.	Rim Dia.	Rim Thck.	Case Length	Ctge. Length	Twist	Primer
40-70 Peabody	A	.408	.428	.551	.581	.662		1.76	2.85	18	L
40-90 Peabody	A	.408	.433	.546	.586	.659		2.00	3.37		B-1
405 Winchester	B	.412	.436		.461	.543	.075	2.58	3.18	14	L
40-75 Bullard	B	.413	.432		.505	.606		2.09	2.54	20	S
40-90 Bullard	A	.413	.430	.551	.569	.622		2.04	2.55	18	L
40-40 Maynard (1882)	B	.415	.450		.456	.532		1.78	2.32	18-20	S
40-60 Maynard (1882)	B	.417	.448		.454	.533		2.20	2.75	18-20	S
40-70 Maynard (1882)	B	.417	.450		.451	.535		2.42	2.88	18-20	B-1
44 Evans Short	**B**	**.419**	**.439**		**.440**	**.513**		**0.99**	**1.44**	**36**	**S**
44 Evans Long	B	.419	.434		.449	.509		1.54	2.00	36	L
40-40 Maynard (1873)	B	.422	.450		.460	.743		1.84	2.34	18-20	B-1
40-70 Maynard (1873)	B	.422	.450		.451	.759		2.45	3.00	18-20	B-1
44 Henry Center Fire Flat	B	.423	.443		.445	.523		0.88	1.36	36	S
40-40 Maynard 1865	B	.423	.450		.458	.766	.058	1.75	2.24	18-20	ext. primed
44 Game Getter/44-40 Marlin/44 Colt Lightning	A	.427	.443	.458	.471	.520	.065	1.31	Varies	36	L
44-40 Extra Long	A	.428	.442	.463	.468	.515		1.58	1.96	36	S
44 Long Center Fire (Ballard)*	B	.439	.440		.441	.506		1.09	1.65	36	S
44 Extra Long Center Fire (Ballard)*	B	.439	.441		.441	.506		1.63	2.10	36	S
44 Wesson Extra Long*	B	.440	.441		.441	.510		1.63	2.19	36	S
44-90 Rem. Special (Necked)	A	.442	.466	.504	.520	.628	.075	2.44	3.08	?	L
44-100/44-90/44-110 Creedmoor	B	.442	.465		.503	.568		2.60	3.97	22-30	L
44-95 Peabody	A	.443	.465	.550	.580	.670		2.31	3.32	?	B-1
44-70 Maynard 1882	B	.445	.466		.499	.601		2.21	2.87	?	B-1
44-75 Ballard Everlasting	B	.445	.487		.497	.603		2.50	3.00	?	B-2
44-100 Ballard	B	.445	.485		.498	.605	.080	2.81	3.25	20	L
44-100 Wesson	B	.445	?		.515-.520	.605-.610		3.38	3.85	?	L
44-77 Sharps & Remington	A	.446	.467	.502	.516	.625		2.25	3.05	?	L-B1
44-85 Wesson	B	.446	?		.515-520	.605-.610		2.88	3.31	?	L
44-90 (44-100) Sharps 2 5/8-inch	A	.446	.468	.504	.517	.625	.065	2.63	3.30	?	B-1
44-60 Sharps & Remington (Necked)	A	.447	.464	.502	.515	.630		1.88	2.55	?	L-B1
44-60 Peabody & Winchester	A	.447	.464	.502	.518	.628		1.89	2.56	?	B-1
45 Remington Thompson	D	.447	.470		.472	.471	.044	1.12	1.45	?	LP
44-60 Sharps & Remington Necked	A	.447	.464	.502	.515	.630		1.88	2.55	?	L-B1
44-100 Maynard 1873	B	.450	.490		.497	.759		2.88	3.46	?	B-1
45-50 Peabody (Sporting)	**A**	**.454**	**.478**	**.508**	**.516**	**.634**	**2.08**	**2.08**	**2.08**	**?**	**?**
45-60 Winchester	B	.454	.479		.508	.629		1.89	2.15(?)	20	L
45-75 Winchester (Centennial)	A	.454	.478	.547	.559	.616		1.89	2.25	20	L
45-100 Ballard	B	.454	.487		.498	.597		2.81	3.25	20	L
45-125 Winchester 45 (Express)	A	.456	.470	.521	.533	.601		3.25	3.63	36	L

Cartridge	Case Type	Bullet Dia.	Neck Dia.	Shoulder Dia.	Base Dia.	Rim Dia.	Rim Thck.	Case Length	Ctge. Length	Twist	Primer
45-70 Van Choate	B	.457		Same as 45-70, see chapter 2				2.25	2.91	22	L
45-75/45-70 Sharps 21/10-inch	B	.457		Same as 45-70, see chapter 2				2.10	2.90	22	L
45-78 Wolcott	B	.457		Same as 45-70, see chapter 2				2.31	3.19	22	L
45-80 Sharpshooter	B	.457		Same as 45-70, see chapter 2				2.40	3.25	20-22	L
45-100 Remington (Necked)	A	.458	.490	.550	.558	.645		2.63	3.26	18-20	L
45-82/45-85/45-90 Winchester & 45-90 Winchester High Velocity	B	.457	.477		.501	.597	.065	2.40	2.88	32	L
45-90/45-100/45-110 Sharps (24/10, 26/10, 23/4, 27/8-inch)	B	.458	.489		.500	.597	.065	2.40, 2.60, 2.75, 2.87	2.85, 3.00	18-20	B-1
45-120/45-125 (31/4-inch) Sharps	B	.458	.490		.506	.597	.065	3.25	4.16	18	L
50-90 Sharps	**B**	**.509**	**.528**		**.565**	**.663**	**.060**	**2.50**	**3.20**	**?**	**L**
50-140 (31/4") Sharps & Winchester	B	.509/ .512	.528		.565	.665	.060	3.25	3.94	?	L
50-115 Bullard	G	.512	.547	.577	.585	.619		2.19	2.56	72	L
50-100/50-105/50-110 Winchester & 50-110 Winchester High Velocity	B	.512	.534		.551	.607	.063	2.40	2.75	54	L
50-50 Maynard 1882	B	.513	.535		.563	.661		1.37	1.91	42	L
50-95 Winchester	A	.513	.533	.553	.562	.627		1.94	2.26	60	L
50-70 Maynard 1873	B	.514	.547		.552	.760		1.88	2.34	42	B-1
50 U.S. Carbine	B	.515	.535		.560	.660		?	?	?	B-1
50-70 Govt. Musket	B	.515	.535		.565	.660	.060	1.75	2.25	24-42	L
50 Sporting							.060				
50 Maynard 1865	B	.520	.543		.545	.770		1.24	1.75	42	none
55-100 Maynard 1882	**B**	**.551**	**.582**		**.590**	**.718**		**1.94**	**2.56**	**?**	**L**
58 Carbine (Berdan)	B	.589	.625		.640	.740		?	?	?	B-2
58 U.S. Musket (Berdan)	B	.589	.625		.646	.740	.062	1.75	2.15	68	B-1
70-150 Winchester	A	.705	.725	.790	.805	.870		2.18	2.63	?	L

Case Type: A = Rimmed, bottleneck. B = Rimmed, straight. C = Rimless, bottleneck. D = Rimless, straight. E = Belted, bottleneck. F = Belted, straight. G = Semi-rimmed, bottleneck. H = Semi-rimmed, straight. I = Rebated, bottleneck. J = Rebated, straight. K = Rebated, belted bottleneck. L = Rebated, belted straight.

Primer Type: S = Small rifle (0.175"). SP = Small pistol (0.175"). L = Large rifle (0.210"). LP = Large pistol (0.210"). 50 BMG = CCI-35/VihtaVuori-110/RWS-8212. B-1 = Berdan #1. B-2 = Berdan #2.

Other codes: V = OAL depends upon bullet used. V = Rifling twist varies, depending upon bullet and application. Belt/Rim Diameter. Unless otherwise noted, all dimensions in inches. Twist (factory) is given as inches of barrel length per complete revolution, e.g., 12 = 1 turn in 12", etc.

* Cartridges so marked used an outside lubricated bullet when originally introduced, and this was of a diameter about the same as the neck or shell mouth. Later, inside lubricated loadings used a much smaller diameter bullet than listed, usually with a long, hollow base. Before the recent advent of effective wax-type lubricants, outside lubricated bullets were never very popular or effective. The inside lubricated hollow-base bullets were cleaner to handle and use and the hollow base was intended to expand the bullet to fit the larger barrel. This never worked very well and accuracy suffered.

** Original 22-10-45 Maynard case length was 1.25".

*** This is a blackpowder primer smaller than the small rifle or pistol size. It has not been made for many years.

Note on blackpowder primers: Not all companies used the same primer type or size in the same cartridge or length case. For example, the 45-70 or its equivalent was usually loaded with the large rifle size primer. However, the Marlin version had the small rifle size and Sharps Co. ammunition had Berdan primers. Primer type and size listed is what appears to have been the most general size and type used. Unless otherwise noted, all dimensions are in inches. So-called 44-caliber blackpowder rifles had groove diameters varying from about 0.446-inch to about 0.460-inch. Most use bullets of about 0.448-inch to 0.452-inch diameter.

Chapter 4

WILDCAT CARTRIDGES

(Rifle and Handgun)

WILDCAT CARTRIDGES have been around for a long time, at least 100 years. Originally, wildcats were developed by some gunsmith or individual experimenter attempting to improve on the ballistics of a commercial cartridge in order to fulfill a personal or special requirement, possibly to increase the effective range for varmint shooting or the knockdown power on big game. I do not know who coined the term "wildcat" to describe these efforts, but for our purposes we will define wildcat cartridges as: cartridge designs and loads not available from major manufacturers as over-the-counter ammunition or cartridges not generally available even in custom loadings. To shoot wildcat cartridges you have to load these yourself or contract that loading with a custom handloader or ammunition producer.

A great proliferation of wildcat cartridge designs has occurred in the past 20 years or so, some of those quite good and some not so good. In some instances the wildcat filled, or was perceived to fill, some niche not accommodated by commercially available ammunition. Good examples include the 35 Whelen and the 458 Alaskan. The former lingered in wildcat limbo for a generation before being commercially adopted. The latter, though certainly useful, will likely never achieve commercialization, chiefly because the only rifle appropriate for it was long ago discontinued. In other instances, the only basis for a wildcat was to offer ballistics previously unavailable in a certain type of firearm, such as the entire genre of current Thompson/Center custom chamberings. Benchresters have long experimented with wildcats, creating designs in which the only criterion is potential inherent accuracy. These wildcats are built to precisely fit a single firearm, and although these are nominally of the same specifications, cannot be interchanged in other so-chambered firearms with impunity.

Several new entries describe recent developments and others describe Australian wildcats from the post-World War II era that are almost unknown in the United States. Still others descibe describe wildcats of historical importance that have not previously appeared. Some older wildcats of historical or developmental interest are retained because many younger or new shooters do not know that these exist. Such ignorance is probably one reason for the development of wildcats that are just a variation on a theme and do not offer anything new.

It is quite impossible to include every known wildcat cartridge because so many exist. Previous editions claimed the number to be in excess of 300. Your current editor suspects the number is now well into the thousands, which seems to be substantiated by Dave Kiff of Pacific Precision reamer manufacturing company, who holds drawings for more than 6000 distinctly-named wildcats!

Wildcat cartridges tend to be regional in nature — what is popular in one area may be completely unknown in the rest of the country — so some viable numbers will never find representation in these pages. Even those wildcats that have been written up and published in gun magazines may have only a limited following. Probably the best indicator of the popularity of a cartridge is the number of loading die sets sold in that particular type. RCBS in Oroville, Calif., is the world's largest manufacturer of wildcat loading and case-forming dies. They make up special-order die sets to customer specifications at relatively modest prices. Quite a few wildcat cartridges have retained sufficient popularity over the years to warrant RCBS carrying those as standard stocked items. Less popular numbers are available on special order, subject to minor delays in delivery.

For many years, the trend in wildcat cartridge development has been toward increased case capacity and higher velocity. Currently, wildcat cartridge design and chambering simply for the sake of improved performance has declined from enthusiastic to almost nonexistent. One explanation for this is a maturity among shooters. We have grown into the realization that there really are no magic cartridges. Within safe pressure parameters, no wildcat chambering in any standard case chambered in any standard gun is going to deliver ballistics significantly different from what is already available in commercial form. Of course, some will disagree, and one must admit that exceptions always exist. However, it is safe to say that the vast majority of recent wildcatting has been directed toward filling target-shooting and gun-type chambering niches, e.g., the aforementioned Thompson/Center chamberings.

Wildcat cartridges are made in a number of ways, from the simple to the more complex. Wildcats can be grouped into basic categories: those with increased case capacity, created by modifying an existing cartridge; those with unusual case capacity for bore diameter, made by necking a case that is larger or smaller than any common commercial example, up or down; those with unusual bullet sizes, created by necking an existing case to accept a different size bullet; and those with unusually close cartridge-to-chamber tolerances, building the rifle and loading dies to match the custom handloaded ammunition. Most recently, we have seen entire new lines of unusually short cases, based upon an unusually large diameter case, which for any given capacity provides a shorter cartridge and powder column, and possibly superior accuracy.

Let us look at some examples. A very early wildcat became the 22 Hornet. In this instance, no change in the case was required, since the cartridge was based on the 22 WCF blackpowder cartridge, and simply loaded with smokeless powder and jacketed 45-grain bullets designed for the 5.5mm Velo Dog revolver cartridge. Early wildcats were rather simple and are good examples of simply necking a standard commercial cartridge case either up or down. The 35 Whelen is an example of the former, the 25-06 the latter, both being based on the standard 30-06 case. Improved cartridges are examples of increasing performance in the original case in an uncomplicated manner. Here, the standard cartridge is fired in the improved chamber, from which it emerges with less body taper and a sharper shoulder. This increases powder capacity, and generally reloading of the improved case provides improved performance over the standard-case load. The Ackley Improved 250 Savage and 257 Roberts chamberings, along with the various improved versions of the 300 H&H Magnum, are good examples of improved wildcats that result in substantial ballistic enhancement over the original cartridge. The same cannot be said of some of the others.

One of the advantages of improved chambers is that these will also chamber and fire factory cartridges designed for the original chambering. This is very handy if you happen to run out of improved reloads in some place far from home. This practice will, of course, result in a slight velocity reduction. Another potentially significant advantage, such as in the 35 Whelen, is improved headspace control.

Several wildcat cartridges are rather complicated to make. These can require extensive reforming and trimming, lathe-turning the rim or neck and even swaging a belt on the base of the case. Such cartridges are, generally, impractical for the average shooter. If a wildcat is to achieve any degree of popularity, cases must be relatively simple and easy to form; otherwise, its use will be confined to a handful of serious tinkerers — something to keep in mind if you happen to be working on a wildcat project you hope will one day become a commercial success.

Some readers might think that someone who develops a popular wildcat that is eventually adopted by one of the big commercial ammunition companies will make a lot of money. Not true. He will be lucky if he even gets credit as the originator. No major company is going to adopt a wildcat cartridge until it has a long-term, proven record. By that time, it will have been around so long it will fall into the category of general public knowledge, and no one will have any claim to it. It is also futile to patent a cartridge design because any slight variation becomes a new cartridge. I mention this because occasionally we hear from someone who thinks developing a "new" cartridge is the road to fame and fortune.

A good number of commercial cartridges originated as wildcats. Some prime examples are: 17 Remington, 22 Hornet, 22-250 Remington, 243 Winchester, 244 Remington, 257 Roberts, 25-06 Remington, 280 Remington, 7mm-08 Remington, 7-30 Waters and the 35 Whelen. Moreover, a large number of commercial cartridges are simply variations of what were originally wildcats. These include practically all of the American 7mm and 30-caliber factory magnum cartridges. Remington has been the leader in adopting wildcat designs, and this has been very beneficial to the shooting sports.

Working with wildcat cartridges is very instructive; those of us who have done so have learned a great deal about the relationship between case size and configuration, bore diameter and powder combustion. One of the areas that has provided some real surprises is in working with short rifle cartridges (case lengths of around 1-1/2 inches). This is a trend begun by the Germans during World War II with the 7.92x33mm assault rifle cartridge, which uses a 1.30-inch long case. The Russians recognized a good idea when they saw one and so developed the 7.62x39mm (M43) cartridge, with a case 1.52 inches long.

As a group, wildcatters tend to be advanced handloaders and true devotees of the shooting sports. Wildcat rifles and cartridges are also a good topic of conversation around the hunting campfire, and if you happen to have a rifle so chambered, it sort of sets you apart — as someone who is at least a little above average in gun knowledge. However, one should never enter lightly into the wildcat arena, because this usually entails a custom-built rifle, plus the investment in forming and loading dies. Rifles chambered for wildcat cartridges are much more difficult to trade or sell in the event you decide that what you have is not exactly what you want. Nevertheless, individuals who have developed wildcat cartridges have spurred major advances to our knowledge of internal ballistics and have spawned a number of very fine cartridges that eventually entered the commercial line. Large companies such as Federal, Remington and Winchester are, by nature, rather conservative and not inclined to market something that will not sell. It is in the area of innovation that the wildcatters make their major contribution, and we have not seen the end yet. No telling what great ideas will come to fruition over the next decade or so.

FCB, with additional text by SS

Pocket Manual for Shooters and Reloaders by Parker O. Ackley. Salt Lake City, 1964.

Practical Dope on the .22 by F.C. Ness. New York and Harrisburg, PA, 1947.

Small Game and Varmint Rifles by Henry F. Stebbins. New York City, 1950.

Twenty-Two Caliber Varmint Rifles by Charles S. Landis. Plantersville, SC, 1947.

Why Not Load Your Own? by Col. Townsend Whelen. Washington, DC, 1949 and later eds.

Wildcat Cartridges by Richard F. Simmons. New York City, 1947.

Woodchucks and Woodchuck Rifles by C.S. Landis. New York City, 1951.

10 Eichelberger Long Rifle

Historical Notes The 10 Eichelberger Long Rifle is the smallest wildcat cartridge known to exist at this time. Pioneering sub-caliber experimenter Bill Eichelberger created this wildcat in 1999 by necking down 22 Long Rifle cases to accept a bullet measuring .103-inch. Over the years, Eichelberger crafted more than 10,000 cartridge cases for the 10 Eichelberger Long Rifle and its bigger siblings in 12-, 14- and 17-calibers. As a rimfire cartridge, each 10 Eichelberger Long Rifle case, after forming, loading and bullet seating, can be fired only one time.

General Comments The 10 Eichelberger Long Rifle cartridge uses Winchester 22 Long Rifle brass as the parent case. Since this cartridge is a rimfire, careful and safe reloading practices are needed to remove the bullet from the internally primed 22 Long Rifle case. Using a series of case forming dies, the live (primed) brass is necked down to 10-caliber and given a 25-degree shoulder––resulting in a diminutive bottleneck shape. After many repetitions of necking down and annealing, the case is trimmed to the final overall length dimension. To avoid excess pressure, extreme care is appropriate in measuring the tiny powder charge. The cartridge works well with 21 inch barrels with a rifling twist of 1:7. Suitable actions to rebarrel and chamber for the 10 Eichelberger Long Rifle include modern 22 LR bolt actions, and single shots such as the Thompson/Center Contender and G2. SSK Industries can supply Contender barrels and 10-caliber bullets for this cartridge on a special order basis. Components, tools and reloading information are available from Bill Eichelberger.

10 Eichelberger LR Loading Data

Bullet (grains/type)	Powder	Grains	Velocity	Energy	Source/Comments
7.2 gr	AA9	1.8`	2160		Bill Eichelberger

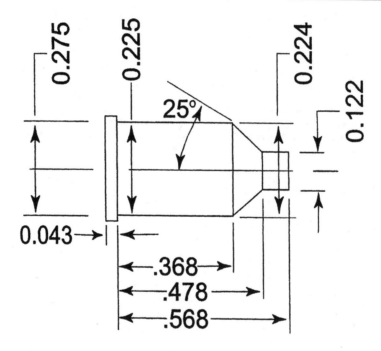

10 Eichelberger Pup

Historical Notes In the diminutive world of experimenter Bill Eichelberger, no cartridge case seems too small to transform into a sub-caliber wildcat. The 10 Eichelberger Pup, built on the less common Cooper CCM brass around 1999, can drive 10-caliber bullets weighing 7.2 grains at velocities over 3600 feet per second. The 10 Eichelberger Pup is intended for small game at ranges approaching 75 to 100 yards. With quality barrels, bullets and shooting techniques, it is capable of MOA or better performance.

General Comments The 10 Eichelberger Pup uses 22 Cooper CCM brass as its parent case. The brass is necked down in a series of dies to accept .103-inch diameter bullets and given a 30-degree shoulder. After many repetitions of necking down and annealing, the case is trimmed to the final overall length dimension. The cartridge uses Federal 205 primers. To avoid excess pressure, extreme care is required in measuring the tiny powder charge. The cartridge works well with 21-inch barrels with a rifling twist of 1:7. Suitable actions for the 10 Eichelberger Pup include the Thompson/Center Contender and G2. SSK Industries can supply Contender barrels and 10-caliber bullets for this cartridge on a special order basis. Components, tools and reloading information are available from Bill Eichelberger.

10 Eichelberger Pup Loading Data

Bullet (grains/type)	Powder	Grains	Velocity	Energy	Source/Comments
7.2 gr	AA9	3.5	3230		Bill Eichelberger
7.2 gr	2400	3.9	3615		Bill Eichelberger
10.0 gr	AA1680	3.9	3134		Bill Eichelberger

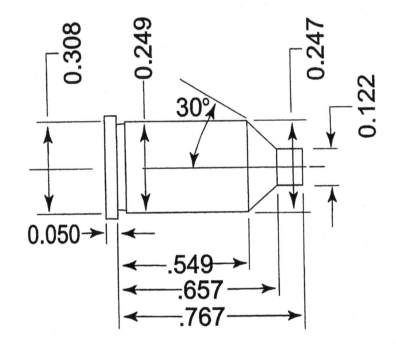

10 Eichelberger Squirrel

Historical Notes In a decades-long quest to explore sub-calibers in small cases, Bill Eichelberger found ways to transform brass cases most folks would consider small into tiny powerhouses. His pre-1999 era 10 Squirrel comes very close to breaking the 4000 feet per second threshold with 7.2-grain, .103-inch diameter bullets. The 10 Squirrel is the fastest 10-caliber cartridge created by Eichelberger; it is suitable for small game at ranges up to 100 yards. Eichelberger also designed 12-caliber and 14-caliber versions of this cartridge.

General Comments The 10 Squirrel uses rimmed Remington 22 Hornet brass as its parent case. The brass is necked down in a series of steps to accept .103-inch diameter bullets and given a 30-degree shoulder. After many repetitions of necking down and annealing, the case is trimmed to the final overall length dimension. The cartridge uses Federal 205 primers. To avoid excess pressure, extreme care is required in measuring the tiny powder charge. The cartridge works well with 21-inch barrels with a rifling twist of 1:7. Suitable actions for the 10 Squirrel include the Thompson/Center Contender and G2. SSK Industries can supply Contender barrels and 10-caliber bullets for this cartridge on a special order basis. Components, tools and reloading information are available from Bill Eichelberger.

10 Squirrel Loading Data

Bullet (grains/type)	Powder	Grains	Velocity	Energy	Source/Comments
7.2-gr	Win 748	6.5	3924		Bill Eichelberger
10-gr	H380	6.4	3290		Bill Eichelberger

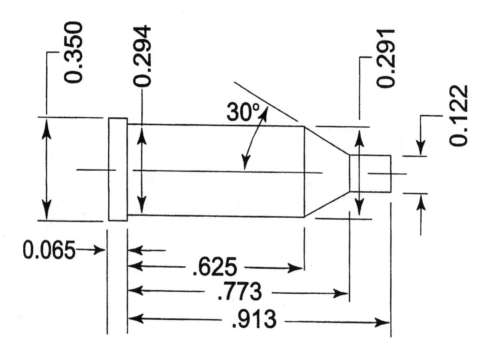

12 Eichelberger LR

Historical Notes In a 21-inch barrel, the 12 Eichelberger Long Rifle can zip a 10-grain, .12-caliber bullet to over 2800 feet per second — blistering performance compared to an ordinary 22 Long Rifle cartridge. Another of Bill Eichelberger's sub-caliber wildcat cartridges dating back to 1982, the 12 Eichelberger Long Rifle was designed for short to mid-range small game and target shooting. Eichelberger also designed 10-caliber and 14-caliber versions of this cartridge.

General Comments The 12 Eichelberger Long Rifle cartridge uses Winchester 22 Long Rifle brass as the parent case. Since this cartridge is a rimfire, careful and safe reloading practices are needed to remove the bullet from the internally primed 22 Long Rifle case. Using a series of case forming dies, the live (primed) brass is necked down to accept .123-inch diameter bullets and given a 25-degree shoulder — resulting in a diminutive bottleneck shape. After multiple cycles of necking down and annealing, the case is trimmed to the final overall length dimension. To avoid excess pressure, extreme care is appropriate in measuring the tiny powder charge. The cartridge works well with 22 inch barrels with a rifling twist of 1:5.5. Suitable actions to rebarrel and chamber for the 12 Eichelberger Long Rifle include modern 22 LR bolt actions, and single shots such as the Thompson/Center Contender and G2. SSK Industries can supply Contender barrels and 12-caliber bullets for this cartridge on a special order basis. Components, tools and reloading information are available from Bill Eichelberger.

12 Eichelberger LR Loading Data

Bullet (grains/type)	Powder	Grains	Velocity	Energy	Source/Comments
10-gr	Accurate Arms 9	2.6	2810		Bill Eichelberger

12 Cooper (CCM)

Historical Notes The 12 Cooper, as designed by Bill Eichelberger in 1996, is a rimmed sub-caliber wildcat cartridge capable of driving 10-grain, 12-caliber bullets to velocities of almost 3800 feet per second. It is suitable for small game hunting and target shooting.

General Comments The 12 Cooper uses rimmed Cooper CCM brass as its parent case. The brass is necked down in a series of dies to accept .123-inch diameter bullets and given a 32-degree shoulder. After multiple repetitions of necking down and annealing, the case is trimmed to the final overall length dimension. The cartridge uses Federal 205 primers. To avoid excess pressure, extreme care is required in measuring the tiny powder charge. The cartridge works well with 15-inch barrels with a rifling twist of 1:5.5. Suitable actions for the 12 Cooper include the Thompson/Center Contender and G2. SSK Industries can supply Contender barrels and 12-caliber bullets for this cartridge on a special order basis. Components, tools and reloading information are available from Bill Eichelberger.

12 Cooper (CCM) Loading Data

Bullet (grains/type)	Powder	Grains	Velocity	Energy	Source/Comments
10-gr	Win 680	6.6	3770		Bill Eichelberger
11.5-gr	Win 680	6.1	3500		Bill Eichelberger

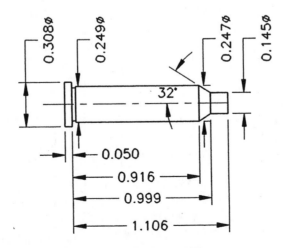

12 Eichelberger Winchester Rimfire Magnum

Historical Notes. Strictly a one-shot proposition, the 12 Eichelberger WRM wildcat cartridge rockets an 11.5-grain, .123-inch diameter bullet to almost 3500 feet per second – stellar performance from a rimfire case. During testing in 1982 of his family of wildcats based on rimfire cartridge cases, designer Bill Eichelberger necked down more than 10,000 rimfire cases (both long rifle and WRM) without one of the internally primed cases discharging. This cartridge is tailored for short to midrange varmint and informal target shooting. Eichelberger also designed a14-caliber version of this cartridge.

General Comments. The 12 Eichelberger WRM cartridge uses Winchester 22 WRM brass as the parent case. Since this cartridge is a rimfire, careful and safe reloading practices are needed to remove the bullet from the internally primed case. Using a series of case forming dies, the live (primed) brass is necked down to accept .123 diameter bullets and given a 25-degree shoulder — resulting in a diminutive bottleneck shape. After multiple repetitions of necking down and annealing, the case is trimmed to the final overall length dimension. To avoid excess pressure, extreme care is appropriate in measuring the tiny powder charge. The cartridge works well with 21 inch barrels with a rifling twist of 1:5.5. Suitable actions to rebarrel and chamber for the 12 Eichelberger WRM include modern 22 WRM bolt actions, and single shots such as the Thompson/Center Contender and G2. SSK Industries can supply Contender barrels and 12-caliber bullets for this cartridge on a special order basis. Components, tools and reloading information are available from Bill Eichelberger.

12 Eichelberger Winchester Rimfire Magnum Loading Data

Bullet (grains/type)	Powder	Grains	Velocity	Energy	Source/Comments
7.2-gr	Win 748	6.5	3924		Bill Eichelberger
10-gr	H380	6.4	3290		Bill Eichelberger

12 Eichelberger Carbine

Historical Notes The original designers of the 30 Carbine cartridge would be amazed to learn sub-caliber experimenter Bill Eichelberger used their military brass to drive knitting-needle-sized bullets to 220 Swift and higher velocities. Conceived in 1997, the 12 Eichelberger Carbine is the fastest wildcat 12-caliber cartridge known to exist. For small game hunting and shooting, it can drive 10-grain bullets to almost 4400 feet per second. Eichelberger also designed a 14-caliber version of this cartridge.

General Comments The 12 Eichelberger Carbine uses Winchester 30 Carbine brass as its parent case. The brass is necked down in a series of dies to accept .123-inch diameter bullets and given a 25-degree shoulder. After multiple repetitions of necking down and annealing, the case is trimmed to the final overall length dimension. The cartridge uses Federal 205 primers. To avoid excess pressure, extreme care is required in measuring the tiny powder charge. The cartridge works well with 15-inch barrels with a rifling twist of 1:5.5. Suitable actions for the 12 Eichelberger Carbine include the Thompson/Center Contender and G2. SSK Industries can supply Contender barrels and 12-caliber bullets for this cartridge on a special order basis. Components, tools and reloading information are available from Bill Eichelberger.

12 Eichelberger Carbine Loading Data

Bullet (grains/type)	Powder	Grains	Velocity	Energy	Source/Comments
10-gr	H335	13.8	4390		Bill Eichelberger
11.5-gr	H335	13.5	4145		Bill Eichelberger

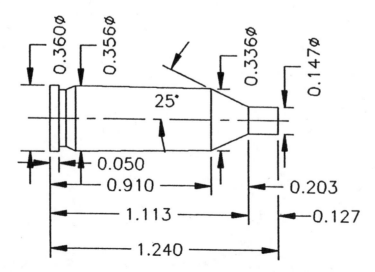

14 Eichelberger Dart

Historical Notes Essentially similar to its smaller 10- and 12-caliber siblings, the 14 Eichelberger Dart turns the 25 ACP pistol case holding a precisely measured powder charge into a velocity powerhouse for 10-grain and 13.0-grain bullets measuring .144-inch in diameter. About 1983, wildcatter Bill Eichelberger designed the 14 Eichelberger Dart to push these micro-sized bullets in the 2330 – 2960 feet per second range – creating a sub-caliber cartridge for small game and paper-punching.

General Comments The 14 Eichelberger Dart uses Winchester 25 ACP brass as its parent case. The brass is necked down in a series of dies to accept .144-inch diameter bullets and given a 30-degree shoulder. After several repetitions of necking down and annealing, the case is trimmed to the final overall length dimension. The cartridge uses Federal 205 primers. To avoid excess pressure, extreme care is required in measuring the tiny powder charge. The cartridge works well with 15-inch barrels with a rifling twist of 1:9. Suitable actions for the 14 Eichelberger Dart include the Thompson/Center Contender and G2. SSK Industries can supply Contender barrels and 14-caliber bullets for this cartridge on a special order basis. Components, tools and reloading information are available from Bill Eichelberger.

14 Eichelberger Dart

Bullet (grains/type)	Powder	Grains	Velocity	Energy	Source/Comments
10.0-gr	Accurate Arms 9	3.5	2967		Bill Eichelberger
12.7-gr	H110	3.2	2614		Bill Eichelberger
13.0-gr	H110	3.3	2692		Bill Eichelberger

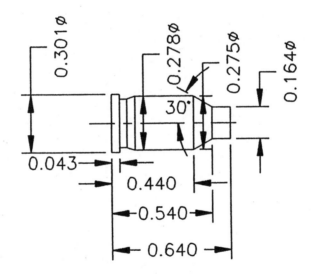

14 Eichelberger Bee

Historical Notes The 218 Bee cartridge, introduced by Winchester in 1938 never achieved great popularity, even though it offered greater case capacity than the contemporary 22 Hornet round. In 1980, Bill Eichelberger exploited the case capacity of the 218 Bee when he modified the brass to accept .144-inch diameter bullets in a cartridge named the 13 Eichelberger Bee. It is capable of driving 15-grain bullets about 150 feet per second faster than Eichelberger's Hornet based wildcat, and can speed the heavier 18.0 grain bullets to more than 3600 feet per second. The 14 Eichelberger Bee fits into the small game and target-shooting niche, and fall within the 100-yard limitation of the sub-caliber wildcats.

General Comments The 14 Eichelberger Bee uses 218 Bee brass as the parent case. The brass is necked down in a series of bushings to accept .144-inch diameter bullets and given a 30-degree shoulder. After several cycles of necking down and annealing, the case is trimmed to the final overall length dimension. The cartridge uses Remington 7-1/2 primers. To avoid excess pressure, extreme care is required in measuring the tiny powder charge. The cartridge works well with 21-inch barrels with a rifling twist of 1:10. Suitable actions for the 14 Eichelberger Bee include the Thompson/Center Contender and G2. SSK Industries can supply Contender barrels and 14-caliber bullets for this cartridge on a special order basis. Components, tools and reloading information are available from Bill Eichelberger.

14 Eichelberger Bee Loading Data

Bullet (grains/type)	Powder	Grains	Velocity	Energy	Source/Comments
13.0-gr	H335	14.6	4124		Bill Eichelberger
15.0-gr	Accurate Arms 2460	14.6	3910		Bill Eichelberger
18.0-gr	Accurate Arms 2495	14.2	3634		Bill Eichelberger

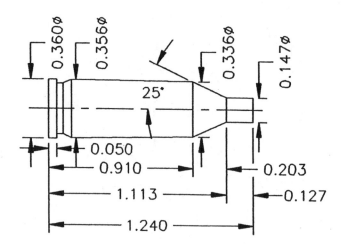

14 Cooper (CCM)

Historical Notes. The 14 Cooper, as designed by Bill Eichelberger in 1993, is a rimmed sub-caliber wildcat cartridge capable of driving 10-grain, 14-caliber bullets to velocities of almost 3900 feet per second. It is suitable for small game hunting and target shooting.

General Comments. The 14 Cooper uses rimmed Cooper CCM brass as its parent case. The brass is necked-down in a series of dies to accept .144-inch diameter bullets and given a 32-degree shoulder. After several repetitions of necking-down and annealing,

the case is trimmed to the final overall length dimension. To avoid excess pressure, extreme care is required in measuring the tiny powder charge. The cartridge works well with 21-inch barrels with a rifling twist of 1:8.75. Suitable actions for the 14 Cooper include the Thompson/Center Contender and G2. SSK Industries can supply Contender barrels and 14-caliber bullets for this cartridge on a special order basis. Components, tools and reloading information are available from Bill Eichelberger.

14 Cooper (CCM) Loading Data

Bullet (grains/type)	Powder	Grains	Velocity	Energy	Source/Comments
10.0-gr	H110	7.4	3895		Bill Eichelberger
12.7-gr	H110	7.1	3491		Bill Eichelberger
13.0-gr	H110	7.0	3443		Bill Eichelberger
15.0-gr	H110	7.5	3487		Bill Eichelberger

14 Walker Hornet

Historical Notes As designed by David Walker, the 14 Walker Hornet combines a straight body, sharp shoulder angle and long neck to drive 10.0-grain bullets to almost 4200 feet per second. It was one of the first 14-caliber wildcats, and served as the basis for the 14 Eichelberger Hornet, which achieves greater case volume and resulting higher velocities. Like all the 14-caliber wildcats, the 14 Walker Hornet is a short range, small game cartridge.

General Comments The 14 Walker Hornet uses Remington 22 Hornet brass as its parent case. The brass is necked down in a series of dies to accept .144-inch diameter bullets and given a 30-degree shoulder. After several cycles of necking down and annealing, the case is trimmed to the final overall length dimension. The cartridge uses Remington 7.5 primers. To avoid excess pressure, extreme care is required in measuring the tiny powder charge. The cartridge works well with 21-inch barrels with a rifling twist of 1:8.75. Suitable actions for the 14 Walker Hornet include the Thompson/Center Contender and G2. SSK Industries can supply Contender barrels and 14-caliber bullets for this cartridge on a special order basis. Components, tools and reloading information are available from Bill Eichelberger.

14 Walker Hornet Loading Data

Bullet (grains/type)	Powder	Grains	Velocity	Energy	Source/Comments
10.0-gr	Accurate Arms 1689	10.3	4198		Bill Eichelberger
13.0-gr	Accurate Arms 1680	9.9	3757		Bill Eichelberger
15.0-gr	Win 748	11.2	3737		Bill Eichelberger

14 Jet Junior

Historical Notes The almost forgotten, 1961 vintage 22 Remington Jet cartridge inspired the 14 Jet Junior. Originally intended as a small game hunting cartridge, the 22 Remington Jet had a long shoulder, tapering gently from case body to the neck. It originally pushed a 40-grain bullet to about 2460 feet per second, and was a solid, but not spectacular cartridge. Sometime before 1998, the late Bud Pylinski transformed it into the 14 Jet Junior, which sends 10-grain bullets screaming downrange at almost twice the velocity of the 22 Jet – 4570 feet per second! In addition, the 14 Jet Junior can handle relative heavy (for a 14-caliber) bullets weighing 18.0 grains. Across the full range of bullets, though, the 14 Jet Junior is best suited for target shooting and small game at ranges up to 100 yards.

General Comments The 14 Jet Junior uses 22 Remington Jet brass as the parent case. The brass is necked down in a series of bushings to accept .144-inch diameter bullets and given a 10-degree shoulder. After several repetitions of necking down and annealing, the case is trimmed to the final overall length dimension. The cartridge uses Remington 7-1/2 primers. To avoid excess pressure, extreme care is required in measuring the tiny powder charge. The cartridge works well with 21-inch barrels with a rifling twist of 1:8.75. Suitable actions for the 14 Jet Junior include the Thompson/Center Contender and G2. SSK Industries can supply Contender barrels and 14-caliber bullets for this cartridge on a special order basis. Components, tools and reloading information are available from Bill Eichelberger.

14 Jet Junior Loading Data

Bullet (grains/type)	Powder	Grains	Velocity	Energy	Source/Comments
10.0-gr	Win 748	14.8	4570		Bill Eichelberger
13.0-gr	Win 748	13.8	4087		Bill Eichelberger
15.0-gr	Win 748	14.3	3925		Bill Eichelberger
18.0-gr	H380	13.3	3479		Bill Eichelberger

Wildcat Resource Directory

Alexander Arms LLC
U.S. Army, Radford Arsenal
PO Box 1
Radford, VA 24143
(540) 639 8356
http://www.alexanderarms.com

William A. Eichelberger
158 Crossfield Road
King of Prussia, PA 19406
(610) 265-8786

E. Arthur Brown Company
(EABCO)
433 State Highway 27 East
Alexandria, MN 56308
(800) 950-9088
www.eabco.com

James Calhoon Manufacturing
4343 U.S. Highway 87
Havre, MT 59501 USA
(406) 395-4079
www.jamescalhoon.com

Cooper Arms of Montana
Stevensville, MT 59870
(406) 777-0373
www.cooperfirearms.com

Guncrafter Industries
171 Madison 1510
Huntsville, AR 72740
(479) 665-2466
www.guncrafterindustries.com

Michael Petrov
923 West 74th Ave.
Anchorage, AK 99518
(907) 522-4628

Quality Cartridge
P.O. Box 445
Hollywood, MD 20636

Reed's Ammunition & Research
1209 SW 129th St.
Oklahoma City, OK 73170
www.reedsammo.com

SSK Industries
590 Woodvue
Wintersville, OH 43953
(740) 264 0176
www.sskindustries.com

Teppo Jutsu LLC
8000 Research Forest Drive,
Suite115-120
The Woodlands, TX 77382
(832) 524-8100
www.teppojutsu.com

Wildey FA, Inc.
45 Angevine Rd.
Warren, CT 06754
(860) 355-9000
www.wildeyguns.com

Z-Hat Custom
4010A S. Poplar St.
Casper, WY 82601
(307) 577-7443

14-222

Historical Notes In the decade following World War II, there was considerable interest and experimentation with sub-caliber cartridges of 14- and even 12-caliber. Although interest subsided, it never completely died out, and a small but persistent group continued to work with the 14-caliber. The 14-222 is among these cartridges. It was originated by Helmut W. Sakschek about 1985. It is based on the 222 Remington case necked-down to 14-caliber. Information covering the cartridge was published in the 1988 issue (20th Edition) of GUNS ILLUSTRATED, DBI Books, Inc., edited by Harold A. Murtz. Mild report and practically zero recoil are characteristics of these small-caliber rifles. With initial velocities of over 4000 fps, these are quite deadly on smaller species of vermin.

General Comments An 11-grain bullet starting out at 4465 fps develops 505 foot-pounds of energy, which does not sound very impressive. However, anything moving at such velocity imparts a sizable portion of that velocity to the molecular structure of whatever it impacts, with devastating results. On the other hand, once remaining velocity drops below about 3500 fps, the effectiveness of these small, lightweight bullets diminishes rapidly, so these are not really all that good for long-range shooting. There are also many problems in working with such small projectiles. For example, metal fouling can be a serious problem and such cartridges generally exhibit extreme sensitivity to charge variations. Wind drift with such light projectiles is also a frequent complaint. Some older 14-caliber cartridges used bullets of 20 to 25 grains which are easier to handle and load, but cannot be pushed at quite the velocity of the lighter projectiles. In any event, the sub-calibers are extremely interesting and represent an area that may see additional development. Barrels in 14-caliber are currently available from Matco Inc., P.O. Box 349, North Manchester, Ind., 46962. Bullet-making equipment is available through Corbin Inc., P.O. Box 2659, White City, Ore., 97503. The advent of cleaner powders, such as those now available from Ramshot, and moly-plated bullets (NECO process) can significantly mitigate bore fouling.

14-222 Loading Data

Bullet (grains/type)	Powder	Grains	Velocity	Energy	Source/Comments
11.4 HP	IMR 4198	20.0	4200	445	NA
11.4 HP	IMR 3031	21.0	4465	505	NA

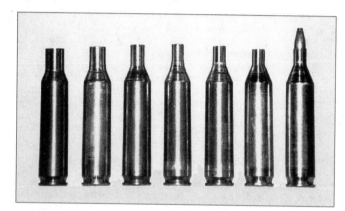

Left to right – factory 222 Rem. case, three stages of progressively swaged necks, resized case with the neck turned to correct thickness, fireformed case trimmed to length, and finished 14-222 with bullet seated.

14/222 Eichelberger Mag

Historical Notes The 14/222 Eichelberger Magnum is the big brother to the 14/221 Eichelberger. As conceived in 1978, Bill Eichelberger adapted the 222 Remington Magnum case, an unsuccessful contender for the small-bore U.S. M-16 rifle, as the dynamo for this sub-caliber wildcat. The 47mm-long case allows for greater powder capacity, enabling heavier bullets to be driven over 3900 fps, and lighter ones to over 4300 fps. The 14/222 Eichelberger Magnum is the ultimate 14-caliber wildcat now available to the serious, curious and dedicated shooter with considerable time and money to invest.

General Comments The 14/222 Eichelberger uses 222 Remington Magnum brass as the parent case. The brass is necked down in a series of bushings to accept .144-inch diameter bullets, and given a 23-degree shoulder with a short neck. After several repetitions of necking down and annealing, the case is trimmed to the final overall length dimension. The cartridge uses Remington 7-1/2 primers. To avoid excess pressure, extreme care is required in measuring the tiny powder charge. The cartridge works well with 21-inch barrels with a rifling twist of 1:8.75. Suitable actions for the 14/222 Eichelberger Magnum include the Thompson/Center Contender and G2. SSK Industries can supply Contender barrels and 14-caliber bullets for this cartridge on a special order basis. Components, tools and reloading information are available from Bill Eichelberger.

14/222 Eichelberger Mag Loading Data

Bullet (grains/type)	Powder	Grains	Velocity	Energy	Source/Comments
13.0-gr	H380	24.5	4368	·	Bill Eichelberger
15.0-gr	Win 780	24.3	4155		Bill Eichelberger
18.0-gr	Accurate Arms 3100	24.4	3959		Bill Eichelberger

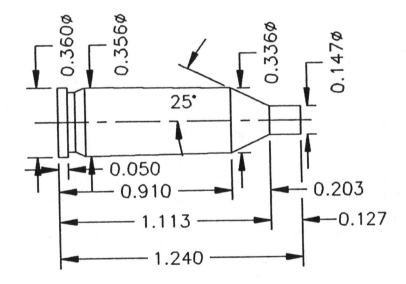

17 Ackley Hornet

Historical Notes The 17 Ackley Hornet is simply the 22 Hornet Improved necked-down to 17-caliber. It was originated by P.O. Ackley in the early 1950s, and he describes this cartridge as one of the most balanced of the 17-caliber cartridges. Although small, it delivers ballistics equal to some of the larger 17-caliber cartridges. It is an effective 200-yard varmint cartridge and is quite accurate. It is normally used in single-shot rifles, although the small Sako bolt-action was favored by many because it was made to handle rimmed cartridges such as the 22 Hornet or 218 Bee.

General Comments The 17 Hornet is a good cartridge for use in settled areas where a mild report and minimum ricochet are desirable characteristics. It is one of the most accurate of the 17-calibers. Its use should be confined to varmint shooting. The standard twist is 1 in 10 inches, the same as most other 17-caliber rifles. Reportedly, IMR 4198 gives the most uniform results, although Ball BL-C2 as well as several of the newer powders should work well. Berger Bullets has recently offered 17-caliber bullets of various styles and weights. This significantly improves the versatility of all 17-caliber cartridges.

17 Ackley Hornet Loading Data

Bullet (grains/type)	Powder	Grains	Velocity	Energy	Source/Comments
25 HP	BL-C2	15.0	3040	510	NA
25 HP	IMR 4198	11.0	3300	600	Ackley
25 HP	IMR 4198	12.0	3585	710	Ackley
25 HP	H4227	11.5	3570	705	Ackley

17 Ackley Improved Bee

Historical Notes The 17 Ackley Bee is a step up from the 17 Hornet as it is based on the 218 Improved Bee case, which has significantly larger powder capacity. This cartridge was developed by P.O. Ackley back in the 1950s, and he considered it the ideal small case for a 17-caliber cartridge. There is relatively little gain in ballistic performance by using cartridge cases larger than the 17 Bee. In fact, cases of very much larger capacity often produce erratic results and poor accuracy.

General Comments The 17 Bee, like the 17 Hornet, is chambered mostly in single-shot rifles, usually of the under-lever type. Bolt-actions are sometimes used, but will not always handle the rimmed case well when feeding from the magazine. The small Sako bolt-action was favored, when available. Like most of the smaller 17-caliber cartridges, the 17 Bee is noted for its mild report and low recoil. This is a good 200- to 225-yard varmint cartridge for use in settled areas. P.O. Ackley recommended IMR 4198, or H4198, as the propellant that produces the most uniform results, and several new choices now available should work as well. Bullets are available from Hornady. Berger Bullets has recently offered 17-caliber bullets of various styles and weights. This significantly improves the versatility of all 17-caliber cartridges.

17 Ackley Bee Loading Data

Bullet (grains/type)	Powder	Grains	Velocity	Energy	Source/Comments
20	H4227	11.0	3845	655	Ackley
25 HP	BL-C2	16.5	3190	565	NA
25 HP	H335	17.0	3285	595	NA
25 HP	IMR 4198	13.0	3180	555	NA

17 Mach IV

Historical Notes Introduced by the O'Brian Rifle Co., Las Vegas, Nev., this cartridge was intended to offer simple case conversion and good ballistics. It succeeded on both counts, but could not compete against a factory chambering, i.e., the 17 Remington.

General Comments This short cartridge can be used in short rifle actions. Efficiency is much better than the various full-power 17s available. This diminutive chambering can produce more than 3850 fps with 25-grain bullets and is fully capable of delivering good varmint accuracy to about 250 yards, perhaps a bit further on a calm day. Muzzle blast is in a different league from larger 17s

and the various high-performance 22s. While by no means "quiet," the 17 Mach IV generates so much less report that this difference is significant. Use of the faster powders listed, while necessitating a slight velocity sacrifice, results in much quieter loads. Since it uses significantly less powder than the 17 Remington, the 17 Mach IV generally produces much less barrel fouling, an important consideration in this diminutive bore size. Berger Bullets has recently offered 17-caliber bullets of various styles and weights. This significantly improves the versatility of all 17-caliber cartridges.

17 Mach IV Loading Data

Bullet (grains/type)	Powder	Grains	Velocity	Energy	Source/Comments
25	2400	13.1	3600	720	Hornady
25	H4227	14.6	3700	760	Hornady
25	H4198	15.6	3700	760	Hornady
25	2015	18.5	3850	820	Accurate
25	2230	20.3	3861	825	Accurate
25	2460	20.5	3883	835	Accurate (Compressed)
25	2520	20.5	3768	785	Accurate (Compressed)

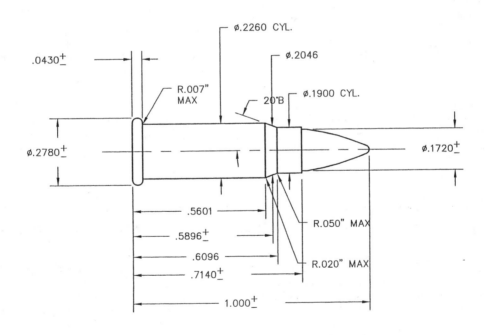

17/222

Historical Notes The 17/222 is simply the 222 Remington case necked-down to 17-caliber. There are several versions of this cartridge, but the one listed here is the most popular. The 17/222 dates back to about 1957, possibly earlier. Many shooters considered the 17/222 more accurate and less sensitive to load variations than the wildcat 17/223, which was the forerunner of the later 17 Remington. P.O. Ackley considered the 222 Remington case about maximum capacity for the 17-caliber and states in his book, *Handbook for Shooters and Reloaders*, that larger cases tend to be inflexible. Those who have experimented with larger cases have usually found he is right.

General Comments The 17/222 did not achieve great popularity, but was well liked by those who worked with it. Performance is practically the same as the 17 Remington, which has a larger case. Best accuracy is usually with IMR 4198 powder and the 25-grain bullet. Recommended twist is 1 in 10 inches. Cases are simple and easy to form by necking-down 222 Remington cases with no other modification. There has been some renewed interest in this cartridge during the past couple of years.

19 Badger

Historical Notes In one shooting day in 2001, Jim Harrison and Jim Leahy shot seven Montana badgers with a 19-caliber cartridge based on the 30 Carbine case. The results from this small-caliber (4.85mm) cartridge effectively ended the search for reliable 300-yard flat-shooting varmint cartridge with low recoil, noise, fouling and barrel heating characteristics, and gave the cartridge its name, the 19 Badger. Harrison, the cartridge designer, previously tested many 19-caliber and parent case combinations, but found most exceeded the "*too large and too fast*" threshold.

General Comments The 30 Carbine parent case, when necked to 19-caliber with a 30-degree shoulder, creates a short powder column with thick case walls at the case neck. Both features contribute to varmint-grade accuracy. Suitable for any firearm capable of accommodating the Hornet case, the 19 Badger works well in 24-inch barrels using a 1:13 twist. Incidentally, the 19 Badger holds about 25 percent more powder than the 19 Calhoon cartridge (which uses the 22 Hornet as its parent case). James Calhoun Mfg offers rifles, barrel kits, loaded ammunition, reloading supplies and components for the 19 Badger cartridge. Cooper Arms also chambers single-shot rifles for this cartridge on special order.

19 Badger Loading Data and Factory Ballistics

Bullet (grains/type)	Powder	Grains	Velocity	Energy	Source/Comments
27-gr Calhoon DBL HP	Accurate Arms 1680	16.3	3775		James Calhoon
32-gr Calhoon DBL HP	FL		3550		James Calhoon

19 Calhoon

Historical Notes Around 1997, Jim Leahy (James Calhoun Mfg) decided to adapt a military cartridge development, the 4.85mm (19-caliber), to varmint cartridges. Their decision reflected two consideration: (1) ballistic superiority over the 22-calibers and (2) consistency and ease of loading over 17-calibers. One of their resulting 19-caliber cartridge offerings, the 19 Calhoon is the most powerful proprietary cartridge based on the 22 Hornet case.

General Comments Occasionally described as a Hornet on steroids, the 19 Calhoon adds an additional 100-yards range over the factory 22 Hornet, and easily drives a 32-grain bullet as fast as the wildcat 17 Hornet cartridge can drive a 25-grain bullet. This

performance translates into a significant range (best at 250 yards and effective to 350 yards) and killing power advantage. Using the parent Hornet case blown out and given a 30-degree shoulder, it can be chambered in any firearm suitable for the Hornet case such as the CZ 527 and Ruger 77. The chambering works well with 24 inch barrels using a 1:13 twist. The 19 Calhoon delivers performance similar to the 17 Mach IV (17-221) in a compact and reliable cartridge. James Calhoun Mfg offers rifles, barrel kits, loaded ammunition, reloading supplies and components. Cooper Arms also chambers single-shot rifles for this cartridge.

19 Calhoon Loading Data and Factory Ballistics

Bullet (grains/type)	Powder	Grains	Velocity	Energy	Source/Comments
27-gr Calhoon DBL HP	Accurate Arms 1680	14.7	3610		James Calhoon
32-gr Calhoon DBL HP	FL		3400		James Calhoon
36-gr Calhoon DBL HP	Accurate Arms 2200	15.0	3165		James Calhoon
40-gr Calhoon DBL HP	Accurate Arms 2200	14.5	3060		James Calhoon

19-223 Calhoon

Historical Notes During 1970 NATO trials to identify a superior infantry cartridge, the 4.85mm Experimental provided exceptional performance to 500+ meters, outperforming other competitors. Essentially a 222 Magnum case adapted to a 19-caliber bullet, the 4.85mm Experimental led to the creation of the 19-223 Calhoon by James Leahy in 1997. Leahy's cartridge, however, used the readily available 223 Remington for its parent case. It offers less recoil and a flatter trajectory than the 223 Remington, and is a superb long-range, flat-shooting varmint cartridge with abundant terminal energy.

General Comments This cartridge offers significant bullet weight versatility, ranging from 32 grains for pelt hunting to 44 grains for improved long-range shooting. The 19-223 Calhoon drives heavier (better ballistic coefficient) bullets than the 17 Remington at similar velocities. The 223 parent case is necked down to 19-caliber in one pass through a forming die and the case shape subsequently formed by fireforming. With a 30-degree shoulder, the fireformed case attains the powder capacity of the 222 Remington Magnum and delivers velocities normally associated with the 220 Swift. The 19-223 Calhoon can be accommodated in firearms suitable for the 223 Remington-length cases. It works well with 26-inch barrels using a 1:13 twist. James Calhoun Mfg. offers rifles, barrel kits, loaded ammunition, reloading supplies, and components. Cooper Arms also chambers single-shot rifles for this cartridge.

19-223 Calhoon Loading Data and Factory Ballistics

Bullet (grains/type)	Powder	Grains	Velocity	Energy	Source/Comments
32-gr Calhoon DBL HP	BLC-2	27.0	4025		James Calhoon
36-gr Calhoon DBL HP	Accurate Arms 2015 BR	24.5	3840		James Calhoon
40-gr Calhoon DBL HP	FL		3750		James Calhoon
44-gr Calhoon DBL HP	VV N550	27.0	3670		James Calhoon

22 Taranah Hornet

Historical Notes The Taranah Hornet was developed by Andy Montgomery, assistant technical editor of *Guns and Game* magazine in Australia. An article appeared in issue 27, Jul-Sept 2000 of the same magazine. The 22 Taranah Hornet is essentially a 22 K-Hornet shortened by .150-inch. The reason for the shorter length is to allow the long-for-weight 40-grain Nosler Ballistic Tip projectile to be used, without running into overall length problems. The cartridge was specifically designed to operate through the ZKW 465 and CZ 527 Hornet detachable magazines. Montgomery reports velocities in excess of the standard Hornet, and only marginally behind the conventional K-Hornet. The original rifle was chambered by Sprinter Arms of South Australia, using one of their 1:10 twist barrels.

General Comments The Taranah Hornet is an ideal small-game cartridge that utilizes ballistically efficient bullets to gain better down range performance. It not only produces higher velocities than the original Hornet, but when 40-grain Nosler Ballistic Tip bullets are used, it also shoots flatter. It is a very efficient cartridge, has a mild report and is economical to shoot. Montgomery has found good case life and excellent accuracy from the cartridge. It would be suitable for most small game and varmints, and it extends the effective range of the standard Hornet a little. The cartridge can be fed through the magazine of popular bolt-action rifles.

22 Taranah Hornet Loading Data

Bullet (grains/type)	Powder	Grains	Velocity	Energy	Source/Comments
40 Nosler BT	Win 680	11.5	2831	712	Andy Montgomery
40 Nosler BT	2400	10.5	2827	710	Andy Montgomery
50 Speer SP	2400	10.0	2489	688	Andy Montgomery
50 Sierra SP	Win 680	11.5	2571	734	Andy Montgomery

22 K-Hornet

Historical Notes Originated by Lysle Kilbourn in 1940, this was one of the first of the so-called "improved" cartridges. It is based on the fire-formed and blown-out 22 Hornet case with straight body, sharp shoulder and short neck. There are other versions, but this is the most popular and is representative of the lot. It has been used for a good many years and is still popular in varmint shooting circles. Extensive experience with this cartridge in the Thompson Contender shows substantial improvements over the 22 Hornet.

General Comments The popularity of the 22 K-Hornet was based on increased performance, plus the fact that any regular factory-loaded ammunition could also be fired in the same chamber. In addition, the conversion is quite cheap and any Hornet rifle can be rechambered. Ammunition is no problem because the round is based on easily obtainable factory ammunition. It brings the 22 Hornet into the same class as the 218 Bee with the added advantage that the 22 Hornet was chambered in several good bolt-action rifles. It is suitable for the same range of varmints and small game as the 218 Bee. Those lucky enough to find an original Kimber rifle chambered for the 22 K-Hornet can pride themselves in owning a superb rifle. The very similar Harvey Kay-Chuck was developed by Jim Harvey about 1956. In that round, loading length was kept short enough so that the ammunition would chamber in modified S&W K-22 revolvers.

22 K-Hornet Loading Data

Bullet (grains/type)	Powder	Grains	Velocity	Energy	Source/Comments
45 SP	IMR 4227	12.5	2875	825	Ackley
45 SP	2400	11.5	2900	840	Ackley
45	IMR 4198	14.5	2800	780	Ackley
50 SP	2400	11.0	2700	810	Ackley

R-2 Lovell

Historical Notes The development of the R-2 Lovell is unusual because it is an example of a wildcat cartridge developed from what was originally a wildcat. It is believed to have been developed in 1937 by Harvey Donaldson of New York. It derived its name from the fact that the second chambering reamer (made by M.S. Risley, Earlville, N.Y.) appeared to be correct in providing what the designer was striving to produce. It is actually an Improved or blown-out version of the original 22 Lovell or 22-3000 developed by Hervey Lovell about 1934. Both are based on the long obsolete 25-20 Single-Shot case necked down, itself a wildcat when it first appeared in 1882.

General Comments The R-2 Lovell is probably the most popular wildcat 22-caliber cartridge ever designed. It was so popular that the late J. Bushnell Smith of Middlebury, Vt., and Griffin & Howe of New York City custom-loaded ammunition in large quantities; when the supply of 25-20 Single-shot cases was exhausted, Griffin & Howe arranged for the manufacture of R-2 cases. This is a fine varmint cartridge and was often chambered in bolt-action and single-shot rifles, where it delivered excellent accuracy. Performance is pretty close to the 222 Remington, but the R-2 Lovell has long since been displaced by this more recent factory chambering, and it is not a good choice, since suitable cases are no longer available. It is included here only for historical significance.

R-2 Lovell Loading Data

Bullet (grains/type)	Powder	Grains	Velocity	Energy	Source/Comments
45 SP	IMR 4227	8.0	1880	350	Ackley
45 SP	IMR 4227	16.0	3280	1070	Ackley
50 SP	IMR 4198	17.0	3050	1030	Ackley
55 SP	IMR 4198	17.0	3050	1135	Ackley

218 Mashburn Bee

Historical Notes The 218 Mashburn Bee is an improved version of the factory 218 Bee. Cases are made by firing factory ammunition in the Mashburn chamber, so no special case-forming dies are required. The cartridge was the work of A.E. Mashburn of the Mashburn Arms Co. in Oklahoma City, Okla. As near as can be determined, the cartridge originated in about 1940 or thereabouts. The improved case produced better ballistics than the original Bee and offered longer case life. There are other Improved versions of the 218 Bee, but all are rather similar. The Mashburn Bee will deliver about the same velocity with the 55-grain bullet as the factory Bee does with the 45-grain bullet.

General Comments The Mashburn Bee was popular until the advent of the 222 Remington. It was, and still is, a very accurate varmint cartridge. The recommended powders for loading these small cartridges are similar to IMR 4198 and IMR 4227.

218 Mashburn Bee Loading Data

Bullet (grains/type)	Powder	Grains	Velocity	Energy	Source/Comments
40 HP	IMR 4227	16.5	3300	960	NA
45 SP	IMR 4227	16.3	3319	1100	Ackley
50 SP	IMR 4198	17.3	3300	1210	Ackley

22 Reed Express

Historical Notes In 2004 Fred Zeglin and Ron Reed, began working on a high-velocity 22-caliber pistol for varminting and for self-defense. As the foundation for their idea, they selected the inexpensive CZ-52 pistol, a quality military pistol currently available from surplus firearm dealers and chambered in the 1930's vintage 7.62x25 Tokarev cartridge. This cartridge was widely used by the former Soviet Union and their allies, before Soviet Bloc countries switched to the 9.x1 Makarov cartridge after WWII. Zeglin and Reed necked the 7.62x25 round to 22-caliber and loaded it with bullets ranging from 30 to 50 grains to create a high-velocity round. Interestingly, the 22 Reed Express achieves velocities with

50-grain bullets that rival those of the FN 5.7x28 cartridge with 26-grain bullets.

General Comments The 22 Reed uses 7.62x25 brass as the parent case. The brass is necked-down to accept .224-inch bullets and the shoulder angle changed. With heavier bullets, the powder charge must be reduced to allow the longer bullets to fit into the CZ-52 pistol magazine. Barrels in 22 Reed Express chambering are available also for the Thompson/Center Contender. Reed's Ammunition & Research offers barrels, reloading components and ammunition.

22 Reed Express Loading Data

Bullet (grains/type)	Powder	Grains	Velocity	Energy	Source/Comments
30 gr. Berger	H110	12.7	2782		Fred Zeglin
35 gr. V-Max	H110	12.6	2721		Fred Zeglin
50-gr	Accurate Arms 9	10.0	2401		Fred Zeglin

22 Waldog

Historical Notes The 22 Waldog was originated by Dan Dowling of Accuracy Gunsmithing in Arvada, Colo., in 1980. He named it after a friend, Waldo G. Woodside, thus the Waldog or Waldo-G. The cartridge is made by running 220 Russian cases through a shortened 22/250 die and trimming the case to a length of 1.375 inches. It is, in effect, a shortened 22 PPC. The idea was to create a more efficient case than the 22 PPC by reducing volumetric capacity to approximately that of the 222 Remington. This cartridge was originally used exclusively in heavy benchrest rifles. Several 100-yard benchrest world records have been broken by the 22 Waldog.

General Comments The 22 Waldog is another effort to develop a super-accurate benchrest cartridge. The current trend is toward smaller, more efficient cases, and the Waldog has proven to be a very accurate cartridge. Best accuracy has been obtained with 52-grain match bullets and 24 grains of H322 powder, but any powder that works well in the 222 Remington should give comparable results in the Waldog. Although not as widely used as the 22 PPC, the Waldog has found a significant following among benchrest shooters. It is reminiscent of the 308x1.5-inch necked down to 22-caliber, also known as the 22 Remington BR, as the two have similar case capacities. However, the 22 Remington BR case is larger in diameter and length is about 0.12-inch longer.

219 Donaldson Wasp

Historical Notes This cartridge originated in 1937, shortly after Winchester introduced the 219 Zipper. It is made by shortening, re-necking and blowing-out 219 Zipper cases. The Donaldson Wasp became the most popular version of such adaptations, and more or less the standard. Many benchrest matches have been won with the 219 Wasp, and it has a well-deserved reputation for excellent accuracy. It has been used mostly in custom-made single-shot rifles because of the rimmed case.

General Comments The 219 Wasp is another 22 wildcat that achieved notable, continued popularity. This is one of the better

wildcat numbers, but like most of the other offbeat 22s, it was overshadowed by the 222 Remington. The 219 Improved Zipper developed by P.O. Ackley in 1938 is a more practical cartridge because it is made by simply fire-forming standard 219 Zipper cases in the Improved chamber. The improved version offers velocities similar to the standard Wasp with significantly lower pressures. Cases for these wildcats can also be made from 25-35 and 30-30 cases. It was claimed by some authorities that breech pressures developed by popular loads in the Wasp ran as high as 55,000 to 60,000 psi, which, in a strong action, is of no consequence.

219 Donaldson Wasp Loading Data

Bullet (grains/type)	Powder	Grains	Velocity	Energy	Source/Comments
45 SP	IMR 3031	30.0	3780	1425	Ackley
45 SP	H380	33.0	3510	1215	NA
50 SP	IMR 4064	32.0	3605	1440	Ackley
50 SP	H380	32.0	3370	1255	NA

22 BR Remington

Historical Notes The 22 BR Remington is based on the 308x1 1/2-inch Barnes case necked-down to 22-caliber and lengthened by 0.020-inch, with the shoulder angle increased to 30 degrees. It is difficult to determine who originated the 22 version of the necked-down 308x1-1/2 because there are a number of versions dating back to about 1963. J. Stekl is credited with having developed the Remington rendition. In any event, Remington standardized the dimensions in 1978 as its 22 BR. It is one of a series of BR cartridges, including the 6mm and 7mm, all based on the same case. The 22 BR is a factory wildcat because loaded ammunition is not available. Cases must be made from special Remington or necked BR cases, which have a small-rifle primer pocket, or from full-size Remington 6mm or 7mm BR cases. The 22 BR has won many honors in benchrest competition and has great accuracy potential.

General Comments The 22 BR is similar to the 22 PPC but has a case of larger base diameter and slightly greater powder capacity with the same case length. Anything one can do, the other can duplicate. Both can push a 55-grain bullet at over 3,000 fps and duplicate the performance of the 223 Remington. Both are extremely accurate and make excellent varmint cartridges as well as competitive benchrest numbers.

22 BR Remington Loading Data

Bullet (grains/type)	Powder	Grains	Velocity	Energy	Source/Comments
53 HP Hornady	2460	32.8	3653	1570	Accurate, 26-inch barrel
55 BT Nosler	2460	32.5	3605	1585	Accurate, 26-inch barrel
60 HP Hornady	2460	31.7	3455	1590	Accurate, 26-inch barrel

224 Texas Trophy Hunter

Historical Notes Every year, Texas hunters take an incredible number of whitetail deer, and more than a few take whitetails with hot 22s. The 224 Texas Trophy Hunter, conceived by gun writer Ralph Lermayer in 1998, uses the greater capacity of the 6mm Remington case to deliver more power than the 22-250 and 220 Swift.

General Comments Following extensive experiments with the 220 Swift, 22/250 and 240 Weatherby cases, Mr. Lermayer settled on the 6mm Remington case as the best balance of case taper, shoulder angle, length and capacity. Necking the 6mm Remington case down to 224 *(with the factory's 26-degree shoulder angle),* the designer created a cartridge that would deliver heavier well-constructed, 70- to 80-grain 224 bullets accurately at relatively high velocities. The 6mm case provides optimum capacity for the 224 bore, brass is readily available, and standard actions and magazines require no modification other than a new barrel. Proper rifling twist for the 224 Texas Trophy Hunter is 1:8 or 1:9. Bullet construction is the key to success; it takes a stout, thick jacket, solid or bonded core bullet to hold up to the velocity potential. Stoutly constructed bullets can be driven in excess of 3500 fps. Dies are available from Redding; Nosler recently endorsed its 22-caliber 60-grain Partition bullet for whitetail deer hunting.

224 Texas Trophy Hunter Loading Data

Bullet (grains/type)	Powder	Grains	Velocity	Energy	Source/Comments
55 Trophy Bonded	H4831	46.5	3840		Ralph Lermayer
60 Nosler Partition	H4831	46.0	3780		Ralph Lermayer
75 Hornady A-Max	Win Mag Rifle	47.0	3780		Ralph Lermayer
79 Lost River	VV N165	45.0	3520		Ralph Lermayer

220 Wotkyns-Wilson Arrow

Historical Notes The 220 Wotkyns-Wilson Arrow was the work of Grosvenor Wotkyns and L.E. Wilson and is the 220 Swift with the shoulder angle increased from 21 degrees to 30 degrees. It dates back to the 1940s. Cases are made by reforming unfired 220 Swift cases in full-length sizing dies. Because of the longer neck, standard Swift ammunition will not fully enter the Arrow chamber and cases cannot be made by fire-forming.

General Comments The 220 Wotkyns-Wilson Arrow represented an effort to remedy a problem by making a minor change in cartridge configuration. Factory Swift cases had the reputation of lengthening after only a few firings, requiring frequent trimming. Changing to a steeper shoulder angle improved headspacing and made for longer case life. The Arrow was a popular benchrest cartridge and a true long-range varmint number. It delivers ballistics comparable to the 220 Swift.

220 Wotkyns-Wilson Arrow Loading Data

Bullet (grains/type)	Powder	Grains	Velocity	Energy	Source/Comments
45 SP	H450	47.0	3985	1580	NA
50 SP	H450	46.0	3850	1640	NA
50 SP	IMR 4064	40.0	3915	1695	NA
55 SP	H380	39.0	3510	1500	NA

220 Weatherby Rocket

Historical Notes The 220 Rocket is the only Weatherby development for which loaded ammunition or empty cases are not available. For this reason, it must be placed in the wildcat category. Developed in 1943 by the late Roy Weatherby, it was the first in the long line of his excellent and successful cartridges. However, it was never very popular. It is important primarily as the beginning of the Weatherby ammunition line and as the initial stimulant to a career of rifle and cartridge manufacture that has had a considerable impact on American thinking.

General Comments The 220 Rocket is actually one of a number of improved wildcat cartridges based on the 220 Swift case. The Ackley and Kilbourn versions are similar to the Weatherby, and none have any particular advantage over any other. In addition, none of these is sufficiently superior to the original 220 Swift to offer anything of outstanding value insofar as performance is concerned. As is typical of improved cartridges in which the original design features significant body taper, the improved Swift extracts somewhat easier and, with proper headspacing, gives longer case life.

220 Weatherby Rocket Loading Data

Bullet (grains/type)	Powder	Grains	Velocity	Energy	Source/Comments
50 SP	IMR 3031	40.0	4005	1775	Ackley
55 SP	IMR 3031	39.0	3767	1730	Ackley
55 SP	IMR 4064	42.0	3860	1820	Ackley

Warning: Start all loads 10 percent below these figures and work up gradually.

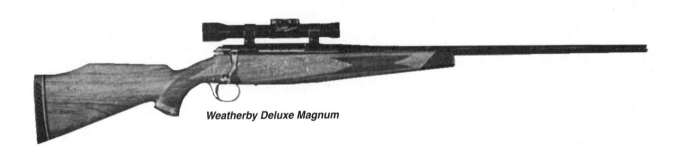

Weatherby Deluxe Magnum

Wildcat Resource Directory

Alexander Arms LLC
U.S. Army, Radford Arsenal
PO Box 1
Radford, VA 24143
(540) 639 8356
http://www.alexanderarms.com

William A. Eichelberger
158 Crossfield Road
King of Prussia, PA 19406
(610) 265-8786

E. Arthur Brown Company
(EABCO)
433 State Highway 27 East
Alexandria, MN 56308
(800) 950-9088
www.eabco.com

James Calhoon Manufacturing
4343 U.S. Highway 87
Havre, MT 59501 USA
(406) 395-4079
www.jamescalhoon.com

Cooper Arms of Montana
Stevensville, MT 59870
(406) 777-0373
www.cooperfirearms.com

Guncrafter Industries
171 Madison 1510
Huntsville, AR 72740
(479) 665-2466
www.guncrafterindustries.com

Michael Petrov
923 West 74th Ave.
Anchorage, AK 99518
(907) 522-4628

Quality Cartridge
P.O. Box 445
Hollywood, MD 20636

Reed's Ammunition & Research
1209 SW 129th St.
Oklahoma City, OK 73170
www.reedsammo.com

SSK Industries
590 Woodvue
Wintersville, OH 43953
(740) 264 0176
www.sskindustries.com

Teppo Jutsu LLC
8000 Research Forest Drive,
Suite 115-120
The Woodlands, TX 77382
(832) 524-8100
www.teppojutsu.com

Wildey FA, Inc.
45 Angevine Rd.
Warren, CT 06754
(860) 355-9000
www.wildeyguns.com

Z-Hat Custom
4010A S. Poplar St.
Casper, WY 82601
(307) 577-7443

22 CHeetah

Historical Notes The 22 CHeetah was developed by Jim Carmichel, shooting editor of *Outdoor Life* magazine, and Fred Huntington of RCBS fame. It appears to have originated in the late 1970s. The cartridge is essentially a full-length Remington 308 BR case — with the small primer pocket — necked-down to 22-caliber, but with the shoulder moved forward. What you end up with is a variation of the 308 Winchester necked-down to 22, but using a special match case. This is not exactly new because there are in existence several slightly different versions made by necking the 243 Winchester case down (such as the 243 Middlestead, which used a 30-degree shoulder angle), and these date back to the early 1960s. However, the 22 CHeetah is an original with regard to the 308 BR case and its small rifle primer pocket.

General Comments The major differences between the 22 CHeetah and its predecessors are the use of the lighter, more uniform BR case, blown-out 40-degree shoulder angle and short neck. In other words, the case has been designed to benchrest specifications. It also has greater powder capacity than any of the older versions. There are actually two case types, the MKI with the 40-degree shoulder angle and the MKII with the original 28-degree shoulder. The 22 CHeetah is somewhat more powerful than the 220 Swift, but ballistics were measured from a 27-inch barrel. The cartridge has proven to be superbly accurate and a very effective 300-yard varmint cartridge.

22 CHeetah Loading Data (MKI)

Bullet (grains/type)	Powder	Grains	Velocity	Energy	Source/Comments
50 SP	IMR 4064	46.0	4285	2040	NA
52 HP	IMR 4064	44.0	4135	1970	NA
55 SP	IMR 4350	49.0	4090	1990	NA

Savage Model 99A lever-action rifle

22 Newton

Historical Notes One of a series of cartridges developed by Charles Newton, this one did not appear in full commercial version. It was designed about 1912, following the introduction of the 22 Savage Hi-Power for the Model 99 lever-action rifle. Newton concluded during his development work on the 22 Savage that it was not entirely adequate for deer. He believed the 70-grain bullet at 2800 fps could be improved by using a larger case. Newton may have used the 7x57mm Mauser case for some of his early experiments. However, the final version of the 22 Newton appears to have been based on the 30-06 case shortened about 1/4-inch and necked-down to take 0.228-inch-diameter bullets. The 22 Newton did not appear as a Newton rifle chambering until about 1914 or later, and did not have a very long life. The original loading had a 90-grain bullet driven at 3100 fps. The 22 Newton was soon displaced by the 256 Newton, which had superior potential as a big game cartridge.

General Comments This is another cartridge somewhat ahead of its time. The new 5.6x57, developed by RWS, is very similar in performance and case capacity. It pushes a 74-grain bullet at 3,400 fps (0.224-inch diameter), and is a necked-down 7x57 case. With a 90-grain bullet, this 5.6mm round would probably just about duplicate 22 Newton performance. Because of the relatively heavy 22-caliber bullet, the 22 Newton would be a satisfactory deer, antelope or similar game cartridge, provided proper bullet construction was used. The 220/257 Gipson is a very similar cartridge based on the 257 Roberts case necked-down to 22-caliber. This latter cartridge was designed by Vernon Gipson, a gunsmith and wildcatter from Worth, Ill. (The 22 Gebby was a similar round on the 257 case.) Rifles for the 22 Newton require a very fast twist (1:8 inches) to stabilize this long, small-caliber bullet.

22 Newton Loading Data

Bullet (grains/type)	Powder	Grains	Velocity	Energy	Source/Comments
70 SP	IMR 4350	40.0	3250	1640	NA
90 SP	IMR 4350	38.0	3100	1920	NA

228 Ackley Magnum

Historical Notes The 228 Ackley Magnum dates back to about 1938 and, although it has been around for a number of years, it developed only a limited popularity. Like the 22 Newton, it was designed as a combination varmint and big game cartridge. Ammunition is made by necking-down and shortening 30-06 or 308 Winchester cases. There are several versions of this cartridge, but Ackley's design is the most popular.

General Comments Rifles for 0.228-inch diameter, heavy-jacketed bullets designed for big game have been used very successfully all over the world. Bullets of this type were made in weights from 70 to more than 100 grains by Fred Barnes, but are now difficult to obtain. Rifles in this class have proven rather conclusively that the difficulties encountered with the 220 Swift and other high-velocity 22s have been mostly a result of improper bullet design. Factory 22-caliber centerfire loads are all made for varmint shooting and do not hold together or penetrate deeply enough on big game. Sometimes these do, and the result is spectacular, but mostly these blow up on contact and inflict a massive, but not immediately fatal, wound. Consequently, hunting deer with any 22-caliber centerfire rifle is illegal in most states. I have witnessed some instant one-shot kills on deer and antelope with high-velocity 22 rifles using proper bullets for the job. Bear this matter of bullet construction in mind next time you get in an argument over the effectiveness of small-caliber rifles on big game.

228 Ackley Magnum Loading Data

Bullet (grains/type)	Powder	Grains	Velocity	Energy	Source/Comments
70 SP	IMR 4350	46.0	3650	2070	Ackley
90 SP	IMR 4350	43.0	3480	2420	Ackley

6x45mm (6mm-223 Remington)

Historical Notes The 6mm-223 Remington, also known as the 6x45mm, came into being in late 1965, shortly after Remington introduced the 223 Remington as a sporting round. Various experimenters built rifles for the cartridge (in order to take advantage of the reduced wind drift offered by the 6mm, as opposed to the original 22-caliber bullet) for benchrest or varmint shooting. Jim Stekl, then manager of Remington's custom shop, set an IBS 200-yard Sporter aggregate record of 0.3069 MOA in 1973 using the 6x45mm. For a time, some owners of AR-15 rifles rebarreled their rifles to this chambering for use in NRA National Match Course competition. However, the 6x45mm cannot compete successfully with the 7.62x51mm NATO (308 Winchester) round at ranges beyond 300 yards. After its brief flurry as a benchrest and match cartridge, the 6x45mm has now been relegated as primarily a varmint cartridge, used by those who want more power than the 223 with the added advantage of being able to utilize inexpensive military cases. Reloading dies are available from RCBS and chambering reamers from Clymer.

General Comments The 6x45mm is one of a series of 6mm benchrest cartridges based on necking-up 223 Remington and 222 Remington Magnum cases. None have any great advantage over the other, and all are capable of extremely fine accuracy. Probably the only advantage of the 6x45mm is that it is based on the 5.56mm (223 Remington) military case, which assures a good supply of cases. On the other hand, its shorter case permits the use of bullets of up to 100 grains to be seated to an overall length that will feed through magazine rifles such as the Colt AR-15, Ruger Mini-14 or Remington 788. In power, the 6x45mm is between the old 25-35 and the 250 Savage, which would make it rather marginal as a deer cartridge except under ideal conditions. It is, however, close to ideal as a varmint and small game cartridge out to 300 yards. This cartridge has become very popular in the Thompson/Center Contender and Remington XP-100 handguns. Bob Milek, the late field editor of *Guns & Ammo* and *Petersen's Hunting* magazines, shot a custom XP-100 in 6x45mm for a number of years. Rifles chambered for cartridges in this group are pleasant to shoot, have a relatively low report and are noted for long barrel life.

6x45mm (6mm-223 Remington) Loading Data

Bullet (grains/type)	Powder	Grains	Velocity	Energy	Source/Comments
70 HP	W748	27.5	2890	1295	NA
75 HP	H335	27.0	2900	1400	NA
80 HP	W748	27.0	2780	1370	NA

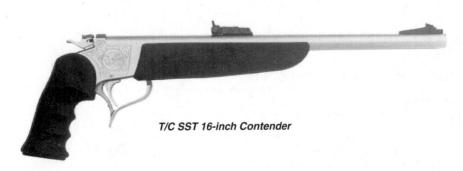

T/C SST 16-inch Contender

6mm Dasher

Historical Notes Early in 1998, this cartridge (based upon the 22 Dasher) was announced in a *Precision Shooting* magazine article that was co-authored by Al Ashton and Dan Dowling. The 22 Dasher was developed as a means of approximating 22-250 ballistics in a shorter case but using cases with the same base diameter. Thinner case walls and the modern Ackley case shape make it possible for the significantly shorter BR case to achieve that goal. This 6mm version is simply the 22-caliber Dasher necked up to accept 6mm bullets with no other changes.

General Comments Lighter 6mm varminting bullets can come very close to matching the trajectory of best 22 Dasher loads; heavier 6mm varmint bullets can exhibit significantly less wind drift. This cartridge will push Nosler's excellent 55-grain BT 150-fps faster than the 22 Dasher will push the same weight bullet. Perhaps a more important advantage is that since the 6mm version is much easier on the barrel, one can expect double the barrel life. Moreover, it is much harder to overheat the barrel during an extended shooting string. The latter fact is a significant consideration to all serious varmint hunters. Concerns over undue barrel heating prompt many varminters to carry several rifles — so they can switch between guns during any extended period of shooting. For this reason alone, the 6mm Dasher is a superior high-performance varminting choice. This cartridge, like the 6mm Norma BR, is finding application in 1,000-yard benchrest events, where it can excel on calm days.

6mm-250 (6mm International) Loading Data

Bullet (grains/type)	Powder	Grains	Velocity	Energy	Source/Comments
55 Nosler BT	H335	39.0	4000	1955	Al Aston (2.175-inch OAL)
70 Nosler BT	H335	36.8	3650	2070	Al Aston (2.175-inch OAL)

6mm-250 (6mm International)
Walker Version

Historical Notes Prior to World War II, the 6mm (24-caliber) was nearly exclusively a British and European development, with some cartridges dating back to the early 1900s. Immediately after World War II, American wildcatters began to work with this caliber. The simple process of necking the 250 Savage case down to take 243 bullets probably occurred to several individuals, but was obscured by other 6mm developments. Several versions exist, but two of these have become popular with benchrest and match shooters. The Donaldson 6mm International was developed by Harvey Donaldson of Fultonville, N.Y., known as the father of modern benchrest shooting. The Remington 6mm International originated with Mike Walker of the Remington Arms Co.

General Comments Cartridges of 6mm based on the 250 Savage case are all similar, but vary slightly in length and shoulder angle.

Original design was the 250 case necked-down with no other change. Donaldson's version used a 1/4-inch shortened case with the shoulder pushed back; on that version, shoulder angle is 30 degrees. The Walker 6mm retains the standard length, but pushes the shoulder back, creating a long neck. Body taper and shoulder angle are the same as the 250. The Remington 40X match rifle has been chambered, on special order, for the Walker cartridge. Robert Hutton, long-time experimenter and gun writer, has worked with these cartridges and his results were presented in the 1962 (16th edition) of GUN DIGEST. The late John T. Amber reported 5/8-inch averages for five-shot, 100-yard groups with the Walker cartridge in the Remington 40X target rifle — impressive performance for that era.

6mm-250 (6mm International) Loading Data

Bullet (grains/type)	Powder	Grains	Velocity	Energy	Source/Comments
60 HP	IMR 3031	32.0	3450	1630	NA
75 HP	IMR 3031	32.0	3390	1910	NA
90 SP	IMR 3031	30.0	3160	2000	NA
100 SP	IMR 3031	28.0	2900	1870	NA

6mm CHeetah

Historical Notes The 6mm CHeetah, designed by *Outdoor Life's* shooting editor Jim Carmichel, is a highly accurate, long-range varmint cartridge. It is best described as a variation of Jim's earlier (and racy) 22 CHeetah cartridge necked up to accommodate 6mm bullets. Based on a modified 243 Winchester parent case, the cartridge employs both fireforming and neck-turning techniques, and requires knowledge of advanced reloading practices.

General Comments The principle advantage of the 6mm CHeetah is accuracy. This performance results from a combination of precise cartridge case preparation steps (especially neck turning to a diameter of .267-inch to achieve precision bullet alignment), and chambering in high quality rifles with target-grade barrels and expert gunsmithing. The case design is not a true improved cartridge, and factory 243 Winchester ammunition cannot safely be fired in the 6mm CHeetah. Loading data for the 243 AI cartridge can be used for the 6mm CHeetah. The fireforming load uses 46.5-grains of Reloader 19 and a Sierra 85-grain bullet seated for an overall loaded cartridge length of 2.747 inches. Rifles using the Remington 40X or modern benchrest-type actions provide the best platform for the 6mm CHeetah. Reamers are available from JGS Precision Tool Mfg; rifles for the 6mm CHeetah can be supplied by gunsmiths specializing in high precision firearms.

6mm CHeetah Loading Data

Bullet (grains/type)	Powder	Grains	Velocity	Energy	Source/Comments
55-gr Nosler Ballistic Tip	H4350	51.0	3627		Jim Carmichel
70-gr Speer TNT	H4350	47.5	3525		Jim Carmichel
100-gr Sierra Boattail Spitzer	H4350	45.0	3074		Jim Carmichel

240 Hawk

Historical Notes Unlike other members of the Hawk cartridge family, Fred Zeglin designed the 240 Hawk as an overbore velocity-addicted varmint cartridge. It is capable of shooting groups as small as .300-inch at 100 yards, and offers one of the flattest trajectories available in 6mm varmint cartridges. Performance comes at a price, however, and 240 Hawk barrel life may be shorter than other 6mm varmint cartridges using lighter powder charges. Devout long-range varmint shooters may decide the trade-off is OK.

General Comments All Hawk cartridges fit into standard 30-06 length actions and use a .473-inch bolt-face. The 240 Hawk uses 280 Remington brass as its parent case. The brass is necked down in a sizing die and fireformed in a 240 Hawk chamber. The 240 Hawk is designed for lighter weight 6mm varmint bullets. Reloading data for the 240 Weatherby can be used as a starting point, as the 240 Hawk enjoys a four percent greater case capacity advantage. However, barrel life will be less than other 6mm varmint cartridges that use lighter powder charges. It is best suited for bolt-action rifles with 28-inch barrels with a 1:14 rifling twist. Z-Hat Custom offers rifles, dies and reloading information. Use caution with the listed loads, as Z-Hat has not conducted pressure tests on them.

240 Hawk Loading Data

Bullet (grains/type)	Powder	Grains	Velocity	Energy	Source/Comments
60-gr Sierra HP	VV N150	53.0	3968		Z-Hat Custom
75-gr Speer HP	H4064	49.0	3652		Z-Hat Custom
80-gr Remington HP	RL-15	53.0	4055		Z-Hat Custom
87-gr Hornady SPT	Win 748	51.0	3954		Z-Hat Custom

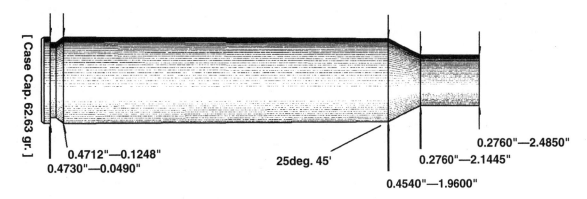

[Case Cap. 62.63 gr.]

0.4712"—0.1248"
0.4730"—0.0490"
25deg. 45'
0.4540"—1.9600"
0.2760"—2.1445"
0.2760"—2.4850"

6mm/30-30 Improved

Historical Notes There are actually two common versions of the 6mm/30-30, one based on the 30-30 Winchester case necked-down without any other change, and the other using the Improved configuration. The Improved version was the most popular and the one recommended. The 6mm/30-30 has the same dimensions as the 22/30-30 except for a larger 0.243-inch neck diameter. The cartridge dates back to the 1940s or earlier, and the version referred to here is the Ackley Improved, although there may be others. One of the original purposes of the 6mm/30-30 was for use in rebored and rechambered 22 Hi-Power Model 99 Savage lever-actions. This chambering has also been used in single-shot actions. Cases can be formed from 30-30 or 32 Special cases, which might require a set of forming dies plus a final fire-forming. More recent versions use a shortened case for application to single-shot pistols.

General Comments The 6mm/30-30, when used in a strong action, can be loaded to almost equal the 243 Winchester. It is a good varmint-through-deer cartridge, but its current usefulness is primarily as a chambering for single-shot actions.

6mm/30-30 Improved Loading Data

Bullet (grains/type)	Powder	Grains	Velocity	Energy	Source/Comments
75 HP	IMR 3031	37.0	3450	1980	Ackley
75 HP	IMR 4895	36.0	3265	1770	Ackley
*85 HP	IMR 4895	37.0	3300	2060	Ackley
90 SP	IMR 4320	38.0	3065	1880	Ackley
*Ackley, op cit.					

6mm-284

Historical Notes It is anybody's guess who might have been first to size Winchester's rebated-rim 284 down to 6mm. The conversion is good for those interested in achieving maximum velocity with this bullet size. This cartridge can be chambered in medium-length actions.

General Comments The 6mm-284 has practically the same capacity as the 240 Weatherby Magnum and the 6mm-06. If loaded to similar chamber pressures, it will produce similar velocity. Therefore, ballistics are indistinguishable. However, it has advantages over the Weatherby offering. Cases are easier to come by and non-belted. The 6mm-284 can also be chambered in medium-length actions.

Just like the 6mm-06 and 240 Weatherby, when loaded with 100-grain bullets, the 6mm-284 produces only about 100 fps more velocity than the 6mm Remington — when loaded to the same peak pressures and fired from equal-length barrels. Likely, with heavier-than-standard bullets, this difference could reach 150 fps. As to whether such an advantage might justify conversion of a 243 Winchester or 6mm Remington rifle to 6mm-284, consider that this performance difference exceeds the performance difference between the 280 Remington and 7mm Remington Magnum!

6mm-284 Loading Data (26-inch barrel)

Bullet (grains/type)	Powder	Grains	Velocity	Energy	Source/Comments
70	IMR 4320	45.0	3600	2015	Hornady
70	IMR 4350	49.5	3600	2015	Hornady
70	H4831	52.5	3600	2015	Hornady
75	H4831	54.1	3600	2155	Hornady
87	H4831	51.7	3400	2230	Hornady
100	IMR 4350	49.0	3200	2275	Hornady
100	H4831	51.4	3200	2275	Hornady

25 Ackley Krag

Historical Notes Ackley offered at least two versions of this cartridge. The 25 Ackley Krag Short holds about 50 grains of IMR type powder, compared to the full-length 25 Ackley Krag, which holds about 55 grains. The shorter version seems to have been Ackley's favorite and he preferred it for chambering in P14 Enfields and various single-shot actions. In the heyday of Ackley's developments, the slowest powders available limited performance gains with case capacity increases much beyond this level in the quarter-bore. This fact explains the similar performance he reported for the two versions.

General Comments The Short version of the 25 Ackley Krag offers very impressive performance when properly loaded in a strong modern action but it is now overshadowed by the full-length version of the 25 Ackley Krag and other larger-capacity cases, such as the 25-06. Nevertheless, either of these cartridges are fully capable as big game cartridges for smaller North American species. These can be highly recommended for single-shot rifle conversions. Very similarly performing 25-caliber versions of the 303 British were championed in Canada and other former British ruled lands for use in the British SMLE (Enfield) or the much stronger P14 Enfield or Martini single-shot action.

25 Ackley Krag Short Loading Data

Bullet (grains/type)	Powder	Grains	Velocity	Energy	Source/Comments
87	H380	49.0	3460	2310	Ackley
100	IMR 4064	43.0	3265	2365	Ackley
100	H380	49.0	3412	2585	Ackley
100	IMR 4350	50.0	3300	2415	Ackley
117	H4831	50.0	3285	2855	Ackley

25 Ackley Krag (full-length 30-40 conversion) Loading Data

Bullet (grains/type)	Powder	Grains	Velocity	Energy	Source/Comments
87	IMR 4064	48.0	3360	2180	Ackley
100	IMR 4350	50.0	3090	2120	Ackley
100	IMR 4895	49.0	3414	2585	Ackley
125	IMR 4350	50.0	3000	2495	Ackley

250/3000 Ackley Improved

Historical Notes The 250/3000 Improved was originated by P.O. Ackley in the late 1940s and, although one of the best of the Ackley "Improved" line of cartridges, has never achieved great popularity. This statement is based upon the observation that it offers the greatest percentage velocity increase of any of the Improved line of wildcats. Increased shoulder angle affects performance chiefly because it increases case capacity. However, it also improves headspacing and decreases case stretching. There are no significant internal ballistic effects related to any particular shoulder design. There are several versions of the 250 Improved, but the Ackley configuration is the best known. The Savage Model 99 lever-action

has recently been offered chambered for the 250/3000, and tens of thousands of these fine rifles are in the hands of hunters. Handloading owners of these rifles should be interested in this excellent conversion, which improves extraction, extends case life and increases performance markedly.

General Comments The 250/3000 Improved offers performance equal to or better than the 257 Roberts. It will, for example, push the 100-grain bullet at a muzzle velocity of 3,200 fps, compared to the factory 257 loading of the same bullet that is listed at 2,900 fps. The commercial 250/3000 loading of the 100-grain bullet, incidentally, is rated at 2,820 fps.

250/3000 Ackley Improved Loading Data

Bullet (grains/type)	Powder	Grains	Velocity	Energy	Source/Comments
87 SP	IMR 4350	42.0	3310	2110	Ackley
100 SP	IMR 4350	41.0	3045	2060	Ackley
100 SP	IMR 4350	42.0	3200	2275	Ackley
120 SP	IMR 4350	40.0	2650	1870	Ackley
120 SP	IMR 4350	41.0	2750	2020	Ackley

250 Humdinger

General Comments The 250 Humdinger is a 243 case expanded to 25-caliber and fire-formed in the Humdinger chamber. The case has absolute minimum body taper and a 45° shoulder angle. This produces about as much capacity as can be squeezed from an improved 243 case. The 25-caliber is ideally suited to hunting wild pigs, feral goats and most deer species in Australia, as well as varmint shooting with lighter bullets. Most short action rifles designed for the 243 or 308 could quite successfully be chambered for this cartridge. Ballistics from a 23-inch barrel exceed factory 25-06 loads, and it could be considered quite an efficient cartridge.

250 Humdinger Loading Data

Bullet (grains/type)	Powder	Grains	Velocity	Energy	Source/Comments
75 Sierra HP	H4350	50.0	3577	2131	Breil Jackson
87 Sierra SP	H4350	48.5	3437	2282	Breil Jackson
100 Nosler BT	H4350	46.0	3194	2266	Breil Jackson
100 Nosler BT	RL 19	48.5	3175	2239	Breil Jackson
117 Hornady SPBT	IMR4831	46.0	3085	2473	Breil Jackson
120 Nosler Partition	IMR4831	45.0	3040	2462	Breil Jackson

257 Ackley Improved

Historical Notes A number of "Improved" versions of the 257 Roberts exist. Most were developed in the late 1940s and early 1950s. The 257 Ackley Improved is one of the best, and certainly the most popular of the crop. This cartridge has rather straight, blown-out case walls with very little taper and a 40-degree shoulder angle. As with the other Ackley Improved cartridges, cases are made by firing factory ammunition in the Improved chamber. The 257 Improved has about the ideal case capacity for the 25-caliber and is quite efficient in the velocity it produces with a given charge of powder. The gains achieved by Improved cartridges are a matter of increasing case capacity by changing shoulder angle and sometimes moving the shoulder forward to lengthen the body, and at the same time reducing body taper. Shoulder angle affects performance chiefly because it increases case capacity. It also improves headspacing and decreases case stretching. However, there are no significant internal ballistic effects related to any particular shoulder design. The 257 Improved will develop from 100 to 300 fps more velocity than the standard 257 Roberts, depending on bullet weight. In fact, velocities are only slightly below those developed by the 25-06 with the same weight bullets (capacities of these two are quite similar).

General Comments The 257 Improved has proven to be an excellent cartridge for long-range varmint shooting and for big game such as deer, antelope, black bear, big horn sheep, etc. This is one of the best of the Improved cartridge line, in terms of useful velocity and energy gain.

257 Improved (Ackley) Loading Data

Bullet (grains/type)	Powder	Grains	Velocity	Energy	Source/Comments
75 HP	IMR 4895	44.0	3570	2365	Ackley
87 SP	IMR 4895	43.0	3352	2160	Ackley
100 SP	IMR 4831	51.0	3200	2280	Ackley
100 SP	IMR 4350	49.0	3160	2220	Ackley
117 SP	IMR 4831	47.0	2850	2112	Ackley
120 SP	IMR 4831	46.0	2875	2210	Ackley

25-284

Historical Notes It is anybody's guess who might have been the first to size the 284 Winchester down to the quarter-bore. This conversion is a good one, offering usable capacity practically identical to the 25-06 in a cartridge that can be chambered in medium-length actions.

General Comments The 25-284 is ballistically indistinguishable from the 25-06, but offers several advantages. First, the sharper case shoulder of the shorter case reduces case stretching and extends case life, compared to the 25-06. Second, the shorter

powder column promises superior accuracy potential. Finally, this more compact cartridge is easier to handle. Nevertheless, the 25-06 was easier to make because 30-06 cases have long been plentiful. Further, the 25-06 enjoyed decades of wildcat history. For these reasons, it is not surprising this was the choice to achieve factory chambering. This is too bad, because the 25-06 offers no ballistic advantages over the 25-284 and the aforementioned facts would tend to suggest the 25-284 as a better all-around choice.

25-284 Loading Data

(Capacity and chamber pressure are essentially identical to the 25-06 and that data can be used, providing a prudent reduction in starting loads and adherence to standard loading practices to ensure against inadvertent use of too-hot loads.)

25 Gibbs

Historical Notes The 25 Gibbs was designed in the 1950s by firearms experimenter R.E. (Rocky) Gibbs. It was a natural follow-on to Gibbs' original 270 Gibbs, which he developed while seeking the optimum case capacity for the 270 bore size in combination with a 150-grain bullet.

General Comments The 25 Gibbs is a blown-out 30-06 (or 270 Winchester) case with a steep shoulder and short neck. The shoulder is pushed forward about .196-inch compared to the standard 270 case, and the case holds about six grains more IMR4350 powder than a standard 270 Winchester. Although Gibbs used this and his other wildcats as front ignition cartridges, the following is a "standard" loading without the front ignition tube.

25 Gibbs Loading Data

Bullet (grain/type)	Powder	Grains	Velocity	Energy	Source/Comments
87 Sierra SP	IMR4350	62.0	3617		R.E. Gibbs

EABCO 6.5mm Bench Rest Magnum (6.5 BRM)

Historical Notes In 1996, Eben Brown lengthened the 219 Donaldson Wasp benchrest cartridge by 1/4-inch, and opened the neck to 6.5mm to create the 6.5 Bench Rest Magnum cartridge. This cartridge was developed to give big-game hunting performance from small frame single-shot rifles and pistols such as the Thompson/Center Contenders and Encores, BF pistols, Ruger Number One rifles and EABCO model 97D rifles.

General Comments Brass is mechanically formed from virgin 30-30 Winchester cases, and given a longer body with a slight taper, sharp 30-degree shoulder and 6.5mm neck. A long, skinny cartridge body keeps bolt thrust manageable for small-frame firearms. In

suitable single-shot firearms, the 6.5mm BRM works well with barrel lengths of 24 inches and 1:8 rifling. The sectional density of 140-grain 6.5mm bullets is similar to 190-grain bullets in 30-caliber cartridges. For large game, such as moose or North American elk, suitable bonded core or partition bullets should be loaded. EABCO provides rifles, barrels, loaded ammunition and reloading supplies for the 6.5 BRM cartridge. In addition, they offer a family of cartridges in 224, 6mm, 7mm and 300 BRM chamberings. All loads listed use EABCO custom-formed brass and CCI BR LR primers.

EABCO 6.5mm Bench Rest Magnum (6.5 BRM) Loading Data and Factory Ballistics

Bullet (grains/type)	Powder	Grains	Velocity	Energy	Source/Comments
100-gr Sierra	VV N150	38.0	2877		EABCO
140-gr Sierra GameKing ®	FL		2400		EABCO
140-gr Sierra GameKing ®	VV N160	38.0	2496		EABCO
140-gr Hornady A-Max ™	H4831SC	39.5	2401		EABCO

6.5 Grendel

Historical Notes The 6.5 Grendel cartridge underwent three years of development before Bill Alexander (Alexander Arms) released it in 2003 as a long-range cartridge specifically intended for the AR-15 family of rifles and carbines. The 6.5 Grendel design transforms the military 7.62x39 parent case by necking it down to 6.5mm, blowing out the shoulder and changing to a Small Rifle primer and flash hole. A close relative of the benchrest-proven 6.5mm PPC, the 6.5 Grendel is the ideal length to seat long ogive 120-grain and 130-grain bullets within the AR-15 magazine length confines.

General Comments Accuracy in the 6.5 Grendel in suitably barreled AR-15 rifles readily attains sub-MOA, making it a great choice for long-range deer and varmint hunting. The 6.5 Grendel accommodates lightweight varmint bullets in the 90-grain class, which offer superb accuracy for competition and small game shooting, mid-weight 108- or 120-grain competition bullets and 130- or 140-grain game bullets for long shots on medium-sized game. Seventeen 6.5 Grendel cartridges will fit into an Alexander Arms-supplied magazine dimensioned to fit into the magazine well in the AR-15's lower receiver. The cartridge performs well in a 24-inch barrel using a 1:9 twist. Factory loads do not exceed 50,000 psi. Alexander Arms supplies rifles, magazines, ammunition, reloading dies and brass.

6.5 Grendel Factory Ballistics

Bullet (grains/type)	Powder	Grains	Velocity	Energy	Source/Comments
90-gr Speer TNT	FL		3030		Alexander Arms
120-gr Nosler BT	FL		2580		Alexander Arms
123-gr Lapua Scenar	FL		2650		Alexander Arms
129-gr Hornady SST	FL		2450		Alexander Arms

264 Hawk

Historical Notes Designed by Wyoming gunmaker Fred Zeglin in 1998, the 264 Hawk, one of the proprietary Hawk cartridge family, is a flat-shooting, open country hunting cartridge. For antelope, mule deer and similar sized game, the 264 Hawk can speed 6.5mm bullets to impressive velocities.

General Comments All Hawk cartridges fit into standard 30-06 length actions and use a .473-inch bolt face. The 264 Hawk uses 280 Remington brass as its parent case. The brass is necked-down in a sizing die and fireformed in a 264 Hawk chamber. The 264 Hawk is can accommodate bullet weights ranging from light 6.5mm varmint bullets up to 140-grain big-game hunting bullets. It is best suited for bolt-action rifles with 26-inch barrels with a 1:14 rifling twist. Z-Hat Custom offers rifles, dies and reloading information.

264 Hawk Loading Data

Bullet (grains/type)	Powder	Grains	Velocity	Energy	Source/Comments
85-gr Sierra HP	H4895	51.0	3575		Z-Hat Custom
120-gr Nosler BP	VV N160	57.0	3440		Z-Hat Custom
129-gr Hornady SP	H4831	56.0	2970		Z-Hat Custom
140-gr Nosler	IMR 7828	54.0	2955		Z-Hat Custom

6.5 Gibbs

Historical Notes The 6.5 Gibbs was designed in the 1950s by firearms experimenter R.E. (Rocky) Gibbs. It was a natural follow-on to Gibbs' original 270 Gibbs, which he developed while seeking the optimum case capacity for the 270 bore size in combination with a 150-grain bullet.

General Comments The 6.5 Gibbs is a blown-out 30-06 (or 270) case with a steep shoulder and short neck. The shoulder is pushed forward about .196-inch compared to the standard 270 case, and the case holds about six grains more IMR4350 powder than a standard 270 Winchester. Although Gibbs used this and his other wildcats as front-ignition cartridges, the following is a "standard" loading without front ignition tube.

6.5 Gibbs Loading Data

Bullet (grains/type)	Powder	Grains	Velocity	Energy	Source/Comments
120 SP	IMR4350	60.0	3325		R.E. Gibbs
140 Speer	H4831	62.0	2967		R.E. Gibbs

6.5mm-06
Ackley Improved

Historical Notes This cartridge was a natural outgrowth from the 6.5-06. After World War II, many military rifles of 6.5mm were surplused by various countries. Most found their way to the shores of the United States as a means of bringing much-needed cash to countries that would have otherwise simply scrapped these. Since ammunition for these chamberings was difficult or impossible to obtain, it was natural for gunsmiths to consider rechambering to 6.5-06, since abundant, inexpensive 30-06 cases are easily necked-down to 6.5 and the conversion offered the promise of more power than the original chambering in the bargain. Similarly, bullet manufacturers responded to the availability of 6.5mm guns by offering component bullets for handloading. This later only served to increase demand for wildcat conversions. It was only reasonable for customers to want to chamber for the improved version of the 6.5mm-06 because this added nothing to the cost of the conversion and promised a ballistic benefit and increased case life. With the powders then available, the latter was delivered; the former was not.

General Comments Ackley's experiences with this chambering are most interesting. He first chambered a 6.5mm barrel to 6.5mm-06 and worked up load data for that. Then he rechambered the same barrel to the improved version and again worked up data. We can only assume that he used the same pressure criteria and the same components for both studies, but perhaps this is an erroneous assumption. The reason for doubt stems from the fact that Ackley reported higher velocities with the standard 6.5-06 than with the improved version. It must be noted that he was limited to powders no slower burning than H4831. Using the slower powders now available, he might have found the improved version to have the ballistic edge. In any case, the difference in ballistics is marginal. It should be noted that the 25-06 and the 6.5mm-06 Improved have almost exactly the same relative case capacity. Therefore, considering bullet availability, including light varmint-style bullets and hunting bullets that are much heavier than anything available in 0.257-inch, the 6.5mm-06 Improved is everything the 25-06 will ever be, and more.

6.5mm-06 Ackley Improved Loading Data

Bullet (grains/type)	Powder	Grains	Velocity	Energy	Source/Comments
120	IMR 4350	53.0	3100	2560	Ackley
140	IMR 4350	51.0	2920	2650	Ackley
140	H4831	53.0	2950	2705	Ackley
150	IMR 4350	49.0	2780	2575	Ackley
150	H4831	51.0	2760	2535	Ackley
165	IMR 4350	46.0	2550	2090	Ackley
165	H4831	48.0	2550	2090	Ackley

6.5mm Leopard

Historical Notes In 2001, *Outdoor Life's* shooting editor Jim Carmichel designed a 6.5mm long-range hunting and target cartridge based on newly available Winchester Short Magnum brass. The resulting cartridge, the 6.5 Leopard, proved successful in long-range competitive shooting, and offers a highly competitive alternative to the 6.5x284 cartridges used by some shooters. At top end loadings the 6.5 Leopard is capable of pushing a Sierra 142-grain Match King bullet to velocities exceeding 3200 fps.

General Comments Following initial experimentation with 300 WSM cases, the 6.5 Leopard case construction became a simple, one-step necking down operation once 270 WSM cases became available. No other case changes are needed because the 270 WSM case length, shoulder diameter and shoulder angle are optimal. The 6.5 Leopard works well in 26-inch barrels with a 1:9 twist. The cartridge is suitable for short action rifles, such as the Remington 700. Reamers are available from JGS Precision Tool Mfg and Redding offers reloading dies. Rifles for the 6.5 Leopard can be supplied by Borden Rifles and other gunsmiths specializing in high precision firearms. Listed loads are starting loads.

6.5 Leopard Loading Data

Bullet (grains/type)	Powder	Grains	Velocity	Energy	Source/Comments
107-gr	IMR 4831	62.0	3404		Jim Carmichel
120-gr	RETUMBO	65.0	3203		Jim Carmichel
140-gr	RETUMBO	60.0	3036		Jim Carmichel

270 REN

Historical Notes Designed in 1985 by Charles Rensing and Jim Rock, this cartridge was developed in response to NRA Hunter Pistol Silhouette competition rules. This category only allows use of straight-walled cartridges. This diminutive number fulfills that requirement while producing minimal recoil, as intended by the inventors.

General Comments The 270 REN is based on the 22 Hornet simply necked straight to accept 270 bullets. Recoil is very mild in typical guns and this little chambering can propel the excellent 90-, 100- and 110-grain bullets available to considerable velocity with modest powder charges. Guns chambered for the 270 REN are currently available from several manufacturers including RPM, Thompson/Center and Merrill.

270 REN Loading Data (10-inch barrel)

Bullet (grains/type)	Powder	Grains	Velocity	Energy	Source/Comments
90	AA No. 7	8.2	1650	540	Accurate
90	AA No. 9	11.1	1888	710	Accurate
90	A1680	14.5	1811	655	Accurate
100 Hornady	H110	10.2	1600	565	Hornady
100 Hornady	AA 5744	10.4	1600	565	Hornady
100 Hornady	W296	11.0	1600	565	Hornady
100 Hornady	AA No. 7	8.2	1566	540	Accurate
100 Hornady	AA No. 9	10.8	1799	715	Accurate
100 Hornady	A1680	14.5	1815	730	Accurate
110 Sierra	AA No. 7	8.0	1474	530	Accurate
110 Sierra	AA No. 9	10.2	1666	675	Accurate
110 Sierra	A1680	14.0	1675	685	Accurate

270 Hawk

Historical Notes Like the 270 Ackley Improved, the 270 Hawk delivers about 50 fps more velocity than the factory 270 Winchester cartridge with identical bullets. Fred Zeglin designed the 270 Hawk as a member of his proprietary Hawk cartridge family about 1998. The 270 Hawk is an excellent deer and antelope cartridge.

General Comments All Hawk cartridges fit into standard 30-06 length actions and use a .473-inch boltface. The 270 Hawk uses 280 Remington brass as its parent case. The brass is necked up to 30-caliber, full length sized and fireformed in a 270 Hawk chamber. The 270 Hawk works well in bolt-action rifles with 24-26 inch barrels and a 1:10 inch rifling twist. Quality Cartridge supplies ammunition and correctly headstamped brass. Z-Hat Custom offers rifles, dies and reloading information.

270 Hawk Loading Data

Bullet (grains/type)	Powder	Grains	Velocity	Energy	Source/Comments
130 gr.	H4350	61.0	3295		Z-Hat Custom
140 gr.	H4350	58.0	3161		Z-Hat Custom
150 gr.	H4350	57.0	3051		Z-Hat Custom

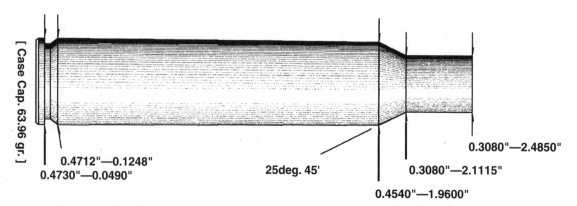

[Case Cap. 63.96 gr.] 0.4712"—0.1248" 0.4730"—0.0490" 25deg. 45' 0.4540"—1.9600" 0.3080"—2.1115" 0.3080"—2.4850"

270 Gibbs

Historical Notes The 270 Gibbs was designed in the 1950s by firearms experimenter R.E. (Rocky) Gibbs. It was developed while seeking the optimum case capacity for the 270 bore size in combination with a 150-grain bullet. Gibbs wanted a case with more capacity than a 270 Ackley, but believed the capacity of "short magnum" 270 cases to be excessive. He wanted to seat a heavy (150 gr.) bullet to "normal depth" and leave very little air space for high loading density maximum loads.

General Comments The 270 Gibbs is a blown-out 30-06 (or 270) case with a steep shoulder and short neck. The shoulder is pushed forward about .196-inch compared to the standard 270 case, and the case holds about six grains more IMR4350 powder than a standard 270 Winchester. Although Gibbs used this and his other wildcats as front-ignition cartridges, the following is a "standard" loading without front ignition tube.

270 Gibbs Loading Data

Bullet (grains/type)	Powder	Grains	Velocity	Energy	Source/Comments
150 gr SPBT	H4831	63.0	3175		R.E. Gibbs

270 IHMSA

Historical Notes Just one of an entire series of cartridges designed by Elgin Gates, the 270 IHMSA (International Handgun Metallic Silhouette Association) is among the more popular of the group, which ranges from 25- through 35-caliber. All are similar and are designed specifically for chambering in single-shot handguns. The intention was to offer competitors a choice of easy-to-make chamberings that could deliver the desired momentum to distant targets. In this endeavor, Gates appears to have been notably successful. Other IHMSA numbers include 7mm & 30-caliber versions.

General Comments The 270 IHMSA is based on the 300 Savage case. Cases are formed by simply necking the case down to accept 270 bullets. The sizing die also drives the inside of the shoulder back to achieve a 38-degree shoulder angle, providing superior headspace control and a longer case neck. The same treatment is utilized for all cases in the IHMSA line.

270 IHMSA Loading Data (14-inch barrel)

Bullet (grains/type)	Powder	Grains	Velocity	Energy	Source/Comments
90	H414	45.0	2691	1445	Hodgdon
90	BL-C(2)	40.0	2719	1475	Hodgdon
100	H414	45.0	2654	1560	Hodgdon
100	H4895	38.0	2654	1560	Hodgdon
110	H414	44.0	2626	1680	Hodgdon
110	H4895	37.0	2590	1635	Hodgdon
130	H414	41.0	2442	1720	Hodgdon
130	H450	44.0	2423	1695	Hodgdon
140	H4831	43.0	2449	1860	Hodgdon
140	H4350	41.0	2394	1780	Hodgdon
150	H4350	40.0	2291	1745	Hodgdon
150	H4895	33.0	2274	1720	Hodgdon

270 Savage
270 Ackley Improved Savage

Historical Notes The 270 Savage was, in its day, a very good cartridge for the Model 99 Savage, and it remains so. With the standard 130-grain bullet, it delivers performance reasonably close to factory 270 Winchester loads. Heavier bullets intrude much of the available powder space and, therefore, do not perform as well. The Ackley improved version comes very close to 270 Winchester ballistics and is a much better Model 99 chambering option in all respects (see discussion at 250-300 Ackley Improved).

General Comments While the 250 Savage is a fine deer cartridge, the 270 version offers the potential to use heavier bullets at about the same velocity. Therefore, this chambering (particularly the Ackley version) is a much better big game hunting option. With properly constructed bullets, this is a much better elk cartridge.

270 Savage Loading Data

Bullet (grains/type)	Powder	Grains	Velocity	Energy	Source/Comments
100 SP	IMR 4064	42.0	3107	2140	Ackley
100 SP	IMR 3031	39.0	2950	1930	Ackley
130 SP	IMR 4064	39.0	2763	2200	Ackley
150 SP	IMR 4350	43.0	2574	2205	Ackley

Savage Model 99R

7mm TCU

Historical Notes The 7mm TCU is another of the series of cartridges developed by Wes Ugalde for Thompson/Center and offered as a standard chambering in the single-shot Contender pistol. All are based on the 223 Remington case necked-up, this one to 7mm (0.284-inch). The 7mm TCU dates back to about 1980, and has become quite popular for metallic-silhouette pistol shooting. It is also known as the 7mmx223. Other TCU numbers include 6mm, 25-caliber and 6.5mm versions of this same basic case.

General Comments The 7mm TCU has a reputation for exceptional accuracy and makes a good varmint cartridge in the T/C Contender pistol, particularly with the 14-inch barrel, which provides an extra couple of hundred fps over the 10-inch barrel. It is on the marginal side for deer or other medium game. The originators recommend that only commercial 223 Remington cases be used for forming cases. Do not use military cases. Cases are easy to make and can be formed in one operation once the dies are properly adjusted. Proper case length is 1.740 inches.

7mm TCU Loading Data

Bullet (grains/type)	Powder	Grains	Velocity	Energy	Source/Comments
100 SP	BL-C2	28.0	2100	980	14-inch barrel
115 SP	IMR 4198	23.0	2185	1220	14-inch barrel
130 SP	IMR 4198	22.0	2050	1215	14-inch barrel
140 SP	H4895	24.0	1880	1100	14-inch barrel
150 SP	BL-C2	25.0	1910	1220	14-inch barrel

7 GNR

Historical Notes The 7 GNR, a 1980s development by Gary Reeder, preceded the production of factory 7x30 ammunition by several years. Originally intended as a long-range, flat-shooting cartridge for the Thompson/Center Contender, the 7 GNR evolved into a popular deer and antelope cartridge for both handguns and rifles.

General Comments Although the 7 GNR originally used rimmed 375 Winchester brass as a parent case, the brass thickness reduced case capacity and ballistic performance. Reeder then tried the 30-30 cartridge cases, necking them down to accept 7mm bullets, shortening the neck and changing the body shape by fireforming. Once Winchester factory 7x30 cases became available, they provided the ideal parent case for the 7 GNR. Firing a round of factory 7x30 ammunition in a 7 GNR chamber produces a perfectly formed case. Existing 7x30 barrels can be rechambered for the 7 GNR. Gary Reeder Custom Guns offers dies, barrels, firearms, reloading components and information.

7 GNR Loading Data

Bullet (grains/type)	Powder	Grains	Velocity	Energy	Source/Comments
120-gr Spitzer	Win 748	40.0	2726		Gary Reeder
125-gr Spitzer	H322	37.0	2600		Gary Reeder
130-gr SSP	H322	37.0	2585		Gary Reeder

7mm ShootingTimes Easterner/(7mm STE)

Historical Notes The 7mm Shooting Times Easterner (7mm STE) was designed in 1987 by gun writer Layne Simpson for Marlin 336 and Winchester Model 94 lever-action rifles. This cartridge is the 307 Winchester case necked down and fire-formed to the Improved configuration with minimum body taper and a 40-degree shoulder. The 307 Winchester is actually a rimmed version of the 308 Winchester, thus providing the 7mm STE with more powder capacity than either the 30-30 Winchester or the 7-30 Waters. Load data for the 7mm STE was developed with the Nosler 120-grain and Hornady 139-grain flat-nosed bullet, as these are compatible with the tubular magazines of the lever guns. Maximum velocities for these bullets in a 22-inch barrel are 2900 fps and 2700 fps, respectively.

General Comments This cartridge has enjoyed fair success on whitetails, mule deer, pronghorns, black bear, caribou and wild hogs. Performance of the Nosler bullet on all of these has been nothing less than outstanding. A favorite open-country "single-shot" recipe, for loading directly into the chamber (not for use in a tubular magazine), is the Nosler 140-grain Ballistic Tip loaded to 2700 fps. Chamber pressures generated by the 7mm STE are comparable to those developed by the 307 Winchester. Consequently, only Model 336 and 94 rifles of recent manufacture and in excellent condition should be considered for this conversion. Those rifles in 30-30 Winchester, 307 Winchester, 356 Winchester and 444 Marlin are easily converted to the 7mm STE by rebarreling with no other modifications necessary.

7mm Shooting Times Easterner (STE) Loading Data

Bullet (grains/type)	Powder	Grains	Velocity	Energy	Source/Comments
120 SP	H414	47.0	2915	2265	Layne Simpson
120 SP	H4895	41.0	2910	2250	Layne Simpson
139 SP	W760	45.0	2710	2265	Layne Simpson
139 SP	RI-22	50.0	2710	2265	Layne Simpson

Marlin 336CS

285 OKH
7mm-06 Mashburn
7mm-06

Historical Notes These cartridges are lumped together because all are practically identical and, except for headspace specification, are very similar to the 280 Remington. The 285 OKH is another O'Neil-Keith-Hopkins development that originally used a "duplex" loading consisting of different powders with different burning rates loaded one on top of the other. It also employed a long flash tube that ignited the powder at the front of the case instead of the rear. This was supposed to improve ballistics and apparently did so, but was a lot of trouble and rather impractical for the average handloader. All of these cartridges originated in the late 1940s and early 1950s.

General Comments Because these cartridges hold about 2 grains less powder than the 280 Remington, maximum 280 Remington loads are not recommended. The various 7mms based on the 30-06 case are worthy of mention because these were the wildcat forerunners of the commercial 280.

285 OKH Loading Data

Bullet (grains/type)	Powder	Grains	Velocity	Energy	Source/Comments
100 SP	IMR 3031	45.0	3110	2150	NA
125 SP	IMR 4350	57.0	3195	2840	NA
150 SP	IMR 4895	48.0	2890	2780	NA
165 SP	IMR 4350	52.0	2820	2920	NA
175 SP	IMR 4350	55.0	2720	2880	NA

7mm Hawk

Historical Notes In 1997, Wyoming gunmaker Fred Zeglin designed the Hawk family of proprietary hunting cartridges, suitable for varminting through dangerous game. Fred's 280 Hawk offers a modest ballistic advantage over factory 280 Remington ammunition. Using the same bullets and barrel length, the 280 Hawk produces about 50 fps more velocity. The cartridge is well suited for most North American big game, except for the Alaskan and Canadian grizzly and brown bears.

General Comments All Hawk cartridges use standard length actions with a .473-inch bolt face. The 280 Hawk uses 280 Remington brass as the parent case. The brass is necked up to 30-caliber, sized in a 280 Hawk die to set the headspace, and fire-formed in a 280 Hawk chamber. The cartridge is well suited for bolt action and modern single-shot rifles. Barrel lengths of 24 to 26 inches with a 1:10 twist are recommended. Loaded ammunition and correctly headstamped brass are available from Quality Cartridge. Z-Hat Custom offers rifles, dies and reloading information.

280 Hawk Loading Data

Bullet (grains/type)	Powder	Grains	Velocity	Energy	Source/Comments
140-gr	H4831	60.0	3015		Z-Hat Custom
154-gr	RL-22	59.0	2827		Z-Hat Custom
160-gr	RL-22	60.0	2845		Z-Hat Custom

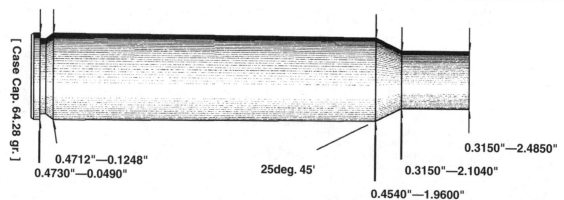

[Case Cap. 64.28 gr.]

0.4712"—0.1248"
0.4730"—0.0490"
25deg. 45'
0.3150"—2.4850"
0.3150"—2.1040"
0.4540"—1.9600"

7mm JRS

Historical Notes The 7mm JRS was designed by Jon R. Sundra. It is based on the 280/7mm Express Remington case, but is more than an Improved 280 in that it cannot be made by fire-forming 280 Remington ammo in a 7mm JRS chamber. Attempting to do so is dangerous because the 7mm JRS pushes a 35-degree shoulder more than 0.050-inch forward of where it would be on the 280 Improved. Therefore, headspace is increased commensurately.

To give some idea of relative case capacities, the 280 Remington/7mm Express holds about 63 grains of water to the base of the neck; the 280 RCBS holds about 66 grains; the 7mm JRS about 70.5 grains (Norma cases). The 7mm Remington Magnum holds about 82 grains.

General Comments Chamber reamers for the 7mm JRS are made by Clymer Mfg. of Rochester, Mich., while reloading dies are made by Hornady. Sundra found that very little load development work was necessary with this cartridge. Norma MRP and Reloder 22 are the best powders, with H4831 and IMR 4831 and IMR 7828 coming in a close second. Other slow burners like IMR 4831 and H450 also do well. Depending on individual rifle and case (Remington, Norma or Winchester), maximum loads range between 60.5 to 63.5 grains

of RI-22 with a 150-grain Nosler. Velocity has ranged from 3060 to 3120 fps in various barrels of 23.5 to 24 inches.

The 7mm JRS is chambered by E.R. Shaw of Bridgeville, Pa. Standard length actions like the Ruger 77 and Mauser (commercial or military) can be used. To take full advantage of case capacity, these loads assume bullet bases seated no deeper than the shoulder (overall length of 3 7/16-inch with a 154-grain Hornady, 3 3/8-inch with a 150 Nosler). Sundra recommends that chambers be throated so a dummy round with either of the above bullets will have a 1/16-inch leade. To accommodate cartridges of this length, you will need a Model 70, Remington 700 or long Sako action. Grayback Wildcats of Klamath Falls, Ore., offers fire-formed (once fired) cases for the 7mm JRS. Similar "pushed shoulder '06-based" improved cartridges exist in 30, 338, 35 and 375 calibers. All are very good, but those in otherwise factory chamberings (280, 30-06 and now the 35 Whelen) create serious safety concerns. Any rifle thus chambered will chamber the factory cartridge of the proper bore diameter, which will then have enough headspace to separate and destroy the gun, and perhaps even the shooter and bystanders.

7mm JRS Loading Data

Bullet (grains/type)	Powder	Grains	Velocity	Energy	Source/Comments
145 SP	RI-22	63.0	3130	3155	Jon Sundra
154 SP	RI-22	61.5	3020	3120	Jon Sundra

7mm Gibbs

Historical Notes The 7mm Gibbs was designed in the 1950s by firearms experimenter R.E. (Rocky) Gibbs. It was a natural follow-on to Gibbs' original 270 Gibbs, which he developed while seeking the optimum case capacity for the 270 bore size in combination with a 150-grain bullet.

General Comments The 7mm Gibbs is a blown-out 30-06 (or 270) case with a steep shoulder and short neck. The shoulder is pushed forward about .196-inch compared to the standard 270 case, and the case holds about six grains more IMR4350 powder than a standard 270 Winchester. Although Gibbs used this and his other wildcats as front ignition cartridges, the following is a "standard" loading without front ignition tube.

7mm Gibbs Loading Data

Bullet (grains/type)	Powder	Grains	Velocity	Energy	Source/Comments
140 Sierra	H4831	67.0	3293		R.E. Gibbs
160 Speer	H4831	67.0	3173		R.E. Gibbs

30 Kurz

Historical Notes The 30 Kurz is made by shortening the 30-06 or 308 Winchester to 1.290 inches. This produces a short cartridge very similar to the German 7.92 Kurz assault rifle cartridge of World War II. The idea originated in the 1960s, and there are other versions of this cartridge. It is intended for use in modified M1 carbines and is the same length as the 30 Carbine case.

General Comments The 30 Carbine cartridge is not very flexible and is not a particularly good choice for hunting. Because of this,

many efforts have been made to improve the performance of the handy little M1 Carbine through wildcat cartridge designs. The 30 Kurz is one of these. The problem is that the cartridge has capabilities beyond the ability of the M1 Carbine. When loaded within the pressure limits of the gun, it does not provide much of an improvement. It is, however, an interesting development as one of the shortest of the short 30-calibers. It is usually loaded with a 110-grain bullet.

308x1.5-inch Barnes

Historical Notes The 308x1.5-inch was developed by the author in March 1961. It is based on the 308 Winchester case shortened from the original 2.01 inches to a length of 1.50 inches. The only other difference is in shoulder diameter, which is 0.003-inch larger than the original cartridge. Two rifles were made up for the developmental work: one on a Swedish Model 96 short military bolt-action (1:12 twist) by Les Corbett, the other on a Remington rolling block single-shot action (1:10-inch twist) by P.O. Ackley. Both rifles proved to be extremely accurate, although the 1:12 twist appears to be the one that has become more or less standard for this cartridge. The 308x1.5 inch is similar to the Russian 7.62x39mm (M43) military round, but is larger in base diameter and has a greater powder capacity. Consequently it can be loaded to produce higher velocity with any given bullet weight. At the time this cartridge was introduced, several gun designers, working on assault rifle designs they hoped to sell to the government, chambered guns to handle the 308x1.5 inch. However, nothing came of these efforts, and the cartridge has never been seriously considered as a military round.

A number of individual experimenters have worked with variations of the original 308x1.5-inch case configuration by lengthening it to 1.6 inches, 1.7 inches, etc., and it has been necked-down to 22, 6mm and 7mm and necked-up to 0.375-inch. Case capacity of the 308x1.5 inch is close to that of the 223 Remington, and if necked-down to 22-caliber, it delivers approximately the same ballistics. The original case-forming and loading dies were made up by RCBS in Oroville, Calif., and these can still be ordered as a regular stock item.

General Comments As originally conceived, the 308x1.5-inch was envisioned by the author as a varmint-through-deer class sporting cartridge that could be chambered in very lightweight, short-action rifles for hunting under conditions in which reduced bulk and heft would be important. As a secondary possibility, it could provide a very efficient 30-caliber match or even a benchrest cartridge. However, it has emerged as more of a special-purpose handgun cartridge for use in custom single-shot pistols for silhouette shooting. Many custom barrels have been made for the popular Thompson/Center Contender single-shot pistol in 308x1.5-inch

chambering, and in addition, the Wichita Silhouette Pistol, made by Wichita Engineering and Supply, Inc. of Wichita, Kan., offers it as a standard chambering. In addition, a number of custom pistolsmiths who make up single-shot pistols based on the Remington XP-100 bolt-action offer it as a chambering choice.

As a rifle cartridge, the 308x1.5-inch delivers initial velocities in excess of the factory-loaded 30-30 Winchester (a true 2530 to 2540 fps with the 150-grain bullet, as opposed to the advertised 2410 fps of the commercial 30-30). Actually, as demonstrated through chronograph tests made by the author and others, the factory 150-grain loading of the 30-30 develops only about 2250 fps from a 22-inch barrel and most of the 30-30s sold have 20-inch barrels. Since the 308x1.5-inch is used exclusively in bolt- or single-shot actions, this allows the use of spitzer bullets, which means that the retained velocity at the longer ranges will also be greater than the flat-pointed 30-30 bullet. The author has had great success with this little cartridge in hunting deer, feral pigs and feral goats. Properly loaded, it has good killing power on animals up to deer-size at ranges out to about 150 yards or so.

Small cartridges such as the 308x1.5-inch are very efficient and deliver performance out of all proportion to their size. However this is only achieved at relatively high pressure levels. When loading the 308x1.5-inch or any similar cartridges to maximum performance levels, adding only a few tenths of a grain of powder can run the pressure up to unsafe pressure levels. Also, if military cases are used, all maximum charges must be reduced because those are generally heavier, which reduces capacity and increases loading density, thereby increasing pressure. A number of shooters have been using the 308x1.5-inch for shooting cast bullets. Lou Delgado of Thousand Oaks, Calif., has been experimenting with cast bullets and various twists from 1 in 12 inches through 1 in 16 inches.

Editor's note: *This cartridge would be a good choice for the "Hunter Benchrest" game, but is not allowed (owing to insufficient case capacity to satisfy the rule requiring that the case must have at least as much capacity as the 30-30 case). Since 308x1.5-inch performance far outclasses any factory 30-30 loading, some might question the common sense of such a rule.*

308x1.5-inch Barnes Loading Data

Bullet (grains/type)	Powder	Grains	Velocity	Energy	Source/Comments
80	IMR 4198	28.0	2875		NA
80	IMR 4198	29.0	2938		NA
93	IMR 4198	28.5	2835		NA
100	IMR 4198	28.5	2810	1755	NA
125	H380	30.0	2015	1125	NA
125	H380	30.0	2015		NA
125	IMR 3031	29.0	2352		NA
125	IMR 4198	27.0	2557		NA
125	IMR 3031	29.0	2350	1535	NA
125	IMR 4198	28.0	2640	1935	NA
150	IMR 4198	27.0	2530	2130	NA
150	H380	23.0	1589		NA
150	IMR 4064	27.0	2032		NA
150	IMR 4198	21.0	2027		NA
150	IMR 4198	26.0	2456		NA
150	IMR 3031	28.0	2370	1870	NA
170	IMR 3031	27.5	2112		NA
170	IMR 4198	24.5	2233		NA
180	IMR 4198	24.0	2180	1900	NA
180	IMR 3031	26.0	2035		NA

30 American

Historical Notes The 30 American is not actually a cartridge. It is, in fact, a specially annealed 30-30 Winchester case with a small primer pocket and small flash hole, made to match-grade tolerances by Federal Cartridge Co. The idea for this originated with David Brennan (editor of *Precision Shooting* magazine), Bill Diefenderfers, David Tooley, et al. The purpose of the special case is to provide the basis for forming a series of wildcat cartridges that are variations of the original 22 Donaldson Wasp. Various versions in calibers from 22 to 35 have been made. All this came about in 1986 and was written up in the 1988, 42nd edition of GUN DIGEST (pp. 154-160).

General Comments The idea behind the 30 American is to field a benchrest cartridge that will beat the 22 and 6mm PPC cartridges developed by Dr. Lou Palmisano and Ferris Pindell. Along the way, it could also provide match-grade cases for making up some of the other wildcats based on the 30-30 case, such as the 30 and 357 Herrett, plus a host of others. Cases are no longer available.

30 Herrett

Historical Notes The 30 Herrett was developed as a handgun hunting cartridge by grip-maker Steve Herrett and the late noted gun writer Bob Milek. It was intended for use in the Thompson/Center single-shot pistol, and the first barrels were made up in 1972, although Thompson/Center did not offer it as a standard chambering until 1973. The cartridge is based on a shortened and reformed 30-30 Winchester case reduced to 1.6 inches as compared to the original length of 2.04 inches. The case is longer and has greater powder capacity than the 30 Carbine, and when fired in the 10-inch barrel of the Thompson/Center pistol, delivers a rather impressive performance. Muzzle velocities of more than 2,000 fps are possible with the 125- or 130-grain bullet.

General Comments Conceived as a superior handgun hunting cartridge, the 30 Herrett has been used successfully on everything from varmints to deer. However, as loaded and used in the Thompson/Center pistol, it develops less velocity and energy than the standard 30-30 rifle and must be considered on the marginal side as a medium-game cartridge in the hands of the average hunter. Much of its success has been due in no small part to the skill of the people who have used it. On the other hand, it offers greater power than the 357 Magnum cartridge, which some consider adequate for big game in the hands of a skilled hunter and good shot. As with all big game hunting with a handgun, it boils down to the question of who is doing the hunting. What Bob Milek or someone in that class can do and what the average person can do are two different things. In any event, the 30 Herrett is an outstanding long-range handgun varmint cartridge, particularly with 110-, 125- or 130-grain bullets. It has also been used with success for silhouette shooting, although most shooters prefer the 357 Herrett for this sport. The 30 Herrett is a good example of a wildcat cartridge designed for a specific purpose not really covered by anything in the commercial line, and one that fulfills its design purpose extremely well.

30 Herrett Loading Data

Bullet (grains/type)	Powder	Grains	Velocity	Energy	Source/Comments
100 SP	2400	19.0	2210	1090	NA
110 HP	2400	20.0	2270	1260	NA
125 SP	IMR 4227	23.0	2205	1350	NA
130 SP	2400	19.0	2000	1160	NA
150 SP	Norma 200	27.0	2100	1470	NA

300 GNR

Historical Notes The 30 Herrett cartridge, originally designed for the Contender action, doesn't work well in revolvers due to cartridge setback, which can prevent cylinder rotation. Arizona gunmaker Gary Reeder developed the 300 GNR to provide near-identical performance in revolvers.

General Comments The 300 GNR uses standard 30-30 brass as its parent case. The case is shortened and the shoulder angle sharpened. The case body taper is removed so the resulting cartridge is straight-sided, with a neck about .100-inch shorter than the 30 Herrett. With 110-grain JHP bullets, the 300 GNR provides excellent performance on deer-sized game. Gary Reeder Custom Guns offers dies, barrels, firearms, reloading components and information. Ballistic data was recorded in a revolver with a 6-inch barrel.

300 GNR Loading Data

Bullet (grains/type)	Powder	Grains	Velocity	Energy	Source/Comments
110-gr JHP	Win 296	23.0	2150		Gary Reeder
125-gr JHP	Win 296	22.0	2100		Gary Reeder
130-gr Spire Point	Win 296	22.0	2080		Gary Reeder

302 Whisper

Historical Notes Developed in 2005 by J.D. Jones, owner of SSK Industries, the 302 Whisper provides an accurate, subsonic-capable round that functions in 308-caliber barrels using the AR-15 family of weapons. The 302 Whisper offers performance similar to the original 308 x 1.5-inch cartridge developed by Frank Barnes in 1961. This cartridge is basically a 30-caliber equivalent of JD Jones' 338 Whisper. Like all of J.D.'s Whisper family, the 302 will launch heavy bullets at subsonic velocities and lighter bullets at high velocities.

General Comments The 302 Whisper is based on the 7mm BR (benchrest) case necked-up to accept 30-caliber bullets. Existing AR-15 rifles can be adapted to the 302 Whisper by the addition of an upper receiver assembly. It can be chambered in suitable bolt-action rifles and the Thompson/Center Encore. SSK Industries offers AR-15 upper receivers, loading dies and information.

302 Whisper Loading Data

Bullet (grains/type)	Powder	Grains	Velocity	Energy	Source/Comments
125-gr Speer	Accurate Arms 1680	33.2	2757		SSK Industries
180-gr Speer	Accurate Arms 1680	32.2	2420		SSK Industries
240-gr Sierra MatchKing	H4227	11.4	1022		SSK Industries

30-30 Ackley Improved

Historical Notes The 30-30 Winchester is one of the most popular sporting cartridges ever produced. It is the standard American deer cartridge, but its popularity is due more to the light, handy carbines that chamber it than to its ballistics. Many hunters have wished that the 30-30 had a little more oomph. The 30-30 Improved does just that by providing an additional 200 to 300 fps within the working pressure limits of the standard Model 94 Winchester action. There are various versions of the 30-30 Improved, but the Ackley version is the most popular. The exact date of introduction is not known, but was probably sometime in the early 1950s or perhaps even earlier.

General Comments Basically, the 30-30 Improved requires only a simple rechambering job. Cases are made by firing standard 30-30 Winchester ammunition in the Improved chamber, then reloading the fire-formed cases. However, anyone who favors the Model 94 Winchester or Marlin 336 and wants more power than the standard 30-30 can simply buy one in 307 Winchester. This would seem to make the Improved 30-30 obsolete for new rifles, but it is still a good modification for older Model 94s and Marlins.

Editor's note: *Since the 307 Winchester appears on its way to obsolescence, perhaps one should not be so hasty in condemning Ackley's solution.*

30-30 Ackley Improved Loading Data

Bullet (grains/type)	Powder	Grains	Velocity	Energy	Source/Comments
100 SP	RI-7	36.0	2750	1680	NA
110 HP	RI-7	35.0	2610	1660	NA
130 SP	W748	36.0	2385	1645	NA
150 SP	RI-7	30.0	2270	1720	NA
150 SP	IMR 3031	37.0	2617	2280	Ackley
170 SP	IMR 3031	35.0	2310	2020	NA

30-06 Ackley Improved

Historical Notes The 30-06 Ackley Improved is made by firing the standard 30-06 in the Improved chamber. Headspace is the same, but the Improved case has a more abrupt shoulder, less body taper and a larger shoulder diameter. The most popular version was developed by P.O. Ackley in 1944, but there are other versions as experiments go back to 1940 or even earlier. This has always been a controversial cartridge with its detractors claiming it was not as good as the standard '06, and its defenders claiming it was better than the 300 H&H Magnum. Actual chronograph tests have proven it definitely superior to the standard 30-06 cartridge with slow-burning powders. However, it could never match the various "Magnums" since usable case capacity is significantly less.

General Comments The advantage of owning a wildcat-chambered rifle that will also shoot standard factory ammunition is obvious. The various Improved cartridges from 22- through 35-caliber are all designed to do exactly that. The idea is to provide superior performance by handloading the Improved case, without preventing use of the standard factory round when an ammunition shortage or other occasion demands.

The 30-06 Ackley Improved is one of the most popular and widely used of the Improved breed. With the proper powder, it will add a little over 100 fps muzzle velocity to any bullet weight, as opposed to the standard factory-loaded cartridge. This does make it equal to the original factory-loaded 300 H&H Magnum with 150-, 180- and 220-grain bullets but, of course, the 300 Magnum can also be handloaded to exceed anything possible in the Improved '06. Best results are obtained with slow-burning powders such as IMR 4350 or Hodgdon 4831. The 30-06 Improved would be adequate for any North American game. As is typical of Ackley's improved series of cartridges, this design exhibits reduced case stretching and easier extraction, compared to the more tapered standard version.

30-06 Ackley Improved Loading Data

Bullet (grains/type)	Powder	Grains	Velocity	Energy	Source/Comments
130 SP	IMR 4895	54.0	3150	2860	Ackley
150 SP	IMR 4350	59.0	3070	3150	Ackley
165 SP	IMR 4350	58.0	2940	3180	Ackley
180 SP	IMR 4350	56.0	2825	3200	Ackley
200 SP	H4831	59.0	2760	3180	Ackley
200 SP	IMR 4350	54.0	2675	3190	Ackley
220 SP	IMR 4350	54.0	2620	3365	Ackley

30 Gibbs

Historical Notes The 30 Gibbs was designed in the 1950s by firearms experimenter R.E. (Rocky) Gibbs. He called it "The world's most powerful 30-06." It was a natural follow-on to Gibbs's original 270 Gibbs, which he developed while seeking the optimum case capacity for the 270 bore size in combination with a 150-grain bullet.

General Comments The 30 Gibbs is a blown-out 30-06 case with a steep shoulder and short neck. The shoulder is pushed forward about .196-inch compared to the standard 30-06 case, and the case holds about seven grains more IMR4350 powder than a standard 30-06 Winchester. Although Gibbs used this and his other wildcats as front ignition cartridges, the following is a "standard" loading without front ignition tube.

30 Gibbs Loading Data

Bullet (grains/type)	Powder	Grains	Velocity	Energy	Source/Comments
150 Hornady	IMR4064	60.0	3285		R.E. Gibbs
180 Barnes	IMR4350	65.0	3139		R.E. Gibbs

30-338 Winchester Magnum

Historical Notes This cartridge was developed specifically for use in 1,000-yard benchrest competition and is now popular in NRA Highpower competition for the long-range events. It was created by simply necking the 338 Winchester Magnum to 30-caliber and almost exactly duplicates the 308 Norma Magnum. (Norma's commercial offering has slightly less case taper and is slightly longer.)

General Comments The 30-338 Winchester Magnum fills a void in Winchester's Magnum line, created when Winchester introduced the 300 Magnum. The 264, 338 and 458 Magnum all share a 2.5-inch case length. Evidently to avoid direct competition with the existing 308 Norma Magnum and to better compete with the well-established and substantially longer 300 Weatherby Magnum, Winchester opted to increase case length and push the shoulder forward on its new 30-caliber magnum (actual usable capacity increase was marginal). The Wildcat 30-338 is likely exactly what Winchester would have offered had Norma not offered it first. Ballistics are very similar to the 300 Winchester Magnum, despite the slight reduction in powder capacity. Compared to that commercial chambering, a slightly longer case neck provides superior purchase for longer bullets. Remington and other mainstream manufacturers have offered rifles chambered for this round as a cataloged item.

30-338 Winchester Magnum Loading Data (26-inch barrel)

Bullet (grains/type)	Powder	Grains	Velocity	Energy	Source/Comments
150 PSP-CL (Rem)	A4350	71.5	3203	3415	Accurate
150 PSP-CL (Rem)	A3100	76.0	3145	3295	Accurate
168 Sierra MK	A3100	68.5	3047	3460	Accurate
168 Sierra MK	A4350	73.5	3076	3530	Accurate
180 Sierra MK	A3100	72.5	2964	3510	Accurate
180 Sierra MK	A4350	66.0	2929	3430	Accurate
190 Sierra MK	A3100	72.3	3006	3810	Accurate
190 Sierra MK	A4350	65.0	2888	3520	Accurate
200 Sierra MK	A3100	71.0	2921	3790	Accurate
200 Sierra MK	A4350	64.0	2811	3510	Accurate
220 Sierra MK	A3100	70.0	2735	3655	Accurate
220 Sierra MK	A4350	63.0	2646	3420	Accurate
220 Sierra MK	AA 8700	80.0	2528	3120	Accurate (Very mild pressure)

8mm-06

Historical Notes Immediately after World War II, many shooters found themselves in possession of 8mm Mauser military rifles for which they could not obtain suitable ammunition. What could have been more natural than to rechamber those rifles for the 30-06 case, with the neck expanded to take 0.323-inch bullets? Presto! The 8mm-06 was born. It is impossible to state positively who first accomplished this as it probably happened at several places about the same time.

General Comments The 8mm-06 in standard or improved form is one of the better wildcat developments. It is similar to the German 8x64mm(S) Brenneke in both dimensions and performance. Using European nomenclature, this would be the 8x63mm(S). With the 125-grain bullet, it makes a very good varmint cartridge, while the 200- to 250-grain bullets are adequate for any North American big game. For those who do not like the performance of the standard 8mm cartridge, the 8mm-06 provides an inexpensive means of altering Mauser military rifles to a more powerful cartridge. However, the conversion eliminates the use of cheap, surplus military ammunition and requires use of handloads. Ballistics of the standard version well exceed 30-06 performance, while the improved version adds another 100 fps and suggests serious big game hunting performance potential.

8mm-06 Loading Data

Bullet (grains/type)	Powder	Grains	Velocity	Energy	Source/Comments
150	IMR 4895	59.0	3026	3050	Ackley
170 SP	IMR 4064	57.0	2930	3240	Ackley
200 SP	IMR 4350	61.0	2700	3260	
225 SP	IMR 4350	58.0	2515	3165	
250 SP	IMR 4831	62.0	2380	3145	Ackley

333 OKH

Historical Notes The 333 OKH was developed by Charles O'Neil, Elmer Keith and Don Hopkins in 1945. It is the 30-06 case necked-up to accept 0.333-inch diameter bullets. At the time the cartridge was developed, 0.338-inch diameter bullets were not generally available, but 0.333-inch bullets were. When the 338 Winchester Magnum was introduced in 1958, a variety of .338-inch bullets became available, which led to rifles made for the 338-06 cartridge.

The difference between the 333 OKH and the 338-06 is miniscule and one can use loading data interchangeably. However, the two bullet diameters are not interchangeable. For additional information, see the 338-06.

General Comments The 333 OKH was a very good cartridge, but is now obsolete.

333 OKH Loading Data

Bullet (grains/type)	Powder	Grains	Velocity	Energy	Source/Comments
250	IMR 4350	62.0	2400	3200	Ackley
275	IMR 4895	45.0	2202	2960	Ackley
275	IMR 4831	57.0	2314	3270	Ackley

334 OKH

Historical Notes The 334 OKH is another development by O'Neil, Keith and Hopkins dating back to the late 1940s. This one is based on the 300 H&H Magnum necked-up to use 0.333-inch bullets. Bullets of this size were made by Fred Barnes in weights from 200 to 300 grains. The 334 OKH is the forerunner of a number of developments leading up to the 338 Winchester Magnum. After the Winchester Magnum was introduced, everyone switched to 0.338-inch diameter bullets.

General Comments The 334 OKH is an excellent big game cartridge for North American hunting and is adequate for most soft-skinned African big game. Like all other 33-caliber cartridges, it was made obsolete by the 338 Winchester Magnum, which used standard 0.338-inch diameter bullets. 0.333-inch diameter bullets are no longer available.

338-223 Straight

Historical Notes The 338-223 Straight originated in 1972 with Max Atchisson of Atlanta, Ga. It was intended as the cartridge for a blow-back semi-auto rifle he designed. It also had a secondary purpose as a possible cartridge for use in rebarreled Model 1907 Winchester self-loading rifles chambered for the 351 Winchester SL. At that time, 351 WSL ammunition was no longer manufactured and was difficult to obtain in shooting quantities. However, Winchester reintroduced 351 WSL ammunition and eliminated that problem.

Although strictly an experimental development, the 338-223 is interesting because it is the ultimate possibility in necking up the 223 Remington or similar cases. There are two versions of the cartridge, one made by necking up the full-length 223 case, the other based on cutting off the 223 case at the shoulder and trimming it to 1.412 inches. The full-length version presented two problems: It is difficult to make without splitting the case neck, and with an overall length of 2.54 inches, it is too long to function through the action of rebarreled Model 1907 Winchester rifles. The short case, on the other hand, is almost the same length as the 351 Winchester SL and can be made to work in the Model 1907 rifle.

General Comments The 351 Winchester SL is loaded with a 180-grain bullet at a muzzle velocity of 1,850 fps. The 338-223 has a 200-grain bullet at 1,820 fps, so the two are ballistically almost identical. Both cartridges are considered marginal for deer, but do very well on coyotes, bobcats, mountain lions or similar predators at close range. The 338-223 project was eventually dropped because the reappearance of 351 Winchester ammunition made such a cartridge non-viable. One problem with the 338-223 is that it is a rimless case, which must headspace on the case mouth. This works well with short pistol cartridges, but not as well with high-powered rifle cartridges. Finally, there seems to be no real need for such a cartridge.

338-223 Loading Data

Bullet (grains/type)	Powder	Grains	Velocity	Energy	Source/Comments
200 SP	2400	18.3	1820	1880	NA
200 SP	IMR 4227	19.0	1750	1370	NA
Loading data for the short case only.					

The 338-223 Straight is a good round for coyotes and other predators.

338/50 Talbot

Historical Notes The 338/50 is the work of Skip Talbot of Talbot's Custom Equipment in Fallon, Nev. Skip began development of the cartridge in 1984 as an outgrowth of working with the 50-caliber Browning Machine Gun cartridge. The 338/50 is the 50 BMG necked-down to 33 caliber and with the shoulder angle increased to 35 degrees. The primary purpose of the 338/50 is long-range target shooting at ranges out to 3000 yards. Forming dies are made by RCBS.

General Comments The 338/50 is a highly specialized cartridge and not intended for hunting. It is of course adequate for any big game. Owing to the unusually large capacity, severe throat erosion occurred within 250 rounds. Talbot also tried a shortened version of the cartridge, about one inch shorter than the full-length case, in order to increase loading density. In the full-length version, a maximum load of 170 grains of Accurate Arms 8700 powder

occupied only about 77 percent of the volumetric capacity. However, the short version was not successful because muzzle velocity was reduced about 500 fps. The full-length case developed a muzzle velocity of 3700 fps with the 250-grain bullet when fired from a 44-inch barrel. By comparison, the 340 Weatherby Magnum pushes the 250-grain bullet at an initial velocity of 2850 fps from a 26-inch barrel, so the 338/50 develops an additional 850 fps with the same bullet. The internal ballistic predictor program, QuickLOAD, shows that 581 fps of this difference results solely from the longer barrel. Equally, given a 44-inch barrel and loaded to similar pressures, the 340 Weatherby would produce 3350 fps. Therefore, these ballistics are not so impressive. However, with a much slower powder and bullets of 300 grains or heavier, the results might be spectacular. It is an interesting cartridge, but not very practical for most purposes until ceramic barrel liners come into vogue.

338/50 Talbot Loading Data

Bullet (grains/type)	Powder	Grains	Velocity	Energy	Source/Comments
250 SP	AA 8700	170.0	3700	7625	NA

9mm Action Express

Historical Notes This is a 1988 innovation by Evan Whildin, who was Vice President of Action Arms, Ltd. at that time. The 9mm Action Express (9mm AE) is the 41 Action Express case necked-down to 9mm. It retains the 41 AE rebated rim, which is the same diameter as the standard 9mm Luger. The advantage of this in the 9mm AE is that the cartridge offers a larger case that can be used in firearms originally designed for the 9mm Luger without the necessity of changing the bolt or breech face. This will allow a number of 41 AE semi-auto pistols and carbines to be changed to the 9mm version by the installation of kits made available for specific guns.

General Comments The 9mm AE has been tested in the Uzi semi-auto pistol and in specially altered 1911 Colt pistols. As a commercial round, it appeared chambered in the Action Arms TZ-75S88. It is a sort of super 9mm and as such is more powerful than the 38 Colt Super Auto. It has an advantage over the 9mm

Winchester Magnum, since it is shorter and most 9mm pistols can be adapted to it. Tests in a 10-inch pressure barrel gave muzzle velocities with a 95-grain bullet of 1,880 fps at 31,760 CUP and 1903 fps with a 100-grain bullet at 34,880 CUP. These pressures are a bit on the high side for some semi-auto pistols. On the other hand, these are top loads and can be reduced and still maintain impressive velocities. A 124-grain bullet was measured at 1590 fps and 28,550 CUP, a load that could be digested by most 9mm autos. The 9mm AE is a potentially good self-defense and field cartridge. Of course, converted auto pistols are not likely to have 10-inch barrels, 5 inches being more normal. However, safe loads of around 1500 fps with the 124-grain bullet have been tested in converted Colt 1911 autos with 5-inch barrels. This beats the 38 Colt Super Automatic and its 130-grain bullet at 1275 fps. Currently, this cartridge is not being commercially manufactured.

9mm Action Express Loading Data

Bullet (grains/type)	Powder	Grains	Velocity	Energy	Source/Comments
115 JHP	AA No. 9	16.1	1825	850	Action Arms
124 JHP	IMR 4227	13.3	1225	415	Action Arms
124 JHP	H110	16.5	1530	645	Action Arms

9x25mm Dillon

Historical Notes Final design of the 9x25mm was completed in 1988, but the cartridge languished until top IPSC competitor Rob Leatham began testing in 1991. This cartridge was developed by a group of people at Dillon, but was chiefly Randy Shelly's concept and he is primarily responsible for the design. Randy's intention was to create a 9mm cartridge that would function through standard pistols and still produce IPSC Major Power Factor without requiring excessive pressures. In an effort to achieve Major Power Factor ratings with light bullets, which reduce recoil, many IPSC competitors have routinely used 38 Super loads generating rifle-type peak pressures! The 9x25mm is based on the 10mm Automatic case necked to 9mm. Its increased capacity allows loads to achieve the Major level with more reasonable pressure.

General Comments The 9x25 Dillon is formed by necking the 10mm Automatic case to 9mm with a sharp shoulder and a short neck. This creates a relatively high-capacity pistol cartridge, which is based on a high-pressure case. With the proper bullet and powder, the 9x25mm Dillon can generate significant muzzle energy and easily achieves IPSC Major-Power levels. VihtaVuori has recently designed a powder (tentatively called Vit N105) specifically for this and similar cartridges. Appropriate 9mm bullets are readily available. The future is bright for this cartridge, which might very well achieve commercialization very soon. Springfield Armory offers guns in this chambering and several custom barrel makers chamber tubes for this round. Representing an increasingly unique example of the breed, the 9x25mm Dillon meets a recognized need. For more information on the 9x25mm and Randy's more recent development, the 9x30mm, contact him at Dillon Precision, Scottsdale, Ariz.

9x25mm Dillon Loading Data (8-inch barrel)

Bullet (grains/type)	Powder	Grains	Velocity	Energy	Source/Comments
100 FMJ RN	AA No. 9	15.3	1751	680	Lyman
100 FMJ RN	W296	17.2	1769	690	Lyman
115 JHP	Her-2400	13.0	1587	640	Lyman
115 JHP	W296	15.0	1566	625	Lyman
124 FMJ FP	W296	14.4	1529	640	Lyman
130 Cast	W296	13.5	1479	630	Lyman (No. 356634)

357 Auto Mag

Historical Notes The 357 Auto Mag is an outgrowth of the 44 Auto Mag and is based on the 44 Auto Mag case necked-down to 35 caliber. The 44 Auto Mag in turn is made by cutting off 30-06 or 308 Winchester case to a length of 1.298 inches and inside reaming to accept a 0.429-inch diameter bullet. The first Auto Mag pistols were announced in 1970 and delivered in late 1971. These were, of course, in 44 caliber. The 357 Auto Mag did not appear until 1973. For an extra $150, one could purchase both the 357 and 44 barrel and slide assembly units to convert the pistol to handle either cartridge with a relatively easy parts change. Auto Mag ammunition was made in Mexico for a time and by Norma in Sweden. Conversion of 44 Auto Mag cases to a smaller caliber is routine. Auto Mag semi-auto pistols are no longer in production.

General Comments The 357 and 44 Auto Mag pistols were made of stainless steel, had a 6 1/2-inch barrel, an overall length of 11-1/2 inches and weighed 3.4 pounds. In other words, these were quite large and heavy, much like the Desert Eagle pistols currently available from Magnum Research. The 357 Auto Mag pushed the 158-grain jacketed bullet at a muzzle velocity of 1600 fps and the 110-grain bullet at over 1900 fps when loaded to maximum performance levels. This is certainly well in excess of anything feasible from a 357 Magnum revolver. Auto Mag pistols in 357 have been used with success on everything from varmints to deer. Like many of the more powerful handgun cartridges, ballistics of the 357 Auto Mag are marginal for big game, but like the others, it can do the job in the hands of a good shot and accomplished hunter. As a self-defense gun, the Auto Mag pistols are a bit unwieldy and overpowered. These are strictly for sporting use.

357 Auto Mag Loading Data

Bullet (grains/type)	Powder	Grains	Velocity	Energy	Source/Comments
110 JHP	BlueDot	19.0	1935	920	NA
125 JHP	BlueDot	18.0	1810	915	NA
140 JHP	BlueDot	17.0	1725	930	NA
158 JSP	BlueDot	16.0	1500	795	NA
158 JSP	H110	22.0	1635	940	NA

357 Herrett

Historical Notes Although the 30 Herrett proved a good handgun hunting cartridge when used in the 10- or 14-inch barrel of the Thompson/Center Contender single-shot pistol, it needed to be improved for hunting heavy game. One solution was to neck it up to 35-caliber to take advantage of larger diameter, heavier bullets. This was done in the initial development. However, it appeared desirable to increase the powder capacity of the original 30 Herrett case and so the final design used a case length of 1.75 inches, which is 0.15-inch longer than the 30 Herrett case. The development of the 357 Herrett was the work of Steve Herrett and gun writer Bob Milek. It was introduced as a standard chambering for the Thompson/Center pistol in 1974. Cases are made by reforming, shortening, and necking-up 30-30 or 32 Winchester Special cases. The case has a 30-degree shoulder angle. After forming, the cases are fire-formed to the final configuration.

General Comments The 357 Herrett is another example of a wildcat cartridge developed for a specific firearm and purpose, filling a gap in the commercial line of ammunition. It was intended primarily as a hunting cartridge for the heavier varieties of medium game, although it also has become quite popular among silhouette shooters. It serves both purposes well, but one must bear in mind that as a hunting cartridge, it delivers ballistics inferior to the 35 Remington fired from a rifle. While it is perfectly capable of handling large animals under average conditions, much depends on the skill of the user, something that is true of all handguns and handgun cartridges when used for hunting. The 357 Herrett is, nevertheless, one of the best of the handgun cartridges for field use on medium or small game and varmints. Nevertheless, all hunting success relies upon either skill or luck — few hunters can successfully rely on the latter.

357 Herrett Loading Data

Bullet (grains/type)	Powder	Grains	Velocity	Energy	Source/Comments
110 JHP	2400	28.0	2600	1650	NA
110 JHP	IMR 4227	33.0	2685	1710	NA
125 JHP	IMR 4227	31.0	2565	1820	NA
150 JHP	IMR 4227	30.0	2380	1910	NA
158 JSP	IMR 4227	29.0	2310	1870	NA
180 JSP	IMR 4227	27.0	2130	1820	NA
180 JSP	Norma 200	32.0	2125	1810	NA

These loads are for the Thompson/Center Pistol with 14-inch barrel.

35-30/30 (35-30)

Historical Notes Although not widely known, the 35-30/30 is one of our oldest wildcats, having originated around the turn of the century. Its original purpose was to salvage worn-out 32-40 and 32 Winchester Special barrels by reboring these to 35 caliber. The idea was also applied to improve the performance of Winchester Model 1894 rifles and carbines while staying within the cartridge length and pressure limitations of that action. While the 35-30/30 cartridge is based on necking-up 30-30 or 32 Winchester Special cases without any other change, a few rifles have been made up to accept the somewhat superior Ackley Improved version. Recently there has been a rebirth of interest in this cartridge by silhouette shooters who like to use cast bullets. In 1976, Arizona gunsmith Paul Marquart built several 35-30/30 silhouette rifles based on the Remington 788 action, and these quickly established a reputation as being both accurate and effective for the intended sport. Information on these rifles was published in *The Fouling Shot*, published by the Cast Bullet Association, and other shooters found it promising as a target and hunting cartridge. The 35-30/30 can be loaded to about equal the ballistics of the 35 Remington, and in fact, if Remington had not introduced its rimless 35 in 1908, it is highly possible that the necked-up 30-30 would have become much more popular than it did.

In any event, it has gained a new but modest following.

General Comments With jacketed bullets there is little, if any, difference between the ballistics and killing power of the 35-30/30 and the 35 Remington. On paper, the 35 Remington appears to have an edge over the 35-30/30 because it has about a 14 percent greater powder capacity, but the factory 200-grain bullet loading rarely attains 2,000 fps except in a 24-inch test barrel, chiefly because of rather anemic loading pressures. As a cast bullet cartridge, the 35-30/30, with its longer neck, permits use of cast bullets as heavy as 270 grains seated to a depth that will feed through magazine rifles designed for the 30-30. This is not possible with the 35 Remington and its short neck. In a strong action, the 35-30/30 can be loaded to deliver performance approaching the 375 Winchester. However, in a strong action, the 35 Remington can be stepped up quite a bit, too. It is possible to attain 1,800 fps with a 300-grain bullet in a strong action chambered for the 35-30/30, which would make it suitable for elk or moose at short range. It is a good cartridge for upping the performance of 30-30 rifles or for salvaging worn-out 32 Special barrels. For a wildcat, it is rather a special-purpose cartridge, but one that may fill the needs of a number of shooters. Dies are available from RCBS and chambering reamers from Clymer.

35/30-30 Loading Data

Bullet (grains/type)	Powder	Grains	Velocity	Energy	Source/Comments
200 JSP	IMR 4198	25.0	1925	1650	NA
208 Lead	IMR 4198	25.0	1895	1660	NA
210 Lead	W630	15.0	1520	1080	Lyman 35875
245 Lead	H335	30.0	1770	1710	Lyman 358318
282 Lead	H335	28.0	1700	1810	Lyman 3589
292 Lead	W748	33.5	1620	1580	NA

35 Sambar

Historical Notes Breil Jackson, Editor of Australia's *Guns and Game* magazine, developed the 35 Sambar. David Stendell built the first rifle on a Model 70 Classic 300 WSM action. The 35 Whelen is a popular sambar deer cartridge in southeast Australia, and Jackson was trying to improve upon its performance while allowing for the use of a short-action compact rifle for hunting in thick brush. The project was launched in 2001 and development of the 35 Sambar was featured in a series of articles in *Guns and Game* magazine throughout 2002.

General Comments The 35 Sambar is the 300 WSM case necked up to 35 caliber, with no other changes. Using 250-grain bullets of good construction, it is a very powerful cartridge in a short-action rifle, suitable for most big game. 2,700 fps can be achieved with 250-grain bullets from a 23-inch barrel. Lighter bullets can also be used for smaller game and longer range, especially the Nosler Ballistic Tip bullets.

35 Sambar Loading Data

Bullet (grain/type)	Powder	Grains	Velocity	Energy	Source/Comments
200 Hornady SP	Varget	65.0	2771	3410	Breil Jackson
200 Hornady SP	Varget	68.0	2920	3787	Breil Jackson
225 Nosler BT	Varget	65.0	2755	3793	Breil Jackson
225 Nosler BT	H4350	75.0	2843	4039	Breil Jackson
250 Speer GS	H4350	72.0	2700	4048	Breil Jackson

358 Ultra Mag Towsley

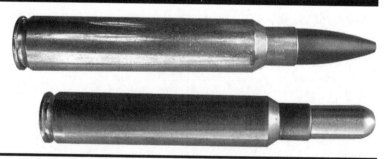

Historical Notes A 1999 idea of *American Rifleman* Field Editor, Bryce Towsley, the 358 Ultra Mag Towsley, puts zip back into the family of 35-caliber cartridges. The 358 UMT shoots flatter than the 7mm Remington Magnum or the 300 Winchester Magnum. The cartridge is intended for elk, big bears, moose and larger African plains game. Mr. Towsley tested the cartridge in Africa, taking kudu, zebra, nyala, gemsbok, and waterbuck at ranges varying from 10 to 450 yards. If Remington ever decided to extend the Ultra Mag series to 35 caliber, odds are the new cartridge would be a spitting image of the 358 UMT.

General Comments Based on necking up the available and affordable 300 Remington Ultra Mag parent case, the 358 UMT maintains the same body taper, 30-degree shoulder and headspacing datum line. Only the larger neck and resulting shorter shoulder distinguish the 358 UMT from its non-belted parent case, and naturally, Remington 700 actions are well-suited for this cartridge. The high velocities possible with this wildcat demand premium bullets such as Barnes X-bullet, Nosler Partition or Swift A-Frame. Many 35-caliber bullets are designed for lower velocity cartridges and may not perform well in the 358 UMT. Loads listed below were tested in the Barnes Ballistic Lab.

358 Ultra Mag Towsley Loading Data

Bullet (grains/type)	Powder	Grains	Velocity	Energy	Source/Comments
180 X-Bullet	MRP	101.5	3408		Barnes/59,000 psi
225 XLC	IMR7828	95.0	3039		Barnes/59,100 psi
250 X-Bullet	RL-25	90.0	2965		Barnes/58,000 psi
250 Nosler Partition	H-1000	102.0	3029		Barnes/61,400 psi
250 Nosler BT	H-1000	104.0	3011		Barnes/57,300 psi

366 DGW

Historical Notes A high performance, medium bore wildcat cartridge crafted by Maine gunsmith Judson Stewart Bailey, the 366 DGW is identified with the initials of its creator, David G. Walker. Mr. Walker's idea was to achieve optimum performance from the 416 Rigby parent case, directly necking it down to accept 366 (9.3mm) bullets. With a 24-inch barrel propelling high sectional density and ballistic coefficient bullets at relatively low pressures, Mr. Bailey believes the 366 DGW will shoot flatter and out-penetrate the Remington Ultra magnums, the 338 Lapua and the 338/378 Weatherby. In 2001, Mr. Bailey successfully hunted the cartridge in South Africa, taking zebra, kudu, warthog, wildebeest, nyala, blesbok and gemsbok.

General Comments Strictly a custom rifle proposition, the 366 DBW cartridge has been chambered in Ruger #1 single-shot and converted Enfield P14 bolt-action rifles. The Beretta/SAKO TRG-s and longer BRNO ZKK 602 and CZ actions would also be suitable for this 416 Rigby-based cartridge. Reloading dies are available from RCBS. Suitably dimensioned bullets are available from various manufacturers, including Nosler®, Woodleigh, Swift™, Barnes and Speer.

366 DGW Loading Data

Bullet (grains/type)	Powder	Grains	Velocity	Energy	Source/Comments
250 Nosler BT	IMR4350	98.0	3253	5875	Judson Bailey
286 Nosler Partition	IMR7828	103.0	3020	5775	Judson Bailey
300 Swift A-Frame	H4831	97.0	2911	5607	Judson Bailey

375 Whelen
375 Ackley Improved

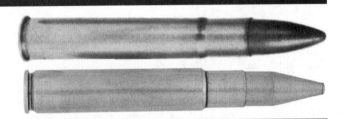

Historical Notes The 375 Whelen, also known as the 375-06, was not developed by the late Col. Townsend Whelen, but was named in his honor. The cartridge was actually the work of the late gunsmith and writer L.R. "Bob" Wallack in 1951 and is based on the 30-06 case necked-up. There are two versions, one based on the standard case and retaining the original 17-degree, 30-minute shoulder angle, the other the Improved case with a 40-degree shoulder angle. The Improved case holds slightly more powder and provides vastly superior headspace control, so it is the more popular version. 0.375-inch is about as far as one can go in expanding the 30-06 case without running into headspace problems, due to lack of a distinct shoulder. Experiments with larger diameter bullets have invariably led to headspace problems. An example of this was the 400 Whelen, which never became popular and is no longer chambered.

General Comments The 375 Whelen is not as powerful as the 375 H&H Magnum but is, nevertheless, a good medium bore for application against most dangerous game. It is certainly adequate for any North American big game. It uses bullets from 200 to 300 grains, and because it is strictly a handloading proposition, can be quite flexible. It can be loaded down with 200- or 250-grain bullets for deer hunting as well as loaded to full-power for larger animals. This is one advantage of wildcat cartridges; these must be handloaded and so can be tailored to fit different game and hunting situations. As with the 338 and 35 versions of the '06, Ackley's improved design is superior. In this instance, it is mandatory to ensure adequate headspace control.

375 Ackley Improved Loading Data

Bullet (grains/type)	Powder	Grains	Velocity	Energy	Source/Comments
200 SP	IMR 4895	58.0	2450	2265	
235 SP	IMR 4064	60.0	2475	3205	
270 SP	IMR 4064	57.0	2380	3400	
300 SP	IMR 4064	52.0	2110	2975	

400 Whelen

Historical Notes Of the various cartridges named after the late Col. Townsend Whelen, recent research indicates that he actually developed both the 35 and the 400. According to Phil Sharpe,* Col. Whelen developed this cartridge while he was commanding officer at Frankford Arsenal during the early 1920s. The 400 Whelen is based on the 30-06 case necked-up with no other changes.

General Comments The 400 Whelen was not a successful development because expansion of the 30-06 case neck to this size leaves only a very slight shoulder. This can give rise to serious headspace problems — particularly with incautious handloading and sloppy chambering practices. Nonetheless, properly built custom rifles in this chambering were used successfully in the United States, Canada and Africa on big game. The 37-caliber bore size is the maximum for the 30-06 case without creating a potential for headspace problems. The combination of careful chambering

and ammunition production can evidently mitigate this potential, because G&H rifles in 400 Whelen were used extensively with no known complaints. J.D. Jones at SSK Industries now offers a 416-06 Improved using a 60-degree shoulder and a body taper similar to Ackley's design. The 400 Whelen works perfectly with no headspace complaints to date. Had Whelen utilized an improved design, perhaps his 400 would have fared better. Good evidence also suggests that one reason for its short popularity was that most shooters considered it both unnecessarily powerful for North American hunting and marginally powerful for the most serious of African applications.

Sharpe, Phillip B., Complete Guide to Handloading, Funk & Wagnalls Co., 1941, p.398.

400 Whelen Loading Data

Bullet (grains/type)	Powder	Grains	Velocity	Energy	Source/Comments
300 JSP	IMR 3031	60.0	2265	3415	
350 JSP	IMR 3031	57.0	2100	3430	

41 Special

Historical Notes It would be impossible to guess who might have been the first to think of this cartridge as a wildcat chambering. Almost certainly, the first gun was completed within a few years of introduction of the 41 Magnum (1964). Basically, the 41 Special is nothing more than the 41 Magnum case shortened to 1.16-inch, which matches case length for both 38- & 44-Special, whence the "Special" moniker. Typically, gunsmiths fit and rechamber a 38 or 357 cylinder to a 41 Magnum gun or install a converted cylinder and new barrel into some other large-frame revolver. Ruger's Flattop & Old Model (three-screw frame) and Smith & Wesson's 586 & 686 are some of the better revolvers for this conversion.

General Comments In 1932, Colt pursued development of a "41 Special" cartridge for police use. At least three versions were tested. These differed only in case length (and ballistics). That 41 Special used a 0.385-inch bullet and, except for the name, had no relationship whatsoever to this wildcat. Commercial production was not pursued.

Compared to the longer-cased 41 Magnum, this cartridge gives better ballistic uniformity with so-called mid-range loads — 200- to 220-grain bullets launched at about 1,000 fps — which is a fine self-defense combination. Top loads can approach the ballistics of 41 Magnum factory levels, but that defeats the intended purpose of providing sufficient energy and velocity for serious self-defense use, or for hunting of smaller big game species up to deer. This is a very good cartridge and deserves more attention than it has heretofore received. Note that bullets as light as 135 grains are offered for 40-caliber pistols. This would suggest that 140-grain, 41-caliber JHP bullets should be workable. Supposing revolvers of essentially the same weight with loads generating about 500 foot pounds of energy, the lighter bullet would generate 15 percent less recoil energy. This is a significant difference and would reduce recovery time and make the gun easier for shooters to manage and master.

41 Special

Bullet (grains/type)	Powder	Grains	Velocity	Energy	Source/Comments
200 Speer JHP	H4227	14.5	1035	475	John Taffin
200 Speer JHP	Unique	7.0	1043	480	John Taffin
200 Speer JHP	2400	12.5	1082	520	John Taffin
215 Cast SWC	Unique	7.0	1027	500	John Taffin
215 Cast SWC	2400	12.5	1063	385	John Taffin
215 Cast SWC	H4227	14.5	1037	500	John Taffin

416 Barnes

Historical Notes The 416 Barnes was the last cartridge design of the late Frank Barnes. In the late 1980s, Barnes began to think about various 40-caliber rifle cartridges. He realized that though there were many available, most were designed for use in Africa. Barnes felt there would be strong interest in a 416 designed for American game and hunting conditions rather than the dangerous African species. Additionally, he felt it would be advantageous if it could be adapted to several different rifle actions, rather than being limited to a single type. After studying the old 40-caliber cartridges, which are too long for today's actions, Barnes settled on the final version, which uses the 45-70 Government cartridge as its base. By using the 45-70, there are a number of current actions available, which would make easy conversions to the 416 Barnes. Readily available and very reasonably priced in particular is Marlin's M-1895 lever-action. Unfortunately, few commercial bullets in 416 are available in the weight range intended and appropriate for use in tubular-magazine rifles.

General Comments The 416 Barnes would be an excellent cartridge for North American big game. Loading data for this cartridge is limited. Barnes recommended using 37 grains of Rl-7 to push a 400-grain bullet at 1625 fps. IMR 3031 is another good general-purpose powder for the 416 Barnes in a lever-action rifle. Barnes found an accurate load of 50 grains of IMR 3031 behind a 330-grain bullet. It gave him a velocity of 2045 fps. This cartridge really comes into its own when used with 270- and 330-grain bullets. Though it provides no real advantage for the deer hunter, it would prove to be an excellent elk, moose or brown bear cartridge.

Editor's note: *It is too bad that Marlin is not chambering this fine round.*

416 Barnes Loading Data

Bullet (grains/type)	Powder	Grains	Velocity	Energy	Source/Comments
300 SP	IMR 4198	52.0	2355	3695	NA
300 SP	Rl-7	54.0	2270	3435	NA
330 Lead	IMR 3031	50.0	2045	3065	NA
400 SP	IMR 4198	44.0	1920	3275	NA
400 SP	IMR 4064	58.0	2140	4070	NA
400 SP	H335	59.0	2155	4125	NA
400 Lead	IMR 4198	39.0	1830	2975	NA

445 Super Magnum

Historical Notes Knocking down metallic silhouettes at 200 meters with a handgun bullet requires delivery of a relatively large dose of momentum. Elgin Gates designed the 445 Super Magnum with this task in mind. The cartridge is essentially a 44 Magnum case with approximately 3/8-inch added to the overall length. As is the case with the 44 Magnum, the name is somewhat misleading as it uses bullets of 0.429-inch diameter. The 445 Super Mag, however, can drive the same bullets nearly 300 fps faster than the 44 Magnum. Dan Wesson Arms Co. was the only company that manufactured a production gun for this cartridge. Starline is the only company that produced cases. Custom loaded ammunition is available from various custom loading companies.

General Comments Due to the pressures involved and overall cartridge length, guns chambered for this cartridge tend to be somewhat large and heavy. This has proven to be a very accurate cartridge and a fine performer with bullets weighing up to 300 grains. There is a price to pay for such performance and it comes in the form of considerable muzzle blast and recoil. The barrel compensator on some of the Wesson firearms has tamed this cartridge considerably, reducing its recoil to that of a 44 Magnum. For those willing to put up with the recoil and muzzle blast, this cartridge could prove to be an excellent choice for competition silhouette shooting or handgun hunting of large game. With more and more bullet manufacturers producing jacketed, 44-caliber bullets of 300 grains and heavier, this cartridge can really come into its own. A note of caution may be advised here. In my experience with this cartridge, I have found that different guns reach maximum loads at different rates. While some work comfortably at the maximum loads listed in loading manuals, others peak out well before this. As with any load, work up to maximum loads with care.

445 Super Mag Loading Data

Bullet (grains/type)	Powder	Grains	Velocity	Energy	Source/Comments
240 JHP	H110	31.7	1400	1045	Hornady
240 JHP	W680	35.2	1500	1200	Hornady
300 SP	H110	28.2	1300	1125	Hornady
300 SP	AA 1680	33.6	1350	1215	Hornady

458x1 1/2-inch Barnes

Historical Notes The 458x1 1/2-inch, which was never intended to be anything except an abstract experiment, has surfaced in a number of roles including a military one (see Chapter 7). It all goes back to 1962, when the author was playing around with the 458 Winchester Magnum and cutting it off to various lengths. That work culminated in the 458x2-inch. All this was reported in the June 1963 issue of *Guns & Ammo* magazine. Nothing noteworthy developed with this very short version as a sporting round until the metallic silhouette game came into bloom, at which point several individuals built up special silhouette pistols based on the Remington XP-100 action and chambered for the 458x1 1/2-inch. One of these was Larry Stevens of Carson City, Nev., who won a number of matches in the unlimited class with this combination. He reports that recoil with bullets over 300 grains is rather heavy.

General Comments The 458x1 1/2-inch will certainly knock down the metallic pigs and rams when fired from either a pistol or a rifle. Also, a 300-grain bullet exiting the muzzle at 1,500 to 1,800 fps is a potent field load and could be effective for anything from small game and varmints on up to deer-size animals. Cases are easy to make by cutting off a standard magnum case to 1.50 inches. No one makes loading dies for the cartridge, but one can improvise by using 45 Colt or other 45 pistol dies. I had this cartridge picked as a loser that would never go beyond the initial test firing, but all in all, it has had a rather interesting history.

458x1 1/2-inch Barnes Loading Data

Bullet (grains/type)	Powder	Grains	Velocity	Energy	Source/Comments
300 JSP	IMR 4198	40.0	1805	2180	24-inch barrel
300 JSP	IMR 4198	40.0	1680	1885	15-inch barrel
*350 JSP	2400	23.0	1376	1470	12-inch barrel
*350 JSP	2400	24.0	1435	1602	12-inch barrel
*430 Lead	IMR 4227	26.0	1348	1740	12-inch barrel

*Loading data furnished by Larry Stevens

45 Silhouette

Historical Notes The 45 Silhouette is an approach to a big-bore silhouette cartridge using the full-length 45-70 government case, which is inefficient when used in 10- or 12-inch barrels. Initial development was carried out by the author and Dick Smith of the Washoe County Crime Laboratory during 1984. The idea resulted from earlier experience with the 458x1 1/2-inch cartridge, which is based on the 458 Winchester Magnum shortened to 1 1/2 inches. The 45 Silhouette is made by cutting back the 45-70 case from 2.1 inches to 1 1/2 inches. Performance of these two is similar, although the 45 Silhouette is a rimmed case, while the 458x1 1/2-inch is a belted case. The rimmed case is better suited to break-open type actions such as the Thompson/Center Contender and might even be used in a revolver. Original testing was in a Siamese Mauser bolt-action rifle with a 20-inch barrel. The idea is neither brilliant nor highly original. The result is very similar to the old 45-50 Peabody sporting cartridge or the 11.75Rmm Montenegrin revolver cartridge, both of blackpowder vintage. In any event, those wanting to work with the 45 Silhouette can obtain a set of trim and loading dies from RCBS in Oroville, Calif.

General Comments The 45 Silhouette is intended primarily to shoot a 300-grain bullet of 0.457- or 0.458-inch diameter. Lighter or heavier bullets can be used, but this detracts somewhat from the original purpose, which is to provide a 45-caliber handgun cartridge that shoots a 300-grain bullet. I think the late Elmer Keith would approve of this, although he did not like some of my other ideas. Although developed as a silhouette cartridge, this would obviously also make a pretty good hunting number for anything from small game on up through deer and black bear, at least when fired from a 20-inch or longer rifle barrel. After all, a 300-grain bullet with a muzzle velocity of over 1,800 fps and 2,100 foot-pounds of energy outperforms a number of popular deer-class cartridges. Loading data listed below was developed in a Siamese Mauser bolt-action rifle with 20-inch barrel and a custom-barreled and modified Thompson/Center Contender pistol with a 10-inch barrel. A twist of 1:16 or 1:18 is recommended with 1/4-inch of freebore.

Editor's note: One could argue that this was the intellectual forerunner of the 475 Linebaugh.

45 Silhouette Loading Data

Bullet (grains/type)	Powder	Grains	Velocity	Energy	Source/Comments
200 Lead	Unique	12.0	1325	785	10" barrel
300 Lead	SR 4759	23.0	1420	1350	10" barrel
300 JHP	IMR 4198	34.0	1240	1030	10" barrel
300 Lead	IMR 4198	36.0	1610	1732	Lyman 456191 20" barrel
300 Lead	Blackpowder	44.0 (FFg)	1170	930	Lyman 456191 20" barrel
300 JHP	IMR 4198	35.0	1485	1470	20" barrel
300 JHP	IMR 4198	38.0	1670	1860	20" barrel
300 JHP	IMR 4198	40.0*	1810	2180	20" barrel

*Compressed charge

416 Aagard

Historical Notes Named as a tribute to the late African professional hunter and writer, Finn Aagard, the 416 Aagard delivers 404 Jeffrey ballistics in a compact cartridge suitable for a medium length action. Fred Zeglin designed this cartridge in 2002 for Frank Selman, a friend and hunting partner of Aagard.

General Comments The 416 Aagard uses Hornady's 376 Steyr brass as the parent case. The modern Hornady brass is necked up to

.416 and sized to create a new shoulder before fire-forming in a 416 Aagard chamber. The cartridge is well suited for bolt-action rifles using a 24-inch barrel and a 1:14 rifling twist. Note the 376 Steyr case requires a special bolt face diameter. Z-Hat Custom offers rifles, dies and reloading information. Hornady sells 376 Steyr brass. Ballistics data cited below was measured in a 21-inch barrel.

416 Aagard Loading Data

Bullet (grains/type)	Powder	Grains	Velocity	Energy	Source/Comments
350-gr Speer	VV N133	62.0	2239		Z-Hat Custom
350-gr Speer	H4895	65.0	2316		Z-Hat Custom
400-gr Hawk	RL-15	64.0	2160		Z-Hat Custom

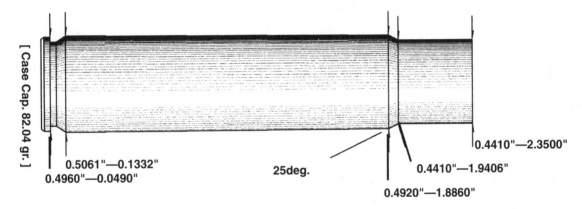

[Case Cap. 82.04 gr.]

0.5061"—0.1332"
0.4960"—0.0490"
25deg.
0.4410"—2.3500"
0.4410"—1.9406"
0.4920"—1.8860"

45 Wildey Magnum

Historical Notes In 1997, the 45 Wildey Magnum became the first big-bore bottleneck magnum cartridge chambered for a production autoloading pistol. Wildey Moore designed the cartridge for a gas-operated, autoloading pistol featuring a three-lug rotary bolt and interchangeable barrel assemblies. Revising the armament planned for the movie "*Death Wish III*", actor Charles Bronson replaced the original 45 Wildey Magnum pistol with its bigger brother, the 475 Wildey Magnum, to maximize the power effect of Wildey's big-bore magnums on the audience.

General Comments Wildey recommends this cartridge for hunting and target shooting, but not for self-defense purposes due to potential for damage or injury to bystanders. The cartridge is suited for barrel lengths of 8 to 18 inches and a 1:16 rifling twist. A 10-inch barrel offers the best blend of performance and carrying convenience. The 45 Wildey Magnum uses readily available .451-inch diameter pistol bullets. Wildey offers pistols, carbines, barrel assemblies, reloading data and dies for the 45 Wildey Magnum.

45 Wildey Magnum Loading Data and Factory Ballistics

Bullet (grains/type)	Powder	Grains	Velocity	Energy	Source/Comments
230	Blue Dot	22.0	Not Given		Wildey/FA
250	FL		1829		Wildey/FA
260	Blue Dot	19.5	Not Given		Wildey/FA

458x2-inch American

Historical Notes This belted cartridge was designed by the author in mid-1962. It uses the 458 Winchester Magnum case, shortened from 2-1/2 inches to 2 inches. It is designed as a medium-power, big-bore cartridge for North American hunting conditions and game. It is short enough to work through either standard- or medium-length rifle actions. The original rifle was made up on the short Remington Model 722 action as a lightweight carbine with 21-inch barrel. This provides an extremely powerful rifle for its size and weight of 7-1/4 pounds. The cartridge also works very well in rebarreled Winchester Model 94 Big Bore rifles.

General Comments The standard 458 Winchester Magnum and the 460 Weatherby Magnum are overpowered for North American big game. Both have very heavy recoil and require heavy, expensive rifles. Efforts have been made by various designers to provide a medium-power, big-bore cartridge more suited to American needs. The 450-348 and 450 Alaskan are examples of this, but those are rimmed cases suitable only for lever-action or single-shot rifles. The 458x2-inch fills the need for a bolt-action round of modern design tailored to game found on the North American continent. The 458x2-inch American is intended for 300- to 405-grain bullets. It gives good performance with these and is adequate for the heaviest North American game at short to medium range. It would also be quite handy for use against any but the more dangerous varieties of African game in close cover. Case dimensions and capacity are similar to the 45-70, but modern rifles permit heavier loads. This cartridge is, in effect, a belted 45-70 rather than just a shortened 458 Magnum. Ammunition can easily be made from 458 Magnum or most other belted Magnum cases. Dies are available from RCBS and chambering reamers from H&M Tool Co. Early in 2000, Marlin began shipping Model 1895 rifles chambered for its version of this cartridge, the 450 Marlin. That case features a different belt and is slightly longer; the 458x2-inch is definitely not safe for use in 450 Marlin-chambered rifles.

458x2-inch Cast Bullet Loading Data

Bullet (grains/type)	Powder	Grains	Velocity	Energy	Source/Comments
210	IMR 4198	23.0	1285	778	Lyman No. 457127
					Light plinking load
250	IMR 4198	28.0	1828	1860	Lyman No. 454485
					gas checked sized 0.457-inch
300	IMR 4198	25.0	1370	1257	Lyman No. 457191
405	IMR 3031	45.0	1535	2120	Lyman No. 457483 gas checked

These loads are economical, accurate and pleasant to shoot. The heavier bullet loads are adequate for deer out to 150 yards.

458x2-inch Jacketed Bullet Loading Data

Bullet (grains/type)	Powder	Grains	Velocity	Energy	Source/Comments
300 H SJ	IMR 4198	36.0	1650	1820	
300 H JHP	IMR 4198	40.0	1825	2223	Very accurate deer load
300 Barnes SP	IMR 4198	55.0	2412	3900	
405 Win SP	IMR 4198	51.0	2110	4005	

Jacketed bullet loads are intended for big game.
Note: All loads fired from 24-inch barrel, average temperature 78 degrees F. Winchester 458 Mag. cases and Federal No. 215 primers used for all loads. Velocity measured with Avtron Model T333 electronic chronograph.

Barnes' original rifle used the Remington Model 722 action and made up a lightweight cabine with 21-inch barrel. Standard model 722 rifle shown.

450 Alaskan
(45-348 Winchester Improved)

Historical Notes The 450 Alaskan was designed by Harold Johnson, a resident of Cooper's Landing, Alaska. This cartridge was designed to meet the demands of hunters who wanted a lever-action rifle that could deliver substantial energy and bullet mass for use against the largest and most dangerous of Alaskan game. Model 71s converted to this chambering are among the most prized rifles in Alaska. Belted Magnum bolt-action rifles are legion on used gun racks in Alaska at certain times of the year. Alaskan-chambered Model 71s are never seen for sale at any price! This is ample testimony to the power, dependability, accuracy and ruggedness this combination delivers.

General Comments Ackley might have been the first to open the hole through the barrel and improve the chamber of a Model 71 Winchester. However, by Ackley's own testimony, Johnson's version of the 45-caliber 348 Improved is a better choice. The 450

Alaskan will function through the Model 71's action with little or no alteration to the feed mechanism, while Ackley's version will not. Ackley's version has slightly less body taper and holds slightly more powder but ballistics are very similar. The 450 Fuller is essentially identical to the 450 Alaskan except for a different shoulder angle. Conversion to any of these cartridges produces a Model 71 lever-action rifle capable of delivering ballistics practically duplicating the 458 Winchester Magnum. Any such conversion necessitates special attachment measures to prevent the magazine and fore end from being separated from the receiver under the stresses of substantial recoil these cartridges generate. The data shown below is based on Ackley's recommendation of reducing 450-348 Ackley Improved data 5 percent for use in the 450 Alaskan chambering (velocities are estimates only).

450 Alaskan Loading Data (26-inch barrel)

Bullet (grains/type)	Powder	Grains	Velocity	Energy	Source/Comments
350	IMR 3031	67.0	2415	4535	Adapted 450-348 Ackley data, see text
400	IMR 4064	67.0	2095	3900	Adapted 450-348 Ackley data, see text
400	IMR 3031	67.0	2215	4360	Adapted 450-348 Ackley data, see text
500	IMR 4064	66.0	2005	4465	Adapted 450-348 Ackley data, see text

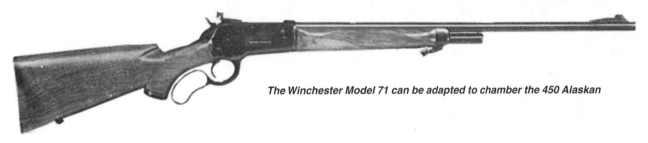

The Winchester Model 71 can be adapted to chamber the 450 Alaskan

450 Howell

Historical Notes The 450 Howell is one of three cartridges designed by Ken Howell. Ken's idea was to design a series of cartridges capable of taking African game that would fit in a standard-length bolt-action. Ken began his design sometime in the mid 1970s when "magnum-length" Mauser actions were prohibitively expensive and relatively rare. The cartridge cases of the 375 H&H Magnum and 416 Rigby were much longer than needed for efficient use with modern smokeless powders. The original version, the 375 Howell, was designed for approximately the optimum smokeless powder capacity for its bore size. All cartridges are based on the 404 Jeffery case, which measures 0.540-inch in diameter at the base versus the 0.532-inch diameter of the H&H base, thus offering a substantial powder capacity in a short

case. The 450 Howell is actually based on Ken's 416 Howell, which was the first of the three he designed. The 450 was just a necked-up version. The design of these non-belted magnums is exceptional and unfortunately was never picked up by any of the commercial cartridge companies, although similar numbers are now offered by Dakota Arms and others.

General Comments With about a 10 percent increase in capacity over the 458 Winchester Magnum, this cartridge can generate fully 100 fps more velocity at the same pressure and with the same cartridge length. It has the further significant advantage of superior accuracy potential because it headspaces on the shoulder rather than a belt and therefore can be aligned better in the chamber.

450 GNR

Historical Notes Gary Reeder developed the 450 GNR in 1990, and hunted it in Africa in 1991 as a dangerous game cartridge. The 450 GNR has dropped at least four elephants and large numbers of African buffalo.The cartridge is well suited for Thompson/Center Encore handguns with custom barrels, or rebarreled Marlin 1895 rifles. In hunting handguns, the recoil of full power loads is fierce, but manageable.

General Comments The 450 GNR performance is about 5 percent below the classic 458 Winchester Magnum. The cartridge can use either the 348 Winchester case necked up, or the 50 Alaskan case necked down. Both the 348 Winchester and 50 Alaskan parent cases require fireforming. Similar to the older 450 Alaskan, the 450 GNR design incorporates a straighter case, sharper shoulder angle and a shorter neck for more case capacity. Loads are optimized for handgun use. The 450 GNR seems to perform well with bullet weights ranging from 300 to 500grains. Gary Reeder Custom Guns offers dies, barrels, firearms, reloading components and information. Ballistics data was recorded in an Encore with a 15-inch barrel.

450 GNR Loading Data

Bullet (grains/type)	Powder	Grains	Velocity	Energy	Source/Comments
300-gr Barnes (Original)	H322	69.0	2180		Gary Reeder
400-gr Speer	IMR 3031	56.0	1710		Gary Reeder

450 Watts Magnum

Historical Notes The 450 Watts Magnum is made by necking-up 375 H&H Magnum cases to accept 0.458-inch diameter bullets. According to P.O. Ackley*, it was originated by Watts and Anderson of Yakima, Wash. It dates back to the 1950s or earlier. The case is 0.35 inch longer than the 458 Winchester Magnum. Because it holds more powder, it can be loaded to slightly higher velocity than the 458 Winchester Magnum.

General Comments The 450 Watts is a powerful cartridge that can push a 500-grain bullet a couple of hundred fps faster than the 458 Winchester. This makes the 450 Watts a fine choice for the handloader. Arizona Ammunition now offers factory-loaded custom ammunition for this and practically any other chambering. Guns so chambered safely shoot 458 Winchester Magnum loads.

*op cit, p. 501

450 Watts Magnum Loading Data*

Bullet (grains/type)	Powder	Grains	Velocity	Energy	Source/Comments
400 SP	IMR 4198	85.0	2670	6320	Ackley
500 SP	IMR 4320	98.0	2500	6920	Ackley
*P.O. Ackley, p. 501					

450 KNR

Historical Notes Developed in 1992 by Kase Reeder for an African safari the following year, the proprietary 450 KNR readily fits into the classic family of big, cigar-sized dangerous-game cartridges. Kase, the son of Arizona gunmaker Gary Reeder, successfully dropped all Africa's Big Five game animals with the 450 KNR. A few hardy souls purchased Thompson/Center Encore pistols in this chambering, but the general consensus suggests the cartridge is too much of a bone-crusher to be shot from a handgun.

General Comments The 450 KNR, essentially a 470 Nitro Express necked down to accept industry standard 458-caliber bullets, works very well in heavy-barreled Ruger #1 rifles. Gary Reeder Custom Guns offers dies, barrels, firearms, reloading components and information. When using Reeder's reloading information for lighter loads, a kapok or facial tissue filler is advisable to hold the powder closer to the primer to prevent misfires.

450 KNR Loading Data

Bullet (grains/type)	Powder	Grains	Velocity	Energy	Source/Comments
500-gr Hornady	H414	105.0	2300		Gary Reeder
510-gr Hornady	IMR 4350	100.0	2300		Gary Reeder

460 G&A Special

Historical Notes On a 1971 Uganda safari, then *Guns and Ammo* magazine publisher and wildcatter Tom Siatos designed the 460 G&A Special to provide the optimum velocity (2350 fps with 500-grain softpoint or solid bullets) for hunting dangerous game. Considered more efficient and effective than the 458 Winchester Magnum, the 460 G&A compiled a most successful track record on African cape buffalo and rhino, and on water buffalo in Brazil and Australia. Professional hunters used the 460 G&A extensively in elephant culling operations. Firearms authority Jeff Cooper considers it suitable medicine for crumpling irritated Cape buffalo at ping-pong table distances, should a hunter step into an unwise circumstance where stopping power means life.

General Comments Testing 500-grain solids against hard pine boards, the 460 G&A cartridge reliably penetrated to a depth of 48 inches before stopping. The 460 G&A uses the beltless 404 Jeffery parent case with the shoulder moved forward, neck expanded to accept .458 bullets, and fire-formed in a 460 G&A chamber. Barrels of 23-24 inches with a 1:14 twist work well with the 460 G&A cartridge. The cartridge adapts readily to magnum Mauser bolt-action rifles, and accepts .458-inch diameter bullets. For tough, nasty and otherwise dangerous game, premium hunting bullets should be the responsible hunter's first consideration.

460 G&A Special Loading Data

Bullet (grains/type)	Powder	Grains	Velocity	Energy	Source/Comments
500-gr Hornady SP	IMR 4064	88.0	2370	6235	J. P. Lott & Bob Forker
500-gr Hornady FMJ	IMR 4064	88.0	2375	6261	J. P. Lott & Bob Forker

475 Wildey Magnum

Historical Notes The 475 Wildey is the brainchild of Wildey J. Moore. This cartridge was designed to be used in a big-bore, gas-operated, semi-automatic handgun, which was also designed by Wildey. The original pistol was chambered for the 45 Winchester Magnum. In order to build the gun, Moore decided to sell stock in his company to raise capital for production. In time, some of the investors wanted to take active roles in production and marketing of this particular handgun. Unfortunately, many of these were not shooters or people knowledgeable about firearms. Moore's share in the Wildey company was diluted to 25 percent, and without his knowledge, other shareholders in the company formed a separate investment company to gain control of Wildey Inc. In January 1983, Moore was fired from his company, but the new management ended up in bankruptcy less than a year later. It took a few years for Moore to get back on his feet. Using this time to advantage, he designed an entirely new pistol with improved ballistics and a new cartridge, the 475 Wildey Magnum. The 475 Wildey is based on the 284

Winchester cartridge shortened to 1.395 inches, then neck reamed to handle 0.475-inch bullets. The cartridge is the same length as the 45 Winchester Magnum, but of greater diameter. Case forming dies for this cartridge are available from RCBS Inc. Bullets for the 475 Wildey are available from Barnes bullets in American Fork, Utah. Several designs are available, both soft points and solids.

General Comments The Wildey is a very heavy handgun designed to handle breech pressures exceeding 48,000 psi. Due to its size and weight, usefulness will most likely be limited to hunting and some sport shooting. Accuracy has proven to be outstanding. Five-shot, 25-yard groups consistently average less than 1 inch. Ballistics are also impressive, with 100-yard remaining energies exceeding 44 Magnum muzzle energy. Load data from Wildey indicates that 18 grains of BlueDot powder should be used with a 300-grain jacketed bullet. With that load, a 300-grain Barnes JSP gives an impressive muzzle velocity of 1610 fps with a muzzle energy of 1727 foot-pounds.

475 Wildey Magnum Loading Data

Bullet (grains/type)	Powder	Grains	Velocity	Energy	Source/Comments
250 SP	BlueDot	21.0	1850	1900	Wildey Inc.
300 SP	BlueDot	18.0	1610	1727	Wildey Inc.

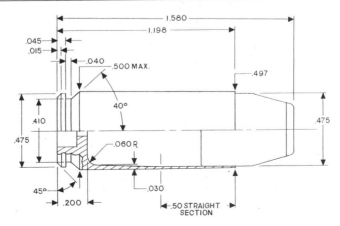

475 Ackley Magnum
475 OKH Magnum

Historical Notes These two cartridges are listed together because they are virtually identical. Both are formed by necking-up 375 H&H cases without any other change. The Ackley 475 Magnum originated in the middle 1950s. The bullet used is the Barnes 600-grain softpoint or solid at a muzzle velocity of 2250 fps. The cartridge is normally chambered in bolt-action rifles.

General Comments A 600-grain bullet at 2250 fps develops 6752 foot-pounds of energy, making for a very powerful cartridge, adequate for any dangerous African game. However, for those who like lots of energy and power, the 475 Ackley/OKH is not as powerful as either the 460 Weatherby or the 475 A&M Magnum. In actual practice, this probably would not make much difference, because any of these cartridges is capable of dispatching an elephant or Cape buffalo with one shot. Of course, this has also been done with smaller numbers developing less energy. Therefore, in the final analysis, a great deal depends on the hunter and his skill. This cartridge is overpowered for North American big game.

475 Ackley Magnum Loading Data

Bullet (grains/type)	Powder	Grains	Velocity	Energy	Source/Comments
600*	IMR 4320	90.0	2250	6750	Ackley
*Ackley, op. cit.					

475 A&M Magnum

Historical Notes This monster round was developed by the Atkinson & Marquart Rifle Co. of Prescott, Ariz., in 1958-59. It is based on the 378 Weatherby case necked-up to 47-caliber. Bullets of this diameter are made by Barnes. Only a few custom-made rifles have been produced in this chambering.

General Comments The 475 A&M Magnum can develop nearly 10,000 foot-pounds of muzzle energy, which makes it one of the most powerful sporting cartridges ever developed. It is not available on a commercial basis and is neither widely used nor known. However, no serious need exists for a cartridge of this power to hunt anything on this planet. Rifles in this class have little practical value for North American hunting conditions. Recoil of a properly built rifle is around 90 foot pounds, so six or eight shots should provide a workout equal to going a couple of rounds with the world's heavyweight boxing champ. What fun!

Editor's note: Around 1960, Fred Barnes (of Barnes bullet fame and no relation to Frank Barnes, the originator of this book) built himself a 475 A&M-chambered rifle, based upon a sporterized Enfield action. With its open sights, that rifle weighed no more than 8 pounds. Being Fred Barnes, his initial handloading effort combined stiff charges of IMR 3031 behind his 600-grain bullets. He, friends and a small group of well-wishers went to an informal shooting range near Grand Junction, Colo. Fred sat down on the pea gravel of the parking area and crossed his legs to fire from the sitting position. He took dead aim at the base of a small juniper tree, which was tenuously hanging on at the top edge of a roadway cutbank.

When Fred pulled the trigger, everyone was watching for the impact. The shot went low. The tree was summarily uprooted! All watchers cheered as the tree fell, then, as a group, they looked around to find what Barnes' reaction might be. There he was, located several feet behind his original position, lying on his back, arms outstretched, holding the rifle above his head. Dust from the muzzle blast and his ignoble recoil-induced slide (he had absorbed well over 110 foot-pounds of energy) was still stirring when Fred asked, matter-of-factly, "Anybody want to buy a rifle?" He found no takers.

—MLM

475 A&M Magnum Loading Data

Bullet (grains/type)	Powder	Grains	Velocity	Energy	Source/Comments
400 SP	IMR 3031	120.0	3227	9250	Ackley
500 SP	IMR 3031	110.0	2980	9860	Ackley
600 SP	IMR 3031	105.0	2502	8340	Ackley

50 McMurdo

Historical Notes Developed by Fifty Caliber Shooter Association member (and later president) Lynn McMurdo in 1995, the 50 McMurdo (12.7x92mm) is a long-range sporting cartridge successfully used for 1000-yard shooting competition. It proved to be a worthy contender in the art of extreme long-range accuracy shooting with 50-caliber rifles. The 50 McMurdo enjoyed wide use by five-time world champion 50-caliber shooter Scott Nye, the late Skip Talbot and other long-range competitive shooters in Fifty Caliber Shooter Association matches.

General Comments The 50 McMurdo is an accurate competition cartridge. For gun control politicians calling for restrictions on fifty caliber rifles to prevent criminal misuse, two facts are relevant. Fifty-caliber rifles are too large, heavy and expensive to be used in routine criminal activities. Fifty-caliber ammo is very expensive, with availability limited to a few retail sales outlets. The 50 McMurdo is strictly a handloading proposition for custom rifles—the 50 BMG parent case is shortened by 7mm and given a 30-degree shoulder. The resulting case was designed to provide optimum loading densities for the 800-grain weight bullets. The 50 McMurdo uses the McMurdo "Ironhand" solid brass projectile.

50 McMurdo Loading Data

Bullet (grains/type)	Powder	Grains	Velocity	Energy	Source/Comments
800-gr McMurdo Ironhand	VV N29	238.0	2650		Lynn McMurdo

510 GNR

Historical Notes The 510 GNR is the largest caliber proprietary handgun cartridge designed by Gary Reeder, who chambers it in specially prepared Ruger Blackhawk and Super Blackhawk revolvers. In 2002, Reeder designed this cartridge to accommodate a loading range varying from the 50 Special to the 500 Linebaugh. At the top end loading, recoil is somewhat less than the 500 Linebaugh. Hunters have used the 510 GNR to take large Alaskan bear and African dangerous game.

General Comments The 510 GNR uses 500 Linebaugh brass as the parent case shortened by .100-inch – about the same length as a

44 Magnum case. The 510 GNR works well in heavy-duty single-action revolvers with five-shot cylinders and five-inch barrels. Custom loaded ammunition (varying from mild to hot) is available from Cartridge Performance Engineering. Correctly headstamped brass, dies, firearms, reloading components and information are available from Reeder Custom Guns. Ballistic data was recorded in a five-inch custom revolver barrel. Note: H4227 loads are based on crimping the LBT bullet at the first lube groove to increase internal powder capacity.

510 GNR Loading Data

Bullet (grains/type)	Powder	Grains	Velocity	Energy	Source/Comments
350-gr LBT	Win 296	30.0	1250		Gary Reeder
350-gr LBT	H4227	34.0	1320		Gary Reeder
435-gr LBT	H4227	32.0	1200		Gary Reeder

510 Nitro Express

Historical Notes The 510 Nitro Express is the brainchild of Bob Schneidmiller and custom gun maker D'arcy Echols. Schneidmiller grew up in the West and from early childhood developed a passion for buffalo hunting. He read virtually everything he could get his hands on and dreamed of owning a 50 Sharps. As he grew up, the boyhood dreams remained and his interests broadened to include the Dark Continent of Africa. On his first trip to Africa, Schneidmiller carried a 50-90 Sharps, with which he took a Cape buffalo, but the performance of the 50-90 left much to be desired. After his return, he met D'arcy Echols and thoughts of building a bigger, more powerful rifle were discussed. Schneidmiller had hoped to build a 500 Nitro, but case supply for that particular cartridge was drying up fast. He had a good supply of Sharps 50-140 3 1/4-inch cases, but D'arcy was not keen about building a custom rifle for an obsolete cartridge. They compromised. They used the same basic case design as the 50-140-3 1/4 Sharps with modern bullets and powders to achieve or better 500 Nitro Express ballistics. Schneidmiller suggested they call the new cartridge the 510 Echols Express, however, Echols did not favor the idea. They finally settled on the 510 Nitro Express. The rifle was built on a Martin Hagn falling-block action and proved superbly accurate. Originally, the rifle was built without a muzzle brake. However, recoil was so heavy that the forearm was torn off with the first shot. The barrel was then so equipped and Schneidmiller claims it is now a pussycat. Some might disagree.

General Comments The 510 Nitro Express is a superb cartridge for anyone desiring a single-shot rifle for dangerous game. This cartridge-and-rifle combination can offer plenty of power without the expense of a double rifle. Though many hunters shy away from the thought of a single-shot rifle for dangerous game, there is still a strong following for the single-shot. For those not wishing to spend the time and money for a custom rifle, the Ruger No. 1 action would probably be an excellent choice for this cartridge.

510 Nitro Express Loading Data

Bullet (grains/type)	Powder	Grains	Velocity	Energy	Source/Comments
500 SP/FMJ	IMR 4895	90.0	2337	6062	Bob Schniedmiller
550 SP	IMR 4895	88.0	2172	5762	Bob Schniedmiller
600 SP	IMR 4831	102.0	2053	5614	Bob Schniedmiller
700 SP	IMR 4350	85.0	1942	5860	Bob Schniedmiller

50 McMillan FatMac

Historical Notes The late Gale McMillan and his son, Rock, developed this cartridge in 1996. Their primary goal was to create a modern (short, fat) case like those now used in benchrest competitive events, but designed to launch 50-caliber match bullets for use in 1,000-yard (or longer-range) Fifty Caliber Shooters Association (FCSA) matches. This case was derived by significantly shortening the bottlenecked 20mm cannon case. The primer pocket has been modified to accept a steel insert. This bushing sizes the primer pocket to accept a 50 BMG primer and doubles as a flash tube. The latter carries the primer blast to near the front of the powder charge, which provides significant internal ballistic benefits, including improved shot-to-shot uniformity and increased muzzle velocity.

General Comments Case capacity exceeds 415 grains of water, which is probably more than is necessary for the intended application (this is comparatively similar to a 30-caliber case of 150-grain capacity). Barrel length in 50-caliber match rifles is commonly quite long — up to about 42 inches. Chronographing showed that this cartridge easily launches 750-grain match bullets in excess of 3,400 fps (using 330 grains of powder) without placing any undue stress on the case. The 50 BMG manages only about 2,700 fps (using about 225 grains of powder). It seems likely that anyone seriously interested in pushing the envelope of 50-caliber performance might do well to consider an even shorter version of this case (perhaps about 350 grains of water capacity). The forward ignition feature is probably a worthwhile addition; this system is routinely used in artillery, where it is more feasible than in small arms. Generally, forward ignition adds measurably to ballistic efficiency (performance) and ballistic uniformity (accuracy). Since McMillan conceived this number strictly as a benchrest cartridge, he used a very short case neck. This could allow one to partially seat a bullet into a case that has been sized to provide very modest neck tension. Then during chambering, the ogive would come to rest against the rifling before the bolt was fully closed. As the bolt was locked, the short, loose case neck would allow the bullet to seat more deeply. As that occurred, the bullet could center and align to the chamber and bore — all are good features for such a cartridge. Shoulder angle is 30 degrees. The rifle uses a custom receiver built by Rock McMillan's, McBros Rifle Co., and a stock built by Kelly McMillan's McMillan Fiberglass Stocks, all of Phoenix, Ariz.

50 McMillan FatMac Ballistic Data

Bullet (grains/type)	Powder	Grains	Velocity	Energy	Source/Comments
750 Hornady A-Max			3425	19,545	McMillan (4.666-inch OAL)

505/530 Woodleigh

Historical Notes The 505/530 Woodleigh was developed by Geoff McDonald of Woodleigh Bullets, Victoria, for an African elephant hunter. Several of these rifles have been built on Enfield P14 actions, which handle the large case head of the 505. BRNO 602 or CZ550 Magnum actions would also be suitable. The rifles are fitted with Ashley ghost ring peep sights, custom-built mercury recoil reducers, and weigh 13.5 pounds. The 505/530 Woodleigh was preceded by the 530 Woodleigh Magnum, created in 1982 by necking up the 460 Weatherby case to fit .530-inch x 750-grain bullets. Its maximum muzzle velocity, with acceptable pressures, is 2,150 fps.

General Comments The 505/530 Woodleigh is the 505 Gibbs case necked up to take .530-inch bullets. With a muzzle velocity of up to 2350 fps (9200 fpe) it is quite a handful. Having a groove and bullet diameter of .530-inch and firing 750-grain FMJ and soft-nose bullets, it is suitable, and more than adequate, for all dangerous game. Field-testing in Zimbabwe in 2001 delivered excellent results on elephant, hippo and buffalo. Woodleigh Bullets of Australia makes .530-inch bullets.

505/530 Woodleigh Factory Ballistics and Loading Data

Bullet (grain/type)	Powder	Grains	Velocity	Energy	Source/Comments
750 Soft Nose or FMJ	H4350	130.0	2100	7346	Geoff McDonald
750 Soft Nose or FMJ	H4350	136.0	2200	8062	Working load
750 Soft Nose or FMJ	H4350	146.0	2352	9215	Geoff McDonald
Use only Federal 215 Magnum Primer.					

585 Nyati

Historical Notes With available muzzle energy exceeding 10,000 foot-pounds, the 585 Nyati deserves mention as very likely the world's most powerful shoulder-gun cartridge. The 50 Browning Machine Gun cartridge is used for sporting purposes, generating vastly more power than the 585 as it launches bullets of the same weight 300 to 400 fps faster. However, the 50 BMG is not by any stretch of the imagination a shoulder firearm cartridge. The 585 is.

This cartridge was created by Ross Seyfried, who modified 577 Nitro cases. Besides case forming, the rim has to be turned down to fit the bolt face. Either standard belted-magnum or 416 Rigby rim size is used, as the bolt requires. Length allows chambering in "magnum-length" Mauser actions with minimal modifications. Modified magazine capacity is three cartridges. Seyfried reports very satisfactory accuracy, no doubt a result of careful chambering and quality workmanship throughout the rifle and load. Nyati (n-ya-te) means "Cape buffalo" in several African languages, and this is certainly a good name for a cartridge delivering so much bullet and energy.

General Comments The 585 gives those who really want power a much more affordable option, compared to the big British double rifles, which can often cost tens of thousands of dollars. However, one must mention recoil. It is an open question as to how many among us can tolerate the kind of recoil this cartridge will generate with full-power loads. In a 10-pound rifle with a good muzzle brake, top loads will generate more than 150 foot-pounds of recoil energy. Compare this to a 30-06, generating a mere 20 foot-pounds. Perhaps a better understanding of what this means is this: Imagine having this 10-pound rifle dropped off a 32-foot cliff and catching it with your shoulder. The originator suggests maximum loads defeat the design purpose. He recommends loads in the 2200 fps range. Sound advice. A quality muzzle brake can significantly mitigate recoil and is almost certainly necessary on such a rifle.

Bullets for the 585 are available from Barnes, Woodleigh and numerous custom manufacturers. This cartridge also performs superbly with pure-lead cast bullets.

585 Nyati Loading Data

Bullet (grains)	Powder	Grains	Velocity	Energy	Recoil Energy*	**	***
650 Barnes TC Solid	IMR 4350	160.0	2402	8325	130	80	65
750 Barnes	IMR 4350	130.0	1925	6175	105	65	58
750 Barnes	IMR 4350	140.0	2040	6935	130	80	65
750 Woodleigh	IMR 4350	140.0	2196	8035	140	90	70
750 Barnes Solid	IMR 4350	140.0	2210	8135	145	92	68
750 Barnes	IMR 4350	150.0	2287	8715	150	95	75
750 Barnes	IMR 4350	160.0	2487	10,300	180	115	90
750 Barnes	RI-15	120.0	2070	7140	115	70	58
750 Barnes	RI-15	130.0	2235	8320	135	85	68
750 Barnes	RI-15	140.0	2420	9755	155	100	78
750 Barnes	RI-15	Max (147.0)	2525	10,620	175	110	88
545 Lead Patched	IMR 4198	72.0	1641	3255	35	25	18
650 Lead Patched	IMR 4198	73.0	1660	3975	55	35	28

All recoil data for vented barrel:

*10-pound rifle,**14-pound rifle,***18-pound rifle

14.5 Whisper

Historical Notes Another 2005 cartridge announced by JD Jones, the 14.5 Whisper uses a shortened and fire-formed 577 Nitro Express case to launch a 14.5mm (.585 inch) bullet. As conceived by SSK Industries, a Whisper cartridge must be capable of sub-sonic extreme accuracy with very heavy bullets for its caliber, plus offer moderate-to-high velocity with excellent accuracy using light bullets in the caliber. To date, the 14.5 Whisper is the largest caliber cartridge using this concept. It can accommodate bullets weights ranging from 750 grains to 1200 grains.

General Comments The 14.5 Whisper uses a 577 NE parent case shortened to just over 2 inches. SSK Industries possesses a BATF destructive device exemption for the rimmed 14.5 Whisper cartridge, enabling the manufacture and sale of rifles and cartridges. The Ruger No 1 single-shot rifle is well suited for the rimmed 14.5 Whisper case. SSK Industries offers rifles, reloading dies, bullets and loading data.

14.5 Whisper Factory Ballistics

Bullet (grains/type)	Powder	Grains	Velocity	Energy	Source/Comments
Barnes 750-gr	FL		1600		SSK Industries

14.5 JDJ

Historical Notes The 14.5 JDJ, the latest in an amazing series of big-bore boomers from JD Jones, uses the 50 BMG case with the neck expanded and case fire-formed to launch .585-inch diameter bullets at high velocities. Using a quality McMillan bolt action built into an SSK rifle, the 14.5 JDJ is capable of achieving sub-MOA groups at 1000 yards using SSK Industries CNC-machined bronze bullets. A 2005 offering from SSK Industries, the 14.5 JDJ cartridge should be considered as the very top end of proprietary cartridges based on the 50 BMG parent case. It can accommodate bullet weights ranging from 750 grains to 1200 grains, and works well with powders suitable for 50 BMG.

General Comments Rifles for the 14.5 JDJ are strictly custom creations, and can use only those actions suitable for the 50 BMG cartridge. The 14.5 JDJ can be expensive to own and shoot as custom rifle prices begin at $5000 (2005 prices). A typical 14.5 JDJ rifle will weigh about 42 pounds with the recommended 36-inch barrel and muzzle brake. SSK possesses a BATF destructive device exemption for the 14.5 JDJ cartridge, enabling the manufacture of rifles and cartridges. Interestingly, the Barnes 750-grain bullet can be driven faster than 3000 feet per second. Listed reloading data are the fireforming loads. SSK Industries offers rifles, reloading dies, bullets and loading data.

14.5 JDJ Loading Data and Factory Ballistics

Bullet (grains/type)	Powder	Grains	Velocity	Energy	Source/Comments
Barnes 750-gr	FL		3000		SSK Industries
Barnes 750-gr	5010	250.0	2900		SSK Industries
SSK 1173-gr Bronze	5010	235.0	2600		SSK Industries

620 JDJ

Historical Notes For those hunters who hold that bullet weight and diameter will trump expansion, the 620 JDJ provides the ultimate cartridge to prove their views. J.D. Jones designed the 620 JDJ in 2005. Chambered in Encore pistols, the cartridge falls under the purview of CFR, Title 27, Volume 1, and is considered a destructive device, requiring payment of the $200 Federal excise tax, along with various law enforcement and BATF approvals. The 620 JDJ may not push big bullets fast enough to ensure expansion. On the other hand, a bullet measuring .620-inch in diameter does not need much expansion. Some shooters might consider the 620 JDJ to be a novelty cartridge, as heavy loads are difficult to manage. Recoil with 900-grain bullets at 1000 feet per second is heavy but tolerable, and actually lighter than some other calibers chambered in the Encore. Accuracy with 900-grain Woodleigh and Barnes bullets is quite good, as is cast bullet accuracy.

General Comments The 620 JDJ uses 577 Nitro Express brass as its parent case, shortened to 2 inches and necked up to accept 600 Nitro Express bullets (.620-inch diameter). The cartridge can be chambered in Thompson/Center Encore single-shot pistols. SSK Industries offers firearms, barrels, reloading dies and information. Ballistics data below was measured in an SSK custom 11-inch Encore barrel.

620 JDJ Loading Data

Bullet (grains/type)	Powder	Grains	Velocity	Energy	Source/Comments
900-gr Jacketed	Accurate Arms 5744	45.0	1000		SSK Industries

729 Jongmans

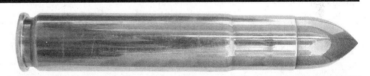

Historical Notes About 1990, Clive Downie of Ripplebrook in Victoria, Australia began experimenting with parallel-sided Browning 50-caliber machine gun cases with the idea of producing a huge-caliber rifle. He gave the project to John Jongmans, a rifle maker with experience with 50-caliber arms, and Jongmans perfected the design by putting a slight shoulder on the case and using a .727-inch bullet. John Jongmans gave it the 729 designation. The rifle was built on a Jongmans action with a 30.5-inch barrel and a huge, homemade muzzlebrake produced by Downie. The gun weighs 21 pounds, bare.

General Comments The 729 Jongmans is needlessly overpowerful for any game on earth, and is perhaps as large a bullet as one could reliably get to work in a Browning 50 case. Loads were worked up with an 896-grain solid copper turned bullet, and then later with a 1048-grain turned copper bullet. Up to 340 grains of powder is used and recoil is brutal. Downie suggests 15 shots maximum in any session is all a seasoned shooter could handle. He estimated the Taylor Knock-Out scale figure is about 250.

729 Jongmans Loading Data

Bullet (grain/type)	Powder	Grains	Velocity	Energy	Source/Comments
895 solid copper	H50BMG	270	1847	6781	Clive Downie
895 solid copper	H50BMG	300	2210	9700	Clive Downie
895 solid copper	H50BMG	340	2367	11137	Clive Downie
1048 solid copper	H50BMG	280	1955	8890	Clive Downie
1048 solid copper	H50BMG	310	2205	11317	Clive Downie
1048 solid copper	H50BMG	330	2265	11941	Clive Downie
	H50BMG	330	2265	11941	Clive Downie

WILDCAT CARTRIDGES
Rifle & Handgun Dimensional Data

Cartridge	Case Type	Bullet Dia.	Neck Dia.	Shoulder Dia.	Base Dia.	Rim Dia.	Rim Thick.	Case Length	Ctge. Length	Twist	Primer
10 Eichelberger LR	A	.103	.122	.223	.225	.275	.043	.568			RF
10 Eichelberger Pup	A	.103	.122	.247	249	.308	.050	..767			S
10 Eichelberger Squirrel	A	.103	.122	.291	.294	.350	.065	.613			S
12 Eichelberger LR	**A**	**.123**	**.140**	**.224**	**.225**	**.275**	**.043**	**.568**			**RF**
12 Eichelberger WRM	A	.123	.140	.238	.241	.293	.050	1.064			RF
12 Cooper	A	.123	.145	.247	.249	.308	.050	1.106			S
12 Eichelberger Carbine	C	.123	.147	.356	.356	.360	.050	1.240			S
14 Eichelberger WRM	**A**	**.144**	**.161**	**.238**	**.241**	**.293**	**.050**	**1.064**			**RF**
14 Eichelberger Dart	A	.144	.164	.274	.278	.301	.043	.640			S
14 Cooper	A	.144	.166	.247	.249	.3085	.051	1.104			S
14 Walker Hornet	A	.144	.170	.285	.294	.350	.065	1.350			S
14 Jet Jr	A	.144	.177	.366	.378	.440	.059	1.260			SP
14 Eichelberger Bee	A	.144	.162	.329	.349.	.408	.065	1.310			S
14/222 Eichelberger	C	.144	.170	.356	.376	.378	.045	1.670			S
14/222 Eichelberger Mag	C	.144	.170	.356	.376	.378	.045	1.850			
14-222	C	.144	.165	.356	.375	.375	.041	1.70	1.92	10	S
17 Ackley Hornet	**A**	**.172**	**.195**	**.290**	**.295**	**.345**	**.060**	**1.39**	**1.47**	**10**	**S**
17 Ackley Improved Bee	A	.172	.201	.341	.350	.408	.060	1.35	1.78	10	S
17 Mach IV	C	.172	.199	.361	.375	.378	.041	1.40	–	10	S
17/222	C	.172	.199	.355	.375	.375	.041	1.69	1.82	10-12	S
17-223	C	.172	.199	.354	.375	.378	.041	1.76	–	10-12	S
MMJ-5.7mm (22 Spitfire)	**C**	**.224**	**.253**	**.332**	**.353**	**.356**	**.046**	**1.29**	**1.65**	**14**	**L**
222 Rimmed	A	.223	.249	.352	.374	.462		1.682	2.144	14	S
224 Kay-Chuk	A	.224	.243	.293	.294	.347	.060	1.35	1.60	10-15	S
22 Kilbourn Hornet	A	.224	.242	.286	.294	.345	.060	1.39	1.70	14-16	S
R-2 Lovell	A	.224	.246	.295	.315	.382		1.63	1.80	16	S
22 Super Jet	A	.224	.248	.372	.379	.440	.055	1.266	1.75	16	S
218 Mashburn Bee	A	.224	.241	.340	.349	.408	.060	1.34	1.75	16	S
224 R-C Maxi	A	.224	.252	.354	.375	.431	.055	1.576	2.048	14	S
223 Ackley Improved	C	.224	.250	.365	.375	.378	.041	1.760	V	7-12	S
22 Waldog	C	.224	.245	.431	.440	.441	.053	1.375	1.820	14	S
22 Dasher	C	.224	.252	.462	.470	.470	.050	1.54	V	12-14	S
219 Donaldson Wasp	A	.224	.251	.402	.418	.497	.058	1.71	2.10	14	L
22 BR Remington	C	.224	.245	.450	.466	.468	.045	1.502	2.00	14-16	S
22/30-30 Ackley Improved	A	.224	.253	.391	.422	.502	.058	2.03	2.48	14	L
22-303	A	.224	.254	.4085	.455	.540	.058	2.031	2.48	14	L
22-250 Ackley Improved	C	.224	.253	.445	.466	.470	.045	1.910	V	7-12	L
220 Wotkyns-Wilson Arrow	G	.224	.261	.402	.443	.472	.045	2.205	2.70	14	L
220 Weatherby Rocket	G	.224	.260	.430	.443	.472	.045	2.21	2.68	14	L
22 Cheetah	C	.224	.250	.451	.466	.470	.048	2.00	2.36	14	S
22-243	C	.224	.260	.454	.471	.473	.048	2.045	V	9-14	L
224 Clark	C	.225	.275	.455	.471	.473	.045	2.237	3.075	9	L
22 Newton	C	.228	.256	.420	.471	.474	.045	2.23	2.85	14-16	L
228 Ackley Magnum	C	.228	.265	.445	.470	.473	.045	2.25	2.55	12	L
6x45mm (6-223 Rem)	**C**	**.243**	**.266**	**.354**	**.376**	**.378**	**.041**	**1.76**	**2.26**	**10-12**	**S**
6mm TCU	C	.243	.265	.354	.376	.378	.041	1.74	2.25	12	L
6mm-47	C	.243	.267	.348	.372	.373	.041	1.81	2.31	12	L
6 BR R	C	.243	.263	.459	.471	.528	.060	1.53	2.44	8	L
6mm Dasher	C	.224	.271	.462	.470	.470	.050	1.54	V	8-16	S
6mm-250 Walker	C	.243	.274	.420	.468	.470	.045	1.91	2.21	12	L
6mm/30-30 Ackley Improved	A	.243	.275	.392	.422	.502	.058	2.03	2.55	9-10	L
6mm Thermos Bottle	C	.243	.275	.576	.580	.578	.060	1.35	V	8	L
243 Ackley Improved	C	.243	.275	.457	.470	.467	.045	2.045	2.80	10	L
6mm/244 Ackley Improved	C	.243	.274	.457	.470	.470	.048	2.230	2.80	9	L
6mm Cheetah	C	.243	.260	.456	.470	.473	.049	2.00			L
240 Hawk	C	.243	.276	.454	.471	.473	.049	2.485			L
6mm-284	I	.243	.276	.475	.500	.473	.049	2.165	2.80	9-10	L
6mm-06	C	.243	.274	.441	.470	.467	.045	2.494	3.34	9-10	L

Cartridge	Case Type	Bullet Dia.	Neck Dia.	Shoulder Dia.	Base Dia.	Rim Dia.	Rim Thick.	Case Length	Ctge. Length	Twist	Primer
243 Catbird	C	.243	.274	.455	.470	.467	.045	2.540	3.34	10	L
25 Ugalde	**C**	**.257**	**.275**	**.368**	**.373**	**.375**	**.041**	**1.76**	**2.27**	**10**	**S**
25 Krag	A	.257	.293	.415	.457	.540	.059	2.24-2.31	V	10	L
25 Ackley Improved Krag	A	.257	.293	.442	.457	.540	.059	2.31	–	10	L
25/303	A	.257	.294	.400	.455	.541	.058	2.22	3.05	10	L
250/3000 Ackley Improved	C	.257	.284	.445	.467	.473	.045	1.91	2.52	10	L
257 Ackley Improved	C	.257	.288	.457	.471	.474	.045	2.23	2.78	10	L
25-284	I	.257	.285	.495	.500	.473	.049	2.17	2.80	10	L
25-06 Ackley Improved	C	.257	.288	.455	.470	.467	.045	2.49	3.34	10	L
6.5 TCU	**C**	**.264**	**.292**	**.368**	**.376**	**.378**	**.041**	**1.749**	**2.60**	**9-10**	**S**
6.5 LBFM	C	.264	.297	.570	.580	.578	.060	1.806	V	8	L
6.5mm-257	C	.264	.297	.429	.470	.467	.048	2.233	2.75	V	L
6.5 Grendel	C	.264	.293	.428	.439	.441	.059	1.526			S
264 Hawk	C	.264	.296	.454	.471	.473	.049	2.485			L
6.5/06-256/06	C	.264	.300	.439	.471	.473	.045	2.50	3.30	9-10	L
6.5mm-06 Ackley Improved	C	.264	.300	.455	.471	.473	.045	2.50	3.30	9-10	L
6.5 Leopard	C	.264	.295	.539	.551	.533	.049	2.093		9	L
270 REN	**B**	**.277**	**.295**		**.298**	**.350**	**.060**	**1.29**		**10**	**S**
270 IHMSA	C	.277	.305	.448	.471	.473	.045	1.866	2.60	10	L
270 Savage	C	.277	.308	.413	.470	.470	.045	1.88	2.62	10	L
270 Ackley Improved Savage	C	.277	.308	.450	.470	.470	.045	1.88	2.62	10	L
270 Hawk	C	.277	.308	.453	.471	.473	.049	2.485			L
7mm TCU	**C**	**.284**	**.302**	**.350**	**.373**	**.375**	**.041**	**1.74**	**2.28**	**10**	**S**
7mm Int-R	A	.284	.311	.402	.422	.502	.058	2.04	2.52	10	L
7mm IHMSA	C	.284	.312	.448	.471	.473	.045	1.866	2.60	9-10	L
7 STE	A	.284	.315	.454	.467	.502	.059	2.1	2.54	10	L
7x57mm Ackley Improved	C	.284	.319	.457	.470	.467	.048	2.235	3.06	8-10	L
285 OKH	C	.284	.315	.442	.470	.472	.045	2.55	3.35	10	L
280 Ackley Improved	C	.284	.313	.455	.470	.467	.045	2.540	3.34	10	L
7mm Hawk	C	.284	.315	.454	.471	.473	.049	2.485			L
7mm JRS	C	.284	.312	.454	.470	.467	.045	2.525	3.455	10	L
7mm-300 Weatherby	E	.284	.313	.490	.511	.532	.048	2.825	3.65	10	L
30 Kurz	**C**	**.308**	**.334**	**.443**	**.470**	**.473**	**.045**	**1.29**	**1.65**	**12**	**L**
308x1.5-Inch Barnes	C	.308	.338	.450	.466	.470	.048	1.50	2.05	10-12	L
30 Herrett	A	.308	.329	.405	.421	.505	.058	1.61	2.01	14	L
30 American	A	.308	.328	.402	.422	.502	.058	2.03	2.53	?	S
30-30 Ackley Improved	A	.308	.328	.405	.422	.502	.058	2.04	2.54	12	L
30 IHMSA	C	.308	.339	.448	.471	.473	.045	1.866	2.60	10-12	L
30-284 Winchester	I	.308	.344	.475	.500	.470	.050	2.017	2.80	10	L
30-06 Ackley Improved	C	.308	.340	.454	.470	.473	.045	2.49	3.35	10	L
30-338 Winchester Magnum	E	.308	.340	.491	.513	.532	.048	2.50		10	L
7.62x74Rmm Meacham	A	.308	.332	.450	.466	.522	.052	2.90	3.95	13	L
300 LBFM	C	.308	.332	.575	.580	.576	.060	2.05	V	8	L
30-8mm Remington	E	.308	.337	.487	.511	.532	.047	2.85	3.65	10	L
308 Baer	E	.308	.334	.494	.511	.532	.048	2.85	V	9-11	L
300 Phoenix	C	.308	?	?	.589	.586	.060	2.50	3.60	?	L
30 Cody	C	.308	.340	.544	.589	.586	.058	2.875	3.67	10	L
8mm-06	**C**	**.323**	**.351**	**.441**	**.470**	**.473**	**.045**	**2.47**	**3.25**	**9-10**	**L**
333 OKH	C	.333	.365	.443	.470	.473	.045	2.49	3.37	10	L
334 OKH	E	.333	.367	.480	.513	.530	.048	2.86	3.65	10	L
338-223 Straight	**D**	**.338**	**.362**		**.376**	**.378**	**.041**	**1.41**	**2.25**	**10**	**S**
338-284 McPherson	I	.338	.365	.486	.500	.467	.050	2.013	2.825	10	L
338-06 Ackley Improved	C	.338	.365	.455	.470	.467	.045	2.49	3.34	12	L
338/50 Talbot	C	.338	.380	.748	.774	.782	.080	3.76	4.25	10	50 BMG
9mm Action Express	**I**	**.355**	**.390**	**.433**	**.435**	**.394**	**.045**	**.866**	**1.152**	**18**	**S**
9x25 Dillon	C	.355	.382	.423	.423	.424	.050	0.99	1.26	10-12	SP
38-45 Hard Head	C	.355	.381	.475	.476	.476	.044	.90	1.20	14	L
357 Auto Magnum	**C**	**.357**	**.382**	**.461**	**.470**	**.473**	**.048**	**1.298**	**1.60**	**18**	**LP**
357/44 B&D	A	.357	.383	.454	.455	.515	.055	1.28	1.55	14	L
357 Herrett	A	.358	.375	.405	.420	.505	.058	1.75	2.10	14	L
35-30/30	A	.358	.378	.401	.422	.506	.058	2.04	2.55	12-14	L
35-284McPherson	I	.358	.385	.486	.500	.467	.050	2.013	2.825	10	L

Cartridge	Case Type	Bullet Dia.	Neck Dia.	Shoulder Dia.	Base Dia.	Rim Dia.	Rim Thick.	Case Length	Ctge. Length	Twist	Primer
35 Ackley Improved Whelen	C	.358	.385	.455	.469	.467	.045	2.494	V	12	L
35 AckleyMagnum	E	.358	.388	.495	.513	.532	.048	?	3.30	12	L
375-284 McPherson	**I**	**.375**	**.399**	**.486**	**.500**	**.050**	**.467**	**2.013**	**2.825**	**10**	**L**
375 Whelen & Ackley Improved Whelen	C	.375	.403	.442/.455	.470	.473	.045	2.50	3.42	12	L
400 Whelen	**C**	**.405**	**.436**	**.462**	**.470**	**.473**	**.048**	**2.49**	**3.10**	**16**	**L**
41 Special	B	.410	.432		.433	.488	.056	1.16	1.60	18	LP
416 Barnes	A	.416	.432	.484	.505	.608	.065	2.112	2.95	14	L
416-284 McPherson	I	.416	.440	.486	.500	.467	.050	2.013	2.825	10	L
416 Prairie Gun Works	C	.416	.446	.606	.637	.637	.058	3.051	3.830	10-14	L
416 Aagaard	C	.416	.441	.492	.506	.496	.049	2.35			L
445 Super Mag	**B**	**.432**	**.456**		**.457**	**.514**	**.055**	**1.60**	**1.985**	**20**	**LP**
451 Detonics	D	.452	.476		.476	.476	.044	.942	1.17	16	L
458x1 1/2-inch Barnes	**F**	**.458**	**.481**		**.513**	**.532**	**.048**	**V**		**14-16**	**L**
45 Silhouette	B	.458	.477		.501	.600	.065	1.51	1.97	18	L
458x2-inch American	F	.458	.478		.508	.532	.048	2.00	2.60	14-16	L
450 Alaskan	A	.458	.480	.515	.547	.605	.062	2.25	2.79	14	L
450 Howell	C	.458	.480	.515	.545	.534	.045	2.5	3.25	14	L
450 Watts Magnum	F	.458	.481		.513	.530	.048	2.85	3.65	14	L
460 G&A Special	C	.458	.480	.530	.545	.545	.049	2.86			L
475 Wildey	**I**	**.475**	**.497**		**.500**	**.473**	**.048**	**1.295**	**1.58**	**?**	**L**
475 Ackley/OKH Magnum	F	.474	.496		.508	.528	.048	2.739	3.518	16-18	L
475 A&M Magnum	E	.475	.502	.560	.589	.603/.580	.060	2.90	3.75	14	L
50 Alaskan	**B**	**.510**	**.532**		**.552**	**.608**	**.065**	**2.10**	**2.50**	**15-20**	**L**
510 Kodiak Express	A	.510	.532	.544	.552	.608	.065	2.33	2.68	12	L
510 Nitro Express	B	.510	.535		.565	.665		3.245	4.185	?	L
50 McMurdo	C	.510	.554	.725	.800	.802	.078	3.700	5.722	15	50 BMG
585 Nyati	**I**	**.585**	**.605**	**.650**	**.660**	**.532/.586**		**2.79**	**3.525**	**?**	**L**

Case Type: A = Rimmed, bottleneck. B = Rimmed, straight. C = Rimless, bottleneck. D = Rimless, straight. E = Belted, bottleneck. F = Belted, straight. G = Semi-rimmed, bottleneck. H = Semi-rimmed, straight. I = Rebated, bottleneck. J = Rebated, straight. K = Rebated, belted bottleneck. L = Rebated, belted straight.

Primer Type: S = Small rifle (0.175"). SP = Small pistol (0.175"). L = Large rifle (0.210"). LP = Large pistol (0.210"). 50 BMG = CCI-35/VihtaVuori-110/RWS-8212. B-1 = Berdan #1. B-2 = Berdan #2.

Other codes: V = OAL depends upon bullet used. V = Rifling twist varies, depending upon bullet and application. Belt/Rim Diameter. Unless otherwise noted, all dimensions in inches. Twist (factory) is given as inches of barrel length per complete revolution, e.g., 12 = 1 turn in 12", etc.

Chapter 5

Proprietary Cartridges

(Rifle & Handgun)

THESE PROPRIETARY cartridges, and guns so chambered, are special. These developments represent the culmination of efforts of serious gunsmiths to provide guns and ammunition that are a cut above the ordinary. All represent a level of hand fitting and precision that is simply not feasible in run-of-the-mill offerings. For those shooters willing and able to pay a premium price, these rifles offer the option of a factory gun that is, in many instances, equal to the best of the fully-custom numbers in both fit and function. The cartridges used in these guns represent an effort toward ballistic perfection. Some are more successful than others.

The concept of the proprietary chamber was well developed in Great Britain beginning in the late 1800s. That tradition continued until quite recently, when unfortunate and thoroughly nonsensical political developments probably destroyed it forever. Under our current definition, many of the reasonably well-known cartridges associated with such firms as Holland & Holland were originally strictly proprietary. Those cartridges were designed to fulfill some specific need in the best possible way. For a fuller understanding of this relationship, one should review the introductory text and cartridge write-ups in Chapter 8, *British Sporting Rifle Cartridges*.

A good example is the belted 375 H&H Magnum. That case was designed to provide solid headspace control while facilitating reliable functioning under extreme and adverse conditions in a bolt-action rifle. Considerations included functionality under extremely hot conditions and when either the ammunition or the rifle chamber might not be perfectly clean. The belt provided for solid headspacing, despite a comparatively loose fit of the case body in the chamber of the rifle. Caliber, capacity, bullet design and loading pressure (case capacity) were also chosen with consideration of the intended applications — in this instance, chiefly short- to medium-range shots on smaller species of dangerous African game.

Similarly, Sharps and many other stateside manufacturers followed the same route during the era of Buffalo exploitation and development of long-range target shooting competitive events. Most of those cartridge developments are long-since obsolete; others moved into the mainstream and are still with us. An example of the former is the 44-50 Peabody; the 38-55 Ballard (now known as the 38-55 Winchester) exemplifies the latter group.

Further, in many instances, cartridges we now think of as standard items were once essentially proprietary. A good example is the 348 Winchester. Here was a cartridge designed by Winchester, which was commercially chambered only by Winchester (in its Model 71 rifle). For many years, Winchester was the only source of 348 ammunition. Similarly, the 444 Marlin was designed for use in only one rifle (Marlin's 444) and (until the advent of Buffalo Bore ammunition's new offerings) was never commercially loaded by anyone other than Remington. While these are SAAMI standard chamberings, both are in some manner proprietary. Other examples abound. In some sense, practically every factory chambering that did not originate as a military cartridge was once proprietary. Nevertheless, we will maintain an arbitrary and perhaps unfair distinction between offerings from mainstream manufacturers and those from smaller producers.

Regarding the wildcat connection, consider the 35 Whelen. While this fine cartridge might seem to fit the proprietary bill, really it does not. For many decades, it was a widely chambered wildcat cartridge but was not commercially loaded. Now it is commercially loaded and chambered as a mainstream offering. Even before that, it was too widely known and chambered for inclusion in this chapter.

While many cartridges discussed in this chapter had antecedents in the wildcat arena (or among European developments), those have not yet achieved standard commercial status. The distinction seems significant. It would be convenient if all proprietary cartridges were unique developments and if no wildcat cartridges fit into this category. However, that is not the situation. Gray areas of overlap are noteworthy and somewhat abundant.

Most proprietary offerings detailed in this chapter followed a developmental path that is similar to the aforementioned historical British proprietary cartridges. Some custom gun manufacturer noted a void in the offerings from major arms manufacturers. That manufacturer then designed a cartridge to fill that void in the best way possible – according to his lights and based upon what basic case types were available for improvement. Here, we might consider the history of the major commercial cartridge offerings with which, in many instances, these proprietary chamberings compete.

Big-bore (50-caliber and up) rifles convey almost romantic images and historic links to the great dangerous game hunters of years past. However, the years between then and now have seen the introduction of legal restrictions on the ownership of these firearms. When proprietary cartridges contain a projectile larger than one-half inch in diameter, they may be considered as destructive devices, according to the United States' Code of Federal Regulations, Title 27, Volume 1. The statuatory authority granted to the BATF allows the director to determine that the device, among other things, is a rifle that the owner intends to use solely for sporting purposes. Certain combinations of firearms actions, barrel lengths and bore diameter may not meet the criteria of "being a rifle that the owner intends to use solely for sporting purposes" and would otherwise constitute a destructive device. Possession of an unauthorized destructive device may subject the possessor to criminal or civil penalties. For shooters interested in purchasing or possessing one of the 50-caliber or larger cartridges documented in this chapter, it is important to confirm the manufacturer of the rifle and cartridge combination has an exemption from the BATF for its manufacture.

226 JDJ

Historical Notes Designed by J.D. Jones in 1979, this cartridge is the 225 Winchester, improved. It provides a reduction in chamber pressure, which improves Contender functioning. Factory 225 Winchester ammunition sometimes gave extraction difficulties in Contender barrels. This design solved that problem while allowing the handloader to achieve 225 Winchester Thompson/Center performance without extraction difficulties. Factory 225 Winchester ammunition can be used.

General Comments As is typical of the JDJ line, this chambering offers 1/2 MOA accuracy potential with proper handloads. New barrels feature a 1 in 9-inch twist for use with heavier bullets, which are gaining popularity in the 22-caliber bore. Typical loads with the 40-grain bullet easily exceed 3600 fps from a 16-inch barrel. The Barnes 45-grain XBT is an effective choice for peccary-size game species. However, use of this bullet requires special handloading techniques (deeper bullet seating and a reduction in powder charge).

226 JDJ Loading Data

Bullet (grains/type)	Powder	Grains	Velocity	Energy	Source/Comments
50 Hornady	IMR 3031	32.0	2864	905	SSK/maximum load, SSK barrel only
55	IMR 4064	33.0	2808	960	SSK/maximum load, SSK barrel only
55 Hornady SX	BL-C(2)	32.0	2637	849	SSK/maximum load, SSK barrel only
60 Hornady SP	H414	35.0	2732	995	SSK/maximum load, SSK barrel only
63 Sierra	H4831	38.5	2831	1115	SSK/maximum load, SSK barrel only

6 Whisper

Historical Notes Created by J. D. Jones, the 6 Whisper uses a modified 221 Fireball case necked up to 6mm to propel heavy bullets at subsonic velocities, and lighter bullets at higher velocities. In a 10-inch-barreled Contender pistol, the 6 Whisper can propel 115-grain bullets to 1054 fps, and lighter 55-grain

bullets to over 3000 fps. Barrels, dies, and cases for the 6 Whisper are available from SSK Industries.

General Comments This cartridge is well suited for Thompson/Center Contender, bolt-action rifles and AR15-type rifles. At subsonic velocities, it functions quietly and accurately in suppressed firearms.

6mm JDJ

Historical Notes This cartridge was designed and developed by noted gun writer and experimenter J.D. Jones, hence the "JDJ" designation. Jones began development of his series of cartridges around 1978, and they are generally fired in barrels furnished by his company, SSK Industries. The purpose of this cartridge is to give added range and power to the Thompson/Center Contender pistol for the primary purpose of hunting varmints and small game. Some of his cartridges have proven to be excellent metallic silhouette numbers as well. The JDJ series of cases is easy to make. All JDJ cartridges are proprietary and SSK neither sells reamers nor permits the reamer maker to duplicate any of the reamers. Should you desire to chamber a JDJ cartridge, contact SSK Industries, 421 Woodvue Lane, Wintersville, OH 43952.

General Comments Based on the 225 Winchester case, itself a modified 30-30 case, this improved chambering provides ample capacity to deliver maximum 6mm velocity from handgun-length barrels (14 to 16 inches). Best applications are in handgun varminting and hunting of the smallest big game species. With the proper 70- to 75-grain bullet, this chambering can deliver 300-yard varmint accuracy and trajectory. Heavier bullets can deliver adequate energy for smaller big game to perhaps 100 yards. The Barnes 75-grain and 85-grain X bullets offer serious hunting performance. However, use of these bullets requires special handloading techniques (deeper bullet seating and a reduction in powder charge).

6 JDJ No. 2 Loading Data

Bullet (grains/type)	Powder	Grains	Velocity	Energy	Source/Comments
70 HP	RI-7	29.0	2845	1260	SSK/maximum load, SSK barrels only
*[70 HP	AA 2700	35.0	2540	1000	SSK/maximum load, SSK barrels only
80 HP	RI-19	37.0	2370	1000	SSK/maximum load, SSK barrels only]

Note: These loads for use only in SSK barrels

6.17 Spitfire

Historical Notes Lazzeroni Arms designed this cartridge in 1997. While somewhat related to an older case, for practical purposes, this is a new case design. This cartridge was created in response to requests (from this editor and others) for a high-performance cartridge that would work in a 2.8-inch action and yet deliver the ballistics of a full-length belted-magnum. Case diameter is similar to conventional belted case rim diameter, so adaptation to a standard action is quite simple.

General Comments Bullet diameter is 0.243-inch (Lazzeroni bases its designations on bullet diameter, instead of bore diameter, which is the common practice). Ballistics are quite impressive for such a short cartridge. The Spitfire comes very close to top 240 Weatherby ballistics. Case design is typical of the Lazzeroni line: moderate body taper, 30-degree shoulder, sufficiently long neck, and thick rim of approximately case-body diameter. In other words, this is a well-designed case.

6.17 Spitfire Factory Ballistics (24-inch barrel)

Bullet (grains/type)	Powder	Grains	Velocity	Energy	Source/Comments
70			3750	2186	Lazzeroni factory load
85			3550	2379	Lazzeroni factory load
100			3350	2493	Lazzeroni factory load

6.17 Flash

Historical Notes Lazzeroni has recently discontinued this as a standard chambering, but still offers it on a special-order basis. Lazzeroni Arms designed this cartridge in 1996. While somewhat related to an older case, for practical purposes, this is a new case design. John Lazzeroni believes that those hunters who will take the time to become competent marksmen can legitimately take game at ranges out to about 500 yards, given a gun with the requisite accuracy and a bullet that will perform properly. This cartridge was created to provide sufficient velocity for medium-weight hunting bullets in order to provide dependable expansion at maximum ranges. Adaptation to standard actions is quite simple.

General Comments Bullet diameter is 0.243-inch (Lazzeroni bases its designations on bullet diameter, instead of bore diameter, which is the common practice). Flash ballistics surpass any other current 6mm cartridge. Case design is typical of the Lazzeroni line: moderate body taper, 30-degree shoulder, sufficiently long neck, and thick rim of approximately case body diameter. In other words, this is a well-designed case. Designed specifically for hunting, with limited barrel life (no more than 500 rounds), this cartridge is not recommended for any other use. While 27-inch barrels are standard, all the smaller-caliber, full-length Lazzeroni numbers would benefit significantly from even longer barrels. Most of Lazzeroni's full-length cartridge loadings use especially lubricated (proprietary process) premium bullets from Nosler, Barnes or Swift. This is a superior performer for those who only hunt the smaller species of big game and who will not abuse the barrel by incautious shooting. The 85-grain Nosler Partition works extremely well.

6.17 Flash Factory Ballistics (27-inch barrel)

Bullet (grains/type)	Powder	Grains	Velocity	Energy	Source/Comments
70			4150	2678	Lazzeroni factory load
85			3900	2871	Lazzeroni factory load
100			3700	3041	Lazzeroni factory load

257 JDJ

Historical Notes This is another cartridge designed and developed by J.D. Jones, hence the JDJ designation. Jones began development of his cartridges around 1978 and they are generally fired in barrels furnished by his company, SSK Industries. The purpose of these cartridges is to give added range and power to the Thompson/Center Contender pistol. Some of his cartridges have also proven to be excellent metallic silhouette numbers. JDJ cartridges are relatively easy to make. All JDJ cartridges are proprietary and SSK neither sells reamers nor has permitted the reamer maker to duplicate any of the reamers for the series. Should you desire a JDJ cartridge, contact SSK Industries, 421 Woodvue Lane, Wintersville, OH 43952.

General Comments Based on the 225 Winchester case, itself a modified 30-30 case, this improved chambering provides ample capacity to deliver near-maximum quarter-bore velocity from handgun-length barrels (14-16 inches). Best applications are in handgun varminting and hunting of smaller big game species. A preferred bullet for the latter application is Nosler's 85-grain Ballistic Tip. This cartridge can launch this bullet to about 2900 fps with top loads from a 14-inch barrel. This combination is said to provide good terminal performance to 300 yards. One can use heavier bullets to deliver more energy. However, reduced velocity limits expansion and trajectory errors increase. Therefore, hunters should limit use of such bullets to shorter ranges. The 75-90 grain Barnes X bullets offer potential advantages for hunting applications. However, use of these bullets requires special handloading techniques (deeper bullet seating and a reduction in powder charge).

257 JDJ Loading Data

Bullet (grains/type)	Powder	Grains	Velocity	Energy	Source/Comments
75 HP	H322	30.0	2310	890	SSK/maximum load, SSK barrels only
75 HP	W748	37.0	2645	1165	SSK/maximum load, SSK barrels only
100 SP	W748	34.0	1405	1285	SSK/maximum load, SSK barrels only
117 SP	IMR 4350	35.0	2195	1250	SSK/maximum load, SSK barrels only

25/06 JDJ

Historical Notes Virtually identical to the 6.5/270 JDJ, the 25/06 JDJ uses a modified 270 Winchester case, necked down to handle 25-caliber bullets. Other changes include shortening the neck, reducing case taper to maximize powder capacity and forming a 60-degree shoulder to achieve ballistics normally associated with belted magnum cartridges in similar length (15-inch) Encore barrels. Barrels, dies, and cases for the 25/06 JDJ are available from SSK Industries.

General Comments The 25/06 JDJ is well suited for Thompson/Center Encore firearms, Ruger #1 rifles or appropriate bolt-action rifles. This cartridge provides long case life, consumes less powder than belted magnum cartridges, and uses relatively inexpensive cases.

257 Mini Dreadnaught

Historical Notes This cartridge was designed by J.D. Jones at SSK Industries. Application is to Thompson/Center Encore *[or Contender] single-shot pistols fitted with a custom SSK barrel. Typical barrel length is 15 inches. Cases are fire formed from empty 220 Swift cases. Neck length is minimal, which is acceptable for a cartridge used in a single-shot gun. Shoulder angle is 60 degrees, which seems to work just fine. Body taper is minimal, similar to Ackley Improved designs much less than "older" rifle cartridge designs. Therefore, this is a maximized, 25-caliber version of the 220 Swift case. Capacity is similar to the 257 Roberts (about 57 grains) and working pressure is higher (about 60,000 psi), so ballistics are quite similar, despite the significant deficit in barrel length.

General Comments Since the Swift case has a rim, it is possible to fire-form necked-up Swift cases to fit this chamber. For this purpose, use loads that are near the maximum level. J.D. Jones recommends 100- to 120-grain bullets for big game hunting applications on smaller species. Nosler's Ballistic Tip and Partition have demonstrated superior performance. However, it would appear that this cartridge is capable of driving 120-grain bullets fast enough to give dependable expansion. While one could use the lightest Barnes X bullets, which can offer impressive terminal performance, the handloader must use X-bullet-specific loading data and special handloading techniques (e.g., the bullet ogive must be seated a minimum of 0.050-inch from the rifling). Further, those bullets work best when a minimum-friction coating (such as moly-plating) is used. For this reason, SSK does not support the use of X-style bullets in its guns. While no bullet substitution is benign, never substitute any X-style bullet in any load — begin with data specifically created for that bullet.

257 Mini Dreadnaught Loading Data

Bullet (grains/type)	Powder	Grains	Velocity	Energy	Source/Comments
100 Nosler BT	AA 4350	48.7	3008	2005	SSK/maximum load, SSK barrels only

6.53 Scramjet

Historical Notes Lazzeroni Arms designed this cartridge in 1996. While somewhat related to an older case, for practical purposes this is a new case design. John Lazzeroni believes that those hunters who will take the time to become competent marksmen can legitimately take game at ranges out to about 500 yards, given a gun with the requisite accuracy and a bullet that will perform properly. This cartridge was created to launch lightweight hunting bullets with sufficient velocity to provide dependable expansion at maximum ranges. Adaptation to standard actions is quite simple. While this case does not sell well, Lazzeroni will continue to handle it, owing to the founder's love for this bore size.

General Comments Bullet diameter is 0.257-inch (Lazzeroni bases its designations on bullet diameter, instead of bore diameter, which is the common practice.). Scramjet ballistics exceed any other current 25-caliber cartridge. Case design is typical of the Lazzeroni line: moderate body taper, 30-degree shoulder, sufficiently long neck, and thick rim of approximately case body diameter. In other words, this is a well-designed case. Designed specifically for hunting, and with limited barrel life, this cartridge is not recommended for any other use. While 27-inch barrels are standard, all the smaller-caliber, full-length Lazzeroni numbers would benefit significantly from even longer barrels. Most of Lazzeroni's full-length cartridge loadings use especially lubricated (proprietary process) premium bullets from Nosler, Barnes or Swift. For hunting, John prefers the 100-grain Nosler Partition and the 90-grain Barnes XBT, while the 85-grain Nosler BT is especially accurate and makes a superb long-range varminting combination. A significant portion of the accuracy and ballistic potential of these cartridges results from the unusually effective reduced-friction coating used.

6.53 Scramjet Factory Ballistics (27-inch barrel)

Bullet (grains/type)	Powder	Grains	Velocity	Energy	Source/Comments
85	FL		4000	3021	Lazzeroni factory load
100	FL		3750	3123	Lazzeroni factory load
120	FL		3550	3219	Lazzeroni factory load

6.5mm Whisper

Historical Notes Designed by J.D. Jones in the early 1990s, this cartridge was intended for use in sound-suppressed M-15s, bolt-action rifles and T/C Contenders. As with most of Jones' line, this cartridge was designed at SSK Industries. This cartridge is based upon the 221 Remington case.

General Comments When combined with a very quick rifling twist, this chambering will deliver 155-grain very low drag (VLD) bullets from SSK Contender barrels with 1/2 MOA accuracy at subsonic velocities (1040 fps). Lighter bullets can achieve a more typical muzzle velocity, but such applications sacrifice the design purpose of this chambering. The 6.5mm Whisper performs well as a short-range deer cartridge.

6.5mm Whisper Loading Data

Bullet (grains/type)	Powder	Grains	Velocity	Energy	Source/Comments
100 Hornady	H110	19.0	2300	1170	Maximum load, SSK barrel only (10")
120 Nosler BT	A-1680	19.0	2150	1230	Maximum load, SSK barrel only (10")
155	H110	8.3	970	320	SSK/M-16 (gas port open)
155	H110	8.3	1051	375	SSK/M-16 (gas port blocked)
155	AA No. 9	8.4	1050	375	SSK/M-16 (gas port open)
155	AA No. 9	8.4	1074	395	SSK/M-16 (gas port blocked)

6.5mm JDJ

Historical Notes Designed by J.D. Jones at SSK Industries, this is the 225 Winchester case improved and necked up to 6mm. The purpose was to provide a Contender hunting cartridge for smaller big game species.

General Comments Excellent bullets are available and with proper loads and in the hands of a good shot, this chambering is capable of 300-yard shots on smaller big game species. Jones considers this cartridge one of the premier small-bore hunting choices. The Barnes 100-grain X offers superior terminal performance for hunting applications. However, use of this bullet requires special handloading techniques (deeper bullet seating and a reduction in powder charge).

6.5mm JDJ Loading Data

Bullet (grains/type)	Powder	Grains	Velocity	Energy	Source/Comments
85 Sierra	IMR 4320	35.0	2644	1315	SSK/maximum load, SSK barrel only (14")
100 Sierra HP	H322	35.0	2714	1635	SSK/maximum load, SSK barrel only (14")
120 Speer	IMR 4350	38.5	2467	1620	SSK/maximum load, SSK barrel only (14")
125 Nosler Part	IMR 4320	33.0	2410	1610	SSK/maximum load, SSK barrel only (14")
129 Hornady	IMR 4320	32.0	2342	1570	SSK/maximum load, SSK barrel only (14")
140 Speer	IMR 4350	34.0	2097	1365	SSK/maximum load, SSK barrel only (14")

6.5mm JDJx30

Historical Notes This J.D. Jones cartridge is the 7-30 Waters necked down to 6.5mm and improved. Its purpose is to meet customer demand for improved performance with readily obtained cases. Since the 7-30 is based on the 30-30 Winchester, one can easily use those abundant cases to form this round. Other than rim diameter and a slight increase in case length, this is essentially identical to the 6.5mm JDJ.

General Comments Excellent bullets are available and with proper loads and in the hands of a good shot, this chambering is capable of 300-yard shots on the smaller species. Jones considers this one of the premier small-bore hunting choices. The Barnes 100-grain X offers superior terminal performance for hunting applications. However, use of this bullet requires special handloading techniques (deeper bullet seating and a reduction in powder charge).

6.5mm JDJ x30 Loading Data

Bullet (grains/type)	Powder	Grains	Velocity	Energy	Source/Comments
85 Sierra	W760	42.0	2710	1385	SSK/maximum load, SSK barrel only (14")
120 Speer	W760	40.0	2477	1635	SSK/maximum load, SSK barrel only (14")
120 Nosler BT	IMR 4064	37.5	2580	1770	SSK/maximum load, SSK barrel only (14")
129 Hornady	IMR 4350	40.7	2481	1760	SSK/maximum load, SSK barrel only (14")
140 Sierra	IMR 4350	40.7	2376	1755	SSK/maximum load, SSK barrel only (14")

6.5 Mini Dreadnaught

Historical Notes This cartridge was designed by J.D. Jones at SSK Industries. Application is to Thompson/Center Encore or Contender single-shot pistols fitted with a custom SSK barrel. Typical barrel length is 15 inches. Cases are formed from empty 220 Swift cases. Neck length is minimal, which is acceptable for a cartridge used in a single-shot gun. Shoulder angle is 60 degrees, which seems to work just fine. Body taper is minimal, similar to the Ackley Improved designs. Therefore, this is a maximized, 6.5mm version of the 220 Swift case. Capacity is similar to the 257 Roberts (about 56 grains) and with a larger bore and higher working pressure (about 60,000-psi), ballistics easily duplicate the Roberts, despite the significant deficit in barrel length.

General Comments Since the Swift case has a rim, it is possible to fire-form necked-up Swift cases to fit this chamber. For this purpose, use loads that are near the maximum level. Jones recommends 120- to 140-grain bullets for big game hunting applications on smaller species. Nosler's Ballistic Tip and Partition have demonstrated superior performance. However, it would appear that this cartridge is capable of driving 155-grain bullets fast enough to give dependable expansion. While one could use 100-grain Barnes X bullets, which can offer impressive terminal performance, the handloader must use X-bullet-specific loading data and special handloading techniques (e.g., the bullet ogive must be seated a minimum of 0.050-inch from the rifling). Further, those bullets work best when a reduced-friction coating (such as moly-plating) is used. For this reason, SSK does not support use of X-style bullets in its guns. While no bullet substitution is benign, never substitute any X-style bullet in any load — begin with data specifically created for that bullet. This cartridge has a significantly shorter case body than the 257 Mini Dreadnaught, so it fails to exceed the ballistic potential of its smaller-bored sibling.

6.5 Mini Dreadnaught

Bullet (grains/type)	Powder	Grains	Velocity	Energy	Source/Comments
120 Sierra	Vit N560	52.0	2852	2165	SSK/maximum load, SSK barrels only
120 Sierra	AA 2700	49.5	2775	2050	SSK/maximum load, SSK barrels only
140 Remington	Vit N560	52.0	2736	2325	SSK/maximum load, SSK barrels only
140 Hornady	AA 2700	48.2	2618	2130	SSK/maximum load, SSK barrels only

6.5mm JDJ No. 2

Historical Notes This J.D. Jones cartridge is the 307 Winchester necked down to 6.5mm and improved. It provides a 6.5mm chambering based upon the 307 Winchester case.

General Comments Excellent bullets are available, and with proper loads and in the hands of a good shot, this chambering is fine for 300-yard shots on smaller species. In handgun-length barrels, ballistics are not significantly superior to the smaller 6.5mm JDJ cartridges to justify the existence of this chambering. The Barnes 100-grain X offers superior terminal performance for hunting applications. However, use of this bullet requires special handloading techniques (deeper bullet seating and a reduction in powder charge).

6.5mm JDJ No. 2 Loading Data

Bullet (grains/type)	Powder	Grains	Velocity	Energy	Source/Comments
120	IMR 4350	43.0	NA	NA	SSK/maximum load, SSK barrel only
129	IMR 4350	42.0	NA	NA	SSK/maximum load, SSK barrel only
140	IMR 4350	41.0	NA	NA	SSK/maximum load, SSK barrel only

6.5/270 JDJ

Historical Notes If anyone produced more successful cartridge designs than J. D. Jones of SSK Industries, they are not very widely recognized. In creating the 6.5/270 JDJ, Mr. Jones used a modified 270 Winchester case, necking it down to handle 6.5mm bullets, shortening the neck, reducing case taper and forming a 60-degree shoulder to achieve ballistics normally associated with belted magnum cartridges in similar length (15-inch) Encore barrels.

Barrels, dies, and cases for the 6.5/270 JDJ are available from SSK Industries.

General Comments The 6.5/270 JDJ is well suited for Thompson/Center Encore firearms, Ruger #1 rifles or appropriate bolt-action rifles. This cartridge provides long case life, consumes less powder than belted magnum cartridges, and uses relatively inexpensive cases.

6.71 Phantom

Historical Notes Lazzeroni Arms designed this cartridge in 1997. While somewhat related to an older case, for practical purposes, this is a new case design. This cartridge was created in response to requests for a high-performance cartridge that would work in a 2.8-inch action and yet deliver the ballistics of a full-length belted magnum. Case diameter is similar to rim diameter of the conventional belted case, so adaptation to a standard action is quite simple.

General Comments Bullet diameter is 0.264-inch (Lazzeroni bases its designations on bullet diameter, instead of bore diameter, which is the common practice). Ballistics are quite impressive for such a short cartridge. The Phantom essentially duplicates 24-inch barrel 264 Winchester Magnum ballistics. Case design is typical of the Lazzeroni line: moderate body taper, 30-degree shoulder, sufficiently long neck, and thick rim of approximately case body diameter. In other words, this is a well-designed case.

6.71 Phantom Factory Ballistics (24-inch barrel)

Bullet (grains/type)	Powder	Grains	Velocity	Energy	Source/Comments
100	FL		3450	2643	Lazzeroni factory load
120	FL		3250	2815	Lazzeroni factory load
140	FL		3050	2892	Lazzeroni factory load

Proprietary Cartridges

6.71 Blackbird

Historical Notes Lazzeroni Arms designed this cartridge in 1996. Lazzeroni no longer routinely chambers this number but will still do so on a special-order basis. While somewhat related to an older case, for practical purposes, this is a new case design. John Lazzeroni believes that those hunters who will take the time to become competent marksmen can legitimately take game at ranges out to about 500 yards, given a gun with the requisite accuracy and a bullet that will perform properly. This cartridge was created to provide sufficient velocity to medium-weight hunting bullets to provide dependable expansion at maximum ranges. Adaptation to standard actions is quite simple.

General Comments Bullet diameter is 0.264-inch (Lazzeroni bases its designations on bullet diameter, instead of bore diameter, which

is the common practice). Ballistics exceed any other current 6.5mm cartridge. Case design is typical of the Lazzeroni line: moderate body taper, 30-degree shoulder, sufficiently long neck, and thick rim of approximately case-body diameter. In other words, this is a well-designed case. Intended specifically for hunting, and with limited barrel life (typically between 700 and 1000 rounds when the rifle is not overheated and is properly cleaned), this cartridge is not recommended for any other use. While 27-inch barrels are standard, all the smaller-caliber, full-length Lazzeroni numbers would benefit significantly from even longer barrels. This is a superior performer for those who only hunt smaller species of big game and who will not abuse the barrel by incautious shooting. The 125-grain Nosler Partitions and 100-Barnes Xs work extremely well.

6.71 Blackbird Factory Ballistics (27-inch barrel)

Bullet (grains/type)	Powder	Grains	Velocity	Energy	Source/Comments
100	FL		4000	3021	Lazzeroni factory load
120	FL		3750	3123	Lazzeroni factory load
140	FL		3550	3219	Lazzeroni factory load

270 JDJ

Historical Notes This is another cartridge designed and developed by J.D. Jones around 1978. It is generally fired in barrels furnished by his company, SSK Industries. The purpose of these cartridges is to give added range and power to the Thompson/Center Contender pistol for hunting medium game. All of the JDJ cartridges are proprietary and SSK neither sells reamers nor has permitted the reamer maker to duplicate any of the reamers for this series. Should you desire a JDJ cartridge, contact SSK Industries, 421 Woodvue Lane, Wintersville, OH 43952.

General Comments Based on the 225 Winchester case (itself a modified 30-30 case) this improved chambering provides ample capacity to deliver impressive velocity from handgun-length barrels, now commonly 14-16 inches. Best applications are in

handgun varminting and hunting of smaller big game species, through mule deer size. For varminting, best performance is probably achieved with bullets of 100 grains. Either Hornady's or Sierra's 110-grain bullets would be good choices for pronghorn hunting. For hunting deer and similar-sized game, the best bullet weight is 130 grains. Heavier bullets can deliver more energy, but expansion is unreliable. This chambering has seen considerable use in various types of handgun competition. This is ample testimony to the potential accuracy of this chambering and the quality of gunsmithing involved in such alterations. Barnes' 100-grain X offers superior terminal performance for hunting applications. However, use of this bullet requires special handloading techniques (deeper bullet seating and a reduction in powder charge).

270 JDJ Loading Data

Bullet (grains/type)	Powder	Grains	Velocity	Energy	Source/Comments
100 SP	RI-7	34.0	2795	1735	SSK/maximum load
110 SP	IMR 4320	36.0	2520	1555	SSK/maximum load
130 SP	RI-7	30.7	2370	1625	SSK/maximum load
130 SP	IMR 3031	35.0	2470	1765	SSK/maximum load (SSK barrels only)

270 JDJ No. 2

Historical Notes Another creation of J. D. Jones, the 270 JDJ #2 uses a modified 30-06-family of cases with a shortened neck, reduced case taper and 60-degree shoulder to achieve ballistics normally associated with belted magnum cartridges in similar length barrels. In a short-barreled Encore pistol, the 270 JDJ #2 can propel 130-grain bullets to 2,487 fps. The cartridge can accommodate a range of 270 bullet weights ranging from 90 grains to 150 grains, including some fine hunting bullets. Barrels,

dies, and cases for the 270 JDJ #2 are available from SSK Industries.

General Comments The 270 JDJ #2 is well suited for Thompson/Center Encore firearms or appropriate bolt-action rifles. Capable of sub-MOA accuracy, this cartridge provides long case life, consumes less powder than belted magnum cartridges, and uses relatively inexpensive cases.

7mm Whisper

Historical Notes Designed by J.D. Jones in the early 1990s, this cartridge was designed for use in sound-suppressed M-15s, bolt-action rifles and T/C Contenders. As with most of the JDJ line, this cartridge was designed at SSK Industries. The 7mm Whisper is based upon the 221 Remington case.

General Comments When combined with a very quick rifling twist, this chambering will deliver heavy 7mm bullets from SSK Contender barrels with 1/2 MOA accuracy at subsonic velocities (1,040 fps). Lighter bullets can achieve velocity that is more typical, but they sacrifice the design purpose of this chambering.

7mm Whisper

Bullet (grains/type)	Powder	Grains	Velocity	Energy	Source/Comments
120	AA 1680	20.0	2250	1345	SSK/maximum load, 16 1/2" brl.
140 Nosler BT	AA 1680	18.5	2060	1315	SSK/maximum load, 16 1/2" brl.
168	AA 1680	9.5	1056	415	SSK/subsonic
168	Vit N540	12.6	1064	420	SSK/subsonic
168	AA 1680				NA

7mm JDJ

Historical Notes This is another cartridge designed and developed by J.D. Jones. Its purpose is to give added range and power to the Thompson/Center Contender pistol for the primary purpose of hunting medium game. This cartridge has also proved to be an excellent choice for metallic silhouette competition. All JDJ cartridges are relatively easy to make. These are proprietary and SSK neither sells reamers nor has permitted the reamer maker to duplicate any of the reamers for the series. Should you desire a JDJ cartridge, contact SSK Industries, 421 Woodvue Lane, Wintersville, OH 43952.

General Comments Based on the 225 Winchester case (itself a modified 30-30 case), this improved chambering provides ample capacity to deliver impressive velocity, especially with longer handgun-length barrels (14-16 inches). Best applications are in

handgun hunting of smaller big game species through mule deer size. Best hunting performance is probably achieved with bullets of 120-140 grains. Experts have tallied many kills at ranges exceeding 200 yards. Heavier bullets can deliver more energy, but expansion is not reliable. Heavier bullets have proven effective in the handgun silhouette game. Bullets of about 150 grains are noted for effectiveness in toppling the silhouette ram target. This chambering has seen considerable use in various types of handgun competition. This is ample testimony to the potential accuracy of this chambering and the quality of gunsmithing involved in such alterations. The Barnes 100-grain and 120-grain X bullets offer superior terminal performance for hunting applications. However, use of these bullets requires special handloading techniques (deeper bullet seating and a reduction in powder charge).

7mm JDJ Loading Data

Bullet (grains/type)	Powder	Grains	Velocity	Energy	Source/Comments
120 SP	H4895	34.0	2480	1640	SSK/maximum load, SSK barrels only
139-140 SP	IMR 4320	34.0	2145	1420	SSK/maximum load, SSK barrels only
150-154 SP	IMR 4320	34.0	2110	1520	SSK/maximum load, SSK barrels only

7mm-30 JDJ

Historical Notes This JDJ cartridge is the 7-30 Waters, improved. The purpose is to meet customer demand for improved performance with readily obtained cases. Since the 7-30 is based on the 30-30 Winchester, one can easily use those abundant cases to form this round. Other than rim diameter and a slight increase in length, this chambering is essentially similar to the 7mm JDJ.

General Comments Excellent bullets are available. With proper loads and in the hands of a marksman, this chambering is capable of

300-yard shots on smaller species. Significantly, it delivers substantially more energy than the 6.5mm JDJ offerings. Despite a shorter barrel, this improved cartridge will drive a 140-grain bullet at about the same velocity as the 7-30 Waters will drive the 120-grain bullet. The Barnes 100-grain and 120-grain X bullets offer superior terminal performance for hunting applications. However, use of X bullets requires special handloading techniques (deeper bullet seating and a reduction in powder charge).

7mm JDJ No. 2

Historical Notes This JDJ cartridge is the 307 Winchester necked down to 7mm and improved. The purpose was to provide a 7mm chambering based upon the 307 Winchester case.

General Comments Excellent bullets are available for this cartridge. With proper loads and in the hands of a good shot, this chambering is capable of 300-yard shots on smaller big game species. In handgun-length barrels, ballistics are not significantly superior to the smaller 7mm JDJ offerings to justify the existence of this chambering. The Barnes 100-grain and 120-grain X bullets offer superior terminal performance for hunting applications. However, use of X bullets requires special handloading techniques (deeper bullet seating and a reduction in powder charge).

7mm JDJ No. 2 Loading Data

Bullet (grains/type)	Powder	Grains	Velocity	Energy	Source/Comments
100 Hornady	W760	47.0	2532	1420	SSK, maximum load, 14" barrel
115 Speer	W760	46.0	2453	1535	SSK, maximum load, 14" barrel
139 Hornady	H4350	45.0	2369	1730	SSK, maximum load, 14" barrel
140 Nosler SB	H414	43.0	2257	1580	SSK, maximum load, 14" barrel
140 Nosler SB	W760	44.0	2303	1645	SSK, maximum load, 14" barrel

280 JDJ

Historical Notes This cartridge was designed by J.D. Jones at SSK Industries. Application is to Thompson/Center Encore single-shot pistols fitted with a custom SSK barrel. Typical barrel length is 15 inches. Cases are formed from empty 280 Remington cases by special means and cannot be fireformed from any other case. Neck length is minimal, which is acceptable for a cartridge used in a single-shot gun. Shoulder angle is 60 degrees, which seems to work just fine. Body taper is minimal, similar to Ackley's improved designs. Therefore, this is a maximized, 28-caliber version of the 280 case. Case capacity is a whopping 76 grains of water, which is only 10 grains less than the 7mm Rem Mag. Working pressure is about 60,000 psi, so ballistics are quite impressive. Best handloads in SSK barrels come close to duplicating 280 (rifle) ballistics.

General Comments Since this case has no rim, it is not generally safe to directly fire-form it in the conventional manner. However, owing to the captive extractor system used in the Encore, it is possible to use a special technique in those guns. In a standard 280 case (sized), seat a jacketed bullet hard against the rifling (so that the gun will just close). The correct powder charge is about 5 percent below the maximum SSK-recommended load. J.D. Jones recommends 140-grain bullets for big game hunting applications on smaller species and bullets up to 175 grains on larger species. With the velocity potential of this chambering, premium bullets are probably a superior choice for hunting applications. While one could use 120-grain Barnes X bullets, which can offer impressive terminal performance, the handloader must use X-bullet specific loading data and special handloading techniques (e.g., the bullet ogive must be seated a minimum of 0.050-inch from the rifling). Further, those bullets work best when a friction proofing (such as moly-plating) is used. For this reason, SSK does not support use of X-style bullets in its guns. While no bullet substitution is benign, never substitute any X-style bullet in any load — begin with data specifically created for that bullet. Speer's 110-grain TNT should provide impressive varminting performance.

280 JDJ

Bullet (grains/type)	Powder	Grains	Velocity	Energy	Source/Comments
120 Nosler BT	IMR 4831	70.0	3119	2590	SSK/maximum load, SSK barrels only
140 Nosler BT	IMR 4831	67.5	2975	2750	SSK/maximum load, SSK barrels only
150 Nosler Part	RI-22	68.4	2775	2565	SSK/maximum load, SSK barrels only
175 Remington	IMR 4831	64.3	2670	2770	SSK/maximum load, SSK barrels only

7.21 Tomahawk

Historical Notes Lazzeroni Arms designed this cartridge in 1997. While somewhat related to an older case, for practical purposes this is a new case design. This cartridge was created in response to requests (from this editor and others) for a high-performance cartridge that would work in a 2.8-inch action and yet deliver the ballistics of a full-length belted magnum. Adaptation to a standard action is feasible but is not recommended.

General Comments Bullet diameter is 0.284-inch (Lazzeroni bases its designations on bullet diameter, instead of bore diameter, which is the common practice). Ballistics are quite impressive for such a short cartridge. Given equal-length barrels, the Tomahawk essentially duplicates top 7mm Weatherby Magnum ballistics, coming very close to the 7mm STW. Case design is typical of the Lazzeroni line: moderate body taper, 30-degree shoulder, sufficiently long neck, and thick rim of approximately case body diameter. In other words, this is a well-designed case.

7.21 Tomahawk Factory Ballistics (24-inch barrel)

Bullet (grains/type)	Powder	Grains	Velocity	Energy	Source/Comments
120	FL		3525	3310	Lazzeroni factory load
140	FL		3300	3386	Lazzeroni factory load
150	FL		3200	3412	Lazzeroni factory load
160	FL		3100	3415	Lazzeroni factory load

7mm Dakota

Historical Notes The 7mm Dakota is based on the 404 Jeffery case. This case is long enough to create standard- or magnum-length cartridges. In any given cartridge length, use of the non-belted 404 Jeffery case offers about 15 percent more case capacity, compared to the standard belted-magnum case. Because maximum case diameter is slightly larger than the standard belted magnum, rechambering to 7mm Dakota often reduces magazine capacity by one cartridge, unless a slight magazine well deepening is accomplished.

General Comments This cartridge functions properly through standard-length (3.35-inch) actions. Guns chambered for the 7mm Remington Magnum are easily converted to 7mm Dakota with only rechambering and slight bolt-face alterations. This chambering offers capacity similar to the much longer 7mm STW (3.65 inches). If loaded to similar pressures with appropriate powders, the 7mm Dakota offers a useful velocity advantage over the 7mm Remington Magnum. With the heaviest bullets, this advantage might be significant. For those interested in getting all the performance possible from the 7mm bore, the 7mm Dakota is worth considering. The 7mm STW has a slight capacity advantage but the ballistic difference is marginal and the STW does require a longer action. Finally, because this cartridge headspaces between case shoulder and bolt face, it is easier to get it to line up properly in the rifle's chamber. This can lead to superior accuracy. It is worth noting that there are no disadvantages to the rimless bottleneck design for most applications.

7mm Dakota Loading Data

Bullet (grains/type)	Powder	Grains	Velocity	Energy	Source/Comments
140	IMR 4831	73.0	3355	3495	Dakota/maximum load
140	H4831	76.0	3295	3375	Dakota/maximum load
140	RI-22	77.0	3365	3515	Dakota/maximum load
140	IMR 7828	80.0	3421	3645	Dakota/maximum load
160	IMR 4831	68.0	3064	3335	Dakota/maximum load
160	H4831	74.0	3156	3535	Dakota/maximum load
160	RI-22	74.5	3212	3660	Dakota/maximum load
160	IMR 7828	75.0	3171	3570	Dakota/maximum load
140	FL		3400	3593	Dakota factory load
160	FL		3200	3637	Dakota factory load

7mm Canadian Magnum

Historical Notes This cartridge was developed about 1989 by North American Shooting Systems (NASS) and is similar to the 7mm Imperial Magnum. This design features a slightly rebated, rimless bottleneck case. Design intent was to provide maximum powder capacity available in a standard action with minimal gunsmithing. (Without deepening the magazine well slightly, magazine capacity is usually reduced by one round.) Bolt face alteration is not necessary. Cartridge feeding and headspacing characteristics are improved.

General Comments The Canadian Magnum series is similar to the Dakota cartridge family in both design and purpose. However, Canadian Magnums all take advantage of the entire 3.65-inch magazine length of the long-action Remington M700 and similar rifles. On these cartridges, body diameter is significantly larger than the standard belted magnum (0.544 inch versus 0.513 inch at the base). Rechambering of nominal belted magnums with the same bore diameter is generally quite simple, requiring no other rifle alterations. For any given case length, capacity is fully 15 percent greater than can be achieved with the belted version. Body taper is minimal and the shoulder is comparatively sharp. However, neck length is sufficiently generous to provide good bullet purchase for hunting ammunition. Performance is commensurate with the generous capacity and pressures used in these loadings. We must note that one should expect this chambering to be rather hard on barrels.

7mm Canadian Magnum Loading Data and Factory Ballistics

Bullet (grains/type)	Powder	Grains	Velocity	Energy	Source/Comments
140	H4831	82.0	3426	3645	NASS/maximum load
140	RI-22	85.0	3523	3855	NASS/maximum load
140	IMR 7828	86.5	3480	3760	NASS/maximum load
160	RI-22	82.0	3264	3780	NASS/maximum load
160	IMR 7828	83.5	3257	3765	NASS/maximum load
160	H1000	87.0	3288	3835	NASS/maximum load
175	IMR 7828	79.0	3018	3540	NASS/maximum load
175	H1000	83.0	3098	3725	NASS/maximum load
175	H870	93.0	3109	3750	NASS/maximum load
140	FL		3525	3860	NASS factory load

7.21 Firehawk

Historical Notes Lazzeroni Arms designed this cartridge in 1996. It was discontinued from standard chambering in 1999, but is still available as a special order item. It was replaced by the 7.21 Firebird. While somewhat related to an older case, for practical purposes, this is a new case design. John Lazzeroni believes that those hunters who will take the time to become competent marksmen can legitimately take game at ranges out to about 500 yards, given a gun with the requisite accuracy and a bullet that will perform properly. This cartridge was created to provide sufficient velocity to medium-weight hunting bullets to provide dependable expansion at maximum ranges. Adaptation to standard actions is quite simple.

General Comments Bullet diameter is 0.284-inch (Lazzeroni bases its designations on bullet diameter, instead of bore diameter, which is the common practice). Until the introduction of the 7.21 Firebird (also from Lazzeroni), ballistics exceeded any other current 7mm cartridge. Case design is typical of the Lazzeroni line: moderate body taper, 30-degree shoulder, sufficiently long neck, and thick rim of approximately case body diameter. In other words, this is a well-designed case. Designed specifically for hunting, and with limited barrel life, this cartridge is not recommended for any other use. While 27-inch barrels are standard, all smaller-caliber, full-length Lazzeroni numbers would benefit significantly from even longer barrels. Most of Lazzeroni's full-length cartridge loadings use especially lubricated (proprietary process) premium bullets from Nosler, Barnes or Swift. These are the only bullets providing the necessary accuracy and terminal performance to meet Lazzeroni's strict requirements. A significant portion of the accuracy and ballistic potential of these cartridges results from the unusually effective, reduced-friction coating used.

7.21 Firehawk Factory Ballistics (27-inch barrel)

Bullet (grains/type)	Powder	Grains	Velocity	Energy	Source/Comments
120	FL		3800	3848	Lazzeroni factory load
140	FL		3600	4030	Lazzeroni factory load
150	FL		3500	4081	Lazzeroni factory load
160	FL		3400	4108	Lazzeroni factory load

7.21 Firebird

Historical Notes Lazzeroni Arms designed this cartridge in 1998 by necking down the 7.82 Warbird. John Lazzeroni believes that hunters who will take the time to become competent marksmen can legitimately take game at ranges out to about 500 yards, given a gun with the requisite accuracy and a bullet that will perform properly. This cartridge was created to eliminate the intermediate Lazzeroni case size in order to stay one step ahead of the competition. Lazzeroni believes that 7mm is the ideal bore size for North American hunting needs and that there is no such thing as too much velocity. This cartridge can provide sufficient velocity to medium-weight hunting bullets for dependable expansion at maximum ranges. Adaptation to standard actions is not recommended.

General Comments Bullet diameter is 0.284-inch (Lazzeroni bases its designations on bullet diameter, instead of bore diameter, which is the common practice). Ballistics exceed any other current 7mm cartridge. Case design is typical of the Lazzeroni line: moderate body taper, 30-degree shoulder, sufficiently long neck, and thick rim of approximately case body diameter, making this a well-designed case. Designed specifically for hunting, and with limited barrel life, this cartridge is not recommended for any other use. While a 27-inch barrel is standard, this number would benefit significantly from use of a longer barrel. Only the best premium bullets provide the necessary accuracy and terminal performance. Factory loads use especially lubricated (proprietary process) premium bullets from Nosler, Barnes or Swift. A 27- or 28-inch barrel with specially prepared Lazzeroni-Barnes 120-grain XBT bullets produces the flattest shooting (shortest time of flight to 1,000 yards) combination of any commercially available hunting or target rifle. One would be hard-pressed to do better with any wildcat.

7.21 Firebird Factory Ballistics (27-inch barrel)

Bullet (grains/type)	Powder	Grains	Velocity	Energy	Source/Comments
120	FL		3950	4155	Lazzeroni factory load
140	FL		3750	4370	Lazzeroni factory load
150	FL		3650	4435	Lazzeroni factory load
160	FL		3550	4475	Lazzeroni factory load
175	FL		3400	4490	Lazzeroni factory load

7.62 Micro-Whisper

Historical Notes Designed by J.D. Jones at SSK Industries in the early 1990s, this is simply the 30 Luger case adapted to use 30-caliber rifle bullets. Case dimensions are identical, but chambering specifications are different. The design intent was for an extremely quiet, sound-suppressed load that would shoot 180-grain bullets to about 1,040 fps.

General Comments This cartridge provides much better subsonic performance than the 308 Winchester. Civilian applications are limited. Nevertheless, performance is startling. For those looking for minimal recoil and noise for short-range use, this is an interesting choice.

7.62 Micro-Whisper Loading Data

Bullet (grains/type)	Powder	Grains	Velocity	Energy	Source/Comments
93 Norma SP	AA No. 9	11.5	1762	640	SSK/maximum load, 8-3/4" barrel
150 Hornady FMJ	H110	7.0	1018	345	SSK/subsonic, 8-3/4" barrel
150 Hornady FMJ	AA No. 9	8.0	1259	525	SSK/maximum load, 8-3/4" barrel
168 Hornady Match	AA No. 9	7.1	1056	445	SSK/subsonic, 8-3/4" barrel
180 Speer	H110	7.0	1025	420	SSK/subsonic, 8-3/4" barrel
180 Speer	H110	8.0	1161	535	SSK/maximum load, 8-3/4" barrel

7.63 Mini-Whisper

Historical Notes Designed by J.D. Jones at SSK Industries in the early 1990s, this is simply the 30 Mauser case adapted to use 30-caliber rifle bullets. Case dimensions are identical, but chambering specifications are different. The design intent was for an extremely quiet, sound-suppressed load that would shoot 200-grain bullets to about 1,040 fps.

General Comments This cartridge provides much better subsonic performance, compared to the 308 Winchester. Civilian applications are limited. Nevertheless, performance is startling. For those looking for minimal recoil and noise for short-range use, this is an interesting choice.

7.63 Mini-Whisper Loading Data

Bullet (grains/type)	Powder	Grains	Velocity	Energy	Source/Comments
93 Norma	Clays	7.5	1727	615	SSK/maximum load, 7" barrel
110 Speer Carb	Clays	7.5	1588	615	SSK/maximum load, 7"barrel (1.415" OAL)
110 Speer Carb	AA No. 7	11.4	1742	740	SSK/maximum load, 7" barrel (1.415" OAL)
150 Hornady FMJ	AA No. 2	4.5	1025	350	SSK/subsonic, 7" barrel
150 Hornady FMJ	AA No. 9	10.5	1445	695	SSK/maximum load, 7" barrel
168 Hornady Match	AA No. 2	5.2	1031	395	SSK/subsonic, 7" barrel
168 Hornady Match	HP-38	5.7	1035	395	SSK/subsonic 7" barrel

300 Whisper

Historical Notes The 300 Whisper is a new concept in the development of small-case-capacity, highly efficient cartridges combined with bullets of extreme ballistic efficiency. This is a special-purpose design by J.D. Jones of SSK Industries based on a 221 Remington case necked up to 308 caliber. It is intended to fire extremely heavy, accurate, ballistically efficient bullets at subsonic velocities in suppressed guns. It delivers more energy more accurately than any other subsonic round at 200 yards. In addition, it has interesting supersonic capabilities above 1160 fps, thus offering greater versatility than any other cartridge capable of performing in these vastly differing arenas. Because powder charges are very small, suppressor size is proportionately smaller.

General Comments Bullet weights from 100 to 240 grains can be used. Best accuracy is obtained with heavier bullets. For silhouette shooting, 220- to 240-grain bullets are best. With 125- or 150-grain projectiles, this cartridge is outstanding for deer and other medium game, offering better performance than the 30-30 Winchester in the T/C Contender pistol with less than one-half the felt recoil. In suppressed guns, noise can be reduced to less than that of a 177-caliber spring-air rifle. Loading data and dies are available from SSK Industries, 590 Woodvue, Wintersville, OH 43953.

300 Whisper Loading Data

Bullet (grains/type)	Powder	Grains	Velocity	Energy	Source/Comments
125 Nosler BT	H110	20.6	2283	1445	SSK/maximum rifle load, AR-15
150 Nosler BT	H110	18.0	2073	1430	SSK/maximum rifle load
165	AA 1680	10.3	1013	375	SSK/subsonic, AR-15
125 Nosler BT	H110	20.6	2283	1445	SSK/maximum load, AR-15
125 Nosler BT	H110	18.0	2014	1350	SSK/maximum load, AR-15
165	AA 2015	12.6	1046	400	SSK/subsonic, AR-15
168	AA 1680	20.2	1906	1355	SSK/maximum load, rifle
200	AA 2015	12.0	1007	450	NA
220	AA No. 9	8.5	1013	500	SSK/subsonic, AR-15
250	H110	8.6	980	530	SSK/subsonic, AR-15

309 JDJ

Historical Notes This cartridge was designed and developed by J.D. Jones about 1978, hence the JDJ designation. It is generally fired in barrels furnished by SSK Industries. Its purpose is to give added power and range to the T/C Contender pistol for hunting medium game. The JDJ series of cartridges is easy to make. All JDJ designs are proprietary rounds and SSK neither sells reamers nor allows the reamer maker to duplicate the reamers for sale. Should you desire to chamber a JDJ cartridge, contact SSK Industries of Wintersville, OH.

General Comments The 309 JDJ is based on a 444 Marlin case necked down to 30-caliber in a 308 full-length sizing die and then fire-formed to obtain the sharp shoulder. This cartridge offers about 2600 fps with a 125-grain bullet, 2450 fps with a 150-grain bullet, and 160-grainers can be driven at 2400 fps. For general use, 165-grain bullets are an excellent choice. Jones has taken large plains game in Africa with this round. In a pinch, it would do for elk with 180-grain bullets. The 309 is easy to shoot and can be extremely versatile. With the proper load and bullet, sighted to shoot about 3 inches high at 100 yards, it will be dead on at about 225-250 yards. It can be very effective on moderate-sized game to that range, with the right bullet and a shooter possessing adequate skills.

309 JDJ Loading Data

Bullet (grains/type)	Powder	Grains	Velocity	Energy	Source/Comments
150 SP	IMR 4320	41.0	2010	1360	SSK/maximum load, SSK barrels only
150 SP	IMR 4350	43.0	2370	1875	SSK/maximum load, SSK barrels only
165 SP	IMR 4350	52.0	2430	1775	SSK/maximum load, SSK barrels only
180 SP	IMR 4350	49.0	2135	1825	SSK/maximum load, SSK barrels only

30-06 JDJ

Historical Notes This cartridge was designed by J.D. Jones at SSK Industries. Application is to Thompson/Center Encore single-shot pistols fitted with a custom SSK barrel. Typical barrel length is 15 inches. Cases are formed from empty Remington 30-06 cases by special means and cannot be fire-formed from any other case. Neck length is minimal, which is acceptable for a cartridge used in a single-shot gun. Shoulder angle is 60 degrees, which works fine. Body taper is minimal, similar to Ackley's improved designs. Therefore, this is a maximized version of the 30-06 case. Capacity is a whopping 75 grains of water, which is significantly greater than the 30-06 (about 70). Working pressure is about 60,000 psi, so ballistics are quite impressive. Best handloads in SSK barrels come very close to duplicating 30-06 (rifle) ballistics.

General Comments Since this case has no rim, it is not generally safe to directly fireform it in the conventional manner. However, owing to the captive extractor system used in the Encore, it is possible to use a special technique in those guns. To fireform, use a standard 30-06 case (sized), seat a jacketed bullet hard against the rifling (so that the gun will just close). Correct powder charge is about 5 percent below the maximum SSK-recommended load. Jones recommends 150-grain bullets for big game hunting applications on smaller species and bullets up to 200 grains on larger species. With the velocity potential of this chambering, premium bullets are probably a superior choice for hunting applications. While one could use 140-grain Barnes X bullets, which can offer impressive terminal performance, the handloader must use X-bullet-specific loading data and special handloading techniques (i.e., the bullet ogive must be seated a minimum of 0.050-inch from the rifling). For this reason, SSK does not support use of X-style bullets in its guns. Further, those bullets work best when a reduced-friction coating (such as moly-plating) is used. While no bullet substitution is benign, never substitute any X-style bullet in any load — begin with data specifically created for that bullet.

30-06 JDJ Loading Data

Bullet (grains/type)	Powder	Grains	Velocity	Energy	Source/Comments
125	IMR 4064	62.0	3167	2785	SSK/maximum load, SSK barrels only
150	IMR 4064	60.0	2930	2860	SSK/maximum load, SSK barrels only
165 Hornady	RI-15	58.3	2790	2850	SSK/maximum load, SSK barrels only
180 Speer	RI-19	66.2	2666	2840	SSK/maximum load, SSK barrels only
200 Speer	Vit N560	63.4	2504	2785	SSK/maximum load, SSK barrels only

308 Cor-Bon

Historical Notes This cartridge was designed by Cor-Bon and announced at the 1999 Shooting, Hunting, Outdoor Trade (SHOT) Show. The purpose was to achieve the greatest feasible performance from an action designed to handle 2.8-inch cartridges, but without the necessity of any significant magazine or action modifications. In a crowded market, Peter Pi (CEO at Cor-Bon) seems to have found a combination that fills a useful niche. Ballistics approximate those of the conventional 30-caliber belted magnum, which is designed to work in a 3.3-inch (or longer) action.

General Comments A significant trend in the wildcat and proprietary arena is toward shorter cartridges. This design promises advantages in both rifle and ballistics. This shorter case chambers in a shorter, lighter, more rigid action that is faster and easier to manipulate. This cartridge might also have intrinsic accuracy advantages; the big push in accuracy competition is toward shorter and fatter cases. Evidently, such a design might promote earlier and more consistent ignition of individual powder granules.

308 Cor-Bon Factory Ballistics

Bullet (grains/type)	Powder	Grains	Velocity	Energy	Source/Comments
165 SPBT	FL		3100	3520	Cor-Bon factory load
180 SPBT	FL		3000	3600	Cor-Bon factory load

7.82 Patriot

Historical Notes Lazzeroni Arms designed this cartridge in 1997. While somewhat related to an older case, for practical purposes, this is a new case design. This cartridge was created in response to requests for a high-performance cartridge that would work in a 2.8-inch action and yet deliver the ballistics of a full-length belted magnum. While feasible, adaptation to a standard action (3.35-inch) is not recommended.

General Comments Bullet diameter is 0.308-inch (Lazzeroni bases its designations on bullet diameter, instead of bore diameter, which is the common practice). Ballistics are quite impressive for such a short cartridge. Given equal-length barrels, the Patriot essentially duplicates 300 Winchester Magnum ballistics. Case design is typical of the Lazzeroni line: moderate body taper, 30-degree shoulder, sufficiently long neck, and thick rim of approximately case body diameter. In other words, this is a well-designed case. This cartridge has already become quite popular and successful in the various 1000-yard target-shooting games. Dick Davis of Lazzeroni Arms is doing quite well with it. This case is the basis for several of my wildcat and target chamberings (6mm Thermos Bottle, 6mm LBFM, 6.5 LBFM, 7mm LBFM & 30-LBFM.)

7.82 Patriot Factory Ballistics (24-inch barrel)

Bullet (grains/type)	Powder	Grains	Velocity	Energy	Source/Comments
130	FL		3550	3635	Lazzeroni factory load
150	FL		3300	3628	Lazzeroni factory load
180	FL		3100	3842	Lazzeroni factory load
200	FL		2950	3866	Lazzeroni factory load

300 Dakota

Historical Notes The 300 Dakota is based upon the 404 Jeffery case. In this application, the case is shortened to create a cartridge of 30-06 length (3.34 inches). The rim of the 300 Dakota is slightly larger than the rim on a standard belted-magnum case, so besides rechambering, the gunsmith must also perform a minor bolt-face alteration. In any given-length cartridge, use of the non-belted 404 Jeffery case provides about a 15 percent increase in usable case capacity, compared to the standard belted case. Because maximum case diameter is slightly larger (0.544-inch versus 0.532-inch), magazine capacity is usually reduced by one round. However, minor gunsmithing alterations will usually remedy that situation.

General Comments The 300 Dakota functions properly through standard-length actions (3.35 inches). This cartridge provides a significant capacity advantage over the 300 Winchester Magnum and comes close to duplicating capacity and performance of the much longer 300 Weatherby Magnum. Rechambering to 300 Dakota is possible in most rifles originally chambered for any standard belted 300 Magnum. One thereby gains the improved feeding and accuracy advantages offered by this non-belted case. If loaded to similar pressures using appropriate powders, the 300 Dakota offers a worthwhile velocity advantage over the 300 Winchester Magnum. For those interested in an all-around 30-caliber hunting cartridge, the 300 Dakota is worth considering. The 300 Weatherby does have a slight capacity advantage, but the ballistic difference is marginal and Weatherby's cartridge requires a longer action.

300 Dakota Loading Data and Factory Ballistics

Bullet (grains/type)	Powder	Grains	Velocity	Energy	Source/Comments
165	IMR 4350	77.0	3247	3860	Dakota/maximum load
165	H4831	82.0	3283	3945	Dakota/maximum load
165	RI-22	83.0	3307	4000	Dakota/maximum load
165	IMR 7828	85.0	3277	3930	Dakota/maximum load
180	H4831	77.5	3114	3875	Dakota/maximum load
180	RI-22	81.0	3249	4215	Dakota/maximum load
180	IMR 7828	82.0	3221	4140	Dakota/maximum load
200	H4831	77.5	2965	3900	Dakota/maximum load
200	RI-22	78.0	3052	4130	Dakota/maximum load
200	IMR 7828	80.5	3026	4060	Dakota/maximum load
200	H1000	82.5	2986	3955	Dakota/maximum load
150	FL		3300	3626	Dakota factory load
180	FL		3100	3840	Dakota factory load

300 Canadian Magnum

Historical Notes This cartridge was developed about 1989 by North American Shooting Systems (NASS) and is somewhat similar to the 300 Imperial Magnum. This design features a slightly rebated, rimless bottleneck case. Design intent was to provide maximum powder capacity available in a standard action with minimal gunsmithing. (Without deepening the magazine well slightly, magazine capacity is usually reduced by one round.) Bolt face alteration is unnecessary. Cartridge feeding and headspacing characteristics are improved.

General Comments The Canadian Magnum series is similar to the Dakota cartridge family in both design and purpose. However, this cartridge takes advantage of the entire 3.65-inch magazine length of the long-action Remington M700 and similar rifles. On the Canadian Magnums, body diameter is significantly larger than the standard belted-magnum (0.544-inch versus 0.513-inch at the base). Rechambering of nominal belted-magnums with the same bore diameter is generally quite simple, requiring no other rifle alterations. For any given case length, capacity is about 15 percent greater than can be achieved with the standard belted-magnum case. Body taper is minimal and the shoulder is comparatively sharp. However, neck length is sufficiently generous to provide good bullet purchase for hunting ammunition. Performance is commensurate with the generous capacity and pressures used in these loadings. Barrel life is a consideration — there are no free lunches.

Editor's note: *This cartridge is similar to Remington's "new" Ultra round.*

300 Canadian Magnum Loading Data and Factory Ballistics

Bullet (grains/type)	Powder	Grains	Velocity	Energy	Source/Comments
165	H4831	86.0	3231	3820	NASS/maximum load
165	RI-22	87.0	3434	4315	NASS/maximum load
165	IMR 7828	89.5	3466	4395	NASS/maximum load
180	RI-22	83.0	3354	4490	NASS/maximum load
180	IMR 7828	87.5	3367	4525	NASS/maximum load
180	H1000	92.0	3163	3995	NASS/maximum load
200	RI-22	79.0	3053	4135	NASS/maximum load
200	IMR 7828	82.0	3093	4245	NASS/maximum load
200	H870	95.0	3070	4180	NASS/maximum load
180	FL		3425	4685	NASS factory load

300 Pegasus

Historical Notes This 1994 chambering is based upon an entirely new case that features a 0.580-inch head size. The rim is essentially identical to the 378 Weatherby case, but the design has no belt. Therefore, case capacity is substantially greater for any given cartridge length. This standard rimless bottleneck design also facilitates proper chambering with tight tolerances. Design intent was the acceleration of 180-grain hunting bullets to a velocity in excess of 3500 fps from a 26-inch barrel without exceeding about 62,000 psi (piezo transducer pressure units) — a typical modern cartridge pressure limit. The 300 Pegasus easily achieves this goal.

General Comments This cartridge seems a good choice for those who feel they need a flat-shooting round that can deliver substantial energy to targets at long range. Rifles originally chambered for the 378 and 460 Weatherby numbers can be rebarreled to accept this cartridge. The slowest handloader powders now available offer the best velocity potential. In a typical rifle, recoil would have to be classed as a bit heavy and barrel life is quite limited.

300 Pegasus Loading Data and Factory Ballistics

Bullet (grains/type)	Powder	Grains	Velocity	Energy	Source/Comments
150 Nosler BT	IMR 7828		3642	4420	A-Square/maximum load
150 Nosler BT	RI-22		3675	4495	A-Square/maximum load
150 Nosler BT	AA 8700		3703	4565	A-Square/maximum load
180 Nosler BT	RI-22		3371	4540	A-Square/maximum load
180 Nosler BT	IMR 7828		3413	4655	A-Square/maximum load
180 Nosler BT	AA 8700		3456	4775	A-Square/maximum load
180 Nosler BT	H870		3505	4910	A-Square/maximum load
150 Nosler BT	FL		3780	4760	A-Square Factory load
180 Nosler BT	FL		3523	4960	A-Square Factory load

A-Square Caesar rifle

7.82 Warbird

Historical Notes Lazzeroni Arms designed this cartridge in 1995. While somewhat related to an older case, for practical purposes this is a new case design. John Lazzeroni believes that those hunters who will take the time to become competent marksmen can legitimately take game at ranges out to about 500 yards, given a gun with the requisite accuracy and a bullet that will perform properly. This cartridge was created to provide sufficient velocity for medium-weight hunting bullets to provide dependable expansion at maximum ranges and to have sufficient energy for taking larger species at longer ranges. Adaptation to standard actions is feasible but is not recommended.

General Comments Bullet diameter is 0.308-inch. (Lazzeroni bases its designations on bullet diameter, instead of bore diameter, which is the common practice.) Ballistics equal or exceed any other factory 30-caliber cartridge. Case design is typical of the Lazzeroni line: moderate body taper, 30-degree shoulder, sufficiently long neck, and thick rim of approximately case body diameter. In other words, this is a well-designed case. Designed specifically for hunting, and with limited barrel life, this cartridge is not recommended for any other use. While 27-inch barrels are standard, all the smaller-caliber, full-length Lazzeroni numbers would benefit significantly from even longer barrels. Most of Lazzeroni's full-length cartridge loadings use especially lubricated (proprietary process) premium bullets from Nosler, Barnes or Swift. These are the only bullets providing the necessary accuracy and terminal performance to meet John's strict requirements. One could argue that this is a superior all-around choice for lighter species. The premium 130-grain bullet will handle most species in North America, while a 200-grain bullet is adequate for most critters anywhere in the world.

7.82 Warbird Factory Ballistics (27-inch barrel)

Bullet (grains/type)	Powder	Grains	Velocity	Energy	Source/Comments
130	FL		4000	4620	Lazzeroni factory load
150	FL		3800	4810	Lazzeroni factory load
165	FL		3600	4750	Lazzeroni factory load
180	FL		3550	5040	Lazzeroni factory load
200	FL		3350	4985	Lazzeroni factory load

8mm JDJ

Historical Notes Designed by J.D. Jones as SSK Industries about 1980, this cartridge uses the 444 Marlin case necked down to 8mm with a sharp shoulder. Design intent was a Thompson/Center chambering that would surpass 35 Remington rifle ballistics.

General Comments With a 200-grain Nosler Partition loaded to top handgun velocity (2100 fps), this chambering can deliver substantial energy within the useful range. The Barnes 180-grain X can deliver superior terminal performance, but its use requires special handloading techniques (deeper bullet seating and a reduction in powder charge). Effectiveness on the lightest of species is improved with Hornady's 150-grain bullet at 2400-fps muzzle velocity.

8mm JDJ Loading Data

Bullet (grains/type)	Powder	Grains	Velocity	Energy	Source/Comments
150 Hornady	IMR 4320	47.5	2286	1740	SSK/maximum load, SSK barrel only (14")
150 Hornady	H322	47.5	2420	1950	SSK/maximum load, SSK barrel only (14")
170 Hornady	IMR 4320	47.5	2254	1915	SSK/maximum load, SSK barrel only (14")
170 Hornady	AA 2520	49.5	2373	2125	SSK/maximum load, SSK barrel only (14")
200 Speer	H4350	52.0	2192	2130	SSK/maximum load, SSK barrel only (14")
225	H4350	51.5	2131	2265	SSK/maximum load, SSK barrel only (14")

338 Whisper

Historical Notes Designed by J.D. Jones at SSK Industries in the early 1990s, this chambering is the 7mm BR opened up to accept 0.338-inch bullets with no other changes. JDJ's intention was the delivery of significant long-range energy from a low-noise rifle. This combination certainly succeeded in attaining that goal.

General Comments Usually this cartridge is chambered in rebarreled 308 Winchester rifles. With a quick rifling twist, 300-grain Sierra MatchKings will deliver superb accuracy past 600 yards. Long-range penetration and energy are surprising.

338 Whisper Loading Data

Bullet (grains/type)	Powder	Grains	Velocity	Energy	Source/Comments
200 Nosler BT	H4227	11.5	1075	510	SSK/Subsonic, 12" barrel
200 Nosler BT	HP-38	8.8	1077	515	SSK/Subsonic, 12" barrel
250 Nosler BT	HP-38	9.6	1029	585	SSK/Subsonic, 12" barrel
250 Nosler BT	Vit N350	10.8	1040	600	SSK/Subsonic, 12" barrel
300 Nosler BT	Vit N350	12.3	1040	720	SSK/Subsonic, 12" barrel
300 Nosler BT	HP-38	10.8	1050	735	SSK/Subsonic, 12" barrel

338 JDJ

Historical Notes Like several other chamberings based upon the same basic case (444 Marlin), this cartridge was designed and developed by J.D. Jones about 1978. Barrels in this chambering are furnished by SSK Industries. The purpose is to provide increased power and range for T/C Contender and other single-shot hunting handguns. Like most of the JDJ line, these cases are easily formed from the parent case. Chambering dimensions are proprietary.

General Comments Based on the 444 Marlin necked down, this chambering provides ample capacity and bullet area to produce impressive muzzle energy, especially with longer handgun-length barrels (14-16 inches). With bullets of only slightly lighter weight, the 338 JDJ offers muzzle velocities similar to the 375 Winchester when fired from a rifle. Since this cartridge uses spitzer bullets, performance at normal hunting ranges is significantly superior to the parent 444 Marlin's rifle ballistics. Conventional bullets of 180-220 grains are good choices. However, the Barnes 160-grain X can deliver superior terminal performance, reduced recoil and a flatter trajectory, but requires special handloading techniques (deeper bullet seating and a reduction in powder charge). With proper hunting bullets loaded to maximum velocity (necessary to assure proper terminal performance), recoil can be rather stiff.

338 JDJ Loading Data

Bullet (grains/type)	Powder	Grains	Velocity	Energy	Source/Comments
225-gr	Win 760	42.5	1561	N/A	SSK 12" barrel
250-gr	Win 760	42.5	1488	N/A	SSK 12" barrel
275-gr	IMR 4831	945.5	1609	N/A	SSK 12" barrel

338-06 JDJ

Historical Notes This cartridge was designed by J.D. Jones at SSK Industries. Application is to Thompson/Center Encore single-shot pistols fitted with a custom SSK barrel. Typical barrel length is 15 inches. Cases are formed from empty 30-06 or 35 Whelen cases by special means and cannot be fireformed from any other case. Neck length is minimal, which is acceptable for a cartridge used in a single-shot gun. Shoulder angle is 60 degrees, which seems to work just fine. Body taper is minimal, similar to Ackley's improved designs. Therefore, this is a maximized, 338-06 case. Capacity is a whopping 76 grains of water, which is significantly greater than the 338-06 (about 71). Working pressure is about 60,000 psi, so ballistics are quite impressive. Best handloads in SSK barrels can approach 338-08 A-Square (rifle) ballistics.

General Comments Since this case has no rim, it is not generally safe to directly fireform it in the conventional manner. However, owing to the captive extractor system used in the Encore, it is possible to use a special technique in those guns: Resize and neck-expand a 30-06 case, then seat a 0.338-inch jacketed bullet hard against the rifling (so that the gun will just close). Correct powder charge is about 5 percent below the maximum SSK-recommended load. Jones recommends 180-grain bullets for big game hunting applications on smaller species and bullets up to 250 grains on larger species. While one could use 160- or 175-grain Barnes X bullets, which can offer impressive terminal performance, the handloader must use X-bullet-specific loading data and special handloading techniques (e.g., the bullet ogive must be seated at least 0.050-inch from the rifling). Further, those bullets work best when a reduced-friction coating (such as moly-plating) is used. For this reason, SSK does not support use of X-style bullets in its guns. While no bullet substitution is benign, never substitute any X-style bullet in any load — begin with data specifically created for that bullet. This cartridge generates sufficient energy for hunting on any continent. Not all shooters have equal abilities and tolerances — while Jones' 9-year old grandson proved capable of handling this combination, recoil may exceed what some adult shooters can handle.

338-06 JDJ Loading Data

Bullet (grains/type)	Powder	Grains	Velocity	Energy	Source/Comments
175 Barnes X	IMR 4064	62.5	2863	3185	SSK/max. load, SSK barrels only
180 Nosler BT	IMR 4064	62.5	2850	3245	SSK/max. load, SSK barrels only
200 Hornady	IMR 4064	61.5	2693	3220	SSK/max. load, SSK barrels only
225 Speer BT	IMR 4064	60.5	2643	3490	SSK/max. load, SSK barrels only
250 Speer GS	IMR 4064	58.0	2481	3415	SSK/max. load, SSK barrels only

8.59 Galaxy

Historical Notes Lazzeroni Arms designed this cartridge in 1997. While somewhat related to an older case, for practical purposes, this is a new case design. This cartridge was created in response to requests for a high-performance cartridge that would work in a 2.8-inch action, yet deliver the ballistics of a full-length belted-magnum. Adaptation to a standard action is feasible but is not recommended.

General Comments Bullet diameter is 0.338-inch (Lazzeroni bases its designations on bullet diameter, instead of bore diameter, which is the common practice.) Ballistics are quite impressive for such a short cartridge. Given equal-length barrels, the Galaxy easily exceeds the 338 Winchester Magnum. Case design is typical of the Lazzeroni line: moderate body taper, 30-degree shoulder, sufficiently long neck, and thick rim of approximately case body diameter. In other words, this is a well-designed case.

8.59 Galaxy Factory Ballistics (24-inch barrel)

Bullet (grains/type)	Powder	Grains	Velocity	Energy	Source/Comments
200	FL		3100	4269	Lazzeroni factory load
225	FL		2950	4349	Lazzeroni factory load
250	FL		2750	4199	Lazzeroni factory load

330 Dakota

Historical Notes The 330 Dakota is based upon a shortened version of the rimless bottleneck 404 Jeffery case. The 330 Dakota is dimensioned to function through a standard-length action (3.35"). Design intent was to offer a factory alternative to the 338 Winchester Magnum with 340 Weatherby performance. This also offers 338 Winchester Magnum rifle owners a simple conversion to improve ballistics and cartridge-feeding characteristics.

General Comments Like the 7mm and 300 Dakota cartridges, the 330 Dakota functions properly through 30-06 length (3.35") actions. This cartridge provides a significant case capacity advantage over the 338 Winchester Magnum (about 15 percent) and comes very close to duplicating capacity and performance of the much-longer 340 Weatherby Magnum. Most rifles chambered for the 338 Winchester Magnum are easily converted to 330 Dakota. This

conversion offers advantages in function, accuracy and ballistics because of the non-belted case. If loaded to similar pressures with appropriate powders, the 330 Dakota should produce 5 percent more velocity (10 percent more energy) than Winchester's 338 Magnum. With the heaviest bullets, the advantage is more significant. For those interested in a hunting cartridge geared to larger big game, the 330 Dakota is a serious contender. Combined with the right bullets, this flat-shooting cartridge can deliver more energy to targets a quarter-mile away than factory 270 ammunition produces at the muzzle! The 340 Weatherby does have a slight capacity advantage, but the ballistic difference is marginal and Weatherby's cartridge requires use of a longer action. For hunters who want maximum performance from the 0.338-inch bore, the Canadian Magnum, A-Square and Lazzeroni offerings are better choices.

330 Dakota Loading Data and Factory Ballistics

Bullet (grains/type)	Powder	Grains	Velocity	Energy	Source/Comments
200	IMR 4350	80.0	3082	4215	Dakota/maximum load
200	RI-22	86.5	3146	4390	Dakota/maximum load
200	H4831	88.0	3200	4545	Dakota/maximum load
200	IMR 7828	88.0	3100	4265	Dakota/maximum load
250	IMR 4350	76.0	2853	4515	Dakota/maximum load
250	RI-22	80.5	2849	4500	Dakota/maximum load
250	H4831	81.5	2878	4595	Dakota/maximum load
250	IMR 7828	82.0	2829	4440	Dakota/maximum load
210	FL		3200	4480	Dakota factory load
250	FL		2900	4668	Dakota factory load

Dakota 76 Classic Bolt-Action Rifle

338 Canadian Magnum

Historical Notes This cartridge was developed about 1989 by North American Shooting Systems (NASS) and is somewhat similar to the 338 Imperial Magnum. This design features a slightly rebated rimless bottleneck case. Design intent was to provide maximum powder capacity available in a standard action with minimal gunsmithing. (Without deepening the magazine well slightly, magazine capacity is usually reduced by one round.) Bolt face alteration is not necessary. Cartridge feeding and headspacing characteristics are improved.

General Comments The Canadian Magnum series is similar to the Dakota cartridge family in both design and purpose. However, this cartridge takes advantage of the entire 3.65-inch magazine length of the long-action Remington M700 and similar rifles. On the

Canadian Magnums, body diameter is significantly larger than the standard belted magnum (0.544-inch versus 0.513-inch at the base). Rechambering of nominal belted magnums with the same bore diameter is generally quite simple, requiring no other rifle alterations. For any given case length, capacity is about 15 percent greater than can be achieved with the standard belted-magnum case. Body taper is minimal and the case shoulder is comparatively sharp. However, neck length is sufficiently generous to provide good bullet purchase for hunting ammunition. Performance is commensurate with the capacity and pressures used in these loadings. As with the 300 Canadian Magnum, one is impressed with the similarity to Remington's "new" Ultra cartridge in the same bore size.

338 Canadian Magnum Loading Data and Factory Ballistics

Bullet (grains/type)	Powder	Grains	Velocity	Energy	Source/Comments
225	IMR 4831	88.0	3083	4745	NASS/maximum load
225	H4831	91.0	3047	4635	NASS/maximum load
250	IMR 4831	88.0	2924	4740	NASS/maximum load
250	RI-19	89.0	2977	4915	NASS/maximum load
250	H4831	91.0	2951	4830	NASS/maximum load
225	FL		3110	4830	NASS factory load

338 A-Square

Historical Notes This 1978 design is a somewhat modified 378 Weatherby Magnum necked down to accept 0.338-inch bullets. The intention was to provide a flat-shooting cartridge capable of delivering substantial energy to medium-sized game animals at normal hunting ranges. With minor modifications, most nominal 3.65-inch bolt-action magazines will handle this cartridge.

General Comments Ballistics are very close to A-Square's 338 Excaliber, but this cartridge will not feed from a magazine as smoothly as that beltless design. The basic design incorporates a sharp shoulder for good headspace control, but features a comparatively generous body taper. Ballistics are impressive. This cartridge can deliver massive doses of energy to long-range targets.

338 A-Square Loading Data and Factory Ballistics

Bullet (grains/type)	Powder	Grains	Velocity	Energy	Source/Comments
200 Nosler BT	H4831	104.0	3259	4715	A-Square/maximum load
200 Nosler BT	IMR 7828	106.0	3353	4990	A-Square/maximum load
200 Nosler BT	RI-22	104.0	3355	4995	A-Square/maximum load
250 Sierra SBT	IMR 7828	95.0	2879	4600	A-Square/maximum load
250 Sierra SBT	RI-22	95.0	2965	4880	A-Square/maximum load
250 Sierra SBT	H870	118.0	3094	5310	A-Square/maximum load
250 Sierra SBT	AA 8700	120.0	3100	5330	A-Square/maximum load
200 Nosler BT	FL		3500	5435	A-Square factory load
250 Sierra SBT	FL		3120	5400	A-Square factory load
250 Triad	FL		3120	5400	A-Square factory load

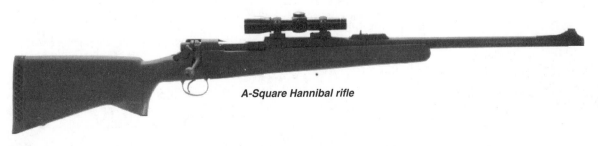

A-Square Hannibal rifle

338 Excaliber

Historical Notes This 1994 chambering is based upon an entirely new case that features a 0.580-inch head size. The rim is essentially identical to the 378 Weatherby case but there is no useless belt. Therefore, case capacity is substantially greater for any given cartridge length. This standard rimless bottleneck design also facilitates proper chambering with tight tolerances. Design intent was acceleration of a 200-grain hunting bullet in excess of 3500 fps without exceeding about 62,000 psi (piezo transducer pressure units) — a typical pressure for modern cartridges. The 338 Excaliber accomplishes this goal.

General Comments This cartridge is a superior choice for those who feel they need a flat-shooting cartridge that can deliver substantial energy to medium-sized game targets at long-range. Rifles originally chambered for the 378 and 460 can be rebarreled to accept this cartridge. The slowest handloader powders now available offer the best velocity potential. In a typical rifle, recoil would have to be classed as heavy, especially when shooting heavier bullets. As is normal with 0.338-inch chamberings, trajectories are essentially indistinguishable from the similar 30-caliber counterpart, but with the delivery of a heavier bullet carrying more energy.

338 Excaliber Loading Data

Bullet (grains/type)	Powder	Grains	Velocity	Energy	Source/Comments
200 Nosler BT	RI-22	113.0	3434	5240	A-Square/maximum load
200 Nosler BT	H870	138.0	3480	5380	A-Square/maximum load
200 Nosler BT	AA 8700	140.0	3493	5415	A-Square/maximum load
200 Nosler BT	IMR 7828	116.0	3497	5430	A-Square/maximum load
250 Sierra SBT	IMR 7827	105.0	2966	4885	A-Square/maximum load
250 Sierra SBT	H5010	128.0	3109	5365	A-Square/maximum load
250 Sierra SBT	RI-22	110.0	3192	5655	A-Square/maximum load
250 Sierra SBT	H870	128.0	3200	5685	A-Square/maximum load
250 Sierra SBT	AA 8700	130.0	3202	5690	A-Square/maximum load

8.59 Titan

Historical Notes Lazzeroni Arms designed this cartridge in 1994, based upon an earlier design (1992). This was the first Lazzeroni cartridge. While somewhat related to an older case, for practical purposes, this is a new case design. John Lazzeroni believes that those hunters who will take the time to become competent marksmen can legitimately take game at longer ranges. This cartridge was created to launch medium- to heavy-weight hunting bullets with sufficient velocity to provide dependable expansion at longer ranges and to have sufficient energy for taking the largest species. Adaptation to standard actions is feasible but is not recommended.

General Comments Bullet diameter is 0.338-inch (Lazzeroni bases its designations on bullet diameter, instead of bore diameter, which is the common practice). Ballistics equal or exceed any factory 33-caliber cartridge. Case design is typical of the Lazzeroni line: moderate body taper, 30-degree shoulder, sufficiently long neck, and thick rim of approximately case-body diameter. In other words, this is a well-designed case. While designed specifically for hunting, this cartridge does have application to long-range target shooting. Standard barrel length is 27 inches, which provides a good measure of the ballistic potential of this cartridge. Most of Lazzeroni's full-length cartridge loadings use especially lubricated (proprietary process) premium bullets from Nosler, Barnes or Swift. These are the only bullets providing the necessary accuracy and terminal performance to meet Lazzeroni's strict requirements. He designed this as the ultimate North American hunting cartridge for the hunter who is interested primarily in elk. His experience with a 33-caliber magnum that would not deliver the accuracy necessary to take an elk cleanly at somewhat beyond 350 yards prompted this development and the subsequent Lazzeroni line.

8.59 Titan Factory Ballistics (27-inch barrel)

Bullet (grains/type)	Powder	Grains	Velocity	Energy	Source/Comments
200	FL		3450	5287	Lazzeroni factory load *
225	FL		3300	5442	Lazzeroni factory load *
250	FL		3150	5510	Lazzeroni factory load *

*RI-25 will produce superior velocity but accuracy has so far been dismal. RI-19 is the preferred powder for this cartridge.

358 JDJ

Historical Notes This is another cartridge designed and developed by J.D. Jones. Jones began development of his cartridges around 1978 to give added range and power to the Thompson/Center Contender pistol. Some of his cartridges have also proven to be excellent metallic silhouette numbers. JDJ cartridges are relatively easy to make. All JDJ cartridges are proprietary and SSK does not sell reamers, nor has it permitted the reamer maker to sell them. Should you desire a JDJ cartridge, contact SSK Industries, 421 Woodvue Lane, Wintersville, OH 43952.

General Comments The first version of this cartridge used the 303 British case, but was later changed to the 444 Marlin necked down. This chambering provides ample capacity and bullet area to produce impressive muzzle energy, especially with longer handgun-length barrels (14-16 inches). Any 357 Magnum, 35 Remington or 35 Herrett Thompson/Center Contender barrel is easily rechambered to use this cartridge. The 358 JDJ offers muzzle velocities similar to the 375 Winchester (rifle loads) with bullets of equal weight. Since this chambering uses spitzer bullets, delivered energy at normal hunting range is significantly higher than the parent 444 Marlin, even when the latter is fired from a rifle. Bullets of 180-225 grains are good choices and the Barnes 180-grain X provides excellent terminal performance. However, use of the Barnes X requires special handloading techniques (deeper bullet seating and a reduction in powder charge). Top loads in this chambering generate significant recoil. An effective muzzlebrake (which increases the already significant muzzleblast effect) is essential. Recoil of top loads compares to top 44 Magnum revolver loads, a recoil level many shooters cannot learn to tolerate. When bullets of proper hunting weight are driven at full velocity (necessary to assure proper terminal performance, even the seasoned handgunner would describe the recoil generated as rather brisk.

358 JDJ Loading Data

Bullet (grains/type)	Powder	Grains	Velocity	Energy	Source/Comments
180 JSP	Rl-7	49.0	2295	2105	SSK/max. load, SSK barrels only
200 SP	Rl-7	48.0	2275	2295	SSK/max. load, SSK barrels only
225 SP	Rl-15	52.5	2145	2300	SSK/max. load, SSK barrels only
250 SP	AA 2520	50.0	2100	2205	SSK/max. load, SSK barrels only

35-06 JDJ

Historical Notes This cartridge was designed by J.D. Jones at SSK Industries. Application is to Thompson/Center Encore single-shot pistols fitted with a custom SSK barrel. Typical barrel length is 15 inches. Cases are formed from empty 30-06 or 35 Whelen cases by special means and cannot be fireformed from any other case. Neck length is minimal, which is acceptable for a cartridge used in a single-shot gun. Shoulder angle is 60 degrees, which seems to work just fine. Body taper is minimal, similar to Ackley's improved designs. Therefore, this is equivalent to a maximized 35 Whelen. Capacity is a whopping 76 grains of water, which is significantly greater than the 35 Whelen (about 72). Working pressure is about 60,000 psi, so ballistics are quite impressive. Best handloads in SSK barrels can approach 35 Whelen (rifle) ballistics.

General Comments Since this case has no rim, it is not generally safe to directly fireform it in the conventional manner. However, owing to the captive extractor system used in the Encore, it is possible to use a special technique in those guns. Resize a 35 Whelen case, and then seat a 0.358-inch jacketed bullet hard against the rifling (so that the gun will just close). Correct powder charge is about 5 percent below the maximum SSK-recommended load. Jones recommends 200-grain bullets for big game hunting applications on smaller species and bullets up to 250 grains on larger species. While one could use 180- and 200-grain Barnes X bullets, which can offer impressive terminal performance, the handloader must use X-bullet specific loading data and special handloading techniques (e.g., bullet ogive must be seated a minimum of 0.050-inch from the rifling). Further, those bullets work best when a reduced-friction coating (such as moly-plating) is used. For this reason, SSK does not support use of X-style bullets in its guns. While no bullet substitution is benign, never substitute any X-style bullet in any load — begin with data specifically created for that bullet. This cartridge generates sufficient energy for hunting on any continent. SSK has not yet fully developed optimal loading data for this number. Recoil may exceed what some shooters can learn to handle.

35-06 JDJ Loading Data

Bullet (grains/type)	Powder	Grains	Velocity	Energy	Source/Comments
180	H335	67.0	2742	3005	SSK/max. load, SSK barrels only
220	IMR 4064	62.8	2584	3260	SSK/max. load, SSK barrels only
225	IMR 4064	62.8	2614	3415	SSK/max. load, SSK barrels only
250	Rl-15	61.8	2415	3235	SSK/max. load, SSK barrels only

9.09 Eagle

Historical Notes Lazzeroni Arms designed this cartridge in 1998. While somewhat related to an older case, for practical purposes this is a new case design. This cartridge was created in response to requests for a high-performance cartridge that would work in a 2.8-inch action and yet deliver the ballistics of a full-length belted magnum. Adaptation to a standard action is feasible but is not recommended. Although standardized, this is essentially a wildcat chambering using the Patriot case. Lazzeroni does offer dies and reamer specifications but does not normally chamber for this cartridge or provide properly headstamped cases.

General Comments Bullet diameter is 0.358-inch (Lazzeroni bases its designations on bullet diameter, instead of bore diameter, which is the common practice). Ballistics are quite impressive for such a short cartridge. Given equal-length barrels, the Eagle essentially duplicates 358 Norma Magnum ballistics. Case design is typical of the Lazzeroni line: moderate body taper, 30-degree shoulder, sufficiently long neck, and thick rim of approximately case-body diameter. In other words, this is a well-designed case.

9.09 Eagle Factory Ballistics (24-inch barrel)

Bullet (grains/type)	Powder	Grains	Velocity	Energy	Source/Comments
250	FL		2850	4510	Lazzeroni factory load

358 Shooting Times Alaskan (358 STA)

Historical Notes This wildcat chambering was originated in 1990 by Layne Simpson, a gun writer for *Shooting Times* magazine. The original version was simply the 8mm Remington Magnum necked up with no other changes. In 1994, a somewhat modified version featuring reduced body taper and a sharper shoulder was adopted for chambering in A-Square rifles. This cartridge takes advantage of the 3.65-inch magazine length of the long-action Remington Model 700.

General Comments The 358 STA has impressive velocity potential and can deliver good ballistics with a variety of bullets and powders. Currently there is little data available, but A-Square provides ammunition and data for a few of the more popular bullet weights and types. It is likely that some of the slower handloader powders would show improved performance in this chambering. A-Square now offers 358 STA ammunition.

358 STA Loading Data and Factory Ballistics

Bullet (grains/type)	Powder	Grains	Velocity	Energy	Source/Comments
125 Sierra JSP	H4831	91.0	3046	2575	A-Square (Practice Load)
225 Sierra SBT	IMR 7828	93.0	3003	4505	A-Square/maximum load
225 Sierra SBT	RI-22	93.0	3041	4620	A-Square/maximum load
225 Sierra SBT	H4831	93.0	3056	4665	A-Square/maximum load
275 A-Square Lion	RI-22	90.0	2835	4905	A-Square/maximum load
275 A-Square Lion	IMR 7828	92.0	2850	4960	A-Square/maximum load
275 A-Square Lion	H4831	90.0	2857	4980	A-Square/maximum load
275 TRIAD	FL		2850	4955	A-Square factory load (3 A-Square bullet types)

9.3mm JDJ

Historical Notes Designed by J.D. Jones at SSK Industries, this chambering is the 444 Marlin case necked down to 9.3mm with no other changes. Design intent was a Thompson/Center chambering that would surpass 35 Remington rifle ballistics and use the newly available U.S.-manufactured 9.3mm bullets.

General Comments Any ballistic difference between this chambering and the 358 JDJ would be very hard to demonstrate. This chambering is reported to deliver impressive performance against deer and black bear-sized game when heavy bullets are

used. The primary market is European, where the 9.3mm bore is quite popular. This chambering generates significant recoil. An effective muzzle brake (which increases the already significant muzzle-blast effect) is essential. Recoil of top loads compares to top 44 Magnum revolver loads, a recoil level many shooters cannot learn to tolerate. When bullets of proper hunting weight are driven at full velocity (necessary to assure proper terminal performance), even the seasoned handgunner would describe the recoil as very brisk.

9.3mm JDJ Loading Data

Bullet (grains/type)	Powder	Grains	Velocity	Energy	Source/Comments
270 Speer	H322	44.0	1906	2175	SSK/max. load, SSK barrel only (14")
270 Speer	H414	57.3	1924	2240	SSK/max. load, SSK barrel only (14")
270 Speer	IMR 4064	52.0	1974	2335	SSK/max. load, SSK barrel only (14")
270 Norma	RI-15	53.0	2027	2465	SSK/max. load, SSK barrel only (14")
270 Speer	RI-15	54.0	2077	2585	SSK/max. load, SSK barrel only (14")

375 Whisper

Historical Notes Created by J. D. Jones, the 375 Whisper, like all other Whisper cartridges, must be capable of subsonic extreme accuracy with very heavy bullets, while maintaining excellent accuracy with light bullets at moderate to high velocity. Barrels, dies, and cases for the 375 Whisper are available from SSK Industries.

General Comments Using a 7mm Bench Rest Remington case necked up to 375-caliber, the 375 Whisper launches a 300-grain Hornady projectile at just under sub-sonic speeds (1050 fps). It can propel 250-grain bullets to 2250 fps. The 375 Whisper can be chambered in suitably barreled Thompson/Center Contender firearms, as well as other single-shot and many bolt-action firearms

375 JDJ

Historical Notes This is another cartridge designed and developed by J.D. Jones, hence the JDJ designation. Jones began development of his cartridges around 1978, and these are generally fired in barrels furnished by his company, SSK Industries. The purpose of these cartridges is to give added range and power to the Thompson/Center Contender pistol for hunting. Some of Jones' cartridges have also proved to be excellent metallic silhouette numbers. JDJ cartridges are relatively easy to make. All JDJ cartridges are proprietary and SSK neither sells reamers nor allows the reamer maker to sell them. Should you desire a JDJ cartridge, contact SSK Industries, 590 Woodvue Lane, Wintersville, OH 43953.

General Comments Based on the 444 Marlin necked down, this chambering provides ample capacity and bullet area to produce muzzle energy similar to what 30-06-chambered rifles deliver, especially with longer handgun-length barrels (14-16 inches). The 375 JDJ loaded to top velocity with 250-grain bullets is fully

capable of taking elk-sized game with proper shot placement. However, the Barnes 210-grain X can deliver superior terminal performance, reduced recoil and a flatter trajectory, but does require special handloading techniques (deeper bullet seating and a reduction in powder charge). With heavier bullets of proper construction, this chambering is adequate for species to the 1-ton class. Jones himself has repeatedly proven this fact. An excellent selection of good bullets that work well when loaded to top 375 JDJ velocity is available. This chambering generates significant recoil. An effective muzzlebrake (which increases the already significant muzzleblast effect) is essential. Top loads generally produce more recoil than top 44 Magnum revolver loads, a recoil level many shooters cannot learn to tolerate. When bullets of proper hunting weight are driven at full velocity (necessary to assure proper terminal performance), even the seasoned handgunner would describe the recoil as very brisk.]

375 JDJ Loading Data

Bullet (grains/type)	Powder	Grains	Velocity	Energy	Source/Comments
220 SP	H4895	51.0	2350	2365	SSK/max. load, *12 – 14 inch SSK barrels only
270 SP	IMR 4064	48.0	2100	2165	SSK/max. load, *12 – 14 inch SSK barrels only
270 SP	IMR 4064	49.2	2100	2400	SSK/max. load, *12 – 14 inch SSK barrels only
300 SP	W748	50.8	1950	2405	SSK/max. load, *12 – 14 inch SSK barrels only

375-06 JDJ

Historical Notes This cartridge was designed by J.D. Jones at SSK Industries. Application is to Thompson/Center Encore single-shot pistols fitted with a custom SSK barrel. Typical barrel length is 15 inches. Cases are best formed from empty 30-06 or 35 Whelen cases by special means. Neck length is minimal, which is acceptable for a cartridge used in a single-shot gun. Shoulder angle is 60 degrees, which seems to work just fine and is probably necessary to maintain headspace against the firing pin blow and primer blast. Body taper is minimal, similar to Ackley's improved designs. Therefore, this is equivalent to a maximized 375 Whelen. Capacity is a whopping 77 grains of water, which is significantly greater than the 375 Whelen (about 73). Working pressure is about 60,000 psi, so ballistics are quite impressive. Best handloads in SSK barrels easily exceed the energy of top factory 35 Whelen (rifle) loads.

General Comments Since this case has no rim, it is not generally safe to directly fireform it in the conventional manner. However, owing to the captive extractor system used in the Encore, it is possible to use a special technique in those guns. Resize and neck

expand a 35 Whelen case, then seat a 0.375-inch jacketed bullet hard against the rifling (so that the gun will just close). Correct powder charge is about 5 percent below the maximum SSK-recommended load. Jones recommends 220-grain bullets at reduced velocity for big game hunting applications on smaller species and bullets up to 300 grains for the largest species. While one could use 210- and 235-grain Barnes X bullets, which can offer impressive terminal performance, handloaders must use X-bullet specific loading data and special handloading techniques (e.g., bullet ogive must be seated a minimum of 0.050-inch from rifling). Further, those bullets work best when a reduced-friction coating (such as moly-plating) is used. For this reason, SSK does not support use of X-style bullets in its guns. While no bullet substitution is benign, never substitute any X-style bullet in any load — begin with data specifically created for that bullet. This cartridge generates sufficient energy for hunting on any continent. SSK has not fully developed optimal loading data for this number at this time. With heavy bullets and top loads, recoil may exceed what even seasoned shooters want to experience.

375-06 JDJ Loading Data

Bullet (grains/type)	Powder	Grains	Velocity	Energy	Source/Comments
220	AA 4350	55.6	1825	1625	SSK/max. load, SSK barrels only
220	VARGET	67.3	2601	3305	SSK/max. load, SSK barrels only
270	Vit N140	65.2	2421	3515	SSK/max. load, SSK barrels only
300	IMR 4320	63.4	2330	3615	SSK/max. load, SSK barrels only

9.53 Hellcat

Historical Notes Lazzeroni Arms designed this cartridge in 1997. While somewhat related to an older case, for practical purposes this is a new case design. The Hellcat was created in response to requests for a high-performance cartridge that would work in a 2.8-inch action and yet deliver the ballistics of a full-length belted magnum. Adaptation to a standard action is feasible but is not recommended.

General Comments Bullet diameter is 0.375-inch (Lazzeroni bases its designations on bullet diameter, instead of bore diameter, which is the common practice.) Ballistics are quite impressive for such a short cartridge. Given equal-length barrels, the Hellcat essentially duplicates the ballistics of the legendary 375 H&H Magnum. Case design is typical of the Lazzeroni line: moderate

body taper, 30-degree shoulder, sufficiently long neck, and thick rim of approximately case body diameter. In other words, this is a well-designed case.

Bill George owns the first Hellcat rifle ever built. With very modest assistance from this editor, George assembled some extremely accurate handloads (well under one-MOA accuracy) using the 300-grain Nosler Partition. He took those to Africa and proceeded to kill everything he shot at, using exactly one round for each animal in almost every instance. This Hellcat load dropped George's Cape buffalo in its tracks, a feat that left his guide practically in shock. The quote was, "Never seen that happen before in my life!" Shot placement and bullet performance count.

9.53 Hellcat Factory Ballistics (24-inch barrel)

Bullet (grains/type)	Powder	Grains	Velocity	Energy	Source/Comments
300	FL		2600	4500	Lazzeroni factory load

375 JRS Magnum

General Comments The 375 JRS was designed by noted gun writer Jon R. Sundra. It is based on the 8mm Remington Magnum case necked up to 0.375 with no other changes. It can be made by fire-forming 375 H&H factory ammunition, or by necking up the 8mm Rem. Mag. using tapered expanders of 0.358-inch, then 0.375-inch, or by fire-forming using blank loads in 8mm Rem. Mag. cases. Of these options, Sundra recommends the latter because only the neck is worked; this procedure requires a load of 35.0 grains of IMR SR 4756, a small over-powder wad of tissue, then filling the remainder of the case to the base of the neck with Cream of Wheat. Seal off the case mouth with a plug of soap by pushing the case neck into a bar of soap. The resultant blank will expand the neck perfectly in a 375 JRS chamber. As of August 1990, the above procedures are no longer necessary because A-Square Co. now offers 375 JRS unprimed cases

as well as loaded ammunition with its headstamp. As of 1992, U.S. Repeating Arms is chambering the Winchester Model 70 Super Grade (the pre-'64 action with controlled round feeding) for the 375 JRS. This cartridge ballistically duplicates the 375 Weatherby Magnum and a host of older wildcats of the same general design.

General Comments Case capacity of the 375 JRS is about 8 percent greater than that of the 375 H&H. The best powder for 270- to 330-grain bullets is IMR 4350. Velocity in 24-inch barrels for a 300-grain bullet will average between 2700 and 2750 fps. Any max load listed for the 375 H&H can be used for a starting load in the 375 JRS. E.R. Shaw and H-S Precision also chamber for the 375 JRS; Hornady and RCBS make reloading dies. A-Square now offers 375 JRS ammunition.

375 JRS Loading Data

Bullet (grains/type)	Powder	Grains	Velocity	Energy	Source/Comments
270 SP	IMR 4350	85.0	2750	4535	Jon Sundra
300 SP	IMR 4350	83.0	2700	4855	Jon Sundra

375 Dakota

Historical Notes The 375 Dakota is a shortened and necked-down version of the basic rebated-rimless 404 Jeffery case, but the rim is enlarged slightly to eliminate the rebated feature. Design purpose was to create a cartridge that would duplicate 375 H&H performance from a 30-06 length action (3.35 inches). The case features a rim that is slightly larger than the standard belted-magnum cases — using this cartridge in a rifle with a standard belted-magnum bolt face will require a slight bolt alteration. Despite its similar capacity, maximum case diameter of this much shorter case is only slightly larger than the 375 H&H Magnum. Typically, magazine capacity is reduced by one cartridge. This is perhaps a significant consideration for a dangerous-game rifle, but a minor magazine alteration will remedy the problem.

General Comments The 375 Dakota, just like the 7mm, 300 and 330 Dakota cartridges, functions properly through standard-length (3.35-inch) actions. Usable case capacity is nearly identical to the 375 H&H Magnum and, if loaded to equal pressures, ballistics are the same. This cartridge provides superior feeding and a potential accuracy advantage over the 375 H&H. Geared toward larger species, this should be a good choice for those who feel lesser calibers are not adequate for the task at hand. Combined with some of the superior bullets now available, this cartridge can rival the long-range trajectory of the best 270 Winchester loads. When loaded with proper dangerous-game bullets, and in the hands of an expert, this cartridge would suffice for any game worldwide.

375 Dakota Loading Data and Factory Ballistics

Bullet (grains/type)	Powder	Grains	Velocity	Energ	Source/Comments
270	RI-15	75.0	2829	4795	Dakota/maximum load
270	IMR 4350	85.0	2895	5020	Dakota/maximum load
270	H4350	85.0	2883	4980	Dakota/maximum load
300	IMR 4350	78.0	2660	4710	Dakota/maximum load
300	H4350	78.0	2648	4670	Dakota/maximum load
300	IMR 4831	79.0	2641	4640	Dakota/maximum load
300	RI-19	83.5	2662	4720	Dakota/maximum load
270	FL		2800	4680	Dakota factory load
300	FL		2600	4502	Dakota factory load

375 Canadian Magnum

Historical Notes This cartridge was developed about 1994 by North American Shooting Systems (NASS) and is simply a 375-caliber version of the 338 Canadian Magnum. This design features a slightly rebated, rimless bottleneck case. Design intent was to provide the maximum feasible powder capacity in a standard action with minimal gunsmithing (without deepening the magazine well slightly, magazine capacity is usually reduced by one round). Bolt face alteration is not necessary. Cartridge feeding and headspacing characteristics are improved.

General Comments The Canadian Magnum series is similar to Dakota's cartridge family in both design and purpose. However, this cartridge (like the entire Canadian line) takes advantage of the full 3.65-inch magazine length of the long-action Remington M700 and similar rifles. On the Canadian Magnums, body diameter is significantly larger than the standard belted magnum (0.544-inch versus 0.513-inch at the base). Rechambering of nominal belted magnums with the same bore diameter is generally quite simple, requiring no other alterations to the gun. For any given case length, case capacity is about 15 percent greater than can be achieved with the belted version. Body taper is minimal and the shoulder is comparatively sharp. However, neck length is sufficiently generous to provide good bullet purchase for hunting ammunition. Performance is commensurate with the capacity and pressures used in these loadings. Actual performance of this number is very close to the vaunted 378 Weatherby Magnum.

375 Canadian Magnum Loading Data and Factory Ballistics

Bullet (grains/type)	Powder	Grains	Velocity	Energy	Source/Comments
270	H4831	103.0	3010	5430	NASS/maximum load
270	FL		3000	5395	NASS factory load

375 A-Square

Historical Notes This is a somewhat modified 378 Weatherby Magnum designed in 1975. The changes were intended to allow duplication of 378 Weatherby Magnum performance in a 375 H&H magazine length (3.65 inches).

General Comments Ballistics duplicate the parent 378 Weatherby Magnum and chambering is easily achieved in any of the many 375 H&H-chambered magazine rifles. Cases are easily converted from 378 Weatherby Magnum cases. This chambering is a viable choice for a light rifle in Africa. The heavier solids offered are certainly capable for use against the heaviest of game, with proper shot placement. Recoil is distinctly less than recoil with any of the 40 caliber and larger dangerous-game chamberings.

375 A-Square Loading Data and Factory Ballistics

Bullet (grains/type)	Powder	Grains	Velocity	Energy	Source/Comments
250 Sierra SBT	IMR 4831	106.0	3184	5625	A-Square/maximum load
250 Sierra SBT	H4831	114.5	3186	5630	A-Square/maximum load
250 Sierra SBT	RI-22	113.0	3217	5740	A-Square/maximum load
300 Monolithic Solid	RI-22	105.0	2839	5370	A-Square/maximum load
300 Monolithic Solid	IMR 4831	101.0	2911	5640	A-Square/maximum load
300 Monolithic Solid	H4831	110.0	2974	5890	A-Square/maximum load
300 Sierra & TRIAD	FL		2920	5675	A-Square factory load (3 A-Square bullet types)

9.53 Saturn

Historical Notes Lazzeroni Arms designed this cartridge in 1996. While somewhat related to an older case, for practical purposes this is a new case design. John Lazzeroni believes that those hunters who will take the time to become competent marksmen can legitimately take game at longer ranges. This cartridge was created to provide sufficient velocity for medium-weight or heavyweight hunting bullets to provide dependable expansion at longer ranges and to have sufficient energy for taking the largest species. Adaptation to standard actions is feasible but is not recommended.

General Comments Bullet diameter is 0.375-inch (Lazzeroni bases its designations on bullet diameter, instead of bore diameter, which is the common practice). Ballistics equal or exceed any factory 37-caliber cartridge. Case design is typical of the Lazzeroni line: moderate body taper, 30-degree shoulder, sufficiently long neck, and thick rim of approximately case-body diameter. In other words, this is a well-designed case. Although designed specifically for hunting, this cartridge does have application to long-range target shooting. While a 27-inch barrel was originally standard, Lazzeroni has recently changed to a 24-inch barrel for this number, there is no significant sacrifice in performance. Lazzeroni's cartridge loadings use premium bullets from Nosler, Barnes or Swift. These are the only bullets providing the necessary accuracy and terminal performance to meet Lazzeroni's strict requirements.

9.53 Saturn Factory Ballistics (24-inch barrel)

Bullet (grains/type)	Powder	Grains	Velocity	Energy	Source/Comments
300	FL		3010	6035	Lazzeroni factory load *

* Lazzeroni has used loads exceeding 3,100 fps, but that is pressing the issue rather hard. Rl-19 is a preferred powder for this number.

400 Cor-Bon

Historical Notes Peter Pi, CEO of Cor-Bon, designed this cartridge in 1995 by simply necking-down the 45 Automatic to 40-caliber using a 25-degree shoulder. Unlike some earlier necked-down 45 Automatic designs, this case has a reasonably long neck. With the advent of plentiful 40-caliber pistol bullets, this was an obvious high-performance cartridge choice. This design offers several advantages. First, in most pistols, conversion is completed by a simple barrel replacement. Second, the feed ramp in the chamber can easily be shortened or eliminated, thus allowing safe use of loads generating significantly higher pressure. Third, owing to the bottleneck design, this case can function better with a wider variety of bullet shapes and is generally more forgiving toward machining, fit and finish tolerances. Finally, for any given energy level, the 400 Cor-Bon produces significantly less recoil than the 45 Automatic (lighter bullets, launched faster).

General Comments This is a very fine cartridge for those who do not like excessive recoil. Factory loads offer significant self-defense ballistics in a package that most shooters can easily learn to handle. Those who are satisfied with the 45 Automatic will probably find little appeal to the 400 Cor-Bon. On the other hand, those who are dissatisfied with 9mm and 40 S&W ballistics might find this a viable option. Cases are easily converted from the ubiquitous 45 Automatic but Starline offers these as a component. Owing to increased case capacity, ballistics of the 400 Cor-Bon approach those of the 10mm Automatic, but with significantly less pressure.

400 Cor-Bon Loading Data and Factory Ballistics

Bullet (grains/type)	Powder	Grains	Velocity	Energy	Source/Comments
135 JHP	Vit N340	9.7	1400	585	Cor-Bon
155 JHP	WAP	10.5	1310	590	Cor-Bon
165 JHP	Vit N105	10.5	1250	570	Cor-Bon
180 Cast	Unique	7.0	1100	480	Cor-Bon
135 JHP	FL		1450	625	Cor-Bon factory load
155 JHP	FL		1350	625	Cor-Bon factory load
165 JHP	FL		1300	615	Cor-Bon factory load

405 Winchester   See Chapter 3 for cartridge information.

40-44 Woodswalker

Historical Notes This cartridge was designed by J.D. Jones at SSK Industries. Application is to Thompson/Center Encore or Contender single-shot pistols fitted with a custom SSK barrel. Typical barrel length is 10 inches. Cases are formed from empty 44 Magnum cases by simply running the case into a full-length sizing die. Neck length is rather short, which is acceptable for a cartridge used in a single-shot gun. Shoulder angle is 30 degrees.

General Comments This is very reminiscent of the 357 Bain & Davis. The only advantage of such a conversion is the ability to launch lighter bullets at higher velocity (compared to the parent cartridge). Working pressure is about 60,000 psi. Energy of top loads approachs that for 454 Casull revolver loads. It is an open question as to whether any readily available JHP bullet will function properly when used at twice the design velocity. However, broadside lung shots on smaller game species (and some not so small) have resulted in spectacular kills when using 180-grain and heavier bullets.

40-44 Woodswalker Loading Data

Bullet (grains/type)	Powder	Grains	Velocity	Energy	Source/Comments
150 Sierra	AA No. 9	30.7	2404	1925	SSK/max. load, SSK barrels only
165 Speer	Vit N110	25.2	2122	1650	SSK/max. load, SSK barrels only
170 Sierra	H110	31.4	2213	1845	SSK/max. load, SSK barrels only
190 Speer	AA No. 9	27.5	2116	1885	SSK/max. load, SSK barrels only

40-454 JDJ

Historical Notes This cartridge was designed by J.D. Jones at SSK Industries. Application is to Thompson/Center Encore and Contender single-shot pistols fitted with a custom SSK barrel. Typical barrel length is 12 inches. Cases are formed from empty 454 Casull cases by simply running the case into the full-length sizing die. Neck length is rather short, which is acceptable for a cartridge used in a single-shot gun. Shoulder angle is 30 degrees.

General Comments This is very reminiscent of the 357 Bain & Davis (the 44 Magnum necked to 35-caliber). The only advantage of such a conversion is the ability to launch lighter bullets at higher velocity (compared to the parent cartridge). Working pressure is about 60,000 psi. Muzzle energy of top loads can exceed any feasible 454 Casull revolver load. It is an open question as to whether any readily available JHP bullet will function properly when used at almost three times the design velocity. Use on smaller game species with broadside lung shots has resulted in spectacular kills when using 180-grain and heavier bullets.

40-454 JDJ Loading Data

Bullet (grains/type)	Powder	Grains	Velocity	Energy	Source/Comments
165 Speer	AA No. 9	36.6	2825	2925	SSK/maximum load
190 Speer	AA No. 9	34.5	2525	2690	SSK/maximum load

408 CheyTac

Historical Notes The 408 CheyTac may just be the ultimate long-range sniper and anti-materiel cartridge. Designed in 2001 by Dr. John Taylor and technical team to fill a gap between the 50 BMG and 338 Lapua, the 408 CheyTac can drive a 419-grain bullet to a supersonic range exceeding 2200 yards. After 400 yards, the retained energy of the 408 CheyTac exceeds that of 50 BMG ball ammunition. With high kinetic energy retention, the 408 can defeat any material that the 50 BMG can defeat, unless an explosive projectile is required. In test firings, the cartridge delivered sub-MOA accuracy at ranges beyond 2500 yards. Doppler radar testing at the U.S. Army Proving Ground in Yuma, Arizona confirmed the 408's ballistics. The 408 CheyTac advantages over the 50 BMG include less weight, a more compact cartridge, improved velocity and accuracy and lower recoil, along with shorter time for the bullet to reach the target. Special operations soldiers tested 408 CheyTac rifles and cartridges in Iraq and Afghanistan (2004)—informal reports of a first-shot hit at ranges exceeding 2300 yards are circulating within the military community.

General Comments Using new, high quality brass, the 408 CheyTac is based on a redesigned and strengthened 505 Gibbs case with a modified web area. The cartridge works well with 25- to 29-inch barrels using a 1:13 rifling twist. The 305-grain and 419-grain bullets for the 408 are CNC-turned bullets from copper-nickel alloy, and encompass a patented "balanced flight" design. A tungsten carbide penetrator (armor-piercing) bullet is also available. CheyTac Associates offers bolt-action and self-loading rifles, ballistic computers, ammunition, and cases.

408 CheyTac Factory Ballistics

Bullet (grains/type)	Powder	Grains	Velocity	Energy	Source/Comments
305-gr Solid	FL		3500		CheyTac
419-gr Solid	FL		3000		CheyTac

411 JDJ

Historical Notes Based upon the 444 Marlin case, this cartridge is designed to take advantage of the plentiful 41-caliber pistol and revolver bullets now on the market. With cast rifle bullets sized properly it provides more versatility than the 0.416-inch bore. J.D. Jones designed this at SSK Industries.

General Comments Various pistol and revolver bullets can be loaded to achieve as high as 2400 fps from a 14-inch Contender barrel. Special cast bullets in the 400-grain range are easily loaded to achieve 1,800 fps in the same guns. This approaches top 45-70 modern rifle ballistics. Even with the best Pachmayr Decelerator grips and the most effective muzzle brake possible, this combination will generate massive recoil. Many otherwise competent shooters simply cannot learn to master such a chambering in a handgun. The Barnes 300-grain X offers reduced recoil with potentially superior terminal performance and a flatter trajectory, but requires special handloading techniques (deeper bullet seating and a reduction in powder charge). With the proper bullets, those who can handle the recoil will find this a serious handgun chambering for use against any species in the world.

411 JDJ Loading Data

Bullet (grains/type)	Powder	Grains	Velocity	Energy	Source/Comments
210 Sierra	H4198	45.0	1878	1640	SSK/maximum load
275 Harrison	H4227	38.0	1990	2415	SSK/maximum load
295 Cast	H322	45.0	1683	1855	SSK/maximum load
330 Harrison	Rl-7	46.0	2000	2930	SSK/maximum load
385 Cast	Rl-7	46.0	1711	2500	SSK/maximum load

411 Express

Historical Notes Created by Z-Hat Custom owner, Fred Zeglin in 2002, the 411 Express is the longest version of the 30-06 case that will function in a standard length action. The 411 Express uses the largest diameter bullet that will fit into the 30-06 case. With good shooting and good bullets, the cartridge is capable (and has done so) of taking North American elk at ranges exceeding 300 yards. The 411 Express is a powerful, large bore cartridge with stout but manageable recoil.

General Comments This cartridge fits into standard length actions with a .473-inch bolt face. The 411 Express uses 30-06 *cylindrical* brass as the parent case. Since the case manufacturer does not neck down cylindrical brass, only experienced handloaders should attempt to form the 411 Express case. The parent brass is necked to .411-inch and then fireformed in a 411 Express chamber. This Z-Hat offering is best suited for bolt-action rifles using 24-inch barrels with a 1:18 or 1:20 rifling twist. Loaded ammunition and correctly headstamped brass are available from Quality Cartridge. Z-Hat Custom offers rifles, dies and reloading information.

411 Express Loading Data

Bullet (grains/type)	Powder	Grains	Velocity	Energy	Source/Comments
300-gr	H4895	66.0	2561		Z-Hat Custom
360-gr	Accurate Arms 2230	60.0	2296		Z-Hat Custom
400-gr	RL-15	59.0	2160		Z-Hat Custom

411 Hawk

Historical Notes The 411 Hawk is the most popular member in the Hawk family of hunting cartridges. Building on an idea by Bob Fulton in 1997, Fred Zeglin created the 411 Hawk to accept the largest diameter bullets that can be loaded into the 30-06 case. With the right bullets, the 411 Hawk can produce over 4000 foot-pounds of energy from a 30-06 case! This is a premier big-game cartridge, suitable for anything on the North American continent, and most game in Africa.

General Comments All Hawk cartridges fit into standard length actions with a .473-inch bolt face. The 411 Hawk uses 30-06 *cylindrical* brass or 35 Whelen brass as the parent case. Since the case manufacturer does not neck-down cylindrical brass, only experienced handloaders should attempt to form the 411 Express

case from 30-06 cylindrical brass. The cylindrical brass is necked down in a cold forming step, and then fireformed in a 411 Hawk chamber. As an alternative, 35 Whelen brass can be expanded using .430 tapered expander, sized in a full length die, and then fireformed in a 411 Hawk chamber. While the 411 Hawk shoulder appears minimal, extensive testing confirmed the shoulder area was ample to safely headspace this powerful cartridge. This Hawk cartridge is suited for bolt action, single-shot and lever action rifles (such as the Browning/Winchester 1895 and BLR) using 24- to 26-inch barrels with a 1:20 rifling twist. Hunters who plan to shoot only 400-grain bullets can use 1:24 twist rifling. Loaded ammunition and correctly headstamped brass are available from Quality Cartridge. Z-Hat Custom offers rifles, dies and reloading information.

411 Hawk Loading Data

Bullet (grains/type)	Powder	Grains	Velocity	Energy	Source/Comments
300-gr Hawk	H4895	64.0	2553		Z-Hat Custom
325-gr North Fork	H4895	64.0	2479		Z-Hat Custom
350-gr A-Frame	IMR 4064	61.0	2366		Z-Hat Custom
360-gr North Fork	Accurate Arms 2230	57.0	2281		Z-Hat Custom
400-gr Hawk	RL-15	57.0	2159		Z-Hat Custom

416 JDJ

Historical Notes Based upon the 444 Marlin case, this cartridge is designed to take advantage of the plentiful 416-caliber rifle bullets now on the market. With cast rifle bullets sized properly, it provides some versatility but is only intended for big game hunting. J.D. Jones designed this at SSK Industries after the advent of 416 handloader bullets.

General Comments Rifle bullets in the 400-grain range are easily loaded to achieve 1800 fps from a 14-inch Contender barrel. This approaches top 45-70 ballistics from a modern rifle. Even with the best Pachmayr Decelerator grips and the most effective muzzle brake possible, this combination will generate massive recoil. Many otherwise competent shooters simply cannot learn to master such a chambering in a handgun. The Barnes 300-grain X offers reduced recoil with potentially superior terminal performance and a flatter trajectory, but requires special handloading techniques (deeper bullet seating and a reduction in powder charge). With the proper bullets, those who can handle the recoil will find this a serious handgun chambering for use against any species in the world.

416 JDJ Loading Data

Bullet (grains/type)	Powder	Grains	Velocity	Energy	Source/Comments
300 Hawk	Rl-7	51.0	2016	2705	SSK/maximum load
350 CB	AA 2230	56.0	1908	2830	SSK/maximum load
400 Hornady	Rl-15	53.5	1727	2650	SSK/maximum load
400 Hawk	Rl-15	56.5	1810	2910	SSK/maximum load

416-06 JDJ

Historical Notes This cartridge was designed by J.D. Jones at SSK Industries. Application is to Thompson/Center Encore single-shot pistols fitted with a custom SSK barrel. Typical barrel length is 15 inches. Cases are formed from empty 35 Whelen cases by special means. Neck length is minimal, which is acceptable for a cartridge used in a single-shot gun. Shoulder angle is 60 degrees, which seems to work just fine. An unusually sharp case shoulder is certainly necessary to maintain headspace against firing pin impact and primer blast. Body taper is minimal, similar to Ackley's improved designs. Therefore, this is equivalent to a maximized, 41-caliber, 30-06 case. Capacity is a whopping 78 grains of water, compared to about 100 grains for the 416 Rem. Mag. Working pressure is about 60,000 psi so ballistics are, nevertheless, quite impressive. Best handloads in SSK barrels far surpass any normal 35 Whelen loads.

General Comments Since this case has no rim, it is not generally safe to directly fireform it in the conventional manner. However, owing to the captive extractor system used in the Encore, it is possible to use a special technique in those guns. Resize and neck-expand a 35 Whelen case, then seat a jacketed 0.416-inch bullet hard against the rifling (so that the gun will just close). Correct powder charge is about 5 percent below the maximum SSK-recommended load. Jones recommends 300-grain bullets for big game hunting applications on medium species and bullets up to 400 grains for the largest species. The 300-grain Barnes X could be used but those require special loading techniques (minimum of 0.050-inch bullet-to-rifling jump) and work best with moly plating. For this reason, SSK does not support use of X-style bullets in its guns. Never substitute any bullet without beginning with specific loading data developed for that bullet. Achieving sufficient velocity to assure bullet expansion is an issue. Lightly constructed bullets would seem to be in order here. On the other hand, velocity is adequate with the 400-grain solid to make this a thoroughly acceptable cartridge for hunting any species on this planet. SSK has not fully developed optimal loading data for this number at this time. With heavy bullets and top loads, recoil probably exceeds what most shooters want to experience or could ever learn to handle. Whether or not this cartridge can have sufficient headspace control seems to be an open question. Do not anneal the case, as doing so will almost certainly allow excessive case stretching.

416-06 JDJ Loading Data

Bullet (grains/type)	Powder	Grains	Velocity	Energy	Source/Comments
300	AA 2015	62.3	2229	3310	SSK/max. load, SSK barrels only
400	AA 2015	60.0	2065	3785	SSK/max. load, SSK barrels only

416 Taylor

Historical Notes The 416 Taylor was developed by Robert Chatfield-Taylor in 1972. It is based on the 458 Winchester Magnum case necked-down to 416 caliber. However, it can also be made by necking-up 338 Winchester Magnum cases. The late Chatfield-Taylor was a writer and hunter of note, and he used the cartridge in Africa and reported very favorably on it. It was also checked out on Cape buffalo, elephant and lion by several others with success, including John Wootters. At one time, there were rumors that the cartridge would be commercialized by Remington or Winchester, but it remained for A-Square to do that. The 416 Taylor is ballistically similar to the 416 Rigby and is adequate for the same range of game, including the tough, dangerous African varieties. It is overpowered for most North American big game, but would be good backup against brown bears.

General Comments The 416 Taylor came about in part because 416 Rigby cartridges and cases were difficult to obtain and partly because the 416-caliber represents a gap in the lineup of American commercial cartridges. The 416 Taylor can be used in a standard-length action. This gap has now been filled by Remington with its 416 Remington Magnum based on the 8mm Remington Magnum case, and by Weatherby with its new 416. In 1988, Federal introduced 416 Rigby ammunition, thus ending the shortage of 416 Rigby ammunition.

The 416 Taylor can be considered something of a forerunner to the Remington 416 because it proved the feasibility and effectiveness of a new 416-caliber to replace the venerable 416 Rigby. The cases are easy to make and RCBS can furnish loading dies. Originally, the problem was the availability of good 0.416-inch bullets. However, that deficiency has been eliminated by Barnes and Hornady. A-Square currently furnishes rifles, cases, bullets and loaded ammunition in 416 Taylor, so it has become a proprietary cartridge.

416 Taylor Loading Data and Factory Ballistics

Bullet (grains/type)	Powder	Grains	Velocity	Energy	Source/Comments
400 SP	IMR 4320	70.0	2270	4595	NA
400 SP	IMR 4320	71.0	2305	4700	NA
400	FL		2350	4905	A-Square factory load

10.57 Maverick

Historical Notes Lazzeroni Arms designed this cartridge in 1998. While somewhat related to an older case, for practical purposes, this is a new case design. This cartridge was created in response to requests for a high-performance cartridge that would work in a 2.8-inch action and yet deliver the ballistics of a full-length belted magnum. Adaptation to a standard action is feasible but is not recommended.

General Comments Bullet diameter is 0.416-inch (Lazzeroni bases its designations on bullet diameter, instead of bore diameter, which is the common practice.) Ballistics are quite impressive for such a short cartridge. Given equal-length barrels, the Maverick easily duplicates 416 Remington Magnum ballistics, although in a short-action rifle. Case design is typical of the Lazzeroni line: moderate body taper, 30-degree shoulder, sufficiently long neck, and thick rim of approximately case-body diameter. In other words, this is a well-designed case. For those who feel 37-caliber rifles are a bit on the light side for dangerous game hunting, this is a fine choice.

10.57 Maverick Factory Ballistics (24-inch barrel)

Bullet (grains/type)	Powder	Grains	Velocity	Energy	Source/Comments
400	FL		2400	5117	Lazzeroni factory load

416 Hoffman

Historical Notes The 416 Hoffman is another of the wildcat cartridges adopted by A-Square Co., with bullets and loaded ammunition currently available there. It originated with George L. Hoffman, of Sonora, Texas, in the late 1970s and is based on the necked-up and improved 375 H&H Magnum case. Ballistically, it duplicates the 416 Rigby and the 416 Taylor, except that the case is about 3/10-inch longer than the Taylor case and holds more powder. The cartridge case is of smaller base diameter than the Rigby, which allows an extra round to be carried in a magazine of equal size. A-Square can also furnish rifles of this caliber.

General Comments The 416 Hoffman is the most practical of the 416 wildcats because one can obtain all of the components without the necessity of reworking 375 H&H cases. With its 400-grain bullet at 2400 fps, it is relatively flat shooting out to 200 yards and is extremely accurate. It would be a good candidate for a one-gun cartridge to use on whatever Africa has to offer. Although overpowered for most North American big game, it would nevertheless do very well on moose or grizzly bear and could be loaded down for use on some of the smaller species. It is a very good cartridge for those who need or favor the 416-bore. A-Square now offers 416 Hoffman ammunition. Being very similar, Remington's 416 seems a superior option.

416 Hoffman Loading Data and Factory Ballistics

Bullet (grains/type)	Powder	Grains	Velocity	Energy	Source/Comments
400 SP	IMR 4064	77.0	2400	5125	NA
400 SP	IMR 4895	74.0	2350	4910	NA
400 SP	IMR 4895	77.0	2425	5230	NA
400 SP	IMR 4320	77.0	2400	5125	NA
400 SP	IMR 4350	88.0	2375	5040	NA
400	FL		2400	5125	A-Square factory load

416 Rimmed

Historical Notes This cartridge was designed by A-Square about 1991, at the behest of several Continental rifle makers. This is essentially a lengthened, rimmed 416 Rigby. Cartridge length (capacity) was chosen to allow 400-grain bullets to reach 2400 fps with pressures that are acceptable in double rifles (about 40,000 psi). The basic design is quite good. For the first time, the hunter who prefers a double rifle in 41 caliber can achieve the vaunted ballistics of typical 41-caliber, bolt-action rifle/cartridge combinations. Older 41-caliber double-rifle numbers fall short of this mark by several hundred fps.

General Comments A-Square specializes in cartridges and bullets intended for dangerous game applications. This new number is an interesting mix of old and new. Professional dangerous-game hunters have long recognized that a muzzle velocity of about 2400 fps seems to be about ideal for these applications. Equally, the 41-caliber bore size launching 400-grain bullets has long been recognized as a fine combination. In guns of reasonable weight, recoil is manageable while both delivered energy and penetration potential are significant.

416 Rimmed Loading Data and Factory Ballistics

Bullet (grains/type)	Powder	Grains	Velocity	Energy	Source/Comments
400 Lion	IMR 7828	112	2437	5275	A-Square
400 Lion	RI-22	108	2402	5125	A-Square
400	FL		2400	5115	A-Square factory load

416 BGA

Historical Notes A large-bore, high performance cartridge, the 416 BGA, was designed in 2003 by Raymond Oelrich, publisher of *Big Game Adventures* magazine, as one of a family of proprietary BGA cartridges. The 416 BGA uses standard length actions, boltfaces and magazines. It is a competent peer to other 416 magnum cartridges. The cartridge should do well on elk, moose, bears and large North American and African game where reach and good retained energy are needed.

General Comments The 416 BGA parent case is the European 9.3x64 manufactured to BGA proprietary specifications. The BGA cartridges are not offered for handloaders. Proprietary ammunition is available from two custom loading ammunition companies, A-Square and Superior Ammo. BGA cartridges are available in high quality custom rifles (crafted by Serengeti Rifle Co.) for GarRay Rifles Ltd. Kelowna, BC, Canada.

416 BGA Factory Ballistics

Bullet (grains/type)	Powder	Grains	Velocity	Energy	Source/Comments
350-gr	FL		2350		Raymond Oelrich
400-gr	FL		2200		Raymond Oelrich

416 Dakota

Historical Notes The 416 Dakota uses a modified full-length 404 Jeffery case, which features a rim that is only slightly larger than the standard belted-magnum rim. In any given length cartridge, use of the non-belted 404 Jeffery case offers about 15 percent more case capacity than the standard belted magnum. Because maximum case diameter is only slightly larger, one can retain full magazine capacity through minor magazine well modifications. Dakota designed its 416 to offer maximum 416-bore ballistics in a standard-size action.

General Comments With about 15 percent more usable capacity, the 416 Dakota offers ballistic performance substantially superior to the 416 Remington Magnum. Lacking the belt, this cartridge also feeds better from the magazine and offers potentially superior accuracy.

This cartridge requires use of a so-called magnum-length action (3.65 inches). Gunsmiths can easily rechamber most 416 Remington Magnum rifles to 416 Dakota. Restrictive laws often prohibit taking of dangerous game with cartridges of lesser caliber (although often there is no restriction on bullet weight, type or velocity!), so the various 416s present themselves as a minimum-caliber alternative in some African countries. Many find the reduction in recoil, compared to larger bores shooting heavier bullets, a worthwhile advantage. When loaded with proper spitzer bullets, the 416 Dakota offers a trajectory similar to the 270 Winchester and can deliver energy levels at extended ranges that rival the muzzle energies of many magnum cartridges. However, even with an effective muzzle brake, recoil becomes a bit stiff in typical rifles.

416 Dakota Loading Data and Factory Ballistics

Bullet (grains/type)	Powder	Grains	Velocity	Energy	Source/Comments
400	IMR 4350	90.0	2489	5500	Dakota/maximum load
400	IMR 4831	95.0	2527	5670	Dakota/maximum load
400	RI-19	100.0	2558	5810	Dakota/maximum load
400	H4831	100.0	2556	5800	Dakota/maximum load
400	FL		2450	5330	Dakota factory load

10.57 Meteor

Historical Notes Lazzeroni Arms designed this cartridge in 1997. While somewhat related to an older case, for practical purposes this is a new case design. This cartridge was created to provide sufficient velocity for heavyweight hunting bullets to provide dependable expansion at intermediate ranges and to have sufficient energy for taking the largest species. Adaptation to standard actions is feasible but is not recommended.

General Comments Bullet diameter is 0.416-inch (Lazzeroni bases its designations on bullet diameter, instead of bore diameter, which is the common practice.) Ballistics equal or exceed any factory 41-caliber cartridge. Case design is typical of the Lazzeroni line: moderate body taper, 30-degree shoulder, sufficiently long neck, and thick rim of approximately case body diameter. In other words, this is a well-designed case. Designed specifically for dangerous game hunting, this cartridge is not recommended for any other use. A 24-inch barrel is standard. A longer barrel will not significantly improve ballistics. Muzzle energy approaches 7000 foot-pounds. Lazzeroni's full-length cartridge loadings use premium bullets from Nosler, Barnes or Swift. These are the only bullets providing the necessary accuracy and terminal performance to meet Lazzeroni's strict requirements.

10.57 Meteor Factory Ballistics (24-inch barrel)

Bullet (grains/type)	Powder	Grains	Velocity	Energy	Source/Comments
300 Barnes X	FL		3100	6400	Lazzeroni factory load
400	FL		2750	6719	Lazzeroni factory load

425 Express

Historical Notes The 425 Express was developed as a joint effort between Cameron Hopkins and Whit Collins, with John French building the original prototype rifle. The entire story was published in the May 1988 issue of *Guns* magazine. The cartridge is based on the 300 Winchester Magnum case shortened from 2.620 inches to 2.550 inches, then fireformed in the 425 chamber. Loading dies are available from Redding Reloading Equipment. The prototype rifle was built on a Ruger Model 77 action.

General Comments The 425 Express fills a gap in the medium-bore cartridge lineup between the 375 Holland & Holland Magnum and the 458 Winchester Magnum. This cartridge fits standard-length bolt actions such as the Winchester Model 70, 1917 Enfield, Mauser 98 or other similar-length actions. This cartridge uses either a 350-grain or a 400-grain bullet and has proven very effective on heavy African game. It is overpowered for most North American hunting, but would provide a margin of safety if going after brown bears in the far North. Col. Charles Askins used the 425 Express very successfully on buffalo in Australia. A-Square now loads 425 Express ammunition.

425 Express Loading Data

Bullet (grains/type)	Powder	Grains	Velocity	Energy	Source/Comments
350 SP	IMR 4064	79.0	2535	5000	Cameron Hopkins
350 SP	H4895	77.0	2490	4825	Cameron Hopkins
350 SP	W760	77.0	2210	3795	Cameron Hopkins
400 SP	H4895	73.0	2420	5210	Cameron Hopkins
400 SP	IMR 4064	76.0	2370	4995	Cameron Hopkins
400 SP	W760	76.0	2155	4120	Cameron Hopkins

440 Cor-Bon

Historical Notes Cor-Bon designed this cartridge in 1997 by the simple expedient of necking down the 50 Action Express to 44 caliber (actually, a 0.429-inch bullet). This case has a reasonably long neck. With the advent of the 50 AE and the existence of plentiful 44-caliber pistol bullets, this was an obvious choice for a high-performance hunting chambering geared toward those who prefer a semi-automatic handgun. Compared to the parent case, this design offers several advantages. First, conversion of the gun is completed by a simple barrel replacement. Second, owing to the bottleneck, this cartridge can give better functioning with a wider variety of bullet shapes and is generally more forgiving toward machining, fit and finish tolerances. Finally, for any given energy level, the 440 Cor-Bon produces significantly less recoil than the 50 AE and shoots flatter (lighter bullets, launched faster). However, with top loads, the 440 cannot match the energy of the 50 AE.

General Comments This is a very fine cartridge for those who do not like excessive recoil. Factory loads offer significant hunting handgun ballistics in a package that most shooters can easily learn to handle (providing only that they have large enough hands to properly hold the gun). Except for a flatter trajectory with the 440 Cor-Bon, those who are satisfied with the 50 AE will probably find little appeal to this conversion. On the other hand, those who are dissatisfied with the 44 Magnum and who can handle the big AE pistol might find this a viable option. Cases are easily converted from 50 AE cases. This chambering offers the handloader a wide selection of bullets, which is not the case with the 50 AE. Ballistics of the 440 Cor-Bon are essentially those of the 454 Casull.

440 Cor-Bon Loading Data and Factory Ballistics

Bullet (grains/type)	Powder	Grains	Velocity	Energy	Source/Comments
240	H110 I W296	30.0	1800	1725	Cor-Bon
260	IMR 4227	27.5	1700	1665	Cor-Bon
240	FL		1900	1920	Cor-Bon factory load
260	FL		1700	1665	Cor-Bon factory load
305	FL		1600	1730	Cor-Bon factory load

458 SOCOM

Historical Notes After a bloody 1993 battle in Mogadishu, Somalia, several individuals addressed the opportunity to increase single-hit stopping power from U.S. military's M-16 and M-4 family of rifles and carbines. Maarten ter Weeme (Teppo Jutsu LLC) developed the 458 SOCOM cartridge to provide the equivalent of 45-70 firepower from M-16 rifles. The 458 SOCOM hurls big chunks of metal at substantial velocity from unaltered lower receivers and magazines—in full auto, and suppressed if desired. During testing, the cartridge defeated Level IIIa protective vests.

General Comments The 458 SOCOM uses the 50 AE as the parent case, lengthened to 1.575 inches (40mm), necked to accept .458-inch bullets, and featuring a rebated .473-inch rim. It accepts readily available 458-caliber bullets ranging from 250 grains to 600 grains, and in a wide variety of bullet styles and construction. Using standard M-16 lower receivers and unmodified magazines, ten 458 SOCOM rounds will fit into a military 30-round M-16 magazine; the 20-round magazine will hold seven rounds. In 16-inch barreled rifles, the 600-grain subsonic load works well with a 1:14 rifling twist. The 300-grain bullets do better with a 1:18 twist. Cor-Bon supplies loaded 458 SOCOM ammunition; Starline offers new brass cases, CH Tool and Die list reloading dies and Teppo Jutsu LLC provides reloading data.

458 SOCOM Factory Ballistics

Bullet (grains/type)	Powder	Grains	Velocity	Energy	Source/Comments
300-gr	FL		2000		Teppo Jutsu LLC
500-gr	FL		1300		Teppo Jutsu LLC

458 Whisper

Historical Notes Designed by J.D. Jones in 1993 at SSK Industries, this chambering uses a shortened 458 Winchester Magnum case. With custom 600-grain very low drag (VLD) bullets, this cartridge will function through standard-length magazines. The design intent was to create a hard-hitting subsonic round with superior penetration potential.

General Comments This is a rather esoteric chambering. For proper use, it requires very expensive custom bullets. Nevertheless, ballistic consistency and accuracy are impressive. When launched at subsonic velocities (1040 fps is typical for the 458 Whisper), this long and heavy VLD bullet loses velocity so slowly that crosswinds have little effect. It also retains much of its muzzle energy beyond one mile!

458 Whisper Loading Data

Bullet (grains/type)	Powder	Grains	Velocity	Energy	Source/Comments
500 H.T.	W231	15.6	1021	1155	SSK/Subsonic
560 H.T.	BlueDot	18.0	1101	1505	SSK/Subsonic
600 H.T.	AA 2015	27.0	1044	1450	SSK/Subsonic

450 Assegai

Historical Notes This cartridge was designed by A-Square, at the behest of several professional African hunters. The 450 Assegai case is similar to a lengthened, rimmed 416 Rigby case. This makes it suitable for application to double rifles. Cartridge length (capacity) was chosen to allow 500-grain bullets to reach 2400 fps with acceptable double-rifle pressures (about 40,000 psi). The basic design is quite good. The hunter who prefers a double rifle in 45-caliber can achieve the vaunted ballistics of the best 45-caliber, bolt-action rifle/cartridge combinations with a case of reasonable capacity. Older 45-caliber double rifle numbers cannot achieve this velocity with acceptable pressures. The assegai (pronounced approximately as *ass-a-guy*) is the ancient stabbing spear of the Zulu, which makes this an interesting moniker for this thoroughly modern cartridge.

General Comments A-Square specializes in cartridges and bullets intended for dangerous game applications. This new number is an interesting mix of old and new. Professional dangerous game hunters have long recognized that a muzzle velocity of about 2400 fps seems to be about ideal for these applications. Some prefer more bullet weight than smaller calibers can manage. Compared to the 41-caliber with a 400-grain bullet, the 45-caliber launching a 500-grain bullet has long been recognized as a fine combination for those who can handle the heavier rifle and increased recoil.

450 Assegai Loading Data and Factory Ballistics

Bullet (grains/type)	Powder	Grains	Velocity	Energy	Source/Comments
500 Lion	H4831	125	2480	6830	A-Square
500 Lion	IMR 4831	117	2379	6285	A-Square
500 Lion	Rl-22	120	2378	6280	A-Square
500	FL		2400	6400	A-Square factory load

450 Ackley Magnum

Historical Notes The late, great gunsmith and master experimenter, Parker Ackley, designed this cartridge about 1960. Ackley describes the genesis of the 458 Ackley as an effort to achieve maximum feasible case capacity using the full-length (2.85-inch) H&H belted magnum case, necked to 45-caliber. Obviously, this required elimination of most of the case body taper and incorporation of a sharp case shoulder with a comparatively short neck. Ackley recognizes that several others had designed very similar cartridges with the same goals and essentially identical results. A-Square, who now offers factory ammunition, adopted this chambering about 1995.

General Comments Compared to the tapered-case 458 Watts, this Ackley-designed number does achieve the same velocity with somewhat less pressure. Conversely, this cartridge does provide for slightly more muzzle velocity when loaded to any given peak chamber pressure. Ackley notes that any difference is essentially academic. All similar numbers can deliver similarly large doses of energy and recoil in guns of reasonable weight. According to Ackley, an advantage the 458 Watts has over this chambering is that one can safely fire 458 Winchester Magnum ammunition in the Watts chamber. Field testing has confirmed this. Further, Ackley reported that some users complained of limited case life with this number. Evidently, the modest case shoulder can allow excessive brass working during the firing and resizing cycle.

450 Ackley Magnum Loading Data and Factory Ballistics

Bullet (grains/type)	Powder	Grains	Velocity	Energy	Source/Comments
465 Solid	H4895	86.0	2422	6055	A-Square
465 Solid	IMR 4064	86.0	2376	5830	A-Square
465 Solid	RI-12	88.0	2395	5925	A-Square
465 Solid	FL		2400	5950	A-Square factory load

458 Canadian Magnum

Historical Notes North American Shooting Systems (NASS) developed this cartridge in about 1994. This cartridge features a slightly rebated, rimless bottleneck case. Design intent was provision of maximum powder capacity in a standard action with minimal gunsmithing. (Without deepening the magazine well slightly, use of this cartridge usually reduces magazine capacity by one round.) Bolt face alteration is not necessary. Cartridge feeding and headspacing characteristics are improved. This particular cartridge is factory loaded to modest pressures to provide assurance of proper functioning in the hottest climes — a worthwhile consideration.

General Comments This cartridge takes advantage of the entire 3.65-inch magazine length of the long-action Remington M700 and similar rifles. This represents the maximum feasible bullet size for use in this beltless case — headspace control, while adequate, is marginal with such a narrow case shoulder (one would be well advised to avoid magnum-strength striker springs). Body diameter is significantly larger than the standard belted-magnum (0.544-inch versus 0.513-inch at the base). Rechambering of nominal belted magnums with the same bore diameter is generally quite simple, requiring no other rifle alterations. For any given case length, capacity is about 15 percent greater than can be achieved with the belted version. Body taper is minimal and the case shoulder is comparatively sharp. However, neck length is sufficiently generous to provide good bullet purchase for hunting ammunition.

458 Canadian Magnum Loading Data and Factory Ballistics

Bullet (grains/type)	Powder	Grains	Velocity	Energy	Source/Comments
500	IMR 4064	89.0	2360	6180	NASS/maximum
350	FL		2575	5150	NASS factory load

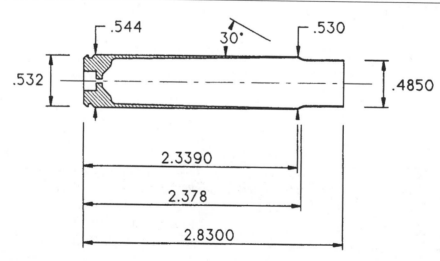

450 Dakota

Historical Notes Formerly, Dakota had based its entire cartridge line on the 404 Jeffery case. However, with the introduction of the 450 Dakota, that changed. Dakota's latest addition to its line, the 450 Dakota, uses an improved 416 Rigby case. Design purpose was to provide a cartridge capable of driving a 500-grain bullet at about 2400 fps with moderate chamber pressures.

General Comments Since the 450 Dakota uses an improved full-length 416 Rigby case, capacity is substantially identical to the 460 Weatherby Magnum. Obviously, if loaded to similar pressures, these two will produce similar ballistics. However, Dakota does not advocate loading this cartridge to full Weatherby pressures. The logic: By slightly reducing peak pressure, one can ease the effort of extracting a fired case. This approach also helps to minimize pressure excursions related to use under extreme tropical heat. Since that is what this cartridge was designed for, such an approach seems reasonable. When loaded to similar peak pressures, the 450 Dakota can propel a 500-grain bullet about 350 fps faster than the 458 Winchester Magnum. The nominal 450 Dakota loading gives up only about 150 fps to full-power 460 Weatherby loads. If one follows Dakota's advice, one ends up with a load propelling a 500-grain bullet at about 2450 fps. Most dangerous game experts agree that 2450 fps is nearly the perfect muzzle velocity for maximizing terminal performance with solid bullets. Because of its non-belted design, this cartridge offers superior functioning from a box magazine and can deliver superior accuracy. However, most would agree that recoil is a bit heavy for a day of shooting holes in paper targets.

450 Dakota Loading Data and Factory Ballistics

Bullet (grains/type)	Powder	Grains	Velocity	Energy	Source/Comments
400	RI-15	105.0	2732	6625	Dakota/maximum load
400	IMR 4064	105.0	2763	6775	Dakota/maximum load
400	IMR 4350	115.0	2650	6235	Dakota/maximum load
500	H4350	110.0	2460	6715	Dakota/maximum load
500	IMR 4350	110.0	2470	6770	Dakota/maximum load
500	IMR 4831	112.0	2444	6630	Dakota/maximum load
500	FL		2450	6663	Dakota factory load

460 A-Square Short

Historical Notes The A-Square series of cartridges was designed in 1974 by Col. Arthur Alphin in response to a hunting incident involving a Cape buffalo and a hunter equipped with a 458 Winchester Magnum. Alphin first designed the 500 A-Square with the purpose in mind of providing maximum stopping power. In order to gain more powder capacity and more power, all original A-Square cartridges were based upon the 460 Weatherby case. The A-Square Co. offers cases and loaded ammunition for each of its A-Square cartridges.

General Comments The 460 A-Square Short provides better ballistics than the 458 Winchester, but with the same length cartridge. It would be an excellent choice for rechambering a 458 Winchester. Aside from rechambering, this would require work on the magazine well and feed ramp as well as opening up the bolt face. This cartridge can easily push a 500-grain bullet at velocities of 2400 fps or more. The 460 Short is an efficient cartridge, as well as being a very accurate one. Groups tighter than 1 inch at 100 yards have been reported on numerous occasions.

460 A-Square Short Loading Data

Bullet (grains/type)	Powder	Grains	Velocity	Energy	Source/Comments
500 SP	IMR 4064	88.0	2385	6315	A-Square
500 SP	IMR 4895	91.0	2450	6670	A-Square
500 SP	IMR 4320	91.0	2435	6580	A-Square
500 SP	IMR 4320	91.0	2435	6580	A-Square

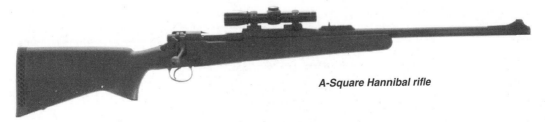

A-Square Hannibal rifle

475 Linebaugh

Historical Notes The 475 Linebaugh is the creation of John Linebaugh of Maryville, Mo. It is the current favorite in the contest to develop the world's most powerful revolver cartridge, a role that, at least at this writing, it fills rather well. The cartridge is based on the 45-70 government case cut off at 1-1/2 inches and loaded with 0.475-inch diameter bullets weighing from 320 to 440 grains. The gun used is a modified, large-frame Ruger Bisley revolver fitted with a five-shot cylinder and 5 1/2-inch barrel. Longer barrels are available if so desired. Freedom Arms now chambers this round.

Cutting 45-70 cases to a length of 1-1/2 inches is not a new idea — the author did this back in 1984 to make the 45 Silhouette, covered elsewhere in this chapter. However, adapting the 1 1/2-inch rimmed case to handle 47-caliber bullets is definitely an innovative move.

The 475 Linebaugh was first announced in an article written by Ross Seyfried in the May 1988 issue of *Guns & Ammo* magazine. Loading dies are available from RCBS.

General Comments The 475 Linebaugh, like all other super-magnum handgun cartridges, is intended primarily for hunting big game or as a backup when confronting dangerous animals. A 370-grain bullet starting out at 1495 fps develops 1840 foot-pounds of energy, and a 440-grain bullet at 1360 fps develops 1800 foot-pounds. This is 108 foot-pounds greater than top 454 Casull loadings, so we can accept the claim that the 475 Linebaugh is the world's most powerful revolver cartridge. However, other factors would probably make it even more effective, because the top energy load for the 454 Casull is a 260-grain bullet at 1723 fps muzzle velocity. If we compare the 300-grain 454 bullet at 1353 fps and 1220 foot-pounds with the 370-grain 475 bullet at 1495 fps and 1840 fpe, the difference is even more pronounced in favor of the 475. In fact, this works out to be 620 foot-pounds more energy on the side of the 475 Linebaugh. On the other hand, if we are talking about handgun cartridges in general, a number of silhouette cartridges fired in single-shot pistols produce more energy than the 475. In any event, the 475 Linebaugh should make a very fine big-game revolver cartridge for those who insist on the biggest or the most. Buffalo Bore (208-756-8085) now offers factory-loaded ammunition.

475 Linebaugh Loading Data and Factory Ballistics

Bullet (grains/type)	Powder	Grains	Velocity	Energy	Source/Comments
370 SP	W296	25.0	1000	825	John Linebaugh
370 SP	H110	29.0	1285	1360	John Linebaugh
370 SP	H110	33.0	1495	1840	John Linebaugh
440 SP	W296	27.0	1280	1605	John Linebaugh
440 SP	W296	29.0	1360	1800	John Linebaugh
420 LFN	FL		950	840	Buffalo Bore factory load
420 LFN	FL		1350	1695	Buffalo Bore factory load
420 WFN	FL		1350	1695	Buffalo Bore factory load
440 ExWN	FL		1300	1650	Buffalo Bore factory load
350 JHP	FL		1500	1745	Buffalo Bore factory load
400 JFN	FL		1400	1740	Buffalo Bore factory load

470 Capstick

Historical Notes This cartridge was designed by Col. Arthur B. Alphin and is named after the famous author and African big-game hunter, Peter Capstick. It delivers the maximum possible power from the 375 H&H Magnum case size while retaining the greater magazine capacity of the H&H over the Weatherby or Rigby cartridges. The 0.475-inch diameter bullets deliver much more shock than the 458-caliber cartridges. The 470 Capstick is designed for heavy game out to 200 yards and dangerous game at close ranges. Trajectory is flat enough to allow taking medium size game at ranges up to 250 yards.

General Comments The 470 Capstick was designed to deliver 500-grain bullets at a muzzle velocity of approximately 2400 fps. It offers a muzzle energy of 6394 foot-pounds and retains well over 5200 foot-pounds of energy at 100 yards. The 470 Capstick is nearly identical in dimensions to the 475 Ackley Magnum, designed quite a few years prior. Probably the most notable difference is the use of a 500-grain bullet in the 470 Capstick (as opposed to a 600-grain bullet), in order to obtain a flatter trajectory. Capstick was a legend in his own time and did much to promote African hunting. He certainly deserves to have a cartridge with his name on it.

470 Capstick Loading Data and Factory Ballistics

Bullet (grains/type)	Powder	Grains	Velocity	Energy	Source/Comments
500 Solid	H4895	85.0	2387	6325	A-Square/maximum load
500 Solid	Rl-12	89.5	2410	6450	A-Square/maximum load
500 Solid	IMR 4064	88.0	2404	6420	A-Square/maximum load
500 Solid	Rl-15	91.0	2385	6315	A-Square/maximum load
500	FL		2400	6400	A-Square factory load

475 JDJ

Historical Notes This cartridge was designed and developed by J.D. Jones, hence the JDJ designation on the cartridge. Jones began development of his series of cartridges in 1978. They are generally fired in barrels furnished by his company, SSK Industries. The purpose of these cartridges is to give added range and power to the Thompson/Center Contender pistol for the primary purpose of hunting. Some of Jones' cartridges have proven to be excellent metallic silhouette cartridges. The JDJ series is relatively simple and easy to make. All of the JDJ cartridges are proprietary and SSK neither sells reamers nor permits the reamer maker to sell them. If you desire a JDJ cartridge, contact SSK Industries, Wintersville, OH.

General Comments The 475 JDJ is the first 475 handgun cartridge. It is made by straightening out the tapered 45-70 Government case to a straight-wall configuration. This is easily done by expanding the neck and firing a 0.475-inch bullet. Cast bullets work very well in this cartridge and many good designs are available. Standard 0.475-inch rifle bullets will not expand reliably. However, a 0.475-inch-diameter, 500-grain bullet pushed at 1650 fps does expand. Big animals fall down quickly. Jones has taken several buffalo with the 475. When properly loaded, it is very impressive on animals in the 2000-pound category. It is noticeably more effective than the 45-70 Government when loaded correctly. Recoil exceeds what most shooters can tolerate. On deer, 400-grain Horrnady pistol bullets deliver excellent results.

475 JDJ Loading Data

Bullet (grains/type)	Powder	Grains	Velocity	Energy	Source/Comments
298-gr Cast	H322	54.0	Fire-forming	N/A	SSK Industries, Inc.
400-gr Hornady	2015BR	53.0	Not Specified	N/A	SSK Industries, Inc.
440-gr	H322	54.0	1727	N/A	SSK Industries, Inc.
500-gr Cast	IMR 3031	48.5	1338	N/A	SSK Industries, Inc.
500-gr Woodleigh	IMR 3031	48.5	1140	N/A	SSK Industries, Inc.

12.04 Bibamufu

Historical Notes Lazzeroni Arms designed this cartridge in 1999 at the request of Col. Craig Boddington. While somewhat related to an older case, for practical purposes this is a new case design. This cartridge was created to provide sufficient velocity for heavyweight hunting bullets to deliver significant doses of energy to the world's biggest and most dangerous game. Adaptation to standard actions is feasible but is not recommended.

General Comments Bullet diameter is 0.475-inch (Lazzeroni bases its designation on bullet diameter, instead of bore diameter, which is the common practice). Ballistics are impressive. Case design is typical of the Lazzeroni line: moderate body taper, 30-degree shoulder, sufficiently long neck, and thick rim of approximately case-body diameter. As produced, the case shoulder is sufficiently hard and thick to provide adequate headspace control. However, the margin of strength is small enough to suggest that one should not anneal these cases. Designed specifically for dangerous game hunting, this cartridge makes no sense for any other purpose. Recoil is significant by any measure. A 24-inch barrel is standard; adding a few inches of barrel length will not significantly improve ballistics. Muzzle energy exceeds 7505 foot-pounds. Ammunition is offered only as a special-order item and can be equipped with any bullet the customer desires.

12.04 Bibamufu Factory Ballistics (24-inch barrel)

Bullet (grains/type)	Powder	Grains	Velocity	Energy	Source/Comments
500	FL		2600	7505	Lazzeroni factory load

50 American Eagle

Historical Notes SSK Industries designed the 50 American Eagle for a single-shot M-16 rifle, used for suppressed applications. Barrels, dies, and cases for the 50 American Eagle are available from SSK Industries.

General Comments Using a 50-caliber, 650-grain projectile in Speer 50 AE cases opened to accept .510-inch bullets, the 50 American Eagle achieves about 1000 fps. Case heads are reduced in diameter to fit 7.62x39-sized bolt faces in the M-16. It is suitable for the Thompson/Center Encore, AR-15, bolt-action firearms and Ruger #1 rifles.

500 Whisper

Historical Notes Designed by J.D. Jones in 1993 at SSK Industries, this chambering is based upon a shortened 460 Weatherby Magnum case. Custom very low drag (VLD) bullets up to 900 grains have been tested. Design intent was to create a very hard-hitting subsonic round with superior penetration potential for use against lightly armored vehicles.

General Comments This is a very esoteric chambering. For proper use, it requires expensive custom bullets. Nevertheless, ballistic consistency and accuracy are impressive when launched at subsonic velocities (1040 fps is typical for the 500 Whisper). Typical heavy VLD bullets lose velocity so slowly that crosswinds have little effect, and retained energy exceeds one-half of muzzle energy well beyond one mile. Yes, such bullets will travel that far with exceedingly good accuracy!

500 Whisper Loading Data

Bullet (grains/type)	Powder	Grains	Velocity	Energy	Source/Comments
650-750	Vit N110	36.6	1050	1590/1835	SSK/Load must be tuned to individual gun

500 Linebaugh

Historical Notes The 500 Linebaugh is the design creation of John Linebaugh, Maryville, Mo. Linebaugh started out by converting a 45 Colt revolver from six-shot to five-shot, thus offering more strength in the cylinder. It was a successful venture, but he continued to search for a more powerful handgun. The result is the 500 Linebaugh. The 500 Linebaugh is based on the 348 Winchester cartridge, which is cut down to 1-1/2 inches and reamed to 50 caliber. He uses a large-frame Ruger Bisley revolver, as he has found the Ruger frame is the only one that can withstand the severe recoil of this cartridge. He replaces the Ruger barrel with one of 50-caliber, usually 5 1/2-inches long. However, he will cut a barrel of any length that the customer desires. The 500 proved to be a very successful round, pushing 500-grain bullets at more than 1200 fps. Accuracy is outstanding, but recoil can only be described as severe. Not long after Linebaugh designed this cartridge, the supply of 348 Winchester cases began to dry up, which is why he designed the 475 Linebaugh based on the readily available 45-70 Government case. Not long after the 475 was designed, Browning reintroduced its Model 1871 rifle in 348 Winchester, and those cases are again readily available.

General Comments There are more powerful pistol cartridges, but primarily for single-shot handguns such as the T/C Contender. When it comes to the revolver, this is close to the ultimate in power. Generally, in these revolvers, the 475 Linebaugh can safely be loaded to higher pressure and, therefore, can deliver more energy. Due to its accuracy and easy handling, this cartridge could prove to be an excellent heavy-game handgun cartridge and possibly a revolver cartridge suitable for taking African game. Specialized bullets are made by Golden Bear of San Jose, Calif. The jackets for these bullets are turned on a screw machine and a lead core is swaged in. I found these bullets excellent performers in terms of both accuracy and penetration. The 500 Linebaugh should find a strong following in the wilds of Alaska or the plains of Africa, where it could be used as a primary hunting gun or a backup. Buffalo Bore (208-756-8085) now offers factory-loaded ammunition.

500 Linebaugh Loading Data and Factory Ballistics

Bullet (grains/type)	Powder	Grains	Velocity	Energy	Source/Comments
400 Cast	H110	27.0	1200	1280	John Linebaugh
410 SP	H110	29.0	1250	1425	John Linebaugh
410 SP	H110	31.0	1320	1590	John Linebaugh
500 SP	FL		1200	1599	John Linebaugh
435 LFN	FL		950	870	Buffalo Bore factory load
435 LFN	FL		1300	1630	Buffalo Bore factory load
440 WFN	FL		1300	1650	Buffalo Bore factory load
400 JHP	FL		1400	1740	Buffalo Bore factory load

495 A-Square

Historical Notes The A-Square series of cartridges was designed in 1974 by Col. Arthur Alphin as a result of a hunting incident with Cape buffalo using the 458 Winchester Magnum. Alphin first designed the 500 A-Square to provide maximum stopping power. In order to gain more powder capacity and more power, all original A-Square cartridges were based on the 460 Weatherby case. The A-Square Co. offers cases and loaded ammunition for each of the A-Square cartridges.

General Comments The 495 A-Square was designed to push 600-grain, 0.510-inch bullets from a cartridge, which could be used in 375 Magnum-length actions. Though the 495 A-Square may not have as much energy as the 460 Weatherby, it does have the advantage of a larger diameter bullet. For a 50-caliber cartridge, recoil is reported as relatively low. It has also been reported that this cartridge does well with cast bullets.

495 A-Square Loading Data

Bullet (grains/type)	Powder	Grains	Velocity	Energy	Source/Comments
600 SP	IMR 4895	100.0	2275	6890	A-Square
600 SP	IMR 4320	103.0	2280	6925	A-Square

50 Beowulf

Historical Notes In 1999, Bill Alexander (Alexander Arms) designed the 50 Beowulf to be the biggest possible cartridge that could be chambered in the AR-15 family of rifles and carbines. No contemporary cartridges existed when Bill reworked the 50 AE parent cartridge case, extended it slightly and rebating the rim to fit an AR-15 bolt face. For close range and brush hunting, the 50 Beowulf is superbly suited for wild hogs and even larger game. Over 5000 rifles have been chambered for the 50 Beowulf.

General Comments The 50 Beowulf delivers exceptional stopping power at short-to-medium ranges using 1/2-inch diameter bullets, ranging in weight from 325 grains to 400 grains at velocities from 1900 to 2050 feet per second. The 50 Beowulf shares the .445-inch case rim dimension with the military 7.63x39 cartridge case. Seven cartridges will fit into an Alexander Arms-supplied magazine dimensioned to fit into the magazine well in the AR15's lower receiver. The cartridge performs well in a 16-inch barrel using a 1:19 twist. Factory loads do not exceed 33,000 psi. Alexander Arms supplies rifles, magazines, ammunition, reloading dies and brass.

50 Beowulf Factory Ballistics

Bullet (grains/type)	Powder	Grains	Velocity	Energy	Source/Comments
300-gr Gold Dot	FL		1900		Alexander Arms
325-gr Unicor	FL		1950		Alexander Arms
334-gr HP	FL		1900		Alexander Arms
334-gr FMJ	FL		1900		Alexander Arms
400-gr SP	FL		1800		Alexander Arms

50 GI

Historical Notes Frustrated by laws in his native Denmark that banned 50-caliber handguns, Alex Zimmerman created the proprietary 50 GI cartridge in 2002 after moving to the United States a decade earlier. First seen publicly at the 2004 SHOT Show, the 50 GI cartridge is not a magnum cartridge. Zimmerman engineered a 1911-style pistol and 50 GI cartridge combination to achieve highly controllable knock-down power for self defense and IPSC shooting.

General Comments One 50 GI factory load drives a 300-grain bullet at 700-725 fps (translating into a 210 power factor) with felt recoil comparable to a 230-grain 45 ACP hardball round. For serious stopping power, a second factory load drives a 275-grain bullet at 875 fps with felt recoil similar to a 10mm. With hotter loads, the 50 GI is suitable for feral hog and deer hunting at moderate ranges. To fit 1911 frames and slides, the 50 GI cartridge features a 45 ACP base and rim on a proprietary cartridge case manufactured by Starline. This feature allows the use of a standard 45 breech face, extractor and ejector on 1911-style pistols. Changing a Guncrafters Industries 50 GI-chambered pistol to 45 ACP requires only a different barrel and magazine. A firm taper crimp must be applied when reloading the 50 GI, and finished cartridges should measure .5235/.5240-inch at the case mouth. Guncrafter Industries offers 1911-type pistols, ammo, empty cases, reloading dies and magazines for the 50 GI cartridge. Hornady and Lee sell reloading dies.

50 GI Loading Data

Bullet (grains/type)	Powder	Grains	Velocity	Energy	Source/Comments
275-gr GI HP (copper clad)	Herco	8.0	875		Factory Load
300-gr GI FP (copper clad)	Titegroup	5.1	700		Factory Load
300-gr IMI JHP	Titegroup	5.9	800		OAL 1.220 "
240-gr Lead SWC	VV N310	4.4	750		OAL 1.230 "
300-gr Speer TMJ	Herco	8.0	875		OAL 1.220 "

500 Wyoming Express

Historical Notes This large capacity revolver cartridge was introduced in 2005 by Freedom Arms to be chambered in the FA Model 83 single-action revolver. The 1.370-inch case is belted to provide reliable headspacing in the Model 83 revolver. Freedom Arms designed the case to minimize forcing cone erosion by matching powder column length, volume and bullet diameter with bullet weights, pressure levels and velocity ranges.

General Comments Case shortening and slight belt expansion is normal with maximum loads. Tests show as much as 0.002-inch expansion on the first firing with much less expansion on subsequent firings for a total expansion of about 0.003-inch after 10 firings with the case still usable. More than 0.004-inch expansion may render the case unusable because of interference between the belt and chamber headspace area. This cartridge was designed to use bullets weighing from 350 to 450 grains. Freedom Arms does not recommend using bullets outside this weight range. Maximum loads should not be exceeded because small increases in the powder charge can cause a dramatic increase in chamber pressure. Powder charges in reduced loads should not be below 90 percent of case capacity. The 500 WE is designed to use a Large Rifle primer for reliable and consistent ignition.

500 Wyoming Express Loading Data

Bullet (grains/type)	Powder	Grains	Velocity	Energy	Source/Comments
350 XTP	TrailBoss	10.0	831	537	Freedom Arms
370WFNGC	Li'lGun	31.0	1528	1918	Freedom Arms
370WFNGC	H4227	34.0	1535	1936	Freedom Arms
370WFNGC	H110	36.0	1607	2122	Freedom Arms
400WFNGC	Li'lGun	31.0	1565	2175	Freedom Arms
400WFNGC	H4227	33.0	1509	2022	Freedom Arms
400FWNGC	H110	34.5	1589	2242	Freedom Arms
440WFNGC	Li'lGun	28.0	1450	2054	Freedom Arms
440WFNGC	H4227	30.0	1413	1951	Freedom Arms
440FWNGC	H110	29.5	1415	1956	Freedom Arms

500 Phantom

Historical Notes In 2005, Marty der Weeme (Teppo Jetsu, LLC) and Garber Supply Co. jointly created the 500 Phantom—specifically for AR-10 firearms. The 500 Phantom is the largest cartridge case that will function through the AR-10 action. The case design accommodates a wide range of 50-caliber bullet weights, including match-grade projectiles and smaller calibers in sabots. It produces velocity levels varying from 2000 fps to subsonic. The 500 Phantom is intended for law enforcement and special operations applications.

General Comments The 500 Phantom cartridge uses a special 50-caliber non-belted short magnum brass case manufactured by Garber Supply Company, with a rebated head and strengthened web for the higher operating pressures. Factory boltfaces for WSM or RSAUM cases readily accept the 500 Phantom cartridge case. Remarkably, unmodified 308 Winchester magazines can accept eight 500 Phantom rounds, and AR-10 lower receivers require no modification. Suitable firearms for the 500 Phantom include the AR-10 and DPMS LR-308 rifles. Teppo Jutsu LLC offers AR-10 upper receivers and information on the 500 Phantom. Both Quality Cartridge and Reed's Ammunition & Research sell loaded ammunition. New brass and loading data are available from Garber Supply Co.

500 Phantom Factory Ballistics

Bullet (grains/type)	Powder	Grains	Velocity	Energy	Source/Comments
525-gr. Barnes RN	FL		2,000	4,664	Teppo Jutsu LLC
750-grHornadyA-Max	FL		1040	1802	Teppo Jutsu LLC

500 A-Square

Historical Notes The A-Square series of cartridges was designed in 1974 by Col. Arthur Alphin after a hunting incident with Cape buffalo using the 458 Winchester Magnum. Alphin first designed the 500 A-Square to provide maximum stopping power. In order to gain more powder capacity and more power, all original A-Square cartridges were based on the 460 Weatherby case. A-Square Co. of Bedford, Ky., offers cases and loaded ammunition for each of the A-Square cartridges.

General Comments The 500 A-Square requires a long magazine (3.77 inches, same as a 416 Rigby and 460 Weatherby). This cartridge delivers high energy and stopping power from a bolt-action rifle. This was Alphin's first design in 1974 and is based on the 460 Weatherby cartridge necked-up and blown out. Alphin reports that this cartridge is the backbone and main reason for the formation of the A-Square Co. in 1979. In addition to custom rifles made for this caliber, A-Square makes its own rifles so chambered. The 500 A-Square is an excellent choice for a backup rifle and has stopping power about equal to the 577 Nitro Express. Naturally, recoil from this dangerous-game cartridge can be extremely heavy.

500 A-Square Loading Data

Bullet (grains/type)	Powder	Grains	Velocity	Energy	Source/Comments
600 SP	IMR 4320	116.5	2475	8155	A-Square

50 Peacekeeper

Historical Notes This cartridge was designed by J.D. Jones at SSK Industries in 1999. This is simply the 460 Weatherby Magnum necked up to 50-caliber with no other changes. Therefore, this is nothing new—this case is essentially identical to the 500 A-Square. What is unique about the 50 Peacekeeper is the loads used and the intended purpose. This combination is specifically designed to launch heavy, long-range match bullets from highly accurate rifles of moderate weight. It is intended to compete directly with the various 30-pound class 50 BMG-chambered rifles. Fired from a rifle of about one-half that weight, recoil energy is similar—bullets are launched at somewhat less velocity using much less powder.

General Comments Muzzle ballistics are sufficient to suggest that this number is worth considering for those who believe they need a 50 BMG-class rifle. Several rifles will easily handle this cartridge in single-shot mode: Ruger M-77 Magnum, Sako large action, Weatherby large action, Ed Brown action, and Prairie Gun Works' new action (which will also feed this round from the magazine). The 50 Peacekeeper can be chambered in the large Sako action.

50 Peacekeeper Loading Data (23-inch barrel)

Bullet (grains/type)	Powder	Grains	Velocity	Energy	Source/Comments
650 Ball	H335	108	2350	7975	SSK/maximum load
700 AP	AA 2700	117	2200	7525	SSK/maximum load
750 A-Max	AA 2520	105	2205	8100	SSK/maximum load

510 Whisper

Historical Notes Created by J. D. Jones, the 510 Whisper, like all other Whisper cartridges, must be capable of subsonic extreme accuracy with very heavy bullets, while maintaining excellent accuracy with light bullets at moderate to high velocity. Barrels, dies, and cases for the 510 Whisper are available from SSK Industries.

General Comments Using a 338 Lapua case shortened to 1.875 inches and necked up to 50-caliber, the 510 Whisper launches a 750-grain Hornady A-Max projectile at just under 1050 fps. The case neck is turned for accuracy and to create a shoulder for headspacing. SSK testing in suppressed, re-barreled SAKO TRG-s rifles achieved MOA accuracy at 600 yards with occasional groups of .5 MOA.

577 Tyrannosaur

Historical Notes This entirely new cartridge was designed in 1993 in response to the demands of two professional African hunting guides who had bad experiences with lesser chamberings as backup guns when clients were hunting dangerous species. There is no secret to the design: This is the longest, largest-diameter case that will properly function through a standard-size, bolt-action rifle. Bullet diameter is limited by the necessity of a sufficient case shoulder to control headspace. Design pressure assures proper functioning even in the hottest climes and will not overstress the action.

General Comments When loaded to 30-30 Winchester pressure levels, this cartridge can develop 10,000 foot-pounds of muzzle energy. When chambered in a 13-pound rifle with a properly designed stock containing three mercury recoil suppressers, recoil of the 577 Tyrannosaur is claimed to be less punishing than Weatherby's Mark V chambered for the much less powerful 460 WM. Nevertheless, by no means should one call this a mildly recoiling combination. However, for those who are looking for the ultimate in affordable repeating-rifle firepower, the 577 is the factory option of choice. Case capacity is on par with the 600 N.E.

For those who can handle the recoil generated, this likely is the best factory option for dangerous game hunting. Price is also a consideration. Compared to purchasing a typical top-quality, big-bore British double rifle, one could buy several 577 Tyrannosaurs, a lifetime supply of 577 ammunition and a new 4x4 pickup to haul the lot around in—with considerable leftover change!

577 Tyrannosaur Loading Data and Factory Ballistics

Bullet (grains/type)	Powder	Grains	Velocity	Energy	Source/Comments
750 Monolithic Solid	Rl-19	177.5	2473	10,180	A-Square/max. load
750 Monolithic Solid	FL		2400	9590	A-Square factory load

600/577 JDJ

Historical Notes Long considered the epitome of big-bore elephant cartridges, the 577 Nitro Express was chambered by premier English gun-makers in top end double rifles. The 600/577 JDJ, as crafted by SSK Industries, expands the 577 Nitro case to a straight taper to accept .620-inch diameter bullets. Barrels, dies, and cases for the 600/577 JDJ are available from SSK Industries.

General Comments The 600/577 JDJ fires a 900-grain bullet at approximately 1800 fps. Muzzle brakes and hydraulic counter-coil recoil-reducing devices are highly recommended in this caliber. It can be chambered in suitably converted Ruger #1 rifles. The ATFE does not classify this cartridge as a destructive device.

700 JDJ

Historical Notes Prolific cartridge designer J. D. Jones created the 700 JDJ in 1995. Using a 50-caliber BMG case necked up to 70-caliber, the 700 JDJ launches an 1100-grain projectile at about 2200 fps. Barrels, dies, and cases for the 700 JDJ are available from SSK Industries.

General Comments The 700 JDJ is still in production and can be chambered in any action suitable for the 50 BMG cartridge. SSK Industries uses special-order Krieger barrels for the 700 JDJ. The ATFE does not classify this cartridge as a destructive device.

950 JDJ

Historical Notes At 95-caliber, this cartridge defines the upper limit of rifle cartridges. As its creator, J. D. Jones, describes the 950 JDJ—it is not for the faint of heart, nor the financially-challenged shooter. The cartridge is based on the 20mm Vulcan case fired in rotary barrel cannon on U.S. Air Force fighter aircraft. Using a shortened, bottlenecked 20mm case, the 950 JDJ launches a 3600-grain projectile at approximately 2200 fps.

General Comments Developed in 1996, the 950 JDJ is no longer in production. SSK Industries developed a few custom rifles in the chambering, using super-sized McMillan single-shot rifles and Krieger special-order barrels. When completed, these bolt-action rifles looked like 50-caliber rifles on steroids, weighing between 100 and 110 pounds. The muzzlebrake alone weighed about 18 pounds, but even so, recoil was brisk. Cartridges cost about $30.00 each (*2002 figures*). The ATFE does not classify this cartridge as a destructive device.

Proprietary Cartridges Rifle & Handgun Dimensional Data

Cartridge	Case Type	Bullet Dia.	Neck Dia.	Shoulder Dia.	Base Dia.	Rim Dia.	Rim Thick.	Case Length	Ctge. Length	Twist	Primer
226 JDJ	A	.224	.256	.410	.419	.467	.045	1.93	V	9	L
224 Weatherby Magnum	E	.224	.247	.405	.413	.425	.045	1.92	2.44	14	L
6mm JDJ	**A**	**.243**	**.272**	**.415**	**.421**	**.470**	**.045**	**1.905**	**2.65**	**V**	**L**
240 Weatherby Magnum	E	.243	.271	.432	.453	.473	.045	2.50	3.06	10	L
6.17 Spitfire	C	.243	.275	.510	.530	.530	.050	2.05	2.8	10	L
6.17 Flash	C	.243	.275	.510	.530	.530	.050	2.80	3.55	12	L
257 JDJ	**A**	**.257**	**.288**	**.415**	**.421**	**.473**	**.045**	**1.905**	**2.81**	**V**	**L**
257 Mini Dreadnaught	G	.257	.290	.425	.445	.467	.045	2.145	V	10	L
257 Weatherby Magnum	E	.257	.285	.490	.511	.530	.048	2.55	3.25	12	L
6.53 Scramjet	**C**	**.257**	**.289**	**.510**	**.530**	**.530**	**.055**	**2.80**	**3.575**	**12**	**L**
6.5mm Whisper	C	.264	.286	.357	.372	.375	.041	1.36	V	V	S
6.5mm JDJ	A	.264	.293	.410	.419	.467	.045	1.93	V	8-9	L
6.5mm JDJx30	A	.264	.285	.409	.419	.497	.058	2.03	V	9	L
6.5 Mini Dreadnaught	G	.263	.296	.425	.445	.467	.045	2.150	V	8-9	L
6.5mm JDJ #2	A	.264	.292	.450	.466	.502	.059	2.00	V	9	L
6.71 Phantom	C	.264	.297	.510	.530	.530	.055	2.05	2.8	10	L
6.71 Blackbird	C	.264	.297	.524	.544	.544	.055	2.80	3.575	10-12	L
270 JDJ	**A**	**.277**	**.305**	**.415**	**.419**	**.467**	**.045**	**1.905**	**2.875**	**10**	**L**
270 Weatherby Magnum	E	.277	.305	.490	.511	.530	.048	2.55	3.25	12	L
7mm Whisper	**C**	**.284**	**.306**	**.357**	**.372**	**.375**	**.041**	**1.36**	**V**	**V**	**S**
7mm JDJ	A	.284	.312	.415	.421	.473	.045	1.905	V	9	L
7mm-30 JDJ	A	.284	.306	.409	.419	.497	.058	2.03	V	9	L
7mm JDJ #2	A	.284	.313	.450	.466	.502	.059	2.00	V	9	L
280 JDJ	C	.284	.312	.455	.470	.467	.045	2.505	V	10	L
7.21 Tomahawk	C	.284	.318	.557	.577	.577	.060	2.05	2.80	10	L
7mm Dakota	C	.284	.314	.531	.544	.544	.042	2.50	3.33	10	L
7mm Canadian Magnum	I	.284	.322	.530	.544	.532	.046	2.83	3.60	9-12	L
7.21 Firehawk	C	.284	.318	.524	.544	.544	.055	2.80	3.55	12	L
7.21 Firebird	C	.284	.318	.557	.577	.577	.060	2.80	3.6	12	L
7.62 Micro-Whisper	**C**	**.308**	**.328**	**.382**	**.389**	**.392**	**.045**	**.846**	**V**	**V**	**SP/S**
7.63 Mini-Whisper	C	.308	.329	.375	.381	.385	.045	.985	V	V	SP/S
300 Whisper	C	.308	.330	.369	.375	.375	.041	1.50	2.575	V	S
309 JDJ	A	.308	.335	.453	.470	.514	.058	2.20	3.16	?	L
30 06 JDJ	C	.308	.335	.455	.470	.467	.045	2.455	V	10	L
308 Cor-Bon	C	.308	.333	.532	.545	.532	.050	2.08	2.80	10	L
7.82 Patriot	C	.308	.340	.557	.577	.577	.060	2.05	2.8	12	L
300 Dakota	C	.308	.338	.531	.544	.544	.046	2.55	3.33	10	L
300 Canadian Magnum	I	.308	.342	.530	.544	.532	.046	2.83	3.60	10	L
300 Pegasus	C	.308	.339	.566	.580	.580	.058	2.99	3.75	10	L
30-378 Wby Magnum	K	.308	.330	.560	.589	.603/.580∂	.060	2.90	3.865	10	L
7.82 Warbird	C	.308	.340	.557	.577	.577	.060	2.80	3.60	14	L
8mm JDJ	A	.323	.356	.455	.470	.514	.058	2.22	V	?	L
338 Whisper	**C**	**.338**	**.360**	**.457**	**.463**	**.466**	**.048**	**1.47**	**V**	**V**	**S**
338 JDJ	A	.338	.365	.453	.470	.514	.058	2.20	V	?	L
338-06	C	.338	.369	.441	.471	.473	.045	2.494	3.34	10	L
338-06 JDJ	C	.338	.370	.455	.470	.467	.045	2.465	V	10	L
8.59 Galaxy	C	.338	.368	.557	.577	.577	.060	2.05	2.80	12	L
330 Dakota	C	.338	.371	.530	.544	.544	.045	2.57	3.32	10	L
340 Weatherby Magnum	E	.338	.366	.495	.513	.530	.048	2.82	3.60	12	L
338 Canadian Magnum	I	.338	.369	.530	.544	.532	.046	2.83	3.60	10-12	L
338 A-Square	K	.338	.367	.553	.582	.603/.580∂	.060	2.85	3.67	10	L
338-378 KT	K	.338	.362	.560	.603	.603/.580∂	.060	2.90	3.865	10	L
338 Excaliber	C	.338	.371	.566	.580	.580	.058	2.99	3.75	10	L
8.59 Titan	C	.338	.369	.557	.577	.577	.060	2.80	3.60	14	L

Cartridge	Case Type	Bullet Dia.	Neck Dia.	Shoulder Dia.	Base Dia.	Rim Dia.	Rim Thick.	Case Length	Ctge. Length	Twist	Primer
358 JDJ	**A**	**.358**	**.362**	**.453**	**.470**	**.514**	**.058**	**.220**	**3.065**	**?**	**L**
35-06 JDJ	C	.358	.385	.455	.470	.467	.045	2.445	V	10	L
9.09 Eagle	C	.358	.387	.557	.577	.577	.060	2.05	2.80	12	L
358 STA	E	.358	.386	.502	.513	.532	.048	2.85	3.65	12	L
9.3mm JDJ	A	.366	.389	.455	.465	.506	.058	2.22	V	?	L
375 JDJ	**A**	**.375**	**.396**	**.453**	**.470**	**.514**	**.058**	**2.20**	**3.13**	**?**	**L**
375-06 JDJ	C	.375	.405	.457	.470	.467	.045	2.435	V	12	L
9.53 Hellcat	C	.375	.404	.557	.577	.577	.060	2.05	2.80	10	L
375 JRS	E	.375	.498	.485	.535	?	.048	2.84	3.69	12	L
375 Dakota	C	.375	.402	.529	.544	.544	.046	2.57	3.32	10	L
375 Canadian Magnum	I	.375	.402	.530	.544	.532	.046	2.83	3.60	10	L
375 A-Square	K	.375	.405	.551	.582	.603/.580∂	.060	2.85	3.65	10	L
378 Weatherby Magnum	K	.375	.403	.560	.584	.603/.580∂	.062	2.92	3.69	12	L
9.53 Saturn	C	.375	.404	.557	.577	.577	.060	2.80	3.60	14	L
400 Cor-Bon	**C**	**.401**	**.423**	**.469**	**.470**	**.471**	**.050**	**.898**	**1.20**	**16**	**LP**
401 Powermag	B	.401	.425		.426	.483		1.29	1.64	18	LP
40-44 Woodswalker	A	.401	.428	.455	.455	.510	.055	1.295	V	14-18	LP
40-454 JDJ	A	.401	.428	.470	.470	.510	.055	1.395	V	14-18	LP
411 JDJ	A	.411	.425	.455	.465	.506	.058	2.235	V	?	L
416 JDJ	**A**	**.416**	**.430**	**.455**	**.465**	**.506**	**.058**	**2.22**	**V**	**?**	**L**
416-06 JDJ	C	.416	.443	.455	.470	.467	.045	2.415	V	16	L
416 Taylor	E	.416	.447	.491	.513	.532	.048	2.50	3.34	10	L
10.57 Maverick	C	.416	.445	.557	.577	.577	.060	2.05	2.80	14	L
416 Hoffman	E	.416	.447	.491	.513	.532	.048	2.85	3.60	10	L
416 Rimmed	A	.416	.446	.549	.573	.665	.060	3.300	4.100	10	L
416 Dakota	C	.416	.441	.527	.544	.544	.042	2.85	3.645	10	L
416 Weatherby	K	.416	.444	.561	.584	.603/.580∂	.062	2.915	3.75	14	L
10.57 Meteor	C	.416	.445	.557	.577	.577	.060	2.80	3.62	14	L
425 Express	**E**	**.423**	**.429**	**.490**	**.513**	**.532**	**.048**	**2.552**	**3.34**	**10**	**L**
440 Cor-Bon	I	.429	.461	.529	.538	.510	.055	1.280	1.59	18	LP
458 Whisper	**F**	**.458**	**.485**		**.506**	**.525**	**.048**	**1.75**	**V**	**V**	**L**
458 Lott	F	.458	.481		.513	.532	.048	2.80	3.60	10	L
458 Canadian Magnum	I	.458	.485	.530	.544	.532	.046	2.83	3.60	10	L
450 Dakota	C	.458	.485	.560	.582	.580	.058	2.90	3.74	10	L
450 Assegai	A	.458	.487	.549	.573	.665	.060	3.300	4.100	14	L
450 Ackley Magnum	E	.458	.487	.503	.512	.532	.048	2.85	3.65	10	L
460 A-Square	K	.458	.484	.560	.582	.603/.580∂	.060	2.50	3.50	10	L
460 Weatherby Magnum	K	.458	.485	.560	.584	.603/.580∂	.062	2.91	3.75	14	L
475 Linebaugh	**B**	**.475**	**.495**		**.501**	**.600**	**.065**	**1.50**	**1.77**	**?**	**L**
470 Capstick	F	.475	.499		.513	.532	.048	2.85	3.65	10	L
475 JDJ	B	.475	.497		.502	.604	.065	2.10	V	14	L
12.04 Bibamufu	C	.475	.500	.557	.577	.577	.060	2.80	3.62	16	L
500 Linebaugh	**B**	**.510**	**.540**		**.553**	**.610**	**.062**	**1.405**	**1.755**	**?**	**L**
495 A-Square	L	.510	.542		.582	.603/.580∂	.060	2.80	3.60	10	L
500 Whisper	K	.510	.549	.563	.580	.603/.580∂	.060	2.90	V	V	L
500 A-Square	K	.510	.536	.568	.582	.603/.580∂	.060	2.90	3.74	10	L
50 Peacekeeper	K	.510	.538	.565	.586	.603/.580∂	.058	2.882	V	15	L
577 Tyrannosaur	**C**	**.585**	**.614**	**.673**	**.688**	**.688**	**.060**	**2.99**	**3.71**	**12**	**L**

Case Type: A = Rimmed, bottleneck. B = Rimmed, straight. C = Rimless, bottleneck. D = Rimless, straight. E = Belted, bottleneck. F = Belted, straight. G = Semi-rimmed, bottleneck. H = Semi-rimmed, straight. I = Rebated, bottleneck. J = Rebated, straight. K = Rebated, belted bottleneck L = Rebated, belted straight.

Primer Type: S = Small rifle (0.175"). SP = Small pistol (0.175"). L = Large rifle (0.210"). LP = Large pistol (0.210"). B-1 = Berdan #1. B-2 = Berdan #2.

Other codes: V = OAL depends upon bullet used. V = Rifling twist varies, depending upon bullet and application. ∂ = Belt/Rim Diameter. Unless otherwise noted, all dimensions in inches. Twist (factory) is given as inches of barrel length per complete revolution, e.g., 12 = 1 turn in 12", etc.

Chapter 6

Handgun Cartridges of the World

(Current & Obsolete—Blackpowder & Smokeless Powder)

IT CAN be stated unequivocally that the United States is the only country where the handgun has developed fully as a sporting arm and is used for hunting as well as various kinds of match and silhouette shooting.

This has had a profound effect on the development of handguns and handgun cartridges in America. Shortly after World War II, for instance, there was renewed interest in the single-action revolver. This resulted in the introduction of new single-action models by Sturm, Ruger & Co. In turn, it became profitable for Colt to reintroduce its single-action revolver, which had been considered obsolete. Now Ruger and several other manufacturers and importers continue the single-action tradition. Handgun hunting was responsible for new cartridges designed primarily for field use, such as the 22 Remington Jet, 221 Remington Fireball, 44 Magnum, 454 Casull, 475 Linebaugh and 500 Linebaugh. The increasing popularity of silhouette pistol competition has given rise to specialized types of handguns designed particularly for this sport, such as the Thompson/Center Contender, Wichita Silhouette Pistol, Merrill Sportsman (now the RPM) and a number of custom handguns based on the Remington XP-100 action and the 7mm BR Remington cartridge. Some of these silhouette pistols chamber cartridges that are suitable for varmint and big game hunting.

The sporting handgun is a uniquely American innovation. Using a handgun for hunting reduces the effective range to about 100 yards, depending on the skill of the shooter. However, it offers the advantages of lightness and easy portability, decided advantages in rough terrain or heavy brush.

Handguns are divided into several types, depending on intended use. Military and police handguns are designed for defensive use at short range. Typical bore sizes vary from 9mm to 45 caliber. The semi-automatic pistol is preferred by the world's military establishments, although the revolver is still used by some military police agencies. In recent years, police organizations in the United States have switched to the 9mm or 40 Auto, and in some instances, the 45 Automatic. Military and police handguns are usually of medium weight and have 3- to 5-inch barrels. Caliber is mostly 9mm, 40 and 45, as represented by the 9mm Luger, 40 S&W and 45 Automatic. Off-duty or special assignment police arms are usually lighter and have shorter barrels than standard arms.

Pocket-type self-defense handguns have generally been small, lightweight and of relatively small caliber, varying from 22 to 38. Some are well made and of good manufacture; others are inexpensive and of lesser quality. Today, the trend is toward pocket-type handguns chambered for cartridges that are more substantial. These high-end models are often of superior quality and capable of surprising accuracy and dependability.

Well-made "pocket" or self-defense handguns can be good small game and plinking guns. Handloading with hunting-type bullets will also help adapt these to field use. However, if one is buying a handgun primarily for hunting, it is better to choose one made for that purpose. Target pistols are characterized by adjustable target sights and usually a barrel of 6 inches or so in length. Match pistols often are so specialized as to be of little use for anything else.

Hunting handguns also tend to be specialized, due to the long barrel and heavy frame. Because most also have adjustable sights, these can be used for target shooting, too. Any handgun can be used for hunting small game at short ranges provided its user can hit with it. Serious hunting handguns vary in caliber from 22 to 50, depending on the game to be hunted. Magnum cartridges are preferred for big game. Some single-shot pistols such as the Thompson/Center Contender are chambered for rifle cartridges like the 30-30 and the 223 Remington.

Because handgun cartridges are limited in velocity, an important consideration is the type of bullet used. The semi-wadcutter, as designed by the late Elmer Keith, is probably the best type of cast-lead bullet. Some modern jacketed handgun bullets with a large area of exposed lead at the nose have also proven highly effective on lighter species. In competent and practiced hands, the 357 Magnum has given a good account of itself on deer-size animals and, in some cases, even larger quarry. One must realize that handgun cartridges used for big game deliver marginal ballistics for that purpose compared to high-powered rifle cartridges. Therefore, shooter skill is particularly critical.

Some handgun cartridges have also become popular as rifle cartridges. This includes the 357 and 44 Magnums as well as the venerable 44-40 Winchester and 45 Colt. These make a good combination for owners of handguns in these chamberings because standard factory ammunition can then be used interchangeably in rifles and pistols. However, some rifles can withstand much higher pressures than most handguns, and handloads that are safe in a rifle may wreck a handgun. Use caution and common sense when handloading.

Handgun cartridges are divided into three major types – those intended for automatic pistols, those to be used in revolvers and those for single-shot pistols. Those designed for automatic pistols are either rimless or semi-rimmed to facilitate feeding from the clip or magazine. Revolver cartridges are, in general, of rimmed construction, although some revolvers have been made to handle semi-rimmed or rimless cartridges such as the 32 Automatic, 30 Carbine, 9mm Luger, 380 Automatic and the 45 Automatic. Single-shot pistol cartridges are often bottlenecked rimmed or rimless. At one time, bullets intended for revolver cartridges were of lead and those for auto-pistol cartridges were jacketed to facilitate feeding. At present, it is common practice to use jacketed bullets in revolvers, particularly for hunting, although match shooters prefer light loads and lead bullets. Lead bullets are also used for target loads in pistols. Jacketed bullets were used in some military revolvers since before World War I because of international agreements.

Owing to limitations in design strength of typical revolvers and pistols, smokeless powder did not improve the performance of handgun cartridges to the extent that it did rifle cartridges. Consequently, blackpowder cartridges of medium to large caliber are almost as effective as modern non-magnum handgun cartridges. In fact, many modern handgun cartridges originated as blackpowder numbers, and their performance with smokeless powder is about the same as it was with the original blackpowder loading.

When selecting a handgun or handgun cartridge, give careful consideration to the gun's intended use. Most individuals have a tendency to overdo it regarding power, following the idea that bigger is better. While a few experts can achieve long-range hits, most handgun hunting is for small game or varmints at ranges of 50 yards or less. It takes a great deal of practice before one can hit a target with any consistency at 100 yards and beyond. Power will not compensate for poor marksmanship, so it is best to start with something you can handle and move up to a larger chambering after proficiency has improved. Remember that the average person must expend hundreds of rounds to develop proficiency with a 22 rimfire pistol, and it takes even more practice with larger chamberings.

The 22 Long Rifle rimfire is probably the most popular handgun cartridge, followed by the 38 Special and 9mm Luger among the centerfires. The 22 rimfire is adequate for small game at close ranges and can serve as a house gun for home protection. The 38 Special has the advantage of reloadability, and by choosing loads it is possible to regulate the power to cover shooting situations from very light target loads to full-power self-defense or field loads. For serious self-defense, the 38 Special and the 380 Automatic are considered minimum. The 38 Special and the 357 Magnum are probably the most widely used revolver cartridges, while the 9mm, 40 S&W and 45 Automatic are the most popular pistol cartridges. For match competition, the 22 rimfire, 38 Special and 45 Automatic may still lead the pack, although other centerfire numbers have recently made gains. — F.C.B.

Current Handgun Cartridges of the World

5.45x18mm Soviet

Historical Notes This modern pistol cartridge was developed in the Soviet Union in the 1970s for the PSM compact semi-automatic pistol. Its design follows Soviet tradition in that the case is bottlenecked and bullet caliber is the same as the service rifle (the 5.45mm AK-74). Case length and overall loaded length are similar to the 9mm Makarov cartridge, although the base and rim diameter of the 5.45x18mm Soviet is smaller. Thus far, Russia is the only country to have adopted this cartridge and the PSM pistol for it.

General Comments The concept behind this cartridge is unknown. By Western standards, this cartridge is a very poor choice for self-defense. Muzzle energy is about the same as the 22 Long Rifle. However, a key to its purpose may be bullet construction, which consists of a gilding metal jacket around a two-piece core consisting of steel front and lead rear halves. If penetration is the purpose, then this bullet should prove effective against body armor. Beyond this, it seems to have little value.

It is one of the few new cartridges to enter production in Russia for many years. Manufactured only in the Commonwealth of Independent States, cases are normally lacquered steel with a Berdan primer. Bullet diameter is about 0.210-inch.

5.45x18mm Soviet Factory Ballistics

Bullet (grains/type)	Powder	Grains	Velocity	Energy	Source/Comments
40 FMJ	FL		1034	95	Factory load

25 (6.35mm) Automatic (25 ACP)

Historical Notes This cartridge was introduced in the United States in 1908 with the Browning-designed, Colt-manufactured 25 Vest Pocket Automatic pistol. It was introduced in Europe a few years earlier in the F.N. Baby Browning, which is practically identical to the Colt. The design of these two pistols has been copied by manufacturers all over the world. Dozens of different pistols have used this cartridge. The original Browning is still made (for European consumption), but Colt did not resume manufacture of its Vest Pocket model after World War II. American Arms, Beretta, Iver Johnson, Jennings, Lorcin, Phoenix Arms, Sundance, Taurus, Ortgies, Astra, Star and Walther have all made pistols in this chambering.

General Comments The 25 Automatic offers surprising velocity for such a small cartridge. However, delivered energy is quite modest. This, combined with the full-metal jacketed bullet of the conventional load, adds up to very poor stopping or killing power on anything. Lighter, expanding bullets lack adequate penetration or delivered energy to suggest any significant improvement. The 25 Auto is not powerful enough for hunting anything but pests, nor is it adequate for serious self-defense. However, 25 Automatic pistols are popular because of their small size and low cost. Their principal usefulness might be as a threat, because no sane person wants to be shot if that can be avoided, not even with the little 25. Winchester and Hornady recently have offered hollowpoint loads in an effort to improve terminal ballistics.

Editor's Note: Three important facts are often overlooked when discussing the value of this cartridge. First, compared to any rimfire chambering, the 25 Automatic provides superior functioning in typical concealable pistols. Despite being very underpowered, well-placed shots from a 25 Auto do beat throwing rocks and will certainly disable or kill. Second, owing to a properly designed case and bullet, this cartridge is dramatically more dependable in a pocket pistol than any rimfire round. Finally, any functional gun that a person can and will carry and use correctly has significant defensive value.

25 (6.35mm) Automatic (25 Automatic) Loading Data and Factory Ballistics

Bullet (grains/type)	Powder	Grains	Velocity	Energy	Source/Comments
50 FMJ	Bullseye	1.2	810	73	Hornady, Sierra
45 JHP	FL		815	66	Factory load, Winchester new
50 FMJ			760	64	NA

25 North American Arms (NAA)

Historical Notes First developed in 1999 by Kentucky firearms writer J.B. Wood, the 25 NAA cartridge is a 32 ACP case necked to 25-caliber. Mr. Wood's goal was to increase reliable expansion of 25-caliber bullets when fired from a short-barreled handgun. The concept of bottleneck cases to drive smaller diameter bullets to greater speeds is more than a century old.

General Comments Fired in a re-barreled Savage model 1908 self-loading pistol with Hornady test ammo, bullet expansion ranged from .360- to .412-inch. With perceived recoil in the 22 Long Rifle range, the improved feeding of a bottleneck cartridge and consistent hollow-point bullet expansion, the North American Arms corporation decided to offer this chambering in its Guardian mini-pistol product line in 2002 or 2003. Cor-Bon will produce the ammo, which will probably bear a *Corbon 25 NAA* headstamp.

25 North American Arms Loading Data

Bullet (grains/type)	Powder	Grains	Velocity	Energy	Source/Comments
35 Hornady XTP	Herco	2.6	1050		Test Load by Hornady
Cor-Bon ballistics not available at press time					

7.62x25mm Russian Tokarev

Historical Notes The 7.62x25mm Tokarev was the official Soviet pistol cartridge adopted in 1930 for the Tokarev Model TT-30 and modified Model TT-33 automatic pistols. The pistols are a basic Browning-type design similar to the Colt 45 Auto pistol. However, these incorporate many original features, to simplify manufacturing processes, and must be considered an advance over Browning's original patented design. These pistols often have a crude finish, but are well made and of excellent design. These have a 4 1/2-inch barrel and a magazine capacity of eight rounds. Large quantities have been sold as military surplus. Some were made in Communist China and Hungary, as well as in Russia. The Hungarian-made Tokarev, in a modified form called the Tokagypt, is chambered for the 9mm Parabellum cartridge. The Chinese began exporting both pistols and ammunition to the United States in 1987 at very reasonable prices.

General Comments The cartridge is very similar in dimension to the 7.63mm (30) Mauser and most brands of Mauser ammunition can be fired in the Tokarev pistol. The 7.62mm Tokarev is a fair field cartridge for small game with good velocity and flat trajectory, but needs softpoint bullets for maximum effectiveness. The handloader can use loading data for the 7.63 Mauser. The Speer 30-caliber plinker bullet of 100 grains makes a good hunting bullet, but because it is slightly heavier than the standard weight, it must be loaded to lower velocity.

Chinese and Russian ammunition are steel-cased and Berdan-primed with corrosive primers. Such ammunition is not reloadable. Recently, Hansen Cartridge has imported quantities of 7.62x25mm ammunition with reloadable cases and non-corrosive Boxer primers.

7.62x25 Russian Tokarev Loading Data and Factory Ballistics

Bullet (grains/type)	Powder	Grains	Velocity	Energy	Source/Comments
86	Bullseye	5.0	1390	365	Duplicate factory ball
87 FMJ	FL		1390	365	Factory load

30 (7.65x21mm) Luger

Historical Notes Introduced in 1900 by Deutsche Waffen u. Munitions Fabriken in Germany, the 7.65mm was designed by Georg Luger for the Luger automatic pistol. The cartridge is still used chiefly in the Luger pistol, although some SIG, Beretta M951, Browning Hi-Power, Ruger P89 and Walther P-38 pistols are chambered for this round. It was adopted as standard issue by the Swiss, Brazilian, Bulgarian and Portuguese armies, but none of them currently issue it for front-line service.

General Comments This is another bottlenecked rimless cartridge, similar to the 30 Mauser, but shorter and not quite as powerful. It is not noted for great stopping power because of the small-diameter, lightweight, full-jacketed bullet. It is used occasionally for small game hunting and will do a fair job on rabbits and the like, provided the bullets are properly placed. The only manufacturer still offering this cartridge is Winchester. Bullet diameter is 0.308-inch.

30 (7.65x21mm, 7.65mm) Luger Loading Data and Factory Ballistics

Bullet (grains/type)	Powder	Grains	Velocity	Energy	Source/Comments
93	Unique	5.0	1115	257	Lyman duplication of factory ball loading
100	Unique	4.8	1210	325	Speer plinker
93 FMJ	FL		1220	305	Factory load

30 (7.63x25mm) Mauser

Historical Notes The 30 Mauser cartridge was developed by American gun designer Hugo Borchardt for the first successful commercial, automatic pistol of the same name. The Borchardt pistol was made by Ludwig Loewe & Co. (later DWM) of Berlin, Germany. Both pistol and cartridge were introduced in 1893. The Borchardt automatic pistol was later redesigned and emerged as the well-known Luger pistol. This cartridge was adopted by Paul Mauser for his famous Model 1896 pistol with increased power for his more rugged design. It has been used mainly in the Mauser M1896 military automatic pistol and various imitations or copies manufactured in Spain and China.

General Comments Until the 357 Magnum cartridge came along, the 30 Mauser was the high-velocity champion of the pistol world. It has a flat trajectory that makes long-range hits possible, but lacks stopping power because of the light, full-jacketed bullet. However, it has been used successfully for hunting small game and varmints at moderate ranges. Handloading with softpoint or hollowpoint hunting bullets improves performance considerably. At one time, both Remington and Winchester loaded this cartridge, but it has been dropped. Fresh supplies of this cartridge were recently imported from Portugal by Century International Arms.

30 (7.63x25mm) Mauser Loading Data and Factory Ballistics

Bullet (grains/type)	Powder	Grains	Velocity	Energy	Source/Comments
86 FMJ	Bullseye	4.5	1160	257	Lyman
86 FMJ	Unique	6.0	1230	289	Lyman
86 FMJ	FL		1410	375	Factory load

32 (7.65mm) Automatic/32 ACP

Historical Notes Designed by John Browning for his first successful automatic pistol, this cartridge was first manufactured by FN in Belgium, and introduced in 1899. It was marketed in the United States when Colt turned out a pocket automatic on another Browning patent in 1903. The 32 Automatic is one of the more popular pistol cartridges ever developed. In the United States, Colt, Remington, Harrington & Richardson, Smith & Wesson and Savage chambered pistols for this cartridge. In Europe, every company that made automatic pistols chambered the 32 ACP (Automatic Colt Pistol). It was also used in the German Pickert revolver. In Europe, it is known as the 7.65mm Browning, while in the United States it is designated 32 Automatic or 32 ACP.

General Comments This cartridge uses a semi-rimmed cartridge case and a 0.308-inch diameter bullet. The 32 Automatic is the minimum cartridge that can be seriously considered for self-

defense. In the United States, it is used exclusively for small pocket-type guns and is not considered adequate for police or military use. However, in Europe it is often used in police pistols and as an alternative but unofficial chambering for military sidearms. As a hunting cartridge, it is not powerful enough for anything larger than small game.

Loading tables generally give bullet diameter of the 32 Automatic as 0.312-inch or 0.314-inch. It is actually closer to 0.308-inch, and this is important if you handload. Effective small game loads can be made by using 100-grain 30-caliber rifle bullets intended for light loads and plinking, such as the Speer 30-caliber Plinker. All major ammunition makers offer this cartridge. Winchester recently introduced a load with a jacketed hollowpoint bullet. Other makers have followed suit.

32 (7.65mm) Automatic/32 ACP Loading Data and Factory Ballistics

Bullet (grains/type)	Powder	Grains	Velocity	Energy	Source/Comments
71 FMJ	Bullseye	2.2	800	100	Sierra, Hornady
71 FMJ	700X	2.0	850	114	Sierra, Hornady
60 JHP	FL		970	125	Winchester factory load
71 FMJ	FL		905	129	Factory load
74 FMJ/JSP	FL				Factory load, early

**Colt Model 1903
Pocket Hammerless**

32 Smith & Wesson

Historical Notes Designed for the Smith & Wesson Model 1 1/2, hinged-frame, single-action revolver introduced in 1878, the 32 S&W is an old and very popular cartridge, widely used in the United States and in Europe for low-priced, pocket-type revolvers. Originally a blackpowder cartridge, it has been loaded with smokeless powder exclusively since 1940. In the United States, Colt, Harrington & Richardson, Hopkins & Allen, Iver Johnson, Smith & Wesson and others have made revolvers for this cartridge. In England, Webley & Scott made revolvers for it and, elsewhere in Europe, the Bayard and Pickert revolvers chambered it. The original loading used 9 grains of blackpowder.

General Comments The 32 Smith & Wesson probably ranks with the 32 Automatic in general popularity, and for the same reason. It is low-powered and adaptable to small, light, inexpensive, pocket-type handguns. Ballistically it is not quite as good as the 32 Automatic. It is very similar to the 32 Short Colt, but the two are not interchangeable because of a difference in bullet and case diameter. Like the 32 Automatic, the 32 S&W is about the minimum cartridge for self-defense. It is considered inadequate for police work. It is used occasionally for hunting small game at very short ranges, but is too underpowered for consideration as a sporting cartridge. This ammunition is still available.

32 Smith & Wesson Loading Data and Factory Ballistics

Bullet (grains/type)	Powder	Grains	Velocity	Energy	Source/Comments
85 Lead	Bullseye	1.1	705	93	NA
85 Lead	Blackpowder (Fg)	9.0	680	90	Factory load
98 Lead	Smokeless powder		705	115	Factory load

32 Smith & Wesson Long
32 Colt New Police
32-44 Target

Historical Notes This cartridge was developed for the Smith & Wesson, First Model, solid-frame, hand-ejector revolver introduced in 1903. The same cartridge, loaded with a flatnose bullet, is called the 32 Colt New Police. Colt, Harrington & Richardson, Iver Johnson and Smith & Wesson were the principal companies making revolvers in this chambering in the United States. Many Spanish and other European revolvers such as the Bayard and Pickert chambered the round. In Europe, it had not been as widely used as the shorter 32 S&W until some ISU centerfire target shooters discovered the 32 S&W Long, and now there are several high-class European target autoloaders for the wadcutter loading of this cartridge.

General Comments The 32 S&W Long is the smallest revolver cartridge deemed adequate for police use in the United States, and it has been fairly popular with detectives or plainclothesmen. It has always been available in a variety of short, light, small-frame revolvers, some of which are very well made. It has a reputation for excellent accuracy and has been used for target and match shooting in the past as well as in ISU shooting. It is as accurate as the 38 S&W Special, but not as versatile. It is the minimum size for sporting use and with handloaded, hunting-type bullets it is quite effective on small game. It is not as popular or widely used for defense as it once was because of the development of compact 38-caliber revolvers. Its range and effectiveness can be increased by handloading. The original load was 13 grains of blackpowder and a 98-grain bullet.

32 Smith & Wesson Long Loading Data and Factory Ballistics

Bullet (grains/type)	Powder	Grains	Velocity	Energy	Source/Comments
90 Lead	700X	1.8	700	98	Hornady
98 Lead	Unique	1.8	665	96	Speer
98 Lead	Blackpowder (Fg)	13.0	780	132	Factory load
98 Wadcutter	Smokeless powder		705	115	Factory load

32 North American Arms (NAA)

Historical Notes Culminating a joint development effort between North American Arms and writer Ed Sanow, the 32 NAA uses an ordinary 380 ACP case, necked-down to house a 32-caliber bullet. In 2002, North American Arms decided to offer this chambering in its Guardian mini-pistol product line.

General Comments Behind the neck, all case dimensions and configurations, including the extractor groove, rimless case, cartridge diameter and bolt face engagement are identical to the 380 ACP. Cor-Bon produces the ammo, which will bear a *Cor-Bon 32 NAA* headstamp. The cartridge uses a proprietary bullet designed by Hornady.

32 North American Arms Factory Ballistics

Bullet (grains/type)	Powder	Grains	Velocity	Energy	Source/Comments
60 JHP	FL		1222	199	Cor-Bon factory load (2.5"bbl)

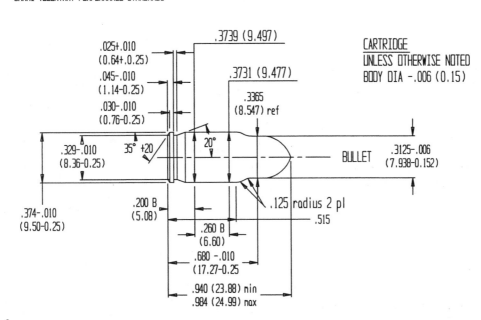

SECTION I – CHARACTERISTICS
CENTERFIRE PISTOL & REVOLVER
SAAMI VOLUNTARY PERFORMANCE STANDARDS

CARTRIDGE & CHAMBER
32 NAA AUTOMATIC

CARTRIDGE
UNLESS OTHERWISE NOTED
BODY DIA -.006 (0.15)

32 H&R Magnum

Historical Notes The 32 H&R Magnum was the result of a joint project between Harrington & Richardson and Federal Cartridge Co. It was introduced in 1984 for the five-shot H&R Model 504, 532 and 586 revolvers. This was followed later in the same year by Charter Arms with its six-shot 32 H&R Magnum Police Undercover revolver and in 1985 by the Ruger New Model 32 Magnum Single-Six and SP101 revolvers. The 32 H&R Magnum is simply the older 32 Smith & Wesson Long case lengthened by 0.155 inch. Therefore, any 32 Magnum revolver will also accept and fire both the 32 S&W and the 32 S&W Long. This makes for a convenient situation because the shooter has a choice of three different cartridges that will work in one handgun. Two loadings of the cartridge were offered — a lead semi-wadcutter bullet of 95 grains or an 85-grain jacketed hollowpoint.

General Comments According to factory ballistics, the 32 Magnum delivers double the energy of the 32 S&W Long and 13

percent more energy than the standard 38 Special load. However, chronograph tests demonstrated that actual velocity at the muzzle ranges 60 to 100 fps below factory-advertised figures. Nevertheless, the cartridge performance level is well above that of any other 32-caliber handgun cartridge currently available. The 32-20 can be handloaded to equal the 32 Magnum in a revolver, but new 32-20 revolvers have not been available since before World War II.

What kept H&R from chambering its revolvers for the 32-20? To do so would have required extensive design changes in its revolvers because the 32-20 is too long. In fact, 32-20 case length is nearly the same as 32 Magnum overall cartridge length.

By the late 1980s, both H&R and Charter Arms had gone out of business (both are again producing firearms, although H&R is not producing handguns as of 2000), leaving Ruger and Dan Wesson as the sole suppliers of revolvers in this chambering. Federal was the only ammunition maker to undertake production.

32 H&R Magnum Loading Data and Factory Ballistics

Bullet (grains/type)	Powder	Grains	Velocity	Energy	Source/Comments
85 JHP	Unique	4.0	900	153	Hornady
90 Lead	Unique	3.4	815	145	Hornady
98 Lead	Unique	3.0	815	145	Speer
85 JHP	FL		1100	230	Factory load
95 SWC Lead	FL		1030	225	Factory load

32-20 (32 Winchester)

General Comments Although designed as a rifle cartridge, the 32-20 became very popular as a revolver cartridge. Historical notes and comments will be found in Chapter 2: Current American Rifle Cartridges.

7.5mm Swiss Army Revolver

Historical Notes This cartridge was adopted by the Swiss Army in 1882 and officially used until 1903. The Swiss Army revolver is based on a modified Nagant system. In the early 1960s, quantities of these revolvers were sold in the American market by surplus dealers. These are quite well made and finished. Both blackpowder and smokeless powder ammunition is encountered.

General Comments The 7.5mm Swiss revolver cartridge is identical to and fully interchangeable with the 7.5mm Swedish and

Norwegian rounds. Modern smokeless powder ammunition was loaded by Norma for the Swedish Nagant, and this can be used in the Swiss revolver. The two cartridges differ only in bullet type. Most Swedish cartridges use an outside-lubricated bullet, whereas the Swiss also used an inside-lubricated type. Ballistics are about the same as the 32 S&W Long. For additional information, see the 7.5mm Swedish Nagant Revolver. Fiocchi now produces this ammunition.

7.5mm Swiss Army Factory Ballistics

Bullet (grains/type)	Powder	Grains	Velocity	Energy	Source/Comments
102-110 Lead	ML		700	115	Military load

8mm Rast-Gasser

Historical Notes The 8mm Rast-Gasser military cartridge was introduced in 1898 for the solid-frame Rast-Gasser military revolver patented in 1873. A number of different revolvers manufactured in Belgium and Germany chambered the round. Although popular in Europe, the 8mm Rast-Gasser was never manufactured in the United States. The round is obsolete and ammunition difficult to obtain.

General Comments The Gasser solid-frame revolver design is noted for simplicity of disassembly. It also has a rebounding hammer and a spring-mounted, separate firing pin. These are usually well made and rather sturdy. Quantities have been sold at various times in surplus stores.

The cartridge resembles the 8mm French Lebel Revolver round quite closely. Bullet diameter is 0.320-inch. Rim and body diameter are nearly identical to the 32 S&W Long. The 32 S&W case is shorter, but both cartridges are of approximately the same power. Lyman cast bullet No. 313445 (95 grains) can be adapted for handloading. Loading data for the 32 S&W can be used as a guide in working up loads. This ammunition is now offered by Fiocchi.

8mm Rast-Gasser Factory Ballistics

Bullet (grains/type)	Powder	Grains	Velocity	Energy	Source/Comments
115-126 Lead	FL		750 - 785	140 - 170	Factory load
125	FL		787	170	1914-1918 factory load
126 Lead	FL		770	166	Fiocchi factory load

8mm Lebel Revolver

Historical Notes This cartridge is for the French 1892 Ordnance Revolver, commonly called the Lebel. This is a six-shot, solid-frame, double-action gun. Bayard and Pieper also made revolvers in this chambering. Small lots have shown up in surplus stores, but these are of interest mostly to military collectors.

General Comments The 8mm Lebel revolver cartridge closely resembles the 32-20 WCF and ammunition can be made by sizing 32-20 cases. This is not a common item, but surplus stores have occasionally offered this ammunition. The 32 Smith & Wesson Long can be fired in these revolvers, but the cases bulge badly and accuracy is poor. When cooking up your own loads, stick to moderate charges and velocity, as the Lebel revolver is not designed for high pressures. For field use, this is another 32 S&W Long-class cartridge suitable only for small game. Bullet diameter is 0.330-inch and one can use the Lyman No. 32359 cast bullet. Fiocchi currently offers this ammunition.

8mm Lebel Revolver Loading Data and Factory Ballistics

Bullet (grains/type)	Powder	Grains	Velocity	Energy	Source/Comments
115 Lead	Bullseye	2.8	700	126	Lyman No. 32359
102 Lead	ML		625	104	Military load

8mm Roth-Steyr

Historical Notes The 8mm Roth-Steyr cartridge and auto pistol were adopted by the Austro-Hungarian cavalry in 1907. No other country or gun employed this cartridge. It was a popular post-World War II surplus item, all but unknown on the American market prior to the war. It is a recoil-operated pistol of rather odd appearance, resembling some modern air pistols.

General Comments The 8mm Roth-Steyr cartridge is similar to the 32 Automatic, but longer and more powerful. It would make a fair field cartridge for small game if loaded with hunting-type bullets. The Roth-Steyr pistol has a non-detachable magazine in the grip that holds 10 shots. As with most Austrian-designed auto pistols of the period, it is loaded by retracting the slide (bolt) and inserting a special charger from the top. It can be loaded without the charger, but this is rather slow and hard on the fingers. Fiocchi still manufactures this cartridge.

8mm Roth-Steyr Loading Data and Factory Ballistics

Bullet (grains/type)	Powder	Grains	Velocity	Energy	Source/Comments
116 Lead	Unique	3.3	1050	283	Lyman No. 313226
113 FMJ	FL		1070	287	Fiocchi factory load
116 FMJ	ML		1090	309	Military load

9mm Ultra

Historical Notes This cartridge was designed for the Walther PP Super semi-auto pistol introduced in 1972-73. This seven-shot autoloader was designed particularly for the West German police. This pistol was not available to the civilian market until 1975 and then only in small numbers. Quite a few guns in this chambering have shown up in the United States as the West German police discontinued using this chambering. In recent years, the Sig-Sauer P230 and the Benelli B76 auto pistols have also been chambered for the 9mm Ultra. The cartridge was actually developed in 1936 for the German Air Force, but was never officially adopted.

The 9mm Ultra is 1 mm longer than the 380 Auto and 1 mm shorter than the 9mm Luger, with the same general case dimensions. In terms of inches, the 380 case length is 0.680-inch, the 9mm Ultra is 0.720-inch and the 9mm Luger is 0.760-inch.

Original loading of the 9mm Ultra (by Hirtenberger of Austria) used a 100-grain full-jacketed bullet at a muzzle velocity of 1060 fps. GECO (Dynamit-Nobel) loads a 94-grain full-jacketed bullet at an initial velocity of 1054 fps. Both bullets are of truncated cone shape. Ammunition is hard to find in the United States, and

American companies do not load it. The case has a slightly rebated rim 0.020-inch smaller than the base.

General Comments European police have traditionally carried small 32 Automatic and 380 Automatic pistols. However, with the increase in crime and attacks by terrorist groups, they found themselves outgunned by those on the other side of the law. There was some reluctance to adopt the full-powered 9mm military auto-pistol, which is heavier and bulkier than the more convenient 32 and 380 autos. The 9mm Ultra was an effort to provide greater stopping power while retaining the small, handy pistols police were used to carrying. This was not successful and most German police now carry 9mm Luger-chambered pistols.

The best that can be said about the 9mm Ultra is that it is as good as and probably more effective than the 380 Automatic. Handloaded with 9mm jacketed hollowpoint bullets, it would certainly be satisfactory for small-game hunting. Hirtenberger, Fiocchi and Dynamit Nobel still offer this cartridge. It is sometimes called the 9mm Police.

9mm Ultra Loading Data and Factory Ballistics

Bullet (grains/type)	Powder	Grains	Velocity	Energy	Source/Comments
100	W231	3.6	1010	225	NA
123 FMJ	FL		1070	350	Fiocchi factory load
124 FMJ	ML		1050	308	Military load

Sig Sauer P230

9mm Browning Long

Historical Notes This Browning-designed pistol cartridge was popular in Europe, but never adopted by American manufacturers. It was introduced with the FN Browning 1903 Model pistol. Sweden used the pistol and cartridge as an official military sidearm starting in 1907 and sold most of these pistols as surplus after World War II. Most were altered to use the standard 380 Automatic for the American market. In addition to the Browning, LeFrancais and Webley & Scott pistols used this cartridge.

General Comments The 9mm Browning Long has been used only to a very limited extent in the United States. In size, it is a shortened 38 Automatic, and in power is between the 380 and 38 Colt Automatic. For field use it would be strictly a small-game number. Bullet diameter is the same as the 9mm Luger. Bullets for reloading are easy to obtain. Like all auto pistol cartridges, killing power can be improved with softpoint or half-jacketed hunting bullets. Even in Europe, this cartridge is essentially obsolete.

9mm Browning Long Loading Data and Factory Ballistics

Bullet (grains/type)	Powder	Grains	Velocity	Energy	Source/Comments
75 Lead	Unique	5.0	1078	192	Lyman No. 358101
95 FMJ	Unique	5.0	1050	230	Estimated Velocity
116 FMJ	Unique	4.8	1000	255	Estimated Velocity
110 FMJ	FL		1100	300	Factory load

9mm Luger (9x19mm Parabellum)
9mm Luger +P

Historical Notes The 9mm Luger, or 9mm Parabellum, was introduced in 1902 with the Luger automatic pistol. It was adopted first by the German Navy in 1904 and then by the German Army in 1908. Since that time, it has been adopted by the military of practically every non-Communist power. It has become the world's most popular and widely used military handgun and submachinegun cartridge. In the United States, Colt, Smith & Wesson, Ruger and many others chamber the 9mm, as do many foreign-made pistols. In 1985, the 9mm Luger was adopted as the official military cartridge by U.S. Armed Forces, along with the Beretta Model 92-F (M-9) 15-shot semi-auto pistol.

General Comments Although the 9mm Luger delivers good performance for police, military or sporting use, it was not popular in the United States until fairly recently. The principal reason was

that no American-made arms were chambered for it initially. In 1954, Smith & Wesson brought out its Model 39 semi-automatic in this chambering and Colt chambered its lightweight Commander for the 9mm Luger in 1951. This, plus the influx of military pistols chambered for the 9mm greatly increased both popularity and acceptance in this country. Currently the 9mm Luger is the most widely used cartridge in the United States. A principal complaint has always been that the 9mm Luger lacks stopping power as a defensive cartridge. However, the only automatic pistol cartridge with proven stopping power is the 45 Automatic. For hunting use, the 9mm Luger is adequate for most small game if hollowpoint bullets are used. Modern premium type JHP loads can dramatically improve performance. A variety of 9mm loadings are offered by every major U.S. ammunition maker.

9mm Luger (9x19mm Parabellum, 9mm Luger +P) Loading Data and Factory Ballistics

Bullet (grains/type)	Powder	Grains	Velocity	Energy	Source/Comments
100	Unique	5.1	1150	294	Hornady
115	Herco	6.0	1200	368	Speer
115	Bullseye	4.8	1250	399	Speer, Hornady, Sierra
115	231	5.2	1150	338	Speer, Hornady, Sierra
124/125	Unique	5.5	1150	364	Speer, Sierra
124/125	700X	4.3	1150	364	Speer, Sierra
88 JHP	FL		1500	440	Factory load
115 FMJ	FL		1160	345	Factory load
115 JHP	FL		1250	399	Factory load
124 FMJ	ML		1299	465	Military load, U.S.
124 FMJ	FL		1120	345	Factory load
147 JHP	FL		975	310	Factory load

9mm Bayard Long
(9mm Bergmann-Bayard Long)

Historical Notes This cartridge is for the 1910 Model Bergmann-Bayard automatic pistol, which was the official Danish military sidearm for many years. The Spanish also used both pistol and cartridge and consequently many Spanish-made pistols were made for this round. The Astra and various Colt-Browning copies or modifications are found in 9mm Bayard chambering.

General Comments The 9mm Bayard has never been manufactured in the United States. Pistols in this chambering are mostly military surplus, which were imported and sold after World

War II. The cartridge is quite similar to the 38 Automatic, but longer. The Astra Model 400 is designed for the 9mm Bayard and will handle the 38 Automatic without any adjustment, but most other pistols will not. It is a potent round and makes a good field cartridge if loaded with hunting-type bullets. Bullet diameter is 0.355-inch and any 9mm Luger bullet can be used, cast or jacketed. Standard loads for the 9mm Luger or the 38 Colt Automatic will work fine in these pistols.

9mm Bergmann-Bayard Long Loading Data and Factory Ballistics

Bullet (grains/type)	Powder	Grains	Velocity	Energy	Source/Comments
116 JSP	Unique	7.0	1280	420	NA
125 FMJ	FL		1120	352	Factory load

9mm Steyr

Historical Notes The standard Austrian military pistol cartridge for the Steyr Model 1912 auto pistol, the case is approximately 23mm long, as compared to the 9mm Luger, which is 19mm. Apparently, the only other countries besides Austria to use this as a military round were Romania and Chile, who adopted both the Steyr pistol and cartridge in 1912. This cartridge is very similar to the 9mm Bergmann-Bayard and these two are often confused. However, 9mm Steyr ammunition is usually found with a nickel-jacketed bullet. The 9mm Bayard case is slightly longer. Quantities of 9mm Steyr pistols have appeared on the United States surplus military market and, for awhile, ammunition was readily available.

General Comments The 9mm Steyr is quite similar to the 9mm Bayard. The Astra Model 400 will sometimes handle both, but other pistols will not. The 9mm Steyr is a good field cartridge, similar to the 38 Colt Automatic in performance. Bullet diameter is the same as the 9mm Luger and one can use Luger bullets for reloading. Any standard load for the 9mm Luger or 38 Automatic will work in the Steyr pistol. Fiocchi of Italy still loads this round.

9mm Steyr Loading Data and Factory Ballistics

Bullet (grains/type)	Powder	Grains	Velocity	Energy	Source/Comments
119 Lead	Unique	6.5	1200	379	Lyman No. 356402
115 FMJ	FL		1200	360	Factory load
116 FMJ	ML		1200	370	Military load

9x23 Winchester

Historical Notes Winchester introduced this cartridge early in 1996, announcing it at the NRA convention. This chambering was designed to meet a specific requirement of the International Practical Shooting Confederation (IPSC) competition, and is not well known outside that discipline. IPSC competitors have struggled for years to concoct the lowest-recoiling load that will qualify for Major Power Factor designation. IPSC Power Factor (PF) is bullet weight (in grains), times muzzle velocity (in feet per second), divided by 1000. To qualify as a "Major Cartridge," a load must generate at least 175 PF units. To qualify as a "Minor Cartridge," it must produce 125 PF units (new rules are now under consideration). Scoring includes a bonus for competitors using a "Major" PF cartridge. Another factor in the IPSC game is the ubiquitous use of muzzle brakes that typically vent a significant portion of the propellant gas out the top of the barrel. A final bit of background, owing to magazine capacity and grip size considerations, the 9mm-bore size is highly preferred. Because of the muzzle-braking devices used, combining a heavy charge of powder with a light bullet to achieve a given PF results in a load that generates less disruption to the shooter's hold, compared to a heavier bullet loaded at lower velocity but generating the same PF. This allows the shooter to get back on target faster. Therefore, the standard approach has been to load unusually light bullets at unusually high velocities. The trouble is, for any given PF, the lighter the bullet, the greater the muzzle energy. Since we have found no free lunches in the world of kinetics, it follows that to achieve more muzzle energy, the load must also generate more chamber pressure. Therefore, IPSC loads tend to generate unusually high chamber pressures—many loads commonly used by top competitors have approached the pressure level of magnum rifle proof-loads! When firing such loads in a conventional pistol, one thing is certain: Eventually, something will give. Winchester's solution to this significant problem was to design a new case.

General Comments While the 9x23 looks like a stretched 9mm Luger, there are significant internal differences. The 9x23 has an unusually thick web section. This prevents the dangerous case-wall blowout that can occur with any conventional pistol cartridge when an unusually high-pressure loading is fired in a gun with a feed ramp in the bottom of the chamber that extends further forward than the "solid" portion of the case (the web). The 9x23mm case has sufficient capacity to allow IPSC shooters to achieve Major power factor using relatively light bullets and without generating gun-wrecking pressures. Nevertheless, IPSC shooters who insist upon using ever-lighter bullets will eventually run into trouble. Ballistics are quite impressive. Given proper loads, this cartridge would seem to qualify as a serious self-defense number.

9x23mm Winchester Factory Ballistics

Bullet (grains/type)	Powder	Grains	Velocity	Energy	Source/Comments
124	FL		1450	577	Winchester factory load
124	FL		1460	585	Winchester factory load

380 Automatic (9mm Kurz/9x17mm/380 ACP)

Historical Notes This cartridge was designed by John Browning and introduced in Europe by FN of Belgium in 1912 as the 9mm Browning Short, and was added to the Colt Pocket Automatic line in 1908. Several governments have adopted it as the official military pistol cartridge. These include Czechoslovakia, Italy and Sweden. It is also much used by European police. Colt, High Standard, Remington and Savage have made pistols in this chambering in the United States. In Europe, Browning, Beretta, Bayard, CZ, Frommer, Astra, Star, Llama, Walther and others made or make 380 Automatic-chambered pistols. This cartridge is also called 9x17mm.

General Comments This is another cartridge that has been very popular because of the light, handy pistols that are chambered for it. The 380 Auto has more stopping power and is a far better cartridge for almost any purpose than the 32 Auto. It is about the minimum pistol cartridge considered adequate for police or military use. For self-defense it is not as powerful as the 9mm Luger, 38 Auto and a few others, but this is offset to a certain extent by the reduced size and weight of the arms it is used in. For hunting or field use, it will do a good job on rabbits, birds or other small game. It offers high velocity, as compared to most light handguns, which is an advantage for field use. With cast or swaged half-jacketed bullets of hunting type, it will do a good job on small game, but not many shooters want to bother handloading it.

380 Automatic (9mm Kurz/9x17mm/380 ACP) Loading Data and Factory Ballistics

Bullet (grains/type)	Powder	Grains	Velocity	Energy	Source/Comments
90 JHP	Bullseye	3.0	900	162	Sierra, Hornady, Speer
95 FMJ	Bullseye	3.2	900	171	Speer, Sierra
95 FMJ	Unique	3.7	900	171	Speer, Sierra
85 JHP	FL		1000	189	Factory load
88 JHP	FL		990	191	Factory load
90 JHP	FL		1000	200	Factory load
95 FMJ	FL		955	192	Factory load

Astra Model 4000 Falcon

38 Short & Long Colt

Historical Notes The 38 Long Colt was once the official United States Army revolver cartridge (1892 to 1911). The short version was used mainly in the Colt Army & Navy Model revolver with swing-out cylinder developed in 1887. The 38 Long Colt was introduced in 1875 as one of several chamberings for Colt's New Line, New Police and New House revolvers.

General Comments Since this was once a military cartridge, a number of Colt and S&W revolvers in this chambering are still around. The 38 Long Colt cartridge can be fired in a 38 Special revolver, but not vice versa. During the Spanish-American War and the Philippine insurrection, the Army found that the 38 Long Colt had insufficient stopping power for combat use. The cartridge was therefore dropped in 1911, in favor of the 45 Automatic. This was the experience that made the U.S. Army reluctant to adopt the 9mm

Luger. It was forced to do so in 1985, largely as a NATO-inspired political decision. Advocates of a smaller caliber admit the superior stopping power of the 45, but point out that extra weight and reduced magazine capacity are detrimental factors that should be considered. The 38 Long Colt is in about the same class as the standard 38 Special loading, but it is not nearly as accurate or as versatile. Some of the old 38 Long Colt revolvers will accept 38 Special or 357 Magnum ammunition, but never fire these in the old 38s. Firing the 357 Magnum would be particularly dangerous, probably wrecking the gun and possibly injuring the shooter or bystanders. Remington has recently manufactured 38 Short Colt ammunition. Black Hills Ammunition has recently reintroduced 38 Long Colt ammunition in response to demands from the Cowboy Action Shooting fraternity.

38 Short & Long Colt Factory Ballistics

Bullet (grains/type)	Powder	Grains	Velocity	Energy	Source/Comments
150 Lead	FL		770	195	Factory load

38 Special (38 Special +P/ 38-44 Target/38-44 High Velocity/ 38 Smith & Wesson Special)

Historical Notes Also known as the 38 Colt Special and, more generally, as simply the 38 Special, this cartridge was developed by S&W and introduced with its Military & Police Model revolver in 1902. This was originally a military cartridge meant to replace the unsatisfactory 38 Long Colt then in use by the Army. Colt brought out its version in 1909, which differs from the original only in bullet shape, a flat-point style. Colt, Smith & Wesson, and others make revolvers specifically for this cartridge. Several Belgian, Brazilian, German and Spanish firms also make 38 Special revolvers. The S&W 52 Target Auto available until 1993 was made for the mid-range wadcutter load. A number of good-quality, lever-action Winchester clones (1866, 1873, 1892) are chambered for the 38 Special.

General Comments The 38 Special is considered one of the best-balanced, all-round handgun cartridges ever designed. It is also one

of the most accurate and is very widely used for match shooting. Any 357 Magnum revolver will also shoot the 38 Special. At one time, it was the standard police cartridge here and largely in Mexico and Canada. It is also usable in lightweight pocket revolvers. Several companies make over/under, two-shot, derringer-type pistols in this chambering that are compact and relatively powerful for close-in self-defense. The 38 Special is also a very popular sporting cartridge for hunting small to medium game and varmint-type animals. With modern hunting bullets, it is effective for this purpose. Because of its moderate recoil, the average person can learn to shoot well with it in a short time, something not true of the 357 or 44 Magnums. The 38 Special is loaded by all major commercial ammunition manufacturers. Bullet weights from 95 to 200 grains have been available.

38 Smith & Wesson Special Loading Data and Factory Ballistics

Bullet (grains/type)	Powder	Grains	Velocity	Energy	Source/Comments
110 JHP	Bullseye	4.7	1000	244	Hornady, Speer, Sierra
125 JHP	231	5.5	1000	278	Sierra, Speer, Nosler
140 JHP	2400	10.4	950	281	Speer, Sierra
158 JHP	Herco	5.0	900	284	Speer, Nosler, Sierra
148 WC	Bullseye	3.1	800	210	Speer, Hornady
95 JHP	FL		1175	291	Factory load
110 JHP	FL		995	242	Factory load
125 JHP	FL		945	248	Factory load
130 FMS	ML		950	260	Military load
148 WC	FL		710	132	Factory load
150 LRN	FL		890	270	Factory load
158 JHP	FL		755	200	Factory load
200 LRN	FL		730	236	Factory load

357 Sig

Historical Notes This cartridge is based upon the 40 S&W case simply necked down with a short neck and a sharp shoulder. The design purpose was to achieve 357 Magnum revolver ballistics from typical semi-automatic pistols. This cartridge design offers several potential advantages. First, its compact nature allows use of a smaller (shorter) grip frame in pistols so chambered. For shooters with smaller hands this is significant; many find guns chambered for the 45 Automatic and 10mm cartridges entirely too big for proper handling and accurate shooting. Second, compared to the parent cartridge, the 357 Sig can effectively launch lighter bullets at greater velocity to achieve similar muzzle energy with less recoil. All of these considerations figured in the development of this cartridge.

General Comments The 357 Sig is loaded to a comparatively high pressure level—the same as top factory 357 Magnum loads and 14 percent higher than the 40 S&W or the 9mm Luger. The combination of high pressure, reasonable case capacity and no barrel venting (as seen in 357 Magnum revolvers) allows this petite cartridge to generate significant ballistics—fully the equal of the 40 S&W in terms of muzzle energy. However, in the typical short pistol barrels used, there is a price to pay for this level of performance: Muzzle blast is significant. Compared to the 40 S&W, which can be chambered in the same pistols, the 357 Sig has only one advantage: a slight reduction in recoil. Time will tell if that will prove sufficient cause to popularize this cartridge.

357 Sig Loading Data and Factory Ballistics

Bullet (grains/type)	Powder	Grains	Velocity	Energy	Source/Comments
88 JHP	AA No. 5	11.1	1616	510	Accurate/1.13" OAL
95 FMJ	AA No. 5	11.0	1572	520	Accurate/1.135" OAL
115 XTP	AA No. 9	13.5	1434	525	Accurate/1.14" OAL
124 XTP	AA No. 9	13.0	1387	530	Accurate/1.14" OAL
147 XTP	Vit N350	6.9	1170	445	VihtaVuori/1.135" OAL
95 FMJ	AA No. 5	11.0	1572	520	Accurate/1.135" OAL
125 JHP	FL		1350	505	Speer & Federal factory load

357 Magnum (357 S&W Magnum)

Historical Notes This chambering was introduced in 1935 by Smith & Wesson for its heavy-frame revolver. Ammunition was developed by Winchester in cooperation with Smith & Wesson. Major Douglas B. Wesson (of S&W) and Philip B. Sharpe are credited with much of the final development work. The 357 Magnum is based on the 38 Special case lengthened about 1/10-inch, so it will not chamber in standard 38 Special revolvers. This was the most powerful handgun cartridge in the world until the 44 Magnum was introduced in 1955. Colt, Ruger, Smith & Wesson and many others manufacture revolvers for this cartridge. There has also been a proliferation of imported single- and double-action revolvers. and several single-shot pistols chamber it. There is even a semi-auto pistol in this chambering. American 357 Magnum revolvers have been used in Canada, Mexico and other countries.

General Comments This is probably the most popular high-velocity handgun cartridge in the United States for police, hunting and target work. The 357 Magnum provides nearly double the velocity and more than three times the energy of standard 38 Special loads. It is noted for its flat trajectory, deep penetration and great knockdown power. It has been used successfully on deer, black bear, elk and even grizzly bear. However, it is not fully adequate for these larger animals unless used by an excellent marksman. It is also used in repeating and single-shot rifles as matched arms to go along with a revolver. In a 20- to 24-inch rifle barrel, standard factory 158-grain loads develop about 1650 fps muzzle velocity and special (rifle only) handloads will develop over 2000 fps. It is considered the best all-round handgun-hunting cartridge for small and medium game and, under proper conditions, for deer at short range. During the Korean conflict, it was very effective against the body armor used by the Communist forces. Nearly every major commercial ammunition manufacturer offers 357 Magnum ammunition.

357 Magnum Loading Data and Factory Ballistics

Bullet (grains/type)	Powder	Grains	Velocity	Energy	Source/Comments
110 JHP	2400	19.0	1500	550	Sierra, Speer
125 JHP	2400	16.0	1200	400	Nosler, Speer, Hornady
140 JHP	W296	16.0	1200	448	Speer, Hornady, Sierra
158 JHP	2400	13.5	1200	505	Hornady, Speer, Sierra, Nosler
110 JHP	FL		1295	410	Factory load
125 JHP	FL		1450	583	Factory load
140 JHP	FL		1360	575	Factory load
158 JHP, Lead	FL		1235	535	Factory load
180 JHP	FL		1090	475	Factory load

38 Super Automatic
38 Super Automatic +P

Historical Notes Introduced by Colt in 1929 as an improved version of the older 38 Auto, the Super Auto is identical to the original cartridge except that it uses a more powerful loading. This is a fine high-speed sporting cartridge for the improved Government Model automatic pistol, but it should not be used in the older Colt pocket models. The Thompson submachine gun was once available in a 38 Super chambering. In Spain, Llama has made pistols for it. It is not popular in Europe, but is very popular in Canada, Mexico and South America where pistols in military chamberings have been prohibited.

General Comments This was for many years the most powerful automatic pistol cartridge made in the United States from the standpoint of both velocity and energy. It makes a good sporting cartridge for hunting small to medium game because the flat trajectory permits accurate long-range shots. However, the original metal-case bullet did not bring out the full potential. With good expanding-type bullets, it is one of our better hunting cartridges for a pistol. It is more powerful than the 9mm Luger, but both are adequate for about the same range of game. It can give greater penetration than the 45 Automatic, but is inferior in stopping power for defense use. For handloading, any 9mm bullet can be used. However, unless proper round-nosed or conical shapes are used, it will be necessary to single load most rounds. This chambering has been extremely popular among IPSC competitors. Both Remington and Winchester offer this cartridge.

38 Super Automatic +P Loading Data and Factory Ballistics

Bullet (grains/type)	Powder	Grains	Velocity	Energy	Source/Comments
115 FMJ	Bullseye	5.0	1200	368	Hornady, Sierra, Speer
125 JHP	231	5.4	1150	500	Sierra, Hornady, Speer
115 JHP	FL		1300	431	Factory load
125 JHP	FL		1240	427	Factory load
130 FMJ	FL		1215	426	Factory load

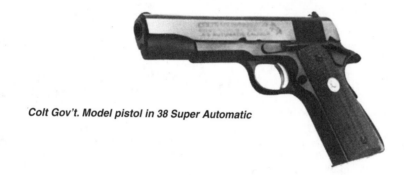

Colt Gov't. Model pistol in 38 Super Automatic

38 Smith & Wesson/38 Colt New Police

Historical Notes Designed by Smith & Wesson for its hinged-frame revolvers introduced about 1877, the 38 S&W is one of the more widely adopted American revolver cartridges; it has been used all over the world. England began using it as an official service cartridge prior to World War II, and it is well-distributed through the British Commonwealth. Large numbers of Spanish-made revolvers in this chambering are used in Mexico and South America, but it has never been very popular in Europe outside the UK. It is also known as the 38 Colt New Police, and with a 200-grain bullet as the 38 Super Police. Colt, H&R, Hopkins & Allen, Iver Johnson, Ruger and S&W have made revolvers in this chambering in the United States. Webley & Scott made many of the British service arms. The British service load is called the 380/200.

General Comments The 38 S&W is another cartridge that owes most of its popularity to the fact that it is well-suited to lightweight pocket guns. It is also a good short-range cartridge for defense use and has better stopping power than any of the 32s and even some of the larger automatic pistol cartridges. The British military figured out that the shocking power of this cartridge with a 200-grain bullet was about the same as its older 455 military cartridge. In actual combat this proved correct, thus permitting the use of lighter guns. The 38 S&W is not a particularly satisfactory hunting cartridge because the curved trajectory limits its use to short ranges. However, it can be improved for hunting through judicious handloading. Remington still offers 38 S&W ammunition.

38 Smith & Wesson Loading Data and Factory Ballistics

Bullet (grains/type)	Powder	Grains	Velocity	Energy	Source/Comments
148 Lead	Bullseye	2.5	700	161	Speer
158 Lead	Unique	3.0	700	172	Speer
145 Lead	FL		685	150	Factory load
200 Lead	ML		630	176	Military load, British

38 Casull

Historical Notes Repeatedly proven for nearly a century, the story of the endurance and reliability of John Browning's 1911 pistol approaches the status of legend. Not well known, however, is the adaptability of the 1911 design to different cartridges. Casull Arms used improved steels and technologies to update their 1911-design pistol to accommodate a new short cartridge, the 38 Casull. Created by Dick Casull in 1998, its case capacity equals or exceeds the 357 Magnum, while fitting in a 45 ACP magazine.

General Comments The cartridge is for long-range target and hunting uses, or for when self-defense needs call for a more powerful cartridge than its parent case, the 45 ACP. The 38 Casull uses a longer case neck and rebated rim for more reliable feeding. For handgun hunters, the 38 Casull demonstrates high accuracy and flat trajectories at 100 yards. The barrel is five inches long, with 1:18 rifling. Shooters are advised that Casull Arms pistols are designed and constructed for this cartridge; chambering in other firearms is strongly discouraged. Loaded ammunition is available from Casull Arms, and initial chronograph testing indicates the factory ammo does attain the specified velocities.

38 Casull Loading Data and Factory Ballistics

Bullet (grains/type)	Powder	Grains	Velocity	Energy	Source/Comments
124 Hornady	FL		1800		Casull Arms
147 Hornady	FL		1600		Casull Arms

9mm Russian Makarov

Historical Notes This is the current Russian military cartridge used in the Makarov and Stechkin auto-pistols. It was adopted shortly after the end of World War II, and its design may have been inspired by an experimental German cartridge called the 9mm Ultra. Other countries from the former Warsaw Pact also use the round. Chinese-made Makarov pistols have recently appeared on the surplus shelves, along with 9mm Makarov ammunition.

General Comments The Soviet 9mm pistol cartridge is intermediate in size and power between the 380 Automatic and the 9mm Luger. Technically, it can be described as a 9x18mm, although it differs dimensionally from the 9x18 Ultra and is not interchangeable with that cartridge. It is a well-designed cartridge for its purpose, although a little underpowered by Western standards. It is satisfactory for small game when loaded with hunting-type bullets, which are now available. Loading data and components are available from various manufacturers. The Makarov pistol is of medium size and is similar to the German Walther. The Stechkin is a selective-fire type that can be used with the holster stock as a submachinegun. Both pistols are well made. Cases are easily formed by passing 9mm Luger cases over an expander ball and then trimming to length.

9mm Russian Makarov Loading Data and Factory Ballistics

Bullet (grains/type)	Powder	Grains	Velocity	Energy	Source/Comments
90 JHP	Unique	4.3	966	185	Lyman
95 FMJ	AA No. 5	5.0	909	173	Lyman
95 Lead	Unique	4.0	1016	215	Lyman No. 364653
100 JHP	Unique	4.1	887	173	Lyman
95 FMJ	ML		1060	237	Military load

38-40 (38 Winchester)

Historical Notes Designed as a rifle cartridge, the 38-40 became a popular handgun chambering. Historical notes and comments will be found in Chapter 2, Current American Rifle Cartridges.

375/454 JDJ Woodswalker

Historical Notes Another big bore, short-range hunting round from SSK Industries, the 375/454 JDJ Woodswalker is based on necking the powerful 454 Casull cartridge to 375-caliber. Barrels, dies, and cases for the 375/454 JDJ are available from SSK Industries.

General Comments Using a 375-caliber, 200-grain Sierra projectile in modified 454 Casull cases and 15-inch SSK barrels, the 375/454 JDJ achieves about 2,375 fps. With 270-grain Hornady Spire Points, it can achieve velocities exceeding 1900 fps. It is suitable for the Thompson/Center Encore.

40 Smith & Wesson

Historical Notes This cartridge was developed as an in-house joint venture between Winchester and Smith & Wesson within six months from the time it was first discussed in June 1989. Mr. Bersett at Winchester and Mr. Melvin at S&W were primarily responsible for this cartridge's development and standardization.

At that time, the FBI had been working with the 10mm Automatic, developing a load that met its criteria for bullet diameter, weight and velocity. The folks at Winchester and Smith & Wesson realized that the power level the FBI had settled on could easily be achieved using a much shorter cartridge. This would facilitate accuracy and allow use of a smaller, more comfortable grip frame.

General Comments Until quite recently, none of the factory loads available actually took full advantage of this cartridge's potential. Several now offered actually generate about 500 fpe in typical guns. This is serious power for such a small package and rivals the best the 45 Automatic can offer. However, such a powerful and compact package requires comparatively high pressures. High peak pressure and a short barrel equate to high noise and muzzle blast. Nevertheless, for its purpose, this has to be considered a superior cartridge design. It has already completely eclipsed the similar 41 Action Express.

40 S&W Auto Loading Data and Factory Ballistics

Bullet (grains/type)	Powder	Grains	Velocity	Energy	Source/Comments
135 JHP	Universal	7.5	1324	524	Hodgdon
155 JHP	Universal	6.6	1186	482	Hodgdon
180 JHP	Universal	5.8	1046	435	Hodgdon
200 JHP	HS 7	7.4	907	363	Hodgdon
155 JHP	FL		1140	447	Factory load
155 JHP	FL		1205	500	Factory load
155 FMJ-SWC	FL		1125	436	Factory load
180 JHP	FL		990	392	Factory load
180 JHP	FL		1015	412	Factory load

10mm Automatic

Historical Notes The 10mm Auto was introduced in 1983 as the cartridge for the Bren Ten semi-auto pistol made by the now-defunct Dornaus & Dixon Enterprises Inc. of Huntington Beach, Calif. Ammunition was loaded by Norma with a 200-grain full-jacketed bullet with a truncated cone shape, similar to some 9mm Luger and 45 Automatic loads of some years back. According to data furnished by Norma, the ammunition is loaded to a mean working pressure of 37,000 psi with a maximum pressure of 44,400 psi. This is getting up in the area of some rifle loads and makes this a rather hot handgun cartridge. Muzzle velocity is listed as 1200 fps and energy at the muzzle as 635 fpe. This makes this cartridge more powerful than the 357 Magnum or the obsolete lead bullet 41 Magnum police load. Muzzle energy is about double that of the 45 Automatic. Gun and cartridge are the creation of Jeff Cooper and associates, who are trying to develop the ideal combat weapon. Colt and several others have offered the 10mm chambering.

General Comments The Bren Ten semi-auto pistol was based on a modification of the much-praised Czech CZ-75 pistol design and had a 5-inch barrel, 11-shot magazine and weighed 39 ounces. It was a full-size combat-type pistol intended primarily for law enforcement/self-defense use but it had many design problems.

The 10mm cartridge is an ideal combat round with good stopping power, particularly with an expanding-type bullet. However, recoil is quite heavy. It would also be a good field cartridge for small to medium game or larger animals in the hands of a good shot and skilled hunter. In the late 1980s, the FBI adopted this cartridge in a slightly reduced loading with a S&W pistol as standard issue. Problems with the guns delayed general issue. Evaluation of stopping power against determined criminals will require much more information than is currently available. Ammunition was initially quite expensive. This discouraged non-handloaders from doing much shooting. Overall, the Bren Ten pistol and cartridge represent an excellent concept for a combat handgun, and it reflects the extensive background and experience of Cooper. Hornady, Speer, Sierra and Nosler offer suitable bullets. The 10mm Auto cartridge has been loaded by Federal, Winchester, Remington, CCI and other U.S. ammunition manufacturers. Actual ballistics are generally about 100 fps slower than early factory claims, so actual 10mm Automatic factory loads do not significantly exceed 45 Automatic +P ballistics.

10mm Automatic Loading Data and Factory Ballistics

Bullet (grains/type)	Powder	Grains	Velocity	Energy	Source/Comments
155 JHP	BlueDot	12.0	1250	538	Hornady, Sierra
180 JHP	BlueDot	10.0	1150	529	Hornady, Sierra
200 FMJ	BlueDot	8.5	1100	537	Hornady
170 JHP	FL		1340	680	Norma factory load
180 JHP	FL		1030	425	Factory load
180 JHP	FL		950	361	FBI factory loading
200 FMC	FL		1200	635	Factory load

41 Remington Magnum

Historical Notes The 41 Remington Magnum revolver cartridge was introduced in June 1964 along with the S&W Model 57 revolver. This is a heavy-frame gun, essentially the same as the older 44 Magnum, but of smaller caliber. The 41 Magnum is very similar to an old, but little-known wildcat cartridge called the 400 Eimer. Bore diameter of the 41 Magnum is a true 0.410-inch rather than the 0.401-inch of the 41 Long Colt. Both a police load and a more powerful softpoint hunting round were originally introduced.

Like most new cartridges, a number of individuals claim to have originated or influenced the design of the 41 Magnum. It might be well in passing to mention that the 400 Eimer appeared around 1924. Possibly, a number of persons working over a span of time convinced Remington that it would be a good idea to bring out such a round. Probably Elmer Keith deserves the major credit.

General Comments There has been much argument as to the need for a police cartridge with greater stopping power than the 357 Magnum. Few understand why a blunt 200-grain bullet for the 357 would not have served this purpose. In addition, a lighter 210-grain police load could have been worked up for the 44 Magnum. However, someone wanted a new cartridge and the 41 Magnum was the result.

Actually, the new round is a more practical all-round hunting cartridge for the average individual than the 44 Magnum. The 357 is not entirely adequate for big game, except in the hands of a good shot and experienced handgun hunter. The 44 Magnum is overpowered for anything but big game and most people do not shoot very well with it. The 41 Magnum covers the small, medium game and varmint-through-deer class quite adequately. Its effectiveness on anything heavier than deer would depend upon who is using it and under what conditions.

Recoil and muzzle blast of the 41 Magnum are slightly less than the 44 Magnum, but still heavy. For the average shooter, mastering either will require about the same amount of training and practice. The 210-grain lead police load with its 1,150 fps is relatively pleasant to shoot and quite adequate for small game or varmints at average handgun ranges. Factory-claimed velocities are for an 8 3/8-inch barrel. Velocity developed from the 6-inch barrel is about 1000 fps for the police load and 1360 to 1400 fps for the softpoint hunting load. In summing up, the 41 Magnum is not quite as powerful as the 44 Magnum, but it is all the gun the average handgun hunter needs. A number of police departments have adopted the 41 Magnum, but most have since dropped it in favor of 9mm Luger or 40 S&W semi-automatic pistols. All major domestic commercial ammunition-makers have offered this cartridge.

41 Remington Magnum Loading Data and Factory Ballistics

Bullet (grains/type)	Powder	Grains	Velocity	Energy	Source/Comments
170 JHP	2400	21.0	1400	740	Sierra
210 JHP	W296	20.0	1200	672	Speer, Nosler, Sierra, Hornady
210 JHP	H110	20.0	1200	672	Speer, Nosler, Sierra, Hornady
170 JHP	FL		1420	761	Factory load
175 JHP	FL		1250	607	Factory load
210 Lead	FL		965	434	Factory load
210 JHP	FL		1300	788	Factory load

10.4mm Italian Revolver

Historical Notes This cartridge was developed for the Italian Model 1874 service revolver, but also used in the Glisenti Model 1889 revolver. It is sometimes listed as the 10.35 Italian Revolver or 10.35 Glisenti. Blackpowder and smokeless powder ammunition is encountered. Both of the above revolvers have been sold from time to time in surplus stores.

General Comments The 10.4 Italian cartridge is similar to the 44 S&W Russian. It would be an effective short-range self-defense or small game hunting number. This ammunition is still commercially available from Fiocchi.

10.4mm Italian Revolver Factory Ballistics

Bullet (grains/type)	Powder	Grains	Velocity	Energy	Source/Comments
177 Lead	Blackpowder		735	212	Military load
177 Lead	Smokeless powder		800	240	Factory load

44-40 (44 Winchester)

Historical Notes Designed as a rifle cartridge, the 44-40 became very popular as a handgun chambering, and many early shooters carried both a rifle and revolver chambered for it. Historical notes and comments will be found in Chapter 2.

44-40 Revolver Loading Data

Bullet (grains/type)	Powder	Grains	Velocity	Energy	Source/Comments
200 SP	Unique	11.1	1125	560	Lyman
205 Lead	Unique	10.9	1095	545	Lyman No. 42798

44 Smith & Wesson Russian

Historical Notes This cartridge was designed by S&W for its Russian Model military revolver in 1870, the first models of which were made for the Imperial Russian Army. A civilian or commercial model was also manufactured beginning in 1878. The Colt Bisley Target Model and its regular single-action were available in this chambering. The German firm of Ludwig Loewe made copies of the S&W Russian Model revolver in the same chambering.

General Comments Originally loaded with blackpowder, the 44 S&W Russian was one of the most accurate and popular cartridges of its day. It was the favorite of Buffalo Bill Cody and many other western characters. Good accuracy to 200 yards was reported, and some of the first precision handgun shooting was accomplished with this cartridge. It was made obsolete by the 44 S&W Special, which was better suited to early smokeless powders. Any gun chambered for the 44 Special or the 44 Magnum will also shoot the 44 Russian. This makes a good field cartridge, but it is not as good as the 44 Special because of the old blackpowder revolvers it was used in, and the fact that it cannot be handloaded to the same level. Cases can be made by trimming 44 Special cases to a length of 0.97-inch. Fiocchi and Black Hills offer 44 Russian ammunition and others may soon offer it for use in Cowboy Action Shooting.

44 Smith & Wesson Russian Factory Ballistics

Bullet (grains/type)	Powder	Grains	Velocity	Energy	Source/Comments
246 Lead	Bullseye	3.6	700	265	NA
246 Lead	Blackpowder (FFFg)	20.0(?)	770	324	Factory load

44 Smith & Wesson Special

Historical Notes With the coming of bulkier smokeless powders, the 44 Russian cartridge case proved too small to permit efficient use of full charges of the new propellants. Though originally a blackpowder cartridge, the 44 Special — which is about 0.2-inch longer than the Russian — eliminated this problem and provided more power, while using the same bullets as the older 44 Russian. This cartridge was introduced about 1907. Both Colt and S&W made revolvers in this chambering and a few Spanish and other European revolvers were made to handle it. There has been a rebirth of interest in the 44 Special in the past few decades.

General Comments The 44 Special is one of the most accurate and powerful big-bore revolver cartridges. However, it was never factory loaded to its full potential. It was left to the handloader to develop truly effective hunting loads. Experiments by men like Elmer Keith, to maximize 44 Special big game hunting potential, culminated in the 44 Magnum. The 44 Special is still popular for target or field use. Revolvers for the 44 Special are not strong enough to handle loads as heavy as those used in Magnum guns. Winchester, Remington, Federal, Black Hills, Cor-Bon and others load this ammunition.

44 Smith & Wesson Special Loading Data and Factory Ballistics

Bullet (grains/type)	Powder	Grains	Velocity	Energy	Source/Comments
180 JHP	231	6.8	900	324	Sierra, Hornady
200 JHP	231	6.0	800	284	Speer, Nosler, Hornady
240 JHP	HS-6	7.5	750	300	Hornady, Speer
200 JHP	FL		900	360	Factory load
200 L-SWC	FL		1035	476	Factory load (very optimistic data)
246 Lead	Smokeless powder		755	310	Factory load

44 Remington Magnum

Historical Notes This cartridge was developed by Smith & Wesson and Remington, and introduced in 1955 for a new heavy-frame 44 Magnum revolver. Ruger, Colt, Smith & Wesson and others make revolvers for this cartridge. Its development was inspired and much preliminary work done by Elmer Keith and that group of hand-cannon fanatics who insisted on the ultimate in handgun accuracy, range and power. Ruger introduced a semi-auto carbine in 44 Magnum chambering in 1961, and Marlin introduced its Model 94 lever-action in 1967.

General Comments In addition to having been the world's most powerful commercial handgun cartridge for many years, the 44 Magnum also has a well-deserved reputation for superb accuracy. It is used more as a field or hunting round than anything else, but a few police officers favor it because of its ability to penetrate an automobile body. It takes a seasoned handgunner to shoot it well as both recoil and muzzle blast are considerable. This is one of the few commercial handgun cartridges that can be considered fully adequate for big game hunting. It has been used to take deer, black bear, elk, moose and the big Alaskan brown bears. It has often been chambered in rifles, with the Model 1894 Winchester or the Remington Rolling-Block action generally used. In a 20- or 24-inch rifle barrel, the standard factory load will develop about 1720 fps at the muzzle and 1580 foot-pounds of energy. This equals the energy of the 30-30 rifle cartridge. It is a very flexible cartridge when handloaded, and can be made to cover any situation within the scope of the modern revolver. Very few, if any, police departments use it because it is simply too much for the average police officer to handle. Its use in police work is largely a personal thing. All major manufacturers of commercial ammunition offer this cartridge in a variety of bullet weights.

44 Remington Magnum Loading Data and Factory Ballistics

Bullet (grains/type)	Powder	Grains	Velocity	Energy	Source/Comments
180 JHP	Unique	14.0	1500	900	Hornady, Sierra
200 JHP	W296	26.0	1450	934	Hornady, Speer
240 JHP	H110	23.0	1350	971	Speer, Hornady, Sierra, Nosler
250 FMJ	2400	21.0	1250	868	Sierra
180 JHP	FL		1610	1035	Factory load
210 JHP	FL		1495	1042	Factory load
210 JHP	FL		1250	729	Factory load
240 Lead	FL		1350	971	Factory load
240 JHP	FL		1180	741	Factory load
240 Lead	FL		1000	533	Factory load
240 Lead	FL		1350	971	Factory load
250 FMJ	FL		1180	775	Factory load

44/454 JDJ Woodswalker

Historical Notes A big-bore, short-range hunting round from SSK Industries, the 44/454 JDJ Woodswalker is based on necking the powerful 454 Casull cartridge to 44-caliber. Barrels, dies, and cases for the 44/454 JDJ are available from SSK Industries.

General Comments Using a 44-caliber, 300-grain Nosler projectile in modified 454 Casull cases and 15-inch SSK barrels, the 44/454 JDJ achieves about 2100 fps. With the Hornady 240-grain XTP bullet, it can reach 2300 fps. It is suitable for the Thompson/Center Encore.

45 Winchester Magnum

Historical Notes The 45 Magnum was first listed in the 1979 Winchester gun and ammunition catalog, although reports of the impending release were circulating some 2 years earlier. The cartridge was chambered in the on-again, off-again Wildey gas-operated semi-automatic pistol and has been adopted as a standard chambering for the Thompson/Center Contender single-shot pistol. The cartridge is essentially an elongated version of the 45 Automatic. Both gun and cartridge were developed initially for silhouette competition, but with the ballistics developed (a 230-grain bullet at a muzzle velocity of 1400 fps), the cartridge should prove an effective hunting round.

General Comments The 45 Winchester Magnum develops 72 percent higher velocity and 200 percent greater muzzle energy than the standard 45 Automatic and is in the same class as the 44 Magnum revolver cartridge. With its rimless case, it is a natural for use in a semi-automatic rifle. Having made this suggestion, if this ever happens, this author can claim that it was all his idea. The Wildey 45 Magnum, along with the 44 Auto Mag, the Desert Eagle and the LAR Grizzly are the only automatic pistols that truly qualify as big-game handguns. The potential is there for a fine combination silhouette and hunting pistol. The price is high, and for strictly silhouette shooting, the much lower-priced Thompson/Center Contender in the same chambering might appeal to many potential buyers. The availability of commercial ammunition with hunting-type bullets would also be a factor, although there is a good variety of such bullets available to the handloader.

45 Winchester Magnum Loading Data and Factory Ballistics

Bullet (grains/type)	Powder	Grains	Velocity	Energy	Source/Comments
185 JHP	BlueDot	20.0	1850	1406	Hornady
200 JHP	2400	22.5	1500	999	Speer
225 JHP	H110	26.0	1500	1124	Speer
230 FMJ	BlueDot	17.0	1550	1227	Hornady
260 JHP	W296	25.0	1500	1300	Speer
230 FMJ	FL		1400	1001	Factory load, Winchester

All of the above loads were developed in a Thompson/Center Contender pistol with a 10-inch barrel. These loads are not recommended for any other handgun.

45 Glock Auto Pistol (45 GAP)

Historical Notes In 2003, Winchester announced ammunition for a new Glock auto pistol. The 45 G.A.P (Glock Auto Pistol) cartridge is 1/8-inch shorter than the timeless 45 ACP cartridge, but delivers similar performance. The shorter cartridge case allows a trimmer, more-ergonomic shape for the Glock Model 37 pistol.

General Comments Many knowledgeable pistol shooters consider the 230-grain bullet to be about the best available for 45-caliber autoloading pistols. For law enforcement use, the frontal area of a 45-caliber bullet offers a stopping power advantage with correct bullet design. During load development, Winchester engineers achieved 45 ACP velocities in the shorter 45 G.A.P. case using 230-grain bullets. Winchester also developed Law Enforcement Only loads for this cartridge for duty use with their proprietary "T-Series" bullets and for training with frangible bullets. Speer offers ammunition in a variety of loads.

45 Glock Auto Pistol (45 GAP) Loading Data and Factory Ballistics

Bullet (grains/type)	Powder	Grains	Velocity	Energy	Source/Comments
175 Frangible	FL		1000		Winchester
185 TMJ FN	FL		1020		Speer
185 SilverTip	FL		1000		Winchester
200 GDHP	FL		950		Speer
230 FMJ	FL		850		Winchester
230 JHP	FL		880		Winchester
185 Hdy XTP	Longshot	7.5	1075		Hodgdon
200 Spr GDHP	Longshot	6.8	1000		Hodgdon

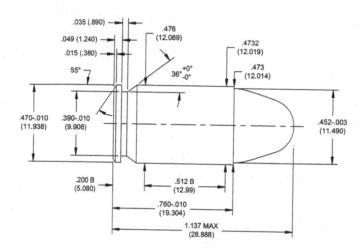

45 Automatic (45 Automatic +P/45 ACP)

Historical Notes This cartridge was developed by John Browning in 1905 and adopted by the United States Ordnance Dept., with the Colt-Browning automatic pistol, in 1911. It has also been made the official military handgun chambering by several other governments, notably Argentina, Mexico and Norway. The 45 Automatic is the most powerful military handgun cartridge in use today. It is also one of the most difficult to master. The Colt Government Model auto-pistol and its copies, as well as the Colt and Smith & Wesson Army Model 1917 revolvers are the principal arms chambered for the 45 Automatic in the United States. Ruger, S&W, Springfield Armory, Glock, Numrich and many other companies now also offer guns in this chambering. Several submachineguns have used it. About 1943, a number of Reising semi-automatic rifles were marketed in this chambering. Imitations of the Colt auto pistol have been made in Argentina, China, Korea, Norway, Spain and the United States. It was replaced as of 1985 as the official U.S. military handgun cartridge by the 9mm Parabellum. However, it remains in U.S. Marine Corps service and has proven increasingly popular with police agencies in the United States.

General Comments The 45 Automatic has been proven in combat all over the world as having excellent stopping power. It has also developed into a first-class match cartridge with accuracy equal to the best. It requires practice for the average person to develop skill with this cartridge, particularly when fired in some untuned semi-automatics. It is used far more for target shooting than hunting, its curved trajectory limiting its effective range. Despite this, it is quite adequate for any small or medium game. Like all the other semi-auto pistol cartridges, it is a better hunting round with softpoint and hollowpoint bullets. A number of police departments have switched from the 38 Special to the 45 Automatic in the last few years. All major and minor commercial ammunition manufacturers offer this cartridge. After several years of declining sales, it is enjoying a resurgence of popularity.

45 Automatic (45 ACP/45 Auto) Loading Data and Factory Ballistics

Bullet (grains/type)	Powder	Grains	Velocity	Energy	Source/Comments
185 JHP	Bullseye	5.0	900	333	Hornady, Sierra, Nosler
200 JHP	BlueDot	10.0	900	360	Speer, Sierra
230 FMJ	Bullseye	5.0	800	327	Nosler, Speer, Sierra
230 FMJ	Unique	6.0	800	327	Speer, Nosler, Hornady, Sierra
185 FMJ SWC	FL		770	244	Factory load
185 JHP	FL		1000	411	Factory load
185 JHP	FL		1140	534	Factory load (+P)
230 FMJ	FL		835	356	Factory load
230 JHP	FL		875	391	Factory load
230 FMJ	ML		855	405	Military load

454 Casull

Historical Notes The 454 Casull, originally called the 454 Magnum Revolver, was developed by Dick Casull and Jack Fulmer in 1957. The first public announcement was made by P.O. Ackley in the November 1959 issue of *Guns & Ammo* magazine. Solid-head 45 Colt cases and specially altered Colt and Ruger single-action revolvers were used for initial development. The 454 Casull employs a special case, originally offered only by Federal, that is 0.1-inch longer than the 45 Colt case, to prevent this round from chambering in 45 Colt revolvers. A five-shot, single-action revolver designed by Dick Casull and manufactured by Freedom Arms Co. is chambered for this cartridge. The revolver is made of stainless steel throughout, has a 7 1/2-inch barrel and weighs 50 ounces in standard configuration. Ammunition is now loaded and marketed by Winchester, Hornady, Buffalo Bore, Cor-Bon and Black Hills Ammunition.

General Comments The 454 Casull is primarily a hunting cartridge, although it will probably also find acceptance among metallic silhouette shooters. The 454 Casull is one of the most powerful revolver cartridges available. Anyone who contemplates hunting dangerous game with a handgun should seriously consider the 454 Casull and the Freedom Arms revolver. For those wishing a reduced load, standard 45 Colt ammunition can be fired in the 454 revolver. There has been a persistent call for a magnum 45 revolver ever since the 44 Magnum was introduced, and the 454 certainly provides all that could be desired in 45-caliber. Firing lead-bullet 45 Colt loads in a 454 can leave a "lead-ring" deposit in the front of the chamber. If this deposit is not removed before chambering and firing full-power 454 loads with the unusually hard bullets used in such rounds, the cylinder can be damaged beyond repair. This is not conjecture — it has happened.

454 Casull Loading Data and Factory Ballistics

Bullet (grains/type)	Powder	Grains	Velocity	Energy	Source/Comments
240 FA JHP	AA No. 9	31.0	1916	1955	Accurate
260 FA JFP	AA No. 9	30.0	1835	1945	Accurate
300 H XTP	AA No. 9	26.0	1623	1755	Accurate
260 JHP	FL		1723	1730	Factory load
300 JHP	FL		1353	1220	Factory load
300 Spr UniCore	FL		1500	1500	Buffalo Bore factory load
325 LBT LFN	FL		1525	1675	Buffalo Bore factory load
360 LBT LWN	FL		1425	1630	Buffalo Bore factory load

455 Revolver MkII
455 Webley Revolver MkII

Historical Notes This is a British military revolver cartridge adopted in 1897 and designated the 455 Revolver MkII. It is a modification of an earlier round originally designed for blackpowder (455 Revolver MkI). Modern revolvers will chamber and fire either the old or the new cartridge. The 455 Webley was used officially in both World War I and II, although it was partly replaced by the 380/200 (38 S&W) adopted in the mid-1930s. In addition to the Webley revolver, both Colt and Smith & Wesson chambered arms for this cartridge. Ammunition was loaded by American companies up to about 1940.

General Comments The 455 Webley Revolver cartridge was never very popular or widely used in the United States because standard American sporting and military arms in 45 Automatic were more easily obtainable. However, after World War II, many obsolete 455 revolvers were sold at low prices in the United States, and this changed the situation somewhat. It is better known and more widely used than previously, but most 455 revolvers have been altered to shoot the 45 Automatic, using half-moon clips or the rimmed 45 Auto-Rim. The 455 Revolver is not a very satisfactory field cartridge because of the low velocity and curved trajectory. On the other hand, it has excellent short-range stopping power. It can be improved by handloading and the use of semi-wadcutter, hunting-type bullets. It is now essentially obsolete. However, Fiocchi of Italy still produces commercial ammunition labeled 455 Webley (MKI).

455 Revolver MkII Loading Data and Factory Ballistics

Bullet (grains/type)	Powder	Grains	Velocity	Energy	Source/Comments
260 Lead	Unique	5.0	610	213	NA
262 FMJ	FL		700	285	Fiocchi factory load
265 FMJ	ML		600	220	Military load

45 Smith & Wesson
(45 S&W Schofield)

Historical Notes This cartridge was introduced in 1875 for the Smith & Wesson Schofield revolver. This revolver was adopted by the U.S. Army in that year and used until 1892 when it, and the 45 Colt Army revolver, were replaced by the Colt Army & Navy Model in 38-caliber. Commercial 45 S&W ammunition was loaded continuously until about 1940 and was reintroduced about 1997 by Black Hills Ammunition, in response to demands from cowboy action shooters for a superior reduced-power 45-caliber cartridge. Some authorities believe Gen. George A. Custer used a Schofield revolver at the Battle of the Little Big Horn.

General Comments The Smith & Wesson Schofield revolver was a single-action, hinged-frame type. It employed a special, heavy barrel latch designed by Gen. Schofield, hence the name. The cylinder of this revolver was not long enough to accept the 45 Colt cartridge, so a shorter round was designed. In addition, to improve extraction, rim diameter was enlarged slightly. Later, to simplify supply contingencies, a 45-caliber cartridge designed with a rim to fit both 45 Colt-chambered revolvers and 45 S&W-chambered revolvers was loaded by government arsenals. A similar commercial loading eventually called the 45 Colt Government followed. This cartridge was used in both the Schofield Model and the Colt Army Model. 45 S&W ammunition can be used in most 45 Colt revolvers, but the reverse is not true. Although the Colt single-action Army revolver is the one always depicted as the universal sidearm of the Old West, the S&W was quite popular. These old guns were made for blackpowder, so heavy smokeless powder charges should never be used. This cartridge and handgun are again in production with Black Hills Ammunition supplying loads that duplicate the original and Navy Arms and others marketing the replica revolver.

45 Smith & Wesson (45 S&W Schofield) Loading Data and Factory Ballistics

Bullet (grains/type)	Powder	Grains	Velocity	Energy	Source/Comments
230 Lead	Bullseye	4.6	740	277	NA
230 Lead	Blackpowder (FFFg)	28.0	730	276	NA
250 Lead	Blackpowder (FFFg)	28.0	710	283	Factory load
230 Lead	Smokeless powder		730	276	Factory load
250 Lead	Smokeless powder		710	283	Factory load

45 Colt

Historical Notes This was introduced in 1873 by Colt as one of the cartridges for its famous "Peacemaker" single-action revolver. Both the cartridge and the revolver were adopted by the U.S. Army in 1875. This served as the official handgun cartridge of the army until 1892 (some 17 years), when it was replaced by the 38 Long Colt. The 45 Colt is one of the cartridges that helped civilize and settle the American West. It was originally a blackpowder number loaded with 40 grains of FFg powder and a 255-grain lead bullet. Recent testing by this editor and others demonstrates that muzzle velocity of the original loading almost certainly exceeded 900 fps in the original revolvers. Various importers offer excellent Italian-made replicas of the original Colt and Ruger and several other makes of more modern single-action revolvers are currently chambered in 45 Colt.

General Comments This is one of the most famous American handgun cartridges and still a favorite with big-bore advocates. As this is written, the 45 Colt has been around for almost 130 years and its popularity is still growing. It is extremely accurate and has more knockdown and stopping power than nearly any common handgun cartridge except the 44 Magnum. It is a popular field cartridge and can be safely handloaded to velocities in excess of 1000 fps with 250-grain cast bullets. Blackpowder revolvers should not be used with any load developing more than about 800 fps muzzle velocity. Although the 45 Colt has a larger case than the 45 Automatic or the 45 Auto-Rim, it is not quite as efficient with factory-duplicating loads using smokeless powder. Using special revolvers, some very heavy loads have been established for the 45 Colt case. These put it in almost the same class as the 44 Magnum. Such loads should not be attempted except by an experienced person who fully understands what he is doing and who will ensure that those loads are only used in a revolver that will withstand the pressures generated. This is another cartridge that has developed a rebirth of interest. Federal, Remington, Winchester, Black Hills Ammunition, Cor-Bon and others all offer 45 Colt loads.

45 Colt Loading Data and Factory Ballistics

Bullet (grains/type)	Powder	Grains	Velocity	Energy	Source/Comments
185 JHP	700X	9.0	1100	497	Sierra
225 JHP	Unique	9.0	950	451	Speer
240 JHP	Unique	8.7	850	385	Sierra
250 JHP	IMR 4227	17.0	800	355	Hornady, Nosler
250 JHP	Unique	7.5	800	355	Hornady
260 JHP	IMR 4227	16.0	850	417	Speer
255 Lead	Blackpowder (FFg)	40.0	930	490	Factory load
225 JHP	Smokeless powder		920	423	Factory load
255 Lead	Smokeless powder		860	420	Factory load

455 Webley Automatic

Historical Notes The 455 Webley semi-rimmed pistol cartridge was adopted by the British Navy in 1912 for use in the 455 Webley self-loading pistol. The pistol was not entirely satisfactory and was replaced by the end of World War I. The cartridge resembles the 45 Automatic, but uses a very blunt-pointed bullet.

General Comments This cartridge has seen very little use in the United States, although a number of Webley pistols in this chambering were sold in military surplus stores after World War II. In performance, it is inferior to the 45 Automatic. Because of the relatively low velocity, it is not as good a field cartridge as the 45 Automatic.

455 Webley Automatic Loading Data and Factory Ballistics

Bullet (grains/type)	Powder	Grains	Velocity	Energy	Source/Comments
200 Lead	Unique	6.2	775	265	Lyman No. 452460
224 FMJ	Smokeless powder		700	247	Military load

455 Revolver MkI
455 Colt/455 Enfield

Historical Notes The 455 Revolver MkI was adopted by the British Army in 1892 to replace the 476 MkIII and the 455 Enfield MkI ammunition. Despite the different designation, these two cartridges actually have the same case dimensions. These differ only in bullet diameter, type and construction. The 476 was a blackpowder cartridge and so was the 455 MkI at its inception. However, in 1894, the propellant was changed to the new Cordite, and after a few years, it was found that the smokeless powder burned more efficiently in a shorter case. Consequently, a shorter case was adopted in 1897, and this altered round was designated the 455 Revolver MkII. This is the 455 Webley, familiar to American shooters. It has a case 0.11-inch to 0.14-inch shorter than the original round.

The 455 Colt is nothing more than Colt's commercial designation of the 455 Revolver MkI, in a somewhat improved loading. It is listed in various publications and was loaded by American companies under this name, but was discontinued in the late 1930s. This is not a Colt-designed cartridge, but it does have different ballistics than the British MkI. Later, new cartridge dimensions were adopted and this round was called the 455 Colt MkII.

General Comments The 455 MkI, 455 MkII, 455 Colt and the original 476 Revolver rounds are all interchangeable and can be fired in early British service arms. The 450 Revolver cartridge can also be fired in 455 revolvers. However, the 455 Webley is the only one still commercially loaded. Use the same bullet and 455 Webley loading data for any of the 455 cartridges listed here. Power and performance are the same. Fiocchi has recently offered this ammunition.

Editor's note: Those not at least slightly confused by the profusion of large-caliber British cartridge designations are a rare breed.

455 Revolver MkI, 455 Colt Factory Ballistics

Bullet (grains/type)	Powder	Grains	Velocity	Energy	Source/Comments
265 Lead	Blackpowder		700	289	Kynoch factory load
265 Lead	Cordite powder		600	212	Kynoch factory load
265 Lead	Smokeless powder		757	337	Factory load, U.S.
262 Lead	FL		850	420	Fiocchi factory load

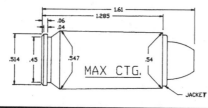
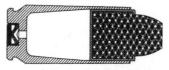

460 Smith & Wesson

Historical Notes Announced in 2005 as a joint Hornady-Smith & Wesson development, the 460 Smith and Wesson (S&W) is the fastest revolver cartridge ever produced, reaching velocities of about 2200 fps with 200-grain bullets. It is chambered in the S&W M460 Extreme Velocity Revolver for long-range handgun hunting. Used by a skilled pistol shooter, the 460 S&W cartridge can achieve MOA accuracy at 100 yards. The CARTRIDGES OF THE WORLD editor took a Wyoming pronghorn at 190 yards with the 460 S&W in late 2005.

General Comments The 460 S&W uses the 454 Casull case lengthened to 1.8 inches as its parent case. It is the first commercial revolver cartridge to use tipped bullets. Hornady and Cor-Bon offer loaded ammunition for the 460 S&W. Hornady and Starline supply reloading components and data for this cartridge. It is well suited for whitetail deer hunting at 150 yard-plus ranges.

460 Smith & Wesson

Bullet (grains/type)	Powder	Grains	Velocity	Energy	Source/Comments
220 Hornady SST	FL		2200	2149	Hornady
225 Barnes X	H110	42.0	2243		Hodgdon
240 Hdy XTP	H4227	45.0	2198		Hodgdon
250 Barnes X	Li'l Gun	42.0	2044		Hodgdon

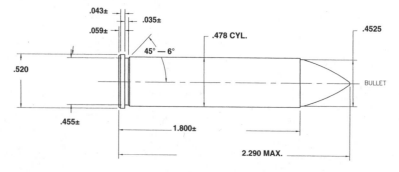

480 Ruger

Historical Notes After a half-century of production, millions of shooters use Bill Ruger's firearms—but only one very special pistol cartridge bears Bill Ruger's name. The 480 Ruger was never intended to be the biggest and heaviest-recoiling handgun cartridge on the block. It splits the difference between the 44 Remington Magnum and 454 Casull cartridges.

General Comments Using a Hornady 325-grain XTP Magnum bullet (diameter .475-inch) and Hornady brass, the 480 Ruger offers a significant velocity and energy increase over the 44 Remington Magnum cartridge, but without the recoil disadvantage of other super-powered handgun cartridges. The key to delivering the two-thirds of a ton of muzzle energy is a well-reasoned balance between bullet weight, velocity and operating pressure, in a cartridge derived from the venerable 45-70 case. The cartridge is chambered in Ruger's rugged double-action six-shooter, the Super Redhawk with an integral scope mounting system on the top strap. It should serve big-game handgun hunters and metallic silhouette target shooters with distinction.

480 Ruger Factory Ballistics

Bullet (grains/type)	Powder	Grains	Velocity	Energy	Source/Comments
325 Hornady XTP	FL		1350	1315	Hornady

50 Action Express

Historical Notes The 50 Action Express (50 AE) was developed in 1988 for the IMI Desert Eagle semi-auto pistol, imported by Magnum Research Inc. It is another development by Evan Whildin, then of Action Arms. It was part of a program to upgrade performance of the semi-auto pistol through new cartridge design. The 50 AE has the same rim diameter, case length and overall length as the 44 Magnum. However, base diameter is 0.547-inch, so, like the 41 AE, the 50 AE has a rebated rim. This allows simple adaptation to the Desert Eagle pistol, which was designed for use with the 44 Magnum. Since the rim is the same, it is possible to change chamberings by the simple process of installing a new barrel, a very practical approach.

General Comments The 50 AE uses a 0.500-inch bullet * weighing 325 grains at a muzzle velocity of 1400 fps. This load develops 1414 fpe, which makes the 50 AE one of the world's most powerful pistol cartridges. This is an excellent field cartridge for deer-size animals or as a backup when hunting dangerous game. Speer now offers factory ammunition.
* The original design featured a standard 50-caliber, 0.510-inch bullet but when a polygonally-rifled bore was adopted, the gauge plug defining the limit of "Sporting Devices" fell through the barrel. This rendered the 50 AE a "Destructive Device," so bore size was reduced and the case was tapered to accommodate the smaller bullet.

50 Action Express Loading Data and Factory Ballistics

Bullet (grains/type)	Powder	Grains	Velocity	Energy	Source/Comments
300 JHP	AA No. 7	27.5	1579	1568	Accurate Arms
325 Speer Uni-Core	AA 1680	37.8	1305	1227	Accurate
325 JHP	FL		1400	1414	Factory load

500 Smith & Wesson

Historical Notes Introduced by Smith and Wesson in 2003 for big game hunting in the first commercial 50-caliber revolver, the 500 S&W became the most powerful factory production cartridge in history. The M500 revolver and 500 S&W cartridge constitute an effective combination for big game hunting at reasonable ranges.

General Comments The 500 S&W uses a rimmed case 1.625 inches long, with a rim diameter of .560-inch. To fit in the M500 revolver's cylinder, the overall length for a loaded cartridge cannot exceed 2.25 inches. The 500 S&W cartridge is best suited to heavy-duty hunting revolvers or modern single-shot pistols and rifles. Factory ammunition is available from Hornady, Cor-Bon and Winchester. Hornady and Starline offer reloading components.

500 Smith & Wesson Loading Data and Factory Ballistics

Bullet (grains/type)	Powder	Grains	Velocity	Energy	Source/Comments
350 Hornady XTP	FL		1900	2805	Hornady
500 Hornady SP	FL		1425	2254	Hornady
275 Barnes XPB	Li'lGun	44.0	2137		Hodgdon
350 Hdy XTP	H110	43.0	1877		Hodgdon
400 Sierra JSP	Li'l Gun	37.0	1725		Hodgdon
500 Hdy SP	H110	32.2	1436		Hodgdon

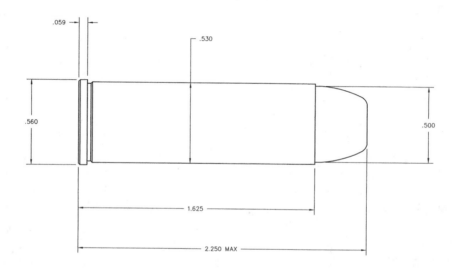

Obsolete Handgun Cartridges

2.7mm Kolibri Auto

Historical Notes The 2.7mm Kolibri Auto is the smallest commercially manufactured centerfire pistol cartridge. It was used in the equally small Kolibri semi-auto pistol introduced about 1914. There was also a single-shot parlor-type pistol chambered for the round. The Kolibri automatic is of conventional blowback design. The cartridge has been obsolete for many years and is a collector's item.

General Comments Small pistols and miniature cartridges may have some value for indoor target practice, but have no other practical use. The tiny 2.7mm Kolibri jacketed bullet is of 0.105-inch to 0.108-inch diameter and weighs about 3 grains. Actual

ballistics are unknown, but muzzle velocity is estimated to be 650 to 700 fps. This would develop an energy of only 3 foot-pounds. When you consider that the 25 Automatic develops 73 foot-pounds at the muzzle, you can see what a pipsqueak this cartridge is. However, it is by no means a toy. It is claimed that the bullet will penetrate 1-1/2 inches of pine, which is sufficient to inflict a serious wound at close range. It should be treated with the same respect accorded any firearm. The 2.7mm Kolibri could not be considered a humane cartridge for hunting anything. However, it might do to dispatch a trapped mouse or eliminate an overly aggressive cockroach. It is not practical to reload these small cartridges.

2.7mm Kolibri Auto Factory Ballistics

Bullet (grains/type)	Powder	Grains	Velocity	Energy	Source/Comments
3 FMJ	FL	650-700		2.8-3.25	Factory load *
*Estimated velocity					

3mm Kolibri

General Comments There is some confusion surrounding the 3mm Kolibri. Some say it is the same as the 2.7mm Kolibri, but physical measurements disprove this. The bullet and case are larger in diameter, compared to the 2.7mm round. In addition, 3mm rounds

have lead bullets, while 2.7mm cartridges use a jacketed projectile. Power and general characteristics would be about the same as the 2.7, which is covered above.

4.25mm Liliput Auto (4.25mm Erika Auto)

Historical Notes Another of the miniature European auto-pistol cartridges, this 4.25mm (17-caliber) cartridge was used in the German Liliput pistol introduced in 1920 and this name stuck to it. However, this cartridge actually originated in Austria about 1913-14 for the Erika auto pistol. Thus, it is sometimes referred to as the 4.25mm Erika. Both gun and cartridge have been obsolete for many years.

General Comments The 4.25mm round is of greater power than the 2.7 or 3mm Kolibri, but that still does not mean it is much of a

cartridge. With a 12- to 15-grain bullet and a muzzle velocity of around 800 fps, it develops only 17 foot-pounds of muzzle energy — still far below the 73 foot-pounds of the 25 Automatic. It could not be considered effective for serious self-defense or any kind of hunting. However, it would kill rats or mice at short range. As with all these miniature cartridges, it is potentially dangerous and could inflict a serious wound at short range. Its principal use would be for indoor target practice. Ammunition is scarce and too expensive to shoot in quantity anyway. This case is not reloadable.

4.25mm Liliput Auto Factory Ballistics

Bullet (grains/type)	Powder	Grains	Velocity	Energy	Source/Comments
12-15	FL		800	17-21.3	Factory load *
*Estimated velocity					

5mm Clement Auto

Historical Notes The 5mm Clement cartridge originated in Spain during 1897 for the obscure Charola-Anitua auto pistol. In 1903, the Belgian-made Clement auto pistol was adapted to the round and this resulted in the change of name. The cartridge is listed in the 1904 and 1934 DWM catalog (No. 484) and was loaded in Germany until about 1938. It was replaced by the more effective 25 Automatic.

General Comments The Clement auto pistol was well made and popular in Europe. The 5mm cartridge is of bottleneck type and the 36-grain bullet has a muzzle velocity of 1030 fps. Because of the high velocity, it develops slightly greater energy than the 25 Automatic. However, it is no more effective. Like the 25 Automatic, it is not entirely satisfactory for self-defense and unsuitable for hunting anything but rats, mice, sparrows or similar pests. It is now a collector's item and ammunition is far too expensive to shoot.

5mm Clement Auto Factory Ballistics

Bullet (grains/type)	Powder	Grains	Velocity	Energy	Source/Comments
36 FMJ	FL		1030	78	Factory load, DWM

5mm Bergmann

Historical Notes A cartridge for the obsolete Bergmann No. 2 auto pistol introduced in 1894 and produced commercially from 1896 until about 1900. This cartridge is listed in the 1904 DWM catalog (No. 416A), but not in the 1934 issue. It has been obsolete since around 1930, being replaced by the 6.35mm Browning (25 Automatic).

General Comments The 5mm Bergmann has a straight, tapered, rimless case. The bullet is of 0.20- to 0.21-inch diameter and was available with a 37-grain lead or 34-grain full-metal jacket or softpoint. According to White and Munhall, muzzle velocity is just a little under 600 fps. Muzzle energy would be about 30 foot-pounds, less than half that of the 25 Automatic. The cartridge has little practical value except for indoor target practice. As originally manufactured, the cartridge had no rim or extractor groove, but after a short time, the extractor groove was added. This is another collector's cartridge, much too expensive to shoot.

5mm Bergmann Factory Ballistics

Bullet (grains/type)	Powder	Grains	Velocity	Energy	Source/Comments
34 FMJ	FL		600	27	Factory load
37 Lead	FL		600	30	Factory load

22 Remington Jet Magnum

Historical Notes The 22 Remington Jet, also known as the 22 Center Fire Magnum, was introduced jointly by Remington and Smith & Wesson. The former developed the cartridge, the latter the revolver. The first news of this cartridge "leaked" out in 1959, but production revolvers and ammunition were not available until 1961. The S&W Model 53 revolver is the only revolver ever to chamber this cartridge, and it was discontinued in 1971. The 22 Jet grew out of popular wildcat handgun cartridges such as the Harvey 22 Kay-Chuk and others based on the altered 22 Hornet case. However, the 22 Jet is actually based on a necked-down 357 Magnum case. Marlin once offered the Model 62 lever-action rifle for the 22 Jet, H&R offered it in the Topper and Thompson/Center offered it in the Contender for a time.

General Comments The 22 Jet is strictly a hunting number intended to provide high velocity and flat trajectory in the field. The M53 revolver will also fire regular 22 Long Rifle ammunition by use of supplemental steel chamber inserts and an adjustable firing pin. This cartridge has ample performance for small game at ranges out to 100 yards, for those who can shoot a revolver that well.

When first announced, most gun writers praised the fantastic performance. A muzzle velocity of 2460 fps was supposed to be developed in an 8 1/2-inch barrel. Chronographed tests by various individuals, including this author, indicated an actual velocity of only around 2000 fps in this barrel length. Quite a letdown, but it is still a good cartridge. The S&W Model 53 in 22 Jet was discontinued because of problems with the cylinder locking up when firing full-powered loads. This ammunition is no longer manufactured commercially.

22 Remington Jet Magnum Loading Data and Factory Ballistics

Bullet (grains/type)	Powder	Grains	Velocity	Energy	Source/Comments
40 HP	2400	10.5	1800	288	Hornady, Sierra
45 SP	2400	12.8	1700	288	Hornady, Sierra
40 HP	FL		2460	535	Factory load

Cartridges and cylinder must be free of grease or oil to prevent setback of case when fired.

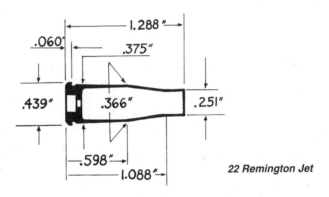

22 Remington Jet

221 Remington Fireball

Historical Notes This cartridge was introduced early in 1963 for the Remington XP-100 bolt-action, a single-shot pistol based on a shortened, lightened 700 series rifle action. The pistol had a streamlined nylon-plastic stock, ventilated barrel rib and adjustable sights. This is the first handgun made by Remington since its pocket automatics were discontinued back in 1935. The Thompson/Center Contender was also available in 221 Remington but has since dropped that chambering. Remington was the only source for 221 Fireball ammunition. It is still available.

General Comments The 221 Fireball follows the modern design in 22-caliber high-velocity pistol cartridges for small game and varmint hunting at long range. The rimless case is a shortened version of the 222 Remington. The cartridge is well adapted to rifles as well as pistols. The bullet is designed for quick expansion on small animals and is very deadly at all practical ranges. The XP-100 pistol has a 10-inch barrel and is intended for use with a scope. It is capable of sub-MOA 100-yard groups when fitted with a scope and fired from a rest. It is much more powerful than the older 22 Remington Jet used in the S&W 22 WMR revolver. Muzzle energy of the 221 Fireball is greater than the 357 Magnum. Despite caliber designation, 0.224 inch is proper bullet diameter.

221 Remington Fireball Loading Data and Factory Ballistics

Bullet (grains/type)	Powder	Grains	Velocity	Energy	Source/Comments
50 SP	IMR 4198	17.0	2610	755	Speer, Hornady, Sierra, Nosler
50 SP	IMR 4227	15.5	2600	750	Speer, Hornady, Sierra, Nosler
55 SP	IMR 4198	16.0	2400	704	Speer, Hornady, Nosler
50 SP	FL		2650	780	Remington factory load

5.5mm Velo Dog Revolver *

Historical Notes This round was introduced in 1894 for the "Velo Dog" revolver, manufactured by Galand of Paris. It derives its name from the French word "velocycle," meaning roughly "bicycle." Later, a number of Belgian and German revolvers also chambered this round. The cartridge was loaded in the United States by Peters, Remington and Winchester up until about 1940. However, no American company made a gun for it. Fiocchi of Italy still loads this cartridge.

General Comments The 5.5mm Velo Dog is a centerfire 22 of slightly less power than the 22 Long Rifle rimfire. It bears some resemblance to the obsolete 22 Extra Long Maynard centerfire rifle cartridge. However, it is easy to distinguish these by the head markings and because the 5.5mm has a metal-cased bullet. The Velo Dog revolver was designed for cyclists to shoot pursuing dogs. This was a unique period in history. Can you imagine what would happen today if some cyclist shot a dog! The cartridge became obsolete because it is ballistically inferior to the popular 22 Long Rifle.

Editor's note: Others might argue that the present period is historically unique. Try to fathom the logic that suggests that it is OK for an unrestricted and untrained "pet" to attack a harmless cyclist or pedestrian, but that it is not OK for that person to effectively defend himself!

*There is some uncertainty as to the proper designation for this cartridge. There is also a loading called the 5.75 Velo Dog which could be the correct name for this cartridge – it would seem that we should have been able to resolve this but that is not yet the case. Maybe we will solve the mystery next edition.

5.5mm Velo Dog Revolver Factory Ballistics

Bullet (grains/type)	Powder	Grains	Velocity	Energy	Source/Comments
45 FMJ	FL		750	55	Fiocchi factory load

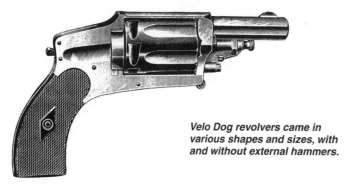

Velo Dog revolvers came in various shapes and sizes, with and without external hammers.

256 Winchester Magnum

Historical Notes The 256 Winchester Magnum handgun cartridge was announced in 1960. However, no arms were available until late in 1962 and most of these were not on the market in quantity before 1963. The Marlin Model 62 lever-action rifle was the first rifle officially announced for this cartridge. This was followed by a new Ruger single-shot pistol named the "Hawkeye," which made the scene ahead of the Marlin. The Ruger "Hawkeye" was discontinued in 1966 and the Marlin 62 was dropped a few years later. The 256 Magnum is based on the 357 Magnum case necked-down to accept 0.257-inch diameter bullets. Some difficulty developed trying to design a revolver for this cartridge due to the cylinder gap and high pressure. The Ruger "Hawkeye" has a completely enclosed breech. Thompson/Center single-shot pistols were also available in this chambering.

General Comments Fired in the Ruger "Hawkeye" with its enclosed breech and 8 1/2-inch barrel, the 256 Magnum develops an average muzzle velocity of about 2360 fps. From a 24-inch rifle barrel, muzzle velocity is over 2800 fps — this with the 60-grain SP bullet originally loaded by Winchester. When first announced, the velocity was listed as 2,200 fps, as the factory used a test barrel shorter than 8-1/2 inches. Although similar to the old 25-20 cartridge, the 256 has greater powder capacity, is loaded to higher pressures and therefore gives superior performance. When used in a rifle, many shooters prefer 75- or 85-grain bullets. The 256 Magnum should be an excellent varmint and small game round at close ranges. In a rifle, it would be effective out to 200 or 225 yards. See the 18th Edition of GUN DIGEST for an excellent report on shooting the 256 by Yard and Helbig. Winchester was the only source of this ammunition. Though Winchester ceased production of this cartridge in the early 1990s, cases are easily formed from 357 Magnums, so the handloader has no problem.

256 Winchester Magnum Handgun Loading Data and Factory Ballistics

Bullet (grains/type)	Powder	Grains	Velocity	Energy	Source/Comments
60 SP	2400	14.6	2300	705	Hornady
60 SP	H4227	16.0	2300	705	Hornady
75 SP	2400	13.0	2000	668	Hornady
60 SP	FL		2200	650	Winchester factory load

6.5mm Bergmann

Historical Notes Another in the series of cartridges developed by Bergmann in the 1894-96 period, the 6.5mm round is listed in the 1904 DWM catalog (No. 413A), but by 1934 had been dropped. Theodor Bergmann designed a number of special cartridges for his auto pistols. These ranged from 5 to 11mm in diameter and practically all of these were obsolete by about 1930. The original version of the 6.5mm was both rimless and grooveless, but because of the problem of extracting an unfired or dud cartridge, this was soon altered to standard rimless design. The more popular Bergmann cartridges were loaded in England as well as on the continent.

General Comments The 6.5mm Bergmann cartridge is a necked, rimless-type that looks very powerful, but really is not. It is actually less powerful than the 32 Automatic. While not an entirely adequate self-defense round, it could be used for shooting small pests or birds. It is more powerful than the 25 Automatic. However, ammunition is scarce and expensive, so no one is likely to do much shooting with it anyway. The 6.5mm Bergmann is one of the few 6.5mm pistol cartridges.

6.5mm Bergmann Factory Ballistics

Bullet (grains/type)	Powder	Grains	Velocity	Energy	Source/Comments
65-88 FMJ	FL		780	94	Factory load

7mm Nambu

Historical Notes This unusual pistol cartridge was manufactured only in Japan for the Japanese "Baby" Nambu semi-auto pistol, which was introduced about 1920. It was not an official Japanese military cartridge, but was specially made for high-ranking officers required to purchase their own sidearms. The 7mm Nambu pistol is a scaled-down version of the original model Nambu, which was developed about 1904. The 7mm Nambu pistol was something of a mystery until after World War II, when quantities were brought back by returning GIs. The 7mm Nambu cartridge is a collector's item and the pistols are scarce.

General Comments By Western standards, the 7mm Nambu would not be considered an adequate self-defense cartridge. For sporting use, it would be effective only on small game or birds. The pistol has a seven-shot magazine, 3 1/4-inch barrel, weighs only 16 ounces, and is extremely well made and of good material and finish. The 1963 (17th) edition of GUN DIGEST includes an article by Roy D. Strengholt, which covers the 7mm Nambu pistol and cartridge in considerable detail. The 7mm Nambu is unusual in that it is one of the very few pistol cartridges to use a 7mm (0.283-inch)-diameter bullet.

7mm Nambu Factory Ballistics

Bullet (grains/type)	Powder	Grains	Velocity	Energy	Source/Comments
56 FMJ	FL		1250	196	Factory load *
*Approximate					

7mm Bench Rest Remington

Historical Notes Originally not a commercial cartridge, but a chambering only for the Remington Model XP-100 Silhouette target pistol, the 7mm BR has graduated to a full-fledged commercial cartridge. It has also become a rifle as well as a pistol round. It is based on the 308x1 1/2-inch Barnes case necked-down to 7mm. Originally the cartridge was made by shortening and necking-down the Remington BR case, a special 308 Winchester case with a Small Rifle primer pocket made especially for this purpose. Mike Walker of Remington was instrumental in developing the 7mm BR.

The idea is not new because the British had developed a similar, although slightly longer, cartridge as an experimental military round as early as 1945. In addition, more than one person has necked the 308x1 1/2-inch case down to 7mm. Elgin Gates worked with a similar cartridge in 1952. The Remington BR line of cartridges originated, according to company literature, in 1978. There is also a 22 BR and a 6mm BR covered elsewhere in this book. This cartridge was designed to provide an out-of-the-box

silhouette cartridge with ballistics calculated to strike the best balance for accuracy, velocity and bullet weight to hit and knock down the metal targets.

General Comments External dimensions of the Remington 308 BR case are identical to the 308 Winchester. However, the walls are thinner and are annealed to facilitate reforming, and the primer pocket is sized for the Small Rifle primer. Ballistics of the factory cartridge showed a 140-grain bullet at a muzzle velocity of 2215 fps and 1525 foot-pounds of energy. This was registered from a 15-inch barrel. It would do better in a slightly longer barrel. These short 1 1/2-inch cartridges often develop maximum velocity in a relatively short barrel, usually about 16 to 18 inches.

The 7mm BR would be a good medium-range varmint and short-range deer cartridge. It cannot be improved to any extent by handloading since the standard factory load is about tops for the 140-grain bullet. Remington no longer catalogs this cartridge.

7mm Bench Rest Loading Data and Factory Ballistics

Bullet (grains/type)	Powder	Grains	Velocity	Energy	Source/Comments
100	W748	34.0	2400	1279	Sierra, Hornady
120	748	32.0	2300	1410	Sierra, Hornady
130	H322	27.0	2100	1277	Sierra, Speer, Nosler
140	748	30.0	2150	1450	Sierra, Hornady, Speer
150	H335	28.0	2000	1333	Sierra, Speer, Nosler
160	748	28.0	2000	1421	Sierra, Hornady, Speer
140	FL		2215	1525	Remington factory load

7.62mm Russian Nagant Revolver

Historical Notes This military revolver cartridge was adopted by Russia in 1895 and used in the Nagant and Pieper revolvers, which were both seven-shot designs as opposed to the usual six. The Nagant design is unique in that when the hammer is cocked, the cylinder moves forward over the barrel shank to form a gas seal. The velocity gain from this arrangement is significant. However, no other revolver has ever used this ingenious, though complicated, system.

General Comments Russian Nagant revolvers have been sold in moderate quantities in the United States, but are more of a

collector's item than a practical gun. Ammunition in shooting quantities is difficult to find, but can be made from 32-20 Winchester cases, which are very similar. Power and effectiveness are about the same as the 32 S&W Long. Most versions of the cartridge have the bullet seated completely inside the case. Velocity of the 108-grain FMJ flat-nose bullet in the Nagant revolver is about 1100 fps, but the conventional Pieper revolver delivers only 725 fps. Bullet diameter is 0.295-inch. Both guns and ammunition were recently in production in Russia. Fiocchi manufactured this cartridge quite recently.

7.62 Russian Nagant Revolver Loading Data and Factory Ballistics

Bullet (grains/type)	Powder	Grains	Velocity	Energy	Source/Comments
115 Cast	Bullseye	3.0	800	165	Lyman No. 311008
98 FMJ	FL		750	122	Fiocchi factory load
108 FMJ	FL		725	125	Factory load – Pieper revolver
108 FMJ	FL		1100	290	Factory load – Nagant revolver

Nagant Model 1895

32 Protector

Historical Notes This cartridge was chambered in the Protector palm pistol that was manufactured by the Minneapolis Fire Arms Co. Winchester offered this cartridge late in 1898 and continued to catalog it until at least 1916. Evidently, despite what must have been very modest power, this combination had some appeal.

General Comments Performance must have been quite anemic. However, just as with similar pocket pistols carried today, there is a certain deterrence value to any gun — very few persons really want to be shot at or hit with anything. When the chips are down, having almost any gun available can far surpass the value of throwing rocks.

32 Protector

Bullet (grains/type)	Powder	Grains	Velocity	Energy	Source/Comments
40	Blackpowder	4.0	550	26	QuickLOAD
Estimated ballistics					

7.65mm Roth-Sauer

Historical Notes The 7.65mm Roth-Sauer originated in 1901 as one chambering for the Frommer pocket-type auto pistol. About 1905, the Roth-Sauer pistol was adapted to a reduced loading of the Frommer cartridge. Due to the popularity of the Roth-Sauer pistol, the name became attached to the cartridge. Winchester loaded the round during the 1920s, but it has been obsolete since 1930.

General Comments The eight-shot Roth-Sauer pistol was a compact pocket, or self-defense, type. Despite the low power of the cartridge, the pistol had a complicated long-recoil locked breech. The 7.65mm Roth-Sauer cartridge looks like the 32 Automatic, but has a shorter case and a bullet of slightly smaller diameter, (0.301-inch). The 70- to 74-grain bullet has a muzzle velocity of 1070 fps, which means it develops a bit more energy than the 32 Automatic. Regardless, both are in the same class and there is not much difference. It is possible to make 7.65mm R-S ammo from 32 Automatic cases by turning down the rim, shortening and reforming.

7.65mm Roth-Sauer Factory Ballistics

Bullet (grains/type)	Powder	Grains	Velocity	Energy	Source/Comments
70-74 FMJ	FL		1070	184	Factory load

30 (7.65mm) Borchardt

Historical Notes Also known as the 7.65mm Borchardt, this is the cartridge for the Model 1893 Borchardt auto pistol. Cartridge and pistol were designed by American Hugo Borchardt, but were manufactured by Loewe in Berlin. The 30 Borchardt is listed in the 1905 and 1918-19 Remington catalogs and was loaded in this country for a number of years.

General Comments The 30 Borchardt is the predecessor of the 7.63 (30) Mauser, 7.65mm Mannlicher and 7.62x25mm Russian Tokarev. These all have similar physical measurements, but the modern rounds are loaded to higher pressures and velocity than the original Borchardt cartridge. The 30 Borchardt fired an 85-grain bullet at 1280 fps, whereas the 30 Mauser fires an 86-grain bullet at 1410 to 1450 fps. Modern ammunition should not he used in the Borchardt or Mannlicher pistols. Borchardt cartridges are now scarce collector's items and should not be fired.

30 (7.65mm) Borchardt Factory Ballistics

Bullet (grains/type)	Powder	Grains	Velocity	Energy	Source/Comments
85 FMJ	FL		1280	312	Factory load

7.63mm (7.65) Mannlicher

Historical Notes This straight-walled rimless cartridge was used in the Model 1900, 1901 and 1905 Mannlicher military automatic pistols. These were manufactured in Austria (Steyr) and in Spain. Austrian guns are well-made and finished, but the Spanish types are sometimes of doubtful quality. These pistols were common military surplus items in the 1950s. Some dealers also had ammunition.

General Comments The 1900 and slightly-modified 1901 and 1905 Mannlicher pistols operate on the delayed-blowback system.

The non-detachable magazine is in the grip and holds eight (1905,10) rounds. These guns are loaded from the top by means of a special charger, after retracting the slide. The 7.63 cartridge is only slightly more powerful than the 32 Automatic and its use in the field would have to be confined to small game. There is also a locked-breech Model 1903 Mannlicher auto pistol that fires a lower-powered cartridge that is otherwise similar to the bottlenecked 7.63 Mauser. The standard Mauser cartridge must not be fired in these Model 1903 pistols, as that will quickly damage the action.

7.63 (7.65) Mannlicher Loading Data and Factory Ballistics

Bullet (grains/type)	Powder	Grains	Velocity	Energy	Source/Comments
86	Unique	3.2	1000	193	Mauser bullet
85 FMJ	FL		1025	201	Factory load

35 Smith & Wesson Auto/35 Automatic

Historical Notes Smith & Wesson introduced this cartridge and a new auto pistol in 1913. The S&W pistol is the only one that ever chambered this cartridge. It was discontinued (in 35 S&W chambering) in 1921. The pistol was based on designs of the Belgian C.P. Clement. Commercial ammunition was loaded until about 1940.

General Comments The 35 S&W Auto is actually a 32-caliber cartridge and is similar to the 32 Automatic. In fact, it is possible to fire 32 Automatic ammo in some 35 semi-auto pistols. The cartridge designation was probably to prevent confusion with the 32 Automatic. However, it has created more confusion than it prevented. The 32 Automatic is a better cartridge and Smith & Wesson eventually chambered its pistol for that more popular round.

35 Smith & Wesson Auto Loading Data and Factory Ballistics

Bullet (grains/type)	Powder	Grains	Velocity	Energy	Source/Comments
76 FMJ	Bullseye	1.6	809	110	Duplicate factory load
76 FMJ	FL		809	110	Factory load

7.65mm MAS (French)

Historical Notes A military cartridge used in the French Model 1935A and 35-S auto pistols and Model 1938 submachinegun. It was replaced in 1950 by the 9mm Parabellum (Luger) cartridge. However, it is still used to a limited extent by French police. Quite a few of these pistols have been sold on the surplus market in the United States. These are of Colt-Browning-type design, but do not have the grip safety.

General Comments The 7.65mm French MAS pistol cartridge must not be confused with the 7.65mm Luger or 7.65mm Browning Long

cartridges. The 7.65mm MAS has an elongated, 19.8 mm straight case that is identical to the .30 Pederson. It is slightly more powerful than the 32 Automatic, but not sufficiently to make it anything but a small game number for field use. For self-defense, it would be a little better than the 32 Automatic. For handloading, any 30-caliber bullet of up to 100 grains can be used. This cartridge was manufactured only in French and Vietnamese arsenals. It will be found with both steel and brass cases. It is no longer in regular production, although small lots of newly produced ammunition will be encountered.

7.65mm MAS (French) Loading Data and Factory Ballistics

Bullet (grains/type)	Powder	Grains	Velocity	Energy	Source/Comments
77	Unique	3.6	1100	206	Lyman No. 311252
85 FMJ	FL		1120	240	Factory load

32 Short Colt – 32 Long Colt 32 S&W Gallery

Historical Notes Introduced by Colt in 1875 along with the New Line model revolvers, this was originally a blackpowder cartridge using a 90-grain outside-lubricated bullet. There is also a 32 Short Colt, which is identical except for a shorter case length. In England and Europe, this is known as the 320 caliber revolver. The 32 Short and Long Colt cartridges are actually obsolete, having been displaced by the 32 S&W and 32 S&W Long. Colt is the only company that used this cartridge in the United States. It was more popular in Europe, where a number of blackpowder 320 revolvers were made.

General Comments The 32 Colt cartridge was originally of the outside-lubricated type, which used a bullet of 0.313-inch diameter. Later this was changed to an inside-lubricated type, which necessitated a bullet of 0.299-inch diameter, so the lubricating grooves would fit inside the case. Bullet weight was reduced from 90 to 80 or 82 grains in the inside-lubricated type and this shortened overall length a little. In power and usefulness, the Colt cartridges are nearly the same as the 32 S&W Short and Long, but not nearly as accurate. Winchester only recently discontinued this loading.

32 Short Colt – 32 Long Colt Loading Data and Factory Ballistics

Bullet (grains/type)	Powder	Grains	Velocity	Energy	Source/Comments
55 Lead	Blackpowder	4.5			Wadcutter lead in 32 Short Colt
80 Lead	Bullseye	1.8	732	94	Approximate Factory Equivalent 32 Short Colt
80 Lead	FL		745	100	Factory Load - Short Colt
82 Lead	FL		755	104	Factory Load - Long Colt

32 Colt

Historical Notes This cartridge was Colt's attempt at solving the problems associated with outside-lubricated cartridges. The 32 Colt utilized a longer case to fully cover the lubricated portion of the bullet and carried a hollow-based bullet to help obturation in the bore. This was necessary because the bullets had to be undersized to fit in the case. Reports were that the effort was not very successful. Loading was an 82-grain lead bullet with 12 grains of blackpowder.

320 Revolver

Historical Notes The 320 Revolver cartridge originated in England about 1870. It was the first used in the Webley revolver, but later a number of other British and European pocket-type guns chambered it. The 320 served as the inspiration for the 32 Short Colt. It is no longer loaded by European ammunition manufacturers. At one time, it was also manufactured in the United States, but was discontinued in the late 1920s.

General Comments The 320 Revolver is nearly identical to the 32 Short Colt in ballistic performance. The 320 is a short-range small game number only. Use the same loading data as given for the 32 Short Colt. Recently 320 Revolver ammunition was offered by Fiocchi.

320 Revolver Factory Ballistics

Bullet (grains/type)	Powder	Grains	Velocity	Energy	Source/Comments
80 Lead	FL		550	54	Factory load

7.5mm Swedish Nagant Revolver

Historical Notes The cartridge listed here is the 7.5mm Swedish designed for the 1887 Swedish Nagant military revolver manufactured by Husqvarna. Since the end of World War II, large quantities of these revolvers have been sold as surplus in the United States. This has a short, rimmed case with an outside-lubricated bullet and is usually loaded with blackpowder. The revolver is long obsolete, but Norma of Sweden loaded this cartridge with Berdan-primed cases and smokeless propellants.

General Comments The 7.5mm Swedish Nagant revolver cartridge was practically unknown in the United States prior to 1948. It is listed here because of the large number of these revolvers

imported. Many Nagant revolvers were altered to use the 22 Long Rifle by lining the barrel and bushing the cylinder. The 32 Short or Long Colt can be fired in these revolvers, but it fits loosely and accuracy is terrible. Cartridge cases can be made from empty 32-20 cases trimmed back to 0.895-inch in length. The Australian 310 Martini cartridge will also work if cut to the proper length. The Swedish Nagant revolver was intended for blackpowder, and only low-pressure, smokeless-powder loads are safe. Ballistically, the 7.5mm cartridge is in the same class as the 32 S&W Long. Fiocchi loads the 7.5mm Swiss, which is essentially the same case with a different loading that can be used in these guns.

7.5mm Swedish Nagant Revolver Loading Data and Factory Ballistics

Bullet (grains/type)	Powder	Grains	Velocity	Energy	Source/Comments
105 Lead	Bullseye	2.0	720	120	Duplicates factory load
105 Lead	Blackpowder (FFFg)	11.5	725	121	Duplicates factory load
104 Lead	FL		725	121	Factory load
107 Lead	FL		710	108	Fiocchi factory load

8mm Nambu

Historical Notes This was the official Japanese military pistol cartridge introduced in 1904 for the Nambu auto pistol, it was also used in the modified 1925 model and the odd-looking 1934 model. This was the official Japanese pistol cartridge in World War II, although other pistols and cartridges were used. It was used only by Japan.

General Comments Quite a few 8mm Nambu pistols were brought back from the Pacific battle areas by returning GIs at war's end. Ammunition has been a problem because most captured stores were destroyed. Externally, the cartridge resembles the 7.65mm Luger,

but uses a larger-diameter bullet and a semi-rimmed case. In power, it is slightly superior to the 32 Automatic. Most Nambu cartridges are collector's items. Bullet diameter is 0.320-inch. Cast 32-caliber revolver bullets sized as close to this as possible would undoubtedly work in weights of 83 to 100 grains. Use only light charges of powder. In the 1980s, Brass Extrusion Laboratories, Ltd. of Bensenville, Ill., manufactured 8mm Nambu cases for Midway Arms Inc. of Columbia, Mo. Midway no longer sells this ammunition. Today this cartridge is commercially loaded by the Old Western Scrounger and the Buffalo Arms Co.

8mm Nambu Loading Data and Factory Ballistics

Bullet (grains/type)	Powder	Grains	Velocity	Energy	Source/Comments
83 Lead	Unique	3.0	950	165	Estimated velocity
102 FMJ	ML		960	202	Military load

Nambu Type 14 (1925)

9mm Glisenti

Historical Notes Adopted for the Italian military Model 1910 Glisenti auto pistol, the 9mm Glisenti was also used in other pistols and submachineguns. It was the official Italian pistol cartridge in World War I and II. It is similar in physical measurement to the 9mm Luger (Parabellum), but is not loaded as heavily. Regular 9mm Luger ammunition should not be fired in pistols intended for the Glisenti cartridge or loading.

General Comments The 9mm Glisenti is in about the same class as the 38 Automatic and is not quite as powerful as the standard 9mm Luger. Quite a few Glisenti pistols have been sold on the American market through military surplus dealers. Ammunition can be made by loading 9mm Luger cases down to the proper velocity-pressure level. Bullet diameter is 0.355-inch, so standard 9mm Luger bullets can be used. This cartridge is now obsolete, but Fiocchi has recently manufactured it.

9mm Glisenti Loading Data and Factory Ballistics

Bullet (grains/type)	Powder	Grains	Velocity	Energy	Source/Comments
116 FMJ	Bullseye	4.0	1070	294	
123 FMJ	FL		1070	350	Fiocchi factory load
124 FMJ	ML		1050	308	Military load

9x21mm

Historical Notes In many countries such as Italy, Mexico and France, it is illegal for private citizens to own semi-automatic pistols in military chamberings such as 9x19mm Parabellum (9mm Luger). Faced with a strong demand for a powerful, semi-automatic pistol in a non-military chambering, the 9x21mm cartridge was developed in the mid-1980s. It is a 9x19mm Parabellum case lengthened 2 mm. However, a blunt, truncated-cone bullet seated deeply in the case mouth is used. Overall loaded length is, therefore, the same as the 9mm Luger cartridge. Thus, magazines, breech faces and feed ramps that are suitable for one cartridge work fine with the other with little or no modification.

General Comments Ballistically, the 9x21mm offers the same performance as the 9mm Luger, so those barrels and recoil springs can be used. Firearms manufacturers find it easy to transition from 9mm to 9x21 to produce this chambering as needed for specialized markets.

For self-defense, the 9x21mm is fully the ballistic equal of the 9mm Luger. It is suitable for small game hunting with expanding bullets. For handloading, 9mm Luger data can be used. Despite its similarity, these two cartridges are not interchangeable.

With the Western European Union consolidating firearms laws, the prohibition against private ownership of pistols in military chamberings will be ended. The purpose for which the 9x21mm was developed will no longer exist. Therefore, the 9x21mm will probably become history. Fiocchi recently offered this ammunition.

9x21mm Loading Data and Factory Ballistics

Bullet (grains/type)	Powder	Grains	Velocity	Energy	Source/Comments
90 JHTP	BlueDot	10.2	1482	437	Lyman
124 FMJ	AA No. 7	9.8	1335	490	Lyman
147 Lead	AA No. 7	8.0	1089	385	Lyman No. 356637
123 FMJ	FL		1181	380	Patronen factory load (Hungarian)
124 FMJ	FL		1110	340	Fiocchi factory load

9mm Federal

Historical Notes The 9mm Federal was developed by Federal Cartridge Co. and first appeared in its 1989 ammunition catalog. It is a rimmed version of the 9mm Luger, intended for use in revolvers. The first handgun specifically chambered for it was the Charter Arms Pit Bull revolver, also introduced in 1989. This was a five-shot double-action revolver with a 2 1/2-inch barrel similar to the older Police Bulldog model. The use of any rimless cartridge in double-action revolvers has never been entirely satisfactory because of extraction difficulties. The 9mm Federal was designed to eliminate this problem in the same way that the 45 Auto Rim removed the need for the half-moon clips in 45 Automatic revolvers. However, the 9mm Federal lacks the very thick rim characteristic of the 45 Auto Rim. Shortly after its introduction, Charter Arms went out of business. No other manufacturer chambered this cartridge.

General Comments Initial loading of the 9mm Federal was a 115-grain jacketed hollowpoint bullet at 1280 fps muzzle velocity from a 4-inch test barrel. Ballistically this equals or exceeds most +P 38 Special loads and is pushing close to 357 Magnum performance.

The principal advantage of the 9mm Federal was the short case length which would allow shortening the length of the cylinder and frame of revolvers designed for it, thus reducing weight and bulk. However, no gun manufacturer ever did this; Charter Arms merely chambered it in a 38 Special-sized cylinder. As a self-defense or field cartridge, this would be equal to the 9mm Luger.

Unfortunately, the 9mm Federal will chamber in most 38 S&W revolvers. Firing such a combination, particularly in the old top-break type, would almost certainly result in destruction of the revolver and injury or death to the shooter and bystanders. Also some lots or makes of 38 S&W ammunition will fit the 9mm Federal chamber, but it might not be safe to fire these in 9mm Federal guns because of the grossly oversize bullet. Last, but not least, 9mm Luger cartridges will chamber and fire in 9mm Federal revolvers, but this can create extraction and other mechanical problems. In all cases, stick to the ammunition for which the gun is chambered. Reloading data for the 9mm Luger can be used as a guide in working up reloads. In 1992, Federal ceased manufacture of this exceedingly ill-conceived cartridge.

9mm Federal Loading Data and Factory Ballistics

Bullet (grains/type)	Powder	Grains	Velocity	Energy	Source/Comments
115	HS 6	7.7	1270	410	NA
115 JHP	FL		1280	420	Factory load

9mm Mauser

Historical Notes Introduced in 1908, this cartridge was developed for the "Export Model" Mauser auto pistol. Both cartridge and pistol had a relatively short life and were discontinued in 1914 with the outbreak of World War I. Production was not resumed after the war. The 9mm Mauser was designed as a more powerful round than the 7.63mm Mauser, in an effort to capture sales in Africa and South America. It failed in this effort and never became popular, although it is potentially a good field cartridge. The 9mm Mauser was revived in 1933-34 when the Swiss-designed Neuhausen submachine gun and later the Austrian Steyr-Solothurn were chambered for this round. Manufacture of this cartridge then resumed in several European countries. Today, the 9mm Mauser (DWM No. 487) is a collector's item.

General Comments The 9mm Mauser is more powerful than the 9mm Luger and has an edge on the 38 Colt Super Automatic. It develops 534 fpe at the muzzle, compared to 465 and 430 for top factory loadings of the 9mm Luger and 38 Colt Super, respectively. According to the DWM catalog, the 9mm Mauser is loaded with a 123- or 128-grain full-jacketed bullet at an initial velocity of 1362 fps. With modern bullets, this would make a good small to medium game hunting cartridge. The case is approximately 0.23-inch longer than the 9mm Luger, is rimless and Berdan-primed. Empty cases are easily reloaded with any standard 9mm (0.355-inch) 100- to 130-grain bullet.

9mm Mauser Loading Data and Factory Ballistics

Bullet (grains/type)	Powder	Grains	Velocity	Energy	Source/Comments
125	BlueDot	10.6	1300	467	Estimated Velocity
128 FMJ	FL		1362	534	Factory load

9mm Winchester Magnum

Historical Notes Reports on the 9mm Winchester Magnum were circulating as early as 1977, but 11 years later, in late 1988, it was still not exactly an over-the-counter item, although a few individuals were using it in Thompson/Center pistols. This cartridge was listed in the 1988 Winchester-Western Sporting Arms and Ammunition Catalog. In any event, the 9mm Magnum is one of two cartridges developed by Winchester for the stainless steel Wildey gas-operated semi-automatic pistol. This is a rather large handgun (weighing over 3 pounds, unloaded), and holding 14 of these 9mm Magnum rounds. That gun was advertised as available in 5-, 6-, 7-, 8- or 10-inch barrel lengths. It had a ventilated, raised rib over the barrel and an adjustable target-type rear sight. This pistol and cartridge are intended primarily for silhouette competition, but have an obvious field application for hunting small to medium game or big game in the hands of an expert.

General Comments The 9mm Winchester Magnum bears some resemblance to the older 9mm Mauser cartridge and develops roughly comparable ballistics. The Mauser 9mm fires a 128-grain bullet at 1,362 fps whereas the Winchester version has a 115-grain bullet that starts out at 1,475 fps. The energies developed are 534 and 556 foot-pounds respectively, so these are not very far apart. A 115-grain bullet with a muzzle velocity of 1,475 fps (5-inch barrel) is impressive, but less than top handloads in the 357 Magnum, which can develop over 1,550 fps with 125-grain bullets. The 9mm Magnum is certainly more powerful than either the 9mm Luger or the 38 Colt Super and, if loaded with hunting-type bullets, should prove to be very effective for a broad range of hunting situations.

9mm Winchester Magnum Factory Ballistics

Bullet (grains/type)	Powder	Grains	Velocity	Energy	Source/Comments
115 FMJ	FL		1475	556	Factory load

357 Remington Maximum

Historical Notes The 357 Maximum was announced as a joint venture between Remington Arms Co. and Sturm, Ruger and Co. This cartridge is a 3/10-inch elongation of the 357 Magnum case. The first handgun to chamber the round was the Ruger Blackhawk 357 Maximum single-action revolver introduced in 1983. This was followed in 1984 by the Dan Wesson double-action, stainless-steel revolver, the Seville single-action stainless-steel revolver and the Thompson/Center Contender single-shot pistol. During the same year, Harrington & Richardson chambered its Model 258 single-shot rifle for the round, as did Savage in its Model 24V and Model 24VS Camper over/under rifle shotgun combination guns. Although Remington developed the commercial 357 Maximum, a similar wildcat cartridge was actually developed earlier by Elgin Gates.

Unfortunately, the 357 Maximum revolvers all developed excessive gas-cutting on the top strap, just forward of the cylinder, within 1000 rounds or so when fired with full factory loads. Ruger withdrew its Blackhawk 357 Maximum revolver from production pending additional research and possible engineering changes. Dan Wesson has eliminated the problem by establishing a 0.002-inch barrel/cylinder gap for its 357 Maximum revolvers, which have interchangeable barrels that are easily replaced and fine-tuned by the customer, using a furnished gap tool. Top strap erosion also is not a problem, of course, with the single-shot Thompson/Center Contender or the rifles chambering the 357 Maximum.

General Comments Efforts to develop ultra high-velocity revolvers have not been crowned with unbridled success. The 22 Remington Jet in the Model 53 Smith & Wesson revolver is another example of a combination that was discontinued because of mechanical troubles. In the case of the 357 Maximum, the cartridge differs from the standard 357 Magnum only in case length, so one can drop back to shooting the 357 Magnum in any Maximum revolver or simply handload to lower velocity levels using the Maximum case. Factory ballistics were taken in a 10 1/2-inch vented test barrel and actual muzzle velocity from a revolver with the same-length barrel is about 200 fps lower than the advertised figure.

The 357 Maximum was conceived primarily as an ultra-velocity, flat-trajectory silhouette cartridge. That it would also make a good field cartridge for hunting small and medium game is obvious. Many would consider it a good deer cartridge, but when used in a handgun, it would be rather marginal for that purpose. Of course, a good deal depends on the skill of the person using it and, as noted elsewhere, the older, less powerful 357 Magnum has killed its share of big game. Certainly, the 357 Maximum has been used as a big game handgun cartridge, but the measure of success has reflected more upon the person behind the gun than upon the cartridge.

357 Remington Maximum Loading Data and Factory Ballistics

Bullet (grains/type)	Powder	Grains	Velocity	Energy	Source/Comments
125 JHP	W296	25.0	1800	900	Hornady, Speer
140 JHP	W296	23.5	1700	899	Hornady, Speer
158 JHP	W296	21.0	1550	843	Hornady, Speer
180 FMJ	H4227	18.4	1300	676	Sierra, Nosler, Speer, Hornady
158 JHP	FL		1825	1168	Factory load
180 JHP	FL		1550	960	Factory load

38 Automatic (38 ACP)

Historical Notes This is another cartridge designed by John Browning and introduced by Colt in 1900 for its 38 Automatic. In its original form, this pistol was designed as a military gun. From this evolved the seven-shot sporting and eight-shot military models of 1902. This cartridge was stepped up in power in 1929 and the improved round called the 38 Super Auto. In the United States, only Colt chambered it. In England, Webley & Scott chambered it in one version of its military automatic. In Spain, a number of automatics have been made for the 38 ACP.

General Comments Although developed for military and self-defense uses, the 38 Colt Auto achieved a degree of popularity for sporting use through its relatively high velocity. The military turned it down because of previous poor results with the 38 Long Colt. No guns designed for this cartridge have been made since 1928, but plenty of the older model Colt pistols are still used. In power, it is about the same as the 9mm Luger, but it has a longer semi-rimmed case. This cartridge is now obsolete and is no longer loaded by any major ammunition maker.

38 Automatic (38 Colt Automatic/38 ACP) Loading Data and Factory Ballistics

Bullet (grains/type)	Powder	Grains	Velocity	Energy	Source/Comments
115 FMJ	Bullseye	5.0	1150	338	Hornady
125 JHP	Bullseye	4.7	1100	336	Hornady
130 FMJ	FL		1040	312	Factory load

380 Short & Long Revolver

Historical Notes The 380 Revolver cartridge is a British innovation for the Webley revolver and originated about 1868-70. It was loaded in the United States until shortly after World War I. The 38 Short Colt was copied from it, and most 380 revolvers will accept the Colt version. It has been largely replaced by the inside-lubricated 38 S&W.

General Comments The 380 is in the same class as the 38 Short Colt or 38 S&W (see for additional information). Use the same loading data. This ammunition recently has been available from Fiocchi.

380 Revolver Factory Ballistics

Bullet (grains/type)	Powder	Grains	Velocity	Energy	Source/Comments
124 Lead	FL		625	110	Factory load

9.8mm Automatic Colt (9.65 Browning Automatic Colt)

Historical Notes This cartridge is also known as the 9.8 Colt Auto Pistol and was developed by Colt in about 1912, probably for the Model 1911 pistol. It was my understanding that this was part of an effort to secure a contract with the Romanian government, whose military did not like the 45 Automatic. In any event, the Romanians opted for the 9mm Steyr Model 1912 automatic pistol produced in Austria. Only a very few Colt pistols chambered in 9.8mm were ever made, and the cartridge was not introduced in this country. However, an identical cartridge appears to have been produced in Belgium, listed as the 9.65mm Browning Automatic Pistol. American cartridges are headstamped WRA and were manufactured by Winchester; the Belgian cases are marked F.N.

General Comments The 9.8mm Colt is a true 38-caliber with a bullet diameter that varies from 0.378- to 0.381-inch and weighs 130 grains. Actual ballistics are not available, but the muzzle velocity must have been in excess of 1,000 fps, which would put it into the same class as the 38 Automatic. It would have made a good military or self-defense cartridge. With all the new handgun cartridges that have appeared in the last few years, it's a wonder that someone has not latched onto this basic design. Increase the bullet weight to 140 grains and start it out at 1,250 fps and you would have a great self-defense and field cartridge. This chambering is long obsolete and 9.8mm cartridges are collector's items.

9.8mm Automatic Colt (9.65 Browning Automatic Colt) Factory Ballistics

Bullet (grains/type)	Powder	Grains	Velocity	Energy	Source/Comments
130 FMJ	FL		1000	289	Factory load *
*Estimated ballistics					

41 Short Colt

Historical Notes The 41 (Short) Colt uses a heel-base bullet of about 0.401-inch maximum diameter. One of an entire line of cartridges designed for application in various revolvers with cylindrical chambers, this was never a very successful cartridge. The chief complaints involved limited case support on the bullet and the problems associated with the necessary external grease grooves, which tended to attract dirt. It was said that this type of cartridge was among the deadliest on the frontier, not because of its ballistic effect but because the dirt and grime it carried into even a minor wound was almost certain to lead to a fatal infection. The historical reason for the invention of heel-based cartridges stemmed from the era of the conversion cap-and-ball revolver. It was a simple matter to bore a hole of cylinder-mouth diameter full-length through the cylinder. The heel-base bulleted cartridge was invented for use in guns so converted. The original loading used a 160-grain lead bullet and 14 grains of blackpowder.

General Comments The 41 Short Colt was never a popular chambering and offered limited ballistics. It was also very difficult to handload properly. Lyman once offered molds that cast hollow-base bullets of inside case diameter. These were easier to load and removed the problem of the external-lube groove but were not sufficiently accurate to engender any following.

41 Long Colt

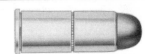

Historical Notes Introduced by Colt with its double-action or Lightning Model revolver in 1877, it was later used in the New Army, New Navy, Army Special, Single Action Army and the Bisley. No revolvers have chambered this cartridge since about the early 1930s. The 41 Short Colt is identical except for case length (0.65-inch) and the 160-grain bullet used. Both rounds were originally blackpowder cartridges using outside-lubricated bullets with a diameter of 0.401-inch. Smokeless powder, inside-lubricated cartridges have hollow-base bullets of 0.387-inch diameter intended to expand into the bore upon exiting the case.

General Comments Although obsolete for a long time, the 41 Long Colt was for some years quite popular. It is largely a short-range number with its slow, heavy bullet, but it has good stopping power. Its performance can be duplicated by using the 200-grain bullet in the 38 Special. It actually is no more powerful than the 38 Special and, in addition, is neither as accurate nor as versatile. It was never popular for hunting, although it would certainly be adequate for small to medium game. These cartridges are now collector's items as there has been no commercial manufacture for many years (Winchester produced a small special-order run about 1970.). Today brass is available from Starline.

41 Long Colt Loading Data and Factory Ballistics

Bullet (grains/type)	Powder	Grains	Velocity	Energy	Source/Comments
200 Lead	Bullseye	3.4	730	235	Duplicate factory load
200 Lead	FL		730	235	Factory load

401 Herter Powermag

Historical Notes This is a proprietary cartridge developed by Herter's Inc. of Waseca, Minn., in 1961. Herter's was a mail-order gun, ammunition and loading supply house that once offered a series of excellent products to the gun trade. The 401 Powermag was chambered in the Herter Powermag single-action revolver. The cartridge is very similar to the 41 Remington Magnum, but the two are not interchangeable. The case of the 41 Remington Magnum is 0.005-inch larger in diameter and 0.009-inch longer than the 401 Powermag. Since the 401 Powermag preceded the 41 Magnum by three years, it is difficult to escape the possibility that it served as the inspiration for Remington. On the other hand, the wildcat 400 Elmer existed in 1924. It is also similar to the 401 and the 41 Magnums, so it is difficult to decide who influenced whom. Ammunition and loading components for the 401 Powermag are no longer available.

General Comments The 401 Powermag is an excellent self-defense or field cartridge. It is capable of doing anything the 41 Magnum can do. It has been used successfully on everything from small game and varmints on up to deer and black bear. With the availability of the commercial 41 Magnum and the many fine guns chambered for it, there is no need for the 401 Powermag, although it was, and still is, a fine cartridge. It is included here for historical significance and perspective.

401 Herter Powermag Loading Data

Bullet (grains/type)	Powder	Grains	Velocity	Energy	Source/Comments
160 JSP	Unique	11.0	1325	625	NA
180 JSP	Unique	10.0	1270	650	NA
200 JSP	Unique	8.5	1140	580	NA
200 JSP	BlueDot	13.0	1280	735	NA

41 Action Express

Historical Notes The 41 Action Express (41 AE) was designed in 1986 by Evan Whildin, vice president of Action Arms. The cartridge is unique among modern handgun cartridges in that it has a rebated rim that will fit 9mm bolt faces and can be used in guns originally designed for the 9mm without the need for extensive changes. The 41 AE is chambered in the Action Arms AT-88, which is a beefed-up copy of the Czech CZ-75 auto pistol. The cartridge was originally developed with a 170-grain JHP bullet at 1130 fps initial velocity. However, the first commercial ammunition, loaded by Samson in Israel and imported into the United States, has a 200-grain flat-nose bullet with a muzzle velocity of 1000 fps, and a 180-grain JHP bullet, also at 1000 fps.

General Comments The 41 AE cannot be readily formed from any other case, although it is possible to make cases from 41 Magnum cases by trimming to 0.866-inch and turning down the rim on a lathe. This is, in fact, how the first experimental cartridges were made by Whildin. According to Bob Olsen of Action Arms, the cross sectional area of the bullet is 33 percent greater than the 9mm, and the bullets are one-third heavier. He also says that the Samson cases have been strengthened to prevent any bulging in blowback guns. Bullet diameter is the same as the 41 Magnum — 0.410-inch.

The 41 AE delivers practically the same ballistics as the 41 Magnum police load, which should make it an effective police or self-defense cartridge. The AT-88 pistol is based on a well-proven design and is accurate and pleasant to shoot. Recoil of the 41 AE is quite noticeably less than the 45 Automatic. The 180-grain load should be a good field load. However, one can handload cases with lighter jacketed or cast bullets. Israel Military Industries (Samson) is the only commercial manufacturer of this round. This concept is so good and performance so nearly ideal for this type of gun that it is quite surprising that this innovative round did not catch on.

41 Action Express Loading Data and Factory Ballistics

Bullet (grains/type)	Powder	Grains	Velocity	Energy	Source/Comments
170 JHP	Unique	6.9	1100	457	Sierra
170 JHP	Herco	7.1	1100	457	Sierra
210 JHP	Unique	5.5	900	378	Sierra, Hornady
180 JHP	FL		1000	400	Factory load
200 FMJ	FL		1000	448	Factory load

44 Merwin & Hulbert

Historical Notes Winchester offered this cartridge beginning in 1882 and continued to catalog it until at least 1916. The Merwin & Hulbert revolver was quite popular and well liked on the frontier. Reproduction guns have even shown up in a few Hollywood productions.

General Comments While this cartridge and gun never received widespread lasting fame, review of the cartridge suggests that it was quite well designed, superior in several ways to many contemporary numbers. Without looking at the headstamp, it would be hard for most shooters to tell that this is not a thoroughly modern cartridge. Ballistics were comparable to the various 44-caliber revolver cartridges of the day.

44 Auto Mag

Historical Notes Introduced late in 1971, this cartridge was developed for the Auto Mag pistol designed by the late Harry Sanford of Pasadena, Calif. The gun was also made and marketed for a few years by High Standard. The cartridge is made by simply cutting off 30-06 or 308 Winchester cases to a length of 1.30 inches, inside reaming the case neck to accept 0.429-inch diameter bullets and finally trimming to a length of 1.298 inches. The newly formed case is then loaded with standard 0.429-inch jacketed bullets of 200 to 240 grains weight. For a time, 44 Auto Mag cases were made in Mexico by Cartuchos Deportivos Mexico and headstamped CDM. Loaded ammunition was later offered by Norma of Sweden. A few custom loaders furnished loaded rounds. Loading and trim dies are made by RCBS. The 44 Auto Mag cartridge was used only in the Auto Mag semi-auto pistol, which is no longer in production.

General Comments The Auto Mag semi-auto pistol operates on the short recoil principle with a six-lug, front-locking rotary bolt. Made almost entirely of stainless steel, it has a 6 1/2-inch barrel, an overall length of 11-1/2 inches and weighs about 3-1/2 pounds. This was the most powerful commercial semi-auto pistol manufactured at that time. When loaded to maximum, a 200-grain bullet can be pushed at over 1500 fps and the 240-grain to 1400 fps. Unfortunately, the Auto Mag pistol had a rather short, stormy career marked by more than its share of manufacturing, marketing and mechanical troubles. The 44 Auto Mag pistol was developed primarily as a sporting gun. It has been used to take all kinds of big game including deer, elk, moose and Kodiak bear. It is in the same class as the 44 Magnum.

44 Auto Mag Loading Data

Bullet (grains/type)	Powder	Grains	Velocity	Energy	Source/Comments
180 JHP	2400	25.0	1600	1024	Sierra
200 JHP	W296	26.5	1500	999	Hornady
240 JHP	W296	24.0	1350	972	Sierra, Hornady
240 JHP	H110	23.0	1400	1045	Hornady

44 Smith & Wesson American

Historical Notes The 44 S&W American was one of the earliest American centerfire revolver cartridges. It was used in the Smith & Wesson single-action Model 3 revolver, known more generally as the 44 S&W American model. It is known to have been in use late in 1870 and was probably introduced as early as 1869. The U.S. Army used this cartridge and revolver for a short time (between 1871 and 1873). The Merwin Hulbert & Co. Army revolver also was made for this round. Commercial ammunition in blackpowder and smokeless powder types was manufactured until about 1940.

General Comments The 44 S&W American is another obsolete blackpowder number that survived an amazing number of years. It used an outside-lubricated bullet of the same diameter as the 44 S&W Russian inside the case, and a slightly larger diameter outside the case. Ammunition with both Boxer- and Berdan-type primers was loaded. Reloadable cases can probably be made by reforming 44 Magnum cases, and dies to do this are available from RCBS. Revolvers for this cartridge are of the older blackpowder type and loads should be kept mild. The 44 American could be used for hunting at short range, but there are better and more modern cartridges available. In power, it is comparable to the 41 Long Colt. These cartridges are now collector's items.

44 Smith & Wesson American Loading Data and Factory Ballistics

Bullet (grains/type)	Powder	Grains	Velocity	Energy	Source/Comments
200 Lead	Unique	5.5	765	259	Lyman No. 419180
205 Lead	FL		682	212	Factory load
218 Lead	Blackpowder (FFg)	25.0	660	196	Factory load

Smith & Wesson New Model No. 3

44 Webley/442 RIC

Historical Notes The 44 Webley originated in 1868 for the Webley Royal Irish Constabulary (RIC) model revolver. In England, it is listed as the 442 Revolver Center Fire. In the United States, it was loaded as the 44 Webley up to about 1940. At least one H&R revolver model chambered it. It was also loaded in Europe, where it is called the 10.5x17Rmm or 442 Kurz (DWM No. 221).

General Comments The 44 Webley was popular for use in pocket-type or self-defense pistols. In power, it is in about the same class as the 41 Long Colt or 44 S&W American. It has much better stopping power than some of the smaller calibers, but is strictly a short-range proposition. Original loading was 15 to 19 grains of blackpowder and a 200- or 220-grain bullet. Late manufactured ammunition used smokeless powder. It is long obsolete and these cartridges are now collector's items.

44 Webley/442 RIC Factory Ballistics

Bullet (grains/type)	Powder	Grains	Velocity	Energy	Source/Comments
200 Lead	FL		715	230	Remington factory load
220 Lead	FL		700	239	Kynoch factory load

44 Bull Dog

Historical Notes The 44 Bull Dog appears to have originated about 1880, perhaps a year or two prior to that. The first reference the author could locate was in the 1880 Homer Fisher gun catalog reproduced in L.D. Satterlee's *Ten Old Gun Catalogs.* British Webley Bull Dog revolvers are advertised therein. American companies loaded the round up to about 1938-39. The 1933 Winchester catalog lists it as for "Webley, British Bull Dog and H&R revolvers."

General Comments The Bull Dog-type pocket revolver was quite popular through the late 1800s. The 44 Bull Dog cartridge was much superior to some of the rimfire cartridges of that period. It provided reasonably good short-range stopping power in a compact gun. However, it is solely a short-range, self-defense round of little value for anything else. It is in the same general class as the 41 Short Colt. The cartridge has been obsolete for a good many years. Both blackpowder and smokeless powder loadings are encountered.

44 Bull Dog Factory Ballistics

Bullet (grains/type)	Powder	Grains	Velocity	Energy	Source/Comments
168-170 Lead	FL		460	80	Factory load

Webley's British Bull Dog

44 Colt

Historical Notes The 44 Colt is yet another blackpowder cartridge of importance primarily because it was once used by the U.S. Army. It was introduced about 1871 and used by the Army from then until 1873. It was used in the metallic cartridge conversion of the Colt 1860 percussion revolver; it could also be fired in the Remington Model 1875 44 Army revolver. Commercial ammunition was loaded in both blackpowder and smokeless powder types up to about 1940.

General Comments The 44 Colt uses an outside-lubricated bullet and is similar to the 44 S&W American, but has a longer case of slightly larger diameter. Early ammunition used the inside Benet cup and Martin folded-type primers. Ammunition has become a collector's item and revolvers for this cartridge are very seldom encountered. Ballistically it is about the same as the 44 S&W American.

44 Colt Factory Ballistics

Bullet (grains/type)	Powder	Grains	Velocity	Energy	Source/Comments
210	Bullseye	4.0	700	226	Lyman No. 429185
210 Lead	Blackpowder (FFg)	23.0	660	206	Factory load
225 Lead	Blackpowder (FFg)	23.0	640	207	Military load
210 Lead	FL		660	206	Factory load
225 Lead	FL		640	207	Factory load

11.75mm Montenegrin Revolver

Historical Notes This cartridge was for the long-obsolete Montenegrin and Austro-Hungarian revolvers based on the Gasser system. The round was introduced about 1870 and is known as the 11mm Austrian Gasser and 11.25x36mm Montenegrin. The revolver for the cartridge is a large, massive hinged-frame type weighing around 4-1/2 pounds. G. Roth manufactured ammunition (No. 287) and apparently so did a number of other companies including a few lots made by Winchester. Both the 11.75mm cartridge and revolver are now in the realm of the collector.

General Comments The 11.75mm is quite a large revolver cartridge, being longer and larger in diameter than the 44 Magnum. The 282- to 313-grain, 0.445-inch bullet is also unusually heavy for a handgun cartridge. As a blackpowder number, it should have knockdown and stopping power on a par with the 44 S&W Special or the 45 Colt, possibly better with the heavier bullet. The author has no loading data, but has been told that ammunition can be made by shortening and extensively reworking empty 45-70 cases.

11.75mm Montenegrin Revolver Factory Ballistics

Bullet (grains/type)	Powder	Grains	Velocity	Energy	Source/Comments
282-313 Lead	FL		700	328	Factory load

11mm French Ordnance Revolver

Historical Notes This was an early French military cartridge for the Model 1873 Ordnance Revolver. It became obsolete in 1892 on adoption of the smaller 8mm Lebel revolver and cartridge. A few of the old M73 revolvers have been sold in surplus stores, although ammunition is very scarce. Evidently, 11mm refers to bore diameter, as barrels measure close to 0.451-inch across the grooves.

General Comments Most military establishments of the period around 1870 used similar handgun cartridges, usually of 43-, 44- or 45-caliber. The 11mm French round is another one not very much different from the 44 S&W Russian. Satisfactory ammunition can probably be made by shortening and reforming 44 S&W Special cases. Lyman No. 42798 (205-grain) cast bullets can be used although undersized. Bullet No. 452460 (200-grain) can also be used if swaged down to about 0.447- to 0.450-inch. There really is not an entirely satisfactory bullet for this particular cartridge. Power is a little less than the 44 S&W Russian, but the 11mm French cartridge would make an effective short-range self-defense or small game field round. This ammunition has been obsolete for many years. Cartridges are scarce collector's items.

11mm French Ordnance Revolver Factory Ballistics

Bullet (grains/type)	Powder	Grains	Velocity	Energy	Source/Comments
180 Lead	Blackpowder		695	195	Military load

11mm German Service Revolver

Historical Notes This cartridge was for the German 1879 and 1883 model service revolvers. It has been obsolete since 1904, but a few of these revolvers were used in World War I and even the last stages of World War II. The cartridge is also listed as the 10.6 or 10.8mm German service or ordnance revolver load (DWM No. 200 & 200A). A moderate number of these revolvers has been sold by surplus dealers in the United States. This cartridge used a heel-based bullet of about 0.451-inch maximum diameter.

General Comments The 11mm German ordnance cartridge bears a close resemblance to the 44 S&W Russian. The two are of the same power. The old German revolvers were designed for blackpowder and only low-pressure smokeless powder loads should be fired in these. Ammunition can be made by shortening and reforming 44 S&W Special cases. This cartridge is obsolete. Ammunition has become a collector's item.

11mm German Service Revolver Factory Ballistics

Bullet (grains/type)	Powder	Grains	Velocity	Energy	Source/Comments
262 Lead	Blackpowder		700	288	Military load

45 Webley

Historical Notes The earliest reference the author could locate regarding the 45 Webley was in the 1876 James Brown & Son gun catalog. * However, it may have originated a year or two earlier. American companies manufactured it up to about 1939. The 1933 Winchester catalog says it is for "Webley and Bull Dog double-action revolvers." It is obsolete.

General Comments The 45 Webley is similar to the 450 Revolver cartridge, but has a slightly longer case. The two will interchange in most revolvers. Originally a blackpowder cartridge, the 45 Webley

was loaded with 20 grains of powder and a 230-grain bullet. Smokeless powder was also used in late loadings. In power, it is in the same class as the 41 Short Colt, but probably has superior stopping power because of the larger, heavier bullet. Ammunition could probably be made by cutting off 455 Webley cases.

L.D. Satterlee op. cit.

45 Webley Factory Ballistics

Bullet (grains/type)	Powder	Grains	Velocity	Energy	Source/Comments
230 Lead	FL		550	150	Factory load, U.S.

45 Automatic Rim (45 Auto Rim)

Historical Notes During World War I, both Colt and Smith & Wesson manufactured revolvers for the 45 Automatic cartridge. This required use of a half-moon clip to support and then eject the rimless 45 Automatic. Thousands of these revolvers were sold on the civilian market after the war ended. In 1920, the Peters Cartridge Co. introduced a rimmed version of the 45 Automatic; this eliminated the need for half-moon clips in the revolver. It was also loaded with a lead bullet, to reduce rifling wear inherent with use of the jacketed 45 Automatic bullets in the unusually soft barrels used.

General Comments Cylinder throats in these revolvers were considerably oversize. Bill Falin, chief ballistician at Accurate Arms, has suggested that this might have been done by design, as a simple means of mitigating chamber pressure when standard 45 Automatic Military rounds were used. Bill's testing demonstrated that heavily jacketed FMJ bullets do not obturate until the rifling is contacted and so a significant amount of gas escapes before peak

chamber pressure occurs. Considering the significant pressure of original 45 Automatic loads, launching 230-grain bullets from the 1911 at an honest 930 fps with powders such as Unique, this might well have been a necessity to keep these somewhat fragile revolvers in one piece. In any case, this is certainly an interesting conjecture.

The 45 Auto-Rim (45 Automatic Rimmed), while similar in performance to the 45 Automatic, is probably a better field or hunting cartridge because it can be handloaded with semi-wadcutter, hollowpoint and other lead hunting bullets. When using such bullets, at slightly increased velocity, it is every bit as good as the 45 Colt revolver cartridge for small through medium game. Many war-surplus 455 Webley revolvers have been altered to shoot the 45 Auto-Rim, and many of these are used in the field. The cartridge is probably more widely used than at anytime since it was introduced. This cartridge is no longer offered by commercial ammunition makers.

45 Automatic Rim Loading Data and Factory Ballistics

Bullet (grains/type)	Powder	Grains	Velocity	Energy	Source/Comments
185 JHP	Bullseye	5.5	850	297	Hornady
200	Bullseye	4.90	750	250	Hornady, Sierra
230	Unique	6.6	800	327	Speer, Sierra
230 Lead	FL		805	331	Factory load

45 Automatic Short

Historical Notes In many countries such as Italy, France and Mexico, it has been illegal for private citizens to own semi-automatic pistols in military chamberings such as 45 Automatic. Gun owners in these countries created a strong demand for a powerful, semi-auto pistol in a non-military chambering. The 45 Automatic Short was developed in response to that demand. It is sometimes called the 45 HP.

This cartridge uses a 45 Automatic case shortened by 1 millimeter. All other case dimensions remain the same. A standard 230-grain FMJ bullet is used, but is seated out so that cartridge overall length and muzzle velocity are identical to the 45 Automatic, using the same loads. Pistols originally designed for the 45 Automatic can quickly be converted to the Short simply by installing a new barrel. All other parts remain the same.

General Comments Because the chamber of the 45 Automatic Short is shorter than the 45 Automatic, the latter round will not chamber in a 45 Short barrel. The letter of the law in the appropriate countries is, therefore, preserved, while shooters can still obtain 45 Automatic performance. The 45 Automatic is famous for its stopping power, and the Short offers identical ballistics. Loading data for the two is interchangeable. With the Western European Union consolidating firearm laws, the prohibition against private ownership of pistols in military chamberings will soon end. Therefore, the purpose for which the 45 Automatic Short exists will end and this cartridge will become obsolete. Only Hirtenberger AG of Austria has commercially loaded this ammunition.

45 Automatic Short Factory Ballistics

Bullet (grains/type)	Powder	Grains	Velocity	Energy	Source/Comments
230 FMJ	FL		835	356	Hirtenberger factory load

45 Colt
45 Colt Government

Historical Notes This was something of a bastardized cartridge, combining the length of the S&W Schofield revolver round with the rim of the Colt SAA round. Army ordnance described at least one version of this cartridge officially as *Revolver Ball Cartridge, Caliber 45.* The Remington-UMC version was labeled (on the box and case heads) as 45 Colt. The evident military incentive for such a loading seems obvious: With both S&W and Colt 45-caliber revolvers (similar, but differently chambered) in use, supplying the correct ammunition to far-flung outposts must have been something of a logistical nightmare. One has to wonder how often troopers found themselves in possession of ammunition that would not work in the gun they had been issued. The 45 Colt ammunition is longer than the Schofield cylinder; chambering Schofield ammunition in the Colt leaves precious little room for rim clearance. It seems likely that some early 45 Colt SAAs would not have chambered some Schofield ammunition, even when the gun was clean. Conversely, the 45 Colt Government, combining the shorter case and smaller

rim, worked (after a fashion) in either gun. Ballistically, it differed little from the standard 45 Colt ordnance loading (which was significantly lighter than the original commercial loading). Available information suggests that this cartridge was available between the late 1870s and the 1930s.

General Comments When the chips are down, having any ammunition that will fit and work in the gun at hand is much better than throwing rocks. However, the Schofield does not function as dependably using the smaller-rimmed 45 Colt Government cases: Incautious manipulation or a somewhat worn gun can result in the extractor slipping past the rim of one or more partially extracted cases. The gun cannot then be closed. Worse, if the cylinder is the slightest bit dirty (blackpowder, remember), removing the offending case can require a dowel, a hammer and at least three hands!

45 Colt Government Factory Ballistics

Bullet (grains/type)	Powder	Grains	Velocity	Energy	Source/Comments
255 LRNFP	Blackpowder (FFFg)	28.0	800	360	Factory load, 1.10-inch case *

*QuickLOAD estimated data. Semi-balloon head sample, headstamped "REM-UMC" over "45 COLT;" slightly rounded primer stamped "U;" 255-grain RNFP bullet appears to match bullets used in original 45 (Long) Colt loads.

450 Revolver/450 Adams

Historical Notes This was the first centerfire revolver cartridge adopted by the British Army. It was adopted for the Adams revolver in November 1868 and saw service until replaced by the 476 Enfield (Mks I & II) in 1880. It was not a satisfactory military round, but became a popular commercial cartridge. American companies loaded it to about 1940 and both Colt and Smith & Wesson chambered revolvers for it. Also loaded in Europe, it is now obsolete. It is often listed as the 450 Short, 450 Adams or 450 Colt. A 450 MkIII was used in World War I as a reserve arm cartridge in Britain.

General Comments The 450 Revolver cartridge was originally a blackpowder round loaded with 13 grains of blackpowder and a 225-grain bullet. Smokeless powder loads were also manufactured. The 450 can be fired in any 455 Webley revolver, and it was often used as a light target-load option. It is in about the same class as the old 44 S&W Russian and makes a good short-range self-defense cartridge. Ammunition can be made from shortened 455 Webley cases. It has been essentially obsolete for decades; however, Fiocchi still occasionally offers this loading.

450 Revolver (450 Adams) Factory Ballistics

Bullet (grains/type)	Powder	Grains	Velocity	Energy	Source/Comments
225 Lead	Blackpowder		650	211	Kynoch factory load
225 Lead	Smokeless powder		700	245	Kynoch factory load
226 Lead	FL		700	245	Fiocchi factory load

476 Eley/476 Enfield MkIII

Historical Notes This was a British military cartridge used from late 1881 to mid-1891, when the 455 Webley Revolver MkI cartridge was introduced. Sometimes called the 455/476, this round has the same case and bullet dimensions as the 455 MkI except that the latter has a 0.05 mm shorter case. Unlike the 476 MkII, the MkIII has a clay plug in the hollow base. The charge was 18 grains of blackpowder. Also known as the 476 Eley and 476 Revolver, the MkIII can be used in any British service 455, but the bullet may be a bit oversized for use in 455 Colts or S&Ws of late manufacture.

General Comments The 476 has caused much confusion among collectors. Here are the facts, we believe: in November 1868, the British Army adopted the 450 Adams revolver cartridge. Generally unsatisfactory, nevertheless the 450 was used in World War I as a reserve weapon, with a MkIII 450 cartridge introduced at the same time. The 450 was officially replaced in 1880 by the 476 Enfield MkI, shortly followed by the 476 MkIII as outlined in the preceding

text. In July 1891, the 455 MkI Webley appeared. Next was a blackpowder load, then a 455 MkI Cordite round (6.5 grains) in September 1894. At about the same time, the 442 cartridge for the R.I.C. was adopted (June 4, 1892), made in only one Mark as a service round. There were also blank cartridges in use — as there were with about all of these British handgun cartridges. The 455 MkII Cordite load was adopted July 1897, this being the first "short" case load, case length being reduced to 19 mm from the original 22mm. Two Cordite loads — a MkIII round approved February 1898 and a MkIV approved May 1912 — were dropped because of bullet form (both were considered of "dum-dum" or "explosive" quality). The last of the 455 ball cartridges was the Mk VI, adopted September 1939, carrying a jacketed bullet and loaded with Cordite (5.5-7.5 grains) or nitrocellulose (5.5 grains). A Mk V had briefly appeared, which was similar to the MkIV, but with antimony in the bullet as a hardening agent.

50 Remington (M71 Army)

Historical Notes This cartridge was introduced in its original version as the 50 Remington Pistol, Navy Model 1867. The cartridge listed here is the 1871 Army modification. Both were used in slightly different models of the Remington single-shot rolling block pistol. The older Navy cartridge had a straight, tapered case, while the Army round had a slight but distinct bottleneck. The Army cartridge also had a larger-diameter rim that prevented it being fired in the Navy pistol. However, the Navy cartridge would chamber and fire OK in the Army pistol. Commercial ammunition was available until about 1920, and used the Navy dimensions. Ammunition was loaded by both Remington and Winchester.

General Comments This is an obsolete blackpowder cartridge of the early centerfire-type originally made with an inside primer. It has been included to complete the record of U.S. military cartridges. The old Remington rolling-block pistols are much esteemed for conversion to modern cartridges and for target shooting. The standard load was 25 grains of FFg blackpowder. This large, heavy bullet should have been a good man-stopper and would certainly be adequate for the usual run of small to medium game at short range. Ammunition for the Army-type pistol can be made from 50-70 cases. Cases with the early inside primers are not reloadable. Some commercial cartridges made with Boxer primers could be reloaded. Both cartridge types are now collector's items.

50 Remington (M71 Army) Loading Data and Factory Ballistics

Bullet (grains/type)	Powder	Grains	Velocity	Energy	Source/Comments
265 Lead	Unique	7.0	750	330	Lyman No. 518144
300 Lead	ML		600	240	Military load

PISTOL & REVOLVER CARTRIDGES OF THE WORLD
Current & Obsolete – Blackpowder & Smokeless Powder
Dimensional Data

Cartridge	Case Type	Bullet Dia.	Neck Dia.	Shoulder Dia.	Base Dia.	Rim Dia.	Rim Thick.	Case Length	Ctge. Length	Twist	Primer
2.7mm Kolibri	D	.107	.139	–	.140	.140		.37	.43	?	B
3mm Kolibri	D	.120	.150	–	.150	.150		.32	.43	?	B
4.25mm Liliput	D	.167	.198	–	.198	.198		.41	.56	?	B
5mm Clement Auto	**C**	**.202**	**.223**	**.277**	**.281**	**.281**	**.025**	**.71**	**1.01**	**?**	**B**
5mm Bergmann	D	.203	.230	–	.273	.274	.020	.59	.96	?	B
5.45x18mm Soviet	C	.210	.220	–	.300	.300		.70	.98	?	SP-B
22 Remington Jet	**A**	**.223**	**.247**	**.350**	**.376**	**.440**	**.055**	**1.28**	**1.58**	**10**	**SP**
221 Fireball	C	.224	.251	.355	.375	.375	.040	1.40	1.82	14	SP
5.5mm Velo Dog	B	.225	.248	–	.253	.308		1.12	1.35	8.2	SP-B
25 Automatic	**D**	**.251**	**.276**	**–**	**.277**	**.298**	**.038**	**.62**	**.91**	**16**	**SP**
256 Winchester Magnum	A	.257	.277	.378	.378	.440	.055	1.30	1.53	14	SP
6.5mm Bergmann	C	.264	.289	.325	.367	.370	.025	.87	1.23	?	B
7mm Nambu	**C**	**.280**	**.296**	**.337**	**.351**	**.359**		**.78**	**1.06**	**12.5**	**B**
7mm Bench Rest				Based on Rem. 308 BR case shortened to 1.50							SP
7.62mm Nagant (Russian)	**B**	**.295**	**.286**	**–**	**.335**	**.388**		**1.53**	**1.53**	**9.5**	**B**
32 Protector	B	.300	.310	–	.310	.352	.040	.350	.555	?	SP
7.65mm Roth-Sauer	D	.301	.332	–	.335	.335		.51	.84	14.2	B
7.62mm Russian Tokarev	C	.307	.330	.370	.380	.390		.97	1.35	10	B
30 Borchardt	C	.307	.331	.370	.385	.390		.99	1.34	?	SP-B
7.63 (7.65) Mannlicher	D	.308	.331	–	.332	.334	.030	.84	1.12	10	B
30 (7.65mm) Luger	C	.308	.322	.374	.388	.391	.045	.75	1.15	9.8	SP-B
30 (7.63mm) Mauser	C	.308	.332	.370	.381	.390	.045	.99	1.36	7.9	SP-B
35 S&W Auto	D	.309	.345	–	.346	.348		.67	.97	12	SP
32 Automatic	H	.309	.336	–	.336	.354	.040	.68	1.03	16	SP
7.65mm MAS (French)	D	.309	.336	–	.337	.337		.78	1.19	?	B
32 S&W	**B**	**.312**	**.334**	**–**	**.335**	**.375**	**.045**	**.61**	**.92**	**16-18**	**SP**
32 S&W Long	B	.312	.335	–	.335	.375	.048	.93	1.27	16-18	SP
32 H&R Magnum	B	.312	.333	–	.333	.371	.050	1.08	1.35	16	SP
32 Short Colt	B	.313	.313	–	.318	.374	.045	.63	1.00	16	SP
32 Long Colt	B	.313	.313	–	.318	.374	.045	.92	1.26	16	SP
32 Colt	B	?	.313	–	.318	.374	.052	.755	1.26	16	SP
320 Revolver	B	.317	.320	–	.322	.350		.62	.90	22	B
7.5mm Swiss Army	B	.317	.335	–	.345	.407		.89	1.29	?	B
8mm Rast-Gasser	**B**	**.320**	**.332**	**–**	**.334**	**.376**		**1.037**	**1.391**	**?**	**?**
8mm Nambu	G	.320	.338	.388	.408	.413		.86	1.25	11	B
8mm Lebel Revolver	B	.323	.350	–	.384	.400		1.07	1.44	9.5	B
7.5mm Nagant (Swedish)	B	.325	.328	–	.350	.406		.89	1.35	18	B
8mm Roth-Steyr	D	.329	.353	–	.355	.356		.74	1.14	10	B
9mm Ultra	**D**	**.355**	**.374**	**–**	**.386**	**.366**		**.72**	**1.03**	**?**	**SP-B**
9mm Browning Long	D	.355	.376	–	.384	.404		.80	1.10	12-16	B
9mm Glisenti	D	.355	.380	–	.392	.393		.75	1.15	10	B
9x21mm	D	.355	.380	–	.392	.393		.830	1.16	10	SP
9mm Bayard	D	.355	.375	–	.390	.392		.91	1.32	?	B
9mm Steyr	D	.355	.380	–	.380	.381		.90	1.30	?	B
9mm Federal	B	.355	.382	–	.386	.435		.754	1.163	9	SP
9mm Luger	D	.355	.380	–	.392	.393	.042	.754	1.16	9.8	SP-B

Cartridge	Case Type	Bullet Dia.	Neck Dia.	Shoulder Dia.	Base Dia.	Rim Dia.	Rim Thick.	Case Length	Ctge. Length	Twist	Primer
9mm Mauser	D	.355	.376	–	.389	.390	.050	.981	1.38	1-12	B
9x23mm Winchester	D	.355	.380	–	.390	.392	.042	.900	1.245	16	LP
9mm Winchester Magnum	D	.355	.379	–	.392	.394	.046	1.16	1.545	1-10	SP
380 Automatic (9mm Browning Short)	**D**	**.356**	**.373**	**–**	**.373**	**.374**	**.040**	**.68**	**.98**	**12-16**	**SP**
38 Short Colt	D	.357	.357	–	.378	.433	.055	.76	1.10	16	SP
38 Long Colt	B	.357	.377	–	.378	.433	.055	1.03	1.32	16	SP
38 Special	B	.357	.379	–	.379	.440	.054	1.16	1.55	16-18	SP
357 S&W Magnum	B	.357	.379	–	.379	.440	.055	1.29	1.51	16-18	SP
357 Maximum	B	.357	.375	–	.375	.433	.055	1.59	1.97	14	SP
357 SIG	C	.357	.381	.424	.425	.424		.865	1.140	16	SP
38 Automatic & 38 Super Automatic	H	.358	.382	–	.383	.405	.045	.90	1.28	16	SP
9.8mm Auto Colt	D	.378	.404	–	.404	.405		.912	1.267	?	SP
38 S&W	B	.359	.386	–	.386	.433	.055	.78	1.20	16-18	SP
9mm Makarov	D	.363	.384	–	.389	.396		.71	.97	?	B
380 Revolver	B	.375	.377	–	.380	.426	.046	.70	1.10	15	SP-B
40 S&W Auto	**D**	**.400**	**.423**	**–**	**.423**	**.424**	**.050**	**.850**	**1.135**	**16**	**SP**
10mm Auto	D	.400	.423	–	.423	.424	.050	.99	1.26	16	LP
41 Short Colt	B	.401	.404	–	.405	.430	.052	?	?	?	SP
41 Long Colt	B	.386/401	.404	–	.405	.430	.052	1.13	1.39	16	SP
41 Action Express	J	.410	.434	–	.435	.394	.045	.866	1.17	16-18	SP
41 Remington Magnum	B	.410	.432	–	.433	.488	.054	1.28	1.58	18	LP
10.4mm Italian	B	.422	.444	–	.451	.505		.89	1.25	10	B
44 Merwin & Hulbert	**B**	**.424**	**.442**	**–**	**.442**	**.502**	**.060**	**1.15**	**1.53**	**?**	**SP**
44 S&W Russian	B	.429	.457	–	.457	.515	.050	.97	1.43	20	LP
44 S&W Special	B	.429	.457	–	.457	.514	.055	1.16	1.62	20	LP
44 Auto Mag	D	.429	.457	–	.470	.473	.048	1.298	1.620	20	LP
44 Remington Magnum	B	.429	.457	–	.457	.514	.055	1.29	1.61	20	LP
44 S&W American	B	.434	.438	–	.440	.506	.050	.91	1.44	20	LP
44 Webley	B	.436	.470	–	.472	.503		.69	1.10	20	LP-B
44 Bull Dog	B	.440	.470	–	.473	.503		.57	.95	21	SP-B
44 Colt	B	.443	.450	–	.456	.483		1.10	1.50	16	LP
11.75mm Montenegrin	**B**	**.445**	**.472**	**–**	**.490**	**.555**		**1.40**	**1.73**	**?**	**B**
11mm French Ordnance	B	.451	.449	–	.460	.491	.035	.71	1.18	16	B
11mm German Service	B	.451	.449	–	.453	.509		.96	1.21	23	B
45 Winchester Magnum	**D**	**.451**	**.475**	**–**	**.477**	**.481**	**.045**	**1.198**	**1.55**	**16**	**LP**
45 Webley	B	.452	.471	–	.471	.504		.82	1.15	?	LP-B
45 Auto-Rim	B	.452	.472	–	.476	.516	.085	.898	1.28	15-16	LP
45 Automatic Short	D	.452	.476	–	.476	.476	.044	.860	1.17	16	LP
45GAP	D	.452	.473	–	.476	.470	.049	.760	1.137	16	LP
45 Automatic	D	.452	.476	–	.476	.476	.044	.898	1.17	16	LP
454 Casull	B	.452	.476	–	.480	.512	.055	1.39	1.70	16	S*
460 Smith & Wesson	B	.452	.478	–	.478	.520	.059	.1.80	2.290		LP
455 Webley Revolver Mk-II	B	.454	.476	–	.480	.535		.77	1.23	16-20	LP-B
45 Colt Government	B	.454	.478	–	.478	.506	.055	1.10	1.44	16-24	LP
45 S&W Schofield	B	.454	.478	–	.478	.522	.055	1.10	1.43	24	LP
45 Colt	B	.454	.476	–	.480	.512	.055	1.29	1.60	16	LP

Cartridge	Case Type	Bullet Dia.	Neck Dia.	Shoulder Dia.	Base Dia.	Rim Dia.	Rim Thick.	Case Length	Ctge. Length	Twist	Primer
450 Revolver	B	.455	.475	–	.477	.510		.69	1.10	16	LP-B
455 Webley Auto	H	.455	.473	–	.474	.500		.93	1.23	10	B
455 Enfield (455 Colt)	B	.455	.473	–	.478	.530	.035	.87	1.35	?	LP-B
476 Enfield	B	.472	.474	–	.478	.530		.87	1.33	?	B
50 Action Express	**J**	**.500**	**.540**	**–**	**.547**	**.514**	**.055**	**1.285**	**1.610**	**?**	**LP**
500 Wyoming Express	F	.500		–				1.370	1.765		LR
500 Smith & Wesson	B	.500	.530	–	.530	.560	.059	2.250			LP
50 Remington Army	A	.508	.532	.564	.565	.665		.875	1.24	?	LP

Notes on handgun primers: Magnum pistol cartridges are usually loaded with Magnum pistol primers and the 22 Remington Jet and 256 Winchester are sometimes loaded with Small Rifle primers. During WWI, Frankford Arsenal made 45 Automatic cases with special #70 primers of .204" diameter instead of the standard .210"

Case Type: A = Rimmed, bottleneck. B = Rimmed, straight. C = Rimless, bottleneck. D = Rimless, straight. E = Belted, bottleneck. F = Belted, straight. G = Semi-rimmed, bottleneck. H = Semi-rimmed, straight. I = Rebated, bottleneck. J = Rebated, straight. K = Rebated, belted bottleneck. L = Rebated, belted straight.

Primer Type: S = Small rifle (0.175"). SP = Small pistol (0.175"). L = Large rifle (0.210"). LP = Large pistol (0.210"). B = Berdan type. B-1 = Berdan #1. B-2 = Berdan #2.

Other codes: V = OAL depends upon bullet used V – Rifling twist varies, depending upon bullet and application. ∂ = Belt/Rim Diameter. Unless otherwise noted, all dimensions in inches. Twist (factory) is given as inches of barrel length per complete revolution, e.g., 12 = 1 turn in 12", etc.

*Full-power loads always use small rifle primers.

Current Military Handguns of the World

Nation	Gun	Chambering	Type	Cap.	Bbl.	Wgt.	Remarks
Argentina	Browning Hi-Power P-35	9mm Luger	S-A	13	5	32	
Austria	Glock 80	9mm Luger	S-A	17	4.5	16	
	Walther P-38	9mm Luger	S-A	8	4.8	34	
Australia	FN35	9mm Luger	S-A	13	5	32	Browning Hi-Power
Belgium	Browning Hi-Power	9mm Luger	S-A	13	5	32	Very good sporting gun
Britain	Browning Hi-Power	9mm Luger	S-A	13	5	32	Adopted by Canada during World War II
Canada	FN 35	9mm Luger	S-A	13	5	32	Browning Hi-Power
China (PRC)	Type 59	9mm Makarov	S-A	8	3.7	19	Similar to Russian PM
	Type 64	7.65x17mm	S/S-A	9	3.7	47	Silenced
	Type 51/54	7.62mm TOK	S-A	8	4.5	33	Tokarav 7F-33
Czech Republic	Cz M-52	7.62mm Russ.	S-A	8	4.7	25	Original design, very good pistol
Slovak Republic	Cz M-83	9mm Makarov	S-A	13	3.8	17	
Denmark	Browning Hi-Power	9mm Luger	S-A	13	5	32	
	SIG P210	9mm Luger	S-A	8	4.7	23 1/2	
Egypt	Helwan	9mm Luger	S-A	8	4.5	23	Beretta 951 Copy
	Beretta M951	9mm Luger	S-A	8	4.5	23	
France	M-1950	9mm Luger	S-A	9	4.4	29	Similar to Browning Hi-Power
	MAB PA-15	9mm Luger	S-A	15	4.7	28	
	SIG P220	9mm Luger	S-A	9	4.7	21.6	
	Beretta	9mm Luger	S-A	15	4.9	25	
Germany	Walther P-38	9mm Luger	S-A	8	4.8	34	A most modern design
Hungary	Model 48	7.65mm Br.	S-A	8	4	24	Mod. Walther PP design
	Model 48	7.62mm Tok.	S-A	7	3.3	22	
India	FN35	9mm Luger	S-A	13	5	32	Browning Hi-Power
Israel	Beretta M951	9mm Luger	S-A	8	4.5	23	
Italy	Beretta M-51	9mm Luger	S-A	8	4.5	31	Very good. Available in U.S.
	Beretta M-34	9mm Br. Short & 7.65mm	S-A	7	3.5	24	Similar model sold in U.S.
	Beretta M-92	9mm Luger	S-A	15	4.9	25	
Japan	SIG P220	9mm Luger	S-A	9	4.7	21.6	
Mexico	Obregon	45 Automatic	S-A	7	5	39	Resembles Colt 45 Auto
New Zealand	FN35	9mm Luger	S-A	13	5	32	Browning Hi-Power
Poland	P7M13	9mm Luger	S-A	13	4.1	25	
	P-64	Makarov	S-A	6	3.3	23	
South Africa	FN35	9mm Luger	S-A	13	5	32	Browning Hi-Power
	Z88	9mm Luger	S-A	15	4.9	25	
Spain	Llama 82	9mm	S-A	15	4.5	29	
	Astra A80	9mm	S-A	15	3.8	25	
	Star 30M	9mm	S-A	15	4.7	30	
Sweden	FN Browning M-07	9mm Brown. (380)	S-A	7	5	32	Similar to Colt Pocket Auto
	SIG P-210	9mm Luger	S-A	8	4.7	24	
Switzerland	SIG P-210	9mm Luger	S-A	8	4.7	24	
Commonwealth of Ind. States	PSM	5.45mm	S-A	8	3.4	12	
	Makarov M-PM	9mm Makarov	S-A	8	3.8	26	Mod. Walther PP
	Stechin-APS	9mm Makarov	S-A	20	5	30	Full auto. fire selector
	Tokarev TT 30 & 33	7.62mm Tok.	S-A	8	4.5	33	Simplified Browning design
Turkey	MKE	9x17mm	S-A	7	3.9	18	
United States	Beretta M-92-S	9mm Luger	S-A	15	4.9	34	Adopted 1985
	Colt M-1911 & M1911A1	45 Automatic	S-A	7	5	39	Military & civilian models

NOTE – Only the principal or official model is listed. Most governments used a variety of alternative types and officers often used nonofficial makes. S-A = Semi-auto Cap. = Magazine capacity Bbl. = Barrel length in inches Wgt. = Weight in ounces.

Chapter 7

Military Rifle Cartridges of the World

(Current & Obsolete—Blackpowder & Smokeless)

THE SALE and use of surplus military firearms in the United States goes back to at least the Civil War and probably earlier. During World War I, American companies manufactured rifles for the British, French and Russian governments. At war's end, when military orders were canceled, they found themselves stuck with undelivered quantities. As a result, a lot of new Enfields, Lebels and Mosin-Nagant rifles showed up in the civilian market, and for a time, 7.62mm Russian and 8mm Lebel sporting ammunition was loaded by American companies. However, nothing in previous history matched the variety and quantity of military arms marketed in the United States after World War II. The first influx occurred about 1947-48. Those were mostly captured enemy guns. However, in the 1950s, practically all of the world powers were in the process of adopting new and more modern military small arms. They sold their older models to surplus dealers who immediately offered those guns in the United States. This period offered unprecedented opportunities to shoot, experiment with and remodel military rifles. Dealers sold many fine and brand new military rifles and handguns at very low prices. Few of these arms sold at prices over $35 to $40 and many sold at $10 to $25. Some of these same guns will bring upward of $300 on today's market. Not a single issue or model ever went down in value.

The Gun Control Act of 1968 ended the importation of surplus guns on such a scale. It is doubtful that we will ever again see anything comparable to the war surplus phenomenon during the period between 1948 and 1968, although recently the surplus market did loosen up again. Consequently, a variety of military rifles are used for target practice, plinking and large and small game hunting in America. Tinkers and gunsmiths can alter most military rifles into first-class sporting arms, and tens of thousands were so altered. Naturally, the cartridges used by these various rifles are of interest to those shooting the guns because, after all, the gun is of no use without the ammunition. That era exposed the American sportsman to chamberings all but unknown prior to World War II, which influenced subsequent cartridge development in this country.

Military ammunition represents one of the most highly developed categories of the metallic cartridge. Military ballisticians have spent untold millions of dollars in research to determine the best and most efficient combination of primer, case, powder and bullet. The resulting degree of perfection explains why military cartridges are so popular for sporting use. This explains why any cartridge adopted as a nation's official military chambering is so likely to become popular in civilian applications. American military cartridges have been highly esteemed in sporting circles and all but the old 6mm Lee and 50-70 are still loaded and used. (Manufacturers have recently reintroduced 50-70 components and sportsmen are again using this cartridge — in Cowboy Action Shooting, for example). Foreign military chamberings do not offer the American sportsman anything new or different, although most are quite good in basic design and performance. These cartridges largely parallel what we already have available. The exceptions are the various 6.5mm and 7mm chamberings, which represent an area that was formerly neglected here.

Middle European, Mediterranean, Scandinavian and Oriental countries have favored 6.5mm cartridges for their military rifles. These cartridges are all quite similar in performance and power and offer little to choose from for sporting use. From the American viewpoint, the 6.5mm Mannlicher-Schoenauer and the 6.5x55mm Swedish are the best choices. However, any of these are good deer and antelope cartridges, superior to anything in the 30-30 class for this purpose. Most are appropriate for use against larger game when loaded with heavier bullets. The 7x57mm Mauser is another cartridge well known in sporting circles. It is well adapted to North American game and hunting conditions. It is listed along with the 8x57mm Mauser and the 303 British under American sporting cartridges because all three are loaded in this country and have been for many years. An interesting recent development has been the widespread availability of the 7.62x53R Russian and 7.62x39mm Soviet cartridges and guns to shoot these cartridges.

A surprising number of obsolete single-shot and repeating blackpowder military rifles have shown up since 1948. Many of these rifles are brand new or in first-class condition. This has spurred shooting interest. The centerfire blackpowder cartridges listed include those that an average neophyte might encounter, along with a few comparatively rare, albeit interesting, examples. Caliber varies from 32 to 60 with bullet weights from 250 to over 500 grains. The original powder used was coarse granulation blackpowder similar to what we know as Fg. The charge ranged from 40 grains to over 80 grains. There was also variation of the powder charge within the same cartridge, owing to use of different bullets and lot-to-lot variation in powder density and performance. Most countries also had a carbine loading, which was lighter than standard. In power, all these old cartridges are similar to our own 45-70 and are adequate for most North American big game at short to moderate range. Standard loadings from these rounds all have a very curved trajectory, which makes it difficult to hit anything beyond 200 yards, although these will kill much further away. However, at known ranges, these are typically quite accurate and will turn in good scores out to 500 or even 1,000 yards.

Continued use of blackpowder military rifles will eventually require reloading of fired cases. All but the American cartridges use Berdan primers, usually of 6.37mm (0.251-inch), 6.46mm (0.254-inch) or 6.5mm (0.256-inch) size. These sizes are available from RWS. Lyman, Hornady, RCBS and others make loading dies for the more popular blackpowder cartridges. It is often possible to make reloadable cases from similar modern cases by trimming and reforming. To produce good ballistics and proper burning, blackpowder charges should fill the case to the base of the bullet; preferably, while seating the bullet, it should slightly compress the charge. When using smokeless powder to load blackpowder cartridges, never exceed original velocity or pressure, as few rifles are strong enough to safely withstand such treatment. Accurate Arms offers simple instructions for loading AA 5744, so as to duplicate the pressure and velocity of the original blackpowder load in any typical rifle cartridge. In brief, begin with a charge that fills 45 percent of the available powder space in the case (room left over with bullet seated normally). Increase the charge, as needed, until the load duplicates the velocity of the original (blackpowder) loading. After firing with blackpowder, cases must be soaked and scrubbed in soap or detergent to remove the fouling, then dried before reloading. A bullet alloy of one part tin to 16 or 20 parts lead is about right for blackpowder, but a mixture of one-to-10 is more satisfactory with smokeless charges. Use of hard, jacketed bullets in blackpowder rifles is not good practice, as these will often rapidly wear the bore, sometimes destroying accuracy within only 100 rounds or so. If you use common sense and exercise reasonable caution, shooting obsolete military rifles is a lot of fun and is perfectly safe if the gun is in good condition.

The subject of military rifles is too broad and involved to be covered adequately in a book devoted primarily to cartridges. However, we have included tables listing the more common smokeless and blackpowder military rifles and their characteristics. In passing, it might be well to at least mention two badly abused phases of the military rifle subject — safety and value. Some authors who should know better have stated bluntly and without qualification that all surplus military arms are unsafe, worthless pieces of junk. This simply is not true. The idea that any military power would arm its troops with guns inherently dangerous to fire is too silly to merit serious discussion. Toward the end of World War II, Germany and Japan turned out some shoddy, makeshift arms for drill, guard or civilian use. Some of these used castings and were definitely not safe to fire. Others looked like hell but were actually quite stout. In any event, these were not standard military issue and the surplus gun market handled very few of these. For marketers to have sold dangerous and unsafe guns would have ended the big surplus military boom long before the Gun Control Act of 1968. That is just a matter of common sense.

I believe it is entirely correct to state that no standard military rifle is any more dangerous than any other if it is in good condition and is fired with the cartridge and load for which it was designed. Use the correct ammunition and exercise common sense in handloading and you will not get in trouble. Alteration of military rifles to other than the original chambering is all right, too, if you know what you are doing. On the other hand, this can be dangerous if mishandled, for it requires knowledge of the relative strength, mechanics and metallurgy of military rifle actions.

Value? Only you can determine the value a certain gun has for you. "Value," as such, has really been beaten to death. Such terms as "good," "bad," "worthless" or a "good buy" are all relative, for their meaning will vary with the buyer and his individual ideas. As late as 1940, one could buy U.S. 1873 45-70 Springfield rifles for $6.50 used and $11 brand new. I owned several and wish I had had both the money and the foresight to have purchased a whole garage full because these rifles are currently worth around $500 in good condition. One must understand, though, that alteration of a military rifle destroys its value as a collector's item. It may then be worthless. Time and availability are big factors in the value of anything.

American-made sporting ammunition included the more popular foreign military chamberings up until about the mid-1930s. The 6.5mm Mannlicher-Schoenauer, 7x57mm Mauser, 7.65mm Mauser, 7.62mm Russian, 8mm Mauser and 8mm Lebel were all made in the United States, along with the 303 British. At present, few American sporting rifles chamber foreign military cartridges and only the 6.5x55mm Swedish, 7mm and 8mm Mauser, plus the 303 British are loaded here. However, Norma and RWS have recently loaded some of these cartridges in sporting version. Most of these are imported through U.S. dealers.

Hunters should not use military ammunition loaded with full-metal-jacket bullets. These bullets are designed to wound, not necessarily kill. Also, bear in mind that full-jacketed bullets will not break up on contact; more often than not, these will ricochet badly. This is also true of the big, low-velocity bullets fired by blackpowder rifles.

Handloading will improve performance of most military cartridges to varying degrees. Most European ammunition is loaded with corrosive Berdan-type primers which (without special tools) are not as quick or easy to decap and reprime as the Boxer-primed cases used by American manufacturers. Many others use steel cases that are not routinely reloadable. Norma continues to import ammunition and cases made for American primers in a number of military chamberings. Availability of reloadable cases is an important consideration because the supply of surplus ammunition is not inexhaustible. The ultimate use of your rifle may depend on just such a small item as this. Some military cartridges have never been loaded as sporting ammunition, but the handloader can correct this deficiency. Some of the old blackpowder military rifles have been relegated as wall hangers because of lack of ammunition, but this situation is changing as small manufacturers now offer these cases to the handloader. Buffalo Arms (208-263-6953) offers many such cases. Many cartridges listed in Chapter 6 are obsolete from the military viewpoint. The United States, the United Kingdom and all NATO countries have adopted the 7.62x51mm NATO round as have Japan, Australia and many Asian countries. In addition, practically all of these countries now use the 5.56x45mm (223 Remington) for their military rifles. The U.S. used this smaller round almost exclusively in Vietnam. Russia and most former satellite countries have adopted the Russian M43 or 7.62x39mm cartridge. In 1974, the Soviet Union adopted a new 22-caliber round designated the 5.45x39mm.

Recent development in military cartridges has been in the realm of caseless cartridges. Efforts to develop caseless small arms ammunition have not been fully successful to date. The word from ordnance circles is, "Happiness is still a cartridge case." — FCB

4.85mm British

Historical Notes An experimental British military cartridge of less than 22 caliber that more or less parallels similar developments by Germany. Although entered in the NATO trials in 1977, none of these small-caliber cartridges were ever adopted, although some of these cartridges developed initial velocities in excess of 4000 fps. The problem with these small, lightweight high-velocity bullets is that all lose velocity and energy rapidly, and, from a military viewpoint, are not very effective beyond moderate range. A gilding metal-clad steel-jacketed bullet of 0.192-inch diameter with lead alloy core and flat base was used. Both Ball and tracer types were made. Further development ended after the 1977 NATO trials.

General Comments The dimensions of the 4.85mm British are practically identical to the wildcat 5mm/223 except that the case is about 1/5-inch longer, due to a longer neck. Muzzle velocity would be similar.

4.85mm British Factory Ballistics

Bullet (grains/type)	Powder	Grains	Velocity	Energy	Source/Comments
56	ML		3117	1210	Military load (L1E1 Ball)

5.7x28mm FN P90 (Belgium)

Historical Notes Developed in the late 1980s by FN for its new P90 personal defense gun, this cartridge is intended to replace the 9x19mm Parabellum pistol cartridge. Claimed ballistic performance is much superior to the 9mm cartridge. As yet, no major country has adopted this new chambering.

General Comments The 5.7x28mm cartridge is somewhat similar in shape to the commercial 221 Fireball cartridge. However, the two are not interchangeable. A sharply pointed Ball bullet weighing only 23 grains is used, as intended range is limited. Despite this, this bullet has been designed to penetrate helmets and body armor at 50 meters without breaking up.

5.7x28mm FN P90 Factory Ballistics

Bullet (grains/type)	Powder	Grains	Velocity	Energy	Source/Comments
23 FMJ-BT Ball	ML		2790	400	Military Load

5.45x39mm Soviet

Historical Notes This is a Russian cartridge introduced about 1974 for use in the new AK-74 assault rifle. There are both fixed-stock and folding-stock versions and the 5.45mm rifle has a redesigned flash reducer/muzzle brake that distinguishes it from the earlier AK-47. The cartridge has a more slender case and a thicker rim than the 7.62x39mm (M43) cartridge. The bullet is 0.221- to 0.222-inch in diameter and weighs from 53 to 54 grains. This bullet is almost 1 inch long and has a very sharp spitzer point, a boattail base, a mild steel core and a short lead filler on top and an air space in the nose. The bullet is designed to be unstable in tissue, producing a more severe wound. The British used somewhat the same idea in the design of their MKVII 303 bullet used in World War II. Casualty reports from Afghanistan, where the new 5.45mm cartridge and rifle first appeared, tend to confirm the lethality of the bullet. Muzzle velocity is approximately 2950 fps.

The first 5.45mm Soviet cartridges publicly available to western military intelligence were brought out of Afghanistan by Galen Geer while on assignment for *Soldier of Fortune* magazine in 1980,

and the first information made public was in the October 1980 issue of *Soldier of Fortune*. Until that time, the existence of a new Russian military cartridge was mostly rumor. Later, the round was withdrawn from service in Afghanistan. Cases are lacquered steel with Berdan primers.

General Comments The Russians apparently designed this cartridge as the result of experience on the receiving end of the U.S. M-16 rifle and 5.56mm round in Vietnam. The 5.45mm Russian is a well-designed cartridge for its intended purpose. The long, thin boattail bullet reduces aerodynamic drag to the minimum and results in higher-retained velocity at long range. The bullet is designed to be stable in flight and provide good accuracy at all ranges out to maximum, but unstable on contact so as to tumble easily, which enhances lethality. It is a better-designed military bullet than the original bullet used in the United States. M193 5.56mm cartridge. However, the new 5.56mm SS109 (M855) NATO standard round with its heavier bullet and improved shape probably has an edge over the Soviet bullet.

5.45x39mm Russian Factory Ballistics

Bullet (grains/type)	Powder	Grains	Velocity	Energy	Source/Comments
54	ML		2950	1045	Military load (SBT Ball)

5.56x45mm NATO

Historical Notes The 5.56x45mm cartridge was originally developed for the Armalite AR-15 rifle and first tested by the U.S. Air Force as a possible replacement for the M-1 Carbine in 1960-1961. The AR-15 later evolved into the selective-fire M-16 adopted by the U.S. military in 1964 after several years of testing by the U.S. Continental Army Command at Fort Monroe, Va. The rifle and cartridge were first combat-tested in Vietnam in the early 1960s.

General Comments As initially loaded, the 5.56x45mm Ball cartridge had a 55-grain spitzer boattail bullet at a muzzle velocity of 3,250 fps. It was the standard U.S. military loading until 1984. In 1980, the 5.56mm FN-designed, 62-grain SS109 bullet was adopted by NATO. Designated the M855 in the United States, the new load

uses a spitzer boattail bullet with a mild steel penetrator in front of the lead base. Muzzle velocity is 3100 fps. Adoption also involved changes in 5.56mm rifles to a quicker rifling twist of one turn in 7 inches to stabilize the longer, heavier bullet. This much-improved bullet resulted in higher retained velocity and greater accuracy at long range. It also has much improved penetration characteristics over the old M193 55-grain projectile at all ranges.

The 5.56mm case is similar in configuration to and interchangeable with the commercial 223 Remington, although SAAMI warns that dimensional differences between military chambers and commercial chambers may make it unsafe to fire military ammunition in sporting rifles. Additional information and loading data can be found under that listing in Chapter 2.

5.56x45mm NATO Factory Ballistics

Bullet (grains/type)	Powder	Grains	Velocity	Energy	Source/Comments
55 FMJ-BT M193 Ball	ML		3250	1325	U.S. Military load, old
62 FMJ-BT M855 Ball			3100	1325	NATO load, new

5.8x42mm Chinese

Historical Notes Surprisingly, in the mid-1990s, the Chinese military introduced a new indigenous 5.8x42mm Small-Caliber High-Velocity (SCHV) assault rifle round and a new family of small arms to use it. This was the result of research spanning more than two decades. Like the Russians, the advantages of SCHV assault rifle ammo observed in Vietnam War battle reports did not go unnoticed by the Chinese military. So, in March, 1971, the Chinese military logistic department commenced a small arms research project known as the "713 Conference" in Beijing to develop the design criteria for an indigenous SCHV assault rifle cartridge.

The design criteria called for a cartridge of approximately 6mm caliber, 1,000 meters per second muzzle velocity with the goals of, reducing recoil and ammo weight while improving accuracy and terminal ballistics over the Type 56/M43 7.62x39mm full-caliber intermediate round. The following "744 Conference" narrowed down the calibers under consideration to 5.8mm and 6mm caliber. The project completed its development in the 1987 and the new SCHV assault rifle cartridge was officially designated as the DBP87.

The Chinese military has since developed a variety of small arms chambered for the new 5.8mm cartridge. The first was the QBZ87 assault rifle primarily used as the test bed for further 5.8mm ammo development. The QBZ87 was an undated 7.62mm Type 81 assault rifle chambered for the new 5.8mm round. The QBZ87 is now largely withdrawn from frontline services and has been handed over to paramilitary, military academies, and reservists.

Next came the QBZ95 assault rifle family comprised of the QBZ95 assault rifle, QBB95 squad automatic rifle/light machine gun and the QBZ95B carbine. The QBZ95 (Qing, Bu-Qiang, Zi-Dong, 1995 Si or Infantry Rifle, Automatic, Model 1995) is a modern looking 7.1 pound (3.25kg) assault rifle in a "bullpup" configuration. Like other bullpup rifles, such as French FAMAS, Austrian AUG and the British SA80, the QBZ has its magazine and action located behind its trigger and pistol grip.

General Comments The 5.8mm ammo is much more conventional than the weapons that are chambered for it. The 5.8mm standard rifle load has a 64 grain (4.15g) bullet with a full metal jacket made of steel and copper-washed coating. The 24.3mm long projectile has a very streamlined external shape with a sharp bullet ogive and a sizeable boat-tail. The 5.8mm bullet has a composite core that consists of a pin shaped hardened steel penetrator located near the base of the bullet, with lead as the filling material between the penetrator and the jacket as well as the tip cavity.

The 5.8mm cartridge has a 42mm long case with a one degree taper in the body from its 10.5mm diameter base. The bottleneck shoulder and the neck are both 4mm long. The shorter but wider 5.8mm case is more space efficient than the long and slim case of the 5.56mm. The tapered case design also helps both ammo feeding and extraction. However, the straight wall case design of the 5.56mm has better accuracy.

5.8x42mm Chinese Factory Ballistics

Bullet (grains/type)	Powder	Grains	Velocity	Energy	Source/Comments
64 gr FMJ BT	Corrosive	approx 28.0	3050	1325	Timothy G. Yan

6mm SAW (U.S.)

Historical Notes In the early 1970s, the U.S. Army began studies to develop a new infantry squad machinegun called the Squad Automatic Weapon (SAW). Frankford Arsenal began computerized parametric design analyses in July 1971 to design a cartridge to meet user requirements. After several experimental designs based on the 5.56x45mm case proved unsuccessful, a new case having a larger 0.410-inch diameter head and a length of 1.779 inches was adopted. A 6mm diameter (0.243-inch), 105-grain FMJ-BT bullet was used.

General Comments Cartridge cases for the 6mm SAW will be found in both steel (with a phenolic varnish finish) and in aluminum (with an anodized finish). The aluminum case is longer than the steel case. The 6mm SAW was never adopted, although considerable quantities of ammunition were loaded experimentally by Frankford Arsenal. This cartridge is frequently encountered in collections. It is historically significant as the first cartridge designed using computerized parametric design analysis. Interestingly, ballistics are quite similar to the circa 1895 Lee Navy cartridge.

6mm SAW Factory Ballistics

Bullet (grains/type)	Powder	Grains	Velocity	Energy	Source/Comments
105 FMJ-BT	ML		2520	1480	Military load, XM732 Ball

6mm Lee Navy

Historical Notes The 6mm Lee cartridge (also known as the 236 Navy) was used in the 1895 Lee Straight Pull bolt-action military rifle manufactured by Winchester for the United States Navy. About 15,000 of these rifles were made and used by the Navy on a trial basis. Winchester, Remington and Blake also chambered sporting rifles for this cartridge. No factory-loaded ammunition has been available since 1935.

General Comments The 244 or 6mm was revived in two cartridges introduced by Remington and Winchester in 1955, the 244 (now the 6mm Remington) and 243. The 6mm Lee cartridge died out mainly because it was too far ahead of its time. The powders available in 1895 were not suitable to this cartridge. A few shooters who have old rifles for this round handload and use it for hunting. It is a good varmint, medium game, deer, black bear and antelope cartridge at moderate ranges. It is not as powerful as the 6mm Remington or the 243 Winchester. By increasing the rim to fit the standard Mauser bolt face and necking the case to accept 0.224-inch bullets, Winchester created the 220 Swift. See Chapter 3 for data.

6.5x50mm Japanese Arisaka

Historical Notes This cartridge, best known for its use in the modified Mauser-type Model 38 Japanese bolt-action rifle of 1905, was actually introduced in 1897 for a discontinued rifle found unsafe in service. It was introduced in the United States after World War II as the result of captured rifles brought back by returning GIs, and later by the surplus arms dealers who sold large numbers of the Model 38 rifles and carbines. 6.5x50mm sporting ammunition has recently been loaded by Norma, using the American-type primer. Military ammunition has a Berdan-type primer, usually of 0.199-inch or 0.217-inch size. Military ball ammunition of recent production with steel cases and Berdan primers has recently been imported from China.

General Comments The 6.5x50mm has a semi-rimmed case, but is otherwise not radically different from other 6.5mm military cartridges. It has the shortest case and least powder capacity of any of the military 6.5mms, but is nonetheless an efficient design with smokeless powder. The Japanese Model 38 rifle has an unusually strong action, which allows the cartridge to be loaded to its full potential. Because commercial sporting ammunition and reloadable cases are available, this is one of the more useful military cartridges. In power, it is on a par with any of the other 6.5 military rounds and is fine for antelope, deer, sheep and black bear. It makes a far more effective deer cartridge than the 30-30. To solve the ammunition problem, some 6.5mm Arisaka rifles have been rechambered to the wildcat 6.5-257 Roberts, which makes a fine conversion.

6.5x50mm Japanese Arisaka Loading Data and Factory Ballistics

Bullet (grains/type)	Powder	Grains	Velocity	Energy	Source/Comments
120 SP	IMR 4350	43	3000	2400	Maximum load
120 SP	H380	36	2680	1918	NA
120 SP	IMR 4895	34	2650	1870	NA
140 SP	IMR 4350	40	2680	2240	NA
140 SP	H380	34	2360	1735	NA
156 SP	IMR 4064	28	2060	1460	Duplicates factory loading
160 SP	IMR 4320	34	2500	2408	NA
139 Ball	ML		2500	1930	Military load
139 SP	FL		2430	1815	Norma factory load
156 SP	FL		2070	1475	Norma factory load

6.5x54mm Mannlicher-Schoenauer (Greek)

Historical Notes This original Greek military cartridge was designed in 1900 and used in the 1903 Mannlicher bolt-action rifle. It is also a popular sporting number in Europe and the United States. All major American ammunition companies loaded the 6.5mm Mannlicher until about 1940. The Austrian-made Mannlicher-Schoenauer sporting rifle was the only rifle routinely available in this chambering. Sporting ammunition is loaded in Europe, and RWS has imported Boxer-primed, reloadable cases and a good variety of sporting loads. European ammunition uses the Berdan primer, usually the 5.5mm or 0.217-inch size.

General Comments The 6.5mm M-S has always had a certain following in the United States, even though American rifle makers do not chamber it as a standard option. It is a very fine cartridge for North American hunting, with far better killing power than the 30-30 or anything in that class. In fact, every species of big game on earth has been taken with this cartridge. A great many elephants were killed by ivory hunters using this little 6.5mm and heavy solid bullets. It did not make enough noise to bother the herd and gave deep penetration for well-placed brain shots. In the hands of an experienced hunter, it will do for any North American big game. However, by today's standards, it is considered primarily a deer, sheep, antelope and black bear cartridge. In power, it is often compared to the 257 Roberts, and there is some validity for this. On the other hand, the 6.5mm M-S is loaded with bullets of around 160 grains in weight, compared to the 120-grain top weight of the 257. It is the long, heavy bullet that makes this a good killer on the tougher varieties of game.

6.5x54mm Mannlicher-Schoenauer (Greek) Loading Data and Factory Ballistics

Bullet (grains/type)	Powder	Grains	Velocity	Energy	Source/Comments
139-140 SP	IMR 3031	35	2510	1950	Antelope, deer
139-140 SP	IMR 4895	36	2400	1790	NA
156 SP	IMR 4350	38	2510	2182	NA
156 SP	IMR 3031	34	2460	2100	Duplicates original military load
160 SP	IMR 4064	38	2450	2140	Heavy game
140 SP	FL		2250	1575	Hirtenberger factory load
159 SP	FL		2330	1740	RWS factory load
159 Ball	ML		2223	1740	Military load

6.5x53.5mm Daudeteau

Historical Notes A collector's item today, this semi-rimmed 1895 design was introduced originally as a military cartridge for the French Navy. It was used in the Daudeteau bolt-action rifle and evidently commercial ammunition was also produced.

General Comments Rifles and ammunition are quite rare, and you are not likely to have one with which to hunt. If you do, it would probably be satisfactory for anything up to deer. According to Aivaro Casal, this cartridge was adopted by Uruguay in 1895 and used until 1898.

6.5x53.5 Daudeteau Factory Ballistics

Bullet (grains/type)	Powder	Grains	Velocity	Energy	Source/Comments
150 RN Ball	ML	40	2395	1922	Military load

6.5x53Rmm Mannlicher (Dutch & Romanian)

Historical Notes This is an earlier, rimmed version of the 6.5x54mm Greek cartridge, designed by Mannlicher and used in the bolt-action Dutch Models 1892 and 1895 and the Romanian Models 1892 and 1893. The cartridge was dropped by both countries after World War II.

General Comments This cartridge delivers ballistics practically identical to the regular 6.5x54mm Mannlicher-Schoenauer, known for many years in the United States and at one time loaded by most cartridge companies. The rimmed version is used in a few single-shot and combination European sporting rifles. Commercial hunting ammunition for rifles so chambered was once loaded in both England and Europe.

This cartridge was introduced in the United States after World War II when quantities of the Dutch and Romanian military rifles and carbines were sold in surplus stores. Only imported sporting ammunition is available, but some dealers have furnished hunting loads based on the military round with the bullet replaced. Rifles in this chambering are suitable for deer, antelope, black bear and the like. The British listed this cartridge as the 256 Mannlicher and many bolt-action rifles were turned out for it by Jeffery and others. It has been popular in parts of Africa. No commercial manufacturer currently offers this ammunition. Brass can be made from 303 British cases.

6.5x53Rmm Mannlicher Loading Data and Factory Ballistics

Bullet (grains/type)	Powder	Grains	Velocity	Energy	Source/Comments
120 SP	IMR 4895	33	2440	1590	NA
120 SP	IMR 4064	35	2650	1875	NA
140 SP	IMR 3031	35	2550	2360	NA
156 SP	IMR 3031	34	2445	2095	Duplicates military ball load
156 SP	IMR 4350	38	2510	2192	NA
160 SP	IMR 3031	34	2250	1810	NA
156 – 159 Ball	ML		2433	2085	Military load
160 SP	FL		2350	1960	Factory load

6.5x55mm Swedish Mauser

Historical Notes A Mauser- and Swedish-designed military cartridge adopted in 1894, the 6.5x55mm was used in the Swedish Models 94, 96 and 38 rifles and carbines. These are based on a modification of the Spanish Mauser-1893 bolt-action. Norway also adopted this cartridge for its 1894 and 1912 Krag-Jorgensen rifles. Ammunition for sporting use is loaded by Norma and others. Military ammunition uses the Berdan primer, usually of 0.199-inch or 0.216-inch diameter. Sporting rifles are currently available on the American market in this chambering. Federal and PMC produce 6.5x55mm ammunition. Remington apparently produced a few rifles in 6.5x55mm some years ago and one version of the Model 70 Winchester was so chambered. The military ball is a spitzer boattail of very advanced design. Both copper and clad steel jacket types exist.

General Comments The 6.5x55 Swedish cartridge is another surplus, post-war immigrant that has become quite popular in the United States. For North American hunting, it is one of the best of the foreign military cartridges. It has been highly developed as a match and hunting round in the Scandinavian countries, and has a reputation for superb accuracy. With lighter bullets (77- to 100-grain), it will do very well for varmint shooting of all kinds. The 120-grain bullet is fine for antelope or deer, and heavier (140 to 160-grain) bullets make it suitable for most types of big game. The Swedish Mauser and the Norwegian Krag are intended for working pressures of only about 45,000 psi and this must be considered when handloading. With a stronger action, maximum loads and performance could be notably increased. Except for a slightly larger rim and base diameter and a shorter neck, this cartridge is very similar to the 6.5x57mm Mauser cartridge. It is not known exactly who designed it, but undoubtedly its design was influenced by Mauser developments.

6.5x55mm Swedish Mauser Loading Data and Factory Ballistics

Bullet (grains/type)	Powder	Grains	Velocity	Energy	Source/Comments
100 HP	IMR 3031	44	3100	2140	Varmint load
120 SP	IMR 4350	50	2780	2062	Deer, antelope
129 SP	IMR 4895	41	2625	1990	NA
140 SP	IMR 4350	45	2520	1980	NA
140 SP	IMR 4831	50	2590	2090	NA
156 SP	IMR 4350	43	2500	2168	NA
160 SP	IMR 4350	42	2430	2100	Heavy game
77 FMJ	FL		3120	1660	Norma bird factory load
139 SP	FL		2790	2395	Norma factory load
156 SP	FL		2490	2150	Norma factory load
139 Ball	ML		2625	2126	Military load

6.5x58mm Portuguese Vergueiro

Historical Notes This was the original Portuguese military cartridge for the Mauser-Vergueiro bolt-action rifle — a basic Mauser-type, but with certain Mannlicher features such as the split-bridge receiver. In 1937, Portugal adopted the 8mm Mauser cartridge and the Model 98 Mauser rifle. Many of the older Vergueiro rifles were then rebarreled to the new round. The military loading used a 155-grain bullet at a muzzle velocity of 2350 fps and 1908 foot-pounds of energy. Sporting ammunition was once loaded by ICI in England and DWM in Germany and imported into the United States. Mauser bolt-action rifles have been chambered for this round in England and Europe, but it has never been used by any American manufacturer.

General Comments This is another early military cartridge that achieved some popularity for sporting use. Its use in the United States has been very limited and confined to the few Mauser-type sporting rifles that were occasionally imported. The cartridge case is similar to the 6.5x57mm Mauser in shape and performance, but is a little smaller in diameter, with a longer neck. It is a good hunting cartridge for North American big game and ranks along with the other military 6.5s. Since the old Vergueiro rifles were largely rebarreled to 8mm, only a relatively few of these in the 6.5mm appeared in the surplus military gun stores. No commercial manufacturers currently offer this ammunition.

6.5x58mm Portuguese Vergueiro Loading Data and Factory Ballistics

Bullet (grains/type)	Powder	Grains	Velocity	Energy	Source/Comments
140 SP	IMR 4831	46	2530	1995	NA
140 SP	IMR 4895	38	2450	1870	Maximum load
156 SP	IMR 4350	43	2510	2183	Approximates factory ballistics
139 SP	FL		2775	2372	Factory load
157 SP	FL		2568	2292	Factory load
155 Ball	ML		2350	1908	Military load

6.5x52mm Italian (Mannlicher-Carcano)

Historical Notes This was the official Italian military cartridge adopted in 1891 for the bolt-action Mannlicher-Carcano rifle. This rifle was a Mannlicher-inspired design in every respect except the bolt, which is a Mauser-type with double locking lugs at the front. It is also the only military rifle of smokeless powder design to use gain-twist rifling. This Italian 6.5mm cartridge is very similar to the 6.5mm Mannlicher-Schoenauer in size, shape and performance. Both unprimed cases and loaded ammunition have been made by Norma.

General Comments The Italian 6.5mm military cartridge was unfamiliar to American shooters until after World War II. Large quantities of Italian Model 91 rifles and carbines have been sold at very low prices, and because we are a great nation of bargain hunters, this is now a fairly widely used cartridge. Many surplus arms dealers furnished hunting ammunition that consisted of the military round with the full-jacketed bullet replaced with a softpoint. Reloadable cases can be made very easily from 6.5x54mm Mannlicher cases. This is a good deer, antelope or black bear cartridge, but the low working-pressure limit of the Carcano rifle prevents loading it as heavily as similar military 6.5mms.

6.5x52mm Italian Mannlicher-Carcano Loading Data and Factory Ballistics

Bullet (grains/type)	Powder	Grains	Velocity	Energy	Source/Comments
140 SP	IMR 4895	33	2250	1570	Maximum for Carcano rifle
140 SP	IMR 3031	34	2320	1730	NA
156 SP	IMR 4064	37	2280	1806	NA
156 SP	IMR 4350	35	2340	1898	NA
160 SP	IMR 4350	35	2320	1919	NA
139 SP	FL		2580	2045	Norma factory load
156 SP	FL		2430	2045	Norma factory load
162 Ball	ML		2296	1902	Military load

6.8x57mm Chinese

Historical Notes While we have no sample cartridge and very little data on this number — we are uncertain even as to the correct name — we feel compelled to include a brief mention of it here. Why? Because other than the 270 Winchester and Roy Weatherby's subsequent 270 Magnum, this is the only other commercial or military cartridge of which we are aware that used a bullet of 0.277-inch diameter. One must speculate that this number might have had something to do with Winchester's decision to use what was an unusual bullet size in what became one of the most successful commercially inspired hunting cartridges of all time. If so, the 6.8x57mm Chinese most assuredly deserves honorable mention.

280 British

Historical Notes This was an experimental cartridge developed by the British army concurrently with a semi-automatic/automatic assault-type rifle, the EM-2. Work began in 1945, immediately after the end of the war, and by 1947, the rifle-cartridge combination was ready for field trials and was tested by both the British and the United States. Its ultimate rejection was mostly a political decision to satisfy the U.S. military brass, who were wedded to the 30 caliber. By 1954, the British had adopted and were manufacturing the 7.62mm NATO round. The EM-2 rifle was a short bullpup design weighing 7 pounds and using a 20-round clip. The British continued field-testing both rifle and cartridge as late as 1951. The cyclic rate of the EM-2 was 600 to 650 rounds per minute.

General Comments In 1948, the rim of the 280 British case was slightly enlarged to match the 30-06 and the name was changed to 280/30. Ballistics remained the same. The 280/30 case was developed by shortening and necking-down the standard 30-06 case so the rim and base diameter of the two cases are the same. The 280/30 case has a slightly-tapered body, probably an aid to feeding and extraction. Various bullet weights were used, ranging from 130 to 140 grains; muzzle velocity of the various loads ranged from 2400 to 2530 fps. When tested in the United States and loaded with American powders, velocity was increased to 2600 fps. The 280/30 would have made a good sporting round, but I do not know of anyone who used it for that purpose. In a good strong bolt- or single-shot action and loaded to maximum performance with American powders, the 280/30 could probably push the 139-grain bullet at something like 2700 to 2800 fps muzzle velocity. For some reason, very little, if any, work has ever been done with this cartridge in the sporting field. It is worth mentioning here because some experimenters, as early as 1962, necked the 308x1.5-inch down to 7mm, creating a very similar round. However, the 280/30 British case is 0.20-inch longer than the 308x1.5-inch and case capacity is probably about 10 percent greater. Remington picked up this idea in its new 7mm BR handgun cartridge used in the XP-100 Silhouette pistol. No commercial sporting ammunition has ever been made.

280 British Military Ballistics

Bullet (grains/type)	Powder	Grains	Velocity	Energy	Source/Comments
139 Ball	ML		2530	1980	Military load, typical

7x57mm Mauser

Historical Notes The 7x57mm Mauser is another cartridge that, although designed as a military round, was widely adapted for sporting purposes. Contrary to what most cartridge books say, it was not introduced in 1893. It was actually developed in 1892 and used in a limited number of Model 1892 Mauser rifles, a modification of the Belgian-Mauser pattern of 1889. In 1893, Mauser introduced an improved bolt-action rifle in 7x57mm that was officially adopted by the Spanish military. Subsequently, with minor modifications, the 7mm-chambered rifle was adopted by other European and many Latin-American governments. The Remington Model 1902 rolling block rifle was also manufactured in 7x57mm Mauser, as was the Model 70 Winchester. More recently, several U.S. gun makers have chambered it in their finest guns.

The original 7mm military round employed a 173-grain bullet with a muzzle velocity of 2296 fps and an energy of 2025 foot-pounds of energy. Other loadings were used by various countries with bullets ranging in weight from 139 grains up to the original 173 grains. Those loads on which data is available are listed below.

Model 93 Mauser rifles in 7mm were used by Spanish troops in Cuba during the Spanish-American war. The effectiveness of this combination against American forces was responsible for the eventual adoption of the Mauser-system 1903 Springfield rifle. San Juan Hill was defended by only about 700 Spaniards armed with the new Mauser 7mm rifles, but they inflicted some 1400 casualties on the 15,000 Americans who attacked their position.

General Comments The United States saw a large influx of surplus 7mm military rifles after World War II. Many who purchased those fine rifles immediately wanted the gun altered to use a more familiar American sporting cartridge. This was foolish, because the 7x57mm is one of the best all-round cartridges available for North American big game hunting. With the proper bullet for the job at hand, the 7mm will handle any big game here. It might not be the choice for grizzly bear in heavy brush, but in the hands of an experienced hunter, it will be far superior to the 30-30 for any purpose. If the barrel is in good shape, it is best to leave a 7mm military rifle in its original chambering. Loading data is in Chapter 2. All major manufacturers offer 7x57mm sporting ammunition.

7x57mm Mauser Factory Ballistics

Bullet (grains/type)	Powder	Grains	Velocity	Energy	Source/Comments
139 Ball	ML		2950	2580	Military load, Brazil & Colombia
142 Ball	ML		2740	2365	Military load, Uruguay
155 Ball	ML		2300	1820	Military load, Mexico
162 Ball	ML		2295	1890	Military load, Mexico
173 Ball	ML		2296	2025	Original military loading used by Spain and others

Model 95 Spanish Mauser short rifle chambered in 7x57mm

276 Enfield

Historical Notes The 276 Enfield was an experimental military cartridge developed by the British beginning in 1909 for what later became the proposed Pattern 13 bolt-action rifle. It is very similar to the Canadian 280 Ross cartridge. Although the rifle and cartridge were issued for troop trials, these were not adopted due to the onset of World War I. However, the rifle was produced in a slightly modified form as the Pattern 14 Enfield, chambered for the 303 British cartridge. Many of these were manufactured in the United States for the British government. Most 276 Enfield ammunition was manufactured by Royal Laboratories at Woolwich, England, and head-stamped R-L. Bullet diameter is 0.282-inch. Bullet weights vary from 144-190 grains.

General Comments The 276 Enfield is primarily a collector's item because it was never officially adopted or used as a military cartridge. Also, it was not used as a sporting cartridge and is interesting mostly as a development that might have replaced the 303 British if World War I had not intervened. After the war, during 1923 to 1932, the United States experimented with a smaller cartridge — the 276 Pedersen. Sporting ammunition has never been made for this chambering.

276 Enfield Loading Data

Bullet (grains/type)	Powder	Grains	Velocity	Energy	Source/Comments
165 Ball	ML		2800	2881	Military load, experimental

276 Pedersen

Historical Notes The 276 Pedersen was a U.S. Army experimental cartridge developed between 1923 and 1932 for the experimental Pedersen semi-automatic rifle. There were actually several variations of this cartridge (perhaps as many as 10) with differences in case length, diameter and other dimensions. It appears that the most common version of this cartridge was developed by necking the 6.5 Carcano up to 7mm. One version, the T2, had the same rim and head dimensions as the 30-06; another (T2-E1) was modified specifically for testing in an early version of the Garand rifle.

The 276 was tested with bullets weighing from 120 grains at 2550 fps to 150 grains at 2,360 fps. Performance was not spectacular but was acceptable for a military cartridge at the time. However, in 1932, Gen. Douglas MacArthur, then Army Chief of Staff, disapproved any caliber reduction and that ended the development program for the 276.

J.D. Pedersen, the originator of the 276 program, was a famous arms designer whose successful designs included the Remington Model 10 shotgun, the Model 12 line of 22 pump-action rifles, the Model 14 and Model 25 centerfire pump-action rifles, and the World War I Pedersen device. The Pedersen semi-auto military rifle design employed a toggle breechblock system similar to the Luger pistol and Maxim machinegun. However, the Pedersen system differed because the barrel did not recoil with the breech block, but rather remained stationary. The Garand system was adopted over the Pedersen rifle prior to World War II.

General Comments The 276 Pedersen was never manufactured as a commercial cartridge and no commercial sporting rifles were chambered for it. It would have made a good deer cartridge, but there were plenty of other cartridges in the same class that served just as well and there was no reason to bring out a sporting version. The 276 ammunition was quite common for a few years after World War II, and it is found in many collections.

276 Pedersen Factory Ballistics

Bullet (grains/type)	Powder	Grains	Velocity	Energy	Source/Comments
120 Ball	ML		2550	1732	Military load, experimental
150 Ball	ML		2360	1858	Military load, experimental
Note: other loadings were tested.					

7.35mm Italian Carcano

Historical Notes The 7.35mm cartridge was adopted by Italy in 1938 to replace the 6.5x52mm round that had been used since 1891. Experience in Ethiopia and other places had demonstrated the desirability of a larger caliber for combat use. The Model 91 Carcano rifle was modified slightly for the new cartridge, but retained the same basic action. That happened about the time Italy became involved in various military actions and the new cartridge created a critical supply problem and was withdrawn from service. Quantities of 7.35mm rifles were used against the Russians by Finnish troops and reportedly gave good service. No sporting ammunition is currently loaded for this chambering, although Norma offered it for many years.

General Comments Many thousands of the Italian Model 38 service rifles and carbines were sold here as surplus. The 7.35mm was unknown to the average shooter until that time. However, these rifles were sold at extremely low prices and are now in rather widespread use all over the country. In power, the 7.35mm is between the 30-30 and the 300 Savage, making it a good deer and black bear cartridge if the proper hunting bullet is used. It is actually a better cartridge than the 30-30 in many respects. Reloadable cases can be made from empty 6.5x54mm Mannlicher cases as imported by RWS. This is done by expanding the neck, running the shell through a full-length sizing die and then trimming back to proper length. The Carcano action is designed for working pressures of only about 38,000 psi and the loads given below should not be exceeded. In a strong, modern action, it would be possible to equal the 300 Savage in performance, but this cannot be done safely in the military Carcano.

7.35mm Italian Carcano Loading Data and Factory Ballistics

Bullet (grains/type)	Powder	Grains	Velocity	Energy	Source/Comments
128 SP	IMR 3031	38	2495	1776	Approximates military load ballistics
128 SP	IMR 4895	40	2500	1782	NA
150 SP	IMR 4320	40	2550	2175	NA
150 SP	IMR 4895	38	2450	2005	NA
150 SP	H380	41	2490	2070	NA
128 Ball	ML		2483	1749	Military load

30 Carbine (30 M-1 Carbine)

Historical Notes In 1940, the U.S. Ordnance Department concluded that a light carbine might have certain advantages over the 45-caliber semi-auto pistol in many combat situations. Various designs were submitted by a number of private manufacturers and, in the end, Winchester's offering was selected. The semi-auto 30 M-1 Carbine was officially adopted in 1941. This cartridge, a modification of the 32 Winchester self-loading round of 1906, was hardly a revolutionary new design, but it served the purpose. At about the same time, the Germans developed their assault rifle and the 7.92mm Kurz (short) cartridge. The M-1 Carbine is not an assault rifle and the military insists it was designed to fulfill a different purpose. A few sporting rifles and handguns have chambered the 30 Carbine (See Chapter 2).

General Comments In mid-1963, the government released 30 M-1 Carbines for sale to civilians through the National Rifle Association at the very moderate price of around $20. Thousands of these rifles, as a result, have been used for sporting purposes. Federal, Winchester and Remington load softpoint sporting ammunition and for the first time, the M-1 Carbine must be considered from other than a strictly military viewpoint. The 30 Carbine cartridge is in the same class as the 32-20 WCF but slightly more powerful. It is wholly a small game and varmint number, despite contrary claims by those who love the short, light and handy M-1 Carbine. The modest accuracy of the Carbine combined with the ballistics of this cartridge limit the effective sporting accuracy range to about 150 yards. The author used an M-1 Carbine to hunt small game and deer as early as 1943, before most people could get their hands on one, so he has a pretty good idea of the capability of this cartridge. Remember that the 32 Winchester self-loading round became obsolete in 1920 because it was ineffective and more or less useless for sporting purposes. The 30 Carbine was derived from it and shares the same shortcomings. However, the 30 Carbine can shoot relatively less expensive military ammunition and this allows use of the gun in many situations not economically feasible with the 32 SL. However, do not kid yourself about the terrific power of the 30 Carbine cartridge — it just is not there. Despite this, it can be a very useful cartridge within its limitations and its use and popularity have increased considerably over the years.

Editor's note: *Had the military adopted a normal modern-rifle-pressure standard, instead of the inexplicably modest 40,000 psi specified, we might have a somewhat different opinion of this cartridge. Loading to normal 30-06 pressures provides about 400 fps more velocity, which seems significant.*

30 Carbine Loading Data and Factory Ballistics

Bullet (grains/type)	Powder	Grains	Velocity	Energy	Source/Comments
100 Plinker	2400	15.5	2170	1045	Speer
110 SP	IMR 4227	15.0	2010	985	NA
125 Lead RN	AA 1680	15.0	1756	855	Accurate Arms
110 Ball	ML		1975	955	Military load, M-1
110 SP	FL		1990	965	Factory load

7.5x54mm French MAS

Historical Notes In 1924, the French army adopted a new cartridge, the 7.5x58mm MLE 1924C, for a new automatic rifle. In 1929, to avoid ammunition mix-ups with the 7.92x57mm, the French changed to a 4mm shorter cartridge of slightly larger diameter, creating the 7.5x54mm MLF 1929C. This cartridge was originally used in light machineguns and automatic arms, but in 1934, the Berthier Model-07/15 bolt-action rifle was modified for this round. In 1936, a newly designed bolt-action rifle (MAS 36) in the new 7.5mm was adopted. This rimless cartridge replaced the rimmed 8mm Lebel, which the French army had used since 1886.

General Comments Fair quantities of French military rifles in this chambering have appeared on the surplus market in the last few years. The French are noted for hanging on to their obsolete military hardware long after it is of any real value. Sporting ammunition for this chambering has never been manufactured. However, A.L.M. Arsenal in France recently produced this cartridge with a Boxer primer. Some of the surplus dealers made up hunting ammunition by replacing the military bullet with a similar softpoint type. The 7.5mm MAS is in the same class as the 30-40 Krag or the 303 British and can be used for the same range of game. Performance can be improved a little in handloading, but only Berdan-primed military cases have formerly been available. The military load develops about 40,000 psi breech pressure.

The initials MAS represent the French arsenal that developed this cartridge and rifle, Manufacture d' Armes de Saint Etienne.

7.5x54mm French MAS Loading Data and Factory Ballistics

Bullet (grains/type)	Powder	Grains	Velocity	Energy	Source/Comments
150 SP	IMR 4831	54	2680	2400	Duplicates military ball
150 SP	IMR 4895	48	2800	2620	NA
180 SP	IMR 4895	44	2590	2692	NA
140 Ball	ML		2600	2100	Military load, MLE 1929C

30 Army (30-40 Krag)

Historical Notes The 30 U.S. Army, or 30-40 Krag, was the first small-bore military cartridge adopted by the U.S. Army. It was adopted in 1892 for the Norwegian-invented, American-modified Krag-Jorgensen bolt-action rifle. Original loads used 40 grains of smokeless powder with a 220-grain full-metal-jacket, round-nose bullet.

The 30-40 Krag cartridge remained in service only a few years before being replaced in 1903 by the rimless 30-03 cartridge, predecessor to the 30-06.

General Comments In 1893, Winchester began offering its High Wall single-shot rifle chambered for the 30-40 Krag, thus becoming the first commercial producer in the United States to offer a small-bore, smokeless-powder sporting cartridge. This was nearly two years before the smokeless powder 30-30 loading was offered.

Editor's note: *A glance at the following ballistics might suggest to the astute reader that original loads used pressures that would today seem excessive for the Krag rifle. Indeed, this seems to have been the case as the rated velocity was routinely achieved in production rifles and, considering the limited case capacity and characteristics of contemporary domestic smokeless powders, pressures had to have been rather brisk, perhaps exceeding 55,000 psi. It seems at least possible that use of such unusually high-pressure loads contributed to the subsequent problems that earned the single-locking-lug Krag action a, perhaps undeserved, reputation for weakness.*

30-40 Krag Factory Ballistics

Bullet (grains/type)	Powder	Grains	Velocity	Energy	Source/Comments
220 FMJ-RN Ball	ML		2200	2365	Military load, special

7.62x51mm NATO (308 Win.)

Historical Notes For the NATO small arms trials in the early 1950s, the U.S. submitted their new T-65 cartridge. This was basically a shortened 30-'06 case using the same caliber bullet and similar case head dimensions. Case length was reduced from 63 mm in the 30-06 to 51 mm for the 7.62mm T-65. This allowed a lighter, more compact cartridge and rifle. Some of the other NATO Allies submitted entries, which were far more advanced than the T-65 cartridge. However, the U.S. used its considerable influence to override all Allied objections in order to have the 7.62x51mm NATO cartridge adopted. This remains a NATO standard to this day.

In 1957, the U.S. Army adopted the M-14 rifle in 7.62x51mm. The M60 machinegun is also chambered for this cartridge, as are various sniper rifles.

General Comments During the Vietnam War, the U.S. military adopted the 5.56x45mm cartridge for the new M-16 rifle, which greatly upset the other NATO Allies. A new series of NATO tests was begun in the late 1970s, which resulted in the 5.56x45mm cartridge being standardized in 1980. Both 7.62x51mm and 5.56x45mm remain NATO standard rounds. Recent tendencies have been to chamber infantry assault rifles for the 5.56x45mm leaving the 7.62x51mm cartridge for machineguns. Nearly all NATO Allies manufacture the 7.62x51mm cartridge. Many non-NATO countries such as Japan, Australia, Brazil, Taiwan, South Africa and many others also use this cartridge. Ball, Tracer, Match, Armor Piercing, and Frangible types exist.

7.62x51mm NATO Factory Ballistics

Bullet (grains/type)	Powder	Grains	Velocity	Energy	Source/Comments
150 FMJ-BT Ball	ML		2750	2520	Military load, M80
168 HP-BT Match	ML		2680	2680	Military load, M852

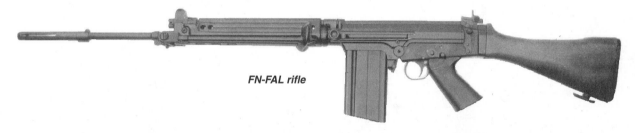

FN-FAL rifle

7.5x55mm Swiss Schmidt-Rubin

Historical Notes The first Swiss 7.5mm cartridge was adopted in 1889 for the Schmidt-Rubin straight-pull rifle of the same year. The original loading used a 0.299-inch diameter, 213-grain paper-patched lead bullet and a charge of 29 grains of semi-smokeless powder. Muzzle velocity was 1970 fps. Later, a steel-capped, hollow-base lead bullet was used, followed by a 190-grain copper or iron-jacketed, round-nose bullet with a smokeless powder loading (Model 90/03). In 1911, the 174-grain spitzer boattail bullet was adopted and the diameter increased to 0.308-inch. Golden State Arms Corp. once imported Japanese-made cases with Boxer primer pockets for loading sporting ammunition. Both unprimed cases and loaded rounds are available from Norma.

General Comments The 7.5mm Swiss military cartridge is another of the surplus items that has become well known to American shooters only since the end of the war. The Swiss army made a number of improvements in the straight-pull, Schmidt-Rubin rifle and the older, less desirable, models were sold off as obsolete surplus. The original Model 89 with rear-locking lugs, a very long receiver and a protruding box magazine was one of those. The improved Model 1911 with shorter receiver, forward-located locking lugs and a less conspicuous magazine is another. The 190-grain load develops about 37,000 psi breech pressure and the 174-grain load about 45,500 psi, and uses a slightly larger-diameter bullet. The 1911 cartridge, considerably more powerful than the older loading, should not be used in the Model 89 rifle. In a suitable action, the 7.5mm Swiss cartridge can be loaded to deliver performance equal to the 308 Winchester and is suitable for the same range of applications. Reloadable cases can be readily made by necking-up 284 Winchester brass. The 284's rebated rim works just fine in the Schmidt-Rubin rifle.

7.5x55mm Swiss Schmidt-Rubin Loading Data and Factory Ballistics
(Model-1911 rifle, or later models, using 0.308-inch diameter bullets)

Bullet (grains/type)	Powder	Grains	Velocity	Energy	Source/Comments
130 SP	IMR 3031	46	3000	2608	Varmint load
150 SP	IMR 3031	45	2820	2658	NA
165 SP	IMR 4895	42	2570	2430	NA
180 SP	IMR 4064	45	2570	2642	NA
200 SP	IMR 4350	49	2460	2700	NA
174 Ball	ML		2560	2540	Military load
180	FL		2650	2805	Factory load

30-06 Springfield (30-06 Government/30-06 U.S.)

Historical Notes The 30-06 Springfield is a United States military cartridge adopted in 1906 for the Model 1903 Springfield service rifle, which was based on the Mauser bolt-action system. The 30-06 is actually a slightly modified version of the original 1903 cartridge, which was loaded with a 220-grain round-nosed bullet at a muzzle velocity of 2300 fps. Because of cartridge developments in Europe, it was considered advisable to change to a lighter weight, pointed 150-grain bullet at an increased velocity (2700 fps). At the same time, the case neck was shortened by 0.07-inch. This improved round was designated the "Ball Cartridge, caliber 30, Model of 1906," but in practice, this cumbersome nomenclature was shortened to 30-06. The 30-06 version can be chambered and fired in any rifle made for the original 1903 round, but the reverse is not true (because of the difference in case neck length). For many years both the 1903 and 1906 configurations were loaded by sporting ammunition manufacturers. Shooting the '06 in the '03 chamber reportedly gave poor accuracy. Old catalogs list both rounds. Occasionally the 1903 version is called the 30-45 because the original loading used 45 grains of smokeless powder. For additional discussion, see the 30-03 listing in Chapter 3.

Again, because of military developments in Europe, the Army switched to a 172-grain bullet with a 9-degree boattail in 1926; the new round being designated the "Ball, caliber 30, M1." Muzzle velocity, originally the same as the 150-grain load of 2700 fps, was later reduced to 2640 fps because of difficulty maintaining pressure specifications at the higher velocity. In 1940, the 150-grain flat-base bullet was re-adopted as the "Cartridge, Ball, caliber 30, M2" and that was the load used in World War II. The return to the lighter bullet came about, at least in part, because of difficulties adapting the new Garand semi-automatic rifle to handle the 172-grain load. The heavier boattail bullet was superior for machinegun use because of its greater maximum range of nearly 6000 yards, compared to about 3500 yards for the 150-grain loading.

The rimless 30-03 and 30-06 replaced the older rimmed 30-40 Krag as the official U.S. military round. The 30-06 has, in turn, been superseded by the 7.62x51mm, also known as the 7.62mm NATO or, in its commercial version, the 308 Winchester. In Europe, the 30-06 is known as the 7.62x63mm and is widely used.

General Comments During World War II, the U.S. government supplied 30-06 arms and ammunition to many Allied nations including Great Britain, Netherlands, France, China, Australia, New Zealand and Brazil. To keep their inventory of guns ready, many countries undertook manufacture of 30-06 ammunition after the war.

In the 1950s and 1960s, vast quantities of surplus 30-06 ammunition were sold on the U.S. market. Shooters will often encounter ball, armor-piercing and tracer types. Ammunition loaded before and during World War II is corrosively primed. Practically all U.S. military ammunition loaded after 1952 has non-corrosive primers. The principal exception is Frankford Arsenal Match ammunition marked FA 53, 54 or 56, which used the old-style corrosive priming because it provided superior accuracy.

30-06 Springfield Factory Ballistics

Bullet (grains/type)	Powder	Grains	Velocity	Energy	Source/Comments
150 FMJ Ball	ML		2740	2500	Military load, M2
172 FMJ-BT Ball	ML		2640	2660	Military load, M1
220 FMJ-RN Ball	ML		2300	2585	Military load, M-1903

Note: Myriad other M-1906 military loadings were adopted for various applications, with differing bullet weights and muzzle velocities.

7.62x45mm Czech M52

Historical Notes This cartridge was independently developed in Czechoslovakia in the late 1940s. It was adopted for official Czech military use in 1952 along with the M52 semi-auto carbine and the M52 machinegun. In the interest of standardization in the Warsaw Pact, the 7.62x45mm cartridge was dropped in the 1960s in favor of the 7.62x39mm Soviet round. The Czech cartridge is of interest historically as it is one of the very few successful independently developed assault rifle rounds outside the 7.62x39mm or 5.56x45mm cartridges. It is now obsolete.

General Comments The 7.62x45mm cartridge offers ballistic performance very similar to the Soviet 7.62x39. A 0.309-inch diameter spitzer, boattail bullet weighing 130 grains was used at a muzzle velocity of 2440 fps. Cases were either brass or lacquered steel with Berdan primers. Both ball and tracer types were made.

The semi-automatic Czech M52 rifle was almost unknown in the United States until recently. About 8000 of the guns have been imported, as well as shooting quantities of ammunition.

AK-47

7.62x39mm
(7.62x39mm Soviet M43)

Historical Notes This "assault rifle" cartridge was adopted by Russia in 1943. It did not come into general use until after World War II, but the Russians now use it as their principal infantry small-arms cartridge. Original use was in the SKS semi-automatic carbine, later replaced by the AK-47 selective-fire assault rifle. The RPD light machinegun also uses the M43 cartridge. Finland and those ex-satellite countries in the Soviet bloc use the M43 cartridge in arms furnished by Russia or of their own design. This cartridge was adopted as the result of Russian military experience against German assault rifles chambered for the 7.92mm Kurz. Ruger introduced its Mini-30 semi-automatic rifle chambered for the 7.62x39mm during 1987, and the bolt-action M77 Mark II

rifle in 1991. Most military ammunition has a steel case and corrosive Berdan primer, but reloadable cases are now readily available.

General Comments The M43 is 1/4-inch longer than the German 7.92mm Kurz and will give substantially better performance with newer powders. This cartridge has been loaded commercially by Federal, Winchester, Remington and Black Hills with Boxer-primed reloadable cases. Better handloads and factory ammunition using soft-point bullets up to about 150 grains place this cartridge far ahead of any reasonable 30-30 load in terms of delivered energy beyond 100 yards.

7.62x39mm Loading Data and Factory Ballistics

Bullet (grains/type)	Powder	Grains	Velocity	Energy	Source/Comments
110 Sierra HP	AA 1680	27.5	2547	1580	Accurate Arms, Maximum load (0.308")
125 Sierra SP	AA 1680	25.5	2368	1555	Accurate Arms, Maximum load (0.311")
150 Sierra SP	AA 2015	26.0	2072	1430	Accurate Arms, Maximum load (0.311")
122 Ball	ML		2329	1470	Military load
123 SP	FL		2300	1440	Black Hills factory load
150 SP	FL		2200	1610	Black Hills factory load

7.62x53Rmm Russian

Historical Notes Sometimes called the 7.62x54Rmm Russian, this cartridge was adopted in 1891 with the Model 1891 Mosin-Nagant bolt-action rifle. Its 150-grain spitzer bullet was adopted in 1909. This cartridge was standard issue in the Russian army during World War II. It is still standard issue for medium machineguns and the SVD sniper rifle. It was also adopted by Finland, China and most ex-satellite nations. It remains one of the few rimmed military cartridges still in standard issue. Early in World War I, Winchester made M95 lefer-action muskets and Remington made rolling block rifles for imperial Russia. Later, Russian Nagant rifles were manufactured in the United States by New England Westinghouse Co. and also by Remington and Winchester. After the war, a large number of surplus rifles were sold commercially and Remington loaded a 150-grain bronze-point hunting round. Additional Russian Nagant rifles and carbines have been sold in surplus stores since the end of World War II. Many of these rifles were captured during the Korean conflict. Surplus Moisin rifles are being imported from China, Finland, Hungary, Poland, Romania and Russia.

General Comments The 7.62x54Rmm Russian cartridge has been kicked around since about 1919 and is fairly well known to

American shooters. Remington discontinued loading this round about 1950. It was recently offered by Norma and Lapua. Various surplus military ammunition (corrosive Berdan primed, steel-cased) has recently been imported into the United States. Russian military cartridges use Berdan primers, usually of 6.45 mm (0.254-inch) diameter.

With the 150-grain bullet, the 7.62mm Russian is in the same class as the 30-06. However, since the rifle has a shorter magazine, it will not do as well as the 30-06 when loaded with heavier bullets. Although military bullets measure 0.309- to 0.311-inch in diameter, rifles with tighter bores will shoot 0.308-inch bullets just fine. However, many rifles have grossly oversized bores (the editor owns a pair with 0.316-inch groove diameter). In such rifles, 0.308-inch jacketed bullets are hopelessly inaccurate; 0.311-inch bullets will shoot with a modicum of accuracy. Properly sized cast bullets will shoot with impressive accuracy (minute-of-angle groups are no problem). Unfortunately, there is no ready source of appropriate commercial jacketed or cast bullets sized large enough for these specimens and others with bores running larger than about 0.313-inch. Standard working pressure is about 45,000 psi.

7.62x53Rmm Russian Loading Data and Factory Ballistics

Bullet (grains/type)	Powder	Grains	Velocity	Energy	Source/Comments
150 SP	IMR 3031	49	2800	2620	Approximates military ball load
180 SP	IMR 4320	48	2630	2772	NA
220 SP	IMR 4350	45	2350	2705	NA
147 Ball	ML		2886	2727	Military load, Type LPS bullet
150 SP	FL		2950	2820	Norma factory load
180 SP	FL		2580	2650	Norma factory load
185 Ball	ML		2660	2910	Military load, Type O bullet

303 British

Historical Notes As a military cartridge, the 303 British must be considered one of the most successful of its type. Developed during 1887 and adopted in 1888, it was the official military cartridge of the British Commonwealth in World War I and II. In 1957, the 7.62x51mm NATO cartridge replaced it.

Originally, the 303 cartridge was loaded with a 215-grain, round-nosed bullet encased in a cupro-nickel jacket. This bullet, backed by 70 grains of compressed blackpowder, developed a muzzle velocity of 1850 fps. Muzzle energy was 1630 foot-pounds. In the 1890s, in response to reports from the frontier that the jacketed round-nose solid bullet was ineffective against tribesmen, Capt. Bertie Clay at the arsenal at Dum Dum, India, perfected an expanding bullet, with the jacket open at the nose to expose the lead core. This bullet mushroomed on impact. Such projectiles became known as Dum Dum bullets, which has led to much confusion and nonsense through the common parlance and lay misunderstanding of what expanding bullets are, how those work, why those are beneficial, etc.

In 1892, propellant charging was changed to use the new Cordite smokeless powder. Muzzle velocity of the new loading was 1970 fps, which produced 1850 foot-pounds of energy. Owing to the efficiency of the new powder, this worthwhile ballistic improvement was accompanied by a significant reduction in peak chamber pressure. In 1910, a load using a 174-grain pointed flat-base bullet was adopted; velocity for that loading was 2440 fps, which produces 2310 foot-pounds of energy. This was the MkVII round, still in use when the 303 was discontinued.

Bullets for the MkVII cartridge had an aluminum- or fiber-filled tip, with a base of conventional lead alloy. This made the bullet longer than normal for its weight. It also produced a stable projectile in flight that would tumble easily on contact, thus increasing wounding potential.

The 303 cartridge was designed for the Lee-Metford MkI magazine rifle, a turn-bolt type invented by James Paris Lee, an American. (In studying these things it is surprising how often significant forearms and cartridge inventors were forced to travel beyond their own shores to find acceptance.) In 1895, the segmental and shallow Metford-type rifling was discontinued in favor of the deeper Enfield-type. (Interestingly, Metford had also patented the so-called Enfield rifling, prior to his segmental form.) From this point on, the rifle was known as the Lee-Enfield. Many variations and types exist.

General Comments The 303 British cartridge has been used extensively in Africa, Canada and India by settlers and government workers. It gained a bad reputation because the full-jacketed military bullets tended to tumble on impact. However, with proper sporting bullets, it does quite well on the lighter, non-dangerous game varieties. Norma offers one loading: a 150-grain soft-nose. U.S. companies now load it with a 180-grain softpoint.

Although usually classed with the 30-40 Krag, the 303 actually has a worthwhile edge over the Krag. For one thing, it has a nominal operating pressure of 45,000 to 48,000 psi, compared to 40,000 to 42,000 psi for the 30-40. In addition, late model Enfield rifles are much stronger than the Krag. Enfield No. 4 MkI rifles have been converted successfully to use the 7.62mm NATO, which has a nominal maximum pressure of 62,000 psi. Finally, the modest increase in bore area gives the edge to the 303.

Ammunition for the 303 loaded in Britain had the Berdan primer, and in older lots usually Cordite powder. Military ammunition loaded by American companies has the Boxer primer and American-type nitrocellulose powder.

Proper jacketed bullet diameter for the 303 is 0.311-inch. Cast bullets may run to 0.312-inch or even 0.313-inch. Loading data will be found in Chapter 2.

303 British Factory Ballistics

Bullet (grains/type)	Powder	Grains	Velocity	Energy	Source/Comments
215 Ball	FFg	70.0	1850	1630	Original blackpowder load
215 Ball			1970	1850	Original Cordite load
175 Ball	ML		2440	2310	Military load, MkVII Ball
215 Ball	ML		2050	2010	Military load, MkVI Ball

7.7x58mm Japanese Arisaka

Historical Notes The 7.7mm cartridge was adopted by the Japanese in 1939 to replace the older 6.5mm, but they ended up using both cartridges during World War II. They also adopted a new rifle, the Model 99 Arisaka, which was a modification of the earlier 1905 gun. Norma has offered empty cases and sporting ammunition for this chambering with American Boxer-type primer pockets. No sporting rifles have ever been manufactured in this chambering.

General Comments The 7.7mm, or 31 Jap as it is sometimes called, is ballistically very similar to the 303 British cartridge and uses the same 0.311-inch diameter bullets. However, it is a rimless type, whereas the British case is rimmed (there is also a semi-rimmed Japanese version for machinegun use). The 7.7mm Japanese can be used for the same kind and size of game as the 303 British. With good Norma sporting ammunition available, this has become one of the more useful military cartridges for North American hunting. Military loads develop about 42,000 psi, which as with the 6.5mm Arisaka seems unusually mild for a modern military chambering, particularly when one considers the unusual strength of these rifles.

7.7x58mm Japanese Arisaka Loading Data and Factory Ballistics

Bullet (grains/type)	Powder	Grains	Velocity	Energy	Source/Comments
130 SP	IMR 3031	46	2950	2510	Duplicates factory loading
150 SP	IMR 3031	41	2680	2400	NA
180 SP	IMR 4064	45	2490	2470	Duplicates factory loading
215 SP	IMR 4064	42	2240	2405	NA
130 SP	FL		2950	2510	Norma factory load
175 Ball	ML		2400	2237	Military load
180 SP	FL		2490	2470	Norma factory load

7.65x53mm Mauser (Argentine)

Historical Notes Mauser-designed for the 1889 Belgian pattern rifle, the 7.65mm was also adopted by Argentina, Bolivia, Columbia, Ecuador, Peru and Turkey. In the United States, Remington and Winchester loaded sporting ammunition and furnished rifles in this chambering until about 1936. It has been obsolete in the United States since that time, but sporting ammunition has always been loaded in Europe. The Remington Model 30 and Winchester Model 54 bolt-action rifles were chambered for the 7.65mm, and it enjoyed a limited popularity for a few years. With the influx of 1891 Argentine Mauser military rifles, it is having another go-around on the American market. Evidently, a very similar but unique Belgian Mauser cartridge also exists. The catalog drawing suggests that it has slightly smaller case head, probably less body taper and perhaps a slightly shorter case neck (the sketch is insufficiently dimensionally denoted to establish facts).

General Comments The 7.65mm is among the best designed of all Mauser cartridges. This number gives excellent performance for North American hunting. In power, its slightly larger usable case capacity and slight bore-size increase place it ahead of the 308 Winchester and quite close to factory 30-06 loads, particularly with bullets up to about 165 grains, which makes it adequate for all medium game.

Arsenal primers are Berdan 5.5mm or 0.217-inch, a size available in several European makes. Occasionally one encounters discontinued American-made cases or ammunition, and these use conventional Boxer, Large Rifle primers. Cases can be made from empty 30-06 cases by using case-forming dies available from several American manufacturers. Bullet size is 0.313-inch, but 0.311-inch or 0.312-inch diameter bullets will give satisfactory accuracy. Norma-made cases and loaded ammunition use Boxer primers.

7.65x53mm Mauser Loading Data and Factory Ballistics

Bullet (grains/type)	Powder	Grains	Velocity	Energy	Source/Comments
150 SP	IMR 4895	47	2810	2638	
150 SP	IMR 4895	42	2550	2172	
174 SP	IMR 489S	45	2590	2600	
175 SP	IMR 4350	49	2560	2550	
175 SP	IMR 4831	53	2456	2346	
180 SP	FL		2590	2685	Norma factory load
150 SP	FL		2920	2841	Norma factory load
155 FMJ-BT Ball	ML		2710	2530	Military load, Type S
174 FMJ-BT Ball	ML		2460	2340	Military load, Type SS
211 FMJ Ball	ML		2130	2150	Military load, Original

8x50Rmm Siamese Mauser (Type 45)

Historical Notes Adopted in 1902, this cartridge derives its name from the Thai year of adoption — 2445. It was a standard Siamese military cartridge from 1902 until World War II. It is historically significant for two reasons. First, the 8x50Rmm Siamese is the first rimmed military cartridge adapted to a unique variation of the popular Mauser rifle. Second, it was the first cartridge to be manufactured in quantity in Thailand (National Arsenal, Bangkok). During World War II, the production machinery was moved to the hills to escape Japanese seizure. The machinery served to supply the guerrilla movement. When the war ended, it was moved back to Bangkok.

General Comments The 8x50Rmm cartridge was loaded with a 0.321-inch-diameter, round-nosed bullet with a copper-nickel jacket in a brass cartridge case with Berdan priming. Only round-nosed bullets were used. Some manufacture of this cartridge was also contracted out to Japan and Germany. In 1923, a new cartridge was adopted, the 8x52Rmm. Rifles for the older round were rechambered and rear sights modified. During the late 1970s, thousands of these surplus rifles were sold in the United States. It is hard to avoid noticing the similarity between this circa-1895 cartridge and the circa-1955 7.62x51mm NATO round.

8x50Rmm Siamese Mauser Factory Ballistics

Bullet (grains/type)	Powder	Grains	Velocity	Energy	Source/Comments
237 Ball	FL		2050 (est.)	2210	NA

8x52Rmm Siamese (Type 66)

Historical Notes In 1923, the Siamese army adopted a new cartridge with a pointed bullet. Case length was 2mm longer than the older 8x50Rmm Siamese cartridge, so the two were not interchangeable. The new round was adapted to a new Mannlicher infantry rifle and carbine, as well as to Madsen, Browning and Vickers machineguns. Older rifles for the 8x50Rmm cartridge were rechambered. The 8x52Rmm cartridge remained in production in Thailand until 1953, after which ball ammunition was contracted out (chiefly to Kynoch in England) until finally discontinued in the late 1960s.

General Comments The pointed, flat-base ball bullet of the 8x52Rmm cartridge will be found with both cupronickel-clad steel and gilding-metal jackets. Cases are of brass with Berdan primers. Boxer-primed cases will also be encountered. In addition to ball loadings, there were tracer, armor-piercing and armor-piercing incendiary types. This cartridge was also made by Kynoch (U.K.), in Japan and Denmark, and recently by Sako of Finland. Surplus rifles in this chambering are often encountered in the United States.

8x52Rmm Siamese Factory Ballistics

Bullet (grains/type)	Powder	Grains	Velocity	Energy	Source/Comments
181 Ball	ML		2250	2615	Military load *
*Estimated ballistics					

8x58Rmm Danish Krag

Historical Notes This Danish-designed military cartridge was adopted in 1889 for the M89 Krag-Jorgensen bolt-action rifle. The cartridge was adopted by Norway in 1888 for a Remington carbine and later adopted by both Denmark and Sweden in 1889. The original loading was the 237-grain round-nosed bullet, but in 1908, this was changed to a 196-grain spitzer bullet at a muzzle velocity of 2460 fps. This was at one time a popular sporting and target cartridge in the Scandinavian countries. Rifles based on the Remington rolling-block action and chambered for this round were once common in Scandinavian countries. A few of those were imported into the United States.

General Comments The Danish 8mm military cartridge has a good reputation for accuracy in the Danish Krag rifle. It is also noted for very satisfactory killing power on European big game. It was practically unknown in the United States until after World War II, when a number of surplus Danish Krags were sold. As a military cartridge, it is in the same class as our own 30-40 Krag or the 303 British. However, the sporting ammunition once offered by Norma was far more powerful than any commercial loads for the 30-40 or 303. In fact, the 198-grain bullet at 2740 fps develops far more energy than any commercial 30-06 load. This is one of the better military cartridges from the point of view of the North American hunter. European sporting cartridges are loaded to pressures of 42,000 to 45,000 psi. This cartridge is no longer commercially loaded and ammunition has become scarce.

8x58Rmm Danish Krag Loading Data and Factory Ballistics

Bullet (grains/type)	Powder	Grains	Velocity	Energy	Source/Comments
159 SP	IMR 3031	52.4	2870	2920	Duplicates factory loading
196 SP	IMR 4895	54	2630	3020	Duplicates factory loading
198 SP	IMR 4895	54.5	2740	3310	Duplicates factory loading
159 SP	FL		2870	2920	Norma factory load
196 SP	FL		2630	3020	Norma factory load
198 SP	FL		2740	3310	Norma factory load
237 Ball	ML		1968	2041	Military load

7.92x33mm Kurz

Historical Notes This cartridge was developed during 1940-41 for use in the newly conceived German MKB42 assault rifle. It first was tested in combat against the Russian army at Cholm, Russia, in late 1942. Several changes and modifications culminated in the *Sturmgewehr* rifle, or Stg-44. This was the first successful assault-rifle cartridge and as such marks an important milestone in military history that has had a profound effect on small-arms development. The 7.92mm Kurz is a short version of the standard 7.92mm (8mm) Mauser cartridge. No commercial sporting rifle has ever been made for this round. Ammunition was manufactured in East Germany for some years for export customers.

General Comments This is a medium-range cartridge designed to increase infantry firepower by permitting more accurate and controlled full-automatic fire. That is not possible with lightweight shoulder guns using full-powered cartridges such as the 30-06 or the German 8x57mm Mauser. This combination must have been quite effective because it was used against the Russians, who almost immediately copied it and brought out a similar assault rifle and cartridge. It has been demonstrated that in close combat in cities, jungles or similar areas, these reduced-power cartridges have all the range and penetration necessary.

The German *Sturmgewehr*, or assault rifle, had a 16-inch barrel, weighed 10 to 11 pounds loaded and used a 30-shot magazine. As a sporting cartridge, the 7.92mm Kurz would be less powerful than the 30-30 and not very well suited for anything but small to medium game. Because guns for this cartridge are capable of full-automatic fire, none have been sold in shooting condition because these come under the National Firearms Act and require a special license to own. This ammunition has never been commercially manufactured. Military ammunition is not reloadable, as it is steel cased and Berdan primed.

7.92x33mm Kurz Loading Data and Factory Ballistics

Bullet (grains/type)	Powder	Grains	Velocity	Energy	Source/Comments
125	4198	20	2070	1193	NA
125	4198	23	2310	1485	Maximum load
125 Ball	ML		2247	1408	Military load

8x50Rmm Austrian Mannlicher

Historical Notes This was an Austrian military cartridge adopted in 1888 for the Mannlicher Model 88 straight-pull rifle, and also used in the later improved Model 95. This cartridge was also used by Bulgaria, Greece and Hungary. It remains fairly popular as a sporting cartridge in Europe, and many Mannlicher rifles have been chambered for it. Sporting ammunition is still loaded in Europe by Hirtenberger, and this cartridge was recently imported to the United States. This was originally a blackpowder design. A smokeless powder loading was adopted about 1890.

General Comments During the 1920s and '30s, a few European sporting rifles chambered for the 8x50Rmm cartridge were imported into the United States and used to a limited extent for big game hunting. This is another cartridge in the 30-40 Krag class, which is adequate for most North American big game. It uses 0.323-inch bullets, of which there is a good variety available for handloading. Berdan-primed cases appear to use the 5.1mm or 0.199-inch primer, although this is variable. Hirtenberger ammunition is Boxer primed and loaded at 40,000 to 42,000 psi.

The Model 88 Mannlicher straight-pull rifle uses a hinged block on the underside of the bolt to lock the action. This design is not noted for great strength and pressures must be kept quite low for safety. The Model 95 has a revolving bolt head and forward-locking lugs, which provide greater strength. Many 95s were altered to shoot the standard German 8mm Mauser service cartridge.

8x50Rmm Austrian Mannlicher Loading Data and Factory Ballistics

Bullet (grains/type)	Powder	Grains	Velocity	Energy	Source/Comments
159 SP	IMR 3031	48	2460	2142	NA
227 SP	IMR 3031	45	2040	2102	NA
244 SP	IMR 3031	45	2010	2200	Approximates military load
196 SP	FL		2310	2320	Hirtenberger factory load
244 Ball	ML		2030	2240	Military load, smokeless powder

Above loads are for the Model 88 action, provided it is in good condition.

Mannlicher Model 1888

8x50Rmm Lebel

Historical Notes The 8mm Lebel was the first smallbore, smokeless-powder military cartridge developed by any world power. The cartridge and the Lebel bolt-action rifle were both adopted in 1886. The original loading used a 232-grain, jacketed flat-nose, flat-base bullet called the Balle M. In 1898, a solid-bronze, spitzer boattail, 198-grain bullet was adopted — the famous Balle D. The cartridge was further updated in 1932 with the adoption of the Balle 32M, which had a cupronickel-clad steel jacket over a lead core. This spitzer boattail bullet weighed 190 grains. Its rimmed case was not well-adapted to automatic arms, so it was replaced by the rimless 7.5x54mm MAS round in 1929. Remington manufactured rolling block and Mannlicher-Berthier chambered in 8x50Rmm Lebel for the French government during World War I. When the war ended, all the surplus was sold commercially and Remington turned out sporting ammunition with a 170-grain, bronze-pointed bullet. Few rifles have been made in this chambering. Military production of this cartridge in France continued, even under German occupation.

General Comments Probably more 8mm Lebel rifles were sold during the 1920s and '30s than after World War II. The Remington factory products were all brand new and in perfect condition, which is more than can be said for the more recent war surplus models that have shown up. The 8mm Lebel cartridge is in the 308 Winchester class and makes a fine cartridge for deer or elk hunting. Modern 8mm Lebel sporting ammunition is difficult to find. Plenty of good 0.323-inch bullets are available and American cases can easily be reloaded. Military cases have Berdan primers of 0.199-inch or 0.216-inch size and are less practical to reload.

8x50Rmm Lebel Loading Data and Factory Ballistics

Bullet (grains/type)	Powder	Grains	Velocity	Energy	Source/Comments
170 SP	IMR 4895	49	2570	2500	NA
198 SP	IMR 3031	46	2380	2481	Duplicates military ball
198 SP	IMR 4895	45	2450	2645	NA
170	FL		2640	2630	Remington factory load
198	ML		2380	2481	Military load, Balle D, Balle 32M

8x53Rmm Japanese Murata

Historical Notes This Japanese service cartridge was adopted in 1887 for the tube-magazine Murata turn-bolt rifle, a modification of the earlier single-shot and repeating 11mm Murata rifles. It is similar to the French Chassepot in design. The 8mm Murata was the principal rifle used by the Japanese in the Sino-Japanese war of 1894. It was known officially as the Meiji 20 8mm rifle and cartridge. Meiji refers to the period of the Emperor Meiji's reign (1868-1912). This cartridge was replaced in 1897 by the 6.5mm round.

General Comments Both 8mm Murata rifles and cartridges are collector's items, and rare ones at that. This cartridge was loaded with smokeless powder and a jacketed, flat-nosed bullet (safe for use in the tubular magazine) that measured 0.320-inch in diameter and weighed 238 grains. No reader is likely to have one of these rifles available for hunting or anything else. However, if you do, the cartridge would be adequate for anything to elk-sized animals at moderate range. The 8x53Rmm is unusual among military cartridges because it has a protected primer that appears as a primer within a primer.

8x53Rmm Japanese Murata Factory Ballistics

Bullet (grains/type)	Powder	Grains	Velocity	Energy	Source/Comments
238 Ball	ML		1850	1810	Military load

7.9x57mmJ and 7.9x57mmJS (8mm German Mauser)

Historical Notes The 8mm Mauser is one of the world's truly great military cartridges. It was the official German military cartridge in both world wars and was also adopted by Czechoslovakia, Poland, China and other countries. It is also a popular sporting round in many parts of the world.

Although designated the 8mm "Mauser," the original military round was designed for the German Model 88 commission rifle, which was a modified Mannlicher-type, not a Mauser design. This rifle was known officially as the Gewehr 88, or German Infantry Model 1888. It was designed by the German Infantry Board or Commission at Spandau Arsenal. It was replaced in 1898 by the superior Mauser model of that year. The original J Patrone cartridge used a round-nosed, 226-grain bullet of 0.318-inch diameter. Muzzle velocity was 2093 fps. In 1905, the Germans adopted an improved cartridge that retained the original 8x57mm case, but employed a larger-diameter bullet (0.323-inch). The new S Patrone bullet was lighter (154 grains) and was pointed or spitzer-type. Muzzle velocity was upped to 2,880 fps. Although the rifle had a significantly longer barrel than the '03 Springfield, the 17 percent muzzle energy advantage that the 7.9x57mmJS load had over the 30-06 ball loading is quite surprising. The editor has evidence that German smokeless powder of that era was vastly superior to anything available in this country and perhaps anywhere else. This no doubt accommodated the above noted ballistic potential of the 7.9x57mmJS loading. External ballistic calculations prove that the German military loading was a significantly superior battlefield cartridge, compared to the U.S. military loading. All German military rifles manufactured since 1905 originated with the 0.323-inch bore. All earlier military and many civilian arms were re-rifled to accommodate 0.323-inch bullets.

The original German 8mm military cartridge was designated by a "J" for "Infanterie." (The story is that U.S. military intelligence officers who were tasked to discover the secret of the superior performance of the German cartridge captured classified German documents toward the end of World War I and then mistook the ornate German script "I" for a "J"; if true, it is indeed ironic that worldwide, including Germany, the designation has been bastardized to J.) The later bullet, for the 0.323-inch diameter groove, is indicated by an "S" for spitzer-type. Sporting ammunition in 8mm is labeled by the same system. The 8x57mmJ or 1888 cartridge can be fired safely in the 1905 or S-bore rifles, though accuracy is poor. However, it is not safe to fire the larger "S" (0.323-inch) bullet in the smaller "J" (0.318-inch) bore.

General Comments Thousands of 8mm military rifles have been sold through surplus dealers since the end of World War II. Most were bought to obtain the 98 Mauser action, which served as the basis for building a sporting rifle for some U.S. cartridge. In many instances, the cost of making up a custom rifle on a military action was not justified. However, if the original chambering was retained and modifications held to the minimum, many of these rifles were a good buy.

The 8x57mmJS Mauser is an outstanding sporting cartridge in its own right, being in the same class as our 30-06. U.S. ammunition companies load only the "S" version of the 8mm, but they hold it to a very mild pressure level so the round could safely be fired in a "J" bored rifle. This has a 170-grain bullet at 2360 fps, which about duplicates the 30-40 Krag in power. Norma makes both 165- and 196-grain sporting loads that bring out the full potential of this cartridge. Sporting loads and handloading data will be found in Chapter 2.

7.9x57mmJ and 7.9mmJS Factory Ballistics

Bullet (grains/type)	Powder	Grains	Velocity	Energy	Source/Comments
154 Ball	ML		2880	2835	Military load, S Patrone
226 Ball	ML		2095	2200	Military load, J Patrone

WARNING! Many "J" bore (0.318-inch) rifles still exist and will fire "S" bore (0.323-inch) cartridges, potentially creating dangerous pressures. When in doubt, check bore diameter CAREFULLY!

8x63mm Swedish

Historical Notes This is a Swedish round introduced in 1932 for use in various Browning air- or water-cooled machineguns, and for the m/40 rifle. Swedish military rifles and light machineguns are chambered for the standard 6.5x55mm cartridge. Its use is confined to Sweden and it is practically unknown outside that area. It was never actually loaded as a sporting cartridge.

General Comments The 8x63mm nearly duplicates the wildcat 8mm/06 cartridge, which is the 30-06 necked-up to accept 0.323-inch bullets. However, the 8x63mm has a larger-diameter case and should be capable of delivering about 15 percent more energy if loaded to the same pressure. (Incidentally, never fire any cartridge in any gun just because it looks similar to, or has a similar designation to, the cartridge the gun is chambered for. This can be extremely dangerous. Almost is not good enough, so if you are at all uncertain about the proper cartridge, have a competent gunsmith check the bullet diameter, case dimensions and headspace. Some British and European cartridges look very much like similar American rounds, but these cartridges absolutely will not interchange safely.) The 8x63mm Swedish is significantly more powerful than the 30-06 Springfield.

8x63mm Swedish Loading Data and Factory Ballistics

Bullet (grains/type)	Powder	Grains	Velocity	Energy	Source/Comments
150 SP	4895	60	3050	3100	NA
170 SP	4320	57	2820	3020	NA
225 SP	4350	57	2450	2960	NA
218 Ball	ML		2493	3025	Military load

8x60Rmm Guedes M85 Portuguese

Historical Notes Portugal adopted the 8mm Guedes rifle and cartridge in 1885; the gun was a single-shot, underlever type based on the Martini-Henry design. These rifles were manufactured by Steyr in Austria and were well-made and finished. One of the last of the military single shots, it had a very short life. A very similar cartridge called the 8x60mm Kropatschek was adapted in 1896 by Portugal. These two may have been generally interchangeable.

General Comments The 8mm Guedes cartridge represented a ballistic advance similar to the 9.5mm Turkish Mauser. However, the Guedes rifle was a step in the wrong direction because all the powers of the time were rapidly developing repeating rifles. Both rifle and cartridge are rare.

The 8mm Guedes was replaced in 1896 by an apparently interchangeable cartridge, the 8x60Rmm Kropatschek (later shortened to 56mm case length). This cartridge was used in the Austrian-made Kropatschek rifle, a tube-magazine repeater. No sporting rifles were made for either of these rounds.

8x60Rmm Guedes M85 Portuguese Loading Data and Factory Ballistics

Bullet (grains/type)	Powder	Grains	Velocity	Energy	Source/Comments
175 Lead	Blackpowder (Fg)	75	1740	1182	Lyman #321232
175 Lead	IMR 4198	28	1670	1090	Lyman #321232
247 Ball	Blackpowder (Fg)	70	1706	1605	Military load

8x59mm Breda

Historical Notes This cartridge was for the Italian Breda Model 1937 and 1938 machineguns. Insofar as can be established, it has never been used as a sporting cartridge.

General Comments Different bullet weights and muzzle velocities are listed for the 8mm Breda and this may reflect the various military loadings. Bullet diameter varies from 0.322-inch to 0.326-inch. The cartridge case is fatter and 1/10-inch longer than the 8mm Mauser. The original purpose of the 8mm Breda was to replace the 6.5mm Italian cartridge as a more effective machinegun round. Since case capacity and published ballistics both suggest that this cartridge came close to matching modern 300 Magnum energy levels, it would seem that it was indeed a significant step up from the 6.5mm Italian Carcano.

8x59mm Breda Loading Data

Bullet (grains/type)	Powder	Grains	Velocity	Energy	Source/Comments
210 Ball	ML		2600	3160	Military load

8x56Rmm Austrian/ Hungarian Mannlicher 8mm Hungarian M31

Historical Notes This cartridge was developed in 1930 for the Solothurn machine gun. It was subsequently adopted by Hungary about 1931. Design goes back to the mid-1920s, when it was developed to replace the 8x50Rmm Austrian round. It was designated the M30 in Austria and the M31 in Hungary. It differs from the older Austrian 8x50Rmm, having a longer, tapered shoulder, plus a bullet of slightly larger diameter. It was used in the Hungarian Model 35 Mannlicher bolt-action rifle and also the modified Model 95 straight-pull Mannlicher. In 1940, Hungary adopted the standard German 8mm military round and many of its rifles were then altered to that chambering. As far as we know, no sporting rifles were turned out in the 8mm Hungarian chambering.

General Comments This cartridge is often confused with the 8x56mm Mannlicher-Schoenauer, which is a rimless sporting cartridge, whereas the Hungarian military round is rimmed. The two are not interchangeable, as there is considerable difference in case dimensions as well as bullet diameter.

Rifles in this chambering are common on the American market and ammunition is also readily available. The 0.329-inch diameter bullet makes handloading a problem because bullets of this size are not normally available. It is possible to use 0.323-inch bullets, but accuracy is poor. Military rifles in this chambering should be considered primarily collector's items because of the ammunition supply problem. In power, the 8x56Rmm Hungarian and the 8x50Rmm Austrian cartridge are in the 30-40 Krag class.

8x56Rmm Hungarian Mannlicher Loading Data and Factory Ballistics

Bullet (grains/type)	Powder	Grains	Velocity	Energy	Source/Comments
198 SP	IMR 3031	46	2310	2358	0.323-inch bullet
206 Ball	IMR 3031	45	2300	2420	Military load

Model 95/34 Mannlicher
(Photo courtesy Century International Arms)

9.5x60Rmm Turkish Mauser

Historical Notes This cartridge was adopted by Turkey in 1887 with the M87 Mauser bolt-action repeating rifle, which was a modification of the German Model 71/84. This last Mauser-designed blackpowder cartridge is one of the most efficient ever developed. Mauser concluded after extensive testing and experimenting that the 9.5mm bullet gave the maximum performance possible with this propellant. The cartridge was used for three years before it was made obsolete by smokeless powder. In 1890, Turkey adopted the 7.65mm Mauser cartridge. The 9.5mm is often referred to as the Turkish Peabody because it was also used extensively in the Peabody-Martini single-shot rifle.

General Comments The Turkish Mauser Model 87 rifle is largely a collector's item because the Turks scrapped most of the original guns when they adopted the 7.65mm in 1890. However, a good number of the single-shot Peabody-Martini rifles in this chambering survived. This cartridge has been obsolete in Europe since the turn of the century. As a hunting number, the 9.5mm Turkish would be adequate for North American big game at moderate ranges.

9.5x60Rmm Turkish Mauser Loading Data and Factory Ballistics

Bullet (grains/type)	Powder	Grains	Velocity	Energy	Source/Comments
290 Lead	IMR 4198	34	1500	1445	Lyman #403173
285 Lead	Blackpowder (Fg)	70	1758	1955	Military load, paper-patched bullet
284 Lead	ML		1758	1950	Military load

10.15x61Rmm Jarmann

Historical Notes This cartridge was adopted by Norway and Sweden in 1881 for use in the Jarmann repeating rifle, featuring a turn bolt and tube magazine. It was officially adopted in 1884, with a modified version adopted in 1887. It was used for only seven years before being replaced by the 6.5x55mm cartridge and the Krag rifle.

General Comments The 10.15mm Jarmann is nearly unknown in the United States and the Jarmann rifle is a collector's item. The cartridge was not used long enough to build much of a following, even in the Scandinavian countries, although it was used to a limited extent in Norway and Sweden for sporting purposes. It is one of the more efficient blackpowder cartridges and is comparable to the 9.5mm Turkish Mauser.

10.15x61Rmm Jarmann Loading Data and Factory Ballistics

Bullet (grains/type)	Powder	Grains	Velocity	Energy	Source/Comments
290 Lead	IMR 4198	32	1430	1315	Lyman #403173
337 Lead	Blackpowder (Fg)	80	1625	1975	Military load, paper-patched bullet
337 Lead	ML		1625	1975	Military load

10.15x63Rmm Serbian Mauser

Historical Notes This cartridge was adopted in 1878 by Serbia for use in the Mauser Model 78/80 single-shot rifle, which was nothing more than a slight modification of the Mauser Model 71 rifle. In the Serbian model, the left receiver wall enclosed the bolt more fully than in the original M71. This modification was later incorporated into the design of the Mauser 71/84 repeating rifle. Quantities of the German 71/84 were also chambered for the Serbian cartridge and sold to that country. It is reported that various 10.15 Serbian Mauser rifles were observed in the Balkans as recently as World War II.

General Comments This is another rare military cartridge not likely to be used for sporting purposes. I do not know of any of these Serbian Mauser rifles being sold in the United States. However, one can never entirely anticipate what some alert arms scout may find hidden away in the future. If any of these rifles do show up, the handloader can make ammunition by sizing 11mm Mauser cases full length in a 10.15mm die.

10.15x63Rmm Serbian Mauser Factory Ballistics

Bullet (grains/type)	Powder	Grains	Velocity	Energy	Source/Comments
290 Lead	IMR 4198	34.0			Lyman #412263, sized to 0.411 inch
340 Lead	Blackpowder		1460	1612	Military load

10.4x38Rmm Swiss Vetterli M69/81

Historical Notes This Swiss cartridge was adopted in 1869 for use in the Vetterli turn-bolt rifle. The official military round is rimfire, but a centerfire version was also loaded in Europe. The cartridge and rifle were discontinued in 1889.

General Comments The 10.4mm, or 41 Swiss, cartridge is quite well known in the United States, and most American companies loaded it until about 1942. Thousands of surplus Swiss Vetterli rifles have been sold in this country, and a surprising number have been used for hunting deer. For a time, there was a good supply of both rifles and cartridges in dealers' stock. American ammunition was loaded with smokeless powder. The 41 Swiss would be a barely adequate short-range cartridge for deer-class animals. The rimfire military version cannot be reloaded. This cartridge is unusual in that it is one of the few rimfire military rounds.

10.4x38Rmm Swiss Vetterli M69/81 Factory Ballistics

Bullet (grains/type)	Powder	Grains	Velocity	Energy	Source/Comments
334 Lead	ML		1345 *	1330	Military load

*Some sources list MV as 1,427 fps, perhaps this refers to a later smokeless loading.

10.4x47Rmm Italian Vetterli M70

Historical Notes This Italian cartridge was adopted in 1870. It was used in the Vetterli single-shot, turn-bolt rifle and later a modified box-magazine repeater (Vitali system). Many of these cartridges were loaded with a brass-coated bullet.

General Comments The 10.4 Italian service cartridge has not been produced for many years, but occasional lots of surplus ammunition have appeared in the surplus arms stores. In performance, it is practically identical to the 10.4mm Swiss Vetterli. Italian Vetterli rifles are fairly common in the United States.

10.4x47Rmm Italian Vetterli M70 Loading Data and Factory Ballistics

Bullet (grains/type)	Powder	Grains	Velocity	Energy	Source/Comments
250 Lead	IMR 4198	27	1300	935	Lyman #429251
313	Blackpowder (Fg)	62	1345	1255	Military load

10.75x58Rmm Russian Berdan (43 Russian Berdan)

Historical Notes The 10.75x58Rmm was adopted by Russia in 1868 and used in the Berdan I and the Krnka M69 rifles. After 1871, it was used in the Berdan II rifle — all single-shot arms. This was the first military cartridge with the outside centerfire Berdan primer and a bottleneck case. Large quantities of these cartridges were manufactured in the United States by Remington and Winchester for the Russian government. Most of the Berdan rifles were made by Colt, but the Russians also manufactured these guns at their Tula arsenal.

General Comments This was primarily a military cartridge and was not used to any great extent for sporting purposes. During the 1950s and '60s, a fair number of the old Colt-made Berdan I and II rifles showed up in various surplus stores along with suitable blackpowder ammunition. In the United States, this was known as the 43 Berdan cartridge.

The Berdan I rifle is a forward-hinged, lift-block type (striker-fired) and the Berdan II is a turn-bolt single-shot, somewhat similar to the Model 71 Mauser. The Krnka is a breech-loading conversion of the Russian muzzleloading rifle. In 1867, the Berdan I-type action was tested by an American military board as a possible means of converting the muzzleloading Springfield to breech-loading.

10.75x58Rmm Russian Berdan Loading Data and Factory Ballistics

Bullet (grains/type)	Powder	Grains	Velocity	Energy	Source/Comments
250 Lead	IMR 4198	33	1400	1085	Lyman #429251
370 Lead	IMR 4198	31	1410	1630	NA
370 Lead	Blackpowder (Fg)	77	1450	1725	Military load, paper-patched bullet

11x60Rmm Japanese Murata

Historical Notes This is the original Japanese military cartridge designed by Major Murata for his single-shot turn-bolt rifle. Different authorities give varying dates for the introduction of the rifle and cartridge. The rifle is called the Meiji 13 11mm by the Japanese, which would make the date of introduction 1880. It was later replaced by an 8mm round. The Japanese purchased obsolete European military rifles until they developed their own. They used quantities of the French Chassepot and the Murata rifle is based on this French design. The 11mm Murata cartridge is also quite similar to the 11mm Gras, which was used in the modified Chassepot.

General Comments The 11mm Murata is another collector's item, too rare and valuable to shoot even if you had several of these cartridges. Less valuable ammunition can be made by reforming 348 Winchester cases. Bullet diameter is 0.432-inch, but Lyman's No. 439186 (370-grain) bullet could probably be sized down and made to work. Use loading data for the 11mm Gras or the 11mm Mauser.

11x60Rmm Japanese Murata Factory Ballistics

Bullet (grains/type)	Powder	Grains	Velocity	Energy	Source/Comments
420 Lead	ML		1487	2060	Military load

11x50Rmm Belgian Albini M67/72

Historical Notes This Belgian military cartridge was adopted in 1867 and used in the Albini-Braendlin single-shot, lift-block rifle. It is often confused with the 11mm Comblain, which it somewhat resembles. It was originally loaded with blackpowder and a paper-patched bullet. Most of the original Albini rifles were sold off and many remodeled into sporter-types or rechambered for sporting cartridges of the late 1800s.

General Comments Moderate numbers of the old Albini Braendlin rifles have been sold in the United States as collector's items. Most of these were in good condition and sold for low prices. Ammunition is very scarce and much too valuable to shoot. Usable cases for blackpowder loads might be converted from modern 470 Nitro Express cases.

11x50Rmm Belgian Albini M67/72 Loading Data and Factory Ballistics

Bullet (grains/type)	Powder	Grains	Velocity	Energy	Source/Comments
370 Lead	IMR 4198	29	1350	1495	Lyman #439186
386 Lead	Blackpowder (Fg)	75	1368	1605	Military load, paper-patched bullet

11x53Rmm Belgian Comblain M71

Historical Notes The 11mm Belgian Comblain was never an official military round, but was used by the Belgian civil guard. It was introduced in 1871 as the cartridge for the falling-block type Comblain single-shot rifle. Rifles in this chambering were used to a limited extent by some of the South American countries. The 11mm Albini was the official Belgian military cartridge.

General Comments The 11mm Belgian Comblain is similar to the Brazilian Comblain, but these cartridges are not interchangeable and should not be confused. However, there is not much difference in the performance or power of the two rounds. Usable cases for blackpowder loads could probably be made from modern 470 Nitro Express cases.

11x53Rmm Belgian Comblain M71 Loading Data and Factory Ballistics

Bullet (grains/type)	Powder	Grains	Velocity	Energy	Source/Comments
370 Lead	IMR 4198	32	1460	1750	Lyman #439186
386 Lead	Blackpowder (Fg)	76	1445	1787	Military load, paper-patched bullet

11.15x58Rmm (43) Spanish Remington (11x53mm Spanish)

General Comments The 11mm (43) Spanish Remington was not seen in the United States until after World War II, when large numbers of Remington rolling-block rifles were sold as surplus. Blackpowder ammunition was available for a short time, but is now a collector's item. Many of these rifles have been rebarreled to some other chambering. It is possible to have these rifles rechambered to accept the full-length 348 Winchester case, which can easily be neck-expanded to take 0.439-inch diameter bullets. This conversion works quite well.

Three distinct blackpowder Spanish military 11.15mm cartridges exist. The one listed here, a carbine version with a case length of 1 7/8 inches was loaded with 60 grains of blackpowder and a 400-grain bullet; the original centerfire cartridge had a straight case and a 0.454-inch-diameter bullet is covered later in this chapter as the "Spanish Reformado." The carbine round had the same case configuration as the standard cartridge and although shorter, could undoubtedly be fired in the standard rifle chamber, but the reverse would not be true. The carbine round is now a rare and valuable collector's item. Like most of the old blackpowder military cartridges, the 43 Spanish would make a good big game hunting cartridge for anything from deer through elk at close range.

11.15x58Rmm (43) Spanish Remington Loading Data and Factory Ballistics

Bullet (grains/type)	Powder	Grains	Velocity	Energy	Source/Comments
387 Lead	IMR 4198	32	1360	1590	Lyman #439186
387 Lead	IMR 3031	40	1310	1475	Lyman #439186
375 Lead	Blackpowder (Fg)	78	1380	1585	Military load

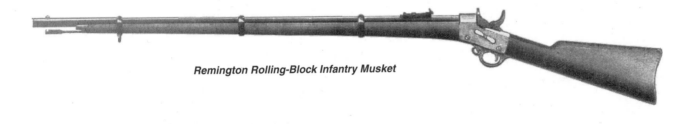

Remington Rolling-Block Infantry Musket

11.15x58Rmm Austrian Werndl M77

Historical Notes This is an improved bottlenecked cartridge adopted by Austria in 1877 to replace the earlier straight case of 11.4 mm. It originally was used in the Werndl rotating block single-shot rifle, but from 1886 to 1888, it was also used in the Mannlicher straight-pull rifle.

General Comments Rifles for the 11.15mm Werndl cartridge are scarce, as is the ammunition. At one time, Winchester and other American companies loaded this round, but it has been used very little in the United States. It is in the same class as the 11mm Mauser for sporting use.

11.15x58Rmm Austrian Werndl M77 Loading Data and Factory Ballistics

Bullet (grains/type)	Powder	Grains	Velocity	Energy	Source/Comments
370 Lead	IMR 4198	32	1360	1520	Lyman #439186
370 Lead	Blackpowder (Fg)	75	1437	1695	Military load; paper-patched bullet

11x59Rmm French Gras
11x59mm Vickers

Historical Notes This French cartridge was adopted in 1874 for the Gras single-shot rifle, a metallic cartridge, breech-loaded conversion of the Chassepot needle gun. This was the first modern French military cartridge. It was replaced in 1886 by the then-revolutionary 8mm Lebel. Many Remington rolling-block rifles were chambered for the 11mm Gras and these, along with the Gras rifle, were used extensively in the Balkans and French colonial areas. Remington loaded this cartridge at one time. The Japanese purchased and used many of the Gras-modified rifles and the 11mm Gras cartridge.

The 11mm Vickers was used by both the British and French during World War I in the Vickers aircraft machinegun to shoot down German artillery observation balloons. This cartridge is also referred to as the 11mm Vickers Balloon Gun cartridge. It uses the same case as the 1874 French Gras rifle cartridge and was actually developed by the French for their Hotchkiss anti-balloon gun. The more reliable Vickers machinegun was later modified to shoot the same cartridge. By 1917, it was found that the standard rifle cartridge was not as satisfactory for shooting down observation balloons as a larger caliber carrying a heavier tracer/incendiary bullet. This was the reason for the development of a special-purpose cartridge. Rather than waste time, the French simply used what was immediately available and adopted the Gras rifle case. Some of these cartridges are head-stamped WESTERN 2-17, indicating that these cartridges were manufactured in the United States by Western Cartridge Co. in February 1917.

General Comments Neither this rifle nor this cartridge have ever been used to any degree in the United States. It would be suitable for North American big game hunting at short range, like most of the other blackpowder military cartridges. It is very similar in performance to the 11mm Mauser.

The 11mm Vickers appears to have a longer, heavier bullet than the original Gras cartridge. It is also of the full-jacketed type and some are brass covered. One should be careful working with these rounds because many have tracer/incendiary bullets.

11x59Rmm French Gras Loading Data and Factory Ballistics

Bullet (grains/type)	Powder	Grains	Velocity	Energy	Source/Comments
365 Lead	IMR 4198	36	1420	1635	Lyman #446109
385 Lead	IMR 4198	33	1400	1675	NA
385 Lead	Blackpowder (Fg)	78	1493	1903	Military load

11.15x60Rmm (43) Mauser
(11x60Rmm Mauser)

Historical Notes This was the first of a long line of military cartridges designed by Paul Mauser. The 11mm Mauser was adopted by the German military in 1871 with the M71 bolt-action, single-shot Mauser rifle. Later this rifle was converted to a tubular magazine repeater as the Model 71/84. This cartridge became a popular sporting cartridge in Europe and East Africa. It is no longer loaded in Europe. Canadian Industries Limited (Dominion Brand) once offered a smokeless powder version that was imported into the United States.

General Comments A popular military and sporting round through the 1870s and '80s, the 11mm Mauser was loaded in the United States by Remington and Winchester. It enjoyed only limited popularity here because our own 45-70 military load was easier to obtain. A modernized version using smokeless powder was produced for H. Krieghoff of Suhl, Germany, and chambered in Mauser bolt-action rifles in the 1920s. A few were imported into the United States. The 11mm Mauser is still a potent short-range cartridge for North American big game. Most military ammunition uses the Berdan primer, usually of 6.5mm (0.254-inch) size. Correct bullet diameter is 0.446-inch.

11.15x60Rmm (43) Mauser Loading Data and Factory Ballistics

Bullet (grains/type)	Powder	Grains	Velocity	Energy	Source/Comments
370 Lead	Blackpowder (Fg)	77	1430	1680	Duplicates military load, paper-patched bullet
387 Lead	IMR 4198	32	1335	1530	NA
387 Lead	IMR 4198	35	1510	1955	Maximum load
385	FL		1360	1580	CIL factory load
386 Lead	ML		1425	1740	Military load

Mauser Model 71/84

11.43x55Rmm Turkish

Historical Notes This cartridge was used by Turkey from 1874 until 1887. It was replaced by the 9.5mm Mauser. This round was used primarily in the Peabody-Martini single-shot rifle, many of which were made in the United States. This cartridge was loaded in England and called the 450 Turkish Peabody-Martini and the 45 Peabody-Martini in the United States. It was popular in the Balkans and on occasion is still used there.

General Comments This is another cartridge that was not distributed very extensively in the United States. A few of the old single-shot, underlever Peabody-Martini rifles have been sold at various times, but 11.43mm ammunition is hard to come by. A Lyman #446187 cast lead bullet weighing 465 grains can be used for handloading.

11.43x55Rmm Turkish Loading Data and Factory Ballistics

Bullet (grains/type)	Powder	Grains	Velocity	Energy	Source/Comments
465 Lead	Blackpowder (Fg)	80	1280	1690	Approximates military load
465 Lead	IMR 4198	36	1410	2050	Lyman #446187
486 Lead	ML		1263	1720	Military load

11.43x50Rmm 43 Egyptian Remington

Historical Notes This cartridge was adopted by Egypt in 1870 for use in the single-shot Remington rolling-block rifle. The Egyptian government ordered 60,000 of these rifles between 1870 and 1876. Remington rifles in this chambering were also used by France in 1870-71 during the Franco-Prussian war. In fact, these rifles were part of a shipment intended for Egypt, but the Egyptians defaulted, so the French bought them. The Egyptians then accepted a later order. Remington loaded huge quantities of this ammunition.

General Comments In appearance, the 43 Egyptian looks similar to the 43 Spanish Remington cartridge. Performance is almost identical, but the two are not interchangeable. The 11mm Egyptian also resembles and is very close to the 11x52Rmm Beaumont in physical measurements. Early Remington catalogs list the 11mm Egyptian as also suitable for the Beaumont rifle, so this cartridge can be fired in both guns.

Obsolete Egyptian rolling-block rifles were sold off in widely scattered places all over the world. Many turned up on the American market. The 11mm Egyptian is adequate for most American game and is comparable in power to the 11mm Mauser.

11.43x50Rmm (43) Egyptian Remington Loading Data and Factory Ballistics

Bullet (grains/type)	Powder	Grains	Velocity	Energy	Source/Comments
465 Lead	Blackpowder (Fg)	70	1280	1690	Lyman #446187
465 Lead	IMR 4198	34	1440	2140	Lyman #446187
400 Lead	Blackpowder (Fg)	75	1330	1570	Military load; paper-patched bullet

11.4x50Rmm Austrian Werndl M73

Historical Notes This was the official Austrian military cartridge from 1873 to 1877. It was used in the Werndl single-shot rifle that featured a breech block that rotated after the hammer was cocked. The block was turned via a protruding thumb-piece so as to expose the loading groove cut on the bottom. Both rifle and cartridge are relatively rare in the United States.

General Comments From time to time, a few Model 73 Werndl rifles are sold as collector's items. The cartridge is a scarce collector's item in the United States. In power, it is on a par with similar blackpowder cartridges. It might be possible to convert 45-70 cases to work in these rifles.

11.4x50Rmm Austrian Werndl M73 Loading Data and Factory Ballistics

Bullet (grains/type)	Powder	Grains	Velocity	Energy	Source/Comments
465 Lead	IMR 4198	29	1300	1745	Lyman #446187
340 Lead	Blackpowder (Fg)	62	1270	1215	Military load

11.4x50Rmm Brazilian Comblain M74

General Comments The Brazilian Comblain cartridge is quite similar in appearance to the Belgian cartridge of the same name. However, the two are not interchangeable. It has seen very little use in the United States. In performance, it is about the same as the 45-70.

11.4x50Rmm Brazilian Comblain M74 Loading Data and Factory Ballistics

Bullet (grains/type)	Powder	Grains	Velocity	Energy	Source/Comments
485 Lead	IMR 4198	27	1280	1765	Lyman #451112
486 Lead	Blackpowder (Fg)	72	1310	1850	Military load

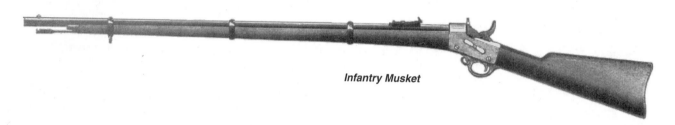

Infantry Musket

11.5x57Rmm Spanish Reformado

Historical Notes This was the original centerfire, Berdan-primed Spanish military cartridge. It was adopted about 1867 and used in early rolling-block rifles manufactured by Remington for the Spanish government. It was also used in some Berdan and Snider conversions of the Spanish muzzleloader. Over a million rounds of this ammunition and many rolling-block rifles were captured by American troops in Cuba during the Spanish-American war. It was replaced by the 11.15mm Spanish Remington cartridge in 1871.

General Comments Although this cartridge is listed as 43-caliber, the bullet has a base band that is actually 0.454-inch in diameter. The bullet is brass covered and has a 10-degree beveled base.

In the tropical climate of Cuba, the brass-covered bullets often turned green with verdigris and were thought to be "poisoned" bullets by American troops. In terms of bacterial count and infectious wounds, these probably were poisoned for all practical purposes. Rim and base diameter and case length are almost identical to the 11.15mm Spanish Remington and cases could be made by expanding and trimming 11.15mm cases.

11.5x57Rmm (43) Spanish Reformado Loading Data and Factory Ballistics

Bullet (grains/type)	Powder	Grains	Velocity	Energy	Source/Comments
250 Lead	IMR 4198	32	1220	825	Lyman #454485
395 Ball	Blackpowder (Fg)	74	1280	1435	Military load

577/450 Martini-Henry

Historical Notes This cartridge was adopted by Great Britain in 1871 for use in the famous Martini-Henry falling-block, single-shot rifle. Originally a rolled-type cartridge case, it was later changed to a drawn case. To some extent, it still is a popular sporting cartridge in England, other parts of the British Commonwealth and Africa. It was loaded in England with both black and smokeless powders with nearly identical ballistics.

The 577/450 cartridge entered history with B Company, 24th Regiment of the British army on January 22-23, 1879. On that day, Lt. John Chard and Lt. Gonville Bromhead, with some 140 men, defended Rork's Drift in Natal, South Africa, from more than 4000 Zulu warriors. When the battle was over, more than 20,000 rounds of 577/450 ammunition had been fired by the defenders.

General Comments Many Martini-Henry rifles were imported into the United States, which has created a mild interest in this cartridge. With its large diameter and heavy lead bullet, it is a good killer on most game at close range. It has been used in Africa and India on all kinds of animals, including the dangerous varieties. It would be adequate for anything in North America out to 100-150 yards or so.

577/450 Martini-Henry Loading Data and Factory Ballistics

Bullet (grains/type)	Powder	Grains	Velocity	Energy	Source/Comments
400 Lead	IMR 4198	38	1450	1865	Lyman #457124
500 Lead	Blackpowder (Fg)	80	1320	1935	Lyman #457125
325 Lead	FL		1600	1845	Kynoch factory load
370 Lead	FL		1450	1725	Kynoch factory load
480 Lead	ML		1350	1940	Military load

11.3x50Rmm Beaumont M71

Historical Notes This was the original Dutch Beaumont cartridge adopted in 1871 for use in the Beaumont single-shot rifle, a turn-bolt type similar to the French Gras. A few years after it was adopted, the rifle was altered to a box-magazine repeater. In 1878, the Beaumont cartridge was redesigned slightly to use a shorter case and a bullet of 0.457-inch diameter.

General Comments Among cartridge collectors there is considerable argument regarding the Dutch Beaumont cartridge. Some claim it is identical to the 11mm Egyptian Remington; others say it is not. The difficulty is caused partly by the fact that both versions of the Beaumont cartridge are similar to the Egyptian Remington. The cartridge listed here is the original version. The slightly modified cartridge is the 11x52Rmm M71/78, which has a longer case and a heavier bullet of 0.457-inch diameter. Old Remington catalogs list the 43 Egyptian as "adapted to Remington, Egyptian model military and Beaumont rifles." Undoubtedly, the 11mm Egyptian can be fired in Beaumont rifles. However, these three cartridges are not identical in physical measurements.

11.3x50Rmm Beaumont M71 Loading Data and Factory Ballistics

Bullet (grains/type)	Powder	Grains	Velocity	Energy	Source/Comments
360 Lead	Blackpowder (Fg)	55	1300	1350	Lyman #509134
360 Lead	IMR 4198	35	1420	1610	Lyman #509134, maximum load
336 Lead	Blackpowder (Fg)	58	1378	1415	Military load

11.63x33mm Belted (458x1-inch Barnes)

Historical Notes To paraphrase the late Robert Ripley, believe it or not, the 458x1 1/2-inch Barnes cartridge was actually used as an experimental military cartridge by U.S. Armed Forces during the Vietnamese war. The cartridge was developed by the author in mid-1962 as part of the work on the 458x2-inch cartridge, which involved cutting the 458 Winchester Magnum case back to various lengths. All of this was duly reported in the June 1963 issue of *Guns & Ammo* magazine, pp. 38-41 and 66. Someone in the military establishment read the article and decided that the short 45-caliber cartridge just might have a certain specialized military application.

It appears there was a problem using the 5.56mm cartridge and the M-16 rifle in jungle ambush situations. The light, high-velocity bullet did not always arrive on target when fired through a lot of intervening jungle growth. It was concluded that because the range of such shooting was fairly short, a proper loading of the 458x1 1/2-inch might solve these problems. The military shortened Barnes, original 1 1/2-inch version to 1.312 inches.

After a short testing period, a load was developed using a 500-grain full-metal-jacket bullet at a muzzle velocity of about 1100 fps, which is below the speed of sound (about 1150 fps). The load was accurate and worked well with a silencer. At least five bolt-action, match-type rifles equipped with heavy barrels, scopes and silencers were built and sent to Vietnam for experimental use. This was probably one of the best-kept secrets of the war, as very few people know about it, even today. The experiment was not an unqualified success because the troops did not like the heavy, cumbersome rifles. A lighter, 20- or 22-inch barrel carbine might have been better accepted in that particular combat environment.

In any event, the 458x1 1/2-inch cartridge must be listed as an unofficial experimental military cartridge. After all, it actually did achieve combat status, which is more than can be said for some other experimental cartridges such as the 276 Pedersen — upon which the military spent considerable time, effort and money, then abandoned. The last of the 458x1 1/2-inch round-nose military ammunition was destroyed in Herlong, Calif., about 1984 or 1985. This is destined to become one of the rarer collector's cartridges because very few got into general circulation. It just goes to show that when you start something, you never know exactly how it is going to end.

11.63x33mm Belted Factory Ballistics

Bullet (grains/type)	Powder	Grains	Velocity	Energy	Source/Comments
500 FMC	ML		1050-1100 *	1225-1340	Military load, experimental
*Estimated velocity					

11.7x51Rmm Danish Remington

Historical Notes This cartridge was adopted by Denmark in 1896. It was used in the Remington rolling-block rifle. This cartridge and guns chambered for it were available as early as 1878. Some were made by Remington and some by the Danes. Remington also loaded this cartridge for many years.

General Comments The 11.7mm, or 45 Danish Remington, has seen considerable use as a target and hunting loading in the Scandinavian countries. It is less known in the United States, only because of the few Danish rolling-block rifles that have trickled in. It is similar to the 45-70, but the case is a little (0.09-inch) shorter. Performance is practically identical. Any load used in the 45-70 will give almost the same results in the 11.7mm. However, such loads should be reduced by at least 1 grain to compensate for the slightly smaller case of the Danish cartridge. It would be adequate for any North American game at short range.

11.7x51Rmm Danish Remington Loading Data and Factory Ballistics

Bullet (grains/type)	Powder	Grains	Velocity	Energy	Source/Comments
300 Lead	IMR 4198	34	1480	1460	Lyman #457191
405 Lead	IMR 4198	29	1340	1615	Lyman #457124
380 Lead	Blackpowder (Fg)	50	1350	1535	Remington factory load
387 Lead	ML		1345	1550	Military load

11x52Rmm Netherlands Beaumont M71/78

Historical Notes The cartridge listed here is the modified version of the Dutch Beaumont military round introduced in 1878. It was used in the turn-bolt single-shot Beaumont rifle, which is very similar to the French Gras. In 1888, the Beaumont single-shot was altered to a box-magazine repeater based on the Italian Vitali system. This employed a vertical single column of cartridges, inserted in the bottom of the action. It is similar to the Lee magazine. For additional information, see the 11.3x50Rmm Beaumont.

General Comments This modification of the original Beaumont cartridge has caused considerable confusion in collecting circles.

The longer 11x52Rmm will chamber in any rifle made for the original 11.3x50Rmm cartridge, but the reverse is not true because of the larger diameter of the case and bullet. The 11mm Egyptian Remington cartridge will chamber in Beaumont rifles and early catalogs list it as being for those. However, the 11.3mm and 11mm Beaumont are not identical to the 11mm Egyptian. The three are very similar and largely interchangeable, but differ in actual physical measurements. The cartridge listed here is the most common and usually found in collections. Beaumont rifles and cartridges were not widely used in the United States and only a few rifles were occasionally sold in surplus stores.

11x52Rmm Netherlands Beaumont M71/78 Loading Data and Factory Ballistics

Bullet (grains/type)	Powder	Grains	Velocity	Energy	Source/Comments
400 Lead	Blackpowder (Fg)	55	1360	1640	Lyman #457124
400 Lead	IMR 4198	31	1430	1815	Lyman #457124, maximum load
345 Lead	Blackpowder (Fg)	60	1476	1670	Military load

50 Browning 12.7x99mm

Historical Notes The German 13mm TUF anti-tank rifle of World War I made quite an impression on U.S. Army brass, who began developing a similar cartridge before the end of the war. Design genius John M. Browning undertook the project, completing his new heavy machinegun and cartridge work in 1921. Both gun and cartridge were adopted by the U.S. Army in 1923. It has remained standard ever since. The cartridge has been adopted and made by at least 30 countries, including the United States, Britain, Canada, France, Belgium, Israel, Netherlands, Japan, Singapore and Taiwan. Many bullet types will be encountered, including ball, armor-piercing, tracer, incendiary, sabot hyper-velocity and others.

General Comments This cartridge is normally found with a Boxer-primed brass case, although steel cases will occasionally be encountered. There are two FMJ-BT ball bullet types, both with mild steel cores. The M2 ball weighs 720 grains and has a muzzle velocity of 2810 fps; the M33 Ball weighs 668 grains with a muzzle velocity of 2910 fps. Recently, long-range target rifles from McMillan, Barrett and others have chambered this round. It has thus moved down from exclusive use in heavy machineguns. The Fifty Caliber Shooters Association (FCSA) holds 1000-yard (and longer) competitive events. In modern rifles, five-shot groups at 1000 yards often fall within a 6-inch circle, and many groups under 3 inches have been recorded. With known wind conditions, it is routine to hit a 55-gallon drum at ranges of about a mile.

50 Browning Factory Ballistics

Bullet (grains/type)	Powder	Grains	Velocity	Energy	Source/Comments
668 FMJ-BT Ball			2910	12,550	Military load, M33
720 FMJ-BT Ball			2810	12,600	Military load, M2

Barrett, Model-82A1

50-70 Government (50 Govt.)

Historical Notes The 50-70 was the United States military rifle cartridge from 1866 to 1873. It was the first centerfire cartridge in general use by the U.S. military. The design was derived from the 50-60-400 Joslyn rimfire. It was used in various models and modifications of the single-shot Springfield rifle until replaced by the 45-70 in 1873. It was also chambered in the Remington single-shot military rifle and in a wide variety of sporting rifles, both single-shot and repeating. The original cartridge had the inside, Benet-type primer. It has been obsolete since the turn of the century.

General Comments The 50-70, or 50 Government, was a popular cartridge through the 1870s and '80s. It was said to be very effective on buffalo and other heavy game. It was the popularity of this cartridge that induced Winchester to bring out the 50-110,

which was, in some sense, an improved and more powerful version of the 50-70. Until recently, very few rifles in this chambering were in use. The recent rise of popularity of the Cowboy Action game has changed that; now both cartridge and gun are once again available. The 50-70 is adequate for any North American big game at short range. Cases with the later Boxer-type priming can be reloaded. Most 50-70 rifles were intended for blackpowder; only very light charges of smokeless powder can be considered safe. In 1934, Francis Bannerman & Sons of New York City advertised both 50-70 Springfield rifles and the ammunition. Rifles were still available as late as 1940. No sporting rifles have chambered this round since the early 1900s. There was also a carbine version with a shorter case (1.35 inches instead of 1.94 inches).

50-70 Government Loading Data

Bullet (grains/type)	Powder	Grains	Velocity	Energy	Source/Comments
300 Lead	Blackpowder (Fg)		1323	1165	QuickLOAD *
450 Lead	Blackpowder (Fg)		1113	1235	QuickLOAD *
*Estimated ballistics					

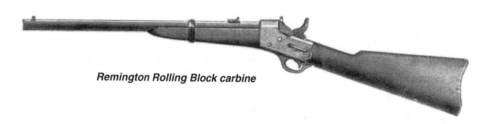

Remington Rolling Block carbine

577 Snider (14.7mm)

Historical Notes This British cartridge was adopted in 1867. It was used in the Snider breech-loading conversion of the Enfield Musket. The Snider system was invented by Joseph Snider, an American, who first offered it to his home country, but was turned down. The converted rifle was usually referred to as the "Snider Enfield." The original cartridge had a cardboard body with a metal base — essentially identical to more recent "paper" shotgun shells. Later, this was improved by using a coiled brass case, designed by Col. Boxer, the man who invented the Boxer-type primer. Modern 577 ammunition has a drawn brass case. Some Martini-Henry single-shot rifles were also chambered for this cartridge. This cartridge was replaced in British military service by the 577/450 in 1871.

General Comments A large number of Snider Enfield rifles were sold in the United States by Francis Bannerman & Sons of New York City. Small numbers were also imported during the 1950s by various surplus military arms dealers. The 577 cartridge was loaded in England with either a solid lead bullet or a lead-base, copper-tube type. The case appears to be straight at first glance, but it has a slight taper and shoulder similar to some American blackpowder cartridges of the same period. The dimensions of the 577 case are very similar to those of the 24-gauge shotgun shell. Brass 24-gauge shells can be used to make ammunition for 577 Snider rifles by trimming about 1/2-inch from the length. Neither the Snider rifle nor the 577 cartridge are very practical for American hunting, but these guns are a lot of fun to shoot. The big bullet has ample power for hunting, but the curved trajectory makes it a short-range proposition.

577 Snider Loading Data and Factory Ballistics

Bullet (grains/type)	Powder	Grains	Velocity	Energy	Source/Comments
350 Lead	Blackpowder (Fg)	73	1310	1330	NA
350 Lead	IMR 4198	31	1380	1480	NA
450 Lead	Blackpowder (Fg)	73	1270	1610	NA
450 Lead	IMR 4198	30	1300	1690	NA
476 Lead	IMR 4198	30	1250	1650	Lyman #575213
480 Lead	Blackpowder (Fg)	70-73	1250	1665	Military load

MILITARY RIFLE CARTRIDGES OF THE WORLD
Current & Obsolete – Blackpowder & Smokeless
Dimensional Data

Cartridge	Case	Bullet Dia.	Neck Dia	Shoulder Dia.	Base Dia.	Rim Dia.	Rim Thick.	Case Length	Ctge. Length	Twist	Primer
4.85 British	C	.197	.220	.353	.375	.376	.041	1.925	2.455		B
5.7x28mm FN	C	.220	.249	.309	.310	.310		1.13	1.71		B
5.45mm Soviet	C	.221	.246	.387	.395	.394	.053	1.56	2.22		B
5.56mm NATO	C	.224	.249	.349	.373	.375	.041	1.76	2.26	9	Bx
6mm SAW	**C**	**.243**	**.273**	**.382**	**.410**	**.410**		**1.779**	**2.58**		**Bx**
6mm Lee Navy	C	.244	.278	.402	.445	.448	.050	2.35	3.11	7.5	Bx
6.5mm Arisaka	**G**	**.263**	**.293**	**.425**	**.455**	**.471**	**.045**	**2.00**	**2.98**	**7.9**	**B**
6.5mm M-S	C	.263	.287	.424	.447	.450		2.09	3.02	7.8	B
6.5 Daudeteau	G	.263	.298	.466	.480	.524	.065	2.09	3.02		B
6.5 Dutch & Romanian	A	.263	.297	.423	.450	.526	.066	2.10	3.03	9.8	B
6.5mm Swedish	C	.264	.297	.435	.480	.480		2.16	3.15	7.9	B
6.5mm Portuguese	C	.264	.293	.426	.468	.465		2.28	3.22	7.8	B
6.5mm Carcano	C	.265	.295	.430	.445	.448	.045	2.05	3.02	19.3/ 8.3*	B
6.8x57mm Chinese	C	.277	?	?	?	?	?	?	2.25	?	?
280 British	**C**	**.283**	**.313**	**.448**	**.470**	**.473**		**1.71**	**2.54**	**?**	**B**
7x57mm	C	.284	.320	.420	.470	.474	.055	2.23	3.06	9	B
276 Enfield	C	.284	.321	.460	.528	.521		2.35	3.25	9	B
276 Pederson	C	.285	.314	.389	.449	.451		2.02	2.85	?	Bx
7.35mm Carcano	C	.298	.323	.420	.445	.449		2.01	2.98	10	B
30 Carbine	**D**	**.308**	**.335**		**.355**	**.360**		**1.29**	**1.65**	**16**	**Bx**
7.5mm French MAS	C	.308	.340	.441	.480	.482	.054	2.11	2.99	10	B
30 Army (30-40 Krag)	A	.308	.338	.415 (0.419)	.457 (0.4577)	.540		2.31	3.10 (3.089)	10	Bx
7.62x51mm NATO (308 Win.)	C	.308	.338	.447	.466	.470		2.01	2.75	12	Bx
7.5mm Schmidt-Rubin	C	.308	.334	.452	.494	.496	.058	2.18	3.05	10.5	B
7.62x63mm U.S. (30-06)	C	.308	.340	.441	.470	.473		2.49	3.34	10	Bx
7.62x45mm Czech M52	C	.309	.334	.412	.441	.440		1.77	2.36		B
7.62X53Rmm (M-43) Russian	C	.310	.340	.394	.443	.445		1.52	2.20	9.4	B
7.62mm Nagant	A	.310	.332	.453	.484	.564	.055	2.11	3.02	9.5	B
303 British	A	.311	.337	.402	.458	.530		2.21	3.05	10	B
7.7mm Arisaka	C	.311	.338	.431	.472	.474	.042	2.28	3.13	9.8	B
7.65x53mm Argentine Mauser	C	.313	.338	.429	.468	.470	.040	2.09	2.95	10	B
8x50Rmm Siamese	**A**	**.321**	**.347**	**.450**	**.480**	**.550**		**1.98**	**2.97**		**B**
8x52Rmm Siamese	A	.321	.347	.460	.500	.550		2.04	2.96		B, Bx
8mm Danish Krag	A	.322	.355	.460	.500	.575	.060	2.28	3.20	12	B
7.92mm Kurz	C	.323	.352	.440	.470	.470		1.30	1.88	10	B
8mm Austrian	A	.323	.351	.462	.501	.553	.040	1.98	3.00	9.8	B
8mm Lebel	A	.323	.347	.483	.536	.621	.068	1.98	2.75	9.5	B
7.9x57mmJS (8mm Mauser JS)	C	.323	.353	.443	.469	.473		2.24	3.17	9 - 10	B
8x63mm Swedish	C	.323	.356	.456	.488	.479		2.48	3.36	?	B
8x60Rmm Guedes M/85	A	.326	.354	.490	.543	.620	.080	2.34	3.25	11	B
8x59mm Breda	C	.326	.357	.433	.491	.469		2.33	3.17	?	B
8mm Murata	A	.329	.361	.485	.492	.558		2.06	2.90		B
8mm Hungarian M-89	A	.329	.365	.473	.491	.554	.060	2.20	3.02	10	B
9.5mm Turkish Mauser	A	.389	.411	.487	.511	.612	.082	2.37	2.97	20	B
10.15mm Jarmann	**A**	**.403**	**.430**	**.540**	**.548**	**.615**	**.078**	**2.40**	**3.06**	**22**	**B**

Cartridge	Case	Bullet Dia.	Neck Dia	Shoulder Dia.	Base Dia.	Rim Dia.	Rim Thick.	Case Length	Ctge. Length	Twist	Primer
10.15mm Serbian Mauser	A	.411	.433	.515	.520	.592	.082	2.46	3.13	22	B
10.4mm Swiss Vetterli	A	.415	.437	.518	.540	.630	.055	1.60	2.20	26	B-RF
10.4mm Italian M/70	A	.430	.437	.517	.540	.634	.058	1.87	2.46	26	B
10.75mm Russian Berdan	A	.430	.449	.506	.567	.637	.080	2.24	2.95	21	B
11mm Murata	**A**	**.432**	**.465**	**.526**	**.542**	**.632**		**2.36**	**3.13**	**20**	**B**
11mm Belgian Albini	A	.435	.472	.535	.580	.678		2.00	2.6	22	B
11mm Belgian Comblain	A	.436	.460	.532	.575	.673	.082	2.10	2.76	22	B
11.15mm Spanish Rem.	A	.439	.458	.512	.516	.635	.082	2.25	2.82	20	B
11.15mm Werndl M/77	A	.441	.466	.536	.545	.617	.100	2.27	3.02	28	B
11mm French Gras 11x59Rmm Vickers	A	.445	.468	.531	.544	.667	.075	2.34	3.00	22	B
11.15mm (43) Mauser	A	.446	.465	.510	.516	.586	.075	2.37	3.00	22	B
11.43mm Turkish	A	.447	.474	.560	.582	.668		2.30	3.12	22	B
11.43mm Egyptian	A	.448	.479	.542	.581	.668	.065	1.94	2.73	20	B
11.4mm Werndl M/73	B	.449	.472		.493	.571		1.97	2.55	29	B
11.4mm Brazilian Comblain	A	.452	.494	.530	.588	.682		2.02	2.62	22	B
11.5mm Spanish Reformado	B	.454	.466		.525	.631		2.26	3.06	20	B
577/450 Martini Henry	A	.455	.487	.628	.668	.746	.050	2.34	3.12	33	B
11mm Beaumont M/71	A	.457	.484	.528	.576	.665	.065	2.04	2.54	30	B
458x1-inch Barnes	**F**	**.458**	**.493**		**.509**	**.530**		**1.50**	**2.19**	**16**	**Bx**
11.7mm Danish Remington	B	.462	.486		.514	.579		2.01	2.45	29 1/2	B
11.3mm Beaumont M/71/78	A	.464	.486	.530	.581	.666	.060	1.97	2.49	29	B
50 Browning	**C**	**.510- (0.511)**	**.555 (0.560)**	**.708 (0.714)**	**.800 (0.804)**	**.800 (0.804)**	**.080**	**3.90 (3.91)**	**5.43 (5.545)**	**16**	**Bx**
50-70 Gov't.	B	.515	.535		.565	.660	.060	1.75	2.25	24 - 42	Bx
577 Snider (14.7mm)	B	.570	.602		.660	.747	.052	2.00	2.45	78	B

Case Type: A = Rimmed, bottleneck. B = Rimmed, straight. C = Rimless, bottleneck. D = Rimless, straight. E = Belted, bottleneck. F = Belted, straight. G = Semi-rimmed, bottleneck. H = Semi-rimmed, straight. I = Rebated, bottleneck. J = Rebated, straight. K = Rebated, belted bottleneck. L = Rebated, belted straight.

Primer Type: B = Berdan. Bx = Boxer. RF = Rimfire.

Other codes: Unless otherwise noted, all dimensions in inches. Twist (factory) is given as inches of barrel length per complete revolution, e.g., 12 = 1 turn in 12", etc. * = Gain twist. Dimensions shown in some instances do not exactly coincide with dimensions found in *The Book of Rifles* (W.H.B. Smith, Harrisburg, Pa., 1960). Differences amount to only a few thousandths of an inch, doubtless attributable to specimen variations. Parentheses indicate maximum cartridge specifications.

Chapter 8

British Sporting Rifle Cartridges

(Current & Obsolete—Blackpowder & Smokeless)

OVER THE past four or five decades, there has appeared a tremendous volume of writings about British cartridges. Much of the writing that has appeared concerns the very biggest and most fascinating of these, the elephant cartridges. However, at best, many of these authors were misinformed. Some of it appeared on these pages.

Part of the reason for the lack of knowledge in years past about the big British cartridges was the great cost and relative scarcity of rifles chambered for these cartridges. Without the gun in hand, it is difficult to discover the truth about these cartridges, much less generate the interest in digging for the truth. If one cannot shoot one's 577 BPE, for example, not much can be learned about its performance. Few writers ever had the chance to examine — and fewer still to shoot — a big British rifle. Therefore, much of their reportage was second-hand.

In recent years, the resurrection of the manufacture of cases and bullets for the great rifles of old Africa has helped bridge the knowledge gap and helped generate enthusiasm. There has never been a lack of firearms to study, stored by collectors who could not shoot the gun. With cases, bullets and even loaded ammunition again available, it is again feasible to shoot these rifles. We have all learned a lot from those who have done so.

A very few writers and gun collectors have come along over the years with enough intense interest in the old British rifles and cartridges to actually make those guns shoot. This required, in times past, a knowledge of what could be expected of the gun, so that one did not blow up a good deer rifle trying to make it into an elephant stopper. One had to know how to get bullets of the right weight and composition, and how to modify or manufacture cases to fit, and know something of the loading techniques involved as well. Without someone to first make a given gun shoot, to prove that it could be done, there would not be enough interest in shooting it to justify the commercial manufacture of appropriate components.

Perhaps every lover of English rifles owes a large debt of gratitude to Ross Seyfried, who did much of the early testing and research with his own rifles; he proved that these guns could be made to shoot, just like new. Seyfried was not alone in those endeavors, but he is unique in that he had the drive, luck, persistence and patience to get his results published.

Seyfried and I experimented together 20 years ago with paper-patch bullets for Cordite-cartridge, double-barrel rifles. (We published our results in the American Rifleman.) There was no other way to get bullets of the correct size, though it was possible to obtain a few types of cases and Berdan primers with difficulty. We both know how pleasant it is today to be able to buy top-quality, Boxer-primed cases or bullets of the correct size and weight for what were, a few years ago, totally obscure British firearms. Such component production and availability were beyond our fondest dreams two decades ago. Today's availability of cases and components would not exist but for the work of early experimenters who helped re-establish a demand for British cartridge cases and bullets.

I have had a very long-term interest in British cartridges and the rifles that shoot those, and had been fortunate enough to have acquired a few British double-barrel rifles, which I shoot as often as possible. That interest and involvement has led me to revise this chapter. While I make no claim to knowing everything about British cartridges, I have attempted here to correct the most grievous errors.

A short time ago, no British producer was loading metallic cartridges. Existing supplies of loaded cartridges were eventually exhausted, and ultimately the metallic cartridge portion of the English ammunition industry ceased to exist. This forced those who wanted to shoot their English rifles into becoming handloaders.

There were a few exceptions. Federal Cartridge Co. came out with 470 Nitro and 416 Rigby rounds. Before that, Jim Bell offered loaded ammunition for some of the more common British numbers. However, for the most part it was impossible to buy loaded ammunition.

Today, we again see the grand old name of Kynoch on new cartridges loaded in England. The company of Kynamco has begun development and loading of ammunition to match double-barrel rifles made in the golden era of British rifle manufacture, specifically those rifles made between World War I and World War II. This is indeed a happy state of affairs.

In previous editions, the author claimed that many, if not most, of the British cartridges were obsolete. I received a nice letter from Ronald Sichel, one of the directors of John Rigby & Co. He kindly informed me that the 275 Rigby (essentially a rather lively loading of the old 7x57) is alive and well and always has been, no matter that we had declared otherwise. He mentioned that Rigby & Co. also offers rifles in a variety of chamberings, including the 450 Rigby, and still makes double-barrel rifles for the 470 as well as for the 577 Nitro and 600 Nitro. We had stated that only Holland & Holland built English-made double-barrel 470s, but that was also incorrect — several other companies are still in this business.

For many decades, uninformed writers have mistakenly compared many of the big double-barrel rifle cartridges, from the 400 Jeffery on up, to the 458 Winchester Magnum. However, the big English double-barrel rifle cartridges worked at relatively low chamber pressure, so the rifles would work perfectly under the blazing hot sun of Africa when one was faced with an unhappy elephant. The 458 was always (until very recently) loaded with a bullet that was too heavy for its small case, and its attendant high pressure led many to curse it in that hot sun in front of that angry elephant. In some cases, those hunters are no longer with us; perhaps if they had used a cartridge designed for the conditions encountered, they would be.

Early British blackpowder cartridges were loaded with lead bullets that were either grooved and lubricated, or without grooves and paper patched. Paper-patching is simply wrapping the bullet with two layers of paper moistened for the application, then allowing it to dry and finally lubing with a waxy substance before loading it into the case. This provided a non-leading bullet of soft lead that was one of the most deadly projectiles ever devised. These are extremely accurate, expand easily, and do not break up, and consequently these bullets perform very well in the hunting field.

The British went hunting in Africa at a time when no suitable rifles or cartridges existed anywhere in the world. Their desperate need for proper dangerous—game rifles and cartridges was unique, because they were just about the only ones hunting in Africa. Incidentally, their development of the double-barrel rifle as the best of the best for hunting dangerous game came out of that need.

The first elephant rifles were muzzleloaders, and the first cartridge-firing elephant guns used blackpowder and lead bullets. These cartridges were so big as to be nearly unbelievable by today's standards. These were the gauge-rifles, ponderous 4-, 6-, or 8-bore guns that weighed up to 25 pounds. A 4-bore rifle, nominally four balls to the pound, has a bore diameter of about 1 inch. Some of these were smoothbores, a holdover from the muzzleloader days, but most were rifled.

These big, lead bullets were not very effective against elephant, as is so well recorded by early African hunter Frederick Courtenay Selous in his writings. To improve performance, manufacturers and handloaders alike often hollowed out these bullets and filled the cavity with explosive compounds; such projectiles are technically shells. These bullets still did not work all that well, as many a severely flattened hunter could attest.

Gauge-rifles for dangerous game were usually 10-bores and larger. Experienced hunters considered the 12-bore a bit small for safe use against the biggest game. The 450s and 500s and even the 577 BPEs (Black-Powder Express) of the latter days of the 19th century were essentially deer and medium-game rifles, not the elephant stompers these numbers became when loaded with Cordite.

Along the way came the Paradoxes (a name copyrighted by Holland & Holland) and their ilk, which were light smoothbores (usually 8- 10-, or 12-bores) with a bit of rifling in what would be termed the choke area of the bore. These fired shotshells quite well, and gave enough spin to round balls or bullets to give adequate accuracy and performance on medium to large game at reasonable ranges.

The coming of smokeless or nitro powder (Cordite in England) brought bullet designers many headaches as they attempted to design bullets to work at the higher velocities provided by the new propellants. Historians have written much on the success or failure of all different types of jacketed bullets that have been, and are still being, developed. The English directed much research toward answering the call from Africa for good bullets to use against dangerous game. It was discovered that "full-patch," or "solid" bullets (the bullet nose fully covered or protected with gilding metal or, with Rigby's bullets, mild steel) would reach the brain of an elephant or Cape buffalo or rhino quite easily, and therefore adequate elephant rifles could be built much lighter than ever before, and of smaller bore size.

Because there were no precedents, the British made some big mistakes in early smokeless cartridge and rifle production. Common among those were building rifles either too heavy or too light for the new smokeless powder loads, and using soft brass cartridges that worked OK with blackpowder, but poorly with smokeless. The 450/400 x 3 1/4-inch NE was one of these blackpowder rounds given a new lease on life through Cordite. It preceded the 375 H&H Magnum as one of the best all-around cartridges for Africa.

Unfortunately, early rifles for the 450/400 x 3 1/4-inch NE often weighed 11 pounds or more, far too much for the performance level of the cartridge. A quarter-century later, gun makers commonly made lighter 465 & 470 Nitro Expresses. Early cases for the 450/400 x 3 1/4-inch were not hard enough for Cordite usage. The cartridge design featured a rather long neck. In addition, the chambers of hunting rifles were commonly pitted from neglect or fouling. The frequent result of this combination was a case stuck in the chamber with the case rim broken or torn off by the extractor. This tied the rifle up until the problem could be resolved. The solution eventually came in the form of better cartridge designs and better-quality brass cases.

The main problem in cartridge development was in determining how small the bore could be for any given game size; a problem that is still with us. Many hunters today believe that the biggest gun is the best, while others try to make the smallest work for everything. Clearly, the biggest guns will be adequate for the smallest game, but the converse has never been true. This, though, is the main reason behind the myriad early British cartridges. The British were hunting worldwide, and were among the very few hunting dangerous game at a time when nothing was known about the new Cordite loads and their jacketed bullets.

Many British cartridges were decades ahead of their time, good ideas that needed better powders and better steels to achieve

fruition. The 275 H&H Belted Rimless Magnum, for instance, came out around 1912 and is a ringer for the 7mm Remington Magnum. Too often, our sense of provincialism restricts us into making comparisons within our immediate sphere of knowledge, with the result that we often overlook originators. Westley Richards, for instance, claims to have been the first to draw brass into cartridges, a fact seldom mentioned in American or German gun journals.

Rigby's 450 Nitro Express (NE) cartridge design eventually became the king of the Cordite elephant slayers. It threw a 480-grain jacketed bullet at just over 2,100 fps. Every maker offered rifles in that chambering, and most of the world's hunters of dangerous game were happy. Then, for political reasons, the British government prohibited the importation of 450-bore rifles into India and the Sudan, so the British gunmakers invented variations on the 450 Nitro theme. The new elephant rifles were designated 465, 470, 476, and a few others. All of these cartridges worked just about like the 450 Nitro had, and you paid your money and took your choice. Each maker had his specialty.

If you wanted somewhat more power than these standard nitro-powered elephant cartridges offered, there were three choices: The 500 NE was just a bit more powerful than all of the 470 class, but the 577 NE and the 600 were tops. These chamberings were the ultimate life-insurance policies for those who were involved in frequent close encounters with elephants. The 700 Nitro did not exist during the golden age of African hunting, which ran from roughly 1900 to the early 1940s.

Today's gun collectors and knowledgeable shooters are no strangers to many British cartridges, as perhaps they were a quarter-century ago. While it was then extremely difficult to get cases or bullets for the British cartridges, today there are several good sources. Bertram, of Australia, offers good, new cases that the handloader can form into most of the cartridges needed to feed British firearms. HDS, A-Square, Bell and Buffalo Bore offer a bewildering selection of cases. Woodleigh, another Australian Company, makes bullets. These are as close as you can get to original shapes and weights, and are of outstanding quality. Bullets are also made for some of the British numbers by Barnes, Ballard, DKT, Hawk, Star, Liberty and a few others.

To add flavor to today's user of British cartridges, Federal Cartridge Co. offers loaded ammunition in 416 Rigby and 470 NE. Ruger chambers its single-shot No. 1 and Express Model 77 in 416 Rigby and, recently, 404 Jeffery. American gunsmith Butch Searcy will make you a double-barrel rifle in 470 or in a variety of chamberings at a reasonably affordable price. Several Italian, French, German and Dutch companies make good double-barrel rifles in classic English chamberings. In England, Holland & Holland, Purdey, Westley Richards, John Rigby & Co., Powell, and a few others still make good rifles in a variety of chamberings, and Rigby even has a brand-new elephant stopper in its 450 Rimless Magnum.

Older rifles chambered for some of the more obscure cartridges pop up from time to time and, because of the happy state of affairs in today's gun-products market, are again permitted to sing their old songs through the loving ministrations of their new owners. Cases and loading components are available through Huntington Die Specialties or the Old Western Scrounger (now owned by Gibbs Rifle Co.). Handloaders can often rework these cases into what they need using custom dies, which are available from RCBS. The *Double Gun Journal* occasionally publishes handloading data. It is no great effort to get just about any oddball British rifle shooting today.

Two books have appeared to help shooters and collectors of English cartridges, one by George Hoyem, *The History and Development of Small Arms Ammunition, Volume Three*; the other by Bill Fleming, *British Sporting Rifle Cartridges*. John "Pondoro" Taylor's classic *African Rifles and Cartridges* has been reprinted many times and is still the best book ever written on the hunting of African game with most of the British cartridges. Today there are many good reference books on British rifles and cartridges, and the collector or shooter has a much easier time finding information on these than ever before.

The 458 Winchester Magnum made its debut after World War II, when folks like John Taylor recommended something similar to it that would be inexpensive, American, and would work OK in

Africa. In spite of its pressure problems, the 458 took care of business in Africa well enough for many years, and it is still widely used there.

Today, with makers like Ruger offering affordable rifles for the 416 Rigby and with the advent of the 416 Remington, there is a swing away from the 458 as more shooters realize its limitations. There has not been too great a swing back to the British cartridges yet except for the 416 and the 470. Those two have remained popular because of ammunition availability and because these are two of the very best big game cartridges ever loaded anywhere, fully capable of keeping the spirit of British cartridges going for another century or so. We may see some of the other old-timers become popular with Kynoch ammunition again available.

For many of the reasons given here, there exists, at least in collections, a great wealth of oddball and never-very-popular British cartridges. Hoyem and Fleming depict many that have popped up, but firearms for some of these cartridges are exceedingly scarce. Here we tell the story of what we feel are the most successful British cartridges.

Many people take their British rifles hunting or target shooting today. If you would do so, please make sure yours is safe to shoot. Be certain to check the size of the bore in your rifle and verify the correct chambering before you attempt to shoot it. We know of some rifles more than 120 years old, yet their owners shoot these guns frequently, and even take these guns hunting. These guns are in perfect condition. The owners shoot loads that are very conservative and thoroughly safe. Because we cannot personally inspect your firearms and advise you on the wisdom of shooting each (and for other reasons), we give very limited loading data.

Another caution might be in order. It is the opinion of David Winks, the now-retired chief barrel maker for Holland & Holland, that no one should ever fire homogeneous bullets of any type through fine rifle barrels, specifically those on British double-barrel rifles. Because of extremely tough construction, these bullets are too hard on the bore, in his expert opinion.

Winks also said he used CARTRIDGES OF THE WORLD nearly every day at the H&H shop, a philosophy echoed by the folks at John Rigby & Co. We sincerely hope this revised chapter will be of some added value to them, and to the many lovers of British rifles and their cartridges worldwide.

We welcome your input to correct any misinformation found here. Please let us know of your ideas for future inclusions or omissions for the next edition of CARTRIDGES OF THE WORLD. We wish you good shooting with your British firearms.

— Ray Ordorica, British cartridge editor

297/230 Morris Short, Long, Extra Long & Lancaster Sporting

297/230 Morris Long

Historical Notes These cartridges are listed together because all are very similar. The Morris Long has a long neck, the Extra Long has a really long neck (1 1/8-inch case length), and the Lancaster Sporting resembles the Short, but its shoulder is farther forward. These first appeared in an Eley ad in 1882. These cartridges are target or practice rounds to be fired from a barrel insert for the British 577/450 Martini-Henry service rifle. The idea originated with Richard Morris and was adopted by the British army. Some models of the 303 Enfield rifle used an insert for the Morris cartridges also. In addition, barrel and chamber inserts were available for the Webley & Scott 450 and 455 revolvers. European-made single-shot pistols and rifles are occasionally found chambered for the Morris cartridges. These cartridges were listed in Eley-Kynoch catalogs as late as 1962. B.S.A. made Martini-action rifles for these cartridges.

General Comments The 297/230 cartridges were used for target practice and small game shooting. Power is about the same as the standard 22 rimfire. These cartridges lost adherents because 22-rimfire ammunition is cheaper, even though the centerfire Morris cartridges can be reloaded. The Morris numbers were originally blackpowder loadings, but late-issue ammunition used smokeless powder. Bullets were of lead in solid or hollowpoint types.

297/230 Morris Short, Long, and Extra Long Loading Data and Factory Ballistics

Bullet (grains/type)	Powder	Grains	Velocity	Energy	Source/Comments
43 lead	Unique	3.0	900	75	Lyman #225438
43 lead	2400	4.0	1200	137	Lyman #225438
37 lead	Blackpowder	3.25	875	62	Eley factory load
37 lead	Blackpowder	5.5	1200	118	Eley factory load

240 Magnum Flanged & 240 Magnum Rimless (H&H 240 Apex)

Historical Notes This pair of 6mm cartridges was introduced by Holland & Holland in the early 1920s. The rimmed cartridge was, of course, designed for double-barrel rifles and the belted rimless version for magazine rifles. H&H also called this the 240 Super Express, but original ammunition boxes from the maker give the names in the header here.

General Comments Performance of these two 240s is similar to that of the 243 Winchester. Holland data gives a velocity of 2,900 fps with a 100-grain bullet for the belted version. In a strong modern single-shot or bolt-action rifle, using modern powders, performance could be increased significantly. However, this usually does not work for double-barrel rifles because those guns are sighted and regulated for a specific loading. If you change things, the rifle may not shoot your loads to the same point of impact as the original load. That is why most rimmed British cartridges have a limited selection of bullet weights and velocities. The British were well ahead of the United States in the development of good 6mm cartridges. Either of these cartridges would do anything that could be done by the 243 or 6mm Remington.

240 Magnum Flanged and Rimless (Holland's 240 Apex) Factory Ballistics

Bullet (grains/type)	Powder	Grains	Velocity	Energy	Source/Comments
100 SP	FL		2900	1865	Factory load

244 Magnum (H&H)

Historical Notes This, the last belted magnum developed by Holland & Holland, was introduced in 1955 for its Mauser-type bolt-action sporting rifles. Custom-made rifles in this chambering are seen occasionally. American loading handbooks have listed it in the past.

General Comments The high-velocity 244 Holland & Holland Magnum is based on the 375 H&H Magnum case necked-down to 6mm. This is a very large capacity case for the caliber. Only very slow-burning powders will develop maximum velocity in a case this big, so the British were forced to use something other than Cordite for this cartridge. American powders such as IMR-4350, IMR-4831 and similar powders give good results with bullets of 100 grains. Holland & Holland advertised a muzzle velocity of 3500 fps with the 100-grain bullet. The 244 H&H Magnum is a long-range, light-game cartridge. It would also be an excellent varmint and small game number under any conditions. Barrel life was extremely limited.

244 Magnum (H&H) Factory Ballistics

Bullet (grains/type)	Powder	Grains	Velocity	Energy	Source/Comments
100 SP	FL		3500	2720	Factory load

297/250 Rook

Historical Notes Introduced by Holland & Holland for its semi-smoothbore rifles, this load dates back prior to 1880. It is a target and small-game cartridge usually used in single-shot rifles based on the small Martini action, though occasionally seen in very fine break-action single and double-barrel rifles. Incidentally, the rook is a bird similar to our crow.

General Comments In performance, the 297/250 is similar to the old 25 Stevens rimfire. However, it is a centerfire, bottlenecked cartridge and can be reloaded. There were a half-dozen or more of these so-called "rook" cartridges. None were very widely used outside Britain. Like the others, this is entirely a small-game cartridge. Bullet diameter is 0.250-inch.

297/250 Rook Factory Ballistics

Bullet (grains/type)	Powder	Grains	Velocity	Energy	Source/Comments
56 lead	Blackpowder	6.5	1150	164	Factory load

242 Rimless Nitro Express

Historical Notes Developed in 1923 by Kynoch for Manton & Co., Calcutta, this cartridge was first called the 242 Manton. It was listed in late postwar Kynoch catalogs.

General Comments The 242 rimless is very similar to the 243 Winchester and 6mm Remington in power and capacity. The case is a little longer than the American 6mms, but not quite as large in diameter. When loaded with American powders and used in a strong modern bolt-action, it will deliver performance very similar to the 243 Winchester. This would be an effective cartridge for the same general range of game and shooting conditions as the 243 Winchester. Bullets are 0.249- to 0.253-inch diameter, so 0.243-inch bullets would not give satisfactory accuracy. One might be able to swage down 25-caliber bullets to fit, but be sure to slug your bore before attempting to handload for this cartridge.

242 Rimless Nitro Express Factory Ballistics

Bullet (grains/type)	Powder	Grains	Velocity	Energy	Source/Comments
100 SP	FL		2800	1740	Factory load, Kynoch

246 Purdey

General Comments A rimmed, necked cartridge designed in 1921 for use in Purdey double-barrel rifles, the 246 Purdey was not popular or widely used and is long-since obsolete. With a 100-grain bullet at 2,950 fps, it is in the same general class as the 243 Winchester or 6mm Remington. As with most cartridges designed for double-barrel rifles, only one loading was available. Bullet diameter ranges from 0.251 to 0.253 inch.

246 Purdey Factory Ballistics

Bullet (grains/type)	Powder	Grains	Velocity	Energy	Source/Comments
100 SP	FL		2950	1930	Factory load

255 Jeffery Rook

Historical Notes This small, rimmed, necked cartridge was introduced by Jeffery and used in Rook rifles. It is long obsolete in Britain and quite rare in the United States.

General Comments This is a small game and target number. Several loadings were provided, with 3 or 9 grains of blackpowder, and several with 3-1/2 to 4-1/4 grains of smokeless powder. The usual bullet was a 65-grain lead solid or hollowpoint bullet at a standard muzzle velocity of 1200 fps. The round may have been used in single-shot pistols as well as in rifles.

255 Jeffery Rook Factory Ballistics

Bullet (grains/type)	Powder	Grains	Velocity	Energy	Source/Comments
65 lead	FL		1200	208	Factory load

256 Mannlicher   See 6.5x53Rmm Chapter 7

Historical Notes There were four target loads developed from the basic shape of the 6.5x54mm Mannlicher-Schoenauer case. These were the 256 Fraser Flanged and Rimless, and the 256 Swift Flanged and Rimless. None achieved any popularity.

256 Gibbs Magnum

Historical Notes This cartridge is a rimless, necked 6.5mm introduced by George Gibbs in 1913 for Mauser-type magazine rifles of his design. The case is very similar to the 6.5x55mm Swedish round in length and other dimensions. Powder capacity and ballistics are also about the same.

General Comments Loading data for the 6.5x55mm could be used as a guide in working up handloads for the 256. Bullet diameter is 0.264-.265, but be sure to slug your bore because there are a great many variations in 6.5mm bore diameter in rifles from all countries. Obtaining bullets of suitable diameter is a problem.

256 Gibbs Magnum Factory Ballistics

Bullet (grains/type)	Powder	Grains	Velocity	Energy	Source/Comments
145 SP	FL		2600	2178	Factory load

26 BSA
(26 Rimless Belted NE)

Historical Notes Introduced by Birmingham Small Arms (BSA) for its bolt-action sporting rifles based on the 1914 Enfield military action, the 26 Rimless Nitro Express originated in 1921. It is actually a belted rimless case of advanced design.

General Comments The 26 BSA was intended to appeal to those interested in high velocity, and it does this well with the light 110-grain bullet. It is also an example of what happens when every other feature is sacrificed for the last fps of velocity. It looks good on paper, but it is not very effective. On the other hand, some other 26-caliber cartridges with heavier bullets at lower velocity have a fine reputation on all kinds of game. As factory loaded, the 26 BSA was not a suitable cartridge for North American hunting conditions. If handloaded with bullets of heavier weight, it can be made as effective as any other 26-caliber cartridge of similar case capacity. Head diameter is close to that of the 300 H&H Magnum, and cases can be made by reforming 300 H&H cases. Bullet diameter of existing cartridge specimens ranges from 0.266-0.269, so be sure to slug your bore. Obtaining bullets of suitable diameter is a problem.

26 BSA Factory Ballistics

Bullet (grains/type)	Powder	Grains	Velocity	Energy	Source/Comments
110 SP	FL		3100	2345	Factory load

275 Rigby (7x57mm)

Historical Notes This round, identical to the 7x57mm Mauser, was adopted by John Rigby & Co. in 1907 for Rigby bolt-action magazine rifles. Rigby was, at that time, the British outlet for Mauser. Rigby's original rifle featured the 175-grain bullet. In its 1924 catalog, Rigby lists three versions of the Mauser, its No. 1 rifle for the 175-grain bullet, and its No. 2 and 3 rifles for the 140-grain bullet, designed for deer stalking. The No. 1 and 2 rifles weighed 7.5 pounds and the No. 3 was built to weigh 6-3/4 pounds.

General Comments This cartridge was made famous by Walter D.M. Bell, the British hunter who killed nearly 1000 elephant with it in the early years of the 20th century. He killed every one using solid bullets of 175-grain weight, usually with one shot apiece. Bell was one of the finest marksmen the world has seen, and you can read about his successes in his *Wanderings of an Elephant Hunter, Karamojo Safari,* and *Bell of Africa.* Unfortunately, many men who read Bell's books and tried to emulate his success with this little cartridge without Bell's skill or luck have gotten themselves killed. The 275 Rigby is a fine deer and medium-game cartridge. A light No. 3 Rigby, stoked with the 140-grain Nosler Partition, is one of the finest all-around rifles available for thin-skinned game in the 200-pound-and-under class.

275 Rigby (7x57) Factory Ballistics

Bullet (grains/type)	Powder	Grains	Velocity	Energy	Source/Comments
140 Solid or LT Capped SN-SPFL			3000	2800	Factory load
175 Solid or SN	FL		2300	2066	Factory load

275 Belted Magnum (H&H)
275 Flanged Magnum (H&H)

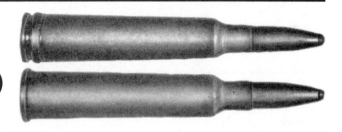

Historical Notes Introduced in England in 1911-12, the belted version for bolt-actions and the flanged for single-shot and double-barrel rifles, these are the first 7mm magnums. These cartridges came out shortly after the 280 Ross created quite a stir in the small-bore, high-velocity field. A fair number of American custom rifles have been made for this round, but no factory rifles. The belted version, known in the United States as the 275 H&H Magnum, was loaded by the Western Cartridge Co. until 1939. The rimmed-version load was slightly reduced from the belted. It was developed by F.W. Jones as an improvement of the 280 Ross. Eley and Kynoch loaded bullets of 105, 140, 143, 150, 160, and 180 grains.

General Comments The 275 H&H Magnum is similar to the 7mm Remington Magnum. With modern powders in a good rifle, this ancient British number will do anything that can be done by the 7mm Magnum. Be sure to slug your rifle to get the correct bore size, and fit your bullets accordingly. This pair is a good long-range duo for mountain or plains hunting of light to medium game.

275 Belted Magnum & Flanged Magnum (H&H) Factory Ballistics

Bullet (grains/type)	Powder	Grains	Velocity	Energy	Source/Comments
140 SP	FL		2650	2184	Factory load, British
160 SP	FL		2700	2600	Factory load, British
175 SP	FL		2680	2800	Western factory load

275 No. 2 Magnum (7mm Rigby Magnum Flanged)

Historical Notes This is a rimmed, necked cartridge designed for Rigby double-barrel rifles. It was introduced in 1927 and was still available in the early 1960s. It is advertised for "deer-stalking and all classes of non-dangerous game." It is another cartridge in about the same class as the 7x57mm Mauser.

275 No. 2 Magnum Factory Ballistics

Bullet (grains/type)	Powder	Grains	Velocity	Energy	Source/Comments
140 SP	FL		2675	2230	Factory load

280 Flanged (280 Lancaster)

Historical Notes Developed by Lancaster, this rimmed 280 cartridge is similar to the rimless 280 Ross and used in single-shot and double-barrel rifles. It was introduced shortly after the Ross cartridge appeared in 1906. It is said to have been a favorite with King George V.

General Comments The rimmed 280 is loaded to slightly lower velocity than the 280 Ross. When the rimless Ross cartridge was introduced in 1906, it created considerable interest all over the world. It was only natural to bring out a rimmed version for the man who preferred the double-barrel rifle. Both cartridges are practically the same power and effectiveness. However, these high-speed 280 cartridges lost popularity after a few big-game hunters were killed while using those on heavy or dangerous game under adverse conditions. One of the most famous of these was Sir George Grey, killed by a lion in Africa.

280 Flanged (280 Lancaster) Factory Ballistics

Bullet (grains/type)	Powder	Grains	Velocity	Energy	Source/Comments
140 SP	FL		2800	2440	Factory load
160 SP	FL		2600	2400	Factory load
180 SP	FL		2400	2300	Factory load

280 Ross (280 Rimless)

Historical Notes This timeless cartridge was designed by F.W. Jones, a consultant to Eley and Sir Charles Ross, and introduced in 1906 for the Canadian straight-pull Ross rifle. This was one of the first modern high-velocity small-bore cartridges. It was originally a military design, but quickly caught the fancy of sportsmen because of high velocity, flat trajectory and excellent killing power. The German 280 Halger Magnum is based on the Ross case. At one time, Remington and Winchester loaded 280 Ross ammunition. American companies discontinued it in 1935. It is actually a semi-rimmed case.

General Comments The 280 Ross is an example of what happens when hunters get overly enthusiastic about something new. It proved to have fantastic killing power on thin-skinned game. Even dangerous species were dispatched, occasionally, as if struck by lightning. However, there is a big difference between killing dangerous game under ideal conditions and stopping those critters cold when conditions get rough. Some men gave their lives to find this out and the 280 Ross hit the skids. The original Ross bullet was made to expand quickly on medium-sized game. No one bullet weight or type will do all things. Other cartridges have been maligned because someone used those on game or under conditions for which those cartridges were not designed.

The 280 Ross is adequate for most North American game and non-dangerous African plains varieties if you select the proper bullet. The early straight-pull Ross rifles gained a bad reputation, because the bolt on those rifles could be assembled incorrectly, which, upon firing, was likely to result in a potentially fatal action failure.

280 Ross Factory Ballistics

Bullet (grains/type)	Powder	Grains	Velocity	Energy	Source/Comments
140 SP	FL		2900	2620	Factory load
150 SP	FL		2800	2610	Factory load
160 SP	FL		2700	2600	Factory load
180 SP	FL		2550	2600	Factory load

280 Jeffery (33/280 Jeffery)

Historical Notes The 280 Jeffery is another of the series of 28-caliber cartridges designed as answers to the 280 Ross. The exact date of introduction is not established but was about 1915. The firm of Jeffery built Mauser-type bolt-action magazine rifles for this cartridge.

General Comments This cartridge is based on the 333 Jeffery case necked-down to accept 0.288-inch diameter bullets. It is a larger case than the 280 Ross and holds more powder, but is not loaded to a much higher velocity. With modern powders, it could be handloaded to deliver a good deal higher velocity within safe pressure limits. However, today there are better and more modern 7mm cartridges available. The 280 Jeffery is a good cartridge for non-dangerous game at moderate to long range with good bullets. However, locating bullets of the correct diameter is no difficult task.

280 Jeffery Factory Ballistics

Bullet (grains/type)	Powder	Grains	Velocity	Energy	Source/Comments
140 SP	FL		3000	2800	Factory load

300 (295) Rook

Historical Notes This is another of the small British Rook cartridges. This one is of rather obscure origin and use. It dates prior to 1874 and was originally a blackpowder cartridge. It was used in single-shot rifles and possibly pistols or revolvers. It was listed in the 1962 Eley-Kynoch catalog.

General Comments Aside from bullet diameter, the 300 Rook closely resembles the obsolete American 32 Extra Long centerfire. The case is shorter than the 32 Extra Long, making it possible to fire 300 Rook cartridges in old rifles for the American cartridge. This might interest owners of old Ballard or Stevens rifles. The 300 is strictly a small game or target number.

300 (295) Rook Factory Ballistics

Bullet (grains/type)	Powder	Grains	Velocity	Energy	Source/Comments
80 lead	Blackpowder	10.0	1100	215	Factory load

300 Sherwood

Historical Notes This was introduced by Westley Richards as its answer to the 310 Greener cartridge in 1901 for use in Martini-action and in Sherwood target rifles. Both solid lead or the amazing LT-capped bullets (designed by Leslie Taylor, then the Director of W-R) were available. About eight years later, W-R came out with a similar cartridge called the 298 Minex, with a slightly shorter and slightly bottlenecked case, and a bolt-action rifle to shoot it.

General Comments This is another British cartridge seldom encountered today. It is of interest primarily to cartridge collectors. In terms of muzzle energy, it is on a par with 357 Magnum revolver ballistics, but has a smaller diameter bullet. It would be useful for small game or pest shooting at short to moderate ranges.

300 Sherwood Factory Ballistics

Bullet (grains/type)	Powder	Grains	Velocity	Energy	Source/Comments
140 JHP	FL		1400	610	Factory load

300 Belted Rimless Magnum (H&H)
30 Flanged Magnum (H&H Super 30)

Historical Notes The belted version here is the 300 Holland & Holland Magnum familiar to most of the world. The flanged version is for double-barrel rifles and is loaded a bit lighter. These cartridges originated in 1925. Additional data on the belted version is located in Chapter 2.

General Comments Performance of this pair with original factory loads is on a par with that of the 30-06, perhaps a bit better. The flanged version must be loaded to give proper regulation in the double-barrel rifle, but the belted version, in a good bolt rifle, easily surpasses 30-06 performance.

300 Belted Rimless Magnum (H&H Super 30) Factory Ballistics

Bullet (grains/type)	Powder	Grains	Velocity	Energy	Source/Comments
150 SP	FL		3000	3000	Factory load, British
180 SP	FL		2750	3020	Factory load, British
220 SP	FL		2300	2115	Factory load, British

30 Flanged Magnum Factory Ballistics

Bullet (grains/type)	Powder	Grains	Velocity	Energy	Source/Comments
150 SP	FL		2875	2755	Factory load
180 SP	FL		2575	2653	Factory load
220 SP	FL		2250	2475	Factory load

303 British

General Comments The 303 British military cartridge is also a popular sporting round throughout the British Commonwealth and much of the world. It is covered in detail under military cartridges and also listed with American sporting cartridges. English and Canadian loads offer greater variety and performance than those loaded in the United States. See Chapter 2 for handloading data.

303 British Factory Ballistics

Bullet (grains/type)	Powder	Grains	Velocity	Energy	Source/Comments
150 SP	FL		2700	2440	Factory load, British
174 SP	FL		2450	2315	Factory load, British
180 SP	FL		2540	2580	Factory load, Canadian
192 SP	FL		2200	2070	Factory load, British
210 SP	FL		2050	1960	Factory load, British
215 SP	FL		2050	2010	Factory load, British

303 Magnum

Historical Notes This cartridge was introduced by Jeffery in 1919 and subsequently adopted by the British Match Rifle Committee. It had a short life, being listed by Kynoch only until 1930. Case configuration is the same as the experimental 276 military round and case capacity is the same as the 30-06.

General Comments This cartridge was designed for target shooting at long ranges. Performance is identical to top 30-06 handloads.

303 Magnum Factory Ballistics

Bullet (grains/type)	Powder	Grains	Velocity	Energy	Source/Comments
174 FMJ	FL		2850	3050	Factory load

375/303 Westley Richards 375/303 Axite

Historical Notes This cartridge was introduced by Westley Richards in 1905, and was listed in its catalogs for several years thereafter. It was also listed in the 1909 Charles Lancaster & Co. catalog. It was used in high-velocity double-barrel rifles by Westley with Lancaster oval-bore rifling, in single-shot falling-block rifles and in Lee-action magazine rifles.

General Comments Power is about the same as the 300 H&H Magnum. It was loaded with Axite, a new Kynoch powder said by the makers to be "comparatively free from erosive and corrosive effects."

375/303 Westley Richards Factory Ballistics

Bullet (grains/type)	Powder	Grains	Velocity	Energy	Source/Comments
215 SP	FL		2500	2981	Factory load
200 SP	FL		2726	2980	Factory load

310 Cadet (310 Greener)

Historical Notes This cartridge was introduced by Greener in 1900 as a target round for the small Martini sporting and training rifles. Many were made for the Australian government as cadet rifles. It also became a popular sporting cartridge for small-game shooting. Thousands of the Australian Martini cadet rifles were imported into the United States after World War II. The 310 cartridge is rather well known in the United States as a result.

General Comments The 310 Cadet cartridge is similar in size and performance to the 32-20. In fact, 310 ammunition can be made from 32-20 cases. Back in the '50s, Winfield Arms Co. and

Klein's Sporting Goods of Chicago sold several hundred 310 Martini rifles and actions. According to a 1955 data circular, these Martini actions were tested with proof loads of up to 60,000 psi in order to determine what range of cartridges those guns would safely chamber. Some were rechambered for the 32 Winchester Special, others were rebored to 357 Magnum. Quite a few have been rebarreled to 22 Hornet or 218 Bee. Ken Warner has one for the 44 Magnum. The 310 Cadet cartridge is a good small game and pest number at moderate ranges, and it also is a good target round.

310 Cadet Factory Ballistics

Bullet (grains/type)	Powder	Grains	Velocity	Energy	Source/Comments
84 lead	FL				Factory load
120 lead	Blackpowder	6.0	1200	385	Factory load
125 lead	FL				Factory load

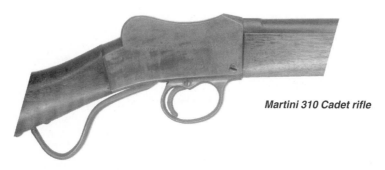

Martini 310 Cadet rifle

318 Rimless Nitro Express (318 Westley Richards/318 Accelerated Express)

Historical Notes This cartridge was developed by Westley Richards in 1910 for its bolt-action, Mauser-type magazine rifles. It was intended for Africa, and it made a fine name for itself there. It was one of the most popular medium-bore cartridges in Africa, even after the advent of the 375 H&H Magnum. Many gunmakers have chambered bolt-action rifles for this round. It is very similar to Elmer Keith's 333 OKH and the current very popular wildcat, the 338-06. There was a square-shouldered version of this cartridge as well, designed to improve headspace control. Because this was not a major problem, the square-shouldered version did not last. It was fired in the standard chamber.

General Comments The 318 can be used in standard-length bolt actions of fairly light weight. This cartridge threw bullets of good weight at respectable velocity that proved very deadly on all sorts of game, and as a result, it became very popular. It worked so well on all African medium game that it got some hunters in trouble when they tried to extend its usefulness to dangerous game, then discovered their mistake, sometimes at the cost of their lives.

The 318 case is very similar to the 30-06 in size, shape and capacity. The 180-grain bullet was used on the lighter animals, while the 250-grain was preferred for all medium to heavy game. Bullet types were solid, softpoint and the Westley Richards copper-capped. Fraser had a "ratchet" bullet load for this cartridge. Bullets of the necessary 0.330-inch diameter for the 318 W-R can be obtained by swaging existing 33-caliber bullets. In addition, Woodleigh makes best-quality bullets in softnose or solid persuasion of the exact size. Cases can be made from 30-06 cases. The 318 W-R has been used with great success on all North American big game, though it is not recommended for use against the biggest bears or any kind of dangerous game in a tight spot.

318 Rimless Nitro Express Factory Ballistics

Bullet (grains/type)	Powder	Grains	Velocity	Energy	Source/Comments
180 SP	FL		2700	2920	Factory load
250 SP	FL		2400	3200	Factory load

333 Jeffery Flanged & Rimless

Historical Notes These are the two versions of the 333 Jeffery introduced in 1908. The rimmed cartridge was intended for double-barrel rifles. The rimless-type, intended for magazine rifles, became more popular. The rimmed 333 was discontinued after World War II. Both have about the same power. German-made Mauser rifles were also chambered for the rimless version.

General Comments The 333 Jeffery earned a fine reputation on all varieties of African big game, including picked shots at elephants. Of course, most professional ivory hunters knew it was on the light side for such animals and used their heavy rifles when in close cover or when they needed to drop dangerous game quickly. On soft-skinned game, it gave excellent penetration, particularly with the 300-grain bullet. This cartridge was the inspiration for the domestic wildcat 333 OKH, designed by Elmer Keith, et al.

333 Jeffery Flanged and Rimless Factory Ballistics

Bullet (grains/type)	Powder	Grains	Velocity	Energy	Source/Comments
250 SP	FL		2500	3480	Factory load, Rimless
300 SP	FL		2200	3230	Factory load, Rimless
250 SP	Cordite	67.0	2400	3200	Factory load, Flanged
300 SP	Cordite	63.0	2150	3090	Factory load, Flanged

Mauser-action magazine rifle by Cogswell & Harrison, London

33 BSA (33 Belted Rimless/330 BSA)

Historical Notes A belted cartridge, this was introduced by Birmingham Small Arms in 1921 for its bolt-action sporting rifles based on the military Enfield. It was never very popular and was discontinued many years ago.

General Comments Like the rimless 26 BSA, the 33 was an effort to furnish a high-velocity cartridge in a popular caliber. Neither effort was a commercial success. The 165-grain bullet starts out at 3000 fps, but its blunt shape and relatively light weight cause it to slow down quite rapidly. At 100 yards, velocity is down to about 2650. The 33 BSA offered good killing power on light game, but failed to penetrate properly on heavy game. For this reason, it was not a successful general-purpose cartridge for African game. Why the manufacturer did not offer a choice of bullets with weights up to about 250 grains is a mystery. Basically, this is a good case design for modern rifles. The handloader can improve this one and put it in the same class as the 338-06 or the 318 Westley Richards. Properly handloaded, the 33 BSA would do well on most North American big game. This cartridge uses 0.338-inch diameter bullets. In fact, if you lengthen the case an 1/8 inch and move the shoulder forward a bit, you have the 338 Winchester Magnum. When handloading this cartridge, remember the British Enfield action will not stand the same high working pressure as will the Mauser 98.

33 BSA Factory Ballistics

Bullet (grains/type)	Powder	Grains	Velocity	Energy	Source/Comments
165 SP	FL		3000	3290	Factory load
175 SP	FL		2900	3265	Factory load *
*Estimated ballistics					

400/350 Rigby

Historical Notes The first of John Rigby & Co.'s 350s, this cartridge was introduced in November 1899. This is the old 400 Purdey case necked-down to 35 caliber. Rigby provided single-shot, double-barrel and bolt-action rifles in this chambering. The cartridge utilized outstanding softpoints and solids of 310 grains at about 2100 fps. The 400/350 was at one time the most popular and widely-used medium-bore cartridge for African hunting. It was succeeded by the 350 No. 2, which is identical in case dimensions but has a bullet of only 225 grains, at somewhat higher velocity. That cartridge was also loaded in a rimless version, but this — the original and some say the best of the 350 Rigbys — was only available as a rimmed case. The magazine boxes of Rigby's bolt rifles were slanted to accommodate the rim.

General Comments The 400/350 is a rimmed case that resembles the old 35 Winchester in general appearance. However, it is longer and uses heavier 0.358-inch diameter bullets. Popularity of the 400/350 was due in a large part to the excellent bullet design, which gave uniform and dependable results. The incomparable John "Pondoro" Taylor had a single-loader in this chambering, and that rifle was a great favorite of his. He used it on lion and other big game. Penetration and overall performance were excellent. The 400/350 would be a good cartridge for most North American big game, particularly where ranges are short.

400/350 Rigby Factory Ballistics

Bullet (grains/type)	Powder	Grains	Velocity	Energy	Source/Comments
310 SP	FL		2100	3035	Factory load

350 No. 2 Rigby & 350 Rigby Magnum

Historical Notes The rimmed version of this cartridge, the 350 No. 2, was the successor to the 400/350 Rigby. Cases are identical. The only difference from the 400/350 is bullet weight and velocity. The rimless 350 Rigby Magnum was designed for bolt-action magazine rifles. Both of these came out in 1908, and both used a bullet of only 225 grains weight in order to increase the velocity of what was already a fully successful cartridge. This, it was felt, was necessary to compete with speedier cartridges that were all the rage at the time.

General Comments The 350 Rigby Magnum and the No. 2 were popular with many African and Asian hunters. Their performance is similar to that of the 35 Whelen. Many hunters preferred the 350 Rigby Magnum over the 375 H&H Magnum because the Rigby had less recoil. Either of these would be a fine cartridge for any North American big game short of big bear, although some hunters who can put up with the poorer trajectory prefer the heavier bullet of the original 400/350. Recently, Rigby chambered its medium-bore double-barrel rifles for the 9.3x74Rmm. Barnes and Speer make bullets of the correct diameter.

350 No. 2 & 350 Rigby Magnum Factory Ballistics

Bullet (grains/type)	Powder	Grains	Velocity	Energy	Source/Comments
225 SP	FL		2625	3440	Factory load, Rimless
225 SP	FL		2575	3312	Factory load, No. 2

400/360 NE (2 3/4-inch) Westley Richards/ Fraser/Evans/Purdey

Historical Notes Although these cartridges have similar names, these are not interchangeable. The Purdey version uses a bigger bullet than the others — 0.367-inch diameter. The other versions have bullets from 0.358- to 0.360-inch diameter. The Purdey is usually marked 400/360P or 400/360B. There are significant variations in bullet weight and in rim thickness as well. In addition, Westley Richards had a rimless version of the 400/360, loaded with a 314-grain bullet.

General Comments These cartridges all generate about the same power. All are fine for use against medium-size game, particularly

for close-range hunting. All appeared about 1900. The Purdey and Evans versions use a 300-grain bullet at 1950 fps, while the Westley Richards version threw a 314-grain bullet at 1900 fps. The Fraser used a 289-grain bullet. Often the correct load is engraved on the rifle in question. Information leading to the correct loading is sometimes given in the proof marks on British firearms. These rifles are quite common today, and correct chambering is often quite difficult to determine. The best way to determine what you have is to make a chamber cast and measure it precisely. Be sure to slug your bore.

400/360 NE (2 3/4-inch) Factory Ballistics

Bullet (grains/type)	Powder	Grains	Velocity	Energy	Source/Comments
289 SP	FL				Fraser factory load
300 SP	FL		1950	2537	Purdey factory load
300 SP	FL		1950	2537	Evans factory load
314 SP	FL		1900	2520	Westley Richards factory load

360 No. 5 Rook

Historical Notes Introduced between 1875 and 1880, this cartridge was loaded until World War II. It was used in handguns and rifles. The 1909 Charles Lancaster & Co. catalog illustrates it for its underlever single-shot rifle and the Webley New "Express" revolver. Many other arms chambered the 360 No. 5.

General Comments In addition to the versions listed below, shot and blank cartridges were also offered. Although ammunition catalogs separate rifle and revolver loadings, in actual practice any version could be used in rifles or in late-model revolvers. The 360 No. 5 cartridge is very similar to the 380 Long and the 38 Long Colt. This is a small game and target load.

360 No. 5 Factory Ballistics

Bullet (grains/type)	Powder	Grains	Velocity	Energy	Source/Comments
82 lead	Blackpowder				Factory load
125 lead	Blackpowder		1050	310	Factory load
134 lead	Blackpowder		1025	312	Factory load
134 lead	Smokeless powder		1025	312	Factory load
145 lead	Smokeless powder		1075	373	Factory load

360 Express (2 1/4-inch)
360 Nitro For Black
360 Nitro Express

Historical Notes The 360 (2 1/4-inch) is a blackpowder cartridge that first appeared before 1873. It was loaded with a great variety of bullet weights as a blackpowder cartridge: from 71 to 215 grains. Cartridge case length also varied considerably. The 2 1/4-inch version was the most common, but a length of 2-7/16 inches was also common — a favorite length of Alexander Henry, who was arguably the best craftsman of the 19th century. Some cases were as long as 2-3/4 inches.

Nitro loadings were with bullet weights of 190, 200, 250, and 300 grains (at least). Nitro versions date from around 1900-1902. Some blackpowder loads were paper patched, others of bare lead.

General Comments This cartridge would be useful for small, thin-skinned game. In power it is about the same as the 38-55 and would not be a bad short-range woods cartridge for deer-size animals. It was used mostly in single-shot and double-barrel rifles. If you have a rifle in this bore size, be sure to make a chamber cast to find out the true dimensions before you attempt to handload for it. Bertram of Australia makes cases for the 360 that are long enough to produce suitable loads for any version of this basic case.

360 Express (2 1/4-inch)/360 Nitro For Black Factory Ballistics

Bullet (grains/type)	Powder	Grains	Velocity	Energy	Source/Comments
134 lead	Blackpowder		1025	312	Factory load
134 lead	Smokeless powder		1025	312	Factory load
190 (360 NBP)	Smokeless powder		1700	1222	Factory load
300 (360 NE)	Smokeless powder	1650	1820	Factory load	

360 No. 2
Nitro Express

Historical Notes This cartridge was introduced by Eley Brothers in 1905 as a cartridge for single-shot and double-barrel rifles. The 360 No. 2 was moderately popular, but could not compete with the 375 H&H Magnum, which appeared on the market only a few years later.

General Comments This is a large, rimmed, bottlenecked case noted for the low pressure it develops. In its day, it was considered a good all-around cartridge for thin-skinned African or Indian game. It would be adequate for any North American big game at moderate ranges and would make a good woods cartridge.

360 No. 2 Nitro Express Factory Ballistics

Bullet (grains/type)	Powder	Grains	Velocity	Energy	Source/Comments
320 SP	FL		2200	3442	Factory load

375 Flanged Nitro Express (2 1/2-inch) (370 Flanged)

Historical Notes Introduced in 1899, this is a straight rimmed case not to be confused with the 375 Flanged Magnum which has a larger necked case. It was used in single-shot and double-barrel rifles, although BSA made a bolt-action Lee magazine rifle in this chambering.

General Comments The straight 375 rimmed cartridge is suitable for much hunting use, and would be adequate for almost any North American big game, particularly for hunting in woods or brush.

Bullets are no problem. This one is very similar in concept to the 375 Winchester, but the two are not interchangeable. This cartridge lends itself to some improvement by handloading, which is okay in a single-shot or magazine rifle. One can make cases from 405 Winchester cases, or seek out Mr. Bertram, of Australia, for new cases. Elmer Keith had a Lancaster oval-bore double-barrel rifle in this chambering which he used for elk on occasion. The grand old master liked the rifle and chambering very much, once he got it regulated properly, which he said was quite a chore.

375 Flanged Nitro Express (2 1/2-inch) Factory Ballistics

Bullet (grains/type)	Powder	Grains	Velocity	Energy	Source/Comments
270 SP	FL		2000	2400	Factory load
300 SP	FL		1900	2405	Factory load *

*Estimated ballistics

400/375 Belted Nitro Express (H&H)

Historical Notes This was the world's first belted case. It was introduced in 1905 by Holland & Holland to compete with the rising popularity of the 9.5mm Mannlicher-Schoenauer. The 400/375 was used mainly in bolt-action rifles, but some double-barrel and single-shot rifles chambered it. It was listed in British ammunition catalogs until 1936-38. Many of Holland & Holland's rifles in this chambering were apparently take-downs, on Mannlicher and, later, on Mauser-98 actions.

General Comments The power of the 400/375 is nearly identical to that of the 9.5mm Mannlicher, or in the same class as the 358 Winchester. It would be adequate for most North American big game at moderate ranges. Cases can be made from 240 Weatherby cases. Bullets designed for 375 Magnum velocities will perform poorly at these low velocities, but one might have good luck with cast bullets or with those designed for the 375 Winchester rifle.

400/375 Belted Nitro Express (H&H) Factory Ballistics

Bullet (grains/type)	Powder	Grains	Velocity	Energy	Source/Comments
270 SP/FMJ	FL		2175	2840	Factory load
320	Cordite	43.0	2000	2840	Factory load *
*Estimated ballistics					

375 Rimless NE (2 1/4-inch) 9.5x57mm MS

General Comments This is the British designation for the 9.5mm Mannlicher-Schoenauer, and it may be listed either or both ways. There is a very slight difference in loading between the two listings, but these cartridges are interchangeable. This cartridge takes bullets of 0.375-inch diameter, and performance is similar to that of the 400/375. The 9.5mm M-S is not listed in late European catalogs. Additional data is in the section on European cartridges.

375 Rimless NE (2 1/4-inch) (9.5x57mm MS) Factory Ballistics

Bullet (grains/type)	Powder	Grains	Velocity	Energy	Source/Comments
270 SP	FL		2150	2771	Factory load, European
270 SP	FL		2100	2643	Factory load, British

369 Nitro Express (Purdey)

Historical Notes This cartridge was brought out in 1922 by Purdey for double-barrel rifles of their manufacture.

General Comments The 369 Purdey was loaded with only one bullet weight (270 grains) and offers ballistics practically identical to the 375 H&H Flanged Magnum with the same bullet. The 369 uses bullets of 0.375-inch diameter. It is a good cartridge suitable for any of the heavier varieties of North American big game. It could be improved by handloading, but because it was only used in double-barrel rifles, it is not normally practical to change performance of the load.

369 Nitro Express (Purdey) Factory Ballistics

Bullet (grains/type)	Powder	Grains	Velocity	Energy	Source/Comments
270 SP	FL		2500	3760	Factory load

375 Flanged Magnum
375 Belted Rimless Magnum
375 H&H Magnum

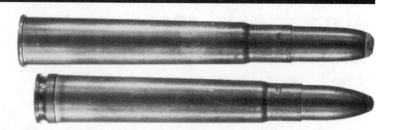

Historical Notes In 1912, Holland & Holland brought out perhaps the most famous pair of cartridges ever devised, the 375 Magnum in belted and flanged versions. The belted version was for magazine rifles and the rimmed for doubles and single-loaders. When these cartridges came out, nothing else similar was available. Their only competitors were the 450/400 in doubles, the 404 Jeffery in magazine rifles, and the smaller 350 Rigby Magnum and No. 2. The 375 offered very flat trajectory, adequate bullet weight, and outstanding performance in handy rifles of top quality. The belted version has always been with us, and Kynoch again loads the rimmed version today.

General Comments This cartridge has been very successful and hence very popular in Africa, India, and of course Alaska. Nearly every manufacturer in the world makes or has made rifles in the belted version of this cartridge. Double-barrel rifles are still occasionally made for the flanged version.

The 375 rimmed is loaded to slightly less velocity than the belted case, but not enough to make any real difference. One can use the same loading data as the 375 belted magnum. However, you cannot change ballistics without causing the barrels of a double-barrel rifle to shoot to different points of impact. You have to regulate your load to the individual rifle by trial and error. A rifle in either version of this cartridge makes a fine all-around hunting rifle for anything on the face of the earth.

375 H&H Flanged Magnum Loading Data and Factory Ballistics

Bullet (grains/type)	Powder	Grains	Velocity	Energy	Source/Comments
270 SP	IMR 4350	83.0	2620	4115	NA
300 SP	IMR 4350	80.0	2500	4160	NA
235 SP	FL		2750	3945	Factory load
270 SP	FL		2600	4050	Factory load
300 SP	FL		2400	3835	Factory load

375 Belted Magnum Factory Ballistics

Bullet (grains/type)	Powder	Grains	Velocity	Energy	Source/Comments
235 SP	FL		2800	4090	Factory load
270 SP	FL		2650	4200	Factory load
300 SP	FL		2500	4160	Factory load

380 Short and Long (Rifle)

Historical Notes These are old blackpowder cartridges dating to the early 1870s. These cartridges were used in single-shot rifles, pistols and revolvers. Ammunition was loaded by DWM, in Germany, and chambered in inexpensive, European-made handguns.

General Comments The 380 Long is similar to the old 38 Long Colt. It is only suitable for short-range target and small game use. If you have a gun chambered for one of these, it is possible to make ammunition from 38 Special cases. The 380 has an outside-lubricated bullet of up to 0.376-inch diameter, but smaller inside-lubricated types can be used for handloading, although accuracy might not be satisfactory. Use the same loading data as for the 38 Long Colt.

380 Short and Long (Rifle) Factory Ballistics

Bullet (grains/type)	Powder	Grains	Velocity	Energy	Source/Comments
124 lead	Blackpowder		1050	304	Factory load

400 Purdey (3-inch)
Light Express
400 Straight 3-inch

Historical Notes Numerous 400 straight cases were chambered in British rifles from the dawn of the breech loading era, including cases made of paper and coiled brass, some as short as 2 inches, others as long as 3-1/4. Purdey's utilized a 3-inch case loaded with "light Cordite" for its double-barrel rifles, around 1905. Kynoch offered a shot cartridge slightly longer than 3 inches, perhaps for use in oval-bored rifles of 40-caliber.

General Comments According to a Purdey catalog, "The light 400 is an excellent firearm for deer, wild boar, etc., and has gained great popularity for tiger shooting in India, having the advantage of being a really powerful firearm and no heavier than a heavy 12-bore gun. The bullet is lead with a nickel base, and at 100 yards, has a striking energy of 1443 foot-pounds." We hope not too many tiger hunters had to defend themselves with this one. A 40-caliber bullet weighing only 230 grains would work fine on deer, as it has about the sectional density of a typical (240-grain) 44 Magnum bullet, though at somewhat greater velocity. Penetration would depend on bullet construction. These rifles require 0.405-inch bullets, which nobody makes, so you will probably have to either cast your own or swage down 41 Magnum bullets.

400 Purdey (3-inch) Factory Ballistics

Bullet (grains/type)	Powder	Grains	Velocity	Energy	Source/Comments
230 lead	Cordite	47.0	2050	2150	Factory load

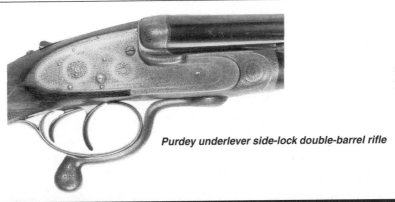

Purdey underlever side-lock double-barrel rifle

400 H&H Magnum

Historical Notes When Holland & Holland began receiving inquiries asking them to develop a cartridge that would increase in power over its legendary 375 H&H Magnum, Technical Director Russell Wilkin began working on the problem. The requests were for a cartridge that could produce 6,000 foot-pounds of energy (fpe) at the muzzle, which is an enormous leap over the 375's 4160 fpe, so Wilkin decided to create two cartridges, a 465 and a more manageable 416-caliber cartridge which could be called the 400 Holland & Holland Magnum. This bore diameter fit neatly between the 375 and the 465 calibers and would be legal in those African countries that require a minimum 40-caliber rifle to hunt dangerous game.

General Comments Holland retained the belted case head of the 375 H&H, mostly for esthetic reasons. The shoulder has been moved back to lengthen the neck, providing plenty of grip on the bullet to withstand inertia under recoil in the magazine of a bolt-action rifle. A shallow shoulder angle ensures a smooth feed from magazine to chamber. Field-testing shows the 400 has a very similar trajectory to the 375 at normal hunting ranges.

400 H&H Magnum Factory Ballistics

Bullet (grains/type)	Powder	Grains	Velocity	Energy	Source/Comments
400 Woodleigh	FL		2400		Holland & Holland

0.400 H&H Magnum Belted Rimless

450/400 3 1/4-inch BPE Nitro for Black Nitro Express

Historical Notes The 450/400 3 1/4-inch uses a necked-down 450 3 1/4-inch case. In blackpowder form, it was loaded with about 110 grains of powder. Bullet weight varied from 230-300 grains. The Nitro for Black version was stoked with 45-48 grains of Cordite and with bullets from 270 to 316 grains. The Nitro Express version was loaded with 400-grain softpoints or solid bullets over 56 to 60 grains of Cordite. Nitro versions of these cartridges were available with rims in two thicknesses. The later, thicker version is 0.042-inch, and exists because of the great length of the case neck. In blackpowder versions, it extracted easily, but on the nitro version, any slight bit of corrosion in the chamber caused the case to stick, and the rim would pull off. Hence the change. Jeffery eliminated the long neck in his version — a good idea, indeed!

General Comments The blackpowder version was considered appropriate for deer hunting and was usually chambered in a lightweight rifle. The nitro version is the smallest of the British cartridges that can be considered as an appropriate dangerous game cartridge. It is practical for all-around use on African game. Before the advent of the 375 H&H Magnum, it was one of the most popular cartridges worldwide. If one is a cool and good shot, he can take this one against the biggest elephant, which is just what John "Pondoro" Taylor did many times. He speaks quite highly of it in his *African Rifles and Cartridges*. Many double-barrel rifles are encountered today for both blackpowder and nitro versions of this cartridge. The nitro rifles tend to be quite heavy for the chambering, probably because rifle makers did not know that such weight was not necessary for this chambering. Jeffery designed a similar 3-inch 40-caliber Nitro round, called the 400 Jeffery, that is not interchangeable with this one (see below). Some of his rifles were quite light, but a great many were built on ponderous actions and weighed more than 11 pounds, when 9-1/2 would have been adequate.

450/400 3 1/4-inch BPE and Nitro Express Factory Ballistics

Bullet (grains/type)	Powder	Grains	Velocity	Energy	Source/Comments
230 - 300 lead	Blackpowder (FFg)		110.0		Factory load
270 - 316 SP	Cordite	45.0 – 48.0			Factory load, Nitro for Black
400 SP	Cordite	56.0 – 60.0	2150	4110	Factory load, Nitro Express

450/400 2 3/8-inch BPE
450/400 2 3/8-inch Nitro For BP
450/400 2 3/8-inch Nitro Express

Historical Notes These are different loadings of the same cartridge — a blackpowder load that originated circa 1880. The nitro-for-black and NE versions originated circa 1899. These are based on the old 450-bore base-diameter case shortened and necked-down to 40 caliber, and loaded with 80 grains of blackpowder and a 210- to 270-grain lead bullet. The nitro-for-black version, made for use in blackpowder rifles, was loaded with 270-grain bullets, and developed very low pressure. The full nitro version featured 300- to 400-grain bullets over 40 to 43 grains of Cordite. There was a similar BP Express cartridge of 2 7/8-inch length, and some other rather rare variations on this theme.

General Comments The British worked up smokeless loads for many of their old blackpowder cartridges. For single-shot rifles, this was not difficult. However, with a double-barrel rifle, the load had to be balanced to shoot to the same point of impact as the original blackpowder load. Just working up the same velocity for the same bullet did not always work. Various bullets and velocities had to be tried to arrive at the right combination. Once that load was found, it provides fine short-range deer hunting performance. The NE version with 43 grains of Cordite and the 400 grain bullet would be quite a bit more powerful and generally more useful.

450/400 2 3/8-inch BPE, Nitro For BP, and Nitro Express Factory Ballistics

Bullet (grains/type)	Powder	Grains	Velocity	Energy	Source/Comments
210 - 270 lead	Blackpowder (FFg)	79.0 - 84.0			NA
270 RN copper-tubed lead	Cordite	38.0	1650	1630	Factory load, Nitro for blackpowder
300 RN HP	Cordite	40.0			Factory load, Nitro Express
400 RN HP	Cordite	42.0-43.0			Factory load, Nitro Express

400 Jeffery NE
450/400 3-inch

Historical Notes This cartridge was designed by Jeffery in 1902. According to Pondoro Taylor*, the short case was brought out because the longer blackpowder cartridge had a tendency to stick in the chamber after firing. Overall length is shorter, but the shoulder is farther forward. The 400 Jeffery was designed exclusively for Cordite; it was never available with black. As with the 3 1/4-inch version, this was very popular before the 375 H&H Magnum appeared. It is still one of the most effective all-around cartridges for Africa.

General Comments The 400 Jeffery throws a 400-grain bullet at adequate velocity, and hence is more effective on the largest game than is the 300-grain 375 H&H Magnum loading. However, it is less versatile as to available guns and loads, and that is where the 375 shines. Taylor wrote that he considered either of the 450/400s, the 3- or 3 1/4-inch version, adequate for any African game under almost any conditions, if used by an experienced hunter. Taylor killed about 1500 elephant. In the process he used just about every available cartridge, so his opinion is something to consider. Elmer Keith wrote that a double-barrel rifle for this cartridge would be his first choice for crawling through an Alaskan alder thicket after big bear. Bullets of proper diameter may be obtained from Barnes or Woodleigh, or from many smaller custom makers. Bertram makes cases that can be formed into either of these two grand 40s. The availability of good bullets in this size (0.411-inch diameter) has made this cartridge newly popular. Good, reasonably light double-barrel rifles for it are becoming hard to find. A-Square used to offer factory 400 NE ammunition.

---

* Op. cit.

400 Jeffery (450/400 NE 3-inch) Factory Ballistics

Bullet (grains/type)	Powder	Grains	Velocity	Energy	Source/Comments
400 SP	Cordite	60.0	2100	3920	Factory load, standard

Loads using 55.0 or 57.0 grains of Cordite were offered for use in extremely hot climates. A 300-grain loading was also offered. It was not particularly popular.

416 Rigby

Historical Notes A proprietary cartridge introduced by John Rigby in 1911 for his magnum Mauser-actioned rifles, both cartridge and rifle established a record of reliability on dangerous game that endures to this day. Magazine rifles were initially offered for this round, but until recently Rigby only made one double-barrel rifle for it, by special order and with lots of monetary persuasion. Today it is chambered by Ruger in single-shot and magazine rifles, and by several other manufacturers. Federal Cartridge Co. offers premium 416 Rigby ammunition. The 416 Rigby is probably the best magazine cartridge for big game ever offered. Recently, two "copies" have appeared — the 416 Remington Magnum and 416 Weatherby Magnum. Both use a belted case, which is a mistake. The clean line of the non-belted case makes for better feeding through a magazine, which adds an extra margin of reliability. (See Chapter 2 for more information.)

General Comments The 416 Rigby delivers greater striking energy than the 404 Jeffery. For those who prefer the bolt-action rifle, it is a great favorite for use against dangerous game in almost any situation. Because the 416 Remington and Weatherby are now standard items, many great bullets are available in this caliber. This cartridge is a handloader's dream. Numerous molds are available for those who would shoot cast bullets.

416 Rigby Factory Ballistics

Bullet (grains/type)	Powder	Grains	Velocity	Energy	Source/Comments
410 SP	FL		2370	5100	Factory load
400 SP	FL		2430	5245	Federal factory load

404 Jeffery
404 Rimless NE

Historical Notes Introduced by W.J. Jeffery in 1909, the 404 Jeffery was vastly popular for many years, then died slowly over many decades. It now has a new lease on life. In 1993, Dynamit Nobel announced it would restart production of 404 Jeffery ammunition, and Ruger announced that the M77 rifle would be chambered for that cartridge. A Canadian company, NASS, recently announced a line of proprietary cartridges ranging from 7mm to 458, based on the 404 case. In the United States, Dakota Arms of Sturgis, S.D., has introduced its own line of proprietary cartridges based on the 404 case, ranging from 7mm to 416. Bullets of 0.423-inch diameter are now available for the 404. Norma, RWS and Bertram make cases. The 404 was designed to be a bolt-action cartridge that would duplicate the ballistics of the rimmed 400 Jeffery and the 450/400 3 1/4-inch. The 404 is also popular on the Continent, and it is metrically named the 10.75x73mm. Today it is loaded a bit hotter than originally.

General Comments The 404 made a great name for itself in Africa, where inexpensive bolt rifles let its performance be experienced by those who could not afford a double-barrel rifle for one of the 400 NE's. At one time, a higher-velocity 300-grain load was available for the 404. It gave good results on thin-skinned game, but proved rather unreliable on the heavier species. With the standard 400-grain bullet, the 404 was a very popular general-purpose cartridge in Africa and India. Properly used, it is adequate for any game found there. It is somewhat overpowered for North American game and lacks the flat trajectory and long-range potential necessary for much of our hunting. The 404 is a good cartridge for hunting bear or other big game at close quarters. The 404 uses 0.423-inch diameter bullets, which are available from Barnes, Woodleigh and RWS.

404 Jeffery Nitro Express Factory Ballistics

Bullet (grains/type)	Powder	Grains	Velocity	Energy	Source/Comments
300 SP	FL		2600	4500	Factory load
400 SP	FL		2125	4020	Factory load
400 SP	FL		2300	4700	Factory load, modern

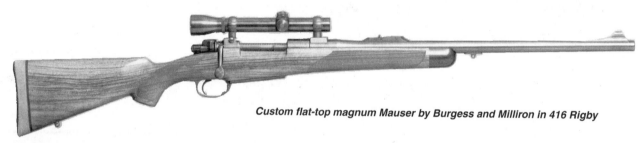

Custom flat-top magnum Mauser by Burgess and Milliron in 416 Rigby

425 Westley Richards Magnum
425 Westley Richards Semi-rimmed Magnum

Historical Notes Westley Richards introduced this cartridge in 1909. The most common and quite successful version has a rebated rim that fits the standard-diameter Mauser bolt face. Westley made double-barrel rifles as well as bolt actions for the 425. It is a very good cartridge and several unsuccessful attempts have been made to resurrect it. The 425 is a sort of poor-man's magnum. Its rebated rim is 30-06 size, so any 30-06 or 8mm Mauser action can be made to accept it with minimal gunsmithing. The result is a very good and powerful big game rifle for reasonable cost. Bullet diameter is 0.428 to 0.435 inch. Barnes and Woodleigh make such bullets.

General Comments The 425 was designed for use against dangerous game. It was intended to take the place of the 450-bore in India, though W-R offered its 476 for Africa. The 425 proved to be a fine cartridge, and was offered with solids and with the Leslie Taylor-designed, capped soft-nose bullets. Taylor was the general manager of W-R at the turn of the century, and he was personally involved in bullet design, among many other things. The so-called LT-capped bullets worked very well and were incorporated into most other W-R cartridges, including the 318 and 476.

425 Westley Richards Magnum Factory Ballistics

Bullet (grains/type)	Powder	Grains	Velocity	Energy	Source/Comments
410 SP	FL		2350	5010	Factory load

500/450 No. 1 Carbine
500/450 No. 1 Express
500/450 No. 1 Musket
500/450 No. 2 Musket

Historical Notes Perhaps no cartridges in the world are more abundant or more confusing than those of British origin labeled 500/450, followed by one or another designator. There are no less than 19 listings of individually identified cartridges in Fleming's *British Sporting Rifle Cartridges*. Many of these cartridges were loaded with a great variety of bullet weights. All of these were bottleneck cartridges, and all originated with blackpowder loadings. The No. 1 Carbine was Westley Richards' first drawn brass case, which appeared just before 1880. W-R was also responsible for the Musket and the 2 3/4-inch No. 1 Express, and possibly others of

this lot. The oldest of the 500/450s used a coiled brass case of 2 1/2-inch length dating to 1871. Some of these cartridges were loaded well into the 20th century.

General Comments All of the 500/450s are in the same class as the 45-70 and would be fairly effective short-range cartridges for North American game. Because of the great variation in designs, the handloader should be careful to determine exactly which of the many variants he has before attempting to build cartridges for it. The 4-D company has a large selection of 500/450 die types in stock.

500/450 No. 1 Express Factory Ballistics

Bullet (grains/type)	Powder	Grains	Velocity	Energy	Source/Comments
270 lead	Blackpowder		1900	2160	Factory load

500/450 No. 2 Musket Factory Ballistics

Bullet (grains/type)	Powder	Grains	Velocity	Energy	Source/Comments
480 lead	Blackpowder		1300	1805	Factory load
480 lead	Smokeless powder		1300	1805	Factory load
500 lead	Smokeless powder		1350	2025	Factory load

577x450 Martini-Henry   See Chapter 7

450 3 1/4-inch BPE

Historical Notes There were a great many "straight" British cartridges of nominal 450 designation, ranging from the 450 No. 1 — barely longer than the 45 Colt — up to the 450 3 1/4-inch. In Fleming's *British Sporting Rifle Cartridges*, there is a progression of no less than nine different lengths illustrated, in coiled paper, coiled brass, and drawn brass. The 3 1/4-inch drawn brass version originated prior to 1877, and coiled brass versions were in existence before 1871. Bullet weights ran from about 270 grains up to 365 in the nitro-for-black versions. Powder charges were from 105 to at least 120 grains of black (Greener indicates 150 grains). Nitro loadings for blackpowder rifles used up to 55 grains of Cordite. The 450 3 1/4-inch was loaded in France, Germany, Austria and Canada,

and most likely elsewhere. It was one of the best blackpowder cartridges in the world.

General Comments The 3 1/4-inch BPE version became one of the most popular cartridges ever devised. It was a deer cartridge, or for medium-size game at best. Selous and Taylor both used this cartridge to take elephant, but they both knew this was something of a stunt. The 450 BP and nitro-for-black versions lasted until well into the 20th century, and many rifles that chamber it are still in use. The editor of this chapter once owned a plain-grade Watson hammer double-barrel that would regulate perfectly with bullets from 300 to 400 grains weight, and shot to its sights at more than a half-mile.

James Purdey & Sons 450 Express Double Rifle

450 3 1/4-inch Nitro Express

Historical Notes When Cordite and suitable full-patch bullets were loaded into what had been one of the world's most popular deer cartridges, the result was the new standard-of-the-world in elephant cartridges. This replaced the ponderous 8-, 6-, and 4-bore blackpowder rifles. John Rigby and Co. introduced this cartridge in 1898. For many years, it was considered the standard elephant or dangerous game cartridge, and enjoyed great popularity. It utilizes 480-grain bullets of 0.458-inch diameter.

General Comments The 450 Nitro is considered adequate for

dangerous African game — or any other game for that matter — under almost any conditions. It would most likely have been the only British cartridge used for big game hunting, except for a British law that prohibited importation of 45-caliber rifles or cartridges into India. British rifle makers had to come up with something new, so the 425, 470, 476, and others came into being. Nevertheless, the 450 NE was and still is a winner, and a great many double-barrel rifles for this cartridge are still in service. A-Square now offers this ammunition.

450 3 1/4-inch Nitro Express Factory Ballistics

Bullet (grains/type)	Powder	Grains	Velocity	Energy	Source/Comments
465 (various)			2150	4770	A-Square
480 lead	Smokeless powder		2150	4930	Factory load

500/450 3 1/4-inch Magnum Express (BPE)

Historical Notes This cartridge originated with a coiled brass case in the 1870s. Loaded with about 140 grains of blackpowder, in drawn brass version, it was once very popular in Africa. Typical express-bullet weight was 325 grains.

General Comments This was popular enough that it was loaded in

both black and smokeless (nitro-for-black) versions until the start of World War II. This must have caused some problems with owners of nitro versions of this cartridge, which was an extremely powerful elephant cartridge, and surely some orders of ammunition arrived in the heart of Africa that would fit the rifle, but did not give the needed performance.

500/450 3 1/4-inch Magnum BPE Factory Ballistics

Bullet (grains/type)	Powder	Grains	Velocity	Energy	Source/Comments
325 SP	Blackpowder		1950	2745	Factory load
325 SP	Smokeless powder		1950	2745	Factory load
365 SP	Smokeless powder		1875	2850	Factory load

500/450 3 1/4-inch Nitro Express

Historical Notes This is a rimmed, necked case introduced (probably by Holland & Holland) around the turn of the century. It is based on the blackpowder 500/450 Magnum Express shell. It was used in single-shot and double-barrel rifles, and made a great name for itself in Africa. It was usually loaded with 480-grain softpoint or solid bullets, but other slightly lighter loadings sometimes appear. It is a fine performer. Theodore Roosevelt had a double-barrel rifle in this chambering. H&H opened this up to become the 500/465 after the ban on 450-bore rifles in India and the Sudan.

General Comments This was a prime competitor of the 450 3 1/4-inch NE. Performance of the two is practically identical. The British developed several 45-caliber large bores, all of which produced

about 5,000 foot-pounds of muzzle energy. These cartridges have about the same killing power and the choice becomes more or less a matter of individual preference. All are large cartridges that develop quite low pressures and are therefore suitable for hot climates where dangerous game abounds. Younger African guides have, in many instances, switched to bolt-action rifles in contemporary chamberings because those rifles are less expensive than the classic English doubles, if not as quick for the second shot. The bullet used in British 45-caliber cartridges varies from 0.454- to 0.458-inch in diameter, so there are plenty of jacketed or cast bullets available to fit almost any of these cartridges.

500/450 Magnum Nitro-Express (3 1/4-inch) Factory Ballistics

Bullet (grains/type)	Powder	Grains	Velocity	Energy	Source/Comments
480 SP	FL		2175	5080	Factory load

450 No. 2 Nitro Express (3 1/2-inch)

Historical Notes This cartridge uses a longer case than the 500/450 Magnum, but uses the same bullet weight loaded to the same velocity. It was introduced in about 1900-1902 by Eley. It was designed to give very low pressure in single-shot and double-barrel rifles, and has a thick rim to aid extraction. It was loaded with 480-grain bullets, 70 to 80 grains of Cordite, and with a great variety of bullet types. It later was opened up to become the 475 No. 2 for importation into India.

General Comments The only logical reason for designing a larger capacity case to deliver the identical ballistics of a smaller cartridge is to reduce breech pressure. It appears that some British cartridges gave extraction difficulties during the era of transition from blackpowder to smokeless powder. At first, this was believed to be the result of the higher pressure developed by smokeless powder. Later, the manufacturers discovered that most of the trouble could be eliminated by making the case walls thicker. Many rifles in this chambering are still around.

450 No. 2 Nitro-Express (3 1/2-inch) Factory Ballistics

Bullet (grains/type)	Powder	Grains	Velocity	Energy	Source/Comments
480 SP	FL		2175	5050	Factory load

450 Rigby

Historical Notes Introduced in 1995, Rigby's newest cartridge is just one more feather in the hat of this very old but still progressive and always innovative company. John "Pondoro" Taylor said that Rigby always had Africa in mind when it brought out a new cartridge. That tradition continues today, with the company under the direction of Paul Roberts. Roberts actually went to Africa himself to test and see the results of the 450 Rigby in the field. The cartridge has already made a good name for itself there and will surely become another of the all-time great classics.

General Comments Rigby offers the 450 Rigby in bolt-action or double-barrel rifle versions. In its standard factory loading, this cartridge throws a 480-grain Woodleigh soft-nose or solid bullet at 2350 fps. This gives it quite a trajectory and terminal-performance edge on the 450-470 group, and it far surpasses the somewhat overstrained 458. The case is basically the same one that the 416 Rigby uses, with a sharp shoulder for good and consistent resistance to the striker blow, and with a 0.458-inch bullet. Similar in size to the 460 Weatherby, this improved design is unhampered by a belt and thus gives smooth, quiet and sure feeding from the magazine. This will be a good choice for the person wanting to take only one rifle to Africa. It will also be right at home with anyone who appreciates a good, powerful rifle.

465 H&H Magnum

Historical Notes When Holland & Holland began receiving inquiries asking them to develop a cartridge that would increase in power over its legendary 375 H&H Magnum, Technical Director Russell Wilkin began working on the problem. The requests were for a cartridge that could produce 6,000 foot-pounds of energy (fpe) at the muzzle, which is an enormous leap over the 375's 4,160 fpe. To achieve this performance goal, it was decided to go to a belted cartridge with a larger head diameter than that of the 375 H&H Magnum. Holland is still fine-tuning this cartridge at press time, but

it appears that the stated performance goal will be reached. If so, the 465 H&H Magnum with a 480-grain Woodleigh bullet will have as much energy at 200 yards as the 375 H&H does at the muzzle.

General Comments The 465 has a head diameter of .580-inch, measured just in front of the belt. The case is 2.89 inches long and has the sloping profile characteristic of Holland offerings. At hunting ranges, the 465's trajectory will be very similar to both the 400 H&H and its predecessor, the 375 H&H Magnum.

465 H&H Magnum Factory Ballistics

Bullet (grains/type)	Powder	Grains	Velocity	Energy	Source/Comments
480 Woodleigh	FL	Not published at press time			Holland & Holland

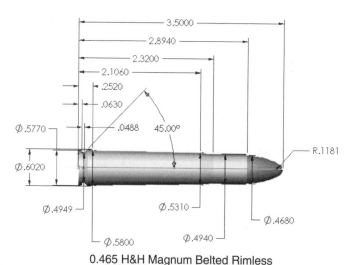

0.465 H&H Magnum Belted Rimless

500/465 Nitro Express

Historical Notes When Holland & Holland began receiving inquiries asking them to develop a cartridge that would offer an increase in power over its legendary 375 H&H Magnum, Technical Director Russell Wilkin began working on the problem. The requests were for a cartridge that could produce 6000 foot-pounds of energy (fpe) at the muzzle, which is an enormous leap over the 375's 4160 fpe. To achieve this performance goal, it was decided to to go a belted cartridge with a larger head diameter than that of the 375 H&H Magnum. Holland is still fine-tuning this cartridge at press time, but it appears that the stated performance goal will be reached. If so, the 465 H&H Magnum with a 480-grain Woodleigh

bullet will have an much energy at 200 yards as the 375 H&H does at the muzzle.

General Comments The 465 is rated as an excellent all-around number for Africa, including heavy or dangerous game. Components are available from U.S. suppliers. It is still tops for African game. Only one bullet weight was used, but those 480-grain slugs were available in solid, softpoint and metal-covered split types. Bullets are available from A-Square, Barnes and Woodleigh, and Bertram and HDS offer cases. A-Square now offers this ammunition.

500/465 Nitro Express Factory Ballistics

Bullet (grains/type)	Powder	Grains	Velocity	Energy	Source/Comments
480 SP	Cordite	73	2150	4930	Factory load
480 (various)	FL		2150	4930	A-Square factory load

470 Nitro Express

Historical Notes The 470 was introduced in 1900 and, according to John Taylor, was designed by Joseph Lang. It is another extremely popular cartridge of the British gun trade, which was adopted by most rifle makers. It was used mostly in double-barrel rifles and was a favorite of elephant hunters. Like most cartridges in this group, it originated as a replacement for the 450 Nitro Express, which was banned in India and the Sudan for a number of years. Holland & Holland, Purdey and others still make guns in this chambering in England. It was (and still is) Rigby's choice when it gave up the 450 NE.

General Comments The 470 Nitro was probably the most popular and widely used of the various 47-caliber cartridges. It is certainly the most enduring. It had plenty of killing power for any of the heavy or dangerous varieties of game and it is potent lion or tiger medicine in a tight spot. It can, like any powerful cartridge, be used for smaller game than that for which it was designed, and that in fact is how most of the big double-barrel rifles are still used today. Federal Cartridge Co. began making loaded ammunition in 1989 using best-quality 500-grain solids and softpoints at 2150 fps. Handloading components are today widely available, and many makers still offer double-barrel rifles in this chambering. It is one of the best choices in any new double-barrel rifle because of ammunition and component availability. Federal does not offer components to the handloader, but bullets are available from A-Square, Barnes, Trophy Bonded Bullets and Woodleigh, and from many smaller custom shops. HDS, Bertram and Norma make cases, and Kynoch again offers ammunition.

470 Nitro-Express Factory Ballistics

Bullet (grains/type)	Powder	Grains	Velocity	Energy	Source/Comments
500 SP/FMJ	FL		2150	5130	Factory load, British
500 SP/FMJ	FL		2150	5130	Federal factory load

Churchill 470 Double Ejector

476 Nitro Express
476 Westley Richards

Historical Notes This cartridge was a Westley Richards development introduced in 1907. It was used in single and double-barrel rifles, but was not as popular as others of the same class. The 520-grain bullets were of 0.476-inch diameter, and the impressive LT capped bullets were available as softpoints.

General Comments Nothing much can be said about the 476 Nitro Express that has not already been mentioned about other cartridges in the same class. These cartridges are all nearly identical in power. The 476 is considered adequate for any and all African or Indian big game. It was a favorite of Elmer Keith's. Barnes and others offer bullets of this size.

476 Nitro Express Factory Ballistics

Bullet (grains/type)	Powder	Grains	Velocity	Energy	Source/Comments
520 SP	FL		2100	5085	Factory load

475 3 1/4-inch Nitro Express

Historical Notes This cartridge, like the 470, was designed to replace 45-caliber British cartridges used in India and the Sudan. Most were introduced between 1905 and 1910. This one came out in about 1900. It is a straight, rimmed shell intended for single-shot or double-barrel rifles, and took a 480-grain bullet of apparently varying diameter. Cartridges with bullets as small as 0.474-inch and as large as 0.483-inch have been encountered.

General Comments The 475 Nitro has about the same performance as the 470, 465, etc., and was considered a good general-purpose round for heavy and dangerous game of all types. Barnes and others offer bullets for loading this cartridge.

475 Nitro Express Factory Ballistics

Bullet (grains/type)	Powder	Grains	Velocity	Energy	Source/Comments
480 SP	FL		2175	5040	Factory load, British

475 No. 2 Nitro Express
475 No. 2 Jeffery

Historical Notes Developed to replace the 450 No. 2 when the British government prohibited 45-caliber cartridges in India and the Sudan. The 475 No. 2 Nitro Express was used, of course, in double-barrel rifles. The standard version used a 480-grain bullet with 80 or 85 grains of Cordite. Jeffrey's load was with a 500-grain bullet and three different powder charges, 75, 80, and 85 grains of Cordite. The various cartridges would interchange but unless the load matched the rifle, it would not regulate properly. There were some bullet variations, but the most common was of 0.489-inch diameter.

General Comments The 475 is a very large, impressive-looking cartridge with an overall length of almost 4-1/2 inches. It undoubtedly gave its user some added bravado or confidence that might have been well-needed in a tight spot, in spite of the fact that performance was about the same as that of shorter cartridges. It has ample power for any African or Indian game, and would also take care of anything in North America. The 475 case is made unusually heavy to reduce expansion and facilitate extraction. Pressure is quite low. A-Square and Barnes offer bullets that are suitable for handloading this cartridge. A-Square offers ammunition.

475 No. 2 Nitro Express Factory Ballistics

Bullet (grains/type)	Powder	Grains	Velocity	Energy	Source/Comments
480 SP	FL		2200	5170	Factory load, standard
480 (various)	FL		2200	5170	A-Square factory load
500 SP	FL		2150	5140	Jeffery factory load

505 Gibbs
(505 Rimless)

Historical Notes The 505 Gibbs was introduced in 1911 as a proprietary cartridge by Gibbs for use in Mauser-type bolt-action magazine rifles. Rifles in 505 Gibbs were imported by American dealers and used to a limited extent here. A few custom-built rifles chambered for the 505 were also turned out by American gunmakers. Most of these big-bore nitro cartridges were developed around 1910 and this one was still available until quite recently. Bullets and cases are still available and a few Ruger M77 Expresses have been rebarreled to this round.

General Comments When the first of the 505 rifles showed up in the United States, there were all kinds of stories floating around about the horrendous recoil. Several individuals were alleged to have suffered broken shoulders or collarbones as a result of firing these cartridges. This sort of nonsense made "heroes" out of those who fired these guns and survived, but hardly contributed to the popularity of the cartridge. The English must have more sturdy frames than we, because none of them appear to have fractured anything. The 505 is slightly less powerful than the 500 Jeffery, but both have an edge over the 458 Winchester. The 505 Gibbs is considered adequate for anything in Africa and has a good reputation against elephant, buffalo and lion. Barnes makes bullets specifically designed for this cartridge.

505 Rimless Magnum (Gibbs) Factory Ballistics

Bullet (grains/type)	Powder	Grains	Velocity	Energy	Source/Comments
525 SP	FL		2300	6190	Factory load
525 (various)	FL		2300	6190	A-Square factory load

577/500 No. 2 BP Express

Historical Notes The 577/500 No. 2 Express is another blackpowder cartridge. It was introduced sometime before 1879. It resembles the 577/500 Magnum Nitro Express, but has a shorter case and is not interchangeable. There were a number of different cartridges bearing the 577/500 designation, though thankfully not as many as with the 500/450. This one has a 3-inch case, and there was a version 1/8-inch longer. Both were loaded with black and nitro-for-black, and the longer version became a full nitro load. Bullet weight in this caliber varied from 300 grains up to 570, with corresponding variances in blackpowder charge, ranging from 130 to about 160 grains. At one time, it was loaded in Germany as the 12.7mm British No. 2.

General Comments The 577/500 No. 2 Express was popular in India for shooting thin-skinned game such as tiger. The blackpowder and nitro-for-black versions were not popular in Africa as these cartridges were not powerful enough for general use there. Bullet diameter is nearly the same as the old 50-caliber Sharps cartridges and Lyman moulds in various weights will work for cast bullets. Keep smokeless loads on the light side as these old rifles do not take kindly to high pressures. Dave Davidson of 4-D Tool & Die explains that some versions of the 577/500 are unique from the 500 No. 2 Express. These 577/500s are bigger than the No. 2 at the case head and rim. In those versions, case-head dimensions match the 577 Nitro.

577/500 No. 2 Express (577/500) Factory Ballistics

Bullet (grains/type)	Powder	Grains	Velocity	Energy	Source/Comments
300 lead	FL		1870	2340	Factory load
340 lead	Blackpowder		1925	2800	Factory load

577/500 3 1/8-inch Nitro Express

Historical Notes This number evolved from a blackpowder cartridge based on the 577 case necked to 50-caliber. It looks like, but is not the same as, the shorter 577/500 No. 2 Express, being about 1/8-inch longer. It enjoyed moderate popularity. The full nitro load utilized Cordite with a 570-grain cupro-nickel bullet.

General Comments This cartridge was more popular in India than Africa. It would be more useful for general big game hunting than any of the more powerful "elephant" cartridges of the same caliber. It would be adequate for deer, bear, elk or moose at moderate ranges and would be fine for woods hunting. The old 45-70 military round is considered capable of killing any American game at short range, and it only develops 2,000 foot-pounds of muzzle energy. The 577/500 is a good deal more potent.

577/500 3 1/8-inch Nitro Express Factory Ballistics

Bullet (grains/type)	Powder	Grains	Velocity	Energy	Source/Comments
440 lead	Axite	58.0			Factory load, Nitro for blackpowder
570 FMJ	Cordite				Factory load, Nitro Express

500 Express (BPE) Nitro-for-Black

Historical Notes The straight 500 was offered in a great variety of lengths, including 1 1/2-, 2-, 2 1/4-, 2 1/2-, 2 5/8-, 3-, and 3 1/4-inch. All were blackpowder cartridges. Some were quite successful and lasted; others faded long before the turn of the century. This cartridge size originated in about the mid-to-late 1860s and over time, a great many lengths were tried and, of course, chambered in rifles that are still around. The most successful of these was the 3-inch version. Bullet weights run from 340 to 440 grains, and the charge was from 123 to 142 grains of blackpowder. Around the beginning of the smokeless era, Westley Richards came out with two versions of this cartridge, one 3-inch, the other in a shorter case, both called the Long Range cartridge. These cartridges utilized heavier bullets and either light charges of Cordite or heavy blackpowder loads.

General Comments The blackpowder 500 was popular in India as a good general-purpose firearm, but was not highly regarded in Africa. This cartridge is similar to the 50-140 Sharps. It would be adequate for any North American big game. Late loads used smokeless powder, but delivered the same ballistics as the original blackpowder load. There is a variety of bullet molds available today that will make just about any of the 500 BP cartridges work. To prevent rapid bore damage, only cast or swaged-lead bullets should be used in these guns.

500 Nitro-for-Blackpowder Express Factory Ballistics

Bullet (grains/type)	Powder	Grains	Velocity	Energy	Source/Comments
400 SP	FL		1900	3530	Factory load

500 Nitro Express (3-inch and 3 1/4-inch)

Historical Notes The 500 Nitro Expresses were derived from what were originally blackpowder cartridges. The smokeless versions were introduced in the 1890s. A 570-grain bullet is used in both case lengths, and ballistics are about identical. The longer case works at a bit lower pressure. There were loadings utilizing a 480-grain bullet and slightly reduced charges of Cordite.

General Comments The 500 NE was considered a real killer on practically anything. John A. Hunter, a game-control hunter for the Kenya Game Department for 26 years considered it his favorite. His book *Hunter* is recommended for those who enjoy reading good firsthand experiences of a guide to African shooting. The 500 Nitro resembles the 50-140 Sharps. This cartridge is a favorite of well-known African professional hunter Mark Sullivan. A-Square and Barnes make appropriate bullets. A-Square now offers the 3-inch loading.

500 Nitro Express (3-inch, 3 1/4-inch) Factory Ballistics

Bullet (grains/type)	Powder	Grains	Velocity	Energy	Source/Comments
570 SP	Smokeless powder		2150	5850	Factory load
570 (various)			2150	5850	A-Square

500 Jeffery

Historical Notes The 500 Jeffery was a proprietary cartridge developed by Schuler in Germany for bolt-action rifles. It was also adopted by Jeffery for his bolt-action magazine rifles based on the Mauser action. It has a rebated, or undercut, rim of smaller diameter than the base to fit the standard-diameter Mauser bolt face. In Germany, the same cartridge was loaded as the 12.7x70mm Schuler and also chambered in Mauser-type rifles.

General Comments The 500 Jeffery is similar to the 505 Gibbs, but it has a shorter case and is loaded to higher velocity and energy. The 500 Jeffery was designed to provide the man who preferred the repeating rifle with the same killing power as some of the popular rimmed double-barrel rifle cartridges. The 500 Jeffery is the most powerful cartridge used in any of the British magazine rifles. The 500 Jeffery is considered adequate for large or dangerous African game under any conditions. It is also quite accurate, and a good shot who can handle the recoil can get 100-yard groups of 2 inches. Most shooters claim the apparent recoil of 500 Jeffery magazine rifles is less than that of similarly-chambered double-barrel rifles. A-Square and Barnes make appropriate bullets and A-Square offers factory ammunition.

500 Rimless Jeffery Factory Ballistics

Bullet (grains/type)	Powder	Grains	Velocity	Energy	Source/Comments
535 SP	FL		2400	6800	Factory load, British
570 (various)			2300	6695	A-Square factory load

577 Snider (14.7 mm)   See Chapter 7

577 BP Express
2 1/2-, 2 3/4-,
3- and 3 1/4-inch

Historical Notes The 577 Express series began in about 1870 with the 2 1/2-inch version. Its predecessors were, of course, the 577 Snider variants, which date from 1866. Numerous shorter coiled-brass and drawn-brass 577-bore cartridges were developed, but the best were the Expresses, specifically those that lasted long enough to become nitro cartridges. The shortest of these is the 2 3/4-inch version. Bore size evolved into 0.585-inch diameter, and the best Express bullets weighed about 520-650 grains. The charge was 135 to 190 grains of blackpowder.

General Comments All of these were for use on the heavier non-dangerous game, though as happens, some hunters used these cartridges against tigers and lions with varying success. There was a great variety of bullets available, and success was directly tied to utilizing the proper bullet. To prevent rapid damage to the bore, only case or swaged-lead bullets should be used in these rifles.

577 Nitro Express
2 3/4-, 3- and 3 1/4-inch

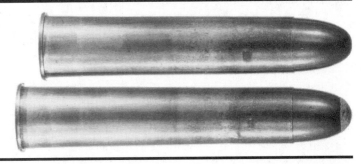

Historical Notes These were all originally blackpowder cartridges, but when loaded with Cordite and proper bullets became some of the best real stoppers for dangerous game. All three originated around the turn of the century. The short case and the 3 1/4-inch shell were overshadowed by the 3-inch version.

General Comments The 577 enjoyed a great reputation as an elephant killer and was a standard chambering found in any battery of African rifles. It was popular with professional ivory hunters for close-cover work. Many claim it is superior to the 600 Nitro because it gave greater penetration. Rifles for the 577 could be made a few pounds lighter than the 62-caliber guns, which also

contributed to its popularity. Cartridges of this size were usually for emergency use under difficult conditions. Most hunters used lighter rifles of smaller caliber for ordinary shooting, but had the big 577 as a backup. Rifles for the 577 weighed 13 pounds or more, and that's a lot of weight if you have to carry it very far at the ready. Gunbearers usually carried the heavy guns until needed, but not because the British were lazy. An exhausted man just cannot handle a rifle of such heft and weight in a pinch. A-Square and Barnes make bullets of this cartridge. A-Square offers factory 3-inch case ammunition.

577 Nitro Express Factory Ballistics

Bullet (grains/type)	Powder	Grains	Velocity	Energy	Source/Comments
750 SP/FMJ	FL		2050	7010	Factory load
750 (various)	FL		2050	7010	A-Square factory load

600 Nitro Express
(2 8/10-inch & 3-inch)

Historical Notes The 600 in either length was the largest and most powerful of the English Cordite elephant cartridges until 1988. These were introduced by Jeffery before 1901. The 2 8/10-inch version came out in 1899. The 600 is of original design and is not based on any earlier blackpowder cartridge. It was used in single-shot and double-barrel rifles. Despite its reputation, only a small number of guns have been made in this chambering. In the early 1990s, Heym of Germany introduced the Magnum Express bolt-action rifle in this chambering. Components for handloading are available from Barnes, Huntington, Old Western Scrounger, Bertram, and Woodleigh.

General Comments At one time, the 600 Nitro Express was the most powerful commercial rifle cartridge in the world, but now the

700 Nitro Express overshadows it. The 600 was designed to deliver the maximum possible stopping power against elephants under the most difficult and dangerous conditions. Even professional ivory hunters considered it overpowered for anything but emergency use. It is said that a head shot that missed the brain of an elephant would still knock it down for a considerable length of time — according to John Taylor, up to 30 minutes. Rifles for the 600 usually weighed 16 pounds or more. There were at least three loadings for the cartridge — at 2050, 1950 and 1850 fps. It is necessary to use the rifle's designated load or the two barrels will not shoot to the same point of impact. The 2.8-inch version of 1899 may have only been a developmental stage of this outstanding big cartridge. A-Square and Barnes offer appropriate bullets and A-Square loads factory 600 NE ammunition.

600 Nitro Express Factory Ballistics

Bullet (grains/type)	Powder	Grains	Velocity	Energy	Source/Comments
900 SP/FMJ	Cordite	120.0	2050	8400	Factory load
900 SP/FMJ	Cordite	110.0	1950	7600	Factory load
900 SP/FMJ	Cordite	100.0	1850	6840	Factory load
900	(various)		1950	7600	A-Square factory load *

*A-Square will custom-load this ammunition to match the velocity of the load for which the rifle was originally regulated.

700 Nitro Express

Historical Notes The 700 Nitro Express is a new cartridge, an original design not based on altering the caliber or configuration of an existing cartridge. It was developed in 1988 by Jim Bell of Bell Basic Brass (formerly Brass Extrusion Laboratories, Ltd.), and William Feldstein of Beverly Hills, Calif. It was chambered in a limited number of double-barrel rifles made by Holland & Holland. It came about because Feldstein wanted H&H to build him a 600 Nitro Express. The company refused because it had already completed its official last 600 NE some years ago and was not interested in reviving the chambering. Bell and Feldstein then decided to approach H&H on the possibility of building a series of rifles in a new chambering, something completely different from anything previously made. Since H&H was looking for a big-bore cartridge, there was really only one way to go, and that was up. Thus the 700 Nitro Express was born. According to Jim Bell, the 700 is based on scaling up the old 600 Nitro using a totally new case, not only of larger diameter but also a full 1/2-inch longer. This bullet is a true 0.700-inch diameter and weighs 1,000 grains. The originators planned to sell cased cartridges to collectors. Although these rifles are very, very expensive, H&H has a continual

backorder amounting to millions of dollars worth of 700 NEs! (Several years after the first 700 NE was built, in response to an unending din of protest from potential customers, H&H – after coming to terms with the owner of the "official last" 600 NE H&H rifle – went back into the business of building 600 NE chambered double-barrel rifles.)

General Comments A 70-caliber bullet weighing 1,000 grains, with a muzzle velocity of 2,000 fps generates a muzzle energy of 8,900 foot-pounds of energy — this is certainly the most powerful sporting cartridge in the world. The Taylor Knockout Value is 200. It will, of course, be more than adequate for any game animal found anywhere on this planet. For those who insist on the biggest, this is it. The 700 H&H double-barrel rifles for this cartridge are very lively and handy, not at all cumbersome. These are fully usable, if costly, tools. However, keeping the weight of such a rifle down to a level that will allow the average hunter to use it properly guarantees that recoil will be quite heavy. A-Square offers bullets, cases and ammunition.

700 Nitro Express Factory Ballistics

Bullet (grains/type)	Powder	Grains	Velocity	Energy	Source/Comments
1000 SP/FMJ	FL		2000	8900	A-Square factory load

Gauge Rifles

WHAT I call the gauge-rifles are from 12- to 4-bores, though a few 2-bores have appeared. These are rifles of full weight and power, rifled through and through, and originally were blackpowder cartridge guns intended for use against large and dangerous game. Bore- or gauge-designated cartridges larger than 8-gauge are seldom of true implied bore size.

4-Bore

The bore designation indicates the number of bore-size lead balls to the pound, hence the 4-bore would nominally accept a round ball that weighed 1/4-pound, or 1750 grains. In actuality, the brass-cased 4-bore was loaded with a round ball of about 1250 grains, or with a blunt or conical bullet that weighed about 1880 grains. The usual propellant charge was 12 to 14 drams (325 to 380 grains) of blackpowder. Muzzle velocity was from 1300 to 1500 fps. Some 4-bore cartridges were loaded with up to 70 grains of Cordite.

The 4-bore saw some use in Africa before the turn of the century, and in India for tiger shooting as recently as 1920. Typical 4-bore rifles weigh from 20 to 25 pounds. There is still quite a bit of interest in these, and at least one outfit is making new double-barrel and single-shot 4-bore rifles today. Variances in cases length were from about 3-1/2 inches up to the 4 1/4-inch version pictured here.

8-Bore

The 8-bore was more popular than the 4 because rifles for it could be built lighter. Typical 8-bores weigh about 15 to 16 pounds, hence were much handier and easier to use. Performance was not far behind that of the 4-bore, either. Typical loads are a 1250-grain conical bullet at about 1500 fps, or a spherical ball of 860 grains at 1650 fps. Case length is from 3 to 3-1/2 inches. Powder charge was about 10 to 12 drams (270 to 325 grains) of blackpowder.

A Paradox-type 8-bore cartridge with lighter loadings was also common. The Paradox was a Holland & Holland invention, which featured rifling in the choke area of its otherwise smooth barrels. These were also sometimes known as ball and shot guns, though some makers used that name for smoothbores that had no rifling in the chokes. Numerous makers turned out variations on this theme, and gave their creations highly individual names. Eight-bore Paradoxes were a bit lighter than fully rifled guns and were thus handier still. The 8-bore Paradox was more of a big game gun, while the 10- and 12-bore Paradoxes were more like heavily-loaded shotguns, and

used only occasionally for big game.

10-Bore

Ten-bore rifles were also taken against dangerous game, and were, like the bigger ones, also loaded with detonating shells and/or lead-covered steel bullets for maximum penetration and performance. Here again the Paradoxes were popular and efficient, and a common load used a 700-grain ball in front of a 5 dram charge for 1300 fps. The full rifle load would give more than 1600 fps to the same round ball or about 1500 fps to a somewhat heavier conical ball.

12-Bore

The 12-bore rifle saw lots of service against big game, but this size cartridge was probably most commonly seen as a Paradox load, either round ball or conical ball. In this guise, it was quite popular. The 12-bore Paradox worked well on medium-size game and was useful with shot loads for filling the pot with birds and small game. Most 12-bore Paradox-types weighed from 7 to 8 pounds. In a fully rifled arm, the weight would be more than 10 pounds and the load significantly more powerful. Case length for fully rifled arms varies from 1 8/10 inches up to 2 3/4 inches. The 1 8/10-inch cartridge is pictured below with a fully rifled, 10 1/4-pound double-barrel 12-bore from this writer's collection, made by James Erskine in approximately 1865-1870. The cartridge fires a 540-grain, hardened-lead round ball.

Gauge rifles were either single-shot or double-barrel. These evolved from muzzle-loading firearms of similar bore size, and while the rapid-fire capability of these early breech-loaders must have been a boon to the early explorers and hunters, it was no panacea.

The usual lead bullet's performance was such that it wasn't a good idea to take head shots on elephant. The skull of that beast consists of honeycombed cellular bone, and a lead ball could not be counted on to penetrate that, much less stay on course and find the brain. Shots to the head that missed the brain had little or no immediate effect on the animal, so the usual and much surer target was the body. A 4-bore ball through the heart would kill the elephant, but apparently not very quickly, as may be determined from the writings of many early African hunters.

The gauge-guns have a fascination matched by few other British or other sporting firearms. The matching cartridges are interesting and greatly varied, well worthy of study, collecting or, if we are lucky enough to find a suitable rifle, shooting.

The 8-bore was probably the best of the dangerous-game gauge rifles. Its conical bullet (above) weighs 1,250 grains. This 12-bore double-barrel rifle was made by Erskine for the 18/10-inch cartridge. The bar-action locks are non-rebounding, and the firing pins are sprung. This rifle features steel barrels with Henry rifling, and shoots extremely well. Circa 1865.

BRITISH SPORTING RIFLE CARTRIDGES
Current & Obsolete – Blackpowder & Smokeless
Dimensional Data

Cartridge	Case	Bullet Dia.	Neck Dia.	Shoulder Dia.	Base Dia.	Rim Dia.	Rim Thick.	Case Length	Ctge. Length	Berdan Primer Size/Kynoch #
297/230 Morris Extra Long	A	.223	.240	.274	.296	.248		1.125	1.45	
297/230 Morris Short	A	.225	.240	.274	.294	.347		0.58	0.89	.177/69
297/230 Morris Long	A	.225	.240	.274	.295	.345		0.80	1.1	.177/69
244 Magnum (H&H)	**E**	**.244**	**.263**	**.445**	**.508**	**.532**		**2.78**	**3.58**	**.217/60**
240 Magnum Flanged	A	.245	.274	.402	.448	.513		2.50	3.25	.217/81
240 Magnum Rimless (240 Apex)	E	.245	.274	.403	.450	467	.035	2.49	3.21	.217/81
297/250 Rook	A	.250	.267	.294	.295	.343		0.82	1.1	.177/69
242 Rimless	C	.253	.281	.405	.465	.465		2.38	3.20	.217/59
246 Purdey	A	.253	.283	.401	.474	.544		2.32	3.03	
255 Rook	**A**	**.255**	**.274**	**.328**	**.344**	**.401**		**1.17**	**1.43**	**.162**
256 Gibbs Magnum	E	.265	.298	.427	.473	.476		2.17	3.04	
26 Rimless BSA	C	.267	.306	.445	.513	.530		2.39	3.24	.217/59
275 Rigby (7x57)	**C**	**.284**	**.324**	**.428**	**.474**	**.475**		**2.24**	**3.07**	**.217**
275 Belted Magnum	E	.284	.325	.454	.513	.532		2.50	3.42	.217/81
275 Flanged Magnum 275 No. 2 Magnum	A	.284	.318	.450	.510	.582		2.50	3.26	217
(7mm Rigby Magnum)	A	.284	.315	.406	.456	.524		2.49	3.24	.243/34
280 Flanged (280 Lancaster)	A	.287	.316	.423	.535	.607		2.60	3.62	.217/60
280 Ross	G	.287	.317	.404	.534	.556		2.59	3.50	.217/59
280 Jeffery (33/280 Jeffery)	C	.288	.317	.504	.542	.538		2.50	3.45	.217/59
300 (295) Rook	**B**	**.300**	**.317**	**–**	**.319**	**.369**		**1.17**	**1.42**	**.177/69**
300 Sherwood	B	.300	.318	–	.320	.370		1.54	2.02	.177/69
300 Belted Magnum (300 H&H)	E	.308	.338	.447	.513	.530		2.85	3.60	.217/60
30 Flanged Magnum (30 Super)	A	.308	.338	.450	.517	.572		2.93	3.69	
375/303 Westley Richards	A	.311	.343	.390	.457	.505		2.50	3.36	
303 British	A	.312	.340	.401	.460	.540		2.21	3.09	
303 Magnum	C	.312	.345	.462	.530	.557		2.35	3.25	
310 Cadet	B	.324	.320	–	.353	.405	.035	1.12	1.72	.177/69
318 Rimless Nitro Express	C	.330	.358	.445	.465	.465		2.39	3.40	.217/81
333 Jeffery Rimless	**C**	**.333**	**.359**	**.496**	**.540**	**.538**		**2.48**	**3.48**	**.217/59**
333 Jeffery Flanged	A	.333	.356	.484	.544	.625		2.50	3.49	.317
33 BSA (33 Belted)	E	.338	.369	.453	.534	.534		2.40	3.10	.217/59
400/350 Rigby	**A**	**.358**	**.380**	**.415**	**.470**	**.520**		**2.75**	**3.60**	**.241/34**
350 Rigby Magnum	C	.358	.380	.443	.519	.525		2.75	3.60	.241/34
350 No. 2 Rigby	A	.358	.380	.415	.470	.520	.050	2.75	3.60	.241/34
400/360 Nitro Express (2Ω-inch)	A	.358	.375	.437	.470	.590		2.75	3.59	.241
360 No. 5 Rook	B	.362	.375	–	.380	.432		1.05	1.45	
360 Express (2 1/4-inch)	B	.365	.384	–	.430	.480	.040	2.25	3.00	.241/34
360 Nitro (2 1/4-inch)	B	.365	.384	–	.430	.480	.040	2.25	2.80	.241/34
360 No. 2 Nitro-Express	A	.367	.393	.517	.539	.631	.045	3.00	3.85	.254/40
375 Flanged Nitro (2 1/2-inch)	B	.375	.397	–	.456	.523		2.50	3.10	.217/34
400/375 Belted Nitro Express (H&H)	E	.375	.397	.435	.470	.466		2.50	3.00	.217
375 Rimless NE (9.5x57mm)	C	.375	.400	.460	.471	.473	0.40	2.25	2.94	.217
369 Purdey	A	.375	.398	.475	.543	.616		2.69	3.60	.254/40
375 Flanged Magnum	A	.375	.404	.450	.515	.572		2.94	3.80	.217/40
375 Belted Magnum	E	.375	.404	.440	.464	.530		2.85	3.60	.217/60
380 Short	B	.375	.379	–	.380	.430		.600	1.11	–
380 Long (Rifle)	B	.375	.379	–	.380	.430		.965	1.33	.177/69
400 Purdey (3-inch)	**B**	**.405**	**.427**	**–**	**.469**	**.516**		**3.00**	**3.60**	**.241/34**
450/400 Nitro Express (3 1/4-inch)	A	.405	.432	.502	.544	.615	.040	3.25	3.85	.254/40
450/400 (2 3/8-inch)	A	.407	.427	.456	.545	.616	.035	2.38	2.95	–
400 Jeffery (450/400 3-inch)	A	.410	.434	.518	.545	.613		3.00	3.75	.254/40
416 Rigby	C	.416	.445	.539	.589	.589	.062	2.90	3.72	Bx
404 Jeffery (404 Rimless)	C	.422	.450	.520	.544	.537	.045	2.87	3.53	.217/81
425 Westley Richards	I	.435	.456	.540	.543	.467		2.64	3.30	

Cartridge	Case	Bullet Dia.	Neck Dia.	Shoulder Dia.	Base Dia.	Rim Dia.	Rim Thick.	Case Length	Ctge. Length	Berdan Primer Size/Kynoch #
500/450 No. 2 Musket	**A**	**.458**	**.486**	**.535**	**.576**	**.658**		**2.36**	**2.90**	
500/450 No. 1 Express	A	.458	.485	.530	.577	.660		2.75	3.38	.241/31A
450 Nitro Express (3 1/4-inch)	B	.458	.479		.545	.624	.040	3.25	4.11	.254/40
500/450 Nitro Express (3 1/4-inch)	A	.458	.479	.500	.570	.644		3.25	3.91	.254/40
500/450 Magnum Express	A	.458	.479	.500	.570	.644		3.25	3.91	.254/40
450 No. 2 Nitro Express (3 1/2-inch)	A	.458	.477	.518	.564	.650		3.50	4.42	.254/40
450 Rigby	B	.458	.475	.539	.589	.589		2.90	3.80	Bx
500/465 Nitro Express	A	.466	.488	.524	.573	.650		3.25	3.89	.254/40
470 Nitro Express	**A**	**.475**	**.500**	**.528**	**.572**	**.646**	**.035**	**3.25**	**4.00**	**.254/40**
476 Nitro Express (W-R)	A	.476	.508	.530	.570	.643		3.00	3.77	.254/40
475 Nitro Express (3 1/4-inch)	B	.483	.502		.545	.621		3.25	4.00	.254/40
475 No. 2 Nitro and Jeffery	A	.489	.510	.547	.576	.666		3.50	4.33	.254/40
505 Gibbs	**C**	**.505**	**.530**	**.588**	**.635**	**.635**		**3.15**	**3.85**	**.254/40**
577/500 No. 2 Express	A	.507	.538	.560	.641	.726	.055	2.83	3.40	.251/31A
577/500 Nitro Express (3 1/8-inch)	A	.508	.526	.585	.645	.717	.055	3.13	3.74	.251/31A
500 Express (3-inch)	B	.510	.535		.580	.660	.055	3.01	3.39	.251/31A
500 Express (3 1/4-inch)	B	.510	.535		.580	.660	.040	3.25	3.63	.251/31A
500 Nitro (3-inch)	B	.510	.535		.580	.660		3.00	3.80	.251/31A
500 Jeffery	I	.510	.535	.615	.620	.575		2.75	3.47	.254/40
577 Blackpowder Express (3 1/4-inch)	**B**	**.584**	**.608**		**.660**	**.748**	**.052**	**3.25**		**.254/40**
577 Nitro Express (3-inch)	B	.584	.608		.660	.748	.052	3.00	3.70	.254/40
600 Nitro Express	B	.620	.648		.697	.805		3.00	3.68	.254/40
700 Nitro Express	B	.700	.728		.780	.890		3.50	4.20	Bx

Case Type: A = Rimmed, bottleneck. B = Rimmed, straight. C = Rimless, bottleneck. D = Rimless, straight. E = Belted, bottleneck. F = Belted, straight. G = Semi-rimmed, bottleneck. H = Semi-rimmed, straight. I = Rebated, bottleneck. J = Rebated, straight. K = Rebated, belted bottleneck. L = Rebated, belted straight.

Primer Type: B = Berdan. Bx = Boxer. RF = Rimfire.

Other codes: Unless otherwise noted, all dimensions in inches. Dimensions shown in some instances do not exactly coincide with dimensions found in *The Book of Rifles* (W.H.B. Smith, Harrisburg, Pa., 1960). Differences amount to only a few thousandths of an inch, doubtless attributable to specimen variations. Parentheses indicate maximum cartridge specifications.

Exterior Ballistic Data for British Centerfire Rifle Cartridges

Cartridge	Bullet weight (grs.)	Powder weight (grs.)	Velocity (ft./sec.) Muzzle	100 yd.	200 yd.	Energy (ft./lb.) Muzzle	100 yd.	200 yd.	Drop (in.)[1] 100 yd.	200 yd.
297/230 Morris Short2	37L	5 B	875	720		63	43		15.0	
297/230 Morris Long2	37L	55 BP	1200	920	760	120	70	48	15.0	71.0
240 Magnum Flanged	100 CP	38 1/2 NC	2800	2570	2355	1740	1470	1230	2.3	10.0
240 Magnum Rimless	100 CP	40 1/2 NC	2900	2665	2445	1870	1580	1330	2.2	9.2
242 Rimless Nitro Exp.	100 CP	42 NC	3000	2740	2490	1970	1635	1355	2.0	8.6
244 H&H Magnum (Belted)	100 CP	74 NC	3500	3230	2970	2725	2320	1980	1.6	5.1
246 Purdey	100	40								
297/250 Rook	56L	8 BP	1150	940	805	165	110	80	15.5	70.0
255 Jeffery Rook	65	9 BP								
256 (6.5mm) Mannlicher	160 SN	36 NC	2350	2045	1765	1960	1490	1110	3.4	15.5
256 Gibbs Magnum	145	35C	2300	2000	1725	1880	1420	1060	3.6	16.0
275 Rigby (7x57)	173 SN	40C	2300	2015	1765	2040	1560	1200	3.9	16.0
275 No. 2 Magnum	140 CP	43 NC	2900	2705	2515	2620	2280	1970	2.2	9.0
275 H&H Magnum (Belted)	160 CP	52 NC	2700	2505	2320	2600	2230	1920	2.5	10.5
275 H&H Magnum Flanged	160 CP	49 NC	2650	2450		2184	1867			
280 Flanged Magnum Nitro Exp.	160 HP	52 NC	2600	2300	2020	2400	1880	1450	2.8	12.0
280 Ross Rimless Nitro	160 HP	54 NC	2700	2395	2110	2600	2040	1580	2.6	11.5
280 Jeffery (33/280)	140 CP	57 NC	3000	2870	2735	2800	2555	2390	2.1	10.0
300 (295) Rook	80L	4 1/2 CH	1100	915	785	215	150	110	16.5	75.0
300 Sherwood	140L	8 1/2 CH	1400	1195	1060	610	445	350	9.9	44.0
300 H&H Magnum	180 SN	55 C	2750	2430	2130	3020	2360	1815	2.8	12.5
30 Super Flanged H&H	180 SN	50 C	2575	2309		2653	2131			
30 Purdey Flanged Nitro	150 SN	42 NC	2700	2385	2090	2430	1900	1460	2.6	11.5
303 British (Mark 6)	215S	31 C	2050	1855	1670	2010	1650	1330	4.4	19.0
303 British (Mark 7)	174S	37 C	2450	2250	2055	2320	1960	1640	3.0	13.0
303 British	150 CP	38 C	2700	2465	2240	2440	2030	1680	2.5	11.0
375/303 W-R (303 Axite)	225	41 AX								
303 Magnum	175 SN	53 NC								
310 Cadet	120L	6 CH	1200	1010	890	385	270	210	14.0	62.0
318 Westley Richards	250 SN	52 NC	2400	2040	1715	3200	2320	1640	3.3	15.0
333 Jeffery	300 SN	65 NC	2200	1950	1720	3230	2540	1980	3.9	17.0
33 BSA	165	60 NC								
400/350 Rigby	310 SN	43 NC	2150	1900		3180	2480		4.7	20.0
350 Rigby Magnum Rimless	225 SN	65 NC	2625	2307		3440	2657			
350 No. 2 Rigby Flanged	225 SN	55 NC	2600			3400				
360 No. 5 Rook	134	15 BP								
360 Nitro Exp. 2 1/4	300 SN	30 C	1650	1490	1355	1820	1480	1210	6.9	29.0
360 2 1/4-inch Nitro for Black	190 CT	22 C	1650	1285	1070	1150	700	485	7.6	36.0
400/360 Purdey Flanged	300 SN	40 C	1950	1776		2537	2102			
400/360 Westley Richards	314 SN	41 C	1900	1724		2520	2072			
360 No. 2 Nitro Exp.	320 SN	55 C	2200	1999		3442	2845			
369 Purdey Nitro Exp.	270 SN	65 NC	2500	2135	1800	3760	2740	1950	3.1	14.0
375 Flanged Nitro Exp.	270 SN	40 C	2000	1735	1405	2400	1810	1190	4.9	22.0
375 Rimless Nitro (9.5x57mm MS)	270 SN	43 C	2100	1870		2640	2100			
400/375 Belted	270	43 C								
375 Flanged Magnum Nitro	235 CP	61 C	2800	2495	2215	4100	3260	2560	2.4	10.5
375 Flanged Magnum Nitro	270 SN	59 C	2600	2280	1980	4060	3120	2360	2.8	12.5
375 Flanged Magnum Nitro	300 SN	56 C	2400	2105	1825	3850	2960	2220	3.3	14.5
375 Belted H&H Magnum	270 SN	61 C	2850	2325	2020	4220	3250	2450	2.9	12.0
375 Belted H&H Magnum	300 SN	60 C	2500	2200	1915	4170	3230	2450	3.0	13.5
380 Long Rifle	124	4 RN								

Cartridge	Bullet weight (grs.)	Powder weight (grs.)	Velocity (ft./sec.) Muzzle 100 yd. 200 yd.			Energy (ft./lb.) Muzzle 100 yd. 200 yd.			Drop (in.)[1] 100 yd. 200 yd.	
400 Purdey 3-inch	230	47 C								
450/400 (2-inch) Nitro Express	400	43 C								
450/400 3-inch (400 Jeffery) Nitro Exp.	400 SN	60 C	2100	1845	1610	3920	3030	2310	4.3	19.0
450/400 3 1/4-inch Nitro Exp.	400 SN	60 C	2150	1890	1650	4110	3180	2420	4.1	18.0
450/400 (3 1/4-inch) BPE	270	110 BP								
404 Jeffery	400 SN	60 C	2125	1885	1670	4020	3160	2480	4.2	18.0
416 Rigby	410 SN	69 C	2371	2110		5100				
425 Westley Richards	410 SN	65 C	2350			5010				
500/450 No. 1 Musket	450	70 BP								
500/450 No. 2 Musket	540	90 BP								
450 3 1/4-inch BPE	365L	120 BP	1700	1510		2240	1570			
450 3 1/4-inch Nitro for Black Powder	365 CT	52 C	2100	1809		3578	2655			
450 3 1/4-inch Nitro Exp.	480 SN	70 C	2150	1900	1665	4930	3860	2960	4.1	18.0
500/450 (3 1/4-inch) BPE	365	140 BP								
500/450 (3 1/4-inch) Nitro for BP	365	60C								
500/450 (3 1/4-inch) Nitro Exp.	480 SN	75 C	2175	1987		5050	4220			
450 Rigby	480									
450 No. 2 Nitro Exp.	480 SN	80 C	2175	1904		5050	3900			
577/450 Martini-Henry	480L	85 BP		1350	1210	1110	1950	1560	1320	10.0
577/450 Martini-Henry Nitro for Black	480L	48 C	1350	1210	1110	1950	1560	1320	10.0	44.0
500/465 H&H Nitro Exp.	480 SN	75 C	2150	1830	1620	4930	3580	2800	4.1	18.5
470 Nitro Exp.	500 SN	75 C	2150	1890	1650	5140	3980	3030	4.1	18.0
475 3 1/4 Nitro Exp.	480 SN	75 C	2175	2000	1830	5040	4260	3580	4.2	18.0
475 No. 2 Nitro Exp.	480 SN	85 C	2200	1925	1680	5170	3960	3020	3.9	17.0
475 No. 2 Jeffery	500 SN	85 C	2150	1880	1635	5140	3930	2970	4.1	18.0
476 Nitro Exp.	520 SN	75 C	2100	1925	1760	5085	4295	3585	4.6	20.0
500 Blackpowder Exp.	440 CT	142 BP	1925	1585		2800	1900			
500 Nitro for Black Powder Express	440 CT	55 C	1900	1570	1290	3530	2410	1630	5.5	25.0
500 Nitro Exp.	570 SN	80 C	2150	1890	1650	5850	4530	3450	4.1	18.0
577/500 No. 2 BPE	380	130 BP								
577/500 (3 1/8-inch) Nitro Express	570									
505 Gibbs	525 SN	92 C	2300			6180				
500 Jeffery	535 SN	95 C	2400			6800				
577 Snider	480L	70 BP	1250	1055	940	1670	1190	940	13.0	57.0
577 (3-inch) BPE	570	167 BP								
577 (3-inch) Nitro for Black	570	75 C								
577 3-inch Nitro Exp.	750 SN	100 C	2050	1795	1570	7010	5380	4110	4.5	20.0
600 Nitro Exp.	900S	110 C	1950	1650	1390	7600	5450	3870	5.1	23.0
700 Nitro Exp.	1000S	180	2000	1700	1430	8900	6419	4542	5.5	24.0

ABBREVIATIONS

AX = Axite
BP or Blackpowder = Blackpowder
C = Cordite
CN = Cadet Neonite
CP = Copper Point
CT = Copper Tube

L = Lead
NC = Nitro-Cellulose
RN = Revolver Neonite
S = Solid (Jacketed)
SN = Softnose

NOTE: [1]Drop is computed from horizontal line of departure for the bullet.

The 8-bore was probably the best of the dangerous-game gauge rifles. Its conical bullet (above) weighs 1,250 grains. This 12-bore double-barrel rifle was made by Erskine for the 18/10-inch cartridge. The bar-action locks are non-rebounding, and the firing pins are sprung. This rifle features steel barrels with Henry rifling, and shoots extremely well. Circa 1865.

Chapter 9

European Sporting Rifle Cartridges

(Current & Obsolete—Blackpowder & Smokeless)

EUROPEAN SPORTING cartridges are, at least nowadays, better known than those of British origin. European arms makers are well represented by a world-wide distributing system and they advertise what they make. They also manufacture products for a mass market at a price that places those within economic reach of hunters who could not possibly afford a fine British double-barrel gun.

The Mauser and Mannlicher turn-bolt systems have been the backbone of European sporting rifle manufacture since the 1890s, long before American companies adopted the type. Because the designers intended these cartridges for the same type of rifle, there is great similarity between many modern European and American cartridge designs. We have borrowed freely from each other and it is often difficult to tell who originated what. Continental gunmakers have also produced very fine handcrafted double-barrel rifles and combination guns as good as anything turned out by the British. Unfortunately, there has always been a certain prejudice against double-barrel rifles not made in Britain. This resulted because some cheap rifles of this type were turned out on the continent that simply did not measure up to the required high standards. The Austrians and Germans, on the other hand, developed the drilling or combination gun — the over/under rifle-shotgun — to a greater extent than anyone else did. These multi-purpose firearms feature various combinations of rifled tubes and shot barrels. When it comes to an all-around gun, nothing is superior to a good combination gun.

Gun makers have produced sporting arms all over Europe, including Russia. Today, guns from the latter country are seeing more use outside the Soviet bloc. For decades, the Japanese have made superb firearms. Many of these are now being sold by their own marketing arms here in the United States. Some of our old-line companies with a tradition as American as Yankee Doodle have been, for years, selling guns under their own names that are actually made in Europe or Japan.

European sporting ammunition originates mostly in Italy, Austria, Germany, Finland, Sweden, and Britain. The French chemist Vieille developed the first commercially successful smokeless powder in 1885. The French adapted this to the 8mm Lebel military cartridge. Commercial manufacture of ammunition started in Germany during 1856 when Heinrich Utendoerffer founded a plant to make percussion caps and later primers. By 1871, he was turning out Berdan-primed centerfire cartridge cases for the Bavarian Werder rifle. This enterprise later grew into the great Rheinisch-Westfällishe-Sprengstoff-AG, or RWS, as we know it today. Early cartridges or cases made by the firm have "H. Utendoerffer" stamped into the head, sometimes with raised letters. RWS developed the non-mercuric, non-corrosive primer in the 1920s and began to market this significantly improved product under the trade name "Sinoxid." Deutsche Waffen und Munitionsfabriken (DWM) is another important German firm that is, unfortunately, no longer in the commercial ammunition business. Hirtenberger-Patronenfabrik, located near Vienna, Austria, was one of the world's largest munitions makers until destroyed during World War II. Organized in 1860 by the Mandl brothers, both fire and acts of war have razed it several times. The company has started production again and has once more become an important source of sporting ammunition. Norma Precision (formerly Norma Projektilfabrik) manufactures sporting ammunition and components in Sweden. Norma has exported products to the United States since shortly after the end of World War II. Norma makes the Weatherby line of cases (and ammunition). It also offers cases for many of the more popular American and European cartridges. The firm of G. Roth manufactured a large variety of sporting ammunition, but did not survive World War II. Lapua of Finland exports to the United States, as does Fiocchi of Italy and Eley of Britain.

European cartridges, with few exceptions, have metric designations, usually expressed in millimeters. By international agreement, 1 millimeter equals 0.03937-inch, or 1 inch equals 2.54 centimeters (which equals 25.4 millimeters). Metric cartridge designation is quite simple, once you understand it. The first figure represents bore diameter; the second figure represents case length. An R indicates a rimmed case; its absence a rimless one. The designer or manufacturer can tack a name on the end of the numeric designation.

Some confusion surrounds two different 8mm cartridges. The original 8mm German military cartridge, adopted in 1888, used a 0.318-inch diameter bullet designed to work in a 7.92mm bore. So did 8mm sporting rounds of the same period. However, in 1905, the German army altered the cartridge and bore design to use a 0.323-inch diameter bullet — bore diameter was unchanged but the grooves were deepened in order to improve accurate barrel life. Shortly thereafter, 8mm sporting cartridges also reflected this change. The old diameter is indicated by a "J" (actually the old German letter form for "I," and standing for "*Infanterie*") and the new one by an S. For example, the 8x57mmJ has a 0.318-inch bullet, and the 8x57mmS (or 8x57mmJS) the 0.323-inch bullet. An R in the designation simply indicates a rimmed shell. This will not hurt anything but accuracy to use the 0.318-inch bullet in a 0.323-inch bore, but it might blow up the gun to do the opposite. The proper designation is always on the box and it is usually stamped on the cartridge head. Read the label! Modern rifles are practically all chambered for the "S" (0.323-inch) bullet. Europeans used single-shot and combination guns that extract better with a rimmed case, so they have a rimmed version of almost all popular rimless cartridges. Ballistics and case dimensions are usually — but not always — identical.

European arms and ammunition firms seized upon many American and British cartridges over the years, but they never took to the British belted-type case as we did. The 22 WCF (5.6x35Rmm), 22 Savage HP (5.6x52Rmm), 25-35 (6.5x52Rmm) and 30-06 (7.62x63) are popular in Europe and listed in late catalogs. The 30-30 WCF is also popular, but they do not currently load it. Cartridges of 6mm and 7mm were highly developed in Europe long before these cartridges became popular here. The 8mm is to Europeans what the 30 caliber is to Americans, and consequently they have a large variety of cartridges in this caliber, some of advanced design. The 8x68mmS, for example, is a magnum round more powerful than the 300 Weatherby or the 300 Winchester Magnum.

German Mauser system bolt-action rifles once competed with the more expensive British rifles for African hunting. They developed some unusually potent cartridges for dangerous game, but currently use American or British magnum cartridges. They have revived few of their African cartridges since the war.

European centerfire ammunition of modern production by RWS, Norma, Hirtenberger, IMI, Fiocchi, Lapua, and Sako use Boxer primers. RWS still offers nine different types of Berdan primers as well as Boxer types to satisfy the needs of handloaders. Ammunition for obsolete cartridge rifles is a problem, but in some instances, handloaders can easily reform available metric or American cases to work satisfactorily. (Buffalo Arms — 208-263-6953 — offers commercially reformed cases that accommodate loading of practically any cartridge you might encounter; these cases, along with a set of custom dies from RCBS will get you shooting in no time.)

European hunting is quite different from that found in the United States. Differences include both game and methods. They have no large, predatory dangerous game, although the wild boar can be a rough customer under certain conditions. Conservation is highly developed and the shooting of game very selective. Weeding out old or undesirable animals is as important as collecting a trophy. In most countries, one must pass a rigid course in gun handling and hunting knowledge before being eligible for a permit or license. The German test is especially difficult. Also in Europe, there is no wide-open hunting. One must get permission or make advance arrangements and a guide of some sort is usually required. Hunters stalk several varieties of deer; these range in size from the 40-pound class roebuck to the hirsch or red stag, which is almost as large as an American elk. The chamois, a prime trophy, is present in the higher mountainous areas. Hunters also pursue small game, mostly hare, and they have good bird shooting opportunities. They do not indulge in formal varmint hunting, although I understand pest shooting has developed some following. Along open fields, long shots are not unusual, but great velocity and flat trajectory are not as important as in some areas of western North America. Great knockdown and killing power is not required for European hunting, and their cartridges reflect this. The more popular hunting cartridges develop from around 2,000 foot-pounds of energy to not much over 2500 foot-pounds of energy, while the trend in the United States is toward energy in excess of 3,000 foot pounds of energy. The Germans once did a great deal of social target shooting, and many older cartridges originated for this. The Schuetzen, or free rifle, arrived here with German immigrants and was highly popular off and on from about 1850 to 1920 — its heyday the 1890-1910 period. Many of our cartridges and bolt-action rifles reflect European ideas and design.

Although more information is available on European cartridges than British, the same problem exists in attempting to establish the exact dates of introduction. I sent letters to the principal European manufacturers requesting such information, but in many instances, records no longer existed. Old catalogs and books were of considerable assistance. If nothing else, these provided sufficient information to establish the period of introduction within a few years. We know that most blackpowder cartridges originated in the 1870s and 1880s, and early smokeless numbers after 1885. Sometimes a cartridge was designed for a specific rifle. The rifle's introduction date then provides a good estimate of cartridge origination date. Individual gunmakers or small companies operated during fixed dates and their designs can often be approximately dated on that basis. Again, if the reader has specific information of this nature and finds what he believes to be an error in dating, let us know. This way, corrections or new data can be included at a future time. — F.C.B.

5.6x33mm Rook & Tesching
5.6x33Rmm Rook & Tesching

Historical Notes Except for rim design (rimmed and rimless), these two cartridges are identical. These cartridges date back to around 1900 or earlier and were originally loaded with blackpowder. Both have been obsolete since about 1936. Like the British, the Germans had a series of rook (a form of crow), or parlor cartridges, for short-range target practice or small-game shooting. These were listed in catalogs as for Tesching Gewehre, i.e., small-game or rook rifles. Although popular in Europe, these cartridges were not used to any extent elsewhere.

General Comments When Winchester introduced the 22 WCF in 1885, it not only replaced most other 22 centerfires in the United States, but also in Europe. The 5.6x33mm is of similar performance and was probably made obsolete by the 22 WCF. Both are strictly small game or target cartridges. The Winchester round is still loaded in Europe, where it is known as the 5.6x35Rmm Vierling. The 5.6x33mm was also listed as the 5.7x33mm. These are said to be for single-shot rifles, but must have also been used in repeating rifles. The rimless 5.6x33mm bears some resemblance to certain wildcat 22 rounds based on necking-down the 30 U.S. carbine.

5.6x33mm Rook, 5.6x33Rmm Rook Loading Data and Factory Ballistics

Bullet (grains/type)	Powder	Grains	Velocity	Energy	Source/Comments
60 Lead	2400	5.0	1600	343 *	Lyman #225462GC
65 Lead	FL		1500	327 *	Factory load

* Approximate ballistics only.

5.6x35Rmm Vierling
22 Winchester Centerfire

Historical Notes This is the European, or metric designation, for the 22 Winchester Centerfire introduced in 1885 and picked up by European gunmakers a year or so later. It was loaded to much higher velocity there than in the United States, thus providing the inspiration for the 22 Hornet, which is based on the same case. Single-shot, combination and repeating rifles of European manufacture have been chambered for the 5.6x35Rmm Vierling.

General Comments The 5.6x35Rmm (22 WCF) is a popular small game and target round in Europe. Although originally a blackpowder number, the Germans adapted it to smokeless powder and stepped up the velocity long before wildcatters created the 22 Hornet in the United States. As loaded in Europe, it is a good 100- to 150-yard, small-game or target cartridge. The 5.6x35Rmm Vierling can easily be formed from 22 Hornet cases.

5.6x35Rmm Vierling (22 Winchester Centerfire) Loading Data and Factory Ballistics

Bullet (grains/type)	Powder	Grains	Velocity	Energy	Source/Comments
48 SP	2400	8.0	2120	480	Lyman #225414
39 SP	FL		1940	325	RWS factory load
39 SP	FL		2630	600	RWS factory load
46 SP	FL		2030	418	RWS factory load

5.6x36Rmm/22 Hornet   See Chapter 2

5.6x50mm Magnum
5.6x50Rmm Magnum

Historical Notes Most authorities agree that the 5.6x50mm Magnum was developed by DWM in cooperation with Friedrick W. Heym, a noted German gun maker, and was introduced in 1968 or 1969. It is an offshoot of the 5.6x47Rmm, which is basically a rimmed version of the 222 Remington Magnum, dating back to about 1967. However, the 5.6x50mm case is 0.118-inch longer than the 222 Remington Magnum and has greater powder capacity, resulting in a higher muzzle velocity. The rimmed version was intended for use in single-shot, combination guns and drillings, with the rimless cartridge for bolt-action rifles. Neither is very well known or used to any extent in the United States.

General Comments In Germany, the 5.6x50mm was used for deer hunting and was loaded with a bullet designed for that purpose. In the United States, it would be primarily a varmint cartridge. Where more power than the 222 or 223 Remington is desired, most Americans would opt for the 22-250 Remington or the 220 Swift because both rifles and ammunition are available here on an over-the-counter basis. Loading dies for the 5.6x50mm are available from RCBS, Forster/Bonanza, and Lyman. RWS and Hirtenberger have recently offered 5.6x50mm Magnum ammunition.

5.6x50mm Magnum, 5.6x50Rmm Magnum Loading Data and Factory Ballistics

Bullet (grains/type)	Powder	Grains	Velocity	Energy	Source/Comments
50 SP	IMR 3031	28.5	3400	1284	Hornady
50 SP	W748	29.5	3500	1360	Hornady
55 SP	IMR 4064	27.5	3300	1330	Hornady
55 SP	W748	28.5	3300	1330	Hornady
60 SP	IMR 4064	27.0	3200	1360	Hornady
50 SP	FL		3590	1430	Factory load – 5.6x50mm
50 SP	FL		3510	1365	Factory load – 5.6x50mm
55 SP	FL		3280	1310	Factory load – 5.6x50Rmm

5.6x57mm RWS
5.6x57Rmm RWS

Historical Notes The 5.6x57mm was introduced by RWS about 1964 as a cartridge for hunting deer and chamois. Germany has a law that requires a minimum remaining energy level at 200 meters in order for a cartridge to be legal for taking these animals. The 5.6x57mm was designed with this in mind. It is also loaded with a properly-designed bullet for these larger animals. There is also a rimmed version.

General Comments The 5.6x57mm is in about the same class as the 220 Swift and as loaded in Europe would probably do very well for American deer or antelope. However, it would be classed as a varmint cartridge here. It is a good cartridge, but the difficulty of finding ammunition would rule out any great popularity in this country. Twist used in rifles of this chambering is 10 inches as opposed to what used to be conventional for 22-caliber centerfires in the United States: 12 to 14 inches (newer 22-centerfires often have 10-inch twists; rifles designed for long-range target shooting often have an 8-inch twist). The cartridge also has an unusually thick neck, which allows the use of 22 rimfire adapter units, but presents problems to the handloader. It is manufactured by RWS and by Hirtenberger. Factory ballistics of both versions are identical.

5.6x57mm, 5.6x57Rmm RWS Loading Data and Factory Ballistics

Bullet (grains/type)	Powder	Grains	Velocity	Energy	Source/Comments
50 SP	IMR 4320	40.0	3900	1689	Hornady
55 SP	W760	42.5	3800	1764	Hornady
55 SP	IMR 4350	41.0	3700	1672	Hornady
55 SP	IMR 4320	39.0	3790	1758	Hornady
60 SP	IMR 4320	38.5	3700	1824	Hornady
74 SP	RI-22	43.0	3400	1890	NA
55 SP	FL		3510	1505	Hirtenberger factory load
74 SP	FL		3410	1910	RWS factory load

5.6x61mm & 5.6x61Rmm Vom Hofe Super Express

Historical Notes These two cartridges were introduced in 1937 by E.A. Vom Hofe for his line of German-made Mauser-action express rifles. Some were exported to the United States between the wars. These chamberings were reintroduced by Stoeger Arms Corp. in 1962. The new rifles were based on the Swedish Husqvarna-Mauser action. Both the rimless and rimmed version were listed in late DWM catalogs. Dimensions and ballistics are identical; these cartridges differ only in the rim.

General Comments The 5.6x61mm Vom Hofe came out two years after the Winchester 220 Swift. It is one of the very few ultra-velocity 22 cartridges developed in Europe. Bullet diameter is identical to the 22 Savage Hi-Power, but the standard bullet is 10 percent heavier. The 22 Savage has remained popular in Europe and is still loaded there. Velocity is close to the 220 Swift, and with its 77-grain bullet, the 5.6 is much more effective on deer-size animals. By American standards, it would be considered a long-range varmint cartridge; in Europe, it is looked on as a proper cartridge for deer or boar. If the bullet is designed for the job, there is no reason why it would not be entirely effective for use in open country. The heavier bullet should also have superior wind-bucking ability at long range. The 5.6 bears some resemblance to the 228 Ackley Magnum, which is made from the necked-down, shortened 30-06 case. Although neither cartridge is now loaded in Europe, new empty cases are available from Old Western Scrounger/Gibbs Rifle Co. and from Huntington's Sportsman Supply. Bullets are available from both sources and from Hornady.

5.6x61mm & 5.6x61Rmm Vom Hofe Super Express Loading Data and Factory Ballistics

Bullet (grains/type)	Powder	Grains	Velocity	Energy	Source/Comments
70 SP	IMR 4895	37.0	2800	1215	RWS
77 SP	H870	61.0	3460	2050	RWS
87 SP	IMR 4350	52.0	3310	2110	RWS
77 SP	FL		3708	2350	RWS factory load (obsolete, very optimistic)
77 SP	FL		3480	2070	RWS factory load (obsolete)

5.6x52Rmm/22 Savage H-P   See Chapter 3

6x29.5Rmm Stahl

Historical Notes This is a small, 6mm, rimmed cartridge for single-shot and combination guns that dates back prior to 1900. It was originally a blackpowder number for guns made by B. Stahl of Suhl, Germany. It has been obsolete for a long time and is largely a collector's item.

General Comments This cartridge resembles the 25-20 WCF, but has a smaller-diameter lead bullet. It is entirely a small game, plinking or target round. Ammunition could probably be made using 25-20 cases, although the rim would have to be turned down to proper diameter. Factory ballistics are unknown, but should be similar to the 25-20-86 blackpowder load.

6x29.5Rmm Stahl Loading Data

Bullet (grains/type)	Powder	Grains	Velocity	Energy	Source/Comments
85 Lead	2400	7.0	1460	405	Lyman #245496

6x57mm Mauser
6.2x57mm RWS

Historical Notes This is a little-known German cartridge that dates back to around 1895. Physical measurements indicate it is the 6.5x57mm Mauser necked-down to 6mm. The 6.5mm, in turn, was based on the 1893 7x57mm Mauser necked-down. This is a very interesting situation because it means the 6x57mm is practically identical to the modern 244/6mm Remington. The two differ only by a minor variation in the shoulder angle. The 244 Remington is the 257 Roberts necked down to 6mm (244) with the shoulder angle increased from 20 degrees, 45 minutes to 26 degrees. The commercial 257 Roberts was originated by necking-down the original 7x57mm Mauser without other notable changes. By a long and devious process, different individuals and companies arrived at practically the same point, but at different

times. It just goes to prove that there is very little new under the sun. For all practical purposes, the 244 Remington originated, or existed, before the turn of the century — it is just that it was 60 years before Remington finally got around to offering the ammunition!

General Comments Records of ballistics or the specific rifle that the 6x57mm was used in are lacking. However, two bullet weights were available: a 120-grain softpoint and a 123-grain hollowpoint. Considering the time and powders available, muzzle velocity was probably near 2600 fps. This would be a fine deer, antelope or black bear cartridge. Standard ballistics are not known and no loading data duplicating the original loads has been developed.

244 Halger Magnum

Historical Notes Although this cartridge has an English cartridge designation, it is a 6mm magnum that originated in Germany. It was introduced in the 1920s by Halger Arms Co. of Hamburg*. The originators were named Halbe and Gerlich, and the Halger was formed by combining the first three letters of each name. The case is rimless (actually no more than the 6.5x57mm case) for use in Mauser bolt rifles, but there were some rimmed cases also made.

General Comments The velocity of the 244 Halger is impressive, at least on paper. However, the Halger line of cartridges turned out

to be somewhat overrated when tested here. Regardless, this would still be a highly effective cartridge even if velocity was a couple of hundred fps below claims. An 87-grain bullet would be mostly for varmint shooting, but heavier bullets could be handloaded for deer or larger animals. In size and general performance, it is very similar to the 6mm Remington. Bullet diameter is 0.243-inch, so any 6mm bullet would be suitable for handloading with proper data.

* *See Halger and His Rifles by Phil Sharpe (*GUN DIGEST*, 7th ed.)*

244 Halger Magnum Loading Data and Factory Ballistics

Bullet (grains/type)	Powder	Grains	Velocity	Energy	Source/Comments
90 SP	IMR 4350	47.0	3270	2142	NA
105 SP	IMR 4350	44.0	3020	2130	NA
87 SP	FL		3770	2745	DWM factory load (optimistic)

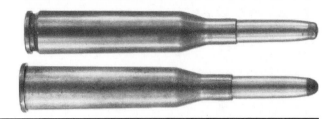

6x58mm Forster
6x58Rmm Forster

Historical Notes These two cartridges are identical except that one is rimless and the other rimmed. These cartridges were introduced about 1904 and have been obsolete for a good many years. Physical measurement indicates this round is based on the 6.5x58mm Mauser necked-down. It is listed for the Forster (forester) stalking rifle. It apparently was used in both bolt-action and single-shot or combination guns.

General Comments The rimless version of the 6x58mm closely resembles the 244 Remington, although these cartridges differ in shoulder angle and length of the neck. Available ballistics list a 127-grain bullet, but at one time a 119-grain and a 123-grain were also available. Performance is a little below the 243 Winchester, but with modern powders and a strong bolt-action one could undoubtedly equal the 243 or the 244 in any given bullet weight. This would be a good deer-class or possibly elk cartridge. Ammunition could be made by necking-down 6.5x58mm cases for the rimless version, but the rimmed type would be a problem.

6x58mm Forster 6x58Rmm Forster Loading Data and Factory Ballistics

Bullet (grains/type)	Powder	Grains	Velocity	Energy	Source/Comments
105 SP	IMR 4320	35.0	2750	1762	NA
108 Lead	IMR 3031	24.0	2200	1165	Lyman #245499GC
127 SP	FL		2788	2176	Factory load

6x62mm Freres
6x62Rmm Freres

Historical Notes This is a recent German development by Metallwerk Elisenhutte GmBH (MEN). While it appears to be based on the 30-06, case-head diameter is greater and 6x62mm should not be made from 30-06 cases — instead use 9.3x62mm cases, which was undoubtedly what was used as a basis for this new number and are available from Norma and others. The 6x62mm is the first new 6mm cartridge developed in Europe for many years. This number is almost unknown in the United States.

General Comments What we have here is a super or magnum 6mm suitable for all types of small and medium game at long range. The 6x62mm offers more performance than the 243 Winchester or 6mm Remington and requires a long action to accommodate its length. For U.S. hunting conditions, the 100-grain SP bullet load should be selected.

6x62mm Freres Factory Ballistics

Bullet (grains/type)	Powder	Grains	Velocity	Energy	Source/Comments
85 SP	FL		3460	2260	MEN factory load
100 SP	FL		3313	2442	MEN factory load

6.5x40Rmm

General Comments An obsolete cartridge for single-shot and combination guns, the 6.5x40Rmm case has considerable body taper. The Germans used a number of similarly shaped cartridges in varying calibers and lengths with a case of similar design. All were blackpowder cartridges, and while one or two made the transition to smokeless powder, most were discontinued after World War I or before 1930. Factory ballistic data is unavailable.

6.5x40Rmm Loading Data

Bullet (grains/type)	Powder	Grains	Velocity	Energy	Source/Comments
100 SP	2400	5.0	1200	324	Lyman #245498GC

6.5x27Rmm
6.5Rmm Ronezewski

General Comments A short, rimmed, bottlenecked cartridge that resembles the 25-20 WCF, the 6.5x27Rmm is fatter and shorter. Performance is practically the same as with the 86-grain loading of the 25-20. The 6.5x27Rmm was listed as the *kal. 6.5mm Einzelladerbüchse* which literally means caliber 6.5mm single-loading gun*. It was used mostly in low-priced, single-shot guns, but apparently also in some combination guns. It dates back to the

1890s or earlier and has been obsolete for a long time.

* Actually, what is meant is a cartridge that is "single-loaded" by the shooter, using powder charges contained in paper envelopes or closed tubes. RWS, for one, offered these for the 8.15x46Rmm cartridge (in the 1934 period), loaded with a variety of powders and in a choice of charge weights.

6.5x27Rmm Loading Data and Factory Ballistics

Bullet (grains/type)	Powder	Grains	Velocity	Energy	Source/Comments
86 SP	2400	7.0	1425	394	25-20 bullet
86 SP	IMR 4227	9.0	1500	434	25-20 bullet
82 SP	FL		1570	465	Factory load

6.5x52Rmm
(25-35 Winchester)

General Comments This is the metric version of the 25-35 WCF. This load was used in European single-shot and combination guns. It is not listed in the latest RWS catalogs, although it has been

popular in Germany for many years. European loading was practically identical to that used by U.S. ammunition companies.

6.5x52Rmm (25-35 Winchester) Factory Ballistics

Bullet (grains/type)	Powder	Grains	Velocity	Energy	Source/Comments
117 SP	FL		2230	1285	RWS factory load

6.5x48Rmm Sauer

General Comments An obsolete blackpowder cartridge developed for use in Sauer-made single-shot and combination guns. Because some samples have jacketed-softpoint bullets, it must have also

been furnished with smokeless powder. This is entirely a target or small-game number.

6.5x48Rmm Sauer Loading Data and Factory Ballistics

Bullet (grains/type)	Powder	Grains	Velocity	Energy	Source/Comments
120 lead	IMR 4198	12.0	1260	428	Lyman #266455GC
126 lead	Blackpowder		1155	378	Factory load

6.5x53Rmm Mannlicher 6.5x54mm MS   See Chapter 7

6.5x54Rmm MS   See Chapter 7

6.5x53.5mm Daudeteau

General Comments A collector's item today, this semi-rimmed type was introduced originally as a military cartridge for the French navy in 1895. It was used in the Daudeteau military bolt-action rifle, but commercial ammunition was also produced. Rifles and ammunition are quite rare, and you are not likely to have one to hunt with. If you do, it would probably be satisfactory for anything up to deer. According to Aivaro Casal, this cartridge was adopted by Uruguay in 1895 and used until 1898.

6.5x53.5mm Daudeteau Factory Ballistics

Bullet (grains/type)	Powder	Grains	Velocity	Energy	Source/Comments
150 SP	FL	40.0	2395	1922	Factory load

6.5x58Rmm Sauer

General Comments This is the longest of the rimmed, tapered 6.5mm cartridges developed for the Sauer-made single-shot and combination guns, as well as some Mauser repeating rifles. The others were the 6.5x40Rmm and the 6.5x48Rmm. All have the same type of tapered case. The 6.5x58Rmm, the most popular, is not listed in recent RWS catalogs. It is less powerful than the 25-35 WCF and by American standards would be underpowered for deer-sized animals.

6.5x58Rmm Sauer Loading Data and Factory Ballistics

Bullet (grains/type)	Powder	Grains	Velocity	Energy	Source/Comments
120 Lead	4198	15.0	1480	588	Lyman #266455GC
120 Lead	4895	21.0	1650	730	Lyman #266455GC
127 SP	3031	24.0	2100	1288	RWS bullet
127 SP	FL		2020	1140	Factory load

6.5x54mm Mauser

Historical Notes This is one of the shortest of the Mauser rimless necked cases and was introduced around 1900. It was chambered mostly in the K Model (Kurz) or short-action carbine. The deluxe type M sporter was also available in 6.5x54. This Mauser cartridge was gradually displaced by the more universally popular 6.5x54mm Mannlicher-Schoenauer. It was once listed in DWM catalogs.

General Comments In both appearance and performance, the 6.5x54mm Mauser is similar to the Mannlicher round. These cartridges are suitable for the same general size and type of big game. Mauser rifles in this chambering were imported into the United States until World War II. The case has a shorter body of slightly larger diameter than the 6.5 Mannlicher. Ammunition can be made by reforming and trimming 308 Winchester or 300 Savage cases. One can use the same loading data as for 6.5 Mannlicher with very similar results. However, when using home-swaged cases, reduce maximum loads by 3 or 4 grains to account for the reduced capacity, compared to original cases.

6.5x54mm Mauser Loading Data and Factory Ballistics

Bullet (grains/type)	Powder	Grains	Velocity	Energy	Source/Comments
120 SP	IMR 4895	36.0	2500	1665	
119 SP	FL		2362	1468	DWM factory load

6.5x55mm Swedish   See Chapter 2 and Chapter 7

6.5x57mm Mauser & RWS
6.5x57Rmm Mauser & RWS

Historical Notes The 6.5x57mm Mauser was developed about 1893-94 as a necked-down version of the 7x57mm Mauser. Listed as a hunting cartridge, it was never adopted as an official military cartridge by any power. However, it undoubtedly influenced the design of many of the 6.5mm military cartridges such as the 6.5x55mm Swedish and 6.5x68mm Portuguese. The three have similar dimensions and performance, but are not the same and cannot be interchanged. The rimmed version is used mostly in combination guns. Both are listed in late RWS and Hirtenberger catalogs.

General Comments As a commercial cartridge, the 6.5x57mm has not been widely used in the United States, although German-made rifles in this chambering have been imported. On the other hand, several virtually-identical wildcat numbers have enjoyed limited popularity. These are based on either necking-down the 7x57mm case or necking-up the 257 Roberts case. The two cases are similar except for shoulder angle and length. The funny thing is that several individuals claim to have "invented" the wildcat version, not knowing that Paul Mauser beat them to it by 100 years. There are a number of chamber configurations used in making up wildcat versions of the 6.5x57, and few, if any, will interchange. Immediately after World War II, a number of Japanese 6.5mm Arisaka military rifles were rechambered to handle various 6.5/257 or 6.5/7mm wildcat cartridges. However, this is a tricky thing that should be checked out by a gunsmith before actually doing any shooting. Better safe than sorry. It should be noted that reforming 6mm Remington, 257 Roberts or 7x57mm cases into 6.5x57mm cases by simply neck sizing the case will not necessarily accommodate proper headspace control. To solve this problem, neck the case up to at least 30 caliber before forming it in the 6.5x57mm full-length sizing die.

6.5x57mm Mauser & RWS, 6.5x57Rmm Mauser & RWS Loading Data and Factory Ballistics

Bullet (grains/type)	Powder	Grains	Velocity	Energy	Source/Comments
129 SP	IMR 4350	44.5	2800	2246	Hornady
140 SP	IMR 4350	43.5	2700	2267	Hornady
160 SP	IMR 4350	41.5	2500	2221	Hornady
93 FMJ	FL		3320	2255	RWS factory load
96 FMJ	FL		3290	2290	Factory load
119 SP	FL		2821	2097	Factory load
123 SP	FL		2683	1967	Factory load
127 SP	FL		2850	2290	RWS factory load
154 SP	FL		2670	2435	RWS factory load
157 SP	FL		2450	2080	DWM factory load

6.5x58mm Portuguese   See also Chapter 7

General Comments The 6.5x58mm Portuguese (used in the Portuguese Mauser-Vergueiro rifle) is often confused with the 6.5x57mm Mauser. Performance is about the same, but these cartridges are not interchangeable. The 6.5x57mm was never adopted as a military round. There is also a 6.5x58Rmm Sauer and a 6.5x58Rmm Krag-Jorgensen, which are distinct cartridges.

6.5x58Rmm Krag-Jorgensen

Historical Notes This Danish target cartridge was developed in 1933 by necking-down the 8mm Model 89 military round. It is used in single-shot match rifles based on the Krag-Jorgensen action. Its use is confined almost entirely to Denmark.

General Comments The 6.5mm is popular in the Scandinavian countries for target and hunting use. This particular round was designed to adapt the local military rifle to that caliber without altering the action in any way. By retaining the same rimmed case, only a new barrel is required. Rifles for this cartridge are quite rare in the United States. However, if you can find the now-obsolete Norma 8x58Rmm Danish Krag cases with Boxer primers, you can neck these down to make ammunition. This would make a good deer cartridge.

6.5x58Rmm Krag-Jorgensen Loading Data and Factory Ballistics

Bullet (grains/type)	Powder	Grains	Velocity	Energy	Source/Comments
140 SP	IMR 4350	46.0	2500	1935 *	
139 SP	FL		2500	1930 *	Factory load
*Approximate ballistics only.					

6.5x61mm Mauser
6.5x61Rmm Mauser

Historical Notes Developed by DWM for various German-made Mauser action rifles, the 6.5x61mm was introduced in the 1930s. There is also a rimmed version for single-shot and combination guns. This cartridge was only moderately popular and has not been revived.

General Comments The 6.5x6lmm is very similar to the 256 Newton. According to the late Phil Sharpe*, it was developed after RWS had imported and tested a 256 Newton rifle. Performance is similar and 256 loading data could be used as a starting point for working up handloads. The 6.5x61mm would be adequate for most North American game under proper conditions.

---

* *Op cit.*

6.5x61mm, 6.5x51Rmm Mauser

Bullet (grains/type)	Powder	Grains	Velocity	Energy	Source/Comments
120 SP	4831	55.0	2860	2180	NA
140 SP	4350	50.0	2640	2170	NA
119 SP	FL		3090	2510	NA
139 SP	FL		2906	2596	NA
157 SP	FL		2749	2617	NA

6.5x65Rmm RWS
6.5x65mm RWS

Historical Notes Developed by RWS about 1988, this is the first new European 6.5mm cartridge in many years. Case-head diameter matches the 9.3x62mm (which is about 0.004-inch larger than the 30-06), but this case is, as indicated, 3mm longer than the 9.3x62mm. A rimmed version is offered for single-shot and combination guns. RWS is the only manufacturer.

General Comments Ballistic performance of this modern 6.5mm is superior to most European 6.5mm cartridges. It is in the same class as the 6.5mm Remington Magnum. This would be a good choice for small and medium game at long range. While the lighter-weight bullets are popular for European hunting, American shooters should select the heavier bullet.

6.5x65mm, 6.5x65Rmm RWS Factory Ballistics

Bullet (grains/type)	Powder	Grains	Velocity	Energy	Source/Comments
108 SP	FL		3460	2260	RWS factory load
127 SP	FL		3313	2442	RWS factory load

6.5x68mm RWS
6.5x68Rmm RWS

Historical Notes This cartridge was developed by RWS about 1938-39 and marketed in the spring of 1940. While this has been called the 6.5x68mm Schuler, such a name is erroneous, because that particular gun maker had nothing to do with its development. It was originally chambered in German-made, Mauser-action rifles. However, the Mannlicher-Schoenauer bolt-action was imported by Stoeger in 6.5x68mm, and Charles Leavell of Sumpter, S.C., also brought in 6.5x68mm and 8x68mm rifles. At one time, the German-made Vom Hofe rifles were available for this round, and it is occasionally referred to as the 6.5mm Vom Hofe Express. It is listed in late RWS and Hirtenberger catalogs and a few American-made custom rifles have been made for it.

General Comments The 6.5x68mm is the most powerful of the many European 6.5mm cartridges. In dimensions and performance,

it is similar to the 264 Winchester Magnum, except that the 264 has a belted case. On paper, the 6.5x68mm boasts a higher velocity with the 93-grain bullet than the 264 with the 100-grain. It has an extremely flat trajectory. With the light bullet, this would be important mostly for long-range varmint shooting. Arguments as to which of the two is more powerful are rather academic because with the same bullet weight, chamber pressure and barrel length, there really is not much difference. It is largely a matter of personal choice and which rifle you prefer. Regardless, the 6.5x68mm is a terrific ultra-velocity small-bore cartridge and would be a good all-round cartridge for North American hunting. It is capable of cleanly killing anything from varmint to grizzly bear if the hunter does his part and uses the proper bullet.

6.5x68mm RWS, 6.5x68Rmm RWS Loading Data and Factory Ballistics

Bullet (grains/type)	Powder	Grains	Velocity	Energy	Source/Comments
87 SP	H4831	73.0	3700	2710	Hodgdon
120 SP	H4831	68.0	3300	2980	Hodgdon
140 SP	H4831	63.0	3000	2800	Hodgdon
93 SP	FL		3950	3180	RWS factory load (optimistic)
123 SP	FL		3450	3255	RWS factory load (optimistic)
140 SP	FL		2920	2651	Hirtenberger factory load

7x33mm Sako
7x33mm Finnish

Historical Notes This cartridge originated in 1942 when Sako was producing 9mm Parabellum cartridges in large quantities. The base of the 7x33mm is the same size as the 9mm, but the case was lengthened to the maximum possible for the available case-making equipment. It was then necked down to 7mm. The original bullet weight was 92.6 gr., but was soon changed to 78 gr., which has been standard ever since. Both SP and FMJ bullets are available.

This caliber was originally developed for capercaillie and black grouse hunting. These birds were widely hunted and were the most important hunting species in Finland following WWII. For bird hunting FMJ bullets were standard.

General Comments The ballistics of the 7x33mm are similar to the 30 Carbine, and velocity at 200 yards is only 1500 fps. Post-WWII hunting in Finland was mostly for food, and the slow, round-nose bullet is a good killer that does not destroy much meat. The 7x33mm is considered effective for bird hunting to about 150 yards. The first rifles chambered for the 7x33mm were the Sako L42 and later L46 models, and about 6000 guns were produced before this caliber was dropped from production in the 1960s. The popularity of the 222 Remington was the principal reason for the demise of the 7x33mm.

7x33mm Sako (7x33mm Finnish) Loading Data and Factory Ballistics

Bullet (grains/type)	Powder	Grains	Velocity	Energy	Source/Comments
78 SP	*N110	16.5	2430	1030	Sako
78 SP or FMJ	FL		2400	998	Sako factory load
*Vihta Vuori					

7x57mm & 7x57Rmm Mauser

General Comments An extremely popular sporting round over much of the world. European loads are much more diverse and useful than those generally provided by American companies. RWS ammunition is available in the larger cities of the United States and many parts of the world.

See Chapter 2 for United States and other load data; see Chapter 7 for military load information, and consult the RWS/DWM ballistic tables for data.

7x57mm, 7x57Rmm Mauser Factory Ballistics

Bullet (grains/type)	Powder	Grains	Velocity	Energy	Source/Comments
123 SP	FL		2955	2390	RWS factory load
139 SP	FL		2625	2125	RWS factory load
154 SP	FL		2690	2473	RWS factory load
177 SP	FL		2460	2385	RWS factory load

7x64mm Brenneke
7x65Rmm Brenneke

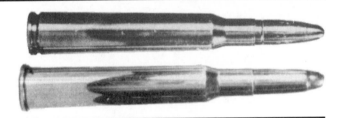

Historical Notes This cartridge was developed by Wilhelm Brenneke in 1917 and used in various Mauser-action sporting rifles. Ammunition is listed in the current RWS, Norma, Federal and Remington catalogs. Brenneke never fabricated ammunition because he was a designer and gun maker, and this task was left to the companies equipped to turn out commercial ammunition. There is a near-identical rimmed version, listed as the 7x65Rmm, used in single-shot or combination firearms.

General Comments Those who think everything new and worthwhile always originates as the result of good old Yankee ingenuity better take a close look at this cartridge. The 7x64mm Brenneke is virtually identical to the 280 Remington or the wildcat

7mm-06 and has been around for more than 75 years. The base diameter of the 7x64mm is a little smaller than the 280, so these cartridges will not actually interchange, but differences are slight. Visibly the only way an expert can tell these cartridges apart without reading the head markings is by the brass texture or the German-type bullet. The 7x64mm Brenneke is adequate for any North American big game with the proper bullet. In its original form, it was loaded with a special bullet designed by Brenneke called the Brenneke Torpedo. Quite a large variety of bullet types are offered in each weight to adapt the cartridge to practically any game or shooting situation.

7x64mm Brenneke, 7x65Rmm Brenneke Loading Data and Factory Ballistics

Bullet (grains/type)	Powder	Grains	Velocity	Energy	Source/Comments
139 SP	IMR 4350	54.5	3000	2810	Hornady (7x65Rmm)
154 SP	IMR 4350	52.5	2900	2877	Hornady (7x65Rmm)
175 SP	IMR 4350	50.5	2700	2833	Hornady (7x65Rmm)
139 SP	FL		2955	2690	Factory load
139			2806	2430	Patronen (Hungarian)
154 SP	FL		2822	2772	Norma factory load
162 SP	FL		2890	3000	RWS factory load
170			2625	2600	Patronen (Hungarian)
173 SP	FL		2790	2990	Factory load

7x66mm Vom Hofe Super Express

Historical Notes This is a rimless 7mm magnum developed for the post-World War II Vom Hofe rifles built on the Swedish Husqvarna-Mauser action. These rifles were first advertised in the United States by Stoeger in 1962, but the 7mm Super Express cartridge was introduced in Germany about 1956. What is apparently the same cartridge has also been listed as the 7x66mm Vom Hofe and also as the 7.6x66mm Vom Hofe. It was once loaded by DWM. E.A. Vom Hofe has been dead for some years and the operation was reactivated by Walter Gehmann, once a world-champion rifle shot, although the Vom Hofe name was retained. Gehmann operates a large gun and sport shop in Karlsruhe, with a branch in Stuttgart. The cartridge he offered differed ballistically and in form from the pre-war type. The case is 66mm long, the rim measures 0.507-inch, the head is 0.544-inch and the shoulder measures 0.504-inch. Thus, it will be seen that the rim diameter is of the type smaller than the head, *a la* the 284 Winchester. The shoulder form is unusual, being of modified venturi-style.

General Comments Ballistics claimed for the 7mm Super Express are quite impressive. With the 170-grain bullet, it beats out the 175-grain load of the 7mm Remington Magnum by almost 300 fps and the 7mm Weatherby Magnum by 164. Not even some of the oversized wildcat 7mm magnum cartridges claim such performance. This makes one wonder what barrel length was used for the velocity tests. American cartridges are usually chronographed from 24- or 26-inch barrels, but Europe ballisticians often use a 30-inch barrel. Regardless, the 7mm Vom Hofe Super Express is as good as any of the other 7mm magnums. It would be an excellent all-round cartridge for North American hunting. It would also do for most non-dangerous African game. It would be at its best for plains or mountain hunting or anytime long shots entered the picture. Case capacity significantly exceeds the 7mm Remington and Weatherby Magnums.

7x66mm Vom Hofe Super Express Loading Data and Factory Ballistics

Bullet (grains/type)	Powder	Grains	Velocity	Energy	Source/Comments
130 SP	IMR 4350	68.0	3350	3250	
175 SP	IMR 4350	60.0	2900	3280	
120 SP	FL		3520	3340	Gehmann factory load
123 SP	FL		3640	3630	Factory load
140 SP	FL		3356	3540	Gehmann factory load
169 SP	FL		3300	4090	Factory load (very optimistic)
170 SP	FL		3052	3540	Gehmann factory load

7x72Rmm

Historical Notes A popular, straight, tapered case for single-shot and combination guns, this load was last listed in the 1960 RWS catalog, but it is not currently available. Date of origin is not determined, but it is also shown in RWS manuals of circa 1934. This is seldom used in the United States, except for an occasional combination gun brought back from Europe. In terms of energy or power, it is in the 30-30 class and would not be satisfactory for anything larger than deer at short to moderate range. Bullet diameter is standard and one can use any American-made 0.284-inch bullets for handloading. This round has occasionally been loaded, as demand dictates.

7x72Rmm Loading Data and Factory Ballistics

Bullet (grains/type)	Powder	Grains	Velocity	Energy	Source/Comments
139 SP	IMR 4198	23.0	1850		NA
139 SP	IMR 4198	28.0	2300	1640	
160 SP	IMR 4895	27.0	1810	1168	
139 SP	FL		2440	1835	Factory load

7x73mm Vom Hofe (Belted)

Historical Notes Developed by E.A. Vom Hofe and his partner Schnienmann in 1931, this cartridge is unusual in that it has a belted case, something German designers normally avoided. Original rifles were based on the Mauser 98 action and made by the firm of Hoffmann in Berlin. After 1936, Vom Hofe made rifles in his own name. The 7x73mm was not as popular as other Vom Hofe cartridges and manufacture was not resumed after World War II.

General Comments The 7x73mm belted delivered the same ballistics as the smaller and shorter 7mm Super Express rimless introduced later. Dimensions of the 7x73mm case are close to the 300 H&H Magnum, but the Vom Hofe has a larger base and belt diameter (about 0.013-inch greater). It is at least possible that the 7x73mm was originally developed by necking-down the full-length 300 H&H case. Some American wildcats, such as the 7mm Mashburn (Long) were made much the same way. Velocity must have been taken in a 30-inch barrel because similar United States cartridges (usually chronographed in 24- to 26-inch barrels) do not achieve such velocities with the same weight bullet.

The 7x73mm is scarce and practically unknown in the United States. It would be entirely adequate for North American big game. In power, it has a slight edge over the 7mm Weatherby Magnum.

7x73mm Vom Hofe (Belted) Factory Ballistics

Bullet (grains/type)	Powder	Grains	Velocity	Energy	Source/Comments
170 SP	FL		3290	4120	Factory load (very optimistic)

7x75Rmm Vom Hofe Super Express

Historical Notes This big cartridge was introduced by Vom Hofe about 1939, and is currently loaded by the Walter Gehmann Co. in Germany. The 7x75Rmm is quite potent, in the same general class as the 7mm Remington Magnum. It is more than adequate for North American game. Cases are imported by Old Western Scrounger. Loading data and factory ballistics are not available.

30R Blaser

Historical Notes Blaser Rifle Works and RWS cooperated in developing this new round in 1990. Being rimmed, it is intended for use in single-shot and combination guns. RWS is the only manufacturer. Note the nomenclature is a combination of European and United States practices.

General Comments Ballistically, this new cartridge fills the slot between the 30-06 and the 300 H&H Magnum. It is suitable for all types of large North American game. Bullet diameter is 0.308-inch. Bullets of 150 to 180 grains work best for most applications.

30R Blaser Loading Data and Factory Ballistics

Bullet (grains/type)	Powder	Grains	Velocity	Energy	Source/Comments
150 SP	RI-22	68.0	3069	3110	RWS
180 SP	RI-22	64.0	2870	3290	RWS
220 SP	RI-22	58.0	2481	3008	RWS
250 SP	RI-22	57.0	2335	3026	RWS
150 SP	FL		3085	3165	RWS factory load
180 SP	FL		2820	3190	RWS factory load

8.15x46Rmm

Historical Notes This is an old, popular target cartridge that was sometimes used for hunting. Exact date of introduction is not established, but it dates back to the period between 1890 and 1900. Single-shot, combination guns and repeating rifles were chambered for the round. It is listed in current RWS catalogs. Modern loads have jacketed bullets, usually flat-nose softpoints, but at one time, lead bullets were commonly used. A variety of diameters were factory offered, designed to fit different rifles. According to Fred Datig, this cartridge was developed by Frohn of Suhl, Germany. For many years, it was the cartridge for 200-meter off-hand target shooting in Germany and Austria.

General Comments The 8.15x46Rmm was practically unknown in the United States until after World War II, when returning GIs brought back various rifles in this chambering (mostly single-shots). Older rifles are intended for low pressure, so one should be careful when handloading and stick to moderate loads if there is any doubt. Ammunition can be made from resized or fire-formed 32-40 cases. In power, the 8.15x46Rmm is comparable to the 32-40. Thus, it is a little underpowered for deer-sized animals but would be fine for any small to medium game. Cases are available from RWS and are imported by Old Western Scrounger.

8.15x46Rmm Loading Data and Factory Ballistics

Bullet (grains/type)	Powder	Grains	Velocity	Energy	Source/Comments
151 SP	IMR 4895	30.0	1900	1240	NA
190 Lead	IMR 3031	23.0	1500	956	Lyman #338237
151 SP	FL		1805	1090	RWS factory load

8x48Rmm Sauer

General Comments This obsolete blackpowder cartridge was used in single-shot and combination guns. It is shown in post-World War II RWS catalogs as a discontinued number. It was popular in its day and rifles in this chambering are common. In power, it is similar to the 32-40 WCF and would qualify as a deer cartridge for short-range shooting.

8x48Rmm Sauer Factory Ballistics

Bullet (grains/type)	Powder	Grains	Velocity	Energy	Source/Comments
155 Lead	IMR 4198	18.0	1500	780	Lyman #316475GC
196 SP	FL		1665	1215	DWM factory load

8x51mm Mauser
8x51Rmm Mauser

Historical Notes An 8mm round designed for the K-Model, or short-action, Mauser rifles. The rimmed version is identical, but made for single-shot or combination guns. Both were introduced in 1888. The rimless cartridge is a shortened version of the German 8x57mm military round developed the same year. It was fairly popular, but has been replaced by the 8x56mm Mannlicher-Schoenauer.

General Comments The 8x51mm Mauser reached its peak popularity before World War I. It was a favorite in Germany for short-action rifles and carbines. Mauser Type A, K and M sporters were imported into the U.S. in this chambering to a limited extent. Ammunition in shooting quantities is almost impossible to find. In power, the 8x51mm is a 30-30-class cartridge and would be good for anything up to deer-size animals. For handloading, 0.318-inch bullets should be used.

8x51mm Mauser, 8x51Rmm Mauser Loading Data and Factory Ballistics

Bullet (grains/type)	Powder	Grains	Velocity	Energy	Source/Comments
125 SP	IMR 4198	30.0	2370	1560	NA
150 SP	IMR 4064	41.0	2350	1840	NA
157 SP	FL		2155	1627	Factory load
158 SP	FL		2380	1990	Factory load
196 SP	FL		2099	1887	Factory load

8x42Rmm – M-88

Historical Notes Introduced in 1888, this is a shortened version of the 8x51Rmm Mauser round. It is listed as a hunting cartridge and was used primarily in single-shot or combination guns. It has been obsolete for many years.

General Comments The need for a less powerful version of the 8x51Rmm must have been rather limited because the 8x42Rmm was not nearly as popular as the longer cartridge. In power, the 8x42Rmm is in the same class as the 32-40 WCF and would just about qualify as a deer cartridge. It would be best for small to medium game at moderate ranges.

8x42Rmm – M-88 Loading Data and Factory Ballistics

Bullet (grains/type)	Powder	Grains	Velocity	Energy	Source/Comments
175 lead	IMR 4227	22.0	1580	975	Lyman #319295GC
157 SP	FL		1780	1110	Factory load

8x57Rmm 360

Historical Notes Based on the 9.3x72Rmm case, this old German cartridge is a copy of the British 360 Nitro Express No. 2. Loaded first with blackpowder and later with smokeless, a fair number of combination guns will be found chambered for this round. Bore diameter is 0.318-inch.

General Comments Due to low breech pressure, ballistic performance of the 8x57Rmm is only moderate. It is suitable for all types of small and medium game at close range but falls off badly at longer ranges. This cartridge is now obsolete. For handloading, use only 0.318 diameter bullets.

8x57Rmm 360 Loading Data and Factory Ballistics

Bullet (grains/type)	Powder	Grains	Velocity	Energy	Source/Comments
196 SP	RI-19	37.5	1893	1561	RWS
196 SP	IMR 3031	26.0	1560	1059	RWS
196 SP	IMR 4350	37.0	1820	1441	RWS
196 SP	FL		1800	1410 *	Factory load

* Estimated ballistics.

8x57mmJ Mauser

Historical Notes This original 8x57mm cartridge was adopted in 1888 along with the Model-88 Commission rifle by the German Army. Many sporting rifles were subsequently chambered for this cartridge. Ammunition is still being manufactured by RWS in Germany. Bullet diameter is 0.318-inch. In 1904, the S Patrone with a 0.323-inch diameter bullet was adopted to replace the I Patrone.

General Comments The later 8x57mmJS uses a 0.323-inch diameter bullet and is loaded to higher pressures. Never fire 8x57mmJS ammunition in rifles chambered for 8x57mmJ ammunition. American manufacturers offer only the 8x57mmJS

load, but it is deliberately loaded down to be safe to fire in 8x57mmJ chambers. The 8x57mmJ would be adequate for any large North American game at medium ranges. Use only 0.318-inch diameter bullets. This cartridge is now universally called the 8x57mmJ Mauser or simply the 8mm Mauser and has caused considerable historical confusion. The story goes that the fancy German script capital I in the German word "Infanterie" (Infantry) was mistaken by interpreters as a capital J. If true, this represents an interesting bit of irony, since even the Germans now routinely refer to this cartridge using the bastardized "J" designation.

8x57mmJ Mauser Loading Data and Factory Ballistics

Bullet (grains/type)	Powder	Grains	Velocity	Energy	Source/Comments
150 SP	IMR 3031	47.0	2800	2611	RWS
170 SP	IMR 3031	45.0	2600	2552	RWS
196 SP	RI-1550	46.0	2225	2145	RWS
196 SP	FL		2391	2488	Factory load
198 SP	FL		2647	3075	Factory load

8x71mm Peterlongo

General Comments Johann Peterlongo was an Austrian gunmaker and designer in Innsbruck. While his products are virtually unknown in the United States, he had a certain following in Europe. He turned out combination guns and other sporting arms of high quality. He designed 8mm and 9mm cartridges based on a long rimless case of necked type. These cartridges are of interest mostly to collectors today. The Peterlongo cartridges were loaded by G. Roth and Hirtenberger-Patronenfabrik.

8x71mm Peterlongo Factory Ballistics

Bullet (grains/type)	Powder	Grains	Velocity	Energy	Source/Comments
200 SP	FL		2650	3132 *	Factory load
154			2854	2785	1932 Catalog (German)
*Estimated ballistics.					

8x75mm
8x75Rmm

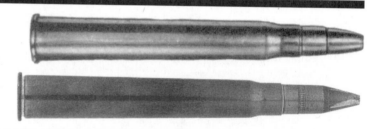

Historical Notes These two cartridges are listed together because one is a rimmed version of the other. These cartridges were introduced around 1910 and are based on the older 9.3x74Rmm case necked-down. These cartridges were intended to provide a powerful 8mm for African use. The rimless version was for bolt-action express rifles, the rimmed for combination guns or single shots.

General Comments At the turn of the century, and until start of World War I, there was considerable competition between German and British gunmakers for the African gun trade. The Germans made good repeating rifles at moderate prices and gained sales by underselling the British. However, the British seemed to always keep one jump ahead in the matter of popular cartridge design. The Germans were constantly trying to come up with something that would compete with the British offerings. The 8x75mm is one of a number of German efforts to produce an express 8mm cartridge. Two bullet diameters were used, the earlier 0.318-inch and the later 0.323-inch, or "S" size. The large diameter bullet should not be used in the smaller bore. Many 8mm cartridges come in two different bullet diameters. One must be very careful about this because the large diameter "S" round is often loaded to higher velocity and pressure. The 8x75mm is in about the same class as the 300 H&H Magnum and is powerful enough for any North American big game.

8x75mm, 8x75Rmm Factory Ballistics

Bullet (grains/type)	Powder	Grains	Velocity	Energy	Source/Comments
180 SP	Rl-22	71.0	2791	3115	RWS
200 SP	Rl-22	68.0	2713	3270	RWS
196 SP	FL		2715	3230	Factory loading for 0.318-inch bore rifles
198 SP	FL		3050	4120	Factory loading for S-bore rifles

WARNING! Many J-bore (0.318-inch) rifles still exist and, depending upon throat and cartridge neck dimension, it can be possible to chamber "S" bore (0.323-inch) cartridges. Firing such a combination can create dangerous pressures.

When in doubt, check bore diameter CAREFULLY!

8x58Rmm Sauer

General Comments This blackpowder cartridge was once used in single-shot and combination guns. A popular schuetzen cartridge in its day, it is long obsolete. It differs from the 8x48Rmm only in length. This cartridge is based on the 9.3x72Rmm case and offers similar performance to the 8x57Rmm 360. Power is about the same as the 32-40 WCF, and it could be used for deer at short range. For handloading, use only 0.318-inch diameter bullets.

8x58Rmm Sauer Loading Data and Factory Ballistics

Bullet (grains/type)	Powder	Grains	Velocity	Energy	Source/Comments
196 SP	IMR 4064	34.0	1942	1642	
196 SP	RI-19	39.0	1877	1533	RWS
196 SP	FL		1690	1248	Factory load

8x54mm Krag-Jorgensen

Historical Notes This cartridge is based on the necked-up 6.5x55mm Swedish-Norwegian military round. The purpose of this chambering was to provide an 8mm cartridge that would operate in the 6.5mm Krag-Jorgensen bolt-action rifle used by Norway. By retaining the original case, this could be done by rebarreling alone with no alteration of the action or magazine. The 8x54mm was used for target shooting and hunting and is seldom encountered outside the Scandinavian countries. It is of practically the same power as the 8x58Rmm Danish Krag military round. It could be used for almost any North American big game. It is no longer in production and this ammunition has become a collector's item. For handloading, use bullets of 0.323-inch diameter.

8x54mm Krag-Jorgensen Loading Data and Factory Ballistics

Bullet (grains/type)	Powder	Grains	Velocity	Energy	Source/Comments
150 SP	IMR 3031	52.0	2850	2718	NA
196 SP	IMR 4895	47.0	2370	2560	NA
196 SP	FL		2295	2300	Factory load

8x56mm Mannlicher-Schoenauer

Historical Notes Introduced about 1908 for various Mannlicher-Schoenauer rifles and carbines, the 8x56mm became quite popular and was picked up by other European gunmakers. It was also manufactured for a short time by American ammunition companies, but no U.S. commercial sporting rifles were chambered for it.

General Comments The 8x56mm Mannlicher has seen only limited use in the United States, although popular in Europe. Ballistically, it is a little more powerful than the 35 Remington. Both shoot approximately the same weight bullet at similar velocity. By American standards, this would be a good short-range cartridge for deer or black bear. While it is a good cartridge, performance is no better than what is available in American chamberings. Western Cartridge Co. discontinued it about 1938. Bullets of 0.323-inch diameter are used for handloading. This cartridge should not be confused with the 8x56mm Hungarian.

8x56mm Mannlicher-Schoenauer Loading Data and Factory Ballistics

Bullet (grains/type)	Powder	Grains	Velocity	Energy	Source/Comments
170 SP	IMR 4895	44.0	2260	1935	NA
200 SP	IMR 3031	40.0	2050	1875	NA
200 SP	FL		2165	1920	Western factory load
200 SP	FL		2200	2150	Eley-Kynoch factory load
202 SP	FL		2170	2105	RWS factory load

8x57RmmJS Mauser

Historical Notes This is the rimmed version of the 8x57mmJS German military round for use in single-shot and combination guns. Introduced in 1888 with the 0.318-inch "J" bullet, it was adapted in 1905 to the larger S-type, or 0.323-inch diameter bullet corresponding to a similar change in the military round. Popular in Europe and listed in the latest RWS and Hirtenberger catalog, it is seldom seen in the United States.

General Comments The 8x57RmmJS gives the same performance as the Rimless 8x57mmJS Mauser familiar to American shooters. It is in the same class as the 30-06 and would do for any North American big game. RWS and Hirtenberger cases and ammunition with American Boxer primers are available, but other European brand cases are made for the Berdan primer. Be sure you use the proper bullet diameter for your particular gun. RWS cartridges for the 0.323-inch, or "S" bore size, have a blackened primer and a cannelured bullet. Bullet diameters are clearly marked on the box. The "S" is available in heavier loading and higher velocity than the "J" (0.318-inch) loading.

8x57RmmJS Mauser Loading Data and Factory Ballistics

Bullet (grains/type)	Powder	Grains	Velocity	Energy	Source/Comments
170 SP	IMR 4895	49.0	2650	2660	8x57mmJR (0.318-inch bullet)
196 SP	IMR 4064	45.0	2440	2600	NA
225 SP	IMR 4350	50.0	2230	2498	NA
170 SP	FL		2591	2535	Hirtenberger factory load, 8x57RmmJS (0.323-inch bullet)
178 SP	FL		2380	2230	Factory load, 8x57RmmJ (0.318-inch bullet)
196 SP	FL		2312	2327	Hirtenberger factory load, 8x57RmmJS (0.323-inch bullet)
227 SP	FL		2130	2290	Factory load, 8x57RmmJ (0.318-inch bullet)

8x57mmJS Mauser

Historical Notes Information on the 8x57mm is given in Chapters 2 and 7. As a military round, the 8mm Mauser is another casualty of World War II, replaced by the 30-06 and the 7.62x51mm NATO round in the West and by the Russian M-43 or 7.62x39mm in the East. As a sporting round, the 8mm Mauser is still popular and many rifles in this chambering are in use. European sporting loads put it in the same class as the 30-06, fully capable of handling any game or situation the 30-06 can. American manufacturers load this cartridge to lower velocity and pressure than European makers. "S" bullet diameter is 0.323-inch.

8x57mmJS Mauser Loading Data and Factory Ballistics

Bullet (grains/type)	Powder	Grains	Velocity	Energy	Source/Comments
150 SP	IMR 4064	50.0	2800	2612	Sierra, Hornady
170 SP	H380	49.0	2500	2360	Hodgdon, Hornady
200 SP	H205	55.0	2500	2776	Speer
220 SP	IMR 4064	39.0	2200	2365	Sierra, Barnes
250 SP	RI-15	42.0	2250	2811	Barnes
165 SP	FL		2854	2985	Norma factory load
170 SP	FL		2657	2666	Hirtenberger factory load
198 SP	FL		2732	3282	RWS factory load

8x60mmJ Mauser & RWS
8x60mmS Mauser & RWS
8x60RmmJ Mauser & RWS
8x60RmmS Mauser & RWS

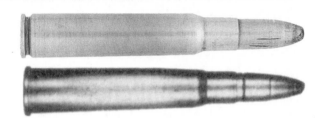

Historical Notes The 8x60mmS and 8x60RmmS were introduced soon after World War I to replace the 8x57mmJS in sporting rifles. After the war, German civilians were forbidden to own rifles in the military chambering, yet many did! Converting these to 8x60mmS was a simple chamber-lengthening job, not costly, and many were so altered in order to be legally licensed. A few years later, the 8x60mm was offered in the old bullet diameter (0.318-inch) as well, probably to add performance to older 8x57mmJ sporting rifles via the same easy conversion.

General Comments The 8x60mm comes in a confusing variety of types and loads. Both rimless and rimmed case are available for the 0.318-inch and "S" (0.323-inch) diameter bullets. There is a standard and a magnum loading and also one called the Magnum-Bombe. Case dimensions are the same, but there is a difference in bullet weight and velocity. In the standard load, the 8x60mm is almost identical to the 30-06 in power, but the magnum loading brings it up to the 300 H&H Magnum performance level. It has sufficient power for North American big game and could be used for anything the 30-06 can handle. On heavy game such as moose, elk or grizzly bear, it would have an edge over the 30-06 if one used maximum loads. It is a popular round in Europe and has been used to some extent in Africa, although most African hunters do not consider it any better than the 300 H&H. It is still loaded by RWS.

8x60mmJ Mauser & RWS, 8x60mmS Mauser & RWS, 8x60RmmJ Mauser & RWS, 8x60RmmS Mauser & RWS Loading Data and Factory Ballistics

Bullet (grains/type)	Powder	Grains	Velocity	Energy	Source/Comments
159 SP	IMR 3031	48.0	2820	2805	NA
196 SP	IMR 4895	49.0	2570	2875	NA
159 SP	FL		2820	2805	Norma factory load, ("S" bore)
187 SP	FL		2810	3275	RWS factory load ("S" bore)
196 SP	FL		2580	2890	RWS factory load

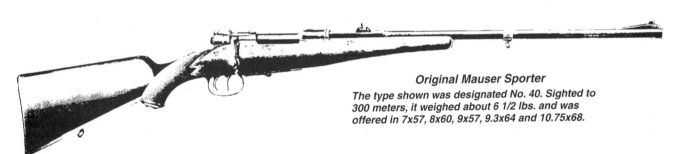

Original Mauser Sporter
The type shown was designated No. 40. Sighted to 300 meters, it weighed about 6 1/2 lbs. and was offered in 7x57, 8x60, 9x57, 9.3x64 and 10.75x68.

8x64mmJ Brenneke
8x64mmS Brenneke
8x65RmmJ Brenneke
8x65RmmS Brenneke

Historical Notes These two cartridges were developed by Wilhelm Brenneke about 1912 for Mauser rifles and combination guns. Originally, loaded ammunition was furnished only by DWM, but RWS made empty cases for Brenneke. Mauser-system Brenneke rifles are again available for the 8x64mmS cartridge, made in Berlin by the original W. Brenneke firm. The 8x64mm cartridge is based on the 9.3x62mm case, while the 8x65Rmm is based on the 9.3x74Rmm case.

General Comments Like most other 8mm cartridges, the 8x64mm and 8x65Rmm are loaded with both 0.318-inch "J" and 0.323-inch "S" bullets. Modern rifles are always chambered for the S-type bullet. This is a constant source of confusion to Americans who own or are interested in 8mm rifles. It is also the principal reason 8mm cartridges are not popular here, because even the sporting goods dealers do not want to bother with two bullet diameters and the difficulty that can cause typical customers. The 8x64mmS is very similar to the wildcat 8mm/06 and has plenty of punch for North American big game.

8x64mmJ, 8x65RmmJ, 8x64mmS & 8x65RmmS Brenneke Loading Data and Factory Ballistics

Bullet (grains/type)	Powder	Grains	Velocity	Energy	Source/Comments
150 SP	IMR 4350	60.0	2770	2560	NA
170 SP	IMR 4064	52.0	2710	2760	NA
225 SP	IMR 4831	61.0	2400	2900	NA
225 SP	IMR 4350	57.0	2450	2955	NA
154 SP	FL		2952	2986	Factory load
185 SP	FL		2890	3420	Factory load
227 SP	FL		2578	3347	Factory load

8x68mmS RWS

Historical Notes First loaded by RWS in 1938-39, for marketing in the spring of 1939, this cartridge is still listed in their latest catalogs as well as in Hirtenberger catalogs. This is one of the most modern and powerful of the 8mm cartridges. After the 9 1/2-inch twist of the standard 8mm barrel was found to be unnecessarily fast, an 11-inch twist was adopted.

General Comments The 8x68mmS is in the same class as the 338 Winchester Magnum, although it has a slightly smaller-diameter bullet of less weight. It is powerful enough for the largest and toughest North American big game and would be superior to the

300 H&H Magnum for African hunting. Some authorities compare it to the 300 Weatherby or the 300 Winchester Magnum, but the 8x68mmS has an edge over both. This is one 8mm that is furnished only in a single bullet size, 0.323-inch. Case dimensions are similar to the belted 300 Magnums, but the 8x68mmS is a rimless cartridge with no belt. It has not been used in the United States very widely to date, but would be popular if more hunters were familiar with it. It is one of the best European cartridges for all-round use in North America. Performance is almost identical to the 8mm Remington Magnum.

8x68mmS RWS Loading Data and Factory Ballistics

Bullet (grains/type)	Powder	Grains	Velocity	Energy	Source/Comments
125 SP	W760	81.0	3500	3401	Hornady
150 SP	W760	76.0	3300	3628	Hornady
150 SP	IMR 4350	73.5	3200	3412	Hornady
170 SP	IMR 4831	75.5	3100	3629	Hornady
170 SP	IMR 4350	72.0	3100	3629	Hornady
200 SP	RI-22	78.0	2971	3920	RWS (optimistic)
220 SP	IMR 4831	67.0	2700	3562	Hornady
187 SP	FL		3180	4195	Factory load (optimistic)
196 SP	FL		2985	3879	Hirtenberger factory load (optimistic)
200 SP	FL		2985	3958	Hirtenberger factory load (optimistic)

8x72Rmm Sauer
8x72Rmm Jugdewehr
8x72R/0.360-inch

Historical Notes This straight, rimmed case was developed by Sauer & Sohn for use in combination guns. The 8x72Rmm is sometimes listed as the 8x72Rmm S&S. Date of introduction is not established, but the old DWM case No. 574 would indicate sometime around 1910. It is obsolete.

General Comments The 8x72Rmm was derived from the older 9.3x72Rmm. The principal difference between the two is caliber.

Instead of having a conventional bottleneck, the 8x72Rmm case is full-length tapered to accommodate an 8mm bullet. Late RWS catalogs list this as a discontinued number. In power, it compares more-or-less with the 35 Remington. The 8x72Rmm would be useful mostly for woods hunting of deer-size animals. For handloading, bullets of 0.323-inch diameter should be used.

8x72Rmm Sauer Loading Data and Factory Ballistics

Bullet (grains/type)	Powder	Grains	Velocity	Energy	Source/Comments
150 SP	RI-15	45.0	2334	1815	RWS
170 SP	RI-15	43.0	2240	1810	RWS
210 Lead	IMR 4198	28.0	1850	1602	Lyman #323471GC
225 SP	IMR 3031	38.0	1910	1830	NA
227 SP	FL		1900	1825	Factory load

9x71mm Peterlongo

Historical Notes This obsolete cartridge was developed by the Austrian gun maker Johann Peterlongo of Innsbruck. His rifles have not been made for a good many years and his products are all but unknown in the United States, except to cartridge collectors. There

is also an 8x71mm Peterlongo cartridge based on this same case. A 227-grain softpoint, round-nose bullet was used in this cartridge. Handloading data is unavailable.

9x71mm Peterlongo Factory Ballistics

Bullet (grains/type)	Powder	Grains	Velocity	Energy	Source/Comments
184	FL		2575	2710	German 1932 Catalog

9x56mm Mannlicher-Schoenauer

Historical Notes The 9x56mm Mannlicher-Schoenauer was one of the early cartridges for the Austrian-made Mannlicher-Schoenauer sporting rifle. The rifle was introduced in 1900 and most of the original cartridges for it were developed between 1900 and 1910. Catalog references indicate that the 9x56mm was added to the line of available chamberings in about 1905. Remington loaded this round until the late 1930s. Modern Mannlicher-Schoenauer sporting rifles were once chambered for the 9x56. The 9x56mm is no longer loaded in Europe.

General Comments The 9x56mm developed a moderate following, but most hunters preferred the more powerful 9x57mm

Mauser. The 8x56mm Mannlicher is still loaded, and one can make 9x56mm ammunition by expanding the neck of the smaller caliber case. The 9x56mm is a notch or two above the 35 Remington, but is largely a short-range woods cartridge for deer or possibly elk. It was never very popular in the United States, because it had little to offer beyond available American cartridges. However, it is a perfectly good cartridge if you do not hunt anything larger than deer and are willing to put up with the difficulty of trying to find the now-obsolete ammunition. For handloading, use 0.356-inch diameter bullets.

9x56mm Mannlicher-Schoenauer Loading Data and Factory Ballistics

Bullet (grains/type)	Powder	Grains	Velocity	Energy	Source/Comments
200 SP	IMR 3031	40.0	2110	1980	NA
205 SP	FL		2114	2234	Factory load
245 SP	FL		2100	2400	Eley-Kynoch factory load
280 SP	FL		1850	2128	Remington factory load

9x57mm Mauser
9x57Rmm Mauser

Historical Notes Shortly after the 8x57mm Mauser military round was introduced in 1888, an entire family of cartridges was developed on this case length by necking it both up and down. The rimless cases were used in bolt-action repeating rifles and a rimmed version was usually made available for combination or single-shot guns. The 9x57Rmm is the rimmed twin of the pictured cartridge. This was a popular round used all over the world and the old Remington Model 30 and Winchester Model 54 bolt-action rifles were available in 9x57mm. Most American ammunition companies loaded it until 1936-38. It is now obsolete both in Europe and the U.S.

General Comments The 9x57mm Mauser is in the same class as the 358 Winchester and would be suitable for all North American big game under most hunting conditions, although it is not a long-range cartridge. African hunters liked it as a meat-getter, but considered it too light for dangerous game. Velocity is moderate, but with the proper bullet, it penetrates well on thin-skinned animals. Bullet diameter is 0.356-inch, but 0.357- to 0.358-inch bullets can be swaged down and used.

9x57mm, 9x57Rmm Mauser Loading Data and Factory Ballistics

Bullet (grains/type)	Powder	Grains	Velocity	Energy	Source/Comments
245 Lead	IMR 3031	38.0	1950	2075	Lyman #358318GC
250 SP	IMR 3031	44.0	2260	2980	
280 SP	IMR 3031	43.0	2030	2570	
280 SP	IMR 4064	46.0	2045	2610	
205 SP	FL		2423	2682	Factory load
245 SP	FL		2150	2520	Eley-Kynoch factory load
275 SP	FL		1850	2090	Remington factory load
281 SP	FL		1920	2285	RWS factory load

9x63mm

Historical Notes At one time, there was a family of metric cartridges based on the rimless 63mm case length. However, all these German or Austrian innovations are currently obsolete. Most of these were introduced after 1905, but little information is available on these cartridges.

General Comments The 9x63mm cartridge is interesting because it is based on the same case length as the 30-06 and is therefore very similar to the 35 Whelen. It has a slightly longer body length and a more abrupt shoulder angle than the American round. Otherwise, there is little difference. Each delivered practically identical ballistics. The 9x63mm would be a good choice for the heavier varieties of North American big game and many African species also. Standard 0.357- to 0.358-inch bullets can he used for handloading. Factory ammunition used a 231-grain bullet.

9x63mm Loading Data and Factory Ballistics

Bullet (grains/type)	Powder	Grains	Velocity	Energy	Source/Comments
231 SP	4320	57.0	2510	3240	NA
250 SP	4320	56.0	2390	3180	NA
231 SP	FL		2550	3336 *	Factory load

*Estimated ballistics

9x70Rmm Mauser

Historical Notes This is the same cartridge as the British 400/360 Westley Richards Nitro Express and has been obsolete for many years. It originated around 1900 and was picked up by German gunmakers for the Mauser action and other rifles intended for the African trade. It was gradually replaced by the 9.3x74Rmm.

General Comments The Germans used a different loading than the British, with a lighter bullet at higher velocity. The German load can be fired in British double-barreled rifles, but is unsatisfactory because the barrels are not regulated for it. The 375 H&H Magnum retired the bulk of the cartridges in this class, and these cartridges are now used mostly in old rifles. The 9x70Rmm would do for any North American big game, but was not satisfactory as an all-round cartridge in Africa. This is not the same as the 360 No. 2 Nitro. Loading data is unavailable.

9x70Rmm Mauser Factory Ballistics

Bullet (grains/type)	Powder	Grains	Velocity	Energy	Source/Comments
217 SP	FL		2477	2970	Factory load, German
314 SP	FL		1900	2520	Factory load, British

9.3x53mm Swiss
9.3x53Rmm Swiss

Historical Notes These two cartridges were popular in Switzerland for target shooting. Rifles of these chamberings are rare in the United States and the cartridge is of interest mostly to collectors. Factory ballistics place these two cartridges in the same class as the 35 Remington. Either would do for any game up to and including deer at short to medium range. Both were introduced in the mid-1920s, possibly 1925. These cartridges use 0.365-inch diameter bullets. Barnes and Speer make appropriate bullets.

9.3x53mm Swiss, 9.3x53Rmm Swiss Factory Ballistics

Bullet (grains/type)	Powder	Grains	Velocity	Energy	Source/Comments
200 SP	FL		2000	1780	Factory load, Swiss 9.3x53mm
200 SP	FL		2054	1960	Factory load, Swiss 9.3x53Rmm

9.3x57mm Mauser

Historical Notes This is a rimless, necked case and is another of the cartridges based on the 8x57mm Mauser expanded to take larger diameter bullets. It dates back to 1900 or earlier and was used in both Mauser and Mannlicher sporting rifles. Except for the larger diameter bullet, it is nearly identical to the 9x57mm. The 9.3x57mm is not listed in the current RWS catalog, but Norma makes cases and loaded ammunition. Apparently, no rifles are currently made for this round. A cartridge designated as the 9.3x57Rmm is not the rimmed version of this cartridge, that number has a straight case.

General Comments The 9.3x57mm is in the same class as the old 35 WCF or the newer 358 Winchester. It would do for any North American big game at short to moderate ranges. It would be good for hunting in brush or heavily-wooded areas. It may also be listed as the 9.2mm Mauser and is often confused with the 9x57mm Mauser because these cartridges differ only in bullet diameter. To further complicate matters, there is a 9.5x57mm Mannlicher, which looks similar, but is not interchangeable. Barnes and Speer make appropriate bullets for handloading this number.

9.3x57mm Mauser Loading Data and Factory Ballistics

Bullet (grains/type)	Powder	Grains	Velocity	Energy	Source/Comments
232 SP	IMR 3031	47.0	2330	2785	NA
286 SP	IMR 3031	43.0	2070	2705	NA
286 SP	FL		2065	2714	Norma factory load

9.3x62mm Mauser

Historical Notes Developed about 1905 by Otto Bock of Berlin, a well-known gun maker, this chambering was introduced to give the farmers and hunters in the German colonies in Africa an adequate cartridge. It was soon used in Europe on wild boar and red deer. Mauser sporters were sold in the United States in this chambering until 1940. It is listed in late RWS and Norma catalogs. Browning and other rifles are available in Europe for this cartridge and Steyr-Mannlicher rifles are currently so chambered.

General Comments The 9.3x62mm is a powerful big game cartridge with a good reputation in Africa and Asia. It is sufficiently powerful for any North American big game and would be a good number for Alaskan bear. At one time, it was one of the most widely-used, general-purpose medium bores in Africa. This was due partly to good performance and partly to the fine, moderately priced bolt-action rifles that chambered it. A-Square and Norma produce ammunition and offer components, while Speer also makes appropriate bullets. The editor used the listed 232-grain Norma Oryx load (bonded-core bullet) to dispatch his first moose. Bullet performance was flawless; at the shot, the bull dropped in his tracks and never so much as wiggled. This type of performance is the basis of the superior reputation this cartridge has earned worldwide. The story goes that when many African countries were in the process of adopting restrictive laws, specifying minimum chamberings for dangerous game hunting, most ruled for a minimum bore size of 40-caliber. Almost universally, the 9.3x62mm Mauser was exempted from the banned classification.

9.3x62mm Mauser Loading Data and Factory Ballistics

Bullet (grains/type)	Powder	Grains	Velocity	Energy	Source/Comments
250 SP	IMR 4350	63.0	2606	3754	Barnes (optimistic)
270 SP	IMR 4350	64.0	2550	3899	Speer (optimistic)
286 SP	H414	57.0	2500	3970	Barnes (optimistic)
232 Oryx	FL		2624	3548	Norma factory load
256 SP	FL		2560	3726	RWS factory load (optimistic)
286 SP	FL		2360	3544	Norma factory load
293 SP	FL		2430	3842	RWS factory load (optimistic)

9.3x64mm Brenneke

Historical Notes This is the largest and most powerful of the various Brenneke cartridges. Wilhelm Brenneke was one of the best-known of the German cartridge designers and many of his ideas were commercial successes. He developed the popular and effective Brenneke-Torpedo bullets*. His career began in the late 1890s, but most of his modern cartridges were perfected in the period around 1910. He was a contemporary of Charles Newton in the development of high-velocity cartridges. There are marked similarities between the Brenneke and Newton cartridges, but it is probably a case of parallel development rather than any influence of one by the other. Brenneke was born in 1864 and died in 1951. The 9.3x64mm is still loaded by RWS. German-made, Mauser-system bolt-action rifles are still available for the 7.8mm and 9.3mm Brenneke cartridges.

General Comments Except in name, the 9.3x64mm has "Magnum" written all over it. This 375 H&H Magnum-class number is certainly adequate for any North American big game and most game worldwide. The estimable John Taylor rated it right along with the 375 H&H Magnum as an excellent all-round cartridge for African hunting. Rifles and ammunition were unavailable for a number of years because of World War II. Now that this cartridge is in production again, its use may increase. Not well known in the United States, it would probably be more of a success here if better publicized. Barnes and Speer make appropriate bullets. A-Square offers ammunition and components.

* For an account of Brenneke's life and developments, see the 14th edition of Gun Digest.

9.3x64mm Brenneke Loading Data and Factory Ballistics

Bullet (grains/type)	Powder	Grains	Velocity	Energy	Source/Comments
286 SP	IMR 4350	76.0	2725	4716	RWS
270 SP	RI-15	67.0	2820	4768	RWS
293 SP	IMR 4350	65.0	2629	4563	RWS
247 SP	FL		2760	4178	RWS factory load
285 SP	FL		2690	4580	RWS factory load
286 Lion	FL		2650	4460	A-Square factory load
293 SP	FL		2570	4298	RWS factory load

9.3x66mm Sako

Historical Notes Sako introduced the 9.3x66mm in 2002. The cartridge was developed for the new Sako 75 family of bolt-action rifles.

General Comments Muzzle energy of the 9.3x66mm is close to the 375 H&H Magnum. For hunting moose and bear at close ranges, Sako has developed a RN Hammerhead bullet with an extremely thick jacket. The 9.3x66mm gets good penetration with the Barnes-X bullet. For dangerous animals, the Barnes solid is an excellent choice. Both bullets are 286 grains, which is virtually the standard weight for the 9.3mm caliber. For long-range hunting the 250-grain Nosler Ballistic Tip performs very well in the 9.3x66mm.

9.3x66mm Sako Factory Ballistics

Bullet (grains/type)	Powder	Grains	Velocity	Energy	Source/Comments
250 Nosler BT	FL		2756	4210	Sako factory load
286 RN Hammerhead	FL		2559	4147	Sako factory load
286 Barnes X-Bullet	FL		2543	4093	Sako factory load
286 Barnes Solid	FL		2559	4147	Sako factory load

9.3x72Rmm Sauer

Historical Notes The 9.3x72Rmm Sauer is an obsolete cartridge developed by Sauer & Sohn for single-shot, double-barrel and combination guns. Rifles in this chambering are scarce, and it is largely a collector's cartridge. It was loaded with a 186-grain bullet. Standard ballistics and loading data are not available. Barnes and Speer make appropriate bullets for handloading.

9.3x74Rmm

Historical Notes The 9.3x74Rmm is a popular German cartridge for single-shot, double-barrel and combination guns. It originated in the early 1900s in answer to the 400/360 Nitro Express, which British gunmakers developed in various versions. It is quite similar to, but slightly longer than, the 400/360 Westley Richards, also loaded and chambered in various rifles by the Germans. The 9.3x74Rmm is listed in the current RWS and Norma catalog. Austrian and German combination guns are still available in this chambering, as are barrels for Thompson/Center rifles from SSK Industries.

General Comments A popular round for heavy game, the 9.3x74Rmm is on par with the 375 Flanged Magnum Nitro Express. It gained a good reputation in Africa for general use against most game, including elephant. It would be more than adequate for North American big game. An over/under combination gun in 9.3x74Rmm chambering and a 12- or 16-gauge shot barrel would be a terrific outfit for the world-wide, one-gun hunter. There is not much of anything, large or small, that it could not handle. For handloading, 0.365-inch diameter bullets should be used. Barnes and Speer make such bullets, which should work well in most rifles. A-Square and Norma offer ammunition and components.

9.3x74Rmm Loading Data and Factory Ballistics

Bullet (grains/type)	Powder	Grains	Velocity	Energy	Source/Comments
250 SP	H380	60.0	2400	3198	Barnes
270 SP	IMR 4895	55.0	2300	3172	Speer
286 SP	IMR 4064	55.0	2300	3360	Barnes
232 SP	FL		2630	3535	Norma factory load
258 SP	FL		2460	3465	RWS factory load
285 SP	FL		2280	3290	RWS factory load
286 SP	FL		2360	3530	Norma/A-Square factory load

9.3x65R Collath

General Comments This is one of a series of obsolete cartridges developed by the European gunsmith whose name appears with the cartridge. He was active in the early 1900s and well known in Europe, but his developments are recognized in the United States only by cartridge collectors. This is a rimmed, bottlenecked case with a long body and short neck. It was loaded with a 193-grain flat-nose, softpoint bullet. Standard ballistics are unknown.

9.1x40Rmm

Historical Notes This is an obsolete cartridge for target and small game shooting that was popular in the early 1900s. It was of blackpowder origin and so probably originated before 1900. It would be OK for small to medium game, but is underpowered for anything else. Loading data not available.

9.1x40Rmm Factory Ballistics

Bullet (grains/type)	Powder	Grains	Velocity	Energy	Source/Comments
140 lead	FL		1800	1014	Factory load

9.5x47Rmm

Historical Notes The 9.5x47Rmm is an obsolete, blackpowder target cartridge that dates back to the 1880s. The Germans used a number of bottlenecked cartridges of 46mm to 47mm in length. These cartridges are all very similar and differ mainly in diameter of the bullet used, which varied from 9mm to 11mm. The 9.5x47Rmm (old DWM case No. 23) appears as though it would be interchangeable with the 9.5x47Rmm Martini (old DWM case No. 179), although there are slight differences in case body diameter.

General Comments Ballistics of these old target cartridges are similar and one wonders over the great variety. There must have been more than 40 of these at one time, with only slight differences in case length, shape or capacity. There would be little to gain in listing these chamberings individually because most are rare collector's gems and rifles for these cartridges are practically nonexistent. Ballistics are in the class of the 40-60 or 44-40 Winchester. As hunting numbers, all of these would be classified as small- to medium-game numbers by today's standards.

9.5x57mm Mannlicher-Schoenauer/9.5x56mm MS

Historical Notes Introduced in 1910 for the Mannlicher-Schoenauer rifle and carbine, this cartridge is also listed as the 9.5x56mm, 9.5x56.7mm, and the 375 Nitro Express Rimless. Old Eley-Kynoch catalogs listed it as the 9.5mm Mannlicher-Schoenauer. It is not listed in current RWS catalogs, and no modern European rifles are being chambered for it, partly because it lacked sufficient headspace control so that incautious chambering or case annealing could lead to dangerous case stretching and potentially case head separations.

General Comments The 9.5 Mannlicher was popular for a number of years with those who liked the light, handy Mannlicher sporting rifles. It did not have a good reputation in Africa for heavy or dangerous game, but was liked by many as a meat-getter and performed well on thin-skinned, non-dangerous game. It is seldom seen in the United States. This is a good short-range cartridge for almost any North American big game. It is in the same general class as the 358 Winchester, but uses a larger diameter bullet that is typically heavier.

9.5x57mm Mannlicher-Schoenauer Loading Data and Factory Ballistics

Bullet (grains/type)	Powder	Grains	Velocity	Energy	Source/Comments
270 SP	IMR 3031	44.0	2150	2780	NA
286 SP	IMR 3031	42.0	2040	2638	NA
270 SP	FL		2150	2780	Eley-Kynoch factory load
272 SP	FL		2148	2791	Factory load

9.5x73mm Miller-Greiss Magnum

Historical Notes A special and relatively little-known cartridge developed for or by Miller and Greiss, two gunsmiths of Munich, Germany, this cartridge is based on the necked-down 404 Jeffery case. Rifles in this chambering were built on the Mauser bolt-action. The date of introduction is not known, but would have been some time between 1910 and the early 1920s. The 9.5x73mm represents another German effort to bring out a cartridge competitive with the British 375 H&H Magnum. This one makes it ballistically, but never got close in popularity. Both rifles and cartridges are quite scarce and are now collector's items.

9.5x73mm Miller-Greiss Magnum Factory Ballistics

Bullet (grains/type)	Powder	Grains	Velocity	Energy	Source/Comments
271 SP	FL		2670	4310	DWM factory load

9.3x48Rmm, 9.3x57Rmm, 9.3x70Rmm, 9.3x72Rmm, 9.3x80Rmm, 9.3x82Rmm

Historical Notes These six cartridges are lumped together because the only real difference is case length. These cartridges all date back to the 1890s; all were originally blackpowder cartridges. Most of these cartridges were still loaded until the start of World War II, but only the 9.3x72Rmm survived the war and is listed in late RWS catalogs. All are of the straight, rimmed type and were used in single-shot and combination guns.

General Comments Old catalogs show the same bullet as suitable for all or most of these cartridges. Despite the difference in case length, there really is not much difference in ballistics or power. All are primarily medium-game cartridges fully adequate only for deer or similar animals. These cartridges can best be compared to the 38-55, although this old American cartridge has a slight edge over most of the various straight-cased 9.3s. Few modern guns are being made for any of these chamberings. Barnes makes one style of jacketed flat-point bullet for the 38-55 WCF that should work well in any of these numbers.

Various 9.3x48Rmm, 9.3x57Rmm, 9.3x70Rmm, 9.3x72Rmm, 9.3x80Rmm, 9.3x82Rmm Factory Ballistics

Bullet (grains/type)	Powder	Grains	Velocity	Energy	Source/Comments
160 SP	FL		1650	973	Factory load
190 SP	FL		1700	1225	Factory load
300 SP	FL		1650	1820	Factory load
193 SP	FL		2020	1750	RWS factory load
193 SP	FL		1640	1155	Factory load

10.25x69Rmm Hunting-Express
10.15x68Rmm Express

Historical Notes This is a long obsolete blackpowder cartridge dating to the 1880-90 period. It was used mostly in single-shot and double-barrel rifles. The Germans had several 40-caliber cartridges that were similar to British rounds in the same class. They also loaded and chambered the various length British 450/400 cartridges popular around the turn of the century. The 10.25x69Rmm is an intermediate-length version between the 450/400 2 3/8-inch and 3-inch. Rifles in this chambering are quite scarce.

General Comments Cartridges of this caliber and class were developed primarily for the African gun trade. In power, these cartridges are similar to the 375 H&H Magnum if loaded with smokeless powder to maximum performance. The 10.25 would probably do for most African game and is certainly ample for North American big game at moderate ranges. Old blackpowder loads are not as effective as later smokeless versions. These cartridges are obsolete and better left to collectors. Bullet diameter is 0.404-inch.

10.25x69Rmm Hunting-Express Factory Ballistics

Bullet (grains/type)	Powder	Grains	Velocity	Energy	Source/Comments
235 SP	FL		2100	2310	Factory smokeless load

10.3x60Rmm Swiss

Historical Notes A Swiss target cartridge originally for single-shot, Martini-action rifles, the 10.3x60Rmm is nothing more than the Swiss version of the obsolete British 450/400 (2 3/8-inch) Blackpowder Express. Some Swiss-loaded ammunition is so marked on the box. Some modern bolt-action rifles have been made in Switzerland in this chambering. The British loaded a 255-grain lead bullet, but the Swiss use heavier bullets of softpoint or full-jacketed type with smokeless powder. The Swiss loading is in the same class as the 405 Winchester and would do for any North American big game at short to medium range. This chambering is still popular in Switzerland and guns and ammunition are still manufactured in Switzerland and in Germany by RWS. In at least one Swiss canton, the 10.3x60Rmm is the only lawful cartridge for big game hunting. Bullet diameter is 0.415-inch.

10.3x60Rmm Swiss Factory Ballistics

Bullet (grains/type)	Powder	Grains	Velocity	Energy	Source/Comments
253 SP	Rl-15	66.0	2432	3324	RWS
330 SP	FL		2070	3143	RWS and Swiss factory loading

10.5x47Rmm

Historical Notes One of a series of obsolete blackpowder target cartridges of varying caliber based on a 47mm bottlenecked case that all date back to the 1880s and '90s, differing only in caliber. Some of these cartridges originated with the Austrian gunsmith Stahl. Bullet weight varied according to caliber. The 10.5x47Rmm used bullets from 260 to 298 grains. Factory ballistics and handloading data not available.

10.75x73mm (404 Rimless Nitro Express, 404 Jeffery)

Historical Notes This is the metric designation for the 404 Jeffery or 404 Rimless Nitro Express. One of the most popular rounds used in Africa, the 404/10.75x73mm is now back in production at RWS. The new RWS loads are assembled with Australian-made Woodleigh bullets with bonded cores and clad-steel jackets. Ruger now offers the bolt-action M77 and the No. 1 single-shot in this chambering.

General Comments Overall length is the same as the popular 375 H&H Magnum, so rifles with magnum-length actions are suitable for this cartridge. Some say it is too powerful for North American game, but as Elmer Keith used to say, "Too much gun always beats the alternative." Bullets for handloading are offered by Barnes and Woodleigh.

10.75x73mm (404 Rimless Nitro Express, 404 Jeffery) Loading Data and Factory Ballistics

Bullet (grains/type)	Powder	Grains	Velocity	Energy	Source/Comments
347 SP	Rl-15	80.0	2335	4200	RWS
400 SP	Rl-15	75.5	2220	4379	RWS
400 SP/FMJ	FL		2315	4761	RWS factory load

10.3x65Rmm Baenziger

Historical Notes This was at one time a popular European target cartridge, particularly in Switzerland. It is now obsolete, but the Swiss manufactured it until after the end of World War II. Swiss Martini-action single-shot rifles were made for the 10.3x65Rmm. This cartridge is actually the brass 2.5-inch .410 (10.35 mm or 36-gauge) shotgun shell loaded with a lead or softpoint bullet. However, the rim is a bit thicker than the average .410 shotshell. DWM case No. 164 is listed in the 1904 catalog under *schrotflinten*, or shotguns. Ammunition can be made from brass .410 cases, although the rim usually has to be built up to the proper thickness. A brass washer is the easiest solution to this.

The equally hard-to-find 405 Winchester case can also be used if trimmed to the right length and the rim turned down. New brass cases from Bertram Bullet Co. are being imported by Huntington. Lyman #412263 (290-grain) cast bullets can be sized and used. Power is about the same as the 44 Magnum revolver cartridge fired in a rifle, so it would make a fairly satisfactory short-range deer number.

There is also a 10.3x65Rmm Swiss target cartridge (old DWM case No. 237A) that is practically identical to the above except for a thin rim. This one has been obsolete for a good many years. Cases are currently made by Bartram Bullet Co.

10.3x65Rmm Baenziger Loading Data and Factory Ballistics

Bullet (grains/type)	Powder	Grains	Velocity	Energy	Source/Comments
290 Lead	3031	43.0	1625	1705	Lyman #412263
285 SP	FL		1785	1940	Factory load

10.75x57mm (Mannlicher)

Historical Notes This obsolete, rimless cartridge is based on the 57mm case length. It dates back to around 1900 or possibly earlier. Ammunition was once made by G. Roth and RWS. It was chambered in sporting rifles based on the Model 88 German military bolt-action and also in later Model 98 Mauser rifles. Some authorities say it originated as a Mannlicher cartridge.

General Comments The 10.75x57mm has such a slight shoulder that one has to look closely to realize is has one at all. The fact that

it was not popular or widely used may have been due in part to headspace trouble such as that encountered with the wildcat 400 Whelen. The Whelen cartridge was made by necking-up 30-06 cases to take 405 Winchester bullets. It had a short life and never got much beyond the experimental stage. The 10.75x57mm would be powerful enough for North American big game and most non-dangerous African game. Rifles for the cartridge are rare. Loading data is not available.

10.75x63mm Mauser

Historical Notes Although generally referred to in literature as a Mauser cartridge, some authorities say this is a Mannlicher development. It was introduced about 1910 and has been obsolete for a number of years. It is not listed in post-World War II German or British catalogs. Except for length, it has practically the same dimensions as the longer 10.75x68. Most samples were made by RWS, but the old DWM case No. 515 (listed as the 10.75x62) is probably the same cartridge. There was also a 10.75x62mm straight

case, whereas the one listed here is bottlenecked, albeit slightly. It was loaded with a 347- or 350-grain bullet at about 2100 fps, but exact ballistics are lacking. It would probably be a little more powerful than the 405 Winchester. Barnes makes a bullet that would work in this round.

10.75x57mm (Mannlicher) Factory Ballistics

Bullet (grains/type)	Powder	Grains	Velocity	Energy	Source/Comments
350 SP	FL		1950	2960	Factory load

10.75x65Rmm Collath

Historical Notes The largest of the Collath-developed cartridges, this one has a straight, rimmed case. It was loaded with a 205-grain softpoint bullet, but the author could find no specific data on the ballistics. The Collath cartridges are collector's items and rifles for these are uncommon. See the 9.3 Collath for additional information. Case dimensions are similar to the 405 Winchester. Barnes makes a bullet that would work in this cartridge.

10.75x68mm Mauser

Historical Notes The 10.75x68mm was a Mauser development and is so listed in German ammunition catalogs. It was introduced in the early 1920s and is still listed in the current RWS catalog. Pre-World War II Mauser magnum-action Type A sporting rifles were chambered for this round and exported to the United States. Post-war Browning and Dumoulin bolt-action rifles were available for this cartridge in Europe. Kynoch of England once made the 10.75x68mm cartridge.

General Comments This was a popular big game cartridge with many African and Indian hunters. The 10.75x68mm has been used on all kinds of dangerous game, including elephant. However, professional ivory hunters did not consider it satisfactory for elephant. This was apparently due to bullet design. The softpoint bullet could not be depended on to hold together and so did not always penetrate properly. In power, it falls short of the British 404 Rimless Nitro Express. With top loads, it approaches 375 H&H Magnum energy levels — no faint praise. However, it is not considered as good a general-purpose cartridge as the 375 H&H. There is no question of it being perfectly adequate for North American big game. Bullet diameter is 0.424-inch. Ammunition is available from Old Western Scrounger and Barnes offers bullets.

10.75x68mm Mauser Loading Data and Factory Ballistics

Bullet (grains/type)	Powder	Grains	Velocity	Energy	Source/Comments
347 SP	IMR 3031	59.0	2250	3900	NA
347 SP	FL		2200	3740	Eley-Kynoch factory load
347 SP	FL		2230	3830	RWS factory load

11.2x60mm Schuler
11.2x60mm Mauser

Historical Notes This cartridge is also listed as the 11.15x59.8 Schuler. It is nothing more than a rimless, smokeless powder version of the popular German 11mm Model-71 Mauser military round. The case has a rebated rim (of smaller diameter than the body), to fit the standard 98 Mauser bolt face. This number appears to have been introduced right after World War I, but may be older. Rifles for the 11.2x60mm were exported to the U.S. in the early 1920s, but it was not popular here. It is obsolete and late German ammunition and gun catalogs do not list it.

General Comments The general popularity of the 11mm Mauser military round was responsible for development of the rimless version. The original cartridge could not be stepped up very much in performance because the Models 71 and 71/84 were blackpowder rifles. The rimless 11.2x60mm was chambered in the stronger Model 98 action. Although it is a considerable improvement over the old blackpowder 11mm military round, it did not catch on in Africa. Most hunters there considered the bullet design unreliable for maximum penetration. In power, it is between the 405 Winchester and the 375 H&H Magnum. Bullet diameter is 0.440-inch.

11.2x60mm Schuler, 11.2x60mm Mauser Loading Data and Factory Ballistics

Bullet (grains/type)	Powder	Grains	Velocity	Energy	Source/Comments
332 SP	IMR 3031	60.0	2130	3360	NA
370 Lead	IMR 3031	45.0	1500	1855	Lyman #439186
332 SP	FL		2198	3575	Factory load

11.2x72mm Schuler
11.2x72mm Mauser

Historical Notes Rifles manufactured by H. Krieghoff of Suhl, Germany, in this chambering were exported to the United States in the early 1920s. The cartridge appears to have been developed about that time, possibly between 1920-22. These Krieghoff-Schuler rifles were based on the Mauser Magnum action with a four-shot magazine. The case has a rebated rim (smaller than the body diameter), to fit the standard Mauser bolt face. The 11.2x72mm was used only to a limited extent by American shooters. It is now obsolete and not listed in the German late catalogs.

General Comments The 11.2x72mm, often confused by gun writers with the shorter and less powerful 11.2x60mm, is a powerful round, equaling the muzzle energy of the 458 Winchester Magnum and 470 Nitro Express. One does not read much about its use in Africa, although it had a small-but-loyal following. For some reason, the German designers never turned out the sturdy, solid bullets demanded by the professional hunters when deep penetration was required. That was the main reason many fine German cartridges were not highly regarded for shooting heavy, thick-skinned African game. This cartridge is listed in the 1911 Alpha catalog.

11.2x72mm Schuler, 11.2x72mm Mauser Loading Data and Factory Ballistics

Bullet (grains/type)	Powder	Grains	Velocity	Energy	Source/Comments
401 SP	IMR 4350	103.0	2360	4975	NA
401 SP	FL		2438	5300	Factory load

460 Steyr (11.64mm)

Historical Notes Certain European countries restrict the sale of military caliber firearms, including those chambering cartridges of .50-caliber. Around 2004, Steyr Mannlicher GmbH developed a proprietary cartridge for the European large caliber market by shortening the 50-caliber Browning Machine Gun cartridge case and sizing it to accept 11.64mm (.458-inch) bullets.

General Comments This cartridge is not currently available in the United States. In the European market, it closely duplicates the performance of the 50 BMG cartridge for non-military applications. The 460 Steyr is well-suited for heavy, single-shot bolt-action target rifles that offer long range, terminal ballistic and other performance advantages, such as the Steyr HS 50 Long Range rifle. Barrel twists used by Steyr are 1:12 and 1:14. Steyr also supplies loaded ammunition.

460 Steyr Factory Ballistics

Bullet (grains/type)	Powder	Grains	Velocity	Energy	Source/Comments
600 Steyr Brass Solid	FL		3000		Steyr

10.8x47Rmm Martini (Target)

Historical Notes This is an obsolete blackpowder cartridge for Martini-action, single-shot target rifles. The 10.8x47Rmm was loaded with a 386-grain paper patched bullet. Ballistics are not known. There were a number of similar rounds used by target shooters during the period 1875 through the 1890s.

12.17x44Rmm Remington M67 (Norway & Sweden) 12x42Rmm Swedish Remington CF

Historical Notes This is the centerfire version of the 12x42mm rimfire military cartridge. It was previously listed as a military cartridge, but was never adopted as such. It was used as sporting round in Norway and Sweden in Remington rolling-block type rifles. It originated in 1867 and was loaded by Remington and also in Germany.

General Comments This is another large-caliber blackpowder cartridge similar to the American 50-70. It would do for any North American big game. However, this cartridge is largely a collector's item and one is not apt to have these in shooting quantities. Bullet diameter is 0.502-inch.

12.17x44Rmm Remington M67 Loading Data and Factory Ballistics

Bullet (grains/type)	Powder	Grains	Velocity	Energy	Source/Comments
345 lead	Blackpowder (Fg)	76.0	1300	1298	Military load
360 lead	Blackpowder (Fg)	75.0	1290	1335	Lyman #509134
360 lead	IMR 4198	32.0	1340	1440	Lyman #509134
345 lead	FL		1300	1298	Factory load

12.5x70mm Schuler 500 Jeffery

Historical Notes This cartridge is the same as, and interchangeable with, the 500 Jeffery Rimless. Some authorities say it was an original Schuler development; others claim Jeffery introduced it. John Taylor said the ammunition was loaded only in Europe, and that would indicate Schuler originated it. Krieghoff-Schuler Magnum rifles were chambered for this round and were exported from the 1920s until World War II. The exact date of introduction is obscure.

General Comments Until introduction of the 460 Weatherby Magnum, this was the most powerful magazine-rifle cartridge in existence. It was used very successfully in Africa on some game. For additional comment and information, see the 500 Jeffery Rimless. Bullet diameter is 0.510-inch. Factory loads were made in both softpoint and full-metal-jacket types. German FMJ bullets had weak jackets and did not perform well against heavy animals. In earlier editions of this text, this cartridge was erroneously listed as the 12.7x70mm. Barnes makes an appropriate bullet.

12.5x70mm (500 Jeffery) Schuler Factory Ballistics

Bullet (grains/type)	Powder	Grains	Velocity	Energy	Source/Comments
535 SP	FL		2400	6800	Factory load

EUROPEAN SPORTING RIFLE CARTRIDGES
Current & Obsolete – Blackpowder & Smokeless
Dimensional Data

Cartridge	Case Type	Bullet Dia.	Neck Dia.	Shoulder Dia.	Base Dia.	Rim Dia.	Rim Thck.	Case Length	Ctge. Length	Twist	Primer: Berdan Dia.	RWS Primer No.	Old DWM Case No.
5.6x33mm & 5.6xR33mm Rook	C/A	.222	.248	.318	.325	.326/ .366		1.31	1.62/ 1.64		.177	1584	467-468
5.6x35Rmm Vierling (22 WCF)	A	.222	.241	.278	.300	.297		1.40	1.62		.177	1584	539
5.6x36Rmm (22 Hornet)	A	.223	.242	.274	.294	.345	.060	1.40	1.72	16	–	–	–
5.6x50mm Magnum 5.6x50Rmm Magnum	C/A	.224	.254	.355	.375	.376	.038	1 97	2.21		–	–	–
5.6x57mm RWS 5.6x57Rmm RWS	C/A	.224	.281	.436	.469	.470		2.24	2.54		–	–	–
5.6x61mm & 5.6x61Rmm Vom Hofe Super Express	C/A	.227	.259/ .260	.468/.470	.476/ .479	.480/ .533	.062	2.39	3.13		.217	5603	431M
5.6x52Rmm (22 Savage High Power)	A	.228	.252	.360	.416	.500	.062	2.05	2.51		.217	5603	545
6x29.5Rmm Stahl	**A**	**.243**	**.262**	**.301**	**.320**	**.370**		**1.16**	**1.44**		**.177**	**1584**	**–**
6x57mm Mauser	C	.243	.284	.420	.475	.476	.045	2.23	2.95		.217	5603	494
244 (6mm) Halger Magnum	A	.243	.287	.435	.467	.470		2.25	3.04		.217	5603	–
6x58mm & 6x58Rmm Forster	C/A	.243	.284/ .285	.437	.470/ .471	.468/ .532	.045	2.26	3.06		.217	5603	489-489A
6x62mm Freres 6x62Rmm Freres	C/A	.243	.271	.451	.474	.470		2.42	3.13		.217	–	–
6.5x40Rmm	**B**	**.250**	**.290**	**–**	**.396**	**.451**		**1.58**	**2.07**		**–**	**–**	**–**
6.5x27Rmm	A	.257	.284	.348	.379	.428		1.06	1.54		.177	1584	476
6.5x52Rmm (25-35 WCF)	A	.257	.280	.355	.420	.500		2.04	2.53		.217	5603	519
6.5x48Rmm Sauer	B	.260	.284	–	.433	.495		1.88	2.43		.217	5603	463A
6.5x53.5mm Daudeteau	G	.263	.298	.466	.490	.524		2.09	3.02		–	–	475A
6.5x58Rmm Sauer	B	.264	.291	–	.433	.501		2.30	3.08		.217	5603	463
6.5x54mm Mauser	C	.264	.289	.432	.468	.463		2.12	2.67		.217	5603	457A
6.5x57mm Mauser & RWS 6.5x57Rmm Mauser & RWS	C/A	.264	.292	.430	.470/ .471	.474/ .521		2.23/ 2.24	3.16/ 3.18		.217	5603	404A
6.5x58mm Portuguese	C	.264	.293	.426	.468	.465		2.28	3.22		.217	5603	457
6.5x58Rmm Krag-Jorgensen	A	.264	.300	.460	.500	.575		2.29	3.25		.217	5603	–
6.5x61mm Mauser 6.5x61Rmm Mauser	C/A	.264	.296/ .297	.452	.477	.479/ .532		2.40	3.55		.217	5603	431L-431M
6.5x65mm RWS 6.5x65Rmm RWS	C/A	.264	.296	.430	.474/ .475	.470/ .531		2.56	3.15		–	–	–
6.5x68mm RWS 6.5x68Rmm RWS	C/A	.265	.295	.481	.520	.510		2.66	3.27		.238	1698	–
7x33mm Finnish/Sako	**C**	**.284**	**.307**	**.365**	**.388**	**.390**		**1.30**	**1.73**		**–**	**–**	**–**
7x57mm Mauser 7x57Rmm Mauser	C/A	.284	.320	.420	.470	.474/ .521	.035/ .056	2.24	3.06/ 3.07		.217	5603	380D-M93A
7x64mm Brenneke 7x65Rmm Brenneke	C/A	.284	.305/ .308	.422	.463	.468/ .521	.055	2.51/ 2.53	3.21		.217	5603	557-557A
7x66mm Vom Hofe Super Express	C	.284	.316	.485	.543	.510	.048	2.58	3.25		.217	?	603
7x72Rmm	B	.284	.311	–	.425	.482		2.84	3.48		.217	5603	573
7x73mm Vom Hofe Belted	E	.284	.315	.483	.527	.533		2.87	3.88		.217	5603	575
7x75Rmm Vom Hofe Super Express	A	.284	.318	.416	.468	.519	.050	2.95	3.68		.217	–	–

Cartridge	Case Type	Bullet Dia.	Neck Dia.	Shoulder Dia.	Base Dia.	Rim Dia.	Rim Thck.	Case Length	Ctge. Length	Twist	Primer: Berdan Dia.	RWS Primer No.	Old DWM Case No.
30R Blaser	A	.308	.343	.441	.480	.531		2.68	3.80		—	—	—
8.15x46Rmm	**A**	**.316**	**.346**	**.378**	**.421**	**.484**		**1.82**	**2.28**		**.250**	**1794**	**455**
8x48Rmm Sauer	B	.316	.344		.432	.500	.040	1.88	2.58		.254	1775	462A
8x51mm Mauser 8x51RmmJ Mauser	C/A	.316	.344	.436	.467	.467/ .515	.045/ .060	1.98	2.67/ 2.68		.217	5603	366L-366L2
8x42Rmm M/88	A	.318	.347	.423	.468	.525		1.66	2.28		.217	5603	88D
8x57Rmm 360	A	.318	.333	.375	.427	.485		2.24	2.96				
8x57mm Mauser	C	.318	.350	.435	.470	.473		2.24	3.17				
8x60mm Mauser & RWS 6x60Rmm Mauser & RWS	C	.318	.345	.431	.470	.468/ .526	.050	2.365	3.11		.217	5603	542
8x64mmJ Brenneke 8x65RmmJ	C/A	.318	.343	.421/.424	.464/ .468	.469/ .520		2.51/ 2.56	3.32/ 3.65		.217	5603	558-558A
8x71mm Peterlongo	C	.318	.349	.422	.462	.468		2.80	3.28		.216	2610	
8x75mm/8x75Rmm	C/A	.318	.345	.411	.466	.467/ .522		2.94	3.50/ 3.51		.217	5603	514A-514
8x58Rmm Sauer	B	.322	.345		.438	.499		2.28	3.00		.254	1775	462
8x54mm Krag-Jorgensen	C	.323	.351	.435	.478	.478		2.12	2.85		.199	1680	
8x56mm Mannlicher-Schoenauer	C	.323	.347	.424	.465	.470	.045	2.21	3.04		.217	5603	528
8x57mmJS Mauser 8x57RmmJS Mauser	C/A	.323	.350	.435	.470	.473/ .526	.043/ .048	2.24/ 2.25	3.17/ 3.55		.217	5603	366D1
8x60mmS Mauser & RWS 8x60RmmS Mauser & RWS	C	.323	.350	.431	.470	.468/ .526	.050	2.365	3.11		.217	5603	542
8x64mmS Brenneke 8x65RmmS Brenneke	C/A	.323	.348	.421/.424	.464/ .468	.469/ .520		2.51/ 2.56	3.32/ 3.65		.217	5603	558-558A
8x68mmS RWS	C	.323	.354	.473	.522	.510		2.65	3.38		.238	1698	
8x72Rmm Sauer	B	.324	.344		.429	.483		2.84	3.40		.254	1775	574
9x71mm Peterlongo	**C**	**.350**	**.386**	**.420**	**.464**	**.466**		**2.80**	**3.26**		**.216**	**2610**	**783**
9x56mm Mannlicher	C	.356	.378	.408	.464	.464		2.22	3.56		.217	5603	491E
9x57mm Mauser 9x57Rmm Mauser	C/A	.356	.380	.424/.428	.467	.468/ .515	.045/ .050	2.24	3.10/ 3.08		.217	5603	491A-491B
9x63mm	C	.357	.384	.427	.467	.468		2.48	3.28		.217	5603	491D
9x70Rmm Mauser	A	.357	.385	.418	.467	.525		2.76	3.37				474B
9.3x53mm Swiss	**C/A**	**.365**	**.389/ .391**	**.453/.455**	**.492/ .494**	**.491/ .563**	**.045**	**2.11**	**2.80/ 2.83**				
9.3x57mm Mauser	C	.365	.389	.428	.468	.469		2.24	3.23		.217	5603	491
9.3x62mm Mauser	C	.365	.388	.447	.473	.470	.044	2.42	3.29		.217	5603	474
9.3x64mm Brenneke	C	.365	.391	.475	.504	.492		2.52	3.43		.217	5603	
9.3x72Rmm Sauer	A	.365	.390	.422	.473	.518		2.83	3.34		.254	1775	
9.3x74Rmm	A	.365	.387	.414	.465	.524	.052	2.93	3.74		.217	5603	474A
9.3x80Rmm	B	.365	.386		.430	.485		3.14	3.50		.254	1775	77B
9.3x82Rmm	B	.365	.386		.430	.485		3.21	3.72		.254	1775	77C
9.3x65Rmm Collath	A	.367	.384	.420	.443	.508		2.56	3.01				
9.3x53Rmm Hebler	A	.369	.398	.462	.484	.550		2.12	2.92				
9.1x40Rmm	B	.374	.385		.404	.446		1.60	2.00				91
9.5x47Rmm	A	.375	.409	.497	.513	.583		1.85	2.37		.254	1775	23
9.5x57mm Mannlicher (9.5x56mm)	C	.375	.400	.460	.471	.473	.040	2.25	2.94		.217	5603	531
9.5x73mm Miller-Greiss Magnum	C	.375	.402	.531	.543	.541		2.86	3.50		.217	5603	473
9.3x48Rmm	B	.376	.382		.433	.492		1.89	2.35		.254	1775	246

Cartridge	Case Type	Bullet Dia.	Neck Dia.	Shoulder Dia.	Base Dia.	Rim Dia.	Rim Thck.	Case Length	Ctge. Length	Twist	Primer: Berdan Dia.	RWS Primer No.	Old DWM Case No.
9.3x57Rmm	B	.376	.389		.428	.486		2.24	2.80		.254	1775	77E
9.3x70Rmm	B	.376	.387		.427	.482		2.75	3.45		.254	1775	77F
9.3x72Rmm	B	.376	.385		.427	.482		2.84	3.27		.254	1775	77D
10.25x69Rmm Hunting-Express	**A**	**.404**	**.415**	**.480**	**.549**	**.630**		**2.72**	**3.17**		**.254**	**1775**	**214**
10.3x60Rmm Swiss	A	.415	.440	.498	.547	.619		2.36	3.08				
10.5x47Rmm	A	.419	.445	.496	.513	.591		1.85	2.40		.254	1775	29
10.75x73mm (404 Jeffery)	C	.421	.450	.520	.544	.537	.045	2.86	3.53		.217		555
10.3x65Rmm Baenziger	B	.423	.431		.462	.505		2.56	3.15				164
10.75x57mm Mannlicher	C	.424	.448	.465	.468	.468		2.24	3.05				
10.75x63mm Mauser	I	.424	.447	.479	.493	.467		2.47	3.22				515-?
10.75x65Rmm Collath	B	.424	.451		.487	.542		2.56	3.02				
10.75x68mm Mauser	C	.424	.445	.470	.492	.488		2.67	3.16		.217	5603	515A
11.2x60mm (Schuler/Mauser)	**I**	**.440**	**.465**	**.512**	**.512**	**.465**		**2.35**	**2.86**		**.217**	**5601**	
11.2x72mm (Schuler/Mauser)	I	.440	.465	.510	.536	.469		2.80	3.85		.217	5601	
460 Steyr	C	.458	.501	.719	.805	.805	.089	3.64	4.80	12, 14		Bx	
12.17x44Rmm Remington M67	**B**	**.502**	**.544**		**.546**	**.624**	**.060**	**1.73**	**2.13**				
12.50x70mm Schuler (500 Jeffery)	I	.510	.535	.615	.620	.578		2.94	3.50		.254	2703	

Case Type: A = Rimmed, bottleneck. B = Rimmed, straight. C = Rimless, bottleneck. D = Rimless, straight. E = Belted, bottleneck. F = Belted, straight. G = Semi-rimmed, bottleneck. H = Semi-rimmed, straight. I = Rebated, bottleneck. J = Rebated, straight. K = Rebated, belted bottleneck. L = Rebated, belted straight.

Other codes: Unless otherwise noted, all dimensions in inches. Twist (factory) is given as inches of barrel length per complete revolution, e.g., 12 = 1 turn in 12", etc. * = Gain twist.

Dimensions shown in some instances do not exactly coincide with dimensions found in *The Book of Rifles* (W.H.B. Smith, Harrisburg, Pa., 1960). Differences amount to only a few thousandths of an inch, doubtless attributable to specimen variations. Parentheses indicate maximum cartridge specifications.

Chapter 10

The Revolutionary Dreyse Needle Gun Cartridge

Though primitive by modern standards, the world's first practical self-contained military round altered the face of warfare.

By Garry James

In the middle of the 19th century breech-loading firearms were nothing special. Neither were paper cartridges. What was exceptional, though, was a paper cartridge that could be chambered in a gun and then fired by pulling the trigger—no flint, no separate percussion cap—nothing. The revolutionary zundnadelgewehr ("needle rifle") invented by German Nikolaus von Dreyse used just such a cartridge—one that a few short decades after its adoption would topple an empire.

The quest for a self-contained cartridge certainly did not originate with von Dreyse. There were many attempts but most, such as the revolutionary and under-appreciated brass round devised by Swiss Samuel Johannes Pauly in 1812, still relied to some degree on external ignition.

The geography in which von Dreyse worked up his invention was quite different from what we're used to today. In the 1830s Germany wasn't a unified country but a collection of separate states whose warlike attitudes and abilities varied with the character of the particular region. Prussia, a northern state which bordered the Russian and Austrian Empires and the Baltic Sea, was the most aggressive of the batch, and it recognized von Dreyse's new system for the hot setup it was. The designer introduced his rifle and cartridge in 1836, and after testing and refinement Prussia adopted them for its infantry in 1840.

Called the "needle gun" because of its unique method of ignition, von Dreyse's concept was simple in some ways, yet complicated in others. The heart of the arrangement lay in the

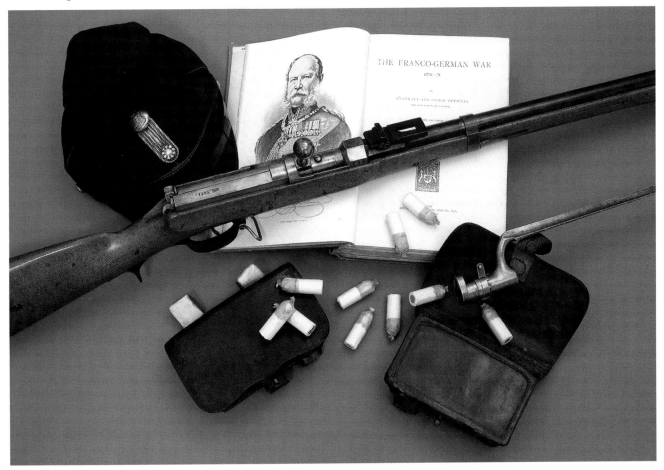

The Dreyse "needle rifle" and its self-contained cartridge was one of the most innovative weapons systems of the 19th century. Even though its use was restricted primarily to Prussia and a few other German states, during the Franco-Prussian War of 1870-71 it was responsible for one of the most lopsided victories in modern history and changed the world forever. Photo credit (not line art) Lynn McCready

Nikolaus von Dreyse devised his innovative rifle and cartridge in 1836. Prussia was the first to adopt it in 1840, and remained its principal user throughout its almost 30-year lifespan.

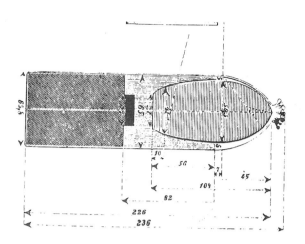

gun's cartridge. It was completely self-contained and incorporated bullet, powder charge and primer all held together in a stout paper wrapper. After some experimentation with bullet configuration, the final cartridge evolved into a load containing (from rear to front) a 65-grain blackpowder charge, priming compound set in the base of a tightly-wrapped paper sabot and an egg-shaped bullet that nestled within a cup at the front of the sabot. Caliber was 15.43 mm (.62.) The rifle itself was a sturdy bolt action, which because of the internally mounted primer, employed a long needle-like striker that passed through the powder charge prior to discharging the round.

Firing the gun was relatively simple. The bolt would be opened, a cartridge inserted in the breech and the bolt closed. The mechanism would then be set by pushing forward on a rear-mounted cocking piece. All that was needed now was to pull the trigger.

It was really ingenious, but it did have its drawbacks. First, like practically all breech-loaders of the period it was hard to seal the action, so von Dreyse came up with a clever solution to the problem by designing the bolt face so that it was enveloped by a cone at the rear of the chamber, directing the gasses forward, out of the shooter's face.

The other problem, and one that would plague the rifle for the 30-odd years it was in service, was the all-important needle itself. To fire the gun, this long, slender firing pin had to go into the powder charge where it was subject to the corrosive effect of the gasses when the round went off.

To solve this difficulty, Prussian soldiers (eventually the system was also adopted to some degree by Hanover, Brunswick, Saxony, Hesse-Kassel, Baden and Wurttemburg) were issued spare needles so they could change them when the older ones became unserviceable. This meant that the delicate needle had to be carefully removed from the rear of the bolt—not a happy thing to do during the heat of battle. Britain's "Chambers Journal" of August 18, 1866 gives an excellent description of how the gun and ammunition were actually employed:

The Dreyse round was the first self-contained cartridge to be a standard military issue. It had a powder charge, primer inset into the base of an internal wrapped paper sabot, and bullet, all contained within a stout paper wrapping.

"Every man going into action is supplied with sixty of these cartridges, which he carries in two pouches moving on a belt, so placed that they balance each other. When he has fired away the contents, of one, he pushes it out of the way, and substitutes the other. As the operation of loading consists merely in dropping the cartridge just as it is in the cavity prepared for it, without biting or any other preliminary, there is no difficulty in firing the gun ten or twelve times a minute; but the soldiers are directed, even in the hottest part of the action, not to fire more than five times a minute. As a matter of fact, they seldom fire even at this rate, and for the very sufficient reason, that, as the picked shots begin firing at the enemy when they are eight hundred yards distance, the whole of their ammunition would be exhausted before they came to close quarters. Much of the destructiveness of the Prussian fire arises from the accurate aim taken by the men. Full confidence in their weapon and its superiority over the muzzle-loaders at close quarters, they watch the approach of their antagonists with calmness, and do not throw away their balls in random shots: the old saying that every bullet has its

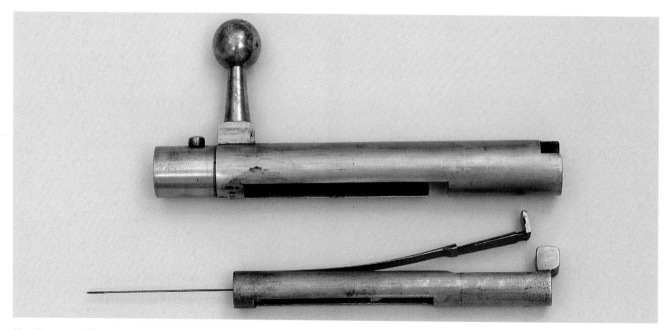

The Dreyse, while not the first bolt-action rifle ever designed, was the first to employ a self-contained cartridge and the first to be used in any quantity by the military. Its mechanism was simple and robust with the exception of the long needle-like firing pin, which could be damaged by repeated firing.

The author's recreation of the Dreyse needle cartridge. It can be made using 20-gauge cardboard shotgun wads for the sabot and cartridge base, a 60-grain blackpowder charge, 62-caliber round ball and musket cap/Large Rifle primer combo for ignition.

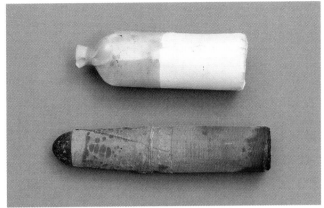

The French Chassepot needle cartridge (bottom) was a considerable improvement over the Dreyse, but as it appeared in 1866 was already virtually obsolete. Despite a superiority in infantry arms, the French were severely drubbed by the Germans during the Franco-Prussian War.

billet, applies with greater truth to Prussian bullets than to those of any other army. To this cause must be assigned the large proportion of Austrians [Austro-Prussian War of 1866] who are to be seen with their arms in slings suffering from what are merely flesh-wounds, of which they speak with a kind of contempt; but inasmuch as these wounds were severe enough to disable them, the shot may be considered to have done its work as effectively as if it had shattered the bone.

"The objections raised against the needle-gun in France, and repeated over here, possibly on no better authority, have been completely met by its performance in the campaign which it has been the principal means of rendering victorious. The gun does not foul rapidly; the cartridge does not explode spontaneously or accidentally; and greatest objection of all, as it was considered, the needle does not easily or often break. When it does, we are told that the remedy is always at hand. Every man carries one or more needles always with him, and is competent to remove the broken fragment and substitute a fresh needle in an exceedingly short space of time."

The gun worked, and worked well, though there were complaints that the round itself was lacking in range and penetration. The curious bullet was actually somewhat ahead of its time having a kind of boattail base, but the powder charge was relatively moderate by the standards of the time though its lack of puissance was offset to some degree by the advantage of the projectile. During its heyday,

the Dreyse was considered something of a super weapon by many of the world's powers, so it is curious that it was not used much outside of Germany. The gun was evaluated by several nations, but most of them stuck to muzzleloaders as their primary infantry weapon. Occasionally it would be seen in other lands but only in limited numbers—such as the Dreyses that were carried by General Charles Gordon's bodyguard during the Chinese Taiping Rebellion of the 1860s. One can largely put the blame on conservative, penurious and shortsighted ordnance departments for this apparent lack of interest. The Dreyse was just too different and too innovative to be appreciated by deeply entrenched, superannuated officers, most of who began their careers dealing with smoothbore flintlock muskets.

There were many models of Dreyses, from pistols through short cavalry carbines and intermediate-sized Jager models to the long Model 1862 infantry rifle that was widely used during the Franco Prussian War. Hunters were not blind to the Dreyse's advantages, and single- and double-barreled sporting rifles were also produced in varying calibers.

Today if you have a Dreyse rifle in good shape and want to shoot it, cartridges can be fabricated, though I must warn you they are rather labor-intensive. I have seen several different methods—some involving actually laboriously rolling the all-important sabots by hand. The one I have found the easiest, though, can actually be made of readily available materials.

The main difficulty, as might be expected, revolves around the sabot/primer setup. I have found that three 20-gauge paper shotgun wads glued together make an adequate sabot. Initially I cemented a musket cap to the rear of the sabot to effect ignition, but found that with today's caps, the needle simply punches through the copper cup, pushing the priming compound/disc out of the way.

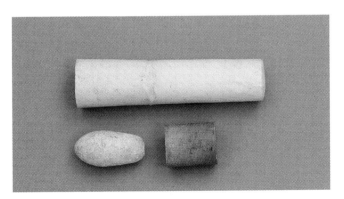

Original Dreyse components showing the original paper wrapper, paper sabot and egg-shaped lead bullet. Enough of these survive separately to indicate that at some point they may have been issued to the troops who then loaded them themselves in the field.

The Dreyse's boattail bullet fit securely within a cavity in the sabot. The fulminate priming compound was inset into the sabot base. Despite its odd appearance, the bullet was found to be fairly accurate—certainly an improvement over the round balls being used by many other armies at the time.

Landwehr Infantry. Pioneers   Horse Artilleryman.

Prussian troops, to include standard infantry, jagers and cavalry, were all issued with arms employing the Dreyse system.

This problem was solved by actually using the cap as a container for a large rifle primer which fits in the cavity perfectly. Now all that is needed is to form a paper tube on a mandrel of the proper diameter and seal the base by gluing on a thin piece of 20-gauge cardboard stripped from one of the wads. Pour in 60 grains of FFg blackpowder, and push the wad down the tube to rest on top of the charge, slightly jiggling the cartridge to allow the primer to settle down into the powder.

One caveat: it may be necessary for you to adjust the powder charge to accommodate your particular rifle. I've found that needle length can vary slightly from model to model, enough that it might not strike the primer or could extend too far into the sabot. A 62-caliber round ball can now be dropped on top of the sabot and the paper cartridge tied off with string (waxed, leather sewing thread works best). The front of the case is then lubricated with the lube of your choice (I try to stay close to the original and use a beeswax/tallow mixture). It may take a bit of adjusting here and there to get your cartridges to ignite properly, but after a modicum of work, it can eventually be accomplished.

Actually the most sophisticated needle cartridge was not developed in Germany, but by the French in their Model 1866 Chassepot. To begin with, the primer was placed at the rear of the sturdy linen-covered cartridge, largely eliminating the erosion problem. The bullet size was reduced to 11mm (43-caliber) while the powder charge was close to 70 grains. The Chassepot had also pretty much solved the breech leakage problem with the adoption of India-rubber sealing washers at the front of the bolt. Velocity, range and stopping power were greater than the Dreyse could muster, so the Chassepot was expected to give the French a decided advantage over the needle guns and muzzleloaders used by Prussia and her allies during the Franco-Prussian War of 1870-71.

Despite such prognostications, bad leadership and an overall general strategy of defense rather than offense more than offset the Chassepot's advantage, and the German victory caused the fall of Napoleon III's comic-opera empire, paving the way for the unification of Germany under Prussia's Kaiser Wilhelm I. Interestingly, by the time of the conflict, both needle rifles were basically obsolete because brass and copper self-contained cartridges had already proved themselves in other conflicts. Accordingly, Germany adopted the centerfire 11mm Mauser in 1871, and in 1874 the French followed suit with the 11mm Gras.

Today the Dreyse might seem to be nothing more than a curious footnote in firearms development. But despite limited use during its lifetime and because of its influence on other, later arms and world history in general, we can now see it was ultimately one of the most important and innovative weapon systems ever devised.

Chapter 11

The Eichelberger 10-, 12- & 14-Caliber Cartridges

What you can do when big-bore cartridges are too much.

By Bill Ball

Elmer Keith wouldn't know what to do with the 12 Eichelberger Squirrel or the 12 Eichelberger Carbine. Under his 10-gallon Stetson hat, the 14 Eichelberger Flea would probably merit a jaded glance and pointed commentary. The late, but still influential, heavy bullet guru once wrote the 222 Remington was just dandy for shooting rats in the local dump. Presumably, Elmer would be hard pressed to find a sporting use for a 10-grain bullet measuring .123- or even .144-inch diameter, even if you could shoot it at more than 4300 fps in either solid or jacketed bullet persuasion.

Even with solid bullets, the 10-, 12- and 14-caliber wildcat cartridges fall outside the performance envelope and legal threshold for belligerent big game, or possibly even annoyed small game. Sub-wildcats from the dean of sub-caliber cartridges, Pennsylvanian Bill Eichelberger, target another niche though — very small game at ranges under 100 yards by virtue of high velocity and inherent accuracy.

Beginning in 1978 when he necked the 222 Remington Magnum case down to 14-caliber, and launched a series of really small bore wildcats, Eichelberger progressively mastered smaller and smaller calibers. After he perfected the 14s, he moved to the 12s and then to 10-calibers. Along the way, he also developed wildcats in 17, 20, 22, 5.75mm and 6mm, but the story of Bill's larger wildcats must await another opportunity.

For sheer ingenuity, it is hard to top the 14 Eichelberger Flea, a radical makeover of the puny 25 ACP cartridge into a tiny powerhouse, capable of speeding 10-grain solid bullets to velocities approaching 3400 fps. If there was a small cartridge case with suitable flexibility and capacity to seat a small bullet, Bill built it into a sub-caliber wildcat. In his exploration of the diminutive side of shooting, Eichelberger appears to be the most prolific creator of wild and extreme, yet safe and very efficient little cartridges.

For more than 30 years, Eichelberger combined an interest in metallurgy, skill in forming metal and a consuming love of labor to produce some exceptional wildcats. In three decades of creating small cartridges from small cases, he bulldozed and then paved the road to a new, microscopic shooting dimension. Mastering these miniature thunderbolts came only after long, tedious and eye-straining experimentation in transforming brass, steel and copper into accurate, reliable and safe, but ever so small, wildcats.

Just for the record, Bill's 12 Eichelberger Carbine wildcat can speed a 10-grain, 12-caliber bullet to almost 4400 fps — greater velocity than any commercially produced American cartridge available in 2006. Eight of the Eichelberger 14-caliber wildcats can speed .144-inch diameter bullets to more than 4000 fps.

The 10 Eichelberger Long Rifle takes a 10-caliber, 7.2-grain bullet in a rimfire case to 2160 fps on just 1.8 grains of powder. Just as my mother did, I'm confident Bill's mom told him not to try to take the bullet out of a 22 Long Rifle because it could blow up in his hand. After transforming a couple of thousand of Long Rifle and Winchester magnum rimfire cases into 10-, 12-, 14-, 17- and 20-caliber Eichelberger cartridges, Bill reports not one ever blew up. This accomplishment doesn't mean the advice of his youth was misguided, but rather that Bill Eichelberger is a thoughtful and careful craftsman, with an eye for safety.

Eichelberger began his professional career as a wood pattern-maker apprentice for the Pennsylvania Railroad's foundry, where a shrink rule became his constant companion. In green sand moulds containing cavities shaped by the patterns, molten iron changed from an orange 3300-degree (Fahrenheit) liquid into a well-dimensioned casting. In making several hundred wood patterns, sculpted from laminated pine and mahogany blocks, he developed a life-long interest in forming metals. Before retiring several decades later to devote near-full-time attention to sub-caliber wildcats, he worked with a team of engineers at General Electric Aerospace Division, developing a variety of aerospace hardware for NASA and the Air Force. Sometime during this working career, Bill began to think big about small cartridges — really small cartridges.

For our purposes, any cartridge firing 15-caliber and smaller diameter bullets is considered to be a sub-caliber. At present, no factory cartridges fall into this spectrum — thus all available sub-caliber cartridges are wildcats.

For the enthusiast, this fact means everything about sub-calibers is a custom proposition, from barrels, reamers and gauges, cases, bullets, cleaning rods, forming dies, reloading dies, powder funnels, and cleaning accessories such as brushes and patches. It also means that creating and shooting sub-caliber wildcats is not for the economy-minded shooter, who could be well (and better) served with white box generic ammo from one of the super-mart stores.

At a time when some shooters considered 17-caliber factory and wildcat cartridges to be small, experimenter Bill Eichelberger developed a new category of sub-caliber wildcats. Based on the concept of very small bullets and small cases, Bill created families of wildcats that seat 10-, 12- and 14-caliber bullets. Although sub-caliber wildcatting does involve a love of labor, the performance of the Eichelberger cartridges borders on spectacular, within their range limitations. Shown here is the 7.2-grain bullet, available in either solid or jacketed construction, and measuring exactly .103-inch in diameter. Eichelberger loads these bullets into 10-caliber cartridges derived from the rimfire Long Rifle, or the centerfire 25 ACP, 22 Hornet, and 32 H&R Magnum parent cases. All are capable of sub-MOA accuracy.

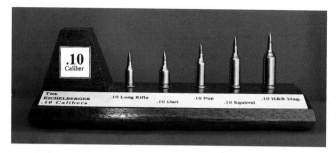

Casting a big shadow on the 95-caliber, 3600-grain solid bullet from the 950 JDJ, the 10-caliber, 7.2-grain bullet from the Eichelberger wildcats can be purchased in either solid or jacketed construction. The Eichelberger bullet measures .103 inches in diameter, and can be loaded into all the 10-caliber Eichelberger wildcats. For those shooters who favor bullet weight over velocity, a 10-caliber, 10-grain bullet is also available.

Pennsylvanian Bill Eichelberger developed a family of 10-caliber wildcat cartridges by carefully and laboriously sizing small factory cartridge cases to accept his .103-inch diameter bullets. Shown on this display are the 10 Eichelberger Long Rifle (22 Long Rifle case), 10 Eichelberger Dart (25 ACP case), 10 Eichelberger Pup (22 Cooper CCM case), 10 Eichelberger Squirrel (22 Hornet case) and 10 Eichelberger H&R Magnum (32 H&R Magnum case). Muzzle velocities from these diminutive wildcats range from 2160 to 3900 fps when firing 10-caliber, 7.2-grain bullets.

In a domain where everything is purpose-built, Eichelberger's 30 years of experimentation resulted in a lot of sub-caliber lessons learned — some easy and others less so. The Cartridges of the World editor recognized that Bill's knowledge merited documentation as an important step in cartridge development.

To start shooting sub-caliber wildcats in 2005, you'll need a goodly number of one hundred dollar bills and a single cartridge drawing. Since Eichelberger deals in very small numbers, the first lesson learned was to use only one, dimensioned drawing from which to have the case-forming dies and sizing bushings, reloading dies, chambering reamers, and the go and no-go gauges manufactured. When 0.001-inch in dimension or 0.1-grain makes a big difference, having the manufacturers of various components work from a common drawing becomes essential. Bill's book, The Eichelberger Small Caliber Cartridges, contains precisely dimensioned engineering drawings for each of his wildcats, and is a great source for the single diagram to send to toolmakers such as Pacific Tool and Gauge, JDS, Neil Jones Tool, or RCBS for dies, bushings, gauges and reamers.

With the precisely-manufactured dies, bushing, gauges and reamers in hand, the next step is to purchase a sub-caliber barrel blank, and have it chambered for the desired cartridge and machined for the selected rifle action.

One of Eichelberger's favorite sub-caliber rifles is built on a Cascade Arms Alpine Cub action, with a 23.5-inch Lawrence barrel and stocked in exquisite French walnut with striking black and brown streaks coursing through the buttstock. The styling is petite, the forend tip is ebony and it wears a LPS scope crafted by Leupold. Naturally, Bill supplied the barrel blank, chambering reamer, and the go and no-go gauges involved in crafting the piece.

For a custom firearm chambered in the 10 Eichelberger Squirrel, accuracy is satisfyingly and predictably sub-MOA. The 10 Eichelberger Squirrel uses a shortened 22 Remington Hornet brass case, and drives 7.2-grain bullets in excess of 4000 fps and 10-grain bullets to almost 3300 fps. Shooting Confederate 13-stripe ground squirrels (a gopher-sized critter) within 50 yards of the muzzle, the combination produces impressive consequences. The cartridge is equally effective on rats, pigeons, starlings, tree squirrels and small mammals.

The popular, but out-of-production flat-sided Thompson/Center Contender or newer G2 action provides an equally good and less expensive action for a sub-caliber firearm. In the interests of legality, the federal requirements for barrel length and overall length

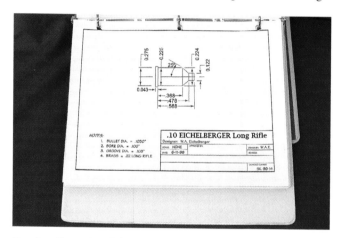

Precise dimensional data for each Eichelberger wildcat cartridge is captured in a set of engineering diagrams, available from Bill Eichelberger in his book, The Eichelberger Small Caliber Cartridges. *This photograph shows the actual drawing for the 10 Eichelberger Long Rifle cartridge.*

Defining the boundaries of little and big centerfire wildcat cartridges, the 10 Eichelberger Dart (left) and the 950 JDJ (right) are real cartridges, capable of being fired in rifles that exist today. The 10 Eichelberger Dart is based on the 25 ACP pistol case used in pocket pistols; the 950 JDJ uses the 20mm Vulcan case, which otherwise would be loaded into rotary-barrel cannon on Air Force fighter aircraft. The 10 Eichelberger Dart can speed bullets to more than 3000 fps, approximately 800 fps faster than the 950 JDJ. As you might expect, though, some recoil and terminal ballistic differences do exist between these two wildcats.

Precise dimensional, loading, performance and safety information on the Eichelberger sub-caliber wildcats in captured in Bill Eichelberger's reloading manuals and engineering drawings. Eichelberger's documents are produced to high quality standards.

Bullets for wildcat and factory cartridges can range from 7.2 grains for the 10-caliber Eichelberger bullet (left), 39-grains for the Sierra 20-caliber Blitz King, 55-grains for the Nosler 22-caliber, and 3600-grains for the proprietary 950 JDJ from SSK Industries. Depending on what you want to shoot, and the money you have available, wildcatting can be an interesting and engaging activity. At either end of the caliber spectrum, pulling the trigger on one of Bill Eichelberger's wildcats or one of J.D. Jones' requires more than a little curiosity, time and money.

Shown to the right of their parent cases are the 14/222 Eichelberger Magnum, based on the now-obsolescent 222 Remington Magnum case, and the 14 Eichelberger Carbine, based on the 30 Carbine case developed by the United States Army in the 1940s. The 14/222 Eichelberger Magnum can speed a 13-grain bullet to over 4300 fps. The 14 Eichelberger Carbine pushes a 10-grain bullet to over 4550 fps — faster than any currently produced factory cartridge available in the United States.

should be respected, since both Contender and G2 actions can be configured as either a pistol or rifle. Many commercial stocking options in synthetic materials or wood of various grades exist for these actions – greatly easing the completion of the firearm.

The Ruger 77/22 series of rifles also provides an excellent starting point to create a sub-caliber wildcat. Interestingly, extensive testing demonstrated the Ruger rotary magazine (in the appropriate size, of course) was 100-percent reliable in feeding sub-caliber wildcats based on the Long Rifle, WRM and Hornet cartridge cases.

Over the years, several barrel makers supplied unturned blanks with diminutive .100-, .120- and .140-inch bore diameters. Obermeyer, MATCO, Walker, and Lawrence supplied barrels at various times during the development of the Eichelberger sub-caliber wildcats. Currently Lawrence supplies most of the sub-caliber barrels used by Eichelberger. Most of the barrels went to Bullberry Barrel Works, and to SSK Industries, where their gunsmiths transformed the bored and rifled blank into a completed Contender or G2 barrel.

In 2005 dollars, the unturned barrel blank will cost about $450, and another $300 or so will get it chambered, tapered, fitted to the action, and drilled and tapped for scope bases and dovetails. For a Contender or G2 action, this cost should include welding the lug on the barrel. Once the firearm is completed and a suitable scope mounted, a supply of cartridges becomes the next priority.

Eichelberger drew great satisfaction in creating small cartridges from existing small cases. Brass cases proven suitable for creating sub-caliber wildcats come from both the rimfire and centerfire

cartridge families. The 22 Long Rifle, 22 WRM, 22 Jet, 22 Hornet, 22 Cooper CCM, 25 ACP, 30 Carbine, 32 ACP and 32 H&R Magnum serve as parent cases for the smaller capacity cartridges in Bill's 10-, 12- and 14-caliber wildcats. The biggest 14-caliber boomers in the Eichelberger family utilize the larger capacity 218 Bee, 221 Remington Fireball, 222 Remington, and 222 Remington Magnum cases as their starting point.

Brass is an alloy with copper and zinc as primary components. Cartridge brass normally contains 70 percent brass and 30 percent zinc for maximum ductility. Under high magnification, cartridge brass looks like grains of rice, separated from each other by spaces called slip planes. When forming a sub-caliber wildcat cartridge case, the case-forming die squeezes the metal grains of brass closer together, and the slip planes become smaller. At room temperatures, the forming process work-hardens the brass, resulting in brittleness and cracking, unless the case is annealed (heated and cooled) periodically during the process. Annealing returns the internal crystalline structure to a normal state, restoring the essential "spring" to the case, and allows the brass once again to flow through the case forming die. Omitting the annealing treatment will cause case forming failures.

Three critically important steps involve using case sizing bushings with (1) highly polished surfaces, (2) keeping the bushings and dies highly polished, scratch-free, and surgically clean, and (3) applying a very light dab of lubricant so the brass will flow easily and without scratching. Excessive amounts of lubricant will cause oil dents in the case body and shoulder.

To create a sub-caliber wildcat cartridge case, the cartridge neck and body must undergo mechanical changes by being pressed into a series of case-forming dies. To change a .25-inch diameter neck to a .10-inch diameter neck can take up to 23 different sizing bushings,

One of the more interesting cartridges listed in the Eichelberger reloading manual, the 14 Jet Junior, was actually designed by the late Bud Pylinski. The obsolescent 22 Remington Jet becomes the basis for the 14-caliber wildcat, which can push a 10-grain bullet to velocities above 4500 fps. The sloping shoulder on the parent case provides an distinctive silhouette for the 14 Jet Junior. On the left is the 14 Eichelberger Bee, based on the Winchester 218 Bee case introduced before WWII. The appealing shape of the 14 Eichelberger Bee cartridge contains a real performer – 13-grain bullets leave the muzzle at speeds over 4100 fps.

The 10 Eichelberger Dart, the 10 Eichelberger H&R Magnum and the 10 Eichelberger Squirrel, pictured from left to right beside their parent case, are accurate (sub-MOA) performers on very small game, such as squirrels, starlings and pigeons at ranges up to 100 yards. In a quality rifle, the Eichelberger sub-caliber wildcats quietly establish an American version of the classic British rook rifle.

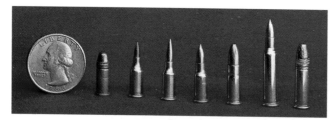

To shoot something well but only once, Eichelberger developed a whole set of rimfire wildcats. Although not reloadable, the Eichelberger rimfire wildcats drive small diameter bullets to remarkable velocities. Shown from the left: Remington 22 Short (factory) 10 Eichelberger Long Rifle, 12 Eichelberger Long Rifle, 14 Eichelberger Long Rifle, 20 Eichelberger Long Rifle, 14 Eichelberger WRM, and 22 Long Rifle (factory). The 14 Eichelberger WRM is a screamer, getting over 3700 fps from a necked-down Winchester Rimfire Magnum case. Naturally, necking-down and powder-charging rimfire (internally primed) cases requires careful and safe methods and practices.

depending upon the ductility of the brass. Each sizing bushing can reduce the case neck diameter by about 0.006- to 0.008-inch. As the case neck draws smaller, the thickness of brass increases, requiring neck reaming at regular intervals.

The sizing, reaming and annealing process, repeated enough times, will finally create an appropriately dimensioned case. Once the bushings to form a specific case to 14-caliber are acquired, only a few additional bushings are needed to size that case down to 12-caliber. A few more bushings will reduce the neck to accept 10-caliber bullets. Did anyone mention that the reckless pursuit of sub-caliber wildcats involves a love of labor?

Quality bullets are the most critical component for sub-caliber wildcatting. Since lightweight bullets respond to wind with acute sensitivity, the sub-caliber wildcats fit a specialized hunting niche, such as shooting at ranges up to 75 yards. For target work and the "let's have fun" shooter, the sub-caliber wildcats are consistently capable of sub-MOA accuracy, provided good bullets, barrels and shooting techniques become part of the shooting equation. For the sub-caliber wildcats, both solid copper and jacketed lead core bullets are available, and when loaded to Bill's recommendations in a good quality barrel, little copper fouling results

Some custom barrel makers seem hesitant to bore and rifle sub-caliber barrel blanks, reflecting real concerns about their reputation. Given a great barrel, mediocre bullets and the resulting poor accuracy, many folks unreasonably blame the barrelmaker, while the real culprit, a dubious quality bullet, skirts responsibility. Any enthusiast intent on exploring sub-caliber wildcats needs to give serious consideration to securing a continuing supply of suitable quality bullets. Fortunately, quantities of good quality sub-caliber bullets are available from Eichelberger and from SSK Industries (on special order).

Loading 10-, 12- and 14-caliber wildcats merits careful and consistent care. Most 10-, 12- and 14-caliber cases accept tiny amounts of powder. Typically, they launch very lightweight bullets

at velocities ranging from moderate to impressive. With tiny-sized bore diameters, exceeding the recommended load by as much as 0.1-grain could create a dangerous, over-pressure result. For safety's sake, powder charges should be measured on a digital scale and again checked, rather than dropped through a powder measure. The smallest caliber wildcat currently known, the 10 Eichelberger Long Rifle, loads 1.8-grains of powder to drive a 7.2-grain bullet at 2160 fps.

The loading technique, once the parent 22 Long Rifle case has been necked down to 10-caliber using decreasing diameter bushings in the case forming dies, calls for measuring out a trivial amount of powder, double-checking the load (including a visual inspection of the charged case) and then carefully flowing the powder down a case neck 0.10- inch in diameter. If a powder measure or scale is accurate to 0.1 grain, and the load is on the high side of the tolerance, the 10-caliber Eichelberger Long Rifle case could now contain a nearly six-percent overload. Two Eichelberger reloading manuals, one for 10- and 12-caliber cartridges and another for 14-calibers, contain precise reloading information to achieve the safety and performance inherent in these cartridge designs. For safety and performance, sub-caliber experimenters should use Bill's tested reloading information with caution, and without any change or substitutions.

With dismaying visions of magnifying glasses and tweezers holding individual powder grains or flakes, the sub-caliber shooter begins to wonder how to get those tiny powder charges through the incredibly small case neck. The answer is both simple and complex, according to Eichelberge—a very small, special powder funnel. In his experimentation, Bill realized funnels made from extruded plastic create tremendous static that bonds the powder to the plastic—making recharging more difficult and tedious. However, he discovered funnels machined from 2-inch cast plexiglass bar stock did not create static. With specially manufactured step bits, the bottom of the funnel could be drilled open to fit one of the different case neck sizes in the Eichelberger 10-, 12- and 14-caliber wildcat family.

Since a chamfered (think about very sharp) 10-, 12- or 14-caliber case mouth can excise a partial circle of flesh with the ease of a surgeon's scalpel, Bill reports that straight-line bullet seating dies (used with a arbor press) produce less wear and tear on the reloader's fingers.

Compared to barrels for larger calibers, sub-caliber rifling is relatively shallow. The lands might be only 0.0015-inch higher than the grooves. While entirely suitable for stabilizing a small-caliber bullet, the small dimensional difference between lands and grooves means that it is entirely possible to scrub the rifling away with aggressive passes with a bronze bore brush. Nylon bore brushes are the cleaning norm, here, along with guides to center the cleaning rod in the bore and assist in reducing angular friction on the lands.

Eichelberger manufactures cleaning rods (in two-rod sets) small enough to fit inside these tiny bores. For the 10-caliber rod, drill rod measuring 0.095 inches is straightened and cut to length. On one rod, a jag shape is ground on one end. The jag shape includes a point to hold the patch, a shoulder sized so the patch engages the rifling, some rings to accommodate the shape of the patch, and an ending taper 0.015-inch smaller. On the second rod, a hole is drilled to accept the shank of a nylon brush and a generous dollop of Loc-Tite adhesive applied. The nylon cleaning brushes are custom-manufactured. Common cotton patches provide the basic cleaning fabric, and an ordinary 3/8-inch leather punch will cleave several sub-caliber-sized patches from a standard rifle patch.

The Eichelberger sub-caliber wildcats are just the ticket for someone inclined to think small. Copious investments of curiosity, money and time are essential prerequisites to shoot the smallest caliber cartridges on the planet. As a practical matter, the sub-caliber wildcats won't challenge the enduring 30-06 as one cartridge that can be adapted to all shooting applications. Within the short-range varmint and target-shooting niche, though, few other endeavors can provide the same sense of accomplishment. Just to pull the trigger on a sub-caliber wildcat cartridge requires the shooter to create and assemble a full spectrum of unique cases, cartridges, barrels, firearms, cleaning items, bullets, dies, reamers and gauges. For the interested and diligent shooter, mastering the sub-caliber domain will deliver a high standard of personal satisfaction and knowledge attained by few others.

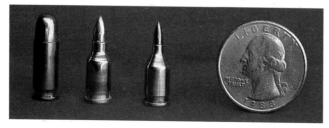

Though some might consider the 25 ACP cartridge on the puny side, when necked down to one of Bill Eichelberger's 10-caliber or 14-caliber wildcats, the case become a pint-sized powerhouse. Shown next to a factory 25 ACP case are the 10 Eichelberger Dart, and its bigger brother, the 14 Eichelberger Dart. The little brother can send a 10-caliber, 7.2-grain bullet to over 3000 fps; the larger sibling pushes a 14-caliber, 10-grain projectile to almost 3000 fps.

Chapter 12

The Chinese 5.8x42mm Small Arms Cartridge

Did the Chinese military find their universal caliber?

By Timothy G. Yan

It has been more than 40 years since Eugene Stoner, the well known post-war American small arms designer, started the Small-Caliber High-Velocity (SCHV) revolution in military rifles. Before Stoner's influential work, the conservative-minded U.S. military rejected the concept of a full-caliber intermediate assault rifle cartridge as pioneered by the Germans (7.92x33mm), Russians (7.62x39) and Czechs (7.62x45mm) during or shortly after World War II.

After being on the receiving end of the Russian 7.62x39mm intermediate round during the American involvement in the Vietnam War, it didn't take long for the U.S. military to change their mind. In realizing their mistake, the U.S. Army hastily adopted Eugene Stoner's unorthodox yet ground-breaking M-16 assault rifle and its 5.56x45mm SCHV round. Other branches of the U.S. military quickly followed the U.S. Army and replaced their leftover World War II rifles with the 5.56mm M-16 marking the beginning of the SCHV era in military small arms.

The small caliber cartridge offers the advantages of reduced ammo and weapon weight, less recoil, flat trajectory, and controllability during full-automatic firing. Also noticing those advantages, the Russian military followed the trend in the mid-1970s by adapting the AK-74 assault rifle and their own version of SCHV in 5.45x39mm. Since then, many other countries' militaries also became SCHV-caliber users.

The 5.56mm was officially adopted by NATO as its standard rifle caliber in the early 1980s. The 5.45mm became the common rifle caliber in many Eastern Bloc militaries. Surprisingly, in the mid-1990s, the Chinese military introduced a new indigenous 5.8x42mm SCHV assault rifle round and a new family of small arms to use it. This article will take an in-depth look at the new Chinese SCHV ammo and to see how it stacks up against the existing American/NATO 5.56mm and Russian 5.45mm.

Like the Russians, the advantages of SCHV assault rifle ammo observed in Vietnam War battle reports did not go unnoticed by the Chinese military. In March, 1971, the Chinese military logistic department commenced a small arms research project known as the "713 Conference" in Beijing to develop the design criteria for an indigenous SCHV assault rifle cartridge.

The design criteria called for a cartridge of approximately 6mm caliber, 1000 meters per second muzzle velocity with the goals of reducing recoil and ammo weight while improving accuracy and terminal ballistics over the Type 56/M-43 7.62x39mm full-caliber intermediate round. The following "744 Conference" narrowed down the calibers under consideration to 5.8mm and 6mm caliber. The cartridge case was to be selected from seven designs with overall cartridge lengths ranging from 56mm to 59.5mm. However, the new small caliber cartridge development was mostly a "paper project" for the initial eight years. The first half of the 1970s was

The 5.8mm small arms family. Top row from L-R: QJY88 belt-fed General-Purpose Machine Gun, QBB95 Squad Automatic Rifle. Bottom row from L-R: QBZ-95B Carbine, QBZ95 Assault Rifle and QBU88 Sniper Rifle. (Photo courtesy *Small Arms Magazine*)

The 5.8x42mm standard rifle load cartridges. (Photo courtesy www. gun-world.net)

The 5.8x42mm (left) **and the 7.62x39mm** (right). **The 5.8mm is intended to replace the 7.62mm as the standard Chinese assault rifle caliber.** (Photo courtesy www.gun-world.net)

a chaotic time for China. The Cultural Revolution and the political infighting for Chairman Mao's succession almost led to an all-out civil war. The actual initiation of the project didn't begin until late 1978 after most of the turmoil had died down. By 1979, the 5.8mm caliber and the 42mm case were chosen as the final design for the new SCHV round. The project completed its development in the 1987 and the new SCHV assault rifle cartridge was officially designated as the DBP87.

The Chinese military has since developed a variety of small arms chambered for the new 5.8mm cartridge. The first was the QBZ87 assault rifle primarily used as the test bed for further 5.8mm ammo development. The QBZ87 was an undated 7.62mm Type 81 assault rifle chambered for the new 5.8mm round. The QBZ87 is now largely withdrawn from frontline services and has been handed over to paramilitary, military academies and reservists.

Next came the QBZ95 assault rifle family comprised of the QBZ95 assault rifle, QBB95 squad automatic rifle/light machine gun and the QBZ95B carbine. The QBZ95 (Qing, Bu-Qiang, Zi-Dong, 1995 Si or Infantry Rifle, Automatic, Model 1995) is a modern looking 7.1 pound (3.25kg) assault rifle in a "bullpup" configuration. Like other bullpup rifles, such as French FAMAS, Austrian AUG and the British SA80, the QBZ has its magazine and action located behind its trigger and pistol grip.

The main benefit of the bullpup layout is that it allows a full-length barrel, needed for long-range shooting, in a short weapon that is good for close-quarters combat. The QBZ95 assault rifle has an 18.2 inch (463mm) cold hammer-forged barrel mounted in a small forged aluminum receiver, enclosed in black polymer housing. Its action uses an adjustable short-stroke gas system and a three-lug rotating bolt. The sight system consists of a hooded post front sight with an aperture rear sight and a proprietary mounting rail inside of the carrying handle for add-on optical sights.

Recently another member of the 5.8mm weapon appeared, the QBZ03 assault rifle. The new rifle seems to use the QBZ95's action. However, instead of the bullpup layout, the QBZ03 is in the "traditional" configuration with its magazine and action in front of the trigger and pistol grip like the American M-16, German G36 and the Russian AK-74.

The 5.8mm ammo is much more conventional than the weapons that are chambered for it. The 5.8mm standard rifle load has a

64-grain (4.15g) bullet with a full metal jacket made of steel and copper-washed coating. The 24.3mm long projectile has a very streamlined external shape with a sharp bullet ogive and a sizeable boattail. The bullet has a physical diameter of roughly 6mm but all small arms bullets in general have a slightly larger actual diameter. The extra thickness is needed by the barrel's rifling to grip on to the projectile and spin it as it travels down the barrel. Similarly, the 5.56mm bullet is actually 5.69mm in diameter and the 5.45mm projectile is really 5.61mm. The 5.8mm bullet has a composite core that consists of a pin-shaped hardened steel penetrator located near the base of the bullet, with lead as the filling material between the penetrator and the jacket as well as the tip cavity. The steel penetrator is 16mm in length, 4mm in diameter, and weights 23 grains (1.5g). In comparison, the M855/SS109 5.56mm's slightly shorter 62 grain (4g) composite core bullet has a cone-shaped steel penetrator followed by a lead core and a copper alloy jacket. The 5.56mm has a cannelure in the middle of the bullet for crimping the metal jacket onto the bullet core. Neither the 5.8mm nor the 5.45mm cartridge has this feature. The 7N6 5.45mm bullet is slightly longer than that of the 5.8mm, and it weights 52 grains (3.43g) with a large empty tip cavity followed by a tiny lead-arsenium alloy plug, then a large mild steel core wrapped by a soft steel jacket. Although a more even comparison could be made with the newer 7N10 enhanced penetration round, which features a small

The 5.8mm round's silver color propellant in small disk-shaped pellets. Also note the projectile size difference between the 7.62mm and the 5.8mm rounds on the upper right.

hardened steel penetrator like that of the other two calibers, most 5.45mm ammo manufacturing today is still of the older 7N6 model.

The 5.8mm cartridge has a 42mm long case with a one degree taper in the body from its 10.5mm diameter base. The bottle-neck shoulder and the neck are both 4mm long. The shorter but wider 5.8mm case is more space-efficient than the long and slim case of the 5.56mm. The tapered case design also helps both ammo feeding and extraction. However, the straight-wall case design of the 5.56mm has better accuracy.

Steel is used as the primary material for the 5.8mm case probably because of the cost. The steel case is less expensive and lighter than the brass case of the 5.56mm. However, it requires extra corrosion protection in the form of a brownish-color lacquer coating which causes many other problems in itself. The lacquer coating tends to leave drips and runs on the case surface during the manufacturing process. These could prevent the ammo from seating properly in the chamber, decrease accuracy, or even stop the bolt from closing on the chamber. The lacquer also leaves residue when it heats up, attracting carbon and grit inside of the weapon. If lacquer residue buildup is severe enough, it may cause the ammo case to fail to extract.

There are other superior processes for rust-proofing steel cartridge cases such as zinc plating, copper wash, and polymer coating but it appears the Chinese military does not want to pay extra for it. Being a harder and more brittle metal, steel tends to form a less-than-perfect seal in the chamber and more easily develops case ruptures that could lead to weapon malfunction. To ensure high extraction reliability, the 5.8mm case has a thick rim and a good-sized extractor groove.

The 5.8mm cartridge uses a silvery dual-base propellant in small dish-shaped pellets. The propellant load is approximately 28 grains (1.8g) which is more than the 5.56mm's 26 grains (1.7g) and the 5.45mm's 25 grains (1.6g). Because of cost-cutting measures, the 5.8mm's propellant is of the corrosive powder variety. In contrast, NATO and other Western nations have not used corrosive propellant since the end of World War II. The 5.8mm's corrosive powder is not particularly hot either. It only generates a 41,500psi (284 MPa) chamber pressure—only marginally higher than that of the old single-base propellant used by the vintage 7.62x39mm. In addition, the 41,500psi (284 MPa) chamber pressure is considered low by contemporary Western ammo standards. For example, the chamber pressure of the 5.56mm M855/SS109 is 55,000psi (380 MPa). A non-reloadable Berdan primer is used to prime the 5.8mm cartridge's propellant. Unfortunately, like the propellant, the primer also contains a corrosive chemical.

Chinese ammo designers claim the 5.8mm cartridge outperforms both the 5.56mm and 5.45mm in ballistics and penetration. The 5.8mm has more muzzle velocity and energy, a flatter trajectory with better velocity and energy retention.

The accompanying velocity curve graph shows the 5.8mm and the 5.56mm have similar ballistic performance out to 400 meters. After 400m, the 5.8mm with its superior ballistic coefficient moves ahead. The 5.45mm cartridge and the 5.56mm fired from the short barrel are simply no match for 5.8mm's ballistics at any range. The M-4 is technically a short carbine version of the M-16 designed for second-line or specialized troops. It's included in the comparison because the U.S. military is issuing the M-4 as the standard rifle for large numbers of its combat troops. Additionally, the supersonic velocity threshold depicted at the bottom of both graphs is important for effective long-range performance. Once the bullet velocity drops below supersonic speed, those small-caliber lightweight rounds do not have enough energy left for reliable penetration of heavily-padded winter clothing, empty ammo magazines, water canteens, and other individual equipment worn by typical infantrymen.

I personally shot the QBZ95 with the 5.8mm standard load, achieving an average three MOA (minute of angle). With a shooter more comfortable with the bullpup layout and a proper zero, a 2.5 MOA or better accuracy should be achievable with the same 5.8mm ammo and rifle combination.

My experience with the M-16A2 shows that the M855/SS109 5.56mm ammo has an average two MOA accuracy when fired from the M-16A2. The newer M-16A4 with its heavier and higher quality barrel should be even more accurate. The best the AK74 and

5.8x42mm Muzzle Velocity and Energy

	Barrel Length	Muzzle Velocity	Muzzle Energy
QBZ95 Assault Rifle	18.2 in (463mm)	3050 fps (930m/s)	1325 ft-lbs (1795j)
QBB95 Squad Auto	21.9 in (557mm)	3181 fps (970m/s)	1441 ft-lbs (1952j)
QBZ95 Carbine	12.8 in (326mm)	2581 fps (790m/s)	956 ft-lbs (1295j)

5.45x39mm Muzzle Velocity and Energy

	Barrel Length	Muzzle Velocity	Muzzle Energy
AK-74 Assault Rifle	16.3 in (415mm)	2952 fps (900m/s)	1025 ft-lbs (1389j)
RPK-74 Squad Auto	23.3 in (590mm)	3150 fps (960m/s)	1166 ft-lbs (1581j)

5.56x45mm Muzzle Velocity and Energy

	Barrel Length	Muzzle Velocity	Muzzle Energy
M-16A2/A4 Rifle	20 in (508mm)	3083 fps (940m/s)	1304 ft-lbs (1767j)
M249/NATO Rifles	18.5 in (470mm)	3018 fps (920m/s)	1249 ft-lbs (1693j)
M-4 Carbine	14.5 in (368mm)	2750 fps (838m/s)	1037 ft-lbs (1405j)

7N5 5.45mm pairing can do is four MOA accuracy. As a whole, the 5.8mm's accuracy is a substantial improvement over the older 7.62x39mm cartridge. Furthermore, it beats out the 1970s-era 5.45mm and approaches the accuracy of the 5.56mm and M-16A2/A4 combination.

Information on the 5.8mm ballistic test was published in the August, 2003 issue of Small Arms, a Chinese-language gun enthusiast magazine from mainland China. 5.56mm and 5.45mm ammo were also used in the test for comparison. All the test plates were shot 22 times with each caliber. Additional test data was available from American small arms writer David M. Fortier's research. The results of hard and soft target tests are as follows:

Test #1: 3.5mm NATO A3 Steel Test Plate at 640 Meters

	Penetration Rate	Impact Velocity	Retained Energy
5.8mm DBP87/QBB95	100%	1575 fps (480m/s)	357 ft-lbs (484j)
5.56mm SS109/FN FNC	100%	1529 fps (466m/s)	320 ft-lbs (434j)
5.45mm 7N6/RPK-74	18.2%	1526 fps (465m/s)	275 ft-lbs (373j)

Test #2: 3.5mm NATO A3 Steel Test Plate at 700 Meters

	Penetration Rate	Impact Velocity	Retained Energy
5.8mm DBP87/QBB95	100%	1389 fps (423m/s)	281 ft-lbs (381j)
5.56mm SS109/FN FNC	72.7%	1345 fps (410m/s)	248 ft-lbs (336j)
5.45mm 7N6/RPK-74	No Penetration	Not Available	Not Available

Test #3: 10mm NATO A3 Steel Test Plate at 300 Meters

	Penetration Rate	Impact Velocity	Retained Energy
5.8mm DBP87/QBB95	100%	2339 fps (713m/s)	787 ft-lbs (1066j)
5.56mm SS109/FN FNC	No Penetration	Not Available	Not Available
5.56mm P112 AP/FN FNC	100%	2254 fps (687m/s)	696 ft-lbs (943j)
5.45mm 7N6/RPK-74	No Penetration	Not Available	Not Available

Test #4: Calibrated Ballistic Soap Block at 85 Meters

	Wound Cavity Size	Impact Velocity	Energy Transfer
5.8mm/QBB95	2.12 cubic in (34.8 cubic cm)	2903 fps (885m/s)	98 ft-lbs (133j)
5.56mm/FN FNC	2.94 cubic in (48.2 cubic cm)	2775 fps (846m/s)	96 ft-lbs (129j)
5.45mm/RPK-74	3.64 cubic in (59.7 cubic cm)	2778 fps (847m/s)	167 ft-lbs (228j)

The first three tests demonstrated the 5.8mm indeed out-penetrates both the 5.56mm and the 5.45mm as Chinese engineers stated. However, the test was manipulated to make the 5.8mm look good. A long-barrel QBB95 squad automatic rifle was used for the test instead of the QBZ95 assault rifle. The 5.8mm rounds fired from the QBB95 have a 164 fps (50m/s) muzzle velocity advantage over the 5.56mm fired from the Fabrique Nationale FNC assault rifle. The 5.45mm rounds were also fired from a squad automatic rifle for the test. Nevertheless, the 5.8mm's 100percent penetration rate of the 10mm steel plate at 300 meters is very impressive. The 5.8mm standard load's armor-piercing performance more or less matches that of the 5.56mm P112 AP. The P112 AP (Armor-piercing) is a NATO-spec. dedicated armor-piercing round of an older steel core design. As for the 5.45mm, evidently the extra velocity from the long-barrel RPK-74 didn't matter much since the 7N6 load is not an enhanced penetration round like the other two cartridges. The large mild steel core inside of the 7N6 is really a low-cost alternative for a lead core, and it doesn't help improve penetration.

Realistically, the penetration performance difference between the 5.56mm and the 5.8mm is much closer. Contrary to the rigged Chinese ballistic test, unbiased tests done by the USMC and U.S. Army's Aberdeen Proving Ground show the 5.56mm M855/SS109 fired from the M-16A2 rifle with the longer 20-inch (508mm) barrel has no problem penetrating the 3.5mm A3 steel test plate at 700 meters. Even so, the 5.8mm is still a better AP round than the 5.56mm. It all comes down to the design of the bullet. In the accompanying cutaway illustration, the 5.8mm bullet's construction resembles the APHC (Armor-piercing Hard Core) projectile design more common to dedicated AP ammo.

It's no coincidence the 5.8mm matches the 5.56mm P112 AP in armor-piercing performance. In comparison, the 5.56mm M855/SS109's bullet has a small cone-shaped steel penetrator added in front of its normal lead core for improved penetration. The 5.8mm penetrates better because it was designed as AP ammo to begin with. Many official and unofficial Chinese sources frequently mention how important the 5.8mm's AP performance is. One possible explanation for the Chinese obsession with AP performance is that the 5.8mm's AP-like core was specially designed for use against opponents who are wearing heavy body armor—such as U.S. forces.

The fourth test conducted by Chinese engineers was the soft target test. Probably to reduce costs, Chinese engineers are still using ballistic soap blocks instead of more appropriate ballistic gelatin for soft target testing. The ballistic gelatin is made from animal products capable of simulating the elasticity and reflexes of muscle and other body tissue, something that the soap block can't do.

The cavity generated in the soap block is of the temporary kind instead of the more significant permanent cavity. The temporary cavity is formed by the stretching of body tissues as the bullet starts to yaw. However, body tissue will quickly bounce back and leave a smaller wound profile, called the permanent cavity. The permanent cavity shows the permanent cuts and tears in the tissues which typically lead to massive internal bleeding and a much more lethal wound. The energy transfer measurements from the test were probably taken from the soap block's base where the amount of force the whole soap block received when it was stricken by bullet is determined.

The side profile illustration of three current small-caliber high-velocity rifle rounds of the world. (Special thanks to Anthony G. Williams)

5.56mm M855   5.8mm DBP87   5.45mm 7N6

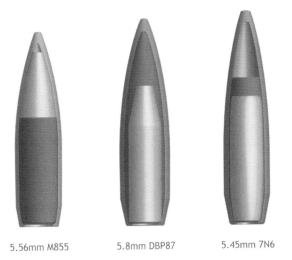

5.56mm M855   5.8mm DBP87   5.45mm 7N6

The projectile cutaway illustration of the three current SCHV calibers. Notice the significant difference in the bullet designs between the three SCHV rounds. (Special thanks to David M. Fortier)

Like most AP ammo, the test showed the 5.8mm bullet left a rather unimpressive wound cavity in the ballistic soap block. The 5.8mm's wound cavity is almost one-third smaller than of the 5.56mm's and close to one-half smaller than that of the 5.45mm's cavity. The 5.8mm lacks the special wound-producing mechanisms that are in use by the 5.56mm and the 5.45mm.

For the 5.56mm, the mechanism is fragmentation by the thin copper alloy jacket and the cannelure that further weakens it.

Once the 5.56mm bullet begins to tumble in the tissue, the bullet breaks apart at the cannelure and produces fragments that cut into surrounding tissues. The size of the permanent cavity is enlarged substantially through this fragmentation process.

The 5.45mm's wounding mechanism is a very clever combination of its hollow tip, lead plug, and the "Gaspolster effect" working with the "sliding ballast" principle. Upon the firing of the 5.45mm cartridge, hot propellant gas leaks through the open base of the bullet and melts the small lead-arsenium plug in front of the mild steel core. The melted lead alloy is then pushed into the empty tip cavity by the hot gas and solidifies asymmetrically when the bullet leaves the barrel. The 5.45mm bullet yaws quickly in tissues due to the weight imbalance caused by the hollow point and tumbles erratically from the unevenly deposited lead in the tip. The thick steel jacket of the 5.8mm bullet prevents any fragmentation. The more balanced weight distribution of the solid lead tip with the steel core in the back also prevents the 5.8mm bullet from tumbling early and erratically. Nonetheless, Chinese sources claim the 5.8mm has 60 percent increase in lethality over the old 7.62x39mm it replaces.

To date, there are some known issues with the 5.8mm ammo and most of them trace back to the use of low-cost material or poor quality control in the manufacturing process. The propellant load and bullet weight could be inconsistent depending on the lot. The propellant leaves corrosive residue in the gas system and the barrel. And the primer has a tendency of rusting through after it has been in storage for a long period of time.

There are other special loads for the 5.8mm caliber. The 5.8mm tracer is marked with a blue-violet color tip. The two different 5.8mm training blanks are the star-crimped case blank and a frangible PVC bullet blank that feeds better and doesn't require the use of a blank-firing adapter. Its plastic bullet breaks up at the muzzle and the safe distance is seven meters from the muzzle. The

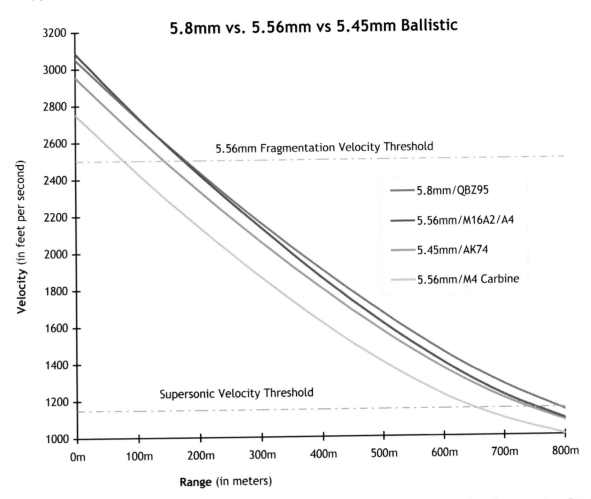

5.8mm vs. 5.56mm vs 5.45mm Ballistic

5.56mm Fragmentation Velocity Threshold

— 5.8mm/QBZ95

— 5.56mm/M16A2/A4

— 5.45mm/AK74

— 5.56mm/M4 Carbine

Supersonic Velocity Threshold

Velocity (in feet per second)

Range (in meters)

All ballistic data were compiled by using Robert Persson's software ballistic calculator with corrections from Aberdeen Proving Ground data and Chinese range test data. Estimated +/- 5 percent margin of error. (Illustrated by Timothy Yan©)

The bullet base and the headstamp of the Chinese DBP87 5.8x42mm assault rifle round. This particular cartridge was manufactured by ammo factory 71 in 1996. (Photo courtesy David M. Fortier)

The bullet entrances in the front of the ballistic soap blocks from the soft target test. (Photo courtesy *Small Arms Magazine*)

The wound cavities generated by the three current SCHV rounds in the ballistic soap blocks. The 5.8mm generated a much smaller cavity than the other two calibers. The 5.8mm bullet exited the soap block without producing much tumbling. (Photo courtesy *Small Arms Magazine*)

latest is the non-lethal 5.8mm rubber bullet load which was shown at the recent Beijing Police Equipment Expo. It has a full-size, round-nose, black rubber projectile in place of the full metal jacket bullet.

A good question is: "How will the 5.8mm perform in combat?" According to China's Xinhua news agency, the 5.8mm round scored its first combat kill recently in Haiti during a firefight between Chinese United Nations peacekeepers and the local rebels. The performance of the 5.8mm in urban combat operation will likely be a mixed bag. On one hand, its superb penetration will be suitable for punching through brick walls, metal doors, automobile bodies, and masonry debris. On the other hand, the 5.8mm's unimpressive terminal ballistics may require multiple hits to neutralize an opponent. In the jungle, the 5.8mm should perform about the same as in urban combat since its high penetration characteristics are also good for perforating trees and other kinds of foliage. The 5.8mm will fare better in open environments such as desert and mountainous terrain with its longer effective range.

Is developing the 5.8x42mm cartridge really worth the effort? Politics and national pride probably had as much to do with its development as the Chinese military. It seems the Chinese engineers did a decent job in designing the 5.8mm cartridge. The problem is that the Chinese military went on the cheap in manufacturing it. We would only see the real potential of the 5.8mm if it is made with the same material and high manufacturing standards, such as using a brass case, hotter and non-corrosive propellant, tight tolerance and good quality control, as the American and European 5.56mm rounds. As of now, whatever edge the 5.8mm cartridge has over the 5.56mm is not enough to make the difference in real combat. The 5.8mm may excel in some areas because it has a slightly heavier bullet, a larger cartridge case, and more propellant. However, the performance improvements are small, in most cases just 5 to 10 percent. In other areas, such as accuracy and lethality, the American/NATO 5.56mm is still a better round by a comfortable margin over the 5.8mm.

Perhaps, during its early development, the 5.8mm SCHV ammo should have been made a little larger—into the 6mm class.

The Chinese 5.8x42mm's case design has a strong resemblance to that of the American experimental 6x45mm SAW (left)*, the Russian 5.45x39mm* (center) *and the 6.5x38mm Grendel* (right)*. The shorter but wider cartridge case offers more internal volume for the propellant and it also allows the use of a long bullet with high ballistic coefficient.* (Photo courtesy David M. Fortier)

A rare group photo of a Chinese special forces team operating in the desert environment somewhere in Northwestern China. The special 7.62mm sound-suppressed submachine gun holding by the Master Corporal team leader (kneeling at the center) *will be replaced shortly by a new sound-suppressor-equipped 5.8mm submachine gun.*

The two current assault rifles in service with the Chinese military. The new Chinese 5.8mm QBZ95 bullpup (bottom) *and the older 7.62mm QBZ81 in the traditional layout* (top)*. Eventually, the QBZ95 will replace all the QBZ81 in the services.*

Chapter 13
The 6.8 SPC

A 21st century Special Forces Assault Rifle cartridge.

By Bill Ball

A popular television science fiction series, the *X-Files*, built thrilling episodes on the theme, "*The truth is out there — somewhere.*" In the first decade of the 21st century, the U.S. 5.56x45mm combat cartridge jumped into a real-world reality check in Iraqi cities and deserts, and in Afghanistan's mountain passes and valleys. Versions of the truth under battlefield conditions ranged from "All is well with the 5.56x45mm cartridge." to "Why stay with the ineffective 5.56x45mm cartridge when better assault rifle cartridges are available now for American soldiers?"

Reports from current combat operations suggest a different cartridge could increase combat lethality and reduce friendly casualties. However, if good and believable reasons exist for change, sound reasons not to change are irrefutable facts of life.

You might recall the British Army's consideration of the 276-caliber Enfield cartridge before WWI, the U.S. Army's recommendation to deploy the 276 Pederson cartridge with the M-1 Garand rifle around 1936, and the post-WWII British efforts to introduce the 280 (7x43mm) cartridge as a standard NATO round. These events confirm that making changes to a fundamental war-fighting element, the infantry rifle and cartridge, can be both divisive and difficult to achieve. In fact, none of these cartridges made the transition to active military service.

Groups of 5.56x45mm status quo supporters might enthusiastically attempt to persuade everyone that if John Browning, John Garand, Eugene Stoner and every other firearms genius that ever lived had to design the perfect combat cartridge, they would universally re-invent the 5.56x45mm cartridge now used by the United States and many other nations, and field it in M-16A2 rifles and the shorter-barreled M-4 carbines. Logistics, life-cycle cost,

training and inertia all contribute to this viewpoint. After all, the M-16 and 5.56x45mm cartridge combination has outlasted every other infantry shoulder arm and cartridge fielded by the U.S. Army.

Advocates for change might describe the 5.56x45mm as a poodle shooter, best suited for making mediocre marksmen out of urban city youths who have no firearms experience and the ever-increasing numbers of female soldiers. The really effective combat cartridges, they'd reason, would be something along the lines of the WWII 7.92x33mm Kurz round and MP-44 Sturmgewehr combination that brought a new level of combat effectiveness and lethality to the Eastern Front, or post-war efforts including Fabrique Nationale's initial chambering of the same 7.92x33mm Kurz cartridge in the original FAL rifle, the British 280 experimental cartridge in the EM-2 assault rifle, or possibly the former Soviet Union's AK47 and M-43 (7.62x39mm) cartridge pairing.

Essential elements of the debate seem to focus on bullet diameter, weight, design and velocity, along with the supporting weapon's reliability, accuracy and ergonomics in the anticipated combat environment.

Since the truth has to be out there somewhere, just waiting to be re-discovered, what combination of circumstances constitutes the big beef with the 5.56x45mm cartridge and M-16 weapons family?

Anecdotal comments from U. S. soldiers deployed during the 1992 riots in Somalia, where 7.62x39mm bullets joined the stones, bats, and crowbars flung at friendly soldiers, suggested when hit repeatedly with the 5.56x45mm bullets, bad guys didn't reliably drop.

From Afghanistan and Iraq, many confirmed and unconfirmed stories describe how multiple upper torso hits failed to disable or incapacitate hostile combatants, when the M-4 carbine and 5.56x45mm cartridge were used. The 5.56x45mm cartridge achieves primary incapacitation through bullet yaw and fragmentation. The standard military loading uses a 62-grain, M855 FMJ bullet. Short-barreled weapons slow bullet velocities to a level where failure to yaw and fragment can often occur.

Modern combat-tested cartridges from the last half of the 20th century and the beginning of the 21st include (left to right) **the Soviet-developed 5.45x39 used in the AK 74 and AKM74 weapons, the U.S.-developed 5.56x45 used in M-16 and M-4 rifles and carbines, the 5th Special Forces Group developed the 6.8 Special Purpose Cartridge used in M-16 and M-4 firearms, the legendary 7.62x39 cartridge for the AK-47 and the NATO-standard 7.62x51 used in a wide variety of rifles and machineguns.**

The primary competitor of the 6.8 Special Purpose Cartridge (left), **developed to improve the combat performance of short-barreled M-4 carbines by MSG Steve Holland, 5th Special Forces Group (ABN), remains the legendary Soviet M43 cartridge for the AK47, otherwise known as the 7.62x39. Cartridge shown on the right is of Yugoslavian manufacture.**

Following the September 11, 2001 attacks, 5th Special Forces Group (Abn) soldiers deployed to Afghanistan discovered the 77-grain bullet in their Mk12 Mod 0 special-purpose rifles was more effective in combat than the standard 62-grain M855 ball ammo. Black Hills Ammo supplied the production 77-grain MK 262 Mod 0 (with Sierra Match King bullets) and Mod 1 (with Nosler Open Tip Match bullets) cartridges used by the 5th Special Forces soldiers. In the 5.56x45mm cartridge, the heavier bullets seemed to perform better. Not perfectly, just better. The absence of a cannelure on Match King bullets may have caused some bullet setback problems.

America's special operations soldiers face different circumstances and missions from other infantry units. For one, they fire many more rounds through their M-4 rifles, perhaps 5000 to 6000 rounds annually, to achieve and maintain high standards of personal and professional excellence. A Special Forces soldier's rifle gets more use and wear in one year than most rifles get in five normal years. When their M-4 rifles began to have failures to extract, failures to feed, double feeds and even burst barrels, weapons reliability questions joined concerns about 5.56x45mm cartridge performance. An obvious couple of questions surfaced about improving reliability, along with terminal ballistic performance of the bullet. The problem might be traced to the reduction in barrel diameter beneath the handguard for weight reduction, or bad magazines, or the high cyclic rate. Whatever the causes, concern arose that the M-4 carbine would not handle the ops tempo needed by Special Forces teams.

The U.S. Army has an active program to improve infantry small arms, and has tested firearms available from many sources. Special Forces soldiers constitute just a fraction of the total number of troops in the Army equipped with shoulder-fired weapons. Whether or not it makes sense to field a unique weapon and cartridge combination for the small numbers of special operations troops is a question where the answer varies depending upon where one hangs their hat. For the special operations guy with camo paint on his face, the answer is pretty clear. The logistician and big picture guy might have a different outlook.

One possible solution could be replacing the 5.56-chambered M-4 carbines and M-16A2 rifles with the universally distributed AK47, with its highly effective 7.62x39mm cartridge. Ballistics for the 7.62x39mm show a 122-grain FMJ bullet, launched at about 2300 feet per second. The United States routinely produces 7.62x39mm ammunition as a standard military item for military and other training programs, so ammunition supply and logistics would not be an insurmountable issue.

The AK47 is a simple, reliable and effective combat firearm. For the last half of the 20th century, it appeared in one variant or another in the inventories of friendly and unfriendly nations, and countless groups of irregular forces, terrorists and individuals. The tough little AK47, with production in tens of millions or even

Remington (left), **Hornady** (center) **and Silver State Armory** (right) **produce factory 6.8 SPC ammunition. Interestingly, the Remington and Hornady cases are stamped** 6.8mm Rem SPC, **while the Silver State Armory brass bears** 6.8 SPC **markings. Typically, factory ammo is loaded with 110-grain V-MAX or with 115-grain Match King and open-tip match bullets.**

greater numbers, survived neglect and indifferent treatment across the mountainous environs of Afghanistan, the deserts and jungles of Africa, the tundra and taiga of Russia and Finland, the swamps and hills of Vietnam, and about every difficult piece of terrain on the planet. Why couldn't it find a home with the United States' Special Forces? After all, it works and it works every time the trigger is pulled. The combat effectiveness of the Soviet M-43 cartridge *(and other nations' similar ammunition)* is substantial.

On an East African operation to train three battalions of Ethiopian infantry, American Special Forces soldiers located crates of Soviet AK47s, stored in dockside warehouses by the Red Sea for several years. Through poor long-term storage, the rifles were rusted badly and the bolts would not cycle. Needing almost 800 rifles for their trainees, the American sprayed five rifles with WD-40, and rapped the bolt handles with leather mallets until the bolt popped free. After emptying several 30-round magazines, the Americans concluded the rifles could be restored to service. Handed to the Ethiopian soldiers detailed to a production line, each rifle was disassembled, cleaned with brake cleaner, wiped with WD-40, reassembled and test-fired with a 30-round magazine. Of 788 rifles serviced by the Ethiopian troopers, only three could not be returned to service.

During the Vietnam War in the 1960s and 1970s, the introduction of the M-16A1 and the 5.56x45mm cartridge into Southeast Asia combat operations caused the then-Soviet Union's military ordnance establishment to revisit the 7.62x39mm cartridge. The United States' fielding of a 22-caliber cartridge with increased velocity, greater lethality, and increased combat loads for the same weight impressed some of the Soviet military establishment.

The 1906-era, virtually obsolete 30 Remington cartridge (right) *became the parent case for the 6.8 Special Purpose Cartridge, primarily because the head size of the case could easily be adapted to the bolt dimensions of the U.S. Army's M-4 carbines, and the shape of the case worked well with existing military issue magazines.*

Remington provided significant assistance in the development of the 6.8 Special Purpose Cartridge. Shown next to the loaded 30 Remington cartridge are Remington factory-stamped cartridge cases, marked (left to right)**:** *7.62mm SPC, 7mm SPC, 6.8mm SPC, and 5.56mm SPC.*

In response, the former Soviet military authorities developed and deployed the AK74 *(and variants)* and the 5.45x39mm cartridge. This Soviet small-bore cartridge pushed a 54-grain bullet at velocities around 2,950 fps, placing the Soviet soldier behind the muzzle of a small-bore cartridge for the first time since designer F.V. Tokarev experimented with the M-1916 Federov *"Avtomat"* selective-fire rifle (chambered for the Japanese 6.5 Arisaka cartridge) in the early 1900s.

Essentially identical to the AK47 except for changes needed for the smaller caliber, the AK74 was used extensively during the Soviet Union's military operations in Afghanistan during the late 1970s and 1980s, where it established a very credible track record. After the introduction of modern U.S.-supplied shoulder-fired, surface-to-air missiles into the conflict, extensive Soviet use of helicopters decreased, and their tactics changed.

In the two years preceding the Soviet withdrawal from Afghanistan, the deployment of Soviet Special Forces units increased greatly. The revised tactics meant small-sized *Spetsnaz* units conducted many engagements without supporting fires from artillery, machine guns or aircraft. Although more effective than earlier tactics, the change came too late to influence the overall political and strategic conditions leading to the Soviet withdrawal in 1989.

Interestingly, available information suggests during the final years of the Afghan war, Soviet *Spetsnaz* soldiers preferred the AK47 and the 7.62x39mm cartridge to the smaller 5.45x39mm cartridge in the AK74 and AK74M rifles.

However, one reason not to introduce the AK47 into the U.S. Special Forces inventory as the primary combat weapon lies in the weapon's ergonomics. For folks who have fired both AK47 and M-16 rifles, there is little doubt Eugene Stoner thought more about shooter convenience than did Mikhail Kalashnikov.

The AK47 places the safety and fire selector in one pivoting (and noisy) control on the right side of the receiver. The magazine release uses a lever operated catch in front of the trigger guard. Neither control is easily manipulated without repositioning the shooting hand. Unlike the AK-family of rifles that use a side-mounted optical rail to position sights above and left of bore centerline, the M-16A2 and M-4 weapons adapt easily to centerline-mounted optical and red dot sights. Happily, the M-16 rifle uses a convenient rotating safety and fire selector control on the left side of the receiver, and the magazine release falls easily to the trigger finger.

Changing to AK-type weapons with different safety, selector, magazine release and sighting systems in the midst of a shooting war, such as now underway in Iraq and Afghanistan, seems at best not very smart. But, as the saying goes, if you can't bring Mohammed to the mountain, perhaps you can bring the mountain to Mohammed. Could, some U.S. Special Forces folks wondered, the 7.62x39mm cartridge be adapted to the M-16 weapons family?

The answer turned out to be *yes* — and *sort of*. M-16 bolts suitable for the 7.62x39mm cartridge have been manufactured for years. Barrels, buffers, springs and gas tubes were easy. The challenge turned out to be magazines, because the U.S. military owns millions of magazines that chamber 5.56x45mm rounds. The introduction of a new type magazine into the U.S. inventory causes incredible logistics problems. Any new assault rifle cartridge that fits a reasonable number of cartridges into the existing M-16 magazines will attain a significant advantage. The 7.62x39mm cartridge did not fit into existing M-16 magazines.

When 5th Special Forces Group (Abn) S5 Force Modernization office — specifically MSG Steve Holland — seriously considered the reliability, accuracy and lethality needs unique to special operations, the magazine consideration proved paramount. Whatever the other cartridge attributes were, it had to fit and function in existing 30-round military magazines. Other desired attributes seemed to include bullet weights and velocities in the 115-grain bullet and 2,800 fps range. Any new cartridge must function with M-16 lower receivers, display suitable accuracy (1.5 MOA or better) out to 600 meters, avoid excessive recoil, and achieve complete reliability.

Armed with a copy of CARTRIDGES OF THE WORLD, MSG Holland checked the cartridge drawings and dimensional data, looking for a parent case that could be modified. Mr. Cris Murray, USAMU Master Gunsmith, thought the 30 Remington cartridge, an obsolete

Remington produced special runs of SPC headstamped brass cases. Shown from the left, along with an older 30 Remington case (stamped Rem-UMC) are the 7.62mm SPC, 7mm SPC, 6.8mm SPC and 5.56mm SPC. Note the 7.62mm and 7mm SPC cases are dummy cases without flash holes drilled in the primer pocket.

rimless cartridge introduced by Remington in 1906 for its Model 8 autoloading rifle, appeared promising. About equivalent to the more popular 30-30 Winchester round in performance, the 30 Remington features a case head measuring .420-inch, slightly smaller (by .025-inch) than the 7.63x39 cartridge. At this dimension, bolts for the M-16 rifle could readily be machined to accept the 30 Remington case. With a shoulder diameter of .402-inch, the case taper was almost straight.

With greatly appreciated assistance from the Army's Special Purpose Rifle program and the Army Marksmanship Unit, barrels in various calibers were procured and fitted to M-16 upper receivers. Unfired 30 Remington cases proved more difficult to obtain than barrels and upper receivers. MSG Holland finally located 100 cases on the back shelf (along with 30 Remington and 25 Remington reloading dies) in a distant Tennessee gun store. One hundred unfired brass cases, in older style, dust-covered boxes, cost exactly $12. Machined shorter to size cartridge cases 45mm long (identical to the 5.56x45mm cartridge), the sizing dies reduced the shortened 30 Remington brass so that, in a stroke of genius or flash of luck, exactly 25 cases fit into an existing M-16 30-round magazine.

The Army Marksmanship Unit crafted prototype upper receivers by opening the bolt face from .378-inch (used by 5.56x45mm ammo) to .422-inch. Under the watchful eye of Mr. Cris Murray, AMU armorers chambered and contoured the 6.5mm, 7mm and 30-caliber barrels. Dave Kiff of Pacific Tool and Gauge, supplied the reamers for the project.

By progressively opening the neck of the 25 Remington sizing die, MSG Holland created new cartridges in 6.5mm, 7mm and 30 calibers, using shortened 30 Remington cases. After some adjustments so the bullet did not intrude into the powder space, an overall cartridge length of 2.26 inches and case length of 43mm was selected. With the newly barreled M-4 upper receivers and handcrafted cartridges, MSG Holland and bus loads of Special

Along with the 6.8 SPC (left), other cartridges tested by 5th Special Forces Group include the 6.5 Grendel® (center) from Alexander Arms and the benchrest standard 6 PPC (right) by Norma. Each of these cartridges can be made to function in M-16 rifles and M-4 carbines, albeit with differences in performance and magazine capacity.

Forces operators started pulling triggers and recording results. Thousands of rounds sped down range from 14.5-, 16-, 18- and 20-inch barrels, thumping steel targets with vigor and punching though paper ones. By all reports, the cartridge performed well, both on the range, and against 10-percent ordnance gelatin blocks.

In testing, the 30-caliber version proved less desirable than either the 7mm or 6.5mm cartridges. The 7mm version produced a larger wound channel, compared to the 6.5mm cartridge. However, 7mm velocities were lower than those of the 6.5mm, reflecting the heavier bullet weights needed to maintain a specific ballistics coefficient. Then, in another bit of genius, Mr. Troy Lawton, USAMU Ballistic Technician observed that the 270-caliber bullets had been overlooked. Since a .277-inch bullet (measuring 6.8mm) was halfway between 6.5mm and 7mm, MSG Holland wondered if it could be driven close to the 6.5mm velocities, while delivering the wound channel of the 7mm.

The gel block was still quivering from Holland's first 6.8mm cartridge, when someone observed they had a winner. The wound channel almost equaled the 7mm version's, and the velocity was very close to the 6.5mm with equivalent ballistic coefficient bullets. After many more test firings, the answer was obvious—the .277 bullet in the shortened 30 Remington case produced the best balance of velocity and wound ballistics.

In the accuracy department, the 6.8 cartridge proved to be no dud. At an AMU 600-yard range, a 12-inch barreled M-4 carbine neatly placed 10 shots into a 10-inch group. With these results, nobody needed a committee decision to pursue the 6.8 version and stop work on the other calibers. Since the 43mm long cartridge was intended for special operations soldiers, MSG Holland named it the 6.8 Special Purpose Cartridge, or 6.8 SPC.

As a potential contender for special missions and operations, the 6.8x43mm cartridge was never intended to replace the standard 5.56x45mm cartridge, now in wide use. Rather, the 6.8 SPC was slated to go head-to-head with the 7.62x39mm cartridge used by hostile forces and enemy soldiers. Even if some shooters became confused on this point, a side-by-side range session with 5.56 M-4 carbines and 6.8 SPC M-4s, produced consistent results—the 6.8's performance was described as "phenomenal!"

When fired into chest pouches containing loaded AK-47 magazines at three meters as might typically be worn by hostile combatants, the 6.8 SPC (115-gr bullet at 2670 fps) delivered significantly more severe results than the 5.56x45mm ammo using the M855's 62-grain FMJ bullet and the MK262 Mod 1's 77-grain open-tip, match projectile. When hit with the 6.8 projectile, the loaded AK47 magazine burst dramatically into flames.

Picatinny Arsenal analysts compared the 6.8 SPC data and dimensions to their computer simulations about an ideal assault rifle cartridge, based on the same considerations of magazine fit, compatibility with M-4 lower receivers and ballistics performance. Their resulting cartridge design, based on thousands of dollars of computer simulation, departed from the 6.8 SPC dimensions by less than .001-inch in any direction.

In 2003, a Judge Advocate General review declared the 6.8 SPC cartridge using the 115-grain open tip match bullet from Hornady or the Sierra Match King was legal for land warfare use and authorized for combat employment. Presumably, special operations soldiers headed into harm's way may well be armed with the 6.8 SPC as this article is prepared.

The 6.8x43 SPC, chambered in M-16, M-4, Mk12 or Mk18 firearms delivers an arguably advantageous outcome—dramatic increase in combat performance at a trivial procurement cost. The total cost to develop and test the cartridge with suitable M-16 weapons was less than $10,000—a remarkable accomplishment in the current military procurement environment. An even more remarkable fact is that the 6.8 SPC development came from seasoned professional soldiers, in a bottom-up approach, based on real-world experience about what a special operations soldier needs.

As the 6.8 SPC cartridge matures, other bridges remain uncrossed. Among many other considerations, any new assault rifle cartridge should also work in the M249 squad automatic weapon. The 6.8 SPC is scheduled for future testing with the M249, and while it appears promising, only comprehensive testing can establish whether the cartridge can function reliably in the SAW. The cartridge may have excellent applications in law enforcement, too, and the FBI is known to be testing the 6.8 SPC at its Quantico, Virginia Ballistic Research Facility. Barrett Firearms Manufacturing, DPMS, Robinson Armaments and Precision Reflex now sell AR-15 rifles chambered in 6.8 Remington SPC for military and law enforcement applications.

While its military and law enforcement futures are being pondered and tested, the 6.8 SPC has found a home in the civilian market. First, Remington, then later, Hornady, decided to produce the cartridge commercially. Remington chambered the 6.8 in its Model 700 bolt-action rifle line. Later, folks discovered the petite CZ 527 bolt-action rifles chambered in 7.62x39mm convert easily to the 6.8 SPC. Thompson/Center's Contender, G2 and Encore actions are naturals for the 6.8 SPC, and factory 6.8 SPC barrels are offered by Thompson/Center and their custom shop. Another source of custom 6.8 firearms, J.D. Jones at SSK Industries, delivered an engraved 6.8 SPC Contender (ordered and paid for by MSG Holland), which turned out so elegantly that Holland decided not to take it hunting. Later Holland killed a number of whitetail deer using an SSK Industries Encore rifle, also chambered in 6.8 SPC. The 6.8 SPC turned out to be a first-rate whitetail deer cartridge, by the way.

Interestingly, other companies are developing assault rifle cartridges, focusing on the same opportunity as the 6.8 SPC developers. Alexander Arms chambers the 6.5 Grendel® cartridge in its own M-16-type weapons. The 6.5 Grendel is almost identical to the 6.5 PPC cartridge, and 17 of them will fit into an Alexander Arms-manufactured M-16 magazine. J.D. Jones, owner of SSK Industries, recently sent the author a cartridge suitable for the M-16, which J.D. named the 6.5 *Idonnowhattocallit*. This cartridge uses the 5.56 case necked up to accept 6.5mm bullets. It appears similar to the earlier 6.5 TCU cartridge. Marty der Weeme of Teppo Jetsu, LLC is developing the 30 HRT (Hostage Rescue Team) cartridge, which uses the 6.8 SPC case necked up to accept 30-caliber bullets. Because the 6.8 SPC began its life as the 30 Remington cartridge necked down, the 30 HRT development proves again the old adage––what goes around, comes around.

In the quest for the ideal cartridge for Special Forces soldiers, a number of viable cartridges are jostling around as hopeful contenders. In the final measure, any future assault rifle cartridge adopted by the U.S. military has to pass some incredibly tough hurdles, real and imaginary. The chances for adoption improve significantly, though, if it is blessed with more than a little luck and good feedback from the soldiers. The bottom line of the decision should always be the foremost consideration—best equipping American men and women fighting insurgents and fanatics in the global war on terrorism.

On the development path to the final 6.8 SPC configuration, MSG Holland resized the 30 Remington cases to different bullet sizes, case lengths and rim dimensions. Shown here are some of the cartridges that didn't perform as well as the 6.8 SPC when tested for accuracy, penetration, reliability and other performance factors. From the left: (1) the 7.62x44, (2) 7.62x41, (3) 7.62x39, (4) 7x44, (5) 7x41, (6) 6.5x45, (7) 6.5x43, and (8) 5.56x43. When the testing concluded, the 6.8 SPC (not shown) demonstrated the best balance between penetration in ordnance gelatin blocks, velocity, accuracy, and the ability to use existing U.S. military magazines. To convert existing M-16 and M-4 weapons to the 6.8 SPC requires only a new upper receiver, bolt and barrel.

Chapter 14

50 BMG Wildcats, and Others

This big competitor has gone on to raise a family.

By Gary Paul Johnston

Having been a late bloomer by today's standards, I fired my first 50 BMG (12.7x99mm) rifle 30 years ago in 1975 at the age of 34. It was a World War II British Boys bolt action that had been converted from the belted 55-caliber Boys down to 50 BMG using a surplus Browning M2 machinegun barrel. Back then the Boys was pretty much the only 50 BMG game in town, but today there are at least a dozen 50 BMG rifles used for hunting and long-range competition. I've shot most of them, along with the Browning M2HB machinegun where it all started.

Designed by small arms genius, John Moses Browning, in 1916, the 50 BMG cartridge was adopted by the U.S. military in 1921 along with the M2 Heavy Machine Gun (HMG) and has remained in service ever since. This makes it the longest running small arms cartridge in U.S. history. For at least half that time, the 50 BMG has also lived a life of its own as a civilian sporting cartridge.

Designed essentially by scaling up the 30-06 cartridge, the 50 BMG, like its smaller parent cartridge and others, came about during the transition from blackpowder to smokeless powder. Like the 30-06, the 50 BMG was thus perhaps longer than necessary, the '06 later being shortened to create the more efficient 7.62mm NATO (308 Win.) cartridge.

For a few statistics, a 700-grain bullet fired from the 50 BMG case has a sectional density (SD) in the 385 range and a ballistic co-efficient of friction (BC) starting at about .835. Muzzle velocity (MV) is normally in the range of 2600 to 2900 feet per second (fps). Chamber pressure in pounds per square inch (PSI) runs from about 42,000 to almost 49,000 in military loads and from almost 51,000 to over 53,000 in proof loads.

The fact that the 50 BMG continues to be used by the military has caused it to remain high in popularity with long-range competitors. However, where necessity and — sometimes — desire is the mother of invention, the 50 BMG has spawned a number of offspring. This has largely occurred through the Fifty Caliber Shooters Association (FCSA), which has over 3500 members in 22 countries. A number of wildcat 50-caliber cartridges based on the 50 BMG have been developed, as well as others of different calibers, using a different parent cartridge case, or both. Let's take a look at some of them.

Skip Talbott

In addition to many others, FCSA pioneer and all-around great guy, the late Skip Talbott did a tremendous amount of experimentation with 50 BMG load development, and Skip also designed the 338/50 Talbott back in the mid-1980s. Nicknamed the "Plenty Go Faster," this round uses a shortened 50 BMG case necked to 338-caliber. Loaded with 170 grains of IMR 5010, this round produced 3680 fps from a 44-inch barrel, at the cost of dramatically shortened barrel life. About the same time experimentation began using 375-caliber bullets in similar 50 BMG parent cases and 50-caliber bullets in cases smaller than the 50 BMG.

The 50 FCSA and 50 BMG Improved

By 1992, two 50 BMG wildcat cartridges had appeared and were written about by Eric Williams in the FCSA newsletter. Both rounds were based on the 50 BMG case with one, the 50 FCSA (12.7x77mm Improved) using a surplus 50-caliber Spotter cartridge case. This round can also be made by shortening and resizing a 50 BMG case to 3.00 inches and then fire-forming to produce an "improved" shoulder angle of 40 degrees. With a case capacity of 230 grains, as compared with 270 grains for the BMG, the 50 FCSA has a more efficient short, fat powder train, and maintains good MV of about 2,850 fps.

In 1991, Skip Talbott, designer of the 50 FCSA, shot the World Record five-shot group with his 33-inch barreled 50 FCSA rifle with five shots measuring 4.25 inches at 1000 yards. In the early 1990s, Skip Talbott did extensive testing of the 50 FCSA cartridge using standard 50 BMG boattail bullets, Zero Index Leadloy steel projectiles and new Beiber steel bullets with copper bore-riders. His conclusion was that he would recommend changing the 40-degree shoulder angle to 35 degrees.

The second cartridge was the 50 BMG Improved. Developed by Eric Williams, the 50 BMG Improved (12.7x99mm) is to the 50 BMG cartridge as the 30-06 Ackley Improved is to the 30-06 cartridge. With a length of 3.89 inches, this case is .003-inch shorter than that of the standard 50 BMG, but has a .779-inch shoulder width as compared with .714-inch for the 50 BMG. The improved round also has a 40-degree shoulder angle as compared with the 15.44 degree angle of the regular 50 BMG and has a 300-grain case capacity vs. 270 grains for the BMG with an MV of 2,930 fps from a 34-inch barrel. However, propellant availability was the major problem with the 50 BMG Improved, as it relies on slower-burning powders, such as those used in 25mm and 30mm cannon ammunition. As with the 50 FCSA cartridge, the 50 BMG Improved necessitated fireforming.

About the same time solid 50-caliber bullets became popular. Made of brass, these bullets are either turned or swaged and provide increased accuracy because of their homogenous makeup. Included among them were the Beiber and TCCI, each weighing 700 grains, the 750-grain TCCI and Barnes and the 800-grain VLD. However, although extremely accurate, these bullets require exacting bore dimensions to prevent pressure spikes and prevent excessive wear.

(L/R), **the 308 Winchester, 338 Lapua, 408 CheyTac with 419- & 305-grain solid bullets, 416 Barrett, 460 Steyr, the 50 DTC loaded with a Hornady AMAX, and the 50 BMG loaded with a Beiber solid brass bullet.**

(L/R): **the 300 Winchester Magnum, 338 Lapua, 408 CheyTac, 460 Steyr and 50 BMG.**

The 50 DTC Euro

By 2000 the FCSA had spread around the world, but in a number of European countries shooters are not allowed to own or use firearms in military calibers. This inspired Eric Dantis, of France, to design a new 50-caliber cartridge based on the 50 BMG cartridge case, but not interchangeable with it. He called it the 50 DTC Euro (12.7x96mm) and markets it through his company, DAN-TEC.

Having an overall case length .125-inch shorter than that of the 50 BMG, the 50 DTC's case measures 3.8000 inches. The 50 DTC also has a shoulder angle of 18.5 degrees as compared with 15 degrees for the 50 BMG, and the 50 DTC's case is less tapered, having a width of 0.7600-inch at the shoulder. These dimensional changes prevent both cartridges from fitting in a barrel chambered for the other.

With all performance measurements being virtually identical to those of the 50 BMG, the 50 DTC cartridge seems an ideal substitute for its parent 50 BMG, and virtually any 50 BMG rifle can easily be converted to use this cartridge. At least academically, because of its shorter powder train, the 50 DTC has an edge in accuracy over the 50 BMG.

However, the main advantage of the 50 DTC is that it is "California legal." This is because when California passed its 50-caliber ban, it specified only the 50 BMG. While currently owned California 50 BMG rifles were grandfathered, we can expect to see the popularity of the 50 DTC grow in that state and elsewhere. Existing 50 BMG caliber rifles can be easily rebarreled or rechambered for the 50 DTC. Currently, the 50 DTC is being marketed in the U.S. by EDM and at least one EDM Windrunner rifle chambered for it was used in the 2005 FCSA National Championship Matches at Whittington Center.

The 11.6x90mm Steyr

Faced by the same European 50 BMG restrictions that led to the development of the 50 DTC, another alternative has been developed by Horst Grillmayer, of Germany. Called the 11.6x90mm (.460) Steyr, this 458-caliber round is also based on the 50 BMG case, but is not currently available in the U.S. However, in late 2005 I was able to examine a single new, unfired 460 Steyr empty case, which measured as follows:

OAL: 3.54" (89.9mm).
Length of Neck: .480" (12.2mm).
Width at Shoulder: .72" (13.2mm).
Shoulder to Head: 2.80" (71.1mm).
Angle of Shoulder: 24 degrees (approx.).

Being an early 460 Steyr case, the sample was made in Yugoslavia with a headstamp that bears the name of the designer and that of the company, as follows: GRILLMAYER 04 11.6X90 460 STEYR. Current cases reportedly read only 460 Steyr.

The bullet weight of the 460 Steyr was designed to be 600 grains with a muzzle velocity of up to 3000 fps loaded with Vitavouri or Hodgdon propellant. Initial tests included boattail and flat-base bullets, but accuracy was poor. Using experimental turned heavy

metal "red cast" 458-caliber bullets of 560 grains and 51mm (1.3 inches) long, groups measuring 70mm (1.8 inches) were reported from a hammer-forged barrel in a fixture at 500m (547 yards). All 460 Steyr bullets are reported to have been moly-coated monolithic brass solids. Hornady Mfg. Co. has been approached about making an AMAX projectile for 460 Steyr.

The Kyser Thunderbolts

In 2002 a whole new family of cartridges based on the 50 BMG casing emerged. Designed by Monte R. Kyser, almost all of these rounds carry the designation Kyser Thunderbolt (KTB). Starting with 375 caliber the KTB family includes calibers .416, .450, .50 and .70. Using the 50 BMG case as a parent, case KTB case lengths include 3.300 inches and 3.910 inches in each caliber, except the 70 KTB, which was only made in the 3.910-inch case length. The 50 KTB using the 3.300-inch length case (12.7x84mm) was the most successful. A performance chart of loadings for it is as follows:

Bullet	Powder	Charge Wt.	MV
Hornady 750 gr. AMAX	V24N41	220 gr.	2753 fps
	H-5010	212 gr.	2656 fps
	T-5070	215 gr.	2606 fps
IMI 647 gr. FMJ	V24N41	235 gr.	2992 fps
	H-5010	225 gr.	2869 fps
	T-5070	230 gr.	2860 fps

The 50 Longson and 50 McMurdo

The 50 Longson (12.7x83mm) was designed by Bruce Longson. This round is loaded with a Zero Index Leadloy steel projectile. The 50 McMurdo (12.7x92mm) uses the McMurdo "Ironhand" solid brass projectile. The 50 McMurdo is still in fairly wide use by five-time world champion 50-caliber shooter Scott Nye and others.

The 338 Lapua

In an effort to remain somewhat chronological, we must jump back and forth with regard to those cartridges that were developed from the parent 50 BMG case and those that have, let us say, been inspired by it. Of particular interest here is a little known fact about the 50 BMG connection with the development of the renowned 338 Lapua cartridge. In the early 1980s Research Armaments, the designer of AMAC sniper rifles for the U.S. Navy, experimented with a U.S. military 50-caliber Spotter case necked down to 375-caliber. The results of AMAC's experiments are not known, but the company's intermediate range sniper rifle was soon introduced in 338/416 Rigby, the forerunner to the 338 Lapua Magnum, or the 8.58x71mm.

Being effective to at least 1,500 meters, the 338 Lapua Magnum is based on a 416 Rigby parent case, and has a muzzle velocity of 2,950 fps in its factory military loading with a 250-grain bullet. A similar hunting load produces 2,855 fps.

The development and proliferation of the 338 Lapua cartridge is probably the ideal example of how the reputation and popularity of the 50 BMG cartridge has influenced other cartridges using different parent cases. Usually smaller than the venerable 50 BMG casing, these rounds have often been designed around parent cases that are better suited to using modern propellants and lighter projectiles. These cartridges have also been designed to perform in smaller, shorter actions and at ranges which, in comparison to those of the 50 BMG, might seem intermediate, but not necessarily.

The 408 CheyTac

Although it remains a magnificent cartridge and one that is extremely fun to shoot, the 80-year old 50 BMG has long been the subject of improvement, to which the many wildcats based on it will attest. However, seeing a need to improve this traditional long-range military cartridge, Professor John D. Taylor spearheaded a group of extremely talented people to form a new company in 1999. It was called CheyTac Associates (an acronym for Cheyenne Tactical) and its goal was to develop the ideal very long-range (VLR) sniper cartridge to replace the 50 BMG cartridge.

The development centered on the concept of "Balanced Flight," the premise of which is that a projectile retaining stability throughout its flight will go farther with greater accuracy. Warren

Jensen, of Lost River Ballistic Technologies, a sister company to CheyTac Assoc., identified the conditions that could be translated into projectile design that would allow very long distance accuracy, and the concept of Balanced Flight was patented.

Working with PRODAS software, Jensen designed projectiles where the linear and rotational drag is matched to eliminate the precession and overspin that are a cause of inaccuracy in conventional projectiles. The result is a balanced forward and axial rate of deceleration with a gyroscopic stability remaining constant, and the projectile remaining on its original trajectory path.

In addition to bullet design and material, a major component of Balanced Flight is barrel design and quality with very exacting tolerances. The purpose is to impart an ideal axial surface friction upon launching, which produces a trajectory characterized by a steadily decreasing rate of axial deceleration. Although major improvements were also made in 30-caliber projectiles, and others, during development, Balanced Flight in 40-caliber projectiles is reported to have gone far beyond expectations, resulting in the 408 being chosen for further refinement.

After studying a number of parent case candidates, CheyTac Associates chose the 505 Gibbs. This case was redesigned for optimum strength both in web thickness and material composition. The case was shortened from 3.15 inches to 3.037 inches and necked to 408-caliber. The result was the 408 CheyTac (1037x77mm).

Bullets for the 408 CheyTac are CNC-machined by Lost River Ballistics of a proprietary solid copper-nickel alloy using a special hardness. Cartridges are available loaded with a 419-grain bullet with a MV of 3000 fps and a 305-grain bullet with a MV of 3500 fps, and each was designed for mission-specific performance. The 419-grain bullet has a reported BC of .945 out to 3500 meters. CheyTac Associates lists a starting load for the 419-grain bullet as 126.5 grains of Reloader #2.

The 416 Barrett

Like the 408 CheyTac, the 416 Barrett (10.57x83mm) was designed as an improvement over the 50 BMG cartridge. It was also designed as a mission-specific cartridge for anti-personnel work with some anti-material capability, uses a solid brass bullet and remains supersonic past 2500 yards. However, that's where physical similarities between the 408 CheyTac and the 416 Barrett pretty much end as, unlike the CheyTac, the 416 Barrett was developed from the 50 BMG case.

Loaded with 200 grains of yet unspecified propellant, the 416 Barrett fires a 395-grain solid brass boattail spitzer bullet at 3300 fps from a 29-inch barrel. This gives the bullet a BC of .989 with external ballistics that are equally impressive. Beginning its flight at mach 3+ speed, the 416 Barrett bullet remains supersonic past 2500 yards — that's 13 miles—and produces 1/2-MOA accuracy.

Where hunting is concerned, there is an endless selection of 416 bullets that can be fired in an envelope with the speed and

trajectory of a 22-250. With regard to competitive shooting, the 416 is also expected become a top contender, but military application is perhaps its brightest future, especially in the wake of the official adoption of the Barrett Model 82A1 as the Army's M107.

This is because the parent case for the 416 Barrett is the 50 BMG. Should the military adopt the 416 Barrett cartridge for any purpose, it requires less than five minutes to replace the M107's 50 BMG barrel with one in the 416 Barrett chambering. Nearly all other aspects of the M107 are the same, such as the bolt and magazine, leaving perhaps only the additional replacement of the recoil spring.

As this is written, there are no plans to manufacture the 416 projectile in configurations especially suited for use as an anti-material cartridge, although it could conceivably fill such a role to a lesser degree than the 50 BMG. However, its anti-personnel application seems endless.

During the 2005 FCSA National Championships, I was able to testfire the 416 Barrett using pre-production ammunition from a Barrett M99 bolt-action rifle. Recoil was sharp, but mild, and in spite of 30-mph gusting wind, the rifle produced MOA accuracy off the bipod. Barrett data on the 416 Barrett follows:

> Case Capacity: 200 grains.
> Projectile: Solid brass boattail spitzer.
> Projectile Weight: 395 grains.
> Projectile Length: 2.0 inches.
> Ballistic Coefficient: .989.
> Cartridge OAL: 4.58".
> Max. PSI: 62,500 PSI.
> Muzzle Velocity: 3,300 fps.
> Accuracy in Prototype: 0.5 MOA.

As this is written, Barrett has not divulged all pertinent information about the 416 Barrett cartridge, such as the propellant, which remains experimental, and no drawings of the round are yet available. However, measurements taken of a loaded 416 Barrett pre-production cartridge are as follows:

> Cartridge OAL: 4.66".
> Case OAL: 3.27".
> Neck Length: .480".
> Shoulder Length: 338".
> Shoulder Angle: 25 degrees.
> Shoulder to Head: .2.49".
> OD at Shoulder: .735".

The future of the 416 Barrett cartridge will be interesting to watch. If it performs up to its promise, it should surpass anything in its class, and could lead the way in cartridges under 50-caliber used in long-range competition. For the time being, Barrett will control the 416 Barrett's production. Of course any military adoption would catapult its success.

As the Fifty Caliber Shooter's Association grows, so will the development of new cartridges with which to compete, even if they are of smaller calibers in their own special classes. For information on the Fifty Caliber Shooter's Association, contact the FCSA at PO Box 111, Monroe, UT 84754-0111, (435) 527-9245, (www.fcsa. org).

Semi-auto rifles, such as this Barrett Model 82 in 50 BMG, are also used in long-range competition. An efficient muzzle brake minimizes muzzle rise; note the just-ejected case caught in mid-air. Barrett also now offers rifles in 416 Barrett, a wildcat designed for maximum efficiency and accuracy at extreme long range.

Long-range target competition for 50-caliber rifles is increasingly popular. Most rifles, such as this bolt-action single-shot, are chambered for 50 BMG, but many shooters have turned to a wildcat cartridge in search of improved performance and accuracy.

Chapter 15

Bullets and Ammo

Evolution becomes revolution.

By Chub Eastman

Shortly before the turn of the 20th century—thanks in large part to the military—hunters and shooters were blessed with major changes in firearms and ammunition. This evolution transformed firearms and ammunition into the forms we see today.

A stronger bolt action came into being to answer the military's need for a more powerful issue rifle for the troops. This change allowed the development of higher pressure cartridges using smokeless power. A major change in bullet construction was also needed to withstand stresses caused by the velocities the new cartridges achieved. A lead bullet didn't get the job done anymore.

Lead continued to be a major component in bullet development, but a new approach and new materials were needed. The final result was the use of a copper/tin compound that had the lubricity to allow the bullet to travel down the bore at high velocity without fouling, yet keeping the lead core intact.

Over the next 40-plus years much advancement in technology and material emerged. New cartridge designs, new developments in smokeless powder and primers yielded a steady improvement in performance.

The basic bolt action design didn't change much, but what did change was the use of materials such as nickel steel and advancements in heat treating. This allowed higher chamber pressures in the 50- to 60,000-psi range.

As performance of new cartridges and velocities increased, demands on components increased. The only component that didn't change much was bullet design. The basic design was a copper disc formed into a jacket that encased the lead core. This worked in most situations as long as velocities were kept to a moderate level.

In 1947 things changed in the civilian market when John Nosler had trouble getting a 30-caliber, 180-grain bullet, shot out of a 300 H&H, to penetrate the mud-caked hide of a bull moose in British Columbia. John decided he needed a better bullet so he sat down

over the winter, and most of the next summer, designing what he thought would get the job done. The next fall a close relative of the bull that John failed to collect the year before became the first victim of the revolutionary new "Partition" bullet.

It didn't take other bullet manufacturers long to realize there was a better way to skin the cat, and they needed to start thinking outside the box to produce bullets that were accurate, reliable—and with more predictable terminal performance. However, for some unknown reason, the major ammunition manufacturers did not think reloading was going to be around very long. As a result, supplying components to the shooting consumer was not high on their priority list.

This opened the door for small manufacturers such as Sierra, Hornady, Speer, Sisk, Bitterroot, Nosler, Barnes, Swift, Berger and others to develop specialized bullets for the reloader.

During this era, shooters/hunters reloaded for four reasons. One, reloading was the only way you could get premium bullets in loaded ammunition. Two, reloaded ammo was more accurate than factory ammo. Three, reloading was fun, and four, you could save a little money. All but three and four were about to change.

In 1977, Federal was the first major ammunition manufacturer to discover a definite demand for high-grade, accurate ammunition loaded with quality bullets made by independent bullet manufacturers. This was the first time loaded ammunition was offered with bullets made by manufacturers other than themselves. Federal's "Premium" ammunition was such a success that the other major ammo manufacturers couldn't ignore it. In short order, Winchester introduced "Supreme" ammunition and Remington offered a "Premier" line of ammo.

In a way, the reluctance of major ammunition manufacturers to recognize that reloading was a viable part of shooting sports was what made independent bullet manufacturers as successful as they are today.

Loaded ammunition and the premium bullets that are available today would boggle the mind of a serious hunter/shooter and reloader back in the 1950s. It used to be that a given bullet was used for everything from varmints to big critters, such as elk or moose. Not any more. Now bullets and ammunition are available that are designed for specific applications. Here is what we have today.

Ammunition

Federal continues to expand their Premium line loaded with bullets from Nosler, Woodleigh, Trophy Bonded and Barnes. Almost all cartridges are designed to be used for a specific application from the 223 Remington loaded with fast expanding Ballistic Tip bullets for varmints to Barnes solids in the big calibers for big critters in Africa.

Federal's newest addition is the "Fusion" line of ammunition, which is loaded with a new bullet designed in-house. The Fusion bullet is manufactured by a process different from the traditional cup-and-draw method. The lead core is plated onto, rather than inserted into the jacket. The result is a bonded bullet for big game that is accurate and reliable.

Winchester's top of the line Supreme ammunition not only looks sexy with its nickel cases and black lubalox-coated bullets, but it performs as good as it looks. Loaded with Ballistic Silver Tip bullets for varmints and Fail Safes or Partition Golds for big game, they offer a loading for any kind of game you are going to pursue. Each load even says on the box what it is designed for.

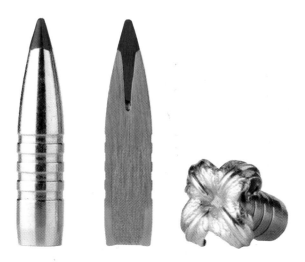

Barnes has added a tungsten core at the rear of the MRX bullet to improve stability in flight. Combined with the relief grooves similar to the Barnes TSX bullet, the MRX has exceptional long-range ballistic and terminal performance.

This XP3 bullet mushroomed perfectly with near-100 percent weight retention.

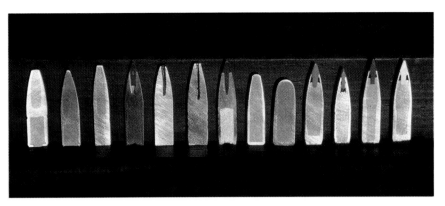

A lineup of premium bullets (l/r): Swift A-Frame, Nosler Partition, Trophy Bonded, Winchester XP³, Barnes X, Barnes Triple-Shock, Barnes MR-X, Norma Oryx, Woodleigh, Nosler Ballistic Tip, Hornady InterBond, Swift Scirocco II and Nosler AccuBond.

Winchester's newest loaded ammunition introduction is loaded with a new bullet they call "XP." It is similar to the Fail Safe bullet, but has a translucent red polycarbonate tip and boattail to give it a high ballistic coefficient and reliable expansion. They also bonded the rear lead core to ensure maximum weight retention.

The Premier line of ammunition from Remington includes loadings using Hornady and Swift bullets. They have even developed a new bullet which is a bonded "Core-Lokt;" extremely accurate with predictable bullet performance.

Remington has also developed a reduced-recoil load for some of the most popular chamberings. Imagine a 30-06 or 7mm Remington Magnum with half the recoil, yet which has enough punch to take to the deer stand. This makes a great load for young shooters or ladies who are a little gun-shy.

Hornady got into the ammunition business a few years ago, and they seem to be growing at a steady, innovative pace. Their "InterBond" bullets and magnum loadings for most calibers placed Hornady ammunition on equal footing with offerings from the Big Three.

The newest introduction from Hornady should have the other manufacturers asking "Why didn't I think of that?" It's called "LEVERevolution" and designed strictly to solve one of the drawbacks to shooting a lever-action rifle with a tubular magazine. Loaded for 30-30 Win., 35 Rem., 444 Marlin, 45-70 and 450 Marlin, it is performance ammunition using an innovative spitzer

bullet with a soft elastomer "Flex Tip™". The problem with all spitzer bullets used in a tubular magazine is the bullet nose rests against the primer of the cartridge in front of it. A recipe for disaster as the pointed tip acts like a firing pin and will set off the rounds ahead of it. With the new "Flex Tip," a mass of soft, rubbery material called "elastomer," when recoil occurs the tip deforms to a round profile against the primer in front of it and absorbs enough of the recoil force to where there is no mark on the primer. Yet, when the next round is levered into the chamber, it has enough memory to return to the original spitzer point.

What this accomplishes, when teamed with newly-developed powders, is a round that packs more punch at a longer range because of the higher ballistic coefficient of the bullet. This new ammunition will turn a short-range brush gun into a medium-range rifle that can be confidently used out to 200 yards, and a little beyond.

Black Hills Gold is another line of excellent quality ammunition. Using Nosler and Barnes bullets, it performs as accurately as most any match-grade ammunition on the market today. Teamed with premium hunting bullets, it is a confidence builder when going afield. The only drawback is the Gold line is limited to the most popular cartridges. However, each year they expand their loadings and it won't be long before they have something for everyone.

There are smaller ammunition manufacturers that literally handload their products for the consumer. Three that produce ammunition equal in accuracy and performance to any of the others

Hornady LEVERevolution ammo has a soft "Flex Tip" that permits the shooter to use pointed bullets in a tube-magazine lever gun.

are Nosler, Superior and Jarrett. All three use premium bullets in their offerings and perform as expected—excellent.

Any of these ammunition lines will test the talents of an accomplished handloader trying to duplicate the performance and accuracy. It took a while, but when ammunition manufacturers finally realized the consumer demand for quality ammunition, they all did a great job. After all, the ammunition is the cheapest part of the hunt, so why not use the best you can get your hands on?

Bullets

From the time John Nosler smacked that bull moose in the wilds of British Columbia to the present, the demand for an accurate, reliable hunting bullet has been gaining momentum. What makes a premium bullet is not only accuracy, but the ability of the bullet to retain the majority of its weight. This quality achieves reliable penetration no matter what the impact velocity or how much bone and tissue the bullet must pass through.

Nosler was the first with the Partition bullet. The basic design has not changed over the years and is still one of the most popular premium bullets on the market today. Its dual lead cores separated by a partition ensures the front of the bullet will expand and shed secondary projectiles throughout the wound channel, while the rear portion stays intact to accomplish the penetration needed to reach the boiler room.

In the 1980s Nosler introduced the Ballistic Tip. This bullet has an impact-extruded jacket with a thick base and tapered side walls to help control the expansion. A pointed polycarbonate tip in the mouth of the jacket not only initiates the expansion quickly, but teamed with a boattail, gives the bullet a very high ballistic coefficient. The Ballistic Tip is one of the most accurate hunting bullets on the market.

Nosler's latest introduction is the AccuBond bullet, which is basically a Ballistic Tip-type bullet with a bonded core. The new Accubond is not only very accurate with a high ballistic coefficient, but it will retain most of its weight because of the bonded core.

The Swift A-Frame is very similar to the Partition in design, but the front and rear core are both bonded to the jacket. This ensures weight retention well over 90-percent, which yields reliable penetration.

The other bullet offered by Swift is the Scirocco. This is a sleek, polycarbonate-tipped, boattail bullet with a very high ballistic coefficient, and the core is bonded to the jacket to ensure weight retention. The new Scirocco II has basically the same design, but the jacket is considerably thicker at the rear portion. This slows the expansion slightly for optimum close-range performance in the new hyper-velocity magnums.

Hornady has always been an innovator in bullet design. Their new InterBond bullets have a polycarbonate tip and bonded core for accuracy and weight retention. Reliable expansion over any realistic range can be expected.

The Trophy Bonded bullet is designed for deep penetration on big critters. The back half of the bullet is solid copper, and the front half has a bonded lead core. The jacket is also tapered to ensure reliable expansion.

Woodleigh, an Australian company, produces large-caliber bullets for the big boomers. Woodleigh bullets use a copper jacket bonded to a pure lead core that ensures everything stays together. Woodleigh's popularity is based in the large-caliber bullets but they also have a complete line that even includes some of the European bore sizes.

Norma also produces a bullet that falls into the premium category. It's called Oryx and is designed with the pure lead core bonded to the jacket. The Oryx can also be obtained in Norma's loaded ammunition in almost all popular chamberings.

The only "green" bullet on the market is the X-Bullet produced by Barnes. It's made of copper with no lead to taint the environment. The pointed nose has a hollow point and a deep recess down the center. The inside of the cavity is scored to ensure expansion, delivering four petals that fold back to form the mushroom.

Shooters can expect 100-percent weight retention with the X-Bullet. Its only drawback was a tendency to foul the bore with copper after a few shots. This was attributed to the fact it was

A large selection of premium bullets is available to the handloader. There now is a bullet designed for any kind of hunting.

constructed from pure soft copper and that it had a long bearing surface. Performance on game in the field was excellent.

Recently Barnes introduced the "Triple Shock," an X-Bullet that eliminated the fouling problem with multiple driving bands around the bullet. This greatly reduced the bearing surface that came into contact with the bore and virtually eliminated the copper fouling problem.

The latest introduction from Barnes is the MRX bullet, still a lead-free "green" bullet, which incorporates a blue polycarbonate tip and a tungsten rear core. The polycarbonate tip and slight boattail give the new bullets a very high ballistic coefficient, despite the heavy tungsten core that makes the MRX a bit shorter than an X-Bullet of similar weight. The new TSX also incorporates the multiple driving bands that make the Triple Shock so successful.

Fail Safe bullets are manufactured by Winchester and sold as a component through Combined Technology, which is a brand name of Nosler. This design was developed for maximum penetration, using a Barnes X-Bullet-like nose section and a rear section with a steel insert and lead core. The design of the rear section ensures the integrity of the bullet while retaining nearly 100-percent of its weight.

When you look back over the years on what was available to shooters and hunters and compare it to what we are blessed with today, it makes you realize the excuses for missed shots and bad bullet placement might have a little truth to them. With the ammunition—and components—we have today, there is no excuse for poor field performance that can be blamed on anyone other than he who pulls the trigger.

Winchester's XP3 bullet is similar to the earlier Fail Safe bullet. But with a polymer tip, boattail and bonded rear core for top performance.

Chapter 16

American Rimfire Cartridges

(Current & Obsolete—Blackpowder & Smokeless)

RIMFIRE CARTRIDGES differ from centerfire cartridges in that the priming compound is contained in the rim. Ignition occurs when the firing pin crushes the rim. Rimfire cartridges are of historical as well as practical interest. Although only one of a number of ignition systems leading to the modern centerfire, the rimfire was the first truly successful system and is still alive and well, almost 150 years later. The common 22 rimfire had its origin with the Flobert BB Cap in 1845, which led to the Smith & Wesson-developed 22 Short of 1857. The idea of rimfire ignition goes back to Roberts' French patent of 1831. This provided for the priming compound covering the entire head interior. The rimfire evolved by leaving the primer mix out of the center. After Smith & Wesson introduced its First Model revolver — a 22 Short chambering in 1857 — development of rimfire arms and cartridges bloomed. The New Haven Arms Co. began manufacturing 44 Henry ammunition in 1861, and 56-56 Spencer ammunition was made in quantity beginning about 1862, although the Spencer rifle design dates back to 1860. Both of these cartridges were used by Federal troops in the Civil War. Chambering of the first successful metallic-cartridge repeating arms was for rimfire cartridges. By the end of the Civil War, numerous rimfire cartridges in various calibers were available.

A great many rimfire cartridges have been developed for rifles and handguns here and in Europe. In the late 1800s, something like 75 different rimfire cartridges had been loaded by American compa-nies, but only about 42 were still around by 1900. The decline in the number of rimfire cartridges occurred because many early types put on the market were really experimental and so had a very short life. These are of academic interest primarily to collectors. Space limita-tions rule out any effort to list all of these here. The criteria for inclusion of a cartridge is that it was loaded by American compa-nies and survived to the turn of the century. The more obscure num-bers and those of British or Continental origin have been covered fairly well elsewhere. The more popular rimfires lasted well past the turn of the century and a few are still in use. The 22 Short rimfire is, in fact, the oldest American cartridge, having survived since 1857. It will probably still be around as long as we own and shoot fire-arms. The decline in the number of rimfire cartridge types can be illustrated by a review of old catalogs. Forty-two U.S. types were in common production in 1900; by 1918 that number had dwindled to 32. By the 1930s, the number was down to a mere 17. After World War II, the count was less than 10. Some older rimfires are still loaded in Europe and from time to time when available, these are imported here. Many of the cartridges listed here were available on an over-the-counter basis up through the 1920s. One or two of the obsolete rimfires would probably be useful to modern shooters, but it is unlikely ammunition manufacturers will revive these car-tridges. While many shooters would welcome a return of the 25 Stevens Long; it seems unlikely that this will ever happen.

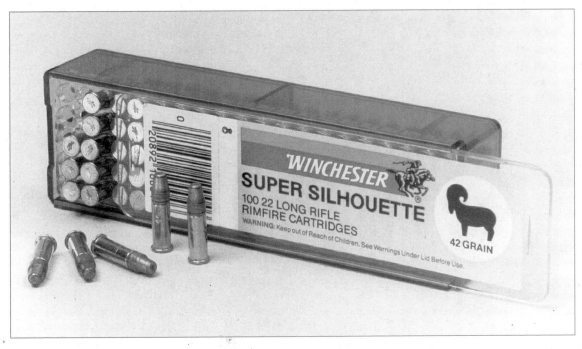

Rimfire cartridges have advantages as well as weaknesses when compared to centerfire cartridges. In smaller calibers, the rimfire is cheaper to manufacture and within equivalent pressures just as good as the centerfire. One important disadvantage of the rimfire is that it is not practical to reload. This was a big consideration with early buffalo hunters and pioneers of the Old West. It was also no small consideration among match shooters who developed top accuracy by loading their own. The rimfire will not stand up under the pressures of modern high-velocity centerfire loads. Solid-head centerfires can be made much stronger. Large-caliber rimfire cartridges cost nearly as much as similar centerfire rounds, so there is an economic point beyond which the rimfire just is not worthwhile.

If any statements made before this give the impression the rimfire cartridge is about to become extinct, don't worry. Nothing could be further from the truth. As recently as 1959, Winchester introduced the 22 Magnum Rimfire, and in 1970 Remington introduced the 5mm Remington Rimfire Magnum. The 22 Magnum caught on immediately and is well into its fifth decade of popularity. The 5mm Magnum did not fare so well despite ballistics that were somewhat superior to the 22 Magnum. It was discontinued after only a few years.

Despite the failure of the 5mm Magnum in the 1970s, Harnady introduced the 17 Hornady Magnum Rimfire in 2002. It is similar in appearance to the earlier 5mm Magnum, but with a 17-grain V-Max bullet at 2,550 fps, its trajectory is more nearly similar to the centerfire 22 Hornet. Already more than a dozen rifle makers are

chambering for the 17 HMR, and it seems destined for a long life.

The 22 Long Rifle has become the most accurate and highly developed sporting cartridge in existence. Its popularity for match shooting and small game or varmint hunting remains undiminished — and is increasing, if anything. There are dozens of makes, models and types of 22 rimfire arms currently manufactured, and new models appear in a steady stream. The 22 Long Rifle has established a place so secure it will be with us as long as guns are made. Those designs that died out just did not fill any particular need.

Modern rimfire cartridges are intended for target, plinking or small game hunting. The 22 Long Rifle does very well out to 75 yards on rabbit-sized animals and on coyote or fox with a well-placed bullet. The 17 Hornady Magnum will extend this range to nearly 200 yards. The 22 Short is a good plinking round and is used in Olympic pistol competition. The high-velocity Long Rifle is a useful self-defense round. It will penetrate better than the 32 Smith & Wesson when fired from a handgun. The 22 WMR develops handgun energies nearly equal to some 38 Special loads.

It would surprise many to know how many deer are killed each year by poachers using the 22 Long Rifle. However, it is not to be considered a deer cartridge. There is reportedly a case of an elephant that was killed with a 22 Long Rifle, but that hardly qualifies it as an elephant cartridge, either. Within their capabilities and limitations, modern rimfire cartridges are among the most useful we have.

— FCB with additional text by SS

17 Mach 2

Historical Notes A 2004 joint rimfire cartridge development between Hornady and CCI, the 17 Mach 2 cartridge delivers higher velocities and flatter trajectories than the 22 Long Rifle cartridge. Hornady designed the 17 Mach 2 for plinking, varminting and small game hunting. In quality firearms, the 17 Mach 2 is capable of MOA or better accuracy.

General Comments The 17 Mach 2 cartridge is not reloadable. It uses the rimfire 22 Stinger case as its parent. Exactly .100-inch longer that the 22 Long Rifle case, the Stinger case is necked down to accept .172-inch diameter bullets weighing 17 grains. The 17 Mach 2 is well suited to 18/22-inch barrels with a 1:9 rifling twist. Ruger, Marlin, Thompson Center and other manufacturers offer rifles chambered for the 17 Mach 2. Hornady, CCI, Remington and Eley supply loaded ammunition.

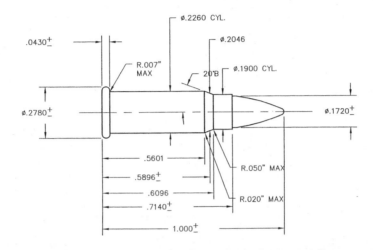

17 Hornady Magnum Rimfire (17 HMR)

Historical Notes In 2002, Hornady provided shooters with serious reasons to consider a rimfire cartridge for medium-range (200-yard) varmint hunting. Their new 17 HMR is the fastest rimfire commercially available; it pushes a 17-grain bullet on trajectories very similar to the larger 22 Hornet centerfire cartridge.

General Comments Launching a 17-grain V-Max™ bullet at 2550 fps, Hornady's bottleneck rimfire cartridge printed five-shot groups measuring .460-inch at 100 yards, and 1.005 inches at 200 yards using a Wiseman-barreled Marlin rifle in factory tests. Flattening the 22 WMR's trajectory by more than 10 inches at 200

yards, the flat-shooting 17 HMR also drifts 15 inches less in a 10 mph wind. Contributing to this fine performance is the boattail V-Max™ bullet with a polymer tip engineered for dramatic expansion. Hornady achieves this performance at pressures slightly greater than the 22 WMR, which suggests existing 22 WMR rifle designs can be readily adapted to the 17 HMR. As a measure of popularity of the new 17 HMR cartridge, rifles and pistols are available from Anschutz, Cooper, H&R 1871, Marlin, New England Arms, Remington, Ruger, Rogue River, Savage and Thompson/Center.

5mm Remington Rimfire Magnum (Obsolete)

Historical Notes The 5mm Remington Rimfire Magnum was announced in 1969, but not actually introduced until 1970. Only the Remington bolt-action Model 591 clip-loading and Model 592 tubular-magazine repeating rifles were available for the round. It was not adopted by other ammunition manufacturers. For a time, Thompson/Center furnished barrels for the Contender pistol in 5mm Remington. This was the only modern bottlenecked rimfire case; however, a number of the obsolete blackpowder rimfires were necked so it is not an entirely new development. Bullet diameter is 0.2045-inch with a weight of 38 grains and a muzzle velocity of 2100 fps. This round developed the highest velocity of any rimfire at the time (newer, 30-grain 22 WMR loads offer greater muzzle velocity).

General Comments The 5mm Remington represented an interesting development that exceeds the performance of some of the early 22 centerfires. Its effective killing range on small varmint-type animals

is 25-50 yards greater than the 22 Winchester Magnum Rimfire. This is due to the better sectional density of the smaller-diameter bullet combined with 150 fps higher initial velocity. Both are essentially varmint cartridges. In both, the hollowpoint-type bullets ruin too much edible meat for small game shooting. However, the 22 WMR is available with a non-expanding full-jacketed bullet, or one could switch to the interchangeable 22 WRF for small game hunting. In summary, the 5mm Remington has the edge for varmint shooting, but the 22 WMR is more versatile for small game. On the other hand, a good FMJ small-game bullet for the 5mm Remington might have changed that analysis. The choice would be largely a matter of use and personal preference. Remington has long since discontinued the Model 591 and 592, and no rifles are currently made in 5mm RFM. Ammunition is no longer made by Remington. The 5mm RFM is another good idea that did not catch on, although it had a lot to recommend it.

22 BB Cap (Current)

Historical Notes The rimfire 22 BB Cap, or Bulleted Breech Cap, is one of the oldest successful, self-contained cartridges. It originated in 1845 for the Flobert indoor target rifle. These guns were also known as saloon (salon) or parlor rifles and were quite popular through the turn of the century. A great many individuals and companies have made both rifles and pistols for the 22 BB Cap. This type of social, indoor shooting has become virtually extinct. American companies loaded the 22 BB Cap up to World War II, but discontinued it after the war. The original cartridge had only a priming charge and a 22-caliber lead round ball, but American ammunition contained a small charge of powder and a conical bullet in many makes. The original case was a tapered percussion cap without a well-defined rim. RWS (in Germany) is the only firm who loads the 22 BB Cap at the present time.

General Comments Many insist the 22 BB Cap is completely worthless, but this author does not agree. Rainy afternoons of target practice in the basement or garage will create a certain appreciation for this little pipsqueak. These cartridges are also handy for a preliminary sighting-in of 22 rimfire rifles or pistols. Modern loads have sufficient power to kill rats, mice, sparrows or other pests out to 40 yards or so. At close range, RWS BB Caps will penetrate 1 inch of soft pine. These could seriously injure or even kill a human, so one should be careful. These are not toys. There is considerable variation in case length and dimensions between different makes. The CCI "Mini-Cap" loaded in 22 Short and Long Rifle cases duplicates performance of the older 22 BB and CB cap for indoor target practice.

22 CB Cap (Current)

Historical Notes The 22 CB Cap, or Conical Bullet Cap, is something of a cross between the 22 BB Cap and 22 Short. It has been manufactured in various sizes. In original form, it was supposed to combine the 29-grain 22 Short bullet with the 22 BB Cap case and a light charge of blackpowder. In actual manufacture, some CB Cap cases have a length about halfway between the BB Cap and Short. It is not a transitional design leading to the 22 Short, but rather a more powerful version of the BB Cap. Earliest catalog reference appears to be about 1888, although it probably originated prior to this. American companies loaded it up to 1942, but most discontinued it after World War II. CCI occasionally catalogs this load and RWS has offered these rounds continuously.

General Comments The 22 CB Cap managed to combine about all the disadvantages of the 22 BB Cap and Short into one generally useless cartridge. It was no more accurate than either of the other two and made enough noise to nullify the indoor virtues of the BB Cap. It also required almost as heavy a backstop as the Short and was just as dangerous indoors. In killing power, it wasn't that much better than the BB Cap to make any real difference, although it might provide an additional 10 or 15 yards of effective range. In recognition of this, almost everyone quit making it with few laments from the shooting public. The original charge was 1-1/2 grains of blackpowder, but after 1920, smokeless powder was used exclusively. CCI in Lewiston, Idaho, currently loads the 29-grain CB Cap bullet in the 22 Short and Long Rifle case at velocities of 727 to 830 fps. Remington offers its CBee, which is a low-velocity round based on the 22 Short and Long case, with a 30-grain bullet at a muzzle velocity of 700 fps. These loads are intended for indoor target practice, gallery or pest shooting.

22 Short (Current)

Historical Notes The 22 Short is the oldest American, commercial, self-contained, metallic cartridge and has been in continuous production for more than 143 years! It was introduced in 1857 for the Smith & Wesson First Model revolver and is still widely used all over the world. Although now popular as a short-range gallery or plinking round, the 22 Short was originally intended for self-defense. It is still used for Olympic match shooting and heavy target pistols are built specifically for it. Initial loading was a 29-grain bullet and 4.0 grains of a fine-granulation blackpowder (probably similar to what we would now call FFFFg). After 1887, it was available with semi-smokeless powder and within a short time, smokeless powder. Remington introduced non-corrosive (Kleanbore) priming for its rimfire line in 1927 and the first high-velocity type in 1930. The 22 Short can be fired in any arm chambered for the Long Rifle, but most semi-auto guns will not function properly with the 22 Short. Since the end of World War II,

a number of small 22 Short pocket-automatic pistols and revolvers have appeared on the market.

General Comments In the high-velocity loading, the Short is quite adequate for small game or bird hunting. However, killing power declines rapidly beyond 50 yards. Hunting should be confined to animals not over 2 pounds in weight. The 22 Short can be deceiving because it looks small and relatively harmless. When fired from a rifle it can penetrate 2 inches of soft pine and has an extreme range of almost 1 mile. It can seriously wound or kill a person right up to the limit of its range. Be careful! Make sure of your backstop before shooting any 22 rimfire. The hollowpoint bullet weighs 27 grains and has about 25 fps higher velocity than the solid and is a particularly effective squirrel load. CCI is the only remaining manufacturer of the hollowpoint load. Although sales today are vastly overshadowed by the less expensive 22 Long Rifle, the 22 Short cartridge was king during this cartridge's first century of production.

22 Short/40-grain (Obsolete)

Historical Notes We have almost no information on this interesting variation. The sample is labeled as an RWS 22 Short case loaded with a 22 Long Rifle bullet. The case appears to be pure copper, which suggests that this round is quite old. Headstamp is an RWS crest with a centered uppercase "R."

General Notes We have included this number, because it will serve to demonstrate that rimfire ammunition is as varied and numerous in design as any other type. As we gain further information, we hope to improve the historical details included with this entry.

22 Long (Current)

Historical Notes The 22 Long is usually referred to as a combination of the Long Rifle case and the Short bullet. This is not true for several reasons. Foremost, the 22 Long happens to be 16 years older than the Long Rifle. It is listed in the 1871 Great Western Gun Works catalog for the seven-shot Standard revolver. A few years later, it was also listed in Remington and Stevens catalogs as a rifle cartridge. The 22 Long Rifle was not on the market until 1887. The Long was originally a blackpowder number loaded with a 29-grain bullet and 5.0 grains of a fine granulation blackpowder (probably similar to what we now call FFFFg). Smokeless powder was available for a time in standard and high-velocity loads. At present, only the high-velocity load is available. A shot load was also offered.

General Comments The original blackpowder loading of the 22 Long had a slightly higher velocity than the 22 Short or Long Rifle, but this was not true of later smokeless loads. The present high-velocity Long has a velocity between the Short and Long Rifle. The 22 Long is not as accurate as the Short or Long Rifle and has outlived any useful purpose it might have once had. I think the reason it hangs on is that a great many people still think it has a higher velocity and greater killing power than the Long Rifle.

Editor's note: Others believe that 1) firing enough 22 Short rounds in a 22 Long Rifle chambered gun will damage the chamber and that 2) the 22 Long gives similar performance to the 22 Short, but without the potential for chamber damage. Old ideas, true or not, are tenacious because people will not readily accept concepts in opposition to what they believe. In any event, the 22 Long is strictly a small game, short-range cartridge ballistically just a notch above the 22 Short. Only Remington and CCI still offer the 22 Long.

22 Long Rifle (Current)

Historical Notes Information available indicates that the 22 Long Rifle was developed by the J. Stevens Arms & Tool Co. in 1887. It is the 22 Long case with a 5.0-grain blackpowder charge (likely with a granulation similar to what we would now call FFFFg) and a 40-grain bullet instead of the original 29-grain. The Peters Cartridge Co. is supposed to have first manufactured it, especially for Stevens. If this is true, then why does the 1888 Stevens catalog refer to a UMC 22 caliber Long rimfire rifle cartridge? This would be a gross ingratitude at best. This 1888 catalog lists the No. 1, 2, 9 and 10 model break-open rifles as available in the new chambering with increased rifling twist. The New Model Pocket or Bicycle rifle also chambered it. The 1888 Marlin-Ballard catalog recommends the new 22 Long "Rifle" cartridge for its No. 3 Gallery rifle as being more accurate than the common 22 Long or Extra Long.

At one time, the 22 Long Rifle was available in black, semi-smokeless and smokeless-powder loads. Remington introduced the first high-velocity type in 1930. Both the 40-grain solid and a 35/38-grain hollowpoint bullet have been available for many years. The original case was not crimped, a feature that did not appear until 1900. Space does not permit a discussion of the different loads and types of 22 Long Rifle cartridges or the rifles and handguns that

chamber it. Suffice to say, it is the most accurate and highly developed of any rimfire cartridge ever.

General Comments The 22 Long Rifle is the most popular match cartridge in existence, and also the most widely used small game and varmint cartridge. The high-velocity hollowpoint is the best field load and will do a good job on rabbit-sized animals out to 75 yards. Beyond that, it is unreliable. The Long Rifle is a great favorite of poachers for killing game out of season with close-up head shots. The modest report does not alarm or alert passersby or officials. At close range, the high-velocity load with the solid-lead bullet will penetrate 6 inches of soft pine and has a maximum range of nearly two miles. Maximum range is achieved at the relatively low angle of between 25-30 degrees, so one must be very careful. Humans shot with the 22 Long Rifle often show little immediate distress, survive without complications for several days, then die very suddenly. This is mentioned because many individuals regard 22 rimfires as playthings, not powerful enough to be dangerous. Careless shooting with the 22 rimfire has probably led to the closure of more areas to hunting and caused more trouble than any other cartridge. Use your head and be careful! There is also a 22 Long Rifle shot cartridge, loaded by most companies and useful mostly for rat and other pest control.

22 Stinger, Spitfire, Viper, Yellow Jacket, Super-Max, Xpediter, etc.

Historical Notes The 22 Stinger was the first of a series of developments aimed at improving the performance of the 22 Long Rifle. Introduced by CCI early in 1977, the concept was an immediate success and was quickly copied by Winchester with their Xpediter, by Remington with their Yellow Jacket and by Federal with their Spitfire. All of these cartridges are much the same and are based on reducing the weight of the hollowpoint bullet from 36 to around 30 grains and loading this into a case full of relatively slow-burning powder. The result is a 30 percent increase in muzzle velocity and 25 percent increase in muzzle energy as compared to the standard 22 Long Rifle hollowpoint high-velocity loading. The overall loaded length of these rounds is the same as the regular 22 Long Rifle and so are all other dimensions except the case length. Some use a standard length 22 Long Rifle case and settle for a somewhat lower muzzle velocity and some use a longer length case to achieve maximum velocity. As a group, these are referred to as hyper-velocity 22s. Only Stinger, Yellow Jacket, and Viper are still in production.

General Comments I have fired all of the increased velocity 22 Long Rifle cartridges, available at the time, in both rifles and handguns and at the same time compared the performance with the standard line of 22 rimfires as well as the 22 WMR. When fired into parafin blocks and soap bars, the hypervelocity hollowpoints demonstrate superior expansion and energy transfer as compared to the regular high-velocity hollowpoints.

Malfunctions can occur when firing the hypervelocity Long Rifles in auto pistols, and I don't think they are well suited to this type of handgun. However, they work fine in revolvers.

Field-testing does not demonstrate any great advantage of one over the other in shooting jackrabbits nor any great superiority over the 22 WMR or over the standard Long Rifle high-velocity hollowpoint. The hypervelocity cartridges do inflict greater tissue damage than the 22 LRHP. However, dead is dead and you can't accomplish anything beyond that.

These cartridges do provide increased velocity and energy for 22 rimfire rifles. They probably extend the effective range on varmints or small game by a few yards. These cartridges cost some 65 percent more than regular 22 Long Rifle HVHP, which is a negative factor. They certainly have a place in the 22 rimfire lineup, but their increased performance is most pronounced when they are fired from a rifle rather than a handgun. In some instances, particularly in short-barreled pistols and revolvers or any revolver with a large barrel-cylinder gap, these loads can generate much less energy than standard 22 Long Rifle high-velocity loads. The bullets actually exit the muzzle slower.

22 Hyper-Velocities Factory Ballistics

Bullet (grains/type)	Powder	Grains	Velocity	Energy	Source/Comments
29	FL, Win.		1680	182	Xpediter (obsolete)
32	FL, CCI		1640	191	Stinger
33	FL, Fed.		1500	164	Spitfire (obsolete)
33	FL, Rem.		1500	164	Yellowjacket
34	FL, Win.		1500	169	Super-Max. (obsolete)
36	FL, Fed.		1410	158	Spitfire (obsolete)
36	FL, Rem.		1410	158	Viper
36	FL, CCI		1425	162	CCI, HP+V

22 Extra Long (Obsolete)

Historical Notes Introduced about 1880, the 22 Extra Long was used in Ballard, Remington, Stevens, Wesson and late (1916) versions of the 1902 and 1904 Winchester bolt-action 58 rifles, as well as S&W revolvers. It was listed in ammunition catalogs as late as 1935. It used the same 40-grain, outside-lubricated bullet that was later adapted to the 22 Long Rifle, but the longer case held more (6.0 grains) blackpowder. It was more powerful than the Long Rifle but not noted for great accuracy. Smokeless powder loads had nearly the same velocity as the modern Long Rifle loadings.

General Comments The 22 Extra Long will not chamber in arms made for the Long Rifle, but since the only dimensional difference is case length, the Short, Long or Long Rifle can be fired in the Extra Long chamber. In terms of killing power, the Extra Long is in the same class as the standard-velocity Long Rifle. At one time, the 22 Extra Long was advertised as a 200-yard target cartridge, but it certainly would not qualify for this by today's standards. Case length and overall cartridge length made the Extra Long unsuitable to most repeating actions, which is another reason it became obsolete. Never fire any high-velocity or hyper-velocity 22 cartridge in any blackpowder gun.

22 Winchester Rimfire (WRF) (Obsolete)

Historical Notes Introduced for the Winchester Model 1890 pump- or slide-action rifle, the original Winchester loading had a flat-nosed bullet, while Remington used a round-nosed type and called it the 22 Remington Special. The two are identical and interchangeable. Bullet can be either a 45-grain solid or 40-grain hollowpoint in standard- or high-velocity loading. This cartridge uses a flat base, inside-lubricated bullet rather than the "heel" type of outside-lubricated bullet of the Short, Long, Long Rifle and Extra Long. The 22 WRF was chambered in various Remington, Stevens and Winchester single-shot and repeating rifles and Colt revolvers. It is no longer routinely loaded by the ammunition manufacturers, and no one makes rifles for it. However, in late 1986, Winchester made a special run of 22 WRF ammunition. This must have been aimed more at collectors than shooters.

General Comments The 22 WRF was the first notable improvement in the killing power of the various 22 rimfires. It is not as accurate as the Long Rifle, but in field use, this is of no consequence. Out to 75 yards, it will kill small animals more reliably than the Long Rifle. Although there is little difference in bullet diameter between the WRF and the standard 22 rimfires, the WRF has a larger case diameter to accept the bullet's full diameter. It is much too large to fit the standard 22 Long Rifle chamber. The 22 Short or Long Rifle fits the WRF chamber quite loosely and will not fire or extract in many guns. When these do fire, the case often splits, which allows particles to escape the action with possible danger to the shooter and bystanders, and accuracy is extremely poor. The 22 WRF can be safely fired in any gun chambered for the 22 Winchester Magnum Rimfire. Winchester produced one batch of these cartridges in 1995.

22 Winchester Magnum Rimfire (WMR) (Current)

Historical Notes The 22 Magnum Rimfire was introduced in 1959 by Winchester, but they didn't market a gun to shoot it until well into the following year. However, Ruger and Smith & Wesson advertised revolvers for the new round before the end of 1959 and Savage chambered their Model 24, a 22-410 over/under combination gun, for the Magnum Rimfire shortly thereafter. The discontinued slide-action Winchester Model 61 was the first rifle of their manufacture available for the new round. At present there is a wide variety of single shot and repeating rifles, pistols and revolvers of American and European manufacture available in 22 Magnum Rimfire caliber. Standard bullet is a jacketed 40 grain type although Federal introduced a 50 grain bullet in 1988 and CCI has recently introduced a hyper-velocity loading with a 30-grain bullet and Federal soon joined the "hyper-velocity" fray with their similar loading.

General Comments The 22 Winchester Magnum Rimfire is an elongated and more powerful version of the older 22 WRF. Case dimensions are the same except for length, and the WRF can be fired in any gun chambered for the Magnum Rimfire. It is not a safe practice to rechamber older guns for the new round. The 22 WRF is loaded with outside lubricated lead bullets while the 22 WMR is loaded with jacketed bullets. With a 40-grain thin-jacketed bullet at about 1900 fps, this is the most potent rimfire cartridge currently available. It is more powerful than the 22 Winchester Centerfire, forerunner of the 22 Hornet. Claimed ballistics in a 6-inch pistol barrel exceed any other rimfire fired from a rifle. Thus it is a very effective 125-yard varmint or small game cartridge, although overly destructive of animals intended for the pot unless solid bullets are used. CCI also loads a shot version.

22 Winchester Automatic (Obsolete)

Historical Notes Used only in the Winchester Model 1903 semi-auto rifle, the 22 Winchester Automatic round was dropped from standard Winchester production in the 1970s. The rifle has been obsolete since 1932. This cartridge has a 45-grain inside-lubricated bullet and will not chamber in any standard 22 Long Rifle gun. It was designed at a time when blackpowder and semi-smokeless-powder 22 rimfires were still loaded and popular. The purpose was to prevent use of anything but smokeless powder ammunition in the semi-auto rifle so as not to foul the action. Blackpowder will gum up such actions and render these inoperable in short order. Remington later brought out a similar cartridge for the same reason. The two are not interchangeable.

General Comments The 22 Winchester Automatic had little to offer over the standard Long Rifle except smokeless powder and the semi-auto rifle in which it was fired. In killing power and range, it was on a par with the 22 Long Rifle. This cartridge is now a collector's item.

22 Remington Automatic (Obsolete)

Historical Notes This cartridge was developed for the Remington Model 16 Autoloading rifle, actually introduced in 1914, and discontinued in 1928. Ammunition has not been loaded since the end of World War II. The purpose of the cartridge was the same as the Winchester 22 Automatic — to prevent use of action-gumming blackpowder ammunition in a semi-auto rifle. No other gun used this round and it is not interchangeable with the 22 Winchester. This is an example of senseless jealous rivalry if ever there was one.

General Comments This was another 22 Long-Rifle-class cartridge. It had an inside-lubricated 45-grain bullet in solid or hollowpoint type, both of the same weight and ballistics. It was neither as accurate nor as effective (generally) as the Long Rifle.

22 ILARCO 22 Short Magnum Rimfire (Obsolete)

Historical Notes The 22 ILARCO Rimfire originated in 1987 and was manufactured in experimental quantities by Winchester for Illinois Arms Co. It is the 22 Winchester Magnum Rimfire shortened to the same loaded length as the 22 Long Rifle. It was chambered in the Illinois Arms Co.'s Model 180 auto/semi-auto rifle that features a 165-round drum-type magazine. The full-auto version was available only to law-enforcement agencies. The reason for the shorter cartridge was that the Model 180 was designed for the 22 Long Rifle and the action would not handle the longer 22 WMR. Illinois Arms Co. was bought out by Feather Industries of Boulder, Colo., and the 22 ILARCO was discontinued. The cartridge is sometimes referred to as the 22 WMR Short.

General Comments Shortening the 22 WMR made sense even though there is some velocity loss. For one thing, the short case uses the same jacketed bullet as the parent cartridge and doesn't pick up dirt and debris the way sticky, outside-lubricated 22 Long Rifle cartridges can. With a 165-round magazine and full-auto fire, this is a matter of some importance. Also, the 22 WMR is too long to function in practically any 22 semi-automatic pistol, but many of these could be adapted to fire the 22 ILARCO. However, this cartridge never went into production and existing specimens are now collector's items.

22 ILARCO 22 Short Magnum Rimfire Factory Ballistics

Bullet (grains/type)	Powder	Grains	Velocity	Energy	Source/Comments
40 FMJ	FL		1350	160	Winchester factory load

25 Short (Obsolete)

Historical Notes Originally this pistol cartridge was developed for the F.D. Bliss revolver and also known as the 25 Bacon & Bliss. It was chambered in other cheap handguns of the period. Date of introduction was around 1860 and both Remington and Winchester listed it in catalogs up to 1920. It is a collector's item now.

General Comments The 25 Short had a 43-grain, outside-lubricated bullet and 5 grains of powder. Bullet diameter is actually 0.245- to 0.246-inch and it closely resembles the 22 Short. In power, it is similar to the blackpowder 22 Long Rifle fired from a short pistol barrel. There is no record of any rifle having been chambered for the 25 Short. It should not be confused with the 25 Stevens Short.

25 Stevens Short (Obsolete)

Historical Notes Introduced in 1902, this cartridge was intended as a shorter, cheaper and less powerful version of the 25 Stevens. The original loading used 4.5 to 5.0 grains of blackpowder, but only smokeless powder was used when it was discontinued in 1942. Remington, Winchester and Stevens rifles chambered this round. It could be fired in any rifle chambered for the 25 Stevens.

General Comments The 25 Stevens Short was not nearly as effective a field cartridge as the longer version. However, it was somewhat cheaper and certainly as good or better than the 22 Short for small game at close range. More expensive than the 22 Long Rifle and no better for hunting purposes, it was never popular.

25 Stevens (Obsolete)

Historical Notes Various dates can be found for the introduction of the 25 Stevens, with most authorities agreeing on 1900. Reference in old books and catalogs would indicate an actual date of 1890, but this is not certain. In any event, this cartridge was developed jointly by the J. Stevens Arms & Tool Co. and the Peters Cartridge Co. The Stevens "Crack Shot" No. 15 rifle came out in 1900, and one of its original chamberings was the 25 Stevens. However, the Stevens "Favorite" rifle, manufactured from 1894 to 1935, may have been the first model available in this chambering. Both of these are underlever single-shots. Remington and Winchester also chambered rifles for the 25 Stevens. Original load was a 67-grain bullet and 10 to 11 grains of blackpowder. Semi-smokeless powder was also used, but smokeless was the only propellant offered when the round was discontinued in 1942. Remington did preliminary work on an improved, high-velocity loading prior to World War II, but the project was dropped after the war. The improved round, called the

267 Remington Rimfire, was rumored to have had a muzzle velocity of 1400 fps with the 67-grain bullet.

General Comments The 25 Stevens had an excellent reputation on small game without ruining edible meat. Most complaints centered around the high cost of ammunition as compared to the 22 Long Rifle and the high trajectory, which made hits beyond 60-70 yards difficult. For years, gun writers called for a high-velocity version, but the ammunition companies did not respond. With modern powder and a longer case, a velocity of 1600 to 1800 fps might be possible.

Rifles are no longer chambered for this round, and ammunition is no longer manufactured, so it appears to be a dead number. Many who used the 25 Stevens were sorry to see it go, but with the 22 Magnum Rimfire, there is not much need for it. It had an inside-lubricated bullet and was available with solid and hollowpoint bullets.

30 Short (Obsolete)

Historical Notes This old-timer originated in the early 1860s and was used mostly in low-priced handguns such as the Sharps four-barrel, the Standard revolver and various single shots. Colt New Line revolvers were also made in 30 Short and 30 Long chamberings. The 30 Short was listed in ammunition catalogs as late as 1919.

General Comments The 30 Short had a 50- to 58-grain lead bullet and 5 to 6 grains of blackpowder. Not a powerful round by any standard, its use was confined to pocket or house guns. It was not as good of a cartridge as the 32 Short rimfire and one wonders why it survived for so long a time. It is now a collector's item.

30 Long (Obsolete)

Historical Notes This rimfire was cataloged as early as 1873, but may have originated earlier. Adapted to Colt, Standard X.L. and Sharps handguns, it was also used in some single-shot rifles. The 30 Short survived until 1920; the 30 Long disappeared before WWI.

General Comments The 30 Short and 30 Long were interchangeable in most guns. The bullet was actually 0.290- to 0.295-inch and of outside-lubricated type. Power of the 30 Long was about the same as the 32 Short rimfire.

32 Extra Short (Obsolete)

Historical Notes This cartridge was made for the Remington magazine pistol and the Chicago Firearms Co.'s "Protector" palm pistol. The Remington pistol was manufactured from 1871 until 1888 and the odd palm pistol originated sometime in the 1880s. This fixes the date of introduction for the 32 Extra Short at 1871, though some authorities indicate a later date. The cartridge was listed in Remington catalogs until 1920. It was also known as the 32 Protector.

General Comments The 32 was a popular chambering for both handguns and rifles for many years. The 32 Extra Short was probably designed to increase the magazine capacity of the Remington-Rider magazine pistol. Since it held five short rounds, it

would have held only three of the standard 32 Short rimfires. A longer pistol would have been unhandy and a reduced magazine capacity not competitive with the five- and seven-shot revolvers of the day. Sales departments have to consider all these angles. The Remington magazine pistol had a tubular magazine below the barrel and a "lever" that protruded slightly above the hammer. Lever and hammer were drawn back together which cocked the gun and extracted the empty shell. Release of the lever chambered a new round as it returned to the forward position. It was of limited popularity. The original load was 5.0 to 5.5 grains of blackpowder with a 54- to 60-grain lead bullet.

32 Short (Obsolete)

Historical Notes The 32 Short rimfire originated under a Smith & Wesson patent of 1860 and early cartridge boxes were so marked. It was first used in the Smith & Wesson New Model 1-1/2 and Model 2 revolvers. It was later adapted to Colt revolvers and others with names such as Allen, Blue Jacket, Enterprise, Favorite, Whitney, X.L. and many, many others. It was also used in a variety of rifles including Remington, Stevens and Winchester. It was loaded and listed in some ammunition catalogs as late as 1972. Navy Arms had 32 Rimfire ammunition made in Brazil in 1990. Until recently, 32 Short ammunition has been available from that source.

General Comments Rifles and pistols using the 32 Short rimfire were popular up to the early 1900s. Stevens single-shot rifles were available in this chambering until 1936. There are tens of thousands of guns around for this cartridge. It actually was a good small-game cartridge out to 50 yards, as it would kill cleanly with hits in the forward body area and not spoil meat. Accuracy is not outstanding, but adequate for field use. However, ammunition costs more than 22 Long Rifle loads, which is a consideration in choosing a rimfire gun. The 32 rimfire is obsolete. The original load had an 80-grain bullet and 9.0 grains of blackpowder.

32 Long (Obsolete)

Historical Notes The 32 Long was originally a revolver cartridge, which was later used extensively in various rifles. It was introduced for the Smith & Wesson New Model 2 revolver in 1861. It was quickly picked up by other manufacturers and offered in such makes as the Allen, Enterprise, Favorite, Forehand & Wadsworth, Harrington & Richardson, Pioneer, Webley, X.L. and many others. The Colt New Line revolvers were available in this chambering also. Stevens single-shot pistols and rifles featured it, as did Marlin, Ballard, Maynard, Remington and Winchester single-shot rifles. It is no longer produced in the United States. Navy Arms had 32 Long ammunition made in Brazil in 1990. Until recently, this ammunition was available from that source.

General Comments The 32 Long rimfire has a heavier bullet and delivers more energy than the 32 Short, although velocity is about the same. Original load had an outside-lubricated, 90-grain lead bullet with 12 to 13 grains of blackpowder. It was a good short-range, small-game number because, like other cartridges in the same class, it killed cleanly without ruining edible meat. However, it was not effective beyond 50 yards because of the relatively high trajectory, making bullet placement difficult at long range. Single-shot Stevens rifles in this chambering were made until 1936.

32 Long Rifle (Obsolete)

Historical Notes This cartridge has an inside-lubricated bullet and a longer case than the regular 32 Long rimfire. It appears on cartridge lists from 1900 into the early 1920s. Both Remington and Winchester loaded it. Some say it was a smokeless powder improvement over the older 32 Long, but the 1918-19 Remington catalog lists it as available in blackpowder loading only. It has been obsolete for many years and is a collector's item.

General Comments Case length of the 32 Long Rifle is between that of the 32 Long and Extra Long rimfire; other dimensions are practically identical. It could be fired in any rifle chambered for the Extra Long and most rifles or revolvers made to handle the Long.

The outside-lubricated bullet was messy to carry in the pocket or loose in a container. These bullets picked up lint and dirt, greased and stained the pocket, etc. Inside-lubricated bullets are much cleaner to handle under any conditions, which is the reason efforts were made to produce such versions of the outside-lubricated types. However, this required a smaller diameter bullet, which gave unacceptable accuracy in the original barrel. That may have been why the 32 Long Rifle had a short life. No one seems to have made a gun specifically for it, or at least the author found no reference to such. The original load was an 81- or 82-grain lead bullet with 13 grains of blackpowder.

32 Extra Long (Obsolete)

Historical Notes Exact date of introduction of this cartridge is obscure. It is listed in various catalogs of 1876, so it probably originated in the mid-1870s. Ballard, Remington, Stevens and Wesson single-shot rifles chambered it. It does not appear in post-World War I catalogs. Many gun companies charged extra for rifles chambered to shoot any of the extra-long rim or centerfire cartridges. Some authorities place the date of introduction as 1866.

General Comments Original load for the 32 Extra Long rimfire was a 90-grain outside-lubricated lead bullet and 18 to 20 grains of blackpowder. The bullet is the same as that used in the ordinary 32 Long, but there were variations, depending on who manufactured the ammunition. The 32 Extra Long was not a very accurate cartridge and never established itself as a match round. It extends the effective hunting range of the rimfire 32 out to perhaps 65-75 yards, but doesn't possess appreciably greater killing power than the 32 Long.

38 Short (Obsolete)

Historical Notes When the Civil War ended in 1865, a number of rimfire cartridges had been developed and used successfully in battle. Most were large-caliber rifle cartridges. After the war, there was a demand for smaller-caliber metallic cartridges for revolvers and sporting rifles. Both the 38 Short and Long rimfire date from this period. These are listed in the 1869 Folsom Bros. & Co. gun catalog. The Remington Model 1866 revolving rifle was available in 38 rimfire. In 1871, the Remington New Model revolver was advertised as available with an extra 38 rimfire cylinder. The 38 Short rimfire was listed in the 1876 J. Brown & Son catalog as for Ballard, Remington and Wesson rifles and Allen, Colt, Enterprise, Whitney, X.L. and other pistols. This is now an obsolete cartridge, but it was manufactured until 1940.

General Comments The 38 Short rimfire is in the same class as the centerfire 38 Short Colt. Original loading was a 130-grain lead bullet and 18 grains of blackpowder. Like most older rimfires, the bullet is outside-lubricated. Bullet diameter is 0.375-inch, the same as the ball fired in 36-caliber cap-and-ball revolvers. The 38 Short probably originated as a cartridge for breech-loading conversions of these old revolvers. Many catalogs listed the 38 Short as for pistols and revolvers, whereas the 38 Long is shown as a rifle type. The Rollin White patent covering the bored-through cylinder, held by Smith & Wesson, did not expire until 1869. This undoubtedly had an effect on the use of the rimfire 38 Short for revolvers.

38 Long (Obsolete)

Historical Notes The rimfire 38 Long is another old-timer dating back to before 1865 and the end of the Civil War. The Remington-Beals single-shot rifle was available in 38 Long from 1867 until it was discontinued in 1875. The Remington revolving rifle of 1866 was also made for it. It was used in Allen, Ballard, Remington, Stevens and Wesson rifles of later date and in Enterprise, Favorite, Forehand & Wadsworth and Colt revolvers. It was a popular rifle and pistol chambering up to the turn of the century. It was replaced by similar centerfire rounds. American companies stopped loading it in the late 1920s.

General Comments The rimfire 38 Long is in the same general class as the centerfire 38 Long Colt. Original load was a 150-grain outside-lubricated bullet and 18 grains of blackpowder. However, loads varied with different manufacturers from a 140- to 150-grain bullet and up to 21 grains of powder with the light bullet. In a rifle, it was a good short-range, small-game load, but accuracy was only fair. No one has made rifles in this chambering since the end of World War I.

38 Extra Long (Obsolete)

Historical Notes The rimfire 38 Extra Long appeared about 1870 and was chambered in Ballard, Howard, Remington, Robinson and F. Wesson single-shot rifles. It was not a standard Ballard chambering, but a special-order item that cost 50 cents extra. It was strictly a rifle chambering, being too long for most revolvers. Because of mediocre accuracy, plus the development of similar centerfire cartridges, the 38 Extra Long rimfire did not have a long life. It was not carried in the 1918-19 Remington catalog, but was listed in the 1916 Winchester catalog.

General Comments The 38 Extra Long is in a class well below the centerfire 38-40 WCF blackpowder loading. The original load was a 150-grain, outside-lubricated bullet and 30-31 grains of blackpowder. However, some companies loaded lighter bullets down to 140 grains, with slightly more powder. It was not a bad small- to medium-game cartridge out to about 80 yards or so. It was introduced at a time when the centerfire was emerging as the dominant type, so it did not build up a following. The centerfire 38 Extra Long was developed by Ballard in 1855-56 and was preferred because it was reloadable.

41 Short (Derringer) (Obsolete)

Historical Notes This is an old and once very popular rimfire because of the light, handy arms that chambered it. The 41 Short was introduced with the National Arms Co. breech-loading derringer in 1863. It was originally called the 41-100 rimfire. The National derringer was patented by Daniel Moore in 1861 and 1863. It was made by National from its introduction to 1870, when the company was purchased by Colt. From 1872 to 1890, this rotating-barrel, single-shot derringer was manufactured by Colt. They also adapted the 41 Short to the Thuer-patented or Third Model derringer and the House pistol or "Cloverleaf" cylinder model of 1871. Derringers made by Allen, Enterprise, Williamson, X.L. and others were also of 41 Short chambering. The Remington over/under or double-barrel derringer manufactured from 1866 to 1935 was the most famous and popular of the lot. Several low-priced pocket revolvers were also chambered for the 41 Short. It has been obsolete since World War II, but special lots of ammunition have been loaded since the war.

General Comments The 41 rimfire Short is so underpowered as to be worthless for anything but rats, mice or sparrows at short range. Fired from the average derringer at a tree or hard object 15 to 25 yards away, the bullet will often bounce back and land at your feet. Nevertheless, it was a popular self-defense cartridge and at point-blank range could inflict a severe wound or kill a human being. These 41 derringer pistols were more of a threat or morale builder than anything else. Original load was a 130-grain, outside-lubricated lead bullet and 13 grains of blackpowder. Late loads used smokeless powder.

41 Long (Obsolete)

Historical Notes This is a longer and slightly more powerful version of the 41 Short. It originated in 1873 and the Colt New Line revolvers appear to be the first to chamber it. The Enterprise No. 4, Favorite No. 4, Forehand & Wadsworth, Webley and other revolvers were available in this chambering. A few cheap, single-shot rifles also chambered it. It has been obsolete since the 1920s.

General Comments The rimfire 41 Long is a better cartridge than the Short, but not by much. There was some variation in bullet weight and powder charge, but the original load used a 163-grain bullet and 13 to 15 grains of blackpowder. The centerfire 41 Short is an outgrowth of this cartridge. Guns chambered for the Long could also shoot the 41 Short rimfire. In power, this cartridge is in about the same class as the 38 S&W centerfire in blackpowder loading.

41 Swiss   See Chapter 7 for the 10.4x38Rmm (Obsolete)

44 Short (Obsolete)

Historical Notes The 44 Short was a handgun cartridge, although it could be fired in arms chambered for the 44 Long rimfire. It is well-established in old catalogs dating from 1870, and was chambered in popular pistols and revolvers, including those made by Allen, Forehand & Wadsworth and Remington. It is best noted as being the cartridge for the single-shot Hammond "Bulldog" pistol made by the Connecticut Arms & Mfg. Co. of Naubuc, Conn. This pistol is believed to have been marketed before the end of the Civil War, which would place the date of origin of the 44 Short at about 1864-65. It has been obsolete since the 1920s.

General Comments The rimfire 44 Short is a better handgun cartridge than the 41 Short or Long, but was not generally as popular. The type and variety of guns that chambered it was rather limited. The original load was a 200- or 210-grain, outside-lubricated bullet and 15 to 17 grains of blackpowder. While velocity was low, with the 200-grain bullet, short-range stopping power was fairly good. Performance was similar to the centerfire British 44 Webley cartridge.

44 Long (Obsolete)

Historical Notes The rimfire 44 Long originated with the Ethan Allen carbine patented in 1860 and manufactured by Allen & Wheelock of Worcester, Mass. It was later adapted to rifles made by Ballard, Howard, Remington, Robinson and F. Wesson. It was fairly popular, but replaced by similar centerfire types. It became obsolete in the early 1920s.

General Comments With a 220-grain bullet and 28 grains of blackpowder, the 44 Long was a potent short-range cartridge for small game. The 44-40 WCF rapidly became the dominant 44-caliber cartridge after it was introduced in 1873. It could be reloaded and was available in repeating rifles and revolvers, important factors on the western frontier. Other 44 cartridges, particularly the rimfire, gradually declined in use and popularity. The 44 Long was neither as powerful nor as accurate as the 44-40.

44 Extra Long (Obsolete)

Historical Notes This Ballard-developed cartridge is a longer, more powerful version of the rimfire 44 Long. Unfortunately, it was introduced about 1869 and soon the 44-40 Winchester Center Fire was establishing a reputation in the West. This number had a very short life and was obsolete by the 1880s. The exact date of introduction is vague, but probably between 1870-75. It is listed in the 1876 catalogs as adapted to Ballard, Remington and F. Wesson rifles.

General Comments The 44 Extra Long is not as good a general-purpose cartridge as the 44-40 Winchester. For one thing, it used an outside-lubricated bullet and in addition, overall length was too long for many repeating actions. It was loaded with a 218-grain bullet and 46 grains of blackpowder. It was not noted for great accuracy. In power, it would be primarily a small-game number. Effective range was not much over 75 yards or so.

44 Henry Flat (Obsolete)

Historical Notes This old and particularly historic cartridge is one of the milestones in the development of modern arms and ammunition. It was developed by B. Tyler Henry for the lever-action repeating rifle bearing his name, the forerunner of the original Winchester lever-action rifle and conceptually and functionally similar to all models up to the 1876. The Henry rifle was manufactured by the New Haven Arms Co. from 1860 to 1866, at which time it was reorganized as the Winchester Repeating Arms Co. The 44 Henry cartridge was manufactured from 1860-61 to 1934. Two versions of the cartridge were offered. The early case was 0.815-inch long. Bullet and powder charge were the same. Colt revolvers were also made in 44 Henry chambering. The Henry rifle and cartridge saw limited use in the Civil War.

General Comments The 44 Henry, although quite successful, was not a powerful round. Barely adequate for deer and certainly no match for buffalo or grizzly bear, its principal advantage was in the 15-shot repeating rifle. This provided undreamed-of firepower, something that could be decisive in combat. In recognition of this fact, Winchester brought out an improved rifle chambered for the 44-40 cartridge in 1873. From that date on, Winchester was in continuing competition with the makers of single-shot rifles and their big, powerful buffalo cartridges. The 44 Henry used a 200-grain bullet and 26-28 grains of blackpowder.

46 Short (Obsolete)

Historical Notes The 46 Short rimfire is usually listed for the Remington Single Action Army revolver. However, the 1878 and 1891 Winchester catalogs both describe this cartridge as: "For Remington, Smith & Wesson and other Army revolvers." Both Remington and Winchester loaded this cartridge and it was carried in their catalogs up to World War I, but did not appear after the war. Date of introduction was circa 1870.

General Comments The 46 Short rimfire was listed in Remington catalogs as having a 227-grain bullet and 20 grains of blackpowder. Winchester's loading was a 230-grain bullet and 26 grains of powder. As a revolver cartridge, it would have been less powerful than the 44-40 WCF.

46 Long (Obsolete)

Historical Notes The 46 Long rimfire was listed in an advertisement by Schuler, Hartley & Graham's in 1864. It is listed in the 1887 Remington catalog as a short-range chambering for the Remington rolling block single-shot Sporting Rifle No. 1 and also for Ballard rifles. The cartridge was loaded by Remington, Winchester and others and carried in ammunition catalogs up to World War I, but did not survive the war. It originated in the early 1870s.

General Comments The 46 Long was loaded by Remington, with a 305-grain bullet and 35 grains of blackpowder. Winchester listed a 300-grain bullet and 40 grains of powder. There may have been other loadings by other companies. It was a marginal short-range deer cartridge.

46 Extra Long (Obsolete)

Historical Notes The 46 Extra Long rimfire was a Ballard cartridge for its single-shot rifle and may also have been used by others. It does not appear in the Remington 1871 catalog, so it originated sometime after that date. Remington appears to have been the only one who loaded this cartridge and it was carried in later catalogs up to World War I, but did not reappear after the war.

General Comments Remington listed the 46 Extra Long as being loaded with a 305-grain bullet and 57 grains of blackpowder. There was never a smokeless loading. It would have been somewhat more powerful than the 46 Long and a better short-range deer cartridge. None of the 46-caliber rifle cartridges enjoyed a reputation for great accuracy. However, since these cartridges survived for quite a few years, these evidently did have a fair following.

50 Remington Navy (Obsolete)

Historical Notes Developed for the single-shot, rolling block, Remington Navy pistol of 1865, this load was replaced within a year by an identical inside-primed, centerfire type. The final commercial version, Boxer primed, was manufactured until World War I. The Remington Navy pistol has been obsolete since the early 1870s.

General Comments The 50-caliber rimfire was a rather potent handgun round. Velocity was low, but the big, heavy bullet would have had considerable effectiveness. However, 44- or 45-caliber handguns are more efficient and the military eventually standardized on 45-caliber cartridge arms. The original load was a 290-grain bullet and 23 grains of blackpowder.

56-46 Spencer (Obsolete)

Historical Notes This post-Civil War sporting cartridge was introduced by Spencer in 1866 for his repeating small carbine and sporting rifle. It was also listed as the No. 46 or 46/100 caliber. Spencer lever-action sporting arms were manufactured from 1866 until the firm failed in 1868-69. Winchester bought up the surplus guns and Spencer patents, but did not manufacture those rifles. However, the company sold off surplus rifles through its agents from 1869 to 1872. The cartridge has been obsolete since before World War I, but was cataloged until 1919.

General Comments The 56-46 Spencer is actually a 44-caliber, bottlenecked cartridge. It was considerably more powerful than the 44-40 WCF. A 320- to 330-grain bullet and 45 grains of blackpowder was the standard load. It was a fairly good short-range deer cartridge, but not satisfactory for larger game. The actions of early repeating rifles were not suited to large or long cartridges. This lack of power caused many hunters and the military to adopt the single-shot rifle, even though the repeater was well-proven. Full-powered repeating rifles, able to compete with the single-shot rifle on any basis, did not appear until 1880.

56-50 Spencer (Obsolete)

Historical Notes This cartridge was actually designed by Springfield Armory late in 1861. It was used in the 1865 model Spencer repeating carbine, a seven-shot, lever-action arm with 20- or 22-inch barrel. The magazine was in the buttstock, and it was loaded through a trap as with modern 22 rimfire rifles. This particular rifle and cartridge was manufactured too late for use in the Civil War, but was issued to troops fighting Indians on the western frontier. The 56-50 cartridge was listed in ammunition catalogs until 1920. The 1918-19 Remington catalog illustrated it as: "adapted to Spencer, Remington UMC, Sharps, Peabody and other rifles and carbines." The 1865 Spencer incorporated the Stabler magazine cutoff not present on earlier models. Spencer did not like the 56-50 cartridge because he thought it had an excessive crimp and it is not advertised in Spencer catalogs. He designed a slightly different version, which became known as the 56-52.

General Comments The 56-50 cartridge was loaded with a 350-grain bullet and 45 grains of blackpowder. It could penetrate almost a foot of soft pine at a range of 15 feet and was a potent short-range cartridge. It was adequate for deer-sized animals, but not satisfactory against larger game. Most western hunters preferred the more powerful single-shot rifles and their big, long-range cartridges. The Spencer action was not adaptable to the long centerfire cartridges that were developed in the years immediately after the Civil War.

56-52 Spencer (Obsolete)

Historical Notes Dating from 1866, this is an alteration of the army-designed 56-50, which Spencer believed had too much crimp. His approach was to incorporate a slight bottleneck, but many manufacturers omitted this, so it is difficult to distinguish between these two rounds. However, these cartridges are interchangeable and any arm chambered for one will fire the other. Spencer 56-52 ammunition was listed in ammunition catalogs up to 1920.

General Comments The 56-52 is more a sporting than a military round. Power is the same as the 56-50, but some companies loaded a heavier bullet. Remington produced a cartridge with 45 grains of powder and a two-groove, flat-point, 400-grain bullet. The 56-50 was always loaded with a 350-grain bullet. By modern standards, the 56-52 would barely qualify as a short-range deer cartridge. It was more powerful than modern smokeless factory 44-40 WCF loads.

56-56 Spencer (Obsolete)

Historical Notes This is the original cartridge for the first Spencer rifle and carbine, patented March 6, 1860, and manufactured in quantity beginning in 1862. Despite great opposition from the U.S. Army Ordnance Department, these guns were finally adopted and used during the Civil War. These first appeared at the battle of Antietam in September 1862, and later played a decisive role in other important engagements. The Spencer is credited as having provided the Union armies with an advantage in firepower that gave them a critical edge in turning back the Confederate forces at Gettysburg. President Lincoln tested the Spencer rifle in 1863 and insisted that the Army place substantial orders with Christopher M. Spencer. Many authorities insist that if the Spencer rifle had been adopted at the onset of the war and issued in quantity, it would have shortened the Civil War by a year or more and greatly reduced the ultimate number of casualties. Editor's note: Since more combatants died from dysentery than from battlefield wounds and injuries, it would seem that this contention probably has even more merit than the originators might have realized. The 56-56 cartridge was loaded by ammunition manufacturers until 1920.

General Comments The Spencer rifle was a seven-shot repeater of lever-action type with the magazine located in the buttstock and loaded through a trap in the buttplate. It could be fired at the rate of seven shots in 12 seconds, faster in the hands of a real expert. Parts were interchangeable, and the gun could be disassembled with only a screwdriver. The 56-56 cartridge was loaded with a 350/60-grain bullet and 42 to 45 grains of blackpowder. Bullet diameter varies from 0.540- to 0.555-inch between various makes of ammunition. Ballard and Joslyn carbines also used this cartridge. It was a short-range number, not very effective on anything larger than deer.

58 Miller, 58 Allin (Obsolete)

Historical Notes This cartridge was used in the 1867 Miller breech-loading conversion system of the muzzle-loading Springfield rifled musket. It was listed in an advertisement by Schuyler, Hartley & Graham's in 1864. It came in two case lengths, 1-3/16 inches and 1-7/16 inches, and was used chiefly in first-model Allin conversions. The Miller swinging-block conversion was one of a number of experimental alterations used by the military in an effort to salvage the million-plus 58-caliber muskets left over from the Civil War. The idea was to convert those guns to some viable breech-loading system rather than into scrap. Although some of the conversion units worked quite well, the effort was not entirely successful and most of these guns were eventually sold off as surplus or scrap metal. There must have been a fair number of the Miller conversions around though, because the cartridge was listed in ammunition catalogs at least as late as 1910. This cartridge is also called the 585 Springfield, 58 Musket, 58 Allen and 58 Ball.

General Comments The 58 Miller rimfire featured a 500-grain bullet backed by 60 grains of blackpowder for a muzzle velocity of approximately 1150 fps. It would have been a pretty good short-range deer cartridge. Some specimens have a heavy crimp, which affects the measurable length of the unfired case, resulting in variations in published figures for the case length. Remington, Winchester and others listed this round.

The Hyper-Velocity 22s

THE 22 rimfires are our oldest self-contained metallic cartridges, originating with the 22 Short back in 1857. From time to time, various improvements have been introduced by manufacturers, starting with smokeless powder loadings in 1888. Non-corrosive priming was adopted in 1927, and high-velocity loadings began in 1930. About 1965, Remington marketed a super-velocity 22 Short called the Rocket, which featured a compressed-composition 15-grain bullet with a muzzle velocity of 1,710 fps. These were intended primarily as a shooting-gallery load with a frangible bullet that would pulverize on striking a metal backstop. The author used this ammunition in a small auto pistol chambered for 22 Short and various 22 revolvers, and found that this load was very deadly on rodents and other small animals at close range. The 22 Rocket was discontinued after about five years, probably because of a poor sales record. In 1977, CCI introduced its Stinger 22 Long Rifle loaded with a 32-grain hollowpoint bullet starting out at 1,640 fps, which provides an increase in muzzle velocity of 360 fps over the older high-velocity type. Federal, Remington and Winchester quickly jumped on the bandwagon with their own versions. These have been collectively designated as hyper-velocity 22s to indicate their greater or increased velocity as compared to high-speed or high-velocity 22s. These are only manufactured in the basic 22 Long Rifle configuration.

The original loading of the 22 Long Rifle was a 40-grain bullet with 5 grains of blackpowder for an initial velocity of 1,150 fps. When smokeless powder was first loaded, the same velocity/pressure relationship as blackpowder was used to avoid problems with existing firearms. This continued for 42 years, until Remington introduced the high-velocity load with the same bullet stepped up to 1,250 fps. There was also a 36-grain HP bullet with a muzzle velocity of 1,280 fps. These ballistics have remained fairly constant right up to the present, except for minor variations between makes. CCI's Stinger pushed velocity up to 1,640 fps, but with a lighter 32-grain hollowpoint bullet. To some extent, this is a sort of hyper-velocity 22 Long, because the bullet weighs only 3 grains more than the 22 Short bullet. Federal, Remington and Winchester versions have muzzle velocities from 1,410 to 1,680 fps, and bullets that vary from 32 to 36 grains. Variations in bullet weight depend on the type of bullet: solid or hollowpoint. There is also a difference in bullet shape, some being conventional round-nosed, while others have a truncated cone. The increase in performance is achieved by several means, including a lighter bullet, modern slower-burning powder and a slight lengthening of the case, which combined with the lighter/shorter bullet leaves more room for powder. This allows an increase in velocity with only a slight increase in pressure. Therefore, hyper-velocity cartridges can be used in any modern firearm in good condition made specifically to handle 22 Long Rifle cartridges. On the other hand, these cartridges should not be used in alloy revolvers, and also these cartridges do not function well in some semi-auto pistols. This is particularly true for the Llama Model XV, which has an undersize bore, and may cause hazardous case ruptures. It is possible to order barrels with standard-bore dimensions for these pistols; this will eliminate the problem. The author has test fired the various makes of 22 hyper-velocity in a variety of rifles and handguns with no problems.

The author's test-firing was both on the range and in the field. This has demonstrated that like most everything else, hyper-velocity 22s have both good and, a few, bad points. Accuracy testing was conducted at 50 yards using a benchrest and a scope-sighted 22 bolt-action rifle with the capability of shooting 1/2-inch groups at 50 yards. It is necessary to establish some sort of base line or standard of comparison in order to evaluate the hyper-velocity 22s. The only way to do this is to also test some standard and high-velocity 22s and see how the hyper-velocities compare with those. The author has a number of boxes of old Remington standard-velocity Long Rifles (1,150 fps) that consistently shoot 1/2-inch or better at 50 yards, plus a variety of high-velocity Long Rifles; these were tested first. The hyper-velocity 22s were then tested in the same rifle and under the same conditions. The results are compared in Table No. 2. Test firing consisted of five, five-shot groups with each brand and type of ammunition listed in the tables. Results of these five-shot groups were then averaged for each type of cartridge. For the purpose of this test, high and low are not of any particular value, so are not recorded. Average of each of the five, five-shot groups provides a good basis for comparison because a single five-shot group doesn't necessarily mean much. Averaging multiple groups helps to reduce the effects of human error. The first groups fired were with standard-velocity Remington ammunition that has a 40-grain bullet at 1,150 fps. This was the most accurate of all ammunition tested and produced an average group size of 3/4-inch. The high-velocity types with either 40-grain solid bullets or 36-grain hollowpoints at from 1,250 to 1,280 fps all managed to average 1-inch. This provided a reasonably good yardstick against which to measure the comparative accuracy of hyper-velocity 22s. Firing conditions were ideal throughout the test with almost dead calm and sun to the rear. Naturally, with a different rifle, results would not necessarily be the same, but time did not permit repeating this test with different rifles.

TABLE 1
Ballistics of Ammunition Used in the Test Series

Cartridge	Bullet Type	Wt. (grs.)	Velocity (fps) Muzzle	Velocity (fps) 100 yds.	Energy (ft lbs.) Muzzle	Energy (ft lbs.) 100 yds.	Mid-Range Traj. (in.) 100 yards	Remarks
Remington Standard Velocity	Solid	40	1150	976	117	85	4.0	Standard Velocity
Remington Thunderbolt	Solid	40	1255	1017	140	92	3.6	High Velocity
Federal HiPower	HP	38	1280	1020	138	88	3.1	High Velocity
Winchester-Western Super X	HP	37	1280	1015	135	85	3.5	High Velocity
CCI Mini Mag	HP	36	1280	1012	135	84	3.5	High Velocity
HYPER VELOCITY								
CCI Stinger	HP	32	1640	1132	191	91	2.6	
Federal Spitfire	Solid	36	1410	1055	160	90	2.6	Truncated Cone
Federal Spitfire	HP	33	1500	1075	165	85	2.3	Truncated Cone
Remington Viper	Solid	36	1410	1055	165	90	2.6	Truncated Cone
Remington Yellow Jacket	HP	33	1500	1075	165	85	2.3	Truncated Cone
Winchester Super-Max	HP	34	1500	1056	170	84	2.8	
Winchester Xpediter	HP	29	1680	1145	182	95	2.4	

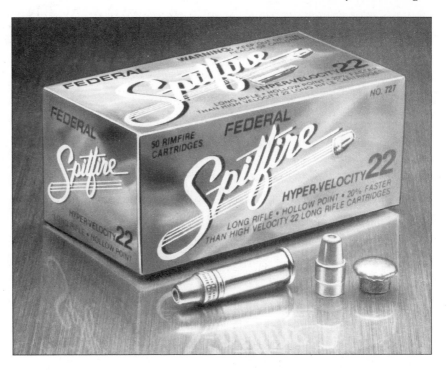

Moving to the hyper-velocity 22s, CCI's Stingers were the first tested. These have a 32-grain hollowpoint bullet at a muzzle velocity of 1,640 fps and made a group average of 2 1/4 inches. Federal's Spitfires were next. The 36-grain solid at 1,410 fps averaged 2 3/4 inches, with the 35-grain hollowpoint at 1,500 fps doing better with an average of 2 1/2 inches. Remington's Viper solids and Yellow Jacket hollowpoints have the same bullet weights and ballistics as Federal's Spitfires. The Viper averaged 1 3/4 inches and the Yellow Jacket 2 1/4 inches. Finally were Winchester's Super-Max, with a 34-grain bullet at 1,500 fps, and Xpediter, with a 29-grain bullet at 1,680 fps, both hollowpoints. The Super-Max produced an average group of 1 3/4 inches, but the Xpediter opened up to 2 1/2 inches. The two most accurate of the hyper-velocities proved to be Remington's Viper truncated cone hollowpoints and Winchester's Super-Max with its conventional round-nosed hollowpoint bullet. All the others grouped to over 2 inches. Clearly, hyper-velocity 22s are not as accurate as the older standard-velocity and high-velocity types. If we extrapolate these results out to 100 yards, which is about the maximum effective range of any 22 Long Rifle ammunition, the older types are all capable of grouping into about 2 inches, while the hyper-velocities are not going to do any better than 3 1/4 to 4 1/2 inches. Actually, this is not bad for practical hunting accuracy, but might be a disadvantage when shooting at very small targets. It is also worth noting that the various brands and types of hyper-velocities did not all shoot to the same point of impact. It is therefore important to find the one that is most accurate in your rifle and then sight-in for that particular cartridge. Another factor that should be considered is cost. The hypers sell for about twice what the high-velocity types do, so it doesn't make good sense to buy these loads for just plinking or casual shooting.

On the other hand, hyper-velocity cartridges are not intended as match ammunition. These cartridges are specifically designed for the hunter, and it is here that these have definite advantages. The author made some preliminary expansion tests with these hollowpoints, shooting into clay, wet telephone books and soap bars. Results indicated that the hypers have a much greater destructive potential than high-velocity hollowpoints. This is born out in the field. Other pluses are flatter trajectory and reduced lead on moving targets. The western ground squirrel is difficult to anchor, and at least 60 percent will make it back into their holes after being hit with high-velocity hollowpoints. However, the hyper-velocity hollowpoints practically eliminate this. These squirrels usually go down and stay down after any solid hit with one of these. The same is true of jackrabbits and other pests I tried these loads on, and it is my observation that hyper-velocities have superior stopping power. These are, however, overly destructive if you intend to eat what you are shooting. Another field observation is that the advantage in killing power disappears out around 100-yards; these loads do not really provide much extended effective range.

In any event, I rate the 22 hyper-velocity hollowpoint as the most effective 22 Long Rifle cartridge currently available for pest or varmint shooting. I would not, at this time, pick any one brand as superior to all the rest because I have had rather good results with all types. Try several makes since accuracy is rifle-dependent.

Not all hyper-velocity 22s had a good sales record and some listed here are now discontinued. However, this account provides a record of how these cartridges compared. — F.C.B.

TABLE 2
An Accuracy Comparison of the Hyper-Velocity 22s

Cartridge	Type	Bullet Wt. (grs.)	Average Group Size * (inches)
Remington Standard Velocity	Solid	40	3/4
Remington Thunderbolt	Solid	40	1
Federal Hi-Power	HP	38	1
Winchester-Western Super X	HP	36	1
CCI Mini Mag	HP	36	1
CCI Stinger	HP	32	2 1/4
Federal Spitfire	Solid	36	2 3/4
Federal Spitfire	HP	33	2 1/2
Remington Viper	Solid	36	1 3/4
Remington Yellow Jacket	HP	33	2 1/4
Winchester Super-Max	HP	34	1 3/4

*Average of five 5-shot groups. Range – 50 yards

Rimfire Cartridges – Factory Ballistics

Cartridge	Pistol Bullet (grs.)	MV	ME	Rifle MV	50 (yds.)	100 (yds.)	ME	50 (yds.)	100 (yds.)	Mid Range Trajectory	Remarks
17 Mach 2	17			2100			166				Hornady factory load (V-Max)
	17			2100			166				Remington factory load (Accu-Tip)
17 Hornady Magnum Rimfire	17			2550			245				Hornady factory load (V-Max)
5mm Remington Magnum	38			2100			372				Obsolete Remington loading
22 BB Cap	20			780			26			12.0	Obsolete U.S. loading
	18			780			24			12.5	CIL Dominion, load
	16			750			20			13.2	RWS load
22 CB Cap	29	760	31	727	667	610	33	28	24	9.3	Typical U.S. loading
	30			725			34			9.3	Eley-Kynoch
22 Short	15			1710			97			3.5	Obsolete gallery load
	27	1077	68	1164	1013	920	81	62	50	4.3	CCI hollowpoint
	29	786	38	830	752	695	44	36	31	6.8	CCI target
	29			1045			70			5.6	Obsolete standard velocity
	29	1065	72	1132	1004	920	83	65	54	4.1	CCI, Remington & Winchester
22 Long	29	706	31	727	667	610	33	28	24		CCI CB
	29	1031	67	1180	1038	946					CCI
22 Long Rifle	29			1680			182				Winchester Xpediter (Obsolete)
	32	1395	136	1640	1277	1132	191	115	91	2.6	CCI Stinger
	33			1500			164				Remington Yellowjacket
	34			1500			169				Winchester Supermax (Obsolete)
	36			1410			158				Remington Viper/Federal Spitfire
	36	1089	94	1280	1126	1012	130	100	81	3.5	CCI hollowpoint
	36	1180	110	1425	1261	1136	162	127	103	2.7	CCI hollowpoint
	37			1280	1127	1015	135	103	85	3.5	Winchester/Remington
	38			1280	1120	1020	138	105	88	3.5	Federal
	38	1089	94	1280	1115	999	138	104	85	3.7	CCI game bullet
	40	940	78	1070	970	890	100	80	70	4.6	Match/Target
	40	1060	98	1255	1110	1016	140	109	92	3.6	High velocity
	42	1025	97	1220		1003	139		94	3.6	Winchester Silvertip
22 Extra Long	40			1050			97				Late smokeless loading
22 Winchester Automatic	45			882			77				Early load
	45			1055			110				20-inch barrel
22 Remington Automatic	45			950			89				22-inch barrel
22 ILARCO	40			1380			168				Winchester data
22 Winchester Rimfire (WRF)	40			1440			183			2.8	High velocity HP (Obsolete)
	45			1450			209			2.7	High velocity solid (Obsolete)
	45			1050			109			5.0	Standard velocity
	45			1320		1055	173		110	3.3	Current Winchester load
22 Winchester Magnum Rimfire	30	1610	171	2200	1750	1373	322	203	127	1.4	Federal JHP/CCI Maxi-Mag+V HP
	40	1428	180	1910	1490	1326	324	197	156	1.7	CCI/Fed./Winchester FMJ CCI/Winchester JHP
	50			1650	1450	1280	300	23 5	180		Federal JHP

Rimfire Cartridges – Factory Ballistics

Cartridge	Bullet (grs.)	Mid Range Trajectory			Remarks
		Muzzle Velocity	Muzzle Energy	100 yards (inches)	
25 Short	43	750	53	6.10	Handgun ballistics
25 Stevens Short	65	950	130	5.4	Smokeless loading
25 Stevens	65-67	1180	208	5.1	Smokeless loading
30 Long	75	750	81		8 grains blackpowder
30 Short	58	700	62		Approximate handgun ballistics
32 Extra Short	54	650	51		Approximate ballistics
32 Short	80	950	160	5.6	Late smokeless load, rifle ballistics
32 Long	90	180	5.2		Modern smokeless load
32 Long Rifle	81-82	960	186	4.9	Approximate rifle ballistics
32 Extra Long	90	1050	221	4.7	Approximate ballistics
38 Short	125-130	725	150		Handgun ballistics
38 Long	150	750	190		Handgun ballistics
	150	980	320	4.5	Rifle ballistics
38 Extra Long	150	1250	526	3.8	3-inch barrel ballistics
41 Short	130	425	52		3-inch barrel ballistics
41 Long	163	700	180		Handgun ballistics
41 Swiss	300	1325	1175	4.7	Blackpowder
	334	1345	1330	4.3	Smokeless load
44 Short	200-210	500	112		Approximate handgun ballistics
44 Long	220	825	332	4.5	Approximate rifle ballistics
44 Extra Long	218	1250	763	3.5	Approximate rifle ballistics
44 Henry Flat	200	1125	568	3.9	Approximate rifle ballistics
50 Remington Navy	290	600	234		Approximate ballistics
56-46 Spencer	330	1210	1080		Approximate ballistics
56-50 Spencer	350	1230	1175		Approximate ballistics
56-52 Spencer	340, 386, 400	1200	1300		Approximate ballistics
56-56 Spencer	350	1200	1125		Approximate ballistics
58 Miller/Allin	500	1150	1468		Approximate ballistics

The following rimfire cartridges are not included above because ballistic data could not be located; the same group, (except the 61 and 69 rimfires) is, however, listed in the Dimensional Data table: 35 Alcan, 9mm Ball, 42 Forehand & Wadsworth, 46 Ex. Short, 46 Short, 46 Remington-Carbine, 56-46 Ex. Long, 46 Hammond Carbine, 50 Ball Carbine, 50 Remington Navy, 50 Remington Pistol, 50 Warner Carbine, 50-60 Peabody, 61 rimfire and 69 rimfire.

AMERICAN RIMFIRE CARTRIDGES
Current & Obsolete
Dimensional Data

Cartridge	Case Type	Bullet Dia.	Neck Dia.	Shoulder Dia.	Base Dia.	Rim Dia.	Rim Thck.	Case Length	Ctge. Length
17 Mach 2	A	.172	.195	.224	.225	.275	.040	.594	
17 Mach 2	A	.172	1900	.2046	.2260	.2780	.007	.7140	1.000
17 Hornady Magnum Rimfire	A	.172	.195	.240	.241	.291	.046	1.052	
5mm Remington Magnum	A	.205	.225	.259	.259	.325	.050	1.020	
22 BB Cap	B	.222	.224		.224	.270	.040	.284	.343
22 CB Cap	B	.222	.225		.225	.271	.040	.420	.520
22 Winchester Auto	B	.222	.250		.250	.310	.040	.665	.915
22 Short	B	.223	.224		.225	.273	.040	.423	.686
22 Short/40-grain RWS load	B	.223	.224		.225	.272	.042	.415	.798
22 Long	B	.223	.224		.225	.275	.040	.595	.880
22 Long Rifle	B	.223	.224		.225	.275	.040	.595	.975
22 Stinger	B	.223	.224		.225	.275	.040	.694	.975
22 Extra Long	B	.223	.225		.225	.275	.040	.750	1.16
22 Remington Auto	B	.223	.245		.245	.290		.663	.920
22 WRF & Remington Special	B	.224	.242		.243	.295	.046	.960	1.17
22 Winchester Magnum RF	B	.224	.240		.241	.291	.046	1.052	1.35
25 Short	B	.246	.245		.245	.290		.468	.780
25 Stevens Short	B	.251	.275		.276	.333		.599	.877
25 Stevens	B	.251	.276		.276	.333		1.125	1.395
30 Short	B	.286	.292		.292	.346		.515	.822
30 Long	B	.288	.288		.288	.340		.613	1.020
32 Long Rifle	B	.312	.318		.318	.377		.937	1.223
32 Extra Short	B	.316	.318		.317	.367		.398	.645
32 Short	B	.316	.318		.318	.377		.575	.948
32 Long	B	.316	.318		.318	.377		.791	1.215
32 Extra Long	B	.316	.317		.318	.378		1.150	1.570
9mm Ball	B	.337	.350		.350	.402		.417	.560
35 Allen	B	.342	.342		.342	.407		.865	1.388
38 Short	B	.375	.376		.376	.436		.768	1.185
38 Long	B	.375	.376		.376	.435		.873	1.380
38 Extra Long	B	.375	.378		.378	.435		1.480	2.025
41 Short	B	.405	.406		.406	.468		.467	.913
41 Long	B	.405	.407		.407	.468		.635	.985
42 Forehand & Wadsworth	B	.417	.416		.416	.485		.847	1.496
41 Swiss	A	.418	.445	.517	.539	.620		1.519	2.205
44 Short	B	.446	.445		.445	.519	.066	.688	1.190
44 Henry Flat	B	.446	.445		.446	.519	.066	.875	1.345
44 Extra Long Ballard	B	.446	.456		.457	.524		1.250	1.843
44 Long	B	.451	.455		.458	.525		1.094	1.842
46 Long	B	.454	.456		.456	.523		1.25	1.876
46 Remington Carbine	B	.455	.455		.455	.529		.990	1.635
46 Extra Short	B	.456	.458		.458	.530		.633	1.125
46 Short	B	.456	.458		.458	.530		.836	1.336
50 Ball Carbine **	B	.456	.476		.560	.640		.859	1.134
46 Extra Long	B	.459	.457		.457	.525		1.534	2.285
56-46 Spencer	A	.465	.478	.555	.558	.641		1.035	1.595
56-46 Extra Long	A	.475	.468	.551	.563	.638		1.200	1.757
46 Hammond Carbine	B	.481	.500		.518	.590		1.625	2.175
50-60 Peabody **	B	.499	.508		.559	.645		1.456	1.919
50 Warner Carbine	B	.505	.526		.526	.604		.850	1.514
50 Remington Navy	B	.510	.535		.562	.642		.860	1.280
50-70 Govt.	B	.512	.532		.557	.655		1.720	2.191
56-50 Spencer Carbine	B	.512	.543		.556	.639	.065	1.156	1.632
56-52 Spencer Rifle	B	.512	.540		.559	.639	.065	1.035	1.500
56-52 Spencer Necked	A	.525	.547	.558	.560	.642	.065	1.020	1.660
50 Remington Pistol	B	.529	.536		.558	.638		.875	1.300
56-56 Spencer Carbine	B	.550	.560		.560	.645	.065	.875	1.545
58 Miller	B	.585	.620		.628	.709		1.193	1.701

A = Rim, bottleneck. B = Rim, straight. Unless otherwise noted, all dimensions are in inches. These cases have slight taper at case mouth-to-neck juncture, neck diameter measurement is taken at case mouth.

Note: Rimfire cartridges dimensions show considerable variation, depending upon manufacturer, specific production lot and production era.

Chapter 17

Shotgun Shells

(Current & Obsolete—Blackpowder & Smokeless)

SHOTGUNS, OR fowling pieces as these guns were originally called, were among the earliest firearms to achieve sporting status. Of course, the use of a number of small pellets of varying sizes for military and hunting purposes predates what we would consider true sporting firearms made primarily for that pursuit. Originally, all guns were smooth-bored because rifling was unknown until around 1500. American colonists used shot in their flintlock muskets because it was easier to hit small moving targets such as birds or rabbits. Single-barrel and side-by-side double-barrel flintlock shotguns reached a high state of development in the late 18th and early 19th centuries.

In England, Joseph Manton and others turned out high-quality flintlock shotguns that were the equal of any made today. When percussion replaced the flintlock, fine shotguns of this type were also manufactured. As a matter of fact, single- and double-barrel muzzleloading percussion shotguns were still popular until the early 20th century. This was not due to reluctance by hunters to accept the new breechloaders, but because muzzleloaders were cheaper and did not require expensive shotgun shells. For a largely rural population, it was simple economics.

The first breech-loading shotguns appeared in the late 1840s, although some experimental types go back much earlier. The Lefaucheaux pinfire shotshell was patented in France in 1836. In 1852, Charles Lancaster marketed an improved breech-loading shotgun, which was followed by others, leading gradually to our modern break-open type. The 1864 Schuyler, Hartley and Graham catalog illustrates several breech-loading shotguns.

The general acceptance of the breech-loading shotgun depended on the development of a gun that was affordable by middle-class hunters, rather than only the wealthy. One disadvantage of the flintlock, percussion lock and the pinfire is that these guns all require external hammers. As soon as breechloaders firing self-contained centerfire ammunition became available, a number of internal-lock shotguns began to appear, starting in the 1870s. The first modern hammerless, breech-loading double-barrel gun was the Anson and Deeley introduced in England in 1875. This shotgun incorporated the self-cocking principle — which operated when the breech was opened — typical of all present-day doubles.

The pump-action shotgun was developed in the United States in the late 1800s and is today the most popular type in this country. This is a matter of economics because one usually can purchase a good pump-action shotgun for less than half the price of a double. The principal of choke boring was long recognized by 1871, but was not widely known or used prior to that time. In that year, it was further developed and publicized by the American Fred Kimble. Shortly thereafter, choke boring became standard on practically all shotguns. Walter Roper, an American, was issued the first patent for choke boring in 1866. However, his screw-on device was for single-barrel guns only and did not become popular. By 1990, screw-in chokes had become the practice on nearly all shotguns.

The type of shotgun used is largely a matter of personal preference and one has no great advantage over another as a practical matter. As to gauge, the 12 will cover the widest variety of game and hunting conditions. For the man on a limited budget, the repeating 12-gauge with an adjustable or interchangeable choke system is the way to go. The 16-gauge is almost as good, but very few guns are still made in this gauge. Actually, the best shotgun is the one in which you have the most confidence and can shoot the best. There is nothing wrong with the 20, 28 or even the .410, except that these relatively small bore sizes impose limits on what you can hunt effectively. At one time, smaller-gauge shells were less expensive, but today, those shells cost the same or even more than the larger gauges, so economy is no reason to pick one over the other, unless you are a handloader.

Bore and Gauge Defined

The gauge or bore diameter of a shotgun is designated differently from that of a rifle or pistol. The system used goes back to earliest muzzleloading days. It was the custom then to give the "gauge" of muskets in terms of how many lead balls of the bore diameter weighed 1 pound. A 12-gauge, thus, had a bore of such diameter that a round lead ball weighing 1/12-pound would just enter the barrel. Sometimes gauge was given as a 12th-pounder or 20th of a pounder (20-gauge). In England, modern terminology often uses "12 bore" or "20 bore," rather than gauge, although the two mean the same thing. The gauge system has persisted to the present. However, there are exceptions such as the .410-"bore" which is actually 68-gauge or 0.410-inch (41-caliber) and the 9mm rimfire shotshell, which is also a bore-size designation, not a gauge. At one time, shotguns were made in every gauge from about 1-gauge down to 32-gauge. Shotguns above 4-gauge were usually punt guns mounted on some type of support or swivel and used in boats for market hunting of waterfowl. In addition, "gauge designations" larger than 10-gauge size were often misrepresented, e.g., the bore of a 4-gauge gun would not accept a 1/4-pound pure lead sphere. American manufacturers no longer load shotshells larger than 10-gauge for sporting use, but some European companies still turn out 8-gauge shells.

Shotgunning Myths

There are all sorts of odd ideas in regard to shotguns. It is at least worth some effort to stamp out a few of these. For example, there is the idea that some shotguns shoot "harder" than others of the same gauge. The idea may arise in part from the fact that some shotguns have poorly fitted stocks. Since apparent recoil is more severe than with similar guns, the owner decides he has a harder-shooting gun. On the other hand, a shooter who has a gun that fits and handles exceptionally well may conclude he has a "hard shooter" because he does such good work with it.

Another outdated belief is that the longer the barrel, the longer the effective range. Modern smokeless powder shotshells develop maximum velocity in about 20 to 22 inches of barrel. Anything over that is just for balance and looks. If the barrel is too long, it will actually reduce velocity slightly through friction or drag. A shotgun with a 26-inch barrel will kill just as far away as one with a 40-inch barrel. In addition, the short barrel will be much faster in

getting on target. In deference to those who refuse to accept this, some shotgun manufacturers provide at least one model available with extra-long tubes! If it takes a 36-inch barrel to make you happy or build your confidence, by all means use one. However, beyond placing the muzzle 10 inches closer to the target, it does not give you any ballistic advantage over the fellow using a much shorter barrel.

The effective range of shotguns is another matter usually subject to much argument and misunderstanding. Some people believe the larger the gauge, the higher the velocity; others believe that the smaller the gauge, the higher the velocity. Obviously, there is room for all sorts of confusion here. Actually, both are wrong. The average muzzle velocity of a similar 10-, 12-, 16- or 20-gauge load is nearly the same. Why then does a larger gauge have a greater effective range? It is a matter of pattern density. For example, if you fire a .410 at a dove flying 40 or 50 yards away, the chances are he will fly right through the pattern without being touched. If he is hit, the pellet or pellets will do as much damage as if fired from a 12-gauge. On the other hand, if you fired at this same bird with a 20-gauge, your chances of bringing him down would be greater, because you have thrown more pellets in his path. With a 12-gauge at this same range, the pattern density is great enough that the chances of the bird slipping through are even more reduced. We are assuming here the same degree of choke for all guns, because choke controls pattern size and density at a given range. There is not much difference in the actual diameter of the pattern thrown by different gauges at the same range if all other factors are equal. However, pattern density (the number of pellets in the pattern) will vary according to gauge with the advantage going to the larger bore. This is also contrary to common belief, so if you disagree, go out and pattern a number of guns of different gauges, but similar choke. Be sure you use the same size shot and type of load in all guns.

Modern Shotshells

Shotgun shells were originally made from wound paper or drawn brass, although these cases have also been made from drawn aluminum, cast zinc and molded or drawn plastic, which is currently the most popular system. Paper shotshells consisted of a laminated paper tube made by winding glue-impregnated paper sheets around a mandrel. The tube was then coated with paraffin wax to make it moisture-resistant, cut to proper length and one end plugged with a tightly rolled paper or composition base wad. The final step was to add a crimped-on brass (or other metal) head, which incorporated the rim and primer pocket. The height of the internal base wad determined the volumetric capacity of the hull and therefore loading density. Cases were divided into high-base and low-base types, depending upon intended loading.

In general, the low base wad was used with black or bulk smokeless powder, because these powders required more volume. The high base wad was used with dense smokeless powders that required less volume. The term high-base or low-base does not refer to the heights of the brass head. Over the years, shells with a high-brass head have become associated with high-velocity or magnum loads and shotshells with low metal heads are associated with target or light field loads.

Almost all modern shotgun shells are made from some variety of polyethylene plastic. Such shells were first introduced by Remington in 1958. Most plastic shells have metal heads of brass, brass-plated steel or anodized aluminum. A few makers have marketed all-plastic shells without metal heads

Smokeless powder has completely replaced blackpowder for loading shotshells. Early smokeless powders were termed "bulk" powders because these could be loaded bulk-for-bulk with blackpowder. However, these powders did not weigh the same, even though ballistics were similar with equal volume. A system of nomenclature evolved to accommodate this. Regardless of the powder type, the charge is given in "drams equivalent." Thus, a shotshell marked 3-1/4 — 1-1/4 means the ballistics are the same as 3-1/4 drams of blackpowder and 1-1/4 ounces of lead shot, and so on. Ballistics will be approximately the same regardless of brand or powder used by the manufacturer.

Shotgun-shell primers differ from rifle primers in size and type. The three-or four-piece No. 209 battery-cup primer is used in most modern shells. Until recently, some European shotshells used Gevelot-type primers. Brass shotshells usually take Large Rifle primers. Brass shells are shorter, but have the same volume as those of paper or plastic. These cases require larger wad diameters as well.

There has been more meaningful development of high performance shotshells in the past couple of decades than there was previously in the history of arms. Shotshells now shoot payloads farther, hit game harder and are manufactured more precisely than ever. But it has come at a price: It's not uncommon to pay $1, $2 or even more per round.

Considering what one gets in the deal, the new high-performance shotshells are well worth their price. Yet there is a dichotomy. Concurrently, low-tech "shootin' shells" are comparatively cheaper than ever in the history of shotshells. That's because of the global "dumping" of low-grade ammo from countries where their manufacture is subsidized. That's right, some shells sell for less in the U.S. than they can be manufactured for, even in their countries of origin. Global economy—most interesting.

The Lead Toxicity Issue

It has been recognized since the late 1800s that ingestion of lead shot by bottom-feeding waterfowl can cause a toxic reaction leading to the death of the bird. In 1959, a wildlife biologist named Frank Bellrose completed a 15-year study on the possible effects of lead shot ingestion and resultant lead poisoning (plumbism) on North American waterfowl. The results of this study were released in a bulletin known as the Bellrose Report. One of the conclusions in this report is that between 2 percent and 3 percent of the population in each waterfowl species in North America is lost each year through lead poisoning. This was actually only a very rough estimate based upon incomplete data. The Bellrose study was based on the examination of bird gizzards furnished by hunters who removed these from formerly live, healthy birds they had just shot. In other words, none of the wildfowl in the study were suffering from or had died from lead poisoning.

The Bellrose Report was not intended to be a final conclusion, but rather an effort to point out a potential problem in a limited area, possibly requiring further study. Unfortunately, this report was seized on by the U.S. Fish and Wildlife Service and the National Wildlife Federation as a *cause celebre*, something that would demonstrate their deep concern for wildfowl and the ecology.

The original study encompassed a relatively small area in the Midwest, but this did not stop the extrapolation of the data to cover all of North America, although there was no valid basis for such a conclusion. Whatever the merits of the argument, the fact is that Federal law now bans lead shot for virtually all waterfowl hunting. Furthermore, the outlook for the future is extension of the lead shot ban to encompass other kinds of hunting as well.

Waterfowl Loads

To be classified as a "waterfowl" load these days, ammo must contain non-toxic shot. This means that rather than the traditional lead, waterfowl cartridges now contain other metals such as bismuth, iron/steel and/or tungsten. Steel shot was the first widely used substitute for lead shot in shotshells intended for waterfowl hunting, but as it turns out, steel shot has a lot of bad features, not the least of which is the ability to ruin the bores of older shotguns now in the hands of hunters. It is as hard as the barrel steel of many high-grade shotguns and can dig grooves in the bores if allowed unprotected contact. Also, steel shot will not compress the way lead shot does as it passes through the choke and so will eventually bulge the choke area.

Steel shot also has poor ballistic properties compared to lead shot of the same diameter. Lead shot of equal size is 44 percent denser. This means that steel shot does not carry as well as lead shot and loses velocity and energy at a faster rate.

In descending order of actual use, today's shot payloads typically contain steel, tungsten and iron or tungsten and polymer (in a matrix), or bismuth.

There has been relatively little, if any, actual development of late on the bismuth front. And there is good reason. Bismuth works

great just as it is. Bismuth ammo offers two major advantages. First, it acts almost exactly like traditional lead. This means it works great, since lead was/is the single finest material for shot (not withstanding the controversy over toxicity). Also, bismuth lends itself superbly to use in the older, finer shotguns that cannot handle the steel or tungsten loads. Thanks for this product availability goes to Bob Petersen, the former publisher and general gun guru. Incidentally, Bob's affinity for the .410 bore also has resulted in the availability of these diminutive cartridges in the Bismuth line for the waterfowler.

Tungsten is a very heavy (heavier than lead), and extremely hard metal. This means that to match a lead load, tungsten must be "watered down" with something else. This watering down is usually accomplished by mixing the tungsten with iron, steel, or some kind of plastic (polymer). In the tungsten/polymer shot, powdered tungsten is suspended in a plastic matrix and then formed into round pellets.

Although the Brits generally are credited with brainstorming tungsten/polymer shot, there have been a couple of North American companies that have offered such ammunition to the general trade. One was Federal, but the sales numbers and sales velocity of Federal's tungsten/polymer loading were not enough to keep that superb offering in the line. Without question, Federal's tungsten/polymer load was a great performer. Meanwhile, Kent Cartridge Co., headquartered in Canada, continues to offer tungsten/polymer ammunition, and it works great, as well.

Most recent developments in non-toxic waterfowling ammunition has been with regular steel shot and with tungsten/other metal combinations. The metal combo shot used by the various companies comes in a variety of proprietary names such as Hevi-Shot (formerly a Remington product, now marketed independently) or High Density shot from Federal.

LEAD SHOT
1. TUBE
2. SHOT
3. WAD
4. POWDER

STEEL SHOT
5. PRIMER
6. BASE WAD
7. HEAD
8. Cushion (lead only)

LEAD VERSUS STEEL PELLET WEIGHT

Lead Pellet		Steel Pellet	
Size	Weight Grains	Size	Weight Grains
BBB	10.4	F(TTT)	11.0
BB	8.8	TT	9.6
BB	8.8	T	8.3
B	7.3	BBB	7.1
1	6.1	BB	6.1
2	5.0	B	5.0
3	4.1	1	4.3
4	3.2	2	3.5
5	2.6	3	2.9
5	2.6	4	2.3
6	1.9	5	1.8
7 1/2	1.3	6	1.4

TYPICAL LEADS FOR STEEL SHOT LOADS AND WATERFOWL CROSSING AT RIGHT ANGLE

MV (fps)	Shot Size	Lead in Feet at Range		
		30 yards.	40 yards.	50 yards.
12-gauge, 3-inch, 1 1/4-ounce 12-gauge, 2 3/4-inch, 1 1/2-ounce 1375/1365	BB	4.7	6.7	9.0
	1	4.8	6.9	9.3
	2	4.8	7.0	9.5
	3	4.9	7.1	9.7
	4	5.0	7.3	10.0
	6	5.2	7.7	10.7
12-gauge, 3 1/2-inch, 9/16-ounce 20-gauge, 3-inch, 1-ounce 1335-1330	2	4.9	7.2	9.7
	3	5.0	7.3	9.9
	4	5.1	7.4	10.1
	6	5.3	7.8	10.9
10-gauge, 3 1/2-inch, 1 5/8-ounce 12-gauge, 2 3/4-inch, 1 1/4-ounce 1285/1275	T	4.9	6.9	9.2
	BBB	4.9	7.0	9.3
	BB	4.9	7.1	9.5
	1	5.0	7.2	9.8
	2	5.1	7.4	9.9
	3	5.2	7.5	10.2
	4	5.2	7.6	10.4
10-gauge, 3 1/2-inch, 1 3/4-ounce 12-gauge, 3-inch, 1 3/8-ounce 1260	T	4.9	7.0	9.3
	BBB	5.0	7.1	9.4
	BB	5.0	7.1	9.6
	1	5.1	7.3	9.9
	2	5.2	7.4	10.1
	3	5.2	7.6	10.3
	4	5.3	7.7	10.6

Actual leads can vary with target speed. Lesser angles will require lesser leads.

EQUAL PELLET COUNT COMPARISONS

Steel Pellet		Lead Pellet	
Size	# Per oz.	Size	# Per oz.
F(TTT)	39	T	34
TT	46	BBB	42
T	52	BB	50
BBB	62	B	60
BB	72	1	72
B	87	2	87
1	103	3	106
2	125	4	135
3	154	5	170
4	192	6	225
5	243	6	225
6	317	7	299

The trend for the metal combo loads has been for companies to offer payloads per volume that are heavier than lead, which, in theory, means they are ballistically superior. This trend is so evident with the heavier metal combos that, in addition to waterfowl loads, companies now are offering this kind of shot in high-density turkey hunting ammunition.

Throughout history, developers have attempted to figure out ways to send heavier and heavier shot payloads out of the barrel at higher and higher velocities.

And on the steel shot front, most development has been a form of fine-tuning in which velocities are increased while pattern uniformity is improved. Without question, velocity is the prime determinant in the success of steel shot load. And, it doesn't hurt with the combo metal loads, either.

There are several reasons why velocity is so crucial for loads that contain super-hard payloads. With respect to steel, the higher velocity stretches the effective distance a bit. But with all super-hard pellets, it is the way they take game that makes velocity so crucial.

Because the pellets are so hard, they do not deform like lead (even plated, hardened lead deformed a bit). This means that each individual pellet acts similarly to a full metal jacket rifle bullet. It puts a small hole in its wake, but does little other damage on the way. This was the characteristic that caused many hit with steel shot in the early days to be hit hard, yet limp off through the air, only to fall dead a mile or so away after they had bled-out. Higher velocity helps preclude this kind of problem.

Years ago, really high velocity (over 1300 feet per second) was achieved with non-toxic loads only when the payload was relatively light for the bore diameter. In 12-gauge, this generally meant one-ounce payloads. Since then, companies have offered many heavier payloads at the higher velocities, thus removing one more negative variable from the equation.

And, to make things even better, changes in wads and manufacturing techniques have taken waterfowling loads to new highs in every respect. And, not insignificantly, virtually all commercial non-toxic waterfowling ammunition these days is as close to being waterproof as is possible. That's nice.

Turkey Loads

Developments in wild turkey hunting loads have focused on ways to deliver the densest patterns at the longest distances. This means developing ammunition that patterns superbly at high velocity. In the long ago, muzzle velocities of 1200 to 1300 fps were typical for shotshells. Now, it is common to find loads, some even with quite heavy payloads, that send the shot out of the barrel at 1400 fps, or faster.

Most of the turkey loads, however, continue to keep the muzzle velocity in the 1300 to 1400 fps arena, but deliver that speed with heavier shot charges. And what shot charges! Although Federal and Mossberg originally developed the 3 1/2-inch 12-gauge shell as a way to put more of the lighter steel shot into waterfowl ammunition, the 3 1/2-inch 12-gauge shell has found a welcome home among many turkey hunters who don't mind the recoil of a gun that shoots 2-1/2 ounces or more of shot out of the barrel at high velocity.

Federal Cartridge Co. upped the ante a bit in recent times with the development of what it calls the Flitecontrol wad. By its very design, this wad keeps the shot swarm together longer, which extends the density of the pattern downrange.

Major breakthroughs in ammunition seem to be happening with regularity these days, and Federal's new Mag-Shok turkey hunting load with its all-new wad design take patterning for big toms to a whole new level. Initial tests in the author's gun resulted in roughly twice as many pellets in the head/neck kill zone as was common with more traditional ammunition from the same gun/choke combination.

At the heart of Federal's new turkey ammunition is an ingenious wad that keeps the pellet swarm tighter. Couple that with hard, copper-plated shot and the world just got a lot easier.

The new wad is thick and made of a plastic that is about the same hardness as that used for steel shot loads for waterfowling. However, that is about where any similarity to most wads ends. A cross-section of the wad itself would remind one of the Nosler Partition bullet jacket design, with the front partition area being about twice the length of the back partition. The front partition holds the buffered shot, while the rear encapsulates the top of the powder charge. Truly it is quite different from the typical wad.

The front section of the wad literally is a cup that holds the shot all the way out the barrel, and then some. There are no petals, slices or slots in the front part of the wad, as is normal in most modern designs. Yet, at the bottom of the front part of the wad, there are three partial cutouts that, upon firing, merely relieve the bottom area of the front, shot-containing cup. They flare out, but almost not at all, during the firing process. It looks like they are there more to relieve some kind of pressure effect on the wad itself than anything else.

Most intriguing is the base, or skirt, of the long, orangish, one-piece wad. The skirt has six major petals that, upon exiting the barrel, flare out, causing major wind drag, which in turn pulls the wad away from the shot that continues at normal velocity. This means the shot doesn't leave the wad until it is long gone from the barrel, which means that the pattern begins to open up much later, making it much tighter at any distance.

Upland Game Loads

There has not been the dramatic development in the upland game loads that there have been in other arenas. About the biggest news in the past few years is that where 1300 fps was common for upland loads a decade or longer ago, 1400 fps, or even a little more, is now in vogue with the latest offerings.

Although the higher speed loads work well, their primary advantage, if any, is that they mitigate at least a bit the amount of "lead" necessary when shooting at moving targets. This probably translates into a few more pattern-edge hits for those whose timing is a little rusty. Other than that, there is an increase in felt recoil that naturally goes with the higher velocity.

Also recently, there has been a slight level of advancement in upland game loads for the smaller gauges. One must consider that in the general shotgunning world, there are the 12- and 20-gauges, and then there is everything else, in which everything else doesn't add up to the volume of either of the top two.

But there still is "everything else." Generally speaking, companies are now offering comparatively heavy shot charges for the 28 gauge and .410-bore guns. For example, there are 28-gauge loads with one-ounce of shot (classically the shot charge weight of the 16-gauge), and Winchester, at least, now offers a three-inch .410 with 3/4-ounce of shot (classically the shot charge weight of the 28-gauge). Although the heavier 28-gauge loading maintains velocity at slightly above 1200 fps, which is classic, the heavier .410 load does not. For example, the classic 1/2-ounce target loading for the .410 has a muzzle velocity of 1200 fps. The traditional three-inch .410 loading with 11/16-ounce of shot has a muzzle velocity of around 1135 fps, and the 3/4-ounce loading goes out at an even 1100 fps. This data suggests that hitting relatively tough targets at relatively close ranges is where the heavier payloads shine.

Deer Hunting Loads

It was common practice with muzzleloading shotguns to load a solid roundball for big-game hunting. This worked fine if the range was short, but accuracy beyond 40 yards was poor. It could be improved by using a patched ball, but the lack of proper sights limits what can be accomplished with a smooth-bored gun. When self-contained shotshells arrived, those were furnished in all gauges with a roundball loading. However, when choke boring became common, it was necessary to use an undersized ball to prevent possible choke damage. Therefore, it became common practice to load a ball sized one or two gauges smaller than the bore. Thus, a 13-gauge ball was loaded in 12-gauge shells, a 17-or 18-gauge ball in the 16-gauge and so on. These undersize lead balls usually were deformed when passing through the choke, so were even less accurate than bore-size balls. Roundball loads in 12-and 16-gauge were

useful in heavy cover where those offered good short-range power on deer-size animals. In addition, 4-, 8-and 10-gauge balls were used on dangerous game in Africa and India. Roundball loads were discontinued in 1941.

The rifled slug has an accuracy potential that will allow one to hit deer at ranges of 100 yards — provided your shotgun is equipped with a set of rifle sights and is properly sighted in. Rifled slugs were introduced by RWS in Germany in 1898. This slug, the Brenneke, is still available under the Rottweil label. The American, or Foster-type slug, was introduced by Winchester in 1936. The two differ in that the Brenneke is a solid-lead with a series of felt and card wads screwed to the base, whereas the Foster type has a deep, hollow base similar to the old Minie-projectile used during the Civil War. Both have a series of angular grooves swaged into the outer circumference. Both work on the same principal as the badminton shuttlecock in that most of the weight is forward of the center of air pressure, which causes these projectiles to fly point forward.

The newest slug design is a saboted copper solid, designed to work in rifled shotgun bores, which have become common in specialized shotguns intended only for use with slugs. When fired from these rifled barrels, these slugs (made by Remington and others) can provide rifle-like accuracy and terminal performance.

Without question, effective range for shotgun ammunition in the deer/big game hunting world took a giant step forward with the use of rifled barrels in conjunction with saboted slugs. Briefly, this move alone doubled (or even more in some instances) the effective range of the shotgun slug. Where credible distance for the more traditional shotgun slugs was somewhere around 50 yards, now 100 yards or more are common distances for successful shots.

Rifling the barrels of shotguns spins the projectile, allowing it to fly more truly to the target— as is the case with bullets in rifles and handguns. But with modern shotgun ammunition, the maximum in accuracy and velocity for shotgun slugs has been achieved by using a sub-bore-diameter slug (bullet) that is cradled in a sabot (French for *shoe*). The plastic sabot engages the rifling, transferring the spin to the slug. After exiting the barrel, the sabot, due to air resistance, falls away from the slug, which continues at high velocity to the target.

Advances in plastics and resultant manufacturing techniques have allowed ammo makers to offer loads that are extremely accurate for shotguns and up the velocity several notches in the process. Some modern slug loads deliver a projectile weight and velocity similar to, if not in some cases superior to, the blackpowder express rifle cartridges used against dangerous game in Africa and India at the end of the 19th century.

Depending upon the gun/ammo combination, it is relatively easy to achieve groups of four inches or less at 100 yards, with a projectile that delivers above the traditional minimum of 1000 foot/pounds of energy for deer-killing performance. In some combinations, groups of two inches or less at 100 yards are achievable. This was considered to be good delivered rifle accuracy several decades ago.

This means that the deer hunter in the woods now can use a shotgun as effectively as his ancestor did the venerable Winchester Model 1894 rifle in 30 WCF.

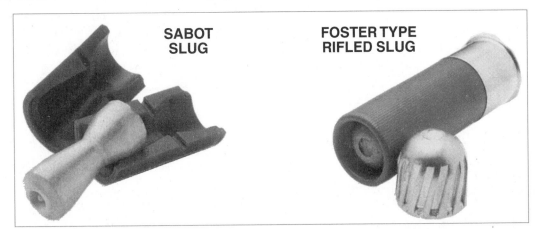

SABOT SLUG

FOSTER TYPE RIFLED SLUG

But development has not been limited only to the saboted slug loads for rifled barrels (saboted slug loads typically do not work very well in smoothbores). There also has been some advancement in ammunition for shotgun slug hunters who continue to use smooth-bore guns Nothing smaller than the 12-gauge slug can be considered adequate for any North American big game. The .410 slug is useless for anything but small game at short range. The 12-gauge Brenneke slugs have proven effective on thin-skinned African game including some dangerous species such as lion and leopard. Shotgun slugs can be compared to the old large-bore blackpowder cartridges such as the big 45-and 50-caliber numbers.

If you could only own one gun, consider a 12-gauge shotgun with an extra slug barrel. It will cover a greater range of game and hunting conditions than any other single gun. — F. C. B.

Additional text by Steve Comus

I WOULD LIKE to thank the many shotshell collectors who provided facts and shotshells from their collections for photography. In particular, I'd like to thank Mr. Russell Hooper and Mr. Frank Napoli for providing information, photographs and sample shotshells and for their invaluable assistance. We intend to further enhance this chapter as information on the more interesting oddball shotshells becomes available. — F.C.B.

1- to 4-Gauge

Historical Notes In most instances, gauges larger than 8-gauge were somewhat misnamed. Two-gauge shells are actually 4-gauge and 4-gauge shells actually 5-or 6-gauge. Guns chambered for such cartridges were generally either punt guns, permanently or semi-permanently mounted on movable platforms, or very heavy smoothbore or fully-rifled arms used by African hunters for taking the biggest and most dangerous species. In the former instance, the guns were used by market hunters who were an important part of

the expanding U.S. economy, as they provided much-needed protein for those who came to occupy new communities. The theory was to launch a vast charge of shot against large flocks of birds that were on the water. In this way, the market gunner killed scores of birds with only one shot. Those used in Africa against dangerous game were quite effective and more so when the cartridge was filled with a charge of shot. These are interesting cartridges that are well worth collecting and studying.

4-Gauge

Historical Notes The 4-gauge was popular as a long-range waterfowl chambering used in unusually heavy shotguns. Toward the later part of the last century, it saw significant application in market hunting. This shotshell saw very little use in any other application in the United States. However, both smoothbore and rifled versions were made for African hunting in that same era.

General Comments New guns in this bore size have been produced recently in both England and Belgium. It seems unlikely that any significant hunting need exists for such a gun, which suggests that the "Magnum" syndrome is not limited to North

America. Guns chambered for the paper-cased version are actually bored between 5-and 6-gauge size, while those chambered for the brass version can have a full 1.052-inch bore, which is true 4-gauge. Pictured is a 3.93-inch long, never-loaded casing featuring a steel head and paper body. This type of shell has no important length limitation — cutting the paper tube an inch longer adds very little cost. Therefore, in all the larger gauges (12-gauge on up), very long cases and matching chamberings were quite common. One is intrigued to speculate just how much shot might safely be fired at what velocity from such artillery-class combinations.

8-Gauge

Historical Notes This was a very popular chambering from the late 1880s through 1917 (in 1918, U.S. legislation prohibited waterfowl hunting with this or any larger gauge). In the United States and elsewhere, this was prized as a long-range duck and goose gun. While "8-gauge" sounds impressively huge, performance of factory loads was quite similar to that of modern 10-and 12-gauge Magnums – 1 3/4-2 1/4 ounces of shot launched at about 1200 fps. Since those original 8-gauge loads lacked any system to protect the shot from bore abrasion and propellant gas sealing was not particularly effective, it is quite unlikely that the best 8-gauge loads

of 100 years ago were anywhere nearly as effective as the best modern 12-gauge offerings.

General Comments Although prohibited for waterfowl hunting in the United States, there is no prohibition against other applications. Therefore, the 8-gauge is making a significant comeback for other purposes, particularly turkey hunting, where it excels. The 8-gauge shells came in 3-, 3 1/4-, 3 3/4-and 4-inch lengths. Bore diameter is 0.835-inch. Game Bore Cartridge Co. of England currently offers 3 1/4-inch cased loads.

10-Gauge

Historical Notes This is the only shotshell larger than the 12-gauge still commercially produced in the United States. Larger gauges were outlawed for sporting use in 1918. American-made single-and double-barreled guns in 10-gauge were manufactured until World War II. Then, after a short hiatus, several arms companies reintroduced the big-10 and, for awhile, these guns gained popularity. However, two things have worked to completely eliminate any sporting benefit offered by the 10-gauge for migratory bird hunting. First was the introduction of the 3 1/2-inch 12-gauge shell with a higher pressure standard than the 10-gauge. Second was the adoption of mandatory steel shot loads for hunting migratory species. There is nothing the 10 can do with steel shot that the higher-pressure 12-gauge loading cannot do better. However, the 10-gauge still has an advantage for turkey hunting, where large doses of lead shot are preferred medicine and velocity is not so important as it is with steel-shot loads. The most commonly seen shell sizes are 2 9/16-, 2 5/8-, 2 7/8-, and 3 1/2-inch. In England, Game Bore recently produced both the 2 7/8-and 3 1/2-inch shells. Here in the United States, 2 7/8-inch 10-gauge shells are available from New England Arms with the 3 1/2-inch widely available from a variety of sources. Bore diameter is 0.775-inch.

11-Gauge

Historical Notes There is very little information on this oddball shotshell. Both Parker Brothers and UMC Co. headstamps are known producers both listed in West Meridan, Conn. The Parker shell featured a large American-type Berdan primer with three holes inside the case. The UMC loading evidently featured an internal primer, as it had no external opening to accept a primer. Best information is that two double-barrel guns and about 200 shells were made in the 1890s. Dimensions for the 11-gauge are: Rim, 0.835-inch; base, 0.790-inch; mouth, 0.782-inch; length, 2.5-inch. 11-gauge bore diameter is 0.751-inch.

12/14-Gauge Martini Shotgun

Historical Notes We have almost no information on this interesting shotshell. The sample is labeled as Caliber 12/14 Martini Shotgun, for Police. The headstamp does have lightly etched markings but those appear to be in Cyrillic or some other stylized system. The case head includes a 0.85-inch-wide by 0.95-inch-deep, square-bottomed annular groove located around the approximately 0.3-inch diameter primer. Outside diameter of this groove is about 0.540 inches — the groove's purpose is unknown.

General Comments We have included this number because it will serve to demonstrate that shotshell ammunition is as varied and numerous in design as any other type. As we gain further information, we hope to improve the historical details included with this entry.

12-Gauge

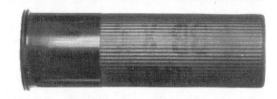

Historical Notes If there is one shotshell that holds all titles as most versatile, most popular and most varied in loading, the 12-gauge is it. Except for the 22 rimfire, by almost any measure, the 12-gauge is the most popular sporting chambering ever offered. It is commonly available loaded with shot made of lead, steel or bismuth. Current shot charges range from about 7/8-ounce to 2 1/2 ounces. Common shot sizes range from No. 9 through 000 Buck. Slugs are typically 1 ounce or 1-1/4 ounces, but other weights are available. Further, it is relatively simple to have a moderate-sized batch of custom-loaded 12-gauge ammunition (with either an odd-sized shot or reduced velocity) produced by a major manufacturer. To gain a true perspective, just consider that at one time in this country, there were literally thousands of distinct 12-gauge loadings offered. In 1995, 12-gauge commercial offerings from only the big three shotshell manufacturers total 435 unique manufacturer and component combinations. Further, other significant commercial manufacturers offer hundreds more loadings, especially in steel and bismuth shot. In fact, commercially available unique 12-gauge loadings exceed the total of all currently available high-powered rifle loadings for all cartridges by a significant margin. The 12-gauge has been and is still used for police and military applications and, as recently as the Vietnam conflict, was the preferred gun of front-line troops for jungle combat. No gun is more intimidating or more effective for home-defense situations. The 12-gauge is at home, given proper loads, hunting big game up through whitetail deer at ranges to about 100 yards with some shotguns and loads stretching useful range a bit further. For sporting use, the 12-gauge performs admirably on clay pigeons. The key word here is versatility. If any chambering offers that characteristic, this is the one. In 1866, a rebated-rim, reloadable-steel 12-gauge shell was patented by Thomas L. Sturtevant. Revolving magazine four-shot guns chambered for this shell were offered by the Roper Sporting Arms Co. until the early 1880s. Eley in England currently produces 2- and 2 1/2-inch shells while here in the United States, the 2 3/4-, 3- and 3 1/2-inch lengths are most common and available from a variety of sources. Longer and shorter versions exist and a rebated rim 2 3/8-inch steel case is known to have been produced. Bore diameter for the 12-gauge is 0.729-inch.

14-Gauge

Historical Notes This chambering was generally available between 1880 and the early 1900s. Shells were domestically available until sometime after World War I and generally available in Europe until the 1970s. Original loads included a 3-dram, 1-ounce shot-charge load. Shells in this gauge are again domestically available from specialty importers. The 14-gauge was experimented with in the 1950s by Winchester in an aluminum casing using both roll and modified-roll crimps. There was also a modified version using a 12-gauge case head and lower body. Both brass and plastic versions of the latter are known. Most commonly seen shell lengths are 2, 2-1/2 and 2-9/16 inches. The French still produce empty hulls for the 2 9/16-inch version. Bore diameter for the 14-gauge is 0.693-inch.

15-Gauge

Historical Notes Winchester's 1877 catalog listed brass shells in this gauge. That was the only year these were listed. Obviously, the 15-gauge is extremely rare. Examples are found only in the best collections. The 15-gauge would have a bore diameter of 0.677-inch.

16-Gauge

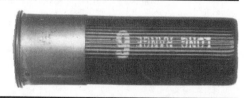

Historical Notes The 16-gauge lingers on, in what seems to be a nearly perpetual state of surprising continued existence. Introduction of 3-inch 20-gauge loadings should have sounded the 16's death knell since the 20-gauge can launch the same shot charge at just about the same velocity and, with modern plastic shot cups, patterning is substantially equivalent. However, there are just too many perfectly good 16-gauge guns still in use and the shells, in surprising variety, are still commonly stocked at the retail level. The 16-gauge is even available in steel shot loadings. In 1866, a rebated-rim, reloadable-steel, 16-gauge shell was patented by Thomas L. Sturtevant. Revolving magazine four-shot guns chambered for this shell were offered by the Roper Sporting Arms Company until the early 1880s. The most common shell lengths in this gauge are 2 1/2- and 2 3/4-inch, both currently produced by various European manufacturers, and the latter in U.S. production. The bore diameter for 16-gauge is 0.662-inch.

64 Maynard

Historical Notes Brass shells of this description were loaded for various models of Maynard sporting guns. The Model 1865 used a 2 5/16-inch shell with a Boxer primer. The 1873, adapted to both the No. 3 and No. 4 breech-loading shotguns used a 2 7/16-inch case featuring a modified Berdan primer. The Model 1882 was adapted to a reloadable case of 2 7/16-inch length. This gun, when equipped with interchangeable barrels, also fired the 40-40 Maynard cartridge. All Maynard shotshells were made with brass cases. This bore diameter corresponds to about 18-gauge.

18-Gauge

Historical Notes This European gauge was loaded for use in custom shotguns. This ammunition was manufactured by Braun & Bloem, Kynoch and Gustave Genschow. United Metallic Cartridge Co. produced a small batch for use in an experimental Browning shotgun. These UMC shells were 1-7/8 inches long and sometimes featured a 20-gauge headstamp. European pinfire versions of the 18-gauge in 2 9/16-inch length also exist. This gauge has a 0.637-inch bore.

20-Gauge

Historical Notes Very much alive and well, the 20-gauge has always been popular because it can be chambered in a smaller, lighter gun compared to the 12-gauge and offers sufficient punch for use against most sporting fowl. It is also completely at home breaking clay pigeons. Usefulness of the 20-gauge has improved dramatically since the blackpowder era, when the top loading was 2-3/4 drams with 7/8-ounce of shot. The comparatively recent standardization of the 3-inch loading brings 20-gauge performance into a new class with shot charges up to 1-1/4 ounces at higher velocity. Loaded with modern shot-protecting cups, the 20-gauge 3-inch Magnum practically duplicates the performance of top 16-gauge loads. Current loadings range from 1 to 1-1/4 ounces of shot and include several buckshot combinations and the 5/8-ounce slug. Steel shot loadings up to 1 ounce are gaining in utility and popularity. By a wide margin, the 20-gauge is the second most popular U.S. chambering. The 2 1/2-inch version is currently available from various European manufacturers. Bore size is 0.615-inch.

24-Gauge

Historical Notes Single-shot shotguns in this bore size were produced in the United States until the late 1930s by Stevens and Harrington & Richardson. The standard load was 2 drams equivalent and 3/4-ounce of shot. Shells in this gauge, and the double-barrel guns that shoot these rounds, are still manufactured in Europe. These have recently been available in the United States. Through American Arms Company and Beretta. Both CBC and Fiocchi have made this ammunition available domestically. Current loads launch 11/16-ounce of shot. The most common shell lengths in this gauge are 2 and 2-1/2 inches. The 2 1/2-inch version is still produced by Fiocchi. Bore size is 0.580-inch.

55 Maynard

Historical Notes Brass shells of this description were loaded for the various models of Maynard sporting guns. The Model-1865 used a 2 1/4-inch shell with a Boxer primer. The Model 1873, adapted to both the No. 1 and No. 2 breech-loading shotguns used a 2 3/8-inch case featuring a modified Berdan primer. The 1882 loading used a reloadable case of 2 5/16-inch length and was adapted to the No. 1 and No. 2 breech-loading guns. This bore size corresponds to the 28-gauge.

28-Gauge

Historical Notes The 28-gauge 2 3/4-inch is currently manufactured in the United States. The original blackpowder loading used a 2 1/2-inch shell with 1 3/4 drams of powder and 5/8-ounce of shot. Federal Cartridge now lists a 2 3/4-inch, 2 1/4-dram, 3/4-ounce load with either No. 6, 7 1/2 or 8 shot and a velocity of 1295 fps. The 28-gauge is perfectly adequate for use in hunting upland birds and is at home breaking clay pigeons. However, recent innovations in shotshell technology have limited the 28-gauge's popularity since 3-inch .410 loadings can practically duplicate 28-gauge performance. Nevertheless, light, easy handling and graceful guns still attract shotgunners; the 28-gauge hangs on to a small but dedicated following, chiefly for this reason. Bore size is 0.550-inch.

32-Gauge

Historical Notes American manufacturers offered 32-gauge guns well into the 1930s. The Winchester Model 1886 rifle was routinely offered on a custom basis especially chambered and barreled for the 32-gauge shotshell, which is essentially a 52-caliber bore. The standard loading was 1/2-ounce of shot but a 5/8-ounce shot load and a 158-grain roundball loading were offered. Loads in this gauge have been continuously available in Europe and shells are domestically available through Fiocchi loaded with either No. 6 or No. 8 shot. Guns in this chambering have recently been imported through the American Arms Co. Even before World War II, the .410 practically duplicated 32-gauge performance. Nevertheless, light, easy-handling guns with graceful lines still attract European shotgunners; the 32-gauge hangs on to a small but dedicated following there, chiefly for this reason. Currently Fiocchi offers the 2 1/2-inch shell. Actual 32-gauge bore size is 0.526-inch.

11.15x52mm

Historical Notes This European brass shotshell was popular in the early 1900s. It was generally loaded with shot but was also available in a ball-loading for use in rifled barrels. Performance of this loading would be quite similar to the modern 44 Magnum shot loadings offered by CCI/Speer. The intended purpose was small game hunting. For targets the size of rabbits and hares, the 11.15x52mm was reasonably effective. This bore size corresponds to 0.439-inch and would be called a 55-gauge.

44 XL (1 9/16-inch)

Historical Notes Made in the early 1900s, shotguns in this bore size were intended solely for use in hunting small game. This could be considered a forerunner to the .410 shotshell. Brass cases and paper shot containers were used. Overall, length was 2 1/32-inch with a case length of 1-9/32 inches. The standard loading used No. 8 shot in a folded paper container, which protruded substantially from the brass case. Both single-barrel and double-barrel shotguns were offered in this chambering. Actual bore diameter was similar to the 44-caliber rifle cartridges (0.425-inch) and would be called 61-gauge.

410 Bore

Historical Notes Though gun and load selection are somewhat limited, the .410 bore (12 mm) is a perfectly good dove and quail chambering and can be argued as the ideal small-game combination. A light, handy .410 breech-break shotgun is a pleasure to carry on long hunts and top 3-inch loads deliver all the punch necessary to cleanly anchor rabbits and smaller species. Many use this diminutive chambering for breaking clay pigeons. Interestingly, it is possible to fire .410 shells in 45/70-chambered rifles. There is also a slug loading, but its value for any purpose is certainly moot. The .410 follows the 12 and 20 gauges in popularity. Many young shooters have learned to shoot with a .410 and that tradition continues. The 0.410-inch bore would be called 68-gauge.

360 Centerfire

Historical Notes Similar to the more popular 9mm rimfire, this chiefly European chambering is strictly in the small game and pest control genre. Shells are found in both paper and brass and are 1-3/4 inches long. While it might be possible to dispatch smaller species of small game with this and other of the various diminutive shotshell chamberings, such use is questionable. Nevertheless, none of these are toy cartridges. All high-velocity shot pellets are equally dangerous, regardless of source. The chief problem with the various diminutive shotshells is the lack of sufficient shot volume to achieve useful hunting pattern density with shot of sufficient size to get the job done. A 0.360-inch bore would be called a 99-gauge.

9.1x40mm

Historical Notes The 9.1x40mm (0.358-inch x 1.575-inch) was an early European shotshell intended for small game hunting. It was also offered in a ball-loading for use in rifles. While it might be possible to dispatch smaller species of small game with this and other of the various diminutive shotshell chamberings, such use is questionable. The chief problem with the various diminutive shotshells is lack of sufficient shot volume to achieve useful hunting pattern density with shot of sufficient size to get the job done. This corresponds to a 0.358-inch bore and would be called a 101-gauge.

9mm Rimfire

Historical Notes This cartridge was offered by Winchester for use in the Model 36 shotgun, which was introduced in 1920 and discontinued in 1927. Only 20,306 such shotguns were made. While that is a surprisingly small production total for a mainline arms manufacturer, this represents a surprising number of guns, considering the limited usefulness and market. The only viable use for such a chambering is pest control. While it might be possible to dispatch smaller species of small game with this and other of the various diminutive shotshell chamberings, such use is questionable. The chief problem with this and other diminutive shotshells is the lack of sufficient shot volume to achieve useful hunting-pattern density with shot of sufficient size to get the job done. The shotshell length was 1-9/16 inches. This corresponds to a 0.354-inch bore and would be called a 105-gauge. Fiocchi again offers 9mm rimfire shotshells.

9mm Centerfire

Historical Notes Recently available in Europe (Spanish manufacture), these are found with plastic bodies and a metal head. The only viable use for such a chambering is pest control. While it might be possible to dispatch smaller species of small game with this and other of the various diminutive shotshell chamberings, such use is questionable. The chief problem is the lack of sufficient shot volume to achieve useful hunting pattern density with shot of sufficient size to get the job done. This corresponds to a 0.354-inch bore and would be called a 105-gauge.

32 Rimfire

Historical Notes Stevens offered its No. 20 Favorite shotgun in this chambering. Shell casings were copper or brass and shot containers were wood or paper. Case length was 7/8-inch for copper rolled rim or 25/32-inch for those with wooden shot containers. Overall, length for the wooden container shotshells was 1-7/32 inches. Remington UMC and WRA manufactured these shells. The only viable use for such a chambering is pest control. While it might be possible to dispatch smaller species of small game with this and other of the various diminutive shotshell chamberings, such use is highly questionable. The chief problem is lack of sufficient shot volume to achieve useful hunting-pattern density with shot of sufficient size to get the job done. A 0.320-inch bore would be called a 142-gauge.

310 Remington

Historical Notes This brass-cased, rimfire shotshell was made by Remington for a mini-skeet shooting game. The shotgun was a bolt-action used to shoot miniature clay pigeons. Shell length was 1 1/16-inch.

7mm

Historical Notes This is a European shotshell and long obsolete. It was also available in a ball loading. Shells are usually copper-based with a paper body. The only potential value of such a chambering is pest control. The 7mm shotshell corresponds to a 0.276-inch bore and would be called a 223-gauge. Most commonly seen length is 1-1/4-inch.

6mm

Historical Notes Little is known about this diminutive chambering. The example seen has a metal case head and paper body. The only potential value of such a chambering is pest control. The 6mm corresponds to a 0.236-inch bore and would be called a 353-gauge.

20-Caliber Wingo

Historical Notes These straight-walled rimfire shells were loaded by Winchester in the 1970s for use in special single-shot, lever-action shotguns used in special indoor Wingo skeet-shooting galleries. The shells feature a 22 rimfire rim size but have a smaller case body to prevent chambering of standard 22 rimfire ammunition in these guns. Wingo ammunition was assembled with 2.1 grains of ball powder and approximately 113 No. 12 shot pellets. Winchester-Western was the sole manufacturer of this cartridge. The 20-caliber Wingo corresponds to a 0.200-inch bore and would be called a 582-gauge.

Collath Gauges

Historical Notes Available in 0, 1, 3, 4, 5, 6, 7 and 8-gauge, these were an early 1900s European development. The shells used a unique gauging system. The 1-gauge is somewhat smaller than the common 12-gauge. Pinfire versions also existed. Collath ammunition was cataloged as late as 1911. The 5-gauge shell in Frank Napoli's collection has a metal band around the outer brass and paper joint. The empty shells were made in Frankfurt, Germany, and available in the *Alfa Arms Catalog of 1911*. Although never very popular, specimens are sometimes seen in collections and at gun shows. The unusual sizings and headstamps can cause significant confusion.

General Comments on Shotshell Dimensional Table

This table is not exhaustive; it does not include many of the rarer but known casing lengths and types. It should, however, provide sufficient information to help the reader identify 99 percent of those shotshells or casings he might come upon. If the example does not fit any of these data, likely it is sufficiently rare to merit advisement from a serious collector.

In many instances, data in this table represents approximations or estimates. In addition, you will note a significant number of "?" entries. We anxiously await reader input toward improving the provided dimensional data and filling in the remaining blanks. The purpose of including estimates is to help the reader make a preliminary identification of either a loaded shell or a fired casing. We believe the included estimated dimensional data will be sufficiently close to accommodate that end.

Note that loaded shell lengths can vary quite dramatically, especially in those shells using a folded or roll crimp. However, such variance is always toward the shorter side. In the larger gauges, current SAAMI specifications provide for a "minus" variance as great as one-quarter inch.

Note also that all case length and diameter measurements include surprisingly generous tolerances, typically about 0.010-inch for length and about 0.020-inch for diameter. Numbers given for case base diameter are representative of a value somewhere near the middle of the radius of the fold where the case body blends into the rim. Generally, diameter of the cylindrical portion of the case head is somewhat smaller.

Shotshell Cartridges
Dimensional Data

Gauge or Bore	Possible Separate Shot Container	Crimp Types	Likely Case Body Material Types (not including case head)	Diameter (inch) Rim	Diameter (inch) Base	Diameter (inch) Mouth	Length (inches) Closed Fold	Length (inches) Closed Roll	Length (inches) Open	Normal Bore Diameter (inches)	Priming Type	Comments
Collath 3-gauge	None	Roll w/Card	Paper	?	?	?		?	2.91	?	Pinfire	Rare
Collath 5-gauge	None	Roll w/Card	Paper	0.803	0.731	0.666			2.56	?	Centerfire	Rare
20-Caliber Wingo	None	Star(?)	Brass	0.270	0.21	0.21	?	?	?	0.200	Rimfire	
6mm	None	Roll w/ Card	Paper	?			?	?	?	0.236	?	Rare
7mm	None	Roll w/ Card	Paper	?	?	?	?	1.20	1.25	0.276	?	
310 Remington	None	Taper w/Card	Brass	0.378	0.320	0.315		1.05	1.06	0.310	Rimfire	
32 Centerfire	Wood or Paper	Tape w/Card	Copper or Brass	?	?	?	?	0.85	0.88	0.320	Rimfire	
32 Centerfire	Wood or Paper	Taper w/Card	Copper or Brass	?	?	?	?	0.78	1.22	0.320	Rimfire	
9mm Centerfire	None	Roll or Taper	Paper, Plastic or Brass	0.436	0.391	0.370		1.67	1.75	0.354	Centerfire	.
9mm Rimfire	None	Taper w/Card	Brass	0.385	0.323	0.320		1.65	1.66	0.354	Rimfire	
9mm Rimfire	None	Taper	Paper or Brass	0.410	0.344	0.326		0.40	0.40	0.354	Rimfire	Single Ball Load
9mm Rimfire	None	Roll or Taper	Paper or Brass	0.410	0.344	0.326		1.44	1.45	0.354	Rimfire	
9.1x40mm	None	Taper w/Card	Brass	?	?	?		1.55	1.58	0.358	Centerfire	
9.1mm Long	None	Taper w/Card	Brass	?	?	?		?	?	0.358	Centerfire	
360 Centerfire	None	Roll or Taper	Paper, Plastic or Brass	0.474	0.422	0.417		1.70	1.75	0.360	Centerfire	
410-Bore	?	Star	Paper, Brass or Aluminum	0.525	0.470	0.465	1.84	1.90	2.00	0.410	Centerfire	
410-Bore	Plastic	Star	Paper, Plastic or Brass	0.525	0.470	0.465	2.36	2.40	2.50	0.410	Centerfire	
410-Bore	Plastic	Taper w/Card	Brass	0.525	0.470	0.465		2.85	2.88	0.410	Centerfire	
410-Bore	Plastic	Roll or Star	Paper or Plastic	0.525	0.470	0.465	2.84	2.90	3.00	0.410	Centerfire	
44 XL	Paper or Wood	Taper w/Card	Brass	0.525	0.471	0.443		1.57	2.03	0.425	Centerfire	
11.15x 52mm	None	Taper w/Card	Brass	?	?	?		2.00	2.05	0.439	Centerfire	
32-Gauge	Plastic	Roll or Taper	Paper, Plastic or Brass	0.640	0.580	0.575	2.30	2.35	2.50	0.526	Centerfire	Pinfire also
28-Gauge	None	Taper/Roll/ Star	Paper or Brass	0.680	0.620	0.615	2.25	2.31	2.50	0.550	Centerfire	Pinfire also
28-Gauge	Plastic	Roll or Star	Paper or Plastic	0.680	0.620	0.615	2.50	2.56	2.75	0.550	Centerfire	
55 Manard '65	None	Taper w/Card	Brass	?	?	?		2 1/4	2 1/4	0.550	Boxer	
55 Manard '73	None	Taper w/Card	Brass	?	?	?		2 3/8	2 3/8	0.550	Berdan	
55 Manard '73	None	Taper w/Card	Brass	?	?	?		2 5/16	2 5/16	0.550	Berdan	Reloadable
24-Gauge	None	Roll or Star	Paper or Plastic	0.725	0.655	0.640	1.70	1.80	2.00	0.580	Centerfire	
24-Gauge	None	Taper/Roll/ Star	Paper, Plastic or Brass	0.725	0.655	0.640	2.20	2.30	2.50	0.580	Centerfire	Pinfire also
20-Gauge	Plastic	Roll or Star	Paper or Plastic	0.760	0.690	0.675	2.20	2.30	2.50	0.615	Centerfire	Pinfire also
20-Gauge	Plastic	Taper w/Card	Brass	0.760	0.690	0.675		2.60	2.63	0.615	Centerfire	
20-Gauge	Plastic	Roll or Star	Paper or Plastic	0.760	0.690	0.675	2.45	2.55	2.75	0.615	Centerfire	
20-Gauge	Plastic	Taper w/Card	Brass	0.760	0.690	0.675		2.85	2.88	0.615	Centerfire	
20-Gauge	Plastic	Roll or Star	Paper or Plastic	0.760	0.690	0.675	2.71	2.80	3.00	0.615	Centerfire	
18-Gauge	None	Roll w/Card	Paper	0.782	0.712	0.697		?	1.88	0.637	Centerfire	Cases only, factory loads never seen

Gauge or Bore	Possible Separate Shot Container	Crimp Types	Likely Case Body Material Types (not including case head)	Diameter (inch) Rim	Base	Mouth	Length (inches) Closed Fold	Closed Roll	Open	Normal Bore Diameter (inches)	Priming Type	Comments
18-Gauge	None	Roll or Taper	Paper or Brass	0.782	0.712	0.697		?	2.56	0.637	Pinfire	
18-Gauge	None	Roll or Taper	Paper or Brass	0.782	0.712	0.697		?	2.56	0.637	Centerfire	
64 Manard '65	None	Taper w/Card	Brass	?	?	?		2 5/16	2 5/16	0.640	Boxer	
64 Manard '73	None	Taper w/Card	Brass	?	?	?		2 7/16	2 7/16	0.640	Berdan	
64 Manard '82	None	Taper w/Card	Brass	?	?	?		2 7/16	2 7/16	0.640	Berdan	Reloadable
16-Gauge		Taper/Roll/ Star	Paper or Brass	0.810	0.740	0.720	2.19	2.23	2.50	0.662	Centerfire	
16-Gauge		Roll w/Card	Paper	0.810	0.740	0.720	2.25		2.56	0.662	Centerfire	Pinfire also
16-Gauge	Plastic	Roll or Star	Paper or Plastic	0.810	0.740	0.720	2.44	2.48	2.75	0.662	Centerfire	
16-Gauge	None	Roll w/Card	Paper	0.810	0.740	0.720		2.73	3.00	0.662	Centerfire	
15-Gauge	None	Roll w/Card	Paper	0.813	0.743	0.728	?	?	?	0.678	Pinfire	Very Rare
15-Gauge	None	Taper w/Card	Brass	0.813	0.743	0.728	?	?	?	0.678	Centerfire	Very Rare
14-Gauge	None	Roll or Star	Paper	0.839	0.769	0.754	1.70	1.75	2.00	0.693	Centerfire	
14-Gauge	None	Taper/Roll/ Star	Paper or Brass	0.839	0.769	0.754	2.20	2.25	2.50	0.693	Centerfire	
14-Gauge	None	Roll w/Card	Paper	0.839	0.769	0.754		2.31	2.56	0.693	Centerfire	Pinfire also
14-Gauge	Plastic (?)	Taper w/Card	Aluminum	?	?	?		?	?	0.693	Centerfire	Experimental
14-Gauge	Plastic (?)	Roll or Taper	Plastic or Brass	0.875	0.805	0.754		?	?	0.693	Centerfire	Experimental
12/14 Martini	None	Partial Star	Brass	0.892	0.792	0.735	2.86		2.88	?	Berdan	Police Load
12-Gauge	Plastic	Roll w/Card	Plastic	0.875	0.805	0.790		1.25	1.50	0.729	Centerfire	
12-Gauge	Plastic	Roll w/Card	Plastic	0.875	0.805	0.790		1.64	1.88	0.729	Centerfire	Pinfire also
12-Gauge	Plastic	Roll w/Card	Paper, Plastic	0.875	0.805	0.790		1.76	2.00	0.729	Centerfire	Pinfire also
12-Gauge	None	Taper w/Card	Steel	?	?	?		2.35	2.38	0.729	Centerfire	Pinfire also
12-Gauge	Plastic	Taper/Roll/ Star	Paper, Plastic or Brass	0.875	0.805	0.790	2.16	2.26	2.50	0.729	Centerfire	Pinfire also
12-Gauge		Taper w/Card	Brass	0.875	0.805	0.790		2.60	2.63	0.729	Centerfire	Pinfire also
12-Gauge *	Plastic	Taper/Roll/ Star	Paper, Plastic or Brass	0.875	0.805	0.790	2.41	2.45	2.75	0.729	Centerfire	Pinfire also
12-Gauge		Taper w/Card	Brass	0.875	0.805	0.790		2.85	2.88	0.729	Centerfire	Pinfire also
12-Gauge *	Plastic	Taper/Roll/ Star	Paper, Plastic or Brass	0.875	0.805	0.790	2.66	2.76	3.00	0.729	Centerfire	Pinfire also
12-Gauge *	Plastic	Roll or Star	Paper or Plastic	0.875	0.805	0.790	3.16		3.50	0.729	Centerfire	
12-Gauge	None	Roll w/Card	Paper	0.875	0.805	0.790		3.76	4.00	0.729	Centerfire	
12-Gauge	None	Roll w/Card	Paper	0.875	0.805	0.790		4.76	5.00	0.729	Centerfire	
11-Gauge	None	Roll w/Card	Paper ?	0.835	0.790	0.782		2.36	2.50 ?	0.751	?	Very Rare
11-Gauge	None	Taper w/Card	Brass	0.835	0.790	0.782		2.48	2.50	0.751	Berdan	Very Rare
11-Gauge	None	Taper w/Card	Brass	0.835	0.790	0.782		2.48	2.50	0.751	Inside	Very Rare
10-Gauge	None	Roll w/Card	Paper	0.925	0.850	0.830		2.36	2.57	0.775	Centerfire	Pinfire also
10-Gauge	None	Roll w/Card	Paper	0.925	0.850	0.830		2.42	2.63	0.775	Centerfire	Pinfire also
10-Gauge *	Plastic	Taper/Roll/ Star	Paper, Plastic or Brass	0.925	0.850	0.830	2.49	2.67	2.89	0.775	Centerfire	Pinfire also
10-Gauge *	Plastic	Taper/Roll/ Star	Paper, Plastic or Brass	0.925	0.850	0.830	3.11	3.29	3.50	0.775	Centerfire	Pinfire priming is also seen
8-Gauge *	None	Roll or Taper	Paper or Brass	0.998	0.913	0.902		2.75	3.00	0.835	Centerfire	
8-Gauge *	Plastic	Roll or Taper	Paper or Brass	0.998	0.913	0.902		3.00	3.25	0.835	Centerfire	
8-Gauge *	None	Roll or Taper	Paper or Brass	0.998	0.913	0.902		3.13	3.38	0.835	Centerfire	
8-Gauge *	None	Taper/Roll/ Star	Paper, Plastic or Brass	0.998	0.913	0.902		3.25	3.50	0.835	Centerfire	
8-Gauge *	None	Roll w/Card	Paper	0.998	0.913	0.902		3.75	3.93	0.835	Centerfire	
8-Gauge *	None	Roll w/Card	Paper	0.998	0.913	0.902		4.00	4.25	0.835	Centerfire	
4-Gauge *	None	Roll w/Card	Paper or Plastic	1.127	1.041	1.114	2.0-4.2	Various 2.5-4.25	0.918 0.975 **	Berdan & Pin- fire	Often a Slug
4-Gauge *	None	Roll w/Card	Paper or Plastic	1.127	1.041	1.114	2.0-4.2	Various 2.5-4.25	0.918 0.975 **	Berdan & Pin- fire	Often a Slug
3-Gauge	None	Taper or Roll	Paper or Brass	1.515	1.388	1.350	4.12	3.875	4.125	1.157	Centerfire	
2-Gauge *	None	Taper or Roll	Paper or Brass	1.888	1.735	1.715		4.500	4.875	1.325 **	Berdan	Usually a Slug

Collath/Gauge Comparisons (Collath #/Gauge #): 0 = 10; 1 = 12; 2 (not used); 3 = 14; 4 = 16; 5 = 18; 6 = 20; 7 = 24; 8 = 28

Brass shotgun shells often use Berdan primers.

* These were also used for dangerous game hunting in Africa. The larger sizes were also used for market hunting in various places. See Chapter 8 for a more complete discussion. Guns were also built with both fully rifled and "paradox" (smooth, excepting the very end, which was rifled) bores. Choking was not used.

** Bore diameters are estimates. These "gauges" were never properly described or standardized. Bore diameter measurements indicate that what various manufacturers described as a 4-gauge (bore) was closer to 5-or 6-gauge (at least three bore diameters are known). Similarly, the "2-gauge (bore)" was actually a 4-gauge (bore).

NOTE: 6 drams = 1 ounce = 437.5 grs.

TABLE 1

40-Yard Patterns
Full, Modified and Improved Cylinder Chokes
Lead and Steel Shot
12-Gauge, 2³/₄-Inch Loads, 1979

Load	Choke	Pellets per oz. Nominal	Approx. Number Pellets in Load	Pattern Per Cent
1¹/₈-oz. #2 Steel	Full	120	135	76
1¹/₈-oz. #2 Steel	Mod.	120	135	68
1¹/₈-oz. #2 Steel	Imp. Cyl.	120	135	44
1¹/₄-oz. #2 Steel	Full	120	150	76
1¹/₄-oz. #2 Steel	Mod.	120	150	68
1¹/₄-oz. #2 Steel	Imp. Cyl.	120	150	44
1¹/₄-oz. #4 Lead*	Full	135	169	72
1¹/₄-oz. #4 Lead*	Mod.	135	169	56
1¹/₄-oz. #4 Lead*	Imp. Cyl.	135	169	34
1¹/₂-oz. #4 Lead*	Full	135	202	73
1¹/₂-oz. #4 Lead"XX"	Full	135	202	87

*This is a standard, non-buffered load

TABLE 2

Pellet Count and Distribution in Patterns
Full, Modified and Improved Cylinder Chokes
Lead and Steel Shot
12-Gauge, 2³/₄-Inch Loads, 1979

Load	Choke	Approx. Number Pellets in Load	Pattern Percent 40 Yards			Pellets in Pattern 40 Yards		
			30" Circle	20" Circle	Annular Area, 30"-20" Circle	30" Circle	20" Circle	Annular Area, 30"-20" Circle
11/8-oz. #2 Steel	Full	135	76	47	29	103	64	39
11/8-oz. #2 Steel	Mod.	135	68	40	28	92	54	38
11/8-oz. #2 Steel	Imp. Cyl.	135	44	22	22	60	30	30
11/4-oz. #2 Steel	Full	150	76	47	29	114	71	43
11/4-oz. #2 Steel	Mod.	150	68	40	28	102	60	42
11/4-oz. #2 Steel	Imp. Cyl.	150	44	22	22	66	33	33
11/4-oz. #4 Lead*	Full	169	72	43	29	122	73	49
11/4-oz. #4 Lead*	Mod.	169	56	29	27	95	49	46
11/2-oz. #4 Lead*	Full	202	73	44	29	147	89	58
11/2-oz. #4 Lead"XX"	Full	202	87	59	28	176	119	57

*This is a standard, non-buffered load

Notes: Area of 30" Circle:707 sq. in.
Area of 20" Circle:314 sq. in.
Annular area:707 - 314:393 sq. in.

TABLE 3

Downrange Velocities and Energies
Lead and Steel Shot
12-Gauge, 2³/₄-Inch Loads

Load	Velocity @ 3 ft. Nominal ft/sec.	Measured ft/sec.	Downrange Velocity, Measured at 40 yd. ft/sec.	Energy p/Pellet at 40 yd. ft-lb.
11/8-oz. #2 Steel	1365	1350	773	4.84
11/4-oz. #2 Steel	1300	1305	761	4.69
11/4-oz. #4 Lead	1330	1319	803	4.64
11/2-oz. #4 Lead	1260	1252	778	4.35
11/2-oz. #4 Lead*	1260	1240	793	4.52

*Buffered load

TABLE 4

40-Yard Penetration
20 Percent Ordnance Gelatin
Lead and Steel Shot
12-Gauge, 2³/₄-Inch Loads

Load	Velocity At 3 ft. ft/sec.	Energy Per Pellet At 40 yd. ft-lb.	Energy Density At 40 yd. ft-lb/sq. in.	Penetration in Gelatin inches
11/8-oz. #2 Steel	1350	4.84	274	2.0
11/4-oz. #2 Steel	1305	4.69	265	1.9
11/4-oz. #4 Lead	1319	4.64	350	2.5
11/2-oz. #4 Lead	1252	4.35	328	2.4
11/2-oz. #4 Lead*	1240	4.52	341	2.5

*Buffered load

COMPARATIVE SHOTGUN SLUG PERFORMANCE

Gauge	Shell Length ins./mm	Slug Weight oz./grs.	Slug Type	Velocity (fps) MV	50 yds	100 yds	Energy (fpe) MV	50 yds	100 yds
10	31/2/89	13/4/766	Foster	1280	1080	970	2785	1980	1605
12	3/76	11/4/547	Foster	1600	1320	1130	3110	2120	1785
12	3/76	13/8/600	Brenneke	1502	1144	936	3017	1749	1240
12	3/76	1/437.5	Foster	1760	1345	1075	3009	1396	891
12	3/76	1/437.5	Sabot	1550	1410	1190	2400	1665	1220
12	23/4/70	11/4/547	Foster	1520	1260	1090	2805	1930	1450
12	23/4/70	11/10/490	Brenneke	1590	1190	975	2745	1540	1035
12	23/4/70	1/437.5	Foster	1680	1285	1045	2741	1605	1061
12	23/4/70	1/437.5	Foster	1610	1330	1140	2520	1725	1255
12	23/4/70	1/437.5	Sabot	1450	1320	1130	2100	1475	1120
12	23/4/70	1/437.5	Foster	1560	1175	977	2364	1342	927
16	23/4/70	4/5/350	Foster	1600	1180	990	1990	1075	755
16	23/4/70	9/10/415	Brenneke	1590	1190	975	2320	1300	875
20	23/4/70	3/4/328	Foster	1600	1270	1070	1865	1175	835
20	23/4/70	7/8/370	Brenneke	1590	1190	975	2080	1165	780
410	21/2/63.5	1/5/88	Foster	1830	1340	1060	650	345	215
410	3/76	1/4/110	Brenneke	1755	1162	917	780	342	213

Chapter 18

Cartridge Identification

CARTRIDGE IDENTIFICATION is important to anyone who works with cartridges, whatever the reason. It is of particular consequence to those involved in forensic firearms identification, military intelligence or serious collecting. In addition to the information presented here, the collector of old, obsolete cartridges has special problems involving ignition systems and types not manufactured for 100 years or more. Much of this is beyond the scope of this book, but the basic procedures are still the same.

In teaching classes in firearms identification, I always tell my students that the easiest way to identify a cartridge is to look at the headstamp, if there is one, because in many instances that will tell you exactly what it is. Unfortunately, it isn't always that simple since some cartridges don't have headstamps, or if it is a military or foreign round, the headstamp may not be readily decipherable. Additionally, the headstamp may be misleading. You might be dealing with a wildcat cartridge, something made by necking an original case up or down or otherwise changing the configuration. For example. the 30-06 case is used as the basis for a variety of wildcats using both military and commercial cases, so the headstamp would only indicate the original case, not the actual cartridge. Cartridge identification may range from a simple determination of caliber to the more complex ascertainment of the country of origin, date of origin, place of manufacture and type of gun involved.

The various factors and problems involved in cartridge identification can be summarized as follows:

I. What is the caliber and/or other designation of the cartridge? For example, 38 Special, 9mm Luger, 250 Savage, 7.62x39mm (M43) Russian, 303 British, etc.
II. What type of cartridge is it, handgun, rifle, sporting or military? Is it modern or obsolete?
III. What is the country of origin, who made it and when was it made? The headstamp is usually the clue to these questions, but it may not answer all of them.
IV. What is the functional character of the cartridge – ball, tracer, incendiary, explosive, sporting, match, etc.
V. Is the cartridge functional? This usually requires actual testing and is important primarily to those in the forensic field. Obviously, one does not test fire rare and valuable collectors cartridges.

Cartridges are classified on the basis of ignition type, case shape, and rim type. Combustion of the propellant charge is initiated by the primer. If the priming compound is distributed around the rim of the cartridge, it is a rimfire. If the priming compound is contained in a separate cup in the center of the case head, it is a centerfire. Until the advent of Remington's new EtronX® ammunition and rifle system featuring electronic ignition (as announced in the company's 2000 literature), all small arms cartridges are percussion-fired; that is, the primer is detonated by the blow or impact of a hammer or firing pin. However, some military ammunition, usually of 20mm or greater, is electrically fired. There are two types of centerfire primers currently in general use, Boxer and Berdan. The Boxer primer is entirely self-contained with the anvil as a part of the primer. The Berdan type lacks the anvil that is produced as a small "teat" or protrusion in the primer pocket. Boxer-primed cases have a single flash hole in the center of the primer pocket, whereas Berdan-primed cases have two or more flash holes surrounding the anvil. The Boxer-type primer is used almost exclusively in the United States at the present time, although some Berdan-primed cartridges were manufactured here in the 1800s and early 1900s. The Berdan type is preferred by many European manufacturers and is usually an indication of such origin.

The cartridge base and rim type are important identifying features. These also serve an important functional purpose in feeding and extraction of the cartridge within the gun mechanism. There are five rim types: rimmed, semi-rimmed, rimless, belted and rebated. *(See illustration on page 510.)*

Rimmed cartridges have a rim or extractor flange of larger diameter than the case base often with a grooved or undercut area immediately ahead of the rim. Semi-rimmed cartridges have a rim that is only slightly larger in diameter than the base and usually also a distinct undercut area between rim and case base. It is sometimes difficult to recognize a semi-rimmed cartridge without actually measuring rim and base diameter, and these can easily be mistaken for a rimless case. Rimless cartridges have a rim and base of the same diameter although the rim may actually be .001- or .002-inch larger than the base. These are the most common type of military cartridges. Belted cartridges have a distinct belt or flange at the base, just forward of the rim, and an extractor groove between the rim and the belt. Rebated cartridges have a rim of significantly smaller diameter than the case body at the base, plus a definite extractor groove between rim and base or belt. Only a few rebated cartridges have been commercialized with success, and those are usually easy to identify. In several rebated rim designs, the rim is only very slightly smaller than the case head. The 404 Jeffery and its derivatives (chiefly the Imperial and Canadian Magnums) are the best examples. These can be difficult to identify without taking careful measurements. Also, note that naming a case design "semi-rimmed" versus "rimmed" is strictly a subjective call – there is no specified difference in base diameter and rim diameter that automatically separates these two styles. However, cases described as semi-rimmed are usually visually distinguishable from similar rimless cases.

The shape or configuration of the cartridge case is also an important identifying characteristic. Cartridges can be divided into the following 12 case types:

A. Rimmed bottleneck	G. Semi-rimmed bottleneck
B. Rimmed straight	H. Semi-rimmed straight
C. Rimless bottleneck	I. Rebated bottleneck
D. Rimless straight	J. Rebated straight
E. Belted bottleneck	K. Rebated belted bottleneck
F. Belted straight	L. Rebated belted straight

Each of these types has a letter designation that is used in the cartridge dimensional tables at the end of each chapter. Note that cases described as "straight" are often tapered; case diameter can be considerably larger at the base, compared to the neck.

The bullet or projectile also provides a clue to the identity of a cartridge, its functional use and the gun it is fired in. Based on the material or construction, bullets are divided into two major types: lead and jacketed. Lead bullets are used for low-velocity guns, such as handguns or blackpowder arms. However, these may also be used for target practice in more powerful guns. Training cartridges may have wooden, fiber, composition or plastic bullets. The shape of the projectile is also important and can be round-nose, flat-nose, conical or spitzer (sharp pointed). Because of the Hague Convention, military bullets do not have lead exposed at the point and are restricted to full-metal-jacketed types. Sporting ammunition or that intended for civilian use can have a variety of bullet tips with varying degrees of lead exposed, hollowpoint, plastic tips and bronze or other metal tips to control expansion in the target.

Bullets for military use can also be classified in terms of special functional design, such as ball; tracer (T); armor-piercing (AP); incendiary (I); high explosive (HE); and observation/ranging, or spotter-tracer types. There can also be two or more of these combined in the same bullet, such as APT, API-T, HEI or HE-T. Not all types are made in every cartridge, since their function is developed to fulfill a specific military requirement. In addition, makeup depends to some extent on the gun for which each is loaded. In general, ball, or full-metal jacketed (FMJ), bullets are intended for use against personnel or unarmored vehicles. These usually have a lead core covered by a cupro-nickel jacket, or a mild steel jacket plated with some copper alloy. These can be easily identified with a magnet. At one time, the French 8mm Lebel military bullet was made of solid bronze. Tracer bullets are used for fire correction or target designation. These cannot be distinguished from ball unless some identifying marking, such as a colored tip (usually, but not always, red), is included. Armor-piercing bullets are also similar to ball except they have a hardened steel or tungsten alloy core. They may or may not have a colored tip. Incendiary bullets contain an incendiary mixture that ignites on impact. Visual identification depends on the color-coding system used. High-explosive bullets are uncommon, but do exist. These are made to explode on impact and can only be recognized by the color-coding. Observation and ranging bullets are intended to produce a flash and/or a puff of smoke to mark the point of impact. Again, these are recognizable only when color-coded. One should handle any ammunition with a colored bullet tip with great care, as appropriate.

The headstamp is the stamped markings on the head of the cartridge. Information that can be obtained from the headstamp is extremely varied and depends on the intended purpose or use of the cartridge and who manufactured it. Headstamps consist of one or more parts or information elements. Cartridges intended for sporting or civilian use usually have two elements; one identifies the specific chambering, the other identifies the manufacturer. Military cartridges can have from one to five elements, including cartridge, date and place of manufacture plus other identifying markings. Some headstamps are segmented, that is, these have one or more segment lines that divide the head into two to four equal parts. This usually indicates an older cartridge, since most countries discontinued segment lines shortly after World War I. The location of the elements is most conveniently indicated by its clock-face orientation, with 12 o'clock at the top, 3 o'clock at the right, 6 o'clock at the bottom and 9 o'clock at the left. The basic U.S. military headstamp prior to World War II had two elements, with the factory code at 12 o'clock and the date at 6 o'clock. Rapid expansion of ammunition manufacturing facilities as the result of the war introduced many new designs without any effort at standardization. Some used three elements spaced equidistant from each other while others adopted a four-element system located at 12, 3, 6 and 9 o'clock. Also the location of the factory code was changed, in some instances, to 6 o'clock or other locations.

Worldwide, there are over 800 military headstamps in existence plus some 400 or more commercial headstamps that have existed at various times. Obviously, this is a complex and highly specialized field. Several volumes have been published on headstamps including at least three by various U.S. governmental agencies. In addition, some books for cartridge collectors include headstamp data on obsolete cartridges. Since it would require another whole book to adequately cover the subject, it is quite impossible to include more than a few basics here. However, we have listed several sources for such data to assist those readers who find a need for it.

The procedure for identifying a cartridge, using the tables in CARTRIDGES OF THE WORLD, are as follows:

1. First look at the headstamp and see what, if any, information is provided there.
2. Look at the cartridge and determine what type it is: straight, necked, rimmed, rimless, etc.
3. Measure the dimensions of the cartridge and make up a table as follows:

Type (A, B, C, D, etc., as shown in the tables)
Bullet Diameter
Neck Diameter
Shoulder Diameter (if there is one)

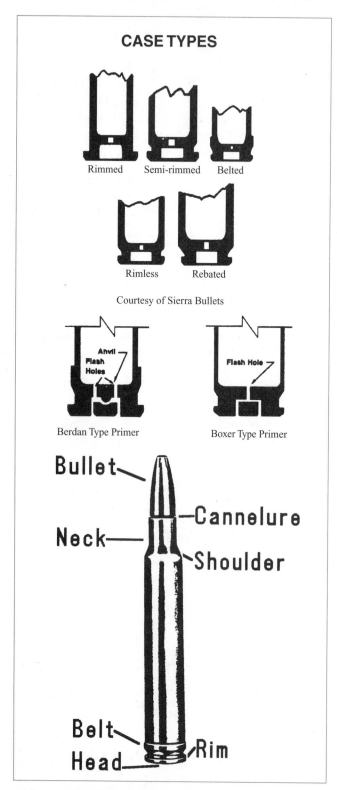

CASE TYPES

Rimmed   Semi-rimmed   Belted

Rimless   Rebated

Courtesy of Sierra Bullets

Anvil
Flash
Holes

Flash Hole

Berdan Type Primer   Boxer Type Primer

Bullet
Cannelure
Neck
Shoulder
Belt
Head
Rim

Base Diameter

Rim Diameter

Case Length

Cartridge Length

Now go to the cartridge measurement tables in chapter 20 and compare your data with the dimensional data.

Check bullet diameters under the proper type, then compare case length and finally other dimensions with your measurements. Type of cartridge case, caliber and case length are the key elements to start with. For practice, two examples are shown below. See if you can identify the cartridges.

Example #1		Example #2	
Type: C		Type: B	
Bullet Diameter:	.308"	Bullet Diameter:	.410"
Neck Diameter:	.340"	Neck Diameter:	.432"
Shoulder Diameter:	.441"	Shoulder Diameter:	n/a
Base Diameter:	.470"	Base Diameter:	.433"
Rim Diameter:	.473"	Rim Diameter:	.488"
Case Length:	2.490"	Case Length:	1.280"
Cartridge Length:	3.340"	Cartridge Length:	1.580"

Bear in mind that there is a certain amount of manufacturing tolerance to be allowed for and your measurements may vary .001- to .002-inch plus or minus from some dimensions in the table. The cartridge in Example 1 will be found in the chapter on modern rifle cartridges; Example 2 is in the chapter on handgun cartridges. Not every known cartridge is listed in CARTRIDGES OF THE WORLD, particularly the more obscure blackpowder types. However, practically all modern sporting and military are included so most readers will not have any difficulty. The idea here is to help you to determine what the cartridge is rather than where it originated or when.

In trying to identify cartridges, there are a couple of things the reader should know. For one thing, the major ammunition manufacturers have, from time to time, made up batches of ammunition on special order with the purchaser's headstamp. Anyone can do this if your order is large enough and you have the money. Then there is the matter of commercial-reloading firms that turn out ammunition for police departments and others using recycled cases of varying make and loaded with powder and bullets never used by the original company. Last, but not least, you have the individual handloader whose imagination is unbounded and who may turn out a few wondrous and non-standard products.

Headstamp Markings Of The Principal American Ammunition Manufacturers

Federal Cartridge Co.	Rimfire, AL EP, G or G, HP, F, XL, XR and WM Centerfire, FC
General Electric Co.	GE plus date (military)
Newton Arms Co.	NA plus caliber (Made by Rem.)
Peters Cartridge Co.	Rimfire, P or PETERSHV Centerfire, P, PC, P.C., PCCO, PETERS
E. Remington & Sons (1870-1890)	E. REMINGTON & SONS
Remington Arms Co.	U, UMC, REM, REM* UMC, R-P, RAH
Robin Hood Ammunition Co.	R, RHA, R.H.A. Co.
Savage Arms Co.	S.A. Co. (made by U.S. Cartridge Co.)
Savage Repeating Arms Co.	S.A. Co., S.R.A.C.O.
Richard Speer Manufacturing Co.	SPEER WEATHERBY
Union Metallic Cartridge Co. Purchased by Remington in 1911	U, UMC or R B
United States Cartridge Co. (1869 to 1936)	US, U.S., *U.S CARTRIDGE CO*, U.S.C. CO. or RL

Headstamp Markings Of The Principal American Ammunition Manufacturers

Western Cartridge Co.	SUPER X, SUPER-X, W, WCC, W.C. Co. WESTERN
Winchester	W, H, SUPER SPEED, W. C. Co.,
Winchester-Western	W-W, super speed

There were about 15 other companies that manufactured ammunition at various times, particularly during the 1860-1900 period. Also a number of private firms manufactured military ammunition during World War I and II.

United States Arsenal Headstamp Markings

Alleghany Ordnance Plant	KS plus date
Denver Ordnance Plant	DEN plus date
Des Moines Ordnance Plant	DM plus date
Eau Claire Ordnance Plant	EW plus date
Evansville Ordnance Plant	ECS plus date
Frankford Arsenal	CF plus date (45-70)
	F plus date
	FA plus date
Lake City Arsenal	LC plus date
Lowell Ordnance Plant	LM plus date
Milwaukee Ordnance Plant	M plus date
Saint Louis Ordnance Plant	SL plus date
Twin Cities Ordnance Plant	TW plus date
Utah Ordnance Plant	U or UT plus date

U.S. Small Arms Ammunition Color Codes

Bullet Tip Marking	Functional Type
Black	Armor piercing (AP)
Red	Tracer
White	Tracer, aircraft type
Blue	Incendiary

Bibliography of Cartridge Identification Publications

Jane's Directory of Military Small Arms Ammunition, by Ian V. Hogg. Jane's Publications, Inc., N.Y., N.Y., 1988.

Cartridges For Collectors, by Fred A. Datig. The Fadco Publishing Co., Vol. I, 1956 and Vol. 2, 1958.

Cartridges For Collectors, by Fred A. Datig. Borden Publishing Co., Los Angeles, Calif., Vol. 3, 1967.

Handbuch der Pistolen und Revolver Patronen, Vol. 1, by Hans A. Erlmeier und Jakob H. Brandt. E. Schwend GmbH, West Germany, 1967.

History of Modern U.S. Military Small Arms and Ammunition, by F.W. Hackley, W.H. Woodin, and E.L. Scranton. The Macmillan Co., N.Y., N.Y., 1967.

Cartridges, by Herschel C. Logan. The Stackpole Co., Harrisburg, PA, 1959.

Cartridge Guide 11/71, by Dr. Manfred R. Rosenberger, and Lilla E. Rosenberger. Sporting Goods GmbH, Bremen, West Germany, 1971.

The American Cartridge, by Charles R. Suydam. G. Robert Lawrence, Santa Ana, CA, 1960.

Centerfire Metric Pistol and Revolver Cartridges, Volume 1 of Cartridge Identification, H.P. White and B.D. Mundhall. The Infantry Journal Press, Washington, DC, 1948.

Centerfire American and British Pistol and Revolver Cartridges, Volume 2 of Cartridge Identification, by H.P. White and B.D. Munhall. The Combat Force Press, Washington, DC, 1950.

Cartridge Headstamp Guide, by H.P. White and B.D. Munhall. H.P. White Laboratory, Bel Air, MD, 1963.

Small-Caliber Ammunition Identification Guide, Volume 1 & 2; Army Material Development and Readiness Command, DST-1160G-514-78-Vol. I & II.

Recognition Guide of Ammunition Available to, or Used by, The Viet Cong; Dept. of the Army Pamphlet #381-12, 1966.

Small Arms Ammunition Identification Guide; U.S. Army Foreign Science Technology Center, FSTC-CW-7-68, Washington, DC 20315.

— Frank C. Barnes

EXAMPLES OF HEADSTAMP STYLES

**SINGLE ELEMENT
6 O'CLOCK**

**DOUBLE ELEMENT
6 & 12 O'CLOCK**

**TRIPLE ELEMENT
2, 10 & 6 O'CLOCK**

**RIMFIRE
FEDERAL CART. CO.**

**QUADRUPLE ELEMENT
3, 6, 9 & 12 O'CLOCK**

**DOUBLE SEGMENTED
3 & 9 O'CLOCK**

**QUADRANGLE SEGMENTED
FOUR ELEMENTS
2, 4, 8 & 10 O'CLOCK**

**MILITARY
DENVER ORDNANCE
PLANT 1943**

**COMMERCIAL
REMINGTON**

**COMMERCIAL
WESTERN CART. CO.**

Chapter 19

U.S. Military Ammunition (5.56 to 20mm)

(Current and Obsolete—Blackpowder and Smokeless)

MUCH OF this information was originally published in our Third Edition. Since then, we have had requests for a reprint of the data covering U.S. military cartridges. The information was compiled to provide a quick and easy-to-use reference source for the identification of the more modern U.S. military ammunition—that is, the post-World War II period. Many of the cartridges listed here are no longer in use, but have become collectors' items of increasing scarcity and value over time.

The identification of armor-piercing, incendiary or explosive-type munitions is a matter of concern to collectors, to shooters of surplus military weapons, and also to police, firemen and others. The data provided here will enable the reader to identify the various types of U.S. military ammunition likely to be encountered on the surplus market or in use by the military. Insofar as the author is aware, this is the only popular publication that has published most of the information contained in this chapter, particularly the identifying color codes.

In addition to the standard military cartridges listed here, the various branches of the service also use a number of commercial cartridges such as the 22 Short and 22 Long Rifle; 22 Hornet; 32 ACP; 38 S&W; 38 S&W Special; 9mm Parabellum (now the official U.S. Military handgun cartridge); 45-70 blank; and the .410-bore, 12- and 10-gauge shotgun shells. Details of all these are not provided in this chapter, but are covered elsewhere in this book. There are a number of new ammunition developments in the U.S. military not listed here, but most of these are experimental or in the developmental stage and have not been officially adopted. The cartridges listed here are those that have been standardized and are–or were–in official use.

This material was, to a large extent, abstracted from two out-of-print government publications: *Small Arms and Small Arms Ammunition, Vol. 2*, Office of the Chief of Ordnance, Washington D.C.; and *Small Arms Ammunition Pamphlet 23-1*, Dept. of the Army Frankford Arsenal, Philadelphia, PA. Don't write to the author or publisher asking where you can get copies of these. We don't know! Such things as industrial or manufacturing codes and drawing numbers have been omitted because they would not be of interest to the great majority of readers of CARTRIDGES OF THE WORLD.

Note: The second figure that appears with some of the data, particularly the weights and pressures, is a manufacturing tolerance and was left in so that the reader will understand that some variations can be expected between different lots and manufacture of ammunition. Also, it should be understood that in some instances the powder type given has been changed from tubular to ball powder in recent years. As an example, 56-2 grs. means a standard weight of 56 grains with no more than a 2-grain variation (±1 gr.) being acceptable. The rest of the data is more or less self-explanatory.

5.56x45MM AMMUNITION

Cartridge, 5.56mm, Ball, M193

Weapon:	Rifle, 5.56mm, M16; M16E1	
Ballistic Perf.:		
Velocity:	3250 ±40 fps at 15 feet; Std. Dev.40 fps max.	
Pressure:	52,000 psi max. avg.; avg. pressure plus 3 Std. Dev. 58,000 psi max.	
Port Pres.:	15,000 psi 2,000 psi	
Accuracy:	2.00" mean radius max. avg. at 200 yards	
Cartridge:	182 - 14 grs.	
Case:	94 - 5 grs.	
Bullet:	56 - 2 grs.	
Primer, Perc.:		
Prim. Wt:	4.0 grs. approx.	
Compos.:	Lead Styphnate	
Propellant:		
Brand:	IMR8208M	WC846
Type:	Single Base	Double Base
Tubular		Spheroidal
Weight:	25.5 grs.	28.5 grs.
Ident.:	Plain tip	

Cartridge, 5.56mm, Ball, M855A1

Weapon:	Rifle, 5.56mm, M16A2, M249	
Ballistic Perf.:		
Velocity:	3020 ±40 fps	
Pressure:	52,000 psi max. avg.; avg. pressure plus 3 Std. Dev.: 58,000 psi max.	
Port Pres.:	15,000 psi 2,000 psi	
Accuracy:	2.00" mean radius max. avg. at 200 yards	
Cartridge:	187 - 14 grs.	
Case:	94 - 5 grs.	
Bullet:	62 - 2 grs.	
Primer, Perc.:		
Prim. Wt:	4.0 grs. approx.	
Compos.:	Lead styphnate	
Propellant:		
Brand:	IMR8208M	WC846
Type:	Single Base Tubular	Spheroidal
Weight:		
Ident.:	Green tip	

Cartridge, Grenade; 5.56mm, M195

Weapon:	Rifle, 5.56mm, XM16E1; M16
Ballistic Perf.:	
Velocity:	140 ± 165 fps at 5.5 ft. (Grenade 1.56 lbs). No individual shot below 140 fps
Cartridge:	127.5 - 4 grs.
Case:	98 - 3 grs.
Primer, Perc.:	
Prim. Wt:	4.0 grs. approx.
Compos.:	Lead Styphnate
Propellant:	
Brand:	IMR4475

Type:	Single Base, Tubular
Weight:	25.0 grs.
Wad:	.5 grs. max., Cardboard, Royal Satin coated (both sides) Booklined Yellow
Ident.:	Case mouth closed with 7 petal rose crimp red tip

Cartridge, 5.56mm, Tracer, M196

Weapon:	Rifle, 5.56mm, M16; XM16E1
Ballistic Perf.:	
Velocity:	3200 ±40 fps at 15 feet; Std. Dev. 40 fps max.
Pressure:	52,000 psi max. avg./avg. pressure plus 3 Std. Dev. 58,000 psi max.
Port Pres.:	15,000 psi 2,000 psi
Accuracy:	5.00" mean radius max. avg. at 200 yards
Trace:	The trace shall be visible from a point not greater than 75 yards from the the muzzle of weapon to a point not less than 500 yards from the muzzle.
Cartridge:	177 - 11 grs.
Case:	94 - 5 grs.
Bullet:	54 - 2 grs.
Point Filler:	28 - .5 grs. - lead-antimony
Base Clos.:	Vinyl
Tracer:	2.7 grs. approx.
Ign.:	1.0 gr.
Sub Ign.	.05 gr.
Primer, Perc.:	
Prim. Wt:	4.0 grs. approx.
Compos.:	Lead Styphnate
Propellant:	
Brand:	IMR 8208M
Type:	Single Base Tubular
Weight:	25.3 grs.
Ident.:	Red Tip

Cartridge, 5.56mm, Test, High Pressure, M197

Weapon:	Used to proof test barrels and weapons (not a service cartridge)
Ballistic Perf.:	
Pressure:	70,000 3,000 psi, max. Std. Dev. 3500 psi
Cartridge:	174 - 11 grs.
Case:	94 - 5 grs.
Bullet:	C10524197 - 56 - 2 grs.
Primer:	4.0 grs. approx.
Propellant:	
Brand:	HPC 3
Type:	Double Base Flake
Weight:	20.0 grs.
Ident.:	Case Stannic Stained or Nickel Plated

Cartridge, 5.56mm, Tracer, M856A1

Weapon:	Rifle, 5.56mm, M16A2, M249
Ballistic Perf.:	
Velocity:	2795 ±40 fps
Pressure:	52,000 psi max. avg./ avg. pressure plus 3 Std. Dev. 58,000 psi max.
Port Pres.:	15,000 psi 2,000 psi
Accuracy:	5.00" mean radius max. avg. at 200 yards
Trace:	The trace shall be visible from a point not greater than 75 yards from the muzzle of the weapon to a point not less than 500 yards from the muzzle.
Cartridge:	177 - 11 grs.
Case:	94 - 5 grs.
Bullet:	63.8 grs.
Primer, Perc.:	
Prim. Wt:	4.0 grs. approx.
Compos.:	Lead Styphnate
Propellant:	
Brand:	

Type:	
Weight:	
Ident.:	Orange tip

Dummy Cartridge, 5.56mm, M199

Weapon:	Rifle, 5.56mm, XM16E1; M16 - Training
Cartridge:	150 - 7 grs.
Case:	94 - 7 grs.
Bullet:	56 - 2 grs.
Primer:	None
Propellant:	None
Ident.:	Impressed upon the case, 6 corrugations, approx. .030-inch deep equally spaced about the periphery.

Cartridge, 5.56mm, Blank, XM200

Weapon:	Rifle, 5.56mm, M16; XM16E1 with blank firing attachment, M13
Ballistic Perf.:	
Screen pert:	No perforations in paper screen at 15 ft.
Cyclic Rate:	Min. 550 rds. per minute, max. 800 rds. per minute
Cartridge:	109.5 - 4 grs.
Case:	98 - 3 grs.
Bullet:	None, Case Mouth closed with 7-petal rose crimp
Primer, Perc.:	
Prim. Wt:	4.0 grs. approx.
Compos.:	Lead Styphnate
Propellant:	HPC 13
Type:	Double Base, Flake
Weight:	7.0 grs.
Wad:	None
Ident.:	Cannelure approx 1/22 from head and mouth closed with 7-petal rose crimp

Dummy Cartridge, 5.56mm, Inert Loaded, M232

Weapon:	Rifle, 5.56mm, XM16E1, M16
Cartridge:	181.5 - 7.0 grs.
Case:	94 - 5 grs.
Bullet:	56 - 2 grs.
Primer:	None
Propellant:	31 grs. Sodium Carbonate Monohydrate
Ident.:	Cartridge, chemical black

Dummy Cartridge, 5.56mm, Inert Loaded, M857

Weapon:	Rifle, 5.56mm, M16A2, M249
Cartridge:	187.5 - 7.0 grs.
Case:	94 - 5 grs.
Bullet:	61 - 2 grs.
Primer:	None
Propellant:	31 grs. Sodium Carbonate Monohydrate
Ident.:	Cartridge, chemical black

.30 CALIBER CARBINE

Cartridge, Cal .30, Carbine, Ball, M1

Weapon:	Carbine, Caliber .30, M1; Carbine., Caliber .30, M2	
Ballistic Perf.:		
Velocity:	1900 ±30 fps	
Pressure:	40,000 psi, max. avg.	
Accuracy:	1.5" mean radius max. avg. at 100 yards	
Cartridge:	146 - 13 grs. (with gilding metal jacketed bullet) 193 - 13 grs. (with gilding metal clad steel jacketed bullet)	
Case:	71 - 6 grs.	
Bullet:	111 - 3 grs. (with gilding metal jacket) 108 - 3 grs. (with gilding metal clad steel jacket)	
Primer, Perc.:	Lead Styphnate	
Propellant:		
Brand:	WC820	HPC5

Type:	Double Base Spheroidal	Double Base Flake
Weight:	13 grs.	13 grs.
Point Ident.:	Plain Tip	

Cartridge, Cal .30, Carbine, M13

Weight:	Carbine Cal .30, M1; Carbine, Caliber .30, M2
Ballistic Perf.:	None
Cartridge:	177 grs.
Case:	66 grs.
Bullet:	111 - 3 grs. - 108 - 3 grs.
Ident.:	Drilled case, no primer

Cartridge, Cal .30, Carbine, Rifle Grenade, M6

Weapon:	Carbine, Caliber .30, M1; Carbine, Caliber .30, M2
Ballistic Perf.:	
Velocity:	Shall propel grenade (AT, Practice, M11A3) with velocity of 145 ±15 fps at 5 feet
Cartridge:	103 grs.
Case:	77 grs.
Wad:	Pressed Paper, Commercial
Primer, Perc.:	
Propellant:	
Brand:	IMR 4809 and Black Powder
Weight:	21 grs.
Ident.:	Case Mouth closed with 5-petal rose crimp

Cartridge, Cal .30, Carbine, Test, High Pressure, M18

Weapon:	Carbine, Caliber .30 M1; Carbine, Caliber .30, M2
Ballistic Perf.:	
Pressure:	47,500 2,500 psi max. avg.
Cartridge:	233 grs. approx.
Case:	71 - 6grs.
Bullet:	152 - 3 grs.
Primer, Perc.:	
Propellant:	
Brand:	HPC-5
Type:	Double Base, Flake
Weight:	14 grs.
Ident.:	Case is stannic stained

Cartridge, Cal .30, Carbine, Tracer, M27

Weapon:	Carbine, Caliber .30, M1; Carbine, Caliber .30, M2	
Ballistic Perf.:		
Velocity:	1800 ±30 fps	
Pressure:	40,000 psi, max. avg.	
Trace:	Bright Trace from 100 to 400 yards	
Accuracy:	3.5" mean radius max. avg. at 100 yards	
Cartridge:	191 - 13 grs.	
Case:	B6200957, 71 - 6 grs.	
Bullet:	103 - 4 grs.	
Tracer:	5.5 grs. approx.	
Igniter:	0.5 gr. approx.	
Primer, Perc.:		
Propellant:		
Brand:	HPC-5	WC 820
Type:	Double Base Flake	Double Base Spheroidal
Weight:	13 grs.	13 grs.
Point Ident.:	Orange Tip	

7.62MM, NATO, AMMUNITION (308 WIN.)

Cartridge, 7.62mm, NATO, Ball, M59

Weapon:	Gun, Machine, 7.62mm, M60; M73 Rifle, 7.62mm, M14
Ballistic Perf.:	

Velocity:	2750 ±30 fps at 78 feet
Pressure:	50,000 psi, max. avg.
Accuracy:	Carton or Clip Pack - 5" mean radius at 600 yards
	Link Pack - 71/2" mean radius at 600 yards
Cartridge:	393 - 27 grs.
Case:	190 - 20 grs.
Bullet:	150.5 - 6.5 grs. (cut cannelure)
	150.5 - 5.5 grs. (knurled cannelure)
Core:	55 - 2 grs. - steel
Fill., Pt.:	24 - 1 grs. - lead-antimony
Fill., Base:	14.5 - 1 grs. - lead-antimony
Primer, Perc.:	
Prim. Wt:	5.430 - 0.520 grs.
Pellet Wt:	.600 - .120 grs.
Compos.:	Lead Styphnate
Propellant	
Brand:	WC 846 — IMR 4475
Type:	Double Base Spheroidal — Single Base Tubular
Weight:	46 grs. — 41 grs.
Point Ident.:	Plain tip

Cartridge, 7.62mm, NATO, Test, High Pressure, M60

Weapon:	Used to proof test barrels and weapons (Not a service cartridge)
Ballistic Perf.:	
Pressure:	67,500 2,500 psi, avg.
Cartridge:	412.0 - 23.5 grs.
Case:	190 - 20 grs.
Bullet:	174.5 - 3.0 grs.
Primer, Perc.:	
Prim. Wt:	5.43 - 0.52 grs.
Pellet Wt:	0.60 - 0.12 grs.
Compos.:	FA-956, Lead Styphnate
Propellant:	
Brand:	IMR 4475
Type:	Single Base Tubular
Weight:	41 grs.
Ident.:	Stannic Stained Case

Cartridge, 7.62mm, NATO, AP, M61

Weapon:	Gun, Machine, 7.62mm, M60; M73 Rifle, 7.62mm, M14	
Ballistic Perf.:		
Velocity:	2750 fps ±30 fps at 78 feet	
Pressure:	50,000 psi, max. avg.	
Accuracy:	7.5" mean radius at 600 yards	
Cartridge:	393 - 27 grs.	
Case:	190 - 20 grs.	
Bullet:	C7553740 - 150.5 - 6.5 grs. (cut cannelure);	
	150.5 - 5.5 grs. (knurled cannelure)	
Core:	55 - 2 grs. - steel	
Fill., Pt:	24 - 1 grs. - Lead Antimony	
Primer, Perc.:		
Prim. Wt:	5.430 - 0.520 grs.	
Pellet Wt:	.600 - .120 grs.	
Compos.:	FA-956, Lead Styphnate	
Propellant:		
Brand:	IMR 4475	WC 846
Type:	Single Base Tubular	Double Base Spheroidal
Weight:	41 grs.	46 grs.
Point Ident.:	Black Lacquer	

Cartridge, 7.62mm, NATO, Tracer, M62

Weapon:	Gun, Machine, 7.62mm, M60; M73 Rifle, 7.62mm, M14
Ballistic Perf.:	
Velocity:	2750 ±30 fps at 78 feet
Pressure:	50,000 psi, max. avg.
Accuracy:	15" mean radius, max. avg., at 600 yards
Trace:	Visible trace between 100 and 850

Cartridge: 383 - 29 grs.
 Case: 190 - 20 grs.
 Bullet: 142 - 4 grs.
 Fill., Pt: 72.0 - 1.5 grs. - Lead Antimony
 Tracer: 6.5 grs.approx.
 Ign.: 1.0 grs. approx.
 Sub-ign.: 1.0 grs. approx.
 Primer, Perc.:
 Prim. Wt: 5.43 - 0.52 grs.
 Pellet Wt: 0.60 - 0.12 grs.
 Compos.: FA-956, Lead Styphnate
 Propellant:
 Type: Double Base Spheroidal
 Weight: 46 grs.
 Point Ident.: Orange Lacquer

Cartridge, 7.62mm, NATO, Tracer, M62
(Overhead Fire Application)

Weapon: Gun, Machine, 7.62mm, M60;
 M73 Rifle, 7.62mm, M14

Ballistic Perf.:
 Velocity: 2680 ±30 fps at 78 feet
 Pressure: 50,000 psi, max. avg.
 Accuracy: 9" mean radius, max. avg. at 600 yards
 Extreme Spread, Max. per target: 45 inches
 Trace: Visible trace between 100 and 850 yards, min.

Cartridge: 387 - 29 grs.
 Case: 190 - 20 grs.
 Bullet: 146 - 4 grs.
 Fill., Pt: 72 - 1.5 grs. - Lead Antimony
 Base Seal: None
 Tracer: 6.5 grs. approx.
 Igniter: 1.0 grs. approx.
 Sub-ign.: 1.0 grs. approx.
 Primer Perc.:
 Prim. Wt: 5.43 - 0.52 grs.
 Pellet Wt: 0.60 - 0.12 grs.
 Compos.: FA-956, Lead Styphnate
 Propellant:
 Type: Double Base Spheroidal
 Weight: 46 grs.
 Ident.: Red Lacquer

Dummy Cartridge, 7.62mm, NATO, M63

Weapon: Gun, Machine, 7.62mm, M60;
 M73 Rifle, 7.62mm, M14

Requirements: Training and Gun Functioning
 Bullet Pull: 175 lb. min.

Cartridge: 258 - 21.5 grs.
 Case: 190 - 20 grs.
 Bullet: 68 - 1.5 grs.
 Ident.: 6 corrugations spaced equally around periphery of case

Cartridge, 7.62mm, NATO, Grenade, Rifle, M64

Weapon: Rifle, 7.62mm, M14
Ballistic Perf.:
 Velocity: Cartridge shall propel a grenade weighing 1.56lbs. 160 ±5 fps at 5.6 feet beyond the forward end of the grenade when fully positioned for launching.

Cartridge: 233 - 21 grs. (HPS 4 Propellant)
 Case: 236 - 21 grs. (IMR8097 Propellant)
 241 - 21 grs. (WC830 Propellant)
 190 - 20 grs. - Copper Alloy
 Primer, Perc.:
 Prim. Wt: 5.430 - 0.520 grs.
 Pellet Wt: .600 - .120 grs.
 Compos.: FA-956, Lead Styphnate
 Propellant:
 Brand: HPC4   1MR8097   WC830

Type:	Double Base Tubular	Single Base Tubular	DoubleBase Spherical
Weight:	37 grs.	40 grs.	45 grs.
Wad:	Pressed Paper		
Ident.:	Rosette Crimp		

Cartridge, 7.62mm, NATO, Ball, M80

Weapon: Gun, Machine, 7.62mm, M60;
 M73 Rifle, 7.62mm, M14

Ballistic Perf.:
 Velocity: 2750 ±30 fps at 78 feet
 Pressure: 50,000 psi, max. avg.
 Accuracy: Carton or Clip Pack - 5" mean radius, max. avg. at 600 yards
 Link Pack - 7.52" mean radius, max. avg. at 600 yards

Cartridge: 392 - 31 grs.
 Case: 190 - 20 grs.
 Bullet: 149 - 3 grs.
 Primer, Perc.:
 Prim. Wt: 5.43 - 0.52 grs.
 Pellet Wt: 0.60 - 0.12 grs.
 Compos.: FA-956, Lead Styphnate
 Propellant:

Type:	Double Base Spheroidal	Single Base Tubular	Single Base Tubular
Weight:	46 grs.	41.5 grs.	41 grs.
Ident.:	Plain Tip		

Cartridge, 7.62mm, NATO, Ball, M80
(Overhead Fire Application)

Weapon: Gun, Machine, 7.62mm, M60;
 M73 Rifle, 7.62mm, M14

Ballistic Perf.:
 Velocity: 2750 ±30 fps at 78 feet
 Pressure: 50,000 psi, max. avg.
 Accuracy: 5" mean radius, max. avg. at 600 yards; Extreme Spread, max. per target - 25 inches

Cartridge: 393 - 31 grs.
 Case: 190 - 20 grs.
 Bullet:
 Primer, Perc.:
 Prim. Wt: 5.43 - 0.52 grs.
 Pellet Wt: 0.60 - 0.12 grs.
 Compos.: FA-956, Lead Styphnate
 Propellant:

Brand:	WC 846	IMR 8138	MIMR4475
Type:	Double Base Spheroidal	Single Base Tubular	Single Base Tubular
Weight:	46 grs.	41.5 grs.	41 grs.
Point Ident.:	Plain Tip		

Cartridge, 7.62mm, NATO, Blank, M82

Weapon: Rifle, 7.62mm, M14, Machine Gun, M60; M73 with blank-firing attachment

Ballistic Perf.:
 Screen Perf.: Perforations in paper screen shall be less than 0.1-inch in diameter at 15 ft. from muzzle of gun

Cartridge: 222 - 225 grs. approx.
 Case: 201 grs. approx.
 Wad: .030-inch tagboard or chipboard
 Primer, Perc.:
 Prim. Wt: 5.430 - 0.520 grs., 5 grs. approx.
 Compos.: Lead Styphnate - FA-956; FA-1023
 Propellant:

Brand:	SR4759	HPC-2	WC818
Type:	Single Base Tubular	Double Base Flake	Double Base Spheroidal
Weight:	17.5 grs.	14.5 grs.	14.5 grs.
Ident.:	No bullet, crimped mouth, double tapered neck and orifice sealed with red lacquer		

Cartridge, 7.62mm, Match, M118

Weapon:	Rifle, 7.62mm, M14 (National Match)
Ballistic Perf.:	
Velocity:	2550 ±30 fps at 78 feet
Pressure:	50,000 psi, max. avg.
Accuracy:	3.5" mean radius, max. avg. at 600 yards
Cartridge:	390 grs. approx.
Case:	190 - 20 grs.
Bullet:	175.5 - 3.0 grs.
Primer, Perc.:	
Prim. Wt:	5.43 - 0.52 grs.; 5.3 grs. approx.; 5 grs. approx.
Pellet Wt:	0.60 - 0.12 grs.; 0.7 - 0.2 grs.; .58 -.08 grs.
Compos.:	FA-956 FA-961 FA-1023
Type:	Lead Styphnate
Propellant:	
Brand:	WC 846 IMR 4895
Type:	Double Base Single Base
	Spherical Tubular
Weight:	44 grs. 42 grs.
Ident.:	Special head stamping-Match stamped on head of case or NM stamped on head of case of cartridges for National Matches

Cartridge, 7.62mm, Match, M852

Weapon:	Rifle, 7.62mm, M14 (National Match)
Ballistic Perf.:	
Velocity:	2550 ±30 fps at 78 feet
Pressure:	50,000 psi, max. avg.
Accuracy:	3.5" mean radius, max. avg. at 600 yards
Cartridge:	383 grs. approx.
Case:	190 - 20 grs.
Bullet:	168 grs. Hollow point boattail
Primer, Perc.:	
Prim. Wt:	5.43 - 0.52 grs.; 5.3 grs. approx.; 5 grs.approx.
Pellet Wt:	0.60 - 0.12 grs.; 0.7 - 0.2 grs.; .58 -.08 grs.
Compos.:	FA-956 FA-961 FA-1023
Type:	Lead Styphnate
Propellant:	
Brand:	IMR 4895
Type:	Single Base Tubular
Weight:	42 grs.
Ident.:	Special head stamping-Match stamped on head of case or NM stamped on head of case of cartridges for National Matches

Cartridge, 7.62mm, Ball, Frangible, M160

Weapon:	Gun, Machine, 7.62mm, M73
Ballistic Perf.:	
Velocity:	1320 ±50 fps
Accuracy:	4.0" mean radius max. avg. at 100 yards
Perf.:	The bullet of the cartridge shall not perforate a 3/162 thick plate Dural .2024 T4 (or equal) with a Brinell hardness of 105 to 125 under a 500 kilogram load at a range of 25 yards.
Cartridge:	315 - 24 grs.
Case:	190 - 20 grs.
Bullet:	108.5 - 3 grs., Bakelite, Natural and powdered lead
Primer, Perc.:	
Prim. Wt:	5.43 - 0.52 grs.
Compos.:	FA-956
Propellant:	
Brand:	SR8074 HPC-8 WC140
Type:	Single Base Double Base Single Base
	Tubular Flake Spheroidal
Weight:	10.5 grs. 8.3 grs. 11.4 grs.
Ident.:	Green tip; White annulus

Dummy, Cartridge, 7.62mm, Inert Loaded, M172

Weapon:	Gun, Machine, M60, Testing Metallic Link Belts and Gun Function
Requirements:	Bullet Extr.: The force required to extract the bullet from the cartridge case shall not be less than 173 lbs.
Cartridge:	385 - 23 grs.
Case:	190 - 20 grs.
Bullet:	149 - 3 grs.
Filler:	Sodium Carbonate Monohydrate or equal
Ident.:	Cartridge, black oxide, no primer or primer vent hole

Cartridge, 7.62mm, NATO, Ball, Duplex, M198

Weapon:	Rifle, 7.62mm, M14
Ballistic Perf.:	
Velocity:	Front Bullet - 2750 ±30 fps at 78 feet Rear Bullet - 2200 fps min. indiv. at 78 feet
Pressure:	52,000 psi, max. avg.
Accuracy:	(Front Bullet) 2" mean radius, max. avg. at 100 yards
Dispersion:	(Rear Bullet) between 5 and 10 inches CEP at 100 yards
Cartridge:	411 - 31 grs.
Case:	190 - 20 grs.
Bullet:	(Front) 84 - 4 grs.
	(Rear) 85 - 4grs.
Primer, Perc.:	
Prim. Wt:	5.43 - 0.52 grs.
Compos.:	FA-956, Lead Styphnate
Propellant:	
Type:	Double Base Spheroidal
Weight:	45.5 grs.
Point Ident.:	Green Lacquer

CALIBER .30 AMMUNITION (30-06)

Cartridge, Cal .30, Tracer M1

Weapon:	Gun, Machine, Cal .30, M37; Gun, Machine, Cal .30 Browning M1919A4; Gun, Machine, Cal .30, M1919A6; Rifle, U.S. Cal .30, M1
Ballistic Perf.:	
Velocity:	2700 ±30 fps at 78 feet GM Bullet 2665 ±30 fps for GMCS Bullet
Pressure:	52,000 psi, max. avg.
Accuracy:	18" mean radius max. avg. at 600 yards
Tracer:	Visible Light from Muzzle to 900 yards
Cartridge:	408 - 27 grs. (GM Bullet) 399 - 27 grs. (GMCS Bullet)
Case:	200 – 20 grs.
Bullet:	152.5 - 3.5 grs.
	143.5 - 3.5 grs.
Tracer:	13 grs. approx.
Igniter:	3 grs. approx.
Primer, Perc.:	
Prim. Wt:	5.43 - 0.520 grs. - Lead Styphnate
Propellant:	
Type:	Double Base, Spheroidal - IMR4895
Weight:	50 grs.
Point Ident.:	Red tip

Cartridge, Caliber .30, Test, High Pressure, M1

Weapon:	(For Proof Testing all Caliber .30 Weapons)
Ballistic Perf.:	
Pressure:	67,500 psi, max. avg.
Cartridge:	432 - 24 grs.
Bullet:	173 - 3 grs.
Primer, Perc.:	
Prim. Wt:	5.5 grs.

Compos.:   FA961 - Lead Styphnate
Propellant:
Brand: IMR 4198
Type: Single Base, Tubular
Weight: 52 grs.
Ident.:   Stannic Stained (tinned) Case

Cartridge, Caliber .30, Ball, M2

Weapon: Gun, Machine, Cal .30, M37;
Gun, Machine, Cal .30, Browning,
M1919A4; Gun, Machine, Cal .30,
M1919A6; Rifle, U.S. Cal .30, M1

Ballistic Perf.:
Velocity: 2740 ±30 fps at 78 ft
Pressure: 50,000 psi, max. avg.
Accuracy: 7.5" mean radius max. avg. at 600 yards
Cartridge: 408 - 23 grs.
Case: 200 - 20 grs.
Bullet: 152 - 3 grs.
Primer, Perc.:
Prim. Wt: 5.43
Compos.:   Lead Styphnate
Propellant:

Brand:	IMR4895	WC852	CMR-100
Type:	Single Base Tubular	Double Base Spheroidal	Single Base Tubular
Weight:	50 grs.	50 grs.	45 grs.
Point Ident.:	Plain Tip		

Cartridge, Caliber .30, Ball, M2
(Overhead Fire Application)

Weapon: Guns, Machine, Caliber .30; M37,
Browning M1919A4 and M1919A6

Ballistic Perf.:
Velocity: 2740 ±30 fps at 78 feet
Pressure: 50,000 psi maximum average
Accuracy: 5.0" mean radius maximum average at 600 yards
Cartridge: 408 - 23 grs.
Case: 200 - 20 grs.
Bullet: 152 - 3 grs.
Primer, Perc.:
Prim. Wt: 5.43
Compos.:   FA956 - Lead Styphnate
Propellant:

Brand:	IMR4895	WC852	CMR-100
Type:	Single Base Tubular	Double Base Spheroidal	Single Base Tubular
Weight:	50 grs.	50 grs.	45 grs.
Point Ident.:	Plain Tip		

Cartridge, Caliber .30, Armor Piercing, M2

Weapon: Gun, Machine, Cal .30, M37; Gun,
Machine, Cal .30, Browning,
M1919A4; Gun, Machine, Cal .30,
M1919A6; Rifle, U.S. Cal .30, M1

Ballistic Perf.:
Velocity: 2715 ±30 fps at 78 feet
Pressure: 54,000 psi, max. avg.
Accuracy: 10" mean radius max. avg. at 600 yards
Cartridge: 424 - 28 grs.
Case: 200 - 28 grs.
Bullet: 166 - 7.5 grs.
Primer, Perc.:
Prim. Wt: 5.43
Compos.:   Lead Styphnate
Propellant:

Brand:	WC852	IMR 4895
Type:	Double Base Spheroidal	Single Base Tubular
Weight:	55 grs.	55 grs.
Point Ident.:	Black tip	

Cartridge, Caliber .30, Rifle Grenade, M3

Weapon: Rifle, U.S. Caliber .30, M1

Ballistic Perf.:
Velocity: Shall propel Grenade (Practice, M11A2)
with a velocity of 180 ±15 fps at 5.5ft
Cartridge: 246 - 20 grs.
Case: 200 - 20 grs.
Wad: Paper
Primer, Perc.:
Prim. Wt: 5.43 - 0.520 grs.
Compos.:   Lead Styphnate
Propellant:
Type: Single Base, IMR 4895
Weight: 40 grs. + 5.0 1.0 gr. Black powder
Ident.:   Case mouth closed with 5-petal rose crimp and sealed with red lacquered disc

Cartridge, Cal .30, API, M14

Weapon: Gun, Machine, Cal .30, M37 (Tank)
Gun, Machine, Cal .30, Browning,
M1919A4; Gun, Machine, Cal .30,
1919A6; Rifle, U.S. Cal .30, M1

Ballistic Perf.:
Velocity: 2780 ±30 fps at 78 feet
Pressure: 54,000 psi, max. avg.
Accuracy: 15" mean radius max. avg. at 600 yards
Incend: Shall produce flash when fired against steel target at 175 yards
Penetra: Avg. penetration depth of .422-in. when fired against steel plate at 100 yards
Cartridge: 407 - 30 grs.
Case: 200 - 20 grs.
Bullet: 151 - 6 grs.
Primer, Perc.:
Compos.:   Lead Styphnate
Propellant:

Brand:	WC 852	IMR 4895
Type:	Double Base Spheroidal	Single Base Tubular
Weight:	50 grs.	50 grs.
Point Ident.:	Aluminum	

Cartridge, Cal .30, Frangible, Ball, M22

Weapon: Gun, Machine, Cal .30, M37; Gun,
Machine, Cal .30, Browning,
M1919A4; Rifle, U.S. Cal .30, M1

Ballistic Perf.:
Velocity: 1320 ±30 fps at 53 feet 1500 fps, max. individual at 53 feet
Accuracy: 2.0" mean radius max. avg. at 100 yards
Perf.:   Shall not perforate aluminum plate at 25 yards 3/162 Dural 2024 T4 with Brinell Hardness of 105 to 125 under 500 Kilogram load
Cartridge: 320 - 24 grs.
Case: 220 - 20 grs.
Bullet: 108.3 grs. Bakelite
Primer, Perc.:
Prim. Wt: 5.5 grs.
Compos.:   Lead Styphnate
Propellant:
Brand: SR 4759
Type: Single Base, Tubular
Weight: 11 grs.
Point Ident.:   Green and white tip

Cartridge, Cal .30, Tracer, M25

Weapon: Gun, Machine, Cal .30 Browning,
M1917A1
Gun, Machine, Cal .30, M37 (Tank)
Gun, Machine, Cal .30 Browning,
M1919A4
Gun, Machine, Cal .30 Browning,
M1919A6 Rifle, U.S. Cal .30 M1

Ballistic Perf.:

Velocity:	2665 ±30 fps at 78 feet
Pressure:	50,000 psi, max. avg.
Trace:	Bright Trace, 75 to 900 yards

Cartridge:	401 - 25 grs.	
Case:	200 - 20 grs.	
Bullet:	145.5 - 4 grs.	
Primer Perc.:		
Prim. Wt:	5.430 - 0.520 grs.	
Compos.:	Lead Styphnate - FA956	
Propellant:		
Brand:	WC 852	IMR 4895
Type:	Double Base	Single Base
	Spheroidal	Tubular
Weight:	50 grs.	50 grs.
Point Ident.:	Orange tip	

Cartridge, Cal .30, Tracer, M25 (Steel Case)

Same as Cartridge, Tracer, Cal .30, M25, except:

Case:	Steel, 180 - 20 grs.

Cartridge, Cal .30, Dummy, M40

Weapon:	For training purposes in all caliber .30 weapons
Ballistic Perf.:	**None**
Cartridge:	268 - 21.5 grs.
Case:	200 - 20 grs.
Bullet:	68 - 1.5 grs.
Ident.:	Corrugated case - no primer

Cartridge, Cal .30, Match, M72

Weapon:	Rifle, U.S. Caliber .30, M1 National Match

Ballistic Perf.:

Velocity:	2640 ±30 fps at 78 feet
Pressure:	50,000 psi, max. avg.
Accuracy:	3.5" mean radius max. avg. at 600 yards

Cartridge:	425 grs. approx.
Case:	200 - 20 grs.
Bullet:	175.5 - 3 grs.
Primer Perc.:	
Prim. Wt:	5 to 5.6 grs.
Compos.:	FA961 or FA1023 - Lead Styphnate
Propellant:	
Brand:	IMR 4895
Type:	Single Base, Tubular
Weight:	50 grs.
Ident.:	MATCH stamped on head of case, and NM stamped on head of case of cartridges for National Matches

Cartridge, Caliber, 30 Blank, M1909

Weapon:	Gun, Machine, Cal .30, Browning M1919A4; Gun, Machine, Cal .30 M1919A6; Rifle, U.S. Cal .30, M1
Ballistic Perf.:	None

Cartridge:	218 - 20 grs.	
Case:	200 - 20 grs.	
Primer Perc.:		
Propellant:		
Brand:	WC Blank	SR 4990
Type:	Double Base	Single Base
	Spheroidal	Flake
Weight:	12 grs.	12 grs.
Wad:	Paper 25 grs.	
Ident.:	No bullet, mouth sealed with red lacquered disc	

Cartridge, Blank, Cal .30, M1909 (Steel Case)

Same as Cartridge, Blank, Cal .30, M1909 except:

Case:	Steel, 180 - 20 grs.

CALIBER 9MM AMMUNITION

Cartridge, Caliber 9mm, Ball, NATO, M882

Weapon:	Pistol, Automatic, Cal 9mm, M9, M11

Ballistic Perf.:

Velocity:	1251 ±25 fps at 16 meters
Pressure:	27,000 psi, max. avg.
Accuracy:	

Cartridge:	179 grs.	
Case:	42 grs.	
Bullet:	124 grs. Copper Alloy	
Primer, Perc.:		
Propellant:		
Brand:	HPC 26	
Type:	Double Base	Flake
Weight:	5 grs.	6 grs.
Point Ident.:	Plain tip	

Cartridge, Caliber 9mm Test, High Pressure, M905

Weapon:	Used to proof test barrels and weapons (Not a service cartridge)

Ballistic Perf.:

Pressure:	50,000 psi, max. avg.

Cartridge:	179 grs.
Case:	42 grs.
Bullet:	124 grs.
Primer, Perc.:	Lead Styphnate
Propellant:	
Brand:	WC 370
Type:	Double Base Ball
Weight:	7.5 grs.
Ident.:	Tinned Case, HPT headstamp

Cartridge, Caliber 9mm, Practice Tracer, M939

Weapon:	AT-4 Subcaliber Trainer

Ballistic Perf.:

Velocity:	885 ±25 fps at 25.5 feet
Pressure:	27,000 psi, max. avg.
Trace:	Visible trace to match AT-4 rocket trajectory

Cartridge:	
Case:	Aluminum
Bullet:	Brass
Tracer:	
Ignit.:	
Primer, Perc.:	Lead Styphnate
Propellant:	
Brand:	
Type:	
Weight:	
Point Ident.:	Red Lacquer over Blue Tip

Cartridge, Caliber 9mm, Dummy M917

Weapon:	Pistol, Automatic, Cal 9mm, M9, M11
Ballistic Perf.:	Not applicable
Cartridge:	179 grs. approx.
Bullet:	124 grs.
Ident.:	Hole in side wall of case

CALIBER .45 AMMUNITION

Cartridge, Caliber .45, Ball, M1911

Weapon:	Pistol, Automatic, Cal .45, M1911A1 Gun, Submachine, Cal. 45, M3A1

Ballistic Perf.:

Velocity:	855 ±25 fps at 25.5 feet
Pressure:	19,000 psi, max. avg.
Accuracy:	7.46" diagonal (max. avg.) at 50 yards

Cartridge:	331 - 17 grs.
Case:	87 - 10 grs.
Bullet:	234 - 6 grs. Copper Alloy .231 grs. Gilding Metal Clad Steel
Primer, Perc.:	

Propellant:

Brand:	SR 7970	HPC 1
Type:	Single Base	Double Base
Flake	Flake	
Weight:	5 grs.	5 grs.
Point Ident.:	Plain tip	

Cartridge, Caliber .45, Ball, M1911, Steel Case

Weapon: Pistol, Automatic, Cal .45, M1911A1
Gun, Submachine, Cal .45, M3A1

Ballistic Perf.:
Velocity: 855 ±25 fps at 25.5 feet
Pressure: 19,000 psi, max. avg.
Accuracy: 7.46" diagonal (max. avg.) at 50 yards
Cartridge: 321 - 20 grs.

Cartridge, Caliber .45, Ball, M1911, Match Grade

Weapon: Pistol, Automatic, Cal .45, M1911A1
National Match

Ballistic Perf:
Velocity: 855 ±25 fps at 25.5 feet
Pressure: 19,000 psi, max. avg.
Accuracy: 3" diagonal (max. avg.) at 50 yards
Cartridge: 334 - 17 grs.
Case: 87 - 10 grs.
Bullet: 234 - 6 grs.
Primer Perc.:
Propellant:

Brand:	SR 7970	HPC 1
Type:	Single Base	Double Base
Flake	Flake	
Weight:	5 grs.	5grs.
Ident.:	Special head stamping - Match - stamped on head of case, and NM stamped on head of case of cartridges for National Matches	

Cartridge, Caliber .45 Test, High Pressure, M1

Weapon: Used to proof test barrels and weapons (Not a service cartridge)

Ballistic Perf.:
Pressure: 22,000 psi, max. avg.
Cartridge: 332-16 grs.
Case: 87 - 10 grs.
Bullet: 234 - 6 grs.
Primer, Perc.: Lead Styphnate
Propellant:

Brand:	SR 7970	HPC 1
Type:	Single Base	Double Base
Flake	Flake	
Weight:	7 grs.	
Ident.:	Stannic Stained Case	

Cartridge, Caliber .45, Blank, M9

Weapon: Pistol, Automatic, Cal .45, M1911A1
Ballistic Perf.:
Screen Perf.: 0.12 dia. max. perforations in paper screen at 15 feet
Cartridge: 104 grs. approx.
Propellant: 7 grs.

Cartridge, Caliber .45, Tracer, M26

Weapon: Pistol, Automatic, Cal .45, M1911A1
Gun, Submachine, Cal .45, M3A1

Ballistic Perf.:
Velocity: 885 ±25 fps at 25.5 feet
Pressure: 19,000 psi, max. avg.
Trace: Visible trace between 15 and 150 yards, min.
Cartridge: 331 - 17 grs.
Bullet: 203 grs. approx.
Tracer: 3 grs. approx.
Ignit.: 2.5 grs. approx.
Primer, Perc.: Lead Styphnate
Propellant:

Brand:	SR 7970	HPC 1
Type:	Single Base	Double Base
Flake	Flake	
Weight:	5 grs.	5 grs.
Point Ident.:	Red Lacquer	

Cartridge, Tracer, Cal .45, M26 (Steel Case)

Same as Cartridge, Cal .45, M26, except:
Case: Steel, 82 - 10 grs.

Cartridge, Caliber .45, Blank Line Throwing M32

Case: Brass
Primer: Non-mercuric, non-corrosive
Propellant: Commercial
Ballistics:
Pressure: 20,000 psi
Ident.: No bullet, rimmed long case, ".45 M32" stamped on head of case
Note: This cartridge used with Lyle life-saving gun, Cal 45/70.

Cartridge, Caliber .45, Match, Wad Cutter (Commercial)

Weapon: Pistol Automatic Cal .45, M1911A1, National Match

Ballistics:
Velocity: The mean velocity of 10 rds. at 15 ft. from the muzzle of the gun shall be 765 ±45 fps
Pressure: The mean pressure of 10 rds. shall not exceed 18,000 psi. The extreme variation shall not exceed 6200 psi.
Accuracy: Average extreme spread of 5-5 shot targets at 50 yards shall not exceed 3.0 inches
Cartridge:
Case: Brass
Bullet: 185 grains Gilding Metal
Propellant: Commercial
Primer: Commercial Lead Styphnate
Ident.: Head stamp in accordance with commercial practice

Cartridge, Caliber .45, Dummy M1921

Weapon: Pistol, Automatic, Cal .45, M1911A1
Gun, Submachine, Cal .45, M3A1
Ballistic Perf.: Not applicable
Cartridge: 313 grs. approx.
Bullet: 234 - 6 grs.
Ident.: Hole in side wall of case

Cartridge, Caliber .45, Dummy, M1921 (Steel Case)

Same as Cartridge, Dummy, Cal .45, M1921, except: Ctg. weight 301 grs. approx.
Case: Steel, 82 - 10 grs.

CALIBER .50 AMMUNITION

Cartridge, Cal .50, Tracer, M1

Weapon: Gun, Machine, Caliber .50, Browning, M2 Heavy Barrel (Turret Type); Gun, Machine, Caliber .50, Browning, M2, Heavy Barrel (Flexible); Gun, Machine, Caliber .50, Tank, M85

Ballistic Perf.:
Velocity: 2700 ±40 fps at 78 feet
Pressure: 52,000 psi, max. avg.
Trace: Bright trace from 250 to 1600 yards
Cartridge: 1785 - 68 grs.
Case: 850 - 50 grs.
Bullet: 676 - 17 grs.
Tracer: 65 grs.
Ignit. Comp. 10 grs.
Primer, Perc.:
Prim. Wt.: 18.5 grs. approx.

Propellant:
Brand: IMR 5010
Type: Single Base, Tubular
Weight: 240 grs.
Point Ident.:   Red tip

Cartridge, Caliber .50, Test, High-Pressure, M1

Weapon: For proof testing all caliber .50 weapons

Ballistic Perf.:
Pressure: 65,000 psi, max. avg.
Cartridge: 2108 - 62 grs.
Bullet: 999 - 11 grs.
Primer, Perc.:
Prim. Wt: 18.5 grs. - Styphnate Cloride
Propellant: WC 860
Type: Double Base, Spheroidal
Weight: 240 grs.
Ident.:   Stannic stained case

Cartridge, Cal .50, Incendiary, M1

Weapon: Gun, Machine, Caliber .50, Browning, M2, Heavy Barrel (Turret Type); Gun, Machine, Caliber .50, Browning, M2, Heavy Barrel (Flexible); Gun, Machine, Caliber .50, Tank, M85

Ballistic Perf.:
Velocity: 2950 ±30 fps at 78 feet
Pressure: 54,000 psi, max. avg.
Cartridge: 1704 grs. approx.
Bullet: 633 - 26 grs.
Incend.:   34 - 2 grs.
Primer, Perc.:
Prim. Wt: 18.5 grs.
Propellant:
Brand: WC860
Type: Double Base Spheroidal
Weight: 240 grs.
Point Ident.:   Blue tip

Cartridge, Blank, Caliber .50, M1

Weapon: Gun, Machine, Caliber .50, Browning, M2, Heavy Barrel (Flexible)

Ballistic Perf.:   None
Cartridge: 891 grs. approx.
Propellant:
Brand: WC-150
Weight: 46 grs.
Type: Double Base, Spheroidal
Wad: 1.5 grs. approx.-Fiberlic No. 2 Kraftboard, or equal (commercial); 256 grs. approx. - Strawboard covered with thin red paper (commercial)
Primer, Perc.:
Prim. Wt: 18.5 grs. approx.
Ident.:   No bullet-mouth sealed with vermilion lacquered wad

Cartridge, Cal .50, Armor Piercing, M2

Weapon: Gun, Machine, Caliber .50, Browning, M2, Heavy Barrel (Turret Type); Gun, Machine, Caliber .50, Browning, M2, Heavy Barrel (Flexible); Gun, Machine, Caliber .50, Tank, M85

Ballistic Perf.:
Velocity: 2810 ±fps at 78 feet
Pressure: 53,000 psi, max. avg.
Accuracy: 10.0" mean radius max. avg. at 600 yards
Cartridge: 1812 - 73 grs.
Case: 850 - 80 grs.
Bullet: 708 - 22 grs.
Primer Perc.:
Prim. Wt: 18.5 grs. approx.
Propellant:

Brand: WC 860   IMR 5010
Type: Double Base Spherodial   Single Base Tubular
Weight: 235 grs.   235 grs.
Point Ident.:   Black tip

Cartridge, Dummy, Cal. 50, M2

Weapon: All Caliber .50 Weapons - for training personnel and testing weapon mechanism
Cartridge: 1215 - 60 grs. (GMCS Bullet Jacket); 1248 - 60 grs. (GM Bullet Jacket)
Ident.:   Three holes in case, no primer

Cartridge, Caliber .50, Ball, M2

Weapon: Gun, Machine, Caliber .50, Browning, M2, Heavy Barrel (Turret Type); Gun, Machine, Caliber .50, Browning, M2, Heavy Barrel (Flexible)

Ballistic Perf.:
Velocity: 2810 ±0 fps at 78 feet
Pressure: 55,000 psi, max. avg.
Accuracy: 9" mean radius max. avg. at 600 yards
Cartridge: 1813 - 73 grs.
Case: 850 - 50 grs.
Bullet: 709.5 - 22 grs.
Primer Perc.:
Prim. Wt: 18.5 grs.
Propellant:
Brand: WC 860
Type: Double Base, Spheroidal
Weight: 235 grs.
Ident.:   Plain tip

Cartridge, Cal .50, Armor Piercing Incendiary, M8

Weapon: Gun, Machine, Caliber .50, Browning, M2, Heavy Barrel (Turret Type); Gun, Machine, Caliber .50, Browning, M2, Heavy Barrel (Flexible); Gun, Machine, Caliber .50, Tank, M85

Ballistic Perf.:
Velocity: 2910 ±30 fps at 78 feet
Pressure: 55,000 psi, max. avg.
Accuracy: 12" mean radius max. avg. at 600 yards
Incen. Fl.:   Incendiary flash must be capable of initiating combustion of flammable liquids
Penetrat.:   Bullet or core must completely perforate armor plate at 100 yards
Cartridge: 1764.5 - 78.5 grs.
Bullet: 662.5 - 27 grs.
Primer Perc.:
Prim. Wt: 18.5 grs. approx.
Propellant:
Brand: WC 860   IMR 5010
Type: Double Base Spheroidal   Single Base Tubular
Weight: 233 grs.   233 grs.
Point Ident.:   Aluminum

Cartridge, Armor Piercing Incendiary, Cal .50, M8, Steel Case

Same as Cartridge, Cal .50, Armor-Piercing Incendiary, M8 except:
Case: Steel, 800 - 50 grs.

Cartridge, Cal .50, Tracer, M10

Weapon: Gun, Machine, Caliber .50, Browning, M2 Heavy Barrel (Turret Type); Gun, Machine, Caliber .50, Browning, M2 Heavy Barrel (Flexible); Gun, Machine, Caliber .50, Tank, M85

Ballistic Perf.:
Velocity: 2860 ±40 fps at 78 feet
Pressure: 54,000 psi, max. avg.
Trace: Bright trace from 225 to 1600 yards

Cartridge:	1752 - 68 grs.
Bullet:	643 - 17 grs.
Tracer:	65 grs.
Ignit.:	11 grs.
Primer Perc.:	
Prim. Wt:	18.5 grs.
Propellant:	
Brand:	IMR 5010
Type:	Single Base, Tubular
Weight:	240 grs.
Point Ident.:	Orange tip

Cartridge, Cal .50, Tracer, M17

| Weapon: | Gun, Machine, Caliber .50, Browning, M2 Heavy Barrel (Turret Type); Gun, Machine, Caliber .50, Browning, M2 Heavy Barrel (Flexible); Gun, Machine, Caliber .50, Tank, M85 |

Ballistic Perf.:

Velocity:	2860 ±40 fps at 78 feet
Pressure:	54,000 psi, max. avg.
Trace:	Bright trace from 100 to 1600 yards
Cartridge:	1737 - 68 grs.
Bullet:	643 - 17 grs.
Ignit.:	11 grs.
Tracer:	40 grs.
Primer Perc.:	
Prim. Wt:	18.5 grs.
Propellant:	
Brand:	IMR 5010
Type:	Single Base, Tubular
Weight:	225 grs.
Point Ident.:	Brown tip

Cartridge, Cal .50, Armor-Piercing, Incendiary, Tracer, M20

| Weapon: | Gun, Machine, Caliber .50, Browning, M2 Heavy Barrel (Turret Type); Gun, Machine, Caliber .50, Browning, M2 Heavy Barrel (Flexible); Gun, Machine, Caliber .50, Tank, M85 |

Ballistic Perf.:

Pressure:	55,000 psi
Incend. Fl.:	Incendiary flash must be capable of initiating combustion of flammable liquids
Penetra.:	Bullet or core must completely penetrate 7/8" armor plate at 100 yards
Trace:	Must exhibit visible trace from 100 to 1600 yards
Cartridge:	1718 - 76.5 grs.
Bullet:	619 - 25 grs.
Primer Perc.:	
Prim. Wt:	18.5 grs.
Propellant:	
Brand:	IMR 5010
Type:	Single Base, Tubular
Weight:	230 grs.
Point Ident.:	Red tip, aluminum

Cartridge, Armor Piercing Incendiary, Tracer Cal .50, M20, Steel Case

Same as Cartridge, Cal .50, Armor-Piercing, Incindiary, Tracer, M20 except:

| Case: | Steel, 800 - 50 grs. |

Cartridge, Cal .50, Tracer, Headlight, M21

| Weapon: | Gun, Machine, Caliber .50, Browning, M2 Heavy Barrel (Turret Type); Gun, Machine, Cal .50, Browning, M2 Heavy Barrel (Flexible); Gun, Machine, Caliber .50, Tank, M85 |

Ballistic Perf.:

| Velocity: | 2840 ±40 fps at 78 feet |
| Pressure: | 55,000 psi, max. avg. |

Trace:	Bright trace from 200 to 500 yards
Cartridge:	1808 - 68 grs. (with gilding metal jacket bullet) 1775 - 68 grs. (with gilding metal clad steel jacket bullet)
Case:	850-50grs.
Bullet:	699 - 17 grs. (with gilding metal jacket); 666 - 17 grs. (with gilding metal clad steel jacket)
Primer Perc.:	
Prim. Wt:	18.5 grs. approx.
Propellant:	
Brand:	IMR 5010
Type:	Single Base, Tubular
Weight:	240 grs.
Point Ident.:	Red tip

Cartridge, Cal .50, Incendiary, M23

| Weapon: | Gun, Machine, Caliber .50 Browning, M2 Heavy Barrel (Turret Type); Gun, Machine, Cal .50, Browning, M2 Heavy Barrel (Flexible); Gun, Machine, Cal .50, Tank, M85 |

Ballistic Perf.:

Velocity:	3400 ±30 fps at 78 feet
Pressure:	58,000 psi, max. avg.
Incend. Fl.:	Incendiary flash must be capable of initiating combustion of flammable liquids
Cartridge:	1581 grs. approx.
Case:	850 - 50 grs.
Bullet:	512 - 24 grs.
Incen.:	90 grs. Max.
Primer Perc.:	
Prim. Wt:	18.5 grs. approx.
Propellant:	
Brand:	IMR 4831
Type:	Single Base, Tubular
Weight:	237 grs. approx.
Point Ident.:	Medium blue tip, slight blue annulus

Cartridge, Cal .50, Ball, M33

| Weapon: | Gun, Machine, Caliber .50 Browning, M2, Heavy Barrel (Turret Type); Gun Machine, Caliber .50, Browning, M2, Heavy Barrel (Flexible); Gun, Machine, Caliber .50, Tank, M85 |

Ballistic Perf.:

Velocity:	2910 ±30 fps at 78 feet
Pressure:	55,000 psi, max. avg.
Cartridge:	1762.5 - 76.5 grs.
Case	850 – 50 grs.
Bullet:	661.5 - 25 grs.
Primer Perc.:	
Prim. Wt:	18.5 grs.

Propellant:		
Brand:	WC860	IMR5010
Type:	Double Base Spheroidal	Single Base Tubular
Weight:	235 grs.	235 grs.
Ident.:	Plain tip	

Cartridge, Cal .50, Spotter-Tracer, M48

| Weapon: | Rifle, Spotting, Caliber .50, M8C |

Ballistic Perf.:

Velocity:	1850 ±20 fps at 78 feet
Accuracy:	10" mean radius at 600 yards
Trace:	Bright trace from 100 to 1500 yards
Pressure:	35,000 psi max. avg.
Spotting:	Must flash and produce smoke upon impact
Cartridge:	1651 grs.
Bullet:	827 - 18 grs.
Primer M26:	
Primer Perc.:	
Prim. Wt:	18.5 grs. approx.

Propellant:	
Brand:	IMR 4831
Type:	Single Base, Tubular
Weight:	120 grs.
Point Ident.:	Yellow tip, red annulus

Cartridge, Cal .50, Spotter-Tracer, M48A1

Weapon:	Rifle, Spotting, Caliber .50, M8C
Ballistic Perf.:	
Velocity:	1745 ±20 fps at 78 feet
Trace:	Bright trace from 100 to 1500 yards
Pressure:	38,000 psi max. avg.
Impact:	Must flash and produce smoke upon impact against steel plate at 175 yards
Cartridge:	1744 - 71 grs. (with GMCS flash tube or steel flash tube), 1714 - 71 grs. (with Al - alloy flash tube)
Case:	740 - 50 grs.
Bullet:	827 - 18 grs.
Primer Perc.:	
Primer Wt.:	18.5 grs. approx.
Propellant:	
Type:	Single Base, Tubular
Weight:	110 grs.
Point Ident.:	Yellow tip, red annulus

Cartridge, Cal .50, Spotter-Tracer, M48A2

Weapon:	Rifle, Spotting, Caliber .50, M8C
Ballistic Perf.:	
Velocity:	1745 ±20 fps at 78 feet
Pressure:	38,000 psi max. avg.
Cartridge:	1744 - 71 grs. (with GMCS flash tube or steel flash tube); 1714 - 71 grs. (with Al - alloy flash tube)
Case:	740 - 50 grs.
Bullet:	828 - 18 grs.
Primer Perc.:	
Prim. Wt.:	18.5 grs. approx.
Propellant:	110 grs. approx.
Type:	Single Base, Tubular
Point Ident.:	Yellow tip, red annulus

Dummy Cartridge, Cal .50, Inert Loaded, XM176

Weapon:	All caliber .50 weapons
Ballistic Perf.:	None
Cartridge:	1752 - 82 grs.
Bullet:	661.5 - 27 grs.
Primer:	No primer
Inert Prop.:	Sodium Carbonate - Monohydrate, 5 grs.
Ident.:	Cartridge coated with black chemical finish

Cartridge, Cal .50, Practice, T249E2

Weapon:	Rifle, Spotting, Caliber .50, M8C
Ballistic Perf.:	
Velocity:	1745 ±20 fps at 78 feet
Pressure:	38,000 max. avg.
Accuracy:	5" mean radius at 600 yards
Cartridge:	1738 - 61 grs. (with GMCS or steel flash tube); 1708 - 61 grs. (with Al - alloy Flash Tube)
Bullet:	817 4 grs.
Primer Perc.:	
Prim. Wt.:	18.5 grs. approx.
Propellant:	
Brand:	IMR 7383
Type:	Single Base, Tubular
Weight:	110 grs. approx.
Point Ident.:	Green tip

Cartridge, Cal .50, Armor Piercing Incendiary, T49

Weapon:	Gun, Machine, Caliber .50, Browning, M2 Heavy Barrel (Turret Type); Gun, Machine, Caliber .50, Browning, M2, Heavy Barrel (Flexible); Gun, Machine, Caliber .50, Tank, M85

Ballistic Perf.:	
Velocity:	3400 ±30 fps at 78 feet
Pressure:	58,000 psi, max. avg.
Accuracy:	10" mean radius at 600 yards
Cartridge:	1597 grs. approx.
Bullet:	501 grs.
Primer Perc.:	
Prim. Wt.:	18.5 grs.
Propellant:	
Brand:	WC 860
Weight:	252 grs.
Type:	Double Base, Spheroidal
Point Ident.:	Blue tip, silver annulus

Cartridge, Caliber .50, Test, High Pressure, T251

Weapon:	Rifle, Spotting, Caliber .50, M8C
Ballistic Perf.:	
Pressure	55,000 psi, max. avg.
Cartridge:	1902 - 50 grs.
Case:	740 - 50 grs.
Bullet:	999-11 grs.
Primer Perc.:	
Prim. Wt.:	18.5 grs. approx.
Propellant:	
Brand:	IMR 4831
Type:	Single Base Tubular
Weight:	142 grs.
Ident.:	Stannic Stained Case

20MM AMMUNITION

Dummy Cartridge, Caliber 20mm, M51A1B1

Weapon:	Guns, Automatic, 20mm, M39, M61, XM168 and GAU-4 (XM130)
Requirements:	Projectile extraction: The cartridge assembly shall withstand a 3900 pound tension force without separation of the projectile from the cartridge case
Cartridge:	3850 grains, min.
Bullet:	Steel, 1520 30 grains
Ident.:	Cartridge chromate finish, marking opaque, color black

Cartridge, 20mm Armor Piercing Incendiary Tracer, M52E1 (USAF)

Weapon:	Gun, Automatic, 20mm, M39, M61 and GAU-4 (XM130)
Ballistic Perf.:	(Single shot - test barrel)
Velocity:	3380 ±50 fps at 78 feet
Pressure:	Not to exceed 60,500 psi
Accuracy:	15-in. mean radius - 600 yards
Cartridge:	3900 grains approx.
Case:	M103, Brass
Prim. Elec:	22 grs.
Propellant:	WC 870, weight to meet ballistic requirements
Projectile:	1530 grains approx. Rotating
Blank:	133 grains approx. Gilding Metal
Ident.:	Projectile black and red - marking opaque; color orange

Cartridge, 20mm, Armor Piercing Incendiary, M53 (USAF)

Weapon:	Guns, Automatic, 20mm, M39, M61 and GAU-4 (XM 130)
Ballistic Perf.:	Single shot - test barrel
Velocity:	3380 ±250 fps at 78 feet
Pressure:	Not to exceed 60,500 psi
Accuracy:	15-in. mean radius max. avg. at 600 yards
Cartridge:	3980 grains approx.
Case:	2150 grs.

Prim. Elec.: 22 grs.
Propellant: WC 870, weight to meet ballistic requirements
Projectile: 1540 35 grs. Rotating
Blank: 133 grains approx., Gilding Metal
Nose: 100 grains approx., Aluminum Alloy
Ident.: Projectile black and band, red marking, opaque color red

Cartridge, 20mm, High Pressure Test, M54A1 (USAF)

Weapon: For use in Proofing Guns, Automatic, 20mm, M39, M61, XM168 and GAU-4 (XM130)

Ballistic Perf.:
Pressure: Shall equal or exceed 62,500 psi and shall not exceed 72,500 psi
Cartridge: 4392 grains approx.
Case: M103, Brass, 2150 grs.
Prim. Elec.: 22 grs.
Propellant: WC 870 or IMR 7013. Weight to meet ballistic requirements
Projectile: 1965 10 grains
Ident.: Projectile, Purple marking, black opaque

Cartridge, 20mm, Target Practice, M55A2 (USAF)

Weapon: Guns, Automatic, 20mm, M39, M61, and XM168 and GAU-4 (XM130)

Ballistic Perf.: (Single shot-test barrel)
Velocity: 3380 ±50 fps at 78 feet
Pressure: Not to exceed 60,500 psi
Accuracy: 15-in. mean radius, max. avg. at 600 yards
Cartridge: 3935 grains approx.
Case: 2150 grs.
Prim. Elec.: 22 grs.
Propellant: WC 870, weight to meet ballistic requirements
Projectile: 1521 30 grs.
Ident.: Projectile blue, opaque black marking

Cartridge, 20mm, High Explosive Incendiary, M6A3 (USAF)

Weapon: Guns, Automatic, 20mm, M39, M61, and GAU-4 (XM130)

Ballistic Perf.: (Single shot - test barrel)
Velocity: 3380 ±250 fps at 78 feet
Pressure: Not to exceed 60,500 psi
Accuracy: 15-in. mean radius at 600 yards
Function: The projectile shall function with high order detonation upon impact.
Cartridge: 2965 grs. approx.
Case: Brass, 2150 grs.
Prim. Elec.: 22 grs.
Propellant: WC 870, weight to meet requirements
Projectile: 1565 grs. approx.
Charged Proj.: 1230 grs.approx.
Charge: 165 grs. min.
Rotating
Blank: 133 grs. approx. (Gilding Metal)
Ident.: Projectile yellow, black opaque marking

Cartridge, 20mm, High Explosive Incendiary, M97A2 (USAF)

Weapon: Guns, Automatic, 20mm, M24 and M24A1
Ballistic Perf.: (Single shot - test barrel)
Velocity: 2680 ±50 fps at 78 feet
Pressure: Shall not exceed 51,000 psi
Accuracy: 15-in. mean radius at 600 yards
Function: Projectile shall detonate high order on impact with the target plate.
Cartridge: 4000 grs. approx.
Case: Brass, 1520 grs.

Prim. Elec.: 22 grs.
Propellant: IMR 7013, WC 875-weight to meet ballistic requirements
Projectile: HEI-2000 40 grs.
Fuze: Point Detonating
Ident.: Projectile yellow, marking black opaque

Cartridge, 20mm, Target Practice, M99A1 (USAF)

Weapon: Guns, Automatic, 20mm, M24 and M24A1

Ballistic Perf.: (Single shot - test barrel)
Velocity: 2680 ±50 fps at 78 feet
Pressure: Shall not exceed 51,000 psi
Accuracy: 15-in. mean radius at 600 yards
Cartridge: 4000 grs. approx.
Case: Brass, 1520 grs.
Prim. Elec.: 22 grs.
Projectile: 2000 35 grs.
Ident.: Projectile blue, marking black opaque

Cartridge, 20mm, Target Practice, M204

Weapon: Gun, Automatic, 20mm, M3
Ballistic Perf.: (Single shot - test barrel)
Velocity: 2680 ±50 fps at 78 feet
Pressure: Shall not exceed 51,000 psi
Accuracy: 15-in. mean radius at 600 yards
Cartridge: 4000 grs. approx.
Case: Brass, 1520 grs.
Prim. Perc.: 26 grs.
Propellant: 4814, IMR 7013 or WC 875 - Weight to meet ballistic requirements
Projectile: TP, M99A1 - 2000 - 35 grs.
Ident.: Projectile blue, marking black opaque

Cartridge, 20mm, Target Practice - Tracer, M206

Weapon: Gun, 20mm, Automatic Gas Operated, Manual or Electric Fired, M139

Ballistic Perf.:
Velocity: 3460 ±50 fps at muzzle
Pressure: 49,500 psi max. avg.
Cartridge: 317 Grams approx.
Case: 134 5.8 Grams, Steel
Primed: 145 Grams
Primer Perc.: 10 Grams
Propellant: 50 Grams, approx.
Projectile: 120 2 Grams
Ident.: Projectile blue, red T's, black letters

Cartridge, 20mm, Target Practice - Tracer, M206E1

Weapon: Gun, 20mm, Automatic Gas Operated, Manual or Electric Fired, M139

Ballistic Perf.:
Velocity: 3460 ±50 fps
Pressure: 49,500 psi max. avg.
Cartridge:
Primer Perc.: 29 grs.
Ident.: Projectile blue, red T's, black letters

Cartridge, 20mm, High Explosive Incendiary M210

Weapon: Gun, Automatic, 20mm, M3
Ballistic Perf.:
Velocity: 2680 ±50 fps at 78 ft.
Pressure: Shall not exceed 51,000 psi
Cartridge: 4000 grains approx.
Case: Brass - 1520 grs.
Primer Perc.: 26 grs.
Propellant: IMR 7013,4815 or WC 875; Weight to meet ballistic requirements
Projectile: 2000 40 grains

Cartridge, 20mm, Armor Piercing Incendiary - Tracer, M601

Weapon: Gun, 20mm, Automatic, Gas operated, Manual or Electric Fired, M139

Ballistic Perf.:
Velocity: 3610 ±50 fps
Pressure: 49,500 psi max. avg.

Cartridge: 310 grains
Case: 134 5.8 Grams, Steel
Primed: 145 Grams
Primer Perc. 10 Grams
Propellant: 53 Grams, approx.
Projectile: 111 2 Grams
Ident.: Projectile black, orange T's, red tip and white letters

Cartridge, 20mm, Armor Piercing Incendiary - Tracer, M601E1

Weapon: Gun, 20mm, Automatic, Gas operated, Manual or Electric Fired, M139

Ballistic Perf.:
Velocity: 3610 ±50 fps
Pressure: 49,500 psi max. avg.

Cartridge:
Primer Perc.: 29 grs.
Propellant: To meet ballistic requirements
Projectile: 112.5 Grams
Ident.: Projectile black, orange T's, red tip and white letters

Cartridge, 20mm, High Pressure Test, MK101 Mod O (USN)

Weapon: Gun, 20mm, chambered to fire MK100 series 20mm ammunition

Ballistic Perf.:
Pressure: Not to exceed 72,500 psi

Cartridge: 4285 50 grs.
Case: 1880 grs. (Steel)
Prim. Elec.: 22 grs.
Propellant: Tubular or ball, nitrocellulose, weight to meet ballistic requirements
Projectile: 1700 grs., inert
Ident.: Green or blue projectile with brown nose and 1/42black letters reading "High Pressure Test Round"

Cartridge, 20mm, Low Pressure Test, MK102 Mod O (USN)

Weapon: Gun, 20mm, chambered to fire MK100 series ammunition

Ballistic Perf.:
Pressure:

Cartridge: 4285 50 grs.
Case: 1880 grs. (Steel)
Prim. Elec.: 22 grs.
Propellant: Tubular or ball, nitrocellulose, weight to meet ballistic requirements
Projectile: 1700 grs., inert
Ident.: Blue or green projectile with brown nose and 1/4" black letters reading "Low Pressure Test Round"

Cartridge, 20mm, Dummy, MK103 Mod O (USN)

Inert round. Has empty primer pocket and holes in case; or when made up from rejected service case, has primer pocket plugged with brass or empty primer cup staked with three equally spaced crimps. Case may be empty or loaded with inert material. Projectile is usually brass or bronze plated.

Cartridge, 20mm, Target Practice, MK105 Mod O (USN)

Weapon: Guns, Automatic, 20mm, MK11 and MK12

Ballistic Perf.: (Single shot - test barrel)
Velocity: 3350 fps at muzzle
Pressure: 60,000 psi
Accuracy: 15-in. mean radius at 600 yards

Cartridge: 4285 50 grs.
Case: 1880 grs. (Steel) 20mm, MK5 Mod O
Prim. Elec.: 22 grs., MK47 Mod O
Propellant: Tubular or ball, nitrocellulose, 650 grs. approx.
Projectile: 1700 grs., inert
Ident.: Green or blue projectile with black lettering or blue projectile with brown nose and black lettering

Cartridge, 20mm, High Explosive Incendiary MK106 Mod O and 1 (USN)

Weapon: Guns, Automatic, 20mm, MK11 and MK12
Ballistic Perf.: (Single shot - test barrel)
Velocity: 3350 fps at muzzle
Pressure: 60,000 psi
Accuracy: 15-in. mean radius at 600 yards

Cartridge: 4285 50 grs.
Case: 1880 grs. (Steel) 20mm, MK5 Mod O
Prim. Elec.: 22 grs., MK47 Mod O
Propellant: Tubular or ball, nitrocellulose, 650 grs. approx.
Projectile: 1700 50 grs., Impact detonating
Ident.: Unpainted fuze, red and yellow projectile

Cartridge, 20mm, Armor Piercing-Incendiary, MK107 Mod O (USN)

Weapon: Guns, Automatic, 20mm, MK11 and MK12
Ballistic Perf.: (Single shot - test barrel)
Velocity: 3350 fps at muzzle
Pressure: 60,000 psi
Accuracy: 15-in. mean radius at 600 yards

Cartridge: 4285 50 grs.
Case: 1880 grs. (Steel) 20mm, MK5 Mod O
Prim. Elec.: 22 grs., MK47 Mod O
Projectile: 1700 50 grs.
Ident.: No fuze. Nose of projectile blue or brown with red band. Body of projectile black with white lettering

Cartridge, 20mm, Armor Piercing-Tracer, MK108 Mod O (USN)

Weapon: Guns, Automatic, 20mm, MK11 and MK12
Ballistic Perf.: (Single shot - test barrel)
Velocity: 3350 fps at muzzle
Pressure: 60,000 psi
Accuracy: 15 inch mean radius at 600 yards

Cartridge: 4285 50 grs.
Case: 1880 grs. (Steel) 20mm, MK5 Mod O
Projectile: 1700 50 grs.
Ident.: No fuze. Hollow windshield. Brown or yellow nose, black projectile body with white lettering

Designation	Description
M1	Cartridge, Ball, Carbine, Caliber .30
M1	Cartridge, Blank, Caliber .50 (T40)
M1	Cartridge, Incendiary, Caliber .50
M1	Cartridge, Test, High Pressure, Caliber .50
M1	Cartridge, Test, High Pressure, Caliber .45
M1	Cartridge, Test, High Pressure, Caliber .30
M1	Cartridge, Tracer, Caliber .30
M1	Cartridge, Tracer, Caliber .50 (AN-MI)
M1E1	Cartridge, Incendiary, Caliber .50 (M1 loaded to 3100 f/s)
M1911	Cartridge, Ball, Caliber .45
M1911	Cartridge, Ball, Match Grade, Caliber .45
M1909	Cartridge, Blank, Caliber .30
M1921	Cartridge, Dummy, Caliber .45
M2	Cartridge, AP, Caliber .50
M2	Cartridge, AP, Caliber .30
M2	Cartridge, Ball, Caliber .50 (AN-M2)
M2	Cartridge, Ball, Caliber .30
M2	Cartridge Dummy, Caliber .50
M2	Cartridge, 12 Gage
M3	Cartridge, Grenade, Rifle, Caliber .30
M3	Cartridge, Igniter, Caliber .38 (for Igniter, Grenade, Frangible M3
M6	Cartridge, Grenade Carbine, Caliber .30 (T6)
M7	Cartridge, Grenade, Auxiliary (T18)
M8	Cartridge, Armor-Piercing-Incendiary, Caliber .50 (T16)
M8E1	Cartridge, Armor-Piercing Incendiary, Caliber .50, Loaded with Double Base Powder to a Higher Velocity
M9	Cartridge, Blank, Caliber .45 (T31)
M10	Cartridge, Tracer, Caliber .50 (T12)
M10E1	Cartridge, Tracer, Caliber .50, Loaded to an Increased Velocity with Double Base Powder
M12	Cartridge, Shot, Caliber .45 (T23)
M13	Cartridge, Dummy, Carbine, Caliber .30
M14	Cartridge, Armor-Piercing-Incendiary, Caliber .30 (T15)
M14A1	Cartridge, Armor-Piercing-Incendiary, Caliber .30 (T15 with T1E48 Bullet)
M15	Cartridge, Shot, Caliber .45 (T29)
M16	Cartridge, Tracer, Carbine, Caliber .30 (T24)
M17	Cartridge, Tracer, Caliber .50 (T9)
M18	Cartridge, High Pressure Test, Carbine, Caliber .30 (T27)
M19	Shell, Shot Gun (All Brass), 12 Gage - 00 Buck
M20	Cartridge, Armor-Piercing-Incendiary-Tracer, Caliber .50 (T28)
M21	Cartridge, Tracer, Headlight, Caliber .50 (T1E1)
M22	Cartridge, Ball, Frangible, Caliber .30 (T44)
M23	Cartridge, Incendiary, Caliber .50 (T48)
M24	Cartridge, Ball, Caliber .22, Long Rifle (T42)
M25	Cartridge, Tracer, Caliber .30 (T10)
M26	Cartridge, Tracer, Caliber .45 (T30)
M27	Cartridge, Tracer, Carbine, Caliber .30 (T43)
M32	Cartridge, Blank, Line Throwing, Caliber .45 (T124)
M33	Cartridge, Ball, Caliber .50 (T122)
M33E1	Cartridge, Ball, Caliber .50
M33E2	Cartridge, Ball, Caliber .50
M35	Shell, Shot Gun .410 (T135)
M39	Cartridge, Ball, Caliber .22 (Hornet) (T200)
M40	Cartridge, Dummy, Caliber .30
M41	Cartridge, Ball, Caliber .38, Special
M48	Cartridge, Spotter-Tracer, Caliber .50 (T189E1)
M48A1	Cartridge, Spotter-Tracer, Caliber .50 (T189E3)
M48A1E1	Cartridge, Spotter-Tracer
M51	Cartridge, Dummy, 20mm
M51E3	Cartridge, Dummy, 20mm
M51E5	Cartridge, Dummy, 20mm (T272E4)
M51E6	Cartridge, Dummy, 20mm
M52	Cartridge, Armor-Piercing, Incendiary Tracer, 20mm (T230)
M53	Cartridge, Armor-Piercing Incendiary, 20mm (T221E3)
M54	Cartridge, High Pressure Test, 20mm
M55	Cartridge, Ball, 20mm (T199E1)
M56	Cartridge, High Explosive Incendiary, 20mm (T198E1)
M58	Cartridge, High Explosive Incendiary, 20mm (T241)
M59	Cartridge, 7.62mm, NATO, Ball (T104E2)

Designation	Description
M60	Cartridge, 7.62mm, NATO, High Pressure Test(T17E1)
M61	Cartridge, 7.62mm, NATO, Armor-Piercing (T93E2)
M62	Cartridge, 7.62mm, NATO, Tracer (T102E2)
M62	Cartridge, 7.62mm, NATO, Tracer (Overhead Fire Application)
M63	Cartridge, 7.62mm, NATO, Dummy (T70E5)
M64	Cartridge, 7.62mm, NATO, Grenade, Rifle (T116E1)
M65	Cartridge, Ball, Caliber .22 Hornet (T200E1)
M72	Cartridge, Match, Caliber .30 (T291)
M80	Cartridge, 7.62mm, NATO, Ball, (T233)
M80	Cartridge, 7.62mm, NATO, Ball, (Overhead Fire Application)
M80E1	Cartridge, 7.62mm, NATO, Ball (Canadian C1)
M82	Cartridge, 7.62mm, NATO, Blank
M95	Cartridge, Armor-Piercing Tracer, 20mm
M96	Cartridge, Incendiary, 20mm
M97E2	Cartridge, High Explosive Incendiary, 20mm
M97A1	Cartridge, High Explosive Incendiary, 20mm
M99A1	Cartridge, Target Practice, 20mm
M118	Cartridge, 7.62 Match
M160	Cartridge, 7.62mm, Ball, Frangible
M172	Cartridge, Dummy, 7.62mm (Inert Loaded)
M181	Cartridge, 14.5mm (with fuze sec) Tracer Low Charge
M182	Cartridge, 14.5mm (with fuze 6 sec) Used with M31 Field
M183	Cartridge, 14.5mm (with fuze PD) Used with M31 Field
M193	Cartridge, 5.56mm Ball
M196	Cartridge, 5.56mm Tracer
M197	Cartridge, 5.56mm High Pressure Test
M198	Cartridge, 7.62mm Ball Duplex
M199	Cartridge, Dummy 5.56mm
M200	Cartridge, 5.56mm Blank
M204	Cartridge, 20mm Target Practice
M206E1	Cartridge, 20mm Target Practice Tracer
M210	Cartridge, 20mm High Explosive Incendiary
M274	Cartridge, 12 Gage Shotgun, No. 4, Hard Chilled Shot
M601El	Cartridge, 20mm Armor Piercing Incendiary Tracer
M855A1	Cartridge, 5.56mm, Ball
M856A1	Cartridge, 5.56mm, Tracer
M857	Cartridge, 5.56mm, Dummy
M882	Cartridge, 9mm, Ball
M905	Cartridge, 9mm, High Pressure Test

EXPERIMENTAL (XM) SERIES
U.S. MILITARY CARTRIDGES

Designation	Description
XM75	Cartridge, Spotter, 10mm
XM101	Cartridge, Spotting, 20mm
XM106	Cartridge, Practice, 20mm
XM107	Cartridge, High Pressure, 20mm
XM108	Cartridge, Spotter, 15mm
XM108E1	Cartridge, Spotter, 15mm
XM115	Cartridge, 7.62mm, Ball
XM142	Cartridge, Caliber .38 Special, Ball
XM147	Dummy Cartridge, 20mm
XM156	Cartridge, Caliber .50 Spotter-Tracer
XM157	Cartridge, Spotter-Tracer, 15mm
XM162	Cartridge, 12 Gage Shotgun; Plastic #00 Buckshot
XM170	Cartridge, Ball, 15mm
XM171	Cartridge, High Presure Test, 15mm
XM176	Dummy Cartridge, Cal. .50, Inert Loaded
XM177	Dummy Cartridge, 15mm
XM178	Cartridge, 7.62mm, Ball, Overhead Fire
XM179	Cartridge, 7.62mm, Tracer, Overhead Fire
XM180	Cartridge, 7.62mm, Tracer, Overhead Fire
XM192	Cartridge, 7.62mm Blank (Short Case)
XM195	Cartridge, 5.56mm, Grenade
XM202	Cartridge, 8.94mm Select
XM205	Cartridge, 20mm High Explosive Incendiary
XM207	Cartridge, 20mm Armor Piercing
XM220	Cartridge, 20mm Target Practice Tracer
XM232	Dummy Cartridge, 5.56mm Inert Loaded

Designation	Description
XM239	Cartridge, 20mm High Pressure Test
XM240	Dummy Cartridge, 20mm
XM242	Cartridge, 20mm High Explosive Incendiary Tracer
XM243	Cartridge, 20mm High Explosive Incendiary Tracer
XM244	Cartridge, 20mm High Explosive Incendiary Tracer
XM246E3	Cartridge, 20mm High Explosive Incendiary Tracer
XM254	Dummy Cartridge, 20mm, Plastic
XM257	Cartridge, Shotshell, 12 Gage No. 4B Special

EXPERIMENTAL (T) SERIES
U.S. MILITARY CARTRIDGES

Designation	Description
T1	Cartridge, Explosive, Caliber .50
T1	Cartridge, Armor-Piercing, Caliber. 276
T1	Cartridge, Tracer, Caliber .30
T1E1	Cartridge, Tracer, Headlight, Caliber .50 (M21)
T1E2	Cartridge, Tracer, Headlight, Caliber .50
T5	Cartridge, Armor-Piercing, Anti-Tank, Caliber .30
T6	Cartridge, Grenade, Carbine, Caliber .30 (M6)
T7	Cartridge, Grenade, Carbine, Caliber .30 (Long Case)
T8	Cartridge, Tracer, Caliber .50 - 1000 yds.
T9	Cartridge, Tracer, Caliber .50 - 2500 yds. (M17)
T10	Cartridge, Tracer, Night, Caliber .30 (Dim lgniter) (M25)
T12	Cartridge, Tracer, Caliber .50 (M10)
T13	Cartridge, Tracer, Caliber .30 Delay
T14	Cartridge, Tracer, Caliber .50
T15	Cartridge, Armor-Piercing-lncendiary, Caliber .30 (M14)
T15E1	Cartridge, Armor-Piercing-lncendiary Caliber .30
T16	Cartridge, Armor-Piercing-lncendiary, Caliber.50 (M8)
TI7	Cartridge, Tracer, Caliber .30 (Clad Steel Jacketed for Improved Accuracy)
T18	Cartridge, Auxiliary, Grenade (M7)
T19	Cartridge, Explosive, Caliber .60
T19E1	Cartridge, Explosive, Caliber .60
T19E2	Cartridge, Explosive, Caliber .60
T19E3	Cartridge, Explosive, Caliber. 60
T19E4	Cartridge, Explosive, Caliber .60
T20	Cartridge, Tracer, Caliber .50 (Spot) 500 yds.
T21	Cartridge, Tracer, Caliber .50 (Spot) 1000 yds.
T22	Cartridge, Ball, Caliber .30 with Steel Case (M2 Alternate)
T23	Cartridge, Shot, Caliber .45 (M12)
T24	Cartridge, Tracer, Carbine, Caliber .30 (M16)
T25	Cartridge, Ball, Caliber .50 with Steel Case (M2 Alternate)
T26	Cartridge, Igniter, Caliber .38 (Component for Igniter, Grenade, Frangible, M3)
T27	Cartridge, Carbine, High Pressure Test, Caliber .30 (M18)
T28	Cartridge, Armor-Piercing-Incendiary-Tracer, Caliber .50 (M20)
T28E1	Cartridge, Armor-Piercing-Incendiary-Tracer, Caliber .50 (Dim Igniter)
T29	Cartridge, Shot, Caliber .45 (M15)
T30	Cartridge, Tracer, Caliber .45 (M26)
T31	Cartridge, Blank, Caliber .45 (M9)
T32	Cartridge, Ball, Caliber .60-1196 grain bullet
T32E1	Cartridge, Ball, Caliber .60 - 1137 grain bullet
T32E2	Cartridge, Ball, Caliber .60
T33	Cartridge, High Pressure Test, Caliber .60
T33E1	Cartridge, High Pressure Test, Caliber .60 (T33 with M36A1 Primer)
T34	Cartridge, High Explosive Incendiary, Caliber .50
T35	Cartridge, Dummy, Caliber .60
T35E1	Cartridge, Dummy, Caliber .60
T36	Cartridge, Incendiary, Caliber .60
T36E1	Cartridge, Incendiary, Caliber .60
T36E2	Cartridge, Incendiary, Caliber .60 (With #28 Primer)
T36E3	Cartridge, Incendiary, Caliber .60 (T36E2 with M36A1 Percussion Primer)
T37	Cartridge, Tracer, Caliber .50 with trajectory to match 3.5-inch Forward Firing Rocket
T38	Cartridge, Armor-Piercing-Tracer, Caliber .50
T38E1	Cartridge, Armor-Piercing-lncendiary, Caliber .50
T39	Cartridge, Armor-Piercing-lncendiary, Caliber .60
T39E1	Cartridge, Armor-Piercing-lncendiary, Caliber .60 (T39 with M36A1 Percussion Primer)
T39E2	Cartridge, Armor-Piercing-lncendiary, Caliber .60
T39E3	Cartridge, Armor-Piercing-lncendiary, Caliber .60
T39E4	Cartridge, Armor-Piercing-Incendiary, Caliber .60
T39E5	Cartridge, Armor-Piercing-lncendiary, Caliber .60
T39E6	Cartridge, Armor-Piercing-lncendiary, Caliber .60
T40	Cartridge, Blank, Caliber .50 (M1)
T41	Cartridge, Incendiary, High Velocity, Caliber .60
T41E1	Cartridge, Incendiary, High Velocity, Caliber .60
T42	Cartridge, Ball, Caliber .22, Long Rifle Jacketed Bullet (M24)
T43	Cartridge, Tracer, Carbine, Caliber .30 (M27)
T44	Cartridge, Ball, Frangible, Caliber .30 (M22)
T44E1	Cartridge, Ball, Frangible, Caliber .30
T45	Cartridge, Armor-Piercing, Caliber .60
T45E1	Cartridge, Armor-Piercing, Caliber .60
T46	Cartridge, Armor-Piercing-Tracer, Caliber .60
T46E1	Cartridge, Armor-Piercing-Tracer, Caliber .60
T47	Cartridge, High Explosive, Incendiary, Caliber .60
T48	Cartridge, Incendiary, Caliber .50 (500 grain bullet) M23
T48E1	Cartridge, Incendiary, Caliber .50 (500 grain bullet)
T48E2	Cartridge, Incendiary, Caliber .50 (500 grain bullet)
T49	Cartridge, Armor-Piercing-Incendiary, Caliber .50 (500 grain bullet)
T50	Cartridge, Incendiary, Caliber .60 - .50
T51	Cartridge, Armor-Piercing-Incendiary, Caliber .60-.50
T52	Cartridge, Tracer, Caliber .60 - .50
T53	Cartridge, Tracer, Caliber .30
T54	Cartridge, Tracer, Caliber .50
T55	Cartridge, Tracer, Caliber .60
T56	Cartridge, Blank, Caliber .50 with Electric Primer
T57	Cartridge, Grenade, Auxiliary, High Pressure Test
T58	Cartridge, Incendiary, Caliber .50 (White Phosphorus Loading)
T59	Cartridge, Carbine, Spotting, Caliber .30
T60	Cartridge, Armor-Piercing-Incendiary-Tracer, Caliber .60
T60E1	Cartridge, Armor-Piercing-Incendiary-Tracer, Caliber .60 (T60 with M36A1 Percussion Primer)
T61	Cartridge, Antenna Erecting
T62	Cartridge, Armor-Piercing, Carbine, Caliber .30
T63	Cartridge, Armor-Piercing-Incendiary-Tracer, Caliber .50 (500 grain) R. V.
T64	Cartridge, Tracer, Caliber .50 (Rocket Fire Control, 2000 100 yds; Dim 500 yds bright)
T65	Cartridge, Ball, Caliber .30, Short Case (7.62mm NATO)
T65E1	Cartridge, Ball, Caliber .30, Short Case
T65E2	Cartridge, Ball, Caliber .30 (for Light Rifle)
T65E3	Cartridge, Ball, Caliber .30 (for Light Rifle)
T65E4	Cartridge, Ball, Caliber .30, Short Case, 10 Caliber, 145 grain, Minimum Boattail
T66	Cartridge, Incendiary-Tracer, Caliber .60, Light Weight Bullet, High Velocity
T67	Cartridge, Grenade, Caliber .45
T68	Cartridge, High Explosive Incendiary, Caliber .60, Light Weight Bullet
T69	Cartridge, Ball, Frangible, Caliber .30 (Carbine Case, Ball Frangible Bullet) (Velocity 1300 30f/s at 78ft)
T70	Cartridge, Dummy, Caliber .30, Short Case (to match Cartridge, Ball, Caliber .30, T65)
T70E1	Cartridge, Dummy, Caliber .30 (FAT1El Case, .030 Wall Ball Bullet)
T70E2	Cartridge, Dummy, Caliber .30 (FAT1El Case, 020 Wall Ball Bullet)
T70E3	Cartridge, Dummy, Caliber .30 (FAT1El Case and Based Tracer Jacket)
T70E4	Cartridge, Dummy, Caliber .30 (FAT1E3 Case, 20 Wall Ball Bullet)
T70E5	Cartridge, Dummy, Caliber .30 (M63)
T71	Cartridge, Test, High Pressure, Caliber .30, Short Case (To match Cartridge, Ball, Caliber .30, T65)

Designation	Description
T71E1	Cartridge, Test, High Pressure, Caliber .30 (T71 with case, brass, FAT1E3; 183 grains approx.) (M60)
M72	Cartridge, Tracer, Caliber .30 (25 yds dim igniter trace)
M72E1	Cartridge, Tracer, Caliber .30
T73	Cartridge, Signal, Caliber .45
T73E1	Cartridge, Signal, Caliber .45
T73E2	Cartridge, Signal, Caliber .45
T74	Cartridge, Frangible, Caliber .30, Loaded with SR-4990 Powder (Point Identification is Green with Tan Tip)
T75	Cartridge, Armor-Piercing-Incendiary, Caliber .50/.60 Assembled w/Bullet, Armor-Piercing-Incendiary, Caliber .50, T49
T76	Cartridge, Armor-Piercing-Incendiary-Tracer, Caliber .60 with Bright Igniter
T76E1	Cartridge, Armor-Piercing-Incendiary-Tracer, Caliber .60 (T60 with Primer, Percussion, M36A1)
T77	Cartridge, Ball, Caliber .60
T77E1	Cartridge, Ball, Caliber .60 (T77 w/Primer, Percussion, M36A1)
T78	Cartridge, Incendiary, Caliber .30, Assembled with Bullet, Incendiary, Caliber .30
T79	Cartridge, Blank, Carbine, Caliber .30
T80	Cartridge, Ball, Caliber .60 (T77 Assembled with M52A3 Electric Primer)
T80E1	Cartridge, Ball, Caliber .60 (T77 Assembled with FAT38 Electric Primer)
T80E2	Cartridge, Ball, Caliber .60 (T77E1 with Cut Cannelure in Sabot)
T81	Cartridge, Incendiary, Caliber .60 (T36E2 Assembled w/Remington T41 Electric Primer)
T81E1	Cartridge, Incendiary, Caliber .60 (T36E2 with Electric Primer, M52A3 and Double Crimp)
T82	Cartridge, Armor-Piercing-Incendiary, Caliber .60 (T39 Assembled with Remington T41 Electric Primer)
T82E1	Cartridge, Armor-Piercing-Incendiary, Caliber .60 (T39E1 with Electric Primer, M52A3 and Double Crimp)
T83	Cartridge, Armor-Piercing-Incendiary-Tracer, Caliber .60 (T60 Assembled with Remington T41 Electric Primer)
T83E1	Cartridge, Armor-Piercing-Incendiary-Tracer, Caliber .60 (T60 Assembled with M52A3 Primer)
T84	Cartridge, Armor-Piercing-Incendiary-Tracer, Caliber .60 (T76 Assembled with Remington T41 Electric Primer)
T84E1	Cartridge, Armor-Piercing-Incendiary-Tracer, Caliber .60 (T76 Assembled with Remington T41 Electric Primer)
T85	Cartridge, High Pressure Test, Caliber .60 (T33 Assembled with Remington T41 Electric Primer)
T85E1	Cartridge, High Pressure Test, Caliber .60 (T33 Assembled with Remington T41 Electric Primer)
T86	Cartridge, Lachrymatory, Caliber .50 (T78 Bullet Charged with LI#2)
T87	Cartridge, Incendiary, Caliber .50 (T78 Bullet Charged with White Phosphorus)
T88	Cartridge, Incendiary, Caliber .30 (Prototype of T87 Charged with White Phosphorus)
T89	Cartridge, Tracer, Caliber .30 (Headlight)
T90	Cartridge, Armor-Piercing, Caliber .30 (Short Case)
T91	Cartridge, High Explosive-Incendiary, Caliber .60
T92	Cartridge, Signal, Caliber .45 (National Fireworks)
T92E1	Cartridge, Signal, Caliber .45 (National Fireworks)
T93	Cartridge, Armor-Piercing, Caliber .30 (140-5 grains AP Bullet for Light Rifle)
T93E1	Cartridge, Armor-Piercing, Caliber .30 (T93 with Case, Brass, 183 grains approx.)
T93E2	Cartridge, Armor-Piercing, Caliber .30 (T93E1 with Bullet, AP, Caliber .30) (M61)
T94	Cartridge, Ball, Caliber .50 (Ball M2 w/aluminum case)
T96	Cartridge, Signal, Carbine, Caliber .30 (National Fireworks)
T97	Cartridge, Armor-Piercing-Incendiary, Caliber .60 (5.25 radius Ogive)
T98	Cartridge, Tracer, Smoke, Caliber .50
T99	Cartridge, Observing, Caliber .30
T100	Cartridge, Release, Life Vest
T101	Cartridge, Armor-Piercing-Incendiary, Caliber .30 (Light Rifle)
T101E1	Cartridge, Armor-Piercing-Incendiary, Caliber .30 (T101 w/Case, Brass, 183 grains approx)
T101E2	Cartridge, Armor-Piercing-Incendiary, Caliber .30 (T101E1 with 10 Caliber Ogive Bullet)
T102	Cartridge, Tracer, Caliber .30 (Light Rifle)
T102E1	Cartridge, Tracer, Caliber .30 (T102 with Case, Brass, 183 grains approx)
T102E2	Cartridge, Tracer, Caliber .30 (T102E1 with10 Caliber Ogive Bullet) (M62)
T103	Cartridge, Observing, Caliber .30 (Light Rifle)
T103E1	Cartridge, Observing, Caliber .30 (T103 with Case, Brass, 183 grains approx)
T103E2	Cartridge, Observing, Caliber .30 (T103 with Case, Brass, 183 grains approx)
T104	Cartridge, Ball, Caliber .30 (Light Rifle)
T104E1	Cartridge, Ball, Caliber .30 (T104 with Case, Brass, 183 grains approx)
T104E2	Cartridge, Ball, Caliber .30 (T104E1 with 10 Caliber Ogive Bullet) (M59)
T106	Cartridge, Ball, Caliber .60 (High Velocity)
T107	Cartridge, Multiple Bullet, Caliber .30
T116	Cartridge, Grenade, Rifle, Caliber .30
T116E1	Cartridge, Grenade, Rifle, Caliber .30
T116E2	Cartridge, Grenade, Rifle, Caliber .30
T117	Cartridge, Ball, Caliber .35 Pistol
T117E1	Cartridge, Ball, Caliber .35 Pistol
T118	Cartridge, Tracer, Caliber .50 (Short Dim Igniter)
T119	Cartridge, Armor-Piercing-Incendiary, Caliber .30 (Tungsten Carbide Core)
T119E1	Cartridge, Armor-Piercing-Incendiary, Caliber .30 (T119 w/Cast, Brass, FAT 1E2, 183 gr. approx)
T120	Cartridge, Ball, Caliber .60
T122	Cartridge, Ball, Caliber .50 (M33)
T124	Cartridge, Blank, Line Throwing, Caliber .45
T128	Cartridge, Guard, Caliber .30
T130	Cartridge, Practice, 20mm (T118 Gun)
T131	Cartridge, High Pressure Test, 20mm, (T118 Gun)
T132	Cartridge, Dummy, 20mm, Inert Loaded
T133	Cartridge, Armor-Piercing-Incendiary, 20mm (T118 Gun)
T134	Cartridge, High Explosive, 20mm (T118 Gun)
T135 (M35)	Shell, Shot Gun, .410 Aluminum Case #6 Shot
T136	Shell, Shot Gun Slug, .410, 220 Grain Slug
T137	Cartridge, Spotting. Caliber .50 (Winchester Centrifugal Armed)
T138	Cartridge, Spotting, Caliber .50 (Winchester Inertia Armed)
T139	Cartridge, Tracer, Caliber .50 (BAT Rifle)
T140	Cartridge, Spotting, Caliber .30 (BAT Rifle)
T142	Cartridge, Practice, 27mm
T143	Cartridge, Dummy, 27mm
T144	Cartridge, High Explosive, 27mm
T145	Cartridge, High Pressure Test, 27mm
T147	Cartridge, Incendiary, 27mm
T148	Cartridge, High Explosive-Incendiary, 20mm (Percussion Primer; 1600 grain shell)
T148E1	Cartridge, High Explosive-Incendiary, 20mm (Percussion Primer; 1600 grain shell)
T149	Cartridge, High Explosive-Incendiary, 20mm (Electric Primer; 1600 grain shell)
T150	Cartridge, Armor-Piercing-Incendiary, 20mm (Percussion Primer; 1600 grain shell)
T150E1	Cartridge, Armor-Piercing-Incendiary, 20mm (Percussion Primer; 1600 grain shell)
T151	Cartridge, Armor-Piercing-Incendiary, 20mm (Electric Primer; 1600 grain shell)
T152	Cartridge, Dummy, 20mm (1600 grain shell)
T53	Cartridge, Practice, 20mm (Percussion Primer; 1600 grain Projectile)
T153E1	Cartridge, Practice, 20mm (Percussion Primer; 1600 grain Projectile)
T154	Cartridge, Practice, 20mm (Electric Primer; 1600 grain shell)

Designation	Description
T155	Cartridge, High Pressure Test, 20mm (Percussion Primer; Modified M99 Projectile)
T155E1	Cartridge, High Pressure Test, 20mm (Percussion Primer; Modified M99 Projectile)
T156	Cartridge, High Pressure Test, 20mm (Electric Primer; Modified M99 Projectile)
T158	Cartridge, Practice, 30mm (Velocity 2000 f/s; 4220 grains; HF1070 grains; pressure 40,000 psi - T121 Gun)
T159	Cartridge, Dummy, 30mm
T160	Cartridge, High Explosive-Incendiary, 30mm w/Shell, T239E6
T160E1	Cartridge, High Explosive-Incendiary, 30mm with Shell, T239E7
T161	Cartridge, High Pressure Test, 30mm
T162	Cartridge, Incendiary, 30mm
T163	Cartridge, High Explosive-Incendiary, 20mm (Length 7.190 in.; T39E3 Projectile)
T164	Cartridge, Armor-Piercing-Incendiary, 20mm
T165	Cartridge, Practice, 20mm
T166	Cartridge, Ball, 20mm using T114 Projectile
T167	Cartridge, Test, High Pressure, 20mm
T168	Cartridge, Dummy, 20mm
T169	Cartridge, Test, Low Pressure, 20mm
T170	Cartridge, Warning Flash
T170	Cartridge, Warning Flash
T170E1	Cartridge, Photoflash
T172	Cartridge, Ball, Caliber .30 (T65E3 with 172 grain M1 Bullet)
T173	Cartridge, Ball, Caliber .30 (T65E3 with all-steel serrated bullet)
T174	Cartridge, Ball, Caliber .30 (Standard Caliber .30 Round with all-steel serrated bullet)
T175	Cartridge, Spotting, Caliber .50 (Used with BAT weapon)
T176	Cartridge, Spotting Caliber .50 (Used with BAT weapon)
T177	Cartridge, Tracer, Caliber .50 (Used with BAT weapon)
T178	Cartridge, Practice, Caliber .50 (Used with BAT weapon)
T185	Cartridge, Bomb Release
T188	Cartridge, Tracer, Caliber .50
T189	Cartridge, Spotter-Tracer, Caliber .50
T189E1	Cartridge, Spotter-Tracer, Caliber .50 (M48)
T189E2	Cartridge, Spotter-Tracer, Caliber .50
T189E3	Cartridge, Spotter-Tracer, Caliber .50 (M48A1)
T190	Cartridge, Spotting, Caliber .50
T191	Cartridge, Spotting, Caliber .50
T192	Cartridge, Tracer, Caliber .50
T193	Cartridge, Tracer, Caliber .50
T194	Cartridge, Practice, Caliber .50
T195	Cartridge, Spotter-Tracer, Caliber .50
T196	Cartridge, Spotter-Tracer, Caliber. 50
T197	Cartridge, Spotter-Tracer, Caliber .50
T198	Cartridge, High Explosive-Incendiary, 20mm
T198E1	Cartridge, High Explosive-Incendiary, 20mm (M56)
T199	Cartridge, Practice, 20mm
T199E1	Cartridge, Practice, 20mm (M55)
T200	Cartridge, Ball, Caliber .22 (M39)
T200E1	Cartridge, Ball, Caliber .22 (M65)
T201	Cartridge, Ball, Caliber .60
T202	Cartridge, Armor-Piercing-Incendiary, Caliber .60
T203	Cartridge, Incendiary, Caliber .60
T204	Cartridge, Practice, 30mm
T205	Cartridge, Dummy, 30mm
T206	Cartridge, High Explosive-Incendiary, 30mm
T206E10	Cartridge, High Explosive-Incendiary, 30mm
T206E11	Cartridge, High Explosive-Incendiary, 30mm
T206E12	Cartridge, High Explosive-Incendiary, 30mm
T206E13	Cartridge, High Explosive-Incendiary, 30mm
T206E14	Cartridge, High Explosive-Incendiary, 30mm
T207	Cartridge, Test, High Pressure, 30mm
T208	Cartridge, Incendiary, 30mm
T221	Cartridge, Armor-Piercing-Incendiary, 20mm (with anvil)
T221E1	Cartridge, Armor-Piercing-Incendiary, 20mm (without anvil)
21E2	Cartridge, Armor-Piercing-Incendiary, 20mm
T221E3	Cartridge, Armor-Piercing-Incendiary, 20mm (M53)
T222	Cartridge, High Explosive-Incendiary, 30mm
T223	Cartridge, Test, High Pressure, 30mm
T224	Cartridge, Target Practice, 30mm
T225	Cartridge, Dummy, 30mm
T228	Cartridge, Dummy, 20mm (M51)
T230	Cartridge, Armor-Piercing-Incendiary-Tracer, 20mm (M52)
T232	Cartridge, Armor-Piercing-Incendiary-Tracer, 20mm
T233	Cartridge, Ball, Caliber .30 (Light Rifle) (M80)
T239	Cartridge, Ball, 30mm
T239E1	Cartridge, Ball, 30mm
T240	Cartridge, High Explosive-Incendiary, 30mm
T241	Cartridge, High Explosive-Incendiary, 20mm (M58)
T249	Cartridge, Practice, Caliber .50 (Used w/BAT weapon)
T249E1	Cartridge, Practice, Caliber .50 (Used w/BAT weapon)
T249E2	Cartridge, Practice, Caliber .50 (Used w/BAT weapon)
T251	Cartridge, High Pressure Test, Caliber .50 (Used w/BAT weapon)
T252	Cartridge, Dummy, Caliber .50 (Used w/BAT weapon)
T252E1	Cartridge, Dummy, Caliber .50 (Used w/BAT weapon)
T252E2	Cartridge, Dummy, Caliber .50 (Used w/BAT weapon)
T253	Cartridge, Test, High Pressure, 30mm
T266	Cartridge, High Explosive-Incendiary, 30mm
T267	Cartridge, Test, High Pressure, 30mm
T268	Cartridge, Ball, 30mm
T269	Cartridge, Dummy, 30mm
T270	Cartridge, High Explosive-Incendiary, 30mm
T271	Cartridge, Ball, 9mm
T272	Cartridge, 20mm, Dummy
T272E1	Cartridge, 20mm, Dummy
T272E2	Cartridge, 20mm, Dummy
T272E3	Cartridge, 20mm, Dummy
T272E4	Cartridge, 20mm, Dummy
T275	Cartridge, 7.62mm, Ball, NATO
T275E1	Cartridge, 7.62mm, Ball, NATO
T275E2	Cartridge, 7.62mm, Ball, NATO
T276	Cartridge, Caliber .38, Special
T283	Cartridge, 20mm, Armor-Piercing-Incendiary-Tracer
T291	Cartridge, Caliber .30, Match (M72)
T334	Cartridge, Practice, 30mm
MK101 Mod 0	Cartridge, 20mm, High Pressure Test
MK102 Mod 0	Cartridge, 20mm, Low Pressure Test
MK103 Mod 0	Cartridge, 20mm, Dummy
MK105 Mod 0	Cartridge, 20mm, Target Practice
MK106 Mod 0 and Mod 1	Cartridge, 20mm. High Explosive-Incendiary
MK107 Mod 0	Cartridge, 20mm, Armor Piercing-Incendiary
MK108 Mod 0	Cartridge, 20mm, Armor Piercing-Tracer

Chapter 20

Cartridge Identification by Measurement

THE PURPOSE of this table is to assist the cartridge collector, and other interested persons, in the identification of unknown cartridges or cartridge cases – based upon dimensional information. The following chart contains all cartridges found in this book, organized by order of increasing bullet diameter, then increasing case length. With only minor variations, these dimensions are constant within any specific cartridge type. Once these dimensions are known, other details will allow identification of the unknown cartridge or case. Those details (rim type, neck diameter, base diameter, shoulder diameter and cartridge length) are listed in separate columns of this table.

By measuring and eliminating options, the interested party can rapidly learn the proper name of the cartridge or case in hand. Once the user knows the cartridge name, he or she can look to the rightmost column and find the page where that cartridge is discussed in this tome.

Consider a hypothetical identification:

We take the case or cartridge in hand and measure bullet diameter or case neck internal diameter (assuming a fired case that is not damaged, this will usually be no more than about 0.004" larger than bullet diameter). This measurement is easily accomplished to about 0.001" accuracy with a dial caliper. We look in the third column of this table and find the approximate bullet diameter. This limits our search to a reasonable number of cartridges.

Next, we note case length, again measured with sufficient accuracy using a dial caliper. In most instances, this will narrow our search to one or, at most, a few choices. We will then review rim type and other aspects of the cartridge, in order to eliminate options. Eventually only one cartridge will remain.

As a specific example of this process, consider the following. We have a loaded cartridge, which has a military headstamp that is meaningless to us. The exposed bullet measures about 0.244". We cannot be certain of exact bullet diameter. Nevertheless, we can narrow our search to those listings with bullets of 0.243", 0.244" and 0.245" diameter – the bullet is clearly larger than 0.228" and smaller than 0.249". The case measures about 2.35" in length. This narrows our search to only two possibilities (within the specified range of bullet diameters) – 6x62mm Freres and 6mm Lee Navy. The base of the case measures about 0.445". This eliminates the 6x62mm Freres (0.474"). Further, the rim is about the same diameter as the base (rimless, case type C). We are satisfied with our identification – 6mm Lee Navy.

Cartridge	Case type	Bullet Dia.	Neck Dia.	Shoulder Dia.	Base Dia.	Rim Dia.	Rim Thick.	Case Length	Ctge. Length	Twist	Primer
10 Eichelberger Long Rifle	A	.1030	.122	.223	.225	.275	.043	.568			RF
10 Eichelberger Pup	A	.1030	.122	.247	.249	.308	.050	.767			SR
10 Eichelberger Squirrel	A	.1030	.122	.291	.294	.350	.065	.613			SR
2.7mm Kolibri	D	.107	.139		.140	.140		.37	.43	?	B
3mm Kolibri	D	.120	.150		.150	.150		.32	.43	?	B
12 Eichelberger Long Rifle	A	.1230	.140	.224	.225	.275	.043	.568			RF
12 Eichelberger Win Mag RF	A	.1230	.140	.238	.241	.293	.050	1.064			RF
12 Cooper	A	.123	.145	.247	.249	.308	.050	1.106			SR
12 Eichelberger Carbine	C	.123	.147	.356	.356	.360	.050	1.240			SR
14 Eichelberger Win Mag RF	A	.144	.161	.238	.241	.293	.050	1.064			RF
14 Eichelberger Dart	C	.144	.164	.274	.278	.301	.043	.640			SP
14 Cooper	A	.144	.166	.247	.249	.3085	.051	1.104			SR
14 Walker Hornet	A	.144	.170	.285	.294	.350	.065	1.350			SR
14 Jet Junior	A	.144	.177	.366	.378	.440	.059	1.260			SP
14 Eichelberger Bee	A	.144	.162	.329	.349	.408	.065	1.310			SR
14/222 Eichelberger	C	.144	.170	.356	.376	.378	.045	1.670			SR
14222	C	.144	.165	.356	.375	.375	.041	1.70	1.92	10	S
14/222 Eichelberger Mag	C	.144	.170	.356	.376	.378	.045	1.850			SR
4.25mm Liliput	D	.167	.198		.198	.198		.41	.56	?	B
17 Ackley Hornet	A	.172	.195	.290	.295	.345	.060	1.39	1.47	10	S
17 Remington	C	.172	.198	.355	.374	.377	.041	1.79	1.86	9	S
17223	C	.172	.199	.354	.375	.378	.041	1.76		10-12	S
17/222	C	.172	.199	.355	.375	.375	.041	1.69	1.82	10-12	S
17 Mach IV	C	.172	.199	.361	.375	.378	.041	1.40		10	S
17 Ackley Bee	A	.172	.201	.341	.350	.408	.060	1.35	1.78	10	S
4.85 British	C	.197	.220	.353	.375	.376	.041	1.925	2.455		B
5mm Clement Auto	C	.202	.223	.277	.281	.281	.025	.71	1.01	?	B

Cartridge	Case type	Bullet Dia.	Neck Dia.	Shoulder Dia.	Base Dia.	Rim Dia.	Rim Thick.	Case Length	Ctge. Length	Twist	Primer
5mm Bergmann	D	.203	.230		.273	.274	.020	.59	.96	?	B
204 Ruger	C	.204	.2310	.360	.375	.378	.045	1.850	2.260		SR
5mm Remington Magnum	A	.205	.225	.259	.259	.325	.050	1.020			
5.45x18mm Soviet	C	.210	.220		.300	.300		.70	.98	?	SB
5.7x28mm FN	C	.220	.249	.309	.310	.310		1.13	1.71		B
5.45mm Soviet	C	.221	.246	.387	.395	.394	.053	1.56	2.22		B
22 BB Cap	B	.222	.224		.224	.270	.040	.284	.343		
22 CB Cap	B	.222	.225		.225	.271	.040	.420	.520		
5.6x35Rmm Vierling (22 WCF)	A	.222	.241	.278	.300	.297		1.40	1.62		.177/1584/539
5.6x33mm & 5.6xR33mm Rook	C/A	.222	.248	.318	.325	.326/.366		1.31	1.62/1.64		.177/1584/467/468
22 Winchester Auto	B	.222	.250		.250	.310	.040	.665	.915		
22 Short	B	.223	.224		.225	.273	.040	.423	.686		
22 Short/40-grain RWS load	B	.223	.224		.225	.272	.042	.415	.798		
22 Long	B	.223	.224		.225	.275	.040	.595	.880		
22 Long Rifle	B	.223	.224		.225	.275	.040	.595	.975		
22 Stinger	B	.223	.224		.225	.275	.040	.694	.975		
22 Extra Long	B	.223	.225		.225	.275	.040	.750	1.16		
297/230 Morris Extra Long	A	.223	.240	.274	.296	.248		1.125	1.45		
22 Hornet	A	.223	.242	.274	.294	.345	.060	1.40	1.72	16	S
5.6x36Rmm (22 Hornet)	A	.223	.242	.274	.294	.345	.060	1.40	1.72	16	
22 Remington Auto	B	.223	.245		.245	.290		.663	.920		
22 Remington Jet	A	.223	.247	.350	.376	.440	.055	1.28	1.58	10	SP
222 Rimmed	A	.223	.249	.352	.374	.462		1.682	2.144	14	S
22 Winchester Magnum RF	B	.224	.240		.241	.291	.046	1.052	1.35		
218 Bee	A	.224	.241	.331	.349	.408	.060	1.35	1.68	16	S
218 Mashburn Bee	A	.224	.241	.340	.349	.408	.060	1.34	1.75	16	S
22 WRF & Remington Special	B	.224	.242		.243	.295	.046	.960	1.17		
22 Kilbourn Hornet	A	.224	.242	.286	.294	.345	.060	1.39	1.70	14-16	S
224 KayChuk	A	.224	.243	.293	.294	.347	.060	1.35	1.60	10-15	S
22 PPC	C	.224	.245	.430	.440	.441	.050	1.52	1.96	14	S
22 Waldog	C	.224	.245	.431	.440	.441	.053	1.375	1.820	14	S
22 BR Remington	C	.224	.245	.450	.466	.468	.045	1.502	2.00	14-16	S
R2 Lovell	A	.224	.246	.295	.315	.382		1.63	1.80	16	S
224 Weatherby Magnum	E	.224	.247	.405	.413	.425	.045	1.92	2.44	14	L
22 Super Jet	A	.224	.248	.372	.379	.440	.055	1.266	1.75	16	S
223 Remington	C	.224	.249	.349	.373	.375	.041	1.76	2.10	12	S
5.56mm NATO	C	.224	.249	.349	.373	.375	.041	1.76	2.26	9	Bx
223 Ackley Improved	C	.224	.250	.365	.375	.378	.041	1.760	V	7-12	S
22 Cheetah	C	.224	.250	.451	.466	.470	.048	2.00	2.36	14	S
221 Fireball	C	.224	.251	.355	.375	.375	.040	1.40	1.82	14	SP
219 Donaldson Wasp	A	.224	.251	.402	.418	.497	.058	1.71	2.10	14	L
224 RC Maxi	A	.224	.252	.354	.375	.431	.055	1.576	2.048	14	S
219 Zipper	A	.224	.252	.364	.421	.497	.058	1.94	2.26	16	L
22 Dasher	C	.224	.252	.462	.470	.470	.050	1.54	V	12-14	S
MMJ5.7mm (22 Spitfire)	C	.224	.253	.332	.353	.356	.046	1.29	1.65	14	L
222 Remington	C	.224	.253	.355	.375	.375	.041	1.70	2.15	14	S
222 Remington Magnum	C	.224	.253	.355	.375	.375	.041	1.85	2.21	14	S
22/30-30 Improved	A	.224	.253	.391	.422	.502	.058	2.03	2.48	14	L
22-250 Ackley Improved	C	.224	.253	.445	.466	.470	.045	1.910	V	7-12	L
5.6x50mm Magnum/ 5.6x50Rmm Magnum	C/A	.224	.254	.355	.375	.376/(?)	.038	1.97	2.21		?
22-303	A	.224	.254	.4085	.455	.540	.058	2.031	2.48	14	L
22-250 Remington	C	.224	.254	.412	.466	.470	.045	1.91	2.33	14	L
226 JDJ	A	.224	.256	.410	.419	.467	.045	1.93	V	9	L
220 Swift	G	.224	.260	.402	.443	.472	.045	2.20	2.68	14	L
225 Winchester	A	.224	.260	.406	.422	.473	.045	1.93	2.50	14	L
220 Weatherby Rocket	G	.224	.260	.430	.443	.472	.045	2.21	2.68	14	L
22-243	C	.224	.260	.454	.471	.473	.048	2.045	V	9-14	L

Cartridge	Case type	Bullet Dia.	Neck Dia.	Shoulder Dia.	Base Dia.	Rim Dia.	Rim Thick.	Case Length	Ctge. Length	Twist	Primer
220 Wotkyns Wilson Arrow	G	.224	.261	.402	.443	.472	.045	2.205	2.70	14	L
223 WSSM	I	.244	.272	.544	.555	.535	.054	1.67	2.175 (2.360)	10	L
6mm Dasher	C	.224	.271	.462	.470	.470	.050	1.54	V	8-16	S
5.6x57mm RWS 5.6x57Rmm RWS	C/A	.224	.281	.436	.469	.470/(?)		2.24	2.54		?
297/230 Morris Short	A	.225	.240	.274	.294	.347		0.58	0.89		.177/69
297/230 Morris Long	A	.225	.240	.274	.295	.345		0.80	1.1		.177/69
5.5mm Velo Dog	B	.225	.248		.253	.308		1.12	1.35	8.2	SPB
224 Clark	C	.225	.275	.455	.471	.473	.045	2.237	3.075	9	L
22-15-60 Stevens	B	.226	.243		.265	.342		2.01	2.26	12	S
5.6x61mm & 5.6x61Rmm Vom Hofe Super Express	C/A	.227	.259/.260	.468/.470	.476/.479	0480/.533	?/.062	2.39	3.13		.217/5603/431M
22 Winchester CF	A	.228	.241	.278	.295	.342	.058	1.39	1.61	16	S
22 Extra Long (Maynard)**	B	.228	.252		.252	.310		1.17	1.41	16	SO***
22 Savage High Power	A	.228	.252	.360	.416	.500	.056	2.05	2.51	12	L
5.6x52Rmm (22 Savage High Power)	A	.228	.252	.360	.416	.500	.062	2.05	2.51		.217/5603/545
22 Newton	C	.228	.256	.420	.471	.474	.045	2.23	2.85	14-16	L
228 Ackley Magnum	C	.228	.265	.445	.470	.473	.045	2.25	2.55	12	L
6mm PPC	C	.243	.260	.430	.441	.442	0.50	1.50	2.12	12	S
6x29.5Rmm Stahl	A	.243	.262	.301	.320	.370		1.16	1.44		.177/1584
6mm Bench Rest Remington	C	.243	.263	.457	.466	.468	.045	1.52	2.19	12	S
6 BR R	C	.243	.263	.459	.471	.528	.060	1.53	2.44	8	L
6mm TCU	C	.243	.265	.354	.376	.378	.041	1.74	2.25	12	S
6mm223	C	.243	.266	.354	.376	.378	.041	1.76	2.26	10-12	S
6mm47	C	.243	.267	.348	.372	.373	.041	1.81	2.31	12	L
6mm Cheetah	C	.243	.260	.456	.470	.473	.049	2.00			LR
240 Weatherby	E	.243	.271	.432	.453	.473	.045	2.50	3.06	10	L
6x62mm Freres/ 6x62Rmm Freres	C/A	.243	.271	.451	.474	.470/(?)		2.42	3.13		.217
240 Hawk	C	.243	.276	.4540	.4712	.473	.049	2.485			
6mm Norma BR	C	.243	.271	.458	.469	.470	.051	1.56	2.44	8	S
6mm JDJ	A	.243	.272	.415	.421	.470	.045	1.905	2.65	V	L
6mm SAW	C	.243	.273	.382	.410	.410		1.779	2.58		L
6mm-250 Walker	C	.243	.274	.420	.468	.470	.045	1.91	2.21	12	L
6mm-06	C	.243	.274	.441	.470	.467	.045	2.494	3.34	9-10	L
243 Catbird	C	.243	.274	.455	.470	.467	.045	2.540	3.34	10	L
6mm/244 Ackley Imp	C	.243	.274	.457	.470	.470	.048	2.230	2.80	9	L
6mm/30-30 Improved	A	.243	.275	.392	.422	.502	.058	2.03	2.55	9-10	L
243 Ackley Improved	C	.243	.275	.457	.470	.467	.045	2.045	2.80	10	L
6.17 Spitfire	C	.243	.275	.510	.530	.530	.050	2.05	2.8	10	L
6.17 Flash	C	.243	.275	.510	.530	.530	.050	2.80	3.55	12	L
6mm Thermos Bottle	C	.243	.275	.576	.580	.578	.060	1.35	V	8	L
244 Remington	C	.243	.276	.429	.470	.472	.045	2.23	2.90	12	L
6mm Remington /244 Remington	C	.243	.276	.429	.470	.472	.045	2.23	2.91 2.825	9 12	L
243 Winchester	C	.243	.276	.454	.470	.470	0.49	2.05	2.71	10	L
6mm-284	I	.243	.276	.475	.500	.473	.049	2.165	2.80	9-10	L
6x57mm Mauser	C	.243	.284	.420	.475	.476	.045	2.23	2.95		.217/5603/494
244 (6mm) Halger Magnum	A	.243	.287	.435	.467	.470		2.25	3.04		.217/5603
6x58mm & 6x58Rmm Forster	C/A	.243	.285/.284	.437	.470/.471	.468/.532	.045	2.26	3.06		.217/5603/489/ 489A
244 Magnum (H&H)	E	.244	.263	.445	.508	.532		2.78	3.58		.217/60
6mm Lee Navy	C	.244	.278	.402	.445	.448	.050	2.35	3.11	7 1/2	L
240 Magnum Flanged	A	.245	.274	.402	.448	.513		2.50	3.25		.217/81
240 Magnum Rimless (240 Apex)	E	.245	.274	.403	.450	467	.035	2.49	3.21		.217/81
243 WSSM	I	.243	.287	.544	.555	.535	.054	1.67	2.060 (2.360)	10	L
25 Short	B	.246	.245		.245	.290		.468	.780		
297/250 Rook	A	.250	.267	.294	.295	.343		0.82	1.1		.177/69

Cartridge	Case type	Bullet Dia.	Neck Dia.	Shoulder Dia.	Base Dia.	Rim Dia.	Rim Thick.	Case Length	Ctge. Length	Twist	Primer
6.5x40Rmm	B	.250	.290		.396	.451		1.58	2.07		?
25 Stevens Short	B	.251	.275		.276	.333		.599	.877		
25 Automatic	D	.251	.276		.277	.298	.038	.62	.91	16	SP
25 Stevens	B	.251	.276		.276	.333		1.125	1.395		
242 Rimless	C	.253	.281	.405	.465	.465		2.38	3.20		.217/59
246 Purdey	A	.253	.283	.401	.474	.544		2.32	3.03		
255 Rook	A	.255	.274	.328	.344	.401		1.17	1.43		.162
25-20 Marlin	A	.257	.274	.329	.349	.405		1.33	?	13-14	S
25-20 Winchester	A	.257	.274	.329	.349	.405	.060	1.33	1.60	13-14	S
25-20 Single Shot	A	.257	.275	.296	.315	.378		1.63	1.90	12-15	S
25 WSSM	I	.257	.299	.5443	.555	.535	.040	1.670	2.360		LR
25 Ugalde	C	.257	.275	.368	.373	.375	.041	1.76	2.27	10	S
256 Winchester Magnum	A	.257	.277	.378	.378	.440	.055	1.30	1.53	14	SP
25-21 Stevens	B	.257	.280		.300	.376		2.05	2.30	14	S
25-35 Winchester	A	.257	.280	.355	.420	.500 (.506)	.059	2.04	2.53	8	L
25 Remington	C	.257	.280	.355	.420	.421	.045	2.04	2.54	10	L
6.5x52Rmm (2535 WCF)	A	.257	.280	.355	.420	.500		2.04	2.53		.217/5603/519
25-36 Marlin	A	.257	.281	.358	.416	.499	.056	2.12	2.50	9	S
25-25 Stevens	B	.257	.282		.323	.376		2.37	2.63	14	S
256 Winchester Magnum	A	.257	.283	.370	.378	.440	.055	1.30	1.53	14	S
6.5x27Rmm	A	.257	.284	.348	.379	.428		1.06	1.54		.177/1584/476
250/3000 Improved	C	.257	.284	.445	.467	.473	.045	1.91	2.52	10	L
257 Weatherby Magnum	E	.257	.285	.490	.511	.530	.048	2.55	3.25	12	L
25-284	I	.257	.285	.495	.500	.473	.049	2.17	2.80	10	L
250 Savage	C	.257	.286	.413	.468	.470	.045	1.91	2.52 (2.515)	14	L
25-06 Remington	C	.257	.287	.441	.470	.471	.045	2.49	3.00	10-12	L
257 JDJ	A	.257	.288	.415	.421	.473	.045	1.905	2.81	V	L
25-06 Ackley Improved	C	.257	.288	.455	.470	.467	.045	2.49	3.34	10	L
257 Improved	C	.257	.288	.457	.471	.474	.045	2.23	2.78	10	L
6.53 Scramjet	C	.257	.289	.510	.530	.530	.055	2.80	3.575	12	L
257 Mini Dreadnaught	G	.257	.290	.425	.445	.467	.045	2.145	V	10	L
257 Roberts (257 Roberts +P)	C	.257	.290	.430	.468	.473	.045	2.23	2.74	10-12	L
25 Krag	A	.257	.293	.415	.457	.540	.059	2.242.31	V	10	L
25 Ackley Krag	A	.257	.293	.442	.457	.540	.059	2.31		10	L
25/303	A	.257	.294	.400	.455	.541	.058	2.22	3.05	10	L
6.5x48Rmm Sauer	B	.260	.284		.433	.495		1.88	2.43		.217/5603/463A
6.5mm MS	C	.263	.287	.424	.447	.450		2.09	3.02	7.8	B
6.5mm Arisaka	G	.263	.293	.425	.455	.471	.045	2.00	2.98	7.9	B
6.5 Mini Dreadnaught	G	.263	.296	.425	.445	.467	.045	2.150	V	8-9	L
6.5 Dutch & Romanian	A	.263	.297	.423	.450	.526	.066	2.10	3.03	9.8	B
6.5 Daudeteau	G	.263	.298	.466	.480	.524	.065	2.09	3.02		B
6.5x53.5mm Daudeteau	G	.263	.298	.466	.490	.524		2.09	3.02		475A
6.5mm JDJx30	A	.264	.285	.409	.419	.497	.058	2.03	V	9	L
6.5mm Whisper	C	.264	.286	.357	.372	.375	.041	1.36	V	V	S
6.5mm Grendel	C	.264	.293	.428	.439	.441	.059	1.526			SR
6.5mm Bergmann	C	.264	.289	.325	.367	.370	.025	.87	1.23	?	B
6.5 Leopard	C	.264	.295	.539	.551	.533	.049	2.093		9	LR
6.5x54mm Mauser	C	.264	.289	.432	.468	.463		2.12	2.67		.217/5603/457A
264 Hawk	C	.264	.296	.454	.471	.473	.049	2.485			LR
264 (6.5mm) Win. Magnum	E	.264	.289	.490	.515 (.5127)	.532	.047	2.52	3.29	9	L
256 (6.5mm) Newton	C	.264	.290	.430	.469	.473	.045	2.44	3.40	10	L
6.5x58Rmm Sauer	B	.264	.291		.433	.501		2.30	3.08		.217/5603/463
6.5 TCU	C	.264	.292	.368	.376	.378	.041	1.749	2.60	9-10	S
6.5x57mm Mauser & RWS 6.5x57Rmm Mauser & RWS	C/A	.264	.292	.430	.471/.470	.474/.521		2.23/2.24	3.16/3.18		.217/5603/404A(?)
6.5mm JDJ #2	A	.264	.292	.450	.466	.502	.059	2.00	V	9	L
6.5mm JDJ	A	.264	.293	.410	.419	.467	.045	1.93	V	8-9	L
6.5mm Portuguese	C	.264	.293	.426	.468	.465		2.28	3.22	7.8	B
6.5x58mm Portuguese	C	.264	.293	.426	.468	.465		2.28	3.22		.217/5603/457

Cartridge	Case type	Bullet Dia.	Neck Dia.	Shoulder Dia.	Base Dia.	Rim Dia.	Rim Thick.	Case Length	Ctge. Length	Twist	Primer
6.5mm Swedish	C	.264	.294	.420	.480	.480		2.16	3.15	7.9	B
6.508 A-Square/260 Rem	C	.264	.294	.452	.468	.467	.045	.025	2.80	9-10	LR
6.5x65mm RWS 6.5x65Rmm RWS	C/A	.264	.296	.430	.474/.475	.470/.531		2.56	3.15		?
6.5mm-257	C	.264	.297	.429	.470	.467	.048	2.233	2.75	V	L
6.5x55 Swedish	C	.264	.297	.435	.480 (.477)	.480 (.479)	.050	2.16	3.15	7.9	L
6.5284 Norma	I	.264	.297	.475	.500	.470	.051	2.17	3.23	8-9	SR
6.71 Phantom	C	.264	.297	.510	.530	.530	.055	2.05	2.8	10	L
6.71 Blackbird	C	.264	.297	.524	.544	.544	.055	2.80	3.575	10-12	L
6.5 LBFM	C	.264	.297	.570	.580	.578	.060	1.806	V	8	L
6.5-06/256-06	C	.264	.300	.439	.471	.473	.045	2.50	3.30	9-10	L
6.506 Improved	C	.264	.300	.455	.471	.473	.045	2.50	3.30	9-10	L
6.5x58Rmm Krag/Jorgensen	A	.264	.300	.460	.500	.575		2.29	3.25		.217/5603
6.5 Remington Magnum	E	.264	.300	.490	.512	.532	.047	2.17	2.80	9	L
6.5x61mm Mauser 6.5x61Rmm Mauser	C/A	.264	.297/.296	.452	.477	.479/.532		2.40	3.55		.217/5603/431/L431M
6.5mm Carcano	C	.265	.295	.430	.445	.448	.045	2.05	3.02	19.3/8.3*	B
6.5x68mm RWS 6.5x68Rmm RWS	C/A	.265	.295	.481	.520	.510/(?)		2.66	3.27		.238/1698
256 Gibbs Magnum	E	.265	.298	.427	.473	.476		2.17	3.04		
26 Rimless BSA	C	.267	.306	.445	.513	.530		2.39	3.24		.217/59
6.8x57mm Chinese	C	.277	?	?	?	?	?	?	2.25	?	?
270 REN	B	.277	.295		.298	.350	.060	1.29		10	S
6.8 SPC	C	.277	.306	.401	.421	.417	.049	1.686	2.260		LR
270 JDJ	A	.277	.305	.415	.419	.467	.045	1.905	2.875	10	L
270 IHMSA	C	.277	.305	.448	.471	.473	.045	1.866	2.60	10	L
270 Hawk	C	.277	.308	.453	.471	.473	.049	2.486			LR
270 Weatherby Magnum	E	.277	.305	.490	.511	.530	.048	2.55	3.25	12	L
270 Winchester	C	.277	.307	.440	.468	.470	.045	2.54	3.28	10	L
270 Savage	C	.277	.308	.450	.470	.470	.045	1.88	2.62	10	L
270 WSM	I	.277	.314	.538	.555	.535	.054	2.10	2.56 (2.860)	10	L
7mm Nambu	C	.280	.296	.337	.351	.359		.78	1.06	12.5	B
280 British	C	.283	.313	.448	.470	.473		1.71	2.54	?	B
7mm TCU	C	.284	.302	.350	.373	.375	.041	1.74	2.28	10	S
7mm Whisper	C	.284	.306	.357	.372	.375	.041	1.36	V	V	S
7mm Hawk	C	.284	.315	.454	.471	.473	.049	2.485			LR
6.8 SPC	C	.277	.306	.401	.421	.417	.049	1.686	2.260		LR
730 Waters	A	.284	.306	.399	.422 (.4215)	.506	.058	2.04	2.52	9 1/2	L
7mm-30 JDJ	A	.284	.306	.409	.419	.497	.058	2.03	V	9	L
7x33mm Finnish/Sako	C	.284	.307	.365	.388	.390		1.30	1.73		?
7x72Rmm	B	.284	.311		.425	.482		2.84	3.48		.217/5603/573
7mm IntR	A	.284	.311	.402	.422	.502	.058	2.04	2.52	10	L
7mm JDJ	A	.284	.312	.415	.421	.473	.045	1.905	V	9	L
7mm IHMSA	C	.284	.312	.448	.471	.473	.045	1.866	2.60	9-10	L
7mm JRS	C	.284	.312	.454	.470	.467	.045	2.525	3.455	10	L
280 JDJ	C	.284	.312	.455	.470	.467	.045	2.505	V	10	L
7mm Weatherby Magnum	E	.284	.312	.490	.511	.530	.048	2.55	3.25	12	L
7x64 Brenneke	C	.284	.313	.422	.463	.468	.045	2.51	3.21		L
7mm JDJ #2	A	.284	.313	.450	.466	.502	.059	2.00	V	9	L
280 Ackley Improved	C	.284	.313	.455	.470	.467	.045	2.540	3.34	10	L
7mm-300 Weatherby	E	.284	.313	.490	.511	.532	.048	2.825	3.65	10	L
7mm Dakota	C	.284	.314	.531	.544	.544	.042	2.50	3.33	10	L
(7mm Rigby Magnum)	A	.284	.315	.406	.456	.524		2.49	3.24		.243/34
280 Remington 7mm Express Remington	C	.284	.315	.441	.470	.472	.045	2.54	3.33	10 1/2	L
285 OKH	C	.284	.315	.442	.470	.472	.045	2.55	3.35	10	L
7 STE	A	.284	.315	.454	.467	.502	.059	2.1	2.54	10	L
7mm-08 Remington	C	.284	.315	.454	.470	.473	.050	2.04 (2.035)	2.80	9	L
7x73mm Vom Hofe Belted	E	.284	.315	.483	.527	.533		2.87	3.88		.217/5603/575

Cartridge	Case type	Bullet Dia.	Neck Dia.	Shoulder Dia.	Base Dia.	Rim Dia.	Rim Thick.	Case Length	Ctge. Length	Twist	Primer
7mm Remington Magnum	E	.284	.315	.490	.511	.525	.047	2.50	3.24	9 1/2	L
7x66mm Vom Hofe Super Express	C	.284	.316	.485	.543	.510	.048	2.58	3.25		.217/?/603
7mm STW	E	.284	.316	.487	.513	.532	.048	2.85	3.65	9-9.5	L
7x75Rmm Vom Hofe Super Express	A	.284	.318	.416	.468	.519	.050	2.95	3.68		.217
275 Flanged Magnum 275 No. 2 Magnum	A	.284	.318	.450	.510	.582		2.50	3.26		.217
7.21 Firehawk	C	.284	.318	.524	.544	.544	.055	2.80	3.55	12	L
7.21 Tomahawk	C	.284	.318	.557	.577	.577	.060	2.05	2.80	10	L
7.21 Firebird	C	.284	.318	.557	.577	.577	.060	2.80	3.6	12	L
7x57mm Ackley Improved	C	.284	.319	.457	.470	.467	.048	2.235	3.06	8-10	L
284 Winchester	I	.284	.320	.465 (.4748)	.495 (.500)	.470	.049	2.17	2.75	10	L
7mm Mauser	C	.284	.320	.420 (.4294)	.470	.474	.046	2.24 (2.235)	3.06	8-10	L
7x57mm	C	.284	.320	.420	.470	.474	.055	2.23	3.06	9	B
7x57mm Mauser/7x57Rmm Mauser	C/A	.284	.320	.420	.470	.474/.521	.035/.05 6	2.24	3.06/3.07		.217/5603/ 380DM93A
7x61 Sharpe & Hart	E	.284	.320	.478	.515	.532	.048	2.40	3.27	12	L
276 Enfield	C	.284	.321	.460	.528	.521		2.35	3.25	9	B
7mm Canadian Magnum	I	.284	.322	.530	.544	.532	.046	2.83	3.60	9-12	L
275 Rigby (7x57)	C	.284	.324	.428	.474	.475		2.24	3.07		.217
275 Belted Magnum	E	.284	.325	.454	.513	.532		2.50	3.42		.217/81
275 H&H Magnum	E	.284	.375	.375	.513	.532	.048	2.50	3.30	9 1/2	L
7x64mm Brenneke 7x65Rmm Brenneke	C/A	.284	.305/.308	.422	.463	.468/.521	.055	2.51/2.53	3.21		.217/5603/557/ 557A
7mm Bench Rest	C	.284	Based on Rem. 308 BR case short- ened to 1.50	SP							
28-30-120 Stevens	B	.285	.309		.357	.412		2.51	2.82	14	L
276 Pederson	C	.285	.314	.389	.449	.451		2.02	2.85	?	Bx
30 Short	B	.286	.292		.292	.346		.515	.822		
280 Flanged (280 Lancaster)	A	.287	.316	.423	.535	.607		2.60	3.62		.217/60
280 Ross	G	.287	.317	.404	.534	.556		2.59	3.50		.217/59
7mmRem. SAUM	I	.284	.320	.534	.550	.534	.050	2.035	2.450 (2.825)	9.5	L
7mm WSM	I	.284	.321	.538	.555	.535	.054	2.10	2.560 (2.860)	9.5	L
7mm Rem. UltraMag	I	.284	.322	.525	.550	.534	.050	2.85	3.450 (3.600)	9.5	L
30 Long	B	.288	.288		.288	.340		.613	1.020		
280 Jeffery. (33/280 Jeffery)	C	.288	.317	.504	.542	.538		2.50	3.45		.217/59
7.62mm Nagant (Russian)	B	.295	.286		.335	.388		1.53	1.53	9.5	B
7.35mm Carcano	C	.298	.323	.420	.445	.449		2.01	2.98	10	B
32 Protector	B	.300	.310		.310	.352	.040	.350	.555	?	SP
300 (295) Rook	B	.300	.317		.319	.369		1.17	1.42		.177/69
300 Sherwood	B	.300	.318		.320	.370		1.54	2.02		.177/69
7.65mm Roth Sauer	D	.301	.332		.335	.335		.51	.84	14.2	B
30 Remington	C	.307	.328	.402	.420	.421	.045	2.03	2.525	12	L
7.62mm Russian Tokarev	C	.307	.330	.370	.380	.390		.97	1.35	10	B
30 Borchardt	C	.307	.331	.370	.385	.390		.99	1.34	?	SPB
300 Phoenix	C	.308	?	?	.589	.586	.060	2.50	3.60	?	L
30 (7.65mm) Luger	C	.308	.322	.374	.388	.391	.045	.75	1.15	9.8	SPB
7.62 MicroWhisper	C	.308	.328	.382	.389	.392	.045	.846	V	V	SP/SR
30-30 Winchester	A	.308	.328	.402	.422 (.4215)	.502	.058	2.03 (2.039)	2.53	12	L
30 American	A	.308	.328	.402	.422	.502	.058	2.03	2.53	?	S
30-30 Ackley Improved	A	.308	.328	.405	.422	.502	.058	2.04	2.54	12	L
30-30 Wesson	A	.308	.329	.330	.380	.440		1.66	2.50	12	L
7.63 MiniWhisper	C	.308	.329	.375	.381	.385	.045	.985	V	V	SP/SR
30 Herrett	A	.308	.329	.405	.421	.505	.058	1.61	2.01	14	L
300 Whisper	C	.308	.330	.369	.375	.375	.041	1.50	2.575	V	S
30-378 Wby Mag	K	.308	.330	.560	.589	.603/.580	.060	2.90	3.865	10	L
7.63 (7.65) Mannlicher	D	.308	.331		.332	.334	.030	.84	1.12	10	B

Cartridge	Case type	Bullet Dia.	Neck Dia.	Shoulder Dia.	Base Dia.	Rim Dia.	Rim Thick.	Case Length	Ctge. Length	Twist	Primer
30 (7.63mm) Mauser	C	.308	.332	.370	.381	.390	.045	.99	1.36	7.9	SPB
7.62x74Rmm Meacham	A	.308	.332	.450	.466	.522	.052	2.90	3.95	13	L
300 LBFM	C	.308	.332	.575	.580	.576	.060	2.05	V	8	L
30 USA Rimless	C	.308	.333	.417	.454	.456	.054	2.31	3.10	?	L
308 CorBon	C	.308	.333	.532	.545	.532	.050	2.08	2.80	10	L
30 Kurz	C	.308	.334	.443	.470	.473	.045	1.29	1.65	12	L
7.5mm Schmidt-Rubin	C	.308	.334	.452	.494	.496	.058	2.18	3.05	10.5	B
300 Winchester Magnum	E	.308	.334	.4891	.5126	.530	.046	2.60 (2.62)	3.30	10	L
308 Baer	E	.308	.334	.494	.511	.532	.048	2.85	V	9-11	L
30 Carbine	D	.308	.335		.355	.360		1.29	1.65	16	Bx
30 Carbine	D	.308	.335		.355	.360	.046	1.29	1.65	16	S
309 JDJ	A	.308	.335	.453	.470	.514	.058	2.20	3.16	?	L
30-06 JDJ	C	.308	.335	.455	.470	.467	.045	2.455	V	10	L
30-8mm Remington	E	.308	.337	.487	.511	.532	.047	2.85	3.65	10	L
300 Weatherby Magnum	E	.308	.337	.495	.513 (.5117)	.530	.048	2.82 (2.825)	3.56	12	L
30 Army (30-40 Krag)	A	.308	.338	.415 (0.419)	.457 (0.4577)	.540		2.31	3.10 (3.089)	10	Bx
30-40 Krag	A	.308	.338	.415 (.419)	.457 (.4577)	.540	.059	2.31	3.10 (3.089)	10	L
7.62x51mm NATO (308 Win.)	C	.308	.338	.447	.466	.470		2.01	2.75	12	Bx
300 Belted Magnum (300 H&H)	E	.308	.338	.447	.513	.530		2.85	3.60		.217/60
300 H&H Magnum	E	.308	.338	.447	.513	.530	.048	2.85	3.60	10	L
308x1.5Inch	C	.308	.338	.450	.466	.470	.048	1.50	2.05	10-12	L
30 Flanged Magnum (30 Super)	A	.308	.338	.450	.517	.572		2.93	3.69		
300 Dakota	C	.308	.338	.531	.544	.544	.046	2.55	3.33	10	L
300 Savage	C	.308	.339	.443 (.4466)	.470	.470	.045	1.87	2.62	12	L
30 IHMSA	C	.308	.339	.448	.471	.473	.045	1.866	2.60	10-12	L
300 Pegasus	C	.308	.339	.566	.580	.580	.058	2.99	3.75	10	L
7.5mm French MAS	C	.308	.340	.441	.480	.482	.054	2.11	2.99	10	B
7.62x63mm U.S. (3006)	C	.308	.340	.441	.470	.473		2.49	3.34	10	Bx
30-06 Springfield	C	.308	.340	.441	.470	.473	.045	2.49	3.34	10	L
30-03 Government	C	.308	.340	.441	.470	.473	.045	2.54	3.34	10	L
306 Ackley Improved	C	.308	.340	.454	.470	.473	.045	2.49	3.35	10	L
308 Norma Magnum		.308	.340	.489	.514	.529	.048	2.56	3.30	10-12	L
30-338 Winchester Magnum	E	.308	.340	.491	.513	.532	.048	2.50		10	L
300 Rem. SAUM	I	.308	.344	.534	.550	.534	.050	2.015	2.450 (2.825)	10	L
300 WSM	I	.308	.344	.538	.555	.535	.054 (2.860)	2.10	2.560	10	L
30 Newton	C	.308	.340	.491	.523	.525		2.52	3.35	10-12	L
30 Cody	C	.308	.340	.544	.589	.586	.058	2.875	3.67	10	L
7.82 Patriot	C	.308	.340	.557	.577	.577	.060	2.05	2.8	12	L
7.82 Warbird	C	.308	.340	.557	.577	.577	.060	2.80	3.60	14	L
300 Canadian Magnum	I	.308	.342	.530	.544	.532	.046	2.83	3.60	10	L
30R Blaser	A	.308	.343	.441	.480	.531		2.68	3.80		?
307 Winchester	G	.308	.344	.454	.470	.506	.059	2.02 (2.015)	2.60 (2.56)	12	L
308 Winchester	C	.308	.344	.454	.470	.470	.049	2.01 (2.015)	2.75	12	L
30-284 Winchester	I	.308	.344	.475	.500	.470	.050	2.017	2.80	10	L
300 Rem. UltraMag	I	.308	.344	.525	.550	.534	.050	2.085 (3.600)	3.450	10	L
32-40 Remington	A	.309	.330	.358	.453	.535		2.13	3.25	16	S
7.62x45mm Czech M52	C	.309	.334	.412	.441	.440		1.77	2.36		B
32 Automatic	H	.309	.336		.336	.354	.040	.68	1.03	16	SP
7.65mm MAS (French)	D	.309	.336		.337	.337		.78	1.19	?	B
35 S&W Auto	D	.309	.345		.346	.348		.67	.97	12	SP
7.62mm Nagant	A	.310	.332	.453	.484	.564	.055	2.11	3.02	9.5	B
7.62X53Rmm (M43) Russian	C	.310	.340	.394	.443	.445		1.52	2.20	9.4	B
7.62x39mm	C	.311	.340 (.337)	.344 (.396)	.438 (.433)	.440	.053	1.52 (1.528)	2.20	9.4	S
303 British	A	.311	.337	.402	.458	.530		2.21	3.05	10	B

Cartridge	Case type	Bullet Dia.	Neck Dia.	Shoulder Dia.	Base Dia.	Rim Dia.	Rim Thick.	Case Length	Ctge. Length	Twist	Primer
303 British	A	.311	.338	.401	.458	.530	.062	2.21 (2.222)	3.05 (3.075)	10	L
7.7mm Arisaka	C	.311	.338	.431	.472	.474	.042	2.28	3.13	9.8	B
375/303 Westley Richards	A	.311	.343	.390	.457	.505		2.50	3.36		
32 Long Rifle	B	.312	.318		.318	.377		.937	1.223		
32-20 Winchester	A	.312	.326	.338 (.3424)	.353	.405	.058	1.32 (1.315)	1 59	20	S
32-20 Marlin	A	.312	.326	.338	.353	.405		1.32	?	20	S
32-30 Remington	A	.312	.332	.357	.378	.437		1.64	2.01	16	S
32 H&R Magnum	B	.312	.333		.333	.371	.050	1.08	1.35	16	SP
32 S&W	B	.312	.334		.335	.375	.045	.61	.92	16-18	SP
32 S&W Long	B	.312	.335		.335	.375	.048	.93	1.27	16-18	SP
32-35 Stevens & Maynard	B	.312	.339		.402	.503		1.88	2.29	16	S
303 British	A	.312	.340	.401	.460	.540		2.21	3.09		
303 Magnum	C	.312	.345	.462	.530	.557		2.35	3.25		
32 Short Colt	B	.313	.313		.318	.374	.045	.63	1.00	16	SP
32 Long Colt	B	.313	.313		.318	.374	.045	.92	1.26	16	SP
7.65x53mm Argentine Mauser	C	.313	.338	.429	.468	.470	.040	2.09	2.95	10	B
32-40 Bullard	A	.315	.332	.413	.453	.510		1.85	2.26	16	S
32 Extra Long	B	.316	.317		.318	.378		1.150	1.570		
32 Extra Short	B	.316	.318		.317	.367		.398	.645		
32 Short	B	.316	.318		.318	.377		.575	.948		
32 Long	B	.316	.318		.318	.377		.791	1.215		
8x48Rmm Sauer	B	.316	.344		.432	.500	.040	1.88	2.58		.254/1775/462A
8x51mm Mauser/8x51RmmJ Mauser	C/A	.316	.344	.436	.467	.467/.515	.045/.06 0	1.98	2.67/2.68		.217/5603/366/ L366L2
8.15x46Rmm	A	.316	.346	.378	.421	.484		1.82	2.28		.250/1794/455
32 Long, CF*	B	.317	.318		.321	.369		0.82	1.35	20	S
32 Ballard Extra Long*	B	.317	.318		.321	.369		1.24	1.80	22	S
320 Revolver	B	.317	.320		.322	.350		.62	.90	22	B
7.5mm Swiss Army	B	.317	.335		.345	.407		.89	1.29	?	B
8x57Rmm 360	A	.318	.333	.375	.427	.485		2.24	2.96		
8x64mmJ Brenneke/8x65RmmJ	C/A	.318	.343	.424/.421	.468/.464	.469/.520		2.51/2.56	3.32/3.65		.217/5603/558/ 558A
8x75mm/8x75Rmm	C/A	.318	.345	.411	.466	.467/.522		2.94	3.50/3.51		.217/5603/514/ A514
8x60mm Mauser & RWS 6x60Rmm Mauser & RWS	C	.318	.345	.431	.470	.468/.526	.050	2.365	3.11		.217/5603/542
8x42Rmm M/88	A	.318	.347	.423	.468	.525		1.66	2.28		.217/5603/88D
8x71mm Peterlongo	C	.318	.349	.422	.462	.468		2.80	3.28		.216/2610
8x57mm Mauser	C	.318	.350	.435	.470	.473		2.24	3.17		L
8mm Rast Gasser	B	.320	.332		.334	.376		1.037	1.391	?	?
32-40 Ballard & Winchester	B	.320	.338		.424	.506	.058	2.13	2.59	16	L
8mm Nambu	G	.320	.338	.388	.408	.413		.86	1.25	11	B
32 Winchester SL	H	.320	.343		.346	.388		1.28	1.88	16	S
32 Remington	C	.320	.344	.396	.420	.421	.045	2.04	2.57	14	L
32 Winchester Special	A	.321	.343	.396 (.4014)	.422 (.4219)	.506	.058	2.04	2.55 (2.565)	16	L
8x50Rmm Siamese	A	.321	.347	.450	.480	.550		1.98	2.97		B
8x52Rmm Siamese	A	.321	.347	.460	.500	.550		2.04	2.96		B, Bx
8x58Rmm Sauer	B	.322	.345		.438	.499		2.28	3.00		.254/1775/462
8mm Danish Krag	A	.322	.355	.460	.500	.575	.060	2.28	3.20	12	B
325 WSM	I	.323	.358	35381	.555	.535	.054	2.10	2.560		LR
8mm Remington Magnum	E	.323	.351 (.3541)	.485 (.4868)	.509 (.5126)	.530	.047	2.85	3.57 (3.600)	10	L
8mm Mauser	C	.323	.353 (.3493)	.431	.469	.473	.046	2.24	3.17 (3.25)	9-10	L
32 Ideal	B	.323	.344		.348	.411		1.77	2.25	18	S
8x56mm Mannlicher Schoenauer	C	.323	.347	.424	.465	.470	.045	2.21	3.04		.217/5603/528
8mm Lebel	A	.323	.347	.483	.536	.621	.068	1.98	2.75	9.5	B
8x64mmS Brenneke 8x65RmmS Brenneke	C/A	.323	.348	.424/.421	.468/.464	.469/.520		2.51/2.56	3.32/3.65		.217/5603/558/ 558A
8mm Lebel Revolver	B	.323	.350		.384	.400		1.07	1.44	9.5	B

Cartridge	Case type	Bullet Dia.	Neck Dia.	Shoulder Dia.	Base Dia.	Rim Dia.	Rim Thick.	Case Length	Ctge. Length	Twist	Primer
8x60mmS Mauser & RWS 8x60RmmS Mauser & RWS	C	.323	.350	.431	.470	.468/.526	.050	2.365	3.11		.217/5603/542
8x57mmJS Mauser 8x57RmmJS Mauser	C/A	.323	.350	.435	.470	.473/.526	.043/.048	2.24/2.25	3.17/3.55		.217/5603/ 366D1
8x54mm Krag Jorgensen	C	.323	.351	.435	.478	.478		2.12	2.85		.199/1680
8mm-06	C	.323	.351	.441	.470	.473	.045	2.47	3.25	9-10	L
8mm Austrian	A	.323	.351	.462	.501	.553	.040	1.98	3.00	9.8	B
7.92mm Kurz	C	.323	.352	.440	.470	.470		1.30	1.88	10	B
7.9x57mmJS (8mm Mauser JS)	C	.323	.353	.443	.469	.473		2.24	3.17	9-10	B
8x68mmS RWS	C	.323	.354	.473	.522	.510		2.65	3.38		.238/1698
8mm JDJ	A	.323	.356	.455	.470	.514	.058	2.22	V	?	L
8x63mm Swedish	C	.323	.356	.456	.488	.479		2.48	3.36	?	B
310 Cadet	B	.324	.320		.353	.405	.035	1.12	1.72		.177/69
8x72Rmm Sauer	B	.324	.344		.429	.483		2.84	3.40		.254/1775/574
7.5mm Nagant (Swedish)	B	.325	.328		.350	.406		.89	1.35	18	B
8x60Rmm Guedes M/85	A	.326	.354	.490	.543	.620	.080	2.34	3.25	11	B
8x59mm Breda	C	.326	.357	.433	.491	.469		2.33	3.17	?	B
8mm Roth Steyr	D	.329	.353		.355	.356		.74	1.14	10	B
8mm Murata	A	.329	.361	.485	.492	.558		2.06	2.90		B
8mm Hungarian M89	A	.329	.365	.473	.491	.554	.060	2.20	3.02	10	B
318 Rimless Nitro Express	C	.330	.358	.445	.465	.465		2.39	3.40		.217/81
333 Jeffery Flanged	A	.333	.356	.484	.544	.625		2.50	3.49		.317
333 Jeffery Rimless	C	.333	.359	.496	.540	.538		2.48	3.48		.217/59
33 Winchester	A	.333	.365	.443	.508	.610	.065	2.11	2.80	12	L
333 OKH	C	.333	.365	.443	.470	.473	.045	2.49	3.37	10	L
334 OKH	E	.333	.367	.480	.513	.530	.048	2.86	3.65	10	L
9mm Ball	B	.337	.350		.350	.402		.417	.560		
338 Whisper	C	.338	.360	.457	.463	.466	.048	1.47	V	V	S
338-223 Straight	D	.338	.362		.376	.378	.041	1.41	2.25	10	S
338 Federal	C	.338	.369	.454	.470	.473	.049	2.01	2.75		LR
338-378 KT	K	.338	.362	.560	.603	.603/.580	.060	2.90	3.865	10	L
338 JDJ	A	.338	.365	.453	.470	.514	.058	2.20	V	?	L
338-06 Ackley	C	.338	.365	.455	.470	.467	.045	2.49	3.34	12	L
338-284 McPherson	I	.338	.365	.486	.500	.467	.050	2.013	2.825	10	L
340 Weatherby Magnum	E	.338	.366	.495	.513	.530	.048	2.82	3.60	12	L
338 A-Square	K	.338	.367	.553	.582	.603/.580	.060	2.85	3.67	10	L
8.59 Galaxy	C	.338	.368	.557	.577	.577	.060	2.05	2.80	12	L
338 Winchester Magnum	E	.338	.369	.480 (.491)	.515 (.5127)	.530	.047	2.49 (2.50)	3.30 (3.34)	10	L
338-06 A-Square	C	.338	.370	.441	.470	.473	.049	2.494	3.240 (3.440)	10	L
33 BSA (33 Belted)	E	.338	.369	.453	.534	.534		2.40	3.10		.217/59
338 Canadian Magnum	I	.338	.369	.530	.544	.532	.046	2.83	3.60	10-12	L
8.59 Titan	C	.338	.369	.557	.577	.577	.060	2.80	3.60	14	L
338-06 JDJ	C	.338	.370	.455	.470	.467	.045	2.465	V	10	L
338 Lapua Mag	C	.338	.370	.540	.590	.590	.060	2.72	3.60		L
338 Rem. UltraMag	I	.338	.371	.526	.550	.534	.050	2.76 (3.600)	3.450	10	L
330 Dakota	C	.338	.371	.530	.544	.544	.045	2.57	3.32	10	L
338 Excaliber	C	.338	.371	.566	.580	.580	.058	2.99	3.75	10	L
338/50 Talbot	C	.338	.380	.748	.774	.782	.080	3.76	4.25	10	50 BMG
35 Allen	B	.342	.342		.342	.407		.865	1.388		
348 Winchester	A	.348	.379 (.3757)	.485	.553	.610	.062	2.26 (2.255)	2.80 (2.795)	12	L
9x71mm Peterlongo	C	.350	.386	.420	.464	.466		2.80	3.26		.216/2610/783
35 Winchester SL	H	.351	.374		.378	.405	.045	1.14	1.64	16	S
351 Winchester SL	H	.351	.374	.378	.407	1.38	.045	1.91	16	S	
9mm Ultra	D	.355	.374		.386	.366		.72	1.03	?	SPB
9mm Bayard	D	.355	.375		.390	.392		.91	1.32	?	B
9mm Browning Long	D	.355	.376		.384	.404		.80	1.10	12-16	B
9mm Mauser	D	.355	.376		.389	.390	.050	.981	1.38	12	B
9mm Winchester Magnum	D	.355	.379		.392	.394	.046	1.16	1.545	10	SP

Cartridge	Case type	Bullet Dia.	Neck Dia.	Shoulder Dia.	Base Dia.	Rim Dia.	Rim Thick.	Case Length	Ctge. Length	Twist	Primer
9mm Glisenti	D	.355	.380		.392	.393		.75	1.15	10	B
9mm Luger	D	.355	.380		.392	.393	.042	.754	1.16	9.8	SPB
9x21mm	D	.355	.380		.392	.393		.830	1.16	10	SP
9x23mm Winchester	D	.355	.380		.390	.392	.042	.900	1.245	16	LP
9mm Steyr	D	.355	.380		.380	.381		.90	1.30	?	B
38-45 Hard Head	C	.355	.381	.475	.476	.476	.044	.90	1.20	14	L
9mm Federal	B	.355	.382		.386	.435		.754	1.163	9	SP
9x25 Dillon	C	.355	.382	.423	.423	.424	.050	0.99	1.26	10-12	SP
9mm Action Express	I	.355	.390	.433	.435	.394	.045	.866	1.152	18	S
380 Automatic (9mm Browning Short)	D	.356	.373		.373	.374	.040	.68	.98	12-16	SP
9x56mm Mannlicher	C	.356	.378	.408	.464	.464		2.22	3.56		.217/5603/491E
9x57mm Mauser/9x57Rmm Mauser	C/A	.356	.380	.428/.424	.467	.468/.515	.045/.05 0	2.24	3.10/3.08		.217/5603/491/ A491B
38 Short Colt	D	.357	.357		.378	.433	.055	.76	1.10	16	SP
357 Maximum	B	.357	.375		.375	.433	.055	1.59	1.97	14	SP
38 Long Colt	B	.357	.377		.378	.433	.055	1.03	1.32	16	SP
357 S&W Magnum	B	.357	.379		.379	.440	.055	1.29	1.51	16-18	SP
38 Special	B	.357	.379		.379	.440	.054	1.16	1.55	16-18	SP
357 SIG	C	.357	.381	.424	.425	.424		.865	1.140	16	SP
350 Griffin & Howe Magnum	E	.357	.382	.446	.511	.528	.048	2.848	3.64	12	L
357 Auto Magnum	C	.357	.382	.461	.470	.473	.048	1.298	1.60	18	LP
357/44 B&D	A	.357	.383	.454	.455	.515	.055	1.28	1.55	14	L
9x63mm	C	.357	.384	.427	.467	.468		2.48	3.28		.217/5603/491D
9x70Rmm Mauser	A	.357	.385	.418	.467	.525		2.76	3.37		474B
358 JDJ	A	.358	.362	.453	.470	.514	.058	.220	3.065	?	L
357 Herrett	A	.358	.375	.405	.420	.505	.058	1.75	2.10	14	L
400/360 Nitro Exp. (2")	A	.358	.375	.437	.470	.590		2.75	3.59		.241
35-30/30	A	.358	.378	.401	.422	.506	.058	2.04	2.55	12-14	L
35 Winchester	A	.358	.378	.412	.457	.539		2.41	3.16	12	L
400/350 Rigby	A	.358	.380	.415	.470	.520		2.75	3.60		.241/34
350 No. 2 Rigby	A	.358	.380	.415	.470	.520	.050	2.75	3.60		.241/34
350 Rigby Magnum	C	.358	.380	.443	.519	.525		2.75	3.60		.241/34
38 Automatic & 38 Super Automatic	H	.358	.382		.383	.405	.045	.90	1.28	16	SP
35 Newton	C	.358	.383	.498	.523	.525		2.52	3.35	12	L
35 Remington	C	.358	.384	.419 (.4259)	.458 (.4574)	.460	.046	1.92	2.52	16	L
358 Norma Magnum	E	.358	.384	.489	.508	.526	.048	2.52	3.22	12	L
35-06 JDJ	C	.358	.385	.455	.470	.467	.045	2.445	V	10	L
35 Ackley Whelen	C	.358	.385	.455	.469	.467	.045	2.494	V	12	L
35-284 McPherson	I	.358	.385	.486	.500	.467	.050	2.013	2.825	10	L
358 STA	E	.358	.386	.502	.513	.532	.048	2.85	3.65	12	L
9.09 Eagle	C	.358	.387	.557	.577	.577	.060	2.05	2.80	12	L
35 Whelen	C	.358	.388	.441	.470	.473	.045	2.50 (2.494)	3.34	12-14	L
356 Winchester	G	.358	.388	.454	.4703	.508	.058	2.02 (2.015)	2.56	12	L
358 Winchester	C	.358	.388	.454	.4703	.473	.048	2.01 (2.015)	2.78	12	L
350 Remington Magnum	E	.358	.388	.495	.5126	.532	.046	2.17	2.80	16	L
35 Ackley Magnum	E	.358	.388	.495	.513	.532	.048	?	3.30	12	L
38 S&W	B	.359	.386		.386	.433	.055	.78	1.20	16-18	SP
35-30 Maynard (1882)	B	.359	.395		.400	.494		1.63	2.03	16-18	S
35-40 Maynard (1873)	B	.360	.390		.400	.492		2.06	2.53	16-18	S
35-40 Maynard (1882)	B	.360	.390		.400	.492		2.06	2.53	16-18	S
360 No. 5 Rook	B	.362	.375		.380	.432		1.05	1.45		
9mm Makarov	D	.363	.384		.389	.396		.71	.97	?	B
38-45 Stevens	B	.363	.395		.455	.522		1.76	2.24	16-18	S
35-30 Maynard 1873	B	.364	.397		.403	.765		1.63	2.10	16-18	B1
360 Nitro (2")	B	.365	.384		.430	.480	.040	2.25	2.80		.241/34
360 Express (2")	B	.365	.384		.430	.480	.040	2.25	3.00		.241/34
9.3x80Rmm	B	.365	.386		.430	.485		3.14	3.50		.254/1775/77B
9.3x82Rmm	B	.365	.386		.430	.485		3.21	3.72		.254/1775/77C

Cartridge	Case type	Bullet Dia.	Neck Dia.	Shoulder Dia.	Base Dia.	Rim Dia.	Rim Thick.	Case Length	Ctge. Length	Twist	Primer
9.3x74Rmm	A	.365	.387	.414	.465	.524	.052	2.93	3.74		.217/5603/474A
9.3x62mm Mauser	C	.365	.388	.447	.473	.470	.044	2.42	3.29		.217/5603/474
9.3x57mm Mauser	C	.365	.389	.428	.468	.469		2.24	3.23		.217/5603/491
9.3x72Rmm Sauer	A	.365	.390	.422	.473	.518		2.83	3.34		.254/1775
9.3x64mm Brenneke	C	.365	.391	.475	.504	.492		2.52	3.43		.217/5603
9.3x53mm Swiss	C/A	.365	.389/.391	.453/.455	.492/.494	.491/.563	.045	2.11	2.80/2.83		?
9.3mm JDJ	A	.366	.389	.455	.465	.506	.058	2.22	V	?	L
9.3x65Rmm Collath	A	.367	.384	.420	.443	.508		2.56	3.01		?
360 No. 2 Nitro Express	A	.367	.393	.517	.539	.631	.045	3.00	3.85		.254/40
9.3x53Rmm Hebler	A	.369	.398	.462	.484	.550		2.12	2.92		?
35-30 Maynard 1865	B	.370	.397		.408	.771/1.07	.037	1.53	1.98	16	Externally primed
38-40 Remington Hepburn	B	.372	.395		.454	.537		1. 77	2.32	16	S
38-45 Bullard	A	.373	.397	.448	.454	.526		1.80	2.26	16-18	S
9.1x40Rmm	B	.374	.385		.404	.446		1.60	2.00		91
38 Short	B	.375	.376		.376	.436		.768	1.185		
38 Long	B	.375	.376		.376	.435		.873	1.380		
380 Revolver	B	.375	.377		.380	.426	.046	.70	1.10	15	SPB
38 Long, CF*	B	.375	.378		.379	.441		1.03	1.45	36	S
38 Ballard Extra Long*	B	.375	.378		.379	.441		1.63	2.06	36	S
38 Extra Long	B	.375	.378		.378	.435		1.480	2.025		
380 Short	B	.375	.379		.380	.430		.600	1.11		
380 Long (Rifle)	B	.375	.379		.380	.430		.965	1.33		.177/69
375 JDJ	A	.375	.396	.453	.470	.514	.058	2.20	3.13	?	L
375 Flanged Nitro (2 1/2")	B	.375	.397		.456	.523		2.50	3.10		.217/34
400/375 Belted Nitro Express (H&H)	E	.375	.397	.435	.470	.466		2.50	3.00		.217
376 Steyr	I	.375	.398	.472	.501	.494	.048	2.35	3.075	12	L
369 Purdey	A	.375	.398	.475	.543	.616		2.69	3.60		.254/40
375-284 McPherson	I	.375	.399	.486	.500	.050	.467	2.013	2.825	10	L
375 Winchester	B	.375	.400		.415 (.4198)	.502	.046	2.02	2.56	12	L
375 Rimless NE (9.5x57mm)	C	.375	.400	.460	.471	.473	0.40	2.25	2.94		.217
9.5x57mm Mannlicher (9.5x56mm)	C	.375	.400	.460	.471	.473	.040	2.25	2.94		.217/5603/531
38-35 Stevens	B	.375	.402		.403	.492		1.62	2.43		S
375 H&H Magnum	E	.375	.402	.440 (.4478)	.521	.530	.046	2.85	3.60	12	L
375 Dakota	C	.375	.402	.529	.544	.544	.046	2.57	3.32	10	L
375 Canadian Magnum	I	.375	.402	.530	.544	.532	.046	2.83	3.60	10	L
9.5x73mm Miller Greiss Magnum	C	.375	.402	.531	.543	.541		2.86	3.50		.217/5603/473
375 Weatherby Magnum	E	.375	.402	.492	.512	.531	.051	2.85	3.540 (3.800)	12	L
375 Rem. UltraMag	I	.375	.405	.525	.550	.534	.050	2.85	3.540 (3.600)	12	L
378 Weatherby Magnum	K	.375	.403	.560	.584	.603/.580	.062	2.92	3.69	12	L
375 Whelen & Improved	C	.375	.403	.442/.455	.470	.473	.045	2.50	3.42	12	L
375 Belted Magnum	E	.375	.404	.440	.464	.530		2.85	3.60		.217/60
375 Flanged Magnum	A	.375	.404	.450	.515	.572		2.94	3.80		.217/40
9.53 Hellcat	C	.375	.404	.557	.577	.577	.060	2.05	2.80	10	L
9.53 Saturn	C	.375	.404	.557	.577	.577	.060	2.80	3.60	14	L
375-06 JDJ	C	.375	.405	.457	.470	.467	.045	2.435	V	12	L
375 A-Square	K	.375	.405	.551	.582	.603/.580	.060	2.85	3.65	10	L
9.5x47Rmm	A	.375	.409	.497	.513	.583		1.85	2.37		.254/1775/23
38-50 Maynard (1882)	B	.375	.415		.421	.500	.069	1.97	2.38		S
375 JRS	E	.375	.498	.485	.535	?	.048	2.84	3.69	12	L
9.3x48Rmm	B	.376	.382		.433	.492		1.89	2.35		.254/1775/246
9.3x72Rmm	B	.376	.385		.427	.482		2.84	3.27		.254/1775/77D
9.3x70Rmm	B	.376	.387		.427	.482		2.75	3.45		.254/1775/77F
9.3x57Rmm	B	.376	.389		.428	.486		2.24	2.80		.254/1775/77E
38-50 Remington Hepburn	B	.376	.392		.454	.535		2.23	3.07	16	S
38-50 Ballard	B	.376	.395		.425	.502		2.00	2.72	20	S

Cartridge	Case type	Bullet Dia.	Neck Dia.	Shoulder Dia.	Base Dia.	Rim Dia.	Rim Thick.	Case Length	Ctge. Length	Twist	Primer
38-90 Winchester Express	A	.376	.395	.470	.477	.558		3.25	3.70	26	L
38-56 Winchester	A	.376	.403	.447	.506	.606	.065	2.10	2.50	20	L
38-72 Winchester	A	.378	.397	.427	.461	.519		2.58	3.16	22	L
38-70 Winchester	A	.378	.403	.421	.506	.600		2.31	2.73	24	L
9.8mm Auto Colt	D	.378	.404		.404	.405		.912	1.267	?	SP
38-55 Winchester/38-55 Ballard	B	.379	.392	.3938	.422	.506	.058	2.12 (2.085)	2.51	18	L
41 Long Colt	B	.386/4 01	.404		.405	.430	.052	1.13	1.39	16	SP
9.5mm Turkish Mauser	A	.389	.411	.487	.511	.612	.082	2.37	2.97	20	B
40 S&W Auto	D	.400	.423		.423	.424	.050	.850	1.135	16	SP
10mm Auto	D	.400	.423		.423	.424	.050	.99	1.26	16	LP
41 Short Colt	B	.401	.404		.405	.430	.052	?	?	?	SP
38-40 Winchester	A	.401	.416	.438 (.4543)	.465	.520	.058	1.30	1.59	36	LP
38 Colt Lightning	A	.401	.416	.438	.465	.520	.058	1.30	?	36	LP
38-40 Marlin	A	.401	.416	.438	.465	.520	.058	1.30	?	36	LP
400 CorBon	C	.401	.423	.469	.470	.471	.050	.898	1.20	16	LP
401 Powermag	B	.401	.425		.426	.483		1.29	1.64	18	LP
40-44 Woodswalker	A	.401	.428	.455	.455	.510	.055	1.295	V	14-18	LP
40-454 JDJ	A	.401	.428	.470	.470	.510	.055	1.395	V	14-18	LP
40-70 Sharps (Straight)	B	.403	.420		.453	.533	.078	2.50	3.18	18-20	L
40-50 Sharps (Straight)	B	.403	.421		.454	.554	.078	1 88	2.63	18	B1
40-50 Sharps (Necked)	A	.403	.424	.489	.501	.580		1.72	2.37	18-20	B1
40-60 Marlin	B	.403	.425		.504	.604		2.11	2.55	20	S
40-85 (40-90) Ballard	B	.403	.425		.477	.545		2.94	3.81	18-20	S
40-90 Sharps (Straight)	B	.403	.425		.477	.546		3.25	4.06	18	B1
40-60 Colt	A	.403	.425	.445	.504	.604	.065	2.09	2.55	?	S
40-70 Sharps (Necked)	A	.403	.426	.500	.503	.595		2.25	3.02	18-20	L
40-110 Winchester Express	A	.403	.428	.485	.565	.651		3.25	3.63	28	L
40-63 (40-70) Ballard	B	.403	.430		.471	.555		2.38	2.55	20	S
10.15mm Jarmann	A	.403	.430	.540	.548	.615	.078	2.40	3.06	22	B
40-65 Ballard Everlasting	B	.403	.435		.508	.600		2.38	2.55	18-20	B1
40-90 Sharps (Necked)	A	.403	.435	.500	.506	.602		2.63	3.44	18-20	B1
10.25x69Rmm Hunting Express	A	.404	.415	.480	.549	.630		2.72	3.17		.254/1775/214
40-60 Winchester	A	.404	.425	.445	.506	.630		1.87	2.10	40	S
41 Short	B	.405	.406		.406	.468		.467	.913		
41 Long	B	.405	.407		.407	.468		.635	.985		
400 Purdey (3")	B	.405	.427		.469	.516		3.00	3.60		.241/34
40-70 Winchester	A	.405	.430	.496	.504	.604		2.40	2.85	20	L
450/400 Nitro Express (3 1/4")	A	.405	.432	.502	.544	.615	.040	3.25	3.85		.254/40
40-70 Remington	A	.405	.434	.500	.503	.595		2.25	3.00	18-20	L
400 Whelen	C	.405	.436	.462	.470	.473	.048	2.49	3.10	16	L
40-65 Winchester	B	.406	.423		.504	.604		2.10	2.48	20-26	L
401 Winchester SL	H	.406	.428		.429	.457	.055	1.50	2.00	14	L
40-82 (40-75) Winchester	A	.406	.428	.448	.502	.604	.060	2.40	2.77	28	L
40-72 Winchester	B	.406	.431		.460	.518		2.60	3.15	22	L
450/400 (2 3/8")	A	.407	.427	.456	.545	.616	.035	2.38	2.95		
40-70 Peabody	A	.408	.428	.551	.581	.662		1.76	2.85	18	L
40-90 Peabody	A	.408	.433	.546	.586	.659		2.00	3.37		B1
41 Remington Magnum	B	.410	.432		.433	.488	.054	1.28	1.58	18	LP
41 Special	B	.410	.432		.433	.488	.056	1.16	1.60	18	LP
41 Action Express	J	.410	.434		.435	.394	.045	.866	1.17	16-18	SP
400 Jeffery (450/400 3")	A	.410	.434	.518	.545	.613		3.00	3.75		.254/40
408 Cheytac	C	.408	.438	.601	.637	.640	.065	3.04	4.307		LR
411 JDJ	A	.411	.425	.455	.465	.506	.058	2.235	V	?	L
10.15mm Serbian Mauser	A	.411	.433	.515	.520	.592	.082	2.46	3.13	22	B
405 Winchester	B	.412	.436		.461	.543	.075	2.58	3.18	14	L
40-90 Bullard	A	.413	.430	.551	.569	.622		2.04	2.55	18	L
40-75 Bullard	B	.413	.432		.505	.606		2.09	2.54	20	S
10.4mm Swiss Vetterli	A	.415	.437	.518	.540	.630	.055	1.60	2.20	26	B-RF

Cartridge	Case type	Bullet Dia.	Neck Dia.	Shoulder Dia.	Base Dia.	Rim Dia.	Rim Thick.	Case Length	Ctge. Length	Twist	Primer
10.3x60Rmm Swiss	A	.415	.440	.498	.547	.619		2.36	3.08		?
40-40 Maynard (1882)	B	.415	.450		.456	.532		1.78	2.32	18-20	S
416 Aargaard	C	.416	.441	.492	.506	.496	.049	2.35			LR
416 Rigby	C	.416	.445 (.4461)	.539 (.5402)	.589	.586	.058	2.90	3.75	16.5	L
416 JDJ	A	.416	.430	.455	.465	.506	.058	2.22	V	?	L
416 Barnes	A	.416	.432	.484	.505	.608	.065	2.112	2.95	14	L
416-284 McPherson	I	.416	.440	.486	.500	.467	.050	2.013	2.825	10	L
416 Dakota	C	.416	.441	.527	.544	.544	.042	2.85	3.645	10	L
416 06 JDJ	C	.416	.443	.455	.470	.467	.045	2.415	V	16	L
416 Weatherby	K	.416	.444	.561	.584	.603/.580	.062	2.915	3.75	14	L
416 Rigby	C	.416	.445	.539	.589	.589	.062	2.90	3.72		Bx
10.57 Maverick	C	.416	.445	.557	.577	.577	.060	2.05	2.80	14	L
10.57 Meteor	C	.416	.445	.557	.577	.577	.060	2.80	3.62	14	L
416 Rimmed	A	.416	.446	.549	.573	.665	.060	3.300	4.100	10	L
416 Prairie Gun Works	C	.416	.446	.606	.637	.637	.058	3.051	3.830	10-14	L
416 Remington Magnum	E	.416	.447	.487	.509	.530	.046	2.85	3.60	14	L
416 Taylor	E	.416	.447	.491	.513	.532	.048	2.50	3.34	10	L
416 Hoffman	E	.416	.447	.491	.513	.532	.048	2.85	3.60	10	L
42 Forehand & Wadsworth	B	.417	.416		.416	.485		.847	1.496		
40-60 Maynard (1882)	B	.417	.448		.454	.533		2.20	2.75	18-20	S
40-70 Maynard (1882)	B	.417	.450		.451	.535		2.42	2.88	18-20	B1
41 Swiss	A	.418	.445	.517	.539	.620		1.519	2.205		
44 Evans Long	B	.419	.434		.449	.509		1.54	2.00	36	L
44 Evans Short	B	.419	.439		.440	.513		0.99	1.44	36	S
10.5x47Rmm	A	.419	.445	.496	.513	.591		1.85	2.40		.254/1775/29
10.75x73mm (404 Jeffery)	C	.421	.450	.520	.544	.537	.045	2.86	3.53		.217/555
10.4mm Italian	B	.422	.444		.451	.505		.89	1.25	10	B
40-40 Maynard (1873)	B	.422	.450		.460	.743		1.84	2.34	18-20	B1
40-70 Maynard (1873)	B	.422	.450		.451	.759		2.45	3.00	18-20	B1
404 Jeffery (404 Rimless)	C	.422	.450	.520	.544	.537	.045	2.87	3.53		.217/81
425 Express	E	.423	.429	.490	.513	.532	.048	2.552	3.34	10	L
10.3x65Rmm Baenziger	B	.423	.431		.462	.505		2.56	3.15		
44 Henry Center Fire Flat	B	.423	.443		.445	.523		0.88	1.36	36	S
40-40 Maynard 1865	B	.423	.450		.458	.766	.058	1.75	2.24	18-20	Externally primed
44 Merwin & Hulbert	B	.424	.442		.442	.502	.060	1.15	1.53	?	S
10.75x68mm Mauser	C	.424	.445	.470	.492	.488		2.67	3.16		.217/5603/515A
10.75x63mm Mauser	I	.424	.447	.479	.493	.467		2.47	3.22		515?
10.75x57mm Mannlicher	C	.424	.448	.465	.468	.468		2.24	3.05		?
10.75x65Rmm Collath	B	.424	.451		.487	.542		2.56	3.02		?
44 Game Getter/44-40 Marlin/44 Colt Lightning	A	.427	.443	.458	.471	.520	.065	1.31	Varies	36	L
44-40 Extra Long	A	.428	.442	.463	.468	.515		1.58	1.96	36	S
444 Marlin	B	.429	.453	.4549	.469	.514	.058	2.16 (2.225)	2.57	38	L
44 S&W Russian	B	.429	.457		.457	.515	.050	.97	1.43	20	LP
44 Remington Magnum	B	.429	.457		.457	.514	.055	1.29	1.61	20	LP
44 S&W Special	B	.429	.457		.457	.514	.055	1.16	1.62	20	LP
44 Auto Mag	D	.429	.457		.470	.473	.048	1.298	1.620	20	LP
440 CorBon	I	.429	.461	.529	.538	.510	.055	1.280	1.59	18	LP
10.4mm Italian M/70	A	.430	.437	.517	.540	.634	.058	1.87	2.46	26	B
10.75mm Russian Berdan	A	.430	.449	.506	.567	.637	.080	2.24	2.95	21	B
445 Super Magnum	B	.432	.456		.457	.514	.055	1.60	1.985	20	LP
11mm Murata	A	.432	.465	.526	.542	.632		2.36	3.13	20	B
44 S&W American	B	.434	.438		.440	.506	.050	.91	1.44	20	LP
425 Westley Richards	I	.435	.456	.540	.543	.467		2.64	3.30		?
11mm Belgian Albini	A	.435	.472	.535	.580	.678		2.00	2.6	22	B
11mm Belgian Comblain	A	.436	.460	.532	.575	.673	.082	2.10	2.76	22	B
44 Webley	B	.436	.470		.472	.503		.69	1.10	20	LPB
44 Long Center Fire (Ballard)*	B	.439	.440		.441	.506		1.09	1.65	36	S

Cartridge	Case type	Bullet Dia.	Neck Dia.	Shoulder Dia.	Base Dia.	Rim Dia.	Rim Thick.	Case Length	Ctge. Length	Twist	Primer
44 Extra Long Center Fire (Ballard)*	B	.439	.441		.441	.506		1.63	2.10	36	S
11.15mm Spanish Rem.	A	.439	.458	.512	.516	.635	.082	2.25	2.82	20	B
44 Wesson Extra Long*	B	.440	.441		.441	.510		1.63	2.19	36	S
11.2x72mm (Schuler/Mauser)	I	.440	.465	.510	.536	.469		2.80	3.85		.217/5601
11.2x60mm (Schuler/Mauser)	I	.440	.465	.512	.512	.465		2.35	2.86		.217/5601
44 Bull Dog	B	.440	.470		.473	.503		.57	.95	21	SPB
10.8x47Rmm Martini Target	A	.441	.463	.512	.516	.591		1.75	2.23		.254/1775/146
11.15mm Werndl M/77	A	.441	.466	.536	.545	.617	.100	2.27	3.02	28	B
44-100/44-90/ 44-110 Creedmoor	B	.442	.465		.503	.568		2.60	3.97	22-30	L
44-90 Rem. Special (Necked)	A	.442	.466	.504	.520	.628	.075	2.44	3.08	?	L
44 Colt	B	.443	.450		.456	.483		1.10	1.50	16	LP
44-95 Peabody	A	.443	.465	.550	.580	.670		2.31	3.32	?	B1
44-100 Wesson	B	.445	?		.515.520	.605.610		3.38	3.85	?	L
44-70 Maynard 1882	B	.445	.466		.499	.601		2.21	2.87	?	B1
11mm French Gras 11x59Rmm Vickers	A	.445	.468	.531	.544	.667	.075	2.34	3.00	22	B
11.75mm Montenegrin	B	.445	.472		.490	.555		1.40	1.73	?	B
44-100 Ballard	B	.445	.485		.498	.605	.080	2.81	3.25	20	L
44-75 Ballard Everlasting	B	.445	.487		.497	.603		2.50	3.00	?	B2
44-85 Wesson	B	.446	?		.515.520	.605.610		2.88	3.31	?	L
44 Short	B	.446	.445		.445	.519	.066	.688	1.190		
44 Henry Flat	B	.446	.445		.446	.519	.066	.875	1.345		
44 Extra Long Ballard	B	.446	.456		.457	.524		1.250	1.843		
11.15mm (43) Mauser	A	.446	.465	.510	.516	.586	.075	2.37	3.00	22	B
44-77 Sharps & Remington	A	.446	.467	.502	.516	.625		2.25	3.05	?	LB1
44-90 (44-100) Sharps 2 5/8"	A	.446	.468	.504	.517	.625	.065	2.63	3.30	?	B1
44-60 Sharps & Remington (Necked)	A	.447	.464	.502	.515	.630		1.88	2.55	?	LB1
44-60 Peabody & Winchester	A	.447	.464	.502	.518	.628		1.89	2.56	?	B1
45 Remington Thompson	D	.447	.470		.472	.471	.044	1.12	1.45	?	LP
11.43mm Turkish	A	.447	.474	.560	.582	.668		2.30	3.12	22	B
11.43mm Egyptian	A	.448	.479	.542	.581	.668	.065	1.94	2.73	20	B
11.4mm Werndl M/73	B	.449	.472		.493	.571		1.97	2.55	29	B
44-100 Maynard 1873	B	.450	.490		.497	.759		2.88	3.46	?	B1
11mm French Ordnance	B	.451	.449		.460	.491	.035	.71	1.18	16	B
11mm German Service	B	.451	.449		.453	.509		.96	1.21	23	B
44 Long	B	.451	.455		.458	.525		1.094	1.842		
45 Winchester Magnum	D	.451	.475		.477	.481	.045	1.198	1.55	16	LP
45 GAP	D	.452	.473	NA	.476	.470	.049	.760	1.137		LP
45 Webley	B	.452	.471		.471	.504		.82	1.15	?	LPB
45 AutoRim	B	.452	.472		.476	.516	.085	.898	1.28	15-16	LP
45 Automatic Short	D	.452	.476		.476	.476	.044	.860	1.17	16	LP
45 Automatic	D	.452	.476		.476	.476	.044	.898	1.17	16	LP
451 Detonics	D	.452	.476		.476	.476	.044	.942	1.17	16	L
454 Casull	B	.452	.476		.480	.512	.055	1.39	1.70	16	S
460 S&W	B	.452	.478	NA	.478	.520	.059	1.80	2.290		LP
11.4mm Brazilian Comblain	A	.452	.494	.530	.588	.682		2.02	2.62	22	B
46 Long	B	.454	.456		.456	.523		1.25	1.876		
11.5mm Spanish Reformado	B	.454	.466		.525	.631		2.26	3.06	20	B
455 Webley Revolver MkII	B	.454	.476		.480	.535		.77	1.23	16-20	LPB
45 Colt	B	.454	.476		.480	.512	.055	1.29	1.60	16	LP
45 S&W Schofield	B	.454	.478		.478	.522	.055	1.10	1.43	24	LP
45 Colt (Government)	B	.454	.478		.478	.506	.055	1.10	1.44	16-24	LP
45-50 Peabody (Sporting)	A	.454	.478	.508	.516	.634		1.54	2.08	?	?
45-75 Winchester (Centennial)	A	.454	.478	.547	.559	.616		1.89	2.25	20	L
45-60 Winchester	B	.454	.479		.508	.629		1.89	2.15(?)	20	L
45-100 Ballard	B	.454	.487		.498	.597		2.81	3.25	20	L
46 Remington Carbine	B	.455	.455		.455	.529		.990	1.635		
455 Webley Auto	H	.455	.473		.474	.500		.93	1.23	10	B

Cartridge	Case type	Bullet Dia.	Neck Dia.	Shoulder Dia.	Base Dia.	Rim Dia.	Rim Thick.	Case Length	Ctge. Length	Twist	Primer
455 Enfield (455 Colt)	B	.455	.473		.478	.530	.035	.87	1.35	?	LPB
450 Revolver	B	.455	.475		.477	.510		.69	1.10	16	LPB
577/450 Martini Henry	A	.455	.487	.628	.668	.746	.050	2.34	3.12	33	B
46 Extra Short	B	.456	.458		.458	.530		.633	1.125		
46 Short	B	.456	.458		.458	.530		.836	1.336		
45-125 Winchester/45 Express	A	.456	.470	.521	.533	.601		3.25	3.63	36	L
50 Ball Carbine **	B	.456	.476		.560	.640		.859	1.134		
45-75/45-70 Sharps 2 1/10"	B	.457						2.10	2.90	22	L
45-78 Wolcott	B	.457						2.31	3.19	22	L
45-80 Sharpshooter	B	.457						2.40	3.25	18-22	L
45-82/45-85/45-90 Winchester & 45-90 Winchester High Velocity	B	.457	.477		.501	.597	.065	2.40	2.88	32	L
11mm Beaumont M/71	A	.457	.484	.528	.576	.665	.065	2.04	2.54	30	B
45-70 Van Choate	B	.457	Same as 45-70, See Chapter 2					2.25	2.91	18-22	L
45-70 Government	B	.458	.475 (.480)	.4813	.500	.600 (.608)	.065	2.105	2.55	18-22	L
460 G&A Special	C	.458	.480	.530	.545	.545		2.86			LR
458 Winchester Magnum	F	.458	.478 (.4811)	.4825	.513	.532	.046	2.50	3.34	14-16	L
450 Rigby	B	.458	.475	.539	.589	.589		2.90	3.80		Bx
45 Silhouette	B	.458	.477		.501	.600	.065	1.51	1.97	18	L
450 No. 2 Nitro Express (3 1/4")	A	.458	.477	.518	.564	.650	.	3.50	4.42		.254/40
458x2inch American	F	.458	.478		.508	.532	.048	2.00	2.60	14-16	L
450 Nitro Express (3")	B	.458	.479		.545	.624	.040	3.25	4.11		.254/40
450 Nitro Express (3")	B	.458	.479		.545	.624	.040	3.25	4.11		.254/40
500/450 Nitro Express (3")	A	.458	.479	.500	.570	.644		3.25	3.91		.254/40
500/450 Magnum Express	A	.458	.479	.500	.570	.644		3.25	3.91		.254/40
450 Marlin	F	.458	.480		.511	.532	.047	2.09	2.55	22	L
450 Alaskan	A	.458	.480	.515	.547	.605	.062	2.25	2.79	14	L
450 Howell	C	.458	.480	.515	.545	.534	.045	2.5	3.25	14	L
458x1 1/2" Barnes	F	.458	.481		.513	.532	.048	V		14-16	L
458 Lott	F	.458	.481		.513	.532	.050	2.80	3.400 (3.600)	14-16	L
460 A-Square	K	.458	.484	.560	.582	.603/.580	.060	2.50	3.50	10	L
458 Whisper	F	.458	.485		.506	.525	.048	1.75	V	V	L
500/450 No. 1 Express	A	.458	.485	.530	.577	.660		2.75	3.38		.241/31A
458 Canadian Magnum	I	.458	.485	.530	.544	.532	.046	2.83	3.60	10	L
450 Dakota	C	.458	.485	.560	.582	.580	.058	2.90	3.74	10	L
460 Weatherby Magnum	K	.458	.485	.560	.584	.603/.580	.062	2.91	3.75	14	L
500/450 No. 2 Musket	A	.458	.486	.535	.576	.658		2.36	2.90		
450 Ackley Magnum	E	.458	.487	.503	.512	.532	.048	2.85	3.65	10	L
450 Assegai	A	.458	.487	.549	.573	.665	.060	3.300	4.100	14	L
45-90/45-100/45-110 Sharps (2 4/10, 2 6/10, 2 3/4")	B	.458	.489		.500	.597	.065	2.40, 2.60, 2.75, 2.87	2.85, 3.00	18-20	B1
45-120/45-125 (3") Sharps	B	.458	.490		.506	.597	.065	3.25	4.16	18	L
45100 Remington (Necked)	A	.458	.490	.550	.558	.645		2.63	3.26	18-20	L
458x1 1/2" Barnes	F	.458	.493		.509	.530		1.50	2.19	16	Bx
46 Extra Long	B	.459	.457		.457	.525		1.534	2.285		
11.7mm Danish Remington	B	.462	.486		.514	.579		2.01	2.45	29 1/2	B
11.3mm Beaumont M/71/78	A	.464	.486	.530	.581	.666	.060	1.97	2.49	29	B
56-46 Spencer	A	.465	.478	.555	.558	.641		1.035	1.595		
500/465 Nitro Express	A	.466	.488	.524	.573	.650		3.25	3.89		.254/40
476 Enfield	B	.472	.474		.478	.530		.87	1.33	?	B
475 Ackley/OKH	F	.474	.496		.508	.528	.048	2.739	3.518	16-18	L
56-46 Extra Long	A	.475	.468	.551	.563	.638		1.200	1.757		
475 Linebaugh	B	.475	.495		.501	.600	.065	1.50	1.77	?	L
475 JDJ	B	.475	.497		.502	.604	.065	2.10	V	14	L
475 Wildey	I	.475	.497		.500	.473	.048	1.295	1.58	?	L
470 Capstick	F	.475	.499		.513	.532	.048	2.85	3.65	10	L
470 Nitro Express	A	.475	.500	.528	.572	.646	.035	3.25	4.00		.254/40

Cartridge	Case type	Bullet Dia.	Neck Dia.	Shoulder Dia.	Base Dia.	Rim Dia.	Rim Thick.	Case Length	Ctge. Length	Twist	Primer
12.04 Bibamufu	C	.475	.500	.557	.577	.577	.060	2.80	3.62	16	L
475 A&M Magnum	E	.475	.502	.560	.589	.603/.580	.060	2.90	3.75	14	L
470 Nitro Express	A	.475	.504	.528 (.5322)	.5728	.655	.037	3.25	3.98	20	L
476 Nitro Express (WR)	A	.476	.508	.530	.570	.643		3.00	3.77		.254/40
46 Hammond Carbine	B	.481	.500		.518	.590		1.625	2.175		
475 Nitro Express (3")	B	.483	.502		.545	.621		3.25	4.00		.254/40
475 No. 2 Nitro and Jeffery	A	.489	.510	.547	.576	.666		3.50	4.33		.254/40
50-60 Peabody **	B	.499	.508		.559	.645		1.456	1.919		
50 Action Express	J	.500	.540		.547	.514	.055	1.285	1.610	?	LP
500 Wyoming Express	F	.500		NA				1.370	1.765		LR
500 S&W	B	.500	.530	NA	.530	.560	.059	1.625	2.250		LP
12.17x44Rmm Remington M67	B	.502	.544		.546	.624	.060	1.73	2.13		?
50 Warner Carbine	B	.505	.526		.526	.604		.850	1.514		
505 Gibbs	C	.505	.530	.588	.635	.635		3.15	3.85		.254/40
577/500 No. 2 Express	A	.507	.538	.560	.641	.726	.055	2.83	3.40		.251/31A
577/500 Nitro Express (3 1/8")	A	.508	.526	.585	.645	.717	.055	3.13	3.74		.251/31A
50 Remington Army	A	.508	.532	.564	.565	.665		.875	1.24	?	LP
50-90 Sharps	B	.509	.528		.565	.663	.060	2.50	3.20	?	L
50 Alaskan	B	.510	.532		.552	.608	.065	2.10	2.50	15-20	L
510 Kodiak Express	A	.510	.532	.544	.552	.608	.065	2.33	2.68	12	L
500 Express (3")	B	.510	.535		.580	.660	.055	3.01	3.39		.251/31A
500 Express (3")	B	.510	.535		.580	.660	.040	3.25	3.63		.251/31A
50 McMurdo	C	.510	.554	.725	.800	.802	.078	3.700	5.722	15	Bx
500 Nitro (3")	B	.510	.535		.580	.660		3.00	3.80		.251/31A
510 Nitro	B	.510	.535		.565	.665		3.245	4.185	?	L
50 Remington Navy	B	.510	.535		.562	.642		.860	1.280		
500 Jeffery	I	.510	.535	.615	.620	.575		2.75	3.47		.254/40
12.50x70mm Schuler (500 Jeffery)	I	.510	.535	.615	.620	.578		2.94	3.50		.254/2703
500 A-Square	K	.510	.536	.568	.582	.603/.580	.060	2.90	3.74	10	L
50 Peacekeeper	K	.510	.538	.565	.586	.603/.580	.058	2.882	V	15	L
500 Linebaugh	B	.510	.540		.553	.610	.062	1.405	1.755	?	L
495 A-Square	L	.510	.542		.582	.603/.580	.060	2.80	3.60	10	L
500 Whisper	K	.510	.549	.563	.580	.603/.580	.060	2.90	V	V	L
50 McMillan FatMac	C	.510	.550	1.111	1.152	1.158	.090	2.645	V	15	50 BMG
50-70 Govt.	B	.512	.532		.557	.655		1.720	2.191		
50-100/50-105/50-110 Winchester & 50-110 Winchester High Velocity	B	.512	.534		.551	.607	.063	2.40	2.75	54	L
56-52 Spencer Rifle	B	.512	.540		.559	.639	.065	1.035	1.500		
56-50 Spencer Carbine	B	.512	.543		.556	.639	.065	1.156	1.632		
50-115 Bullard	G	.512	.547	.577	.585	.619		2.19	2.56	72	L
50-95 Winchester	A	.513	.533	.553	.562	.627		1.94	2.26	60	L
50-50 Maynard 1882	B	.513	.535		.563	.661		1.37	1.91	42	L
50-70 Maynard 1873	B	.514	.547		.552	.760		1.88	2.34	42	B1
50 U.S. Carbine	B	.515	.535		.560	.660		?	?	?	B1
50-70 Govt. Musket	B	.515	.535		.565	.660	.060	1.75	2.25	24-42	L
50-70 Gov't.	B	.515	.535		.565	.660	.060	1.75	2.25	24-42	Bx
50 Maynard 1865	B	.520	.543		.545	.770		1.24	1.75	42	none
56-52 Spencer Necked	A	.525	.547	.558	.560	.642	.065	1.020	1.660		
50 Remington Pistol	B	.529	.536		.558	.638		.875	1.300		
56-56 Spencer Carbine	B	.550	.560		.560	.645	.065	.875	1.545		
55-100 Maynard 1882	B	.551	.582		.590	.718		1.94	2.56	?	L
577 Snider (14.7mm)	B	.570	.602		.660	.747	.052	2.00	2.45	78	B
577 Blackpowder Express (3")	B	.584	.608		.660	.748	.052	3.25			.254/40
577 Nitro Express (3")	B	.584	.608		.660	.748	.052	3.00	3.70		.254/40
585 Nyati	I	.585	.605	.650	.660	.532/.586		2.79	3.525	?	L
577 Tyrannosaur	C	.585	.614	.673	.688	.688	.060	2.99	3.71	12	L
58 Miller	B	.585	.620		.628	.709		1.193	1.701		
58 Carbine (Berdan)	B	.589	.625		.640	.740		?	?	?	B2

Cartridge	Case type	Bullet Dia.	Neck Dia.	Shoulder Dia.	Base Dia.	Rim Dia.	Rim Thick.	Case Length	Ctge. Length	Twist	Primer
58 U.S. Musket (Berdan)	B	.589	.625		.646	.740	.062	1.75	2.15	68	B1
600 Nitro Express	B	.620	.648		.697	.805		3.00	3.68		.254/40
700 Nitro Express	B	.700	.728		.780	.890		3.50	4.20		Bx
70-150 Winchester	A	.705	.725	.790	.805	.870		2.18	2.63	?	L
303 Savage	A	.308/.311	.334 (.3322)	.408 (.4135)	.439	.501	.058	2.00 (2.015)	2.52	12	L
50-140 (3 1/4") Sharps & Winchester	B	.509/.512	.528		.565	.665	.060	3.25	3.94	?	L
44-40 Winchester	A	.427/.429	.443	.4568	.471	.525	.058	1.31	1.92	20-36	LP
50 BMG	C	.510/.511	.560	.714	.804	.804	.080	3.91	5.545	16	50 BMG
50 Browning	C	.510 (.511)	.555 (0.560)	.708 (0.714)	.800 (0.804)	.800 (0.804)	.080	3.90 (3.91)	5.43 (5.545)	16	Bx
50 Sporting							.060				

Key To Abbreviations

Notes: Bullet diameter can vary by several thousandths. The sizes listed are those that are most commonly encountered or are as specified in appropriate standards.

Cartridge length is not a particularly useful measure for identifying cartridges: This often varies widely, depending upon load type and bullet weight; it can vary between manufacturers; and it can vary with time, standard length from one era might not hold in another. An example is the 45-70 cartridge: 405gr. loads from the 1870s are about 2.625" long while current standards call for a maximum length of 2.55". Similar examples abound.

Case type: (For simplicity the various common rimmed/rimless pairs are listed together but with separate dimension, where variation occurs): **A** = Rimmed, bottleneck. **B** = Rimmed, straight. **C** = Rimless, bottleneck. **D** = Rimless, straight. **E** = Belted, bottleneck. **F** = Belted, straight. **G** = Semi-rimmed, bottleneck. **H** = Semi-rimmed, straight. **I** = Rebated, bottleneck. **J** = Rebated, straight. **K** = Rebated, belted bottleneck. **L** = Rebated, belted straight.

Primer type: **S** = Small rifle (0.175"). **SP** = Small pistol. (0.175"). **L** = Large rifle (0.210"). **LP** = Large pistol (0.210"). **Bx** = Boxer. **B** = Berdan type. **B-1** = Berdan #1. **B-2** = Berdan #2. **50 BMG** = CCI-35/VihtaVuori-110/RWS-8212.

Note on blackpowder primers: Not all companies used the same primer type or size in the same caliber or length case. For example, the 45-70 or its equivalent was usually loaded with the standard Large Rifle-diameter primers. However, Marlin's version used Small Rifle-diameter primer and Sharps Co., ammunition used Berdan primers. Primer type and size listed is what appears to have been the most general (common?) size and type used.

Finally, earliest loadings for the military and possibly other cartridges used an internal primer and were not reloadable. This practice continued until about 1877, perhaps later with some manufacturers. In some instances the earliest outside primers were 0.250" in diameter. Some early 30-06 military loading also used a 0.250" primer. It is possible other oddball primer sizes might be encountered, for example, both the 38-40 and the 45 Automatic have sometimes been loaded with small-diameter Boxer primers. Likely this is true of the 44-40 and perhaps many other chamberings, too.

Notes on handgun primers: Magnum pistol cartridges are usually loaded with special Magnum primers and the 22 Remington Jet and 256 Winchester are sometimes loaded with Small Rifle primers. The 454 Casull is always loaded with Small Rifle primers. During WWI, Frankford Arsenal made 45 Automatic cases with special #70 primers of .204" diameter instead of the standard .210". Recently, at least one foreign manufacturer produced 45 Automatic ammunition using Small Pistol primers.

* Cartridges so marked used an outside lubricated bullet when originally introduced; these bullets were heel-based. The front was about the same diameter as the outside of the case neck (shell mouth) just like a modern 22 rim fire cartridge. Later, inside-lubricated loadings used an inside case mouth diameter bullet: these bullets usually had a long, hollow base intended to expand to fill the rifling while providing a cleaner-to-handle load. (This system was never particularly successful.)

V** Various versions exist, these differ chiefly in length of the case and loaded cartridges.

** Original 22-10-45 Maynard case length was 1.25".

*** This is a blackpowder primer smaller than standard Small Rifle or Pistol size. It has not been used or available for decades.

**** The 8x60mm, 8x60Rmm (dimensionally similar to the 8x60mm Mauser, except for the rim) and 8x64mm Brenneke, are dimensionally the same as "S" designated series, shown, excepting use of bullets of .318" diameter.

Other codes: Belt/Rim Diameter. Twist (standard factory) is given as inches per complete revolution, e.g., 12 means 1 turn in 12 inches of barrel, etc. 25.4mm, exactly, equals 1 inch. Unless otherwise noted, all dimensions are in inches. Data in parenthesis represents SAAMI maximum specifications.

Index To Cartridges

About the Author

IT IS not given to many of us in the bookish trades to create perennials, books that go on and on. Fellow named Webster did it with dictionaries and a woman named Irma Rombauer hit a good lick with *Joy of Cooking* and Frank C. Barnes made the grade with this very book, CARTRIDGES OF THE WORLD.

Actually, Barnes was not, at the beginning, very deeply into bookish stuff. He was more of a doer. However, COTW caught him well and truly and held him, one edition after another, for decades.

Barnes died in 1992 and was sick awhile before that. It was then he handed over the job, sure that the book would go on for decades.

He was born in Chicago June 25, 1918. He began collecting cartridge data about age 12, which would be about 1930.

Before he began to write of guns and ammunition, he made a living as a geologist-engineer and spent a lot of time in the field in the West and Southwest. He did not "go hunting," he said many times, because he was already there. This experience made Barnes a practical hunter-rifleman, entitled to his opinions on rifles and shotguns and their cartridges. Barnes came to the same sort of competence with handguns even earlier — his father was a police officer who let his son shoot his sidearms if he kept them clean.

The net result was a practical sort of fellow and his principal creation, CARTRIDGES OF THE WORLD, is a practical sort of book. He decided it should cover all the cartridges that count, that it should be a great guide to all of those and not get lost in the esoteric worlds of headstamps and variations. It proved a good plan.

Barnes was a pilot and raced sports cars and rode motorcycles. Eventually he received a Master's Degree in Justice, and taught law enforcement matters at the college level.

And he designed cartridges, too, becoming a respected wildcatter. When he generated the 458 American by cutting 1/2 inch off the redoubtable 458 Winchester Magnum, Barnes put it into a practical rifle. His shortened big bore fit very nicely into a short-actioned 722 Remington, stocked to the muzzle.

Barnes' last project, his last wildcat, was another practical sort of thing. It involved a 416 on the 45-70 case fitted into the Marlin Model 1895 lever-action rifle. This one was not to be, however — he just didn't get it finished. He did finish enough in his 74 years, however. If he's remembered as long as his book lasts, that's a lot longer than the rest of us ever count on.

About the Editor

STAN SKINNER'S interest in guns and hunting began during his childhood years when his Uncle Joe introduced him to squirrel hunting in rural Oklahoma. He soon became an avid reader of hunting stories by John Hunter, Robert Ruark, Elgin Gates, Elmer Keith, and others. Articles about firearms, ballistics and handloading fascinated him, and by his early teens, he often surprised his elders with his knowledge of guns and related subjects.

Skinner attended the University of Oklahoma where he was a member of the varsity rifle and pistol teams. His education was interrupted by the Vietnam War, and during his service in the U.S. Army, he became a Lifetime Master in Outdoor Pistol as a member of the Fort Sill Pistol Team. Following his release from active duty, he continued his education and earned a degree in Journalism. In 1969, Skinner accepted a commission in the U.S. Army Corps of Engineers and served in Vietnam as a helicopter pilot and editor of the *USARV Aviation Safety magazine*.

Following a total of eight years of active military service, Skinner became Associate Editor of *National Guardsman* magazine, later *National Guard* magazine. In 1981, he joined the staff of the National Rifle Association as Managing Editor of *American Hunter* magazine. As Technical Editor for *Guns & Ammo* magazine, he writes a regular reloading feature and technical articles on reloading and ballistics. He is Managing Editor of *SAFARI* Magazine and is a Life Member of Safari Club International.

Skinner has worked and traveled on five continents and has hunted in Africa, Australia, Alaska and the "Lower Forty-Eight." He has several African, South Pacific and North American species listed in *Rowland Ward's Records of Big Game* and the *SCI Record Book of Trophy Animals*.